ETHICAL CONFLICTS IN PSYCHOLOGY

IMPORTANT NOTICE

The statements and opinions published in this book are the responsibility of the authors. Such opinions and statements do not represent official policies, standards, guidelines, or mandates of the American Psychological Association (APA), the APA Ethics Committee or Ethics Office, or any other APA governance group or staff. Statements made in this book neither add to nor reduce requirements of the APA's *Ethical Principles of Psychologists and Code of Conduct* (2017), hereinafter referred to as the APA Ethics Code or the Ethics Code, nor can they be viewed as a definitive source of the meaning of the Ethics Code standards or their application to particular situations. Each ethics committee or other relevant body must interpret and apply the Ethics Code as it believes proper, given all the circumstances of each particular situation. Any information in this book involving legal and ethical issues should not be used as a substitute for obtaining personal legal and/or ethical advice and consultation prior to making decisions regarding individual circumstances.

FIFTH EDITION

ETHICAL CONFLICTS IN PSYCHOLOGY

ERIC Y. DROGIN

AMERICAN PSYCHOLOGICAL ASSOCIATION
Washington, DC

Published by
American Psychological Association
750 First Street, NE
Washington, DC 20002
www.apa.org

APA Order Department
P.O. Box 92984
Washington, DC 20090-2984
Phone: (800) 374-2721; Direct: (202) 336-5510
Fax: (202) 336-5502; TDD/TTY: (202) 336-6123
Online: http://www.apa.org/pubs/books
E-mail: order@apa.org

In the U.K., Europe, Africa, and the Middle East, copies may be ordered from
Eurospan Group
c/o Turpin Distribution
Pegasus Drive
Stratton Business Park
Biggleswade, Bedfordshire
SG18 8TQ United Kingdom
Phone: +44 (0) 1767 604972
Fax: +44 (0) 1767 601640
Online: https://www.eurospanbookstore.com/apa
E-mail: eurospan@turpin-distribution.com

Typeset in Meridien by Circle Graphics, Inc., Reisterstown, MD

Printer: Sheridan Books, Chelsea, MI
Cover Designer: Beth Schlenoff, Bethesda, MD

Library of Congress Cataloging-in-Publication Data
Names: Drogin, Eric York, author.
Title: Ethical conflicts in psychology / by Eric Y. Drogin.
Description: Fifth Edition. | Washington, DC : American Psychological
  Association, [2019] | Revised edition. | Includes bibliographical
  references and index.
Identifiers: LCCN 2018031897 (print) | LCCN 2018033754 (ebook) | ISBN
  9781433830518 (eBook) | ISBN 1433830515 (eBook) | ISBN 9781433829871
  (pbk.) | ISBN 1433829878 (pbk.)
Subjects: LCSH: Psychology—Moral and ethical aspects. |
  Psychologists—Professional ethics.
Classification: LCC BF76.4 (ebook) | LCC BF76.4 .D76 2019 (print) | DDC
  174/.915—dc23
LC record available at https://lccn.loc.gov/2018031897

British Library Cataloguing-in-Publication Data
A CIP record is available from the British Library.

Printed in the United States of America

http://dx.doi.org/10.1037/0000125-000

10 9 8 7 6 5 4 3 2 1

CONTENTS

PREFACE TO THE FIFTH EDITION

This fifth edition of *Ethical Conflicts in Psychology* is a tribute not only to the enduring relevance of its subject matter but also to the long shadow cast over the field of psychological ethics by the author of the first four editions, Donald N. Bersoff.

It is entirely to the reader's benefit that, when I was asked to continue this project, APA made it clear how successful the book's ongoing format had been and how indispensable so much of its previous content would be. When Don penned the first version in 1995—perhaps he actually used a pen—there was nothing like it. The same is true nearly a quarter of a century later. I would never have accepted an invitation to "replace" *Ethical Conflicts in Psychology*, but the current arrangement feels instead like an appropriate act of stewardship.

I'm not sure that APA Books has always felt the same way. There must have been times when the real concern appeared to be not whether I would remain true to Don's legacy but whether it would take me *another* quarter of a century to do so. For her unflaggingly cheerful support, peerless editorial acumen, and astonishing patience, I would like to single out Susan Reynolds, senior acquisitions editor of APA Books.

PREFACE TO THE FIRST EDITION

This book represents the final common pathway of over 3 decades of professional work. My experiences as a psychologist working with inpatients and outpatients, collecting data from human subjects in research, or scrutinizing the research proposals of others while serving on institutional review boards; my work as an attorney defending psychologists against claims of malpractice and unethical conduct, or acting as a consultant to state psychology licensing boards seeking to discipline errant professionals; and my service to the American Psychological Association (APA) as its legal counsel for 10 years and, currently, as a member of its Board of Directors—all of this has taught me that there is a need to better inculcate ethical values and virtues in all those who practice, teach, and do research in psychology. In particular, however, it was my role as an academician—directing programs in law and psychology, discussing and debating ethical issues with colleagues and graduate students, and, specifically, teaching ethics to graduate students—that led me to develop this book.

As a teacher, I found that books providing narrative overviews of ethics, although educational, did not always stimulate lively discussion, sometimes failed to adequately represent several sides to the ethical conflicts and dilemmas that contemporary psychologists face, and did not easily facilitate a career-long commitment to treating clients, employees, academic institutions, or research participants with fidelity and integrity. In actuality, students who read published materials, such as journal articles or book chapters, seemed more inspired to invest in particular topics. However, many of these excellent selections often either were burdensomely long or contained information irrelevant to psychology graduate students who were taking their first course in ethics. Moreover, readings alone could not provide the structure, context, and balance that students needed to comprehend the breadth of issues in the field, to understand the conflicts inherent in ethical decision making, and to integrate this material in a meaningful way.

As a result, for a number of years I experimented in the classroom with a hybrid approach—attempting to combine the best of both worlds. First, I gleaned materials from a wide variety of sources, including psychology journals and books, law reviews, legal decisions, statutes, and official policy documents of the APA. When appropriate, I presented only excerpts of the publications to focus attention on their most relevant and salient points, which allowed for comprehensive coverage over the course of a semester of the major ethical conflicts in psychology.

To the articles previously published, I added original explanatory writings before or after some readings as well as provided introductions to each of the topics. In this book, my comments within excerpted articles are called *Editor's Notes,* or *Ed. Notes,* whereas my notes before and after articles are offered as *Commentary.* I added these comments to illuminate the issues raised by readings, to provide thought-provoking questions, and, at times, to direct the reader to other important sources. I found that the topical organization helped to structure learning and the brief introductions to the topics provided readers with an overview and context for both the readings and the notes.

I have used successive editions of these materials since 1990, when I began teaching a course in ethics and professional issues through Hahnemann University's Department of Clinical and Health Psychology. Each year I have revised and improved the materials on the basis of informative and candid critiques by students themselves. Once I felt satisfied that they were indeed inculcating sensitivity and awareness of ethical issues and fostering the kind of ethical decision-making strategies that are respectful of the complexity of such issues, I decided to offer them to a broader audience. This book is the result.

Being fully aware of the professional need for guidance in this area, I also designed this book to be of interest and value to psychologists who have finished their formal training and are engaged in teaching, practice, and research. It is in the conduct of day-to-day professional life in psychology that ethical principles become truly compelling. It is then that perception of and sensitivity to ethical issues become paramount and that ethical decision-making skills are put to the test. Most important, it is in these practical situations that ethical problems fully reveal their ambiguity and in which psychologists may feel at sea. At such times, a book such as this can serve as an anchor—allowing psychologists a brief respite on stormy waters to study the scholarly constellations and landmarks before navigating further on their particular ethical voyage. It is my hope that this book will serve this purpose well.

For psychologists as well as students of psychology, the book is particularly timely, as it reflects the major changes that were made by the APA in 1992 to its Ethics Code, when it was renamed the *Ethical Principles of Psychologists and Code of Conduct.* I take complete responsibility for my interpretation of the past and current Ethics Codes and for the views expressed throughout the book, while applauding the APA for courageously publishing a volume that is at times critical of official APA policy. I do wish to emphasize, however, that my past and current affiliations with the APA do not imply APA endorsement of or agreement with the views expressed herein.

I now offer some words of appreciation for those who helped in the development of this book. First and foremost, I owe the greatest debt of gratitude to my students for their thoughtful and honest critiques of the material over the years. I also wish to acknowledge the support of the APA Publications and Communications Program. Executive director Gary VandenBos encouraged me early on to do this project, despite its unusual format. Julia Frank-McNeil, director of acquisitions and development for APA Books, helped shape the contours of the text during its formative stages and secured helpful, early reviews from colleagues whom I can only thank anonymously. Development editor Margaret Schlegel not only applied just the right amount and mixture of positive reinforcement and necessary prodding but also provided essential suggestions for improving the book's organization and structure. Production editor Molly Flickinger significantly improved its language and readability, with the assistance of Sarah Trembath, production assistant. Both Stan Jones, director of the APA Office of Ethics, and Ken Pope, one of the most prolific and thoughtful ethics scholars in psychology, prepared detailed critiques of the content and structure of drafts. Each of these contributions immeasurably enhanced this text. Of course, I am fully accountable for the flaws that remain.

Back home, Steven P. Frankino, dean of the Villanova Law School, sustained me with research grants for four summers while I wrote, edited, and revised the book. The Medical College of Pennsylvania—Hahnemann University, my other academic setting, provided me with Robin Lewis—one of the most efficient, intelligent, and helpful secretaries that a faculty member could hope for. Finally, I wish to thank Lowell Burket, Adam Rosen, Steve Anderer, Drew Messer, Natacha Blain, and Trudi Kirk, all of whom served as my research assistants during the writing of this text and, as such, did the "scut work"—tracking down the materials, securing readable copies, and obtaining the necessary permissions to reprint—that faculty members assiduously attempt to avoid.

If students, psychologists, or other readers have favorite articles relevant to the issues covered in this text that were not included and serve its goals, I would very much like to hear from them. Please provide me with an appropriate reprint or, at least, a citation to the reference. I will be happy to consider your suggestions for future editions.

ETHICAL CONFLICTS IN PSYCHOLOGY

Introduction

thical Conflicts in Psychology, now in its fifth edition, still maintains the same primary purpose propounded by its founding author, Donald N. Bersoff: "to help readers develop sensitivity to the ethical aspects of their work as present or future psychologists."

However, much has changed across ethical practice in psychology, particularly with regard to the American Psychological Association's (APA's; 2017) *Ethical Principles of Psychologists and Code of Conduct* (the "Ethics Code"), since the first edition of this book was published in 1995. At that time, psychologists were still determining how to incorporate into their practices sweeping changes in a document that had been revised twice in the preceding five years—more than doubling in length during that period—to include not just "Principles" but an enforceable "Code" as well.

In 2003, the third edition of *Ethical Conflicts in Psychology* surfaced in the wake of very substantial 2002 Ethics Code revisions that, for example, added "gender identity" and "culture" as foci for nondiscrimination, made distinctions between "test data" and "test materials" that greatly affected the ability of third parties to access them both, and simply deleted a slew of Standards pertaining to forensic psychological services.

In recent years, there have been some minor but nonetheless impactful changes to the Ethics Code. Perhaps the most visible of these has been the revision of Standard 3.04, Avoiding Harm, which now mandates that "psychologists do not participate in, facilitate, assist, or otherwise engage in torture."

http://dx.doi.org/10.1037/0000125-001
Ethical Conflicts in Psychology, Fifth Edition, by E. Y. Drogin

There has also been a steady increase in the number of "guidelines"—aspirational in nature, and not, like the Ethics Code, enforceable—since the first edition of *Ethical Conflicts in Psychology*. Currently, there exist 23 APA guidelines that address general practice, clinical practice, and further guidelines development. Many of these are reproduced, in whole or in part, in this fifth edition.

This book contains a collection of both recently published and recognizably classic sources of ethical guidance. Some sources—for example, the latest version of the APA's aforementioned Ethics Code—appear in their entirety, while others are excerpted for critical content. In every instance, readers receive full citation information for the original document, which can be retrieved via the APA PsycNET online research tool. Each of the accompanying commentaries is augmented with five of the most up-to-date references on a given topic, so that readers can quickly supplement their newly acquired knowledge.

Special care has been taken to cater in a balanced fashion to the overlapping interests and professional identities of clinicians, researchers, and teachers. For this purpose, retaining the prior overall format of this book has been particularly apt. First, in Chapter 1, readers learn what ethics codes actually are, how they are enforced, and how they are applied. Then, the process of learning ethics—and, by extension, teaching ethics—is explored in depth in Chapters 2 and 3.

From that point on, this book addresses in turn a series of standard notions in psychological ethics, including confidentiality, privilege, and privacy (Chapter 4), and multiple relationships (Chapter 5). Particular attention is paid to various professional service contexts, including assessment (Chapter 6), therapy (Chapter 7), research, academia, and clinical supervision (Chapter 8), and forensic settings (Chapter 9). Finally, the business aspect of psychology is examined in detail in Chapter 10.

Throughout this edition, there has been an attempt to focus more on "ethical" conflicts per se than on those having to do primarily with law, politics, or public policy—important considerations, to be sure, but ones that in a book of this nature are properly consigned to secondary status.

Just as psychological ethics are in a constant state of evolutionary flux, so has *Ethical Conflicts in Psychology* evolved over the years to become as much of a living document as possible. I hope this book will be responsive to your needs and inspire dialogue about the future of ethical practice in psychology.

REFERENCE

American Psychological Association. (2017). *Ethical principles of psychologists and code of conduct* (2002, Amended June 1, 2010 and January 1, 2017). Retrieved from http://www.apa.org/ethics/code/index.aspx

1

Ethics Codes and How They Are Enforced

In an ideal world, ethical conduct would flow naturally from one's twin dedications to mission and to craft. The entire notion of ethics enforcement would be superfluous—perhaps even oxymoronic. Why should it be necessary for someone personally committed to helping others and educationally steeped in professional responsibility to be subjected to the oversight of peer organizations and governmental institutions?

The answer primarily lies not in some abstract notion of lamentable human frailty or of a slavering beast hidden within all of us, ready to pounce, but rather in the complex and continually evolving nature of ethical obligations themselves. Rare indeed is the psychologist who entered the field to make a lot of money or to locate a ready source of fellow human beings to exploit. The rates are too low and the penalties too high for this to be a plot that was subjected to even the most cursory of investigations. Simply put, ethics are hard.

Just as ethical comportment is a practically and intellectually challenging endeavor, so is ethics enforcement. Similar to scientific journal editing and professional guild promotion, ethics committee and board members are compensated—at best—with honoraria, and frequently find the process bewildering. There is no magical spell that confers insight upon one's statement of willingness to monitor ethical conduct. Board members remain prey to the same logical complexities, emotional blind spots, and experiential deficits as the rest of us.

Understanding the ethics enforcement process is of critical importance to psychologists, for two reasons. The first is that proper ethical comportment

http://dx.doi.org/10.1037/0000125-002
Ethical Conflicts in Psychology, Fifth Edition, by E. Y. Drogin

flows handily from a thorough grasp of what those setting and applying the rules are attempting to accomplish. Graduate students learn quickly that although professional ethics presuppose the existence of an internal moral compass in good working order, possessing such in instrument does not guarantee that we know the specific direction in which we need to travel. Exposure to the enforcement decision-making scheme shows us what the enforcers think is necessary, and applied sanctions impute the comparative seriousness of potential transgressions.

The second reason is reflected in the time-honored legal admonition that one should "always practice the other person's case." There is nothing wrong in attempting to defend oneself—and, by extension, one's colleagues, clients or patients, and personal dependents—against what might be a disproportionately severe penalty for alleged ethical misconduct. Knowing which methods can and will be used after the fact to challenge our professional decision-making is a highly effective means not only of avoiding problems in the first place, but of making the best of what can follow from a false step, however inadvertently taken.

Among its other features, this chapter addresses the development of standard sources of ethical guidance, reproduces the American Psychological Association's (2017) *Ethical Principles of Psychologists and Code of Conduct* (APA Ethics Code) in its entirety, identifies the most recent amendments to the Ethics Code, and provides excerpts from bylaws, rules, and procedures that govern the enforcement process.

(*Note.* Although some articles in this chapter refer to earlier versions of the APA Ethics Code, the insights and analysis remain just as relevant today.)

REFERENCE

American Psychological Association. (2017). *Ethical principles of psychologists and code of conduct* (2002, Amended June 1, 2010 and January 1, 2017). Retrieved from http://www.apa.org/ethics/code/index.aspx

1.1. A Short History of the Development of APA's Ethics Codes

Donald N. Bersoff

The American Psychological Association (APA) was founded in 1892, but it took 60 years before it produced its first code of ethics (APA, 1953), and that occurred only after considerable debate (see, e.g., Hall, 1952). Although a Committee on Scientific and Professional Ethics was created as early as 1938, it acted informally and in the absence of any written code. It was not until a decade later that the Committee suggested that a formal code be developed. Finally, on September 4, 1952, the APA's Council of Representatives, its legislative body, adopted what it called the *Ethical Standards of Psychologists* as official policy of the APA. The standards that it promulgated were to be provisional and used for only 3 years until the membership of APA voted, principle by principle, to make them permanent.

The group drafting the first code of ethics was denominated the Committee on Ethical Standards for Psychology. Its chair was Nicholas Hobbs, and its seven other members included such luminaries as Stuart Cook, Helen Sargent, and Donald Super. It went about its task in a unique way. An earlier committee headed by Edward Tolman decided that the preparation of ethical standards should be research based:

> Many psychologists responded favorably to the proposed procedure for developing the code, because it rejected an a priori approach in favor of an empirical approach in which ethical principles would be based on the raw data of experience of psychologists in solving their ethical problems. (APA, 1953, p. viii)

Thus, in 1948, the then 7,500 APA members were asked in a letter to describe anonymously a situation they knew from personal experience in which a psychologist made a decision having ethical implications. The drafting committee received more than 1,000 of these reports. It then placed these ethical problems into six categories: (a) Ethical Standards and Public Responsibility, (b) Ethical Standards in Client Relationships, (c) Ethical Standards in Teaching, (d) Ethical Standards in Research, (e) Ethical Standards in Writing and Publishing, and (f) Ethical Standards in Professional Relationships.

Although the APA was by the 1950s becoming more populated by professional psychologists, it is noteworthy that only one category of the standards (client relationships) pertained to clinicians (compare this to the current Code, reprinted later in this chapter).

From *Ethical Conflicts in Psychology* (4th ed., pp. 10–13), by D. N. Bersoff, 2008, Washington, DC: American Psychological Association. Copyright 2008 by the American Psychological Association.

Drafting of the standards on the basis of the critical incidents gleaned from the 1,000 responses began shortly after 1948 and went through several revisions and publication, category by category, in the *American Psychologist* as well as after presentations at APA conventions. As noted, the final draft was submitted to the Council of Representatives for passage in September 1952.

Recent commentators have raised concerns that the two most recent versions of the Ethics Code are worded vaguely and ambiguously. The committee drafting the original Code not only had similar concerns but, more broadly, "whether to concern itself only with issues that were clearly a matter of ethics, in the sense of bearing moral implications, or whether to extend its concern to include matters of professional practice and of courtesy" (APA, 1953, p. ix). It decided on the latter course but identified these differing layers by the precision with which the standards were drafted:

> In general, principles involving issues with clear ethical import are worded strongly, in such phrases as, "it is unethical," "the psychologist is obligated," "the psychologist should," "the psychologist must." Principles involving issues of good practice are worded less strongly, in such phrases as, "it is unprofessional," "the psychologist is expected," "good practice requires," "the psychologist should in general." Principles involving issues of courtesy or of etiquette are worded with modifying phrases which clearly indicate their nature, such as "Professional courtesy suggests," "as a matter of courtesy," etc. (APA, 1953, ix)

It would be worthwhile to peruse the original standards, which are too long to reproduce here. Many of those standards would today be considered illegal (e.g., prohibitions on advertising in newspapers or on radio), and although there are cautionary principles regarding dual relationships, there is no explicit bar against sexual relationships with current or former clients, which did not appear until 1979. But the most singular aspect of the initial Code was that its drafters eschewed an "armchair approach" (Hobbs, 1948, p. 82) in favor of "an empirically developed code" (p. 83) gleaned from critical incidents reported by members of APA itself. Or, as Golann (1969) commented, "The *Ethical Standards of Psychologists* is unique in the sense that it was based on the day-to-day decisions made by psychologists in the practice of their professions, rather than prescribed by a committee" (p. 454).

Nevertheless, as Pope and Vetter (1992) noted, "APA never again conducted a mail survey of a representative sample of the membership as the basis for revising the general code" (p. 398). The last two versions were developed by an appointed task force, although its drafts were published for comment and recommendations by the APA membership. As the 1992 Code was being drafted, however, Pope and Vetter sought to replicate the critical incident method of constructing the original Code. They sent a survey to 1,319 randomly selected APA members and fellows asking them to anonymously describe a recent ethically troubling incident. They received replies from 679 psychologists (return rate = 51%). Before the reader looks below, can you guess what were the five most troubling categories of troubling incidents?

The five categories of most concern (Pope & Vetter, 1992, p. 399) with their percentages are as follows: (a) confidentiality, 18%; (b) blurred, dual, or conflictual relationships, 17%; (c) payment sources, plans, setting, and methods, 14%; (d) academic settings, teaching dilemmas, training, 8%; and (e) forensic psychology, 5%. Readers may want to study the current Code and consider if these concerns are given proper weight in the enforceable standards.

No other category, including sexual issues, ethics codes, ethnicity, treatment records, or supervision received more than 4% of responses. Interestingly, of the five categories with the highest percent of responses, only three-dual relationships, payment issues, and one form of forensic psychology-led to a significant number of complaints to the APA Ethics Committee (see American Psychological Association, Ethics Committee, 2006). Confidentiality and academic issues, rarely, if ever, result in ethics complaints to APA.

REFERENCES

American Psychological Association. (1953). *Ethical standards of psychologists.* Washington, DC: Author.

American Psychological Association, Ethics Committee. (2006). Report of the Ethics Committee, 2005. *American Psychologist, 61,* 522–529.

Golann, S. E. (1969). Emerging areas of ethical concern. *American Psychologist, 24,* 454–459.

Hall, C. S. (1952). Crooks, codes, and cants. *American Psychologist, 7,* 430–431.

Hobbs, N. (1948). The development of a code of ethical standards for psychology. *American Psychologist, 3,* 80–84.

Pope, K. S., & Vetter, V. A. (1992). Ethical dilemmas encountered by members of the American Psychological Association: A national survey. *American Psychologist, 47,* 397–411.

COMMENTARY: Dr. Bersoff's concise summary and analysis of the history of our foundational source of ethical guidance rings as true today as it did a decade ago. Of particular interest here is the observation of a potential imbalance in emphasis between what surveyed American Psychological Association members perceive as an "ethically troubling incident" and what our Ethics Code has historically chosen to adopt as "enforceable standards."

Perfect synchrony of what those in the field—clinically, academically, and in other professional pursuits—and those writing our rules find significant is a goal that can never fully be realized, but it is a necessary pursuit and one that mirrors each psychologist's personal, career-long ethical journey. For those who may question why the Ethics Code is (and will be revised) again and again, the answer lies in the fact that ethical conflicts are a permanent aspect of each and every one of the helping professions, and the obligation to deal with them at the institutional level should not be ascribed to fluctuating resolve or exercises in guild politics.

The following references are recommended for those interested in further investigation of the perpetually evolving nature of ethics codes, the moral imperatives underlying them, and the profession's obligation to respond to societal as well as institutional concerns.

Allen, L. R., & Dodd, C. G. (2018). Psychologists' responsibility to society: Public policy and the ethics of political action. *Journal of Theoretical and Philosophical Psychology, 38,* 42–53.

Joyce, N. R., & Rankin, T. J. (2010). The lessons of the development of the first APA ethics code: Blending science, practice, and politics. *Ethics & Behavior, 20,* 466–481.

Nagy, T. F. (2011). A brief history and overview of the APA Ethics Code. In *Essential ethics for psychologists: A primer for understanding and mastering core issues* (pp. 29–48). Washington, DC: American Psychological Association. http://dx.doi.org/10.1037/12345-002

Stark, L. (2010). The sciences of ethics: Deception, the resilient self, and the APA code of ethics, 1966–1973. *Journal of the History of the Behavioral Sciences, 46,* 337–370.

Teo, T. (2015). Are psychological "ethics codes" morally oblique? *Journal of Theoretical and Philosophical Psychology, 35,* 78–89.

1.2. Ethical Principles of Psychologists and Code of Conduct

American Psychological Association

From *Ethical Principles of Psychologists and Code of Conduct* (2002, Amended June 1, 2010 and January 1, 2017), by the American Psychological Association, 2017. Retrieved from http://www.apa.org/ethics/code/index.aspx. Copyright 2017 by the American Psychological Association.

The American Psychological Association's Council of Representatives adopted this version of the APA Ethics Code during its meeting on August 21, 2002. The Code became effective on June 1, 2003. The Council of Representatives amended this version of the Ethics Code on February 20, 2010, effective June 1, 2010, and on August 3, 2016, effective January 1, 2017. (see p. 16 of this pamphlet). Inquiries concerning the substance or interpretation of the APA Ethics Code should be addressed to the Office of Ethics, American Psychological Association, 750 First St. NE, Washington, DC 20002-4242. This Ethics Code and information regarding the Code can be found on the APA website, http://www.apa.org/ethics. The standards in this Ethics Code will be used to adjudicate complaints brought concerning alleged conduct occurring on or after the effective date. Complaints will be adjudicated on the basis of the version of the Ethics Code that was in effect at the time the conduct occurred.

The APA has previously published its Ethics Code, or amendments thereto, as follows:

American Psychological Association. (1953). *Ethical standards of psychologists.* Washington, DC: Author.
American Psychological Association. (1959). Ethical standards of psychologists. *American Psychologist, 14,* 279–282.
American Psychological Association. (1963). Ethical standards of psychologists. *American Psychologist, 18,* 56–60.
American Psychological Association. (1968). Ethical standards of psychologists. *American Psychologist, 23,* 357–361.
American Psychological Association. (1977, March). Ethical standards of psychologists. *APA Monitor,* 22–23.
American Psychological Association. (1979). *Ethical standards of psychologists.* Washington, DC: Author.
American Psychological Association. (1981). Ethical principles of psychologists. *American Psychologist, 36,* 633–638.
American Psychological Association. (1990). Ethical principles of psychologists (Amended June 2, 1989). *American Psychologist, 45,* 390–395.
American Psychological Association. (1992). Ethical principles of psychologists and code of conduct. *American Psychologist, 47,* 1597–1611.
American Psychological Association. (2002). Ethical principles of psychologists and code of conduct. *American Psychologist, 57,* 1060–1073.
American Psychological Association. (2010). 2010 amendments to the 2002 "Ethical Principles of Psychologists and Code of Conduct." *American Psychologist, 65,* 493.
American Psychological Association. (2016). Revision of ethical standard 3.04 of the "Ethical Principles of Psychologists and Code of Conduct" (2002, as amended 2010). *American Psychologist, 71,* 900.

Request copies of the APA's Ethical Principles of Psychologists and Code of Conduct from the APA Order Department, 750 First St. NE, Washington, DC 20002-4242, or phone(202) 336-5510.

INTRODUCTION AND APPLICABILITY

The American Psychological Association's (APA's) *Ethical Principles of Psychologists and Code of Conduct* (hereinafter referred to as the Ethics Code) consists of an Introduction, a Preamble, five General Principles (A–E), and specific Ethical Standards. The Introduction discusses the intent, organization, procedural considerations, and scope of application of the Ethics Code. The Preamble and General Principles are aspirational goals to guide psychologists toward the highest ideals of psychology. Although the Preamble and General Principles are not themselves enforceable rules, they should be considered by psychologists in arriving at an ethical course of action. The Ethical Standards set forth enforceable rules for conduct as psychologists. Most of the Ethical Standards are written broadly, in order to apply to psychologists in varied roles, although the application of an Ethical Standard may vary depending on the context. The Ethical Standards are not exhaustive. The fact that a given conduct is not specifically addressed by an Ethical Standard does not mean that it is necessarily either ethical or unethical.

This Ethics Code applies only to psychologists' activities that are part of their scientific, educational, or professional roles as psychologists. Areas covered include but are not limited to the clinical, counseling, and school practice of psychology; research; teaching; supervision of trainees; public service; policy development; social intervention; development of assessment instruments; conducting assessments; educational counseling; organizational consulting; forensic activities; program design and evaluation; and administration. This Ethics Code applies to these activities across a variety of contexts, such as in person, postal, telephone, Internet, and other electronic transmissions. These activities shall be distinguished from the purely private conduct of psychologists, which is not within the purview of the Ethics Code.

Membership in the APA commits members and student affiliates to comply with the standards of the APA Ethics Code and to the rules and procedures used to enforce them. Lack of awareness or misunderstanding of an Ethical Standard is not itself a defense to a charge of unethical conduct.

The procedures for filing, investigating, and resolving complaints of unethical conduct are described in the current Rules and Procedures of the APA Ethics Committee. APA may impose sanctions on its members for violations of the standards of the Ethics Code, including termination of APA membership, and may notify other bodies and individuals of its actions. Actions that violate the standards of the Ethics Code may also lead to the imposition of sanctions on psychologists or students whether or not they are APA members by bodies other than APA, including state psychological associations, other professional groups, psychology boards, other state or federal agencies, and payors for health services. In addition, APA may take action against a member after his or her conviction of a felony, expulsion or suspension from an affiliated state psychological association, or suspension or loss of licensure. When the sanction to be imposed by APA is less than expulsion, the 2001 Rules and Procedures do not guarantee an opportunity for an in-person hearing, but generally provide that complaints will be resolved only on the basis of a submitted record.

The Ethics Code is intended to provide guidance for psychologists and standards of professional conduct that can be applied by the APA and by other bodies that choose to adopt them. The Ethics Code is not intended to be a basis of civil liability. Whether a psychologist has violated the Ethics Code standards does not by itself determine whether the psychologist is legally liable in a court action, whether a contract is enforceable, or whether other legal consequences occur.

The modifiers used in some of the standards of this Ethics Code (e.g., *reasonably, appropriate, potentially*) are included in the standards when they would (1) allow professional judgment on the part of psychologists, (2) eliminate injustice or inequality that would occur without the modifier, (3) ensure applicability across the broad range of activities conducted by psychologists, or (4) guard against a set of rigid rules that might be quickly outdated. As used in this Ethics Code, the term *reasonable* means the prevailing professional judgment of psychologists engaged in similar activities in similar circumstances, given the knowledge the psychologist had or should have had at the time.

In the process of making decisions regarding their professional behavior, psychologists must consider this Ethics Code in addition to applicable laws and psychology board regulations. In applying the Ethics Code to their professional work, psychologists may consider other materials and guidelines that have been adopted or endorsed by scientific and professional psychological organizations and the dictates of their own conscience, as well as consult with others within the field. If this Ethics Code establishes a higher standard of conduct than is required by law, psychologists must meet the higher ethical standard. If psychologists' ethical responsibilities conflict with law, regulations, or other governing legal authority, psychologists make known their commitment to this Ethics Code and take steps to resolve the conflict in a responsible manner in keeping with basic principles of human rights.

PREAMBLE

Psychologists are committed to increasing scientific and professional knowledge of behavior and people's understanding of themselves and others and to the use of such knowledge to improve the condition of individuals, organizations, and society. Psychologists respect and protect civil and human rights and the central importance of freedom of inquiry and expression in research, teaching, and publication. They strive to help the public in developing informed judgments and choices concerning human behavior. In doing so, they perform many roles, such as researcher, educator, diagnostician, therapist, supervisor, consultant, administrator, social interventionist, and expert witness. This Ethics

Code provides a common set of principles and standards upon which psychologists build their professional and scientific work.

This Ethics Code is intended to provide specific standards to cover most situations encountered by psychologists. It has as its goals the welfare and protection of the individuals and groups with whom psychologists work and the education of members, students, and the public regarding ethical standards of the discipline.

The development of a dynamic set of ethical standards for psychologists' work-related conduct requires a personal commitment and lifelong effort to act ethically; to encourage ethical behavior by students, supervisees, employees, and colleagues; and to consult with others concerning ethical problems.

GENERAL PRINCIPLES

This section consists of General Principles. General Principles, as opposed to Ethical Standards, are aspirational in nature. Their intent is to guide and inspire psychologists toward the very highest ethical ideals of the profession. General Principles, in contrast to Ethical Standards, do not represent obligations and should not form the basis for imposing sanctions. Relying upon General Principles for either of these reasons distorts both their meaning and purpose.

Principle A: Beneficence and Nonmaleficence

Psychologists strive to benefit those with whom they work and take care to do no harm. In their professional actions, psychologists seek to safeguard the welfare and rights of those with whom they interact professionally and other affected persons, and the welfare of animal subjects of research. When conflicts occur among psychologists' obligations or concerns, they attempt to resolve these conflicts in a responsible fashion that avoids or minimizes harm. Because psychologists' scientific and professional judgments and actions may affect the lives of others, they are alert to and guard against personal, financial, social, organizational, or political factors that might lead to misuse of their influence. Psychologists strive to be aware of the possible effect of their own physical and mental health on their ability to help those with whom they work.

Principle B: Fidelity and Responsibility

Psychologists establish relationships of trust with those with whom they work. They are aware of their professional and scientific responsibilities to society and to the specific communities in which they work. Psychologists uphold professional standards of conduct, clarify their professional roles and obligations, accept appropriate responsibility for their behavior, and seek to manage conflicts of interest that could lead to exploitation or harm. Psychologists consult with, refer to, or cooperate with other professionals and institutions to the extent needed to serve the best interests of those with whom they work. They are concerned about the ethical compliance of their colleagues' scientific and professional conduct. Psychologists strive to contribute a portion of their professional time for little or no compensation or personal advantage.

Principle C: Integrity

Psychologists seek to promote accuracy, honesty, and truthfulness in the science, teaching, and practice of psychology. In these activities psychologists do not steal, cheat, or engage in fraud, subterfuge, or intentional misrepresentation of fact. Psychologists strive to keep their promises and to avoid unwise or unclear commitments. In situations in which deception may be ethically justifiable to maximize benefits and minimize harm, psychologists have a serious obligation to consider the need for, the possible consequences of, and their responsibility to correct any resulting mistrust or other harmful effects that arise from the use of such techniques.

Principle D: Justice

Psychologists recognize that fairness and justice entitle all persons to access to and benefit from the contributions of psychology and to equal quality in the processes, procedures, and services being conducted by psychologists. Psychologists exercise reasonable judgment and take precautions to ensure that their potential biases, the boundaries of their competence, and the limitations of their expertise do not lead to or condone unjust practices.

Principle E: Respect for People's Rights and Dignity

Psychologists respect the dignity and worth of all people, and the rights of individuals to privacy, confidentiality, and self-determination. Psychologists are aware that special safeguards may be necessary to protect the rights and welfare of persons or communities whose vulnerabilities impair autonomous decision making. Psychologists are aware of and respect cultural, individual, and role differences, including those based on age, gender, gender identity, race, ethnicity, culture, national origin, religion, sexual orientation, disability, language, and socioeconomic status, and consider these factors when working with members of such groups. Psychologists try to eliminate the effect on their work of biases based on those factors, and they do not knowingly participate in or condone activities of others based upon such prejudices.

ETHICAL STANDARDS

1. Resolving Ethical Issues

1.01 Misuse of Psychologists' Work

If psychologists learn of misuse or misrepresentation of their work, they take reasonable steps to correct or minimize the misuse or misrepresentation.

1.02 Conflicts Between Ethics and Law, Regulations, or Other Governing Legal Authority

If psychologists' ethical responsibilities conflict with law, regulations, or other governing legal authority, psychologists clarify the nature of the conflict, make known their commitment to the Ethics Code, and take reasonable steps to resolve the conflict consistent with the General Principles and Ethical Standards of the Ethics Code. Under no circumstances may this standard be used to justify or defend violating human rights.

1.03 Conflicts Between Ethics and Organizational Demands

If the demands of an organization with which psychologists are affiliated or for whom they are working are in conflict with this Ethics Code, psychologists clarify the nature of the conflict, make known their commitment to the Ethics Code, and take reasonable steps to resolve the conflict consistent with the General Principles and Ethical Standards of the Ethics Code. Under no circumstances may this standard be used to justify or defend violating human rights.

1.04 Informal Resolution of Ethical Violations

When psychologists believe that there may have been an ethical violation by another psychologist, they attempt to resolve the issue by bringing it to the attention of that individual, if an informal resolution appears appropriate and the intervention does not violate any confidentiality rights that may be involved. (See also Standards 1.02, Conflicts Between Ethics and Law, Regulations, or Other Governing Legal Authority, and 1.03, Conflicts Between Ethics and Organizational Demands.)

1.05 Reporting Ethical Violations

If an apparent ethical violation has substantially harmed or is likely to substantially harm a person or organization and is not appropriate for informal resolution under Standard 1.04, Informal Resolution of Ethical Violations, or is not resolved properly in that fashion, psychologists take further action appropriate to the situation. Such action might include referral to state or national committees on professional ethics, to state licensing boards, or to the appropriate institutional authorities. This standard does not apply when an intervention would violate confidentiality rights or when psychologists have been retained to review the work of another psychologist whose professional conduct is in question. (See also Standard 1.02, Conflicts Between Ethics and Law, Regulations, or Other Governing Legal Authority.)

1.06 Cooperating With Ethics Committees

Psychologists cooperate in ethics investigations, proceedings, and resulting requirements of the APA or any affiliated state psychological association to which they belong. In doing so, they address any confidentiality issues. Failure to cooperate is itself an ethics violation. However, making a request for deferment of adjudication of an ethics complaint pending the outcome of litigation does not alone constitute noncooperation.

1.07 Improper Complaints

Psychologists do not file or encourage the filing of ethics complaints that are made with reckless disregard for or willful ignorance of facts that would disprove the allegation.

1.08 Unfair Discrimination Against Complainants and Respondents

Psychologists do not deny persons employment, advancement, admissions to academic or other programs, tenure, or promotion, based solely upon their having made or their being the subject of an ethics complaint. This does not preclude taking action based upon the outcome of such proceedings or considering other appropriate information.

2. Competence

2.01 Boundaries of Competence

(a) Psychologists provide services, teach, and conduct research with populations and in areas only within the boundaries of their competence, based on their education, training, supervised experience, consultation, study, or professional experience.

(b) Where scientific or professional knowledge in the discipline of psychology establishes that an understanding of factors associated with age, gender, gender identity, race, ethnicity, culture, national origin, religion, sexual orientation, disability, language, or socioeconomic status is essential for effective implementation of their services or research, psychologists have or obtain the training, experience, consultation, or supervision necessary to ensure the competence of their services, or they make appropriate referrals, except as provided in Standard 2.02, Providing Services in Emergencies.

(c) Psychologists planning to provide services, teach, or conduct research involving populations, areas, techniques, or technologies new to them undertake relevant education, training, supervised experience, consultation, or study.

(d) When psychologists are asked to provide services to individuals for whom appropriate mental health services are not available and for which psychologists have not obtained the competence necessary, psychologists with closely related prior training or experience may provide such services in order to ensure that services are not denied if they make a reasonable effort to obtain the competence required by using relevant research, training, consultation, or study.

(e) In those emerging areas in which generally recognized standards for preparatory training do not yet exist, psychologists nevertheless take reasonable steps to ensure the competence of their work and to protect clients/patients, students, supervisees, research participants, organizational clients, and others from harm.

(f) When assuming forensic roles, psychologists are or become reasonably familiar with the judicial or administrative rules governing their roles.

2.02 Providing Services in Emergencies

In emergencies, when psychologists provide services to individuals for whom other mental health services are not available and for which psychologists have not obtained the necessary training, psychologists may provide such services in order to ensure that services are not denied. The services are discontinued as soon as the emergency has ended or appropriate services are available.

2.03 Maintaining Competence

Psychologists undertake ongoing efforts to develop and maintain their competence.

2.04 Bases for Scientific and Professional Judgments

Psychologists' work is based upon established scientific and professional knowledge of the discipline. (See also Standards 2.01e, Boundaries of Competence, and 10.01b, Informed Consent to Therapy.)

2.05 Delegation of Work to Others

Psychologists who delegate work to employees, supervisees, or research or teaching assistants or who use the services of others, such as interpreters, take reasonable steps to (1) avoid delegating such work to persons who have a multiple relationship with those being served that would likely lead to exploitation or loss of objectivity; (2) authorize only those responsibilities that such persons can be expected to perform competently on the basis of their education, training, or experience, either independently or with the level of supervision being provided; and (3) see that such persons perform these services competently. (See also Standards 2.02, Providing Services in Emergencies; 3.05, Multiple Relationships; 4.01, Maintaining Confidentiality; 9.01, Bases for Assessments; 9.02, Use of Assessments; 9.03, Informed Consent in Assessments; and 9.07, Assessment by Unqualified Persons.)

2.06 Personal Problems and Conflicts

(a) Psychologists refrain from initiating an activity when they know or should know that there is a substantial likelihood that their personal problems will prevent them from performing their work-related activities in a competent manner.

(b) When psychologists become aware of personal problems that may interfere with their performing work-related duties adequately, they take appropriate measures, such as obtaining professional consultation or assistance, and determine whether they should limit, suspend, or terminate their work-related duties. (See also Standard 10.10, Terminating Therapy.)

3. Human Relations

3.01 Unfair Discrimination

In their work-related activities, psychologists do not engage in unfair discrimination based on age, gender, gender identity, race, ethnicity, culture, national origin, religion, sexual orientation, disability, socioeconomic status, or any basis proscribed by law.

3.02 Sexual Harassment

Psychologists do not engage in sexual harassment. Sexual harassment is sexual solicitation, physical advances, or verbal or nonverbal conduct that is sexual in nature, that occurs in connection with the psychologist' s activities or roles as a psychologist, and that either (1) is unwelcome, is offensive, or creates a hostile workplace or educational environment, and the psychologist knows or is told this or (2) is sufficiently severe or intense to be abusive to a reasonable person in the context. Sexual harassment can consist of a single intense or severe act or of multiple persistent or pervasive acts. (See also Standard 1.08, Unfair Discrimination Against Complainants and Respondents.)

3.03 Other Harassment

Psychologists do not knowingly engage in behavior that is harassing or demeaning to persons with whom they interact in their work based on factors such as those persons' age, gender, gender identity, race, ethnicity, culture, national origin, religion, sexual orientation, disability, language, or socioeconomic status.

3.04 Avoiding Harm

(a) Psychologists take reasonable steps to avoid harming their clients/patients, students, supervisees, research participants, organizational clients, and others with whom they work, and to minimize harm where it is foreseeable and unavoidable.

(b) Psychologists do not participate in, facilitate, assist, or otherwise engage in torture, defined as any act by which severe pain or suffering, whether physical or mental, is intentionally inflicted on a person, or in any other cruel, inhuman, or degrading behavior that violates 3.04a.

3.05 Multiple Relationships

(a) A multiple relationship occurs when a psychologist is in a professional role with a person and (1) at the same time is in another role with the same person, (2) at the same time is in a relationship with a person closely associated with or related to the person with whom the psychologist has the professional relationship, or (3) promises to enter into another relationship in the future with the person or a person closely associated with or related to the person.

A psychologist refrains from entering into a multiple relationship if the multiple relationship could reasonably be expected to impair the psychologist's objectivity, competence, or effectiveness in performing his or her functions as a psychologist, or otherwise risks exploitation or harm to the person with whom the professional relationship exists.

Multiple relationships that would not reasonably be expected to cause impairment or risk exploitation or harm are not unethical.

(b) If a psychologist finds that, due to unforeseen factors, a potentially harmful multiple relationship has arisen, the psychologist takes reasonable steps to resolve it with due regard for the best interests of the affected person and maximal compliance with the Ethics Code.

(c) When psychologists are required by law, institutional policy, or extraordinary circumstances to serve in more than one role in judicial or administrative proceedings, at the outset they clarify role expectations and the extent of confidentiality and thereafter as changes occur. (See also Standards 3.04, Avoiding Harm, and 3.07, Third-Party Requests for Services.)

3.06 Conflict of Interest

Psychologists refrain from taking on a professional role when personal, scientific, professional, legal, financial, or other interests or relationships could reasonably be expected to (1) impair their objectivity, competence, or effectiveness in performing their functions as psychologists or (2) expose the person or organization with whom the professional relationship exists to harm or exploitation.

3.07 Third-Party Requests for Services

When psychologists agree to provide services to a person or entity at the request of a third party, psychologists attempt to clarify at the outset of the service the nature of the relationship with all individuals or organizations involved. This clarification includes the role of the psychologist (e.g., therapist, consultant, diagnostician, or expert witness), an identification of who is the client, the probable uses of the services provided or the information obtained, and the fact that there may be limits to confidentiality. (See also Standards 3.05, Multiple Relationships, and 4.02, Discussing the Limits of Confidentiality.)

3.08 Exploitative Relationships

Psychologists do not exploit persons over whom they have supervisory, evaluative, or other authority such as clients/patients, students, supervisees, research participants, and employees. (See also Standards 3.05, Multiple Relationships; 6.04, Fees and Financial Arrangements; 6.05, Barter With Clients/Patients; 7.07, Sexual Relationships With Students and Supervisees; 10.05, Sexual Intimacies With Current Therapy Clients/Patients; 10.06, Sexual Intimacies With Relatives or Significant Others of Current Therapy Clients/Patients; 10.07, Therapy With Former Sexual Partners; and 10.08, Sexual Intimacies With Former Therapy Clients/Patients.)

3.09 Cooperation With Other Professionals

When indicated and professionally appropriate, psychologists cooperate with other professionals in order to serve their clients/patients effectively and appropriately. (See also Standard 4.05, Disclosures.)

3.10 Informed Consent

(a) When psychologists conduct research or provide assessment, therapy, counseling, or consulting services in person or via electronic transmission or other forms of communication, they obtain the informed consent of the individual or individuals using language that is reasonably understandable to that person or persons except when conducting such activities without consent is mandated by law or governmental regulation or as otherwise provided in this Ethics Code. (See also Standards 8.02, Informed Consent to Research; 9.03, Informed Consent in Assessments; and 10.01, Informed Consent to Therapy.)

(b) For persons who are legally incapable of giving informed consent, psychologists nevertheless (1) provide an appropriate explanation, (2) seek the individual' s assent, (3) consider such persons' preferences and best interests, and (4) obtain appropriate permission from a legally authorized person, if such substitute consent is permitted or required by law. When consent by a legally authorized person is not permitted or required by law, psychologists take reasonable steps to protect the individual' s rights and welfare.

(c) When psychological services are court ordered or otherwise mandated, psychologists inform the individual of the nature of the anticipated services, including whether the services are court ordered or mandated and any limits of confidentiality, before proceeding.

(d) Psychologists appropriately document written or oral consent, permission, and assent. (See also Standards 8.02, Informed Consent to Research; 9.03, Informed Consent in Assessments; and 10.01, Informed Consent to Therapy.)

3.11 Psychological Services Delivered to or Through Organizations

(a) Psychologists delivering services to or through organizations provide information beforehand to clients and when appropriate those directly affected by the services about (1) the nature and objectives of the services, (2) the intended recipients, (3) which of the individuals are clients, (4) the relationship the psychologist will have with each person and the organization, (5) the probable uses of services provided and information obtained, (6) who will have access to the information, and (7) limits of confidentiality. As soon as feasible, they provide information about the results and conclusions of such services to appropriate persons.

(b) If psychologists will be precluded by law or by organizational roles from providing such information to particular individuals or groups, they so inform those individuals or groups at the outset of the service.

3.12 Interruption of Psychological Services

Unless otherwise covered by contract, psychologists make reasonable efforts to plan for facilitating services in the event that psychological services are interrupted by factors such as the psychologist's illness, death, unavailability, relocation, or retirement or by the client's/patient's relocation or financial limitations. (See also Standard 6.02c, Maintenance, Dissemination, and Disposal of Confidential Records of Professional and Scientific Work.)

4. Privacy and Confidentiality

4.01 Maintaining Confidentiality

Psychologists have a primary obligation and take reasonable precautions to protect confidential information obtained through or stored in any medium, recognizing that the extent and limits of confidentiality may be regulated by law or established by institutional rules or professional or scientific relationship. (See also Standard 2.05, Delegation of Work to Others.)

4.02 Discussing the Limits of Confidentiality

(a) Psychologists discuss with persons (including, to the extent feasible, persons who are legally incapable of giving informed consent and their legal representatives) and organizations with whom they establish a scientific or professional relationship (1) the relevant limits of confidentiality and (2) the foreseeable uses of the information generated through their psychological activities. (See also Standard 3.10, Informed Consent.)

(b) Unless it is not feasible or is contraindicated, the discussion of confidentiality occurs at the outset of the relationship and thereafter as new circumstances may warrant.

(c) Psychologists who offer services, products, or information via electronic transmission inform clients/patients of the risks to privacy and limits of confidentiality.

4.03 Recording

Before recording the voices or images of individuals to whom they provide services, psychologists obtain permission from all such persons or their legal representatives. (See also Standards 8.03, Informed Consent for Recording Voices and Images in Research; 8.05, Dispensing With Informed Consent for Research; and 8.07, Deception in Research.)

4.04 Minimizing Intrusions on Privacy

(a) Psychologists include in written and oral reports and consultations, only information germane to the purpose for which the communication is made.

(b) Psychologists discuss confidential information obtained in their work only for appropriate scientific or professional purposes and only with persons clearly concerned with such matters.

4.05 Disclosures

(a) Psychologists may disclose confidential information with the appropriate consent of the organizational client, the individual client/patient, or another legally authorized person on behalf of the client/patient unless prohibited by law.

(b) Psychologists disclose confidential information without the consent of the individual only as mandated by law, or where permitted by law for a valid purpose such as to (1) provide needed professional services; (2) obtain appropriate professional consultations; (3) protect the client/patient, psychologist, or others from harm; or (4) obtain payment for services from a client/patient, in which instance disclosure is limited to the minimum that is necessary to achieve the purpose. (See also Standard 6.04e, Fees and Financial Arrangements.)

4.06 Consultations

When consulting with colleagues, (1) psychologists do not disclose confidential information that reasonably could lead to the identification of a client/patient, research participant, or other person or organization with whom they have a confidential relationship unless they have obtained the prior consent of the person or organization or the disclosure cannot be avoided, and (2) they disclose information only to the extent necessary to achieve the purposes of the consultation. (See also Standard 4.01, Maintaining Confidentiality.)

4.07 Use of Confidential Information for Didactic or Other Purposes

Psychologists do not disclose in their writings, lectures, or other public media, confidential, personally identifiable information concerning their clients/patients, students, research participants, organizational clients, or other recipients of their services that they obtained during the course of their work, unless (1) they take reasonable steps to disguise the person or organization, (2) the person or organization has consented in writing, or (3) there is legal authorization for doing so.

5. Advertising and Other Public Statements

5.01 Avoidance of False or Deceptive Statements

(a) Public statements include but are not limited to paid or unpaid advertising, product endorsements, grant applications, licensing applications, other credentialing applications, brochures, printed matter, directory listings, personal resumes or curricula vitae, or comments for use in media such as print or electronic transmission, statements in legal proceedings, lectures and public oral presentations, and published materials. Psychologists do not knowingly make public statements that are false, deceptive, or fraudulent concerning their research, practice, or other work activities or those of persons or organizations with which they are affiliated.

(b) Psychologists do not make false, deceptive, or fraudulent statements concerning (1) their training, experience, or competence; (2) their academic degrees; (3) their credentials; (4) their institutional or association affiliations; (5) their services; (6) the scientific or clinical basis for, or results or degree of success of, their services; (7) their fees; or (8) their publications or research findings.

(c) Psychologists claim degrees as credentials for their health services only if those degrees (1) were earned from a regionally accredited educational institution or (2) were the basis for psychology licensure by the state in which they practice.

5.02 Statements by Others

(a) Psychologists who engage others to create or place public statements that promote their professional practice, products, or activities retain professional responsibility for such statements.

(b) Psychologists do not compensate employees of press, radio, television, or other communication media in return for publicity in a news item. (See also Standard 1.01, Misuse of Psychologists' Work.)

(c) A paid advertisement relating to psychologists' activities must be identified or clearly recognizable as such.

5.03 Descriptions of Workshops and Non–Degree-Granting Educational Programs

To the degree to which they exercise control, psychologists responsible for announcements, catalogs, brochures, or advertisements describing workshops, seminars, or other non–degree-granting educational programs ensure that they accurately describe the audience for which the program is intended, the educational objectives, the presenters, and the fees involved.

5.04 Media Presentations

When psychologists provide public advice or comment via print, Internet, or other electronic transmission, they take precautions to ensure that statements (1) are based on their professional knowledge, training, or experience in accord with appropriate psychological literature and practice; (2) are otherwise consistent with this Ethics Code; and (3) do not indicate that a professional relationship has been established with the recipient. (See also Standard 2.04, Bases for Scientific and Professional Judgments.)

5.05 Testimonials

Psychologists do not solicit testimonials from current therapy clients/patients or other persons who because of their particular circumstances are vulnerable to undue influence.

5.06 In-Person Solicitation

Psychologists do not engage, directly or through agents, in uninvited in-person solicitation of business from actual or potential therapy clients/patients or other persons who because of their particular circumstances are vulnerable to undue influence. However, this prohibition does not preclude (1) attempting to implement appropriate collateral contacts for the purpose of benefiting an already engaged therapy client/patient or (2) providing disaster or community outreach services.

6. Record Keeping and Fees

6.01 Documentation of Professional and Scientific Work and Maintenance of Records

Psychologists create, and to the extent the records are under their control, maintain, disseminate, store, retain, and dispose of records and data relating to their professional and scientific work in order to (1) facilitate provision of services later by them or by other professionals, (2) allow for replication of research design and analyses, (3) meet institutional requirements, (4) ensure accuracy of billing and payments, and (5) ensure compliance with law. (See also Standard 4.01, Maintaining Confidentiality.)

6.02 Maintenance, Dissemination, and Disposal of Confidential Records of Professional and Scientific Work

(a) Psychologists maintain confidentiality in creating, storing, accessing, transferring, and disposing of records under their control, whether these are written, automated, or in any other medium. (See also Standards 4.01, Maintaining Confidentiality, and 6.01, Documentation of Professional and Scientific Work and Maintenance of Records.)

(b) If confidential information concerning recipients of psychological services is entered into databases or systems of records available to persons whose access has not been consented to by the recipient, psychologists use coding or other techniques to avoid the inclusion of personal identifiers.

(c) Psychologists make plans in advance to facilitate the appropriate transfer and to protect the confidentiality of records and data in the event of psychologists' withdrawal from positions or practice. (See also Standards 3.12, Interruption of Psychological Services, and 10.09, Interruption of Therapy.)

6.03 Withholding Records for Nonpayment

Psychologists may not withhold records under their control that are requested and needed for a client' s/patient' s emergency treatment solely because payment has not been received.

6.04 Fees and Financial Arrangements

(a) As early as is feasible in a professional or scientific relationship, psychologists and recipients of psychological services reach an agreement specifying compensation and billing arrangements.

(b) Psychologists' fee practices are consistent with law.

(c) Psychologists do not misrepresent their fees.

(d) If limitations to services can be anticipated because of limitations in financing, this is discussed with the recipient of services as early as is feasible. (See also Standards 10.09, Interruption of Therapy, and 10.10, Terminating Therapy.)

(e) If the recipient of services does not pay for services as agreed, and if psychologists intend to use collection agencies or legal measures to collect the fees, psychologists first inform the person that such measures will be taken and provide that person an opportunity to make prompt payment. (See also Standards 4.05, Disclosures; 6.03, Withholding Records for Nonpayment; and 10.01, Informed Consent to Therapy.)

6.05 Barter With Clients/Patients

Barter is the acceptance of goods, services, or other nonmonetary remuneration from clients/patients in return for psychological services. Psychologists may barter only if (1) it is not clinically contraindicated, and (2) the resulting arrangement is not exploitative. (See also Standards 3.05, Multiple Relationships, and 6.04, Fees and Financial Arrangements.)

6.06 Accuracy in Reports to Payors and Funding Sources

In their reports to payors for services or sources of research funding, psychologists take reasonable steps to ensure the accurate reporting of the nature of the service provided or research conducted, the fees, charges, or payments, and where applicable, the identity of the provider, the findings, and the diagnosis. (See also Standards 4.01, Maintaining Confidentiality; 4.04, Minimizing Intrusions on Privacy; and 4.05, Disclosures.)

6.07 Referrals and Fees

When psychologists pay, receive payment from, or divide fees with another professional, other than in an employer employee relationship, the payment to each is based on the services provided (clinical, consultative, administrative, or other) and is not based on the referral itself. (See also Standard 3.09, Cooperation With Other Professionals.)

7. Education and Training

7.01 Design of Education and Training Programs

Psychologists responsible for education and training programs take reasonable steps to ensure that the programs are designed to provide the appropriate knowledge and proper experiences, and to meet the requirements for licensure, certification, or other goals for which claims are made by the program. (See also Standard 5.03, Descriptions of Workshops and Non–Degree-Granting Educational Programs.)

7.02 Descriptions of Education and Training Programs

Psychologists responsible for education and training programs take reasonable steps to ensure that there is a current and accurate description of the program content (including participation in required course- or program-related counseling, psychotherapy, experiential groups, consulting projects, or community service), training goals and objectives, stipends and benefits, and requirements that must be met for satisfactory completion of the program. This information must be made readily available to all interested parties.

7.03 Accuracy in Teaching

(a) Psychologists take reasonable steps to ensure that course syllabi are accurate regarding the subject matter to be covered, bases for evaluating progress, and the nature of course experiences. This standard does not preclude an instructor from modifying course content or requirements when the instructor considers it pedagogically necessary or desirable, so long as students are made aware of these modifications in a manner that enables them to fulfill course requirements. (See also Standard 5.01, Avoidance of False or Deceptive Statements.)

(b) When engaged in teaching or training, psychologists present psychological information accurately. (See also Standard 2.03, Maintaining Competence.)

7.04 Student Disclosure of Personal Information

Psychologists do not require students or supervisees to disclose personal information in course- or program-related activities, either orally or in writing, regarding sexual history, history of abuse and neglect, psychological treatment, and relationships with parents, peers, and spouses or significant others except if (1) the program or training facility has clearly identified this requirement in its admissions and program materials or (2) the information is necessary to evaluate or obtain assistance for students whose personal problems could reasonably be judged to be preventing them from performing their training- or professionally related activities in a competent manner or posing a threat to the students or others.

7.05 Mandatory Individual or Group Therapy

(a) When individual or group therapy is a program or course requirement, psychologists responsible for that program allow students in undergraduate and graduate programs the option of selecting such therapy from practitioners unaffiliated with the program. (See also Standard 7.02, Descriptions of Education and Training Programs.)

(b) Faculty who are or are likely to be responsible for evaluating students' academic performance do not themselves provide that therapy. (See also Standard 3.05, Multiple Relationships.)

7.06 Assessing Student and Supervisee Performance

(a) In academic and supervisory relationships, psychologists establish a timely and specific process for providing feedback to students and supervisees. Information regarding the process is provided to the student at the beginning of supervision.

(b) Psychologists evaluate students and supervisees on the basis of their actual performance on relevant and established program requirements.

7.07 Sexual Relationships With Students and Supervisees

Psychologists do not engage in sexual relationships with students or supervisees who are in their department, agency, or training center or over whom psychologists have or are likely to have evaluative authority. (See also Standard 3.05, Multiple Relationships.)

8. Research and Publication

8.01 Institutional Approval

When institutional approval is required, psychologists provide accurate information about their research proposals and obtain approval prior to conducting the research. They conduct the research in accordance with the approved research protocol.

8.02 Informed Consent to Research

(a) When obtaining informed consent as required in Standard 3.10, Informed Consent, psychologists inform participants about (1) the purpose of the research, expected duration, and procedures; (2) their right to decline to participate and to withdraw from the research once participation has begun; (3) the foreseeable consequences of declining or withdrawing; (4) reasonably foreseeable factors that may be expected to influence their willingness to participate such as potential risks, discomfort, or adverse effects; (5) any prospective research benefits; (6) limits of confidentiality; (7) incentives for participation; and (8) whom to contact for questions about the research and research participants' rights. They provide opportunity for the prospective participants to ask questions and receive answers. (See also Standards 8.03, Informed Consent for Recording Voices and Images in Research; 8.05, Dispensing With Informed Consent for Research; and 8.07, Deception in Research.)

(b) Psychologists conducting intervention research involving the use of experimental treatments clarify to participants at the outset of the research (1) the experimental nature of the treatment; (2) the services that will or will not be available to the control group(s) if appropriate; (3) the means by which assignment to treatment and control groups will be made; (4) available treatment alternatives if an individual does not wish to participate in the research or wishes to withdraw once a study has begun; and (5) compensation for or monetary costs of participating including, if appropriate, whether reimbursement from the participant or a third-party payor will be sought. (See also Standard 8.02a, Informed Consent to Research.)

8.03 Informed Consent for Recording Voices and Images in Research

Psychologists obtain informed consent from research participants prior to recording their voices or images for data collection unless (1) the research consists solely of naturalistic observations in public places, and it is not anticipated that the recording will be used in a manner that could cause personal identification or harm, or (2) the research design includes deception, and consent for the use of the recording is obtained during debriefing. (See also Standard 8.07, Deception in Research.)

8.04 Client/Patient, Student, and Subordinate Research Participants

(a) When psychologists conduct research with clients/patients, students, or subordinates as participants, psychologists take steps to protect the prospective participants from adverse consequences of declining or withdrawing from participation.

(b) When research participation is a course requirement or an opportunity for extra credit, the prospective participant is given the choice of equitable alternative activities.

8.05 Dispensing With Informed Consent for Research

Psychologists may dispense with informed consent only (1) where research would not reasonably be assumed to create distress or harm and involves (a) the study of normal educational practices, curricula, or classroom management methods conducted in educational settings; (b) only anonymous questionnaires, naturalistic observations, or archival research for which disclosure of responses would not place participants at risk of criminal or civil liability or damage their financial standing, employability, or reputation, and confidentiality is protected; or (c) the study of factors related to job or organization effectiveness conducted in organizational settings for which there is no risk to participants' employability, and confidentiality is protected or (2) where otherwise permitted by law or federal or institutional regulations.

8.06 Offering Inducements for Research Participation

(a) Psychologists make reasonable efforts to avoid offering excessive or inappropriate financial or other inducements for research participation when such inducements are likely to coerce participation.

(b) When offering professional services as an inducement for research participation, psychologists clarify the nature of the services, as well as the risks, obligations, and limitations. (See also Standard 6.05, Barter With Clients/Patients.)

8.07 Deception in Research

(a) Psychologists do not conduct a study involving deception unless they have determined that the use of deceptive techniques is justified by the study's significant prospective scientific, educational, or applied value and that effective nondeceptive alternative procedures are not feasible.

(b) Psychologists do not deceive prospective participants about research that is reasonably expected to cause physical pain or severe emotional distress.

(c) Psychologists explain any deception that is an integral feature of the design and conduct of an experiment to participants as early as is feasible, preferably at the conclusion of their participation, but no later than at the conclusion of the data collection, and permit participants to withdraw their data. (See also Standard 8.08, Debriefing.)

8.08 Debriefing

(a) Psychologists provide a prompt opportunity for participants to obtain appropriate information about the nature, results, and conclusions of the research, and they take reasonable steps to correct any misconceptions that participants may have of which the psychologists are aware.

(b) If scientific or humane values justify delaying or withholding this information, psychologists take reasonable measures to reduce the risk of harm.

(c) When psychologists become aware that research procedures have harmed a participant, they take reasonable steps to minimize the harm.

8.09 Humane Care and Use of Animals in Research

(a) Psychologists acquire, care for, use, and dispose of animals in compliance with current federal, state, and local laws and regulations, and with professional standards.

(b) Psychologists trained in research methods and experienced in the care of laboratory animals supervise all procedures involving animals and are responsible for ensuring appropriate consideration of their comfort, health, and humane treatment.

(c) Psychologists ensure that all individuals under their supervision who are using animals have received instruction in research methods and in the care, maintenance, and handling of the species being used, to the extent appropriate to their role. (See also Standard 2.05, Delegation of Work to Others.)

(d) Psychologists make reasonable efforts to minimize the discomfort, infection, illness, and pain of animal subjects.

(e) Psychologists use a procedure subjecting animals to pain, stress, or privation only when an alternative procedure is unavailable and the goal is justified by its prospective scientific, educational, or applied value.

(f) Psychologists perform surgical procedures under appropriate anesthesia and follow techniques to avoid infection and minimize pain during and after surgery.

(g) When it is appropriate that an animal's life be terminated, psychologists proceed rapidly, with an effort to minimize pain and in accordance with accepted procedures.

8.10 Reporting Research Results

(a) Psychologists do not fabricate data. (See also Standard 5.01a, Avoidance of False or Deceptive Statements.)

(b) If psychologists discover significant errors in their published data, they take reasonable steps to correct such errors in a correction, retraction, erratum, or other appropriate publication means.

8.11 Plagiarism

Psychologists do not present portions of another' s work or data as their own, even if the other work or data source is cited occasionally.

8.12 Publication Credit

(a) Psychologists take responsibility and credit, including authorship credit, only for work they have actually performed or to which they have substantially contributed. (See also Standard 8.12b, Publication Credit.)

(b) Principal authorship and other publication credits accurately reflect the relative scientific or professional contributions of the individuals involved, regardless of their relative status. Mere possession of an institutional position, such as department chair, does not justify authorship credit. Minor contributions to the research or to the writing for publications are acknowledged appropriately, such as in footnotes or in an introductory statement.

(c) Except under exceptional circumstances, a student is listed as principal author on any multiple-authored article that is substantially based on the student's doctoral dissertation. Faculty advisors discuss publication credit with students as early as feasible and throughout the research and publication process as appropriate. (See also Standard 8.12b, Publication Credit.)

8.13 Duplicate Publication of Data

Psychologists do not publish, as original data, data that have been previously published. This does not preclude republishing data when they are accompanied by proper acknowledgment.

8.14 Sharing Research Data for Verification

(a) After research results are published, psychologists do not withhold the data on which their conclusions are based from other competent professionals who seek to verify the substantive claims through reanalysis and who intend to use such data only for that purpose, provided that the confidentiality of the participants can be protected and unless legal rights concerning proprietary data preclude their release. This does not preclude psychologists from requiring that such individuals or groups be responsible for costs associated with the provision of such information.

(b) Psychologists who request data from other psychologists to verify the substantive claims through reanalysis may use shared data only for the declared purpose. Requesting psychologists obtain prior written agreement for all other uses of the data.

8.15 Reviewers

Psychologists who review material submitted for presentation, publication, grant, or research proposal review respect the confidentiality of and the proprietary rights in such information of those who submitted it.

9. Assessment

9.01 Bases for Assessments

(a) Psychologists base the opinions contained in their recommendations, reports, and diagnostic or evaluative statements, including forensic testimony, on information and techniques sufficient to substantiate their findings. (See also Standard 2.04, Bases for Scientific and Professional Judgments.)

(b) Except as noted in 9.01c, psychologists provide opinions of the psychological characteristics of individuals only after they have conducted an examination of the individuals adequate to support their statements or conclusions. When, despite reasonable efforts, such an examination is not practical, psychologists document the efforts they made and the result of those efforts, clarify the probable impact of their limited information on the reliability and validity of their opinions, and appropriately limit the nature and extent of their conclusions or recommendations. (See also Standards 2.01, Boundaries of Competence, and 9.06, Interpreting Assessment Results.)

(c) When psychologists conduct a record review or provide consultation or supervision and an individual examination is not warranted or necessary for the opinion, psychologists explain this and the sources of information on which they based their conclusions and recommendations.

9.02 Use of Assessments

(a) Psychologists administer, adapt, score, interpret, or use assessment techniques, interviews, tests, or instruments in a manner and for purposes that are appropriate in light of the research on or evidence of the usefulness and proper application of the techniques.

(b) Psychologists use assessment instruments whose validity and reliability have been established for use with members of the population tested. When such validity or reliability has not been established, psychologists describe the strengths and limitations of test results and interpretation.

(c) Psychologists use assessment methods that are appropriate to an individual's language preference and competence, unless the use of an alternative language is relevant to the assessment issues.

9.03 Informed Consent in Assessments

(a) Psychologists obtain informed consent for assessments, evaluations, or diagnostic services, as described in Standard 3.10, Informed Consent, except when (1) testing is mandated by law or governmental regulations; (2) informed consent is implied because testing is conducted as a routine educational, institutional, or organizational activity (e.g., when participants voluntarily agree to assessment when applying for a job); or (3) one purpose of the testing is to evaluate decisional capacity. Informed consent includes an explanation of the nature and purpose of the assessment, fees, involvement of third parties, and limits of confidentiality and sufficient opportunity for the client/patient to ask questions and receive answers.

(b) Psychologists inform persons with questionable capacity to consent or for whom testing is mandated by law or governmental regulations about the nature and purpose of the proposed assessment services, using language that is reasonably understandable to the person being assessed.

(c) Psychologists using the services of an interpreter obtain informed consent from the client/patient to use that interpreter, ensure that confidentiality of test results and test security are maintained, and include in their recommendations, reports, and diagnostic or evaluative statements, including forensic testimony, discussion of any limitations on the data obtained. (See also Standards 2.05, Delegation of Work to Others; 4.01, Maintaining Confidentiality; 9.01, Bases for Assessments; 9.06, Interpreting Assessment Results; and 9.07, Assessment by Unqualified Persons.)

9.04 Release of Test Data

(a) The term *test data* refers to raw and scaled scores, client/patient responses to test questions or stimuli, and psychologists' notes and recordings concerning client/patient statements and behavior during an examination. Those portions of test materials that include client/patient responses are included in the definition of *test data*. Pursuant to a client/patient release, psychologists provide test data to the client/patient or other persons identified in the release. Psychologists may refrain from releasing test data to protect a client/patient or others from substantial harm or misuse or misrepresentation of the data or the test, recognizing that in many instances release of confidential information under these circumstances is regulated by law. (See also Standard 9.11, Maintaining Test Security.)

(b) In the absence of a client/patient release, psychologists provide test data only as required by law or court order.

9.05 Test Construction

Psychologists who develop tests and other assessment techniques use appropriate psychometric procedures and current scientific or professional knowledge for test design, standardization, validation, reduction or elimination of bias, and recommendations for use.

9.06 Interpreting Assessment Results

When interpreting assessment results, including automated interpretations, psychologists take into account the purpose of the assessment as well as the various test factors, test-taking abilities, and other characteristics of the person being assessed, such as situational, personal, linguistic, and cultural differences, that might affect psychologists' judgments or reduce the accuracy of their interpretations. They indicate any significant limitations of their interpretations. (See also Standards 2.01b and c, Boundaries of Competence, and 3.01, Unfair Discrimination.)

9.07 Assessment by Unqualified Persons

Psychologists do not promote the use of psychological assessment techniques by unqualified persons, except when such use is conducted for training purposes with appropriate supervision. (See also Standard 2.05, Delegation of Work to Others.)

9.08 Obsolete Tests and Outdated Test Results

(a) Psychologists do not base their assessment or intervention decisions or recommendations on data or test results that are outdated for the current purpose.

(b) Psychologists do not base such decisions or recommendations on tests and measures that are obsolete and not useful for the current purpose.

9.09 Test Scoring and Interpretation Services

(a) Psychologists who offer assessment or scoring services to other professionals accurately describe the purpose, norms, validity, reliability, and applications of the procedures and any special qualifications applicable to their use.

(b) Psychologists select scoring and interpretation services (including automated services) on the basis of evidence of the validity of the program and procedures as well as on other appropriate considerations. (See also Standard 2.01b and c, Boundaries of Competence.)

(c) Psychologists retain responsibility for the appropriate application, interpretation, and use of assessment instruments, whether they score and interpret such tests themselves or use automated or other services.

9.10 Explaining Assessment Results

Regardless of whether the scoring and interpretation are done by psychologists, by employees or assistants, or by automated or other outside services, psychologists take reasonable steps to ensure that explanations of results are given to the individual or designated representative unless the nature of the relationship precludes provision of an explanation of results (such as in some organizational consulting, preemployment or security screenings, and forensic evaluations), and this fact has been clearly explained to the person being assessed in advance.

9.11 Maintaining Test Security

The term *test materials* refers to manuals, instruments, protocols, and test questions or stimuli and does not include *test data* as defined in Standard 9.04, Release of Test Data. Psychologists make reasonable efforts to maintain the integrity and security of test materials and other assessment techniques consistent with law and contractual obligations, and in a manner that permits adherence to this Ethics Code.

10. Therapy

10.01 Informed Consent to Therapy

(a) When obtaining informed consent to therapy as required in Standard 3.10, Informed Consent, psychologists inform clients/patients as early as is feasible in the therapeutic relationship about the nature and anticipated course of therapy, fees, involvement of third parties, and limits of confidentiality and provide sufficient opportunity for the client/patient to ask questions and receive answers. (See also Standards 4.02, Discussing the Limits of Confidentiality, and 6.04, Fees and Financial Arrangements.)

(b) When obtaining informed consent for treatment for which generally recognized techniques and procedures have not been established, psychologists inform their clients/patients of the developing nature of the treatment, the potential risks involved, alternative treatments that may be available, and the voluntary nature of their participation. (See also Standards 2.01e, Boundaries of Competence, and 3.10, Informed Consent.)

(c) When the therapist is a trainee and the legal responsibility for the treatment provided resides with the supervisor, the client/patient, as part of the informed consent procedure, is informed that the therapist is in training and is being supervised and is given the name of the supervisor.

10.02 Therapy Involving Couples or Families

(a) When psychologists agree to provide services to several persons who have a relationship (such as spouses, significant others, or parents and children), they take reasonable steps to clarify at the outset (1) which of the individuals are clients/patients and (2) the relationship the psychologist will have with each person. This clarification includes the psychologist's role and the probable uses of the services provided or the information obtained. (See also Standard 4.02, Discussing the Limits of Confidentiality.)

(b) If it becomes apparent that psychologists may be called on to perform potentially conflicting roles (such as family therapist and then witness for one party in divorce proceedings), psychologists take reasonable steps to clarify and modify, or withdraw from, roles appropriately. (See also Standard 3.05c, Multiple Relationships.)

10.03 Group Therapy
When psychologists provide services to several persons in a group setting, they describe at the outset the roles and responsibilities of all parties and the limits of confidentiality.

10.04 Providing Therapy to Those Served by Others
In deciding whether to offer or provide services to those already receiving mental health services elsewhere, psychologists carefully consider the treatment issues and the potential client's/patient's welfare. Psychologists discuss these issues with the client/patient or another legally authorized person on behalf of the client/patient in order to minimize the risk of confusion and conflict, consult with the other service providers when appropriate, and proceed with caution and sensitivity to the therapeutic issues.

10.05 Sexual Intimacies With Current Therapy Clients/Patients
Psychologists do not engage in sexual intimacies with current therapy clients/patients.

10.06 Sexual Intimacies With Relatives or Significant Others of Current Therapy Clients/Patients
Psychologists do not engage in sexual intimacies with individuals they know to be close relatives, guardians, or significant others of current clients/patients. Psychologists do not terminate therapy to circumvent this standard.

10.07 Therapy With Former Sexual Partners
Psychologists do not accept as therapy clients/patients persons with whom they have engaged in sexual intimacies.

10.08 Sexual Intimacies With Former Therapy Clients/Patients
(a) Psychologists do not engage in sexual intimacies with former clients/patients for at least two years after cessation or termination of therapy.

(b) Psychologists do not engage in sexual intimacies with former clients/patients even after a two-year interval except in the most unusual circumstances. Psychologists who engage in such activity after the two years following cessation or termination of therapy and of having no sexual contact with the former client/patient bear the burden of demonstrating that there has been no exploitation, in light of all relevant factors, including (1) the amount of time that has passed since therapy terminated; (2) the nature, duration, and intensity of the therapy; (3) the circumstances of termination; (4) the client's/patient's personal history; (5) the client's/patient's current mental status; (6) the likelihood of adverse impact on the client/patient; and (7) any statements or actions made by the therapist during the course of therapy suggesting or inviting the possibility of a posttermination sexual or romantic relationship with the client/patient. (See also Standard 3.05, Multiple Relationships.)

10.09 Interruption of Therapy

When entering into employment or contractual relationships, psychologists make reasonable efforts to provide for orderly and appropriate resolution of responsibility for client/patient care in the event that the employment or contractual relationship ends, with paramount consideration given to the welfare of the client/patient. (See also Standard 3.12, Interruption of Psychological Services.)

10.10 Terminating Therapy

(a) Psychologists terminate therapy when it becomes reasonably clear that the client/patient no longer needs the service, is not likely to benefit, or is being harmed by continued service.

(b) Psychologists may terminate therapy when threatened or otherwise endangered by the client/patient or another person with whom the client/patient has a relationship.

(c) Except where precluded by the actions of clients/patients or third-party payors, prior to termination psychologists provide pretermination counseling and suggest alternative service providers as appropriate.

COMMENTARY: The American Psychological Association's (APA's) *Ethical Principles for Psychologists and Code of Conduct* (APA Ethics Code) is its flagship source of professional guidance and to this day remains its only directly enforceable authority, on the basis of which members can ultimately be expelled for noncompliance. Thus, it is worth noting that the tone of the document is affirming, encouraging, and heuristic as opposed to shrill, chiding, or dismissive; this says a great deal about the profession and its most highly recognizable and well-subscribed, national-level society.

The enforceability of the Ethics Code extends beyond the boundaries of APA in two key aspects. The first of these is the fashion in which licensing boards, courts, state-level societies, and caregiving institutions recognize it as the profession's most authoritative collection of core value statements—and they are certainly encouraged in this regard when it comes to the careful, limiting language that accompanies various secondary "guidelines" promulgated by APA and its internal entities. The second of these is the extent to which the Ethics Code is "incorporated by reference" into codified licensure and certification laws and regulations.

The following references are recommended for those interested in further investigation of the impact of the 2002 Ethics Code, the ways in which it differs significantly from its predecessors, and the extent to which critics and proponents continue to identify growing edges to this guidance and their implications.

Erard, R. E. (2004). Release of test data under the 2002 Ethics Code and the HIPAA privacy rule: A raw deal or just a half-baked idea? *Journal of Personality Assessment, 82*, 23–30. http://dx.doi.org/10.1207/s15327752jpa8201_4

Knapp, S., & VandeCreek, L. (2003). An overview of the major changes in the 2002 APA Ethics Code. *Professional Psychology: Research and Practice, 34*, 301–308. http://dx.doi.org/10.1037/0735-7028.34.3.301

Knapp, S., & VandeCreek, L. (2004). A principle-based analysis of the 2002 American Psychological Association Ethics Code. *Psychotherapy: Theory, Research, Practice, Training, 41*, 247–254. http://dx.doi.org/10.1037/0033-3204.41.3.247

Lees-Haley, P. R., Courtney, J. C., & Dinkins, J. P. (2005). Revisiting the need for reform in the disclosure of tests and raw test data to the courts: The 2002 APA Ethics Code has not solved our dilemma. *Journal of Forensic Psychology Practice, 5*, 71–81. http://dx.doi.org/10.1300/J158v05n02_05

Report of the Ethics Committee, 2015. (2016). *American Psychologist, 71*, 427–436.

1.3. Amendments to the 2002 "Ethical Principles of Psychologists and Code of Conduct" in 2010 and 2016

American Psychological Association

2010 AMENDMENTS

The following amendments to the 2002 "Ethical Principles of Psychologists and Code of Conduct" (the Ethics Code; American Psychological Association, 2002) were adopted by the APA Council of Representatives at its February 2010 meeting. The changes involve the last two sentences of the final paragraph of the Introduction and Applicability section and Ethical Standards 1.02 and 1.03. The amendments became effective June 1, 2010. A history of these amendments to the Ethics Code is provided in the "Report of the Ethics Committee, 2009" in this issue of the American Psychologist (American Psychological Association, Ethics Committee, 2010).

Following are a clean version of the revisions and a version indicating changes from the 2002 language (inserted text is underlined; deleted text is crossed out). The full Ethics Code with the amendments is available at http://www.apa.org/ethics/code/index.aspx; a print copy may be obtained from the APA Ethics Office.

FINAL AMENDMENTS

Introduction and Applicability

If psychologists' ethical responsibilities conflict with law, regulations, or other governing legal authority, psychologists make known their commitment to this Ethics Code and take steps to resolve the conflict in a responsible manner in keeping with basic principles of human rights.

1.02 Conflicts Between Ethics and Law, Regulations, or Other Governing Legal Authority

If psychologists' ethical responsibilities conflict with law, regulations, or other governing legal authority, psychologists clarify the nature of the conflict, make known their commitment to the Ethics Code, and take reasonable steps to resolve the conflict consistent with the General Principles and Ethical Standards

38

of the Ethics Code. Under no circumstances may this standard be used to justify or defend violating human rights.

1.03 Conflicts Between Ethics and Organizational Demands

If the demands of an organization with which psychologists are affiliated or for whom they are working are in conflict with this Ethics Code, psychologists clarify the nature of the conflict, make known their commitment to the Ethics Code, and take reasonable steps to resolve the conflict consistent with the General Principles and Ethical Standards of the Ethics Code. Under no circumstances may this standard be used to justify or defend violating human rights.

ORIGINAL LANGUAGE WITH CHANGES MARKED

Introduction and Applicability

If psychologists' ethical responsibilities conflict with law, regulations, or other governing legal authority, psychologists make known their commitment to this Ethics Code and take steps to resolve the conflict in a responsible manner. ~~If the conflict is unresolvable via such means, psychologists may adhere to the requirements of the law, regulations, or other governing authority~~ in keeping with basic principles of human rights.

1.02 Conflicts Between Ethics and Law, Regulations, or Other Governing Legal Authority

If psychologists' ethical responsibilities conflict with law, regulations, or other governing legal authority, psychologists <u>clarify the nature of the conflict,</u> make known their commitment to the Ethics Code, and take <u>reasonable</u> steps to resolve the conflict <u>consistent with the General Principles and Ethical Standards of the Ethics Code</u>. ~~If the conflict is unresolvable via such means, psychologists may adhere to the requirements of the law, regulations, or other governing legal authority.~~ <u>Under no circumstances may this standard be used to justify or defend violating human rights.</u>

1.03 Conflicts Between Ethics and Organizational Demands

If the demands of an organization with which psychologists are affiliated or for whom they are working <u>are in</u> conflict with this Ethics Code, psychologists clarify the nature of the conflict, make known their commitment to the Ethics Code, and ~~to the extent feasible, resolve the conflict in a way that permits adherence to the Ethics Code.~~ <u>take reasonable steps to resolve the conflict consistent with the General Principles and Ethical Standards of the Ethics Code. Under no circumstances may this standard be used to justify or defend violating human rights.</u>

REFERENCES

American Psychological Association. (2002). Ethical principles of psychologists and code of conduct. *American Psychologist, 57,* 1060–1073.
American Psychological Association, Ethics Committee. (2010). Report of the Ethics Committee, 2009. *American Psychologist, 65,* 483–492.

2016 AMENDMENT

3.04 Avoiding Harm

(a) Psychologists take reasonable steps to avoid harming their clients/patients, students, supervisees, research participants, organizational clients, and others with whom they work, and to minimize harm where it is foreseeable and unavoidable.

(b) Psychologists do not participate in, facilitate, assist, or otherwise engage in torture, defined as any act by which severe pain or suffering, whether physical or mental, is intentionally inflicted on a person, or in any other cruel, inhuman, or degrading behavior that violates 3.04(a).

1.4. Examining the Personal–Professional Distinction: Ethics Codes and the Difficulty of Drawing a Boundary

Randolph B. Pipes, Jaymee E. Holstein, and Maria G. Aguirre

. . .

GENESIS OF THE BOUNDARY

How has there come to be, expressed in so many ways, including the APA Ethics Code, a boundary between the personal and the professional? Does it make sense to talk about such a boundary? The relationship between the individual and the group (often society) was of interest to the Greek Hellenic philosophers and extends through the Age of Enlightenment with political philosophers such as Hobbes, Locke, and Rousseau. Discussion of related issues continues through the present era, framed in a variety of ways including (but certainly not limited to) individualism versus collectivism (e.g., Oyserman, Coon, & Kemmelmeier, 2002; Sampson, 2000), the self (definitions and threats to identity in the postmodern era; e.g., Gergen, 1991; Smith, 1994), and broad sociological discourses on individualism and civic life in the United States (Bellah, Madsen, Sullivan, Swidler, & Tipton, 1985; Putnam, 2000).

This distinction between the personal and the professional (and the related distinction between the private and the public) is rooted deeply in cultural values. Particularly in United States culture (to the extent one can talk about one U.S. culture), there is enduring emphasis on one's right to a personal life little constrained by other individuals, organizations, or government. Justice William O. Douglas expressed a part of this philosophy when he said, "The right to be let alone is indeed the beginning of all freedom." Similarly, one of the popular mantras of the 1960s was "do your own thing," a paean to individuality and to one's right to live a life unfettered by the expectations or control of others. In the legal arena, even such fundamental rights as freedom of the press may be substantially limited when a newspaper criticizes a person deemed to be a private individual as opposed to a public figure (for related case law, see *Franklin Prescriptions, Inc. v. New York Times Co.*, 2003). In general, numerous amendments to the United States Constitution, including but not limited to the Bill of Rights, stand as a bulwark against capricious government

From "Examining the Personal–Professional Distinction: Ethics Codes and the Difficulty of Drawing a Boundary," by R. B. Pipes, J. E. Holstein, and M. G. Aguirre, 2005, *American Psychologist, 60*, pp. 325–334. Copyright 2005 by the American Psychological Association.

activity and in general help protect minority viewpoints, however unpopular or out of fashion. Even psychologists advocating what many other psychologists might call "snake oil" treatments may find protection under the First Amendment (Kennedy, Mercer, Mohr, & Huffine, 2002). Within the profession of psychology, the frequency with which psychologists invoke the broad, culturally constructed ethical principle of autonomy and the related concept of informed consent is further evidence of the influence, value, and expression of free choice for the individual whenever possible. In turn, in their purely private lives, psychologists could be expected to steadfastly guard their own free choices and freedom of expression.

In addition to the political and constitutional roots that helped develop the construct of the personal–professional boundary, the philosophical and psychological notion of the autonomous self, existing apart from the group, also helps underpin the distinction. In this view, individuals are capable of functionally separating themselves and their behavior from the groups (including professions) in which they are embedded. Both what the individual is capable of doing in terms of separation as well as the individual's responsibility to the group becomes of interest. Furthermore, role theory, which has a long history in the social sciences (e.g., Getzels & Guba, 1954), assumes that individuals can carry out multiple, although sometimes conflicting, roles. Thus, the construct of roles allows one set of obligations or activities to be defined and then contrasted with a different set of obligations or activities. Taken together, the idea of the autonomous self and the idea of roles, when combined with the political, philosophical, and constitutional issues, allow us to talk about the boundary between the personal and the professional.

. . .

WHAT IS PERSONAL? WHAT IS PROFESSIONAL?

The 1992 APA Ethics Code was apparently the first APA Code to draw a distinction between the personal and the professional behavior of psychologists in terms of the applicability of the Code. The Introduction section of this Code states, "These work-related activities can be distinguished from the purely private conduct of a psychologist, which *ordinarily* [italics added] is not within the purview of the Ethics Code" (APA, 1992, p. 1598).

Fisher and Younggren (1997) noted that the issue of whether particularly egregious behavior outside one's role as a psychologist should fall under the purview of the Code was a subject for discussion in future revisions of the Code (for a discussion of changes reflected in the 2002 APA Code, see Fisher, 2003; Knapp & VandeCreek, 2003a, 2003b). In fact, the limitation of the Code's applicability to professional (as opposed to personal) behavior actually appears to have been strengthened in the new (2002) Ethics Code. As noted above, the 2002 APA Code says, "These activities shall be distinguished from the purely private conduct of psychologists, which *is not* [italics added] within the purview of the Ethics Code" (p. 1061). Despite the clear statement about the purview of the Code, Section 2.06 (Personal Problems and Conflicts) suggests that psychologists' personal behaviors might be at least partially at issue when considering whether the Code has been violated. Standard 3.06 (Conflict of Interest) also brings into focus the potential intermingling of personal activity and professional obligations. The distinction between the personal and the professional is made difficult when the Code both places personal behavior off the table for consideration yet recognizes that personal problems, which may at times be evidenced primarily in nonwork-related activities, are likely correlates of poor performance in the work setting. The distinction between the personal and the professional has been implicitly criticized by Payton (1994), who noted the following:

> The distinction [between personal and professional behavior] provokes rethinking of my role. Until now, I have always considered myself a psychologist regardless of my job title. Social acquaintances view me as such. Are there any psychologists who have not been greeted with a "Oh, you can read my mind," when introduced as a psychologist? The new code [i.e., the 1992 Code] frees me to leave my professional identity at the office at the close of business. (p. 319)

Of particular note in Payton's position is the emphasis on the perception of others. From this standpoint, such perception is an important criterion in determining whether psychologists can in fact, in Payton's words, "leave . . . [their] professional identity at the office at the close of business" (p. 319).

In their book on the 1992 Code, Canter, Bennett, Jones, and Nagy (1994) gave the example (still relevant for the 2002 Code) of the psychologist who sits on a library board and makes statements about the effects of certain kinds of books on children. Is such behavior subject to the Ethics Code? On the one hand, the psychologist may argue that she volunteered to be on the board as a private citizen and that as a member of the board she is entitled to express opinions about children's books. On the other hand, an observer might argue that the individuals who made the board appointment were likely aware that the individual was, in fact, a psychologist. Such an observer might also argue that it is a matter of common sense to link the appointment, the role the psychologist plays as a university professor with, for example, a specialty in child psychology, and the opinions being expressed by the psychologist.

Psychologists who substantially quote psychological literature and freely comment on it in public are arguably engaging in activity that is a part of their "scientific, educational, or professional roles as psychologists," even if they do not specifically identify themselves as psychologists (APA, 2002, p. 1061). It is interesting to note that the Canadian Code of Ethics for Psychologists (Canadian Psychological Association, 2000), the Principles of Medical Ethics With Annotations Especially Applicable to Psychiatry (American Psychiatric Association, 2001), and the ethics code of the American Counseling Association (1995) each contain a section that is quite applicable here. Each of these codes notes that professionals have an affirmative duty to indicate when they are speaking as a matter of personal opinion as opposed to speaking as experts.

This distinction between speaking as a matter of personal expression versus speaking as a representative of a profession or an institution is addressed by the American Association of University Professors (1940) Statement of Principles on Academic Freedom and Tenure:

> College and university teachers are citizens, members of a learned profession, and officers of an educational institution. When they speak or write as citizens, they should be free from institutional censorship or discipline, but their special position in the community imposes special obligations. As scholars and educational officers, they should remember that the public may judge their profession and their institution by their utterances. Hence they should at all times be accurate, should exercise appropriate restraint, should show respect for the opinions of others, and should make every effort to indicate that they are not speaking for the institution. (Section: Academic Freedom [c])

Even though the APA Ethics Code does not contain a standard requiring that psychologists clarify statements that might be ambiguous along the dimension of speaking privately versus speaking as a professional, such a standard could indeed help prevent misunderstanding. Obviously, claims by psychologists that they are acting as private citizens, in the face of clear and convincing evidence that they were functioning within a professional role, are fraudulent.

Although the purpose of this article is not to suggest new APA ethical standards, we do believe that in making future revisions of the APA Ethics Code, psychologists should consider slightly altering current standards in the area of public statements, so as to provide additional guidance to psychologists seeking to make clear that they are speaking for themselves in a given arena. In turn, such a standard, when applied to a particular situation, would directly address the question of the distinction between the personal and the professional. Not all difficulties in distinguishing between personal and professional behavior can be solved by a statement; nonetheless, in our view, a standard outlining one's obligation to clarify roles would make a reasonable addition to the Ethics Code. Perhaps it would be helpful to point out here that one of the purposes of the APA Code is to set forth enforceable standards, but another purpose is to educate psychologists. By outlining a standard in the area of public statements, the Code would be alerting psychologists to the importance of being clear about one's role (speaking as a professional vs. speaking personally).

Consider two more examples that draw further attention to the issue of the personal and the professional:

> *One night, while drinking with friends at a bar, Dr. Rodriguez, a clinical psychologist, sees two of his long-term clients sitting just a few feet away. Even though he knows his clients are there, he becomes very intoxicated, to the point of slurred speech.* Is his behavior subject to the Ethics Code? Would it make any difference if one of his clients had a problem with alcohol abuse or if Dr. Rodriguez ran the local alcohol treatment facility? What if the same incident was repeated a number of times?

> *Dr. Green, a psychologist who is a statistician, is a player–manager for a softball team and she has invited her doctoral student, Lois, to play on the team with her. On the ball field, and in front of the other players, Dr. Green repeatedly belittles her student's athletic skills. She also frequently makes substitutions in a way that limits Lois's playing time. In the role of doctoral advisor, Dr. Green is supportive and fair.* Is Dr. Green's behavior on the softball field subject to the Code?

Explicit guidance concerning such behavior is not in the Code, although Standard 3.04 (APA, 2002) does admonish psychologists to avoid harming students and others with whom they work. It is unlikely that any ethics code will be able to answer clearly questions about all of the many complicated situations that could conceivably arise in distinguishing between the personal and the professional. Nonetheless, later in this article, we turn to the problem of determining the tilt (toward the personal or toward the professional) a behavior takes as a function of several variables, including some raised by the examples just cited.

Perhaps as much as any area of psychology, feminist theory and practice (e.g., Worell & Johnson, 1997) raises the question of the personal versus the professional life of the psychologist. One of the mantras of feminist psychology has been the belief that "the personal is political." . . . In turn, political issues (e.g., social justice) are seen as part and parcel of the psychological enterprise. One need only pick up any of several books on feminist ethics (e.g., Brabeck, 2000; Rave & Larsen, 1995) to see that personal values and personal identity are inextricably interwoven with the idea of professional values and ethics.

Another example highlighting the ambiguous relationship between the personal and the professional, especially from a feminist perspective,[1] is that of hate speech. Vasquez and de las Fuentes (2000) have discussed the issue of hate speech and the issues involved in balancing the need for autonomy and feminist ethics. They concluded that faculty and student speech codes were needed (and also discussed a number of relevant court cases). As they pointed out, freedom of speech is by no means absolute. At the same time, however, courts have been rather reluctant to endorse speech codes, often finding them too broadly drawn. Although the issue of hate speech on campus is not the same as, for example, hate speech in one's personal life, nonetheless, the issue is raised as to the interaction between one's personal life and one's professional life. If a therapist sees a large caseload of clients who identify their ethnicity as African American, should the profession merely say in essence, "we have nothing to say" if the therapist writes letters to the editor that are racist? Is such (perhaps) personal behavior outside the scope of the APA Ethics Code?

The confusion between the personal and the professional is also indirectly addressed by those writers (e.g., Kitchener, 1996, 1999, 2000; Meara, Schmidt, & Day, 1996) who advocate virtue ethics as an alternative or addendum to principle ethics. Virtue ethics, with its emphasis on, among other things, character, suggests that the kind of person someone is (in some total sense) drives what the person does and how the person thinks in the professional as well as in the personal realm. Hence, individuals who advocate for virtue ethics as an effective tool in thinking about ethical dilemmas, although not necessarily ruling out the distinction between the personal and the professional, certainly add complexity to psychologists' thinking.

---

[1] It is inaccurate to speak of a single feminist position on, for example, ethics or hate speech. As Enns (1993) has pointed out, there are several schools of feminist thought, not to mention individual variation among feminists.

The question of character and fitness for duty has been raised directly in the literature by Johnson and Campbell (2002, 2004) who suggested that training programs and licensure boards should give more attention to these two issues. In their view, there should be more screening along character dimensions (e.g., integrity, prudence, and caring) and fitness (e.g., personality adjustment, psychological health, and use of substances). Although their articles focused on screening, as opposed to discipline, the implication is clear that variables outside one's immediate performance of duties can and should be considered if there is a rational link between a deficiency and one's fitness or capacity to practice psychology. Likewise, training programs often seek out students who possess the ability to be self-reflective. For example, in their predoctoral internship materials, the Ball State University Counseling Center (2004) states the following:

> An important component of our training program is the intersection between the personal and professional. . . . We believe that effectiveness in all aspects of professional functioning is related to one's ability to reflect on oneself, one's interpersonal and personal dynamics and the history from which these dynamics emerge. Thus, professional functioning can be either enhanced or hindered by one's development, or lack thereof, in these essential areas. (¶ 16)

From this perspective, a personal skill, self-reflection, is implicitly a professional skill.

Discussions about virtue ethics, character and fitness requirements for duty, the importance of self-reflection, and the challenges of impairment suggest that psychologists really do in fact want it both ways. We are committed to honoring a separate personal life, yet in our hearts, we really believe that the personal and the professional are often inseparable.

. . .

INTERROGATING THE BOUNDARY

We now pose [a question], and make related comments, which we believe help interrogate this boundary between the personal and the professional. Space does not permit a detailed discussion of these items. What follows is not meant to provide definitive answers but rather is to be thought of as a set of beginning heuristics as we think about this boundary.

. . .

What Might Impact the Tilt a Behavior Takes Toward Either the Personal or the Professional?

Despite our comments above about the importance of focusing on the appropriate integration of the personal and the professional, we understand that psychologists at times may want more clarity about whether a behavior tilts toward the professional or toward the personal. We emphasize that when a behavior is ambiguous enough to be near the personal–professional boundary, we seek to know the tilt the behavior is taking rather than aiming for a categorization. Our overall bias is to help sensitize psychologists to situations in which the welfare of clients, students, research participants, or even the public at large might be at risk. Whether such welfare is at risk is by no means the sole determinant of whether a behavior is to be considered professional. At the same time, we believe that psychologists should proceed with great caution when the behavior under consideration is somewhat personal but poses significant risk of harming or seriously confusing those with whom they work. Such behavior that is repeated or done in a highly public manner bears special scrutiny.

Drawing on the contents of the ethics codes discussed above, the examples cited, and on heuristic guides published on multiple relationships (e.g., Anderson & Kitchener, 1998; Gottlieb, 1993), we suggest a series of questions that might be asked to help determine whether an action is tilting toward the professional: (a) Does the behavior, on its face, seem at least partially professional? (b) Is there a high probability that students, research participants, or clients will be directly, significantly, and negatively affected? (c) Is the action under discussion linked to a role played by psychologists? (d) Has a client, student, or research participant expressed confusion about whether the behavior is personal or professional? (e) Is there a high probability that the action will be viewed or discovered by research participants, students, or clients currently receiving services? (f) Does the action threaten the credibility of the psychologist or the field of psychology? (g) Given the opportunity, did the psychologist fail to clarify that the action was a personal one? (h) Was the behavior repeated, especially if the answer to one of the first four questions was yes?

Although not listed as one of the guiding questions, we would also note that if the behavior seems likely to violate the spirit or letter of either the Ethical Standards, the Ethical Principles, or any APA guidelines, obviously this should be a signal to engage in further thoughtful analysis, even if all other indicators suggest that the behavior is personal. It is important to emphasize that answers to these questions, as noted above, do not provide an automatic categorization. Rather, they provide a framework to help think about the degree to which a behavior might be slipping into the professional realm.

. . .

REFERENCES

American Association of University Professors. (1940). *1940 statement of principles on academic freedom and tenure with 1970 interpretive comments.* Retrieved December 29, 2004, from http://www.aaup.org/statements/Redbook/1940stat.htm

American Counseling Association. (1995). *Code of ethics.* Alexandria, VA: Author.

American Psychiatric Association. (2001). *The principles of medical ethics with annotations specially applicable to psychiatry.* Arlington, VA: Author.

American Psychological Association. (1992). Ethical principles of psychologists and code of conduct. *American Psychologist, 48,* 1597–1611.

American Psychological Association. (2002). Ethical principles of psychologists and code of conduct. *American Psychologist, 57,* 1060–1073.

Anderson, S. K., & Kitchener, K. (1998). Nonsexual posttherapy relationships: A conceptual framework to assess ethical risks. *Professional Psychology: Research and Practice, 29,* 91–99.

Ball State University Counseling Center. (2004). *Training model and underlying values*. Retrieved from http://www.bsu.edu/students/cpsc/training/trgmodelvalues/

Bellah, R. N., Madsen, R., Sullivan, W. M., Swidler, A., & Tipton, S. M. (1985). *Habits of the heart: Individualism and commitment in American life*. Berkeley: University of California Press.

Brabeck, M. (Ed.). (2000). *Practicing feminist ethics in psychology*. Washington, DC: American Psychological Association.

Canadian Psychological Association. (2000). *Canadian code of ethics for psychologists* (3rd ed.). Retrieved from http://www.cpa.ca/ethics2000.html

Canter, M. B., Bennett, B. E., Jones, S. E., & Nagy, T. F. (1994). *Ethics for psychologists: A commentary on the APA ethics code*. Washington, DC: American Psychological Association.

Enns, C. Z. (1993). Twenty years of feminist counseling and therapy: From naming biases to implementing multifaceted practice. *The Counseling Psychologist, 21*, 3–87.

Fisher, C. B. (2003). *Decoding the ethics code: A practical guide for psychologists*. Thousand Oaks, CA: Sage.

Fisher, C. B., & Younggren, J. N. (1997). The value and utility of the 1992 ethics code. *Professional Psychology: Research and Practice, 28*, 582–592.

Franklin Prescriptions, Inc. v. New York Times Co., 267 F. Supp. 2d 425 (E.D. Pa. 2003).

Gergen, K. J. (1991). *The saturated self: Dilemmas of identity in contemporary life*. New York, NY: Basic Books.

Getzels, J. W., & Guba, E. G. (1954). Role, role conflict, effectiveness. *American Sociological Review, 19*, 164–175.

Gottlieb, M. C. (1993). Avoiding exploitive dual relationships: A decision-making model. *Psychotherapy, 30*, 41–48.

Johnson, W. B., & Campbell, C. D. (2002). Character and fitness requirements for professional psychologists. Are there any? *Professional Psychology: Research and Practice, 33*, 46–53.

Johnson, W. B., & Campbell, C. D. (2004). Character and fitness requirements for professional psychologists: Training directors' perspectives. *Professional Psychology: Research and Practice, 35*, 405–411.

Kennedy, S. S., Mercer, J., Mohr, W., & Huffine, C. W. (2002). Snake oil, ethics, and the First Amendment: What's a profession to do? *American Journal of Orthopsychiatry, 72*, 5–15.

Kitchener, K. S. (1996). There is more to ethics than principles. *The Counseling Psychologist, 24*, 92–97.

Kitchener, K. S. (1999). *Foundations of ethical practice, research, and teaching in psychology*. Mahwah, NJ: Erlbaum.

Kitchener, K. S. (2000). Reconceptualizing responsibilities to students: A feminist perspective. In M. M. Brabeck (Ed.), *Practicing feminist ethics in psychology* (pp. 37–54). Washington, DC: American Psychological Association.

Knapp, S., & VandeCreek, L. (2003a). *A guide to the 2002 revision of the American Psychological Association's ethics code*. Sarasota, FL: Professional Resource Press.

Knapp, S., & VandeCreek, L. (2003b). An overview of the major changes in the 2002 APA Ethics Code. *Professional Psychology: Research and Practice, 34*, 301–308.

Meara, N. M., Schmidt, L. D., & Day, J. D. (1996). Principles and virtues: A foundation for ethical decisions, policies, and character. *The Counseling Psychologist, 24*, 4–77.

Oyserman, D., Coon, H. M., & Kemmelmeier, M. (2002). Rethinking individualism and collectivism: Evaluation of theoretical assumptions and meta-analyses. *Psychological Bulletin, 128*, 3–72.

Payton, C. R. (1994). Implications of the 1992 ethics code for diverse groups. *Professional Psychology: Research and Practice, 25*, 317–320.

Putnam, R. (2000). *Bowling alone: The collapse and revival of American community*. New York, NY: Simon & Schuster.

Rave, E. J., & Larsen, C. C. (Eds.). (1995). *Ethical decision making in therapy: Feminist perspectives*. New York, NY: Guilford Press.

Sampson, E. E. (2000). Reinterpreting individualism and collectivism: Their religious roots and monologic versus dialogic person–other relationship. *American Psychologist, 55*, 1425–1432.

Smith, M. B. (1994). Selfhood at risk: Postmodern perils and the perils of postmodernism. *American Psychologist, 49*, 405–411.

Vasquez, M. J. T., & de las Fuentes, C. (2000). Hate speech or freedom of expression? Balancing autonomy and feminist ethics in a pluralistic society. In M. M. Brabeck (Ed.), *Practicing feminist ethics in psychology* (pp. 225–247). Washington, DC: American Psychological Association.

Worell, J., & Johnson, N. G. (Eds.). (1997). *Shaping the future of feminist psychology: Education, research, and practice*. Washington, DC: American Psychological Association.

COMMENTARY: As with any brand of applied science—social or otherwise—psychology as a profession is ultimately conducted by human beings, not machines. In addition, the human beings in question do not reside solely in their offices, treating patients/clients or engaging in research around the clock. This having been acknowledged, to what extent is it fair, desirable, or even feasible to judge the ethical adherence and service capability of a psychologist based on his or her extracurricular activities?

Certain recreational activities, of course, will lead to impairment that cannot help but affect the capacities of a clinician or researcher during normal work hours. Similarly, conviction of serious criminal offenses not only brings the profession into disrepute but can also compromise a psychologist's ability to function effectively, with respect, and with moral authority as a result of some combination of reputational harm, substantial fines, and even incarceration. Balancing these factors with the optimal degree of personal freedom will remain an ongoing source of ethical conflict.

The following references are recommended for those interested in further investigation of the ethical ramifications of work–life balance, issues or personal freedom of expression and political affiliation, and the ways in which such notions are best address in the course of professional training instead of waiting until a solution may come far too late.

Barnett, J. E. (2009). The complete practitioner: Still a work in progress. *American Psychologist, 64*, 793–801. http://dx.doi.org/10.1037/0003-066X.64.8.793

Carter, L. A., & Barnett, J. E. (2014). *Self-care for clinicians in training: A guide to psychological wellness for graduate students in psychology*. New York, NY: Oxford University Press.

Haeny, A. M. (2014). Ethical considerations for psychologists taking a public stance on controversial issues: The balance between personal and professional life. *Ethics & Behavior, 24*, 265–278. http://dx.doi.org/10.1080/10508422.2013.860030

Lehavot, K. (2009). "MySpace" or yours? The ethical dilemma of graduate students' personal lives on the Internet. *Ethics & Behavior, 19*, 129–141. http://dx.doi.org/10.1080/10508420902772728

Lehavot, K., Barnett, J. E., & Powers, D. (2010). Psychotherapy, professional relationships, and ethical considerations in the myspace generation. *Professional Psychology: Research and Practice, 41*, 160–166. http://dx.doi.org/10.1037/a0018709

1.5. Bylaws of the American Psychological Association

American Psychological Association

. . .

ARTICLE XI: BOARDS AND COMMITTEES

. . .

5. The Ethics Committee shall consist of not fewer than eight persons, at least seven of whom shall be Members of the Association, elected from different geographical areas, for terms of not less than three years. Members of the Ethics Committee shall be selected to represent a range of interests characteristic of psychology. The Ethics Committee shall have the power to receive, initiate, and investigate complaints of unethical conduct of Members (to include Fellows), Associate members, and Affiliates; to report on types of cases investigated with specific description of difficult or recalcitrant cases; to dismiss or recommend action on ethical cases investigated; to resolve cases by agreement where appropriate; to formulate rules or principles of ethics for adoption by the Association; to formulate rules and procedures governing the conduct of the ethics or disciplinary process for approval by the Board of Directors acting on behalf of Council; and to interpret, apply, and otherwise administer those rules and procedures.

    The work of the Ethics Committee, including information and recommendation on all cases before it, shall be kept confidential, except as provided by the Ethics Committee in rules and procedures approved by the Board of Directors, consistent with the objectives of the Committee and the interest of the Association.

6. The Election Committee shall consist of the Past President, acting as Chair, and the two other most recently retired Presidents of the Association. The Election Committee shall be responsible for the conduct of elections by voting Members of the Association, shall determine the results of all such elections, shall investigate complaints about APA elections, and shall certify the outcome of elections to the Board of Directors and Council. The Election Committee shall also oversee the voting Bylaws amendments and shall certify the results.

From "Bylaws and Association Rules," by the American Psychological Association, 2017, pp. 19–24. Retrieved from http://www.apa.org/about/governance/bylaws/index.aspx

7. The Policy and Planning Board shall consist of not fewer than nine Members of the Association, three of whom shall be elected each year and each of whom shall serve for an initial term of not less than three years. The Policy and Planning Board shall be selected to represent the range of active interests within the Association. No person shall be eligible to serve more than two consecutive terms. The Policy and Planning Board's function shall be the consideration of current and long-range policy. As a continuing body, it shall recommend to the Members, Board of Directors, and Council such changes in existing policy and such extensions or restrictions of the functions of the Association, its Divisions, or State/Provincial/Territorial Psychological Associations as are consonant with the purposes of the Association. The Policy and Planning Board shall report annually by publication to the membership. It shall review the structure and function of the Association as a whole in every fifth year and shall make recommendations by written report to Council and by publication to the Association.

8. The Publications and Communications Board shall consist of no fewer than nine Members of the Association. Members of the Board shall serve for staggered terms of six years. In addition, the Treasurer and chief staff officer shall be ex-officio members, without vote, of the Publications and Communications Board. It shall be the function of this Board to make recommendations on current and innovative plans and policies on the acquisition, management, initiation, or discontinuance of journals, separates, bibliographic and related publications, and information services. It shall appoint Editors, except the Editor of the official organ of the Association.

9. The Board of Educational Affairs shall consist of not fewer than twelve Members of the Association, one of which may be an APA Teacher Affiliate member, who shall serve for terms of not less than three years each. It shall have general concern for all educational and training affairs which transcend more than one Division or group of psychologists. Members of the Board of Educational Affairs shall be selected to represent the range of interests characteristic of psychology in all its aspects.

10. The Board of Professional Affairs shall consist of no fewer than nine Members of the Association, who shall serve for terms of three years each, except when filling a vacancy on the Board. The Board of Professional Affairs shall be responsible for developing recommendations for and monitoring the implementation of APA policy, standards and guidelines for the profession of psychology, maintaining relationships with other professional organizations and groups appropriate to its mission, recognizing contributions to the profession of psychology through awards and honors, proposing to the Association ways to enhance the profession of psychology, and fostering the application of psychological knowledge in order to promote public welfare. Insofar as possible, members of the Board of Professional Affairs shall be elected to represent the range of interests characteristic of the profession of psychology.

11. The Board of Scientific Affairs shall consist of not fewer than nine Members of the Association, who shall serve for terms of not less than three years. It shall have general concern for all aspects of psychology as a science, including the continued encouragement, development, and promotion of psychology as a science; scientific aspects of the program at the Annual Convention; and psychology's relations with other scientific bodies. It shall have particular responsibility for liaison with agencies giving financial support to scientific projects, for awards and honors in recognition of scientific achievement, and for seeking new ways in which the Association can assist scientific activities. Members of the Board of Scientific Affairs shall be selected to represent the range of interests characteristic of psychology in all its aspects.

12. The Board for the Advancement of Psychology in the Public Interest (BAPPI) shall consist of not fewer than ten members elected for three-year terms. Nine of the members must be Members of the American Psychological Association. The tenth member shall be a public member appointed by BAPPI for up to a three-year term. The mission of the Board shall be to encourage the generation and application of psychological knowledge on issues important to human well-being. It shall have general concern for those aspects of psychology that involve solutions to the fundamental problems of human justice and that promote equitable and just treatment of all segments of society. BAPPI shall encourage the utilization and dissemination of psychological knowledge to advance equal opportunity and to foster empowerment of those who do not share equitably in society's resources. The Board shall be concerned with increasing scientific understanding and training in regard to those aspects that pertain to, but are not limited to, culture, class, race/ethnicity, gender, sexual orientation, age and disability. The Board shall support improving educational and training opportunities for all persons in psychology and continue the promotion of culturally sensitive models for the delivery of psychological services. The Board shall be sensitive to the entire range of APA activities as they pertain to the mission of this Board and make recommendations regarding ethically and socially responsible actions by APA when appropriate. The composition of the Board shall reflect diversity in terms of ethnic minorities, gender, sexual orientation, disabilities and religion, as well as the range of interests characteristic of psychology in all its aspects.

1.6. Rules and Procedures: October 1, 2001

Ethics Committee of the American Psychological Association

. . .

PART II. GENERAL OPERATING RULES

. . .

11. Available Sanctions

On the basis of circumstances that aggravate or mitigate the culpability of the member, including prior sanctions, directives, or educative letters from the Association or state or local boards or similar entities, a sanction more or less severe, respectively, than would be warranted on the basis of the factors set forth below, may be appropriate.

11.1 Reprimand
Reprimand is the appropriate sanction if there has been an ethics violation but the violation was not of a kind likely to cause harm to another person or to cause substantial harm to the profession and was not otherwise of sufficient gravity as to warrant a more severe sanction.

11.2 Censure
Censure is the appropriate sanction if there has been an ethics violation and the violation was of a kind likely to cause harm to another person, but the violation was not of a kind likely to cause substantial harm to another person or to the profession and was not otherwise of sufficient gravity as to warrant a more severe sanction.

11.3 Expulsion
Expulsion from membership is the appropriate sanction if there has been an ethics violation and the violation was of a kind likely to cause substantial harm to another person or the profession or was otherwise of sufficient gravity as to warrant such action.

From "Rules and Procedures: October 1, 2001," by the Ethics Committee of the American Psychological Association, 2002, *American Psychologist, 57*, pp. 626–645. Copyright 2002 by the American Psychological Association.

11.4 Stipulated Resignation

A stipulated resignation may be offered by the Committee following a Committee finding that the respondent has committed a violation of the Ethics Code or failed to show good cause why he or she should not be expelled, contingent on execution of an acceptable affidavit and approval by the Board of Directors, under Part IV, Section 12 or Part V, Subsection 7.6.

12. Available Directives

12.1 Cease and Desist Order

Such a directive requires the respondent to cease and desist specified unethical behavior(s).

12.2 Other Corrective Actions

The Committee may require such other corrective actions as may be necessary to remedy a violation, protect the interests of the Association, or protect the public. Such a directive may not include a requirement that the respondent make a monetary payment to the Association or persons injured by the conduct.

12.3 Supervision Requirement

Such a directive requires that the respondent engage in supervision.

12.4 Education, Training, or Tutorial Requirement

Such a directive requires that the respondent engage in education, training, or a tutorial.

12.5 Evaluation and/or Treatment Requirement

Such a directive requires that the respondent be evaluated to determine the possible need for treatment and/or, if dysfunction has been established, obtain treatment appropriate to that dysfunction.

12.6 Probation

Such a directive requires monitoring of the respondent by the Committee to ensure compliance with the Ethics Committee's mandated directives during the period of those directives.

13. Matters Requiring the Concurrence of the Chair of the Committee and Director of the Ethics Office

Whenever matters entrusted by these Rules and Procedures to the Chair and Director require the concurrence of those officers before certain action may be taken, either officer in the event of disagreement may refer the matter to the Vice Chair, who, together with the Chair and Director, shall make a final determination by majority vote.

. . .

PART V. COMPLAINTS ALLEGING VIOLATION OF THE ETHICS CODE

. . .

7. Review and Resolution by the Committee

The Ethics Committee may assign a member of the Committee or an Ethics Committee Associate to serve as a case monitor. The monitor may provide assistance to assure that an adequate record is prepared for Ethics Committee review and in such other respects as necessary to further the objectives of these Rules and Procedures.

Upon conclusion of the investigation, the case shall be reviewed by the Ethics Committee. Members of the Ethics Committee and Ethics Committee Associates may be assigned to review and summarize the case. Members and Associates may also be assigned to participate on a panel to review and make a preliminary recommendation prior to review by the full Ethics Committee. Ethics Committee Associates may also attend and participate in the full Ethics Committee meetings, but shall not vote on the full Committee's disposition of a case. When review of a case has been completed, the Ethics Committee shall vote to take one of the following actions described below: remand, dismiss the charges, recommend reprimand or censure, recommend expulsion, or recommend stipulated resignation. In addition to any of these actions, the Committee may vote to issue an educative letter. The Committee may choose to dismiss some charges but find violation and take disciplinary action on the basis of other charges in the charge letter. The respondent shall then be notified of the Committee's action, the ethical standard(s) involved, if any, the rationale for the Committee's decision, any sanction, and any directives.

7.1 Remand

The Committee may remand the matter to the Director for continued investigation or issuance of a new charge letter according to Subsection 6.1.3 of this part.

7.2 Dismiss the Charges

7.2.1 No Violation. The Committee may dismiss a charge if it finds the respondent has not violated the ethical standard as charged.

7.2.2 Violation Would Not Warrant Further Action. The Committee may dismiss the complaint if it concludes that any violation it might find (a) would constitute only a minor or technical violation that would not warrant further action, (b) has already been adequately addressed in another forum, or (c) is likely to be corrected.

7.2.3 Insufficient Evidence. The Committee may dismiss a charge if it finds insufficient evidence to support a finding of an ethics violation.

7.3 Educative Letter

Where the Committee deems it appropriate, the Committee may issue an educative letter, to be shared only with the respondent, concerning the behaviors charged or other matters. An educative letter may be issued whether the Committee dismisses the charges or recommends finding violations.

7.4 Recommend Reprimand or Censure

If the Committee finds that the respondent has violated the Ethics Code, but decides that the nature of the respondent's behavior is such that the matter would be most appropriately resolved without recommending loss of membership, the Committee will recommend reprimand or censure of the respondent, with or without one or more available directives. See Part II, Subsections 11.1, 11.2, and Section 12.

7.5 Recommend Expulsion

The Committee may recommend expulsion if it concludes that there has been an ethics violation, that it was of a kind likely to cause substantial harm to another person or the profession, or that it was otherwise of such gravity as to warrant this action.

7.6 Recommend Stipulated Resignation

In lieu of the other resolutions set forth in this section, with the agreement of the respondent, the Committee may recommend to the Board that the respondent be permitted to resign under stipulations set forth by the Committee, according to the following procedure:

7.6.1 Offer of Stipulated Resignation by the Committee. When the Committee finds that the respondent has committed a violation of the Ethics Code, the Committee may offer to enter into an agreement with the respondent, contingent upon approval by the Board of Directors, that the respondent shall resign from the Association under mutually agreed upon stipulations. Such stipulations shall include the extent to which the stipulated resignation and underlying ethics violation shall be disclosed and a minimum period of time after resignation during which the respondent shall be ineligible to reapply for membership. The Committee may also vote to recommend and inform the member of an alternative sanction chosen from among Subsections 11.1–11.3 of Part II of these Rules in the event the member does not accept the offer of stipulated resignation.

. . .

1.7. Professional Practice Guidelines: Guidance for Developers and Users

American Psychological Association

This policy document is intended to assist the developers and users of "Professional Practice Guidelines" that become policy of the American Psychological Association (APA). It is a revision and integration of two earlier policy documents from APA: "Criteria for Practice Guideline Development and Evaluation" (APA, 2002c) and "Determination and Documentation of

From "Professional Practice Guidelines: Guidance for Developers and Users," by the American Psychological Association, 2015, *American Psychologist, 70,* pp. 823–831. Copyright 2015 by the American Psychological Association.

This policy document is a revision and integration of two prior documents: "Criteria for Practice Guideline Development and Evaluation" (APA, 2002c) and "Determination and Documentation of the Need for Practice Guidelines" (APA, 2005). It has been drafted by members of the APA Board of Professional Affairs (BPA) and APA Committee on Professional Practice and Standards (COPPS). Special thanks to Mary Ann McCabe, PhD (2010 Chair [COPPS] and 2013 Chair [BPA]) for her leadership and tireless efforts in the review and revision of these APA guidelines policy documents. Thanks and special recognition to Lois O. Condie, PhD, ABPP (2012 Chair [COPPS]); Julia Ramos-Grenier, PhD, ABPP (2011 Chair [COPPS]); April Harris-Britt, PhD (2013 Chair [COPPS]); John A. Zervopoulos, PhD, JD; Terry S. Gock, PhD (2012 Chair [BPA]); and Cynthia A. Sturm, PhD (2009 Chair [BPA]) for their insights and careful review. Thanks and recognition to members of BPA during the development and review process, including Judith S. Blanton, PhD (2011 Chair); Susan G. O'Leary, PhD; Lydia P. Buki, PhD; Susan D. Cochran, PhD, MS; Elaine Clark, PhD; Ruth E. Fassinger, PhD and Cathy McDaniels Wilson, PhD, ABPP (BPA Liaisons to COPPS); Karen S. Budd, PhD; Stewart E. Cooper, PhD, ABPP (2014 Chair [BPA]); Anderson "A.J." Franklin, PhD; Patricia Arredondo, EdD (2015 Chair [BPA]); Vickie M. Mays, PhD, MSPH; and Helen L. Coons, PhD, ABPP. Thanks and recognition to members of COPPS during the development and review process, including Robert Kinscherff, PhD, JD; Bonita G. Cade, PhD, JD; Michael H. Fogel, PsyD, ABPP; Robin M. Deutsch, PhD, ABPP; Daniel C. Holland, PhD, MPH, ABPP; Scott J. Hunter, PhD (2014 Chair [COPPS]); and Jorge Wong, PhD. Sincere appreciation to APA Practice Directorate staff from the Governance Operations Department, in particular, Mary G. Hardiman, MS, who facilitated both the work of BPA and COPPS and this revision effort, and Sheila Kerr-Wilson for her support. BPA and COPPS also appreciate helpful consultation from the Practice Research and Policy Department, in particular Lynn F. Bufka, PhD, and Legal and Regulatory Affairs, and from the Office of General Counsel. Finally, BPA and COPPS wish to thank the many other APA members, colleagues, and governance groups who offered insights and comments on earlier drafts of this document.

This document is scheduled to expire in February 2025, 10 years from the date of approval by APA Council of Representatives. After this date, users are encouraged to contact the APA Practice Directorate to confirm that this document remains in effect.

Correspondence concerning these guidelines should be addressed to the Practice Directorate, American Psychological Association, 750 First Street, NE, Washington, DC 20002-4242 the Need for Practice Guidelines" (APA, 2005), which are better understood as unified policy. This new policy document provides updated guidance for and examples[1] of "Professional Practice Guidelines" that have evolved over the past decade, as well as current scholarly literature specific to these guidelines. It has been drafted by the APA Board of Professional Affairs (BPA) and APA Committee on Professional Practice and Standards (COPPS).

This guidance is intended for professional practice guideline development groups composed entirely of psychologists and for multidisciplinary efforts in which psychologists are involved. (There may be other situations where APA is asked to endorse guidelines developed by another organization. While these documents undergo a similar review process in accordance with Association Rule 30–8 Standards and Guidelines, they are not addressed here.)

The landscape is changing for the practice of professional psychology, within a climate of increasing accountability. Psychologists and other professionals have greater access than ever before to examples of best practices and formal guidelines from various sources. However, there are critical differences across guidelines in terms of terminology, content, goals, evidence, and impact.

The APA Council of Representatives approved a critical terminology change in August 2012 to bring its labeling of guidelines in accord with other health care organizations. There are two types of practice guidelines in development as APA policy: "Professional Practice Guidelines" and "Clinical Practice Guidelines." The guidance contained here pertains only to "Professional Practice Guidelines."

APA "Professional Practice Guidelines" (previously named "Practice Guidelines") are designed to guide psychologists in practice with regards to particular roles, populations, or settings and provide them with the current scholarly literature. These guidelines reflect consensus within the field since the very process of guideline development helps to resolve areas of disagreement. In contrast, APA "Clinical Practice Guidelines" are focused on specific disorders and interventions and are recommendations founded on systematic reviews. (For further information on APA "Clinical Practice Guidelines," please see http://www.apa.org/about/offices/directorates/guidelines/clinical-practice. aspx.) For additional information on "Clinical Practice Guidelines" across health care, please see resources from APA, APA, 2002b; the Institute of Medicine (2011a, 2011b, http://www.iom.edu/reports/2011/clinical-practice-guidelines-we-can-trust.aspx and http://www.nap.edu/catalog.php?record_id=13059; and the Agency for Health Care Research and Quality, www.guideline.gov/).

---

[1] Guidelines that have been approved as APA policy that are cited throughout this document may have been revised or may be currently under revision. Please see "Guidelines for Practitioners" (http://www.apa.org/practice/guidelines/index.aspx) on the official website of the American Psychological Association for the most current version.

DEFINITIONS

As it is used in APA policy, the term *guidelines* refers to statements that suggest or recommend specific professional behavior, endeavor, or conduct for psychologists. Guidelines differ from standards. Standards are mandatory and, thus, may be accompanied by an enforcement mechanism; guidelines are not mandatory, definitive, or exhaustive. Guidelines are aspirational in intent. They aim to facilitate the continued systematic development of the profession and to promote a high level of professional practice by psychologists. A particular set of guidelines may not apply to every professional and clinical situation within the scope of that set of guidelines. As a result, guidelines are not intended to take precedence over the professional judgments of psychologists that are based on the scientific and professional knowledge of the field (Ethics Code, Std. 2.04, APA, 2002d; APA, 2010a).

The primary purpose of "Professional Practice Guidelines" is to educate, to facilitate competence (Wise et al., 2010), and to assist the practitioner in the provision of high-quality psychological services by providing well-supported practical guidance and education in a particular practice area. "Professional Practice Guidelines" also "inform psychologists, the public, and other interested parties regarding desirable professional practices" (APA, 2002c, Section 2.5). Guidelines are not to be promulgated as a means of establishing the identity of a group or specialty area of psychology, nor are they to be created with the purpose of excluding any psychologist from practicing in a particular area (APA, 2002a). Stakeholders for a given set of guidelines include psychologists, students of psychology, consumers of psychological practice, members of the public, policymakers, regulatory bodies, other health care professionals, and other professionals.

ESTABLISHING NEED: REASONS FOR THE DEVELOPMENT OF GUIDELINES

APA policy states that "Professional Practice Guidelines" should be written only when there is a clearly demonstrated and documented need (APA, 2005). It is in the best interests of the profession to avoid the unnecessary proliferation of guidelines, particularly those which may be advocacy based rather than scientifically based. Prospective developers of "Professional Practice Guidelines" should begin the process by considering the specific need, purpose, and intended audience or stakeholders for guidelines. Although the need must be well established, the basis for establishing and documenting need will depend on the impetus for the particular set of guidelines. This section is a revision of the earlier policy document, "Determination and Documentation of the Need for Practice Guidelines" (APA, 2005).

It is essential that "Professional Practice Guidelines" provide a clear justification for focusing on a singular topic apart from the rest of psychological practice. Guidelines that focus on a particular client population or characteristic must explain why and how psychological practice with this population is suffi-ciently different from sound practice with all clients to justify separate guide-lines. Guidelines could potentially be written for any number of client characteristics (e.g., age, gender, sexual orientation, religion, ethnicity). Good psychological practice requires that practitioners be sensitive to all these client characteristics and their interactions, and it is generally not clinically useful to conceptualize clients' problems according to a singular personal attribute. Although evidence of past and present injustice in the broader sociocultural context is likely to be relevant, it is not sufficient as a justification for "Profes-sional Practice Guidelines."

There are three broad categories of potential need for "Professional Practice Guidelines": (a) legal and regulatory issues, (b) public benefit, and (c) profes-sional guidance (APA, 2005). While these distinctions are conceptually useful, the categories are likely to overlap in regard to the need for any particular guidelines document.

Legal and Regulatory Issues

Legal and regulatory issues in response to which "Professional Practice Guide-lines" may be written include the following:

Laws
Changes in state, federal, or international laws or statutes may generate the need for "Professional Practice Guidelines." Guidelines are not written to interpret laws, which are mandatory. However, in areas in which laws are silent, unclear, or conflicting, guidelines may assist psychologists to consider appropriate practice options for a given situation or to seek legal advice on how to manage that situation.

Court Decisions and Case Law
Federal circuit court and U.S. Supreme Court decisions may require changes in professional practice. For example, the U.S. Supreme Court decision in *Daubert v. Merrell Dow Pharmaceuticals* (1993) prompted significant changes in how psy-chologists in affected jurisdictions prepare for and deliver expert opinions in court. Guidelines might educate psychologists about evidentiary requirements and how to respond more effectively to them.

Professional Interaction With the Legal System
Psychologists are called on to respond to various types of requests from judges, lawyers, and administrative bodies. These requests may require psy-chologists to provide information in the form of records or sworn testimony. Examples of guidelines relevant to professional interaction with the legal system include the "Guidelines for Child Custody Evaluations in Family Law Proceedings" (APA, 2010b), the "Guidelines for the Practice of Parenting Coordination" (APA, 2012c), the "Guidelines for Psychological Evaluations in Child Protection Matters" (APA, 2013c), and the "Specialty Guidelines for

Forensic Psychology" (APA, 2013b). Guidelines can also educate and inform psychologists about specific legal concepts and requirements.

Changes in Regulatory and Administrative Systems

Psychologists are subject to regulation by state licensing boards and federal health regulatory systems. Although the agencies that promulgate regulations sometimes write explanatory documents, there are areas in which regulations are silent or not fully clarified. In those cases, guidelines might help psychologists adapt generally accepted practice and procedures to meet these standards. For example, state or federal record keeping regulations may be vague or conflicting. Psychologists required to keep records in a setting with such regulations may seek guidance from the APA's "Record Keeping Guidelines" (APA, 2007b; see also Drogin, Connell, Foote, & Sturm, 2010).

Public Benefit

Guidelines may be written to benefit the public in ways that include the following:

Improved Service Delivery

"Professional Practice Guidelines" may be developed to improve service-delivery models, as "Guidelines for Psychological Practice With Girls and Women" (APA, 2007a). Or, psychologists' education in specific areas may prompt positive changes in treatment, evaluation or assessment procedures. For example, "Guidelines on Multicultural Education, Training, Research, Practice, and Organizational Change for Psychologists" (APA, 2003) heightens awareness of special considerations for service delivery to diverse populations.

Avoidance of Harm

The development of "Professional Practice Guidelines" may be supported when there is empirical evidence or professional consensus of bias, discrimination, or harm to clients. For example, the development of "Guidelines for Psychological Practice With Lesbian, Gay, and Bisexual Clients" (APA, 2012d) was prompted by evidence of misguided treatment of these clients.

Emerging, Underserved, or Vulnerable Client Populations

"Professional Practice Guidelines" may be developed to meet the psychological needs of emerging, underserved, and/or vulnerable client populations. Emerging populations may include client groups identified by shifting demographics (e.g., immigrant populations); underserved groups may include certain rural, homeless, or undocumented immigrant individuals; vulnerable populations are those less able to advocate for themselves with regard to access to and utilization of health services (e.g., minors, victims of interpersonal violence). See, for example, "Guidelines for Psychological Practice With Older Adults" (APA, 2004) and "Guidelines for Assessment of and Intervention With Persons With Disabilities" (APA, 2012a).

Professional Guidance

Guidelines may offer professional guidance in relation to issues such as the following:

Advances in Theory and Science

Advances in psychological theory and science may lead to the development of new approaches with which psychologists need guidance or which point to emerging consensus. For instance, advances in theory and science are reflected in "Guidelines for the Evaluation of Dementia and Age-Related Cognitive Change" (APA, 2012b) and "Guidelines for Prevention in Psychology" (APA, 2014).

New, Expanded, or Complex Multidisciplinary Roles

Psychologists may require guidance when providing novel services or working in new contexts or emerging areas of practice. "Guidelines Regarding Psychologists' Involvement in Pharmacological Issues" (APA, 2011) and "Guidelines for Psychological Practice in Health Care Delivery Systems" (APA, 2013a) are examples of guidance regarding expanded roles.

Specialized Areas of Practice in Need of Clarification

For areas of specialization within psychological practice, it is sometimes helpful to provide updated guidance (e.g., "Guidelines for Psychological Practice With Older Adults," APA, 2004; "Specialty Guidelines for Forensic Psychology," APA, 2013b). When developing guidelines for areas of specialized practice, it is helpful to include guidance related to assessment when there is an appropriate scholarship base.

Professional Risk-Management Issues

"Professional Practice Guidelines" may be developed in response to professional risk-management issues. For example, APA "Record Keeping Guidelines" (APA, 2007b) may protect psychologists in the absence of clear guidance from state and federal regulations.

Development of New Technology

The development of new technology may necessitate reconsideration of existing processes and procedures. For example, the increasing use of electronic devices enables psychologists to deliver health services via telephone and computer when appropriate or where it may not be possible in person ("Guidelines for the Practice of Telepsychology," Joint Task Force, 2013). Electronic transmission of medical records require psychologists to modify their practices concerning control and confidentiality of records ("Record Keeping Guidelines," APA, 2007b; Drogin et al., 2010).

Changing Social Norms

"Professional Practice Guidelines" may be developed to address the changing needs of professionals that stem from the dynamic nature of social norms. For example, the construct of privacy has changed in recent years due to new communication techniques that make public what traditionally were private venues of communication, warranting new consideration of the need to preserve confidentiality (Joint Task Force, 2013). "Guidelines for the Practice of Telepsychology" (Joint Task Force, 2013) have been developed, in part, in response to changing social customs in the use of technology for communication.

Evidence Supporting Guidelines

Each guideline document as a whole, and each of its component guidelines, must be accompanied by an explicit rationale and supporting evidence appropriate to its range of application. Developers of guidelines should describe each source of evidence used in guideline formulation so that a reader can evaluate the guidelines' base of support. Documentation of empirical and broad-based professional consensus in developing guidelines will protect against the appearance of advocacy for particular policy positions or theoretical perspectives or restrictive attempts to regulate professional behavior and judgment.

Not all guidelines are alike in terms of the need for, availability of, and type of evidence. Timing and context matter. For example, guidelines developed for legal or regulatory reasons will have different types of evidentiary support than guidelines developed for professional reasons. Decisions about the nature and scope of evidence to be cited in a particular set of guidelines may be made in accordance with features of the guidelines themselves, such as the purpose (e.g., education, emerging professional consensus), stakeholders (e.g., students, users not familiar with the area of study), focus on a specific population, setting, or key role/function, inclusion of controversial statements or definitive statements, and timing. The aforementioned examples of guidelines that have been approved as APA policy illustrate these various features and can be helpful to developers for deciding the scope of evidence required for acceptance and approval.

Not all scholarly references should be considered equal. The quality of the literature cited to support guidelines is the most important consideration. Developers have the duty to explain the choice of literature, but it is recommended that references be current, broad, empirical where possible, and inclusive of seminal works and reviews when available.

In all instances, guideline developers should strive to be comprehensive and representative in their selection of theoretical and empirical sources and should consider the positions of other relevant stakeholders as applicable. Developers should examine relevant evidence, including that which may contradict their point of view. Direct empirical support for recommending specific professional behavior is always a strong form of evidence, though such support is not always available.

In some areas, expert professional consensus is the strongest form of evidence available. A variety of forms of information may reflect professional consensus, depending on the nature of the guidelines being developed. These include, but are not limited to, agreement among recognized subject-matter experts, practitioner surveys, incidence of inquiries to APA or other professional or regulatory bodies, reviews of professional literature, and general agreement among psychologists regarding responsible professional conduct.

Guidelines that make reference to a single theoretical perspective or a narrow body of literature are less useful than guidelines that integrate multiple perspectives. The wider the intended application of guidelines, the more developers should seek to integrate perspectives from across (and outside) the profession. For example, the scope of the "Guidelines on Multicultural Education, Training, Research, Practice, and Organizational Change for Psychologists" (APA, 2003) required the integration of a broad base of evidence and perspectives. In contrast, there are contexts (e.g., forensic) for which guidelines are appropriately based on a narrower range of evidence and expertise, such as "Guidelines for Psychological Evaluations in Child Protection Matters" (APA, 2013c).

It is expected that guidelines approved as policy by APA will have relevance to a significant segment of APA membership. APA represents psychologists from diverse theoretical perspectives functioning in a broad array of professional settings. The processes for development, review, and revision of guidelines allows for input from those holding the full range of views.

To be adopted by the APA Council of Representatives, guidelines must have strong support across constituencies. The nature of the guidelines development process, the need to develop aspirational language (rather than determinative), the need for evidence, and the format of guidelines (rationale, application) all sharpen thought, encourage dialog, and drive consensus. The resultant coherence is critical for APA governance approval of new guidelines as policy.

CRITERIA FOR "PROFESSIONAL PRACTICE GUIDELINES"

The following guidance aims to ensure deliberation and care in the process of developing "Professional Practice Guidelines." The guidance promotes quality and consistency in "Professional Practice Guidelines" and identifies, in advance, the specific criteria by which they will be evaluated and reviewed. Proposed "Professional Practice Guidelines" are not considered APA policy until they have been reviewed and approved in accordance with Association Rule 30–8.

The specific criteria outlined below are designed to assist the development of guidelines addressing a range of practice areas and issues yet also educate the practitioner to provide high quality psychological services, including intervention, psychotherapy, testing, assessment and consultation. Examples of "Professional Practice Guidelines" that have already been approved as APA policy can be particularly helpful for developers by illustrating adoption of the criteria (See "Guidelines for Practitioners" at http://www.apa.org/practice/guidelines/index.aspx.)

The following criteria are an affirmation and revision of the "Determination and Documentation of the Need for Practice Guidelines" (APA, 2005) and the "Criteria for Practice Guideline Development and Evaluation" (APA, 2002c) that, in turn, revised the "Criteria for Guideline Development and Review" (APA, 1995).

Guideline Attributes

The following attributes will assist practice guideline developers and will be considered during review (see "Professional Practice Guidelines Checklist," available online at http://www.apa.org/practice/guidelines/practice-criteria-checklist.pdf):

Need
As noted earlier, "Professional Practice Guidelines" are encouraged (and approved) only for areas with a clearly demonstrated and documented need.

Respect for Human Rights and Dignity
"Professional Practice Guidelines" reflect sensitivity to cultural, individual, and role differences among psychological service providers and their client populations, including but not limited to those due to age, gender, race, ethnicity, national origin, religion, sexual orientation, disability, language, and socioeconomic status (APA, 2002c, 2010a).

Delineation of Scope
"Professional Practice Guidelines" have a clearly defined scope in terms of content, users, and context. "Professional Practice Guidelines" are focused on professional practice rather than specific disorders or treatments.

Avoidance of Bias
"Professional Practice Guidelines" avoid bias or appearance of bias through consideration and/or integration of alternative views during the development and review process, when guideline developers are expected to provide the reasoning behind their decisions and judgments and ensure citations of relevant literature.

Educational Value
"Professional Practice Guidelines" inform psychologists, the public, and other interested parties regarding desirable professional practices.

Internal Consistency
No part of the practice guideline conflicts with any other part in intent or application.

Basis

"Professional Practice Guidelines" take into account the best available sources on current theory, research, and professional literature and the APA Ethics Code so as to provide a defensible basis for recommended conduct.

Flexibility

"Professional Practice Guidelines" recognize the importance of professional judgment and discretion and do not unnecessarily or inappropriately limit the practitioner.

Feasibility

Implementation of the particular "Professional Practice Guidelines" is feasible in the current practice environment. Following the guidelines should not place an excessive educational or financial burden on psychologists beyond that of commonly agreed upon best practices.

Compatibility

"Professional Practice Guidelines" take into account current APA policies and must be consistent with the APA Ethics Code (APA, 2002d, 2010a).

Guidelines Language

Clarity

"Professional Practice Guidelines" are clear, succinct, and unambiguous in their use of language and avoid jargon. Developers should try wherever possible to use generally accepted terminology, whether within APA or the broader health or policy community. Clarity of guideline language is greatly aided by the guideline review process, described below.

Aspirational Language

"Professional Practice Guidelines" avoid words such as *should* and *must* because those words connote mandatory intent. (Such intent is appropriate for standards rather than guidelines.) Instead, "Professional Practice Guidelines" use words such as *encourage*, *recommend*, and *strive* because these words connote the aspirational intent consistent with the broad purposes and educative goals. The guideline review process assists with this aspirational language. Aspirational language has been noted to stimulate dialog, identify and resolve disagreement, encourage consensus, and lead to a more coherent statement for the field.

Recommended Language for Common Situations

There are a number of common situations with "Professional Practice Guidelines" where standardized or "boiler plate" language can be very helpful for guideline developers. For example, the use of lists is quite common yet can be particularly cumbersome and/or problematic; lists can never be exhaustive or incorporate future developments during the life span of guidelines. Phrasing such as "including but not limited to" is recommended in lieu of attempting to be all inclusive.

A Few Additional Common Phrasing Situations Warrant Mention

When describing multicultural issues, it is recommended that "diverse backgrounds and needs" be considered. When lists are made for the various types of diversity, guideline developers might consider using the reference "Dimensions of Personal Identity" as described in the APA "Multicultural Guidelines" (currently under revision). In addition, the Council of National Psychological Associations for the Advancement of Ethnic Minority Interests has published three documents on working with ethnic/minority populations specific to education and training, research, and practice. These resource documents would be of benefit to educators in all areas and might provide useful terminology and guidance (http://www.apa.org/pi/oema/resources/cnpaaemi-pubs.aspx). Guideline developers should consider whether groups with unique needs (e.g., underserved, under-recognized, understudied, overrepresented, vulnerable) are included in the guideline or in supporting evidence. Finally, experience with guidelines has shown the term *objective* to be preferred over *impartial*.

Recommended Elements Within Guidelines

The following outline of recommended elements can assist in the development of "Professional Practice Guidelines"; these elements form the basis for review (see also "Practice Guideline Checklist," http://www.apa.org/practice/guidelines/practice-criteria-checklist.pdf). (To facilitate review, it is recommended that practice guideline proposals contain page numbers and line numbers and not be right justified.) The recommended elements for "Professional Practice Guidelines" can be seen in Figure 1.

Introduction

"Professional Practice Guidelines" are accompanied by a general introductory section that explains the need for the proposed guidelines and the process by which the proposed guidelines were developed. This section informs reviewers about the justification for creating the proposed guidelines and the steps taken in their development. "Professional Practice Guidelines" contain review and citation of the literature sufficient to inform and to justify both a set of proposed "Professional Practice Guidelines" and individual guideline statements therein. (See previous discussion of Evidence Supporting Guidelines.)

Purpose

Guideline authors articulate a clear statement of purpose. This statement includes the subject matter of the guidelines, beneficiaries of the guidelines, the boundaries of applicability, and intended degree of specificity.

**FIGURE 1. Recommended Elements of Professional
Practice Guidelines**

Introduction
- Statement of purpose
- Documentation of need
- Identification of those for whom the guidelines have been created (audience/stakeholders)
- Statement distinguishing between guidelines and standards
- Statement that federal and state laws supersede the guidelines
- Definition of terms
- Statement regarding consistency with APA Ethics Code and other policy

Background
- Background/history of development for this guidelines proposal (including developers of the guidelines proposal and any source(s) of financial support)
- Selection of evidence

Guidelines
- The set of guidelines with associated text (see Figure 2)
- Date of expiration
- Author's note – if applicable

References

Documentation of Need

This portion of the proposed guideline document describes the impetus for them. It documents the need for the guidelines and their relevance to current practice. Relevant sources of information may include demonstrated patient or client need, practitioner demand, or legal and regulatory requirements that justify the necessity for the proposed guidelines. (See previous discussion of Establishing Need.)

Users

The intended audience/stakeholders of the "Professional Practice Guidelines" are explicitly identified.

Distinction Between Standards and Guidelines

A statement is included in the guidelines clarifying the distinction between standards and guidelines. The APA Office of General Counsel has recommended that the following language be included in every practice guideline document:

> The term *guidelines* refers to statements that suggest or recommend specific professional behavior, endeavor, or conduct for psychologists. *Guidelines* differ from

standards. *Standards* are mandatory and, thus, may be accompanied by an enforcement mechanism; guidelines are not mandatory, definitive, or exhaustive. *Guidelines* are aspirational in intent. They aim to facilitate the continued systematic development of the profession and to promote a high level of professional practice by psychologists. A particular set of *guidelines* may not apply to every professional and clinical situation within the scope of that set of guidelines. As a result, *guidelines* are not intended to take precedence over the professional judgments of psychologists that are based on the scientific and professional knowledge of the field (see Ethics Code, Std. 2.04).

Definitions

Terms are clearly defined, particularly when some are not commonly used or when common usage varies or is imprecise. Definitions may be provided in the text or in a glossary of terms.

Compatibility

A statement must be included that asserts the consistency of the proposed guidelines with the current APA Ethics Code (APA, 2002d, 2010a). "Professional Practice Guidelines" also acknowledge other relevant APA policy.

Background

Practice guideline development process. The review process is documented so that others can evaluate both the process itself and the sources utilized. Potential conflicts of interest are disclosed. Individuals, groups, and represented organizations that developed the guidelines are identified. Sources of direct and indirect financial support for practice guideline development are identified. There is also full disclosure of any potential financial benefit to the guideline developers that may result from the development or implementation of the guidelines.

Selection of Evidence

Guideline developers describe the process by which supporting professional literature or other evidence was selected, reviewed, included, and excluded. Literature included in the "Professional Practice Guidelines" document's reference section is generally limited to current or seminal publications or other writings recognized in the field as important to the proposed guideline's subject matter. (See previous section on Evidence Supporting Guidelines. In addition, existing "Professional Practice Guidelines" can be helpful illustrations for describing how evidence/professional literature was selected, etc.)

Necessary Components of Each Guideline

The necessary components of "Professional Practice Guidelines" are illustrated in Figure 2.

Guidelines should have adequate documentation and provide clear examples of recommended professional practice. Each practice guideline statement has a three-part structure: the practice guideline statement, which is a specific recommendation for professional conduct, typically one sentence and a single

FIGURE 2. Necessary Components of Each Guideline

```
┌─────────────────────────────────────────────────┐
│                                                   │
│               Guideline Statement                 │
│                                                   │
└─────────────────────────────────────────────────┘
                        ↓
┌─────────────────────────────────────────────────┐
│               Rationale/Justification             │
│     (Knowledge upon which the guideline is founded) │
│                                                   │
└─────────────────────────────────────────────────┘
                        ↓
┌─────────────────────────────────────────────────┐
│                                                   │
│                   Application                      │
│          (Suggestions for the practitioner)        │
│                                                   │
└─────────────────────────────────────────────────┘
```

idea; the guideline statement rationale, which may include relevant literature, intended audience, and intended benefits or goals, typically a short
paragraph; and the practice guideline application, or commentary to facilitate
the reader's understanding about how the guideline may be applied in practice, typically one or more paragraphs in length.

Status and Expiration Date

"Professional Practice Guidelines" must include a proposed expiration date.
Under no circumstances may an expiration date of more than 10 years be
proposed. This maximum time frame is appropriate for practice areas in
which the knowledge base, practice patterns, and relevant legal and regulatory climate are stable. In many practice areas, an earlier expiration date
will be more appropriate (e.g., 5 or 7 years), particularly for an emerging
area or one where there is rapidly developing research base or policy landscape. In all cases, developers provide a rationale for the proposed time
frame. All "Professional Practice Guidelines" documents include the following statement:

> This document is scheduled to expire [*insert date*]. After this date, users are encour-
> aged to contact the APA Practice Directorate to confirm that this document
> remains in effect.

Guidelines Review Process

The process of developing guidelines according to the format described above
(i.e., rationale and application) has been found to drive clear articulation and
precise wording of what is intended. Similarly, the process for editing drafts of
guidelines following mandatory periods for public (and governance) comment raise and sharpen areas of disagreement and drive greater consensus for
the final guidelines document.

Documentation and Review

The "Professional Practice Guidelines" proposal undergoes both preliminary and formal levels of review. (This process may differ somewhat for revising existing guidelines documents that are nearing expiration.)

Preliminary Review

Guideline developers are strongly encouraged to consult with the APA BPA early in the "Professional Practice Guidelines" development process. BPA's mission includes developing recommendations for standards and guidelines and monitoring the implementation of standards and guidelines for the profession of psychology. BPA will assist guideline developers in obtaining consultation from the APA COPPS (of which BPA is the parent board) as well as appropriate APA legal review in order to determine any risk to APA and its members that may be posed by any particular guidelines project. The developers are also encouraged to contact other groups or organizations that could have an active interest or stake in the proposed "Professional Practice Guidelines" (e.g., APA divisions, committees, task forces).

Record Keeping for Preliminary Review

All correspondence and documents generated by both the reviewers and the guideline developers must be maintained.

Formal Review (APA Approval Process)

After the "Professional Practice Guidelines" proposal has been edited in the preliminary review process, a proposal is submitted for formal APA governance review. It is also disseminated for a public comment period of at least 60 days, which is a highly participatory process for APA members and others outside the organization. Guideline developers are required to respond to all comments and incorporate changes where appropriate; it is this process that develops the base of professional consensus that strengthens the final guidelines document. The approval process is outlined in Figure 3. APA divisions, committees, or other APA entities or stakeholders wishing to develop guidelines are referred to APA's "Association Rules" (APA, 2002a), which describes additional review requirements.

Record Keeping for Formal Review

As in the record keeping for preliminary review, guideline developers must maintain records of the correspondence and documents generated by reviewing committees and boards. Text additions and deletions are made in accordance with APA's policies and procedures for documenting revisions. When suggestions are not integrated, the developers respond in writing to the reviewer(s) with an explanatory comment. Both the reviewer feedback and the response to it then become part of the record and are submitted with the proposal.

FIGURE 3. Review Process for Proposed Guidelines or Standards

Lead Board or Committee

Relevant Boards or Committees (All reviews must include the Committee on Legal Issues. If Professional Practice Guidelines, must also include the Board of Professional Affairs; and, if Education or Training Guidelines, must also include the Board of Educational Affairs.) All guidelines must meet <u>all</u> stated requirements of Association Rule 30–8.

Cross Cutting Agenda (If the guidelines affect more than one group or constituency)		**Conference Committee** (If appropriate)

Public Comment (60-day public comment period, in accordance with Association Rule 30–8)

Legal Counsel Review/Central Office Staff Review (Including Office of General Counsel, relevant departments and staff)

Board of Directors Reviews for appropriateness and performs a risk assessment.

Council Leadership Team Performs content review, reviews risk assessment, and makes recommendations on approval for Council consideration.

Council of Representatives Considers for approval and adoption as APA policy

Publication in *American Psychologist* (Dissemination through appropriate media)

Guidelines Expiration and Revision

"Professional Practice Guidelines" reaching expiration routinely are reviewed by members of COPPS and BPA for relevance. Guidelines are monitored to minimize overlap between sets of guidelines, and to identify and respond to changing needs for professional guidance or evolving evidence for/against guideline statements. (Note: New APA policies and procedures have been developed by the Policy and Planning Board, in collaboration with BPA, COPPS, APA parent boards, and other governance groups, to better administer and document the review process for existing guidelines that are within 3 years of expiration.)

In cases in which there is no clear rationale for updating a set of guidelines, a decision may be made to sunset the guidelines. Two examples are illustrative. First, a set of guidelines might be allowed to expire without revision when practice norms are firmly established and guidelines for practice have been sufficiently incorporated into the conventions of practice. Second, the need for guidelines may be less necessary because of coverage elsewhere. An example of coverage elsewhere would be the incorporation of a set of guidelines into legislation, other forms of APA policy, or cross-organizational guidelines that obviate the need for a specific set of APA guidelines for practice.

The decision process for updating guidelines involves a review of the following elements: the introduction section of guidelines, the purpose of guidelines, the appropriateness of the existing distinction within the document between guidelines and ethical standards, intended users, definitions, whether an updated needs assessment is indicated, continued compatibility with other guidelines and with APA policies, continued compatibility with APA Ethics Standards (APA, 2002d, 2010a), member support for renewal of the document, fit with the APA strategic plan, availability of funding to support a revision, and whether an appropriate group of designees have been or will be appointed to complete the process of updating and renewing the guidelines. Because of the dynamic nature in which guidelines are developed, designees to update and renew the guidelines may be appointed from BPA, COPPS, the governance of an APA division, or some other relevant body. If appropriate and feasible, members of the original development group may participate in updating those guidelines.

Roles of Guideline Developers

When psychologists begin the process of developing "Professional Practice Guidelines," they are committing to develop the guidelines in accordance with the aforementioned criteria, collaborate with key stakeholders, participate in the review process, maintain documentation of comments and revisions, contribute to the dissemination process, and anticipate a mechanism for deciding whether and how to revise the guidelines before they expire. The developers of guidelines must consider the broader implications and the range of applications of guidelines, which are likely to extend beyond the group by which they are developed. In some instances, guidelines may affect groups outside the profession of psychology (e.g., other health professionals, test developers, public stakeholders); this should be considered in advance of developing guidelines. In these cases, a broader development and review process that solicits comment from individuals and groups outside APA is appropriate. Developers may need to consider and comment on guidelines adopted by other organizations for the same or related areas.

Common Challenges With Guidelines Development

The most common challenges for developers include decisions regarding the length of the guidelines document and the scope of evidence; as noted previously, it helps to identify features of guidelines that might aid decision-making in this regard (e.g., timing, purpose, special populations, roles/functions, settings, emerging areas, inclusion of controversial and/or definitive statements). For example, effective dissemination of guidelines and implementation in practice may be aided by a shorter, rather than longer, document. It is important that guidelines developers anticipate if any proposed guidelines statements may become "dated" prior to when their practice guidelines document will expire; this can occur, for example, when very recent or proposed (but not approved) public policy is featured.

It is also a common challenge for developers to anticipate both intended and unintended consequences for guidelines, yet this can be invaluable in the process of guideline development. In some contexts (particularly forensic ones), where the notion of professional judgment might be defined differently, guidelines can represent "peer review." As a result, psychologists may find themselves in a situation where they must be prepared to justify why their judgment deviates from "Professional Practice Guidelines." Again, guidelines are aspirational rather than mandatory and do not trump professional judgment. However, it may be that the more immediate and consequential the impact (e.g., vulnerable population), and the more psychologists have control over their work (e.g., forensic role vs. multidisciplinary team), the greater impact a prospective set of guidelines has for public welfare. Psychologists in such situations may be asked to justify a deviation in practice from existing guidelines. Note that when psychologists' professional conduct and judgments do not conform to practice guidelines statements, they should base their conduct and judgments on the scientific and professional knowledge of the field (see Ethics Code, Std. 2.04, APA, 2002d, 2010a).

A final challenge for guideline developers is to consider how best to disseminate guidelines among professionals who may benefit from their implementation. Developers should carefully identify prospective stakeholders both within and outside psychology for "Professional Practice Guidelines," and then consider what types of products reach them, with what timing. It is helpful to anticipate the obstacles to dissemination or implementation and consider potential solutions in the guidelines where possible. It is also important to consider how to advance new guidelines into training and educational programming. When they embark on the process of guideline development and approval, developers make a commitment to a long-term process that rewards effort with enhanced professional practice and public benefit.

Resources for Guideline Development and Review

The APA website, www.apa.org, lists existing "Professional Practice Guidelines" on the "APA Guidelines for Practitioners" page (see http://www.apa.org/practice/guidelines/index.aspx.) For guideline developers, this web page includes documents that illustrate the typical trajectory of work tasks, committee activities, reporting structures, the process of seeking public comment on proposed guideline drafts, feedback loops and mechanisms for communicating with members of COPPS, and the process for gaining final approval by the APA Council of Representatives. Additional information is found under the heading "Policy Documents on Developing APA Guidelines."

SUMMARY

When psychologists begin the process of developing "Professional Practice Guidelines," they commit to development, collaboration with key stakeholders, participation in the review process, and contribution to the dissemination process. Guidelines serve as valuable educational tools but there must be a demonstrated and documented need. There is enormous value in the guidelines review and approval process. It enables the evolution of guidelines documents with desired attributes, recommended precise and aspirational language, supporting evidence, and required elements. The review process also clarifies what guidelines are not, and prevents the proliferation of unnecessary guidelines. The result is "Professional Practice Guidelines" that serve the best interests of the field of psychology and the public.

REFERENCES

American Psychological Association (APA). (1995). *Criteria for guideline development and review*. Washington, DC: Author.

American Psychological Association (APA). (2002a). *Association rules of the American Psychological Association*. Washington, DC: Author.

American Psychological Association (APA). (2002b). Criteria for evaluating treatment guidelines. *American Psychologist, 57*, 1052–1059. http://dx.doi.org/10.1037/0003-066X.57.12.1052

American Psychological Association (APA). (2002c). Criteria for practice guideline development and evaluation. *American Psychologist, 57*, 1048–1051. http://dx.doi.org/10.1037/0003-066X.57.12.1048

American Psychological Association (APA). (2002d). Ethical principles of psychologists and code of conduct. *American Psychologist, 57*, 1060–1073. http://dx.doi.org/10.1037/0003-066X.57.12.1060

American Psychological Association (APA). (2003). Guidelines on multicultural education, training, research, practice, and organizational change for psychologists. *American Psychologist, 58*, 377–402.

American Psychological Association (APA). (2004). Guidelines for psychological practice with older adults. *American Psychologist, 59,* 236–260.

American Psychological Association (APA). (2005). Determination and documentation of the need for practice guidelines. *American Psychologist, 60,* 976–978. http://dx.doi.org/10.1037/0003-066X.60.9.976

American Psychological Association (APA). (2007a). Guidelines for psychological practice with girls and women. *American Psychologist, 62,* 949–979. http://dx.doi.org/10.1037/0003-066X.62.9.949

American Psychological Association (APA). (2007b). Record keeping guidelines. *American Psychologist, 62,* 993–1004. http://dx.doi.org/10.1037/0003-066X.62.9.993

American Psychological Association (APA). (2010a). 2010 Amendments to the 2002 "Ethical principles of psychologists and code of conduct." *American Psychologist, 65,* 493. http://dx.doi.org/10.1037/a0020168

American Psychological Association (APA). (2010b). Guidelines for child custody evaluations in family law proceedings. *American Psychologist, 65,* 863–867. http://dx.doi.org/10.1037/a0021250

American Psychological Association (APA). (2011). Practice guidelines regarding psychologists' involvement in pharmacological issues. *American Psychologist, 66,* 835–849. http://dx.doi.org/10.1037/a0025890

American Psychological Association (APA). (2012a). Guidelines for assessment of and intervention with persons with disabilities. *American Psychologist, 67,* 43–62. http://dx.doi.org/10.1037/a0025892

American Psychological Association (APA). (2012b). Guidelines for the evaluation of dementia and age-related cognitive change. *American Psychologist, 67,* 1–9. http://dx.doi.org/10.1037/a0024643

American Psychological Association (APA). (2012c). Guidelines for the practice of parenting coordination. *American Psychologist, 67,* 63–71. http://dx.doi.org/10.1037/a0024646

American Psychological Association (APA). (2012d). Guidelines for psychological practice with lesbian, gay, and bisexual clients. *American Psychologist, 67,* 10–42. http://dx.doi.org/10.1037/a0024659

American Psychological Association (APA). (2013a). Guidelines for psychological practice in health care delivery systems. *American Psychologist, 68,* 1–6. http://dx.doi.org/10.1037/a0029890

American Psychological Association (APA). (2013b). Specialty guidelines for forensic psychology. *American Psychologist, 68,* 7–19. http://dx.doi.org/10.1037/a0029889

American Psychological Association (APA). (2013c). Guidelines for psychological evaluations in child protection matters. *American Psychologist, 68,* 20–31. http://dx.doi.org/10.1037/a0029891

American Psychological Association (APA). (2014). Guidelines for prevention in psychology. *American Psychologist, 69,* 285–296. http://dx.doi.org/10.1037/a0034569

Daubert v. Merrell Dow Pharmaceuticals, 509 U.S. 579 (1993).

Drogin, E. Y., Connell, M., Foote, W. E., & Sturm, C. A. (2010). The American Psychological Association's revised "Record Keeping Guidelines": Implications for the practitioner. *Professional Psychology: Research and Practice, 41,* 236–243. http://dx.doi.org/10.1037/a0019001

Institute of Medicine. (2011a). *Clinical professional practice guidelines we can trust.* Washington, DC: The National Academies Press.

Institute of Medicine. (2011b). *Finding what works in health care: Standards for systematic reviews.* Washington, DC: The National Academies Press.

Joint Task Force for the Development of Telepsychology Guidelines for Psychologists. (2013). Guidelines for the practice of telepsychology. *American Psychologist, 68,* 791–800. http://dx.doi.org/10.1037/a0035001

Wise, E. H., Sturm, C. A., Nutt, R. L., Rodolfa, E., Schaffer, J. B., & Webb, C. (2010). Life-long learning for psychologists: Current status and a vision for the future. *Professional Psychology: Research and Practice, 41*, 288–297. http://dx.doi.org/ 10.1037/a0020424

COMMENTARY: Over the course of the past approximately two decades, the American Psychological Association has grappled with sort of dilemma that many of its national professional organization counterparts—for example, the American Bar Association and the American Psychiatric Association—might indeed have welcomed: a burgeoning level of contribution from several internal entities, all seeking to contribute lasting, impactful guidance for colleagues in a host of specialty research and practice areas.

Despite this phenomenon's positive reflection on institutional vitality, the Association's justifiable concern has been that encouraging psychologists, licensing boards, or attorneys to view these as having the same requisite import and enforceability as the "Ethics Code" would saddle clinicians and researchers with an unreasonable burden of checklist-driven pressure and enhanced legal liability. As a result, what Association members have taken to calling the "Guidelines on Guidelines" provides direction to those promulgating these advisory resources to make it clear that the guidance in question is aspirational, not mandatory.

The following references are recommended for those interested in further investigation of ways in which "Guidelines" are properly styled and identified as such, making use of recent examples not included in other chapters of this book:

American Psychological Association. (2013). *Guidelines for psychological practice in health care delivery systems*. Retrieved from http://www.apa.org/practice/guidelines/ delivery-systems.aspx

American Psychological Association. (2014). Guidelines for prevention in psychology. *American Psychologist, 69*, 285–296. Retrieved from https://www.apa.org/pubs/ journals/features/amp-a0034569.pdf

American Psychological Association. (2016). *Professional practice guidelines for integrating the role of work and career into psychological practice*. Retrieved from http://www.apa.org/ about/policy/work-career-practice.pdf

American Psychological Association. (2017). *Clinical practice guideline for the treatment of posttraumatic stress disorder*. Retrieved from http://www.apa.org/ptsd-guideline/ index.aspx

American Psychological Association. (2017). *Professional practice guidelines for occupationally mandated psychological evaluations*. Retrieved from http://www.apa.org/ practice/guidelines/occupationally-mandated-psychological-evaluations.pdf

2

How Ethics Are Applied

After perhaps half a dozen years of classroom-based study through which ethical issues have been routed like a fine filament, and in the wake—for clinically oriented programs—of numerous cautiously monitored practicum and internship experiences, how will the newly minted psychologist find a way to put these lofty, still largely theoretical principles into practice?

Fear not; ethical conflicts will come knocking of their own accord, and in short order. A student supervisee—scarcely younger than the psychologist—wants to meet over dinner to discuss "a personal matter." A research colleague leaves a voice-mail message, with slurred diction, to explore a "brand new idea" for a study that was actually discussed in detail a few weeks ago. The parent of a 15-year-old client/patient demands delivery of "all the notes and test results" from the child's file because "we're going to get divorced now, as if you didn't know."

An ethical conflict doesn't afford us the courtesies of advanced warning, banker's hours, or patiently waiting until the *last* ethical conflict to come over the transom has been addressed to our satisfaction. To wish that these problems would stop occurring is, in effect to wish, for early retirement—the only foolproof method for ensuring that no more ethical conflicts will ensue.

Peer support is a critical factor in preparation for these perpetual distractions. As the preceding paragraph implies, developing such a network is not merely an early-career priority. Once the transition is made from calling up one's recent professors and supervisors for advice ("Didn't you graduate last spring?") to seeking out a cadre of like-minded colleagues via informal

http://dx.doi.org/10.1037/0000125-003
Ethical Conflicts in Psychology, Fifth Edition, by E. Y. Drogin

consultation and scheduled peer supervision groups, it becomes the psychologist's agenda, at times seemingly in the blink of an eye, to perpetuate and maintain such arrangements as a senior participant.

Just as a deep bench of fellow professionals is needed, so is a finely tuned yet flexible paradigm for addressing ethical conflicts on one's own. Not every research and practice conundrum is one that can be managed by committee. Ultimately, the final decision rests with the psychologist in question. When conflicts loom, seldom is there time to rescan the American Psychological Association's (2017) *Ethical Principles of Psychologists and Code of Conduct* (the "Ethics Code") in its entirety and order a book or two on the subject in question before at least some initial form of action is required.

Supplementing one's ongoing reading program is one way to maintain ethical readiness. For licensed clinicians, most jurisdictions require proof of having engaged in a certain number of hours of ethically oriented continuing education experiences, but it would be a mistake to rely on these periodic tune-ups as the sole means of remaining current. Mandatory continuing education is designed to ensure a minimally sufficient level of competency, not to serve as a substitute for a lifelong commitment to self-directed study.

Among its other features, this chapter addresses various tried-and-true ethical decision-making models, ethical ambiguities specific to practice with child clients/patients, the surveyed ethical beliefs and behaviors of psychologists, and methods for dealing with the inevitable collision of ethical and legal requirements.

REFERENCE

American Psychological Association. (2017). *Ethical principles of psychologists and code of conduct* (2002, Amended June 1, 2010 and January 1, 2017). Retrieved from http://www.apa.org/ethics/code/index.aspx

2.1. Ethical Decision Making in Mental Health Contexts: Representative Models and an Organizational Framework

R. Rocco Cottone

. . .

DEFINING ETHICAL DECISION MAKING IN PSYCHOLOGY

As used in this chapter, the term *ethical decision making* (sometimes referred to by others as *ethical problem solving* or *ethical choice making*) relates to the use of formal models or processes to address *professional ethical dilemmas within a mental health context*. Ethical choice and moral choice philosophy often address decisions, but those decisions are focused on choices that involve a moral dilemma (whether stealing to survive is justified or whether one should kill in self-defense, as examples). Literature also addresses decision making on matters of choices that have little to do with mental health practice—like choosing to buy a certain product when alternatives are available. The literature addressed in this chapter is limited to those publications or works that specifically attend to choices mental health professionals must make when facing a professional ethical dilemma. Literature outside of the mental health realm may be relevant to professional ethical decision making, but readers must be alerted to the specific contexts within which certain models or terminology apply. . . .

MAJOR INTELLECTUAL MOVEMENTS IN DECISION MAKING IN PSYCHOLOGY

Three major intellectual movements are relevant to the ethical decision making in psychology. An intellectual movement, as defined here, refers to a unique philosophical framework that excludes easy application of ideals from another competitive philosophy. For example, relying on a decision maker who rationally applies accepted standards is different than relinquishing a decision to someone based primarily on his or her character. Similarly, committee decision making and individual decision-making are mutually exclusive. As applied to decision making, an intellectual movement must have a unique

From *APA Handbook of Ethics in Psychology: Vol. 1. Moral Foundations and Common Themes* (pp. 99–121), by S. J. Knapp (Ed.), 2012, Washington, DC: American Psychological Association. Copyright 2012 by the American Psychological Association.

Special thanks to Hsin-hsin Huang for her assistance in producing this chapter.

philosophy on which decision making stands. Given this definition, the three major intellectual movements in the area of ethical decision making in psychology are principle ethics, virtue ethics, and relational ethics. Additionally, the theme of multicultural sensitivity represents an overarching framework within which decisions may be generated. Multicultural sensitivity does not rise to the level of a full-fledged movement, but it does provide a general theme within which decisions are framed. The next sections address the three intellectual movements and the theme of multicultural sensitivity as applied to ethical decision making in psychology.

Principle Ethics: The First Intellectual Movement in Psychology Decision Making

Some outstanding works on ethics in the health professions have influenced decision making in psychology. One of the most influential is a text entitled *Principles of Biomedical Ethics by Beauchamp and Childress* (2009), now in its sixth edition. The first edition was published in 1979. In keeping with the foundational work of R. W. Ross (1930) on principle ethics, Beauchamp and Childress defined four ethical principles to guide medical professionals in decision making. The principles were autonomy (the patient's right to make choices on his or her own), beneficence (the idea that medical professionals should primarily be concerned with the well-being of patients), nonmaleficence (the idea that medical professionals should do no harm), and justice (the idea that professionals should treat people fairly and without discrimination). They also defined an ethical rule (not as prominent as a principle) entitled "fidelity," meaning that medical professionals should be faithful to their patients. It was Kitchener, in 1984, who firmly brought psychology's attention to the biomedical ethical standards defined by Beauchamp and Childress. Kitchener (1984), in a seminal work, embraced the biomedical ethical principles, and she elevated Beauchamp and Childress's ethical rule of fidelity to an ethical principle in psychology (following the lead of Drane, 1982). (Beauchamp and Childress later defined *professional–patient relationships* as a principle, addressing concerns such as fidelity, privacy, and confidentiality.) Kitchener further heralded the works of Hare (1981) applying his two levels of moral thinking: intuition and critical evaluation. Kitchener's work is highly cited, and she succeeded in establishing the foundation for what can be called *principle ethics* in psychology. Principle ethics is the logical application of identified and highly accepted principles (overarching standards) that are crucial to any decision in psychology. Kitchener defined the ethical principles as prima facie, meaning they hold weight and should be set aside only for compelling reasons. (See Ross, 1930, seminal analysis of prima facie responsibility.) Kitchener stated,

> While the problems of applying ethical principles in decision making need to be acknowledged, this does not keep them from being useful or important. By accepting them as prima facie valid, we imply that their relevance always needs to be considered in ethical situations. (Kitchener, 1984, p. 53)

Kitchener's work (1984), specifically, and principle ethics, in general, lay the groundwork for defining one philosophical framework for understanding ethical decision making in psychology. Decision making is viewed as a process of an individual who considers ethical principles while deliberating an ethical dilemma. Principle ethics fits nicely within the context of a psychology that views the individual as a decision maker—a singular person who weighs options and makes choices.

Virtue Ethics: The Second Intellectual Movement in Psychology Decision Making

A competing view to principle ethics is *virtue ethics*. Initially, virtue ethics (which focuses on the character of the decision maker) was viewed as a complement to principle ethics. In the 21st century, virtue ethics often is described in general textbooks on ethics as a different or as an alternative approach to ethical judgment (Sommers-Flanagan & Sommers-Flanagan, 2007; Sperry, 2007; Welfel, 2006). Originally, Meara, Schmidt, and Day (1996) proposed that the virtue of the ethical agent (the decision maker) is crucial in decision making and worthy of study in tandem with the study of ethical principles. They proposed that personal character should be a major component in the decision process. The issue of virtue raises the discussion of making decisions from the simple means of defining right and wrong (e.g., means to avoid punishment for breaching an ethical standard or principle) to the means of an ethical ideal (virtuous professional psychologists). The proponents did not propose that virtue ethics should replace principle ethics, but they did make the case that virtue ethics complement principle ethics, and they even went so far as to call for an expansion of ethics research to encompass the character of the decision maker. They demonstrated that one cannot fully understand an ethical decision on the basis of principles alone: Some people will do the minimum only to avoid punishment or will not act ethically at all, whereas other people will embrace an ethical lifestyle regardless of ethical dictates. In either case, the decision maker is the crucial variable. This helps to explain why people bound by the same code of ethics act differently in similar circumstances.

Relational Ethics: The Third Intellectual Movement in Psychology Decision Making

A third philosophical or theoretical movement that has affected the decision-making literature is what can be identified as relational ethics. Relational ethics, which focuses on social context, has put principle ethics in perspective, just as virtue ethics provided another way to view the decision process. One of the first publications to address contextual factors was a chapter by Hill, Glaser, and Harden (1995). In that chapter, the authors argued that consideration of contextual factors enters into value judgments, and therefore context affects decision making. They stated,

> Time in a particular setting or working from a certain theoretical base represents at least a certain amount of exposure to specific values and often a personal investment in those values. Factors such as gender, ethnicity or race, religious

background, geographic location, and so forth, are even more obviously related to values. The therapist's personal experiences of oppression and the uses of power (e.g., through race, sexual orientation, gender, size, disability, class, and age) will sensitize that individual in certain ways. Those same factors and others (such as religious background, family or living situation, or geographic location) will influence the therapist's priorities and assumptions. In order to make a feminist model for decision making, these aspects of who the therapist is cannot be separated from the decisions that she or he makes. If therapists turn to ethical decision-making models that do not address these factors, they then run the risk of making these factors invisible and thus not open to scrutiny. (1995, p. 25)

Hill et al. made a case for consideration of the social–cultural context in decision making, "particularly as it relates to issues of power" (1995, p. 36). They provided a stepwise model for decision making, which they called "a feminist model for ethical decision making." The steps are as follows: (a) recognizing a problem, (b) defining the problem, (c) developing solutions, (d) choosing a solution, (e) reviewing process, (f) implementing and evaluating the decision, and (g) continuing reflection. They argued that through the decision-making process the feminist must consider "the emotional-intuitive responses of the therapist; the sociocultural context of the therapist, client, and consultant particularly as it relates to issues of power; and the client's participation in the decision making process" (1995, p. 36). The call for a feminist ethics is a call for placing principle ethics in the context of social (and specifically social power) considerations.

Betan (1997) also made a significant contribution to the decision-making literature by introducing a hermeneutic model of ethical decision making. Hermeneutics is a philosophical framework through which knowledge is viewed as residing in the context of human relationships. Betan stated, "Hermeneutics involves an awareness that the process of inquiry is affected by and in turn affects the person seeking knowledge" (1997, p. 352). Therefore, all historical, personal, and circumstantial factors are involved in every decision. Even ethical principles are viewed as historical and circumstantially situated— they are not standards that come from some objective source of knowledge— they are reflective of the cultural context from which they emerge and the situation in which they are applied. Betan did not provide a stepwise model for decision making. He attempted, however, to demonstrate that hermeneutics "allows the therapist to remain part of the situation, and it places authority not in abstract, externally imposed principles but rather in the connection between therapist and patient" (1997, p. 362). Social and relational considerations are prominent in this model. Still, in hermeneutics, there is an individual decision maker. The decision is not made by a committee. In other words, the model is not so extreme as to situate the mind of the individual in the social matrix. Some (one) person does weigh the social factors that are involved in a decision, and the decision is still a psychological process for the decision maker.

Cottone's (2001) model is much more extreme. Guided by social constructivism as a philosophical movement in the human services, Cottone took an extreme relational stance, claiming that decisions are not made in the head of the apparent decision maker—rather they reflect a consensualizing process that is culturally, socially, and interpersonally imbedded. He built on the works of Gergen (1985) on the constructionist movement in modern psychology, and he used the works of Maturana (1980) on the biology of cognition (as lauded by Dell, 1985) as representing a fully relational view of the human condition. Using these foundational works, Cottone developed a social constructivism model of ethical decision making, which is completely interpersonal. Decisions are taken out of the decision maker's head and placed within the social interactive context. Decision making involves negotiating, consensualizing, and arbitrating, rather than individual deliberation. . . .

THE ETHICAL DECISION MAKER'S DECISION-MAKING DILEMMA

Beyond the issue of autonomy, the profession of psychology must also be alert to another issue that may compromise easy application of standards. Professional psychology has arrived at a place at which a psychologist, confronted with an ethical dilemma, must not only address the dilemma, but also make a decision as to which ethical decision-making model to apply.

For Canadian psychologists, the CPA's *Canadian Code of Ethics for Psychologists* (CPA, 2000) provides a recommended decision-making model. The CPA model is clearly a model of individual choice—providing logical steps for applying the CPA ethical standards. It is not attuned to the influence of relational or multicultural factors (group influence is given lip service) or to the relative weight applied to professional consultation (which is addressed only as a postscript to the model). Although there are weaknesses in the model, at least Canadian psychologists know what is expected of them when applying standards from their code of ethics. Members of the APA comparatively have much more flexibility in applying decision-making models to an ethical dilemma, for better or for worse.

It is ironic that the profession of psychology, which prides itself on its scientific foundation, has little in the way of scientific data to offer the practitioner attempting to discern which decision-making model to use. Only a few studies have empirically assessed ethical decision-making models (e.g., Dinger, 1997; Garcia, McGuire-Kuletz, Froehlich, & Dave, 2008; Garcia, Winston, Borzuchowska, & McGuire-Kuletz, 2004). The number of published studies is surprisingly small; this may be true, in part, because ethical decision-making processes have derived their meaning from the study of ethics, which is a branch of philosophy. It is easy to see that the nature of decision-making models is aligned with the study of moral philosophy and the literature of moral choice. Theories of philosophy underpin some of the best known models (e.g., utilitarianism). The application of logic (another branch of philosophy) also pervades existing decision-making models. There is, therefore, more of a philosophical than empirical basis for decision-making model development. Decision-making models, only recently and by means of virtue ethics and the relational movements, are breaking from the classic philosophical mode. The newer models offer distinctions that may serve researchers well, as they begin to define real and measurable differences in the processes involved in decision making. For example, Cottone's (2001) social constructivism model provides an opportunity to measure observable interpersonal processes in the decision process, in contrast to the isolated weighing of options (based on some criterion) of the typical model of individual choice. In effect, the decision-making knowledge base has expanded to the degree that empirical studies may prove fruitful.

A question that logically flows from this analysis is, "Does it really matter what model is chosen?" It is fair to ask, "Aren't most decision-making models going to lead to the same conclusions?" The answer is that it does matter because decisions may be quite different depending on the model. For instance, a model that operates on the extreme of one of the intellectual movements of psychology decision making (principle, virtue, relational) or that takes a purist philosophical position (utilitarianism, social constructivism) likely will produce outcomes that are different and perhaps unique to the model. . . .

REFERENCES

Beauchamp, T. L., & Childress, J. F. (2009). *Principles of biomedical ethics* (6th ed.). New York, NY: Oxford University Press.

Betan, E. J. (1997). Toward a hermeneutic model of ethical decision-making in clinical practice. *Ethics and Behavior, 7,* 347–365. http://dx.doi.org/10.1207/s15327019eb0704_6

Canadian Psychological Association. (2000). *Canadian code of ethics for psychologists* (3rd ed.). Ottawa, Canada: Author.

Cottone, R. R. (2001). A social constructivism model of ethical decisionmaking in counseling. *Journal of Counseling and Development, 79,* 39–45.

Dell, P. F. (1985). Understanding Bateson and Maturana: Toward a biological foundation for the social sciences. *Journal of Marital and Family Therapy, 11,* 1–20. http://dx.doi.org/10.1111/j.1752-0606.1985.tb00587.x

Dinger, T. J. (1997, April). *Do ethical decision-making models really work? An empirical study.* Paper presented at the American Counseling Association World Conference, Orlando, FL.

Drane, J. F. (1982). Ethics and psychotherapy: A philosophical perspective. In M. Rosenbaum (Ed.), *Ethics and values in psychotherapy* (pp. 15–50). New York, NY: Free Press.

Garcia, J., McGuire-Kuletz, M., Froehlich, R., & Dave, P. (2008). Testing a transcultural model of ethical decision making with rehabilitation counselors. *Journal of Rehabilitation, 74,* 21–26.

Garcia, J. G., Winston, S. M., Borzuchowska, B., & McGuire-Kuletz, M. (2004). Evaluating the integrative model of ethical decision-making. *Rehabilitation Education, 18,* 147–164.

Gergen, K. J. (1985). The social constructionist movement in modern psychology. *American Psychologist, 40,* 266–275. http://dx.doi.org/10.1037/0003-066X.40.3.266

Hare, R. (1981). The philosophical basis of psychiatric ethics. In S. Block & P. Chodoff (Eds.), *Psychiatric ethics* (pp. 31–45). Oxford, England: Oxford University Press.

Hill, M., Glaser, K., & Harden, J. (1995). A feminist model for ethical decision-making. In E. J. Rave & C. C. Larsen (Eds.), *Ethical decision-making in therapy: Feminist perspectives* (pp. 18–37). New York, NY: Guilford Press.

Kitchener, K. S. (1984). Intuition, critical evaluation and ethical principles: The foundation for ethical decisions in counseling psychology. *The Counseling Psychologist, 12,* 43–55. http://dx.doi.org/10.1177/0011000084123005

Maturana, H. R. (1980). Biology of cognition. In H. R. Maturana & F. J. Varela (Eds.), *Autopoiesis and cognition: The realization of the living* (pp. 5–58). Boston, MA: Reidel. (Original work published 1970)

Meara, N. M., Schmidt, L. D., & Day, J. D. (1996). Principles and virtues: A foundation for ethical decisions, policies, and character. *The Counseling Psychologist, 24,* 4–77. http://dx.doi.org/10.1177/0011000096241002

Ross, W. D. (1930). *The right and the good.* Oxford, England: Oxford University Press.

Sommers-Flanagan, R., & Sommers-Flanagan, J. (2007). *Becoming an ethical helping professional: Cultural and philosophical foundations.* Hoboken, NJ: Wiley.

Sperry, L. (2007). *The ethical and professional practice of counseling and psychotherapy.* Boston, MA: Pearson/Allyn & Bacon.

Welfel, E. R. (2006). *Ethics in counseling and psychotherapy: Standards, research, and emerging issues* (3rd ed.). Belmont, CA: Thompson Brooks/Cole.

2.2. Ethical Ambiguities in the Practice of Child Clinical Psychology

Carole I. Mannheim, Michael Sancilio, Susan Phipps-Yonas, Donald Brunnquell, Peter Somers, Georganne Farseth, and Fred Ninonuevo

This might have happened to you. In 1991 an article appeared in the *Minneapolis Star Tribune* in which it was noted that a licensed psychologist had been disciplined by the Minnesota Board of Psychology because, among other infractions, she had taken a preschool-age client to the restroom during a therapy session; she had also had dinner in the hospital cafeteria with a young adolescent client (who had missed her bus after a session and had to wait an hour in the early evening for the next one). Many practicing child psychologists reacted with surprise, questioning why such behaviors were deemed problematic, much less unethical. Concerns were raised as to whether the state licensing board was sensitive to the problems that surface regularly for practitioners who work with children and adolescents. Although it may seem obvious on an abstract level that developmental factors affect the types of assessment and interventions that can be applied to a client, it does not follow that professionals who work exclusively with adults readily appreciate the added complexities of working with a younger clientele. For example, a competent adult psychologist would never propose that a 9-year-old take the Minnesota Multiphasic Personality Inventory, but that psychologist also might not recognize the fact that giving treats to or accepting hand-made presents from a young child has a very different meaning (and an inherent ethical propriety) for the child than it would for an adult client under identical circumstances.

A task force of child psychologists in Minnesota was formed to address what seemed to be a void in the consideration of ethical dilemmas unique to professionals who provide services to minors and their families. In 1992 a survey was conducted among a small sample of child psychologists in Minnesota, and the findings (Child Psychology Task Force, 1992) highlighted the difficulties that such practitioners face in their day-to-day work.

The present study came about as an effort to expand upon those findings. Its objectives were to (a) assess the prevalence of specified professional practices

From "Ethical Ambiguities in the Practice of Child Clinical Psychology," by C. I. Mannheim, M. Sancilio, S. Phipps-Yonas, D. Brunnquell, P. Somers, G. Farseth, and F. Ninonuevo, 2002, *Professional Psychology: Research and Practice, 33*, pp. 24–29. Copyright 2002 by the American Psychological Association.

uniquely salient in clinical work with children and their families, (b) survey the professional community's perception of the ethical propriety of those designated practices, (c) explore the extent of ethical ambiguity when applying professional standards and ethical guidelines to clinical work with children, and (d) examine the extent to which specialization in adult as opposed to child clinical practice affects the perception of ethical propriety.

THE MINNESOTA CHILD PSYCHOLOGISTS' SURVEY

The survey instrument for this study was constructed by the Ethics and Standards of Practice Committee of the Minnesota Child Psychologists. This group of six clinical child psychologists represents a diverse array of practice settings. They began with a pool of 45 practice behaviors taken from an earlier, local survey developed by the Minnesota Child Psychology Task Force (1992). Additional items were culled from other published surveys on ethical issues (Borys & Pope, 1989; Gibson & Pope, 1993; Pope, Tabachnick, & Keith-Spiegel, 1987, 1988; Rae & Worchel, 1991; Tabachnick, Keith-Spiegel, & Pope, 1991) and adapted to reflect ethical dilemmas frequently encountered in child practice settings.

Certain survey items were drafted in parallel forms in order to permit comparisons of the ethical propriety of a particular practice across developmental levels (i.e., preschool, school age, adolescent, and/or adult). Thus, a single professional practice could be presented for two, three, or four ratings. Parallel forms were also developed to permit comparisons between various contexts, such as service mode (i.e., assessment vs. therapy), relationships (e.g., treating a sibling vs. a parent of a child client), and levels of consent. After conducting a pilot survey to ensure that the final survey could be completed in 30 min and did not include items lacking special salience for practitioners working with minors, we included in the final version of the survey 33 numbered practice behavior items, 22 of which were presented in parallel forms, resulting in a total of 76 items.

To facilitate presentation of the data, we clustered the 76 survey items into four rationally derived thematic groups. These groups, delineated in the Appendix, include the following:

1. Clinical boundary issues involving practices that are not an intrinsic part of clinical intervention but may coincidentally occur within the context of a clinical intervention.

2. Professional relationship issues involving possible dilemmas with multiclient families and potential dual relationships with current and former clients.

3. Confidentiality issues.

4. Forensic opinions pertaining to custody and other placement issues for a child or an adolescent being seen in individual therapy.

Each of the items required ratings on two 5-point Likert-type scales. The first rating scale, My Practice, measured the prevalence of each practice. Here, respondents were directed to identify the frequency with which they personally engaged in the identified practice (*never, rarely, sometimes, fairly often, very often*, and *not applicable*). A second scale, Ethical Propriety, asked respondents to designate "your judgment about the ethics of such a practice, whether you actually do it or not. For example, you may make it a practice never to shake a client's hand, but you might not judge it unethical for another clinician to do so." The response options for this scale included the following: *unquestionably not ethical, ethical under rare circumstances, ethical under some circumstances, ethical under many circumstances, and unquestionably ethical.* Another response option was *don't know/uncertain.*

Three types of ethical ambiguity, all derived from the respondents' ratings of ethical propriety, were investigated in this study:

1. *Individual uncertainty,* the extent to which individuals are unable to decide about the ethical propriety of a practice, was operationally defined as the percentage of *don't know/uncertain* responses to each item.

2. *Group variability,* reflecting the degree of consensus or controversy among those offering an opinion about the ethical propriety of a practice, was indicated by both the standard deviation of the item's ethical ratings and the shape (kurtosis) of the rating distribution.

3. *Situational variability,* or the degree to which ethical propriety is viewed as dependent on the specific circumstances in which the behavior occurs, was reflected in the effect of contextual variables on the ethical ratings for a given professional activity. One measure of situational variability was the degree to which respondents rated a practice as ethical *under some circumstances* (the middle response option, as opposed to either of the more positive or negative sets of response options). A second indicator of situational variability was derived by contrasting ratings from parallel forms of a practice item that varied only on a single contextual dimension (e.g., the developmental level of the client).

Survey participants came from two sources: (a) the roster of licensed psychologists maintained by the Minnesota State Board of Psychology and (b) the roster of school psychologists maintained by the Special Education Division of the Minnesota Department of Families, Children, and Learning. The former source included an undifferentiated pool of child and adult clinicians, industrial-organizational psychologists, and academic psychologists. The latter source included only certified school psychologists in public schools (kindergarten through Grade 12). When psychologists' names appeared on both rosters, they were categorized as school psychologists. We then randomly selected 700 psychologists from the pool of licensed psychologists to receive the survey. We sent the survey to all 368 psychologists on the roster of school psychologists, yielding a total potential pool of 1,068 respondents. The final survey was mailed under cover of the sponsoring professional association (Minnesota Child Psychologists) but with an explicit request and rationale for participation by those who were not child practitioners. Stamped, self-addressed return envelopes were included in this mailing, along with the names and telephone numbers of contact resources. Approximately 10 days following the initial mailing, we mailed follow-up postcards requesting completion and return of the surveys. Of the 1,068 surveys sent out, 354 (33%) were returned. The response rates were equivalent across the pools of licensed and school psychologists.

SURVEY FINDINGS

Notwithstanding the size of this data set and the wide array of possible analytical approaches, this article limits its focus to general trends, developmental comparisons, and ethical ambiguity. Analyses of rating differences between principally adult and child practitioners and between rural and urban practitioners will be reported in future articles.

Clinical Boundary Issues

When we compared ethical ratings in this category with the developmental level of the client, evidence emerged for a significant age-related gradient on all of the items, with Items 1 and 2 showing significant differences among all age groups. Whether the practice concerned accepting a hug or attending a client's major life event, the younger the client was, the more the practice in question received positive ethical ratings and fewer negative ratings.

Individual uncertainty, averaging 6.8% across all items in this cluster, was lower than that in the other item clusters, but not uniformly so: Only 3.5–4.4% of respondents were unsure about the propriety of accepting client hugs; the percentage rose to 17.1% in the case of assisting preschoolers with toileting. Ethical uncertainty was unrelated to the developmental status of the client except in the single case of restraining out-of-control clients. Here, McNemar's Test revealed greater uncertainty ($p = .02$) about restraining an adolescent (vs. a school-aged) client from damaging property.

In spite of respondents' relative confidence about the ethical propriety of practices in this category, group consensus, whether measured by standard deviation (ranging from 0.90 on Item 5b to 1.20 on Item 3c) or kurtosis of the response distribution (ranging from −0.93 on Item 21 to 1.00 on Item 8c), was the most fragile among the four content clusters. The likeliest practices to spark ethical controversy included restraining young clients (Items 2a, 2b, and 3c) and escorting preschoolers to the restroom (Item 8a).

Contextual considerations (as measured by endorsement of the middle response option, *ethical under some circumstances*) figured prominently (as the modal response category) in 46% of all 76 practices enumerated in this survey.

In the case of clinical boundary practices, 41% of the rated practices produced this modal endorsement, including accepting hugs from clients (Items 1a, 1b), restraining out-of-control clients (Items 2a–2c), rewarding clients with special food-outings (Item 4a), buying fund-raiser items from child clients (Item 6a), and giving gifts to child clients (Item 7a).

Professional Relationship Issues

Evidence for an age-related gradient in ethical ratings reappeared in all of the items contained in this cluster, which focused on multiclient families and other potential client conflicts.

Individual uncertainty averaged 9.5% in this cluster. Respondents displayed the least uncertainty about the propriety of social relationships with former clients or their parents (Items 15a–15c) and accepting child clients who had indirect social connections to the psychologist (Items 14a–14c; *don't know* percentages ranged from 2.4 to 5.3). The greatest uncertainty (15.0–16.2%) was associated with the practice of accepting as a private client someone with whom professional contact was first made in another setting, adding concurrent family therapy when already providing individual therapy to a member of the family, and adding concurrent individual therapy with a family member already being seen in family therapy. Although uncertainty in this cluster was not generally related to the developmental status of the client, more respondents indicated uncertainty about the propriety of diagnostically assessing the parent of a current child or adolescent client than doing the same assessment with a sibling (McNemar's Test, $p < .01$) or other relative ($p = .04$).

In this cluster, ethical confidence better coincided with consensus. Respondents as a group were in close agreement about the ethical impropriety of engaging in social relationships with former clients or with parents of current child clients ($SD = 0.79$ and 0.80, respectively; kurtosis = 1.95 and 2.79, respectively).

Contextual considerations were perceived as critical in 74% of the 27 items in this cluster, although they played a notably minimal role when respondents evaluated the propriety of social relationships with a client's parents or with a former client.

Confidentiality

Strong evidence for the operation of an age-related gradient reappeared in items constituting this cluster; rating differences suggest that protecting the privacy of adolescent clients is viewed as more ethically imperative than protecting that of younger clients.

Among the practices in this cluster, uncertainty was lowest (at 3.2–6.5%) about reporting significant behaviors of a young client over the client's objection. Uncertainty was highest about two record-keeping issues: maintaining individual records for each participating member in family therapy (Item 26;

20.9%) and filing parent test data in a child's clinical record (Item 23; 18.8%). Developmental status had no bearing on ethical uncertainty.

Group consensus and controversy were wide-ranging (SDs = 0.83–1.27; kurtosis = −0.94 to 2.96) in this cluster. Five practices from this cluster produced the greatest response variability survey-wide, including placement of parental data in the child's clinical record; refusal to share the contents of a therapy session with a parent when doing so is viewed as being in the client's best interests; sharing the contents of a therapy session with a parent after informing the child but not obtaining the child's consent; and exchanging information regarding a client with an agency colleague who is working with another member of the client's family, after obtaining a signed release. Other items with similar content also produced rating distributions with relatively high standard deviations, suggesting similarly high levels of potential controversy. Two practices that produced relatively little rating variation concerned the report of dangerous behaviors to parents (Items 18a and 18b).

Few behaviors in this cluster produced high percentages of respondents who perceived situational factors to have a significant influence on ethical propriety. Only 5 of the 20 practices produced modal responses suggesting situational leeway. These included reporting antisocial behavior to parents, honoring a child's request to refuse parental disclosure, engaging in collegial exchanges about client families, and recording parental data in a child's clinical record (Items 18c, 19b, 20b, 21b, and 22).

Forensic Opinions

Forensic practices elicited the highest levels surveywide of individual uncertainty, averaging 17.6% of the sample across the items in this category.

Forensic practice items also elicited the five highest levels of group concurrence about ethical propriety surveywide. Those items pertained to conducting custody evaluations without attempting to see all the parties (Items 32a, 32b, and 32c) and proffering recommendations about visitation or family reunification without attempting to see all the parties (Items 33a and 33b).

Only two of the seven practices in this cluster produced modal endorsements of situationally qualified ethical ratings (Items 24 and 25). The remaining five practices produced the lowest level of endorsement survey wide of contextual qualifiers, suggesting that most survey respondents perceived the ethical propriety of forensic practices to be relatively unamenable to the influence of case-specific factors.

IMPLICATIONS

Were you aware that the majority of your professional colleagues report that they will commonly overrule a young client's objection about reporting dangerous behaviors or instances of personal victimization to the child's parent but will rarely, if ever, otherwise report a young client's disclosures to a parent without first seeking the child's consent or at least informing the client? Such knowledge about normative standards, as Pope et al. (1987) noted 15 years ago, is essential for psychologists to be able to regulate their own professional behavior. Those researchers decried the relative absence of comprehensive data that could inform decision making, and they called for further work. Although the present survey answered that call, the results suggest that little may have changed since that first groundbreaking survey, insofar as actual practice varies so widely among clinicians. With few exceptions, the majority of the psychologists who responded implemented the practices under consideration in this survey at least on occasion. Nevertheless, certain practices (taking adult clients out for food or rewards; maintaining social relationships with former child clients or their parents) appeared to be relatively rare; others (overriding young clients' objections to parental disclosure, as noted previously) appeared commonplace. Although frequency data can assist practitioners in identifying what constitutes standard practice, such data are less useful in informing practitioners about what they should and should not do.

In terms of ratings of ethical propriety, even here their guidance value is far from clear-cut, particularly in the case of boundary-related and professional relationship practices, where situational considerations seemed to hold sway with the largest group of survey respondents. Indeed, situational considerations predominated respondents' ethical ratings in nearly half of the practices surveyed.

One specific contextual variant—developmental status of the client— emerged as a robust factor in the perceived ethical propriety of given practices. In all three practice categories where this factor was varied, evidence of an age-related gradient uniformly appeared. Generally, the younger the client, the greater the leniency when evaluating the propriety of the specified practice. Thus, 49% of survey participants viewed accepting an adult client's hug as only rarely, if ever, ethical, whereas one fourth that number, or 12% of the sample, maintained that stance when the client was a preschooler. Age-dependent ethical ratings appeared to be particularly relevant with practices related to clinical boundary issues, such as rewarding clients with food-outings, attending client celebrations, or providing them with gifts, not unlike the sanctioned practices described in the introduction to this article. In light of these data, rigidly holding child practitioners accountable to the same standards designed with an adult clientele in mind may be undesirable, if not inappropriate, from a developmental perspective. Context was less influential when judging the ethical propriety of practices related to client confidentiality and forensic assessments, perhaps because of the abundance of state and federal statutes, as well as rules, regulations, and agency policies relating to these issues (see Hansen & Goldberg, 1999, for a thoughtful discussion of how such considerations influence ethical decision-making strategies).

The guidance value of ethical ratings may be further undercut by their distributional variations. When there is relative consensus in the ratings, as in the case of participating in social relationships with former clients or with parents of current child clients and reporting dangerous behaviors to parents, the ratings can more reliably guide practitioners' ethical practice. However, in instances in which controversy has been reflected in high variances, as in the case of restraining young clients, escorting preschoolers to the restroom, or placing parent data in child clinical records, the practitioner may discover that the ratings constitute a less reliable basis for defending a practice.

Given the contextual and conditional instability of ethical perceptions, there should be little wonder that the average practitioner can easily become confused or lack confidence when ethical choices emerge in day-to-day practice. Interestingly, in this survey, consensus and controversy appeared unrelated to the level of individual ethical uncertainty except in the area of forensic practice. There, however, the relationship that emerged was counterintuitive. Those forensic practices enjoying the highest levels of rating consensus also produced the highest levels of ethical uncertainty among responding practitioners. Perhaps the limits of one's competence become more evident in areas of high-profile practice, where the professional community, under the pressure of external scrutiny, has developed relatively unequivocal standards. A practitioner is then likelier to be aware that a standard exists, even if its specifics have never personally been mastered.

What has been referred to as individual uncertainty in this study (expressed in *don't know/uncertain* responses) has been characterized by other researchers (Pope et al., 1987; Tabachnick et al., 1991) as "difficult judgments." It should be noted, however, that the percentages reported in this study may underestimate the actual level of individual uncertainty, because this number reflects only a subset of those not providing a positive or negative ethical rating. An additional subset of participants (ranging from 4.4% to 13.8% across all survey items, with a mean of 8.3%) failed to endorse any response. It appears likely that many, if not most, of these omissions also reflect uncertainty. The correlation (.61) between the subsets suggests considerable overlap.

The predominantly negative view among this survey's participants on the issue of developing social relationships with clients or their parents merits comment. Such relationships were viewed by a majority of this survey's respondents as unquestionably not ethical in the case of former clients and the parents of current child clients; the proportion dipped slightly to 44% of the sample in the case of socializing with the parents of a former child client. Only 6.4% of the psychologists surveyed by Pope et al. (1987) had offered such a negative assessment. In a similar vein, almost one fifth of the respondents in the present study proscribed the practice of attending a client's special event, up from the 5% of the Pope et al. (1987) sample that rated such behavior as never ethical. These disparities suggest that Minnesota psychologists may differ from colleagues in other states or, alternatively, that there has been a major shift in beliefs. The disparities also serve to highlight the potential limitations of this survey: Our data reflect the behaviors and opinions of psychologists from a single, midwestern state, where the response rate (one in three) was less than optimal and information about the representativeness of the participating sample was unavailable. Additionally, no reliability estimates exist for the measures.

Notwithstanding any cautionary limitations on the generalizability of our data, this study constitutes an important step in what should become an ongoing process of elaborating and qualifying professional standards so they can more effectively guide both the psychologist engaged in professional practice, as well as the psychologist who has been entrusted with responsibility for professional oversight. These survey results specifically caution psychologists to be mindful of the various contextual factors that may affect the ethical propriety of a specific practice or relationship. They further suggest that psychologists may need to consider developing different sets of standards to address the situational specifics encountered in different types of practices. The robust age-related gradient evident in this study, for example, strongly argues against the blanket application of standards developed with an adult clientele in mind to clinical practice with children. Psychologists who serve children and adolescents may need to construct an independent set of ethical guidelines that, while adhering to the same general principles of their colleagues, more realistically addresses the many special circumstances and considerations that are unique to their work. Because ethical ambiguities and uncertainty are certain to survive the refinement of more population-specific standards, psychologists will also need to recognize that their empirical data can never fully replace the professional decision-making process. The successful application of our aspirational standards to the day-to-day work of clinical practice will most likely remain a complex and stimulating challenge for coming generations of professional practitioners.

APPENDIX
SURVEY ITEMS GROUPED THEMATICALLY

CLINICAL BOUNDARY ISSUES

1. I accept hugs from clients if they are:
   a. Preschool age
   b. School age
   c. Adolescent
   d. Adult

2. I restrain tantrumming clients who are damaging property if they are:
   a. Preschool age
   b. School age
   c. Adolescent

3. I restrain tantrumming clients who are in danger of hurting themselves or others if they are:
   a. Preschool age
   b. School age
   c. Adolescent

4. I take clients out for food or other rewards during a therapy hour if they are:
   a. Children/adolescents
   b. Adult

5. I accept invitations to clients' outside events (e.g., school plays, recitals, graduations, weddings) if they are:
   a. Children/adolescents
   b. Adult

6. I buy things from clients (e.g., Girl Scout cookies, raffle tickets) if they are:
   a. Children/adolescents
   b. Adult

7. I give gifts to clients for special events (e.g., termination) if they are:
   a. Children/adolescents
   b. Adult

8. I escort clients to the restroom if they are:
   a. Preschool age
   b. School age
   c. Adolescent

9. I assist preschool-aged, outpatient clients with toiletting.

PROFESSIONAL RELATIONSHIP ISSUES

10. I take as a separate client for individual *therapy* a current child or adolescent client's:
    a. Sibling
    b. Parent
    c. Other relative(s)
    d. Close personal friend

11. I take as a separate client for individual *therapy* a current adult client's:
    a. Child
    b. Spouse or partner
    c. Relative(s)
    d. Close personal friend

12. I take as a separate client for *diagnostic evaluation* a current child or adolescent client's:
    a. Sibling
    b. Parent(s)
    c. Other relative(s)
    d. Close personal friend

13. I take as a separate client for *diagnostic evaluation* a current adult client's:
    a. Child
    b. Spouse or partner
    c. Relative(s)
    d. Close personal friend

14. I accept as a client, a child:
    a. Of a personal friend
    b. Of a professional colleague with whom I have periodic professional contact
    c. Who attends my child's school, church, etc.

15. I initiate or maintain social relationships with:
    a. A former client
    b. A parent of a current child client
    c. A parent of a former child client

27. I agree to conduct ongoing family therapy when I already have a current psychotherapy relationship with a child or adolescent member of the family.

28. I agree to conduct ongoing family therapy when I already have a current psychotherapy relationship with an adult member of the family.

29. I agree to conduct individual therapy with a child or adolescent member of a family for whom I currently provide family therapy.

30. I agree to conduct individual therapy with an adult member of a family for whom I currently provide family therapy.

31. I accept as private patients, clients with whom I first had professional contact in another, current job setting (full- or part-time consultation, etc.).

CONFIDENTIALITY ISSUES

16. I disclose information from a *child* client's individual therapy to a parent or legal guardian who requests it:
    a. Without informing the child or seeking the child's consent
    b. After informing the child but without asking for the child's consent
    c. After informing the child and even if the child objects

17. I disclose information from an adolescent client's individual therapy to a parent or legal guardian who requests it:
    a. Without informing the adolescent or seeking the adolescent's consent
    b. After informing the adolescent but without asking for his/her consent
    c. After informing the adolescent and even if the adolescent objects

18. I would report to the parents or legal guardian, over the objections of my child or adolescent client their report of:
    a. Behaviors that are dangerous to themselves
    b. Behaviors that are dangerous to others
    c. Antisocial behaviors
    d. Victimization

19. I refuse to disclose information from a *child* client's individual therapy to a parent or legal guardian who requests it when:
    a. I believe it is in the child's best interests
    b. The child requests that I do so

20. I refuse to disclose information from an *adolescent* client's individual therapy to a parent or legal guardian who requests it, when:
    a. I believe it is in the adolescent's best interests
    b. The adolescent requests that I do so

21. I exchange information about my client with colleagues at my agency who work with a family member of my client:
    a. Without informing my client
    b. With oral permission from my client but without a signed release
    c. With a signed release from my client (or my client's legal guardian)

22. I record details of the parent's personal life, such as mental health history, in the child's clinical record.

23. I file parent test data (e.g., MMPI [Minnesota Multiphasic Personality Inventory]) in the child's clinical record.

26. I maintain individual records for each family member participating in ongoing family therapy.

FORENSIC ISSUES

24. I offer expert opinions to the Court about *specific* custody/visitation placements for children and adolescents I see in psychotherapy.

25. I offer opinions about other legally mediated matters about children and adolescents I see in psychotherapy, such as out-of-home placements, juvenile court dispositions, personal injury, etc.

32. I perform a custody evaluation without attempting to see:
    a. The child
    b. Either parent
    c. Both parents

33. I make recommendations regarding visitation and/or reunification between a child in out-of-home placement and his or her parent(s) without attempting to see:
    a. The child
    b. The parent(s)

REFERENCES

Borys, D. S., & Pope, K. S. (1989). Dual relationships between therapist and client: A national study of psychologists, psychiatrists, and social workers. *Professional Psychology: Research and Practice, 20*, 283–293.

Child Psychology Task Force. (1992). *Community standards for child and family practice in Minnesota*. Unpublished manuscript.

Gibson, W. T., & Pope, K. S. (1993). The ethics of counseling: A national survey of certified counselors. *Journal of Counseling and Development, 71*, 330–336.

Hansen, N. D., & Goldberg, S. G. (1999). Navigating the nuances: A matrix of considerations for ethical-legal dilemmas. *Professional Psychology: Research and Practice, 30*, 495–503.

Pope, K. S., Tabachnick, B. G., & Keith-Spiegel, P. (1987). Ethics of practice: The beliefs and behaviors of psychologists as therapists. *American Psychologist, 42*, 993–1006.

Pope, K. S., Tabachnick, B. G., & Keith-Spiegel, P. (1988). Good and poor practices in psychotherapy: National survey of beliefs of psychologists. *Professional Psychology: Research and Practice, 19*, 547–552.

Rae, W. A., & Worchel, F. F. (1991). Ethical beliefs and behaviors or pediatric psychologists: A survey. *Journal of Pediatric Psychology, 16*, 727–745.

Tabachnick, B. G., Keith-Spiegel, P., & Pope, K. S. (1991). Ethics of teaching: Beliefs and behaviors of psychologists as educators. *American Psychologist, 46*, 506–515.

COMMENTARY: Ethical issues in practice with children are immeasurably complicated by the fact that minor clients/patients are often minimally communicative, hampered by some combination of conditions and circumstances that make them appear even less functional than their chronological age, and subject to the directions, demands, and sometimes conflicting needs of parents, guardians, or treatment providers. The American Psychological Association's (2017) *Ethical Principles of Psychologists and Code of Conduct* addresses much of what may transpire in these and similar situations but affords comparatively little direct guidance concerning ethical issues of children per se.

Dr. Mannheim and her colleagues have conducted a survey that—over a decade and a half later—still continues to highlight notions of critical importance to the contemporary clinician. It is no less true today that with respect to the child client/patient "the average practitioner can easily become confused or lack confidence when ethical choices emerge in day-to-day practice." Perhaps more than in any other specialty area, psychologists treating this population need recourse to regular peer supervision on ethical issues and continuing education that is supplemented by reference to prevailing legal requirements.

The following references are recommended for those interested in further investigation of the unique ethical concerns arising in service provision to minor children, with particular attention to highly specialized contexts.

Becker-Blease, K. A., & Freyd, J. J. (2006). Research participants telling the truth about their lives: The ethics of asking and not asking about abuse. *American Psychologist, 61,* 218–226. http://dx.doi.org/10.1037/0003-066X.61.3.218

Byars, K. C., & Simon, S. L. (2016). Behavioral treatment of pediatric sleep disturbance: Ethical considerations for pediatric psychology practice. *Clinical Practice in Pediatric Psychology, 4,* 241–248. http://dx.doi.org/10.1037/cpp0000149

Cardona, L. (2017). Ethical considerations in the care of children with life-limiting conditions: A case illustration of the role of a pediatric psychologist on a hospital ethics committee. *Clinical Practice in Pediatric Psychology, 5,* 287–293. http://dx.doi.org/10.1037/cpp0000205

Edwards, V. J., Dube, S. R., Felitti, V. J., & Anda, R. F. (2007). It's OK to ask about past abuse. *American Psychologist, 62,* 327–328. http://dx.doi.org/10.1037/0003-066X62.4.327

Morrissey, M. B., & Whitehouse, P. (2016). From suffering to holistic flourishing: Emancipatory maternal care practices—A substantive notion of the good. *Journal of Theoretical and Philosophical Psychology, 36,* 115–127. http://dx.doi.org/10.1037/teo0000039

2.3. Practical Ethics

Jeffrey N. Younggren

Since this is my last column in the *Clinical Psychologist*, I would like to take a little liberty with the subject area and discuss a series of suggestions I have for clinical psychologists who are struggling with ethical issues. I think that this might be a helpful summary of what I have tried to address over the past two years in my quarterly column. I also know that it is a summary that might generate some controversy, which is fine with me. Ethics should not always be easy and ethicists do not always agree.

1. Avoid getting stuck on rules.

It appears to me that psychologists are more and more concerned with finding the "right answer" to an ethical question. While the attempt to do this likely comes from laudable intentions, this is not always a wisest approach to problem solving when one is confronted with an ethical dilemma. I would advise my colleagues to pay attention to ethical fundamentals when confronting a professional dilemma and try to generate answers to problems based upon an understanding of these principles. This will usually lead to the solution. It seems to me that it is very unwise to spend endless hours searching for the "right answer" to complex questions that have unclear answers. I tend to believe that if you find a concrete "right answer" to an ethical question, someone else will find the exception. So, when you are confronting an ethical question, examine the fundamental principles of beneficence, nonmaleficence, autonomy, fidelity, and justice and try to come up with the solution. Finding an answer to a dilemma based on this approach is harder for sure, but I believe it is a better way to problem solve than just looking for a rule to a complex question.

2. Be aware that some problems do not have good answers.

Every so often you will be confronted with a situation that does not have a good answer because it pits moral principles against each other. For example, taking action to prevent someone from engaging in self-harm violates that individual's autonomy and confidentiality rights. Or, you might find yourself having to report child abuse on a patient with whom you have a very positive relationship, an uncomfortable state of affairs that pits confidentiality against social policy designed to protect children. So, because a solution causes you some discomfort, does not mean that your answer is wrong. It just means that you have been forced to make a compromise between completing ethical and moral principles a circumstance that almost always creates discomfort in those who have to deal with it.

3. Because something is not in the Ethical Principles of Psychologists or a part of some policy does not make it right.

The Ethical Principles of Psychologists and Code of Conduct are not comprehensive. University policies are not comprehensive. Laws and ethics evolve. Throughout your career you will be confronted with dilemmas that have unclear answers. For example, power differentials that occur in therapy do also occur elsewhere in the world. Patients and students and colleagues and friends and employees can be exploited. Just because somebody has failed to tell you not to do something, does not make it ok. Just because there is not a concrete policy about it does not make it ethical or the right thing to do.

4. Make use of the myriad of resources available to you for guidance.

This profession is filled with professionals who can assist you when you are dealing with an ethical dilemma. While some few individuals are prone to hang their colleagues out when they disagree with them, most professional psychologists are not that way. Make use of these resources but also do not assume that everybody will agree with your reasoning regarding an ethical decision. Seek out qualified colleagues, consult with them and, if you disagree with their position on an issue, continue to consult until some level of clarity begins to surface regarding the answer to your dilemma. Oh, by the way, be sure to write these consultations down since this is a strong defense should someone choose to officially question your conduct in a matter.

5. Good therapy can have a bad outcome.

A psychologist can provide the best treatment in the most ethical of ways and still things can go wrong. This does not mean you have made a mistake. Simply put, good psychotherapy can have a bad outcome. What this reality teaches is that you must engage in good risk management when you provide professional services in complex cases. Doing good risk management will help you prove to others that you did the best you could and that your conduct was consistent with professional standards. A reality here is that a bad outcome can create administrative and legal problems, but that is the cost of doing business. However, if you practice good risk management and conduct yourself ethically, you will prevail if someone questions your conduct.

6. Do not be surprised if you get sued or if your licensing board investigates you.

The data are pretty compelling that sometime throughout your career you will find yourself confronting a legal action that questions your professional conduct. This is simply likely to happen. This is also why you have insurance. The good news here is that most psychologists prevail when this happens to them, and the ones that do not prevail, probably should not. One important thing to remember when this happens is that this is an adversarial legal matter and you should never try to resolve this yourself. Retain competent legal assistance and follow your lawyer's advice.

7. Be aware that patients have responsibilities in the treatment setting.

One of my major objections to where we currently find ourselves is that many psychologists believe that the only person in treatment setting that has duty and responsibility is the psychologist. This is simply wrong. Patients have duties too and when they violate those duties, your obligations to them are reduced. Moral treatment of each other is good for both sides of the desk, if you will. So, patients cannot do whatever they want to you and expect you to stay loyal to the psychotherapy. Examples of these include boundary violations on the part of the patient, threats to you, nonpayment of fees and lack of compliance with a treatment plan, to name a few. Bringing these types of impasses and problems to the attention of the patient is most appropriate but, if this does not resolve the matter, termination and referral are in order.

This is my list. While many of the issues I raise here might seem somewhat unrelated, I am convinced that if psychologists would adhere to them, their professional lives would be much more secure let alone happier.

2.4. Ethics of Practice: The Beliefs and Behaviors of Psychologists as Therapists

Kenneth S. Pope, Barbara G. Tabachnick, and Patricia Keith-Spiegel

The American Psychological Association (APA) has developed elaborate ethical principles and standards of practice to guide the behavior of its membership (APA, 1973, 1981a, 1981b, 1986, 1987a, 1987b; *Standards*, 1985). However, we still lack comprehensive, systematically gathered data about the degree to which members believe in or comply with these guidelines. Consequently, such data are not available to inform either the clinical decisions of individual practitioners or the attempts of the APA to revise, refine, and extend formal standards of practice.

No implication is intended that norms are the equivalent of ethical standards. In many situations, the formulation and dissemination of formal standards are intended to increase ethical awareness and to improve the behaviors of a professional association. For example, many of the standards set forth in the ancient and still honored Hippocratic Oath were held by a minority of the physicians at the time. But those who are charged with developing, disseminating, and enforcing professional codes can function much more effectively if they are aware of the diverse dilemmas confronting the membership and of the membership's varied personal codes and behaviors.

METHOD

Survey Questionnaire

A survey questionnaire, a cover letter, and a return envelope were sent to 1,000 psychologists (500 men and 500 women) randomly selected from the 4,684 members of Division 29 (Psychotherapy) as listed in the 1985 *Directory of the American Psychological Association* (APA, 1985).

From "Ethics of Practice: The Beliefs and Behaviors of Psychologists as Therapists," by K. S. Pope, B. G. Tabachnick, and P. Keith-Spiegel, 1987, *American Psychologist, 42*, pp. 993–1006. Copyright 1987 by the American Psychological Association.

We appreciate the assistance of Barbara Nicholson, who transferred the initial survey responses to a computer data file. We also wish to thank the California State University, Northridge, Computer Center for the use of the facility. This project was supported by the California State University, Northridge, Foundation small grants program.

Ed. Note: Some of the material in this article is irrelevant to the major point, that is, the variability in how psychologists judge certain behavior as ethical. But, the senior author of the article required that no editing take place as a condition for its publication. The most important material is in Table 3 and its related discussion.

TABLE 1. Demographic Characteristics of Psychologists Providing Usable Data

Characteristic	Category	*N*	%
Sex	Male	231	50.7
	Female	225	49.3
Age group	45 and under	230	50.4
	Over 45	226	49.6
Primary work setting	Private office	330	72.4
	Clinic	35	7.7
	Hospital	26	5.7
	University	48	10.5
	Other	14	3.1
	No answer	3	0.7

The survey questionnaire was divided into three main parts. The first part consisted of a list of 83 behaviors. Participants were asked to rate each of the 83 behaviors in terms of three categories.[1] First, to what extent had they engaged in the behavior in their practice? Participants either could indicate that the behavior was *not applicable* to their practice or they could rate the behavior's occurrence in their practice as *never, rarely, sometimes, fairly often,* or *very often.* Second, to what extent did they consider the practice ethical? In rating whether each behavior was ethical, participants could use five categories: *unquestionably not, under rare circumstances, don't know/not sure, under any circumstances,* and *unquestionably yes.*

The second part of the questionnaire presented 14 resources for guiding or regulating practice. Participants were asked to rate each resource in terms of "the effectiveness . . . in providing education, direction, sanctions, or support to regulate the practice of psychologists (i.e., to promote effective, appropriate, and ethical practice)." Five options were available for rating each of these resources: *terrible, poor, adequate, good,* and *excellent.*

The third part of the questionnaire asked participants to provide information about their own age, sex, primary work setting, and major theoretical orientation.

RESULTS

Demographic Characteristics of the Participants and Ratings of the 83 Behaviors

Questionnaires were returned by 456 respondents (45.6%). Table 1 presents descriptions of the respondents in terms of sex, age, and primary work setting. Table 2 presents the theoretical orientations of the respondents. Table 3

---

[1] The third category in the survey asked participants to rate the extent to which they considered each of the behaviors to constitute "good practice." Due to space limitations, analyses of these data and their relationships to the other ratings have been omitted from this article. However, these analyses are being prepared for separate publication.

TABLE 2. Theoretical Orientation of Psychologists Providing Usable Data

Orientation	*N*	%
Psychodynamic	150	32.9
Eclectic	117	25.7
Cognitive	33	7.2
Gestalt	25	5.5
Humanistic	21	4.6
Existential	18	3.9
Systems	17	3.7
Behavioral	12	2.6
Other	53	11.7
No answer	10	2.2

presents the percentage of respondents' ratings for each of the 83 behaviors in terms of occurrence in their own practice and the degree to which they believe the behavior to be ethical.[2]

Resources for Regulating Psychology

Table 4 presents the respondents' ratings of each of the 14 resources for regulating psychology. A mixed between-between-within analysis of variance was performed on ratings of the 14 resources. Between-subjects factors were the two age groups and sex. The within-subjects factor was composed of the 14 resources. With a Huyn-Feldt adjustment for heterogeneity of covariance, a highly significant difference in ratings was found as a function of type of resource, $F(13, 4316) = 55.24$, $p < .001$. Type of resource accounted for 14% of the variance in ratings, using η^2.[3] Scheffé-adjusted pairwise comparisons among the 14 means revealed that 48 of the 91 differences were statistically reliable, $p < .01$. Means for the 14 resources and differences among those means appear in Table 5.

On the average, older clinical psychologists rated the resources higher (mean rating = 3.36) than those who were younger (mean rating = 3.17), $F(1, 32) = 8.88$, $p < .01$, $\eta^2 = .03$. No statistically significant main effect of sex was found.

---

[2] Duplication of the item "Being sexually attracted to a client" as both Item 66 and Item 82 provided an informal check on reliability. Correlations between Items 66 and 82 were .84 for responses relevant to "your practice" and .83 for "ethical."

On the assumption that there might be some consistency of responses across certain groups of items, 78 of the 83 behaviors were grouped, on an a priori basis, into 10 potential factors. After the data were collected, separate factor analysts were run on the three types of responses ("your practice," "ethical," and "good or poor practice") by choosing transformations that most effectively normalized variables, including log or square root transforms or dichotomization of variables (Tabachnick & Fidell, 1983). Seven factors, involving 45 of the behaviors, emerged. Due to space limitations, these analyses are not presented here, but a summary is available, upon request, from the authors.

[3] Because of the magnitude of the design, an alternative form of n^2 was used in which the denominator is the sum of the effect being described and its error term.

TABLE 3. Percentage of Psychologists (N = 465) Responding in Each Category

Item	Rating											
	Occurrence in your practice?						Ethical?					
	1	2	3	4	5*	NA		1	2	3	4	5*
1. Becoming social friends with a former client	42.1	45.2	9.2	1.8	1.1	0.7		6.4	51.1	13.4	21.9	6.8
2. Charging a client no fee for therapy	33.3	47.4	15.8	1.1	1.8	2.9		4.6	25.2	14.5	24.8	29.6
3. Providing therapy to one of your friends	70.4	25.2	2.2	0.2	0.7	2.2		47.6	40.1	2.9	4.4	3.7
4. Advertising in newspapers or similar media	72.4	13.2	10.1	2.4	0.4	5.5		12.9	14.7	17.8	33.3	20.6
5. Limiting treatment notes to name, date, and fee	48.2	18.4	13.8	6.6	12.1	1.5		18.6	22.4	21.7	20.8	14.7
6. Filing an ethics complaint against a colleague	61.6	25.2	7.5	0.7	1.1	10.7		2.4	11.8	3.1	22.8	57.9
7. Telling a client you are angry at him or her	9.6	45.0	36.8	5.7	2.2	0.7		3.1	26.8	8.3	35.5	25.4
8. Using a computerized test interpretation service	39.0	21.7	20.8	7.9	7.5	13.2		2.0	9.0	12.9	39.3	34.9
9. Hugging a client	13.4	44.5	29.8	7.7	4.2	0.2		4.6	41.2	8.3	35.5	9.2
10. Terminating therapy if client cannot pay	36.2	36.2	20.0	3.7	2.0	5.3		12.1	27.4	15.4	32.7	11.0
11. Accepting services from a client in lieu of fee	66.9	27.0	3.5	0.2	0.4	7.9		22.6	39.3	14.5	16.0	6.4
12. Seeing a minor client without parental consent	65.8	22.4	5.5	0.2	0.7	14.0		23.5	45.6	13.4	11.6	3.7
13. Having clients take tests (e.g., MMPI) at home	43.9	27.0	16.0	4.8	3.5	10.7		20.2	25.9	19.5	22.1	10.1
14. Altering a diagnosis to meet insurance criteria	36.4	26.5	27.0	5.5	2.6	2.9		37.3	28.9	16.0	14.0	2.0
15. Telling client: "I'm sexually attracted to you."	78.5	16.2	3.5	0.2	0.2	4.8		51.5	33.1	5.5	6.8	2.4
16. Refusing to let clients read their chart notes	33.1	21.3	13.6	5.7	14.9	23.2		14.5	28.3	14.9	21.5	16.0
17. Using a collection agency to collect late fees	48.0	21.9	19.7	5.9	1.8	8.6		5.0	15.1	15.6	35.5	27.4
18. Breaking confidentiality if client is homicidal	15.6	9.6	6.6	24.6	17.3	35.7		1.1	5.0	3.5	18.9	69.1
19. Performing forensic work for a contingency fee	67.3	7.0	6.8	0.9	0.7	42.1		35.5	11.0	29.8	7.0	10.3
20. Using self-disclosure as a therapy technique	5.9	22.1	38.6	19.7	12.9	0.7		2.2	17.1	7.9	43.0	29.2

21.	Inviting clients to an office open house	76.3	9.6	5.0	0.7	2.0	19.3	28.9	25.7	23.2	12.1	8.3
22.	Accepting a client's gift worth at least $50	72.1	19.1	2.4	0.4	0.0	16.7	34.2	36.2	15.8	8.6	3.3
23.	Working when too distressed to be effective	38.8	48.5	10.5	0.4	0.2	5.3	46.7	38.4	8.6	4.4	1.3
24.	Accepting only male or female clients	83.8	3.7	2.4	0.2	1.1	18.2	11.0	16.2	18.6	16.9	34.6
25.	Not allowing client access to testing report	45.0	23.5	13.6	5.9	6.6	14.3	21.7	32.9	14.0	20.6	8.8
26.	Raising the fee during the course of therapy	27.6	23.9	29.4	11.8	5.7	3.5	8.3	15.8	13.2	32.5	28.9
27.	Breaking confidentiality if client is suicidal	16.2	24.6	25.0	9.6	19.3	11.8	2.0	10.1	5.5	23.5	57.5
28.	Not allowing clients access to raw test data	32.2	10.5	9.0	7.9	30.0	1.8	12.1	12.9	11.2	22.8	36.8
29.	Allowing a client to run up a large unpaid bill	12.5	44.1	34.4	5.7	1.5	2.9	7.2	35.3	22.8	16.9	16.4
30.	Accepting goods (rather than money) as payment	65.1	24.8	6.4	0.2	0.4	12.7	15.8	33.8	21.3	18.2	9.6
31.	Using sexual surrogates with clients	81.8	5.7	1.1	0.7	0.2	33.1	36.2	25.7	23.7	8.6	4.6
32.	Breaking confidentiality to report child abuse	25.0	16.2	15.1	8.3	22.6	29.4	1.3	4.4	5.3	20.8	64.9
33.	Inviting clients to a party or social event	82.9	13.2	2.2	0.2	0.4	4.6	50.0	34.0	8.1	6.1	1.5
34.	Addressing client by his or her first name	2.0	2.6	9.4	20.8	65.1	0	0.7	0.9	2.6	30.7	65.1
35.	Crying in the presence of a client	42.5	41.5	12.5	1.8	0.7	4.6	5.9	32.0	14.5	18.4	27.6
36.	Earning a salary which is a % of client's fee	46.3	4.4	10.1	3.5	5.3	41.0	12.1	8.1	34.2	16.0	16.4
37.	Asking favors (e.g., a ride home) from clients	60.5	35.7	2.4	0	0.2	5.0	27.0	45.2	12.3	10.1	4.4
38.	Making custody evaluation without seeing the child	76.8	7.2	1.3	0.2	0.2	36.0	64.0	22.8	5.3	2.4	0.9
39.	Accepting a client's decision to commit suicide	73.9	16.4	3.7	0.4	0	15.4	45.2	36.6	8.8	4.8	2.9
40.	Refusing to disclose a diagnosis to a client	49.8	30.9	10.1	4.6	2.4	4.2	21.5	43.2	13.2	13.4	6.8
41.	Leading nude group therapy or "growth" groups	88.6	2.2	0.9	0.2	0	24.3	59.6	16.4	14.9	3.9	2.9
42.	Telling clients of your disappointment in them	46.9	39.0	11.4	1.1	0.4	2.6	19.7	37.1	18.0	15.4	7.9
43.	Discussing clients (without names) with friends	22.8	46.3	22.4	5.7	2.0	0.9	32.9	38.6	13.8	9.4	4.6
44.	Providing therapy to your student or supervisee	63.8	22.4	6.8	0.9	0.9	12.3	45.8	33.6	6.1	8.8	4.2
45.	Giving gifts to those who refer clients to you	78.5	11.4	7.0	1.5	1.1	4.2	47.8	21.7	15.6	10.3	4.2

(table continues)

TABLE 3. (continued)

| | Occurrence in your practice? | | | | | | Rating | | | | |
| | | | | | | | Ethical? | | | | |
Item	1	2	3	4	5*	NA	1	2	3	4	5*
46. Using a law suit to collect fees from clients	62.7	21.3	10.3	0.2	0.4	15.4	10.1	28.3	19.3	19.7	21.1
47. Becoming sexually involved with a former client	88.2	10.5	0.4	0	0.2	7.5	50.2	34.4	7.2	3.9	3.3
48. Avoiding certain clients for fear of being sued	48.9	30.3	13.4	1.3	0.9	13.8	7.9	23.0	23.7	23.9	19.7
49. Doing custody evaluation without seeing both parents	63.8	16.9	6.6	0.7	0.2	30.5	47.1	31.6	10.7	3.9	2.6
50. Lending money to a client	73.7	23.9	1.5	0	0	4.4	40.6	38.8	10.7	5.9	3.3
51. Providing therapy to one of your employees	79.6	12.9	2.0	0	0.7	15.6	55.0	31.1	6.8	2.9	2.4
52. Having a client address you by your first name	3.5	10.5	21.9	21.9	41.9	0.4	1.3	3.3	7.9	23.5	63.6
53. Sending holiday greeting cards to your clients	61.4	16.2	12.9	3.1	4.8	5.3	10.5	12.9	26.8	20.4	28.5
54. Kissing a client	70.8	23.5	4.4	0.2	0.4	2.2	48.0	36.6	4.6	7.7	2.2
55. Engaging in erotic activity with a client	97.1	2.4	0.2	0	0	3.9	95.0	3.5	0.4	0.4	0.4
56. Giving a gift worth at least $50 to a client	95.0	3.7	0.4	0	0	4.6	69.7	16.0	8.1	2.9	2.6
57. Accepting a client's invitation to a party	59.6	34.9	4.4	0.2	0.4	2.9	25.7	46.1	10.1	10.7	6.8
58. Engaging in sex with a clinical supervisee	95.0	2.9	0.4	0	0	8.8	85.1	9.0	3.5	1.5	0.2
59. Going to client's special event (e.g., wedding)	23.5	50.7	20.4	3.3	1.5	0.4	5.3	34.0	13.8	28.7	17.5
60. Getting paid to refer clients to someone	98.0	0.4	0.2	0	0	7.2	88.4	7.2	3.3	0	0.2
61. Going into business with a client	95.6	1.5	0.2	0	0.2	9.9	78.5	12.7	5.5	1.1	1.1
62. Engaging in sexual contact with a client	97.8	1.5	0.4	0	0	4.2	96.1	2.6	0.2	0.7	0.2
63. Utilizing involuntary hospitalization	30.5	42.1	16.7	2.4	1.1	17.1	3.1	28.9	8.8	24.3	31.8
64. Selling goods to clients	90.6	5.9	2.0	0	0.4	7.5	71.1	18.4	4.4	29	2.0
65. Giving personal advice on radio, t.v., etc.	66.0	18.6	9.2	1.5	0.2	18.6	18.4	28.3	22.1	23.7	6.4

		Occurrence					Ethical				
		1	2	3	4	5	NA / 1	2	3	4	5
66.	Being sexually attracted to a client*	9.2	38.8	43.9	5.5	1.3	1.1	11.2	11.0	19.5	19.1	33.3
67.	Unintentionally disclosing confidential data	36.0	58.6	3.3	0	0	2.9	75.2	14.3	4.6	1.8	1.8
68.	Allowing a client to disrobe	94.5	2.9	1.5	0	0	5.0	81.4	12.1	3.1	1.5	1.3
69.	Borrowing money from a client	97.1	1.8	0	0	0	4.4	86.2	10.7	1.1	0.4	0.9
70.	Discussing a client (by name) with friends	91.2	7.5	0.4	0.2	0	3.5	94.5	3.5	0.7	0.4	0.4
71.	Providing services outside areas of competence	74.8	22.8	1.8	0	0	2.0	80.7	16.9	0.2	0.9	0.7
72.	Signing for hours a supervisee has not earned	89.0	7.2	0.9	0	0	9.9	92.5	5.5	0.4	0.4	0.7
73.	Treating homosexuality per se as pathological	75.0	12.7	6.4	2.6	1.8	4.4	55.7	12.9	17.3	6.6	5.3
74.	Doing therapy while under influence of alcohol	92.8	5.7	0.2	0	0	3.5	89.5	7.7	1.1	0	0.9
75.	Engaging in sexual fantasy about a client	27.0	46.3	22.4	2.4	0.7	3.5	18.9	15.1	26.8	13.2	21.9
76.	Accepting a gift worth less than $5 from a client	8.6	31.8	45.0	9.4	3.7	0.7	5.0	20.0	16.2	36.4	20.2
77.	Offering or accepting a handshake from a client	1.3	3.3	17.5	28.1	48.2	1.1	0.7	1.1	3.3	21.7	71.9
78.	Disrobing in the presence of a client	97.8	0.9	0	0.2	0.2	4.6	94.7	3.3	0	0.2	0.7
79.	Charging for missed appointments	11.8	15.4	26.3	22.6	22.6	2.4	1.1	6.8	7.2	38.2	45.8
80.	Going into business with a former client	83.1	10.1	2.0	0	0.4	15.6	36.8	28.9	17.5	9.0	5.9
81.	Directly soliciting a person to be a client	89.3	8.6	0.9	0	0.2	4.4	67.5	22.6	5.7	1.8	1.5
82.	Being sexually attracted to a client	9.2	39.5	41.0	6.1	0.9	1.3	9.2	13.4	21.9	18.0	30.0
83.	Helping client file complaint re a colleague	52.9	19.4	9.4	1.1	1.1	20.0	6.4	22.6	14.9	29.2	25.2

Note. Rating codes: Occurrence in your practice? 1 = never, 2 = rarely, 3 = sometimes, 4 = fairly often, 5 = very often, NA = not applicable. Ethical? 1 = unquestionably not, 2 = under rare circumstances, 3 = don't know/not sure, 4 = under many circumstances, 5 = unquestionably yes.

* Responses 1 through 5 sum to less than 100% due to missing data.

TABLE 4. Percentage of Respondents Rating Effectiveness of Sources of Information About Regulating the Practice of Psychologists

Source	Terrible	Poor	Adequate	Good	Excellent
Your graduate program	5.3	19.1	27.0	29.6	18.2
Your internship	2.0	11.4	25.4	35.7	24.1
Agencies for which you've worked	5.0	16.2	31.4	30.7	12.9
State and federal laws	3.9	32.7	39.0	18.4	1.8
Court decisions (case law)	4.6	30.5	29.6	25.4	4.2
State licensing board	5.9	21.7	35.7	25.9	6.8
APA *Ethical Principles*	1.1	5.9	26.3	45.8	19.1
APA Ethics Committee	2.0	11.4	32.9	36.8	12.9
State ethics committee	3.3	20.8	32.9	28.5	7.0
Local ethics committee	6.4	22.8	29.4	20.8	4.8
Published research	7.2	28.5	30.7	21.3	5.0
Published clinical and theoretical work	4.8	20.0	33.1	29.2	7.2
Continuing education programs	2.4	19.1	29.6	33.6	9.2
Colleagues (informal network)	1.1	6.6	18.9	43.4	28.1

Note. Rows may not sum to 100% due to missing data or rounding.

The interaction between age group and resource was reliable, $F(13, 4316)$ = 2.29, $p < .05$, but of small magnitude, $\eta^2 < .01$. Applying a Scheffé criterion at $\alpha = .01$, differences between younger and older psychologists were statistically reliable for only three resources: state licensing board (older, $M = 3.25$; younger, $M = 2.86$), state ethics committee (older, $M = 3.36$; younger, $M = 2.97$), and local ethics committee (older, $M = 3.12$; younger, $M = 2.77$). None of the other interactions was statistically significant.

Behaviors Systematically Related to Sex of Psychologist

In order to assess the degree to which male and female psychologists might be differentially engaging in the 83 behaviors, chi-square analyses were performed on these data. To help eliminate seemingly significant findings actually due to chance—in light of the large number of analyses—a very strict significance level ($p < .001$) was used. Table 6 presents the items significantly related to sex, using this criterion.

DISCUSSION

Validity and Interpretation Issues

Caution is essential in interpreting these data. First, this is an initial study, and it awaits attempts at replication. Second, it is unclear how the behaviors and beliefs of this sample of Division 29 members compare with those of the over 60,000 APA members, of the close to 50,000 individuals (both APA and non-APA members) who are licensed or certified by the states to practice psychology (Dörken, Stapp, & VandenBos, 1986), or of the approximately 63% of

TABLE 5. Means and Mean Differences for Rated Effectiveness of Sources of Information About the Practice of Psychologists

Source	M							Mean differences						
		1	2	3	4	5	6	7	8	9	10	11	12	13
1. Graduate program	3.36													
2. Internship	3.71	.35*												
3. Agencies	3.30	.06	.40*											
4. State and federal laws	2.64	.52*	.67*	.46*										
5. Court decisions	2.98	.38*	.73*	.32	.14									
6. State licensing board	3.06	.30	.65*	.25	.22	.07								
7. APA *Ethical Principles*	3.77	.41*	.06	.46*	.93*	.79*	.71*							
8. APA Ethics Committee	3.47	.11	.24	.17	.63*	.49*	.42*	.29						
9. State ethics committee	3.17	.19	.54*	.14	.33*	.18	.11	.60*	.31					
10. Local ethics committee	2.95	.41~	.76*	.36*	.11	.04	.11	.62*	.53*	.22				
11. Published research	2.84	.52~	.87*	.46*	.00	.14	.22	.93*	.63*	.33*	.11			
12. Published clinical and theoretical work	3.10	.26	.61*	.21	.26	.11	.04	.67*	.38*	.07	.15	.26		
13. Continuing education programs	3.25	.11	.46*	.06	.41*	.26	.19	.52*	.23	.08	.30	.41*	.15	
14. Colleagues	3.93	.57*	.22	.62*	1.09*	.94*	.87*	.16	.45*	.76*	.98*	1.09*	.83*	.66*

*p < .01. Scheffé criterion.

TABLE 6. Items Significantly Related to Sex (p < .001)

Item	Direction	χ^2	df
9. Hugging a client	Female more likely	18.70	4
15. Telling a client: "I'm sexually attracted to you."	Male more likely	16.29	2
52. Having a client address you by your first name	Female more likely	20.00	4
73. Treating homosexuality per se as pathological	Male more likely	19.26	4
75. Engaging in sexual fantasy about a client	Male more likely	40.39	4
81. Directly soliciting a person to be a client	Male more likely	11.24	1

licensed, doctoral psychologists who identify clinical psychology as their current major field (Stapp, Tucker, & VandenBos, 1985). Third, the behavior of the majority may not reflect what the majority themselves believe to be ethical. For example, almost two thirds of the participants reported that they have disclosed confidential material unintentionally, yet three fourths identify this behavior as unethical. Fourth, specific ethical standards may not be reflected in majority belief. Most psychologists, for example, may be unfamiliar with the procedures, research, or complexities of such special areas as treating minors, performing forensic work, engaging in sex with former clients, or working with suicidal clients. As previously mentioned, the formulation and dissemination of formal ethical standards can represent attempts to improve ethical awareness and behavior. Empirical data about the behavior and beliefs of a general sample should inform—not determine—our ethical deliberations. Finally, most of the questionnaire items involve enormously complex issues. The following discussion is meant only to highlight some of the major themes, patterns, and dilemmas emerging from these initial data.

Relationship Between Behavior and Beliefs

The data suggest that the psychologists' behavior was generally in accordance with their ethical beliefs. This inference is based on the fact that for all but four items, the frequency with which the respondents reported engaging in a behavior was less than the frequency of instances in which the behavior was ethical in their judgment. Of the four exceptions, three involved confidentiality: "discussing a client (by name) with friends," "discussing clients (without names) with friends," and "unintentionally disclosing confidential data." The fourth exception was "providing services outside areas of competence."

Behaviors That Are Almost Universal

For 7 of the 83 items, at least 90% of the respondents indicated that they engaged in the behavior, at least on rare occasions (see Table 3). Two of these almost universal behaviors involved self-disclosure to the clients: "using self-disclosure as a therapy technique" and "telling a client that you are angry at him or her." Thus, it appears that the more extreme versions of the therapist as "blank screen" are exceedingly rare among psychologists. Similarly, the models of the therapist as a distant, almost stand-offish authority figure—which, like the "blank screen" approach, are derived from the classical psychoanalytic tradition—are infrequently practiced. Fewer than 10% of the respondents indicated that they never engaged in "having a client address you by your first name" (as Table 6 shows, it is mainly male therapists who insist on being addressed by their last names), "addressing your client by his or her first name," "accepting a gift worth less than $5 from a client," and "offering or accepting a handshake from a client." Finally, only 9.2% of the respondents indicated that they had never been sexually attracted to a client. This finding may be compared to a survey of APA Division 42 (Psychologists in Independent Practice) in which 13% indicated that they had never been sexually attracted to a client (Pope, Keith-Spiegel, & Tabachnick, 1986).

Behaviors That Are Rare

One of the most surprising results was that only 1.9% of the respondents reported engaging in sexual contact with a client and that only 2.6% reported engaging in erotic activity (which may or may not involve actual contact) with a client. Previously, there have been three national surveys of sexual intimacies between psychologists and their patients. Holroyd and Brodsky (1977) reported 7.7% respondents "who answered positively any of the questions regarding erotic-contact behaviors or intercourse during treatment." Pope, Levenson, and Schover (1979) found that 7% of the therapists in their survey reported engaging in sexual contact with their clients. Pope et al. (1986) reported that 6.5% of their respondents acknowledged engaging in sexual intimacies with clients.

It is difficult to explain the discrepancy between the current findings and those of the previous three studies. It may be that respondents are now less willing to admit, even on anonymous survey, to a behavior that is a felony in some states, or it may be that these findings are reflective of random sampling error or bias in return rate rather than of a change in behavior.

However, the current findings may indicate an actual decrease in the percentage of psychologists engaging in sexual intimacies with their patients. The increasing publicity given to the Therapist–Patient Sex Syndrome (Pope, 1985, 1986) and other devastating consequences of therapist–patient sexual intimacy (Bouhoutsos, Holroyd, Lerman, Forer, & Greenberg, 1983; Feldman-Summers & Jones, 1984; Pope & Bouhoutsos, 1986), as well as the vivid first-person accounts of patients who have been sexually involved with their therapists (Freeman & Roy, 1976; Plaisil, 1985; Walker & Young, 1986), may be significantly altering the behavior of psychologists who are tempted in this area. Clinical strategies developed to help therapists at risk to refrain from sexual contact with their patients may also be contributing to this decline (Pope, in press).

Some other items concerning sexual behaviors—such as nudity as part of therapy or using sexual surrogates with clients—also had extremely low rates. Engaging in sex with a clinical supervisee was reported by only 3.4% of the respondents. This figure corresponds closely to the 4.0% in a prior survey of

APA Division 29 members who reported engaging in sexual intimacies with their clinical supervisees (Pope et al., 1979).

Dishonesty in helping candidates to become degreed or licensed without the requisite supervised experience is relatively rare; it was reported by 8.1%.

A number of the rare practices concerned financial or business practices, such as borrowing money from a client, selling goods to clients, going into business with a client, or giving a gift worth at least $50 to a client. The most infrequently reported behavior was getting paid to refer clients to someone (0.6%). It is heartening to note that psychologists are not putting their judgment and influence up for sale.

Although over a fourth (26.1%) of the respondents advertise in newspapers and similar media, only 9.7% report directly soliciting a person to be a client. As Table 6 indicates, men were more likely than women to engage in this practice.

Few psychologists blatantly breach the confidentiality of their clients. However, 8.1% have discussed a client (by name) with friends.

Doing therapy while under the influence of alcohol is also rare (5.9%).

For the most part, psychologists are careful to interview the child when making a custody evaluation, although 8.9% fail to do so.

A gender-based criterion for admission to treatment is rare. Accepting only male or female clients was reported by 7.4%.

Although rare, some of these practices—such as discussing clients by name with friends or doing therapy while under the influence of alcohol—so clearly undermine the rights and welfare of patients that they need to be addressed much more forcefully and effectively by the profession.

Difficult Judgments

We defined a difficult judgment as one in which at least 20% of the respondents indicated "don't know/not sure." There were 12 behaviors that posed difficult judgments in terms of whether they were ethical: "performing forensic work for a contingency fee," "accepting goods (rather than money) as payment," "using sexual surrogates with clients," "earning a salary which is a percentage of client fees," "avoiding certain clients for fear of being sued," "sending holiday greeting cards to your clients," "giving personal advice on radio, t.v., etc.," "engaging in sexual fantasy about a client," "being sexually attracted to a client," "limiting treatment notes to name, date, and fee," "inviting clients to an office open house," and "allowing a client to run up a large unpaid bill." It is interesting that one third of these directly concerned financial issues, and one fourth concerned sexual issues. The profession may need to develop practical guidelines in these areas.

Topic Areas

Redlich and Pope (1980) have suggested seven principles for meaningfully coordinating ethical guidelines with other standards of professional practice in a way that can be most useful to psychologists and psychiatrists attempting to carry out their professional tasks responsibly. These are (1) above all, do no harm; (2) practice only with competence; (3) do not exploit; (4) treat people with respect for their dignity as human beings; (5) protect confidentiality; (6) act, except in the most extreme instances, only after obtaining informed consent; and (7) practice, insofar as possible, within the framework of social equity and justice. The first five are ancient and are mentioned explicitly in the Hippocratic Oath. The sixth and seventh are of recent origin, express patients' rights, and have not yet been universally accepted. This seven-part framework organizes the following discussion of the questionnaire items.

1. Do No Harm

Lending money to a client. It is ironic that lending money to a client—an act that might seem to be generous and helpful—would be viewed as so harmful to the therapeutic enterprise as to be clearly unethical by 40.6% of the respondents and unethical under most circumstances by an additional 38.8%. Nevertheless, about one fourth of the respondents acknowledged that they had lent money to a client (23.9% rarely; 1.5% sometimes).

Signing for unearned hours. A clear majority (92.5%) believe that signing for hours that a supervisee has not earned is unethical. Producing graduates and licensees whose credentials were fraudulently obtained may subject numerous future clients to harm.

Filing ethics complaints. The injunction to do no harm can be construed to include the mandate not to remain passively acquiescent when fellow professionals are violating ethical principles and standards of practice. A surprising finding was that one fourth of the respondents reported that they had, on a rare basis, filed an ethics complaint against a colleague. An additional 9.3% reported that they did so more frequently.

The view that it is unethical always (2.4%) or under most circumstances (11.8%) to file an ethical complaint against a colleague may reflect the difficulties experienced by an association (the APA) charged with the task of promoting the profession when it also attempts to monitor and discipline the behavior of its members. Furthermore, the practical steps for effective peer monitoring may need to be more widely disseminated (see Keith-Spiegel & Koocher, 1985).

Helping a client file an ethics complaint was a behavior performed by over one third of the respondents on a rare (19.4%) or more frequent (11.6%) basis. Over one fourth believed that this action was unethical (6.4%) or unethical under most circumstances (22.6%). Although Principle 7g of the current *Ethical Principles* (APA, 1981a) speaks to this general issue, the *Principles* may need to address more specifically situations in which the allegations of unethical behavior are brought to the attention of psychologists by their clients.

2. Practice Only With Competence

Providing services outside areas of competence. Both the *Ethical Principles of Psychologists* (APA, 1981a) and the *Specialty Guidelines for the Delivery of Services by Clinical Psychologists* (APA, 1981b) make clear statements that psychologists are to practice only within the limits of demonstrable expertise. Nevertheless, almost one fourth of the respondents indicated that they had practiced outside their area of competence either rarely (22.8%) or sometimes (1.8%).

Impaired performance. Psychology has turned increased attention to the impaired or distressed professional (Kilburg, Nathan, & Thoreson, 1986; Laliotis & Grayson, 1985). The results of this survey suggest that those efforts are needed. Over half (59.6%) of the respondents acknowledged having worked— either rarely or more often—when too distressed to be effective. About 1 out of every 15 or 20 (5.7%) respondents acknowledged, on a rare basis, doing therapy while under the influence of alcohol.

Competence in carrying out assessments. In the area of assessment, what seem like efficient and competent short-cuts or innovative strategies to some may seem questionable to others. Sending tests home with clients is said, by its advocates, to be more convenient and to allow clients to fill out the test in more familiar, less stressful surroundings. Critics of the practice argue that psychologists should monitor the administration of such tests—for example, to prevent clients from relying on the advice of friends and family about how to fill out the test. Furthermore, maintain the critics, should the test results become part of important legal proceedings, the psychologist would be unable to testify that the test responses were those of the client unaided by friends or family. The current study indicates that over half of the respondents send such tests home with clients either on a rare (27.0%) or more frequent (24.3%) basis. This practice is viewed as unethical by 20.2% and unethical in most circumstances by 25.9%.

The use of computerized psychological test interpretations has been harshly criticized (Matarazzo, 1986) but seems to have been accepted by the APA, which has issued guidelines for their use (APA, 1986). The current findings indicate that a majority of the respondents have used such services either rarely (21.7%) or more often (36.2%). Few believe that they are unethical (2.0%) or unethical under most circumstances (9.0%).

The literature in the field of child-custody conflicts indicates that a competent custody evaluation cannot be conducted without interviewing both parents. Shapiro (1984), for example, wrote that "under no circumstances should a report on child custody be rendered to the court, based on the evaluation of only one party to the conflict" (p. 99). About half of the respondents agree that doing a custody evaluation without seeing both parents is unethical. Only 16.9% reported that they had done this rarely, 7.5% more frequently.

3. Do Not Exploit

Sexual issues and physical contact. As mentioned earlier, the rates of sexual contact and erotic activities with patients are significantly lower than in the three previously reported national studies of psychologists. Over 95% of the respondents believed that both of these behaviors were unethical.

About half of the respondents believed that becoming sexually involved with a *former* client was unethical. (This figure may be compared to the 6.4% who believe that becoming friends with a former client is unethical.) These beliefs seem consistent with the harm associated with these relationships (Pope & Bouhoutsos, 1986), with the awarding of general and punitive damages in malpractice suits in which the sexual intimacies occurred only after termination (e.g., *Whitesell v. Green*, 1973), and with a multiyear study of the adjudications of state licensing boards and state ethics committees (Sell, Gottlieb, & Schoenfeld, 1986). The study found "that psychologists asserting that a sexual relationship had occurred only after the termination of the therapeutic relationship were more likely to be found in violation than those not making that claim" (p. 504). It is also interesting to note that the $25,000 cap on coverage in regard to sexual intimacies in the APA professional liability policy specifies sex with former as well as current clients.

The focus on erotic contact in therapy has raised questions about the legitimacy and effects of ostensibly nonerotic physical contact (Geller, 1980; Holroyd & Brodsky, 1977, 1980). Holroyd and Brodsky (1980) pointed out that it "is difficult to determine where 'nonerotic hugging, kissing, and affectionate touching' leave off and 'erotic contact' begins" (p. 810). About one fourth of our respondents reported kissing their clients, either rarely (23.5%) or more often (5.0%). About half viewed this practice as unethical. An additional 36.6% believed it to be unethical in most circumstances.

Hugging clients was practiced by 44.5% of the respondents on a rare basis, and by an additional 41.79b more frequently. Few (4.6%) believed the practice to be clearly unethical, but 41.2% believed it to be ethical only under rare circumstances.

The findings in the previous two categories may be compared to the results reported by Holroyd and Brodsky (1977) in which 27% of the therapists reported occasionally engaging in nonerotic hugging, kissing, or affectionate touching with opposite-sex patients, and 7% reported doing so frequently or always.

Almost all respondents offered or accepted a handshake from a client, either rarely (48.9%) or more frequently (48.2%). Very few found the behavior to be ethically questionable.

As mentioned earlier, using sexual surrogates with clients was a difficult ethical judgment for almost one fourth of the respondents. A little over one third believed that the behavior was unethical. An additional one fourth believed it was ethical only under rare circumstances. The use of surrogates has been frequently challenged on ethical bases (Redlich, 1977), but so far no complaint has been filed with the APA Ethics Committee concerning the use of a sexual surrogate.

A large majority (85.1%) believe that sexual intimacies with clinical supervisees are unethical, a finding consistent with published analyses of this practice (Pope & Bouhoutsos, 1986; Pope, Schover, & Levenson, 1980).

Over 1 out of every 10 respondents believed that simply "being sexually attracted to a client" was unethical. Approximately an additional one tenth believed that feeling such attraction was ethical under rare circumstances. These findings seem consistent with the results of a prior survey in which 63% of the respondents reported that experiencing sexual attraction to clients made them feel guilty, anxious, or confused (Pope et al., 1986).

Almost half (46.3%) of the respondents reported engaging in sexual fantasy about a client on a rare basis, an additional one fourth (25.5%) more frequently. These figures may be compared to the 28.7% of psychologists in a previous study who answered affirmatively the question, "While engaging in sexual activity with someone other than a client, have you ever had sexual fantasies about someone who is or was a client?" (Pope et al., 1986). Both the current and previous survey found that male psychologists were significantly more likely to engage in sexual fantasies about clients. This difference is consistent with research regarding sexual fantasizing in general, which shows higher rates for men (Pope, 1982).

Financial issues. The vulnerability, dependency, and sometimes confusion of so many who seek help from psychologists call for a strong ethic against financial exploitation, as well as extensive research to determine which financial arrangements work best for therapist and patient. Yet until the 1970s, the subject was virtually absent from the research literature. Volumes attempting comprehensive collection, review, and evaluation of research in psychotherapy (Bergin & Garfield, 1971; Rubinstein & Parloff, 1959; Shlien, 1968; Strupp & Luborsky, 1962) cited no research on financial arrangements, prompting one contributing author to comment:

> As a footnote, I would like to remark that if a Martian read the volumes reporting the first two psychotherapy conferences and if he read all the papers of this conference it would never occur to him that psychotherapy is something done for money. Either therapists believe that money is not a worthwhile research variable or money is part of the new obscenity in which we talk more freely about sex but never mention money. (Colby, 1968, p. 539)

Mintz (1971) likewise labeled fees a "tabooed subject" and suggested that "a varied set of guidelines" concerning fee payment has "functioned to inhibit therapists from inquiring too closely into the financial side of psychotherapeutic practice and into the actual effects it may have on the therapeutic enterprise" (p. 3).

In the last 15 years such factors as the increase in third-party payments have brought financial issues into the open. As the results of this study reveal, psychologists have developed a consensus of opinion about the acceptability of some—but by no means all—of the financial approaches to their work.

Over half of the respondents reported altering an insurance diagnosis to meet insurance criteria, either rarely (26.5%) or more frequently (35.1%). This action—which can be legally construed as insurance fraud—is viewed by slightly more than one third as unethical. An additional one fourth viewed it as ethical under rare circumstances. This widespread practice—in light of its legal implications and the use of dishonesty in the therapeutic endeavor—is in need of open discussion among professionals.

Charging for missed appointments seems an acceptable practice to virtually the entire psychological community. Raising a fee during the course of therapy also seems widely accepted. Principle 6d of the *Ethical Principles* (APA, 1981a) stresses that clients must be aware of such financial aspects of the services in advance and that they thus have a right to informed consent to or informed refusal of the financial arrangements.

About half (49.3%) of the respondents have used a collection agency to collect late fees, at least on a rare basis. Only 5% view this practice as unethical.

About one third (21.3% rarely; 10.9% more often) of the respondents have filed a lawsuit to collect fees. One out of 10 (10.1%) view this as unethical. It may be useful for psychologists to be aware that the current APA professional liability policy specifically excludes "disputes concerning fees charged by any Insured, including but not limited to third party reimbursements sought or received by any Insured" (American Home Assurance Company, undated, p. 3). In addition, psychologists must be aware of the ways in which fee-collection attempts that involve third parties (e.g., collection agencies, the courts) affect both the psychological welfare of the clients as well as such aspects of therapy as privacy and confidentiality.

Accepting a salary that is a percentage of client fees—a practice sometimes known as "kick-backs" or "fee-splitting" (Keith-Spiegel & Koocher, 1985)—was reported by 23.3% of the respondents. It is viewed as unethical by 12.1%. This was the item with the lowest response rate by far, suggesting that many respondents may have been unsure of the meaning of the question.

In another area, forensic psychology, psychologists may be tempted to accept a contingency fee. Standard texts have made clear statements concerning the unacceptability of such arrangements. "The psychologist should never accept a fee contingent upon the outcome of a case" (Blau, 1984, p. 336). "The expert witness should never, under any circumstances, accept a referral on a contingent fee basis" (Shapiro, 1984. p. 95). Only about 15% of the respondents report engaging in this practice either rarely (7.0%) or more often (8.4%).

Bartering of services for therapy has customarily been viewed by the profession as a dual relationship, hence unethical. The APA Ethics Committee took up the question of bartering at its February 18–20, 1982 meeting and formally approved a policy statement that "bartering of personal services is a violation of Principle 6a" (APA, 1982). However, about one fourth of the respondents reported that they had engaged in such bartering, at least on a rare basis. Over half viewed the practice as either unethical or unethical under most circumstances.

Other dual relationships. Both sexual intimacy with clients and bartering for services are dual relationships. However, Principle 6a of the *Ethical Principles* (APA, 1981a) lists other dual relationships that are to be avoided: "Examples of such dual relationships include, but are not limited to, research with and treatment of employees, students, supervisees, close friends, or relatives" (p. 636). The current study inquired into three of these areas: therapy with employees, students/supervisees, and friends. The most frequent dual relationship involved students and supervisees (22.4% rarely; 8.6% more frequently), followed by friends (25.2% rarely; 3.1% more frequently) and employees (12.9% rarely; 2.7% more frequently).

Dual relationships can also be initiated once therapy begins, as happens when a therapist engages in sexual contact with a patient. According to the respondents, initiating business relationships with clients (1.5% rarely; 0.4% more frequently) and former clients (10.1% rarely; 2.4% more frequently) is not a widespread practice.

Advertising for and soliciting clients. Currently, advertising per se is not considered unethical, although direct solicitation of clients can be viewed as potentially exploitive (Keith-Spiegel & Koocher, 1985). About one fourth of the respondents report advertising in newspapers and similar media, either rarely (13.2%) or more frequently (12.9%).

Fewer than 10% of the respondents (generally male psychologists) directly solicit clients. At least two thirds view this practice as unethical.

4. Treat People With Respect for Their Dignity as Human Beings

To some extent, the history of psychotherapy has reflected the struggle to arrive at the most effective way in which to express respect. For example, Thompson (1950) discussed the ways in which, because of suspicions about countertransference,

> the feeling grew that even a genuine objective feeling of friendliness on his part was to be suspected. As a result many of Freud's pupils became afraid to be simply human and show the ordinary friendliness and interest a therapist customarily feels for a patient. In many cases, out of a fear of showing countertransference, the attitude of the analyst became stilted and unnatural. (p. 107)

In this study, we found that many of the walls that prevented therapists from engaging in simple human interactions—for example, therapists revealing their emotions—have come down, although therapists are still in a quandary about some of these issues.

An overwhelming majority of the respondents are on a first-name basis with their clients and do not view this as ethically questionable. Three fourths have attended a client's social event, such as a wedding, although only about one third have accepted an invitation to a party. About one fourth view accepting a party invitation as unethical. About the same percentage have invited clients to an office open house, but slightly more (28.9%) view this as unethical.

A large majority (93.3%) use self-disclosure. More specifically, over half tell clients that they are angry with them (89.7%), cry in the presence of a client (56.5%), and tell clients that they are disappointed in them (51.9%). The most questioned of these was telling clients of dis-appointment: 56.8% viewed it as unethical or unethical under most circumstances.

5. Protect Confidentiality

Breaking confidentiality to prevent harm. The results of this study suggest that psychologists have accepted the legitimacy of breaking confidentiality in order to prevent danger. Fewer than 10% view this action as unethical in cases involving homicide, suicide, or child abuse.

The data also indicate that such situations are a customary part of general practice for psychologists: 78.5% report having broken confidentiality in regard to suicidal clients, 62.2% in cases of child abuse, and 58.1% when the client was homicidal.

Informally or unintentionally breaking confidentiality. About three fourths discuss clients—without names—with friends. Only 8.1% discuss clients—with names—with friends. Surprisingly, over half (61.9%) have unintentionally disclosed confidential data.

The widespread disclosure of confidential information—whether or not with names—is a practice that needs attention from the profession. Discussion of client information with friends seems to be a clear violation of Principle 5a: "Information obtained in clinical or consulting relationships, or evaluative data concerning children, students, employees, or others, is discussed only for professional purposes and only with persons clearly concerned with the case" (APA, 1981a, p. 636). It also appears to violate the *General Guidelines for Providers of Psychological Services:*

> Psychologists do not release confidential information, except with the written consent of the user involved, or of his or her legal representative, guardian, or other holder of the privilege on behalf of the user, and only after the user has been assisted to understand the implications of the release. (APA, 1987b, p. 21)

Public psychology. When psychological services are performed in a public forum, of course, there is no confidentiality. Giving personal advice on radio, TV, and so forth, is a very difficult issue. More than one in five indicated that they did not know or were not sure if it was ethical. The *Ethical Principles* (APA, 1981a, p. 635) appear to indicate that giving such advice is not in itself unethical by stating,

> When personal advice is given by means of public lectures or demonstrations, newspaper or magazine articles, radio or television programs, mail, or similar media, the psychologist utilizes the most current relevant data and exercises the highest level of professional judgment.

Surprisingly, over one fourth of the respondents reported giving such advice in the media either rarely (18.6%) or more frequently (10.9%).

6. Acting Only With Informed Consent

Seeing a minor without parental consent. A major ethical, as well as legal, dilemma is faced by many psychologists when the client is not empowered to give adequate consent to treatment (Koocher, 1976; Melton, 1981; Morrison, Morrison, & Holdridge-Crane, 1979; Plotkin, 1981). Over one fourth of the respondents have elected to see a minor without parental consent either rarely (22.4%) or more frequently (6.4%). Over half of the respondents believe such treatment to be either unethical (23.5%) or unethical under most circumstances (45.6%).

Withholding access to data. Should the clients have full access to assessment and treatment data that concern them? On the one hand, access to data about the client's condition may be important to the client's reaching a truly informed decision about initiating or continuing treatment. For example, if clients are not honestly told the diagnosis, it may be hard for them to know whether they want to be treated without knowing what they are to be treated for. On the other hand, psychologists may feel that certain technical terms or raw data may actually exacerbate the client's condition.

About one in five believe that it is unethical to refuse to disclose the diagnosis (21.5%) or to refuse access to a test report (21.7%). Fewer believe that refusing to allow clients to read their chart notes (14.5%) or that denying clients access to raw test data (12.1%) is unethical. Around half of the respondents have denied their clients access to the diagnosis (48.0%), to the testing report (49.6%), to their chart notes (55.5%), or to raw test data (57.4%).

Access to chart notes may have differential meaning and usefulness depending on how much information is contained in the chart. Over half (50.9%) of the respondents indicated that they had, at least rarely, limited treatment notes to name, date, and fee. The *General Guidelines for Providers of Psychological Services* (APA, 1987b) mandate that "accurate, current and pertinent records of essential psychological services are maintained" (p. 19). Lack of adequate documentation of assessment, interventions, and responses to interventions have contributed to successful malpractice actions by establishing lack of care. One court held:

> The hospital record maintained by the State was about as inadequate a record as we have ever examined. We [the court] find that . . . the inadequacies in this record militated against proper and competent psychiatric and ordinary medical care. . . . Therefore, to the extent that a hospital record develops information for subsequent treatment, it contributed to the inadequate treatment this claimant received . . . it was so inadequate that even a layman could determine that fact. (*Whitree v. State*, 1968, p. 487)

Interventions against the client's wishes. Some of the most difficult and painful judgments psychologists must make concern under what, if any, conditions informed consent can be waived. One area of such judgments involves involuntary hospitalization, an area filled with controversy. Over half of the respondents have utilized involuntary hospitalization, either rarely (42.1%) or more often (20.2%). Fewer than 5% view it as unethical.

Whether to accept a client's decision to commit suicide is likewise a difficult and painful dilemma for many psychologists. Some have argued that the informed consent of the patient to accept or to refuse treatment in such cases must be absolute (Szasz, 1986). Only about one in five of the respondents has accepted, either rarely (16.4%) or more frequently (4.1%), a client's decision to kill himself or herself. Almost half (45.2%) believe it to be unethical. An additional 36.6% believe it to be unethical under most circumstances.

7. Promoting Equity and Justice

Homosexuality. The profession's struggle to eliminate the stigma and pathologizing of homosexuality has been long, difficult, and not yet complete (Baer, 1981; Malyon, 1986a, 1986b). Slightly more than one in five of the respondents reported treating homosexuality per se as pathological, either rarely (12.7%) or more often (10.8%). However, over half (55.7%) viewed such a practice as unethical.

Sex of client. Whether to make access to one's practice dependent in any way upon the making of discriminations about a potential client's sex, race, religion, and so forth, is another of the very difficult judgments for many psychologists. On the one hand, discrimination as the term is customarily used is abhorrent. On the other hand, psychologists may wish to specialize, and such specialty areas may be founded in part upon such characteristics as sex, race, or religion. Fewer than 10% engaged in this practice either rarely (3.7%) or more often (3.7%).

Financial barriers. To what extent are people without sufficient funds denied access to needed psychological services? Ever since Freud's (1913/1958) statement that "the absence of the regulating effect offered by the payment of a fee makes itself very painfully felt" (pp. 131–132), there have been strong advocates for the therapeutic necessity of charging fees (e.g., Davids, 1964; Kubie, 1950; Menninger, 1961). Such claims have been made in the absence of empirical support, because systematic studies have found, in general, no therapeutic effect exerted by the fee and no harm to the therapy caused by an absence or lowering of the fee (Balch, Ireland, & Lewis, 1977; Pope, Geller, & Wilkinson, 1975; Turkington, 1984).

Almost half (47.4%) of the respondents report providing free therapy on a rare basis, an additional 18.7% more frequently.

Over half of the respondents had terminated therapy due to the client's inability to pay, either rarely (36.2%) or more often (25.7%). The potential legal liability of the therapist's terminating therapy for other than "therapeutic" reasons may expose the psychologist to a malpractice suit for "abandonment."

Fear of being sued. Do certain clients whose condition may make therapists wary of being sued find access to therapy shut off? Avoiding certain clients for fear of being sued was acknowledged by 30.3% on a rare basis and by 15.6% more often. Fewer than 10% viewed this practice as unethical.

Resources for Regulating the Practice of Psychology

It is interesting that informal networks of colleagues are viewed as the most effective source of guidance, but it is heartening that both the *Ethical Principles* and the APA Ethics Committee are highly valued resources. The fact that both state and local ethics committees received significantly lower ratings suggests that state and local associations may need to devote increased time, financial backing, and program planning and evaluation to these efforts if they are to be judged as valuable by psychologists.

In light of psychology's identity as an empirically based discipline (Singer, 1980), the low ratings accorded to published research are troubling. It is possible that research too rarely addresses ethical concerns and standards of practice in a way that is useful for psychologists.

CONCLUSION

The lack of comprehensive normative data about the behaviors of psychologists and their relationship to ethical standards leaves psychologists without adequate guidelines to inform their choices (Rosenbaum, 1982). Ethical issues in general may be relatively neglected in the professional literature. For example, Baldick (1980) reviewed 250 psychotherapy and counseling texts and found that only 2.8% discussed ethical issues encountered in professional practice.

These data would also be useful to psychology in the formulation of formal standards (APA, 1973, 1981a, 1981b, 1986, 1987a, 1987b; *Standards*, 1985) and in the deliberations of the APA Ethics Committee. In this age of increasing accountability, the formal means by which we psychologists hold ourselves accountable for our behavior is the APA Ethics Committee. Although the Committee participates in a variety of tasks, a major activity is the attempt to resolve complaints against APA members. If the Committee can adjudicate these complaints in a sensitive, fair, and informed manner and can demonstrate a legitimate system of accountability, four consequences are likely to follow.

First, those who file complaints may believe that the perceived wrongs have been corrected or at least seriously addressed. The relationship between the psychologist-complainee and the client or colleague may be reestablished on a more positive, constructive level. At a minimum, those who may have been harmed by the unethical actions of a psychologist may feel that they have been heard and respected. Second, the psychologist-complainee may be at less risk for future unethical behavior and at less risk for harming others. Third, the integrity of the profession is affirmed. Fourth, if the profession can demonstrate a sound process of accountability, that task will not fall by default to external agencies, such as the courts and legislatures, that are ill-equipped for such monitoring.

The integrity of psychology is contingent to a great degree on the extent to which we—both as a discipline or profession and as individuals—can regulate our own behavior. Our ability to engage in effective and ethical regulation, in turn, is contingent on our willingness to study our own behavior and our beliefs about that behavior.

REFERENCES

American Home Assurance Company (undated). *Psychologists' professional liability policy* [Insurance policy]. New York: Author.

American Psychological Association. (1973). Guidelines for psychologists conducting growth groups. *American Psychologist, 28,* 933.

American Psychological Association. (1981a). *Ethical principles of psychologists* (rev. ed.). Washington, DC: Author.

American Psychological Association. (1981b). *Specialty guidelines for the delivery of services by clinical psychologists.* Washington, DC: Author.

American Psychological Association, Ethics Committee. (1982, February 18–20), *Policy statement.* Statement presented at the meeting of the Ethics Committee of the American Psychological Association, Washington, DC.

American Psychological Association. (1985). *Directory of the American Psychological Association.* Washington, DC: Author.

American Psychological Association. (1986). *Guidelines for computer-based tests and interpretations.* Washington, DC: Author.

American Psychological Association. (1987a). Guidelines for conditions of employment of psychologists. *American Psychologist, 42,* 712–723.

American Psychological Association. (1987b). General guidelines for providers of psychological services. *American Psychologist, 42,* 724–729.

Baer, R. (1981). *Homosexuality and American psychiatry.* New York: Basic Books.

Balch, P., Ireland, J. F., & Lewis, S. B. (1977). Fees and therapy: Relation of source of payment to course of therapy at a community mental health center. *Journal of Consulting and Clinical Psychology, 45,* 504.

Baldick, T. L. (1980). Ethical discrimination ability of intern psychologists: A function of training in ethics. *Professional Psychology, 11,* 276–282.

Bergin, A. E., & Garfield, S. L. (Eds.). (1971). *Handbook of psychotherapy and behavior change: An empirical analysis.* Oxford, England: John Wiley.

Blau, T. H. (1984). *The psychologist as expert witness.* New York: Wiley Interscience.

Bouhoutsos, J. C., Holroyd, J., Lerman, H., Forer, B. R., & Greenberg, M. (1983). Sexual intimacy between psychotherapists and patients. *Professional Psychology: Research and Practice, 14,* 185–196.

Colby, K. (1968). Commentary: Report to plenary session on psychopharmacology in relation to psychotherapy. In J. M. Shlien, (Ed.), *Research in psychotherapy* (Vol. 3, pp. 536–540). Washington, DC: American Psychological Association.

Davids, A. (1964). The relation of congitive-dissonance theory to an aspect of psychotherapeutic practice. *American Psychologist, 19,* 329–332.

Dörken, H., Stapp, J., & VandenBos, G. R. (1986). Licensed psychologists: A decade of major growth. In H. Dörken (Ed.), *Professional psychology in transition: Meeting today's challenges* (pp. 3–19). San Francisco: Jossey-Bass.

Feldman-Summers, S., & Jones, G. (1984). Psychological impacts of sexual contact between therapists or other health care practitioners and their clients. *Journal of Consulting and Clinical Psychology, 52,* 1054–1061.

Freeman, L., & Roy, J. (1976). *Betrayal.* New York: Stein & Day.

Freud, S. (1958). Further recommendations in the technique of psychoanalysis: On beginning the treatment. In J. Strachey (Ed. & Trans.), *The standard edition of the complete psychological works of Sigmund Freud* (Vol. 12). London: Hogarth. (Original work published 1913)

Geller, J. D. (1980). The body, expressive movement, and physical contact in psychotherapy. In J. L. Singer & K. S. Pope, (Eds.), *The power of human imagination: New methods in psychotherapy* (pp. 347–378). New York: Plenum.

Holroyd, J. C., & Brodsky, A. M. (1977). Psychologists' attitudes and practices regarding erotic and nonerotic physical contact with patients. *American Psychologist, 32,* 843–849.

Holroyd, J. C., & Brodsky, A. M. (1980). Does touching patients lead to sexual inter-course? *Professional Psychology, 11,* 807–811.

Keith-Spiegel, P., & Koocher, G. (1985). *Ethics in psychology: Professional standards and cases.* New York: Crown Publishing Group/Random House.

Kilburg, R. R., Nathan, P. E., & Thoreson, R. W. (Eds.). (1986). *Professionals in distress: Issues, syndromes, and solutions in psychology.* Washington, DC: American Psychological Association.

Koocher, G. P. (Ed.). (1976). *Children's rights and the mental health professions.* New York: Wiley.

Kubie, L. S. (1950). *Practical and theoretical aspects of psychoanalysis.* Oxford, England: International Universities Press.

Laliotis, D., & Grayson, J. (1985). Psychologist heal thyself: What is available for the impaired psychologist? *American Psychologist, 40,* 84–96.

Malyon, A. K. (1986a). *Brief follow-up to June 24, 1986 meeting with the American Psychiatric Association work group to revise DSM–III.* Unpublished manuscript.

Malyon, A. K. (1986b). *Presentation to the American Psychiatric Association work group to revise DSM–III.* Unpublished manuscript.

Matarazzo, J. D. (1986). Computerized clinical psychological test interpretations: Unvalidated plus all mean and no sigma. *American Psychologist, 41,* 14–24.

Melton, G. B. (1981). Effects of a state law permitting minors to consent to psycho-therapy. *Professional Psychology, 12,* 647–654.

Menninger, K. (1961). *Theory of psychoanalytic technique.* New York: Science Editions.

Mintz, N. L. (1971). Patient fees and psychotherapeutic transactions. *Journal of Consulting and Clinical Psychology, 36,* 1–8.

Morrison, K. L., Morrison, J. K., & Holdridge-Crane, S. (1979). The child's right to give informed consent to psychiatric treatment. *Journal of Clinical Child Psychology, 8,* 43–47.

Plaisil, E. (1985). *Therapist.* New York: St. Martin's/Marek.

Plotkin, R. (1981). When rights collide: Parents, children, and consent to treatment. *Journal of Pediatric Psychology, 6,* 121–130.

Pope, K. S. (1982). *Implications of fantasy and imagination for mental health: Theory, research, and interventions* (Report commissioned by the National Institute of Mental Health, Order No. 82M024784505D). Bethesda, MD: National Institute of Mental Health.

Pope, K. S. (1985, August). *Diagnosis and treatment of Therapist–Patient Sex Syndrome.* Paper presented at the annual meeting of the American Psychological Association, Los Angeles.

Pope, K. S. (1986, May). *Therapist–Patient Sex Syndrome: Research findings.* Paper presented at the annual meeting of the American Psychiatric Association, Washington, DC.

Pope, K. S. (in press). Preventing therapist–patient sexual intimacy: Therapy for a therapist at risk. *Professional Psychology: Research and Practice.*

Pope, K. S., & Bouhoutsos, J. C. (1986). *Sexual intimacy between therapists and patients.* New York: Praeger.

Pope, K. S., Geller, J. D., & Wilkinson, L. (1975). Fee assessment and outpatient psychotherapy. *Journal of Consulting and Clinical Psychology, 43,* 835–841.

Pope, K. S., Keith-Spiegel, P. C., & Tabachnick, B. (1986). Sexual attraction to clients: The human therapist and the (sometimes) inhuman training system. *American Psychologist, 41,* 147–158.

Pope, K. S., Levenson, H., & Schover, L. R. (1979). Sexual intimacy in psychology training: Results and implications of a national survey. *American Psychologist, 34,* 682–689.

Pope, K. S., Schover, L. R., & Levenson, H. (1980). Sexual behavior between clinical supervisors and trainees: Implications for professional standards. *Professional Psychology, 11,* 157–162.

Redlich, F. C. (1977). The ethics of sex therapy. In W. H. Masters, V. E. Johnson, & R. D. Kolodny (Eds.), *Ethical issues in sex therapy and research* (pp. 143–157). Boston: Little, Brown.

Redlich, F. C., & Pope, K. S. (1980). Ethics of mental health training. *Journal of Nervous and Mental Disease, 168*, 709–714.

Rosenbaum, M. (Ed.). (1982). *Ethics and values in psychotherapy*. New York: Free Press.

Rubinstein, E. A., & Parloff, M. B. (Eds.). (1959). *Research in psychotherapy*. Washington, DC: National.

Sell, J. M., Gottlieb, M. C., & Schoenfeld, L. (1986). Ethical considerations of social/romantic relationships with present and former clients. *Professional Psychology: Research and Practice, 17*, 504–508.

Shapiro, D. L. (1984). *Psychological evaluation and expert testimony: A practical guide to forensic work*. New York: Van Nostrand.

Shlien, J. M. (Ed.). (1968). *Research in psychotherapy* (Vol. 3). Washington, DC: American Psychological Association.

Singer, J. L. (1980). The scientific basis of psychotherapeutic practice: A question of values and ethics. *Psychotherapy: Theory, Research & Practice, 17*, 372–383.

Standards for educational and psychological testing. (1985). American Psychological Association. Washington, DC.

Stapp, J., Tucker, A. M., & VandenBos, G. R. (1985). Census of psychological personnel: 1983. *American Psychologist, 40*, 1317–1351.

Strupp, H. H., & Luborsky, L. (Eds.). (1962). *Research in psychotherapy* (Vol. 2). Baltimore, MD: French-Bray.

Szasz, T. (1986). The case against suicide prevention. *American Psychologist, 41*, 806–812.

Tabachnick, B. G., & Fidell, L. S. (1983). *Using multivariate statistics*. New York: Harper & Row.

Thompson, C. (1950). *Psychoanalysis: Evolution and development*. New York: Hermitage House.

Turkington, C. (1984, April). Austin study questions tenet that free therapy lacks value. *APA Monitor*, p. 6.

Walker, E., & Young, T. D. (1986). *A killing cure*. New York: Henry Holt.

Whitesell v. Green, No. 38745 (Dist. Ct. Hawaii filed November 19, 1973).

Whitree v. State (1968). 290 N. Y. S. 2nd 486.

COMMENTARY: Psychologists give of themselves in therapy. Commonality of experience, relatability, and genuineness are balanced against overdisclosure, ingratiation, and boundary violation. All of this presupposes that psychologists, too, are unique individuals, just like clients/patients. It should not surprise us, however, to learn that there are shared elements, such as motivating factors, cultural indoctrination, and professionally imposed ethical standards, that tend to make most psychologists more alike than different.

The survey conducted by Dr. Pope and his colleagues more than 30 years ago is a testament to not only presumptively valid research design but also the durability of certain beliefs and behaviors that, based on what one observes in day-to-day practice, persist in force to this day. Here, one learns that the typical clinical psychologist is anything but a "blank screen" for his or her clients/patients, and that the respect of others' "dignity as human beings" is paramount. Although psychologists should not conclude that their role in the face of this evidence is to become even more like their colleagues, they should be inspired to consider just what impact the verbal or behavioral expression of such traits may have on recipients of treatment.

The following references are recommended for those interested in further investigation of ethical implications of the attitudes and beliefs of psychologists providing clinical services, including those situations in which, during these culturally and politically fraught times, a lack of fit may have more profound consequences than previously encountered in general practice.

Barnett, J. E. (2008). Impaired professionals: Distress, professional impairment, self-care, and psychological wellness. In M. Hersen & A. M. Gross (Eds.), *Handbook of clinical psychology: Vol. 1. Adults* (pp. 857–884), Hoboken, NJ: Wiley.

Branstetter, S. A., & Handelsman, M. M. (2000). Graduate teaching assistants: Ethical training, beliefs, and practices. *Ethics & Behavior, 10*, 27–50. http://dx.doi.org/10.1207/S15327019EB1001_3

Helbok, C. M., Marinelli, R. P., & Walls, R. T. (2006). National survey of ethical practices across rural and urban communities. *Professional Psychology: Research and Practice, 37*, 36–44. http://dx.doi.org/10.1037/0735-7028.37.1.36

Redding, R. E. (2001). Sociopolitical diversity in psychology: The case for pluralism. *American Psychologist, 56*, 205–215. http://dx.doi.org/10.1037/0003-066X.56.3.205

Schneller, G. R., Swenson, J. E., III, & Sanders, R. K. (2010). Training for ethical situations arising in Christian counseling: A survey of members of the Christian Association for Psychological Studies. *Journal of Psychology and Christianity, 29*, 343–353.

2.5. The Ethical Decision-Making Model

Samuel J. Knapp, Michael C. Gottlieb, and Mitchell M. Handelsman

From the standpoint of principle-based ethics, the term *ethical dilemma* applies to situations in which two or more overarching ethical principles appear to conflict such that psychologists cannot fulfill one ethical principle without offending the other (Beauchamp & Childress, 2009). Dilemmas may occur when the relevant standards from the American Psychological Association (APA, 2010) Ethics Code conflict with one another or require psychologists to use their professional judgment when the Code's standards conflict with a law or an organizational policy. Sometimes, psychologists encounter situations in which neither the APA Ethics Code nor the law provides adequate direction. We discuss each of these areas later in more detail.

In this chapter, we use the five-step model (identify relevant principles, generate alternatives, select the optimal intervention, act, and review; Knapp & VandeCreek, 2012) to review decision making from the perspective of principle-based ethics. We describe principle-based ethics, identify the principles important in problem analysis and resolution, give examples of how the model may be applied, and pay special attention to creative ways to resolve apparent ethical conflicts. We view ethics decision making as a process that is more than a thought experiment—it is a process that also is influenced by emotions and other nonrational factors. We contend that awareness of these factors can improve the quality of decision making.

Almost every decision-making model is an example of slow, deliberate, and effortful System 2 thinking (see Chapter 1). Here, we present the five-step model of Knapp and VandeCreek (2012; see also Weinstein, 2000), which borrows from others models, such as the IDEAL system (identify, develop, explore, act, and look back; Bransford & Stein, 1993) and the SHAPE system (scrutinize,

From *Ethical Dilemmas in Psychotherapy: Positive Approaches to Decision Making* (pp. 25–45), by S. J. Knapp, M. C. Gottlieb, and M. M. Handelsman, 2015, Washington, DC: American Psychological Association. Copyright 2015 by the American Psychological Association.

Portions of this chapter are adapted from *Practical Ethics for Psychologists: A Positive Approach, Second Edition* (pp. 35–48), by S. J. Knapp and L. D. VandeCreek, 2012, Washington, DC: American Psychological Association. Copyright 2012 by the American Psychological Association.

Note that chapter cross-references herein refer to the book in which this chapter original originally appeared, *Ethical Dilemmas in Psychotherapy: Positive Approaches to Decision Making*.

develop hypothesis, analyze proposed solution, perform, and evaluate; Härtel & Härtel, 1997). Our labels for the five steps include the mnemonics of both Bransford and Stein (1993) and Härtel and Härtel (1997).

The IDEAL and SHAPE systems are general decision-making models and are not specific to ethics. Many of the factors related to decision making in general apply to ethical decision making, too (Elm & Radin, 2012). We review the basics of principle-based ethics and then go through each of the five steps to show how they are linked to principle-based ethics. We want to emphasize right at the beginning, though, that ours is a dynamic model in; depending on the circumstances of a problem, the decision maker may need to skip steps, repeat steps, move backward, or otherwise alter the sequence of decision making.

PRINCIPLE-BASED ETHICS

As noted in Chapter 1, the English philosopher William David Ross (1930/1998) developed principle-based ethics, and American philosophers Thomas Beauchamp and James Childress (2009) expanded and applied it to health care. The influence of principle-based ethics is clear in APA's (2010) "Ethical Principles of Psychologists and Code of Conduct," in which the General (aspirational) Principles are modeled largely after W. D. Ross.

W. D. Ross (1930/1998) developed principle-based ethics after reflecting on two of the dominant philosophies of his time: deontology and utilitarianism. *Deontological ethics* focuses on the importance of following rules dealing with obligations and prohibitions. W. D. Ross appreciated the emphasis that deontological ethics gave to following overriding values, but he disliked that it did not allow for exceptions under unique circumstances, and that it had no ethical decision-making process to follow when two or more obligations appeared to collide.

In contrast, *utilitarianism* focuses on the importance of looking at the effect of behavior on all affected people. W. D. Ross (1930/1998) appreciated utilitarianism, because it had an ethical decision-making process and it emphasized the welfare of all people affected by the decision maker's behavior. But he disliked that utilitarianism weighed the effect on all people equally—that is, in making moral judgments, the well-being of strangers had the same weight as the well-being of families, friends, or others to whom the moral agent has special obligations. As a result, W. D. Ross tried to develop a philosophy that maximized the strengths and minimized the limitations of deontological and utilitarian ethics. Thus, the principle-based ethics that he developed retained an emphasis on moral obligations as found in deontological ethics and included a decision-making process, as did utilitarianism.

W. D. Ross (1930/1998) identified six *prima facie duties*, those that people should generally follow and that represent a reasonable claim or obligation that can be expected of an individual. He identified the duties in no particular order or priority and without claiming "completeness or finality" (p. 269): fidelity, gratitude, justice, beneficence, self-improvement, and non-maleficence. Later, Beauchamp and Childress (2009) identified those principles that apply more directly to health care professionals, including *beneficence* (to act to promote the well-being of another person), *nonmaleficence* (to avoid harming another person), *respect for patient autonomy* (to respect the decisions made by patients and to promote circumstances that help the patient make informed decisions), *justice* (either *procedural justice*—treating people fairly—or *distributive justice*—the notion that everyone in society has access to some of the goods of society necessary for life), and *physician–patient relationships* (dealing with the obligations to keep promises). Knapp and VandeCreek (2012) added *general* or *public beneficence* (dealing with obligations to the public). Brief definitions and examples of these principles appear in Exhibit 1.

Authors vary slightly in how they formulate or discuss these over-arching ethical principles. For example, the General Principles of the APA Ethics Code combine beneficence and nonmaleficence. However, we concur with Beauchamp and Childress (2009) that nonmaleficence should be separated from beneficence, because there is a human tendency to give more weight to negative than positive events, even when they are of equal valence.

EXHIBIT 1

Definitions and Examples of Ethical Principles

Respect for patient autonomy: Respecting the decision-making capacities of autonomous people

Examples:
- Respecting a patient's wishes for the goals of therapy
- Refraining from pushing a personal political agenda onto the patient

Nonmaleficence: Avoiding the causation of harm

Example: Not using a therapy technique that has a background of unwanted side effects

Beneficence: Providing benefits and balancing benefits, risks, and costs

Example: Selecting the best treatments for the patient

Fidelity (or doctor–patient relationship): Loyalty to the patient; placing a patient's interest first, keeping promises

Example: Avoiding taking patients when a possible conflict of interest could compromise effectiveness of therapy

Justice: People are treated fairly

Example: Not discriminating on the basis of age, gender, racial or ethnic group, national background, sexual orientation, socioeconomic status, and so forth

General (public) beneficence: Concern for the welfare of society

Example: Ensuring that information psychologists write in an article for a local newspaper is accurate and up to date

---

FIVE-STEP DECISION-MAKING PROCESSES

In this section, we go through the five steps sequentially.

Step 1: Identify or Scrutinize the Problem

Psychologists first identify the ethical dilemma or conflict by identifying the most relevant overarching ethical principles and how they may conflict. Here is an example of applying Step 1 to the situation introduced in the Introduction to this book:

> **A Conflict in Values**
>
> Dr. Yasuto was treating a patient who had made a serious attempt to kill himself. After a thorough discussion with the patient and a review of situational factors, Dr. Yasuto determined that the patient was at a high risk to die from suicide, yet the patient resisted hospitalization. Dr. Yasuto needed to decide whether to initiate procedures for an involuntary psychiatric hospitalization.

The most relevant overarching ethical principles in this example are beneficence (patient's well-being), nonmaleficence (avoiding harm to the patient), and respect for patient autonomy (generally following the wishes of the patient in setting the goals and agreeing on the procedures in treatment).

Step 2: Develop Alternatives or Hypothesize Solutions (Listen and Talk)

Often, psychologists reach the best decisions after they have considered a range of useful alternatives. Psychologists can improve the number and quality of their options if they listen and talk to patients and others who may be influenced by their decisions. That is, they need to discuss the issues with others—including conversations with patients and other affected people, and formal consultations—and consider the cognitive and emotional influences on their decision-making process.

A long line of evidence supports the importance of listening to and talking in social networks to generate good ideas. In his review of the history of technology and science, S. Johnson (2010) debunked the popular belief that a lone genius produces great innovations through sudden insights that advance the state of knowledge by years or decades. In contrast, he argued that most innovators have a close network of collaborators (or a network through which ideas are exchanged freely) and that scientific advances are almost always incremental improvements on existing ideas. Few great leaps occur. Similarly, psychologists can use networks and connections to improve the quality of the ideas they generate. Ideas gained from free exchange with patients, members of patients' social circles, and by consulting professionals may lead to insights or interventions that psychologists could not have generated on their own. For example, consultation groups can be a source of such useful ideas. As W. B. Johnson, Barnett, Elman, Forrest, and Kaslow (2013) noted, psychologists increase their competence when they have a network of relationships with colleagues who take an interest in their professional well-being.

Listen and Talk (Benefits of Soliciting Input)

Sometimes input comes through formal consultations with other professionals, who can help address the cognitive and emotional aspects of decision making. From a cognitive perspective, consultants may be able to identify sources of knowledge, neglected questions, types of interventions, or useful resources. From an emotional perspective, they may help psychologists reduce strong emotional influences, allow them to process information more clearly, and provide frameworks for their thinking. For example, consultants may challenge psychologists to explore their perceptions, intuitions, assumptions, logic, and blind spots; the ethics acculturation model (see Chapter 4) may be particularly helpful in this regard. The very process of describing a dilemma to another person may help psychologists to clarify and think through the dilemma for themselves.

With the goals of testing assumptions and identifying options, it can be useful to discuss options with the patients or other affected individuals. In the case of Dr. Yasuto, she needed to consider her patient's reasons for opposing the treatment plan (in this case, a psychiatric hospitalization), such as the lack of availability of child care or fear of losing his job. Dr. Yasuto may find that her patient is rationalizing to mask his true intentions, or he may have legitimate problems getting child care and is trying to balance his need for treatment with other practical concerns. Furthermore, because the patient is seriously depressed, he may be thinking in a rigid manner such that he is unable to consider obvious alternatives to address those concerns. Consider these examples:

Examples of Involving Patients

One psychologist had instituted an involuntary hospitalization of a patient who suddenly dropped her opposition to going to the hospital when he told her that he would respect her wishes not to be sent to a particular one. It turned out that her father had died in that hospital and she still had great anxiety about going there. Another psychologist had a patient who suddenly dropped her opposition to going to the hospital when he told her that he would respect her wishes of going to the hospital in her family car and not an ambulance. The patient was afraid that the neighbors would begin gossiping about her if they saw an ambulance drive away from her house.

Reflect (Cognitive Distortions and Feelings)

As discussed in Chapter 1, nonrational factors influence psychologists' ability to make good decisions (Kahneman & Klein, 2009; Rogerson, Gottlieb, Handelsman, Knapp, & Younggren, 2011). Physician Jerome Groopman (2007) described the effect of thinking errors on physicians. For example, he claimed that the premature foreclosure of other options can cause physicians to select a diagnosis prematurely, and then, through the process of confirmation bias, "[confirm] what you expect to find by selectively accepting or ignoring information" (p. 65)—cherry-picking, without conscious awareness, symptoms that confirm the original diagnosis.

In addition to attending to potential cognitive errors, psychologists may also improve the quality of their decision making by considering the emotional aspects of the process. Although feelings may provide useful insights and motivate people to solve problems, more intense emotions can disrupt the cognitive processes necessary to generate or evaluate sound solutions. For example, high anxiety may cause psychologists to select the first or one of the first solutions that comes to mind only because quickly arriving at a solution immediately, albeit temporarily, reduces distress.

Psychologists may experience cognitive rigidity and view a problem as having only one solution (or one kind of solution) without considering alternative strategies and explanations. For example, when dealing with patients who threaten others, psychologists sometimes jump too quickly to the conclusion that they must warn the identified victim. However, the first halfway reasonable solution that comes to mind may not be the optimal one. It would be more desirable for psychologists to avoid the dichotomous thinking of either "warn" or "do nothing" and consider other ways to diffuse the danger, such as by acting to protect the patient. In this regard, it may be prudent to consider the Aristotelian *golden mean* (Aristotle, circa 330 BCE/1985) when it comes to emotions and decision making. According to the golden mean, too much or too little of a trait could be harmful (e.g., too much courage is recklessness; too little courage is cowardice). As applied to ethical decision making, too little as well as too much emotion can undermine the quality of the decision-making process.

Emotional interference also may prevent psychologists from recognizing cognitive processes, such as the availability heuristic (Kahneman, 2011), which may influence their decision making. For example, after a widely publicized shooting, the threat of mentally ill shooters will be on the minds of many members of the public, including psychologists. As a result, psychologists may become more sensitive to the issue of school shootings and correctly identify potential shooters, but they may also err on the side of overidentifying patients as being at risk for harming others when they are not.

Dr. Yasuto needs to generate potential options for handling her patient, who has strong suicidal thoughts. She has the option of following beneficence/nonmaleficence and hospitalizing the patient, and she also may be tempted to do this just to reduce her own anxiety. On the other hand, she may respect the patient's autonomy and allow him to stay out of the hospital. Ideally, Dr. Yasuto will go beyond these two options by soliciting more detailed information from the patient concerning his wishes. If time permits, it would be helpful to solicit input from others in the patient's social network and other professionals who have contact with him, such as his family physician.

Dr. Yasuto's consultation with other mental health professionals may reduce her distress and cognitive distortions. In the tension and distress caused by this situation, Dr. Yasuto may define the problem as: How do I get the patient into the hospital? She may be substituting this easier question for a more difficult but more important one, such as, How do I ensure the safety of the patient, and at the same time minimize harm to the treatment relationship and generate better solutions? Before acting, Dr. Yasuto can take her *emotional temperature* to assess the extent to which strong emotional reactions could be influencing her thinking (Gino, 2013). On reflection and consultation, she may redefine the problem.

Step 3: Analyze and Evaluate

In Step 3, psychologists analyze, evaluate, and select an optimal intervention. The best solutions often arise when psychologists identify the advantages and disadvantages—which include practical, clinical, and legal considerations—of each potential solution from Step 2. But, from the perspective of principle-based ethics, resolving dilemmas often means that one overarching ethical principle temporarily overrides another (Beauchamp & Childress, 2009; W. D. Ross, 1930/1998). According to W. D. Ross (1930/1998),

> When I am in a situation . . . in which more than one of these *prima facie* duties is incumbent on me, what I have to do is to study the situation as fully as I can until I form the considered opinion (it is never more) that in the circumstances one of them is more incumbent than any other. (p. 268)

No one overarching ethical principle always demands the highest priority; any principle may be trumped by any other, depending on the circumstances. W. D. Ross did not provide an absolute rule for determining when one ethical principle should trump another other than that it seems like the most appropriate thing to do.

Hadjistavropoulos and Malloy (1999) argued that psychologists should rank principles into a hierarchy so that some ethical principles take precedence over others. For example, they argued that respect for people's rights and dignity takes precedence over others. However, that is not the perspective of W. D. Ross or Beauchamp and Childress, and even Hadjistavropoulos and Malloy noted the possibility of exceptions to their hierarchy. Also, Williams et al. (2012) found equivocal evidence for the ease or utility of ranked versus unranked hierarchies of principles.

The saying *primum non nocere* ("above all, do no harm") appears to demand that nonmaleficence should always trump all other ethical principles. But we concur with W. D. Ross and Beauchamp and Childress that no one overarching ethical principle, such as nonmaleficence, should always trump another ethical principle. Instead, the decisions depend on the circumstances of the situation. Beauchamp and Childress (2009) proposed that individuals choose one option over others when several conditions are met. The four most salient of these conditions follow:

1. The decision maker has sufficient reason to act on behalf of one overarching ethical principle rather than another.
2. The action has a realistic chance of success.
3. The decision maker can find no morally preferable alternative.
4. The decision maker seeks to minimize the negative effect of infringing on the offended ethical principle.

According to these conditions, Dr. Yasuto must ask,

1. Is there sufficient justification to allow one ethical principle (beneficence or nonmaleficence) to trump another ethical principle (respect for patient autonomy)?

   Typically, in the case of imminent suicide, beneficence/nonmaleficence trumps respect for patient autonomy. However, Dr. Yasuto needs to assess the imminence and potential lethality of suicidal behavior with attention to many case-specific and contextual factors. If the risk of suicide is low, Dr. Yasuto needs to give greater deference to respecting the patient's autonomous decision making.

2. Does the proposed action have a realistic chance of success?

   Dr. Yasuto may decide that the patient has to go to the hospital, even if the admission is done involuntarily. In this situation, Dr. Yasuto must first determine if the patient's behavior meets the statutory requirements for an involuntary hospitalization in her state to determine whether an effort to obtain it would be successful.

3. Can a morally preferable alternative be found?

   From this brief vignette, it appears that no preferable alternative to hospitalization can be found. However, the general rule is that, whenever possible, psychologists should strive assiduously to find useful alternatives that avoid a direct conflict between two ethical principles.

   In her search for a solution, Dr. Yasuto may consider whether she can mobilize the healthy aspects of the patient, as a matter of respect for his autonomy, to ensure his safety and cooperation with the general treatment goals without the use or threat of force. Because an involuntary psychiatric hospitalization offends respect for patient autonomy so extensively, Dr. Yasuto should only use it as a last resort when she can find no other alternative to save the patient's life. She also would prefer a voluntary hospitalization to avoid making the patient reluctant to seek treatment in the future. Nonetheless, in some situations, no morally preferable alternative may be available.

4. Can Dr. Yasuto minimize the harm to the offended ethical principle?

   If Dr. Yasuto decides to have beneficence/nonmaleficence trump autonomy and institute an involuntary hospitalization, she should attempt to involve the patient in the decision as much as possible. For example, if possible, Dr. Yasuto could give the patient a choice of hospital.

We find that the most common mistake graduate students make is their failure to consider how to minimize harm to an offended moral principle. Nonetheless, this is the feature that often distinguishes excellent ethical decisions from minimally acceptable ones and may be the key to preserving the therapeutic alliance.

A general strategy may be to select a solution that combines the best elements of the different solutions proposed through a process akin to *theory knitting.* In experimental psychology "theory development progresses through the integration of the strongest features of the alternative theories with one's own ideas about the phenomenon under investigation" (Sternberg, Grigorenko, & Kalmar, 2001, p. 107). Similarly, psychologists can knit solutions by comparing alternatives, evaluating the conflicting properties of each, and integrating the best aspects of each.

Step 4: Act or Perform

Step 4 can be quite complex because even the most thorough deliberation does not necessarily lead to action. Here we consider whether and how Dr. Yasuto will implement her solution.

Whether the Solution Will Be Implemented

Some studies have found that many psychology graduate students (Bernard & Jara, 1986) and psychologists (Bernard, Murphy, & Little, 1987) who reached the "right" solution to an ethical dilemma would not act on the solution. The reasons for these findings are unclear. At times, the inability to act may be due to shortcomings of psychologists who may be excessively timid or afraid that the patient may retaliate by giving a negative review online, thus making the psychologist a victim of harmful gossip, or even filing a licensing board complaint. Perhaps other psychologists were inadequately socialized into the ethics of the profession. We may say that some of these psychologists failed to live up to their optimal ethical values. In these circumstances, psychologists need to develop better skills at addressing issues despite their anxiety or to learn more about how to integrate their personal moral beliefs into the ethical requirements of the profession (see Chapter 4). In Chapter 3, we discuss how psychologists can strengthen their resolve or moral courage by grounding themselves in an overarching ethical theory.

We also want to consider that the failure to act may occur because psychologists do not proceed adequately through Steps 1, 2, or 3. Subsequently, they may feel discomfort or uneasiness with their decision. Perhaps their response reflected what they thought the APA Ethics Code, law, or risk management guidelines required of them, but they did not incorporate enough of their personal values into their decision (T. S. Smith, McGuire, Abbott, & Blau, 1991). Or perhaps they did not adequately consider the effect that their personal emotions or contextual factors could have on their actions (Betan & Stanton, 1999).

Psychologists who experience ambivalence about acting in Step 4 may wish to reflect on the reasons for their ambivalence. For example, Dr. Yasuto may reach a decision to treat the patient as an outpatient. However, after she makes that decision, she immediately feels dread and apprehension. At this point, Dr. Yasuto may wish to identify the sources of her discomfort and determine if those feelings reveal something about herself and her fear of making tough decisions, or if those feelings indicate unexamined thoughts about the wisdom of it.

How the Solution Will Be Implemented

Even if Dr. Yasuto reaches a good decision, the manner in which she implements her decision can be as important as the decision itself. That is, it is possible to implement decisions in ways that further reflect or further offend overarching ethical principles.

A Bad Decision Implemented Badly. Perhaps Dr. Yasuto made a hasty decision, with minimal input, to recommend hospitalization (beneficence trumps respect for patient autonomy). She did not listen and talk, solicit meaningful input from the patient, attempt to motivate the patient to accept the reasonableness of the hospitalization decision, solicit input from other members of the patient's social network, seek consultation, consider less intrusive means to reach the goal of patient safety, or review her emotional temperature and the risk of cognitive and affective distortions. In addition to making a bad decision, she may implement it poorly. For example, a lack of emotional competence (excessive worry and fear) may cause Dr. Yasuto to speak to the patient in a manner that he perceives as brusque and insensitive. If so, the patient may then perceive Dr. Yasuto as unconcerned with his well-being (poor beneficence) and more focused on protecting herself. The patient may now view Dr. Yasuto as having trumped his autonomy for selfish reasons, thereby violating her fiduciary duty to him.

A Bad Decision Implemented Well. In another situation, Dr. Yasuto could do an equally poor job of making a decision that allows beneficence to completely trump respect for patient autonomy. Nonetheless, Dr. Yasuto may be able to implement the bad decision well. For example, she may speak to the patient in a caring manner that conveys genuine concern. Thus, the patient may (accurately) perceive that Dr. Yasuto has beneficent motives, even if she trumps respect for his autonomy.

A Good Decision Implemented Badly. Perhaps Dr. Yasuto could reach a conclusion that appears to adequately balance beneficence with respect for patient autonomy. Nonetheless, the value of her decision may be compromised if she discusses it in a manner that fails to convey her concern for the patient's well-being or fails to show her desire to respect his decision-making autonomy.

Step 5: Look Back or Evaluate

The fifth step is to look back and evaluate the solution. In many cases, the five-step model will result in a solution that resolves the ethical dilemma. In other cases, psychologists may look back, evaluate the effectiveness of the intervention, and determine that another intervention is warranted or that they need to modify their original intervention.

The five-step model is dynamic—it is not necessarily linear or fixed. For example, the resolution of one dilemma may give rise to additional, unanticipated dilemmas. Or it may provide more information that causes psychologists to alter their previous interpretation of the problem and return to previous steps. For example, work on the second and third steps (develop and analyze options) may lead psychologists to go back to Step 1 (identify or scrutinize the original problem). Also, sometimes it is not until the fourth or fifth steps (act/ perform and look back/evaluate) that psychologists become aware of contextual factors that would have modified the options generated in Steps 1 and 2. Consider this example:

> **A Patient Responds to Concerns**
>
> A psychologist had a young adult outpatient who had very recently taken an overdose of medication but had been medically cleared. She was sullen, would not look at the psychologist, and would not answer questions or respond to his entreaties to talk with him. Finally, he told her that, given her refusal to speak, he had no option but to err on the side of safety and recommend that she be placed in the psychiatric unit of the local hospital. The psychologist moved to Step 3 and determined that beneficence would trump respect for patient autonomy. He initiated Step 4 (act) in her presence and telephoned the appropriate authority (called a "mental health delegate"), who was on her way to his office to complete the necessary paperwork. Apparently, the patient decided that he was serious about the hospitalization; as soon as he got off the phone, she began to talk to him about her concerns and worries. By the time the mental health delegate arrived to complete the paperwork, the psychologist had enough information and confidence in the young woman that he decided that hospitalization was unnecessary and that she could be safely treated as an outpatient. In this situation, the psychologist moved from Step 4 (implementing) back to Step 2, where he reconsidered the options and ended up with another course of action.

APPLICATION OF THE FIVE-STEP MODEL

The five-step decision-making model is useful in specific situations in which the ethical standards themselves require psychologists to make decisions, when the practices of an agency or institution may conflict with the APA Ethics Code, or when the Code provides insufficient direction.

Ethical Dilemmas Found in the Enforceable Standards

Many standards in the APA Ethics Code use modifiers such as "reasonably," "appropriately," or "potentially," which indicate that psychologists need to use their professional judgment in applying the standard. For example, psychologists may encounter patients in a first session who are in a state of great emotional turmoil. They may have had strong thoughts of suicide or homicide, or they may be faced with a situation that requires an immediate decision.

Standard 3.10, Informed Consent

In this situation, conducting the informed consent process at the start of treatment while patients are essentially in an emergency would result in a conflict between the principles of respect for patient autonomous decision making

and beneficence. Fortunately, the APA Ethics Code anticipates such situations
and specifically allows one ethical principle temporarily to trump another, as
long as psychologists attempt to minimize harm to the offended ethical principle. Standard 10.01a states that "psychologists inform clients/patients as
early *as is feasible* [emphasis added] in the therapeutic relationship about the
nature and anticipated course of therapy, fees, involvement of third parties,
and limits of confidentiality. . . ." The standard thus permits psychologists
discretion in delaying the informed consent process. Next, we explore each
alternative and discuss how the principles may be balanced.

Respect for Patient Autonomy

It is possible to respond to these situations by focusing only on respect for
patient autonomy. One can imagine a scenario in which a patient has strong
suicidal ideation but the psychologist deflects some of the patient's dis-
tress-filled comments to talk about office protocols, billing forms, and fees. In
this scenario, the psychologist may allow the formalities of respecting patient
autonomy to trump patient beneficence. We use the phrase "formalities of
respecting patient autonomy" because it is unlikely that a patient in such a
crisis would be able to pay much attention to the presentation on billing and
office procedures to begin with. Thus, the psychologist would be upholding
the letter of respect for patient autonomy but violating its spirit.

Beneficence

We could also envision a scenario in which the psychologist focuses entirely on
the patient's immediate concerns and does nothing to explain billing procedures, limits of confidentiality, or other topics typically addressed in the informed
consent process. In this case, beneficence completely trumps respect for patient
autonomy, with no effort to minimize harm to the offended ethical principle.
This scenario involves some risk because some of the topics covered in the
informed consent process, such as confidentiality, may influence what the
patient decides to tell the psychologist. For example, if the patient knew that
the psychologist had an obligation to break confidentiality in cases of suspected
child abuse, the patient may not be forthcoming about parenting behaviors.

Beneficence/Respect for Patient Autonomy

Standard 10.01 of the APA Ethics Code allows psychologists to trump temporarily the overarching principle of respect for patient autonomy to promote
beneficence or avoid nonmaleficence. Consistent with principle-based ethics,
psychologists should make an effort to minimize harm to the offended ethical
principle (respect for patient autonomy) by engaging in the informed consent
process as early as is feasible or by giving patients a truncated version of the
informed consent process ahead of time (perhaps only focusing on limits to
confidentiality if that is likely to be a concern), and then completing the process later. Psychologists can provide information gradually, much like a hospital patient receives doses of medication gradually through a titration process
(Gottlieb, Handelsman, & Knapp, 2013).

Informed Consent With Children and Parents

Balancing beneficence and respect for autonomy has unique aspects when working with children. Generally, psychologists must obtain the informed consent of patients, or, in the case of children, the parents or their legal guardians. In some states, adolescents may consent to treatment without parental consent, at least in some circumstances. Even when adolescents do not have the legal authority to consent to treatment, the APA Ethics Code requires psychologists to attempt to obtain the child's assent or agreement to treatment. Standard 3.10b, Informed Consent states,

> For persons who are legally incapable of giving informed consent, psychologists nevertheless (1) provide an appropriate explanation, (2) seek the individual's assent, (3) consider such persons' preferences and best interests, and (4) obtain appropriate permission from a legally authorized person, if such substitute is permitted or required by law.

Generally, parents have the best interests of their children in mind, and psychologists may generally assume that parents are making adolescents do something that they believe will be good for them. That is, the parents may require treatment, because they see beneficence as trumping respect for the autonomy of their child. The APA Ethics Code recognizes that the wishes of the decision maker (usually the parent) may trump those of the child or adolescent patient. Nonetheless, psychologists try to minimize the violation of adolescents' autonomy by seeking their assent and considering their preferences, because doing so can be essential to successful treatment. Adolescent patients, however, may not want treatment. They, sometimes accurately, may see therapy as an attempt to control their behavior or make them do things that they would not ordinarily want to do (Oetzel & Scherer, 2003), or they may feel that being the identified patient stigmatizes them as the "sick one" in the family, when others also may have problems.

Many psychologists balance the ethical principles of beneficence and respect for patient autonomy for adolescents by using a flexible standard. That is, they consider the consequences for the adolescent or other family members in making these decisions. If the threat to the welfare of the child or other family members is high, then psychologists may give greater importance to treatment and allow beneficence and public beneficence to trump respect for patient autonomy. On the other hand, if the threat to the welfare of the patient or others is less serious or less imminent, then psychologists may defer more to the adolescent's wishes. Consider one psychologist who uses a "three strikes, you're out" rule: She requires the adolescent to have three sessions, and if the adolescent does not like it or see the value in it, then she will not continue. The three strikes rule give beneficence a chance to work but also minimizes the harm to the adolescent's autonomous decision-making ability.

In addition to the basic agreement on whether to be involved, parents and children may disagree on the goals or focus of treatment. McGillicuddy,

Rychtarik, Morsheimer, and Burke-Storer (2007) found that parental awareness of the extent to which adolescents abused alcohol or other drugs varied considerably. Hawley and Weisz (2003) found that more than three fourths of child–parent–therapist triads failed to have consensus on a single problem at the start of treatment. For example, parents may view their child's behavior as disrespectful and offensive, whereas the child views the behavior of parents as intrusive and unwarranted. Or parents may want their daughter to become more respectful to them, but the daughter is only interested in better relationships with her peers at school.

At times, parents, adolescents, and psychologists also may all have differing goals. For example, the parents may want their son to stay out of trouble with the police, the son wants to get his parents off his back, and the psychologist believes that the adolescent has a rather serious but unacknowledged depression that needs treatment. Sometimes mixed agreement and disagreement on goals exist: The parents want their son to do better in school and excel in athletics, even though the son agrees with doing better in school but has little interest in athletics.

Questions of how to balance the needs of, and obligations to, all the members of the family do not have simple answers. However, psychologists often can serve their patients best by avoiding dichotomizing goals and by facilitating better communication among family members and helping them to reach mutually acceptable solutions. Robbins et al. (2006) found that the alliance between parents and psychologists and the alliance between adolescents and psychologists predicted dropout rate; that is, psychologists may encounter treatment failure unless they are able to build alliances with both adolescents and parents. One of the goals of therapy may be to get parents and adolescents to understand the effect of their behavior on each other. Psychologists should neither blindly acquiesce to, nor dismiss, the concerns of parents or adolescents. Principle-based ethics does not always mean immediately trumping principles as much as it means balancing them.

There is a lot to be said for listening carefully to patients' concerns. For example, when asked about how they felt about their encounters with psychiatrists, children responded that they appreciated when the psychiatrists listened, asked questions, and actively exchanged ideas with them (Hartzell, Seikkula, & von Knorring, 2009). More detailed interviewing may result in the development of mutually compatible goals. That is, although parents and children initially may disagree on what the presenting problem is, it may be possible to develop common areas of agreement. For example, children initially may agree that the goal of "getting my parents off my back" is something they would be willing to work on, and that may lead to actions on their part that may indirectly address some legitimate concerns of the parents.

This perspective is consistent with the idea of *ethical gradualism* or *ethical incrementing* proposed by Francis (2009). According to this perspective, a psychologist does not always have to take an uncompromising moral stance on every ethical issue that arises. Although there can be no compromise on some basic issues, at times, psychologists can balance overarching ethical principles gradually or incrementally, according to the patient's needs.

Boundaries of Competence

Similar balancing occurs with other standards. For example, psychologists may provide services to patients in emergencies, even if they lack the expertise that would ordinarily be needed to help those patients (Standard 2.02). In an emergency, psychologists may be unable to help patients (fulfilling the overarching principle of beneficence) without risking harm (offending the overarching principle of nonmaleficence), but the APA Ethics Code allows psychologists the option of having beneficence temporarily trump nonmaleficence. However, psychologists should try to minimize harm to the offended principle by referring patients to appropriate services as soon as practically possible. In Chapter 3, we discuss in more detail the importance of anticipating problems.

In emergencies and other similar situations, psychologists have little time to think through a detailed response as would occur with System 2 thinking. Ideally, however, psychologists would have considered these types of dilemmas ahead of time and could be more prepared to respond appropriately and quickly, as needed.

Ethical Dilemmas Outside of the Enforceable Standards

Sometimes psychologists encounter situations for which the APA Ethics Code provides no direction. For example, the 1992 APA Ethics Code did not anticipate the widespread use of electronic media and was silent on how psychologists should respond to those new technologies. Until APA released its guidelines on telecommunications (APA, 2013), psychologists had to rely primarily on peer-reviewed articles and their own discretion regarding how or when to apply these technologies.

Another example deals with hate-filled speech.[1] Psychologists typically encourage patients to express opinions freely, thereby promoting the overarching ethical principle of respecting patient autonomy. However, some patients may express opinions that disparage members of ethnic or sexual minorities, or other marginalized groups. It could be argued that psychologists should challenge hateful speech on the basis of general beneficence, because such speech creates an atmosphere that permits, encourages, or condones victimization of certain groups. Also, the quality of life in society, in general, diminishes when any one group becomes marginalized or a victim of unfair discrimination. This is an example in which the relevant overarching

---

[1] Portions of this section are adapted from "How Should Psychologists Respond to Hate-Filled Comments?" by S. Knapp, 2011, Pennsylvania Psychologist, October 2011, p. 7. Copyright 2011 by the Pennsylvania Psychological Association. Adapted with permission.

ethical principles could overlap because an argument also could be made that the hate-filled language offended the ethical principle of justice to the extent that psychologists have an obligation to ensure that people are treated fairly. Although psychologists may not be engaging in the unjust act themselves, they could be seen as complicit by accepting an environment that condones injustices and harm to marginalized people. We discuss this issue in more detail in Chapter 9.

Conflicts Between Overarching Ethical Principles and Organizational Policies or Laws[2]

If the APA Ethics Code conflicts with an organizational policy, then psychologists are required to "make known their commitment to the Ethics Code, and take reasonable steps to resolve the conflict consistent with the General Principles and Ethical Standards of the Ethics Code" (Standard 1.03). However, the Code does not permit obedience to an organization policy that involves violations of basic human rights.[3] The APA Ethics Code—appropriately, we believe—adopts a middle position. On one hand, it does not permit psychologists to follow unethical practices of an organization blindly and without protest. On the other hand, the Code does not require psychologists to resign their positions; rather, it requires them to make a reasonable effort to address the problem. As a practical matter, it is too difficult for any ethics code to prescribe appropriate and detailed actions when what constitutes a "reasonable" action usually depends on circumstances and available options. Consider this example:

An Indignant Psychologist

A psychologist at a public facility was told that he had to start treating older adults, even though he had little training or experience with this population. The psychologist immediately went into his supervisor's office with a copy of the APA Ethics Code and highlighted the various standards that he thought he would violate if he were to follow the supervisor's instructions. He pounded his fist on the desk, described all of the violated standards, and uttered the refrain "You are unethical" with every standard he pointed to.

Although the APA Ethics Code does not tell psychologists exactly how to address organizational conflicts, we know that conflicts, in general, are best addressed if both parties make an effort to understand the perspectives and concerns of the other and to try to find common ground. In this case, the

---

[2] Portions of this section are adapted from "When Laws and Ethics Collide: What Should Psychologists Do?" by S. Knapp, M. Gottlieb, J. Berman, and M. M. Handelsman, 2007, Professional Psychology: Research and Practice, 38, pp. 54–59. Copyright 2007 by the American Psychological Association.
[3] This issue received prominence after reports emerged and stated that psychologists participated in the torture of detainees at Guantanamo Bay. These psychologists were acting as consultants to interrogators and not as psychotherapists, so their actions were not directly related to the focus of this book. Nonetheless, we believe that this important human rights issue requires at least some acknowledgment.

agency had just lost a funding stream dedicated to pay for its geropsychologist, and the agency was uncertain when it could restore the position. The supervisor offered the reassigned psychologist additional training and supervision in geropsychology. Also, if the psychologist had read the APA Ethics Code more carefully, he would have noted that the Code does make exceptions to competence in unusual situations (e.g., Standard 2.01e). Although it may be possible to find some situations in which it may be necessary to go into supervisors' offices and accuse them of being unethical, this should be the last resort after exhausting other options.

At other times, a law (statute, regulation, or court order) may conflict with one of the standards of the APA Ethics Code. Standard 1.02 states that when the relevant standards of the Code create obligations greater than the obligations found in the law, psychologists must follow the Code. If the ethics standard conflicts with a particular law, then psychologists need to make an effort to address the problem.

When psychologists encounter situations involving conflicts with laws or organizational policies, it is possible to use the decision-making model by treating the law or the standards of the organization in a manner similar to describing conflicts between overarching ethical principles. That is, psychologists review options and determine if an overarching ethical principle should trump the offending law. Consider this example:

Is This a Case of Child Abuse?

A seriously depressed adolescent patient confided to a psychologist that she thought, but was not certain, that her grandfather had sexually abused her. The psychologist lived in a state that mandated the report of sexual abuse of a child under the age of 18. However, the patient stated that she would kill herself if the psychologist reported this abuse to the local child protective services agency. The psychologist had had contact with the agency in the past and lacked confidence in its ability to handle the situation with adequate sensitivity to the adolescent's emotional needs. Neither the patient nor her parents had heard from her grandfather for many years (it is likely that he had died), and there was no foreseeable likelihood that she would have any future contact with him.

The child presented information that, on further inquiry, may cause a reasonable psychologist to suspect abuse. If the psychologist did, she would be required to report it. However, the psychologist feared that reporting the abuse would precipitate the suicide that she was trying to prevent. Although the APA Ethics Code assures psychologists that they will not be found in violation for following the law, this conscientious psychologist wanted to choose the best way to act consistent with the ethical principles that are most salient in this vignette: beneficences, or helping the patient stay alive and live well; and nonmaleficence, or avoiding harming her.

The initial reaction of many psychologists may be to engage in dichotomous thinking and to consider either reporting or not reporting, weigh the benefits and risks of each, and decide which one to follow. Nonetheless, as in other situations, psychologists can ask themselves whether the information is sufficient to have reason to suspect abuse. Are the statements of the child credible (are there any secondary gains or manipulation)? How realistic is the threat of suicide? Is there a predator who is putting other children at risk?

However, after addressing the questions above, the psychologist may determine that the conflict continues between beneficence (providing optimal care) and obeying the law (reporting). Once again, the decision-making process provides one way to balance the demands of a particular situation. Beauchamp and Childress (2009) would allow one moral value to trump another, as long as the infringement is the least possible and is consistent with achieving the primary goal, and efforts are made to minimize the negative effect of the infringement. The same process may be used when considering how to respond to a problematic law.

When Obeying the Law Trumps Beneficence

If the psychologist in the preceding example decides to obey the law and report the suspicion of abuse, she may limit the harm to the offended ethical principle by attempting to include the patient in the process as much as possible. She may inform the patient of the legal obligation and give her input into how the report will be handled. The psychologist could enlist the support of family, school, or friends to take other actions to reduce the risk of a suicide attempt.

When Beneficence Trumps Obeying the Law

Most proponents of civil disobedience would agree with John Woolman (Moulton, 1971), Mohandas Gandhi (Fischer, 1983), or Martin Luther King, Jr. (1967) that individuals should obey the law, except under limited circumstances. Moral agents should disobey a law only if it is necessary to uphold an important moral principle—and never solely for personal gain.

When psychologists encounter an apparent conflict between laws and the standards of the APA Ethics Code, they should consider alternatives that would allow them to follow the law while still upholding their values. If they decide to disobey the law, we recommend that they limit their disobedience as much as possible. For example, psychologists should only disobey that portion of the law that violates an ethical standard. In the preceding case, if clinically and ethically indicated, the psychologist may continue treatment with the possibly abused girl until her mental state has improved, and then involve her in the decision to make a report, even though the failure to report the abuse within a reasonable period violates the child abuse reporting law. The psychologist should document the reasons why she chose the action she did. If there were a disciplinary hearing, the documentation of the circumstances may lead the disciplinary body to mitigate the punishment.

We know of a few situations in which psychologists have deliberately violated a law for conscientious reasons. Consider this example:

Conscientious Civil Disobedience

A psychologist was treating a teenager who had confessed to the police that he was driving while drunk when, in fact, he was not the driver. He and his older friend were stopped by the police and the older friend, who was driving while drunk, told the teenager quickly to change seats. The police then arrested the teenager for drunk driving. The older man had two previous DUIs and would have been sent to jail for a third one. The court appearance for the teenager was approaching soon. The treating psychologist had encouraged the teenager to come forth and tell the truth—noting, among other things, that his older friend probably had a serious drinking problem and was on a tragic trajectory of a life of alcoholism unless he could take responsibility for his actions and be forced into treatment. Although the teenager agreed that he needed to tell the truth, he never followed through. Then, in violation of state law that gives teenagers the right to control confidentiality, the psychologist brought the young man's mother into the treatment room with the young man present and told her what really happened. In this case, the young man appeared relieved and later thanked the psychologist.

Of course, there is no guarantee that all actions in defiance of the law would have the same positive consequences. Under different circumstances or with different patients, the psychologist might have faced a licensing board complaint or a malpractice suit. But, in this case, he determined that his values required him to take this risk.

SUMMARY

At times, psychologists will encounter situations in which they cannot fulfill one obligation without violating another. The five-step model presented in this chapter describes how psychologists can balance these obligations by selecting one moral principle to trump another, while attempting to minimize harm to the offended moral principle. Future chapters will illustrate the application of this model.

REFERENCES

American Psychological Association. (2010). *Ethical principles of psychologists and code of conduct* (2002, Amended June 1, 2010). Retrieved from http://www.apa.org/ethics/code/index.aspx

American Psychological Association. (2013). *Guidelines for the practice of telepsychology.* Retrieved from https://www.apa.org/practice/guidelines/telepsychology.aspx

Aristotle. (1985). *Nichomachean ethics* (T. Irwin, Trans.). Indianapolis, IN: Hacket. (Original work published circa 330 BCE)

Beauchamp, T. L., & Childress, J. F. (2009). *Principles of biomedical ethics* (6th ed.). New York, NY: Oxford University Press.

Bernard, J. L., & Jara, C. S. (1986). The failure of clinical psychology graduate students to apply understood ethical principles. *Professional Psychology: Research and Practice, 17,* 313–315. http://dx.doi.org/10.1037/0735-7028.17.4.313

Bernard, J. L., Murphy, M., & Little, M. (1987). The failure of clinical psychologists to apply understood ethical principles. *Professional Psychology: Research and Practice, 18,* 489–491. http://dx.doi.org/10.1037/0735-7028.18.5.489

Betan, E. J., & Stanton, A. L. (1999). Fostering ethical willingness: Integrating emotional and contextual awareness with rational analysis. *Professional Psychology: Research and Practice, 30,* 295–301. http://dx.doi.org/10.1037/0735-7028.30.3.295

Bransford, J. D., & Stein, B. S. (1993). *The ideal problem solver: A guide to improving thinking, learning, and creativity.* New York, NY: Freeman.

Elm, D. R., & Radin, T. J. (2012). Ethical decision making: Special or no different? *Journal of Business Ethics, 107*, 313–329. http://dx.doi.org/10.1007/s10551-011-1041-4

Fischer, L. (1983). *The life of Mahatma Gandhi.* New York, NY: Harper & Row.

Francis, R. D. (2009). *Ethics for psychologists* (2nd ed.). Chichester, England: British Psychological Society/Blackwell. http://dx.doi.org/10.1002/9781444306514

Gino, F. (2013). *Sidetracked: Why our decisions get derailed and how we can stick to the plan.* Boston, MA: Harvard Business Review Press.

Gottlieb, M. C., Handelsman, M. M., & Knapp, S. (2013). A model for integrated ethics consultation. *Professional Psychology: Research and Practice, 44*, 307–313. http://dx.doi.org/10.1037/a0033541

Groopman, J. (2007). *How doctors think.* Boston, MA: Houghton Mifflin.

Hadjistavropoulos, T., & Malloy, D. C. (1999). Ethical principles of the American Psychological Association: An argument for philosophical and practical ranking. *Ethics & Behavior, 9*, 127–140. http://dx.doi.org/10.1207/s15327019eb0902_4

Härtel, C. E. J., & Härtel, G. F. (1997). SHAPE-assisted intuitive decision making and problem solving: Information-processing-based training for conditions of cognitive busyness. *Group Dynamics: Theory, Research, and Practice, 1*, 187–199. http://dx.doi.org/10.1037/1089-2699.1.3.187

Hartzell, M., Seikkula, J., & von Knorring, A.-L. (2009). What children feel about their first encounter with child and adolescent psychiatry. *Contemporary Family Therapy: An International Journal, 31*, 177–192. http://dx.doi.org/10.1007/s10591-009-9090-x

Hawley, K. M., & Weisz, J. R. (2003). Child, parent, and therapist (dis)agreement on target problems in outpatient therapy: The therapist's dilemma and its implications. *Journal of Consulting and Clinical Psychology, 71*, 62–70. http://dx.doi.org/10.1037/0022-006X.71.1.62

Johnson, S. (2010). *Where good ideas come from: The natural history of innovation.* New York, NY: Penguin.

Johnson, W. B., Barnett, J. E., Elman, N. S., Forrest, L., & Kaslow, N. J. (2013). The competence constellation model: A communitarian approach to support professional competence. *Professional Psychology: Research and Practice, 44*, 343–354. http://dx.doi.org/10.1037/a0033131

Kahneman, D., & Klein, G. (2009). Conditions for intuitive expertise: A failure to disagree. *American Psychologist, 64*, 515–526. http://dx.doi.org/10.1037/a0016755

Kahneman, D. (2011). *Thinking fast and slow.* New York, NY: Farrar, Straus and Giroux.

King, M. L., Jr. (1967). *Where do we go from here: Chaos or community?* New York, NY: Harper & Row.

Knapp, S. J., & VandeCreek, L. D. (2012). *Practical ethics for psychologists: A positive approach* (2nd ed.). Washington, DC: American Psychological Association.

McGillicuddy, N. B., Rychtarik, R. G., Morsheimer, E. T., & Burke-Storer, M. R. (2007). Agreement between parent and adolescent reports of substance use. *Journal of Child & Adolescent Substance Abuse, 16*, 59–78. http://dx.doi.org/10.1300/J029v16n04_04

Moulton, P. P. (Ed.). (1971). *The journal and major essays of John Woolman.* New York, NY: Oxford University Press.

Oetzel, K. B., & Scherer, D. G. (2003). Therapeutic engagement with adolescents in psychotherapy. *Psychotherapy: Theory, Research, Practice, Training, 40*, 215–225. http://dx.doi.org/10.1037/0033-3204.40.3.215

Robbins, M. S., Liddle, H. A., Turner, C. W., Dakof, G. A., Alexander, J. F., & Kogan, S. M. (2006). Adolescent and parent therapeutic alliances as predictors of dropout in multidimensional family therapy. *Journal of Family Psychology, 20,* 108–116. http://dx.doi.org/10.1037/0893-3200.20.1.108

Rogerson, M. D., Gottlieb, M. C., Handelsman, M. M., Knapp, S., & Younggren, J. (2011). Nonrational processes in ethical decision making. *American Psychologist, 66,* 614–623. http://dx.doi.org/10.1037/a0025215

Ross, W. D. (1998). What makes right acts right? In J. Rachels (Ed.), *Ethical theory* (pp. 265–285). New York, NY: Oxford University Press. (Original work published 1930)

Smith, T. S., McGuire, J. M., Abbott, D. W., & Blau, B. I. (1991). Clinical ethical decision making: An investigation of the rationales used to justify doing less than one believes one should. *Professional Psychology: Research and Practice, 22,* 235–239. http://dx.doi.org/10.1037/0735-7028.22.3.235

Sternberg, R. J., Grigorenko, E. L., & Kalmar, D. A. (2001). The role of theory in unified psychology. *Journal of Theoretical and Philosophical Psychology, 21,* 99–117. http://dx.doi.org/10.1037/h0091200

Weinstein, B. (2000). *What should I do? 4 simple steps to making better decisions in everyday life.* New York, NY: Perigee.

Williams, J., Hadjistavropoulos, T., Fuchs-Lacelle, S., Malloy, D. C., Gagnon, M., & Sharpe, D. (2012). A mixed methods investigation of the effects of ranking ethical principles on decision making: Implications for the Canadian Code of Ethics for psychologists. *Canadian Psychology, 53,* 204–216. http://dx.doi.org/10.1037/a0027624

2.6. When Laws and Ethics Collide: What Should Psychologists Do?

Samuel Knapp, Michael Gottlieb, Jason Berman, and Mitchell M. Handelsman

Laws governing psychologists come from a variety of sources such as court decisions, federal and state statutes (including psychology licensing laws and regulations), and the enforceable standards of the American Psychological Association's "Ethical Principles of Psychologists and Code of Conduct" (American Psychological Association, 2002; hereinafter referred to as the Ethics Code) if they are adopted by state psychology licensing boards. For the most part, the laws regulating the practice of psychology are consistent with generally recognized ethical values. For example, almost every ethical psychologist would agree that, among other things, psychologists should (a) not have sex with patients, (b) keep information about patients confidential (except in a few unusual circumstances), (c) be competent when delivering services, and (d) refrain from insurance fraud. When Knapp and VandeCreek (2004) examined the Ethics Code from the standpoint of principle-based ethics, they found that almost all of its enforceable standards could be justified from the perspective of overarching ethical principles.

The consistency between ethical and legal requirements generally allows practitioners to adhere to both without disruption of their daily functioning. Nevertheless, circumstances may arise in which a law (broadly defined to include state and federal laws and regulations, binding case law, administrative rules, or court orders) may require psychologists to do something that could harm patients, limit patient autonomy, and/or otherwise offend the personal and professional ethical values of most psychologists (Knapp & VandeCreek, 2006). When such conflicts arise, psychologists need to engage in an ethical decision-making process to evaluate the alternatives available to them and determine the best possible (or least harmful) course of action.

If a conflict arises between a specific law and an enforceable standard of the Ethics Code, Standard 1.02 provides the following guidance:

> If psychologists' ethical responsibilities conflict with law, regulations, or other governing legal authority, psychologists make known their commitment to the Ethics Code and take steps to resolve the conflict. If the conflict is unresolvable via such means, psychologists may adhere to the requirements of the law, regulations, or other governing legal authority.

Nevertheless, Pope and Bajt (1988) surveyed senior-level psychologists, including those knowledgeable about ethics, and found that 57% of the respondents acknowledged intentionally breaking a law or a formal ethical standard at least once "in light of client welfare or another deeper value" (p. 828). Of the 34 instances reported, 7 involved the refusal to report child abuse, 7 entailed illegally divulging confidential information, 3 involved having sex with a patient, 2 concerned unspecified dual relationships, 2 involved refusing to fulfill a legal mandate to warn about a dangerous patient, and the remainder fell into no clear category. When these situations arise, they may cause *moral distress* or "a situation where one is constrained from acting on a moral choice" (Austin, Rankel, Kagan, Bergum, & Lemermeyer, 2005, p. 199). These findings demonstrate that the guidance provided in Standard 1.02 is not sufficient in many cases and that ethical decision making is seldom as simple as we would like it to be.[1]

Furthermore, when some legal requirements arise, the Ethics Code may be silent or ambiguous regarding how psychologists should proceed. In these cases, psychologists turn to a variety of additional resources for assistance in their decision making. One resource that is seldom mentioned is that of one's personal values. As Handelsman, Knapp, and Gottlieb (2002) have noted, psychologists can think of ethics not only in terms of the ethical "floor," or the enforceable minimal standards of the profession, but also in terms of how they can practice to the best of their ability and in a manner consistent with their own ethical values and highest ethical aspirations.

The purpose of this article is to show how psychologists' personal values can be of assistance in addressing some of these vexing situations. In this article, we offer a decision-making process for psychologists facing conflicts between the law and their personal ethical values.

A DECISION-MAKING PROCESS

Consider the following clinical situation:

> *Example 1.* A psychologist in solo practice who was compliant with the Health Insurance Portability and Accountability Act of 1996 (HIPAA) terminated a patient for nonadherence with treatment. Shortly after treatment terminated, the patient made harassing and threatening phone calls to the psychologist. The psychologist refused to respond to these phone calls, believing that doing so would harm the patient by reinforcing her preoccupation with him. Later, citing HIPAA requirements, the patient demanded a face-to-face meeting with the privacy officer (who was the psychologist himself).

In this situation, the law appears to demand so much respect for the patient's autonomy that it might violate the ethical principle of nonmaleficence (seeking to avoid harming patients) and the virtues of compassion and prudence. The psychologist feared that meeting with the patient, regardless of the reason,

---

[1]It is worth noting that the current article was published in 2007, prior to the 2010 Amendments to the Ethics Code that updated Standard 1.02.

would only enhance her preoccupation with him and make it more difficult for her to accept a referral to another practitioner.

The APA Ethics Code states, "If this Ethics Code establishes a higher standard of conduct than is required by law, psychologists must meet the higher ethical standard" (p. 1062). In addition, Standard 1.02 instructs us to "adhere to the requirements of the law, regulations, or other governing legal authority." Thus, psychologists who follow the law will not be subject to disciplinary action by the APA Ethics Committee as long as they have taken steps to resolve the law–ethics conflict responsibly. Although this guidance is somewhat helpful, it does not absolve psychologists of the need to choose whether to violate their ethical values and follow the law or to violate the law to uphold their values.

Using this example as well as others below, we offer a decision-making process for psychologists who may find themselves in a conflict between the law and their personal system of values (see summary in Table 1). First, psychologists should ensure that they understand what the law requires of them. Sometimes psychologists misunderstand or misconstrue their legal requirements and assume a conflict between the law and ethical values when, in fact, no such conflict exists. Second, psychologists should ascertain if they understand their ethical obligations correctly. Third, if a genuine conflict is found to exist, psychologists can seek creative ways to satisfy both their legal and ethical obligations. Fourth, if the conflict between the law and ethics is real and cannot be avoided, psychologists should either obey the law in a manner that minimizes harm to their ethical values or adhere to their ethical

TABLE 1. Considerations to Address

Question	Action to reflect upon
1. What does the law require?	1. Consultation or research may be needed.
2. What are your ethical obligations? Will the standards of the APA Ethics Code inform you of your obligations? If not, how can you use your personal values to frame your response?	2. You may need to explore your underlying values (e.g., gain clarity about the overarching virtues that you want to characterize your professional and personal life). This is often best done in the context of a supportive, yet honest consulting relationship.
3. How can you reconcile the demands of the law and your ethical concerns?	3. Search for ways to meet both your legal and ethical obligations.
4. Should you follow the law or your ethical values? How do you balance your legal obligations with the consequences to the patient or other interested parties?	4. If the law is followed, seek ways to minimize infringement of the ethical values; if ethical values are followed, seek ways to minimize the infringement of the spirit or letter of the law.
5. Can you anticipate conflicts and take preventive measures?	5. Anticipate and appreciate the ethical nuances and complications of your work (e.g., use practical wisdom). Emphasizing informed consent often helps circumvent or reduce law–ethics conflicts.

values in a manner that minimizes the violation of the law. In either situation, psychologists should anticipate and be prepared to live with the consequences of their decisions. Finally, psychologists can avoid or mitigate many of these ethical conflicts by anticipating potential conflicts between laws and ethics and taking proactive measures. Examples of proactive or preventive measures are described below.

What Does the Law Require?

In Example 1, the psychologist determined that it was clinically contraindicated to intermittently reinforce the patient by allowing her to meet with him under the pretense that she was meeting with the privacy officer. Doing so might violate the ethical principle of nonmaleficence, as well as Standard 3.04 (Avoiding Harm) and Standard 1.02 (Conflicts Between Ethics and Law, Regulations, or Other Governing Legal Authority). Thus, the psychologist was left with an apparent conflict between ethics and the law. However, Example 1 does not represent an actual conflict between ethics and the law. The HIPAA Privacy Rule does not require privacy officers to meet face-to-face with complainants, although the privacy officer has to review the complaint (45 C.F.R. 164.524; U.S. Department of Health and Human Services, 2002). The psychologist does have to communicate to the patient, but it does not have to be a face-to-face meeting.

Also, consider the following:

> *Example 2.* A patient states that he feels strong urges to harm a third party with whom he had a fight the week before over a former girlfriend. The treating psychologist, who works in a state that has a duty-to-protect law, believes that notifying the threatened third party would precipitate the very violence that the psychologist wants to prevent.

Here is another case in which the relevant standard of the Ethics Code (Standard 4.05b) does not provide clear direction in that it permits disclosures if mandated by law but fails to provide guidance for an extenuating ethical circumstance such as that seen in Example 2. Thus, a response to this situation requires a thorough knowledge of the relevant state law and illustrates the need for legal consultation. Standards regarding the duty to warn or protect vary from state to state. In some states, psychologists must warn whenever a patient presents an imminent danger to identifiable third parties. In other states, psychologists have more flexibility and may take protective actions to prevent harm to third parties that may include actions other than warning the intended third party.

The issuance of a verbal threat by a patient may or may not, depending on the totality of the circumstances, context, and clinical features, indicate imminent danger. Psychologists who are aware of the clinical literature on assessing risk of violence are better able to determine whether the threshold for immediate harm has been reached. Even if the threshold is reached, competent psychologists can often use clinical interventions other than warning

intended victims (hospitalizations, partial hospitalization, referral for medication, increased frequency of outpatient sessions, family therapy, between-
session phone contacts, etc.) to diffuse the immediate danger. From the
information given in Example 2, it is not clear if the psychologist has a legal
duty to warn. Consequently, the treatment might proceed on the basis of
clinical considerations and appropriate safeguards without a clinically and
ethically questionable warning.

Discerning Ethical and Clinical Obligations

Sometimes self-interest, prejudice, ignorance, personal distress, or other factors can cause psychologists to misconstrue the application of their ethical values or simply to act unethically. In the study by Pope and Bajt (1988), for
example, is a description of three psychologists who believed that the prohibition against having sex with their patients conflicted with their ethical obligations. It is unlikely that an objective third party would have reached such a
conclusion, given that sexual relationships typically harm patients and degrade
the profession. In other less obvious and more common situations, it is possible that other psychologists can have their perception of their ethical obligations clouded by a number of extraneous factors. Such situations require
"moral perceptions" (Fowers, 2005, p. 117), or the ability to separate the critical ethical issue in a situation from extraneous factors such as personal satisfaction or anxiety reduction. Consequently, whenever psychologists believe
that a law requires them to violate an ethical value, they are wise to seek consultation as to whether they are, in fact, construing the clinical situation, the
law, and their ethical values accurately.

In other situations in which psychologists act unethically, they might be
motivated by overidentification with the patient's suffering, a failure to appreciate the total ethical impact of their decisions, or unwise compassion (when
their desire to be helpful becomes a personal need that leads them to clinically
contraindicated interventions). For example, a psychologist motivated by a
desire to assist a member of a historically disenfranchised group might, in an
effort to be helpful, act in a disempowering and paternalistic manner (Gottlieb
& Tjeltveit, 2006). Or psychologists could become too emotionally involved
with patients and fail to maintain appropriate therapeutic distance and perspective, thus compromising their therapeutic effectiveness.

Taking Steps to Avoid Conflicts

At times there may only appear to be a conflict between the demands of the
law and the enforceable standards of the APA Ethics Code or the personal
values of a psychologist. Consider this example:

> *Example 3.* A psychologist was treating a man who, among other problems, was
> accused of assaulting his wife. In one session that the wife attended as a collat-
> eral contact, the husband acknowledged that he had struck her. Months later
> the psychologist received a court order stating that she was to appear in court to

testify that the husband admitted to striking his wife. The husband did not want the psychologist to testify.

This example deals with privileged communications laws that can be complex and vary from jurisdiction to jurisdiction. It is not our intent to review the complexities of these laws but only to illustrate where the law, in the form of a court order, appears to require the psychologist to do something contrary to her promise of confidentiality and good public policy. That is, testifying would limit the willingness of this patient to be honest in his communications with future psychotherapists, and other patients or prospective patients who learn of this breach of confidentiality may be reluctant to seek treatment or if they did seek treatment, might not be forthcoming about their concerns. Although the psychologist appreciated the wife's desire to seek a judicial remedy, she was concerned that confidentiality was being threatened. In this case the psychologist went to court and followed the course of action required in Standard 1.02 (attempting to resolve conflicts between the law and the Ethics Code). After she respectfully explained her dilemma, the judge excused her from testifying.

When the Conflict Between Law and Ethics Cannot Be Avoided

As with many situations, the response of the psychologist in Example 4 below cannot be determined by relying only on the Ethics Code, which permits disclosure without patient consent if mandated by state law (Standard 4.05b). The psychologist was forced to consult with other sources of moral and ethical guidance (beyond the Ethics Code) if she wanted to act in an ethically praiseworthy manner toward her client and with future psychotherapy patients in mind.

> *Example 4.* A seriously depressed adolescent patient confided to a psychologist that she thought, but was not certain, that her father had sexually abused her. The psychologist lived in a state that mandated the report of all sexual abuse by a parent against any child under the age of 18. However, the patient stated that she would kill herself if the psychologist reported this to the local child protective services agency. The psychologist had contact with the agency in the past and lacked confidence in its ability to handle the situation with adequate sensitivity to the emotional needs of the child. The patient had not seen her father for many years, and there was no foreseeable likelihood that she would have any future contact with him.

In Example 4, the child presented information that may, upon further inquiry, cause a reasonable psychologist to suspect abuse. If the psychologist did suspect abuse, according to the laws in many states, she would be required to report it. However, the psychologist believed that reporting the abuse would precipitate the suicide that she was trying to prevent. Although the Ethics Code assures the psychologist that she would not be found in violation of the Ethics Code for following the law, this conscientious psychologist wanted to choose the best way to act, consistent with her overall virtuous aims of helping the client stay alive and live well.

The initial reaction of many psychologists may be to engage in dichotomous thinking and to consider either one option (reporting) or another (not reporting), weigh the benefits and risks of each, and decide which one to follow. Nonetheless, it may be prudent to consider a series of sequential steps before deciding how to respond. The first step is for psychologists to consult with knowledgeable colleagues who can provide them with useful information, encourage them to think through the issues (e.g., including ways the psychologists can advance virtuous aims), and challenge their clinical, legal, and ethical assumptions, if necessary. As noted above, sometimes conflicts are more apparent than real and psychologists may have more flexibility in responding than they originally thought, or they may have misinterpreted the ethical issues or legal requirements involved.

In Example 4, the psychologist needed to assess carefully whether the information she was given was sufficient for a reasonable psychologist to suspect abuse or whether more information was needed. Sometimes in cases of abuse it can be difficult to determine whether the requisite threshold of certainty has been reached. The legal standard for reporting in her state ("reason to suspect") is a vague and poorly defined state of mind that exists somewhere between a passing thought and certainty (Levi & Loeben, 2004). Also, creative clinical solutions can often allow psychologists to meet both their legal and ethical obligations. For example, the psychologist first needed to ensure that the threat was not a manipulation motivated by a secondary gain. Assuming the threat was genuine, the psychologist might bring the mother or another trusted relative into the therapy to obtain more information. Additional clinical information from other sources may clarify the extent of the danger of self-harm, make more clear the likelihood that the abuse occurred, or suggest additional options for dealing constructively with the apparent conflict.

If no viable clinical solution emerges, psychologists must determine how to resolve the conflict between providing optimal care and the duty to report on the basis of their individual value systems. The decision-making process of principle-based ethics provides one way to balance the demands of a particular situation. Beauchamp and Childress (2001) would allow the trumping of one moral value over another after a thorough assessment of the dilemma. But doing so requires that the infringement is the least possible, that it is consistent with achieving the primary goal, and that efforts are made to minimize the negative impact of the infringement. The same process might be used when one is considering disobeying a law. The disobedience should be the least possible, consistent with the primary goal, and done with efforts made to limit the negative effects of the infringement. That is, the disobedience to the law should be restricted only to that portion that violates the ethical standards of the psychologist.

The perspective of virtue ethics provides another way for psychologists to address this conundrum. Psychologists relying on virtue ethics would identify the virtues most relevant to this situation (e.g., kindness, fairness, responsibility, trustworthiness, honesty), deliberate or know what actions would be most likely to reach the desired goal (e.g., help the patient live, heal, and eventually flourish), and respond in a manner that a virtuous or morally out-standing person would, given this situation (e.g., rely on collateral sources of information and consult with ethically outstanding colleagues).

If the Decision Is Made not to Obey the Law

Civil disobedience has a long history, dating from Sophocles (440 BCE/2006), in whose play, *Antigone*, the heroine (Antigone) defies the orders of the tyrant Creon and openly performs a burial ceremony for her brother, Polyneices, even though it means her death. Proponents of civil disobedience may disagree on particulars, but most would agree with Woolman (1772/1971), Gandhi (Fisher, 1983), King (1958), and others that individuals should obey the laws except only under very limited circumstances to comply with a higher value and be willing to accept whatever punishments may occur.

When psychologists are considering disobeying a law, we recommend that they follow the sequential steps enumerated above: (a) Seek consultation to ensure that the law requires them to do what they believe it requires, (b) make certain that they understand their ethical obligations clearly, (c) consider alternatives that would allow them to follow the law while still upholding their values, and (d) contemplate violating a law only if no viable alternative is available. If a decision is made to disobey the law, the psychologist must ask, "If I disobey the law, how can I limit my disobedience to the minimum necessary to fulfill my higher goal?" Or, "How should I act to support or advance the most relevant virtue?" For example, if clinically and ethically indicated, the psychologist may continue treatment with the possibly abused girl until her mental state improves and then involve her in the decision to make a report. Psychologists should document the reasons why they chose the action they did. If there is a disciplinary hearing, the documentation of the circumstances may lead the disciplinary body to mitigate the punishment.

If the Decision Is Made to Obey the Law

If the decision is made to obey the law, the psychologist needs to ask, "How can I minimize the harm to the offended ethical values?" For example, the psychologist can act to minimize the negative impact of the decision by including the patient in the process as much as possible. The psychologist might inform the patient of the legal obligation and give her the opportunity to have input into the manner in which the disclosure is made. Or the psychologist could ask the child protective services agency to interview the girl in her office with the mother present, if that is what the girl prefers.

Anticipate Conflicts

> *Example 5.* A mother of a patient wants a copy of her child's test results. The background information from social service agencies is accurate and relevant to the needs of the child but might create great distress for the mother if she sees it. The psychologist is a covered entity under HIPAA and, accordingly, her patients (or their legal representatives) are permitted copies of their psychological test reports except in limited circumstances that do not apply here.

Psychologists can avoid many disputes between law and ethics by antici-pating potential conflicts. In Example 5 the psychologist feels torn between her duty to provide accurate information and avoid disclosing information that could cause pain or embarrassment to the parent. According to the HIPAA Privacy Rule, the results of psychological tests are not considered "psy-chotherapy notes" and therefore may be seen by the patient or the patient's legal representative except in narrow circumstances such as when there is domestic abuse and, in the opinion of the treating psychologist, it would be harmful to the child (45 CFR 164.524 [3]; U.S. Department of Health and Human Services, 2002).

Assuming that the limited exceptions enumerated in the HIPAA Privacy Rule do not apply, psychologists can minimize the likelihood of this conflict occurring by maximizing parental involvement in the assessment process as early as possible. Some psychologists, such as Brenner (2003) and Fischer (2004), conceive of psychological assessment as a cooperative or collabora-tive process that seeks to increase the patient's or parent's role in the assess-ment process, including developing the referral questions, selecting the tests, and writing the report. The psychologist could inform the agency of her policy of involving the parent in all aspects of the report, including viewing a near-final draft. Such a procedure could be described during the psychologist's informed-consent process.

In cooperative or collaborative assessments, concerns about the parent or family functioning can be brought up early in the assessment process. Although discussion of these frank concerns may be uncomfortable, it may be better for the parent to hear them early in the process rather than to read about them later in a report. In addition, the open discussion of these issues may be therapeutic for the patient or parent, and it may help the psychologist better understand the life circumstances and perspectives of the patient's family.

If this process had been followed in Example 5, the parent would have had input into the phrasing used in the history or background section of the report. Although there is no guarantee that the process would avoid anger-ing the parent, the likelihood of an extreme reaction would be reduced, and the parent would not have felt blindsided or betrayed by the content of the final report. Even when no good alternative can be found, it may be possible to mitigate the consequences of the law by anticipating the conflict. Gottlieb (1997) urged "each practitioner [to] investigate the ethical dilemmas that commonly occur in his or her practice area and create an individualized ethics policy to address them" (p. 266). This recommendation is especially helpful regarding those dilemmas that are not explicitly addressed by the Ethics Code. Virtuous psychologists who demonstrate practical wisdom will cultivate a habit of deliberating about the salient ethical issues that they are likely to encounter, anticipate them, and develop policies to proactively address them.

In Example 4, dealing with suspected child abuse, the virtuous psychologist might have been able to minimize the conflict by being especially explicit with the patient at the start of psychotherapy concerning her obligation to report suspected child abuse and explaining what that means. This process entails more than just having the patient or parent sign the HIPAA privacy notice or providing a cursory description of the exceptions to confidentiality. Rather, it would mean explaining the common exceptions to confidentiality, giving the patient (or parent) an opportunity to ask questions, and revisiting the issues throughout the course of treatment as needed. In this way, the patient would have known the consequences of such a disclosure and could have made a better decision about what information to reveal.

SUMMARY AND CONCLUSIONS

Fortunately, the laws governing the practice of psychology are, for the most part, based on readily justifiable ethical values. At times, however, psychologists may perceive a conflict between the law and their personal ethical values, especially in situations in which the standards of the Ethics Code do not provide explicit direction. Psychologists need to verify what the law requires and determine the nature of their ethical obligations. Often apparent conflicts between the law and ethics can be avoided if psychologists anticipate problems ahead of time or engage in integrative problem solving. At times, however, psychologists may need to choose between following the law and protecting the welfare of their patients or an ethical value. We suggest careful practical wisdom or deliberation when such decisions are made.

REFERENCES

American Psychological Association. (2002). Ethical principles of psychologists and code of conduct. *American Psychologist, 57*, 1060–1073.

Austin, W., Rankel, M., Kagan, L., Bergum, V., & Lemermeyer, G. (2005). To stay or to go, to speak or stay silent, to act or not to act: Moral distress as experienced by psychologists. *Ethics and Behavior, 15*, 197–212.

Beauchamp, T., & Childress, J. (2001). *Principles of biomedical ethics* (5th ed.). New York, NY: Oxford University Press.

Brenner, E. (2003). Consumer-focused psychological assessment. *Professional Psychology: Research and Practice, 34*, 240–247.

Fischer, C. (2004). Individualized assessment moderates the impact of HIPAA privacy rules. *Journal of Personality Assessment, 82*, 35–38.

Fisher, L. (1983). *The life of Mahatma Gandhi*. New York, NY: Harper & Row.

Fowers, B. (2005). *Virtue and psychology: Pursuing excellence in ordinary practices*. Washington, DC: American Psychological Association.

Gottlieb, M. (1997). *An ethics policy for family practice management*. In R. Magee & D. Marsh (Eds.), *Ethical and legal issues in professional practice with families* (pp. 257–270). New York, NY: Wiley.

Gottlieb, M., & Tjeltveit, A. (2006). *Overcoming ethical vulnerabilities and developing ethical resilience: The DOVE model*. Manuscript in preparation.

Handelsman, M. M., Knapp, S., & Gottlieb, M. C. (2002). Positive ethics. In C. R. Snyder & S. J. Lopez (Eds.), *Handbook of positive psychology* (pp. 731–744). New York, NY: Oxford University Press.

King, M. L. (1958). *Stride toward freedom*. San Francisco, CA: Harper & Row.

Knapp, S., & VandeCreek, L. (2004). A principle-based analysis of the 2002 American Psychological Association's Ethics Code. *Psychotherapy: Theory, Research, Practice, Training, 41*, 247–254.

Knapp, S., & VandeCreek, L. (2006). *Practical ethics for psychologists: A positive approach*. Washington, DC: American Psychological Association.

Levi, B., & Loeben, G. (2004). Index of suspicion: Feeling not believing. *Theoretical Medicine, 25*, 277–310.

Pope, K., & Bajt, T. R. (1988). When laws and values conflict: A dilemma for psychologists. *American Psychologist, 43*, 828–829.

Sophocles. (2006). *Antigone*. Retrieved January 18, 2006, from http://classics.mit.edu/Sophocles/antigone.html (Original work produced circa 440 BCE)

U.S. Department of Health and Human Services. (2002, August 14). Standards for privacy of individually identifiable health information: Final rule. *Federal Register, 67*, 53182–53277.

Woolman, J. (1971). *The journal and major essays of John Woolman* (P. Moulton, Ed.). New York, NY: Oxford University Press. (Original work published 1772)

COMMENTARY: As the reader has likely already surmised, this book strives to maintain a distinction between mental health law and psychological ethics—a distinction muddied in recent years from both practice-based and pedagogical perspectives, due to the persistent popularity of forensic psychology and the significant professional consequences of ethical lapses that may bear legal consequences.

Although distinct, ethics and law will always be practically intertwined, and the topic should not be dismissed simply to compel recognition of their separate identities and imperatives. The critical point to keep in mind is that legal consequences inform ethical conclusions but do not ultimately dictate them. The best laws are drafted in the service of predictability and are designed to anticipate all circumstances. The best ethical guidelines are promulgated in recognition of the fact that one simply cannot know in advance what situations may arise, and when. As proof, we need only to consider how often something has occurred in our own practices that neither we nor our colleagues have ever experienced in precisely the same way.

The following references are recommended for those interested in further investigation of the collision of legal and ethical considerations, reflecting the perspectives of both independent disciplines.

Barnett, J. E., & Scheetz, K. (2003). Technological advances and telehealth: Ethics, law, and the practice of psychotherapy. *Psychotherapy: Theory, Research, Practice, Training, 40*, 86–93. http://dx.doi.org/10.1037/0033-3204.40.1-2.86

Breiger, D., Bishop, K., & Benjamin, G. A. H. (2014). Law, ethics, and competence. In *Educational evaluations of children with special needs: Clinical and forensic considerations* (pp. 21–27). Washington, DC: American Psychological Association.

DeLeon, P. H., Robinson Kurpius, S. E., & Sexton, J. L. (2001). Prescriptive authority for psychologists: Law, ethics, and public policy. In M. T. Sammons & N. B. Schmidt (Eds.), *Combined treatment for mental disorders: A guide to psychological and pharmacological interventions* (pp. 33–52). Washington, DC: American Psychological Association.

Gelles, M. D., & Palarea, R. (2011). Ethics in crisis negotiation: A law enforcement and public safety perspective. In C. H. Kennedy & T. J. Williams (Eds.), *Ethical practice in operational psychology: Military and national intelligence applications* (pp. 107–123). Washington, DC: American Psychological Association.

Williamson, A. A., Raglin Bignall, W. J., Swift, L. E., Hung, A. H., Power, T. J., . . . Mautone, J. A. (2017). Ethical and legal issues in integrated care settings: Case examples from pediatric primary care. *Clinical Practice in Pediatric Psychology, 5,* 196–208. http://dx.doi.org/10.1037/cpp0000157

3

Learning Ethics

Charity begins at home, but professional ethics begin in the classroom. True, students must possess an innate sense of right and wrong and a certain philanthropic and altruistic bent to be suited in any way to assaying psychology as a profession, but it is just those colleagues who rely on untutored good intentions at the expense of true educationally instilled insight who are most likely to run afoul one day of ethics committees and licensing boards.

Opportunities lost at both undergraduate and graduate levels to inculcate not just ethical knowledge but ethical thinking will pay dark dividends over the course of what is likely to become a tragically foreshortened professional career. It is difficult, if not impossible, to overemphasize the necessity for every university-based program to construct a carefully planned, content-intensive, periodically manifested arc of classroom instruction and integrated clinical training in professional ethics.

The teaching of ethical thinking is optimally vignette driven. This is not to suggest that rote, code-based instruction does not have its place, but ethics really come to life for the student when he or she can visualize an active role in conducting psychotherapy, assessment, or scientific research. The highly variable nature of vignette-driven fact patterns and their resolutions drives home a secondary message: There is no way truly to predict just what sorts of ethical conflicts may arrive and what the best way of managing them may be for a particular client/patient, subject, or institution.

In addition to memorized watchwords and memorable examples, what all students need—and what the most highly motivated and ultimately successful

http://dx.doi.org/10.1037/0000125-004
Ethical Conflicts in Psychology, Fifth Edition, by E. Y. Drogin

students crave—is not just instruction but acculturation. Professional service rests on more than an intellectual exercise and an accumulation of technical skills. To become a psychologist is to learn to view the world *like* and ultimately *as* a psychologist—not in terms of politics or societal goals but in terms of the needs of psychology as a discipline and of every individual, group, and organization that our shared discipline is intended to serve.

It would be a mistake to focus solely on what innate student qualities and programming concerns lend to the process of learning ethics while neglecting to mention critical issues of faculty recruitment and assignment. Just as not every academic psychologist is equally suited to teaching statistics, test-based assessment, or psychotherapy, there are those faculty members whose efforts are better directed to other tasks than ethics instruction. This is not to suggest that some teachers are "ethically challenged," but rather to stress that those who have truly studied the topic and who have applied it themselves in clinical and research settings cannot be absent from the mix.

Among its other features, this chapter addresses defining and applying acculturation models, distinguishing between education and training, using *competency* as a metric for gauging the success of a program of ethics instruction, the notion of *virtue ethics*, and the perspectives of students themselves on what constitutes ethical conduct.

3.1. Training Ethical Psychologists: An Acculturation Model

Mitchell M. Handelsman, Michael C. Gottlieb, and Samuel Knapp

How do students develop a sense of themselves as ethical professionals? How do they develop a "professional ethical identity" as a part of the process of becoming psychologists? We ask these questions to help improve ethical behavior in our students and better prepare them to be more responsive to an increasingly complex and diverse professional world. . . .

There are at least three reasons ethics training is not so simple. First, the rules embedded in ethics codes are sometimes vague and conflicting (Keith-Spiegel, 1994). Second, learning about the ethics of the profession of psychology by watching models is incomplete at best (Branstetter & Handelsman, 2000; Handelsman, 1986). Third, ethics is the study of right and wrong but is often taught as the study of wrong. Many ethics courses are devoted to laws, disciplinary codes, and risk management strategies and do not focus on best practices.

If ethics training is limited primarily to learning rules, then students may not appreciate the extent to which the need for sound ethical thinking will permeate their professional lives. The development of an identity as an ethical psychologist is a far more complex matter that deserves greater attention. To do so requires that ethics training be considered in a new way, as a process of acculturation. . . .

The "culture" of psychology is larger than ethics, and an acculturation model could be used more broadly than we attempt here. We focus on ethics because it transcends all aspects of the discipline and because ethics training has been neglected relative to other aspects of professional preparation. In this article we propose that ethics training is an acculturation process, and we present some resulting implications and practical suggestions. . . .

BERRY'S MODEL OF ACCULTURATION

Berry (1980, 2003; Berry & Sam, 1997) conceived of acculturation as a process of adaptation that includes two dimensions that lead to four possible strategies of acculturation or types of adaptation. The first dimension, which Berry and Sam (1997) called *cultural maintenance*, refers to identification with the culture of origin: "Is it considered to be of value to maintain cultural identity and characteristics?" (p. 296). When people enter a new culture (either voluntarily or by force) and need to adapt, they vary in their desire to retain their original cultural values and traditions. At one end of the continuum are those who give up their culture of origin completely. At the other extreme are those who want to fully preserve their heritage.

The second dimension, *contact and participation*, refers to identification with the adopted culture: "Is it considered to be of value to maintain relationships with dominant society?" (Berry & Sam, 1997, p. 296). Individuals high in identification see great value and potential in the traditions of their new culture. Those low in identification refuse to accept a culture of which they are ignorant or in which they place little value. . . .

The acculturation choices trainees make are influenced by many factors, not all of which are consciously recognized. External factors include the conditions of both the culture of origin and the new culture. For example, how supportive of cultural maintenance is a particular training program or agency? Another factor influencing adaptation is cultural distance (Berry & Sam, 1997, p. 307), or the degree of difference between the two cultures. Among the internal or psychological factors that influence acculturation strategies are trainees' coping styles (Berry, 2003), their sense of how voluntary their acculturation is, and their orientation to moral and ethical issues and judgment (Forsyth, 1980). In the next sections we consider each of the four strategies. Although some of the more extreme features of these strategies are presented here, it should be recognized that each strategy comprises a continuum of behaviors.

Integration

People who adopt an *integration* strategy retain important aspects of their heritage but they also adopt what their new culture has to offer. Integration appears to be the most effective acculturation strategy (Berry, 2003; Berry & Sam, 1997). "Evidence strongly supports a positive correlation between the use of this strategy and good psychological adaptation during acculturation" (Berry & Sam, 1997, p. 298). Applied to ethical acculturation, people choosing integration would adopt the ethical values of psychology while understanding and maintaining their own value tradition. . . .

Assimilation

Berry (2003; Berry & Sam, 1997) called the strategy of relatively high contact and relatively low cultural maintenance *assimilation*. At the extreme of the assimilation strategy, the new culture is adopted totally, and the values and traditions from the culture of origin are discarded. In this mode, students adopt professional standards but do so with little personal sense of a moral base. . . .

When pursuing an assimilation strategy, external trappings may become more important than substance; this can lead to a false sense of competence.

The degree, license, and well-furnished office all signify entry into the profession. Certificates, memberships, and offices in professional associations may be sought because of the purely personal satisfaction they bring rather than the professional accomplishments they are supposed to represent. These outward signs are meaningless and potentially harmful without a firm personal grounding in and an appreciation for the ethics and value traditions of the professional culture. . . .

Separation

The *separation* strategy describes relatively high cultural maintenance and relatively low contact and participation. Applied to psychology training, students might have a well-developed ethical sense from their own upbringing, or the values of other professions to which they may have belonged, but they do not identify as strongly with the values of psychology. Those choosing the separation strategy may feel that their own way of expressing their morals, ideals, and compassion are sufficient for helping others or doing good research and that they do not need additional rules. . . .

Marginalization

Marginalization is the most problematic acculturation strategy, comprising low identification with both cultures. Sometimes this may be a temporary strategy—for example, when people move to a new culture and give up their culture of origin before they attempt to adopt the new culture. However, marginalization may also constitute an enduring state of alienation, or a failure of attempts at other strategies (Berry, 2003). In terms of ethics, psychologists using the marginalization strategy do not have a well-developed personal moral sense; neither have they (yet) internalized a sense of professional ethics. Such persons may be at greatest risk for ethical infractions. The extreme of this dimension is represented by psychopaths, although such persons represent a very small percentage of psychologists. . . .

IMPLICATIONS AND APPLICATIONS OF AN ACCULTURATION MODEL FOR INSTRUCTORS AND SUPERVISORS

Berry's (2003; Berry & Sam, 1997) model of acculturation and adaptation provides a framework for ethics education that may allow one more effectively to understand the transition from person to professional. Although a full explication of Berry's model is beyond the scope of this article, in this section we explore how viewing ethics training as an acculturation process may help those who train psychologists, and we provide some specific suggestions.

Two major ideas underlie an acculturation approach to ethics training. The first is that an acculturation model may provide a more positive approach to teaching ethics. An explicit focus on acculturation in the classroom or

supervision may make it easier to see that trainees' decisions and disagreements with instructors and supervisors about appropriate courses of action
can be considered and discussed as an acculturation task (or stress) rather than
evidence of inadequate learning. The educational task may be more easily
viewed as one of helping students make transitions; thus, some of the problems
of indoctrination may be avoided or mitigated. Exploring the gap between
students' two (or more) cultures respects their personhood and may allow
them to be more receptive to altering their judgments without feeling like they
are giving up parts of themselves. Trainees will be engaged in active integration.

Integration may best occur when instructors and supervisors view ethics
not only as a set of prohibitions but also as a way to actualize students' visions
of what it means to be a psychologist. Codes of conduct, licensing board rules,
and other disciplinary documents are certainly necessary, but they represent
only the ethical floor, or minimum standards. Teaching these documents by
themselves may lead students to separation choices; they may feel that the codes
and rules are external to their sense of ethical identity. (After all, applicants
do not say they want to become psychologists so they can obey the law.). . . .

The second underlying idea is that acculturation is a long-term developmental process. . . . We believe that becoming an ethical professional is also a
developmental process (de las Fuentes et al., 2003). In regard to acculturation,
Berry and Sam (1997) noted that "during the course of development (and even
in later life) individuals explore various strategies, eventually settling on one
that is more useful and satisfying than the others" (p. 297). In regard to ethics,
faculty who select and teach graduate students, and clinical supervisors, can
periodically assess and facilitate the acculturation of students. The fact that
acculturation is a lifelong adaptation means that continuing education can also
be viewed as part of the process.

. . .

Ethics Courses

Ethics courses present an excellent opportunity for students to explore their
acculturation and to begin developing an ethical identity. It may be useful in
such courses to have students engage in some reflection about their backgrounds, value traditions, and ethical cultures of origin, before or as they
learn the relevant codes and discuss cases. Also, instructors may be more
effective when they understand how their instruction fits within the values
and skills of their students. One way to accomplish this may be to have trainees write an *ethics autobiography* in which they outline how they came to their
present notion of what it means to be an ethical professional. In addition
to being a good early assignment in an ethics class, such a paper could be
assigned at the beginning of supervision, or even as part of an application to
graduate school. Indeed, the assignment can be done several times during the
course of training, and beyond.

A variation on the ethics autobiography could be *ethics ethnograms* or
genograms (de las Fuentes et al., 2003), in which students explore the moral

or professional orientation of their family members and other important people in their lives. Having a good sense of where they come from may help students understand and make good use of other class activities, such as studying case vignettes, narrative approaches, first-person accounts of clients, families, and professionals, and exploring the contextual and emotional factors that influence ethical behaviors (Knapp & Sturm, 2002).

Ethics autobiographies or genograms may also make it easier for students to understand that one's ordinary moral sense is not a sufficient basis for ethical behavior in many professional situations (Kitchener, 2000). . . . Similarly, trainees must see relationship boundaries, privacy, conflicts of interest, respect, and other issues not only from the vantage point of friendship but also from that of a well-defined set of professional principles. Understanding one's own implicit moral principles may make it easier to appreciate the philosophical principles behind ethics codes. Having students critique or debate the APA Ethics Code (see, e.g., Keith-Spiegel, 1994) may be an effective way to juxtapose principles from both cultures and thus move students toward integration. . . .

Practicum Supervision

As trainees progress from the classroom to their practicum placements, the acculturation tasks include putting their new ethical identities to the test in real situations. It may be important to prepare students for the types of dissonance that may occur and to encourage openness not only in the classroom but also in their ongoing supervision. Ethics instructors may have a difficult balancing act to perform. On the one hand, it might be useful to try to "immunize" students by warning them that people in complex real life situations do not always live up to their highest professional aspirations. On the other hand, this message may communicate to students that at least some level of ethically questionable activity is tolerated by professionals in positions of authority. Instructors and supervisors may want to reflect on how they first encountered this conflict and how they think about it now.

Caring about clients, students, or research participants, and knowing that their interests come first, are good starting points for ethical decision making. However, such first principles may not be sufficient in all situations. Stoltenberg and Delworth (1987) noted that it is only the more advanced trainees who "expect—rather than are confused by—the reality that different principles of their professional code seem to contradict each other" (p. 99). This appreciation of complexity and inherent ambiguity is a goal that trainers strive to facilitate, but for some students it remains elusive. . . .

Practicum supervisors might want to create an environment in which ethical issues and choices can be discussed openly. Again, it may be useful to approach such discussions as acculturation tasks rather than indications of ethical weakness or an ineffective ethics course. Supervisors may want to have trainees update (or write) their ethics autobiographies, to ask about the acculturation tasks their new trainees have already faced, and to anticipate some of the adaptations that they will face. Consider this example: A trainee has a spouse who insists that good dinner conversation include details of sessions with therapy clients. Although this may seem like a small issue, the resolution of the trainee's dilemma reflects an initial acculturation strategy. The trainee may accede to the spouse's request to maintain marital harmony (isn't that what good people do?) but does so at the expense of violating patient confidentiality. Such a decision may be indicative of a nascent separation strategy. Alternatively, the trainee may choose assimilation and berate the spouse for being insensitive to transcendent professional obligations. The best, and most difficult, resolution comes from integration of the professional value of confidentiality with personal values of mutual respect and caring. In this case, the trainee might explain why such requests cannot be honored but find other ways to talk about his or her work.

. . .

REFERENCES

Berry, J. W. (1980). Acculturation as varieties of adaptation. In A. M. Padilla (Ed.), *Acculturation: Theory, models, and some new findings* (pp. 9–25). Boulder, CO: Westview Press.

Berry, J. W. (2003). Conceptual approaches to acculturation. In K. M. Chun, P. B. Organista, & G. Marin (Eds.), *Acculturation: Advances in theory, measurement, and applied research* (pp. 17–37). Washington, DC: American Psychological Association.

Berry, J. W., & Sam, D. L. (1997). Acculturation and adaptation. In J. W. Berry, M. H. Segall, & C. Kagitcibasi (Eds.), *Handbook of cross-cultural psychology* (pp. 291–326). Needham Heights, MA: Allyn & Bacon.

Branstetter, S. A., & Handelsman, M. M. (2000). Graduate teaching assistants: Ethical training, beliefs, and practices. *Ethics & Behavior, 10,* 27–50.

de las Fuentes, C., Willmuth, M. E., & Yarrow, C. (2003, August). *Knowledge is not enough: Training for ethical competence.* In N. J. Kaslow (Chair), 2002 Competencies Conference: Update and future directions. Symposium conducted at the 111th Annual Convention of the American Psychological Association, Toronto, Ontario, Canada.

Forsyth, D. R. (1980). A taxonomy of ethical ideologies. *Journal of Personality and Social Psychology, 39,* 175–184.

Handelsman, M. M. (1986). Problems with ethics training by "osmosis." *Professional Psychology: Research and Practice, 17,* 371–372.

Keith-Spiegel, P. (Ed.). (1994). The 1992 ethics code: Boon or bane? [Special section]. *Professional Psychology: Research and Practice, 25*(4).

Kitchener, K. S. (2000). *Foundations of ethical practice, research, and teaching in psychology.* Mahwah, NJ: Erlbaum.

Knapp, S., & Sturm, C. (2002). Ethics education after licensing: Ideas for increasing diversity in content and process. *Ethics and Behavior, 12,* 157–166.

Stoltenberg, C. D., & Delworth, U. (1987). *Supervising counselors and therapists: A developmental approach.* San Francisco: Jossey-Bass.

COMMENTARY: Those who do not come to the study of psychology with a suitable moral foundation are not going to find one in the context of their undergraduate and graduate school educations merely by being exposed to this sort of material. It would be untrue, however, to suggest that professional ethics are going to come easily and accurately to everyone who approaches interpersonal relationships with the proper frame of mind. Ethics are more than feelings. Ethically informed clinical services and scientific research are just that—informed.

It is also true, however, that "information" and "knowledge" are distinct but closely related phenomena. Students can be taught what codes and guidelines contain and what professionals tend to do in certain situations, but it is the notion of "ethical acculturation" that most compellingly conveys what schooling in professional ethics requires for a successful outcome. In this context, Dr. Handelsman and his colleagues incorporate a graphically appealing depiction of "ethical identity" to excellent effect, as "personal ethics of origin" and "identification with psychological ethics" are combined to lay the groundwork for optimal professional induction.

The following references are recommended for those interested in further investigation of how instructors and supervisors can draw on the existing literature for background information consistent with the model of ethical acculturation.

Bashe, A., Anderson, S. K., Handelsman, M. M., & Klevansky, R. (2007). An acculturation model for ethics training: The ethics autobiography and beyond. *Professional Psychology: Research and Practice*, *38*(1), 60–67. http://dx.doi.org/10.1037/0735-7028.38.1.60

Berry, J. W. (2003). Conceptual approaches to acculturation. In K. M. Chun, P. B. Organista, & G. Marin (Eds.), *Acculturation: Advances in theory, measurement, and applied research* (pp. 17–37). Washington, DC: American Psychological Association.

Crowley, J. D., & Gottlieb, M. C. (2012). Objects in the mirror are closer than they appear: A primary prevention model for ethical decision making. *Professional Psychology: Research and Practice*, *43*, 65–72. http://dx.doi.org/10.1037/a0026212

Gallardo, M. E., Johnson, J., Parham, T. A., & Carter, J. A. (2009). Ethics and multiculturalism: Advancing cultural and clinical responsiveness. *Professional Psychology: Research and Practice*, *40*, 425–435. http://dx.doi.org/10.1037/a0016871

Knapp, S. J., Gottlieb, M. C., & Handelsman, M. M. (2015). The ethics acculturation model. In *Ethical dilemmas in psychotherapy: Positive approaches to decision making* (pp. 67–84). Washington, DC: American Psychological Association.

3.2. Some Principles for Ethics Education: Implementing the Acculturation Model

Michael C. Gottlieb, Mitchell M. Handelsman, and Samuel Knapp

. . .

SOME PRINCIPLES OF ETHICS EDUCATION

Ethics Education Is Positive

We have been concerned for some time that ethics education has become too heavily focused on rule adherence in order to help students avoid professional sanctions and civil litigation. In that sense, ethics education can inadvertently reinforce an assimilation strategy. Ethics education should include information regarding the ethics code (APA, 2002); state statutes, regulations, and court decisions; federal statutes and regulations; and risk management principles. Learning this information is essential, but it is not sufficient, in and of itself, to help students reach the goal of using the integration strategy, in which students and professional psychologists maximize their personal virtues and values within the context of what the law and professional standards allow.

The advent of the positive psychology movement (e.g., Snyder & Lopez, 2002) provided an opportunity to pursue our view that ethics can and should be taught from a more positive and aspirational perspective. Based on this premise, we proposed that the profession refocus its efforts in the direction of what we termed *positive ethics* (Handelsman, Knapp, & Gottlieb, 2002). The goal of positive ethics is to shift the primary emphasis from avoiding professional discipline to a "more balanced and integrative approach that includes encouraging psychologists to aspire to their highest ethical potential" (p. 731). . . .

An explicit and comprehensive emphasis on positive ethics can contribute to effective ethics education in several ways. First, a positive emphasis might expand students' awareness of the ways that the profession's enforceable rules are based on its higher aspirational principles. Second, a positive emphasis may help students consider ethical issues in a broader context, for example, by more explicitly including their highest personal and professional values, virtues, and motivations into their decision making. Third, positive ethics can contribute to a greater degree of openness so that students and colleagues feel more free to explore difficult issues (e.g., Pope, Sonne, & Greene, 2006) and seek the assistance of others. In an atmosphere of increasing anxiety over professional liability, this openness may help professionals avoid feeling that they cannot seek consultation from a trusted colleague precisely at a time when they most need it.

Ethics Education Is a Life-Long Process

If we assume that ethics education is complete when it is taught only as a fixed body of knowledge covered in a single academic course, students may be at risk for adopting assimilation strategies. It is as if one were to say, "I had the ethics course; I know all the rules. What else do I need to worry about?" This approach is problematic for at least three reasons.

First, contemporary professional practice is far too complex for such an attitude to be adequate. Contemporary risk management procedures (e.g., Bennett et al., 2007) rely on sophisticated clinical and ethical decision making skills that go well beyond simple rule adherence.

Second, assimilation strategies ignore the larger context in which future psychologists will function as both professionals and individuals. Assimilation strategies cannot anticipate changes in our personal circumstances, predict social change, or take account of how we will choose to actualize our personal values in a constantly shifting professional context. Alternatively, the acquisition and enhancement of integration strategies may be accomplished more effectively when ethics education is considered a lifelong process in which psychologists continually reconsider their personal and professional values. Therefore, we contend that professional preparation should establish the basis for this lifelong process by integrating ethics education at all levels of training.

Third, we hear a great deal about lifelong learning but fear the idea has become trite. Experience is a great teacher, but it is not the only one. We feel that when explicit ethics training is integrated throughout the professional development process we are more likely to model the behaviors we hope to instill in our students and trainees.

Ethics Education Is Experiential

Experiential exercises may be a particularly effective way to teach ethics. The experiential principle speaks directly to the need to surround oneself with the new culture and its values, traditions, and language. Just as language is effectively taught by immersion, we view experiential exercises as accomplishing a similar purpose.

Traditionally, basic concepts in ethical decision making have been developed as a largely intellectual and quasi-legal reasoning process. There is great value in this approach as it helps students explore all relevant sources of knowledge and entertain multiple hypotheses. We support this process and teach it ourselves, but we do not think that it is adequate per se. We disagree with others (e.g., Ford, 2006) who consider emotions to be a distraction to be ignored. Rather, we suggest that emotionally charged experiences are a crucial component of ethical deliberation (Betan & Stanton, 1999) and that students become more fully engaged and effective when they experience the choices they make both intellectually and emotionally. This approach challenges students to go beyond more legalistic reasoning and to consider ways in which they can optimize the good they can do by a reflective balancing of sometimes competing ethical concerns.

Ethics Education Is Social and Supportive

Healthy competition in the marketplace of ideas contributes to learning and knowledge. Critiques of journal articles, rejoinders, and intellectual argument demonstrating superior reasoning and methodology have a time-honored place in our scholarly tradition. Although vigorous debate is vital to the scientific enterprise, we submit that ethics education should be different. Here the goal is not to win an intellectual argument by defeating someone else. Rather, it is to cooperatively shape and sharpen the deliberative skills of all involved. This is what we mean when we state that effective ethics training should be social and supportive.

Sadly, an "I am right and you are wrong" attitude, combined with the apprehensions created by a litigious environment, may impede the willingness of students and professionals to talk with each other about their ethical concerns. This reluctance may be exacerbated when we teach ethical decision making based only on the reasoned, intellectual, and quasi-legal thinking noted above.

Experiential and positive ethics training may help psychologists hone their integration skills by being more open about their values, motivations, conflicts, and aspirations (Pope et al., 2006), which is necessary if they are to develop an integration strategy. Furthermore, supportive environments help engender positive emotions. According to Frederickson's "broaden and build" theory (2002), individuals who experience positive emotions are better decision makers than those who experience negative ones, and positive emotions can help build a reservoir of strength and resilience that one can draw upon in times of stress. In short, social support fosters sound ethical decision making, good risk management, and attentive self care.

Ethics Education Is Focused on Students' Backgrounds and Needs

Implementing the foregoing principles requires that instructors consider the personalities, backgrounds, and moral/ethical value traditions of the learners. If we are to do this, ethics educators, practicum supervisors, internship and post doctoral trainers have the responsibility of assessing a trainee's values, reasoning skills, ethical sensitivity, and other relevant attributes to help them integrate these with the demands of professional practice. Such an assessment can be done quickly and informally in the context of case discussions and/or supervision; it can be the focus of an individual session; or it can include certain exercises such as the ethics autobiography that we discuss below.

Progress toward integration may be difficult for some students who are asked to accept professional standards that are confusing or appear counter-intuitive to them. Such obstacles may be particularly problematic for students who have worked in other fields that appear to have similar standards to those of professional psychology but upon closer examination do not. For example, a psychology trainee had worked at a shelter for abused women where counselors were encouraged to share their personal abuse history with their counselees. Another was as a nurse who had worked at a nursing home where beneficence was often given a far higher priority than respecting patient autonomy. Therefore, it is not unusual for trainers to find that some of their best students may briefly become stuck in a separation strategy. These students may need help with "culture shedding" (Berry & Sam, 1997, p. 298) or understanding why they must unlearn rules they previously considered to be virtuous. . . .

IMPLEMENTING THE ACCULTURATION MODEL: THE CASE OF I. C. KLERELY

In this section, we illustrate how the principles we have listed can be put into practice. We do this by following the career of a student through various steps in her training. At each one, we provide examples of challenges students face and recommend a variety of experiential and personal exercises gleaned from the literature.

Ms. Klerely[1] was required by her program to take a full three credit hour course in ethics during her second year of graduate training in clinical psychology. It coincided with her first practicum experience. One goal of the course was to help students reflect on their personal values through an ethics autobiography. . . .

In her ethics autobiography, Klerely wrote, "I am the kind of person who will do whatever it takes to help my patients." She explained that she came from a strong family and religious tradition that placed great value on social justice and helping others. Prior to enrolling in graduate school, she had worked as a para-professional for a publicly funded mental health program that sent workers into the homes of at risk children in underprivileged areas of a large city.

Despite the laudable goals of the program, well-developed treatment plans were often lacking, and the supervision was sporadic at best. Klerely quickly decided to "do whatever it took" to win the acceptance of the families, including buying groceries with her own money, babysitting the children, and cleaning house. Once she even had her boyfriend change the oil in the truck of one family.

---

[1] The trainee in this example represents a composite of many students and trainees whom the authors have taught or trained over the years. It does not and is not intended to represent a specific individual.

After reading her ethics autobiography, her professor became concerned that Ms. Klerely might have extended herself beyond appropriate professional boundaries. Also, her behavior raised questions regarding the extent to which families may have been consenting to treatment based on an implicit agreement that "I will let you come into my house and do things with my children as long as you provide other nonclinical service to me." Although in-home services involve unique boundary issues, the extent of Klerely's behavior appeared to deviate substantially from the more porous boundaries that exist when providing such treatment (Knapp & Slattery, 2004). In psychotherapy situations, Klerely's approach could undercut the patients' perceived value of therapy and their investment in the process.

Klerely's description of her attitudes and behavior suggested that she was using a separation strategy. That is, she had acted upon her deeply held personal beliefs regarding the need to be of service to others and did not appreciate the value of establishing professional boundaries. Her professor saw her goal as helping Klerely move toward an integration strategy.

The professor's approach was to use lecture and class discussion in a supportive, strength-based, and experiential manner. Her goal was to create a safe environment that encouraged mutual support and self reflection. In one exercise, the students studied the General (aspirational) Principles and linked them to enforceable Standards in the APA Ethics Code (APA, 2002). Also the students were asked to keep an ethics diary in which they would address a variety of issues, such as how their class readings and clinical experiences affected their personal values. Other exercises included examining paternalistic versus facilitative ethical decision-making models as well as reading court cases regarding informed consent (Knapp & VandeCreek, 2004). At the end of the course Klerely expressed her appreciation to he professor for what she had learned, but it was not clear that she had integrated this new knowledge into her clinical practice.

Klerely's third-year practicum class followed a model similar to that of her ethics class the previous year, and it seemed that her attitudes had begun to change. The class was asked to do the provocative statements exercise (Plante, 1995) in which students are given the task of challenging basic professional assumptions, such as "The boundaries for professional psychologists are too rigid and are an obstacle to establishing close relationships." Students broke into two groups to develop arguments defending or challenging the provocative statement, and a spokesperson was selected to argue the group's position in front of the class.

During the class discussion that followed, Klerely related her experiences both as a worker before entering graduate school and with patients she had treated the previous year. She acknowledged finding the work stressful and admitted feeling confused about boundary maintenance to the point that she had reconsidered her goal of becoming a psychologist. In the context of a supportive environment that emphasized positive ethics, she volunteered that some of her patients benefited, but others did not. Some even developed a sense of entitlement, and she felt exploited by them. Klerely was quite self-critical and felt that her work had fallen far short of her own expectations. Nevertheless, the group supported her self-examination, empathized with her struggles, and shared their own progress and frustrations with ethical acculturation. Klerely came away feeling that she could be more open about her struggles without being seen as unethical or intellectually inferior.

In Klerely's fourth year practicum class, the students were asked to reread the ethics autobiography they had written two years earlier, revise it as needed, and then comment on the differences and what they had learned in the interim. This time she wrote, "I am the kind of person who will do whatever it takes to help my patients, within the limits of my professional role." Her practicum instructor had been briefed about Klerely by his colleagues and found this statement and other comments she had made in class encouraging. He believed that she was well on the way toward adopting an integration strategy and felt she was ready to leave for internship training.

It was during this year that Klerely experienced another challenge to her professional acculturation. During graduate school, she had developed an interest in anxiety disorders and had become proficient with cognitive behavior therapy. Upon arrival at her internship site, she was assigned a young woman suffering from panic disorder with some avoidant and mixed personality traits and features. The patient responded well, and treatment was terminated in the fall. Several months later, the patient returned, but this time it was to seek Klerely's opinion about whether to marry her fiancé. Part of the reason the patient returned to consult Klerely was that she interviewed him as a collateral contact during the patient's previous treatment. At that time, Klerely felt that he was unhelpful and rather dismissive of her patient's condition. Her view of the fiancé was reinforced by other comments the patient had made about his selfishness.

When the patient presented her dilemma, Klerely had an immediate and strong desire to tell the patient exactly what she thought about the fiance, but she also knew that sharing her strong reactions might constitute a clinically contraindicated and perhaps unethical boundary crossing. She knew this intellectually via her readings, but she also recognized it emotionally because she had explored her feelings about boundaries in previous courses and practicum. She managed to suppress her desire to share her feelings and avoided the question by focusing on getting an update on the patient's progress. They agreed to meet again.

After the session, Klerely was troubled by her intense reaction. She immediately went to her supervisor who took a Socratic approach with her. In the course of their discussion, the supervisor asked questions such as, "What was it that troubled you so much? If you expressed your feelings, what impact would that have had on the patient? Do you think the patient really wants you to tell her what to do, and even if she does, should you?"

Klerely and her supervisor reflected on her reactions, and Klerely quickly realized that some of her reaction was due to the fact that she recently terminated a relationship with an undesirable man herself. At the time, she wished that her friends had been more forthcoming with her regarding their concerns about him.

Once this information was explored in supervision, Klerely was better able to consider how she could be of greater assistance to her patient. Klerely concluded that the issue was not so much offering the patient her opinion about marrying this man as it was helping her to clarify her goals for and values about marriage, and whether this man was an appropriate choice for her. As a result of the supervision, Klerely felt far more secure in her professional role, confident that she could set appropriate boundaries around the treatment, and able to help her patient gain insight into her situation. . . .

REFERENCES

American Psychological Association. (2002). Ethical principles of psychologists and code of conduct. *American Psychologist, 57,* 1060–1073.

Bennett, B. E., Bricklin, P. M., Harris, E., Knapp, S., VandeCreek, L., & Younggren, J. (2007). *Assessing and managing risk in psychological practice: An individualized approach.* Rockville, MD: American Psychological Association Insurance Trust.

Berry, J. W., & Sam, D. L. (1997). Acculturation and adaptation. In J. W. Berry, M. H. Siegel, & C. Kagitcibasi (Eds.), *Handbook of cross-cultural psychology* (pp. 291–326). Needham Heights, MA: Allyn & Bacon.

Betan, E. J., & Stanton, A. L. (1999). Fostering ethical willingness: Integrating emotional and contextual awareness with rational analysis. *Professional Psychology: Research and Practice, 30,* 295–301.

Ford, G. G. (2006). *Ethical reasoning for mental health professionals.* Thousand Oaks, CA: Sage.

Frederickson, B. (2002). Positive emotions. In S. Lopez & R. Snyder (Eds.), *Handbook of positive psychology* (pp. 120–139). New York: Oxford.

Handelsman, M. M., Knapp, S. J., & Gottlieb, M. C. (2002). Positive ethics. In C. R. Snyder and S. J. Lopez (Eds.), *Handbook of positive psychology* (pp. 731–744). New York: Oxford University Press.

Knapp, S., & Slattery, J. (2004). Professional boundaries in non-traditional settings. *Professional Psychology: Research and Practice, 35,* 553–558.

Knapp, S., & VandeCreek, L. (2003, Fall). Do psychologists have supererogatory obligations? *Psychotherapy Bulletin, 38*(3), 29–31.

Knapp, S., & VandeCreek, L. (2004). Using case law to teach professional ethics. *Teaching of Psychology, 31,* 281–284.

Plante, T. G. (1995). Training child clinical predoctoral intern and post-doctoral fellows in ethics and professional issues: An experiential model. *Professional Psychology: Research and Practice, 26,* 616–619.

Pope, K. S., Sonne, J. L., & Greene, B. (2006). *What therapists don't talk about and why.* Washington, DC: American Psychological Association.

Snyder, C. R., & Lopez, S. J. (Eds.). (2002). *Handbook of positive psychology.* New York: Oxford University Press.

COMMENTARY: The initial "acculturation model" article by Gottlieb and colleagues—and the training paradigm it proposed—were so well received by the academic and training communities that a follow-up article was soon published to address implementing that model. Now touted as the ethics acculturation model (EAM), this approach is appropriately conceptualized as a lifelong endeavor with a pronounced experiential component.

A particular strength of the EAM is its articulation not just of a relatable set of values or a culturally appropriate perspective on professional issues but of a definable collection of guiding principles that include positivity, supportiveness, and a focus on alignment with the student's background and needs. Also helpful is the reliance on vignette-driven training that humanizes the process and supplements it with a healthy dose of memorable human interest. It is easy to see that internalization of the EAM can be, over the arc of a professional career, as impactful as the lessons it is initially employed to convey.

The following references are recommended for those interested in further investigation of how instructors and supervisors, as well as active practitioners seeking to extend their own skills, can utilize the EAM and/or its guiding principles on an ongoing basis.

Barnett, J. E. (2009). The complete practitioner: Still a work in progress. *American Psychologist, 64*, 793–801. http://dx.doi.org/10.1037/0003-066X.64.8.793

Gottlieb, M. C., & Younggren, J. N. (2009). Is there a slippery slope? Considerations regarding multiple relationships and risk management. *Professional Psychology: Research and Practice, 40*, 564–571.

Knapp, S., Handelsman, M. M., Gottlieb, M. C., & VandeCreek, L. D. (2013). The dark side of professional ethics. *Professional Psychology: Research and Practice, 44*, 371–377. http://dx.doi.org/10.1037/a0035110

Tirpak, D. M., & Lee, S. S. (2012). Navigating peer-to-peer multiple relationships in professional psychology programs. *Training and Education in Professional Psychology, 6*, 135–141. http://dx.doi.org/10.1037/a0029234

Tjeltveit, A. C., & Gottlieb, M. C. (2010). Avoiding the road to ethical disaster: Overcoming vulnerabilities and developing resilience. *Psychotherapy: Theory, Research, Practice, Training, 47*, 98–110. http://dx.doi.org/10.1037/a0018843

3.3. Ethical Issues in Education and Training

Jennifer A. Erickson Cornish

With the advent of *Training and Education in Professional Psychology* (*TEPP*) in 2006, the literature on the education and training of professional psychologists has simultaneously expanded and become more organized. As the field has moved toward defining and assessing the competencies needed by health-service psychologists, the importance of integrating ethics into education, training, and supervision has become increasingly clear. For instance, the *2013 Education Leadership Conference* was devoted to Ethics and Education. Participants discussed ethical dilemmas in education, training, supervision, and research, and highlighted the importance of mentoring and innovative teaching approaches (Clay, 2013).

Due to the inherent power differential and the prevalence of multiple relationships between faculty/supervisors and students/trainees, there is a wide range of potential ethical dilemmas within education and training. A student's dissertation chair may also be his or her professor in a class and a member of the faculty internship advisory committee; if a boundary violation occurs in any of these relationships, the student not only has to deal with an unethical situation, but one that is difficult to report.

The American Psychological Association's *Ethical Principles of Psychologists and Code of Conduct* (Ethics Code; APA, 2010) rests on five overarching principles (beneficence and nonmaleficence, fidelity and responsibility, integrity, justice, and respect for people's rights and dignity) all of which are seemingly related to education and training. In addition, Standard 7 (Education and Training) explicitly outlines ways in which education and training programs should be designed and described, and how students and supervisees are to be assessed. This standard prescribes accuracy in teaching, the importance of access to practitioners unaffiliated with the program if individual or group psychotherapy is mandated, and prohibits student disclosure of personal information (except in restrictive circumstances), as well as sexual relationships with students and supervisees. While the Ethics Code is always the place to begin when considering ethical issues, it simply cannot address all the potential dilemmas within education and training.

From "Ethical Issues in Education and Training," by J. A. Erickson Cornish, 2014, *Training and Education in Professional Psychology, 8,* pp. 197–200. Copyright 2014 by the American Psychological Association.

COMPETENCE

The competency movement in professional psychology has gained momentum, particularly since the 2002 *Competencies Conference: Future Directions in Education and Credentialing in Professional Psychology*, resulting in a "culture shift" toward competencies (Roberts, Borden, Christiansen, & Lopez, 2005) and away from simply accruing hours of experience. Competence is generally defined as including knowledge, skills and attitudes/values in foundational and functional activities performed by health-service psychologists. Several approaches to defining and describing the competencies necessary for professional psychologists have been proposed, including the Competency Benchmarks (Fouad et al., 2009); the *Revised Competency Benchmarks for Professional Psychology* (APA, 2011); the *Association of State and Provincial Psychology Boards* (ASPPB; n.d.) *Competencies Expected of Psychologists at the Point of Licensure*; the *Blueprint for Health-Service Psychology Education and Training* (Health-Service Psychology Education Collaborative, 2013); and the current ongoing revision of the APA Accreditation Guidelines and Principles, *Standards of Accreditation in Health-Service Psychology* (APA, Commission on Accreditation, in press).

Although ethics has been recognized in professional psychology as central to education and training since at least the 1970s (Welfel, 2012), and is listed as a competency area (sometimes combined with legal standards and policy) across all the approaches in professional psychology, supervision became a distinct competence more recently (Grus, 2013). In addition to ethics and supervision, the original and revised *Competency Benchmarks* (APA, 2011) include teaching and management/administration, two other competencies that are central to education and training. The *Blueprint* (Health-Service Psychology Education Collaborative, 2013) redefines professional psychology as health-service psychology, and includes, among its list of 16 competencies, ethical legal standards and policy, teaching, and supervision. There is no mention of management/administration, but professional leadership development is included, and teaching and supervision are combined into the Education section. The ASPPB *Competencies Expected of Psychologists at the Point of Licensure* (ASPPB; n.d.) include ethical practice as one of six competency areas, but are silent regarding supervision, teaching, or administration (although clearly, supervision and teaching are crucial to education and training, and administration is a competency needed for any director of a doctoral, practicum, internship, or postdoctoral program). The 10 competencies listed in the proposed standards of accreditation for doctoral and internship programs include ethical and legal standards as well as supervision and learning, but do not include either teaching or administration, whereas the competencies for postdoctoral programs include ethics as an advanced profession-wide competency, with no mention of supervision, teaching, or administration, presumably due to the specialty focus of fellowship training.

In addition to the attempts to describe a set of comprehensive competencies for health-service psychology, de las Fuentes, Willmuth, and Yarrow (2005) describe core ethical competencies and strategies for ethics education and training. They observe that, because ideals and rules may conflict with each other, it is important that psychologists develop competencies to address ethical dilemmas. Finally, the new focus on competency-based supervision (Falender, Shafranske, & Falicov, in press) is reflected in the *Guidelines for Competency-Based Clinical Supervision in Health-Service Psychology Education and Training Programs* (APA, Board of Educational Affairs, in press). These guidelines include the notion that supervisors should be ethical role models, uphold their primary ethical and legal obligation to protect clients, serve as gatekeepers for the profession, provide informed consent through a contract, and maintain accurate and timely documentation of supervisee performance.

ETHICAL ISSUES IN EDUCATION AND TRAINING

Noting these developments in the field, the *TEPP* editorial team issued a call for articles addressing ethical issues in education and training, including ethical issues in individual and group supervision, ethics as a competency necessary in the education and training of psychologists, best practices and evidence-based approaches to teaching and training ethics, and outcomes related to ethics in education and training. The result was a large number of submissions; 12 articles were chosen for this special section.

IN THIS SECTION

The articles in this special section illustrate the current breadth of ethics in education and training within health-service psychology, representing a wide variety of approaches from the conceptual (including a paradigm shift) to the practical and the more empirical. The section begins with "Ethical Supervision: Harmonizing Rules and Ideals in a Globalizing World" by Pettifor, Sinclair, and Falender (2014, pp. 201–210). This article includes a description of the history and evolution of ethics and multiculturalism related to supervision in the United States and Canada and offers important suggestions for educators, including expanding education and training for supervisors/supervisees, continuing to develop ethical guidelines for supervision, and emphasizing globally accepted ethical principles (e.g., *Universal Declaration of Ethical Principles*, 2008, which focuses on ethical principles rather than behavioral mandates). Noting that the development of modern ethics codes for psychologists, starting in the mid-20th century, have been primarily individually focused (a problem for many cultures that are non-Western), the article sets the stage for the next article in the section that describes a paradigm shift in the way we educate and train students to become ethically competent.

Expanding on their previous work related to developing a communitarian approach to psychology ethics (Johnson, Barnett, Elman, Forrest, & Kaslow,

2013a, 2013b), Johnson et al. (2014, pp. 211–220) have proposed a fundamental change in educating and training ethics in "Preparing Trainees for Lifelong Competence: Creating a Communitarian Training Culture." These authors note the problems that can occur when training psychologists emphasize individualistic conceptions of competence, and they propose instead a communitarian training culture that infuses existing competency models with an emphasis on interdependence and community, and extends ethical education and training throughout the career.

"Using the *Ethical Context* to Enhance Practicum Training" by Wise and Cellucci (2014, pp. 221–228) provides a general conceptualization and specific strategies for integrating professional and ethical competence into practicum programs, especially those that serve as in-house training clinics for doctoral programs. Applying a competency-based approach that is closely tied to the APA Ethics Code, these authors provide many helpful recommendations for the profession.

A second article primarily pragmatic in nature is "Fostering the Ethical Sensitivity of Beginning Clinicians" by Moffett, Becker, and Patton (2014, pp. 229–235). These authors expand on Welfel's (2012) recommendation for teaching ethical sensitivity and describe a mnemonic checklist to help students consider ethical issues, particularly when learning to perform intakes.

Recognizing the importance of using contracts for individual supervision, Smith, Erickson Cornish, and Riva (2014, pp. 236–240) make the case for also using contracts for group supervision in "Contracting for Group Supervision." Such contracts may not only be useful, but essential to the delivery of ethical and impactful group supervision. The authors also provide a sample group-supervision contract.

Moving from the conceptual and practical to more empirical approaches, "Ethics Education in Professional Psychology: A Survey of American Psychological Association Accredited Programs" by Domenech Rodriguez et al. (2014, pp. 241–247) and the companion piece "Graduate Ethics Education: A Content Analysis of Syllabi" by Griffith, Domenech Rodriguez, and Anderson (2014, pp. 248–252) seek to describe the current state of ethics education in the United States. Of the 136 instructors who completed a survey, nearly all reported a required ethics course at their institution, and most endorsed lectures as a teaching method, reading as the most common type of assignment, "teaching by example," and an overarching goal of advancing students' critical thinking. Syllabi for 53 ethics courses were analyzed and noted to be quite varied in the information they included, with no consistent pedagogical structure or consistent content across programs, and in some cases, the use of sources that were older than 5 years. Suggestions from these studies include the following: teaching practical applications of ethical principles and standards in creative ways, considering research and teaching in addition to clinical issues, learning from each other, using peer evaluation such as that provided by APA Division 2 (Society for the Teaching of Psychology), and potentially developing specific content guidelines for coursework.

"Promoting Ethical Behavior by Cultivating a Culture of Self-Care During Graduate Training: A Call to Action" by Bamonti et al. (2014, pp. 253–260) uses the creative method of analyzing references to student self-care in departmental and/or clinical training area handbooks from clinical psychology doctoral programs associated with the Council of University Directors of Clinical Psychology (CUDCP). Because self-care has been described as an ethical obligation (Barnett, Baker, Elman, & Schoener, 2007), the importance of incorporating it into graduate training is crucial, yet results of this study indicate that most handbooks only include references to psychotherapy or mental health services for students experiencing problems.

A second CUDCP-based study by January, Meyerson, Reddy, Docherty, and Klonoff (2014, pp. 261–268), "Impressions of Mis-conduct: Graduate Students' Perception of Faculty Ethical Violations in Scientist-Practitioner Clinical Psychology Programs," addresses how perceived faculty ethical violations affect graduate students and their training environment. Results of an online survey ($N = 374$) indicated a wide range of perceived unethical faculty behaviors that was associated with decreased confidence in the faculty, and a lower perceived program climate.

Brown, Murdock, and Abels (2014, pp. 269–276) have written "Ethical Issues Associated with Training in University Counseling Centers," a collaborative effort between faculty and practicum/internship staff members. Seventy-two internship directors from the Association of Counseling Center Training Agencies responded to a brief Internet survey, with the results indicating that there were two main ethical issues prevalent in these settings: balancing supervision time with other activities, and providing counseling to students who might be eligible for practicum/internship placement.

An example of a unique approach to researching ethics education is the "Effects of Experience and Surface-Level Distraction on Ability to Perceive Ethical Issues" by Fialkov, Jackson, and Rabinowitz (2014, pp. 277–284). This study applied cognitive science research to psychology ethics training through the use of ambiguous scenarios in an Internet survey. Due to the low response rate, the significance of the conclusions is difficult to determine, but the attempt to study awareness and skills related to potential distractions, using cognitive science research methods is a useful first step.

Lougherty, Hamilton, and Magistro (2014, pp. 285–291), in the final article in this special section, attempted to combine a practical approach with an outcome evaluation. The authors describe a small-group format as an adjunct to traditional classroom pedagogy, with doctoral students teaching aspects of professional ethics to master's students in "Psychology Ethics Education in a Peer-Facilitated Laboratory Setting." Although their results need replication over time and across other programs, the article may serve as an example to others seeking to better describe and evaluate their own teaching approaches.

Taken together, these articles both advance the literature in ethics in health-service-psychology education, training, and supervision, and underscore the need for considerable future research. Although the conceptual and practical articles challenge the profession to develop best practices, they are as yet unsupported by empirical study. Most of the studies relied on Internet surveys, in which the demographics of the respondents may be skewed, and the response rates were generally unknown or too low to produce significant results. Although ethical issues in doctoral, practicum, and internship programs have been represented in the section, postdoctoral programs are missing, possibly due to the emerging nature of literature related to postdoctoral fellowships.

NEXT STEPS

Roberts, Campbell, Erickson Cornish, Klonoff, and Siegel (2014) have called for developing the evidence base in education and training. This special section certainly illustrates that need. Staff from practicum, internship, and postdoctoral programs could collaborate with faculty members (as did Brown et al., 2014) to better research the integration of ethics education and training throughout the developmental trajectory. The two articles based on CUDCP samples (Bamonti et al., 2014; January et al., 2014) could serve as models to students and faculty from other training councils seeking to study the application of ethics education by the recipients of that training. It would also be useful to go beyond single training councils to conduct more omnibus (and fully representative) sampling of students, faculty, and programs. More robust studies focusing on outcomes, perhaps involving direct observation rather than Internet surveys, could be useful. Finally, broadening the proposed competencies in the APA's accreditation standards to include teaching and administration may be an important consideration for the profession. The literature related to ethics in health-service-psychology education, training, and supervision has increased, but to truly change the paradigm, to educate, train, and supervise psychologists to become ethically competent over the course of their careers, there is clearly considerable work ahead.

REFERENCES

American Psychological Association. (2010, June). *Ethical principles of psychologists and code of conduct* (Original published 2002, amended June 1, 2010). Retrieved from http://www.apa.org/ethics/code/index.aspx

American Psychological Association. (2011). *Revised competency benchmarks for professional psychology.* Retrieved from http://www.apa.org/ed/graduate/competency.aspx

American Psychological Association, Board of Educational Affairs. (in press). *Guidelines for competency-based clinical supervision in health-service psychology education and training programs.*

American Psychological Association, Commission on Accreditation. (in press). *The standards of accreditation in health-service psychology.* Retrieved from http://www.apa.org/ed/accreditation/newsletter/2014/05/standards-accreditation.aspx

Association of State and Provincial Psychology Boards. (n.d.). *ASPPB competencies expected of psychologists at the point of licensure.* Retrieved from https://cdn.ymaws.com/www.asppb.net/resource/resmgr/eppp_2/2017_ASPPB_Competencies_Exp.pdf

Bamonti, P. A., Keelan, C. M., Larson, N., Mentrikoski, J. M., Randall, C. L.,
   Sly, S. K., . . . McNeil, D. W. (2014). Promoting ethical behavior by cultivating a
   culture of self-care during graduate training: A call to action. *Training and Education
   in Professional Psychology, 8*, 253–260. http://dx.doi.org/10.1037/tep0000056

Barnett, J. E., Baker, E. K., Elman, N. S., & Schoener, G. R. (2007). In pursuit of
   wellness: The self-care imperative. *Professional Psychology: Research and Practice, 38*,
   603–612. http://dx.doi.org/10.1037/0735-7028.38.6.603

Brown, C., Murdock, N. L., & Abels, A. (2014). Ethical issues associated with training
   in university counseling centers. *Training and Education in Professional Psychology, 8*,
   269–276. http://dx.doi.org/10.1037/tep0000063

Clay, R. A. (2013). Education Leadership Conference: Ethics and Education. *Educator,
   12*, 1–15.

de las Fuentes, C., Willmuth, M. E., & Yarrow, C. (2005). Competency training in
   ethics education and practice. *Professional Psychology: Research and Practice, 36*,
   362–366. http://dx.doi.org/10.1037/0735-7028.36.4.362

Domenech Rodriguez, M. M., Erickson Cornish, J. A., Thomas, J. T., Forrest, L.,
   Anderson, A. J., & Bow, J. N. (2014). Ethics education in professional psychology:
   A Survey of American Psychological Association accredited programs. *Training
   and Education in Professional Psychology, 8*, 241–247. http://dx.doi.org/10.1037/
   tep0000043

Falender, C. A. Shafranske, E. P., & Falicov, C. P. (Eds.). (in press). *Clinical supervision:
   Foundation and praxis.* Washington, DC: American Psychological Association.

Fialkov, E. M., Jackson, M. A., & Rabinowitz, M. (2014). Effects of experience and
   surface-level distraction on ability to perceive ethical issues. *Training and Education
   in Professional Psychology, 8*, 277–284. http://dx.doi.org/10.1037/tep0000067

Fouad, N. A., Grus, C. L., Hatcher, R. L., Kaslow, N. J., Hutchings, P. S., Madison,
   M. B., . . . Crossman, R. E. (2009). Competency benchmarks: A model for understanding and measuring competence in professional psychology across training
   levels. *Training and Education in Professional Psychology, 3*, S5–S26. http://dx.doi.org/
   10.1037/a0015832

Griffith, S. M., Domenech Rodriguez, M. M., & Anderson, A. J. (2014). Graduate
   ethics education: A content analysis of syllabi. *Training and Education in Professional
   Psychology, 8*, 248–252. http://dx.doi.org/10.1037/tep0000036

Grus, C. L. (2013). The supervision competency: Advancing competency-based
   education and training in professional psychology. *The Counseling Psychologist, 41*,
   131–139. http://dx.doi.org/10.1177/0011000012453946

Health-service psychology Education Collaborative. (2013). Professional psychology
   in health care services: A blueprint for education and training. *American Psychologist,
   68*, 411–426. http://dx.doi.org/10.1037/a0033265

January, A. M., Meyerson, D. A., Reddy, L. F., Docherty, A. R., & Klonoff, E. A. (2014).
   Impressions of misconduct: Graduate students' perception of faculty ethical violations in scientist-practitioner clinical psychology programs. *Training and Education
   in Professional Practice, 8*, 261–268. http://dx.doi.org/10.1037/tep0000059

Johnson, W. B., Barnett, J. E., Elman, N. S., Forrest, L., & Kaslow, N. J. (2013a).
   Infusing psychology ethics with a communitarian approach. *American Psychologist,
   68*, 479–480. http://dx.doi.org/10.1037/a0033635

Johnson, W. B., Barnett, J. E., Elman, N. S., Forrest, L., & Kaslow, N. J. (2013b).
   The competence constellation: A developmental network model for psychologists.
   Professional Psychology: Research and Practice, 44, 343–354. http://dx.doi.org/10.1037/
   a0033131

Johnson, W. B., Barnett, J. E., Elman, N. H., Forrest, L., Schwartz-Mette, R., &
   Kaslow, N. (2014). Preparing trainees for lifelong competence: Creating a communitarian culture. *Training and Education in Professional Psychology, 8*, 211–220.
   http://dx.doi.org/10.1037/tep0000048

Lougherty, M. J., Hamilton, D., & Magistro, C. (2014). Psychology ethics education in a peer-facilitated laboratory setting. *Training and Education in Professional Psychology*, *8*, 285–291. http://dx.doi.org/10.1037/tep0000053

Moffett, L., Becker, C.-L., & Patton, R. (2014). Fostering the ethical sensitivity of beginning clinicians. *Training and Education in Professional Psychology*, *8*, 229–235. http://dx.doi.org/10.1037/tep0000054

Pettifor, J., Sinclair, C., & Falender, C. (2014). Ethical supervision: Harmonizing rules and ideals in a globalizing world. *Training and Education in Professional Psychology*, *8*, 201–210. http://dx.doi.org/10.1037/tep0000046

Roberts, M. C., Borden, K. A., Christiansen, M. D., & Lopez, S. J. (2005). Fostering a culture shift: Assessment of competence in the education and careers of professional psychologists. *Professional Psychology: Research and Practice*, *36*, 355–361. http://dx.doi.org/10.1037/0735-7028.36.4.355

Roberts, M. C., Campbell, C. D., Erickson Cornish, J. A., Klonoff, E. A., & Siegel, W. G. (2014). Developing the evidence base for training and education in professional psychology. *Training and Education in Professional Psychology*, *8*, 1–2. http://dx.doi.org/10.1037/tep0000011

Smith, R. D., Erickson Cornish, J. A., & Riva, M. T. (2014). Contracting for group supervision. *Training and Education in Professional Psychology*, *8*, 236–240. http://dx.doi.org/10.1037/tep0000075

Universal Declaration of Ethical Principles for Psychologists. (2008). Retrieved from http://www.iupsys.org/ethics/univdec12008.html

Welfel, E. R. (2012). Teaching ethics: Models, methods, and challenges. In S. J. Knapp (Ed.), *APA handbook of ethics in psychology: Vol. 2. Practice, teaching and research* (pp. 277–305). Washington, DC: American Psychological Association.

Wise, E. H., & Cellucci, T. (2014). Using the ethical context to enhance practicum training. *Training and Education in Professional Psychology*, *8*, 221–228. http://dx.doi.org/10.1037/tep0000055

3.4. Competency Training in Ethics Education and Practice

Cynthia de las Fuentes, Mary E. Willmuth, and Catherine Yarrow

The 2002 Competencies Conference was held November 7–9, 2002, in Scottsdale, Arizona. The conference was hosted by the Association of Psychology Postdoctoral and Internship Centers in collaboration with cosponsors from Canada, Mexico, and the United States, including boards, committees, and divisions of the American Psychological Association (APA); education and training groups; credentialing and regulatory bodies; and ethnic minority psychology organizations. Much of the work during the conference was accomplished in small working groups in which dialogue and debate among participants were encouraged. The working group in which we participated was charged with addressing the identification, training, and assessment of the development of competence in ethics, legal, public policy, advocacy, and professional issues. Group members spent most of their time discussing training and assessment of competence in ethics. This article presents an overview of the working group's product, enhanced by relevant literature and organized to address (a) the identification of core components of competence in ethics; (b) the critical educational and training experiences needed to develop the knowledge, skills, and attitudes to become a competent ethical psychologist; and (c) the assessment of ethics competency.

IDENTIFICATION OF CORE COMPONENTS OF COMPETENCE IN ETHICS

Although the working group was not expected to achieve consensus on every issue but rather to create a record of their discussions, noting both areas of agreement and disagreement, there was unanimous agreement on the following core components of competence in ethics. Through lively and collegial discussions and debate and the sharing of instructional models and practices, the working group came to a consensus that psychologists and psychologists in training need knowledge and skills for ethical decision making and intervention, including the following abilities:

1. to appraise and adopt or adapt one's own ethical decision-making model and apply it with personal integrity and cultural competence in all aspects of their professional activities;

From "Competency Training in Ethics Education and Practice," by C. de las Fuentes, M. E. Willmuth, and C. Yarrow, 2005, *Professional Psychology: Research and Practice, 36,* pp. 362–366. Copyright 2005 by the American Psychological Association.

2. to recognize ethical and legal dilemmas in the course of their professional activities (including the ability to determine whether a dilemma exists through research and consultation);

3. to recognize and reconcile conflicts among relevant codes and laws and to deal with convergence, divergence, and ambiguity; and

4. to raise and resolve ethical and legal issues appropriately.

The working group agreed that to accomplish the above identified skills, psychologists and psychologists in training need to obtain knowledge and awareness of the following:

1. the self in community as a moral individual and an ethical professional and

2. the various professional ethical principles and codes; practice standards and guidelines; civil and criminal statutes; and regulations and case law relevant to the practice of psychology.

The above summarized core components of ethics competency were considered by the working group to be the foundation of ethics education and were discussed as neither sequential in development nor discrete, but as overlapping and essential throughout the professional life of the psychologist.

The only area in which the working group did not reach consensus regarded whether *courage* is a core component of ethics education and a competency necessary for ethical action. Although some of the members of the working group maintained that courage is necessary for ethical competence and therefore a significant component of ethics training, others maintained it is a more general attribute.

Following the identification of core components for competence in ethics, the working group focused on its next task: identifying the critical educational and training experiences needed to develop the above identified core components of ethics competency. However, once we began our discussion, it became obvious to us that training for ethics competency necessitated the appropriate selection of applicants for training and an ethical training environment. These two components of ethics training will thus be discussed first.

GATEKEEPING: PROGRAM RESPONSIBILITIES IN THE SELECTION AND ADJUDICATION OF TRAINEES

Of course, ethics training programs are designed to affect the ethical decision making and behaviors of psychologists and psychologists in training; however, it is naive to assume that training programs can develop a specific moral character in its students, given all of the variables involved in creating moral behavior. Therefore, a comprehensive ethics education program obligates itself to (a) appropriately select candidates whose psychological fitness and moral character are not likely to interfere in their abilities to deliver competent and ethical psychological services and, once students are admitted into a training program, (b) monitor their capacity to process ethical and moral issues and dilemmas cognitively, affectively, and behaviorally. It was the consensus of the working group that training programs and the faculty in them have a responsibility to evaluate a student's personal and professional competence to practice in the service of protecting the public, the student body, and the profession. Indeed, the APA (2002) Code of Ethics clearly states that applicants and students may be compelled to disclose elements of their history (those bearing on character and fitness; Johnson & Campbell, 2004) if

> the information is necessary to evaluate or obtain assistance for students whose personal problems could reasonably be judged to be preventing them from performing their training- or professionally related activities in a competent manner or posing a threat to the students or others. (APA, 2002, Section 7.04, pp. 1068–1069)

Additionally, the working group members agreed that programs should develop an ethical training program that includes clear communications about expected conduct, remediation for professionally inappropriate or unethical behavior, termination from the course of study if a remediation plan is not followed or not a viable option (as in the case of impairment or egregious unethical or incompetent behavior), and due process and rights to appeal decisions regarding a change of their status in the training program (see also APA, 2002, Section 7.02: Descriptions of Education and Training Programs). We felt strongly that training programs become emboldened regarding the evaluation and dismissal (if necessary) of students whose conduct, character, or capacity demonstrates an inability to competently and ethically serve the public.

MILIEU AND MODELING

Working group members recalled and discussed many instances from their own training or programs in which ethical standards were required of trainees but not of administrators or educators. Because the most adjudicated offense in psychology is unethical sexual relationships between male therapists and female clients, what attitudes and behaviors are being modeled by psychology faculty who engage in unethical multiple relationships with their students? If people act morally because others have modeled moral behaviors (Rest, 1983), could not the reverse be true? Can what is taught in the classroom be contradicted by faculty–student relationships outside of the classroom? Are we, as trainers and educators, modeling attitudes and behaviors that imply acceptance of multiple relationships with clients, supervisees, students, research participants, subordinates, and others in positions of lesser power? Kitchener (1992) lamented that "silence best characterizes the discussion of the ethical responsibilities of faculty members toward students in higher education in general and psychology education in particular" (p. 190) and argued that the ethical principles should be the foundation of ethics education in psychology.

Training programs are responsible for providing an environment that is safe and nurturing of psychology trainees' exploration of themselves and the ethical issues inherent in psychology (Vasquez, 1988). The working group members believed that teaching ethical concepts and prohibitions, although essential and generally occurring during most training programs, is not sufficient and does not necessarily translate into ethical behavior. A comprehensive ethics training program includes (a) a living self-reflective application of ethical principles in the training environment demonstrated and modeled for trainees in order for it to become an enduring part of their professional identity and (b) a training that focuses not only on the therapeutic environment but also on the social and cultural contexts within which training occurs (Housman & Stake, 1999).

TRAINING FOR ETHICS COMPETENCE

Once the working group members discussed the fact that training for ethics competency necessitates the appropriate selection of applicants for training and an ethical training environment, we proceeded to focus on identifying the critical educational and training experiences needed to develop the identified core components of ethics competency.

The working group discussed our belief that multicultural issues often did not receive the consideration necessary in teaching of ethical behavior and practice. We noted that our ethical codes and ethical practice have evolved in a cultural context and with multicultural influences. We felt that it is essential that all training programs in ethics address the APA's published guidelines on multicultural practice; therapy with gay, lesbian, and bisexual individuals; and therapy with women, in addition to others.

The working group members agreed that training in ethical issues should be infused throughout the training curricula. Although the members agreed that training should be progressive in consideration of trainees' professional development, there was no consensus on a specific sequence for training. The following developmental sequence provides an outline of a set of skills and content areas that programs may consider as they train for ethical competence. The skill sets described below address content and process areas reflecting progressive levels of training.

Beginning students must be able to demonstrate awareness, knowledge, and skills of the following content areas: the development of moral reasoning and moral behavior; values and beliefs as emerging from cultural contexts; ethical codes and practice guidelines; ethical principles, virtues, and orientations; and relevant case law. Beginning students must also be able to demonstrate the following processes skills: the ability to explore one's own moral and ethical values and attitudes, interpersonal skills of flexibility, openness to new ideas and change, nondefensiveness to feedback, and awareness and appreciation of differences in moral and ethical values across cultures.

Teaching Moral Reasoning and Moral Behavior

Ethical behaviors have been seen as arising from several origins, one of which is morals. Although empirical studies have been published that offer a curriculum or model for teaching new professionals how to avoid or address ethically problematic behavior, many authors (e.g., Fly, van Bark, Weinman, Kitchener, & Lang, 1997; Welfel & Kitchener, 1992) have suggested that Rest's (1983, 1986) work provides some guidance. Rest's four stage model of ethical decision making consists of (a) recognition of a moral dilemma and related emotional response, (b) a cognitive understanding of the moral issues involved, (c) a moral course of action that is decided on, and (d) an appropriate ethical behavioral response that is carried out. Fly et al. (1997) suggested that ethics curricula that address all of these stages may be more efficacious in facilitating the ethical development of graduate students as they learn how to avoid ethical transgressions and produce ethical behaviors.

One member of the group, Richard Weinberg, described an innovative instructional tool, a morality genogram, which he uses to encourage trainees to examine the development of their own values and morality. In constructing this genogram, students look for critical incidents and other important influences (e.g., culture and religion) on their own moral development. Although morality is a dimension that is not often articulated in training, it is likely essential for ethical behavior. The genogram introduces this dimension as it helps trainees articulate how morality enters into ethical decision making in the course of one's professional life.

Ethical Principles and Virtues

An example of principle ethics in psychology was described in Kitchener's (1984) two-level theory of ethical decision making. Kitchener proposed that Beauchamp and Childress's (1983) five principles (autonomy, nonmalfeasance, beneficence, justice, and fidelity) make up the basis for the critical evaluation of ethical justification in the context of counseling and psychology. Instructors might consider discussing how the above principles have influenced the evolution of APA's (2002) general principles of beneficence and nonmaleficence, fidelity and responsibility, integrity, justice, and respect for people's rights and dignity.

Virtue ethics focus on the character of the individual rather than on the solution to a particular ethical dilemma. According to Meara, Schmidt, and Day (1996), the unique characteristics of virtue ethics is the identification of the motivation, emotion, character, ideals, and moral habits of a person who functions in the traditions and practices of a culture, group, or community. As ethics educators, we should demonstrate to our students that psychologists are informed by both virtues and principles in our professional practice.

In addition to the above, advanced students must be able to demonstrate culturally appropriate and reasoned ethical decision-making skills and ethical behaviors in (a) content areas including case studies, vignettes, and role plays in didactic situations and (b) process areas such as in their interactions with faculty, peers, clients, supervisors, and the organizations and institutions in which they work and study. These competencies necessitate the skills of knowing when and how to use consultants and supervisors appropriately and, with the information acquired from these sources, pursuing appropriate courses of action to resolve an ethical dilemma.

Many advanced students in psychology training programs teach courses at the undergraduate level. With this in mind, these students need also be able to demonstrate ethical decision-making skills commensurate with this practice. For example, advanced student instructors must address plagiarism or falsification of data by their students because these transgressions violate psychology's ethical principles of honesty and integrity.

Internship and postdoctoral trainees should be able to consistently demonstrate an integration of the above skills in a culturally appropriate, smooth, and compelling manner in all aspects of their professional lives (i.e., not only in the presence of an ethical dilemma) and, with appropriate consultation, recognize and reconcile conflicts among relevant codes and laws to deal with convergence, divergence, and ambiguity. Because most training programs at this level include training in supervision, the trainee should become familiar with the ethical and legal issues involved in this new role.

Working group members discussed that competence acquisition would be enhanced if, during the course of their training, trainees could provide feedback to faculty, training directors, supervisors, and administrators on their ethical conduct. This might facilitate the likelihood that trainees will become ethical and competent trainers for the next generation.

Professional psychologists demonstrate all of the above advanced skills and provide competent ethical consultation to others. The working group members discussed that psychologists are lifelong learners and as a result they join or form peer networks and consultation-study groups in which they receive and provide consultation and feedback on the competent and ethical delivery of services they provide. To encourage and facilitate this process, those jurisdictions not already doing so should be encouraged to consider providing continuing education credit for participation in peer consultation-study groups. These continuing education practices encourage discussion of the scientific bases of decision making in practice and may make it more likely that a psychologist will access appropriate consultation when confronting an ethical dilemma. In addition, psychologists take advantage of the numerous formal continuing education opportunities available that address the continued development and maintenance of their skills and ethical practice.

In summary, ethics and legal competencies are not discrete competencies that begin in the first year of graduate school and are completed by the end of training. These competencies develop along a lifelong continuum, from early moral training in childhood to the end of one's professional career.

ASSESSMENT OF COMPETENCE IN ETHICS

Following the identification of the critical educational and training experiences needed to develop the identified core components of ethics competency, the working group members turned their attention to assessment of competence in ethics. We reached rapid agreement that with regard to the components of competency in ethics, acquisition of knowledge and skills can be readily measured but that values and attitudes may be more difficult to assess as they are not created in graduate school and are not limited to professional spheres of activity. Nonetheless, we strongly believed that values and attitudes need to be identified and assessed for "goodness of fit" to the profession before competence in ethics can be determined.

In its discussions regarding training, the working group considered both formative and summative assessments to be very important. Much assessment throughout training is formative, such as determining whether training objectives in ethics competencies are being met (e.g., in courses and practicum). But at various points during a student's tenure in a graduate program, trainers must make summative decisions, most often occurring at transitions from one stage of training to another or when there is serious concern about the behavior and capacity for change of a trainee. Regrettably, most summative evaluations of ethics competencies occur by ethics committees and state boards that must determine whether a psychologist has violated ethical or legal edicts. Unfortunately, training programs are rarely made aware of these summative judgments made against their former trainees, resulting in a failure of a feedback process for their training curriculum and processes.

The working group members thought that multimodal methods of assessment were necessary to ensure that trainees develop ethical practice skills. Suggestions for modes of assessment included the following methods:

1. Assess for ethical integrity in every course throughout training including monitoring plagiarism, falsification of data, and misrepresentation of one's work or contribution (e.g., in the case of group projects) as these are all reflective of dishonest attitudes and behavior.

2. Assess for ethical competence in clinical training, including violations of confidentiality, sexual and nonsexual boundary violations, compromising the welfare of a client, distortion of information provided to supervisors, and procedural breaches with ethical or legal implications as these transgressions can have harmful effects on clients and reflect a failure to understand or abide by the core ethical values of the profession.

3. Assessments can also be made by the use of a 360°-type of evaluation whereby everyone in the training environment (i.e., peers, support staff, administration, faculty, supervisors, and clients) can evaluate and provide feedback to students and the program regarding students' interpersonal and ethical competence. One member of the working group related a situation of graduate students who did not report incidents of sexual harassment by

one of their peers until after he graduated. We agreed that although we might not be able to catch all cases of interpersonal abuse among peers, a 360° evaluation might provide a venue by which ethical offenses by psychologists in training and psychologists in the training environment may be addressed.

4. Assess how trainees respond to actual ethical dilemmas through the use of critical incident methodology. Such a methodology makes note of the processes by which a trainee has (or has not) recognized an ethical or legal dilemma, used (or did not use) consultation and supervision, used appropriate (or inappropriate) cultural and contextual sensitivity, and addressed (or did not address) the matter in an ethical manner. The working group members thought that this approach could be conducted in a transparent, public, and sensitive manner so that all relevant parties can contribute to the discussion and learn from the training moment.

Working group members identified a further issue with regard to assessment in ethical competence that trainers may want to be alert to. Interns are sometimes cast in the role of evaluating how more junior graduate trainees handle ethical dilemmas. This may place the interns in conflicting roles between the students and the intern's own supervisor or could result in the supervisor having less opportunity to directly evaluate the more junior trainee and address incipient problems. It is important to remember that it remains the responsibility of trainers to directly assess and address any ethical problems that occur during training, as these incidents may well be predictive of future ethical and legal transgressions.

ASSESSMENT OF THE ETHICS TRAINING PROGRAM

Peppered throughout our discussions, the working group members addressed assessment of ethics training programs. We agreed that training programs should request data on their students' scores on the ethics domain of the Examination for Professional Practice in Psychology and use the data to inform their training program development. In addition, working group members thought it would be helpful for licensing boards to provide information to training programs about the adjudication of their graduates. Such information could provide feedback to training programs about their (a) selection of appropriate students to train into the field and (b) the efficacy of their ethics training model.

CONCLUSION

Working group members found the opportunity for trainers and regulators to meet and brainstorm on the topic of ethics competencies extremely helpful. A member of the group recommended that a joint conference of regulators and the training community at the national level be held in the future to discuss innovative models and assessment of training for ethics competency. Such a conference would build on the work of the 2002 Competencies Conference, which has been reported in part here, and the proceedings could be developed into a case book of best practices.

We conclude with a quote from educator and ethicist Melba Vasquez (1992) who wrote "Professionals concerned with the problems of unethical behavior believe that the strongest weapon against professional misconduct may be the education of trainees" (p. 196). The working group underscored this belief and has offered a variety of ways by which ethics education may be improved and the standing of our profession and protection of consumers of psychological services enhanced.

REFERENCES

American Psychological Association. (2002). Ethical principles of psychologists and code of conduct. *American Psychologist, 57*, 1060–1073.

Beauchamp, T. L., & Childress, J. F. (1983). *Principles of biomedical ethics* (2nd ed.). Oxford, England: Oxford University Press.

Fly, B. J., van Bark, W. P., Weinman, L., Kitchener, K. S., & Lang, P. R. (1997). Ethical transgressions of psychology graduate students: Critical incidents with implications for training. *Professional Psychology: Research and Practice, 28*, 492–495.

Housman, L. M., & Stake, J. E. (1999). The current state of sexual ethics training in clinical psychology: Issues of quantity, quality, and effectiveness. *Professional Psychology: Research and Practice, 30*, 302–311.

Johnson, W. B., & Campbell, C. D. (2004). Character and fitness requirements for professional psychologists: Training directors' perspectives. *Professional Psychology: Research and Practice, 35*, 405–411.

Kitchener, K. S. (1984). Intuition, critical evaluation and ethical principles: The foundation for ethical decisions in counseling psychology. *The Counseling Psychologist, 12*, 43–56.

Kitchener, K. S. (1992). Psychologist as teacher and mentor: Affirming ethical values throughout the curriculum. *Professional Psychology: Research and Practice, 23*, 190–195.

Meara, N. M., Schmidt, L. D., & Day, J. D. (1996). Principles and virtues: A foundation for ethical decisions, policies, and character. *The Counseling Psychologist, 24*, 4–77.

Rest, J. R. (1983). Morality. In P. Mussen (Series Ed.), J. Flavell & E. Markham (Vol. Eds.), *Handbook of child psychology: Vol. 3. Cognitive development* (pp. 556–629). New York: Wiley.

Rest, J. R. (1986). *Moral development: Advances in research and theory*. New York: Praeger.

Vasquez, M. J. T. (1988). Counselor–client sexual contact: Implications for ethics training. *Journal of Counseling and Development, 67*, 238–241.

Vasquez, M. J. T. (1992). Psychologist as clinical supervisor: Promoting ethical practice. *Professional Psychology: Research and Practice, 23*, 196–202.

Welfel, E. R., & Kitchener, K. S. (1992). Introduction to the special section: Ethics education—An agenda for the '90s. *Professional Psychology: Research and Practice, 23*, 179–181.

COMMENTARY: It is important to understand ethics, and it is important to know which principles apply, when, and to whom. Then there is the matter of skillful execution, which is the province of "competency training" for students and supervisees. Knowledge, as indispensable as it is, is not enough to ensure that appropriate care will be taken on behalf of clients/patients and research subjects.

As observed by former American Psychological Association President Melba Vasquez and cited in the preceding article, "Professionals concerned with the problems of unethical behavior believe that the strongest weapon against professional misconduct may be the education of trainees." The education envisioned by Dr. Vasquez is not achieved merely through a reading program, as helpful as this component surely is. Trainees need practical exposure to multicultural issues, informed (as noted by Dr. de las Fuentes and her colleagues) by the dissemination of guidelines of the sort promulgated periodically by association entities dedicated to the needs of specific diverse and minority populations.

The following references are recommended for those interested in further investigation of the ways in which competency training has been applied to ethical coursework for students and supervises professing a wide range of clinical and research pursuits.

Dana, R. H., & Allen, J. (Eds.). (2008). *Cultural competency training in a global society.* New York, NY: Springer Science + Business Media.

Kaslow, N. J., Dunn, S. E., & Smith, C. O. (2008). Competencies for psychologists in academic health centers (AHCs). *Journal of Clinical Psychology in Medical Settings, 15,* 18–27. http://dx.doi.org/10.1007/s10880-008-9094-y

Leffingwell, T. R., & Collins Jr., F. L. (2008). Graduate training in evidence-based practice in psychology. In R. G. Steele, D. T. Elkins, & M. C. Roberts (Eds.), *Handbook of evidence-based therapies for children and adolescents: Bridging science and practice* (pp. 551–568). New York, NY: Springer Science + Business Media.

Pettifor, J., Sinclair, C., & Falender, C. A. (2014). Ethical supervision: Harmonizing rules and ideals in a globalizing world. *Training and Education in Professional Psychology, 8,* 201–210. http://dx.doi.org/10.1037/tep0000046

Westefeld, J. S. (2009). Supervision of psychotherapy: Models, issues, and recommendations. *The Counseling Psychologist, 37,* 296–316. http://dx.doi.org/10.1177/0011000008316657

3.5. Impressions of Misconduct: Graduate Students' Perception of Faculty Ethical Violations in Scientist–Practitioner Clinical Psychology Programs

Alicia M. January, David A. Meyerson, L. Felice Reddy,
Anna R. Docherty, and Elizabeth A. Klonoff

Academia is unique in many aspects of its environmental context, and this distinctiveness is perhaps most evident in the relationship that graduate students have with faculty members. . . . More than just the obligation to train students in ethics, implicit in the position is the responsibility to behave and model ethical behavior. However, empirical data related to the ethicality of faculty members' behavior with regard to graduate students have been lacking in the field of clinical psychology. . . .

CURRENT STUDY

The current study sought to (a) explore ethical dilemmas faced by students in faculty relationships; (b) investigate students' responses to these ethical violations, particularly the decision to disclose versus conceal knowledge of the violation; and (c) explore the emotional and academic impact of unethical faculty behaviors on students' perception of the training environment. We hypothesized that knowledge of faculty ethical violations would be uncommon, but that when students reported experience of an ethical violation it would be associated with negative evaluations of the program environment and diminished confidence in department and program effectiveness.

METHOD

Survey Recruitment Procedures and Participants

Participants were clinical psychology graduate students enrolled in Council of University Directors of Clinical Psychology (CUDCP) member programs across the United States and Canada. . . . A total of 165 programs were contacted via student liaisons (n = 114) or through the Director of Clinical Training (DCT, n = 51) who, in turn, disseminated survey information to all clinical psychology students enrolled in that program. The remaining four programs did not have a clearly designated student liaison or DCT, and thus, did not receive the survey. . . .

Although a total of 539 students consented to participate, 165 had substantial missing data and were excluded, and, therefore, final analyses are based on the 374 participants who completed the survey. A majority of the participants (81.5%) were women, on average were 27.18 years of age (SD = 4.33, range 22–55), and enrolled in graduate school for a mean of 3.11 years (SD = 16.81, range 1–10). Students self-identified their ethnicity as Caucasian (82.2%), Hispanic/Latino/a (5.9%), Asian/Asian American (3.8%), African American (3.5%), biracial (1.4%), Native American/Hawaiian (.8%), and 2.4% of participants specified "other" ethnicity. The majority of participants were seeking a PhD (90.9%) with a few expecting to earn a PsyD (5.3%) or a terminal Masters Degree (3.8%).

Measures

. . . The items of interest in the current analysis were developed by the authors to target two domains: (a) student perceptions of faculty problems of professional functioning, particularly ethical misbehavior; and (b) the potential impact of perceived ethical violations on students. . . .

To assess the impact of faculty competence issues on students, participants were asked to rate their level of sympathy (i.e., *How sympathetic are you . . .*) for different faculty problems (i.e., skills-based competence problem, relational competence problem, personal problem, violation of an ethical standard) on a 5-point Likert-type scale (1 = *very unsympathetic* to 5 = *very sympathetic*). Participants were also asked to indicate (1 = *strongly disagree* to 5 = *strongly agree*) how faculty problems might have affected them (i.e., negatively affected my own emotional state, negatively affected my ability to learn, made me lose faith in the faculty in my program, diminished the value of a doctoral degree in clinical psychology).

Students who knew of a faculty member who committed an ethical violation were asked a subset of questions, including the type of violation, their subsequent actions (i.e., did they tell someone, who did they tell, did they switch advisors, did they have direct conflict/argument with the faculty member), and how these actions affected them (e.g., negatively affected their emotional state). Students who did not know a faculty member who violated an ethical standard were asked to hypothesize how they would act if they were to witness a faculty member violating an ethical standard. An open-ended item was included to gain a better understanding of the types of ethical violations that students had either witnessed or experienced. Students who reported knowing a faculty member who violated an ethical standard were asked to briefly describe the ethical violations that their faculty committed. Consistent with qualitative research methodology, an inductive coding approach was used to analyze these responses (Patton, 2002). Specifically, the first and second author examined the responses for common themes and synthesized the data into informative groups that attempted to minimize overlap of categories. Based on participants' answers, the first and second authors independently evaluated and organized the violations into 10 categories, which was later simplified to an 8-category coding scheme (see Table 1). Reliability between coders was adequate (Cohen's κ = .74), and discrepancies between coding were resolved through discussion.

Finally, students' perceptions of program climate were measured using the Graduate Program Climate Scale (Veilleux, January, VanderVeen, Reddy, & Klonoff, 2012b). Climate is defined as students' subjective evaluations of environmental quality, including sense of safety, respectful relationships, and

TABLE 1. Coded Responses of Ethical Violations Committed by Faculty Reported by Students

Category	Actual Examples	Total *N* = 16 *n* (%)
1. Multiple relationships/ Boundary issues	a. Dual/Sexual relationships with students b. Dual/Sexual relationships with clients	26 (22.4%)
2. Research integrity and academic dishonesty	a. Not giving authorship credit when due b. Ghost writing c. Fudging/Fabricating data	24 (20.7%)
3. Respectful treatment	a. Sexual harassment of students b. Asking students to disclose personal information regarding their own treatment experiences c. Favoritism	20 (17.2%)
4. Mentorship/Supervisory competency	a. Refusing to use evidence-based treatments b. Providing grades to students without feedback c. Inadequate and untimely supervision and training d. Substance use at work	
5. Privacy/Confidentiality issues	a. FERPA issues/Disclosure of students' confidential information b. Permitting unofficial parties access to research information c. HIPAA violations (e.g., Talking about a client socially)	15 (12.9%)
6. Administrative issues/ Record-keeping	a. Financial misappropriations b. Poor fund management c. Poor record-keeping	5 (4.3%)
7. Lack of Multicultural sensitivity/Cultural competency	a. Cultural competency b. Discrimination based on cultural backgrounds c. Discrimination based on disability status	3 (2.6%)
8. Other	a. Avoiding harm b. Fidelity and responsibility	4 (3.4%)

Note. FERPA = Family Educational Rights and Privacy Act; HIPAA = Health Insurance Portability and Accountability Act.

effective organizational systems, in their clinical training programs. The Graduate Program Climate Scale is a brief, 20-item, single-factor measure with high internal consistency ($\alpha = .96$).

RESULTS

As can be seen in Table 2, the most common faculty problems (>50%) observed by graduate students tended to be around interpersonal abilities, feedback, and dependability, while more severe personal problems, such as substance abuse, were considerably more rare (<10%). Of central concern to the current study, 121 of the 374 graduate students who completed the study (32.4%) reported either knowledge of a faculty member having committed an ethical violation or having a direct conflict with a faculty member as a result of an ethical violation.

Those who reported knowledge of faculty violations had been enrolled in graduate school significantly longer ($M = 3.52$ years, $SD = 1.58$) than those who did not ($M = 2.92$, $SD = 1.70$; $t(372) = 3.27$, $p < .01$) and were more likely to be female, $\chi^2(1) = 5.55$, $p = .02$ (35.0% of women reported knowledge of an ethical violation vs. 20.3% of males). . . .

Students' knowledge of a faculty member who violated an ethical standard ranged in terms of type (e.g., fabricating data; providing inadequate

TABLE 2. Number of Graduate Students Reporting Faculty Problems of Professional Functioning

Faculty problem	$N = 374$ n (%)
Provide unhelpful/inconsistent feedback	241 (64.4%)
Lacks interpersonal skills	230 (61.5%)
Unavailable	216 (57.8%)
Punitive or critical	216 (57.8%)
Lacks self-awareness	211 (56.4%)
Unreliable	165 (44.1%)
Fatigue or burnout	151 (40.4%)
Lacks interest in students' training and professional development	151 (40.4%)
Lacks statistical skills	145 (38.8%)
Poor judgment	127 (34.0%)
Violated ethical standards	121 (32.4%)
Personality disorder	105 (28.1%)
Mood, anxiety, eating disorders	100 (26.7%)
Anger management problems	80 (21.4%)
Lacks intellectual reasoning	49 (13.1%)
Alcohol abuse/dependence problems	33 (8.8%)
Drug abuse/dependence problems	24 (6.4%)
Reported direct confrontation or conflict attributable to faculty's:	
Lack of relational based competence	110 (29.4%)
Ethical violation	35 (9.4%)
Personal problems	34 (9.1%)
Lack of skill based competence	33 (8.8%)

supervision, etc.) and severity (e.g., publishing poorly collected data; fabricating data). These data are presented in Table 1. Of the 121 who reported knowledge of an ethical violation, 85 reported the specific ethical violation(s) for a total of 116 violations that could be coded. The most commonly reported ethical violations were related to boundary issues and multiple relationships (22.1%), but many students also reported research and academic dishonesty (20.7%), disrespectful treatment (17.2%), and mentorship/supervisory concerns (16.4%).

We were also interested in how faculty violations might affect graduate students. To evaluate whether knowledge of at least one faculty ethical violation had an influence on perceptions of program climate and department effectiveness, we conducted a one-way analysis of variance (ANOVA) across groups, comparing those who reported knowledge of unethical faculty behaviors versus those who did not (see Table 3). Not surprisingly, students who endorsed knowledge or experience with unethical faculty behavior reported significantly lower overall program climate. Additionally, participants who experienced at least one faculty ethical misbehavior reported being less confident in the ability of their department to effectively identify or address issues related to faculty competence. When asked how faculty ethical violations might affect them personally, students who could identify at least one ethical violation believed that ethical violations contributed to a greater loss of faith in graduate program faculty and created more negative emotions (rated directly on a 1 *strongly disagree* to 5 *strongly agree* Likert-type scale) than did students who could not identify unethical faculty behavior. However, students were similar on ratings of how they believed violations of ethical standards contributed to the value of a doctoral degree and affected students' ability to learn. Notably, when asked how sympathetic students were toward faculty problems, students who reported knowledge of unethical faculty conduct reported lower levels of sympathy (1 = *very unsympathetic* to 5 = *very sympathetic*) for not only unethical faculty, but they also were less sympathetic toward faculty problems in unrelated areas, such as personal or relationship problems.

For the next set of analyses, we focused only on participants who indicated knowledge of at least one faculty ethical violation. Of the 121 participants who identified at least one faculty member who had committed an ethical violation, 32.2% ($n = 39$) reported that they told someone else about the violation (e.g., a faculty member, peer, administration, etc.). Moreover, at least 30.6% ($n = 37$) reported that they attempted to address it with the individual concerned or had a direct conflict with a faculty member over the ethical violation. Taken together, only half ($n = 61$, 50.5%) reported disclosing knowledge of the violation to someone else and/or addressing it directly, with a small percentage reporting ($n = 15$, 12.4%) that they shared their knowledge with another individual as well as handled it directly, through discussion or conflict. Using one-way ANOVA, we compared climate scores as well as confidence in department's ability to address issues related to faculty competence

TABLE 3. Comparison of Students Who Did/Did Not Report Experience With or Knowledge of Unethical Faculty Behavior

	Identified faculty ethical violation			
	No, n = 253 M (SD)	Yes, n = 121 M (SD)	F (df)	Cohen's d
Climate	3.14 (0.54)	2.71 (0.61)	F (1, 361) = 46.02**	.77
Effectiveness of department in identifying problems	3.07 (1.00)	2.52 (1.15)	F (1, 369) = 22.69**	.52
Effectiveness of department in addressing problems	2.86 (1.09)	2.08 (1.08)	F (1, 369) = 41.57**	.72
Sympathy for faculty problems	3.10 (0.77)	2.83 (0.78)	F (1, 350) = 9.93**	.36
Sympathy for faculty ethical violations	1.90 (0.89)	1.66 (0.85)	F (1, 317) = 5.42*	.27
Degree that faculty ethical violations:				
Negatively affects emotional state	3.39 (1.02)	3.80 (1.10)	F (1, 316) = 11.26**	.39
Negatively affects ability to learn	3.25 (1.06)	3.43 (1.10)	F (1, 315) = 2.13	.17
Negatively affects faith in the clinical faculty	3.73 (1.10)	4.05 (1.01)	F (1, 315) = 6.63*	.30
Diminishes value of doctoral degree	3.20 (1.23)	3.32 (1.21)	F (1, 317) = 0.72	.10

*$p \leq .05$. **$p \leq .01$.

between the groups of students who either disclosed (directly or with another individual) and those who reported keeping the information to themselves (see Table 4). Surprisingly, students who did not share or disclose the ethical violation rated their departments' climate significantly higher than those who did report the information. Furthermore, compared with the group of students who reported disclosing the information, the nondisclosure group reported greater confidence in the ability of the department to both effectively identify and address faculty problems.

Of the remaining 253 (67.6%) participants who had no reported experience or knowledge of unethical faculty behavior, only a small percent ($n = 6$, 2.4%) reported that if they were ever to gain knowledge of unethical faculty behavior they would not tell someone about it, whereas a vast majority reported that they would share the information ($n = 137$, 54.2%) or did not know how they would respond ($n = 110$, 43.5%).

DISCUSSION

. . . In the current study, nearly a third of the doctoral students reported that they had encountered a faculty ethical violation. This estimate is lower than the estimated 51% of graduate students who reported unethical supervisor behaviors (Ladany et al., 1999), but considerably higher than the reported 5% of unethical mentor behaviors (Clark et al., 2000). The reason for these discrepancies may be the result of sampling differences. Specifically, the Ladany et al. (1999) study included students in both clinical and counseling psychology, and asked about trainee experiences with supervisors at all levels of training (including at practicum and internship sites), whereas the questions in the current study were focused only on clinical psychology faculty within CUDCP member programs. Conversely, Clark et al. (2000) asked graduate students who had finished their degree program to retrospectively report on mentor behavior. The lower estimate found in their study may be related to either the retrospective nature of the questions or the more narrow reference (just mentor, not faculty broadly).

Not surprisingly, students reported slightly higher rates of research/academic dishonesty on the part of faculty in the current study (5.6%) than faculty self-reported the same behavior in previous research by Tabachnik and colleagues (Tabachnik et al., 1991). Interestingly, although multiple relationships, including sexual relationships with students, was one of the most commonly reported ethical violations in the current study, it was reported with less frequency by students (6.9%) than faculty self-report (Tabachnik et al., 1991). It is possible that certain behaviors, even if considered controversial and unethical by both faculty and students, are perceived with a greater degree of shame than others. For example, whereas fabricating data may be universally viewed as unethical, there might be more ambiguity in dual or multiple relationships on the part of a faculty member. Consequently, faculty may feel more comfortable self-reporting inappropriate relationships than disclosing

TABLE 4. Comparison of Students Who Did/Did Not Disclose Knowledge or Experience of Faculty Ethical Violation

| | Disclosed violation | | | |
	No, $n = 60$ M (SD)	Yes, $n = 61$ M (SD)	F (df)	Cohen's d
Climate	2.92 (0.61)	2.50 (0.54)	F (1, 112) = 14.88**	.72
Effectiveness of department in identifying problems	2.78 (1.31)	2.26 (0.89)	F (1, 118) = 6.40*	.46
Effectiveness of department in addressing problems	2.29 (1.23)	1.89 (0.88)	F (1, 118) = 4.28*	.38
Sympathy for faculty problems	2.86 (0.74)	2.79 (0.83)	F (1, 115) = 0.22	.09
Sympathy for faculty ethical violations	1.69 (0.84)	1.63 (0.87)	F (1, 115) = 0.16	.07
Degree that faculty ethical violations:				
Negatively affects emotional state	3.60 (1.21)	3.98 (0.96)	F (1, 112) = 3.54	.35
Negatively affects ability to learn	3.17 (1.10)	3.68 (1.06)	F (1, 111) = 6.37*	.47
Negatively affects faith in the clinical faculty	3.87 (1.10)	4.22 (0.89)	F (1, 111) = 3.48	.35
Diminishes value of doctoral degree	3.15 (1.25)	3.47 (1.15)	F (1, 112) = 2.14	.27

$*p \leq .05.$ $**p \leq .01.$

academic dishonesty. It may also be the case that students would be less aware of inappropriate relationships if they themselves were not involved or that the passage of time has resulted in changing social values and attitudes toward these behaviors.

As would be expected, we found that perception of unethical faculty behavior was related to a number of potentially undesirable outcomes. Students who reported faculty misconduct reported lower perceived program climate, less belief in the effectiveness of their department to identify and address faculty problems, as well as significantly less sympathy for faculty difficulties that were unrelated to ethical behavior (such as personal problems). Despite these relationships, when students who reported no previous knowledge of a faculty ethical violation were asked about their likely response should they encounter unethical faculty behavior, many reported uncertainty regarding how they would handle the situation; only a small minority reported outright that they would keep this knowledge to themselves (6%). Of the students who reported knowledge of or conflict attributable to a faculty ethical violation, almost half (49.6%) reported that they did not disclose the information. Although it is not uncommon for there to be a discrepancy between intentions and actions, it is unclear why, when asked to speculate, so few graduate students believe outright that they would remain silent in response to knowledge of an ethical transgression, but when students are actually confronted with the decision to respond to a violation, a much larger percentage choose inaction. Perhaps this suggests that ideologically, students may feel a responsibility to respond in some way to ethical conflicts and are hesitant to explicitly state they would remain silent when confronted with the knowledge, but in reality, when ethical concerns arise, the challenge of addressing or responding to violations in practice becomes overwhelming. . . .

REFERENCES

Clark, R. A., Harden, S. L., & Johnson, W. (2000). Mentor relationships in clinical psychology doctoral training: Results of a national survey. *Teaching of Psychology, 27,* 262–268. http://dx.doi.org/10.1207/S15328023TOP2704_04

Ladany, N., Lehrman-Waterman, D., Molinaro, M., & Wolgast, B. (1999). Psychotherapy supervisor ethical practices: Adherence to guidelines, the supervisory working alliance, and supervisee satisfaction. *The Counseling Psychologist, 27,* 443–475. http://dx.doi.org/10.1177/0011000099273008

Patton, M. Q. (2002). *Qualitative evaluation and research methods* (3rd ed.). Thousand Oaks, CA: Sage.

Tabachnick, B. G., Keith-Spiegel, P., & Pope, K. S. (1991). Ethics of teaching: Beliefs and behaviors of psychologists as educators. *American Psychologist, 46,* 506–515. http://dx.doi.org/10.1037/0003-066X.46.5.506

Veilleux, J. C., January, A. M., VanderVeen, J. W., Reddy, L. F., & Klonoff, E. A. (2012b). Perceptions of climate in clinical psychology doctoral programs: Development and initial validation of the Graduate Program Climate Scale. *Training and Education in Professional Psychology, 6,* 211–219. http://dx.doi.org/10.1037/a0030303

3.6. Ethics Education in Professional Psychology: A Survey of American Psychological Association Accredited Programs

Melanie M. Domenech Rodriguez, Jennifer A. Erickson Cornish, Janet T. Thomas, Linda Forrest, Austin Anderson, and James N. Bow

. . .

METHOD

Participant and Program Characteristics

Participants were 136 instructors of ethics courses from APA-accredited programs. The vast majority of questionnaires returned were from PhD programs. A substantial number of programs were clinical and followed a scientist practitioner training model. The response rate across specialties ranged from 34.5% to 41.4%. The overwhelming majority of programs required an ethics course. Ethics courses were most commonly offered on an annual basis and taught by core faculty. Instructors were typically experienced in teaching ethics and class size varied substantially. Most classrooms had doctoral students only. See Table 1 for specific data.

Sampling Procedures

The sample was drawn from the total population of APA-accredited doctoral programs. A list of programs was obtained from the annual report in the *American Psychologist* (APA, 2011b). It consisted of 373 programs in the United States and Canada. A team of undergraduate research assistants visited each program website and obtained the name and e-mail address of the Directors of Training (DT). DTs were asked to forward a link to the survey to "whomever teaches the ethics courses in your program." Participants were asked to respond to a brief survey and share their syllabus. An initial e-mail reached 283 DTs. When e-mails were not available, programs were contacted by phone. An additional 79 programs were identified. In all, nine programs were not contacted due to insufficient information. Of the 364 programs successfully contacted, 136 surveys were returned (37%). . . .

TABLE 1. **Frequency and Percentages for Participant and Program Characteristics**

	n	%
Program:		
Clinical	81	59.6
Counseling	29	21.3
School	23	16.9
Combined	3	2.2
Program model:		
Scientist Practitioner	100	73.6
Practitioner Scholar	28	20.6
Clinical Science	7	5.1
Degree offered:		
PhD	106	77.9
PsyD	28	20.6
Other	1	0.7
Ethics curriculum:		
Single course	100	73.5
Part of a sequence of courses	28	20.6
Covered in other courses	8	5.9
Ethics course:		
Required	130	95.6
Elective	4	2.9
Offered:		
Every semester/quarter	10	7.4
Every year	108	79.4
Every other year	15	11.0
Faculty:		
Core	119	87.5
Adjunct	17	12.5

Measures

Because no existing surveys to assess ethics education were identified in the literature, the authors developed the survey for this study. All but one of the authors are current or former members of the APA Ethics Committee, have a combined 80 years teaching ethics, and have published scholarship on ethics topics. The survey consisted of 20 questions. Each question was followed by a list of potential answers as well as an "other" category. Participants were invited to select as many answers as applied. . . .

RESULTS

General descriptive statistics are presented for each of the variables of interest. We analyzed the differences across program specialization (clinical, counseling, school, combined), training model (scientist practitioner, practitioner scholar, clinical scientist), and degree offered (PhD, PsyD). However, when the program characteristics were examined for overlap, we found that nearly all counseling (93.1%) and school (95.7%) programs followed the scientist practitioner model. Clinical programs were more variable with 62.5% scientist practitioner, 28.8% practitioner scholar, and 8.8% clinical science models. Of the three combined programs reporting, two (66.7%) reported a practitioner scholar and one (33.3%) a scientist practitioner model. Similarly, the overwhelming majority of PhD programs (88.6%) followed a scientist practitioner model, whereas the overwhelming majority of PsyD programs (82.1%) followed a practitioner scholar model. Only one program reported an "other" degree and it too followed a scientist practitioner model. Thus, analyses for all of these categories would result in confusing redundancies, so we limited comparisons to either program training model or program specialty.

Educational Strategies

The most commonly used educational strategy was lectures, followed by small group discussions (see Table 2). Over half of respondents used student presentations, large group discussions, and experiential exercises. All other strategies listed were used by less than half of the respondents. Across models, practitioner scholar programs (82.1%) used large group discussions more often compared to scientist practitioner (59.0%) and clinical science (28.6%) programs, $\chi^2(2, N = 135) = 8.54$, $p = .014$.

Educational Content

Topics

Educators reported on 36 topics covered in their ethics courses (see Table S1 in the online supplemental materials). Fully 100% of ethics educators reported teaching about mandated reporting and informed consent to treatment. An overwhelming majority (90% or over) reported teaching the following 11 topics: confidentiality, record keeping and documentation of psychological services, federal/state legal and regulatory issues, boundary issues/challenges, multiple relationships, conflicts between ethics and the law, competence, ethical issues in assessment, principle ethics, diversity/multiculturalism, and ethical issues in individual psychotherapy.

Clinical science programs reported less coverage of (a) principle ethics (57.1%) when compared to scientist practitioner (95.0%) and practitioner scholar (100%) programs, $\chi^2(2, N = 135) = 19.04$, $p < .001$; (b) decision making models (42.9%) as compared to scientist practitioner (89.0%) and practitioner

TABLE 2. Frequency and Percentages of Instructional Strategies Used in Teaching Ethics

Strategy	n	%
Lectures	130	95.6
Guest speakers	63	46.3
Student presentations	94	69.1
Small group discussions	109	80.1
Large group discussions	84	61.8
Experiential exercises	85	62.5
Educational Videos/DVD	48	35.3
Popular media Videos/DVDs	41	30.1

Note. n and % represent "yes" responses. Participants were asked to respond to all that applied.

scholar (92.9%) programs, χ^2(2, N = 135) = 13.61, p = .001; and (c) conflict between ethics and the law (71.4%) as compared to scientist practitioner (96.0%) and practitioner scholar (100%) programs, χ^2(2, N = 135) = 10.94, p = .004.

Practitioner scholar programs reported more coverage of (a) social media (96.4%) than clinical science (85.7%) and scientist practitioner (74.0%) programs, χ^2(2, N = 135) = 6.88, p = .032; and (b) professional issues (96.4%) than clinical science (85.0%) and scientist practitioner (57.1%) programs, χ^2(2, N = 135) = 7.42, p = .024.

Guidelines

Participants were asked about specific guidelines covered in class. The most commonly used document across programs (99.3%) was the *Ethical Principles of Psychologists and Code of Conduct* (APA, 2010). A far second was the *Record Keeping Guidelines* (APA, 2007), used by 72.8% of the sample. All others were used sparingly (see Table S2 in the online supplemental materials). Further analysis on guidelines by the program type revealed the following. Counseling programs were significantly more likely (41.4%) to include the *American Counseling Association Code of Ethics* (ACA, 2005) than clinical (6.2%), school (4.3%), or combined (0%) programs, χ^2(3, N = 136) = 25.56, p < .001. Not surprisingly, school psychology (39.1%) and combined (33.3%) programs were more likely to assign the *National Association of School Psychology Principles for Professional Ethics* (NASP, 2010) than clinical (0%) and counseling (3.4%) programs, χ^2(3, N = 136) = 40.35, p < .001.

There were no significant differences across clinical, counseling, school, and combined programs in their use of the Multicultural Guidelines (APA, 2003) to address diversity issues. However, there were differences in the use of the *Guidelines for Psychological Practice With Lesbian, Gay and Bisexual Clients* (APA, 2012), with clinical programs (54.3%) having the highest use, followed by counseling (34.5%), combined (33.3%), and school psychology (21.7%) programs, χ^2(3, N = 136) = 9.33, p = .025.

Finally, there were significant group differences in the use of *Record Keeping Guidelines* (APA, 2007) among clinical (80.2%), counseling (55.2%), school (65.2%), and combined (100%) programs, χ^2(3, N = 136) = 8.61, p = .035. Similarly, there were significant group differences in the use of the *Guidelines for Psychological Evaluations in Child Protection Matters* (APA, 2011c) among clinical (32.1%), counseling (3.4%), school (21.7%), and combined (0%) programs, χ^2(3, N = 136) = 10.80, p = .013. There were also significant group differences in the use of APA *Guidelines for Psychological Evaluations in Child Protection Matters* among clinical (22.2%), counseling (3.4%), school (30.4%), and combined (0%) programs, χ^2(3, N = 136) = 7.72, p = .052.

Assignments

. . . Half or more of the participants reported assigning a paper analyzing ethics dilemmas/vignettes and individual presentations. Fewer than half

TABLE 3. Frequencies and Percentages of Course Assignments and Activities and Teaching Practices

	n	%
Assignments and activities		
Textbook/s	123	90.4
Other readings (journal articles, newsletters, etc.)	128	94.1
Oral analysis of ethical dilemmas/vignettes	113	83.1
Paper–Analysis of ethical dilemmas/vignettes	93	68.4
Individual presentations	68	50.0
Experiential exercises (e.g., role plays)	62	45.6
Group presentations	54	39.7
Paper–Reaction	53	39.0
Paper–Research	48	35.3
Paper–Essays	33	24.3
Development of practice forms (e.g., informed consent)	30	22.1
Teaching practices		
Teaching by example (e.g., modeling thinking and behavior)	123	90.4
Developing a trusting relationship with your students	117	86.0
Providing learning goals	109	80.1
Using a Socratic method to promote students' independence	109	80.1
Providing corrective feedback to students: written	105	77.2
Having expectations and rules of conduct in the classroom	96	70.6
Providing corrective feedback to students: live/observed	90	66.2

of ethics educators indicated that they assigned research papers, reaction papers, essays, group presentations, or the development of practice forms. See Table 3 for full data.

Some interesting program model differences emerged. Practitioner scholar programs all assigned a text (100%), compared to scientist practitioner (89.0%) and clinical science (71.4%) programs, $\chi^2(2, N = 135) = 6.09, p = .048$. Scientist practitioner (98.0%) and clinical science (100%) programs reported assigning readings more often than practitioner scholar (85.7%) programs $\chi^2(2, N = 135) = 8.02, p = .018$. Nearly half of scientist practitioner programs (45.0%) assigned reaction papers whereas only one quarter (25.0%) of practitioner scholar programs did so. No clinical science programs ($n = 7$) assigned reaction papers, $\chi^2(2, N = 135) = 8.32, p = .016$. No other significant differences were found.

Teaching Practices

The most common teaching practice among ethics educators was "teaching by example (modeling thinking and behavior)." All of the teaching practices identified in the survey were endorsed by the majority of participants (see Table 3). Across program models, there were some differences in providing corrective written feedback, learning goals, and having expectations for classroom behavior. Practitioner scholar programs reported more instances using the three. Specifically (a) almost all (92.9%) provided corrective feedback in written form compared to scientist practitioner (74.0%) and clinical science (57.1%) programs, $\chi^2(2, N = 135) = 6.05, p = .049$; (b) almost all (92.9%)

provided learning goals compared to scientist practitioner (80.0%) and clinical science (42.9%) programs, $\chi^2(2, N = 135) = 9.14$, $p = .010$; and (c) most (82.1%) reported having expectations for classroom behavior compared to scientist practitioner (71.0%) and clinical science (28.6%) programs, $\chi^2(2, N = 135) = 7.83$, $p = .020$.

Teaching Goals

Ethics educators most frequently endorsed the following teaching goals: advancement of critical thinking, providing specific information and resources on ethics, and preparing students to use ethical decision-making models. This last point is interesting because fewer instructors endorsed addressing decision-making models directly under topics. See Table 4 for full data.

When examined by program type, scientist practitioner (71.0%) and practitioner scholar (78.6%) programs reported promoting students' self-discovery more often than clinical science (28.6%) programs, $\chi^2(2, N = 135) = 6.79$, $p = .034$. Practitioner scholar (50.0%) programs reported preparing students for comprehensive examinations more often than scientist practitioner (33.0%) and clinical science (0%) programs, $\chi^2(2, N = 135) = 6.73$, $p = .035$. Finally practitioner scholar (71.4%) programs reported preparing students for licensure more often than scientist practitioner (58.0%) and clinical science (14.3%) programs, $\chi^2(2, N = 135) = 6.73$, $p = .035$.

DISCUSSION

. . . Not surprisingly, nearly all of the ethics educators in this study indicated that lecture is a primary instructional method. The pervasive use of this teaching method likely reflects an understanding that ethical practice is not primarily intuitive and that, in fact, it requires far more than good intentions. Acquiring knowledge of ethics has been likened to learning a new culture (Handelsman et al., 2005), and sometimes unlearning previous assumptions is key to that training. Thus, a significant portion of what professional psychology

TABLE 4. Frequencies and Percentages of Teaching Goals and Objectives

	n	%
Advancing critical thinking	129	94.9
Preparing students to use ethical decision making models	126	92.6
Providing specific information and resources on ethics	126	92.6
Teaching the ability to make difficult decisions	118	86.8
Preparing students for practicum/field experiences/internship	111	81.6
Teaching the ability to tolerate ambiguity	100	73.5
Promoting students' self-discovery	95	69.9
Preparing students for licensure exams	80	58.8
Being a resource to students rather than guide	62	45.6
Preparing students for comprehensive exams	48	35.3
Maximizing empathy	35	25.7

graduate students need to know about ethical behavior is factual. Lectures may be the most efficient and effective strategy for accomplishing this objective. Reading textbooks, articles, ethics codes, licensing board regulations, practice guidelines, and federal and state or provincial statutes are commonly used to complement didactic presentations.

. . . Despite remarkable homogeneity among responses, variability is evident in teaching methods, course goals, assignments, and ethical issues, codes, and guidelines addressed. Differences between practitioner scholar and scientist practitioner programs (e.g., more frequent use of textbooks, less use of reaction papers) may be attributable to larger class sizes in some PsyD programs (Norcross, Kohout, & Wicherski, 2005). It also makes sense that there would be a stronger focus on preparing students for licensure in practitioner scholar than in scientist practitioner or clinical science programs. . . .

REFERENCES

American Counseling Association. (2005). *American Counseling Association code of ethics*. Retrieved from http://www.counseling.org/resources/codeofethics/TP/home/ct2.aspx

American Psychological Association. (2003). *Guidelines on multicultural education, training, research, practice, and organizational change for psychologists*. Retrieved from http://www.apa.org/pi/oema/resources/policy/multicultural-guidelines.aspx

American Psychological Association. (2007). Record keeping guidelines. *American Psychologist, 62*, 993–1004. http://dx.doi.org/10.1037/0003-066X.62.9.993

American Psychological Association. (2010). *Ethical principles of psychologists and code of conduct* (2002, Amended June 1, 2010). Retrieved from http://www.apa.org/ethics/code/index.aspx

American Psychological Association. (2011b). Accredited doctoral programs in professional psychology: 2011. *American Psychologist, 66*, 884–898. http://dx.doi.org/10.1037/a0026057

American Psychological Association. (2011c). *Guidelines for psychological evaluations in child protection matters*. Retrieved from http://www.apa.org/practice/guidelines/child-protection.pdf

American Psychological Association. (2012). Guidelines for psychological practice with lesbian, gay, and bisexual clients. *American Psychologist, 67*, 10–42. http://dx.doi.org/10.1037/a0024659

Handelsman, M. M., Gottlieb, M. C., & Knapp, S. (2005). Training ethical psychologists: An acculturation model. *Professional Psychology: Research and Practice, 36*, 59–65. http://dx.doi.org/10.1037/0735-7028.36.1.59

National Association of School Psychologists. (2010). *Principles for professional ethics*. Retrieved from http://www.nasponline.org/standards-and-certification/professional-ethics

Norcross, J. C., Kohout, J. L., & Wicherski, M. (2005). Graduate study in psychology: 1971 to 2004. *American Psychologist, 60*, 959–975. http://dx.doi.org/10.1037/0003-066X.60.9.959

COMMENTARY: There is no more foundational, consequential, and forward-looking setting for future psychologists, when forging an understanding of—and commitment to—the principles espoused by the American Psychological Association's Ethics Code, than those clinical and research training programs that the association has chosen to accredit. Identifying the presence of at least one course that is devoted in full (not a few courses devoted in part) to the substantive examination of ethical issues is a requisite component of the accreditation process.

Prominent in the survey conducted here by Dr. Domenech Rodriguez and her colleagues is an emerging focus on "where an ethics course is placed in the sequence of graduate studies." On the one hand, it is valuable to expose students to notions of professional responsible as soon as is feasible in their classroom-based training; on the other hand, there is much that would make relatively little sense to them before they have gained any practical exposure to the treatment and assessment of clients/patients. A requirement that there be at least one course in ethics does not suggest that there could (or should) not be two or even more.

The following references are recommended for those interested in further investigation of methods for inculcating ethical appreciation and adherence at that point where future psychologists are taking their first steps on the journey to professionalism.

Bingham, R. P. (2015). The role of university and college counseling centers in advancing the professionalization of psychology. *American Psychologist, 70,* 792–796. http://dx.doi.org/10.1037/a0039638

Erickson Cornish, J. A. (2014). Ethical issues in education and training. *Training and Education in Professional Psychology, 8,* 197–200. http://dx.doi.org/10.1037/tep0000076

Miller, S. A., & Byers, E. S. (2010). Psychologists' sexual education and training in graduate school. *Canadian Journal of Behavioural Science, 42,* 93–100. http://dx.doi.org/10.1037/a0018571

Moffett, L. A., Becker, C.-L. J., & Patton, R. G. (2014). Fostering the ethical sensitivity of beginning clinicians. *Training and Education in Professional Psychology, 8,* 229–235. http://dx.doi.org/10.1037/tep0000054

Regas, S. J., Kostick, K. M., Bakaly, J. W., & Doonan, R. L. (2017). Including the self-of-the-therapist in clinical training. *Couple and Family Psychology: Research and Practice, 6,* 18–31. http://dx.doi.org/10.1037/cfp0000073

3.7. Psychology Ethics Education in a Peer-Facilitated Laboratory Setting

Mary Jo Loughran, Deanna Hamilton, and Cynthia Magistro

. . .

This article describes a unique format for graduate education in professional ethics that integrated doctoral- and master's-level instruction in "ethics laboratory" activities for the mutual benefit of both groups of graduate psychology students. . . . In an effort to maximize student engagement in the ethical decision-making process, traditional lecture and seminar classroom sessions were held separately for students enrolled in either the master's- or doctoral-level courses in professional ethics, but were supplemented by laboratory sessions in which counseling psychology doctoral students served as team leaders for small discussion groups comprised of counseling psychology master's students. . . .

METHOD

Participants

In two successive years, two sections of a master's-level class and one section of a doctoral-level class in professional ethics were offered simultaneously during the summer term. Students in the master's courses were enrolled in either Chatham University's MS program in Counseling Psychology or MA program in Psychology. The MS program is designed for students to pursue licensure as professional counselors in the Commonwealth of Pennsylvania following graduation, whereas the MA program prepares students for doctoral study in psychology or related fields. . . .

The doctoral students were enrolled in Chatham University's PsyD program in Counseling Psychology, a program intended to prepare graduates for licensure as psychologists. The doctoral ethics course focused exclusively on the ethics code of the APA (2010). The program requires a master's degree in psychology or a related field for admission; thus, all doctoral students had at least one previous graduate-level course in professional ethics prior to their entrance into the PsyD program. . . .

Instruments

Tomcho and Foels (2008) conducted a meta-analysis of psychology teaching effectiveness studies and argued against reliance upon course grades in outcome assessment. Accordingly, we designed alternative measures to assess impact of the laboratory experience. At the end of the first year of the project, students were asked to evaluate their satisfaction with the experience by completing eight items on a 5-point Likert scale (1 = *strongly disagree*, 5 = *strongly agree*). For example, one item read, "The ethics lab on models of ethical decision making effectively presented content that I am likely to remember." Students also completed open-ended questions asking them the benefits or strengths of the experience and also their recommendations for future changes to the experience.

At the end of the second year, we modified the assessment instruments in response to concerns that satisfaction ratings might not accurately assess pedagogical effectiveness (e.g., Johnson, Aragon, & Shaik, 2000). Instead, we used three instruments to assess the effectiveness of the lab program: (a) an anonymous 16-item multiple-choice test to assess knowledge of the four topics covered in the laboratory component (eight items assessing knowledge related to ethical decision-making models, assessment and diagnosis, informed consent, and boundaries) as well as four classroom components (eight items assessing knowledge related to confidentiality, diversity, competence, and responsibility to the profession); (b) an 11-item Likert scale asking students for self-assessment ratings of their confidence in handling ethical dilemmas covered in the lab and classroom sessions; and (c) a set of four open-ended questions about students' experiences participating in the ethics laboratory: (a) How did the lab experiences in this class prepare you to be a member of an ethical decision-making team? (b) How did the lab discussions prepare you to practice ethically? (c) How did the lab experiences contribute to your development as a leader? and (d) Suggestions for improving the lab experience?

The instructors designed the assessment instrument to have content validity by drawing from the subject matter covered in the classroom and laboratory sessions, and common to the ethics textbooks used in both courses. In the interest of brevity, the assessment included only two items per domain, with the quiz items constructed with input and agreement from all three of the course instructors. Although this could not assess the breadth of student learning, the three instructors concurred that the ethics codes- and textbook-derived items captured core content from each domain. . . .

Procedure

Four laboratory sessions were conducted during the term on the following topics: (a) application of an ethical decision-making model, (b) ethical issues in assessment and diagnosis, (c) informed consent, and (d) boundary issues and multiple relationships. The remainder of the material for both courses was covered separately, thus allowing for a direct comparison of outcome assessments for the laboratory activities with traditional instruction methods.

For each of the laboratory sessions, the students at both levels completed reading assignments from their respective textbook on the topic prior to the group meetings. The doctoral students also read the master's-level assigned readings and familiarized themselves with the ACA Code of Ethics (2005). The doctoral students ($n = 9$) were divided into three teams of two and one team of three, and prepared the specifics of the laboratory activities in advance. In each of the four laboratory sessions, the master's students ($n = 30$) were divided into groups of seven or eight and assigned to a team headed by the doctoral students. For each laboratory session, each team was given an experiential task to complete in their breakout groups, such as a hypothetical ethical dilemma to discuss and resolve. Following completion of the assigned activity, the students attended a debriefing session cochaired by the faculty instructors for both courses. A more detailed description of each laboratory session follows. Case study transcripts and other course materials used in the laboratory exercises can be obtained by contacting the first author.

Session 1: Application of an Ethical Decision-Making Model

Students read and discussed a hypothetical scenario in which they assumed the role of the clinical supervisor in an agency in which one graduate student trainee reported another trainee for numerous violations, including alcohol consumption at the work site. The accused trainee countered that the complaints were unfounded and were, in fact, made in retaliation for a rebuffed romantic advance that had occurred in the week prior to the allegation. The students were charged with using an ethical decision-making model (Knapp & VandeCreek, 2012) to identify the issues for consideration and to outline a plan of action for dealing with the situation.

Session 2: Ethical Issues in Assessment and Diagnosis

This laboratory activity consisted of the analysis of a hypothetical case example in which a counselor is faced with the dilemma of assigning an inaccurate diagnosis to a client for the purposes of having the beneficial treatment paid for by the client's health insurance (Welfel, 2010, p. 99). In the case example, the client no longer met the criteria for a reimbursable diagnosis but wished to continue in treatment because it continued to be a rewarding and productive experience. The counselor concurred about the continuing benefit of treatment, but the client was unable to afford the counseling sessions "out of pocket" and the agency setting would not permit the client to pay less than the full fee for each session. In their small group sessions, doctoral students led their teams through each step of a decision-making model (Knapp & VandeCreek, 2012) to process the most appropriate course of action for the counselor to take.

Session 3: Informed Consent

In this laboratory session, the students reviewed and critiqued an informed consent policy for a hypothetical counseling agency that contained numerous errors, including descriptions of questionable business practices, misleading guarantees for positive outcomes, and omissions of important information. Students were charged with identifying problems with the hypothetical policy, citing specifics from the ACA (2005) and APA (2010) codes of professional ethics. The student groups then constructed revisions to the policy that were in line with the professional ethics code.

Session 4: Boundary Issues and Multiple Relationships

To explore the topics of boundary issues and multiple relationships, the doctoral students constructed a series of skits in which they role-played situations during which a helping professional might encounter the potential for a multiple relationship or a boundary crossing. For example, in one case scenario, the "psychologist" encounters his "client" in a coffee shop, with varying situational complexities that would potentially impact the most appropriate course of action for the psychologist to take. After processing the issues stemming from the skits, the doctoral students introduced a decision-making model tailored to address multiple relationships (Gottlieb, 1993). The student groups then used this model, in addition to the more general model introduced in earlier lab sessions, to come to a consensus about the most appropriate course of action for additional hypothetical situations, for example, what to do if the client presents the counselor with a token gift or invites the counselor to his or her wedding or graduation ceremony.

At the conclusion of each of the laboratory sessions, all students came together for a debriefing session conducted by the three course instructors. Each of the student groups reported their decision or resolution for the laboratory tasks to the larger group, and all students engaged in a question-and-answer session with the instructors in a town hall format to clarify remaining uncertainties.

RESULTS

Student Evaluation of the Laboratory Experience, Year One

At the end of the first year of the project, students evaluated the ethics laboratory experience quite positively ($\bar{x} = 4.11/5$). Responses to the open-ended questions were also positive. One master's student reported, "Master's students can see first-hand what the doctoral students have learned; doctoral students have the opportunity to demonstrate their skills to master's students and to themselves." These evaluation data were used to refine the content of the laboratory sessions.

Knowledge of Course Material, Year Two

In the second year of the project, the outcome assessments were designed to gauge the effectiveness of the ethics laboratory compared with the traditional instruction methods used in the remainder of the course. Our primary outcome variable was knowledge of the pertinent sections of the ethics code. We hypothesized that there would be no difference between students' demonstrated knowledge of content covered in the laboratories and the remainder of the courses. A dependent-samples t test comparing all students' mean scores on the laboratory-based multiple-choice questions with their scores on multiple-choice questions focusing on the classroom-based discussions found no significant difference between the means of the two content areas, $t(38) = -.41$, $p > .05$. The mean of the students' laboratory scores ($\bar{x} = 7.15$, $SD = .93$) was not significantly different from the mean of the students' classroom scores ($\bar{x} = 7.23$, $SD = .74$). Although our design precludes completely disentangling these effects, because we taught different content in the two settings, these nonsignificant results suggest that laboratory teaching of ethics may be as effective as traditional classroom teaching of ethics.

Confidence in Ethics Competence

In addition to students' demonstrated knowledge of the course content, we were also interested in how the experience of serving as leaders of a decision-making team impacted the doctoral students' perceived confidence in their competence in areas of ethical practice. We asked the doctoral students to complete self-assessment Likert-scale ratings to assess perceived confidence in managing 11 professional practice areas (five items covered in the laboratories and six items covered in the classroom discussions). Students' confidence ratings were compared for topics covered in the laboratory versus those covered in the classroom setting. Surprisingly, confidence ratings were higher for classroom-covered topics than the laboratory topics, $t(38) = -10.52$, $p < .001$.

Benefits of the Laboratory Experience

A qualitative analysis using a modification of consensual qualitative research (CQR-M; Spangler, Lui, & Hill, 2012) was conducted to explore students' perception of the laboratory experience. Two of this article's authors independently coded students' anonymous responses to open-ended questions for domains and categories, and discussed their analyses until reaching consensus. Most categories did not adhere to only one question but emerged in responses to several questions.

Doctoral Students

Analysis of doctoral students' ($n = 9$) responses to these qualitative questions yielded the domain of Benefits of the Laboratory Experience, with the following five categories, in order of frequency:

1. Students ($n = 7$) reported that they engaged with the ethics material more deliberately, reflectively, and systematically in the labs than in individual work. One student commented, "[The discussions] increased my awareness

of the multitude of options/courses of action that can be taken in any given circumstance, with some options being more desirable and ethical than others."

2. Students learned from hearing others' perspectives and came to consider possibilities they would not have generated on their own ($n = 6$). According to one comment, "It also helped to work with others who may take a different perspective on situations that I may not have initially considered, or initially opposed."

3. Students attributed an increased sense of familiarity and comfort with the language, content, and ambiguity of ethical decision making ($n = 5$) to the lab discussions. Specifically, one student noted, "I feel that the lab experiences have prepared me to become fluent in speaking the ethical language. I have developed a comfort in the new area of ethics." Another student commented, "They [the labs] helped to exemplify just how gray the areas are in competing standards with some difficult scenarios."

4. The lab experience provided an opportunity to develop leadership skills ($n = 6$). One comment read, "To lead a group of professionals in critical discussion takes a different skill set. The lab helps us start to develop these skills." A subtheme emerged related to students' perception of increased accountability resultant from their role as lab leaders ($n = 3$). One student remarked, "I feel that as a 'teacher' I am accountable for being knowledgeable, experienced, and up-to-date on the APA ethic code, state laws, statutes, and so forth."

5. The lab experience taught students to value the process of consultation or supervision ($n = 4$). An illustration of this theme can be found in the following comment, "[Working with the team] solidified and put into practice the idea of peer consultation."

Master's Students

In addition to the benefits that doctoral students who led the labs gleaned from the experience, the master's students also described ways that the labs helped their development as ethical clinicians. In fact, there was a great deal of overlap between the responses provided by master's- and doctoral-level students. Both groups reported that the lab experiences fostered a deliberative approach to ethical decision making, including use and knowledge of ethics codes, thinking through complex dilemmas in a systematic way, and wrestling with the many sides to ethical dilemmas. Additionally, both groups of students felt that their understanding of ethical issues was broadened by hearing a variety of perspectives from the other members of their lab teams.

Two of the authors coded master's student responses to the questions "How did the laboratory experience prepare you to be a member of an ethical decision-making team?" and "How did the lab discussions prepare you to practice ethically?" Two major categories emerged across their responses to these questions. First, many students ($n = 21$) felt it was useful to discuss ethical dilemmas in small groups in which they could hear and consider the perspectives and values of their peers and the group leaders. As one student put it, "The labs allowed me to hear and be open to other perspectives and opinions on the same topic. They enhanced my understanding about the procedures or steps to take but clarified how messy situations can be within the field." The second major category was related to the development of ethical skills ($n = 21$). Students felt that the labs provided opportunities to practice thinking about ethical situations in a systematic way that included practice applying ethical decision-making models, engaging with the code of ethics, and tolerating ambiguous situations. According to one student, "It made me think about ethical situations in a more organized and comprehensive way." Other students shared, "The discussions prepared me by helping me understand the process of ethical decision making," and, the labs "fostered greater understanding of the ACA code." It should be noted that although the vast majority of the students cited specific ways that the ethics labs helped their development as counselors, four students wrote comments indicating that they did not find the labs to be any more useful than classroom discussions.

DISCUSSION

Our outcome evaluations appear to offer preliminary support for the argument that participation in a student-led ethics laboratory can be at least as effective as traditional instructional methods in conveying requisite knowledge for ethical practice to both master's and doctoral students. In addition to the original competency objectives for the courses, prior to the start of the semester, we identified three goals specific to the ethical laboratories. First, it was expected that the lab experience would provide all students (both master's and doctoral) the opportunity to discuss ethical issues in a small group setting, similar in size to a typical treatment team in many practice settings. This goal was achieved based on how the laboratories were carried out. On average, there were two or three doctoral student group leaders and seven or eight master's students per team. Further, student comments supported the idea that the small size of the teams simultaneously exposed teammates to new ideas and created a safe, supportive space for them to process the ethical implications of the contributions made by each member. This level of detailed exploration is often not possible in a traditional classroom with 20 or more students, some of whom participate a great deal, while others remain relatively quiet. A second goal of the labs was to reinforce the value of peer consultation in the ethical decision-making process. This goal was achieved based on the nature of the lab assignments. That is, as part of the labs, students were asked to consult with the team leaders and team members to generate a variety of responses to the complicated scenarios that served as a starting point for each of the labs. Additional evidence in support of the second goal's achievement came from the qualitative analysis of the open-ended questions on the student assessment forms that specifically mentioned the promotion of peer consultation as an outcome of the laboratories. The third and final goal was to provide doctoral students with the opportunity to practice leading discussions of challenging ethical dilemmas. Again, we met this goal by the very nature of the lab design, which required doctoral students to lead, facilitate, and conclude each lab session. Student comments supported the achievement of this goal; for example, they reported that the labs provided valuable leadership opportunities that they otherwise would not have had. . . .

REFERENCES

American Counseling Association. (2005). *ACA code of ethics*. Alexandria, VA: Author.

American Psychological Association. (2010). *American Psychological Association ethical principles of psychologists and code of conduct*. Retrieved April 6, 2014, from http://www.apa.org/ethics/code/index.aspx

Gottlieb, M. C. (1993). Avoiding exploitive dual relationships: A decision-making model. *Psychotherapy: Theory, Research, Practice, Training, 30*, 41–48. http://dx.doi.org/10.1037/0033-3204.30.1.41

Johnson, S. D., Aragon, S. R., & Shaik, N. (2000). Comparative analysis of learner satisfaction and learning outcomes in online and face-to-face learning environments. *Journal of Interactive Learning Research, 11*, 29–49.

Knapp, S. J., & VandeCreek, L. D. (2012). *Practical ethics for psychologists: A positive approach* (2nd ed.). Washington, DC: American Psychological Association.

Spangler, P. T., Lui, J., & Hill, C. E. (2012). Consensual qualitative research for simple qualitative data: An introduction to CQR–M. In C. E. Hill (Ed.), *Consensual qualitative research: A practical resource for investigating social science phenomena* (pp. 269–283). Washington, DC: American Psychological Association.

Tomcho, T. J., & Foels, R. (2008). Assessing effective teaching of psychology: A meta-analytic integration of learning outcomes. *Teaching of Psychology, 35*, 286–296. doi:10.1080/00986280802374575

Welfel, E. R. (2010). *Instructor's guide: Ethics in counseling and psychotherapy: Standards, research and emerging issues* (4th ed.). Belmont, CA: Cengage.

3.8. Evaluating Continuing Professional Education in Ethics

Richard F. Ponton

Psychologists can expect to spend 36 hours or more in the course of their career involved in continuing education regarding ethics in 31 of the 50 states (Health Care Training Institute, n.d.). However, in 19 states, psychologists may not spend a single one hour in such activities during their career. Managers in medical facilities, mental health facilities, and other-care providing organizations will find that their multidisciplinary staffs will have varying requirements for continuing education, most with some ethical components. Psychologist-managers employed in government, education, and industry will similarly find a variety of requirements for ethics training across disciplines.

Perhaps as a reasoned approach to societal change or perhaps as a knee jerk reaction to ethical breaches that were both widespread and broadly impacting, such mandates have proliferated over the past three decades. The training mandates as well as other legislative mandates at the state and federal level reveal assumptions about the nature of ethical behavior. The training requirement suggests a belief that the likelihood of a moral or ethical choice is enhanced by continuing education. In states where the training delivery is limited to face to face delivery modalities, there is an implied assumption that ethics training cannot effectively be transmitted via distance learning or print media. The considerable time and money that is dedicated to continuing ethics education programs both by individuals and by organizations may lead the psychologist-manager to question the goals, assumptions, methods, and success of such programs. Such questions illuminate the need for a systematic evaluation of continuing education in ethics and provides the basis of empirical investigations focusing on both process and outcome. This article reviews the existing literature of ethics training in psychology and applies a model of program evaluation to the conceptualization of continuing education in ethics.

Both the importance and the challenges of evaluation can be highlighted through the lens of one hypothetical psychologist-manager, the C.E.O. of a small outpatient clinic. Dr. Doright lives in a state which requires 3 hours of ethics training for each two year license renewal period. He manages a staff of five psychologists, five mental health counselors, two nurses, and a psychiatrist.

From "Evaluating Continuing Professional Education in Ethics," by R. F. Ponton, 2015, *The Psychologist-Manager Journal, 18*, pp. 12–30. Copyright 2015 by the American Psychological Association.

Assuming a 40 year career, Dr. Doright will spend 60 hours in continuing education training. Dr. Doright wonders about the impact of ethics training on professional development and the outcome of professional service rendered to clients. Hearing the same conversations every two years, Dr. Doright contemplates the difference between 60 hours of training and three hours of training repeated 20 times. As a manager, Dr. Doright is aware that each of the professional staff members has similar requirements for ethics training. The organization compensates the staff for training and underwrites the cost of the training. Dr. Doright wonders whether indeed the needs of the staff for ethics training might better be addressed in a different way. As a manager does of all expenditures, Dr. Doright asks, *What is the return on this investment?*

The challenge of such questions is that psychologist-managers do not have a framework with which to approach them. With regard to ethical training, the goal, the process and the expected outcome is unclear. The purpose of this article is to review the literature of ethics training and apply an evaluation model to a discussion of continuing education in ethics.

ETHICAL DECISION MAKING

A fundamental question in the evaluation of any educational program is the identification of the domain. For continuing professional education (CPE) in ethics, that question is not as simple as it may appear. There are multiple approaches to understanding ethics and multiple assumptions about the nature and causes of ethical and unethical behavior (see Sommers-Flanagan & Sommers-Flanagan, 2007). Although a discussion of the nature of these assumptions is beyond the scope of this article, it is important to acknowledge that ethical systems differentially value reason versus emotion, the individual versus the group, objectivity versus subjectivity, and the transcendent versus the immanent. These differential values demonstrate themselves in both the development of ethical codes and the training and continuing education of professionals.

Rest (2008) suggested that a four-component model of moral behavior brings together the myriad of approaches to moral decision making by defining what must take place psychologically for one to act ethically. Rest's original model (1986) builds on Kohlberg's (1984) cognitive–developmental work which views the individual as progressing through a stage-like hierarchy in moral decision making and assumes that in normative development, knowing what is moral leads to moral action. Rest, however, acknowledged that moral action requires more than knowing. His model includes four components, with the first two focusing on knowing and the second two focusing on choosing and acting on moral decisions. Table 1 describes the four components of Rest's model: moral sensitivity, moral judgment, moral motivation, and moral character and provides exemplars of "ethical fitness" for each. . . .

TABLE 1. Individual and Organizational Components of Moral Decision Making

Rest's component	Mnemonic	Individual ethicality	Individual ethical fitness	Organizational ethicality	Organizational ethical fitness	Educational task
Sensitivity to moral issues	"See it"	The individual is aware of the ethical considerations of particular behaviors and responds affectively to moral questions. The individual can think creatively about the morality of a situation, beyond the concrete and immediate circumstance. The individual has not dulled his/her moral senses by gradual and incremental ethical transgressions.	Deepening and broadening ethical awareness through self-monitoring and authentic "ethic informing" relationships with others.	The organization at all levels understands the moral implications of its actions and has not dulled its understanding through gradual and incremental transgressions.	Organization has a code of ethics. Open channels for authentic discussion of ethics. Promotes ethical climate. Is aware of and calls out ethical slippage.	Promote the knowledge of ethical codes and standards of practice. Provide a framework for the individual and organization to develop awareness of challenges and slippage.
Moral judgment	"Think about it"	The individual is able to evaluate a course of action using cognitive skills that are related to decision making. The individual may apply a decision making model and effectively resolve the dilemmas of competing moral priorities.	Engaging in a planned and systematic process of decision making. Understanding the cognitive skills involved in moral decision making	The organization has processes in place that promote a shared rational approach to ethical decision making and a post hoc evaluative process.	Organization identifies a process of decision-making that includes all levels of personnel. Organization has formal ethics training program. Organization promotes an ethical culture.	Teach decision making process. Provide opportunity to practice the cognitive skills of decision making. Develop and maintain ethical processes for organizations.

(table continues)

TABLE 1. (Continued)

Rest's component	Mnemonic	Individual ethicality	Individual ethical fitness	Organizational ethicality	Organizational ethical fitness	Educational task
Moral intent	"Choose It"	The individual gives priority to the values that are associated with the moral ideal over other competing values	Engaging in clarification of values. Reflection on the systemic and interactionist influence on valuing. Acknowledging one's competing values.	The organization is aware of what its values and mission, takes active steps to announce them publicly and measures all ethical decisions in regard to their compliance with the mission and values.	Intentionally looking beyond the ethic of compliance to a organizational choice behaviors which are congruent with the organizational mission and values. Providing opportunities for employees to discuss the values that are driving organizational decisions.	Identify shared professional values and individual's personal values. Announce the organizational values. Examine congruence between the values and ethical decisions. Teach reflection skills.
Moral character	"Do it"	The individual has the capacity and is in the habit of choosing and acting on moral choices.	Reflecting on the congruence between one's moral decisions and one's behaviors. Announce one's intentions for a specific moral behavior.	The organization has a sense of its identity, values and mission and acts congruently with that knowledge.	The organization seeks to hire for mission and evaluates all decisions in the light of its covenantal ethical responsibility.	Promote individual and organizational reflection. Move beyond the ethic of compliance.

EVALUATING CONTINUING PROFESSIONAL EDUCATION IN ETHICS

. . . Continuing professional education (CPE) is often evaluated on the basis of the stated objectives of the program. Objectives are statements of what will happen to the participants as a result of attending the program. CPE programs are chosen for inclusion in conferences and training programs or as part of an organized in-service education program based on some assessment of the appropriateness and quality of the objectives. The participants often evaluate the program based on those objectives and plans for future continuing education are developed in response to such evaluations. Objectives clearly help to clarify not only what can be expected from a CPE program but also what was accomplished by it. However, the sole use of objectives in the evaluation of a CPE program is not enough to demonstrate its efficacy. Ottoson (2000) proposed the Situated Evaluation Framework (SEF), an evaluation model for CPE based on a theory of program evaluation that connects the components of evaluation, programming, valuing, knowledge, and use. It extends the objective-based evaluation model and provides a systematic foundation for the discussion of continuing professional education in ethics. Ottoson's framework for evaluation of continuing education will be explained and applied to a discussion of ethics training in the continuing education of psychologists.

SEF PROGRAMMING COMPONENT

The first evaluation component of SEF is labeled programming. This component provides information regarding how the continuing education program addresses the goal(s) of the training. According to Ottoson (2000), this component, "attends to a couple of deceptively simple questions. What is the CPE program? How is it intended to work?" (p. 46). The American Society for Training and Development estimates that more than $164 billion is spent annually on training in the United States (ASTD Research, 2013), indicating that the answers to these "simple questions" are of great significance. Specifically, the questions address the objectives and methodology of the CPE experience. The criteria extend the traditional evaluation of objective by evaluating the match among the purpose, ethical philosophy, learning theory, and pedagogy of the program. Additionally, these criteria concern the implications of the training on the work setting and the work setting on the training. . . .

SEF VALUING COMPONENT

Theories of subjective valuing in economics suggest that the value of something is not intrinsic, but is rather determined by the meanings and purposes ascribed to it by both the sellers and the purchasers (von Mises, 1949/1998). Closely related to this economic theory, Ottoson's model (2000) suggests that the valuing component in SEF examines how the evaluation process addresses

the priorities of CPE and applies those priorities to the evaluation of programs. She suggests that although all evaluation is a judgment of value against
a criterion, the priorities of the criterion are an important consideration in
evaluating CPE.

One such criterion of evaluation is participant satisfaction. In much of the
CPE in psychology, satisfaction has been the sole criterion. Following a CPE
program, participants complete a questionnaire that asks about their satisfaction
with various aspects of the CPE including how well satisfied they are with
how the objectives were met. Those responses are collated and provided as
"evidence" of the value of the program. This reliance on the value of satisfaction
is true in ethics education. Indeed, participant satisfaction is a readily measurable variable that lends itself well to Likert scales and quantitative data analysis,
but is it actually a variable that is valued in CPE in ethics? VandeCreek, Knapp,
and Brace (1990) said of the satisfaction criteria that "it would be surprising if
participant satisfaction were anything but favorable . . . studies of this type add
little to our evaluation of the effectiveness of CE" (p. 136). When accrediting
bodies and licensing agencies mandate ethics training, the goal is not to satisfy
the professional who will attend. When the leadership in organizations decide
to invest in any CPE program, participant satisfaction is a means, not an end.
Rather than participant satisfaction, other values drive the mandates and investment in ethics CPE. Sometimes aligned and sometimes competing, these values
represent social, political, ideological, personal, and professional inclinations
of the stakeholders. Thus, in establishing the evaluative process, recognition
of its value-laden nature requires both inclusivity and transparency. . . .

SEF KNOWLEDGE COMPONENT

Ottoson's (2000) third component of SEF is knowledge, in which she posits
that a fundamental element of CPE evaluation is "knowledge about how the
value of CPE is constructed" (p. 50). She explains that there is a bias in our
culture toward a positivist construction of knowledge which suggests that
quantifiable change is valued more highly that qualitative change. Thus,
those CPE programs which demonstrate increases in measures of quantifiable
variables are valued more highly than those which do not. For example, a
human resources manager might evaluate a health-benefits survey with data
demonstrating increases in employee participation in a 401(k). However,
Ottoson proposes that limiting evaluation in such a manner also limits the
type of knowledge (i.e., change) that CPE can hope to measure. . . .

SEF UTILIZATION COMPONENT

Ottoson's fourth component of SEF is utilization, which highlights an understanding of the use of the evaluation of CPE as foundational to the entire
evaluation process. The purposes for which the evaluation will be used will

direct what information will be collected and attended to throughout the process. An evaluation of a CPE program can have many uses, including program selection, program improvement, and program elimination. CPE evaluations can be used to promote change in a particular CPE course or in an organization's CPE program. According to Ottoson (2000), utilization can be instrumental, in which the evaluation is used by stakeholders to make direct changes. Conversely, utilization can be conceptual, in which the evaluation is used to enlighten stakeholders and change is gradually shaped by the information as part of a larger context. . . .

In psychology, there is a significant absence of data to support the impact of CPE on the work of the psychologist. Neimeyer, Taylor, and Wear (2009) summarized more than 30 years of literature regarding continuing education: "little attention has been paid to assessing actual levels of learning, the translation of learning into practice, or the impact of CPE on actual professional service delivery outcomes" (p. 619). Responding to this lack of outcome data, they surveyed 6,095 psychologists of the 40,000 members of the American Psychological Association regarding (among other things) their satisfaction and with and beliefs about the impacts of CPE in psychology. Their data suggested that respondents supported continuing education, with nearly 75% indicating it should be mandated and about 80% indicating that they perceived CPE to have helped them become more effective as a psychologist. Notwithstanding, there remains no objective indication of the effectiveness or impact of CE in psychology. . . .

CONCLUSION

Psychologist-managers approach the question of ethics training from several perspectives, including (a) as individual consumers of continuing education, (b) as leaders of organizations with internal or external training providers, (c) as training providers, and (d) as members of psychological associations. From each of these perspectives both an understanding of the components of moral decision making and a systematic approach to the evaluation of CPE will assist in making informed choices about ethics CPE. The hypothetical Dr. Doright illustrates the application of the model.

As an individual, Dr. Doright's, choices of ethics CPE program will be guided by a perception of the components of moral decisions on which Dr. Doright chooses to focus and an understanding of which components are being addressed by the program. Although variables such as convenience and cost will remain important (Neimeyer, Taylor, & Wear, 2010), a thoughtful understanding of the match between program and need may enhance the value of the program. Kilburg (2012) has noted that the APA Code of Ethics (American Psychological Association, 2010) is more applicable to psychologists working with clients in clinical settings than to those working in organizations. Thus, the program and value components would suggest that Dr. Doright would be more intentional about seeking ethics CPE with organizational and managerial content.

As a psychologist-manager, Dr. Doright may be making decisions about the content and processes of CPE for the organization. This challenge is compounded by the leadership role Dr. Doright plays in an interdisciplinary organization. Like many psychologist-managers, Dr. Doright will need a CPE program that balances and integrates professional values, ethical perspectives, and competing priorities (Sitley Brown & Folen, 2005; Mendelberg, 2014). An understanding of the nature of moral decision making and an informed process of evaluation will allow Dr. Doright to insure that the goals of the organization's training program are achievable. The SEF allows for the evaluation of the ethics CPE program as it is situated in the organization and in broader global and community contexts. . . .

REFERENCES

American Psychological Association. (2010). *Ethical principles of psychologists and code of conduct*. Washington, DC: Author. Retrieved from http://www.apa.org/ethics/code/principles.pdf

ASTD Research. (2013). *2013 state of the industry*. Alexandria, VA: American Society of Training and Development.

Health Care Training Institute. (n.d.). *Online continuing education approvals for psychologists*. Retrieved from http://www.onlineceucredit.com/continuing-education-approvalspsychologist.php

Kilburg, R. (2012). Ethical thinking: Beyond compliance to wisdom. In R. Ponton & I. M. Thorn (Fac.), *Conversation in ethics for psychologist managers* [Video series]. Washington, DC: American Psychological Association. Retrieved from http://apa.bizvision.com/product/PDP/conversationinethicsforpsychologistmanagers%286823%29

Kohlberg, L. (1984). *The psychology of moral development* (Vol. 2). San Francisco, CA: Harper & Row.

Mendelberg, H. (2014). The integration of professional values and market demands: A practice model. *The Psychologist-Manager Journal, 17*, 159–177. http://dx.doi.org/10.1037/mgr0000018

Neimeyer, G. J., Taylor, J. M., & Wear, D. M. (2009). Continuing education in psychology: Outcomes, evaluations, and mandates. *Professional Psychology: Research and Practice, 40*, 617–624. http://dx.doi.org/10.1037/a0016655

Neimeyer, G. J., Taylor, J. M., & Wear, D. (2010). Continuing education in psychology: Patterns of participation and aspects of selection. *Professional Psychology: Research and Practice, 41*, 281–287. http://dx.doi.org/10.1037/a0019811

Ottoson, J. M. (2000). Evaluation of continuing professional education: Toward a theory of our own. *New Directions for Adult and Continuing Education, 2000*, 43–53. http://dx.doi.org/10.1002/ace.8605

Rest, J. R. (1986). *Moral development: Advances in research and theory*. New York, NY: Praeger.

Rest, J. R. (2008). Background: Theory and research. In J. R. Rest & D. Narvaez (Eds.), *Moral development in the professions: Psychology and applied ethics* (pp. 1–27). Hillside, NJ: Erlbaum.

Sitley Brown, K., & Folen, R. A. (2005). Psychologists as leaders of multidisciplinary chronic pain management teams: A model for health-care delivery. *Professional*

Psychology: Research and Practice, 36, 587–594. http://dx.doi.org/10.1037/ 0735-7028.36.6.587

Sommers-Flanagan, R., & Sommers-Flanagan, J. (2007). *Becoming an ethical helping professional: Cultural and philosophical foundations.* Hoboken, NJ: Wiley.

VandeCreek, L., Knapp, S., & Brace, K. (1990). Mandatory continuing education for licensed psychologists: Its rationale and current implementation. *Professional Psychology: Research and Practice, 21*, 135–140. http://dx.doi.org/10.1037/ 0735-7028.21.2.135

von Mises, L. (1998). *Human action: A treatise on economics.* Auburn, AL: Ludwig von Mises Institute. Retrieved from http://mises.org/books/humanactionscholars.pdf (Original work published 1949)

3.9. On Psychology and Virtue Ethics

Frank C. Richardson

Virtue ethics has caused great enthusiasm in many intellectual quarters in recent decades, to say the least. Blaine Fowers' work in *Virtue and Psychology: Pursuing Excellence in Ordinary Practices* and other publications, a program of theory and research gathering a full head of steam at the present time, is the most extensive effort to date to mine the resources of virtue ethics for theory and practice in psychology. In this article, I will describe several key, representative notions and principles of the virtue perspective that I find particularly compelling, revealing, or helpful, and explore a few of their implications for the fields of psychology and psychotherapy.

THE ENLIGHTENMENT PROJECT OF JUSTIFYING MORALITY

One of the most exciting things I ever read was Alasdair MacIntyre's (1981, p. 49 ff.) account, in his celebrated book *After Virtue*, of the collapse of what MacIntyre terms "the Enlightenment Project of justifying morality." Here is how I would retell that story. Many people today look back with some nostalgia on aspects of life in premodern or traditional societies, in which people apprehend themselves in a "pretheoretical" (Berger, 1979) or taken-for-granted manner as being an organic part of a hierarchical and meaningful order of being. In such a life, as Clifford Geertz (1973, p. 90) puts it, myth and ritual tune "human action to an envisioned cosmic order and [project] images of order onto the plane of human existence." This can afford people meaningful roles to play in life and provide what Antonovsky (1979) calls a "sense of coherence" that helps make "affectively comprehensible" the uncontrollable and tragic aspects of human existence. At the same time, very few of us are comfortable with such a vision of life. We are steeped in the kind of modern consciousness and outlook, deeply antiauthoritarian and emancipatory in character that was fashioned in large part by progressively desacralizing the universe in order to undo dogmatism, domination, and irrational constraints on human liberty and creativity.

This kind of nostalgia for something lost coupled with keen ambivalence about it is just one manifestation of an acute cultural and ultimately personal

From "On Psychology and Virtue Ethics," by F. C. Richardson, 2012, *Journal of Theoretical and Philosophical Psychology, 32*, pp. 24–34. Copyright 2011 by the American Psychological Association.

dilemma that touches every part of modern life. Paul Ricoeur (1973, p. 156) called this dilemma the "antinomy of value," the "central antinomy of [modern] moral philosophy." The question is: Are moral or spiritual values created or discovered? In Ricoeur's words, "If values are not our work but precede us, why do they not suppress our freedom? And if they are our work, why are they not arbitrary choices?" (p. 156). We can't live with them but can't live without them, so to speak.

Long interested in moral philosophy, I always thought of modern moral systems like utilitarianism or Kantian/deontological viewpoints as timeless philosophical options whose adequacy we had somehow to evaluate. But MacIntyre (1981) argues persuasively that these systems are based on unquestioned assumptions about the nature of things, that when exposed to the light of day, turn out to be the creatures of a particular historical era. They were fashioned in response to its unique needs and pressures, and in many ways are highly questionable. MacIntyre suggests that these early modern moral philosophers in a posttraditional world genuinely wanted to honor both freedom and responsibility. Their problem was how to construe moral values so that they (1) do not violate hard-won modern ideals of autonomy and political tolerance but (2) still retain enough authority or credibility so as not to appear arbitrary or irrational.[1]

On MacIntyre's (1981) account, quite diverse approaches to modern moral philosophy represent versions of the same basic strategy in attacking this dilemma. First, this strategy attempts to ground morality in some familiar aspect of human nature or functioning, such as reason, feeling, or will, understood as morally neutral or as not defined in terms of its role in some wider cosmic story. Second, each of these approaches then justifies a particular set of moral values—typically a thinned-out version of inherited, traditional ideals—by arguing that it grows naturally out of the full and proper exercise of one of these basic human capacities. This scheme is artfully designed to preserve autonomy and disallow arbitrary authority at all costs. This commitment to autonomy is illustrated by Kant's insistence—even though he held sincere religious beliefs—that in order to conclude reasonably that we should do something commanded by God, we first would have to know that we *ought* to do what God commands, and knowing that, we would require a standard of judgment independent of God's commandments (p. 43).

For example, utilitarian moral theory portrays human beings as engaged in a kind of direct pursuit of happiness or pleasure, notwithstanding the perennial wisdom that genuine happiness comes only as a by-product of seeking the good or doing the right thing for its own sake. This view sees making moral decisions as a matter of calculating the pleasure and pain an action

---

[1] We might think of these philosophers as secular high priests of early modern times, attempting to explain and justify modern culture to its inhabitants. Perhaps, for many, that role is taken over by psychotherapy theorists and therapists in the 20th century, who try to show how the one-sided individualism of that era can nevertheless be harmonized with meaningful social ties and sustaining human relationships.

will cause and pursuing policies that produce the greatest pleasure for the greatest number.

The trouble is, such an approach simply assumes that people will opt for decent, civilized satisfactions and not for whatever they happen to find plea-surable or diverting or even sadistically gratifying at the moment. In other words, utilitarian thought really does not *establish* but rather *presupposes* a way of distinguishing between right and wrong or identifying the good life (MacIntyre, 1981, p. 63).

Similarly, Kantian liberalism takes the inherent dignity of persons more seriously than utilitarian views and argues that human reason, employing "no criterion external to itself" (MacIntyre, 1981, p. 43), dictates a rational test for evaluating the rules or maxims that guide moral choices. By fol-lowing his famous "categorical imperative" to act only on principles that can be consistently universalized without contradiction, he felt that moral autonomy is preserved and ethics no longer depends on either securing worldly benefits or capitulating to whatever we just happen to find pleas-ing. The trouble is, on close examination, it turns out that immoral maxims like "Only keep promises unless it is really quite inconvenient to do so" can be universalized without logical contradiction. It's just that most of us don't admire the way of life or kind of person such a principle allows. So, this approach, too, does not establish but rather presupposes a way of discern-ing the good or right life. The Enlightenment Project of justifying morality fails and we are left with moral ideals or convictions we can neither abandon nor defend.

There is no time for any of the details, but elsewhere (Richardson, Fowers, & Guignon, 1999), we have argued that other modern ethical outlooks, includ-ing Romantic or expressive individualism, modern existentialism, and even to an extent postmodern or social constructionist viewpoints, all represent more or less attenuated versions of this failed Enlightenment Project. Maybe 20th century psychology felt that it could avoid entanglement in this confusing and seeming irresolvable clash of moral visions by adopting a strictly value-neutral approach to investigating human life. But Fowers (2005) points out in *Virtue and Psychology* that this approach hardly amounts to ethical neutrality. It demands a significant, austere "detachment from the scientist's cherished beliefs and outlook" that ironically represents a "central feature of a character ideal" (p. 20), one that scarcely seems applicable to all phases of the search for understanding—which might require emotional sensitivity, ethical engagement, and wisdom, as well as certain kinds of objectivity, to grasp the meaning of human phenomena. Moreover, this ideal amounts to a confusing injunction that one ought to "value being value free" (Slife, Smith, & Burchfield, 2003, p. 60), opening the back door to the surreptitious embrace of one or more of these at least questionable modern moral outlooks that are then used in a consequential way to interpret one's data (or patients). The source of much of this confusion, Fowers believes, is that these diverse visions of human life *all* tend to assume the distinctively modern "fact-value split" or "fact-value" separation, which he feels is "neither possible nor desirable." Recognizing this sets in motion "the search for an alternative ontology that can encompass both facts and values" and offer a more plausible account of human striving for a good or decent life.

INSTRUMENTALISM

Another issue with these modern outlooks, from utilitarianism to existentialism, heirs to the Enlightenment Project, is that they tend to picture human agents as first, determining their goals or ideals in an inward, relatively private fashion and then second, implementing them in a social world that serves mainly either to facilitate or to impede those aims. This leads almost inevitably to the dominance in our culture at large and the social sciences in particular of a narrowly *instrumental* view of mature human behavior. Fowers documents the extent to which instrumentalism pervades the field of psychology, imposing the idea of a sharp separation between means and ends in human activity, with ends or goals in living chosen *subjectively* and most human action portrayed in terms of "strategies, methods, or techniques that are directed toward reaching a goal" (p. 56). He identifies two key features of the instrumental account. One is that there is "no necessary connection between one's goal and the means one adopts" to reach it, so the means can be discarded at no cost if another strategy turns out to be more effective or efficient.[2] The other is that an individual or group's "strategic expertise in reaching their goals" is strictly "independent of the kinds of persons they are," of their ethical quality or character (ibid.).

Fowers notes that the instrumental perspective appears to many to "leave . . . questions of goods and values to the individual," thus freeing researchers and therapists to focus on . . . value-neutral "causal connections and strategies." But he insists that "instrumentalism *is itself* an ethical framework because it dictates that choices of values and goals *should* be left to individuals" (p. 58). That is why ideas like "health," "effectiveness," "functional," and "well-being" function almost like god terms in most psychology. Merely to claim they are what you seek to "maximize" (another one of those god terms) puts your moral or social aims beyond question or doubt. (Who can argue with "well being?")

So, instrumentalism and individualism have to be evaluated as, in part, a moral vision (Christopher, 1996). They can't get by with claiming to undermine *reprehensible* ethical ideals by treating *all* substantive ethical ideals as merely subjective or preferential, especially when doing so is part of the

---

[2] So, for example, if instead of conveying to one's spouse how much one loves and cherishes him or her by taking the time and trouble to find an especially appropriate birthday or anniversary gift one can accomplish the same aim by just dropping a little pill in their drink at dinner, there is no problem or loss with the latter approach. It is merely more efficient.

defining *ethical* credo of modern society, one that many feel is ethically insufficient and begs for critical scrutiny. Indeed, most of us have a strong sense that the instrumental perspective is incomplete and has by itself a coarsening effect on personal and social life. Thus, we might find some merit in Fowers' suggestion that this view "tends to trivialize cultural meaning, dissolve the capacity to respect and cherish others, and undermine the pursuit of common goals, thereby eroding the very social foundations necessary for effective instrumental action," in its proper place, "in a complex and interdependent society" (p. 60).

However, coming up with a credible alternative perspective is another matter altogether. MacIntyre (1981), of course, argues that without an alternative way of enframing the pursuit of social and personal excellence other than a taken-for-granted sense of being embedded in a traditional meaningful cosmos, there is no way to avoid a slide into moral confusion and a deleterious relativism. Virtue ethics might contribute greatly to outlining or discerning such an alternative.

VIRTUE ETHICS

Virtue ethics is not a narrow ethical theory but a wide and deep perspective on human flourishing and the good life. It is ironic that we are as inarticulate as we are about key notions of virtue like character, excellence, flourishing, and practical wisdom, because so much of our common sense, our practical wisdom about living, our most valued relationships, the things we most admire about others and are proud of in ourselves, and our sense of priorities, of what is most important in life are very hard to understand or express except in terms of this sort.

In the late Tim Russert's bestselling last little book, *Wisdom of Our Fathers*, composed of letters from daughters and sons about their fathers, one woman writes that shortly after her parents' retirement, her mother became ill and was bedridden for over a year before she passed away. Her husband spent every day with her until her death. Once she said to him, "I'm so sorry about this, I know we had so many plans for the rest of our life that we won't be able to enjoy now." "What do you mean," he replied. "There's nothing to regret. All I want to do is to be in the same room with you." No philosophical ethic is worth its salt if it can't capture and convey the realities of loyalty and courage, and of human fulfillment that this little story reflects.

Human Excellences

Fowers (2005) stresses that "virtues are, simply, human excellences." There are excellences of things like craftsmanship and artistic endeavor and friendship, which Aristotle asserted was the greatest of the virtues. In *Virtue and Psychology*, Fowers' focus is on ethics and the good life, where the concern is "virtues of character" or "the character strengths that make it possible for individuals to pursue their goals and ideals and to flourish as human beings" (p. 4). This focus on excellence in the pursuit of worthwhile aims in ordinary life seems to me very helpful. Such an approach is distinct from "much contemporary talk about 'values' as an internal, personal possession." Rather, "There is no virtue without concrete activity" (p. 41), or "Virtues are embodied" (p. 67). This is part of how virtue ethics does away with the "fact-value split." Virtue or excellence does not reside in fine ideas located in the heads of social actors. They are embodied and are out there in the practices of ordinary life, which, in addition, "cannot be conceived as a set of individual actions, but are essentially modes of social relation, of mutual action" (Taylor, 1985a, p. 36).

Here is a hodge-podge of examples: the shrewd practice of democratic politics without cynicism or corruption; "good enough" parenting; questioning someone's political or religious beliefs in a respectful manner; cultivating the kind of loyal friendship that goes beyond mutual enjoyment and benefits; recognizing when generosity in the form of gift-giving is called for and selecting and presenting a gift appropriately; discerning whether it is wiser courageously to speak up or wait to join the issue another time, inspiring students to want to learn; exercising leadership among colleagues or in an organization that brings out the best in people; effective, timely psychotherapeutic interpretations; winning someone's trust without flattery or deceit; learning to write well; setting firm limits on a child while causing a minimum of guilt or discouragement; forgiving someone in a whole-hearted manner when at all possible; maximizing the honesty possible in social, political, or professional situations; learning to detect vanity or envy in oneself and dissolve or transform the emotions involved; gaining the ability to put people at ease in various life situations; discriminating when in the pursuit of justice that "the perfect may be the enemy of the good"; and so forth.

Maybe this gives a clue as to why Fowers (2005) writes that "The concept of virtue, [or excellence] encompasses essential features of individuals' psychological lives—disposition, cognitions, affect, motivation, goals, behavior, relationships, communities, and society—and shows how these elements of life can be brought into an integrated whole" (p. 5).

I hasten to add that these examples of internal goods or morally excellent practices are lifted for the purposes of illustration from concrete contexts of living that are presumably familiar to most readers of this article. They make full sense only in those contexts and even there are not unambiguously good, perfect, or final instances of excellent living. There are no such things. The ideals involved lose their meaning and vitality—they become static, stale, or dogmatic—unless they are periodically refined through the challenge of new circumstances or an encounter with heretofore unknown or underappreciated conceptions of the good life from our own or other traditions. These examples are offered in a descriptive, not a prescriptive, spirit. Individuals and communities will find convincing whatever they do in their search for meaning and ethical orientation. This process cannot be influenced by coercion or intimidation without significantly distorting it and the ideals involved. The point is only that *some* such goods and ideas of excellence shape the lives of people in any recognizably human society.

Emotional Experience

Just one example will have to suffice, one which I find particularly interesting and telling; namely, virtue ethics' treatment of emotional experience. According to Fowers (2005), the distinctiveness and appeal of this view comes out when compared with the available alternatives. The Romantic philosophical tradition that has decisively shaped humanistic and many other psychotherapy theories teaches us to see "emotions as spontaneous experiences that are beyond our control and rise naturally out of our inner nature." Emotional experience is a guidepost to exploring and understanding our deepest selves and should be "allowed to unfold naturally and unedited" (p. 44). But this approach affords us absolutely no way to distinguish between loving and cruel impulses and oddly makes us out to be hapless victims of them, whatever they are.

Fowers (2005) writes that, in contrast, "cognitive therapies and cognitive psychology generally, inspired by the Enlightenment tradition that extols rationality over emotionality, see affective life as largely secondary to patterns of thought and behavior," meaning that "emotions are to be regulated [and managed] rather than reverentially received and interpreted" (p. 44). But the positive genius of the Romantic tradition has been to show that this approach fragments the person into terminally warring internal agencies and tends to make a one-sided orientation of instrumental control the last word in human relations, undermining spontaneity and wholeness and completely ignoring the role such virtues as patience, modesty, loyalty, and forgiveness might play in a good life for humans.

The virtue ethical view transcends the dichotomy between such humanistic and cognitive approaches. It holds that emotions reveal "the kind of person one is" (Fowers, 2005, p. 44) and reflect the current state of one's "character strengths" (p. 9) or excellences in living. Character development involves nonjudgmentally and noncoercively schooling one's emotions "so that they are consistent with acting well" and make up an important part of the experience of what one takes to be the best kind of life. The person who has cultivated such character excellences can act "with a concordance of emotion, thought, and action," making possible a degree of "continuity, wholeness, and cumulativeness" (p. 66) in one's life over time.

Internal Goods

Fowers (2005) makes the notion of "internal goods" central to his exposition of virtue ethics. External goods such as wealth, power, prestige, or simple pleasures, comforts, and satisfactions, are the separable outcome of some activity, held as possessions by individuals. Their supply is usually limited and they are typically objects of competition. Internal goods are qualitatively different. They reflect a different kind of purpose and are found meaningful in a different way than external goods. One can attain "internal goods only by acting in the ways that embody those goods" (p. 65). Be it spending unstructured time with a child or friend, acting courageously without certainty about the outcome, creating or appreciating fine art, doing volunteer work in a hospice, or practicing meditation or contemplative prayer, the activity is felt to be good and is enjoyed *for its own sake*, not undertaken to reach any other outcome or product.

The idea is contestable, of course, but it seems that in personal or cultural life *external* goods are always "subsidiary to" and serve chiefly as an "infrastructure" for the pursuit of *internal* goods (Fowers, 2005, p. 60), which in some form seem to be presupposed even by those that deny them. Internal goods are not subject to competition because when realized, they immediately enrich the life of the wider community or anyone who appreciates them. We may, of course, feel envy or worse toward someone else's excellence or the admiration they elicit from others for it, but that occurs only because in addition to any appreciation on our part of the internal goods involved, we also remain unduly attached to external goods of power or prestige as ends in themselves.

It seems worth pondering the implications of this idea that, in the sphere of excellence or virtue, means are not at all separable from ends but are "experienced as central to *constituting* a particular way of life . . ." In "constituent-end" as opposed to "means-end" social practices, the whole activity, more or less excellent, "is undertaken for the sake of being such and such: I run as a part of being a healthy person, or I help someone for the sake of being a good friend" (Guignon, 1993, p. 230). For one thing, this suggests that internal goods do have, in Fowers' (2005, p. 69) words, a certain "primacy" in human life. Fowers states that "people in reasonably coherent societies are always guided by a more or less shared understanding of what is good." Thus, we are always contextualized in and shaped at our core by some moral tradition or traditions along with some internal goods, some shared moral outlook on the business of living that set the very terms of our action, reflection, and emotional experience. Thus, Fowers (2005) writes that "When humans are born, we enter a fully formed social arena in which long-established projects and practices are already underway. . . we are already committed to a form of life and a perspective on how to live it appropriately long before it is possible for us to reflect on whether and how we want to continue our involvement" (p. 92).

This primacy or centrality may be appealing but can seem confining as well to a modern sensibility. It raises the important question as to how we can gain the distance or leverage needed to critically evaluate our moral ideals and internal goods when there is "no possibility of stepping outside the flux of history to obtain a purely objective perspective" (p. 31), or question all of our assumptions at once. Virtue ethics may afford a way to both appreciate deep human limitations and encourage thorough-going ethical critique.

Cultural and moral values are "multivocal and dynamic" and "tend to resist precise formulation" (Fowers, 2005, p. 31). Unless our cultural traditions are dogmatically hardened into what might be termed "traditionalism," such traditions, Alasdair MacIntyre somewhere suggests, might be characterized as the "temporal extension of an argument." There are always tensions among our highest ideals, there are diverse and never fully harmonized versions of them, and they always require reinterpretation in the face of unique situations and unexpected challenges. Open and honest dialogue and reinterpretation of this sort—a never-finished process—may be what most fully can bring underlying assumptions to light and can compel a demanding reworking of them. . . .

REFERENCES

Antonovsky, A. (1979). *Health, stress, and coping.* San Francisco, CA: Jossey-Bass.

Berger, P. (1979). *The heretical imperative.* Garden City, NY: Anchor/Doubleday.

Christopher, J. (1996). Counseling's inescapable moral visions. *Journal of Counseling & Development, 75,* 17–25.

Fowers, B. (2005). *Virtue ethics and psychology: Pursuing excellence in ordinary practices.* Washington, DC: American Psychological Association.

Geertz, C. (1973). *The interpretation of cultures.* New York: Basic Books.

Guignon, C. (1993). Authenticity, moral values, & psychotherapy. In C. B. Guignon (Ed.), *Cambridge companion to Heidegger* (pp. 215–239). Cambridge, England: Cambridge University Press.

MacIntyre, A. (1981). *After virtue.* Notre Dame, IN: University of Notre Dame Press.

Richardson, F., Fowers, B., & Guignon, C. (1999). *Re-envisioning psychology: Moral dimensions of theory and practice.* San Francisco, CA: Jossey-Bass.

Ricoeur, P. (1973). Ethics and culture. *Philosophy Today, Spring,* 153–165.

Slife, B., Smith, A., & Burchfield, C. (2003). Psychotherapists as crypto-missionaries: An exemplar on the crossroads of history, theory, and philosophy. In D. Hill & M. Krall (Eds.), *About psychology: At the crossroads of history, theory, and philosophy* (pp. 55–72). Albany, NY: SUNY Press.

Taylor, C. (1985a). Interpretation and the sciences of man. In *Philosophy and the human sciences: Philosophical papers* (Vol. 2, pp. 15–57). Cambridge, UK: Cambridge University Press.

COMMENTARY: The "virtue ethics" movement in psychological education, practice, and research revolves around the notion that there exist "human excellences" that rely substantially on "internal goods," comprising the satisfaction personally derived from acting a morally supportive manner toward others. "External goods," on the other hand, reflect material rewards and also tangible advantages derived from or potentiated by the positive regard of others and are seen as complicating distractions that erode the purity and focus of internally motivated ethical behavior.

"Duty ethics," by contrast, are driven by adherence to preestablished rules, such as, for example, the American Psychological Association's Ethics Code. Duty ethics are not considered to represent an inferior or less laudable form of ethical comportment, but the "virtue ethics" movement in psychology is dedicated to reminding researchers and clinicians that there is much more to professional ethics than mere compliance with codes and guidelines.

The following references are recommended for those interested in further investigation of the role of "virtue ethics" in educating psychologist-in-training and for perpetuating these values over the course of a professional career.

Aho, K. A. (2012). Assessing the role of virtue ethics in psychology: A commentary on the work of Blaine Fowers, Frank Richardson, and Brent Slife. *Journal of Theoretical and Philosophical Psychology, 32*, 43–49. http://dx.doi.org/10.1037/a0025829

Fowers, B. J., & Davidov, B. J. (2006). The virtue of multiculturalism: Personal transformation, character, and openness to the other. *American Psychologist, 61*, 581–594. http://dx.doi.org/10.1037/0003-066X.61.6.581

Islam, G. (2007). Virtue ethics, multiculturalism, and the paradox of cultural dialogue. *American Psychologist, 62*, 704–705. http://dx.doi.org/10.1037/0003-066X.62.7.704

Sisti, D. A., & Baum-Baicker, C. (2012). A plea for virtue in ethics. *American Psychologist, 67*, 325. http://dx.doi.org/10.1037/a0028162

Slife, B. D. (2012). Virtue ethics in practice: The Greenbrier Academy. *Journal of Theoretical and Philosophical Psychology, 32*, 35–42. http://dx.doi.org/10.1037/a0026443

4

Confidentiality, Privilege, and Privacy

onfidentiality, privilege, and *privacy* are terms that are often used interchangeably but that in fact represent distinct notions with overlapping
features. Taken together, they form essential prerequisites for client/patient
or research subject participation, from practical and ethical standpoints alike.
Who would avail oneself of psychological services knowing that statements
made and data gathered could be broadcast to the world, and who would
attempt to provide such services under such circumstances?

Of the three, *confidentiality* is the notion that resides most squarely within
the territory of professional ethics. It addresses an ethical obligation not to share
information obtained in the contexts of treatment and research. This obligation
is not absolute, for a host of reasons. For one, it is typically the case that more
than one individual may be present or otherwise involved before, during, or
after an initial point of contact. These might include, for example, other group
therapy clients/patients, office staff, cotherapists, and research assistants. For
another, there may those who are potentially involved on varying "need to
know" bases, such as parents of minor children, targets of threatened harm,
and insurance company employees.

Privilege is a legal construct with ethical ramifications. It constitutes an
exception to the usual ability of attorneys and judges to identify, obtain, and
have entered into evidence certain documents, utterances, and other protected
information. Often lost in the last-minute scuffling over legally relevant disclosure is the fact that it is the client/patient or—on occasion—the research
subject who is the true "owner" of the privilege. Typically inhabiting what

http://dx.doi.org/10.1037/0000125-005
Ethical Conflicts in Psychology, Fifth Edition, by E. Y. Drogin

experts acknowledge as a poorly defined nether region between legal and ethical mandates is the extent of the psychologist's obligation to protect that privilege on another's behalf. This is most readily observed in frequently misunderstood shifts, in recent years, in the perspective of the American Psychological Association's (APA's; 2017) *Ethical Principles of Psychologists and Code of Conduct* (APA Ethics Code) on the surrender of either "test data" or "test materials."

Privacy straddles both law and ethics and, beyond that, is a notion that reflects ingrained aspects of social custom as well. Unlike the more technically defined notions of confidentiality and privilege, privacy is usually reflected more in the spirit than in the letter of case law, statutes, regulations, and codes and guidelines for professional responsibility. Laypersons can be sued civilly— or indicted criminally—for an invasion of privacy, as can psychologists, on whom the APA Ethics Code does place a burden to minimize intrusions on privacy and to inform clients/patients of certain risks to privacy that typically the provision of professional services.

Among its other features, this chapter addresses malpractice-related ramifications of confidentiality breaches, risk containment strategies for psychologists facing mandated reporting requirements, special confidentiality considerations in providing services to diverse client/patient populations, the maintenance and protection of electronic health records, and public policy considerations for the field of psychology in matters of confidentiality, privilege, and privacy.

REFERENCE

American Psychological Association. (2017). *Ethical principles of psychologists and code of conduct* (2002, Amended June 1, 2010 and January 1, 2017). Retrieved from http://www.apa.org/ethics/code/index.aspx

4.1. Privacy and Confidentiality

Thomas F. Nagy

A 41-year-old man with depression was referred by his primary care physician to Dr. Teller for treatment. In the first session, the patient revealed that he had recently divorced and was experiencing chronic pelvic pain and many depressing thoughts. Dr. Teller described how therapy would proceed, discussed fees and length of sessions, and gave a general description of his theoretical orientation. He said little about confidentiality and its limits, however.

In the second session, Dr. Teller informed his patient that he had contacted his primary care physician to learn of his medical history. He had also revealed the patient's history to the physician, including disclosures about the man's experiences of childhood sexual abuse. The patient was distressed that the therapist had done so without first obtaining his authorization. It is true that he had consented to contacting his physician and obtaining additional medical history from him, but he did not want Dr. Teller disclosing details of his early sexual abuse to him. He abruptly terminated treatment with Dr. Teller, feeling that the trust had been broken.

INTRODUCTION

Maintaining privacy and confidentiality has long been an essential ingredient in the work of psychologists. This includes psychotherapy, management consulting, research, academic settings, and virtually any situation in which personal information is disclosed to a psychologist with the expectation that it will be held in confidence. Confidentiality was addressed in the very first Ethics Code, informing American Psychological Association (APA) members that safeguarding information about an individual was a "primary obligation of the psychologist" (APA, 1953). . . .

PRIVACY, CONFIDENTIALITY, AND PRIVILEGED COMMUNICATION

. . .

Privacy

Privacy speaks to the relationship between the psychologist and other individuals (e.g., patients, clients, supervisees). As a general concept, privacy is an

From *Essential Ethics for Psychologists: A Primer for Understanding and Mastering Core Issues* (pp. 105–126), by T. F. Nagy, 2011, Washington, DC: American Psychological Association. Copyright 2011 by the American Psychological Association.

integral part of the professional relationship; what is revealed in the consulting office must remain there. Even the fact that the consultation occurred is a private matter if the professional relationship is to be effective and helpful to the client. . . .

Confidentiality

Confidentiality concerns the information that is gathered or held by psychologists. It includes the specific obligation, both ethical and legal, that private information must be safely maintained and never revealed to others, voluntarily or in response to a formal request (e.g., from family members, employers, other interested parties), unless certain conditions are met. . . .

The APA has been in the forefront in defining and promulgating confidentiality in its Ethics Code, casebooks, and ethics committee adjudications since the first Ethics Code was published (Caudill & Kaplan, 2005). However, legal statutes defining confidentiality on a federal or state basis have been relatively recent. These address the concept of privileged communication and form the basis for rules concerning compelled discovery of the clinical records of mental health providers. There are many exceptions to confidentiality as well, such as disclosures concerning one's intention to harm oneself or another or revelations of child abuse; these are explored later. Although the Ethics Code does not specifically require psychologists to disclose these exceptions in writing to new patient and clients, many states do have such a rule.

Privileged Communication

Privileged communication refers to the legal right of an individual to shield confidential disclosures made to a psychologist from any judicial proceedings or court of law. These include trials, depositions, and subpoenas for examining clinical records (Kaplan, 2005). . . .

PRIVACY AND CONFIDENTIALITY IN RESEARCH SETTINGS

Investigators have been obliged to maintain the privacy of individuals and protect the confidentiality of any information gathered about them in the course of data gathering since the very first code was written in 1953. . . . Since then, the concepts of privacy and confidentiality have expanded in scope far beyond protecting the identity of research subjects, as have the threats to safeguarding them, as a result, in part, of the complexity of research and the innovations in technology. To review, privacy pertains to one's interest in controlling others' access to information about one, whereas confidentiality pertains to the psychologist's obligation to safely maintain private information that is revealed in the course of a professional relationship with a researcher. Let us examine these two concepts as well as the risks to each.

Privacy in Research Settings

Privacy is not only a relevant concept for individual research participants but also has implications for the outcome of research and, ultimately, the body of research knowledge in psychology itself. Participants who feel their privacy is not secure may have anxiety about the consequences of revealing their personal information and responses in the course of an investigation, doubting that their anonymity will be respected. And in addition to increased anxiety about participating in research, these participants may be evasive in their responses or withdraw from the research altogether, resulting in biased sampling as well as a threat to the validity and usefulness of the data (Folkman, 2000). . . .

Current understandings of privacy consist of two elements that go far beyond simply protecting the identity of the participant. The first pertains to participants' freedom to select the time and circumstances under which facts about them and the extent to which their attitudes, beliefs, behavior, and opinions will be revealed to or withheld from others (Kelman, 1972). This freedom is largely dependent on providing comprehensive informed consent, allowing prospective participants to learn about any aspect of the research project that might affect their willingness to volunteer as a subject. The second aspect of privacy protects participants' right to avoid receiving information that they might not want to know about (Sieber, 1992). This might include feedback about their own HIV status, their performance or score on a competitive task compared with other participants, personality traits assessed during the course of the investigation, or information that might be considered offensive or anxiety provoking (e.g., learning that they scored higher on measures of paranoid thinking or willingness to lie or cheat compared with the norm). Another example would be receiving information that a participant might consider to be pornographic, such as research involving sexual attitudes or behavior (Folkman, 2000).

Confidentiality in Research Settings

Confidentiality pertains to the agreements psychologists make with research participants about the use of their data. Researchers are expected to protect the privacy of participants' data (i.e., not share with others) unless they are authorized to do so or there is some other justification. For example, investigators commonly assign code numbers instead of using actual names of participants. Video or audio recording of participants presents somewhat more of a challenge to the investigator because the study may involve raters evaluating the recordings and, obviously, the necessity of seeing clear images of the facial expressions or hearing sound recordings that could also clearly reveal the identity of the participant. Here the concept of *informed consent* would be tightly linked to confidentiality because the prospective participant would be made aware early in the explanation of the research protocol that his or her image will not only be captured but also revealed to others. It would also add an additional level of security for the participant to be informed of the identity of those who would actually view or evaluate the video- or audiotapes in advance; in that way, the participant would know if there was a risk of revealing his or her private information to a person already known to him and could opt out of participating in the project. . . .

PRIVACY AND CONFIDENTIALITY IN ACADEMIC SETTINGS

Psychologists who hold academic or training positions are also expected to respect the privacy of their students and supervisees, including instructors, teaching assistants, clinical supervisors in training settings, and anyone else involved in teaching students of any age or stage of development. Those teaching graduate students or supervising training in clinical settings must avoid certain personally sensitive subjects, such as the student's or supervisee's sexual history; history of abuse and neglect; psychological treatment; and relationships with parents, peers, spouses, and significant others (APA, 2010).

There are two exceptions to this ethical rule allowing educators to broach these topics if (a) the training program has disclosed such requirements of self-disclosure in its admission materials or (b) the information being sought is essential to help students with personal problems that are interfering with their current training and professional duties (e.g., the competent rendering of personal counseling or therapy) or pose a threat to fellow students or others. The first exception specifically has to do with informed consent—what the student entering the program or signing up to take a class was informed of about requirements concerning revealing such private information by the instructor at the outset or in the course catalogue. The second exception clearly addresses the situation in which a teaching assistant, practicum student, or therapist trainee under supervision is experiencing impairment in mental health (e.g., major depression, anxiety disorder) or a life event (e.g., illness or chronic pain, divorce, death of a family member) that diminishes his or her ability to carry out his or her work as a psychology trainee. In these situations the trainee's personal stress may prevent a trainee from completing professional responsibilities or impair his or her ability to maintain professional boundaries, resulting in the befriending of clients or patients or seeking solace by engaging them in romantic relationships.

When client or patient information is used for didactic purposes, such as a professor's clinical vignette from his or her therapy practice to describe obsessive-compulsive personality, great care must be taken to adequately disguise the patient whose private information is now being put on display. This can be done by altering identifying information such as the gender, age, ethnicity, and details of the patient's situation before presenting it in public. It is also wise to inform listeners that this necessary deception has occurred, lest they believe that confidentiality is being disregarded. Whenever clinical data are used in publications, such as journal articles or books, it is essential to obtain specific consent from patients to do so; otherwise, the author must carefully disguise salient details of patients' situations to protect their privacy.

PRIVACY AND CONFIDENTIALITY IN CLINICAL AND COUNSELING SETTINGS

. . .

Ethical Rules Concerning Privacy and Confidentiality

Ethically, psychologists must inform new clients and patients about their rights to privacy and the exceptions to confidentiality at the beginning of services, unless this is contraindicated or not feasible (e.g., emergency situations). With individual clients this is a relatively straightforward process. Adult recipients of services are told that, apart from the list of exceptions, everything they discuss and reveal in the course of treatment or psychological assessment will remain confidential, including the fact that the consultations occurred. They are free to discuss any aspect of their treatment with anyone of their choosing, but psychologists must always protect their privacy, refuse to acknowledge the identity of their patients and clients, and reveal nothing of the patient's or client's disclosures, commonly referred to as *protected health information* (PHI), unless at least one of the conditions for such a revelation is met.

When psychologists write psychological reports engage in authorized communications with others about their patients (e.g., other therapists, group or marital; high school teachers of a boy with oppositional defiant disorder; or parents of a minor), they must limit their communications to that information that is germane to the request; no gratuitous information is to be included. For example, a psychologist responding to a request of his or her patient who is filing a worker's compensation claim might reveal information to the employer about his or her patient's cognitive impairment or other metrics of his or her disability that directly impair his or her ability to work but would not reveal his or her patient's positive HIV status or history of childhood physical abuse unless these had a direct bearing on the case. . . .

Providing therapy to children and adolescents offers a different array of privacy concerns to be reviewed at the outset. Therapists should clearly explain privacy and confidentiality to parents as well as the child in treatment at the beginning of therapy: what is required by law and maximizes clinical benefit. Legally a parent or custodian of a minor is entitled to know what occurs in the course of his or her child's treatment, but clinically it is generally considered unwise for the therapist to be fully transparent about every detail of the therapy process.

A simple example of the therapist using his or her judgment about how much to disclose to a parent is the case of an adolescent boy who is actively contemplating suicide and has developed a detailed and specific plan for ending his life. In this case the therapist would have an obligation to take steps to maximize the boy's safety. This might include some combination of the following: informing the parents of the risk of suicide, engaging their cooperation in maintaining his safety, referring the boy for a psychopharmacological evaluation, hospitalizing him on a voluntary basis, or calling the police or emergency psychiatric team for hospitalizing on an involuntary basis. However, the therapist treating a 16-year-old girl who has been experimenting with sexual activity may have less of a clear mandate to inform her parents or none whatsoever. The parents may be legally entitled to have access to the therapist's clinical records on their daughter, but would it serve the best interests of the daughter if she knew that her parents were going to be privy to all that is revealed in treatment? On the other hand, the therapist would also be obliged to assess the potential risk of harm connected with ongoing casual sex, considering the possibilities of physical assault, pregnancy, and sexually transmitted diseases with potentially fatal consequences. In this case, given sufficient risk of harm to the girl, the therapist may opt to include her parents in treatment at some point. . . .

EXCEPTIONS TO PRIVACY AND CONFIDENTIALITY IN CLINICAL AND COUNSELING SETTINGS

. . .

Danger to Self

This includes the client or patient who reveals his or her intent to harm or kill him- or herself. An example is the patient who discloses to his therapist that he or she has a clear intent to inflict harm on him- or herself or commit suicide, that he or she has a detailed plan to do so, and that he or she has the means (i.e., has purchased a weapon, has access to lethal drugs, or has some other obviously risky or lethal plan). In addition, the psychologist would also consider the patient's prior history of suicide attempts, the presence of a psychological disorder such as major depression or a personality disorder, concurrent drug or alcohol abuse, family history and current living situation, and other variables that might be likely to increase the risk of self-harm. But regardless of the presence or absence of other risk factors, the patient's verbalizing his or her serious objective in ending his or her life would be sufficient grounds for intervening rapidly by voluntary hospitalization or other means to maintain the patient's safety. If the patient refused and was actively suicidal, then the therapist would contact the police or an emergency psychiatric team for involuntarily hospitalization, necessarily breaking patient confidentiality by revealing information to law enforcement authorities and hospital personnel.

. . .

Child Victim of a Crime

If a child under 16 years of age has been the victim of a crime, such as assault or rape, and discloses this to his or her psychologist, the child has yielded his or her right to confidentiality because the therapist may be required to report this information to the authorities.

Assisting in Committing a Crime

An individual who seeks psychological services to enable him- or herself or another to commit a crime yields his or her right to privacy concerning the details of the intended crime. This includes an individual seeking psychological services to avoid detection or apprehension concerning a crime.

Court Appointment

Whenever a psychologist is appointed by a court to evaluate an individual, the resulting report is submitted to the court and the individual forfeits his or her right of confidentiality.

Sanity Proceedings

This includes the situation in which a patient has been arrested and is involved in a criminal proceeding. If his or her sanity is directly at issue, a court-appointed psychologist will evaluate him, and a report will be submitted to the court.

. . .

Competency Proceedings

When a patient is being evaluated for his or her competence, such as in a proceeding for guardianship (e.g., child custody) or conservatorship (e.g., a patient with dementia), the patient does not have the right of confidentiality. Again, the psychologist performing the evaluation writes a report that is submitted directly to the court as a guide in making a legal determination about the mental status of the individual being assessed.

Lawsuit Against a Therapist or Patient

Confidentiality is voided in both of these cases: (a) a patient suing a therapist for breach of duty (e.g., the patient sues the therapist for incompetent practice or for having a sexual relationship with the patient) or (b) a therapist litigating against the patient for his or her behavior (e.g., the therapist sues a patient in a small claims court for nonpayment of a bill or sues a potentially violent patient who has been stalking the therapist or damaged his office or car). Information in the psychologist's clinical record sufficient to resolve either dispute will be subject to disclosure.

. . .

Patient Authorization

If a client or patient signs an authorization for release of his or her PHI to a certain entity, the client or patient is consenting to the transmission of his or her PHI to that entity. However, the authorization itself must comply in form and content with (a) state law, if any applies, and (b) the federal regulations of HIPAA [Health Insurance Portability and Accountability Act]. Regulations may include important details such as including an expiration date, stating the rationale for the release of records, including the fact that the patient is entitled to receive a copy of the consent form, and printing the authorization form in 14-point letters, which are easier to read. . . .

REFERENCES

American Psychological Association. (1953). *Ethical standards of psychologists.* Washington, DC: Author.

American Psychological Association. (2010). *Ethical principles of psychologists and code of conduct.* Washington, DC: Author. Retrieved from http://www.apa.org/ethics/code/principles.pdf

Caudill, O. B., & Kaplan, A. I. (2005). Protecting privacy and confidentiality. In S. F. Bucky, J. E. Callan, & G. Stricker (Eds.), *Ethical and legal issues for mental health professionals: A comprehensive handbook of principles and standards* (pp. 117–134). Binghamton, NY: Haworth Maltreatment and Trauma Press/The Haworth Press.

Folkman, S. (2000). Privacy and confidentiality. In B. D. Sales & S. Folkman (Eds.), *Ethics in research with human participants* (pp. 49–57). Washington, DC: American Psychological Association.

Kaplan, A. I. (2005). Therapist–patient privilege: Who owns the privilege? In S. F. Bucky, J. E. Callan, & G. Stricker (Eds.), *Ethical and legal issues for mental health professionals: A comprehensive handbook of principles and standards* (pp. 135–143). Binghamton, NY: Haworth Maltreatment and Trauma Press/The Haworth Press.

Kelman, H. C. (1972). The rights of the subject in social research: An analysis in terms of relative power and legitimacy. *American Psychologist, 27*(11), 989–1016.

Sieber, J. E. (1992). *Applied social research methods series, Vol. 31. Planning ethically responsible research: A guide for students and internal review boards.* Thousand Oaks, CA, US: Sage Publications, Inc.

4.2. Confidentiality and Privacy

David L. Shapiro and Steven R. Smith

. . .

PRIVACY, CONFIDENTIALITY, AND PRIVILEGE

It is helpful to clarify terms. *Privacy* is a generic concept that certain information belongs to the individual and should not be disclosed. *Confidentiality* refers to the ethical and legal obligation of a professional to maintain the private communications concerning a client, absent a specific justification for releasing the information. *Privilege*—or, more accurately, testimonial privilege—is the special legal right to keep from courts (or other bodies) confidential communications from certain relationships, including therapist–client communications. It may, for example, prevent a therapist from being called as a witness in court to repeat what a client said in therapy. . . .

The obligation of confidentiality is significant for malpractice in two ways. First, it defines an important legal obligation of therapists, and breach of that obligation can lead to malpractice liability. Second, the testimonial privilege associated with confidentiality arises with some frequency in the malpractice area. In this chapter, we review the basic principles of privacy, confidentiality, and privilege and how they work to strike a balance between keeping clients' secrets and protecting the public.

LEGAL PROTECTIONS OF CONFIDENTIALITY

The legal protections of the confidences of therapy arise from many sources: the U.S. Constitution and state constitutions, federal and state statutes and regulations, state licensing laws, codes of ethics, and the common law (developed by courts through case law). For the most part, state law has been of primary importance in protecting confidentiality. Now, however, federal law is becoming more important. . . .

The statutes or regulations of many states provide for therapist–client confidentiality and impose damages for the breach of that confidentiality. Even in states in which there is no specific statutory provision creating such liability, it exists by common law or general malpractice or tort principles. The general

From *Malpractice in Psychology: A Practical Resource for Clinicians* (pp. 61–77), by D. L. Shapiro, and S. R. Smith, 2011, Washington, DC: American Psychological Association.

rules of negligence related to psychologists impose liability for the improper disclosure of such information. Other causes of action (depending on the facts) might also result in liability for the improper release of this information, including breach of contract, intentional infliction of emotional distress, invasion of privacy, and defamation. . . .

The right of confidentiality in therapy communications is intended to protect the client. Thus, the client "owns" the right of confidentiality, and the client may choose to waive, or give up, the confidentiality. Unless the law creates an exception (and there are a number of such exceptions), a therapist may not independently decide to waive confidentiality without the client's consent. At the same time, when clients request copies of their own information, the therapist is usually obligated to release the information.

. . .

EXCEPTIONS TO CONFIDENTIALITY

Confidentiality in psychotherapy has many exceptions. Some exceptions are mandatory, in which case the therapist is required to release information. Others are discretionary, in which case the therapist may release information but is not required to do so. Most of the exceptions we discuss in this section are mandatory. We do not deal with every possible exception to confidentiality, only with the major exceptions. For example, in most states a therapist may, without violating confidentiality, consult with another professional for the purpose of receiving assistance or advice related to the care of a client, and many institutions have a quality-improvement process that may include examination of client files.

Consent to the Release of Information

Because the right of confidentiality of psychotherapy belongs to the client, a competent client may waive the confidentiality. The waiver is most often for a limited purpose. A typical waiver, for example, is to obtain reimbursement for services or to transmit information to another health care provider. Therapists are ordinarily obligated to respect the limitations on clients' demands regarding the disclosure of private information. Therefore, the fact that a client has directed the release of specific information does not give a therapist broad authority to release all information. Discussing the disclosure and the extent of the disclosure with the client prior to releasing any information, and confirming this in writing, is a good caution to observe.

HIPAA has imposed several limitations on the release of information subject to the consent of the client. For example, information transmitted to a third party (e.g., an insurance company) that is subject to HIPAA has a form of extended confidentiality in which that third party is precluded from retransmitting the confidential information without additional consent from the client. On the other hand, HIPAA does *not* always require consent for the release of information; for example, it would not be required when child abuse needs to be reported to authorities.

A potential problem arises when a client consents to the release of records that may include copyrighted tests or scoring instructions that could result in a loss of test security. The release of raw psychological test data has been a matter of controversy among psychologists and between the law and psychology. Lees-Haley and Courtney (2000) argued that there is no basis legally or ethically for withholding raw psychological test data from attorneys. Many psychologists disagree with this position.

Lawyers who demand access to such raw data as an essential part of legal discovery argue that they are entitled to anything on which the psychologist has based her or his opinion. Psychologists argue that, to protect the data from misuse, they should provide it only to another psychologist. In the Statement on the Disclosure of Test Data (APA Committee on Psychological Tests and Assessment, 1996) and in "Strategies for Private Practitioners Coping With Subpoenas or Compelled Testimony for Client Records and Test Data" (APA Committee on Legal Issues, 2006), APA has laid out conditions for withholding raw data. . . .

In complying with a client's request to transmit information about therapy to third parties, mental health professionals should take a minimalist approach and transmit the minimum necessary to accomplish the client's purpose. Additional information can always be provided if necessary but, once released, information is usually impossible to recapture. This approach would be modified, of course, when the information is being transferred to other health care providers who need the information to diagnose or treat the client.

Dangerous Clients

Many states now require that therapists take reasonable steps to avoid serious harm or death to identifiable potential victims of dangerous clients (Rogge, 2000). In those states, of course, therapists are not only permitted but also may be legally required to breach client confidentiality to avoid harm. . . .

It is likely that even when the duty to protect is not triggered as a legal requirement—for example, in those circumstances in which there are real (but not identifiable) victims—therapists are permitted to breach confidentiality in order to avoid serious harm. The extent of such a voluntary right, which exists by statute in a number of states, is not always clearly defined. For example, it is not clear how serious the potential harm must be. A therapist who in good faith honestly discloses limited information in order to avoid serious physical harm is generally taking the lesser risk of two evils: serious physical harm versus a violation of confidence. Nevertheless, this is a high-risk situation and, if time and circumstances permit, the therapist should consult with a legal advisor or malpractice insurance carrier. The clinician should consider explaining to the client, perhaps as part of informed consent, that if she or he threatens a third party the therapist may break confidentiality in order to protect that third party.

Child and Other Abuse Reporting Laws

. . . State laws vary somewhat on who is obligated to report suspected or known abuse. Some states place the obligation only on those treating or caring for the individual. Other states require "any person" or "professional" who knows or suspects abuse to report the situation. In those states, a mental health professional treating a client who, for example, reveals that he or she is seeking therapy because he or she needs help to stop abusing a child must report the abuse.

When reporting is required, the therapist does not have the latitude to decide that she or he would rather provide treatment to a client than to report the situation. Reporting is mandatory. The therapist should document decisions regarding required reporting. It is also good practice to communicate to clients, as part of informed consent, that the therapist is obligated to make reports of the abuse of children and others. A misunderstanding of this issue is seen in the following example.

Dr. P was consulted by a client who asked Dr. P if everything he said would be confidential. Dr. P said that it would be unless he felt that the client was dangerous. The client then confided in Dr. P that he had been having sexual relations with his 14-year-old daughter. Dr. P made the mandated report to the Department of Social Services. On the basis of this report, the man was arrested and prosecuted for child abuse. He then filed a complaint against Dr. P alleging breach of confidentiality. The breach of confidentiality, of course, was justified, but the confusion arose from Dr. P's failure to inform his client that he had a mandate to report instances of child abuse. His statement about "dangerousness" was vague.

Because all states require that known or suspected child abuse be reported but vary in details of exactly what must be reported, it is important for therapists to review the relevant statutes in their states and to have a specific plan for dealing with known or suspected abuse. In addition, most states have other mandatory reporting statutes (e.g., regarding abuse of individuals who are elderly or have disabilities), and therapists need to be clear on their obligations under those laws. It is helpful to have the guidance of an attorney who is familiar with the state laws. Practitioners may also receive helpful advice from state psychological associations or their malpractice insurance carrier.

. . .

PRACTICAL SUGGESTIONS

1. Client privacy and confidentiality are among the most important professional values for psychologists. In addition to their ethical commitment to client privacy, therapists should know that the law imposes damages for

the breach of that confidentiality. Most commonly, breach of confidentiality is considered negligence, but other possible causes of action include breach of contract, invasion of privacy, and defamation.

2. The right of confidentiality in therapy communications is intended to protect the client. The client, not the therapist, "owns" the right of confidentiality, and the client may choose to waive the confidentiality. Psychologists should convey these limits to their clients in a carefully crafted informed consent document.

3. Therapists need to be familiar with a major federal law, HIPAA (as amended by HITECH), that has changed the landscape of client information. HIPAA protects confidentiality of health records by significantly limiting the release of these records without client consent and by allowing clients to see their own records. The law provides special protection to psychotherapy notes.

4. Therapists need to understand the laws of their states as well as HIPAA. When the HIPAA Privacy Rule and state health information privacy laws conflict, the one that is more protective of privacy or gives clients greater access to their records will prevail.

5. Therapists need to be HIPAA compliant—not an easy task. HIPAA and similar state obligations are complicated. This is one area in which it is especially important that therapists obtain solid legal advice to stay within the obligations of the law.

6. Clients may waive confidentiality and direct therapists to release information from therapy. Such releases are generally for a limited purpose, and therapists should release the information only to the extent to which they are directed to do so. Discussing the disclosure and the extent of the disclosure with the client prior to release is a good caution to observe.

7. Clients may request to see their own records, and ordinarily therapists should comply with the request. When that could harm the client or result in the violation of testing copyright protection or trade secrets, or when state law allows withholding psychotherapy notes, the therapist may withhold some information.

8. Psychologists should have a process in place to ensure that reports of child or other abuse are made consistent with state law. Therapists are legally obligated to report known or suspected child abuse as defined by state law. Some states require other abuse reporting.

9. In forensic evaluations the limits of confidentiality must be spelled out and included in the informed consent to avoid any misunderstanding by the examinee or others potentially involved in the legal proceeding.

REFERENCES

American Psychological Association, Committee on Legal Issues. (2006). Strategies for private practitioners coping with subpoenas or compelled testimony for client records or test data. *Professional Psychology: Research and Practice, 37,* 215–222.

American Psychological Association, Science Directorate, Committee on Psychological Tests & Assessment. (1996). Statement on the disclosure of test data. *American Psychologist, 51*(6), 644–648.

Lees-Haley, P. R., & Courtney, J. C. (2000). Disclosure of tests and raw test data to the courts: A need for reform. *Neuropsychology Review, 10,* 169–174.

Rogge, S. (2000). Liability of psychiatrists under New York law for failing to identify dangerous patients. *Pace Law Review, 20,* 221–229.

4.3. Privacy and Confidentiality in Psychotherapy

Louis Everstine, Diana Sullivan Everstine, Gary M. Heymann, Reiko Homma True, David H. Frey, Harold G. Johnson, and Richard H. Seiden

. . .

DEFINITIONS

The term *confidentiality*, as defined by the committee, refers to the uses of information. The information in question concerns a particular person rand is unique to that person (as opposed to information that could be about any person qua person). This information is, in addition, linked to the person by a figurative though unambiguous chain; that is, the person and the information referring to the person are inseparably associated, in such a way that the information itself and the person are one entity and to attempt to distinguish one from the other would be absurd reasoning. The root problem of confidentiality, therefore, concerns the restraints that need to be placed on the uses of personal information. At once these kinds of questions arise:

1. What information can be revealed to others?

2. How can "need to know" in respect to that information be established?

3. What restraints will govern the use of that information once it has been revealed?

4. To whom may that information, once revealed, be further revealed?

5. To what extent should the person about whom information has been revealed know about the course that has been followed by the information during the time elapsing since it was first revealed?

6. Should the person know the identity of each and every person who has obtained access to that information?

7. After what passage of time does that information cease to be relevant, and how can it be made to disappear?

These and other basic questions form the background to an understanding of the concept of confidentiality.

The concept of *privacy*, as defined by the committee, refers to persons and personhood. A person is assumed to occupy a certain emotional, cognitive, or psychological "space," the use, management, or control of which properly resides with the person.[1] The concept of privacy is addressed by the Fourth Amendment to the Constitution, which is that portion of the Bill of Rights which protects a person's home against illegal "search and seizure" by the government. And though the framers of the Fourth Amendment could in no way have foreseen present-day dangers to privacy, there is a rich tradition of case law that has applied the basic principle of the amendment (namely, that "a man's home is his castle") to a wide range of contemporary issues. In effect, people are protected against invasion of privacy by their government or by the agents of government. The problems that arise in respect to preserving privacy stem from the difficulty of generalizing to other, nongovernmental attempts to intrude upon personal space. Questions such as these arise:

1. To what extent should psychological or emotional states be protected from manipulation or scrutiny by others?

2. Is a person's "sense of well-being" a possession, such as property, that should be held impervious to trespass?

3. How shall it be decided who may intrude upon privacy and what circumstances must prevail?

4. When privacy has been invaded, what can be done to ameliorate the situation?

5. Does the person have an irrevocable right to waive his or her own privacy, even when the best interests of that person may thereby be threatened (i.e., for some self-punitive motive)?

Some of the foregoing questions will call to mind certain well-known cases that are by no means confined to the realm of psychotherapy. As practitioners we confront many of these conundrums each time we decide that a person requires counseling, therapy, hospitalization, or some other form of "help" in adjusting his or her thoughts, feelings, or behavior to the social orbit within which he or she moves.

---

[1] Although these definitions of *confidentiality* and *privacy* imply that the two concepts are intertwined, it should be noted that privacy is the more basic concept of the two. In fact, breach of confidentiality is properly conceived as only one of many kinds of invasion of privacy, and thus the issue of confidentiality is seen as a subset of the privacy issue. By no means should the terms be used interchangeably. As an example of the misleading assumptions that can be generated when one term is substituted for the other, consider the Federal Privacy Act, which deals almost exclusively with the subject of confidentiality.

OVERVIEW

The following is an identification of and elaboration on a subset of problems that are becoming increasingly salient for the professional practice of psychology. The seriousness of these issues can be brought home by the following case in point: In the July 8, 1977, issue of the *San Francisco Chronicle*, an article appeared whose headline read "Doctor Goes to Jail." This brief account told of a local psychiatrist who was preparing to serve a three-day sentence for refusing to reveal certain information concerning a former client in a court of law, The psychiatrist had taken his case, for the right to refuse to testify, to the U.S. Supreme Court and after five years, had lost his final appeal. Here was an instance in which a therapist took a principled stand on behalf of the preservation of confidentiality; in effect he took upon himself the responsibility not to breach that confidentiality and he lost. This case needs to be contemplated as an exemplar, and the title of that newspaper article warrants sober reflection.

The Hippocratic oath contains the following pledge: "Whatever, in connection with my profession, or not in connection with it, I may see or hear in the lives of men which ought not to be spoken abroad I will not divulge as reckoning that all should be kept secret." For those who have accepted this oath as a guide to their professional conduct, the pledge states a clear and unmistakable "duty of silence." And even though many psychologists do not feel obligated by the oath, most will agree that the duty of silence represents a reasonable standard for ethical responsibility. . . .

INFORMED CONSENT FOR PSYCHOTHERAPY

The need to protect client privacy invokes the issue of consent for treatment. Even when a client seeks out a therapist, he or she may face some risk owing to lack of knowledge concerning some inherent consequence of that decision. In effect, the client may inadvisedly waive his or her right to privacy by entering into a therapeutic relationship. Our committee takes the view that the client should be given an opportunity for reflection on whether or not to waive this right. And in the process by which a therapist shows sensitivity to this issue, it may be that some of the trust necessary for the relationship to be effective can be gained. To the extent that the potential experiences of therapy are revealed to a client early in treatment, the therapeutic relationship will be nurtured. This is our rationale for the discussion of consent procedures that follows.

It is true that most clinicians already make use of some type of informed-consent procedure in their private practices. Nevertheless, in a majority of cases the application of these procedures is haphazard in manner and timing, and the procedures are rarely documented in retrievable form.

This discussion primarily concerns the rights of clients who seek help in non-institutional settings. Naturally, in crisis intervention situations, or when a client needs to be hospitalized, alternative rules concerning when and how informed consent is to be obtained will apply. Nevertheless, clients should be made aware of their rights, and some agreement on a course of treatment should be obtained at the earliest appropriate time. Thus, some general principles apply to both institutional and noninstitutional settings.

What Is Consent?

Consent as a legal concept has three basic elements (Biklen, Boggs, Ellis, Keeran, & Siedor, Note 1): capacity or competence, information, and voluntariness.

Competence

The basic question is, Can the person engage in rational thought to a sufficient degree to make competent decisions about his or her life? Competence is assumed unless a person has been legally declared to be "mentally incompetent." *Direct* consent should be obtained from all competent persons. For persons legally declared incompetent (such as minors under the age of 18), *substitute* consent from parents, guardians, or court-appointed conservators should be obtained. In fact, both the required substitute's consent and the incompetent person's consent should be obtained when possible.

Information

For consent to be "informed," clients must possess relevant information about the procedures that are to be performed. Two major considerations are what information is provided and how the information is communicated. The kind of information that should be provided generally includes (a) an explanation of the procedures and their purpose, (b) the role of the person who is providing therapy and his or her professional qualifications, (c) discomforts or risks reasonably to be expected, (d) benefits reasonably to be expected, (e) alternatives to treatment that might be of similar benefit, (f) a statement that any questions about the procedures will be answered at any time, and (g) a statement that the person can withdraw his or her consent and discontinue participation in therapy or testing at any time. This information should be presented in language that the client can understand (e.g., by means of simple, declarative sentences and the avoidance of jargon).

Voluntariness

At times of extreme crisis, when serious bodily harm or the death of a client or another person is involved, consent is not an issue. In such cases, the law generally operates on the principle of compelling or justifiable interest; that is, society's best interests outweigh the client's right to give or withhold consent. In such cases, it is a good idea to obtain consent as soon as possible after the crisis has subsided. Similarly, when someone is forced to participate in assessment of therapy by order of a court, the concept of consent takes on a different meaning. Our recommendation is that consent be obtained even in these nonvoluntary Situations. And while the consent itself may be legally empty, in many cases it will very likely have a clinical usefulness.

In summary, true consent requires that the person be mentally competent and fully informed and that consent be given voluntarily. In most private-practice cases, both competence to choose therapy and voluntariness are immediately evident. A major concern of the therapist is to make sure that a client is informed about the procedures to be used.

. . .

EROSION OF THE PROFESSIONAL TRUST RELATIONSHIP

A hallmark of psychotherapy is the establishment of a relationship of trust between client and therapist, and this relationship must be carefully protected through the course of the therapeutic experience. Yet a gradual and continuous weakening has occurred in the confidentiality privilege, one legal mechanism by which this professional trust relationship is implemented in our social system. Events during recent years have resulted in the general deterioration of many stabilizing values throughout our culture, particularly in respect to people's ability to trust their social institutions and each other. In the context of this general erosion, it is urgent that we make every effort to reestablish and strengthen the sociolegal nature of the, trust relationship that is so central to our professional work. A brief outline of four legally defined professional trust relationships follows. . . .

There is a physician–patient privilege, which is controlled by the patient. When the patient claims it in regard to some information, the patient can refuse to permit that information to be revealed by the physician. The physician cannot claim the privilege independently; that, is, he or she cannot countermand the patient's decision. If the patient decides to waive the privilege, the physician can then reveal the information only to someone who is designated by the patient—even if, in the physician's judgment, this may be injurious to the patient. The fact that this privilege is not held independently by the physician is an important point. Even so, there are four major conditions under which a physician *must* breach this patient-controlled confidentiality privilege under the law: (a) if criminal action is involved; (b) if the information is made an issue in a court action, for example, in an injury suit initiated by the patient; (c) if the information is obtained for the purpose of rendering an expert's report to a lawyer (thus, when the physician makes a report to an attorney in a legal case, the information is not subsumed under the privilege; the attorney, in fact, has an obligation to share this information with his or her opposite number—the defense or prosecuting attorney—and with the court); and (d) if the physician is acting in a court-appointed capacity. It is worth noting that the physician–patient privilege also extends to such third-party persons as the physician's nurse, a technician, or a clerk/secretary who is working with the physician.

There is a psychotherapist–client privilege. In California law, *psychotherapist* is defined as a clinical psychologist, a school psychologist, a clinical social worker, or a psychiatrist. This privilege is controlled by the client, is not independently held by the psychotherapist, and *must* be breached by the psychotherapist under six legal conditions: (a) when criminal action is involved; (b) when the information is made an issue in a court action; (c) when the information is obtained for the purpose of rendering an expert's report to a lawyer; (d) when the psychotherapist is acting in a court-appointed capacity; (e) when the psychotherapist believes that the client is a danger to himself, herself, or others and feels that it is necessary to prevent an actual threat of danger from being carried out; and (f) when a client is under the age of 16 and the therapist believes that the client has been the victim of a crime (e.g., incest, rape) and judges such disclosure to be in the client's best interest.

There is a lawyer–client privilege, which is controlled by the client or the client's guardian, conservator, personal representative, or successor (here can be seen considerable widening of control beyond the person who originally imparted the information). This privilege is not held independently by the lawyer and *must* be breached by the lawyer under two conditions: (a) if criminal action is involved and (b) if the information is made an issue in a court action.

Finally, there is a clergy privilege, which is very tightly defined by the law. It applies only to those clergy whose church rules specify that they have a duty to keep information secret and that there be no third party present when the information is given. Within those constraints, the privilege is controlled by the "penitent" (equivalent to the client or patient), but it may also be held independently by the clergy. An important distinction which pertains here is that while the penitent can bind the clergy, the penitent is not bound by the clergy's privilege. Thus, if the penitent claims the privilege, the information cannot be revealed by the clergy; but if the penitent waives the privilege and the clergy claims it, the clergy can remain silent even though the penitent reveals the information. A clergy's independently held privilege is established for the benefit of the clergy's personal sense of conscience. There are no exceptions to this privilege arrangement. It cannot be breached for any legal reason whatsoever. It is absolute.

Ironically, it is the psychotherapy client whose privilege of confidentiality is most vulnerable to breach under the law. For this reason, we need a redefinition of the confidentiality privilege for psychotherapy that embodies the following principles. First, information should not be used for purposes that were not intended when it was revealed within the professional relationship. In a divorce action, for example, facts about sexual behavior can be used as evidence that someone is not a fit parent; when this information is offered in the context of treatment, it is not likely that it is intended to be used as court testimony. Thus, it is inappropriate for this information to be made available in a context that is totally different from the one prevailing when the information was revealed. Second, the privilege should be held independently by the professional as well as by the client. If we are to be responsible for helping our clients and protecting them from harm, we need the legal sanction to refrain from revealing that which, in our judgment, is likely to be harmful to the client. Finally, the privilege should be inviolate to breach by external authority, including such intrusions as "security" investigations by governmental agencies of any kind. Court subpoenas, too, are external intrusions upon confidentiality.

In summary, we affirm that existing regulatory and statutory provisions which define our professional trust relationships need to be changed. We are confident that raising consciousness concerning this issue will lead the profession to take action and to ensure that appropriate changes are made. . . .

REFERENCE

Biklen, D. P., Boggs, E. M., Ellis, J. W., Keeran, C. V., & Siedor, G. R. *Consent handbook* (Special Pub. No. 3). Washington, DC: American Association on Mental Deficiency, 1977.

COMMENTARY: It has been nearly 40 years since Dr. Everstine and his colleagues published their classic *American Psychologist* article on these matters. It is, in a way, both sobering and reassuring to realize how much of this material would be deemed current and topical if submitted for publication in the same flagship journal today. We appear as a profession to be grappling with so many of the same old issues, and yet we can be glad that long ago we realized that were and would remain such vital concerns for ethically informed practice.

Establishing which if any parties may have a "need to know" has always been a particularly salient consideration. It is far easier for the overstretched and time-strapped clinician to discern an appropriate way to communicate with those whose inquiries truly merit a weighing of disclosure options instead of with everyone who might or might not require some form of notification. Still highly relevant—and all the more so in light of evolving Health Insurance Portability and Accountability Act (HIPAA) standards—are concerns over "the identities of each and every person who has obtained access."

The following references are recommended for those interested in further investigation of privacy and confidentiality concerns, with pronounced ethical and legal emphases (including those relevant to malpractice).

Bennett, B. E., Bricklin, P. M., Harris, F., Knapp, S., VandeCreek, L., & Younggren, J. N. (2006). Privacy, confidentiality, and privileged communications. In *Assessing and managing risk in psychological practice: An individualized approach* (pp. 105–128). Rockville, MD: The Trust.

Donner, M. B., VandeCreek, L., Gonsiorek, J. C., & Fisher, C. B. (2008). Balancing confidentiality: Protecting privacy and protecting the public. *Professional Psychology: Research and Practice, 39*, 369–376. http://dx.doi.org/10.1037/0735-7028.39.3.369

Fisher, M. A. (2008). Protecting confidentiality rights: The need for an ethical practice model. *American Psychologist, 63*, 1–13. http://dx.doi.org/10.1037/0003-066X.63.1.1

Lustgarten, S. D. (2015). Emerging ethical threats to client privacy in cloud communication and data storage. *Professional Psychology: Research and Practice, 46*, 154–160. http://dx.doi.org/10.1037/pro0000018

Tribbensee, N. E., & Claiborn, C. D. (2003). Confidentiality in psychotherapy and related contexts. In W. O'Donoghue & K. Ferguson (Eds.), *Handbook of professional ethics for psychologists: Issues, questions, and controversies* (pp. 287–300). Thousand Oaks, CA: Sage.

4.4. Some Contrarian Concerns About Law, Psychology, and Public Policy

Donald N. Bersoff

To be given this special recognition by people who know you well, faults and all, makes this an honor that I will cherish for a lifetime. But I have to say I feel a bit guilty. You may recall that Mowrer became severely depressed after being elected president of APA because he believed he did not deserve the honor. I have similar feelings. I have not done the kind of programmatic research or legal analyses that creates cutting edge findings and revolutionizes public policy—the kind of work exemplified by many of my colleagues in law and psychology. Nevertheless, I am deeply grateful for this honor. And, as an exemplar of my dilletantish interests, I will wax wisely and whinely about a half dozen or so topics—thus, Some Contrarian Concerns About Law, Psychology, and Public Policy.

CONCERN NUMBER ONE: CHILDREN AND THE SUPREME COURT

Decisions by the United States Supreme Court in the 1960s and early 1970s were the high water marks in the child advocacy movement. But the current reality, beginning with *Parham* in 1979 (*Parham v. J. R.*, 1979) and the adolescent abortion decisions, is that when it comes to children's rights, the Supreme Court is at best ignorant, at worst duplicitous, and more evenhandedly, simply confused and unprincipled.

One can distinguish between the right of persons to make choices and the right of persons to be protected from the choices or misconduct of others. Translated in the context of this discussion, there are those who could be called "kiddie libbers" and others who could be called "child savers." The child advocacy movement has mainly been populated by the child savers who have secured, I readily concede, important advances.

By and large, however, children remain, like Ralph Ellison's hero, Invisible Persons whose views are infrequently invoked and whose wishes are rarely controlling. Everyone is asked to serve children's best interests even if that means overriding their refusal to participate in testing, research, and therapy, or refusing to honor their preference between two fit parents in custody hearings.

From "Some Contrarian Concerns About Law, Psychology, and Public Policy," by D. N. Bersoff, 2002, *Law and Human Behavior, 26*, pp. 565–574. Copyright 2002 by American Psychology-Law Society/Division 41 of the American Psychological Association.

The child saver function has been the traditional role of parents and the state. At bottom, however, this concern for children's best interests—a term no one can accurately define—has meant that parents and the state have exerted inordinate control over children. The role of protector, acting *in* behalf of the child, is different from acting *on* behalf of, which connotes that the advocate is acting on the part of, another, or as the one represented might act. If we are genuinely to urge the expanded rights of children such advocacy must include the right of children to full-fledged participation in the decision-making process when their significant interests and future hang in the balance. Nevertheless, in light of the Supreme Court's overriding preference for parental control and its distrust of older minors' ability to make adult-like judgments, it is unlikely that children will be granted the right to decide most matters for themselves.

I personally believe that we should reverse our current presumptions. Rather than assume that children are too young emotionally and cognitively to make "appropriate" decisions, we can presume that children are capable of making those decisions no more disastrously than adults. The legal system, however, continues to assume that children are unable to render decisions that approach the level of judgments adults use. What is particularly galling to me, as well as those who have contributed scholarship to this debate, is that the Court justifies its differential treatment on the unsupported assumptions that all children, regardless of age, are particularly vulnerable, unable to make critical decisions in an informed, mature manner, and need the control and guidance of their parents. We know that, by and large this is not true—as recently exemplified in the study of adolescents' adjustment to abortion in last September's *Psychology, Public Policy, and Law* (Quinton, Major, & Richards, 2001).

In light of these comments, I would like to make two recommendations. First, I would urge researchers seeking to assess children's competence and judgment to continue moving out of the laboratory and into more realistic settings, as we began to do in the latter part of the last century. Second, we need to study, in real-life settings and over the long term, what I call "liberating parents and liberated children." Developmental psychologists must first discover parents who foster autonomy, independence, self-determination, and self-reliance and who view those as predominant values to be transmitted to their children. Then, we must study the effects of those overtly expressed values in a sample of these children, along with appropriate comparison groups, along the age span from infancy to later adolescence. Maturity is fostered, not only through parental guidance and restraint, but through the creation by parents of the appropriate context for decisionmaking and offering choices to children, encouraging autonomy, and holding them accountable for their decisions. Until we engage in this kind of longitudinal, naturalistic study we will have a difficult time discerning whether children are genuinely developmentally incompetent for much of their childhood, or whether we have, indeed, subjected them to unnecessary dependency and learned help-lessness. The present status of children's rights will not advance significantly unless there is strong, valid evidence that the "pages of human experience" (read, the subjective views of nine old men and women) are simply wrong.

CONCERN NUMBER TWO: APA AND THE SUPREME COURT

As Michael Saks has pointed out, lawyers are "smart people who do not like math" (Saks, 1989, p. 1115). So, while I decry the Supreme Court's unsupported assumptions about children, its behavior in this regard is understandable. But, our own professional organization, one would hope, would be a bit more sophisticated about data and its meaning. Thus, I find inexcusable and unwarranted the position the American Psychological Association (joined by the American Psychiatric Association and the American Academy of Psychiatry and the Law) took in its amicus brief in *McCarver v. North Carolina* (2001), the case that would have decided whether it is unconstitutional to execute those diagnosed as mentally retarded. However, when North Carolina changed its law to bar the execution of persons with mental retardation, the Court dismissed the writ of certiorari as improvidently granted and replaced *McCarver* with *Atkins v. Virginia* (2002), a case presenting similar issues. The Court heard oral arguments in *Atkins* in late February 2002. APA and its two cosigners were granted permission to resubmit its brief in *McCarver* in *Atkins*. In fact, not only did the *McCarver/Atkins* brief undermine the rights of people with mental retardation but, despite APA's efforts in prior cases, the rights of children as well. Here are two quotes from the APA's brief:

> Th[e] small group of [individuals with mental retardation] represents those whose intellectual limitation substantially restrict their development and adaptive functioning. These limitations are reflected in diminished capacities to understand and process facts and information; to learn from mistakes and from experience generally; to generalize and to engage in logical if–then reasoning; to control impulses; to communicate; to understand the moral implications of actions and to engage in moral reasoning; and to recognize and understand the feelings, thoughts, and reactions of other people.
>
> . . . A comparison with children is instructive [C]hildren and persons with mental retardation share the same critical characteristic: diminished intellectual and practical capacities compared to non-retarded adults.
>
> . . . Inexperience, less education, and less intelligence make the teenager less able to evaluate the consequences of his or her conduct while at the same time he or she is much more apt to be motivated by mere emotion or peer pressure than is an adult. *McCarver v. North Carolina*, 2001, pp. 7–9 [footnotes and citations omitted]

An early hypothetical I was confronted with in my first year of law school concerned the stereotypical little old lady who, after contracting with a major bank to secure a loan, found herself unable to pay the installments because of unfortunate life circumstances. Many of us sided with the poor, aged, and infirm woman against the big bad bank (knee jerk liberals were still going to law school in the early '70s). But, our professor pointed out, if a court permitted this senior citizen to breach her contract, the consequence would be that no bank would lend money to the elderly, an outcome that served no one's purposes. The applicability of this hypo struck me as I was drafting this talk. I believe a bright line rule making the death penalty unconstitutional for all defendants with mental retardation ultimately disserves their interests.

I want to state unequivocally that I am adamantly opposed to the death penalty for anyone. As we have discovered, its imposition is inevitably fraught with caprice and mistake (Black, 1974; *United States v. Quinones*, 2002). Execution by the State, particularly of those with severe intellectual deficits, does not comport with the standards of decency that should be the hallmark of governments, and therefore violates the cruel and unusual punishment clause of the Eighth Amendment.

But, if the death penalty can be meted out to adults and older adolescents, as the Supreme Court has said it can, then it is short-sighted to exclude all mentally retarded people from its imposition, precisely because a constitutional ban for these defendants, on the ground that they deserve special protection and dispensation, is antagonistic to their long range rights and entitlements. It is difficult for me to see how an absolute ban, grounded on the assumption that they are too incompetent to be held morally responsible and criminally culpable serves their ultimate interests. As important as it is to protect those who cannot protect themselves, it is equally important to promote the right of all persons to make their own choices, and, as a corollary, to be accountable for those choices. It is simply untrue that no person with mental retardation is incapable of carrying out a horrible murder with the requisite intent or foresight. If we accept the concept of blanket incapacity, we relegate people with retardation to second class citizenship, potentially permitting the State to abrogate the exercise of such fundamental interests as the right to marry, to have and rear one's children, to vote, or such everyday entitlements as entering into contracts or making a will.

That is why, albeit reluctantly, I agree with Justice Scalia who has argued for individualized decision making in death penalty cases. The concept of individualized decisionmaking comports with the sophisticated and discriminating treatment we should accord all people with intellectual deficits. IQ, after all, is not the factor that renders the imposition of the death penalty against those with mental retardation unjust. Rather, IQ is a proxy, and an imperfect one at that, for a combination of factors, such as maturity, judgment, and the capability of assessing the consequences of one's conduct, that determine the relative culpability of a mentally retarded killer. It is those factors that should be evaluated by a forensic clinician on a case-by-case basis. Culpability, not IQ, should be the benchmark. In this way, defendants with mental retardation will be treated as persons and society can respond to their conduct in a manner that respects the defendant's choice to engage in such conduct.

Incidentally, I raised these concerns with Division 33 representatives at the APA convention in August 2001. As a poignant reminder of the great influence I wield at APA, I discovered that APA refiled the *McCarver* brief, without a single change, in *Atkins* in late February. I will never forgive and will always regret that the APA decided to take such a thoughtless approach to the rights of our fellow citizens.[1]

CONCERN NUMBER THREE: THE DILUTION OF SELF-DETERMINATION

The APA's brief surfaces a larger, more pervasive concern—our strong preference for beneficence over autonomy. In the last century, the English philosopher W. D. Ross (Ross, 1930) propounded a set of prima facie duties underlying ethical behavior. They include nonmaleficence, beneficence, justice, fidelity, and autonomy. These fundamental moral principles have been popularized by Beauchamp and Childress (1994) in their text on research ethics, and play a prominent part in the latest draft of the potentially new APA ethics code. Beneficence refers to our responsibility to help others and act in their best interests. Autonomy requires us to allow others the freedom to think, choose, and act, so long as their actions do not unduly infringe on the rights of others. APA and most of our colleagues display a strong preference for beneficence over autonomy. This is reflected in psychologists' involvement in involuntary civil commitment, restrictive definitions of the capacity to refuse psychotropic medications, and, as I have already discussed, our treatment of children. As a card-carrying autonomist, this preference, in my opinion, undermines the civil liberties of us all.

---

[1] After this talk was delivered in March but before it was set in print, the Supreme Court decided *Atkins v. Virginia* (2002). By a 6–3 vote, the Court held that executions of all mentally retarded individuals violated the eighth amendment's cruel and unusual punishment clause. Justice Stevens, writing for the majority, clearly relied on the APA's amicus brief in grounding his opinion. Justice Stevens, though acknowledging that people with mental retardation "frequently know the difference between right and wrong and are competent to stand trial" (p. 2250), found that their lesser culpability precluded imposition of the death penalty in any case. He based this lesser culpability on their "diminished capacities to understand and process information, to communicate, to abstract from mistakes and learn from experience, to engage in logical reasoning, to control impulses, and to understand the reaction of others" (p. 2250). This quote echoes the excerpt from the APA's brief cited in the text of my talk. In a dissenting opinion, Chief Justice Rehnquist took issue with the majority's reliance on methodologically questionable public opinion polls, and the views of professional organizations to establish a national consensus against executing persons with mental retardation. Justice Scalia, in a separate dissenting opinion, as expected, would have relied on the individualized decisionmaking of sentencers to determine whether a particular defendant deserved the death penalty: "Once the Court admits . . . that mental retardation does not render the offender *blameless* . . . there is no basis for saying that the death penalty is *never* appropriate retribution, no matter *how* heinous the crime" (p. 2266; emphasis in original).

Although I am gratified by any decision that further reduces the imposition of the death penalty (as the majority has done) and do not support Justice Scalia's retributive basis for executing any defendant (see Concern # 6), as I asserted in my talk, I believe that Justice Scalia's particularized approach is, in the long run, more protective of the rights of people with mental retardation, than is the rationale adopted by APA and the Court's majority.

I believe that one of government's overriding social goals should be to promote human dignity and individual autonomy. Individuals should have the right to decide how to live their lives, and more particularly, what types of intrusions they will allow on their bodily integrity. Our society should be committed to respecting each individual's right to choose his or her own fate—even if the choices the individual makes do not serve, in some objective sense, what the majority would consider to be in the individual's best interest. In short, each individual should have the right to make mistakes, and not to have those mistakes forcibly corrected or overridden by the State or its agents.

That is why I have some concern, for example, about prescription privileges for psychologists. I fear that like our psychiatric colleagues, we will become paternalistic, compelling our patients to take drugs even when they do not want to take them. I am not against attempting to influence those we care for to agree to take something that will improve their functioning and there is a role for the State in caring for those citizens incapable of caring for themselves. This interest does not, however, justify every good faith effort to intrude, interfere, intervene, or become involved (you choose your own verb—I opt for intrude) in individual decisionmaking. As Justice Brandeis wrote in a famous dissenting opinion, and his statement is so often quoted that it has become trite, but is so singularly apt in this context that I feel bound to repeat it: "Experience should teach us to be most on our guard to protect liberty when Government's purposes are beneficent" (*Olmstead v. United States*, 1928, p. 479).

CONCERN NUMBER FOUR: *TARASOFF* AND ITS PROGENY

It has been my view for over 25 years (Bersoff, 1974), and I agree totally with Chris Slobogin (Reisner, Slobogin, & Rai, 1999) on this, that *Tarasoff* is bad law, bad social science, and bad social policy. It is bad law because there never has been a duty within the Restatement of Torts to protect private third parties from harm unless there are specific conditions and relationships not present in *Tarasoff* (*Tarasoff v. Regents of University of California*, 1976). Remember Poddar was in outpatient therapy not under the control of a hospital and not eligible for involuntary commitment. Second, it is bad social science because the therapist's duty is based on an evaluation of the patient's propensity to act violently. Although more sophisticated research done by the MacArthur Project's Research Network on Mental Health and the Law has improved risk assessment (Monahan et al., 2001), it is still extremely difficult to make accurate assessments in outpatient, nonpsychotic, nonsubstance abusing populations—the vast majority of patients mental health professionals see. Third, the duty to protect is bad social policy. The crucial fact in this case was not an uttered threat of future violence but that once Poddar knew that his confidences were disclosed by his therapist to the campus police, he never returned for treatment. One wonders if Ms. Tarasoff would be alive today if the psychologist–therapist and his psychiatrist-supervisor were not so quick to call the police but rather worked with their patient for the 2 months between the threat and the killing.

This does not mean that I advocate letting potentially violent patients go unchecked. The truly violent aggressor at some time loses his or her right to absolute protection when he or she threatens to use deadly force. The APA code of ethics (APA, 1992), which permits unconsented to disclosures merely to protect others from harm (left undefined) and not under the more stringent standard required by *Tarasoff* of serious bodily harm, and immunity statutes that protect us from litigation, simply make it too easy to betray our fidelity to our patients and to become society's police force. I think we should be obliged to do all we can to attempt all other viable options before we abrogate the principle of fidelity and unilaterally disclose confidential communications to private third parties.

I would agree in large part with the Supreme Court's view on this issue in *Jaffee v. Redmond* (1996) expressed in a footnote: "[W]e do not doubt that there are situations in which the [psychotherapist–patient] privilege must give way . . . if a serious threat of harm to the patient or others can be averted only by means of a disclosure by the therapist." I find it heartening that Texas in the 1999 case of *Thapar v. Zezulka* rejected the mandatory rule of *Tarasoff* and supported what to me is a more defensible position by recognizing the statutory exception to its privilege statute that allows, but does not require, disclosure and only when the therapist determines that there is a probability of imminent physical injury by the patient to others. This is more in line with the ethical rules binding lawyers. In any event, I would hope that organized mental health would ally themselves with our clients' desire for privacy rather than society's increasingly serious attempts to diminish it. The latest draft of APA's ethics code lamely follows the latter trend, I am sad to say.

Tarasoff, by the way, is also an example of the legal system's tendency, particularly the legislature, to make laws without considering their long term or unintended consequences. A tragedy occurs, most likely some violent death, and lawmakers, driven by some inherent availability heuristic, enact some quick fix to remedy the situation. Current examples are sexually violent predator laws, Megan's laws, and recidivist statutes (I call them three strikes and you are in laws) where three felonies, even nonviolent ones, can lead to life imprisonment, often without parole. So now we will have to take care of the health needs of burnt out senior citizens while they languish with Alzheimer's, cancer, and the like.

CONCERN NUMBER FIVE: THE INCREASING USE OF THE PCL-R IN DEATH PENALTY CASES

My penultimate concern relates to an increasingly invidious practice; the use of the PCL-R in the penalty phase of capital murder cases. You may recall that in 1995 the American Psychiatric Association expelled from its membership James Grigson, the notorious Texas psychiatrist, better known as Dr. Death.

He was tossed out "for arriving at a psychiatric diagnosis without first having examined the individual in question, and for indicating, while testifying in court as an expert witness, that he could predict with 100 [per cent] certainty that the individual would engage in future violent acts" (quoted in Shuman & Greenberg, 1998). Much of the same kind of behavior is, unfortunately, being engaged in, in my opinion, by a few misguided, ignorant, and unethical forensic psychologists who are using the PCL-R to testify, to a reasonable psychological certainty, that capital defendants comprise a continuing threat of violence, even while confined in maximum security prisons. The problem is compounded by the fact that, unlike psychiatric diagnoses propounded on the basis of interviews, the PCL-R is widely regarded as a psychometrically sound instrument. Although it may have some usefulness in predicting future violence, recent articles (Edens, 2001; Edens, Petrila, & Buffington-Vollum, in press; Freedman, 2001) indicate that it is not a valid predictor of the most pertinent forms of violence relevant to determining future dangerousness in capital cases. For example, Sorenson and Pilgrim (2000) reported that of a sample of 6,390 convicted murderers in the Texas prison system, the incidence of homicides over a 40-year period was about 0.2%. Given that the base rate of psychopathy is about 20–30% of the prison population, approximately 1,600 of the prisoners would be psychopaths as defined by the PCL-R. As Edens et al., who cited this study in their about-to-be published article, states, "[e]ven if all of the 13 homicides estimated to occur over this [40 year] time period . . . were to be committed by psychopaths—a highly questionable assumption—the overwhelming majority of these offenders (99%) will not kill again." A table summarizing almost a dozen studies in Freedman's 2001 article in the *Journal of the American Academy of Psychiatry and Law* indicates that false positive rates for violent recidivism are uniformly at or above 50%. The use of the PCL-R in death penalty cases to offer an expert opinion about future lethal violence is therefore, in my humble opinion, negligent, unethical, and inadmissible under any reasonable interpretation of *Daubert v. Merrell Dow Pharmaceuticals, Inc.* (1993) and *Kumho Tire Co., Ltd. v. Carmichael* (1999).

Let me also warn that attorneys who defend death penalty cases are well aware of this literature. I strongly urge all forensic psychologists to read this literature as well. In the unbridled defense of their clients, defense counsel are ready, willing, and able to attack on cross-examination those unwary psychologists who misuse the PCL-R or any psychological instrument and to report this conduct to the appropriate professional associations.

CONCERN NUMBER SIX: THE CLASH BETWEEN SCIENCE AND CRIMINAL LAW

Nowhere is the disconnect between science and law more obvious than in how we define crime and treat criminals. Criminality is commonly defined as conduct that will incur a formal and solemn pronouncement of the moral condemnation of the community. And, while the Supreme Court pays lip service to deterrence and to an even lesser extent, rehabilitation, the predominant theory underlying the punishment of criminals is retribution. Retributivists believe that punishment is justified because people deserve it. Although the tragedies of September 11th have resurrected the rampant concept of evil and its retaliation by moral crusade, there is nothing new in this. Writing 120 years ago in *A History of the Criminal Law in England*, James Fitzjames Stephen (1883) asserted that:

> [T]he infliction of punishment by law gives definite expression and a solemn ratification and justification to the hatred which is excited by the commission of the offense. . . . The criminal law thus proceeds upon the principle that it is morally right to hate criminals and it confirms and justifies that sentiment by inflicting upon criminals punishments which express it. (p. 81)

Retribution is grounded in the belief that behavior is the result of free will. People freely choose, the position claims, to engage in evil behavior and, therefore, deserve the punishments they receive, including execution at the hands of the State. But, any decently trained psychologist knows that behavior is determined as the result of the confluence of genetic endowment and life experiences. For those who do not ascribe to the reality of determinism, one must respond to the question—Would Hitler or bin Laden have acted as they did if they were born to the doubter's parents, lived in their home town, and gotten their doctorate in psychology? Those who ascribe to free will would make human beings the only species whose behavior was not determined by heredity and the reinforcing impact of their daily lives. Free will is a legal fiction, but an enduring one impervious to the findings of science.

I distinguish between responsibility and accountability. We all have the right to self-defense and to be protected from harm. So, those whose genes and environment lead them to engage in acts that we define as criminal should be held accountable and it may be entirely appropriate to segregate them from society. But, that is much different from viewing them as evildoers deserving of hateful retribution. Adopting a deterministic philosophy would result in more humane institutions, greater reliance on empirically-validated interventions, and, of course, the end of the death penalty. These arguments, however, have been made before and to no avail. Unfortunately, like so many other areas of law, this is another example of how unreceptive the law is to science and reality.

It is my hope that this curmudgeonly rendition of some issues will stimulate discussion and rebuttal. As I wrote about them, it was clear what my core preferences are—privacy over intrusion, autonomy over beneficence, science over faith, rehabilitation over retribution. But this is not where the world seems to be going and it saddens me terribly.

REFERENCES

American Psychological Association. (1992). Ethical principles of psychologists and code of conduct. *American Psychologist, 47,* 1597–1611.

Atkins v. Virginia, 122 S. Ct. 2242, 536 U.S. (2002).

Beauchamp, T., & Childress, J. F. (1994). *Principles of biomedical ethics* (4th ed.). New York: Oxford University Press.

Bersoff, D. N. (1974). Therapists as protectors and policemen: New roles as a result of *Tarasoff*. *Professional Psychology, 7,* 267–273.

Black, C. L. (1974). *Capital punishment: The inevitability of caprice and mistake.* New York: Norton.

Daubert v. Merrell Dow Pharmaceuticals, Inc., 509 U.S. 579 (1993).

Edens, J. (2001). Misuses of the Hare Psychopathy Checklist–Revised in court: Two case examples. *Journal of Interpersonal Violence, 16,* 1082–1093.

Edens, J., Petrila, J., & Buffington-Vollum, J. K. (2001). Psychopathy and the death penalty: Can the Psychopathy Checklist—Revised identify offenders who represent "a continuing threat to society?" *Journal of Psychiatry and Law, 29,* 433–481.

Freedman, D. (2001). False prediction of future dangerousness: Error rates and the Psychopathy Checklist—Revised. *Journal of the American Academy of Psychiatry and Law, 29,* 89–95.

Jaffee v. Redmond, 518 U.S. 1 (1996).

Kumho Tire Co., Ltd. v. Carmichael, 526 U.S. 137 (1999).

McCarver v. North Carolina, No. 00-8727, writ of certiorari dismissed as improvidently granted (Sept. 25, 2001).

Monahan, J., Steadman, H., Silver, E., Appelbaum, P., Robbins, P. C., Mulvey, E., et al. (2001). *Rethinking risk assessment.* New York: Oxford University Press.

Olmstead v. United States, 277 U.S. 438 (1928).

Parham v. J. R., 442 U.S. 584 (1979).

Quinton, W. J., Major, B., & Richards, C. (2001). Adolescents and adjustment at abortion: Are minors at greater risk? *Psychology, Public Policy, and Law, 7,* 491–514.

Reisner, R., Slobogin, C., & Rai, A. (1999). *Law and the mental health system* (3rd ed.). St. Paul, MN: West Group.

Ross, W. D. (1930). *The right and the good.* Oxford, England: Clarendon.

Saks, M. (1989). Legal policy analysis and evaluation. *American Psychologist, 44,* 1110–1117.

Shuman, D., & Greenberg, S. (1998, Winter). The role of ethical norms in the admissibility of expert testimony. *The Judges' Journal, 37,* 4–9; 42–43.

Sorenson, J. R., & Pilgrim, R. L. (2000). Criminology: An actuarial risk assessment of violence posed by capital murder defendants. *Journal of Criminal Law and Criminology, 90,* 1251–1270.

Stephen, J. F. (1883). A history of the criminal law in England (Vol. 2), quoted in Dressler, J. (1999). *Cases and materials on criminal law* (2nd ed.). St. Paul, MN: West Group.

Tarasoff v. Regents of University of California, 551 P.2d 334 (1976).

Thapar v. Zezulka, 994 S.W.2d 635 (Tex. 1999).

United States v. Quinones, No. S3 00 CR 761, 2002 WL 1415648 (S.D.N.Y. 2002).

COMMENTARY: What better perspective is there than that of the "contrarian" for identifying ethical conflicts that have been hiding in plain sight—in some cases, for many years? Here, Dr. Bersoff addresses notions that in some cases may have seemed too politically fraught for earnest dissection and that, in other cases, found clinicians and researchers proceeding in lockstep, if only out of a sense that no practical solution appeared feasible. Upon the waning of an initial sense of surprise, quite a few approaches suggested here make one wonder why they hadn't surfaced much earlier.

The welcome movement to exclude persons with intellectual disability from the death penalty may secondarily and unintentionally have served to undercut our recognition of the humanity and autonomy needs of the individuals whose lives such innovations were designed to protect. Diversity and inclusiveness may not have wound up being as easily blended as we expected. The transformation of research measures into clinical ones has yielded policy concerns as well as scientific ones.

The following references are recommended for those interested in further investigation of the perspectives aired in Dr. Bersoff's underlying address—ones that he openly acknowledged "may cut against the majoritarian grain."

Abeles, N. (2010). In the public interest: Intellectual disability, the Supreme Court, and the death penalty. *American Psychologist, 65*, 743–748. http://dx.doi.org/10.1037/0003-066X.65.8.743

Alger, J. R. (2013). A supreme challenge: Achieving the educational and societal benefits of diversity after the Supreme Court's *Fisher* decision. *Journal of Diversity in Higher Education, 6*, 147–154. http://dx.doi.org/10.1037/a0034355

Bushman, B. J., & Pollard-Sacks, D. (2014). Supreme Court decision on violent video games was based on the First Amendment, not scientific evidence. *American Psychologist, 69*, 306–307. http://dx.doi.org/10.1037/a0035509

Duvall, J. C., & Morris, R. J. (2006). Assessing mental retardation in death penalty cases: Critical issues for psychology and psychological practice. *Professional Psychology: Research and Practice, 37*, 658–665. http://dx.doi.org/10.1037/0735-7028.37.6.658

Jeandarme, I., Edens, J. F., Habets, P., Bruckers, L., Oei, K., & Bogaerts, S. (2017). PCL-R field validity in prison and hospital settings. *Law and Human Behavior, 41*, 29–43. http://dx.doi.org/10.1037/lhb0000222

4.5. Limiting Therapist Exposure to *Tarasoff* Liability: Guidelines for Risk Containment

John Monahan

Mention the word *law* in conversation with practicing psychologists, psychiatrists, and social workers, and they will soon speak of *Tarasoff v. Regents of the University of California* (1976). No case is better known or evokes stronger feelings. Initially the subject of vilification by mental health professionals, the California Supreme Court's holding in *Tarasoff*—that psychotherapists who know or should know of their patient's likelihood of inflicting injury on identifiable third parties have an obligation to take reasonable steps to protect the potential victim—has become a familiar part of the clinical landscape. Although a few state courts have rejected *Tarasoff* and others have limited its scope, most courts that have addressed the issue have accepted the essence of the "duty to protect," and several have even expanded that duty to include nonidentifiable victims (for reviews, see Appelbaum, 1988; Beck, 1985, 1990; Schopp, 1991; Smith, 1991). In jurisdictions in which appellate courts have not yet ruled on the question, the prudent clinician is well advised to proceed under the assumption that some version of Tarasoff liability will be imposed (Appelbaum, 1985, p. 426). The duty to protect, in short, is now a fact of professional life for nearly all American clinicians and, potentially, for clinical researchers as well (Appelbaum & Rosenbaum, 1989).

I have served as an expert witness in several dozen cases in which the therapist's duty to protect others from a patient's violence was at issue. In each of these cases, someone had been killed or injured by a patient or former patient of a psychologist, psychiatrist, or social worker. The questions put to me were always the same: Would a reasonable therapist, applying the professional standards that existed at the time of the treatment, have assessed the patient's risk of violence as sufficient to justify preventive intervention, and if so, was an appropriate intervention chosen? Initially, given my view (Monahan, 1976) that violence was virtually impossible to validly assess, I was retained solely by defense attorneys. Later, as I came to believe that risk assessment might be

From "Limiting Therapist Exposure to *Tarasoff* Liability: Guidelines for Risk Containment," by J. Monahan, 1993, *American Psychologist, 48,* pp. 242–250. Copyright 1993 by the American Psychological Association.

Melissa G. Warren served as action editor for this article.

This work was supported by the Research Network on Mental Health and the Law of the John D. and Catherine T. MacArthur Foundation.

I am grateful to Paul Appelbaum, Joel Dvoskin, S. Ken Hoge, and Norman Poythress for their comments on the article.

feasible and appropriate under some circumstances (Monahan, 1981, 1984), referrals began to come equally from defense and plaintiff's attorneys.

In working on these cases and seeing the obvious emotional, financial, and reputational costs that they placed upon the defendant therapists and their institutions (Brodsky, 1988; Poythress & Brodsky, 1992), I often thought about what the therapist could have done to have foreseen and prevented his or her patient's violence, or at least, when the violence was not foreseeable, to have reduced his or her own exposure to civil liability. In this article, I organize those reflections into a series of guidelines for violence prevention and the reduction of exposure to liability that may be useful to practicing mental health professionals. No jurisdiction currently requires adherence to all, or even to most, of these guidelines in order to meet professional standards of care for dealing with potentially violent patients. Thus failure to act as suggested here does not necessarily mean that liability "ought" to be found by a jury. Each of these guidelines, however, has played a prominent role in at least one "failure to predict" case on which I have been retained. The guidelines cluster in five domains: risk assessment, risk management, documentation, policy, and damage control. . . .

RISK ASSESSMENT

Four tasks form the basis of any professionally adequate risk assessment: The clinician must be educated about what information to gather regarding risk, must gather it, must use this information to estimate risk, and, if the clinician is not the ultimate decision maker, must communicate the information and estimate to those who are responsible for making clinical decisions.

Education

The essence of being a "professional" is having "specialized knowledge" not available to the general public. In this context, specialized knowledge consists of both knowledge of mental disorder in general (e.g., assessment, diagnosis, and treatment) and knowledge of risk assessment in particular. In addition, one should be thoroughly conversant with the laws of the jurisdiction in which one practices regarding the steps to follow when a positive risk assessment is made.

Clinical Education

Familiarity with basic concepts in risk assessment (e.g., predictor and criterion variables, true and false positives and negatives, decision rules, and base rates) and with key findings of risk assessment research (e.g., past violence as the single best predictor of future violence) is becoming an important aspect of graduate education in psychology, psychiatry, and social work. For clinicians whose graduate education predated this emphasis or neglected it, many books and articles are readily available (e.g., Appelbaum & Gutheil, 1991; Bednar, Bednar, Lambert, & Waite, 1991; Simon, 1987; Tardiff, 1989). One does not have to commit these works to memory. But I have seen the blood drain from clinicians' faces when a plaintiff's attorney begins a cross-examination by reading a list of well-known titles in the area and asks whether the witness has read them, and the clinician is forced to mumble "no" (see Brodsky, 1991).

It is not enough to learn the basic concepts and classic findings in the field of risk assessment once and consider one's education complete. Research findings evolve and become modified over time, and the conventions of professional practice become more sophisticated. Continuing education in risk assessment through formal programs sponsored by professional or private organizations is one way to keep apprised of developments in the field. Periodically perusing original research journals (e.g., *Law and Human Behavior, Behavioral Sciences and the Law*, the *International Journal of Law and Psychiatry*) is another.

In the context of large facilities for assessing and treating mentally disordered people, the most efficient form of risk education may be to charge one person with the responsibility of being a "risk educator." This person's responsibilities might include maintaining a small reference library of literature on risk, keeping abreast of developments in the field, and communicating his or her conclusions to other staff through in-house workshops, reading groups, or occasional memoranda. This person might be an ideal candidate for a local consultant for cases that present difficult risk issues.

Legal Education

The standards to which clinicians will be held in making judgments on risk are set largely by state law. In the past, these standards were usually articulated by judges who applied common law tort principles to the context of clinical risk assessment. This is what happened in *Tarasoff* and similar cases in other states. Increasingly, and after intense lobbying by professional mental health organizations, state legislatures are passing statutes to make standards for liability and immunity in this area explicit (Appelbaum, Zonana, Bonnie, & Roth, 1989). These statutes, however, will still require much adjudication to interpret inevitably ambiguous terminology (e.g., what counts as a "serious threat" or a "reasonably identifiable victim" in California's, 1990, statute?). The point here is that there is no national legal standard for what clinicians should do when they assess risk (Givelber, Bowers, & Blitch, 1984), and that it behooves clinicians to know precisely what the legal standards in their own jurisdiction are regarding violence prevention. State mental health professional associations ought to have this information readily available.

Information

Once a clinician knows what information, in general, may be relevant to assessing risk, he or she must take efforts to gather that information in a given case. Most of the *Tarasoff*-like cases on which I have worked have faulted clinicians not for making an inaccurate prediction but for failing to gather information that would have made a reasonable effort at prediction possible. There are generally four sources in which relevant information can be found: in the records of past treatment, in the records of current treatment, from interviewing the patient, and from interviewing significant others. In some criminal contexts (e.g., assessments for suitability for release on parole or from insanity commitment) additional records in the form of police and probation reports, arrest records, and trial transcripts may also be available and should be consulted. But in the civil context, these records are generally not available to clinicians.

Past Records

The only cases in which I have been involved that were, in the words of the defense attorneys, "born dead" were those in which the patient had an extensive history of prior violence that was amply documented in reasonably available treatment records, but those records were never requested. In these cases, the clinician has been forced to acknowledge on the witness stand that if he or she had seen the records, preventive action would have been taken.

The emphasis in the previous paragraph should be on the phrase *reasonably available*. At one extreme, I served as an expert witness for the defendant in a case in which a patient was hospitalized for a few days and killed a person shortly after being released. One of the arguments of the plaintiff's attorney to support a finding of negligent release was that the treating clinician had not written to the Philippines, where the patient had briefly been hospitalized many years earlier, to obtain the treatment records. This is clearly absurd (i.e., unreasonable), as the patient would in any event have been discharged long before the records had arrived (and had been translated from Tagalog), assuming that they ever would have been sent.

At the other extreme, however, I was the plaintiff's witness in a case in which an outpatient clinic was on the ground floor of a building that housed an affiliated mental hospital. A patient whose hospital records were replete with extreme violence was transferred from the hospital to the outpatient clinic. The hospital did not send the records with the patient, and the outpatient clinic did not request them, at least not until the staff read in the newspapers that the patient—now *their* patient—had been arrested for murder.

Somewhere between writing to the Philippines and walking upstairs, a line has to be drawn as to what constitutes a reasonable effort to obtain records of past treatment. I know of no standard operating procedure on this question. "Records" does not have to mean the entire hospital file; a discharge summary may often suffice. More of a priority might be accorded to requesting the records of patients whose hospitalization was precipitated by a violent incident, or who exhibited violence in the hospital, than to requesting the records of other patients. In the context of long-term hospitalization, of course, there will be more opportunity to obtain records from distant facilities than would be the case for short-term treatment (this opportunity to obtain records is also present for patients with repeated short-term hospitalizations). Hospitals in the same geographic area or in the same treatment system (e.g., among public hospitals in the same state or between state hospitals and community mental health centers) might be expected to have established procedures for transferring information. Records of more recent hospitalizations (e.g., within the past five years) may be more probative of risk than may older hospital records. But when indications are that the current hospitalization will be brief and when prior hospitalizations were at distant locations or occurred long ago, it is clearly not standard practice to request records. Nor should it be. It takes time and money to request, locate, copy, transmit, and read treatment records—resources that might more profitably be spent providing treatment.

Current Records

Reading the chart of the current hospitalization when making risk judgments about hospitalized patients is essential. I am continually amazed, however, at how often clinicians peruse the chart as if it were a magazine in a dentist's waiting room. In particular, nursing notes, in which violent acts and threats are often to be found, are frequently glossed over. Yet, I have seen plaintiff's attorneys introduce exhibits consisting of eight-foot-by-four-foot photographic enlargements of pages from nursing notes containing statements such as, "assaulted several other patients without provocation tonight," and "patient threatening to kill spouse as soon as released." These exhibits certainly concentrated the jury's attention.

Inquiries of the Patient

Clinicians appear to question patients more often about a history of violence to self or current suicidal ideation, than about a history of violence to others or current violent fantasies. There seems little justification for this inconsistency. Directly asking patients about violent behavior and possible indices of violent behavior (e.g., arrest or hospitalization as "dangerous to others") is surely the easiest and quickest way to obtain this essential information. Open-ended questions such as "What is the most violent thing you have ever done?" or "What is the closest you have ever come to being violent?" may be useful probes, as might "Do you ever worry that you might physically hurt somebody?" The obvious problem, of course, is that patients may lie or distort their history or their current thoughts. This is always a possibility, but often corroborating information will be available from the records (above) or from significant others (below). Quite often, however, patients are remarkably forthcoming about violence. And although there may be reasons to suspect a negative answer in a given case, a positive answer should always be pursued. Unless a question to the patient is ventured, potentially valuable information on risk will not be gained.

Inquiries of Significant Others

Records are often unavailable, and patients are sometimes not reliable informants. A significant other, usually a family member, is frequently available in the case of inpatient hospitalization, however, either in person (accompanying the patient to treatment or seen later in conjunction with the patient's therapy) or at least by telephone. Asking the significant other about any violent behavior or threats in the event that precipitated hospitalization, or in the past, as well as open-ended questions such as "Are you concerned that X might hurt someone?" with appropriate follow-up questions as to the basis for any expressed concern, may yield useful information.

Estimation

I have elsewhere suggested a clinical model for estimating a patient's risk of violent behavior (Monahan, 1981). Although the mental health professions have yet to demonstrate that the accuracy of their estimations of risk is high in absolute terms, it is clearly high relative to chance. For example, Kozol, Boucher, and Garofalo (1972), in one of the most cited prediction studies, identified a group of patients, 35% of whom were found to have committed a violent act within five years of release. The base (i.e., chance) rate of violence was 11%. Thirty-five percent is both much lower than 100% and much higher than 11%. Whether these clinical predictions were any more accurate than those that could have been made by nonclinicians (or actuarial tables) using simple demographic variables, however, is unknown. More recent research (e.g., Klassen & O'Connor, 1988) has demonstrated considerably more accurate predictions with narrowly defined groups of high-risk patients. . . .

Communication

In the individual practice of psychotherapy, the clinician who gathers information on risk is also the clinician who makes decisions based on this information. But in outpatient treatment agencies and in mental hospitals, a division of labor often exists: One person may do the intake, another may be responsible for patient care, a team of several professionals may provide a variety of assessment and treatment modalities, and one person will have formal responsibility for making or approving discharge decisions. Although this division of labor may be an efficient use of resources, it does raise an issue not present in the solo practitioner context: the communication of relevant information from one mental health professional to another. Here, information must be transferred between or among clinicians, and significant information must be made salient to the person responsible for making the ultimate decisions regarding the patient (Klein, 1986).

Placing all relevant information in the chart, of course, is the primary way of transferring information among treatment professionals. As long as the person ultimately responsible for making the institutionalization or discharge decision reads the entire file, the information is thereby communicated to the person who needs to know it.

In the real world of professional practice, however, information is not always effectively communicated by simply passing on a chart. The ultimate decision maker may be a harried senior staff member whose signature is often a pro forma endorsement of the recommendations of line staff, based only on a brief discharge summary. Or the amount of information in the chart, including information from numerous past hospitalizations, may be literally so voluminous that no final decision maker would be expected to read it verbatim.

For example, I was involved in a case in which a private hospital sought to transfer a chronic patient to a community care facility. The hospital "discharge planner" needed a dolly to move several cartons of records on this patient to the office of the community facility's intake director. Numerous violent incidents were recorded throughout this massive record, but none of them were mentioned on the hospital's upbeat discharge summary (the hospital appeared to be trying to sell the patient to the community facility). It was unreasonable, the jury believed, for the hospital to expect the community intake worker to sit down for several days and read the entire record before accepting this patient, especially because the hospital also wanted transfer decisions to be made on a number of other patients by the end of a one-hour meeting.

It is not sufficient to dump undigested information on the desk of the ultimate decision maker and to claim that he or she assumed the risk of liability by taking possession of the file. Rather, information pertinent to risk should explicitly (and in writing, see below) be brought to the attention of the decision maker. Only by making the information salient can one be assured that the decision maker has had the option to make use of it.

From the decision-maker's vantage point, the implications of information overload are equally clear: When the transfer or discharge summary prepared by others makes no explicit positive or negative reference to risk, one should directly ask what information relevant to risk is in the chart and should record the answer. . . .

REFERENCES

Appelbaum, P. (1985). *Tarasoff* and the clinician: Problems in fulfilling the duty to protect. *American Journal of Psychiatry, 142,* 425–429.

Appelbaum, P. (1988). The new preventive detention: Psychiatry's problematic responsibility for the control of violence. *American Journal of Psychiatry, 145,* 779–785.

Appelbaum, P., & Gutheil, T. (1991). *Clinical handbook of psychiatry and the law* (2nd ed.). Baltimore: Williams & Wilkins.

Appelbaum, P., & Rosenbaum, A. (1989). *Tarasoff* and the researcher: Does the duty to protect apply in the research setting? *American Psychologist, 44,* 885–894.

Appelbaum, P., Zonana, H., Bonnie, R., & Roth, L. H. (1989). Statutory approaches to limiting psychiatrists' liability for their patients' violent acts. *American Journal of Psychiatry, 146,* 821–828.

Beck, J. (Ed.). (1985). *The potentially violent patient and the Tarasoff decision in psychiatric practice.* Washington, DC: American Psychiatric Press.

Beck, J. (1990). *Confidentiality versus the duty to protect: Forseeable harm in the practice of psychiatry.* Washington, DC: American Psychiatric Press.

Bednar, R., Bednar, S., Lambert, M., & Waite, D. (1991). *Psychotherapy with high-risk clients: Legal and professional standards.* Pacific Grove, CA: Brooks/Cole.

Brodsky, S. (1988). Fear of litigation in mental health professionals. *Criminal Justice and Behavior, 15,* 492–500.

Brodsky, S. L. (1991). *Testifying in court: Guidelines and maxims for the expert witness.* Washington, DC: American Psychological Association.

Givelber, D., Bowers, W., & Blitch, C. (1984). *Tarasoff,* myth and reality: An empirical study of private law in action. *Wisconsin Law Review, 1984,* 443–497.

Klassen, D., & O'Connor, W. (1988). A prospective study of predictors of violence in adult male mental patients. *Law and Human Behavior, 12,* 143–158.

Klein, J. (1986). The professional liability crisis: An interview with Joel Klein. *Hospital and Community Psychiatry, 37,* 1012–1016.

Kozol, H. L., Boucher, R. J., & Garofalo, R. F. (1972). The diagnosis and treatment of dangerousness. *Crime & Delinquency, 18,* 371–392.

Monahan, J. (1976). The prevention of violence. In J. Monahan (Ed.), *Community mental health and the criminal justice system* (pp. 1334). New York: Pergamon Press.

Monahan, J. (1981). *The clinical prediction of violent behavior.* Washington, DC: U.S. Government Printing Office.

Monahan, J. (1984). The prediction of violent behavior: Toward a second generation of theory and policy. *American Journal of Psychiatry, 141,* 10–15.

Poythress, N., & Brodsky, S. (1992). In the wake of a negligent release suit: An investigation of professional consequences and institutional impact on a state psychiatric hospital. *Law and Human Behavior, 16,* 155–174.

Schopp, R. (1991). The psychotherapist's duty to protect the public: The appropriate standard and the foundation in legal theory and empirical research. *Nebraska Law Review, 70,* 327–360.

Simon, R. (1987). *Clinical psychiatry and the law.* Washington, DC: American Psychiatric Press.

Smith, S. (1991). Mental health malpractice in the 1990s. *Houston Law Review, 28,* 209–283.

Tarasoff v. Regents of the University of California, 131 Cal. Rptr. 14, 551 P 2d 334 (1976).

Tardiff, K. (1989). *Concise guide to assessment and management of violent patients.* Washington, DC: American Psychiatric Press.

COMMENTARY: It is the nagging concern, if not recurrent nightmare, of every psychological treatment provider that one of our clients/patients will next surface not in the waiting room but in the top headline of a 24-hour news channel. How do we walk the line between reporting the stray remarks of every disgruntled, resentful, or reproachful service recipient to the police and simply shrugging off overwrought expressions of vengeful fantasy with the advice to "try to let go of this and we'll meet again next week"?

"Limiting exposure" may present itself to some as an inherently distasteful goal, indicative to some extent of "defensive practice" and its antitherapeutic implications. Such concerns are certainly valid, but professional responsibilities ultimately extend to oneself, one's family, and one's employees as well as to clients/patients and to persons who might otherwise be subjected to harm. Liability emerges due to the failure to maintain articulated standards of practice and care—standards devised to protect everyone, not just the psychological treatment provider.

The following references are recommended for those interested in further investigation of how ethical and legal requirements have been identified, disseminated, perpetuated, and revised in the several decades following the seminal *Tarasoff* decision.

Barnett, J. E., & Kolmes, K. (2016). The practice of tele-mental health: Ethical, legal, and clinical issues for practitioners. *Practice Innovations, 1,* 53–66. http://dx.doi.org/10.1037/pri0000014

Bersoff, D. N. (2014). Protecting victims of violent patients while protecting confidentiality. *American Psychologist, 69,* 461–467. http://dx.doi.org/10.1037/a0037198

Huey, S. R. (2015). *Tarasoff*'s catch-22. *American Psychologist, 70,* 284–285.

Johnson, R., Persad, G., & Sisti, D. (2014). The *Tarasoff* rule: The implications of interstate variation and gaps in professional training. *Journal of the American Academy of Psychiatry and the Law, 42,* 469–477.

Pabian, Y. L., Welfel, E., & Beebe, R. S. (2009). Psychologists' knowledge of their states' laws pertaining to *Tarasoff*-type situations. *Professional Psychology: Research and Practice, 40,* 8–14. http://dx.doi.org/10.1037/a0014784

4.6. Outpatient Psychotherapy With Dangerous Clients: A Model for Clinical Decision Making

Derek Truscott, Jim Evans, and Sheila Mansell

Outpatient psychotherapy with a dangerous client poses a conflict for therapists between therapeutic, ethical, and legal duties to the client and a legal duty to protect any potential victims of the client's violent behavior. If a threat of violence is made known to others, either for the purpose of warning a potential victim or alerting law enforcement officials to prevent the violent act, it violates the client's confidence and could result in the client feeling intense embarrassment or anger; being charged, arrested, and possibly convicted of a criminal offense; or being denied or refusing further treatment. The therapist could also face disciplinary or civil charges for breaching confidentiality. If, on the other hand, the threat is kept confidential, any subsequent violence might have been prevented and the therapist may feel guilt, anxiety, lowered confidence, and a reluctance to treat similar clients; also, the therapist may face a lawsuit.

Before the 1976 California Supreme Court decision of *Tarasoff v. Regents of the University of California*, psychotherapists tended not to be concerned about legal liability for their clients' behavior outside the therapy. The *Tarasoff* court ruled, however, that psychotherapists in California have a duty to exercise reasonable care to protect the potential victims of their clients' violent behavior. Although the ruling was relevant only in California, almost every other jurisdiction in the United States (Fulero, 1988; Kamenar, 1984) as well as Canada (Truscott & Crook, 1993) has applied analogous legal reasoning. Although some jurisdictions differ,[1] the duty to protect generally exists when a client has been (or reasonably should have been) assessed to pose a serious threat of physical violence to a reasonably identifiable victim or victims and when the chain of causation that results in harm is clear (Truscott & Crook, 1993). Of note also is the fact that *Tarasoff* did not establish a duty to warn, as is often incorrectly asserted (Truscott, 1993). An earlier, and much publicized (Gurevitz, 1977), 1974 decision (*Tarasoff v. Regents of the University of California*,

---

[1] Clinicians are advised to be aware of the existing position in their jurisdiction.

From "Outpatient Psychotherapy With Dangerous Clients: A Model for Clinical Decision Making," by D. Truscott, J. Evans, and S. Mansell, 1995, *Professional Psychology: Research and Practice, 26,* pp. 484–490. Copyright 1995 by the American Psychological Association.

Research was conducted with funding from the Social Sciences and Humanities Research Council of Canada. Opinions expressed in this article are solely those of the authors and not necessarily those of the funding agency.

We are indebted to Steve Knish for his contribution to this article.

1974) did rule that California psychotherapists had a duty to warn, but that ruling was reheard by the California Supreme Court and superseded by the 1976 duty-to-protect decision.

Although the duty to protect does not appear to have necessitated a radical change in therapeutic practice (Givelber, Bowers, & Blitch, 1984), it has resulted in an increased fear of liability on the part of some therapists and an avoidance by some of probing into matters of dangerousness (Wise, 1978). It has also forced clinicians to consider more seriously risk for violence and to integrate that consideration into their clinical decision making. The difficulty, however, is that no standard of care for dangerous clients has been established.

In an attempt to establish just such a standard of care, Botkin and Nietzel (1987) surveyed psychologists about their use of therapeutic interventions with dangerous outpatients. Hospitalizing, building rapport, managing the client's environment so that the client would be less likely to attack others, and breaking confidentiality were rated as the interventions psychologists were most likely to employ. Therapists more experienced in the treatment of dangerous clients were more likely than those less experienced to involve significant others in treatment, to manage the client's environment, and to use behaviorally based treatments. Similarly, Monahan (1993) identified three categories of interventions for clients who pose a high risk of physical violence to others: incapacitation (hospitalization), target hardening (warning potential victims), and intensified treatment. The purpose of our article is to present a model for clinical decision making to aid clinicians in selecting interventions for dealing with dangerous clients in the outpatient setting. It is, of course, tentative and exploratory at this point, and we eagerly await its evaluation beyond this paper.

INTERVENTION SELECTION

When a client's potential for violence becomes an issue in outpatient psycho-therapy, the therapist rarely has the time to ponder the finer points of ethics, legal duty, diagnosis, and other issues. We propose that the client be thought of as occupying one of four cells in a 2×2, Violence Risk × Alliance Strength, table. Interventions are then selected to strengthen the therapeutic alliance and reduce the risk of violence as identified by Botkin and Nietzel (1987) and Monahan (1993), thereby "moving" the client to the lower right cell of low violence risk, strong therapeutic alliance. This formulation is presented in Figure 1.

We assert that attending to the degree of violence risk and the strength of the therapeutic alliance is central both to the effective treatment of these clients and to the protection of their potential victims. The therapeutic alliance should be strengthened as much as possible because it is the foundation on which all treatment interventions are built (Whiston & Sexton, 1993); furthermore, if one acts only to prevent a current violent episode without attending to the therapeutic alliance, it may enrage a client and actually increase the risk of violence while simultaneously deterring the client from

FIGURE 1. Model for Decision Making with Dangerous Clients

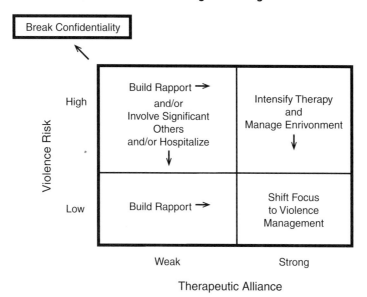

seeking further psychotherapeutic services for dealing with any future violent impulses (Weinstock, 1988). If the risk of violence is low, the therapist should attempt to strengthen the alliance and to shift the focus of therapy to deal more specifically with the violent behavior (as one would with any therapeutic issue).

ASSESSING VIOLENCE RISK

The low degree of certitude in predicting violence on the part of psychotherapists is well documented in the research literature (Wettstein, 1984), but this does not, in and of itself, make all acts of violence unforeseeable on the part of a psychotherapist. The legal test is one of "reasonable foreseeability," not "certainty." That is, would a prudent psychothcrapist have predicted violence on the part of the client (*Barefoot v. Estelle*, 1983)? Our ability to make accurate long-term predictions of any human behavior, particularly a relatively rare behavior such as violence, is poor. This difficulty is because complex human behaviors are rarely, if ever, the result of stable individual traits. Rather, they result from an interaction between characteristics of the individual and his or her environment. Virtually anyone is capable of violent behavior despite being usually nonviolent, whereas even the most violently predisposed individual is not always behaving violently. Stated differently, individual characteristics are neither necessary nor sufficient causes of violent behavior, whereas in most cases situational characteristics can be (cf. Felson & Steadman, 1983). It is for these reasons that psychometric assessment has little to add to the prediction of imminent violence (Monahan, 1981).

Individual characteristics can serve to alter the threshold at which situational characteristics precipitate violence. An individual who possesses many characteristics typical of violence-prone persons would be considered at high risk for violence given relatively fewer situational precipitants. When one is working with a violence-prone individual, therefore, close attention should be paid to situational variables.

Thorough records are critical to document that appropriate procedures were followed and reasonable steps were taken in light of the facts. Liability is usually imposed for failing to follow appropriate procedures (especially in gathering or communicating information), not for errors.in judgment in light of the known facts (Monahan, 1993). The degree to which relevant information can be obtained will depend on the circumstances of the case. If a client presents with problems related to angry or violent behavior, a thorough assessment of violence-related factors should be undertaken at intake. If concerns arise unexpectedly in the course of therapy, every reasonable effort should be made to obtain the information needed without unduly disrupting the therapeutic alliance. The following variables to be considered are adapted from Meloy (1987) and Monahan (1981).

Individual Characteristics

Demographic Variables
Violent behavior is most often perpetrated by non-White males in their late teens or early 20s who have a history of opiate or alcohol abuse, have a low IQ and education, and have an unstable residential and employment history. The more closely an individual resembles this fictional modal violent person, the lower the threshold for current risk.

Violence History
This is the single most powerful predictor of violent behavior. The more recent, severe, and frequent was the past violence, the lower the threshold for current risk. Such indexes as juvenile or adult court involvement for violent acts, hospitalizations for dangerous behavior, and self-reported violence are relevant.

Situational Characteristics

Availability of Potential Victim(s)
The majority of violent crimes occur between people who know each other. Also, does the client have a history of aggressing against a particular type of person (e.g., women or coworkers) or in a particular setting? If the current situation involves the same or similar type of person or setting, the risk for violence is high.

Access to a Weapon
Weapons are both situationally disinhibiting and lethal. An individual with combat or martial arts training, or an individual who possesses great strength, is capable of inflicting greater harm.

Alcohol Use

Alcohol (or other disinhibitors) increase the risk of impulsive behavior.

Stressors

Stress related to family, relationships, peer group, finances, and employment can erode an individual's frustration tolerance as well as provide the motivation for violence.

ASSESSING THE THERAPEUTIC ALLIANCE

. . . Gelso and Carter (1985) developed a three-component model of the therapeutic relationship and later elaborated the interactions among these components (Gelso & Carter, 1994). Their model was based on an earlier three-component model proposed by Greenson (1967) and includes the working alliance, the transference relationship, and the real relationship. Gelso and Carter argued that all components are present in all therapeutic relationships, but emphasis given to the components of the relationship varies according to the therapist's theoretical perspective.

The therapeutic alliance refers to the development of an emotionally warm relationship and an alignment of client and therapist that creates the sense of working together toward common therapy goals. The transference, or unreal, relationship refers to the client's repetition of past feelings, behaviors, and attitudes connected with earlier relationships in his or her interaction with the therapist. This unreal, or distorted, component also includes countertransference: the therapist's responses to the client that are prompted by events in the therapist's own life and past significant relationships. The real relationship refers to the humanistic concepts of therapist genuineness, warmth, authenticity, and congruence and also includes the interchange between client and therapist. It is the therapeutic alliance that is most important to client compliance with treatment and to successful therapy outcome (Horvath & Greenberg, 1994).

Bordin (1994) developed a formulation of the therapeutic alliance that incorporates a mutual understanding and agreement between therapist and client about the goals of therapy, the necessary tasks to move toward these goals, and the establishment of an emotional bond to maintain the work of this partnership. The active collaboration of the therapist with the client in determining goals and tasks and the forming of bonds are central to the development of a strong alliance and promote client compliance to treatment. The development of this therapeutic alliance early in the relationship is crucial and is predictive of a significant proportion of final outcome variance (Henry & Strupp, 1994; Horvath & Symonds, 1991).

Formal Assessment of the Therapeutic Alliance

A number of measures have been developed to assess the therapeutic alliance. They include the Working Alliance Inventory (Horvath & Greenberg, 1989), the Penn Helping Alliance Scale (Morgan, Luborsky, Crits-Christoph, Curtis, & Solomon, 1982), the Vanderbilt Therapeutic Alliance Scale (Hartley & Strupp, 1983), and the California Psychotherapy Alliance Scale (Gaston & Ring, 1992). . . . These measures are primarily research instruments that continue to undergo validation studies, however, and are not suited for use by practicing therapists to assess the status of the therapeutic relationship.

Informal Assessment of the Therapeutic Alliance

To determine what the client perceives as helpful or engaging in therapy, the initial client assessment should include an active inquiry into the client's history of other constructive interpersonal relationships (Whiston & Sexton, 1993). Also it will be relevant to determine the client's expectations of the therapy relationship (Whiston & Sexton, 1993). Because the therapeutic alliance is interactive, it is important to periodically review the alliance and to maintain a record of indicators through careful and detailed case notes. Careful documentation can help address any biases associated with retrospective interpretation of the alliance by enabling a comparison of current experience with previous notes. Consultation may also be helpful in assessing the therapeutic alliance. In addition, the therapist's personal reactions to clients may provide additional insights into how the therapy is progressing and may suggest various interventions that can help a struggling alliance.

The client's view of the therapeutic alliance is regarded as especially predictive of therapy outcome (Luborsky, 1994; Whiston & Sexton, 1993). The following client perceptions to be considered are adapted from Bordin (1994), Gelso and Carter (1985), and Whiston and Sexton (1993).

Trust
The working alliance is based on the client trusting the therapist to place the client's best interest first and help the client face his or her problems no matter what those interests and problems may be. It is also dependent on the client perceiving the therapist as genuine and as an expert. The degree to which the client is able to trust people in general (especially any paranoid tendencies) and any previous experience with trust issues in therapy (e.g., perceived abandonment) are also relevant.

Understanding and Acceptance
Has the client expressed, explicitly or implicitly, positive interpersonal feelings toward the therapist? Does the client perceive the therapist as warm, supportive, concerned, empathic, compassionate, and respectful? Is there an emotional bond with the therapist?

Working Toward Shared Goals
How has the client formulated his or her reason for seeking help? What are the client's change goals and are they consistent and congruent with the therapist's?

Helpfulness of Therapy

Has the client expressed any opinions about the helpfulness of therapy so far? Any missed appointments and reasons for same may be relevant.

Values of Treatment Process

Does the client agree with the therapist as to what tasks and behaviors will be helpful in attaining their shared goals? In particular, to what degree is the client committed to discussing problems in therapy rather than acting on them outside of the therapy? . . .

REFERENCES

Barefoot v. Estelle, 51 LW 5190 (1983).

Bordin, E. S. (1994). Theory and research on the therapeutic working alliance: New directions. In A. O. Horvath & L. S. Greenberg (Eds.), *The working alliance: Theory, research, and practice* (pp. 13–37). New York: Wiley.

Botkin, D. J., & Nietzel, M. T. (1987). How therapists manage potentially dangerous clients: Toward a standard of care for psychotherapists. *Professional Psychology: Research and Practice, 18*, 84–85.

Felson, R. B., & Steadman, H. J. (1983). Situational factors in disputes leading to criminal violence. *Criminology, 21*, 59–74.

Fulero, S. M. (1988). Tarasoff: 10 years later. *Professional Psychology: Research and Practice, 19*, 184–190.

Gaston, L., & Ring, J. M. (1992). Preliminary results on the Inventory of Therapeutic Strategies. *Journal of Psychotherapy Research and Practice, I*, 1–13.

Gelso, C. J., & Carter, J. A. (1985). The relationship in counseling and psychotherapy: Components, consequences, and theoretical antecedents. *The Counseling Psychologist, 13*, 155–244.

Gelso, C. J., & Carter, J. A. (1994). Components of the psychotherapy relationship: Their interaction and unfolding during treatment. *Journal of Counseling Psychology, 41*, 296–306.

Givelber, D. J., Bowers, W. J. & Blitch, C. L. (1984). *Tarasoff*, myth and reality: An empirical study of private law in action. *Wisconsin Law Review, 1984*, 443–497.

Greenson, R. R. (1967). *The technique and practice of psychoanalysis* (Vol. 1). Madison, CT: International Universities Press.

Gurevitz, H. (1977). *Tarasoff*: Protective privilege versus public peril. *American Journal of Psychiatry, 134*, 289–292.

Hartley, D. E., & Strupp, H. H. (1983). The therapeutic alliance: Its relation to outcome in brief psychotherapy. In J. Masling (Ed.), *Empirical studies in analytic theories* (pp. 1–37). Hillsdale, NJ: Erlbaum.

Henry, W. P., & Strupp, H. H. (1994). The therapeutic alliance as interpersonal process. In A. O. Horvath & L. S. Greenberg (Eds.), *The working alliance: Theory, research, and practice* (pp. 51–84). New York: Wiley.

Horvath, A. O., & Greenberg, L. S. (1989). Development and validation of the Working Alliance Inventory. *Journal of Counseling Psychology, 36*, 223–233.

Horvath, A. O., & Greenberg, L. S. (Eds.). (1994). *The working alliance: Theory, research, and practice*. New York: Wiley.

Horvath, A. O., & Symonds, B. D. (1991). Relation between working alliance and outcome in psychotherapy: A meta-analysis. *Journal of Counseling Psychology, 38*, 139–149.

Kamenar, P. D. (1984). Psychiatrists' duty to warn of a dangerous patient: A survey of the law. *Behavioral Sciences and the Law, 2*, 259–272.

Luborsky, L. (1994). Therapeutic alliances as predictors of psychotherapy outcomes: Factors explaining the predictive success. In A. O. Horvath & L. S. Greenberg (Eds.), *The working alliance: Theory, research, and practice* (pp. 38–50). New York: Wiley.

Meloy, J. R. (1987). The prediction of violence in outpatient psychotherapy. *American Journal of Psychotherapy, 41,* 38–45.

Monahan, J. (1981). *Predicting violent behavior: An assessment of clinical techniques.* Beverly Hills, CA: Sage.

Monahan, J. (1993). Limiting therapist exposure to *Tarasoff* liability: Guidelines for risk containment. *American Psychologist, 48,* 242–250.

Morgan, R., Luborsky, L., Crits-Christoph, R., Curtis, H., & Solomon, J. (1982). Predicting outcomes of psychotherapy by the Penn Helping Alliance Rating Method. *Archives of General Psychiatry, 39,* 397–402.

Tarasoff v. Regents of the University of California, 118 Cal. Rptr. 129, 529 P.2d 533 (1974).

Truscott, D. (1993). The psychotherapist's duty to protect: An annotated bibliography. *Journal of Psychiatry & Law, 21,* 221–244.

Truscott, D., & Crook, K. H. (1993). *Tarasoff* in the Canadian context: Wenden and the duty to protect. *Canadian Journal of Psychiatry, 38,* 84–89.

Weinstock, R. (1988). Confidentiality and the new duty to protect: The therapist's dilemma. *Hospital and Community Psychiatry, 39,* 607–609.

Wettstein, R. M. (1984). The prediction of violent behavior and the duty to protect third parties. *Behavioral Sciences & the Law, 2,* 291–317.

Whiston, S. C., & Sexton, T. L. (1993). An overview of psychotherapy outcome research: Implications for practice. *Professional Psychology: Research and Practice, 24,* 43–51.

Wise, T. P. (1978). Where the public peril begins: A survey of psychotherapists to determine the effects of *Tarasoff. Stanford Law Review, 31,* 165–190.

4.7. Factors Contributing to Breaking Confidentiality With Adolescent Clients: A Survey of Pediatric Psychologists

Jeremy R. Sullivan, Eleazar Ramirez, William A. Rae,
Nancy Peña Razo, and Carrie A. George

How do psychologists decide whether to break confidentiality in order to inform the parents of risk-taking adolescent clients about the potential harm that may result from the adolescent's behavior? In order to encourage open communication and trust during treatment, psychologists often assure adolescent clients that confidentiality will be maintained, although there is no legal basis for doing so (Rae, 2001). Parents have the legal privilege to all information about their adolescent, yet in practice this privilege is usually voluntarily waived in order to facilitate the therapy process. Rather than being based on law, this decision is based on the psychologist's desire to build and maintain an honest therapeutic relationship with the adolescent, in which the client feels safe in revealing sensitive information (Gustafson & McNamara, 1987). However, it is clear that psychologists have an ethical and legal responsibility to break confidentiality when a client's behavior is deemed dangerous enough to constitute potential harm to the client or others (American Psychological Association [APA], 1992).

The decision to break confidentiality appears to be one of the most frequently encountered and serious ethical issues in the practice of professional psychology (Haas, Malouf, & Mayerson, 1986; Jacob-Timm, 1999; Pope & Vetter, 1992), and psychologists seem willing to break confidentiality in order to protect the client or others from harm (Pomerantz, Ross, Gfeller, & Hughes, 1998; Rae & Worchel, 1991). However, very little is known regarding the importance that psychologists place on various factors or considerations when faced with the ethical dilemma of whether to break confidentiality and risk damaging the therapeutic relationship. Clinicians working with adolescents and their families are especially likely to encounter this issue, as adolescent clients are likely to engage in a range of what the psychologist may consider

---

From "Factors Contributing to Breaking Confidentiality With Adolescent Clients:
A Survey of Pediatric Psychologists," by J. R. Sullivan, E. Ramirez, W. A. Rae,
N. Peña Razo, and C. A. George, 2002, *Professional Psychology: Research and Practice, 33,*
pp. 396–401. Copyright 2002 by the American Psychological Association.

An earlier version of this article was presented at the 109th Annual Convention of the American Psychological Association, San Francisco, August 2001. We are grateful to Victor L. Willson for his consultation regarding the statistical analysis for this study.

to be potentially dangerous behaviors, thereby making confidentiality a particularly salient issue with this client population (Powell, 1984).

Research has demonstrated the importance that psychologists place on general considerations such as safeguarding the process of therapy and protecting the client when deciding whether to break confidentiality and report adolescent risk-taking behavior (Haas et al., 1988), but the relative influence of more specific factors remains largely unexplored by researchers. Moreover, although these considerations have received some limited attention in areas such as school counseling and school psychology (Chevalier & Lyon, 1993; Isaacs & Stone, 1999), there is a relative paucity of research examining the factors involved in ethical decision-making within other psychological subdisciplines, such as pediatric psychology.

Pediatric psychologists working with risk-taking adolescents are likely to be faced with the decision to break confidentiality to tell parents about adolescent risk-taking behavior in order to protect the teenager from harm. The pediatric psychologist must assess the potential of danger to the adolescent, but it is often difficult to determine if the adolescent's behavior presents a genuine risk of danger to self or others. it is important to note that although psychologists are both legally and ethically bound to protect their clients from harm, and although both legal and ethical guidelines are critical sources of guidance and accountability for practicing psychologists, laws are prescriptive, whereas ethical principles allow for individual differences in decision making. With that said, the purpose of the present investigation was to identify which considerations most contribute to pediatric psychologists' decision to break confidentiality and report risk-taking behavior to parents when working with adolescent clients in the context of a therapeutic relationship.

THE SURVEY OF ETHICAL DILEMMAS IN REPORTING ADOLESCENT RISK-TAKING BEHAVIOR

This study is based on a section of the Survey of Ethical Dilemmas in Reporting Adolescent Risk-Taking Behavior, which was designed to assess psychologists' ethical attitudes and beliefs about the treatment of risk-taking adolescents. In the first part of the survey, participants were asked to read a vignette and then rate the degree to which they believed it was ethical to break confidentiality with an adolescent client engaging in risky and potentially dangerous behaviors (i.e., cigarette smoking, sexual activity, alcohol use, drug use, and suicidal behavior) with varying degrees of frequency, intensity, and duration. The results of the first part of the survey are presented elsewhere (Rae, Sullivan, Razo, George, & Ramirez, in press) and are briefly summarized later in this article.

In the second part of the survey, on which the present study is based, respondents were asked to indicate the importance of 13 factors when faced with the decision of whether to break confidentiality to report adolescent risk-taking behavior to parents. For this section, participants rated their responses on a

5-point scale, ranging from 1 (*extremely unimportant*) to 5 (*extremely important*). This section was independent of the first section, as the items were not based on the vignette, and participants were not asked to consider any specific risk-taking behaviors; rather, the items were designed to assess the importance of *general* considerations when deciding whether to break confidentiality. In reviewing possible items for this section, we reviewed the literature to explore which factors may contribute to ethical decision-making (e.g., Chevalier & Lyon, 1993; Haas et al., 1986, 1988). We then brainstormed additional items based on our own clinical experience in order to generate items more specifically related to the research question (i.e., breaking confidentiality). This set of items was then reviewed by several colleagues in order to ensure that the items were comprehensive in scope. All 13 items are provided in Table 1. Finally, participants were asked to provide basic background information about themselves (e.g., demographics, theoretical orientation, primary work setting, education). These personal and professional characteristics were not included in the present analyses as independent variables due to the relative homogeneity of the sample with regard to these characteristics.

For the purposes of the present study, the survey was mailed to 200 randomly selected members of the Society of Pediatric Psychology (APA Division 54); the survey packet also included a cover letter explaining the purpose of the study, a self-addressed, stamped return envelope, and a postcard for participants who wished to obtain a copy of the results. All responses were anonymous, and two mailings were conducted in order to maximize the response rate. Overall, 85 participants returned the survey, yielding a 43% response rate. Of

TABLE 1. Item Responses: Percentages and Means

Item	% response 1	2	3	4	5	*M*	*SD*
1. Apparent seriousness of the risk-taking behavior	1	4	1	19	74	4.61	0.82
2. The negative effects of reporting on the family	7	24	10	42	18	3.39	1.23
3. Confidence that risky behavior has actually occurred	1	3	4	41	50	4.37	0.81
4. Upholding the law	8	19	10	32	31	3.59	1.32
5. Protecting the adolescent	1	1	5	14	78	4.66	0.76
6. Avoiding legal problems for the adolescent	11	28	16	34	11	3.05	1.23
7. Not disrupting the process of therapy	5	28	10	43	14	3.31	1.18
8. Potential for risk-taking behavior to stop without telling parents	3	8	12	46	28	3.92	1.00
9. Likelihood that family will continue treatment after breaking confidentiality	10	28	18	34	11	3.08	1.20
10. Frequency of risk-taking behavior	3	1	0	43	53	4.42	0.81
11. Intensity of risk-taking behavior	3	1	1	22	73	4.61	0.82
12. Duration of risk-taking behavior	3	3	1	37	57	4.42	0.88
13. Gender of the client	53	23	12	10	3	1.86	1.13

Note. Item responses: 1 = *extremely unimportant*, 2 = *somewhat unimportant*, 3 = *not sure*, 4 = *somewhat important*, 5 = *extremely important*. Percentages that do not add up to exactly 100 are the result of missing data and rounding.

the 85 participants responding to the survey, 11 chose not to complete it, resulting in 74 usable surveys. All participants were full members of APA, with 95% ($n = 70$) having a doctoral degree; 93% ($n = 69$) were also licensed psychologists. In this sample, 51% ($n = 38$) were women, with a mean age of 49.3 years ($SD = 10.32$). The majority of respondents were Caucasian/White (97%, $n = 72$). It is important to note that these demographics appear to be representative of the members of the Society of Pediatric Psychology: 49% male, 96% with a doctoral degree, 93% Caucasian/White (for those reporting), and a mean age of 49.6 years (APA, 1999).

Regarding responses to individual items, protecting the adolescent, intensity of risk-taking behavior, and apparent seriousness of the risk-taking behavior were rated as most important by respondents; gender of the client was seen as the least important. Percentages of item-response frequencies, in addition to the mean rating and standard deviation for each item, are presented in Table 1. . . .

As can be seen in Table 1, responses to the five items (i.e., Items 1, 5, 10, 11, and 12) that constituted the Negative Nature of the Behavior factor were rather linear and did not result in much response variance within these items; the vast majority of respondents rated these items as either somewhat or extremely important. Responses to the four items (i.e., Items 2, 7, 8, and 9) that constituted the Maintaining the Therapeutic Process factor, however, were generally much less consistent, resulting in higher levels of variance within the items. This comparison suggests that there is much less consensus with regard to the importance assigned to the items that constituted the Maintaining the Therapeutic Process factor.

The survey results must be interpreted in light of several limitations. First, 13 items is a relatively small number from which to derive underlying constructs or factors. Second, the items had a narrow range of scores (i.e., from 1 to 5). Finally, the sample size was rather small for a factor analytic study, especially when combined with the previously cited limitations. In order to account for these limitations, we conducted the analyses and interpreted the results rather conservatively: Only the two factors with the largest eigenvalues were retained for the principal-axis-factoring analysis, and each factor consisted of at least 4 items with loadings of .4 or greater. Due to the limitations of the study, however, the results should be considered preliminary. The true value of this work may be its potential to facilitate discussion of practical matters regarding breaking confidentiality with adolescent clients, as well as its potential to serve as a springboard for more focused and rigorous research in this area with larger samples, a larger and more comprehensive set of initial items, and additional professional groups (e.g., school psychologists, clinical child psychologists).

IMPLICATIONS FOR TRAINING AND PRACTICE

Interestingly, the two factors identified in the present study may be seen as competing. That is, there is a tension or push–pull relationship between the factors, such that the Negative Nature of the Behavior factor may push one toward a decision to break confidentiality, whereas the Maintaining the Therapeutic Process factor may pull one away from breaking confidentiality. Although there was more consensus among respondents with regard to the importance assigned to the items within the Negative Nature of the Behavior factor, and although this factor accounted for a greater share of the variance among items, we feel that both factors have important and unique clinical and training implications. In the following sections, we discuss each of the factors separately in terms of these implications.

Negative Nature of the Behavior

The presence of the Negative Nature of the Behavior factor suggests the importance of comprehensively and systematically assessing the degree of potential risk to adolescent clients (and others) that results from their behaviors. This assessment would take into account psychology's knowledge base regarding the nature and consequences of different risk-taking behaviors given the developmental context of adolescence and would likely facilitate planning for intervention and treatment. A systematic process such as this is similar to a process that may be used in order to determine a client's risk for suicide based on suicidal ideation, past attempts, and risk and protective factors (e.g., Baerger, 2001; Sánchez, 2001) and would include (at the very least) an assessment of the frequency, intensity, and duration of the behavior, as well as a consideration of the potential effect of the behavior on the adolescent and others.

With regard to training, the importance of the Negative Nature of the Behavior factor suggests that psychologists-in-training would benefit from developing an informed knowledge base on normative adolescent risk-taking behavior. This knowledge base would stem from empirical data on normative risk-taking behavior during adolescence (e.g., prevalence rates of different risk-taking behaviors) and would facilitate comparisons between normative behavior and the specific client's behavior in order to determine the extent to which the client's behavior deviates from the norm. Several organizations and authors (e.g., Centers for Disease Control, 1997; Department of Health and Human Services, 2000; Lewinsohn, Rohde, & Seeley, 1996; National Institute on Drug Abuse, 1998; Resnick et al., 1997; Sells & Blum, 1996) have systematically gathered and reported prevalence data on such adolescent risk-taking behaviors as sexual activity, substance abuse, suicidal ideation, and suicide attempts, thereby making this information available for practitioners, trainers, and practitioners-in-training. The purpose of developing such a knowledge base would be to facilitate empirically based decision making as opposed to relying solely on intuition or "what feels right" when faced with the difficult decision of whether to break confidentiality with a specific adolescent client.

The great importance that respondents assigned to items composing the Negative Nature of the Behavior factor (e.g., frequency, intensity, and duration of the risk-taking behavior) is consistent with findings from the first part of the survey (Rae et al., in press), which examined the influences of frequency, intensity, duration, and type of risk-taking behavior on the perceived ethicality of breaking confidentiality with a fictitious adolescent client described in a vignette. The five domains of risk-taking behavior examined in the first part of the survey, and the levels of intensity within each domain, were as follows: smoking (one cigarette, more than a pack of cigarettes), alcohol use (one drink, four or more drinks), drug use (marijuana, amphetamines, inhalants, hallucinogens), sexual behavior (sexual activity with steady partner, sexual activity with multiple partners, sexual activity without protection when HIV-positive), and suicidal behavior (suicidal ideation, suicide gesture, suicide attempt). At each level of intensity within each of the five behavioral domains (with the exception of suicide gesture and suicide attempt), there were four levels of frequency/duration: once several months ago, monthly for several months, weekly for several months, and nearly daily for the last year.

Briefly, results from this previous study indicated that across all five domains of risk-taking behavior, psychologists found it more ethical to break confidentiality as the behaviors increased in intensity and frequency/duration. Thus, respondents were generally unlikely to find it ethical to break confidentiality when the behaviors were of low intensity and low frequency/duration. However, when the adolescent in the vignette was reported to be HIV-positive and admitted to engaging in sexual activity without using protection, and when the adolescent admitted to attempting suicide, respondents were likely to find it ethical to report these behaviors even when they were of relatively low levels of frequency/duration. Conversely, even at high rates of frequency/ duration, respondents were unlikely to find it ethical to report the client's smoking more than a pack of cigarettes, using marijuana, and sexual activity with either a steady partner or with multiple partners. Thus, especially intense or severe behaviors appeared to warrant disclosure regardless of frequency and duration, whereas behaviors thought to be common among adolescents were unlikely to lead to disclosure even at high levels of frequency and duration. Finally, respondents were most likely to find it ethical to report suicidal behavior, followed by drug use, sexual behavior, and alcohol use, with cigarette smoking representing the behavior least likely to warrant breaking confidentiality.

In sum, the results from both parts of the survey illustrate the importance of considering the frequency, intensity, duration, and type of behavior when deciding whether to break confidentiality to protect the adolescent client (or others) from harm. Although all of the behaviors included in the survey could be described as risky or dangerous, the extent to which respondents felt that breaking confidentiality was warranted varied as did the intensity and frequency/duration of the behaviors. Although there is no consensus on how to determine whether a certain behavior is potentially dangerous enough to warrant breaking confidentiality, an assessment of the frequency, intensity, and duration of the client's behavior would appear to be a reasonable starting point. The information gained from this assessment can then be used to compare the client's behavior with data regarding typical adolescent behavior in order to reach an informed, empirically based decision.

Maintaining the Therapeutic Process

The emergence of the Maintaining the Therapeutic Process factor suggests the importance of identifying methods with which to maintain the therapeutic relationship even when confidentiality must be broken. Psychologists may fear that once confidentiality has been broken, the adolescent will no longer trust the psychologist and will therefore disclose less information during therapy sessions. Further, psychologists may fear that breaking confidentiality will result in the family's terminating treatment and will cause the family (especially the adolescent) to be less likely to seek help for psychological or behavioral concerns in the future. At the same time, the psychologist may feel pressure from parents to reveal what their adolescent has been up to. These issues point to the importance of a frank and thorough discussion of the limits of confidentiality early in the therapeutic relationship (APA, 1992; Melton, Ehrenreich, & Lyons, 2001). The psychologist should delineate specific behaviors that would warrant breaking confidentiality in order to make the discussion concrete. This process should involve both the adolescent client and the client's parents, and the psychologist should always ensure that everyone comprehends the limits of confidentiality, perhaps by asking follow-up questions to check for understanding (Ford, Thomsen, & Compton, 2001; Gustafson & McNamara, 1987). Including the limits of confidentiality on the consent form to be signed by the parents and adolescent may also serve to avoid misunderstandings (Rae, 2001). Additionally, confidentiality issues should be revisited periodically or as new issues arise in order to ensure continued understanding by the client. . . .

REFERENCES

American Psychological Association. (1992). Ethical principles of psychologists and code of conduct. *American Psychologist, 47,* 1597–1611.

American Psychological Association. (1999). [1997 APA Directory Survey with new member updates for 1998 and 1999]. Unpublished raw data.

Baerger, D. R. (2001). Risk management with the suicidal patient: Lessons from case law. *Professional Psychology: Research and Practice, 32,* 359–366.

Centers for Disease Control. (1997). *Fertility, family planning, and women's health: New data from the 1995 National Survey of Family Growth* (DHHS Publication No. PHS 97-1995). Washington, DC: U.S. Government Printing Office.

Chevalier, N. E., & Lyon, M. A. (1993). A survey of ethical decision making among practicing school psychologists. *Psychology in the Schools, 30,* 327–337.

Department of Health and Human Services. (2000). *Healthy People 2010: Understanding and improving health* (2nd ed.). Washington, DC: U.S. Government Printing Office.

Ford, C. A., Thomsen, S. L., & Compton, B. (2001). Adolescents' interpretations of conditional confidentiality assurances. *Journal of Adolescent Health, 29,* 156–159.

Gustafson, K. E., & McNamara, J. R. (1987). Confidentiality with minor clients: Issues and guidelines for therapists. *Professional Psychology: Research and Practice, 18,* 503–508.

Haas, L. J., Malouf, J. L., & Mayerson, N. H. (1986). Ethical dilemmas in psychological practice: Results of a national survey. *Professional Psychology: Research and Practice, 17,* 316–321.

Haas, L. J., Malouf, J. L., & Mayerson, N. H. (1988). Personal and professional characteristics as factors in psychologists' ethical decision making. *Professional Psychology:
Research and Practice, 19*, 35–42.

Isaacs, M. L., & Stone, C. (1999). School counselors and confidentiality: Factors
affecting professional choices. *Professional School Counseling, 2*, 258–266.

Jacob-Timm, S. (1999). Ethically challenging situations encountered by school
psychologists. *Psychology in the Schools, 36*, 205–217.

Lewinsohn, P. M., Rohde, P., & Seeley, J. R. (1996). Adolescent suicidal ideation
and attempts: Prevalence, risk factors, and clinical implications. *Clinical Psychology:
Science and Practice, 3*, 25–46.

Melton, G. B., Ehrenreich, N. S., & Lyons, P. M. (2001). Ethical and legal issues in
mental health services for children. In C. E. Walker & M. C. Roberts (Eds.),
Handbook of clinical child psychology (3rd ed., pp. 1074–1093). New York: Wiley.

National Institute on Drug Abuse. (1998). *National survey results on drug use from
the Monitoring the Future Study, 1975–1997: Vol. 1. Secondary school students*
(NIH Publication No. 98-4345). Rockville, MD: Author.

Pomerantz, A., Ross, M. J., Gfeller, J. D., & Hughes, H. (1998). Ethical beliefs of psychotherapists: Scientific findings. *Journal of Contemporary Psychotherapy, 28*, 35–44.

Pope, K. S., & Vetter, V. A. (1992). Ethical dilemmas encountered by members of the
American Psychological Association: A national survey. *American Psychologist, 47*,
397–411.

Powell, C. J. (1984). Ethical principles and issues of competence in counseling
adolescents. *Counseling Psychologist, 12*(3), 57–68.

Rae, W. A. (2001). Common teen–parent problems. In C. E. Walker & M. C. Roberts
(Eds.), *Handbook of clinical child psychology* (3rd ed., pp. 621–637). New York: Wiley.

Rae, W. A., Sullivan, J. R., Razo, N. P., George, C. A., & Ramirez, E. (in press).
Adolescent health risk behavior: When do pediatric psychologists break
confidentiality? *Journal of Pediatric Psychology*.

Rae, W. A., & Worchel, F. F. (1991). Ethical beliefs and behaviors of pediatric
psychologists: A survey. *Journal of Pediatric Psychology, 16*, 727–745.

Resnick, M. D., Bearman, P. S., Blum, R. W., Bauman, K. E., Harris, K. M.,
Jones, J., et al. (1997). Protecting adolescents from harm: Findings from
the National Longitudinal Study on Adolescent Health. *Journal of the American
Medical Association, 278*, 823–832.

Sánchez, H. G. (2001). Risk factor model for suicide assessment and intervention.
Professional Psychology: Research and Practice, 32, 351–358.

Sells, C. W., & Blum, R. W. (1996). Current trends in adolescent health. In
R. J. DiClemente, W. B. Hansen, & L. E. Ponton (Eds.), *Handbook of adolescent
health risk behavior* (pp. 5–34). New York: Plenum.

4.8. Confidentiality and Electronic Health Records: Keeping Up With Advances in Technology and Expectations for Access

Britt A. Nielsen

lectronic health records (EHR) and issues of confidentiality of behavioral health records continue to be a focus of discussion in the literature, as well as in professional circles. In the first issue of *Clinical Practice in Pediatric Psychology* (*CPPP*), Smolyansky et al. (2013) described experiences and decisions made related to the implementation an electronic health record (EHR) at four children's hospitals. The Society of Pediatric Psychology (Division 54 of the American Psychological Association) list-serv continues to be a forum for discussion of EHR confidentiality specific to a pediatric medical setting, reflecting the learning curve involved when implementing an EHR. As with most technology, while we are adapting to what is available to us now, developers are continuing to push the envelope of *who* can access a patient's health information, as well as *where*, *when*, and *how* that access can occur. The purpose of this commentary is to highlight unique ethical considerations in the use of electronic health records in an interprofessional pediatric setting, while keeping in mind the ever-evolving advances in technology. Specific issues of EHR documentation related to pediatric patients, interprofessional teams, and trainees will be explored, with some discussion of how psychologists can adapt documentation practices given changes in technology and increasing expectation for information access.

PEDIATRIC PATIENTS AND THE EHR

Pediatric psychology has long dealt with issues of confidentiality and sharing information with parents. Adding an EHR to the mix magnifies these issues. Informed consents typically identify limits of confidentiality; however, patients (and parents) are not always aware of what information is being shared and with whom (Richards, 2009). With paper documentation, information about care provided to minors was stored separately and not readily accessible. Although EHRs integrate information for all health care services provided to allow better coordination of care, one significant downside is that parents potentially could have electronic access to information even from confidential psychology visits. This risk is particularly great when personal health records (discussed below) are utilized. Thus, tension is created between the health benefits that EHRs bring to pediatric care and the threat to confidentiality, particularly when the patient is an adolescent (Bayer, Santelli, & Klitzman, 2015).

Personal Health Records (PHR)

In line with the ongoing push for patient-centered care, patients are given access to notes written in the EHR (Kuhn et al., 2015). Personal Health Records (PHRs) specifically, provide patients with on-demand electronic access to their medical information. For children and adolescents, a parent or a guardian must be identified as a "proxy," essentially defined as someone who is allowed to access the patient's PHR. In the most recent upgrade of the EHR at Metro-Health Medical Center, one new feature allows providers to "share notes" with the patient. Currently, the default for this feature is to "not share notes"; however, it is expected that in the future, the default will be changed so that notes will routinely be shared with patients. Institutions must be careful to assure that confidential information, such as information about sexuality, remains confidential and that parents with proxy access are not inadvertently given permission to view potentially inflammatory progress notes or lab results (e.g., a positive STD screen). Providers also must take extra caution when documenting information that older children or adolescents do not want shared with parents or guardians.

Family Information Documented in the EHR

In a pediatric setting, providers obtain social, substance use, mental health, and medical history about extended family members; however, little attention has been focused on protecting parents' (or extended family members') information in the EHR (Bayer, Santelli, & Klitzman, 2015). This can lead to a variety of problems. For example, in contentious family relationships, one parent may disclose information about a former spouse that may be seen by the former spouse if, for some reason, that person gains access to the child's medical record. In other families, custody of the patient may change, either to family members, or to individuals outside of the family. Again, there is potential for providing individuals with access to information that the reporter most likely did not expect any one else to learn.

Additionally, parents may share information that is unknown to a child and that the parent was unprepared to have revealed. For instance, a parent may disclose the identity of the child's true biological parent, or the fact that they were adopted, without wanting the child to know. Unbeknownst to the parent, there may be a time when this potentially sensitive information is shared with the child in the course of care. In one such example, a teenager I was working with learned that the man she thought was her father was identified as a "stepfather" in the emergency contact list that was reviewed with her before her surgery. In this case, the parent did not expect that the child would ever have access to that information. Ultimately, one can never be sure who will have access to information in the EHR or how it will be shared in the future. These situations highlight the complexities of maintaining confidentiality using the EHR for a pediatric population that were not as obvious in paper records.

INTERPROFESSIONAL TEAMS, STAFF, AND THE EHR

Although our physician colleagues and other team members understand issues around HIPAA, they often do not fully appreciate the added protections for mental health notes, or what information is confidential in the EHR (Richards, 2009). Colleagues may not understand that even though they have access to specific mental health information, it may not be appropriate to share that information verbally, or copy and paste that information into their own documentation. Psychologists should take a role in helping educate physicians and other team members on the confidentiality of mental health notes. The psychologist must proactively discuss with the team what information can be shared and what information must be protected (Richards, 2009).

With EHRs, staff now have access to a large amount of information and field requests for information from parents, caregivers, schools, or community agencies that may come through appropriate channels with documented release of information or through informal requests (Nielsen, Baum, & Soares, 2013). It is important to provide education, even to experienced staff, on policies and procedures related to mental health documentation and release of these records in the EHR. Other institutions protect patient information by requiring the medical records office to contact the mental health provider directly when a request for information is received, the provider must then consent for the release to occur. Providers may not always be aware of automatic functions that institutions may add to the EHR. At our institution, if a patient was referred by an outside provider, a letter is automatically generated and the note associated with the encounter is attached to the letter. These documents get printed at an outside facility for automatic mailing. Typically, our referrals come from inside our institution so, our department does not have to deal with this; however, if there is an error in the entry of the referring provider, a provider with no relationship to our patient could possibly be sent this letter and progress note. There is a way to delete the letter if it is generated; however, if someone unknowingly comes across it, the chance for an accidental breach of confidentiality exists.

TRAINEES AND THE EHR

Typically, in psychology graduate programs, trainees learn to write extensive notes, lengthy reports, and include all the information they obtained from the patient. They get training on confidentiality; however, this training is not necessarily focused on documenting in the EHR. Many trainees learn from their practicum or internship placements about documenting in an EHR. Some training may be more formal than others. At our site, it was originally expected that trainees participate in EHR training with physicians, nurses, and so forth. Our department was able to work with the informatics trainers to get permission to train psychology graduate trainees on the EHR to focus on work flow and confidentiality issues related to the EHR and mental health documentation. In the future, graduate training programs will need to focus on teaching graduate students how to document appropriately in an EHR.

At our institution, information that trainees document in the EHR is immediately visible to others with access to the patient's case. This may happen before the supervisor has a chance to review the documentation or edit it, which can be a cause for concern at times. One possible way around this is to have trainees create a draft note outside of the EHR and upload it after the supervisor has reviewed it. This, of course, has HIPAA-related issues, some of which may be overcome by providing HIPAA-compliant USB storage devices to trainees for this purpose. Another solution is, when creating the security access to the EHR for trainees, psychologists may choose to work with their informatics department to prevent these notes from being visible until the supervisor is able to sign off on the note. Some institutions use documentation templates that meet the standards of the Joint Commission on Hospital Accreditation, insurance companies, and auditors. These templates help guide trainees on what information to include in the note.

PROVIDERS ADAPTING TO THE EHR

To survive the evolution of technology and push for easier access to the health record, providers will need to adapt their own thinking about mental health documentation. Psychologists are used to thinking of notes as the psychologist's record of what occurred in a visit. These more traditional "psychotherapy notes" often contain information about family dynamics and social interactions and may have a more "He said/she said" feel. Now, we need to think of the note as belonging to the patient and learn to write "progress notes" to document medical necessity for billing, symptoms, progress, and plan for treatment. Rather than a verbatim transcription of the clinical interaction, a good note should be a brief synthesis of history, findings, decision making, and plans (Kuhn et al., 2015). Providers may want to read their notes and think, what would a patient think if they read this?

THINK ABOUT NOW AND THE FUTURE

At the beginning of EHR use, the concern was about what level of security to give to mental health information for providers inside an institution. As technology evolves there will be a greater expectation for access to medical information. Now, patients can get access to the EHR and providers at outside institutions are able to share information provided that the patient signs a release of information. As Kuhn et al. (2015) points out, some of the changes may be good, including "avoidance of pejorative language in descriptions of patients, patient behaviors, and findings; increased documentation and clarity in documentation of care plans; and increased efforts for timely completion of notes."

In the future, technology that has not even been developed yet is likely to integrate with, or replace, the EHR as we think of it now (Kuhn et al., 2015). Providers need to think about now, but also be prepared for advances in technology and anticipated shifts in the mind-set about access to records. Who knows? In the future, the stigma about mental health may evaporate and information about mental health care will come to be viewed as nothing more than health care.

REFERENCES

Bayer, R., Santelli, J., & Klitzman, R. (2015). New challenges for electronic health records: Confidentiality and access to sensitive health information about parents and adolescents. *Journal of the American Medical Association, 313*, 29–30. http://jama.jamanetwork.com. http://dx.doi.org/10.1001/jama.2014.15391

Kuhn, T., Basch, P., Barr, M., Yackel, T., & the Medical Informatics Committee of the American College of Physicians. (2015). Clinical documentation in the 21st century: Executive summary of a policy position paper from the American College of Physicians. *Annals of Internal Medicine, 162*, 301–303. http://dx.doi.org/10.7326/M14-2128

Nielsen, B. A., Baum, R. A., & Soares, N. S. (2013). Navigating ethical issues with electronic health records in developmental–behavioral pediatric practice. *Journal of Developmental and Behavioral Pediatrics, 34*, 45–51. http://dx.doi.org/10.1097/DBP.0b013e3182773d8e

Richards, M. M. (2009). Electronic medical records: Confidentiality issues in the time of HIPAA. *Professional Psychology: Research and Practice, 40*, 550–556. http://dx.doi.org/10.1037/a0016853

Smolyansky, B. H., Stark, L. J., Pendley, J. S., Robins, P. M., & Price, K. (2013). Confidentiality and electronic medical records for behavioral health records: The experience of pediatric psychologists at four children's hospitals. *Clinical Practice in Pediatric Psychology, 1*, 18–27. http://dx.doi.org/10.1037/cpp0000009

COMMENTARY: Technology giveth, and technology taketh away. What a boon to the preservation of record confidentiality it is that we can cocoon documents in multiple passwords, redact the names and other identifying information of clients/patients with a simple macro instead of the laborious (and questionably effective) practice of blacking-out with a magic marker and recopying, and transmit encrypted clinical and research data to colleagues through proprietary communications pathways.

What a hindrance to our lofty goals of privacy it is, however, that passwords can be misplaced or purloined, that macros can be confounded by false cognates or variations in punctuation, and that electronic mail transmissions can be hacked or just misdirected by a simple typing error. Not only do psychologists need to remain abreast of the latest technological developments—while avoiding bankrupting ourselves by indulging in every promising fad that comes along—we also need to know what various and sometimes contradictory sources of ethical and legal guidance are setting as enforceable standards for record confidentiality.

The following references are recommended for those interested in further investigation of electronic storage, retrieval, and conveyance expectations in a range of research and clinical service delivery contexts.

Richards, M. M. (2009). Electronic medical records: Confidentiality issues in the time of IIIPAA. *Professional Psychology: Research and Practice, 40*, 550–556. http://dx.doi.org/10.1037/a0016853

Smolyansky, B. H., Stark, L. J., Pendley, J. S., Robins, P. M., & Price, K. (2013). Confidentiality and electronic medical records for behavioral health records: The experience of pediatric psychologists at four children's hospitals. *Clinical Practice in Pediatric Psychology, 1*, 18–27. http://dx.doi.org/10.1037/cpp0000009

Steinfeld, B. I., & Keyes, J. A. (2011). Electronic medical records in a multidisciplinary health care setting: A clinical perspective. *Professional Psychology: Research and Practice, 42*, 426–432. http://dx.doi.org/10.1037/a0025674

Tynan, W. D., & Woods, K. E. (2013). Emerging issues: Psychology's place in the primary care pediatric medical home. *Clinical Practice in Pediatric Psychology, 1*, 380–385. http://dx.doi.org/10.1037/cpp0000042

Wallace, C. E. (2015). Electronic health records: A graduate student's experience. *Clinical Practice in Pediatric Psychology, 3*, 179–181. http://dx.doi.org/10.1037/cpp0000098

4.9. HIV, Confidentiality, and Duty to Protect: A Decision-Making Model

Tiffany Chenneville

What is your duty as a psychologist when treating a client with HIV? Do Tarasoff principles apply? Are ethical guidelines consistent with individual state laws? Questions such as these are all too familiar for mental health professionals who serve clients with HIV. Clinicians may be forced to make difficult decisions about whether to breach confidentiality to protect third parties from HIV exposure. Breaches in confidentiality may result in deterioration of the therapeutic relationship, which may be harmful to the overall well-being of the client. Alternatively, maintaining confidentiality may result in physical, mental, and emotional harm to third parties. . . .

ETHICAL ISSUES

A consensus generally exists regarding the importance of confidentiality within therapeutic relationships. Without an assurance of confidentiality, clients may be hesitant to seek treatment because of fear of stigmatization. Furthermore, mental health professionals generally agree that effective treatment may necessitate full disclosure and that confidentiality is important for the maintenance of the therapeutic relationship.

Confidentiality is particularly important in the area of HIV. Individuals at risk for HIV infection may fear discrimination, lifestyle exposure (e.g., sexual orientation, drug use habits or practices), social rejection, or disruption of existing relationships. These fears may discourage individuals from being tested for HIV or from receiving appropriate medical treatment, psychological treatment, or both. Also, given the correlation between HIV exposure risk and domestic abuse (Molina & Basinait-Smith, 1998), it is possible that fear of relationship violence may result in hesitancy to seek treatment if confidentiality is not ensured.

Confidentiality is the standard except in situations in which there is a conflicting duty to protect. For a duty to protect to exist, a special relationship must be present. Examples of special relationships include parent–child, guardian–ward, and doctor–client. Mental health professionals fall under the special relationship of doctor–client. A duty to protect arises for mental health

From "HIV, Confidentiality, and Duty to Protect: A Decision-Making Model,"
by T. Chenneville, 2000, *Professional Psychology: Research and Practice, 31*, pp. 661–670.
Copyright 2000 by the American Psychological Association.

professionals when they become aware that their client poses a potential threat of harm to others. This duty includes a variety of circumstances such as suspected child abuse or elder abuse.

The ethical codes and standards of the American Psychological Association (APA; 1992) outline provisions for confidentiality and disclosure of confidential information. In reference to maintaining confidentiality, Ethical Standard 5.02 states the following: "Psychologists have a primary obligation and take reasonable precautions to respect the confidentiality rights of those with whom they work or consult, recognizing that confidentiality may be established by law, institutional rules, or professional or scientific relationships" (p. 1606). With regard to disclosure of confidential information, Ethical Standard 5.05 states the following:

> Psychologists disclose confidential information without the consent of the individual only as mandated by law, or where permitted by law for a valid purpose, such as (1) to provide needed professional services to the patient or the individual or organizational client, (2) to obtain appropriate professional consultations, (3) to protect the patient or client or others from harm, or (4) to obtain payment for services, in which instance disclosure is limited to the minimum that is necessary to achieve the purpose. (p. 1606)

LEGAL ISSUES

The general duty to protect is the result of a landmark court case, *Tarasoff v. Regents of the University of California* (1974, 1976). The case involved a client who made statements to his psychologist at the university counseling center indicating that he intended to harm Tatiana Tarasoff. The psychologist notified campus police, who initially detained the client but released him on the basis of a determination that he did not pose a risk to Tarasoff. (Tarasoff was vacationing out of the country when the threat was made.) Neither the victim nor her parents were notified. Two months later, after returning from vacation, Tarasoff was killed by the client. Tarasoff's parents sued the psychologist, as well as other defendants, claiming that their daughter should have been protected in some way (either through a warning or civil commitment of the client).

The Supreme Court of California initially ruled that psychologists have a duty to warn potential victims of imminent danger. However, on appeal, the court replaced a duty to "warn" with a duty to "protect." Specifically, the court ruled that mental health professionals have a duty to take reasonable actions to protect potential victims if it is determined (or should have been determined) that a client presents a serious risk of violence to others. Reasonable actions may include (a) warning the intended victim or others who can then notify the victim of the impending danger, (b) notifying law enforcement, or (c) taking other reasonable steps depending on the situation (e.g., civil commitment or other intervention).

Controversy exists with regard to whether the duty to protect outlined in Tarasoff applies to situations involving HIV. Understated, the duty to protect as applied to HIV is much less definitive than the duty to protect as applied to physical violence. The case law in this area is mixed. Rubenstein, Eisenberg, and Gostin (1996) discussed a case in Kansas in which an HMO was ordered not to breach confidentiality on the basis that duty-to-warn elements did not exist. The case involved a couple who had been separated and had not been involved sexually for several months prior to the proposed disclosure. Furthermore, test results indicated the "potential victim" had not been exposed to the virus. Thus, it was determined that disclosure was not warranted. . . .

Given variations that exist with regard to legal mandates, it is likely that mental health professionals will encounter situations in which their legal obligations contradict their personal and professional ethics. As Sizemore (1995) pointed out, many mental health professionals are more concerned about the ethical and moral ramifications, as opposed to the legal ramifications, inherent in these types of cases. To make decisions that are both legally and ethically sound, mental health professionals need to consider several factors when contemplating whether to disclose confidential information to protect a third party. It is generally agreed that the foreseeability of harm, the identifiability of the victim, and the implications of disclosure should be considered when one is contemplating whether to disclose confidential information to protect a third party from violence. However, although similarities between protection from violent acts and protection from HIV infection exist with regard to these dimensions, there are some significant differences.

Foreseeability of Harm

Who is more dangerous: a person with a physical weapon who verbally threatens the life of another or a person with HIV who engages in high-risk behavior (e.g., unprotected sexual activity, IV drug use)? Some may argue that standing before someone with a loaded gun will produce more predictable outcomes than sharing needles or having sex with someone who is HIV-positive. When determining the level of risk associated with sexual activity, it is necessary for one to examine information available on the transmission of HIV. Existing information suggests that the recipient of semen is at greater risk than the donor, although transmission in both directions is possible (Miner, 1998). As a result, male-to-female transmission is more likely than female-to-male transmission. In addition, individuals with sexually transmitted diseases (e.g., herpes) are at greater risk for transmitting and receiving the virus. Finally, there is a considerable amount of available research showing that condom use reduces transmission. It has been recommended that factors such as these be considered when level of risk is being assessed (Melchert & Patterson, 1999).

Some have argued that the Tarasoff ruling should not apply to dangers associated with legally permissible actions (Schlossberger & Hecker, 1996).

Such arguments seem to be based on the assumption that sexual contact is legal and that sex between two adults is usually consensual. However, one must consider whether consent relieves a mental health professional of the duty to protect and whether consent without knowledge of the partner's health status constitutes true consent.

Another issue in terms of foreseeability of harm relates to the assessment and prediction of dangerousness. The question becomes whether prediction of HIV transmission is a behavioral prediction or a medical prediction. If viewed as a medical prediction, it could be argued that mental health professionals are not in a position to make such predictions. If viewed as a behavioral prediction, mental health professionals are qualified but still must contend with the issue of reliability. Overprediction will result in breaches of confidentiality, and underprediction may result in potential harm to others.

A detailed model of risk assessment has been presented by Melchert and Patterson (1999), who categorized risk into the following levels on the basis of probability of HIV transmission: no risk, negligible risk, high risk, and severe risk. Factors in determining risk level include the extent, type, and frequency of sexual contact: use of safe sex or needle-sharing practices; personality characteristics that may increase risk of transmission; and whether an intent to harm others is present. Expanding on these recommendations, it is important that clinicians assess the actual behavior of their clients, rather than making assumptions about behavior based on association with high-risk groups. Also, it is important to assess substance abuse. Use of substances decreases inhibitions, which can increase risk behaviors for HIV transmission (Winiarski, 1998). Melchert and Patterson also discussed the need to consider the results of HIV testing and whether partners have been informed when making decisions about whether to disclose HIV information. However, this consideration seems redundant because there would be no duty to protect in situations in which a client did not even know he or she was HIV-positive or in which the partner of an HIV-positive client already was informed of the risk of transmission.

Identifiability of the Victim

Are mental health professionals obligated to investigate a potential victim's identity? According to the Tarasoff ruling, the answer is "no." Consistent with Tarasoff, the court ruled in *Thompson v. County of Alameda* (1980) that there is no duty to protect nonspecific victims. However, the court ruled that there is a duty to protect a class of persons at risk, rather than a specific person, in *Lipari v. Sears, Roebuck, & Company* (1983). It seems unlikely that mental health professionals would be expected to investigate the identity of potential victims of an individual who admits to frequenting nightclubs and taking home strangers. However, greater liability is likely to be imposed when the situation involves a client who is married or is involved in a serious relationship, thus making the identity of the victim easily attainable.

DECISION-MAKING MODEL

The following decision-making model is based on a review of the literature in this area. It takes into account the major premises outlined in the Tarasoff decision while emphasizing professional ethics and the best interest of the client. In addition, this model takes into account differences in statutory and case law, representing an expansion of models currently available. Indeed, the APA's HIV/AIDS Office for Psychology Education and Ad Hoc Committee on Psychology and AIDS dictate that psychologists "should abide by state laws and regulations" and "should determine what state statutes and case law require, and permit, in the state in which they practice" (APA, 2000). This model also provides specific information on how to proceed in situations in which disclosure is warranted. . . .

Step I: Determine Whether Disclosure Is Warranted

The first step of the decision-making model involves determining whether disclosure is warranted. As discussed above, making this determination requires an assessment of the foreseeability of harm (i.e., What are the sexual or IV drug use practices of the client?) and the identifiability of the victim (i.e., Are the identities of sexual or needle-sharing partners known?). The following is a list of questions for mental health professionals to consider when determining foreseeability of harm:

To what extent is the client sexually active or engaged in needle-sharing practices?

How often does the client engage in sexual relations or needle-sharing practices and with whom?

Does the client take precautions against HIV transmission during sexual relations and needle-sharing practices? For example,

Does the client use condoms?

Does the client clean needles before and after use?

What personality characteristics exist that may increase risk? For example,
    Is the client impulsive?
    Is the client aggressive?
    Is the client submissive?
    Is the client shy or timid?

Has the client been diagnosed with an Axis I or Axis II disorder?

If so, what symptoms are likely to increase risk of danger to others? Does the client use substances (e.g., alcohol) that decrease inhibitions?

What motivation exists for the client's unwillingness to self-disclose?

Is the client afraid to disclose HIV status because of fear of rejection, discrimination, and so forth?

Is the client intentionally trying to harm others?

If harm is foreseen on the basis of an examination of the aforementioned factors, then it is necessary to determine whether you can identify a third party at risk. The question is whether you, as a clinician, can identify with relative accuracy the identity of one or more potential victims. If you are able to identify a potential victim, then it is necessary to assess the therapeutic alliance. This assessment may be done through a formal or informal examination of the extent to which there is trust, understanding, acceptance, shared goals, perceived effectiveness, and shared values within the therapeutic relationship (see Truscott, Evans, & Mansell, 1995, for specific guidelines on conducting formal and informal assessments of the therapeutic alliance). Keeping in mind the client's best interest, the initial and primary goal of the therapist should be to guide clients to disclose their HIV status to sexual or needle-sharing partners on their own. Not only will this protect the therapeutic relationship but it also may instill in the client a sense of responsibility and personal control. If the client's self-disclosure can be accomplished, there will be no need for a breach in confidentiality. If you are unable to identify a potential victim, it still is advisable that you work with the client to reduce behaviors that increase the risk of transmitting the virus to others.

Step 2: Refer to Professional Ethical Guidelines

The second step of the decision-making model involves an examination of professional ethical guidelines. Mental health professionals who are members of the APA should refer to Ethical Standards 5.02 and 5.05 (APA, 1992). Depending on the discipline, it may be necessary to consult the ethical guidelines set forth by other professional organizations such as the American Medical Association or the National Association of Social Workers.

Step 3: Refer to State Guidelines

The third step of the decision-making model involves an examination of state guidelines. Statutory laws specify one of the following: permissive disclosure, required disclosure, or mandatory confidentiality. . . .

Permissive Disclosure

If state law outlines "permissive disclosure" (i.e., disclosure is allowed but not mandated), mental health professionals need to consider the potential impact of disclosure on the client, the client's amenability to treatment directed at containing the endangering behavior, and the client's willingness to disclose his or her health status to potential victims. The APA (2000), as outlined in a recommendation made by the HIV/AIDS Office for Psychology Education, supports the presumption that "confidentiality on behalf of the client shall be maintained except in extraordinary circumstances wherein individuals are unwilling or incapable of reducing the risk of infection to sexual or needle-sharing partners." In terms of assessing the potential impact of disclosure on the client, mental health professionals need to consider the therapeutic relationship, the emotional well-being of the client, and the potential harm to the client (e.g., in cases in which domestic violence is likely; see Molina & Basinait-Smith, 1998). When assessing a client's amenability to treatment directed at containing endangering behavior, it is important for mental health professionals to consider the client's motivation for engaging in high-risk behaviors. In addition, it is important to consider the attitudes and behavioral characteristics that support at-risk behaviors and the likelihood that they are amenable to treatment efforts. In terms of assessing a client's willingness to disclose his or her health status to a potential victim, it is important to consider the client's motivation for maintaining confidentiality of health status (e.g., fear of discrimination, loss of relationship). Finally, if it is determined that disclosure is necessary after considering the aforementioned factors, mental health professionals should refer to the steps outlined in the next section of this article.

Required Disclosure

If state law requires disclosure, mental health professionals should first encourage the client to disclose his or her HIV status to potential victims. Verification and documentation of self-disclosure are critical at this juncture. If the client refuses to self-disclose, an attempt should be made by the mental health professional to gain the client's consent for disclosure. If the client refuses to consent, the mental health professional must notify the client that information is going to be released. Notification of impending disclosure should be done verbally, preferably in person, and in writing. The basis for the decision (i.e., factors warranting disclosure) and the potential impact on the therapeutic relationship should be discussed with the client. In addition, the client should be given another opportunity to self-disclose. If the client still refuses, thus requiring third-party disclosure, only pertinent information should be provided to potential victims. It is important to remember that the duty outlined in Tarasoff is to protect. Protection may or may not include warning. For example, some states consider notification to a local health department to be sufficient protective action. Health officials then become responsible for warning, or otherwise protecting, potential victims in accordance with state regulations. In cases in which protective action requires warning, disclosure should be limited to notifying a potential victim that he or she may have been exposed to HIV without divulging the name of or other personal information about the client. The disclosure process, including notification to the client, should be documented in writing. This documentation is extremely important for the protection of the clinician. The date, time, content, and outcome of all conversations pertaining to the topic should be maintained. Also, the reasoning behind the clinician's decision to "protect" should be documented. Finally, an attempt should be made to maintain or repair the therapeutic relationship. If this is not possible, the client should be referred to another mental health professional for continued treatment.

Mandatory Confidentiality

If state law requires confidentiality without exceptions, an attempt should be made by the mental health professional to encourage the client to disclose his or her health status to potential victims. If the client refuses to self-disclose, it is important for the mental health professional to address the issues and behaviors that prohibit disclosure. Finally, an attempt should be made to work with the client on changing or altering high-risk behaviors (e.g., encourage the client to use condoms). . . .

REFERENCES

American Psychological Association. (1992). Ethical principles of psychologists and code of conduct. *American Psychologist, 47,* 1597–1611.

American Psychological Association. (2000). *Duty to warn, HIV/AIDS Office for Psychology Education (HOPE)*. Washington, DC: Author. Retrieved January 28, 2000, from the World Wide Web: http://www.apa.org/pi/aids/hope.html

Lipari v. Sears, Roebuck, & Company, 497 F. Supp. 185 (1983).

Melchert, T. P., & Patterson, M. M. (1999). Duty to warn and interventions with HIV-positive clients. *Professional Psychology: Research and Practice, 30,* 180–186.

Miner, K. (1998). The etiology and epidemiology of HIV disease. In M. D. Knox & C. H. Sparks (Eds.), *HIV and community mental healthcare* (pp. 19–36). Baltimore: Johns Hopkins University Press.

Molina, L. D., & Basinait-Smith, C. (1998). Revisiting the intersection between domestic abuse and HIV risk. *American Journal of Public Health, 88,* 1267–1268.

Rubenstein, W. B., Eisenberg, R., & Gostin, L. O. (1996). *The rights of people who are HIV positive*. Carbondale: Southern Illinois University Press.

Schlossberger, E., & Hecker, L. (1996). HIV and family therapists' duty to warn: A legal and ethical analysis. *Journal of Marital and Family Therapy, 22,* 27–40.

Sizemore, J. P. (1995). Alabama's confidentiality quagmire: Psychotherapists, AIDS, mandatory reporting, and Tarasoff. *Law and Psychology Review, 19,* 241–257.

Tarasoff v. Regents of the University of California, 17 Cal.3d 425, 551 P.2d 334 (1976).

Tarasoff v. Regents of the University of California, 118 Cal. Rptr. 129.529 P.2d 533 (1974).

Thompson v. County of Alameda, 614 P.2d 728 (1980).

Truscott, D., Evans, J., & Mansell, S. (1995). Outpatient psychotherapy with dangerous clients: A model for clinical decision making. *Professional Psychology: Research and Practice, 26,* 484–490.

Winiarski, M. G. (1998). Treating persons who use drugs. In M. D. Knox & C. H., Sparks (Eds.), *HIV and community mental healthcare* (pp. 266–278). Baltimore: Johns Hopkins University Press.

5

Multiple Relationships

Far from being subject to a per se ethical proscription, *multiple relationships* are a commonplace and at times virtually unavoidable aspect of research and clinical service provision. This does not, of course, make them a preferred option, and in many instances the ethical problems posed by their existence will prove insurmountable, requiring a permanent sundering of professional or personal contact—and perhaps both. This having been noted, there is an important definitional distinction to be drawn between multiple relationships and outright conflicts of interest.

As a general matter, multiple relationships exist whenever there is a juxtaposition of two or more roles in the psychologist's interactions with other individuals, groups, or organizations. Any of the roles in question could be current, could have occurred in past, or could be contemplated or even predicted with respect to the future. Multiple relationships may reflect a conscious decision on the part of the psychologist or may instead wind up having arisen without warning in a fashion that no amount of foresight would have been likely to identify.

The most extreme manifestation of a multiple relationship transpires when the psychologist engages in a sexual relationship with a client/patient or forensic examinee. Here, the conflict of interest is most blatant and the harm to the other party is most palpable. This incontrovertible ban is not exclusive to psychology but extends to the other helping professions as well. Not surprisingly, the penalties levied in these instances by ethics committees and licensing boards

http://dx.doi.org/10.1037/0000125-006
Ethical Conflicts in Psychology, Fifth Edition, by E. Y. Drogin

are among the most severe, including what may be permanent banishment from clinical practice.

At or near the other end of the ethical spectrum is the prospect of barter, which occurs when the psychologist agrees—or even proposes—that payment should be made for professional services not in cash but in some other commodity instead. Here, it may be that the client/patient may lack monetary funding but, for example, is a farmer who typically makes ends meet by exchanging produce for all manner of products and assistance, in a fashion normally deemed regionally and culturally appropriate. Of course, what is "typical" is not necessarily what is ethical in the context of psychotherapy or assessment, and the psychologist would have much to consider in terms of appropriateness before entering into such an arrangement.

Barter and other multiple relationship concerns are addressed in detail by the American Psychological Association's (APA's; 2017) *Ethical Principles of Psychologists and Code of Conduct* (APA Ethics Code). In each instance, what the Ethics Code requires is that such situations are avoided "if the multiple relationship could reasonably be expected to impair the psychologist's objectivity, competence, or effectiveness in performing his or her functions as a psychologist, or otherwise risks exploitation or harm to the person with whom the professional relationship exists" (Standard 3.05, Multiple Relationships).

Among its other features, this chapter addresses historical perspectives on sexual boundary violations, the complex prospect of nonsexual posttherapy relationships, unique boundary issues in telepsychology, and specific risk management considerations when psychologists are contemplating entry into multiple relationships.

REFERENCE

American Psychological Association. (2017). *Ethical principles of psychologists and code of conduct* (2002, Amended June 1, 2010 and January 1, 2017). Retrieved from http://www.apa.org/ethics/code/index.aspx

5.1. A Preliminary Look at How Psychologists Identify, Evaluate, and Proceed When Faced With Possible Multiple Relationship Dilemmas

Douglas H. Lamb, Salvatore J. Catanzaro, and Annorah S. Moorman

Psychologists who are in professional roles or relationships with clients, supervisees, or students may intentionally, unintentionally, or unforeseeably find themselves in a second role or relationship with that same individual. . . .

Although MRs with clients, supervisees, and students are discussed from a variety of perspectives, they all appear to have five defining characteristics. First, MRs typically take one or more of the following three forms: (a) sexual relationships (e.g., with clients: Bartell & Rubin, 1990; Gabbard, 1989; Garrett, 1999; Lamb et al., 2003; Pope, 1994; Williams, 1992; with supervisees: Bartell & Rubin, 1990; Lamb & Catanzaro, 1998; Lamb et al., 2003; O'Connor-Slimp & Burian, 1994; with students: Blevins-Knabe, 1999; Lamb & Catanzaro, 1998; Lamb et al., 2003; Stamler & Stone, 1998); (b) nonsexual social or professional relationships, such as having dinner with a former client or employing a current supervisee (Anderson & Kitchener, 1996, 1998; Pipes, 1999); and/or (c) financial–business relationships, particularly as they may occur in a rural practice and small communities (Campbell & Gordon, 2003; Faulkner & Faulkner, 1997; Lamb et al., 1994).

Second, there is some evidence that certain activities within the professional relationship itself (e.g., nonsexual touching, self-disclosure by the psychologist) are associated with and may, depending on the circumstances and context of such activities, increase the likelihood of the development of an explicitly sexual MR (see Brodsky, 1989; Folman, 1991; Gabbard, 1989; Lamb & Catanzaro, 1998). Third, MRs, by definition, may occur concurrently, consecutively, or in an overlapping manner with the established professional relationship. For example, a professional relationship may intentionally be discontinued in order to engage in some form of MR, such as terminating psychotherapy in order to develop a sexual relationship with a client (e.g., American Psychological Association [APA], 1988; Gottlieb, 1993; Lamb & Catanzaro, 1998; Lamb et al., 2003). Fourth, MRs are not restricted to the specific individual in the professional relationship (e.g., client, supervisee, student) but may apply to "a person closely associated with or related to the person with whom the psychologist has the professional relationship" (APA, 2002, p. 1065). An example would be a situation in which a therapist learns, in the context of therapy, that she (the therapist) is dating the former spouse of her client.

Finally, engaging in MRs of the nature identified above may or may not be considered unethical, depending on (a) the nature of the MR (e.g., sexual relationships with current clients are prohibited whereas other MRs are not), (b) the degree to which the MR may impair the psychologist's effectiveness, or (c) whether there is a risk of exploitation or harm to the person with whom the professional relationship exists (e.g., Brown, 1994; Gabbard, 1989; Lerman & Rigby, 1990). In fact, the APA (2002) ethics code states that "multiple relationships that would not reasonably be expected to cause impairment or risk exploitation or harm are not unethical" (p. 1065).

Although it may be relatively easy to define MRs conceptually, clinical practice suggests that it may be more difficult to recognize potential MR dilemmas as they develop. Further, there is little consensus about the ethicality of engaging in various nonsexual MRs (Anderson & Kitchener, 1998; Lazarus & Zur, 2002a; Lerman & Rigby, 1990). Although Anderson and Kitchener (1996, 1998) have identified seven categories of new, posttherapy nonsexual MRs that professionals might face, they did not report on the actual incidence of such MRs as revealed by the psychologists. The present study extended the work of Anderson and Kitchener (1996, 1998) by actually surveying psychologists as to what types of nonsexual relationships they found necessary to discuss. Further, we were interested in knowing if these types of MRs occurred at different frequencies for current and former clients, supervisees, and students.

In addition to our goal of identifying the actual nonsexual MR dilemmas faced by psychologists, a second goal of this study was to better understand how psychologists recognize or determine that a sexual MR was possible with a client, supervisee, or student; how these psychologists evaluated the current and potential relationship; and how they proceeded. In this regard, a previous study provided some information on the rationales used by those psychologists who have engaged in sexual MRs, such as "there was no harm, thus I proceeded," "consulted a colleague or negotiated with client (supervisee, student)," and "continued although I knew the behavior was problematic or unethical" (Lamb et al., 2003, p. 105).

Yet the majority of psychologists do not participate in prohibited sexual relationships. What deters them? We were interested in surveying psychologists to learn what actions or behaviors cued the psychologists to a potential sexual relationship (recognition) and what rationales were used by these psychologists to help them prevent, avoid, or otherwise not pursue the potential sexual relationship.

. . .

Participant Response Information

Of the initial 1,000 surveys sent, 28 were returned unopened, so the final possible response number was 972. A total of 298 surveys were completed and returned, for a response rate of 31%. The gender distribution of the respondents was 57% female and 42% male; marital status included married (74%), divorced (9%), partnered (6%), single (8%), and "other" or no response (3%). Almost all of the 298 respondents were Caucasian (95%). The mean number of years providing psychological services was 16.23 ($SD = 8.01$), and the most common work setting was private practice (60%), whereas 9% were in university counseling centers, 8% were in academic settings, and 23% were in a combination of other settings. A PhD was the most frequent degree status (86%), followed by EdD (9%) and PsyD (5%). Fifteen percent of the respondents identified themselves as APA fellows, and 3% self-identified as diplomates. Finally, the discipline distribution was 52% clinical and 46% counseling psychology, percentages very similar to the parent population (50%, 50%).

RESULTS AND DISCUSSION

Frequency of Discussing New Relationships With Current and Former Clients, Supervisees, or Students

Respondents identified which of seven relationships, from a list previously developed by Anderson and Kitchener (1996, 1998), they found themselves having to discuss or address. Information was gathered on types of relationships and whether these relationships were with current or former clients, supervisees, or students.

Regarding types of relationships, Table 1 indicates that respondents reported discussing social interactions and events most frequently (676 times), followed by collegial or professional relationships (301 times). The least frequently discussed relationship was business or financial (41 times). These new relationships were most often discussed, overall, with supervisees (721 times), followed by clients (664 times). Discussing new relationships with students (379 times) occurred much less often than with either supervisees or clients.

When we looked at types of new relationships to be discussed (e.g., social, collegial) as a function of the type of professional relationship, no strong patterns emerged. Social, business or financial, and religious affiliation relationships had to be discussed more frequently with clients, whereas collegial or professional, collegial or professional with social component, supervisory or evaluative, and workplace relationships had to be discussed more frequently with supervisees. In six out of the seven new relationships, discussions with students took place the most infrequently.

Finally, it was possible to identify differences in types of relationships to be discussed as a function of being a current or former client, supervisee, or student. It was clear that discussion with individuals with whom the psychologist had a previous (former) relationship occurred much more frequently (1,165 times) than with individuals who were currently in a professional relationship with the psychologist (599 times). Table 1 also indicates the types of relationships that would most likely have to be discussed with current and

TABLE 1. Frequencies of Negotiating New Relationships With Clients, Supervisees, or Students

| | Type of formal relationship[a] | | | | | | |
| | Client | | Supervisee | | Student | | |
Type of new relationship	n	%	n	%	N	%	Total
1. Social interactions and events							
Current	128	4	94	32	52	17	
Former	180	60	135	45	87	29	
Total	308		229		139		676
2. Business or financial (exchanging dollars or collaborating for financial gain)							
Current	4	1	9	3	0	0	
Former	21	7	1	0.3	6	2	
Total	25		10		6		41
3. Collegial or professional (new, "equal" power relationship)							
Current	22	7	22	7	13	4	
Former	58	20	129	4	57	19	
Total	80		151		70		301
4. Collegial or professional with social component							
Current	19	6	31	10	12	4	
Former	38	13	98	3	40	14	
Total	57		129		52		238
5. Supervisory or evaluative relationship							
Current	6	2	44	15	13	4	
Former	38	13	59	20	29	10	
Total	44		103		42		189
6. Religious affiliation relationship							
Current	46	16	10	3	9	3	
Former	53	18	11	4	12	4	
Total	99		21		21		141
7. Workplace relationship							
Current	10	3	40	13	15	5	
Former	41	14	38	12	34	12	
Total	51		78		49		178
Total[b]							
Current	235		250		114		599
Former	429		471		265		1,165

[a] Total possible $n = 298$. [b] The total frequency is greater than the number of participants and the total percentage is greater than 100 because respondents were allowed to check more than one alternative.

former clients, supervisees, and students. For example, social and religious affiliation relationships were the two relationships that required the most frequent discussion between therapists and current clients. Although respondents were given the opportunity to identify other types of relationships that they had to discuss, less than 1% of the respondents commented on any additional types of new relationships.

Actions Suggesting a Potential Sexual MR Was Possible and Rationales Psychologists Used to Avoid Such Relationships

The above discussion has focused on identifying the frequency with which psychologists face new, nonsexual types of relationships with current or former clients, supervisees, or students. It is also likely that psychologists find themselves in situations, with current or former clients, supervisees, or students, that could eventuate into sexual intimacies. Although sexual relationships do occur in actual practice, the vast majority of these potential situations do not develop into actual sexual intimacies. We thought it was important to better understand how such situations developed or were recognized (i.e., what actions occurred to suggest a potential sexual relationship) and the reasons (rationales) that professionals may have used to prevent the relationship from becoming sexual. To that end, we asked the respondents to indicate, from a list of seven possible actions and 11 potential rationales, "all those actions that indicated that a sexual relationship was possible and the reasons (rationales) you used to prevent the relationship from occurring." We also requested that respondents specify whether those actions and rationales occurred before, during, or after the professional relationship. Individuals were also provided with the opportunity to identify their own actions and rationales. No such additional responses were provided.

Actions

We identified three possible categories of actions. The first included the psychologists' own thoughts about the relationship (e.g., "I thought of initiating a relationship but didn't act in any way"). The second category addressed sexual overtures initiated by either party (e.g., "I tried to initiate a potential sexual relationship but the other person was not interested," or "The other individual initiated a potential sexual relationship but I was not interested"). The third category entailed efforts to prevent or cause the relationship to not be pursued (e.g., "I did initiate a potential relationship but at a particular point I decided not to pursue it," "I did initiate a potential relationship but at a particular point he/she decided not to pursue it," "The other individual initiated a potential relationship, I was interested, but at a particular point I decided not to pursue it," and "The other individual initiated a potential relationship but at a particular point he/she decided not to pursue it").

Overall, only two specific actions were checked with any frequency by the respondents. They were "I thought of initiating a relationship but didn't act in any way" (45% of all respondents) and "The other individual initiated a potentially sexual relationship but I was not interested" (39%). All the remaining actions noted above together accounted for only 16% of the responses.

Then, we analyzed the percentage of psychologists who reported the two most frequently cited actions as a function of type of formal relationship. The results indicated that the responding psychologists "thought of initiating a relationship but didn't act in any way" most frequently with a supervisee (54%) or a student (51%) and less so with a client (38%). Yet the percentage of psychologists who reported that "the other individual initiated a potentially sexual relationship but I was not interested" was highest with a client (49%) and lower for both supervisees (28%) and students (26%).

When one looks at actions as a function of whether the client, the supervisee, or the student was current or former, it was found that the psychologists reported contemplating a relationship more often in the context of a current relationship than after the relationship: current client, 68%, and former client, 32%; current supervisee, 60%, and former supervisee, 40%; current student, 54%, and former student, 46%. Thirty-nine percent of the psychologists also reported that the other individual initiated a potential sexual relationship. Of that 39%, the most frequent individual initiating was a current student (83%); such a relationship was slightly less likely to be initiated by either a current client or a supervisee (77% and 74%, respectively).

Rationales

In contrast to the relatively limited range of reported actions, there were a number of different rationales provided by these professionals as to why they did not ultimately engage in a sexual relationship with their clients, supervisees, or students. Table 2 provides the list of rationales as well as the frequencies and percentages of each rationale's being checked. Overall, respondents checked, on the average, more rationales for not pursing a relationship with clients (3.4) than with either supervisees (1.5) or students (1.1).

Although for any type of relationship, Rationale 1 ("personal ethics/values/morals prohibited me from pursuing it") was cited most frequently by the respondents, that rationale was most frequently cited for clients (89%) and less so for supervisees (47%) and students (39%). The next most frequently checked rationale related to perpetuity (i.e., once a client always a client). The frequency of citing this rationale (Rationale 5) was again highest for clients (65%) followed by students (10% for Rationale 7) and supervisees (9% for Rationale 6).

In addition to the rationales related to ethics and perpetuity, Table 2 indicates that there were two other rationales checked by at least 50% of the respondents. These two rationales were related to (a) the prohibition associated with a dual relationship (Rationale 4) and (b) the existing power relationship between the psychologist and the other individual (Rationale 8). Again, as with the other rationales, the frequency of response for these two rationales was greatest for clients and was less compelling for supervisees and students. Finally, fear of legal, ethical, or collegial repercussions (Rationale 2) was mentioned by relatively few respondents (with respect to clients, 15%; supervisees, 6%; and students, 2%).

Besides identifying rationales as a function of type of formal relationship, respondents also identified the time of the relationship (before, during, or after the formal relationship). In all cases, the number of rationales cited for not engaging in the relationship was greatest during the formal relationship (45%), followed by after (35%) and before (20%), and this order was the same for all three types of formal relationships. . . .

TABLE 2. Frequencies of Rationales Given by Psychologists (*n* = 298) for Not Engaging in Sexual Relationships With Clients, Supervisees, or Students

Rationale	Client *n*	Client %	Supervisee *n*	Supervisee %	Student *n*	Student %
1. My personal ethics/values/morals prohibited me from pursuing it.	265	89	140	47	116	39
2. I was afraid that I would be found out by my colleagues and/or something ethical/legal would develop.	45	15	17	6	5	2
3. I was not personally attracted to the individual.	58	20	16	5	12	4
4. I perceived the possible situation as constituting a dual relationship with possible negative consequences.	165	55	68	23	49	16
5. For clients I believe in the principle of client perpetuity (i.e., once a client always a client).	194	65	N/A	N/A	N/A	N/A
6. For supervisees I believe in the principle of supervisee perpetuity (i.e., once a supervisee always a supervisee).	N/A	N/A	28	9	N/A	N/A
7. For students I believe in the principle of student perpetuity (i.e., once a student always a student).	N/A	N/A	N/A	N/A	29	10
8. Power differential still exists between me and the other individual.	131	44	62	21	51	17
9. Dependency of the individual (or other transference material) was too great.	60	20	19	6	20	7
10. Broader community would have been negatively impacted.	49	16	23	8	20	7
11. Undoing or potentially undoing the good accomplished in the formal relationship.	45	15	20	7	38	13
Total[a]	1,012		393		340	

Note. N/A = not applicable.

[a]The total frequency is greater than the number of participants and the total percentage is greater than 100 because respondents were allowed to check more than one alternative.

REFERENCES

American Psychological Association. (1988). Ethics Committee Report. *American Psychologist, 43*, 897–904.

American Psychological Association. (2002). Ethical principles of psychologists and code of conduct. *American Psychologist, 57*, 1060–1073.

Anderson, S., & Kitchener, K. (1996). Nonromantic, nonsexual posttherapy relationships between psychologists and former clients: An exploratory study of critical incidents. *Professional Psychology: Research and Practice, 27*, 59–66.

Anderson, S., & Kitchener, K. (1998). Nonsexual posttherapy relationships: A conceptual framework to assess ethical risks. *Professional Psychology Research and Practice, 29*, 91–99.

Bartell, P., & Rubin, L. (1990). Dangerous liaisons: Sexual intimacies in supervision. *Professional Psychology: Research and Practice, 21*, 442–450.

Blevins-Knabe, B. (1999). The ethics of dual relationships in higher education. In D. Bersoff (Ed.), *Ethical conflicts in psychology* (2nd ed., pp. 263–265). Washington, DC: American Psychological Association.

Brodsky, A. S. (1989). Sex between patients and therapists: Psychology's data and response. In G. Gabbard (Ed.), *Sexual exploitation in professional relationships* (pp. 15–25). Washington, DC: American Psychiatric Press.

Brown, L. (1994). Boundaries in feminist therapy. *Women and Therapy, 15,* 29–38.

Campbell, C., & Gordon, M. (2003). Acknowledging the inevitable: Understanding multiple relationships in rural practice. *Professional Psychology: Research and Practice, 34,* 430–434.

Faulkner, K., & Faulkner, T. (1997). Managing multiple relationships in rural communities: Neutrality and boundary violations. *Clinical Psychology: Science and Practice, 4,* 225–234.

Folman, R. (1991). Therapist–patient sex: Attraction and boundary problems. *Psychotherapy, 28,* 168–173.

Gabbard, G. (Ed.). (1989). *Sexual exploitation in professional relationships.* Washington, DC: American Psychiatric Press.

Garrett, T. (1999). Sexual contact between clinical psychologists and their patients: Qualitative data. *Clinical Psychology and Psychotherapy, 6,* 54–62.

Gottlieb, M. (1993). Avoiding exploitative dual relationships: A decision-making model. *Psychotherapy, 30,* 41–48.

Lamb, D., & Catanzaro, S. (1998). Sexual and nonsexual boundary violations involving psychologists, clients, supervisees, and students: Implications for professional practice. *Professional Psychology: Research and Practice, 29,* 498–503.

Lamb, D., Catanzaro, S., & Moorman, A. (2003). Psychologists reflect on their sexual relationships with clients, supervisees, and students: Occurrence, impact, rationales, and collegial intervention. *Professional Psychology: Research and Practice, 34,* 102–107.

Lamb, D., Strand, K., Woodburn, J., Buchko, K., Lewis, J., & Kang, J. (1994). Sexual and business relationships between therapists and former clients. *Psychotherapy, 31,* 270–278.

Lazarus, A., & Zur, O. (Eds.). (2002a). *Dual relationships and psychotherapy.* New York: Springer.

Lerman, H., & Rigby, D. (1990). Boundary violations: Misuse of the power of the therapist. In H. Herman & N. Porter (Eds.), *Feminist ethics in psychotherapy* (pp. 51–59). New York: Springer.

O'Connor-Slimp, P., & Burian, B. (1994). Multiple role relationships during internship: Consequences and recommendations. *Professional Psychology: Research and Practice, 25,* 39–45.

Pipes, R. (1999). Nonsexual relationships between psychotherapists and their former clients: Obligations of psychologists. In D. Bersoff (Ed.), *Ethical conflicts in psychology* (2nd ed., pp. 254–257). Washington, DC: American Psychological Association.

Pope, K. (1994). *Sexual involvement with therapists.* Washington, DC: American Psychological Association.

Stamler, V., & Stone, G. (1998). *Faculty–student sexual involvement: Issues and interventions.* Thousand Oaks, CA: Sage.

Williams, M. (1992). Exploitation and inference: Mapping the damaging effects from therapist–patient sexual involvement. *American Psychologist, 47,* 412–421.

5.2. Sexual Boundary Violations: A Century of Violations and a Time to Analyze

Judith L. Alpert and Arlene (Lu) Steinberg

A young female patient was convinced that she was in love with her male therapist. She spoke of her love for him incessantly. The therapist was flattered, scared, and tempted. When the male supervisee discussed this in supervision, the 80-ish year old female supervisor who was clearly disabled from a childhood disease said to her supervisee: "You should see the handsome 20-somethings who are in love with me!" The supervisor then explained that it was the patient's absolute right to try to seduce his analyst and, similarly, it was the analyst's obligation to analyze the behavior.

This special issue focuses on sexual boundary violations. Our intent is clear: We want to promote discussion and clarification on this topic. Underlying this is the belief that a study of sexual boundary violations can potentially avert reenactments. As we are all potentially vulnerable to boundary transgressions, including sexual ones, such study is essential.

In this first overview article, we present a brief (a) summary of some of the major topics relevant to sexual boundary violations and an (b) overview of the articles included in this special issue. A few introductory comments are in order: First, in this volume we use "mental health professionals" and "psychoanalysts" interchangeably. We do so because mental health professionals of every theoretical orientation commit sexual boundary violations. The authors of this special issue are psychoanalysts and they write, for the most part, about sexual boundary violations within *psychodynamic* and *psychoanalytic* treatment. It should be clear, however, that psychoanalysts and psychodynamically oriented therapists are not more prone to boundary violations than other mental health professionals. In fact, psychoanalytic and psychodynamic therapists have lower prevalence rates of misconduct than therapists of other orientations (Celenza, 2007). Regardless of whether it is addressed in treatment and or whether the type of treatment utilized is designed to make use of transference, a transference-based relationship will develop in the course of treatment. The therapy process promotes unresolved transference-based relationships and can contribute to the patient's greater receptiveness to boundary violations.

A second point: While we are considering sexual boundary violations in *treatment*, sexual and other boundary violations occur in other related contexts such as in supervision or in an academic setting. While many of the issues are similar across settings, our focus here is limited to treatment. We refer readers interested in boundary issues in supervision and academia to comprehensive chapters in Gabbard and Lester (1995) and Celenza (2007).

Another associated point: This volume focuses mainly on sexual boundary violations or physical contact occurring in the context of a therapeutic relationship for the purpose of sexual pleasure. Not included in this definition is the occasional handclasp or embrace, when the analyst's intent is other than for sexual pleasure. Of course there are boundaries other than sexual that are violated within treatment. While some reference is made to other violations throughout this volume, these are not the primary focus here. It should be noted, however, that nonsexual boundary violations are more common than sexual ones and that therapist–patient sex may be the result when there is a violation of nonsexual boundaries. This is the "slippery slope" in which boundary violations that begin as inconsequential and nontoxic rocket to major and destructive ones. Further, considerable harm may be done to both the patient and the process even when the culmination of boundary violations is not sexual (Gabbard & Lester, 1995).

Fourth, the literature supports that more violations are committed by male than female therapists (Schoener, Milgrom, Gonsiorek, Luepker, & Conroe, 1989) and more violations are perpetrated on female than male patients. Prevalence studies, for example, indicate that men are the transgressors in 80% of the incidents of sexual boundary violations in the therapy relationship (Garrett, 2002). While female practitioners seldom commit sexual boundary violations, when they do it is usually with female patients. Given this, we will refer to the transgressors as "he" and the victims as "she." However, it should be clear that both male and female therapists may be transgressors and both male and female patients may be victims of transgressions and that violations may occur in same or cross-sex pairs.

And lastly, we have not exhausted the issues related to sexual boundary violations, which are covered in this special issue. Even the chronicled history, which follows, is incomplete.

ABBREVIATED HISTORY

In many ways these violations have been woven into the very fabric of psychoanalytic history. Falzeder (2015) noted, Freud became aware of the risks inherent in the analytic relationship. However, he waffled between acknowledging and distancing. Breuer's reaction to Anna O exemplifies this. Perhaps the blank screen model may have been Freud's suggested remedy.

The study of boundary violations in the history of psychoanalysis is also the study of the evolution of the concepts of transference and countertransference. Freud warned against sexual violations. He stated clearly in his 1915 article on transference love that the analytic situation induces the patient to fall in love and he counseled analysts to keep countertransference in check (Freud, 1915). Other early analysts (e.g., Fromm-Reichmann, 1950) advised similarly.

Nevertheless, our field has a long history of mental health professionals committing sexual violations. For example, Blechner (2014) provides a list of early and renowned psychoanalysts who had sex with patients or married them. This list includes: Carl Jung, Sandor Ferenczi, Erich Fromm, Frieda Fromm-Reichmann, Wilhelm Reich, Victor Tausk, Otto Fenichel, Harry Stack Sullivan, and Karen Horney.

Falzeder (2015) indicates that there are many training analyses that were or became erotic relationships. In addition to presenting a chart documenting this, he mentions many names. We list a few here: Georg Groddeck and his later wife Emmy von Voigt; Michael Balint and his second wife Edna Oakeshott; Otto Rank and his wife Beata; August Aichhorn and Margaret Mahler; Wilhelm Reich and his later wife Annie Pink; Rudolph Lowenstein and Marie Bonaparte; Carl Jung and Sabina Spielrein; and Toni Wolff and Maria Moltzer.

There are many more transgressors who have been identified. For more listings, see Celenza (2007), Falzeder (2015), and Gabbard and Lester (1995). These authors also point to the early blurring of the boundaries between an analytic and a social relationship. Perhaps as a new field the resultant risks of this blurring were not so readily perceivable. Falzeder's work is particularly relevant here and his reportings particularly disturbing. What a study of our history and these lists make clear is that sexual boundary violations were committed by many prominent people in our profession. These boundary violations continue today. Most important, we are all potentially vulnerable to them. Clearly there needs to be discussion about why these violations occur so frequently and why institutes and mental health colleagues, while expressing their disapproval, are lax to end violations. Such discussion occurs in the present volume.

Many of us have observed senior analysts who sexually violated a patient and then, years later, observed that one of his patients who was not violated, violates. Does transmission have to do with the ensuing silence in the aftermath of a violation? Might this silence contribute to the enactment? Is this simply an issue of identification? Might it be that the "copy-cat" analyst saw few if any repercussions and assumed that this behavior would be tolerated and, perhaps, was even expected? Might the copy-cat analyst have been traumatized by the behavior of his analyst and repeated his analyst's behavior in a doomed-to-fail effort to master the trauma? It appears that many generations removed act out split off aspects of their professional parents and professional grandparents unspoken and often unformulated recollections.

SOME FACTS: INCIDENCE, PERPETRATORS, AND VICTIMS

Incidence

Data derived from a national pool of mental health professionals who represent various disciplines, indicate that the incidence of erotic contact between patients and practitioners in the United States ranges from 7–12% (Borys & Pope, 1989;

Jackson & Nuttall, 2001; Pope, Tabachnick, & Keith-Spiegel, 1987). As most of the studies involve self-report, it is reasonable to propose that the true prevalence is much higher. Additional specifics about percentage of psychotherapists who have had sexual contact with their patients can be found in Blechner (2014).

Victims

Usually victims of sexual boundary violations in treatment are female (80% women). While female patients are also abused by female therapists, female mental health professionals account for a relatively low percentage of the occurrence.

Patients who have a history of incest are most at risk for being violated in this way. Pope and Vetter (1991), for example, report that patients who had a history of child sexual abuse comprised 32% of patients who had sexual relations with their therapist.

Victim Effects
Freud stated clearly in his 1915 article on transference love that the analytic situation induces the patient to fall in love and he counseled analysts to keep countertransference in check. Nevertheless, he seemed to blame female patients for analyst's transgressions. In fact, throughout history the profession has minimized the harm to patients and, in fact, often blamed the patients for the therapist's transgression. The transgressed blame themselves as well.

In addition to the blame that victims take on, research indicates other negative effects. Given the substantiation of deleterious effects from a wide-ranging review of the literature, Williams (1992), in an article in *The American Psychologist*, concluded that ethical standards prohibiting sexual boundary violations should be created. For sure, sexual boundary violations are more frequently judged damaging as indicated in the literature and as elaborated in several articles in the current issue (e.g., Charles, Pizer).

Victim Treatment
Victims may not want treatment. They have been violated and they may not trust. Further, like incest victims, they often blame themselves. It is important to remember that false allegations are believed to be rare and that, just as we are all potential transgressors, we are all potential victims. Transference and countertransference are known to be forceful.

Transgressors

Who are the perpetrators of sexual boundary violations? There seem to be different types of transgressors. Gabbard has written a great deal about the perpetrators. While we review Gabbard's typology here very briefly, the reader is referred to his full work (Gabbard, 1994a, 1994b; Gabbard & Lester, 1995).

Based on his experience in evaluating and treating more than 70 cases of therapists who had sex with their patients, Gabbard (1994a, 1994b) developed a typology of perpetrating analysts. He notes four categories of disorder, and we review them very briefly here: (a) psychotic disorders, which are rare; (b) predatory psychopathy and paraphilias, which include true antisocial personality disorders and also severe narcissistic personality disorders with prominent antisocial features; (c) lovesickness; or (d) masochistic surrender.

He points out that the second category (predatory psychopathy and paraphilias) includes antisocial personality disorders and severe narcissistic personality disorders with prominent antisocial features, and that these clinicians are not rare. He elaborates that it is the sexual *behavior* that is predatory and psychopathic. He elaborates that clinicians in this category are not necessarily psychopathic predators. Rather, they act on their perverse impulses with patients and are usually found to have severely compromised superegos associated with character pathology on the narcissistic-to-antisocial continuum. Apparently these transgressions often involve multiple victims, include sadistic behaviors, and involve analysts who often have histories of having been identified in their training as being unethical. Because they threatened to obtain a lawyer, they were often allowed to continue with their training. Gabbard indicates a variant of this predator: The profoundly narcissistic analyst who is recognized and acclaimed and becomes grandiose.

Most analysts who violate sexually fall into the third group (lovesickness) according to Gabbard. Usually the violator is a middle-aged practitioner in solo independent practice, who is in personal distress and believes he is in love with a much younger female patient (Borys & Pope, 1989; Jackson & Nuttall, 2001; Somer & Saadon, 1999).

Transgressors identified as belonging to this last category (masochistic surrender) appear to be highly invested in their own suffering. Gabbard notes that the most common scenario in this latter category involves the analyst feeling controlled by a challenging patient; boundary violations escalate in response to the analyst feeling that this is the only way to avoid the patient's suicide.

In another study of nine cases of transgressors (Dahlberg, 1970) a pattern is noted: The therapist is a male over 40 who is from 10–25 years older than the patient. Further, he is either separating from his wife or recently divorced. He points out that the transgressor is attempting to evoke his youth and is acting out the fantasy of being young, attractive, and pursued by good-looking girls.

Transgressor Rationales

Numerous rationales are offered for sexual boundary violations or "why he does it." While this position is clearly not accepted within the mental health professions, a few (e.g., McCartney, 1966; Shepard, 1971) point to the beneficial effects of such violation. Consider McCartney. He indicated that some patients need a sexual experience within treatment to proceed to mature heterosexuality. Further he stated that men could find professionals to assist them sexually, while women require a male therapist to fill this need. McCartney had sexual relations with many of his female patients, which finally resulted in his expulsion from the American Psychiatric Association. . . .

Transgressor Consequences for Violation

Consistently over time there has been disinclination by institutes, universities, colleagues, and victims to condemn or to punish sexual boundary violators. Overall there have been few strong penalties. Our profession does not seem to enforce its own principles. Often the solution is to tell the accused analyst to return to analysis while the patient's needs were overlooked. Colleagues have often been uncomfortable "blowing the whistle," and sometimes they simply did not have a place to report or know how to report. Institutes were often quiet as well in their desire to protect one of their own and in the fear of facing a lawsuit. In some cases when disciplinary actions were taken, ethics committees were even ostracized. Clearly, in the early days the focus was on protecting one's colleagues rather than the patient. Perhaps it has not changed much since then.

Talking about sexual boundary violations can be more harshly punished than committing a sexual boundary violation (Dimen, 2011). The message that is given to whistle blowers or potential whistle blowers is "close your eyes and bite your tongue." Slochower discusses this in the present volume as well.

Gabbard and Lester (1995) present an aspirational model for dealing with problems of sexual boundary violations. They divide institutional response into four areas: management of complaints, response to the victim, assessment and rehabilitation, and prevention. With respect to management, they encourage therapists to familiarize themselves with the reporting laws in their state. They point to the importance of having an ombudsman or a designated person to whom one can turn around such matters. An ethics committee is also indicated, and the authors consider the process when a violation becomes known. With respect to the response to the victim, they make a strong case for addressing the patient's needs. They also introduce the idea of a mediation process whereby the accused analyst and the accusing patient have an opportunity for dialogue about exploitation and betrayal and apology. Third, they outline the aspirational process of assessment and rehabilitation and, lastly, they consider the rehabilitation plan.

Transgressor Treatment

The issue of how to treat the offender is raised. Gabbard and Lester develop their ideas about treatment, which should include disciplinary measures as well as human rehabilitation based on an understanding of the individual practitioner.

Transgression Prevention

Without question, therapists frequently have sexual and romantic feelings and fantasies. They will occur. And there is no solution for preventing sexual boundary violations. However, we can work toward reducing these violations. Institutes and societies need ethics committee, but they are not enough. Colleagues need to be encouraged to "tell" and to talk. There is a fissure. The dissociation between what is said to others and what is thought privately must be eradicated. We can work toward this by dialogue. Blechner (2014) suggests that training programs should acknowledge the existence of sexual boundary violations and should promote discussion about sexual feelings within psychoanalytic training. In addition, training needs to focus more on dealing with erotic transference. He also reminds us of Fromm-Reichmann's advice: that it is important for the psychotherapist to have adequate sources of personal gratification in life outside the consulting room to avoid seeking such gratification inside the room. Most important, there needs to be education about transference and countertransference, regardless of the theoretical orientation of the training program and regardless of the level of training (graduate school, internship, or postdoctoral training). Clearly there needs to be education about boundaries, transference, the power differential, ethics, and self-care. And as there is no such thing as one trial learning, this should involve more than a one-shot course. These topics need to be integrated into every course and every supervision. . . .

REFERENCES

Blechner, M. (2014). Dissociation among psychoanalysts about sexual boundary violations. *Contemporary Psychoanalysis, 50*, 23–33. http://dx.doi.org/10.1080/00107530.2014.868299

Borys, D. S., & Pope, K. S. (1989). Dual relationships between therapist and client: A national study of psychologists, psychiatrists, and social workers. *Professional Psychology: Research and Practice, 20*, 283–293. http://dx.doi.org/10.1037/0735-7028.20.5.283

Celenza, A. (2007). *Academic and supervisory contexts. Sexual boundary violations: Therapeutic, supervisory, and academic contexts* (pp. 65–76). New York, NY: Aronson.

Dahlberg, C. (1970). Sexual contact between patient and therapist. *Contemporary Psychoanalysis, 6*, 107–124. http://dx.doi.org/10.1080/00107530.1970.10745180

Dimen, M. (2011). Lapsus linguae or a slip of the tongue? A sexual violation in an analytic treatment and its personal and theoretical aftermath. *Contemporary Psychoanalysis, 47*, 35–79. http://dx.doi.org/10.1080/00107530.2011.10746441

Falzeder, E. (2015). *Psychoanalytic filiations: Mapping the psychoanalytic movement.* London, UK: Karnac Books.

Freud, S. (1915). Observations on transference-love. In J. Strachey (Ed.), *The standard edition of the complete psychological works of Sigmund Freud* (Vol. 12, pp. 157–171). London, UK: Hogarth Press.

Fromm-Reichmann, F. (1950). *Principles of intensive psychotherapy.* Chicago, IL: University of Chicago Press.

Gabbard, G. O. (1994a). Commentary on papers by Tansey, Hirsch, and Davies. *Psychoanalytic Dialogues, 4*, 203–213.

Gabbard, G. O. (1994b). On love and lust in erotic transference. *Journal of the American Psychoanalytic Association, 42*, 385–386. http://dx.doi.org/10.1177/000306519404200203

Gabbard, G. O., & Lester, E. (1995). *Boundaries and boundary violations in psychoanalysis.* New York, NY: Basic Books.

Garrett, T. (2002). Inappropriate therapist–patient relationships. In R. Goodwin & D. Cramer (Eds.), *Inappropriate relationships* (pp. 147170). Mahwah, NJ: Erlbaum.

Jackson, H., & Nuttall, R. L. (2001). A relationship between childhood sexual abuse and professional sexual misconduct. *Professional Psychology: Research and Practice, 32,* 200–204. http://dx.doi.org/10.1037/0735-7028.32.2.200

McCartney, J. L. (1966). Overt transference. *Journal of Sex Research, 2,* 227–237. http://dx.doi.org/10.1080/00224499.1966.10749568

Pope, K. S., Tabachnick, B. G., & Keith-Spiegel, P. (1987). Ethics of practice. The beliefs and behaviors of psychologists as therapists. *American Psychologist, 42,* 993–1006. http://dx.doi.org/10.1037/0003-066X.42.11.993

Pope, K. S., & Vetter, V. A. (1991). Prior therapist–patient sexual involvement among patients seen by psychologists. *Psychotherapy: Theory, Research, Practice, Training, 28,* 429–438. http://dx.doi.org/10.1037/0033-3204.28.3.429

Schoener, G. R., Milgrom, J. H., Gonsiorek, J. C., Luepker, E. T., & Conroe, R. M. (1989). *Psychotherapists' sexual involvement with clients: Intervention and prevention.* Minneapolis, MN: Walk-In Counseling Center.

Shepard, M. (1971). *The love treatment.* New York, NY: Wyden.

Somer, E., & Saadon, M. (1999). Therapist–client sex: Clients' retrospective reports. *Professional Psychology: Research and Practice, 30,* 504–509. http://dx.doi.org/10.1037/0735-7028.30.5.504

Williams, M. H. (1992). Exploitation and inference. Mapping the damage from therapist–patient sexual involvement. *American Psychologist, 47,* 412–421. http://dx.doi.org/10.1037/0003-066X.47.3.412

COMMENTARY: This important article by Drs. Alpert and Steinberg is the key offering in a unique special issue of *Psychoanalytic Psychology* devoted specifically to the devastating phenomenon of sexual boundary violations. Although the topic has been a staple of psychological ethical analyses for as long as the field itself has existed, it has rarely if ever been examined in such considerable depth in the context of a contemporary, peer-reviewed scientific journal. On display here are not just explorations of deleterious effects on clients/patients, but also practical advice for avoiding such tragic errors in clinical care and judgment.

Pivotal in successfully navigating these issues is to cultivate a sufficient grasp of the constellation of intrapsychic needs and pressures that can make a client/patient vulnerable to this brand of exploitation, without stereotyping such persons as a class by implying that they are inherently flawed beings for whom sexual boundary violations are a predictable consequence. Additionally, it is necessary to recognize, for purposes of prevention, the quotidian nature of the clinician's early-stage impulses that become unquestionably impermissible and pervasively destructive in their subsequent expression.

The following references are recommended for those interested in further investigation of sexual boundary violations, the circumstances that can potentiate them, and methods for reducing their occurrence.

Demos, V. C. (2017). When the frame breaks: Ripple effects of sexual boundary violations. *Psychoanalytic Psychology, 34,* 201–207. http://dx.doi.org/10.1037/pap0000119

Gabbard, G. O. (2017). Sexual boundary violations in psychoanalysis: A 30-year retrospective. *Psychoanalytic Psychology, 34,* 151–156. http://dx.doi.org/10.1037/pap0000079

McNulty, N., Ogden, J., & Warren, F. (2013). "Neutralizing the patient": Therapists' accounts of sexual boundary violations. *Clinical Psychology & Psychotherapy, 20,* 189–198. http://dx.doi.org/10.1002/cpp.799

Steinberg, A. (L.), & Alpert, J. L. (2017). Sexual boundary violations: An agenda demanding more consideration. *Psychoanalytic Psychology, 34,* 221–225. http://dx.doi.org/10.1037/pap0000105

Tylim, I. (2017). On transference, passion, and analysts' sexual boundary violations. *Psychoanalytic Psychology, 34,* 182–185. http://dx.doi.org/10.1037/pap0000080

5.3. Nonromantic, Nonsexual Posttherapy Relationships Between Psychologists and Former Clients: An Exploratory Study of Critical Incidents

Sharon K. Anderson and Karen S. Kitchener

. . .

Little if any research has examined the types of nonromantic, nonsexual relationships that occur or have the potential to occur between psychotherapists and former clients. The purpose of our study was to explore and describe this type of contact. More specifically, we used the Critical Incident Technique (Flanagan, 1954) to identify the types of nonromantic, nonsexual posttherapy relationships that exist or have the potential to exist between the psychotherapist and former client. In addition, we explored whether or not psychologists believe these posttherapy relationships are ethically problematic and why or why not. In other words, the purpose of the study was, to describe the types of nonromantic, nonsexual relationships psychologists in practice encounter.

METHOD

. . . A total of 63 replies were received from psychologists (including the pilot and final study) for a response rate of 20%. The return rate was low; however, the purpose of the study was not to obtain a random sample for generalization. Rather, the study was exploratory and had two main goals: (a) to identify and classify the types of potential or actual relationships psychologists encounter with former clients, and (b) to explore psychologists' reasons for and against such relationships.

. . .

RESULTS

. . . In the sections that follow, we describe the research results in the following format. First, each of the eight relationship categories is described. Next,

From "Nonromantic, Nonsexual Posttherapy Relationships Between Psychologists and Former Clients: An Exploratory Study of Critical Incidents," by S. K. Anderson and K. S. Kitchener, 1996, *Professional Psychology: Research and Practice, 27*, pp. 59–66. Copyright 1996 by the American Psychological Association.

We wish to thank Bruce Uhrmacher for his assistance in bringing this research study to fruition.

examples drawn from participants' responses are provided to illustrate each category. (To assist the reader, the relationship category is identified after each example.) Because participants' descriptions are reported, the following steps were taken to protect the confidentiality of participants and former clients: (a) pronouns and nouns indicating gender were changed to neutral terms (i.e., *former client, spouse, child, parent*); (b) specific occupational titles of the former clients were changed to more general occupational titles; and (c) descriptive phrases or words that could be used to identify a participant's or former client's place of employment were changed by using more general phrases and words. . . . Last, the participants' perspectives about the ethical nature of these relationships is reported.

Personal or Friendship Relationships

This category included 18 incidents. In these relationships, the therapists and former clients had moved past the position of social acquaintance to a closer or more intimate relationship, and the therapist appeared to be more personally invested in the relationship. It was likely that more of the therapist's personal life was known by the former client. The incidents included in this relationship category reflected either a personal connection between the therapist and former client that had some unique or special quality such that the therapist's private life was accessible to the former client, or a friendship where there was a sense of camaraderie between the therapist and former client. The nine incidents defined as personal relationships spanned a broad range of contexts from the therapist being a neighbor of the former client to the therapist being the parent of a teenager who dated the former client. The following is an example of these incidents:

> Former client marries friend of psychologist's spouse. Former client's spouse and therapist's spouse want to socialize together as couples. (personal relationship)

A majority of the participants (seven out of nine) who described these incidents perceived the relationships as ethically problematic. Some of these participants suggested that an equal, normal friendship between a therapist and former client is improbable if not impossible. Other participants shared their belief that a multiple relationship would occur because the therapist–client relationship continues after termination. . . .[See Table 1.]

Social Interactions and Events

The social interaction and events relationship category also included 18 incidents. Participants described interactions that ranged from a onetime occurrence (e.g., attending the wedding of former clients) to social activities that could have been more ongoing and ranged from casual (e.g., participating in community or neighborhood activities) to sexual (e.g., participating in "swingers" parties). The circumstantial and intentional subcategories emerged during the sorting process. In the following example, the therapist and former client

TABLE 1. Categories of Nonromantic, Nonsexual Relationships With Former Clients and Psychologists' Ethical Evaluations of These Relationships

Relationship category	No. of critical incidents	Ethically problematic	Not ethically problematic	Both ethically problematic and not ethically problematic
Personal or friendship	18	7	7	4
Social interactions and events				
Circumstantial	9	3	6	
Intentional	9	9	0	
Business or financial	12	7	5	
Collegial or professional	12	2	8	2
Supervisory or evaluative				
Circumstantial	2	2	0	
Intentional	8	3	5	
Religious affiliation	9	0	9	
Collegial or professional plus social	7	1	6	
Workplace				
Circumstantial	3	2	1	
Intentional	2	2	0	

Note. Numbers in the fourth column represent the number of participants who saw the incident as being both ethically and not ethically problematic.

seemed to have met each other in a social context with little or no prior planning on either person's part.

> Found myself a fellow competitor at a dog show with a former patient. (social interactions and events—circumstantial)

Different from the circumstantial interactions between the therapist and former client, the following example illustrates a type of social activity where the therapist or former client initiated some action to invite contact or ensure interaction with the other in a social context. The former client initiated a majority of these social interactions.

> While coincidentally vacationing in the same resort area, psychologist and family accepted invitation of former client and family to visit at their vacation house along with several other guests. (social interactions and events—intentional)

Six out of the nine participants who described circumstantial social contacts saw these interactions as not ethically problematic. They provided justifications such as the following: the contact was brief and unplanned; confidentiality remained intact; and the psychologist took preventative measures to minimize potential harm in the posttherapy contact. For example, one psychologist who anticipated the possibility of social contact "discussed [with the former client] the potential uncomfortableness of the relationship after discharge." . . .

Business or Financial Relationships

The common theme in the business or financial category was either (a) exchanging dollars between the therapist and former client for the former client's expertise or assistance or (b) joining areas of expertise that brought in dollars (e.g., hiring a former client, receiving financial assistance or advice from a former client, patronizing the former client's place of business, and having a business together). This category included a total of 12 incidents. The following is an example:

> Psychologist hired a former patient to clean house for psychologist's family on a weekly basis. Was later let go because of poor performance, unreliability. (business or financial relationship)

Seven of the twelve participants saw this type of relationship as ethically problematic. Their reasons for this perspective included the following: dual role issues; negative impact on the former client's internalized image of the therapist; special knowledge about the former client influencing the therapist's objectivity; the power differential; and a limit on the former client's option to return to therapy. The following statements illustrate, from two participants' point of view, the difficulties associated with the business or financial relationships:

> My relationship with the former client as the former therapist causes me to cut this person slack [in two business or financial arrangements]. . . . The former client thrives and appears to benefit greatly, but I'm not always so sure it is good for me. Also it could cause too much dependency on me.

> I couldn't allow myself to see this person as other than a therapist, to move beyond the role we historically had defined between us. I needed this person to be only a therapist and felt I would be losing that.

Five participants did not see the incidents they described as ethically problematic. These participants identified the following reasons for their perspective: the relationship remained a professional relationship without two-way exchange of personal information, and the boundaries of the business relationship remained clear.

Collegial or Professional Relationships

In these 12 incidents, the therapist and former client held positions or took roles potentially equal in power and the relationship was likely to be more externally focused on professional or business issues or problems. An example follows:

> Professor of psychology served as therapist to university colleague (in another department); the two later occasionally worked on university committees together. (collegial or professional relationship)

Nine out of twelve participants said they saw these new relationships as not ethically problematic. Some of the participants argued they could compartmentalize their roles. For example, one participant wrote: "We all have multiple roles. . . . Some degree of compartmentalization is normal in life . . . dual relationships between [the] therapist and client are sensibly managed this way."

The participants who saw the collegial or professional relationship as ethically problematic suggested that the new relationship could produce problems because of dual role conflicts and transference issues. The following is an example of one participant's point of view: "A therapist [might] overlook trans-ferential material as important determinants of relationships long after the 'treatment' aspect has ended."

Supervisory or Evaluative Relationships

In 10 incidents, the new relationship was more supervisory or evaluative in nature. Typically, the therapist took or held a role that required overseeing or evaluating the former client's performance in a clinical or academic setting. As with the social interactions and events incidents, the raters judged that some of these relationships occurred because of an external factor somewhat out of the control of either the therapist or the former client. The following description is an example of the incidents in this category:

> As an instructor for a psychology course occasionally, it is not uncommon to have students previously seen at the counseling center by myself or others I supervise. (supervisory or evaluative relationship—circumstantial)

There were supervisory or evaluative relationships that occurred by more intentional action by either the therapist or former client. Frequently, the intentional action was a request or invitation. The following is offered as a sample of the eight incidents in the intentional subcategory of supervisory or evaluative relationships:

> I provided clinical supervision to a private agency who employed a counsel-or-therapist who had been a client of mine before and during the former client's graduate days. (supervisory or evaluative relationship—intentional)

Half of the participants (five) saw these circumstantial and intentional super-visory or evaluative relationships with former clients as ethically problematic because of conflicting role obligations. For example, a participant who was an administrator of an agency completing a job search commented:

> A former client . . . applied for a . . . clinical position . . . [the former client] was fairly pathological and I felt wouldn't be good in the job . . . I couldn't acknowl-edge my role due to confidentiality. I was very worried [the former client] would be selected by the search committee. . . .

Religious Affiliation Relationships

The religious affiliation category included nine incidents. Although the main theme of this category was attending the same church, most of these incidents included another type of interaction, such as working together on church com-mittees, social contact after a service, or support and assistance in another part of the former client's life (e.g., campaigning for a public office). Note the follow-ing example:

> A former client family joined the religious institution to which I belonged and where I became an officer. The couple who had seen me in short-term family work around their child's problems became active in the institution and we wound up working together on . . . activities sharing responsibility for committee

work and where they were often in a position of reporting directly to me on committee activities. (religious affiliation relationship)

None of the participants who described these incidents saw the contact or relationship as ethically problematic. Their reasons for this perspective included the following: the therapist–client relationship was over; confidentiality was maintained; the posttherapy relationship was discussed prior to entering it; considerable time had elapsed since termination; and it was unethical to ignore or avoid the former client. More specifically, one participant, who described a posttherapy incident in a religious context, stated:

> Given a small community, it is virtually [*sic*] impossible to attend church or social events without contact with present or former clients. . . . The more I practice . . . the more I recognize flexibility is needed with regard to general, social contact with former clients, especially in small communities. . . .

Collegial or Professional Plus Social Relationship

The difference between this category and the category of collegial or professional relationships is the presence of social contact in addition to the collegial or professional connection. The social contacts between therapists and former clients took place in a variety of settings (e.g., parties, social involvement in the psychology community, and meeting for lunch). The following is an example:

> An ex-patient of mine entered training at the same institute where I was a faculty member. . . . Later, this person too became a faculty member of the same institute. We found ourselves on the same committees, at the same faculty meetings and social events. (collegial or professional plus social relationship)

Similar to those participants who described collegial or professional relationships with former clients, a majority of these participants (six out of seven) did not see these relationships as ethically problematic. Their reasons included length of time since termination, the conscious effort to discuss issues related to the new relationship, and the natural evolution of the new relationship from the therapist–former client relationship. Although these six participants did not see the relationships as ethically problematic, two of them did identify the collegial plus social relationships as being "uncomfortable" for them. For example, one participant commented:

> At times [it is] uncomfortable for me (who would like to keep my personal and professional experiences separate) but I see no clear violation of ethical standards. . . . It is extremely important at the outset to discuss potential complications re: overlap of contact with patients in this category. . . .

Workplace Relationships

In this category, participants described five incidents where the therapist and former client found themselves in the same workplace, either as professional peers or as employees of the same clinical practice. In three incidents, these relationships occurred circumstantially. The following is an example of the incidents that were sorted into the subcategory of circumstantial workplace relationships:

> A psychologist left one job to go to work in another setting where a former client had been recently employed as office help. (workplace relationship—circumstantial)

In the other two workplace incidents, the therapist or former client initiated some purposeful action to bring about the workplace relationship. The following is an example:

> A clinic I work at recently hired a former client's parent as office help (over my objections). This parent was involved in several therapy sessions with the child. Presently, the parent has both computer and file drawer access to our files. (Workplace relationship—intentional)

Four out of the five participants saw these workplace relationships as ethically problematic. Some participants identified the ethical problem of dual role relationships; others indicated a strong concern related to "special knowledge" that the therapist might have about the former client and how this could influence the therapist's objectivity in the new relationship or role. For example, one participant stated it might be difficult "to separate work behavior from the psychological knowledge. . . . Anytime [the] employee was late for work or work behavior was decreasing, it would be difficult to remain unbiased."

In summary, the respondents' descriptions of critical incidents with former clients were sorted into eight relationship categories with personal or friendship and social interactions and events relationships being the most frequently described. Furthermore, participants presented a variety of perspectives regarding the ethicality of these posttherapy relationships. The majority of participants who described social interactions and events, business or financial relationships, and workplace relationships perceived these relationships as ethically problematic. On the other hand, the majority of participants who described collegial or professional relationships and collegial or professional plus social relationships perceived these relationships as not ethically problematic. An equal number of those who described personal or friendship relationships and supervisory or evaluative relationships saw these as ethically and not ethically problematic. Only one relationship category, religious affiliation, was perceived unanimously by participants as not ethically problematic. . . .

REFERENCE

Flanagan, J. C. (1954). The critical incident technique. *Psychological Bulletin, 51*, 327–358.

COMMENTARY: When it comes to psychological ethics, the lion's share of professional and popular media attention has been given to romantic and sexual transgressions—failings that raise the most substantial questions about a service provider's suitability for practice or other professional duties, result in some of the most emotionally damaging of consequences for clients/patients, and most readily titillate readers and viewers in the public at large. Nonromantic, nonsexual boundary violations are afforded comparatively minimal shrift.

Some "critical incidents" represent cases of either sublimated erotic desire or a conscious attempt to wander as close as possible to potential disaster without going just that little bit too far. Others are products of singular or mutual interest, of a sort that genuinely does not reflect any prurient motivation on the part of either party. The latter are the incidents that constitute the focus of this highly informative study by Drs. Anderson and Kitchener, who identified "little consensus" among psychologists as to "whether or not nonromantic, nonsexual relationships are ethical" when conducted with former patients/clients.

The following references are recommended for those interested in further investigation of this phenomenon and the institutional reaction it inspires, concerning members of different professions as well as clinicians and researchers at different stages of career development.

Dallesasse, S. L. (2010). Managing nonsexual multiple relationships in university counseling centers: Recommendation for graduate assistants and practicum students. *Ethics & Behavior, 20,* 416–428. http://dx.doi.org/10.1080/10508422.2010.521440

DeJulio, L. M., & Berkman, C. S. (2003). Nonsexual multiple role relationships: Attitudes and behaviors of social workers. *Ethics & Behavior, 13,* 61–78. http://dx.doi.org/10.1207/S15327019EB1301_09

Gutheil, T. G., & Simon, R. I. (2002). Non-sexual boundary crossings and boundary violations: The ethical dimension. *Psychiatric Clinics of North America, 25,* 585–592. http://dx.doi.org/10.1016/S0193-953X(01)00012-0

Miller, R. D., & Maier, G. J. (2002). Nonsexual boundary violations: Sauce for the gander. *Journal of Psychiatry & Law, 30,* 309–329. http://dx.doi.org/10.1177/009318530203000302

Pritchett, S., & Fall, Kevin A. (2001). Post-termination and non-sexual dual relationships: Dynamics and assessment. *TCA Journal, 29,* 72–79.

5.4. Therapeutic Boundaries in Telepsychology: Unique Issues and Best Practice Recommendations

Katherine B. Drum and Heather L. Littleton

. . .

BOUNDARIES, CLINICAL UTILITY, AND SALIENT ISSUES

Boundaries are generally understood to be the rules that govern the therapeutic relationship and which help to differentiate it from that of a business or social relationship (Knapp & Slattery, 2004). Such rules or boundaries include structural elements such as time, place/space, and money, and also content factors such as what actually occurs between the therapist and client (Smith & Fitzpatrick, 1995). Boundaries encompass issues such as who the client is, what payment will be, where and when therapy will take place, when it may be necessary to break confidentiality, how to manage multiple relationships, and issues surrounding termination. Other aspects of boundaries concern how cancellations, rescheduling, and nonpayment issues are handled, whether gifts and bartering are permitted, what types of interactions are acceptable, issues related to therapist self-disclosure, and issues related to proximity (physical distance between client and therapist), clothing, and language use (Gottlieb, Younggren, & Murch, 2009; Gutheil & Gabbard, 1993; Zur, 2007).

In general, boundaries are clinically useful as they serve to provide guidance regarding the nature of the therapeutic relationship and help the client and clinician regulate their behavior in ways that maximize clinical outcomes and minimize harm (Borys, 1994; Zur, 2007). Boundaries can also promote a number of other therapeutic aims including building a trusting working alliance, modeling assertiveness skills to the client, enhancing the client's self-worth (i.e., by respecting the client's rights and autonomy), as well as ensuring the integrity of the relationship (Borys, 1994; Simon, 1992; Smith & Fitzpatrick, 1995). In addition to providing protection for the client, appropriate boundaries also protect clinicians from harm. For example, appropriate boundaries help prevent clinicians from engaging in ethically risky behaviors such as entering into inappropriate multiple relationships with clients. Appropriate boundaries also serve to protect the clinician from being manipulated by clients (e.g., those diagnosed with a personality disorder) who may attempt to lead the therapist toward a more "special" and less professional relationship (Gutheil, 1989; Simon, 1992; Smith & Fitzpatrick, 1995).

Boundaries are highly important in the treatment relationship, yet they can be difficult to operationalize as they are dependent upon a number of unique factors specific to each client and clinician (e.g., the client's diagnosis and the clinician's orientation). Thus, because there is some flexibility in boundaries across clients, contexts, and orientations, the potential exists for boundary issues and challenges to arise. Boundary issues that have been known to arise in traditional settings include those related to place and space, time, money, role, gifts, physical touch, language, clothing, self-disclosure, and sexual contact (Gutheil & Gabbard, 1993).

Furthermore, one can distinguish between two types of boundary transgressions: *boundary crossings* and *boundary violations*. The term boundary crossing refers to departures from typically accepted clinical practice, which may or may not be beneficial to the client (Smith & Fitzpatrick, 1995). Boundary crossings include more minor deviations from typical therapeutic practice such as attending a client's graduation after being invited or giving a client a hug at the final session. Boundary violations on the other hand, are more severe and are departures from acceptable clinical practice which pose a serious risk to the client and/or the therapeutic process (Gutheil & Gabbard, 1993; Simon, 1992; Smith & Fitzpatrick, 1995). Boundary violations commonly include ethical violations such as engaging in a sexual relationship or exploitive business practices with a client (Gutheil & Gabbard, 1993; Williams, 1997; Zur, 2007). Overall, it is generally accepted that boundary crossings have the potential to be therapeutic, neutral, or harmful depending on myriad factors, yet boundary violations are always harmful. Additionally, although the vast majority of psychologists who cross boundaries do so in a way that is considered safe and therapeutic (Gottlieb & Younggren, 2009), the potential exists for successive boundary crossings to lead some down a slippery slope toward boundary violations (Gutheil & Gabbard, 1993). Thus, the provision and maintenance of appropriate therapeutic boundaries is essential and warrants special consideration in telepsychology settings as maintaining boundaries in such settings is likely to present unique challenges.

. . .

BEST PRACTICE RECOMMENDATIONS

Given the potential for unique and challenging boundary issues to arise in telepsychology settings, best practice recommendations for the prevention and management of such issues are offered below. It is our hope that considering the abovementioned issues and observing the following recommendations will lead to the establishment and maintenance of professional boundaries that maximize clinical utility and minimize harm. Additionally, following these recommendations will help to maintain the integrity of the treatment process in the novel and continuously changing context that is telepsychology.

Recommendation 1: Maintain Professional Hours and Respect Timing of Sessions

Although it is acceptable for clients to interact at any hour they choose, clinicians are advised to only conduct therapeutic interactions and schedule telepsychology appointments during normal business hours. A therapist may choose to construct asynchronous feedback for a client at any hour, but that feedback should only be presented during normal business hours. This will help to distinguish therapeutic communications from everyday interactions with others in the client's life. It will also ensure that therapy is perceived as structured, consistent, predictable, and professional. In addition, as one would in a traditional face-to-face setting, clinicians are advised to respect the timing of appointments and sessions. They are advised to arrive to sessions on time and to ensure that technology is working properly before the start of the session. Additionally, clinicians practicing telepsychology should be mindful of cultural variances related to punctuality and not assume underlying therapeutic significance if clients whose cultures do not place great emphasis on punctuality are late to an appointment. Clinicians may, however, wish to discuss the importance of being on time as it relates to ensuring timely access to care to others.

Recommendation 2: Ensure Timely and Consistent Feedback and Manage Excessive Communications

Clinicians should take care to provide consistent and timely feedback. One to three business days for online program feedback and 24 hrs for more instant communications are generally considered acceptable turnaround times (Abbott et al., 2008; Manhal-Baugus, 2001). Clinicians should also discuss feedback turnaround times at the start of treatment so that clients know what to expect. Providing consistent feedback will model accountability and provide clients with a sense of safety, security, and trust. Additionally, in order to avoid showing unintentional favoritism, clinicians should provide feedback in the order that it was received (with the exception of those in immediate crisis or danger). If the client's speed of communication appears excessive and clinically contraindicated, the clinician should slow his or her feedback response in order to model a more appropriate and therapeutic interaction pace.

Recommendation 3: Ensure a Private, Consistent, Professional, and Culturally Sensitive Setting

In order to protect confidentiality, clinicians should refrain from conducting telepsychology services while in public and clients may be advised to do the same. Clinicians should also advise clients to ensure that video-conferencing takes place in a private space within their homes and to take measures to ensure that others do not intrude on the session, perhaps by simply locking the door. Text-based communication may be helpful to include with videoconferencing equipment in the event that privacy is breeched and the client is no longer able to communicate verbally. It is also recommended that clinicians conduct therapeutic services containing a video component from a consistent environment. This will help to ensure privacy, model stability, and convey a safe and reliable place for the therapeutic work to occur. It will also help prevent clinicians from practicing outside of their jurisdictions. Clinicians are also advised to be mindful of what appears in the camera's view when using video components, and ensure that the space appears professional. Suggestions for professional backdrops include artwork such as neutral land and seascapes or one's degrees, diplomas, and certificates (Devlin et al., 2013). In addition, because clients have only a limited view of the therapist's professional space when using video equipment, clinicians should consider the cultural backgrounds of the populations with whom they primarily work and design a setting that promotes cultural acceptance and sensitivity (Devlin et al., 2013). Taking care to prevent excessive background noise when using audio equipment—perhaps via use of a white noise machine outside of one's office door—may also help alleviate privacy concerns and ensure professionalism. Lastly, although this may seem like a given, the therapist should always be dressed in a professional manner when video equipment is used.

Recommendation 4: Ensure Privacy of Nonclients and Prevent Unintentional Self-Disclosures

In addition to ensuring the client's privacy, clinicians may also wish to inform clients to take measures to ensure the privacy and confidentiality of others (e.g., family members, friends, or roommates) who may be in their environments. Clients may wish to remove any identifying information such as family photographs from the camera's view when video services are used. Clients should also be advised to anticipate any unintentional self-disclosures that could occur as a result of using a video camera.

Recommendation 5: Ensure That Telecommunication Technologies Used Convey Professionalism

Clinicians should take great care to ensure that telepsychology services used promote professionalism. Web sites should make use of professional photographs and include descriptions of services that contain professional language that is free from jargon and grammatical errors. Clinicians may also wish to refrain from including detailed personal information such as their likes and interests. Links to the therapist's state licensing board and verification of licensure, the code of ethics, and any professional organizations to which the therapist belongs may also be included in order to establish the therapist's professionalism and credentials as well as help clients to be reassured that the services provided are safe and legitimate. Additionally, clinicians should also consider the professionalism of all of their online activity such as blog, Facebook, and Twitter posts and consider all such activity to be public domain (see Zur, 2008 for suggestions on maintaining professionalism and managing various forms of self-disclosure via the Internet). Additionally, if clinicians do use social media, it will likely be helpful to have a policy in place to be reviewed with clients regarding ways in which they will handle nontherapeutic online contacts such as Facebook friend requests and requests to join a therapist's online forum (for an example of such a policy see Kolmes, 2010).

Recommendation 6: Model Appropriate Self-Boundaries

Clinicians should be mindful of a healthy work–life balance and adhere to boundaries that ensure proper self-care. Clinicians should take leave time when ill or vacationing, rather than continuing to conduct telepsychology services during such times. It is also recommended that clinicians avoid the temptation to check asynchronous communications during nonbusiness hours (e.g., during family time or on weekends). Notifying clients of scheduled leave time in advance, indicating when therapeutic communication will resume, and reminding clients of emergency procedures and coverage of care will help clinicians to avoid the temptation to check on clients during nonbusiness hours or when on leave.

Recommendation 7: Ensure Privacy of the Therapist's Work

In order to promote boundaries related to the therapist's privacy, the clinician may wish to restrict clients' abilities to download asynchronous video and audio files to computers, as well as design written program text so that one is unable to copy and paste the content. Although this will not prevent the client from potentially showing the telecommunications to others, it may prevent any editing and misuse/misrepresentation of the therapist's work. The therapist may also wish to have a policy regarding use and misuse of feedback and make this available to prospective clients prior to the start of treatment. Implementing such boundaries will help reinforce the importance of privacy and confidentiality and also model one's right to set appropriate limits with others.

Recommendation 8: Use Professional Language and Consider Alternative Interpretations

Therapists who engage in telepsychology are encouraged to reread their written feedback to clients and consider word choices in text-based communications. Reviewing text communications prior to making them available to clients will help prevent and minimize confusion as well as help ensure that unintentional boundary crossings do not occur because of miscommunications. Additionally, to help distinguish therapeutic communications from that of social interactions, clinicians are advised to refrain from the use of chat acronyms, text message shorthand, excessive punctuation, and emoticons.

Recommendation 9: Ensure Competence in the Practice of Telepsychology

Lastly, as an overarching recommendation, clinicians are encouraged to take measures to ensure competence in the telepsychology services they provide. This includes acquiring the skills and knowledge necessary to comfortably use the technologies being utilized. At a minimum, this should include consultation with information technology professionals, Web-design developers, expert clinicians in the field, and the like. Ongoing consultation with experts in the field of telepsychology will also be highly important for clinicians new to the practice, and all clinicians are encouraged to seek ongoing consultation regarding any boundary issues that arise at any point in the telepsychology treatment relationship. Additionally, although it is not yet a requirement for those practicing telepsychology, clinicians would also be wise to further their competence in this context by participating in training programs/continuing education courses which specifically address the provision of services related to telepsychology. Such courses can be accessed by visiting the following Web sites: http://www.apa.org, http://www.telehealth.org, http://www.zurinstitute.com, http://www.onlinetherapyinstitute.com, http://drkkolmes.com/for-clinicians/ceus/, and http://www.cce-global.org/DCC. Additionally, some states such as Florida now allow the option for obtaining an add-on credential in telepsychology (for information on this, please see http://onlinetherapyinstitute.com). Lastly, the psychology field at large has begun to stress the importance of including courses related to telepsychology and the development of a professional online identity in clinical training programs and advances in this area should continue.

SUMMARY

Mental health service delivery via the use of telecommunication technologies continues to expand at a rapid pace. With such advances come new challenges and issues that clinicians must consider in order to provide competent and ethical care in this mode of service delivery. Maintaining therapeutic boundaries within the telepsychology treatment relationship is one area in which challenges can occur. Such challenges include issues related to ensuring that the flexibility of service delivery via telepsychology does not lead to interventions that are less professional or high quality, as well as ensuring that the professionalism of the therapeutic relationship is established and maintained. Additional challenges relate to avoiding a number of temptations that could jeopardize the therapeutic relationship and potentially lead to ethical violations such as conducting therapeutic services while in public settings. However, by being aware of the issues related to these challenges and engaging in a number of proactive strategies, the telepsychology clinician can prevent many of these boundary issues from arising. Proactive strategies to prevent such issues include: establishing and maintaining a professional and consistent office environment, maintaining professional hours, ensuring privacy of clients and nonclients, preventing unintentional self-disclosures, providing consistent and timely feedback, managing excessive communications, and modeling appropriate self-boundaries. Being mindful of the unique boundary issues that can arise in telepsychology will aid clinicians who choose to utilize this form of service delivery. Most importantly, careful attention to boundary issues by clinicians will ensure that telepsychology services are conducted in a manner that is both ethical and efficacious.

REFERENCES

Abbott, J. M., Klein, B., & Ciechomski, L. (2008). Best practices in online therapy. *Journal of Technology in Human Services, 26*, 360–375. doi:10.1080/15228830802097257

Borys, D. (1994). Maintaining therapeutic boundaries: The motive is therapeutic effectiveness: Not defensive practice. *Ethics and Behavior, 4*, 267–273. doi:10.1207/s15327019eb0403_12

Devlin, A. S., Borenstein, B., Finch, C., Hassan, M., Iannotti, E., & Koufopoulos, J. (2013). Multicultural art in the therapy office: Community and student perceptions of the therapist. *Professional Psychology: Research and Practice, 44*, 168–176. doi:10.1037/a0031925

Gottlieb, M. C., & Younggren, J. N. (2009). Is there a slippery slope? Considerations regarding multiple relationships and risk management. *Professional Psychology: Research and Practice, 40*, 564–571. doi:10.1037/a0017231

Gottlieb, M. C., Younggren, J. N., & Murch, K. B. (2009). Boundary management for cognitive behavioral therapists. *Cognitive and Behavioral Practice, 16*, 164–171. doi:10.1016/j.cbpra.2008.09.007

Gutheil, T. G. (1989). Borderline personality disorder, boundary violations, and patient–therapist sex: Medicolegal pitfalls. *The American Journal of Psychiatry, 146*, 597–602.

Gutheil, T. G., & Gabbard, G. O. (1993). The concept of boundaries in clinical practice: Theoretical and risk-management dimensions. *The American Journal of Psychiatry, 150*, 188–196.

Knapp, S., & Slattery, J. M. (2004). Professional boundaries in nontraditional settings. *Professional Psychology: Research and Practice, 35*, 553–558. doi:10.1037/0735-7028.35.5.553

Kolmes, K. (2010). *Social media policy.* Retrieved from http://drkkolmes.com/for-clinicians/social-media-policy

Manhal-Baugus, M. (2001). E-therapy: Practical, ethical, and legal issues. *CyberPsychology & Behavior, 4*, 551–563. doi:10.1089/109493101753235142

Simon, R. I. (1992). Treatment boundary violations: Clinical, ethical, and legal considerations. *Bulletin of the American Academy of Psychiatry and the Law, 20*, 269–288. Retrieved from http://www.jaapl.org

Smith, D., & Fitzpatrick, M. (1995). Patient–therapist boundary issues: An integrative review of theory and research. *Professional Psychology: Research and Practice, 26*, 499–506. doi:10.1037/0735-7028.26.5.499

Williams, M. H. (1997). Boundary violations: Do some contended standards of care fail to encompass commonplace procedures of humanistic, behavioral, and eclectic psychotherapies? *Psychotherapy, 34*, 238–249. doi:10.1037/h0087717

Zur, O. (2007). *Boundaries in psychotherapy: Ethical and clinical explorations.* Washington, DC: American Psychological Association. doi:10.1037/11563-000

Zur, O. (2008). The Google factor: Therapists' self-disclosure in the age of the internet. Discover what your clients can find out about you with a click of the mouse. *Independent Practitioner, 28*, 83–85.

5.5. Maintaining Boundaries in the Treatment of Pathological Narcissism

Andrew F. Luchner

It is clear that narcissism is not a unitary construct that is defined solely by grandiosity, entitlement, and selfishness, but that it also manifests as deficits in self-esteem (a depleted or devalued self), lack of confidence, conformity, and hypersensitivity to slights and negativity (Dickinson & Pincus, 2003; Gabbard, 1994; Masterson, 1993; Miller, 1997; PDM Task Force, 2006; Wink, 1991). The two subtypes of narcissism have been termed *grandiose* and *vulnerable*, respectively. . . . Patients with pathological narcissistic characteristics are among the more difficult to treat in psychotherapy because they use others (e.g., therapists) to define themselves, are fragile and easily affected by perceived slights and mistakes, and are perfectionistic in their attempts to elicit admiration from others to neutralize internal experiences of devaluation (Ivey, 1995; McWilliams, 1994). The source of self-satisfaction for narcissistic patients does not exist within themselves; thus, in psychotherapy, therapists are depended on to fulfill absent self-definition and self-worth. The pressure that therapists feel is a function of the demands that narcissistic patients place on them to exist as separate people and to exist as an extension of their devalued and critical self. Because patients with grandiose and vulnerable narcissism lack clearly defined boundaries between themselves and others, therapists can have difficulty managing and maintaining boundaries.

Pathological narcissistic patients may be additionally challenging to treat because of therapists' strivings for admiration, acceptance, and recognition for selflessness—core aspects of vulnerable narcissism. Many therapists tend to be giving, caring, and willing to accommodate to the needs of others, including their patients. It is hyper-responsibility, aversion to wrongdoing, and the wish to provide and take care of others that increases the probability that difficulties maintaining boundaries in psychotherapy will occur. For example, grandiose narcissistic patient characteristics may force therapists to confront their inability to help, whereas vulnerable narcissistic patient characteristics may leave therapists blinded by identification and the fantasy that providing psychotherapy can resolve past and current needs for helpfulness and selflessness. Although vulnerable narcissistic characteristics are not emblematic of all therapists, it is common to hear therapists talk about their special role in personal relationships as the one who has always been the "good listener" or the one whose friends "go to when they need to talk." At the expense of one's own needs and authentic responses in the moment, therapists may have learned early to deny their own self (e.g., denial of their own need to be gratified and attended to) as a way to feel some sense of self-worth, identity, and helpfulness to others. To care more about others than oneself has been linked to the choice of psychotherapy as a profession (Miller, 1997), and therapists are drawn to want to be the most helpful, the most effective, and the most sought out for their ability to engender change.

The interaction between characterological qualities of many therapists and the vicissitudes of therapeutic practice make working with patients with pathological narcissism challenging and taxing. As a result, psychotherapy with narcissistic patients affects therapists' ability to attend to therapeutic boundaries that are a necessary component not only for patient care (e.g., managing the therapeutic relationship) but for therapist self-care as well (Kottler, 2010; McWilliams, 2004). . . .

BOUNDARIES AND BOUNDARY MAINTENANCE

Although there are no specific American Psychological Association (APA) ethical standards that pertain to the maintenance of boundaries, psychotherapists widely agree that boundaries play a crucial role in the therapeutic process (Gelso & Hayes, 1998). The establishment of boundaries is directly related to the professional standards of conduct, notably the importance of upholding the principle of Beneficence and nonmaleficence (APA, 2002). However, clear definitions and clear agreement of what differentiates healthy boundaries from boundary violations are lacking (Gabbard & Lester, 1995; Glass, 2003; McWilliams, 2004). For the purpose of this discussion, boundaries are defined as therapeutic limits that allow for the protection of the patient's best interests, thereby allowing for safety, reliability, and dependability (Gabbard & Lester, 1995; Gelso & Hayes, 1998; Glass, 2003; Gutheil & Gabbard, 1998; Smith & Fitzpatrick, 1995). The psychotherapist attempts to protect boundaries by maintaining focus on the patient's difficulties as they relate to therapeutic goals, reducing or attending to the role of therapist opinion, and enhancing opportunities to increase patient independence and autonomy (Epstein, 1994; Smith & Fitzpatrick, 1995). The purpose of establishing and maintaining boundaries is to ensure that therapy is geared toward helping the patient and not motivated by therapist needs, wishes, or agendas (Smith & Fitzpatrick, 1995). When boundaries are compromised, boundary transgressions occur, which exist on a continuum ranging from *adaptive* (i.e., ethical and therapeutically useful boundary crossings) to *maladaptive* (i.e., antitherapeutic and unethical; Frank, 2002; Zur, 2007). *Boundary violations*, which stand at the maladaptive end of the boundary continuum, are "serious" and "harmful" (Gabbard & Lester, 1995, p. 123), do not involve careful consideration by anyone involved in the therapy, and occur when the therapist crosses the line of appropriate, decent, and ethical behavior (Zur, 2007). Furthermore, boundary violations are characterized by an absence of attenuation, involving the therapist's inability or refusal to address the enactments, being pervasive in nature, and causing harm. Many theorists consider boundary violations as inherently unethical and exploitative, departing from normal practice, involving the misuse of power and influence, and causing harm to the patient (Gabbard & Lester, 1995; Smith & Fitzpatrick, 1995; Zur, 2007). Some examples of boundary violations include establishing romantic and sexual relationships with patients and manipulating patients for financial gain. . . .

PSYCHOTHERAPISTS AND VULNERABLE NARCISSISM

Two important aspects of providing psychotherapy appear to connect to descriptions of vulnerable narcissism: the importance of attunement and the one-sided nature of therapeutic work. Attunement with and interest in the needs of the patient are skills that psychotherapists depend on to form a collaborative therapeutic relationship with patients (Binder, 2004; Gelso & Hayes, 1998). These abilities have been described as "emotional antennae" that allow the therapist to provide important qualities such as "sensibility, empathy" and "responsiveness" (Miller, 1997, p. 19). The qualities that allow therapists to center their attention and suspend focus on themselves also create pressure to feel that they must provide more when patients express or communicate displeasure or dissatisfaction (McWilliams, 2004). Second, psychotherapy is focused on helping one person, which leaves the therapist relatively protected from being known by the patient (Coen, 2007; Epstein, 1994; Smith & Fitzpatrick, 1995; Wolf, 1988). Therapy has the potential to create ongoing and repetitive interpersonal experiences of not getting needs met. For example, psychotherapy depends greatly on a working alliance, which is established by focusing on the needs and goals of the patient in order to establish trust and safety (Gabbard & Lester, 1995; Gelso & Hayes, 1998). Therefore, the necessary conditions for the establishment of a therapeutic alliance (e.g., attunement, establishment of trust and safety) create ample opportunities for the therapist to rescue (Masterson, 1993) and fulfill the need to be selfless, caretaking, giving, and self-sacrificing —aspects of vulnerable narcissism.
. . .

BOUNDARIES AND PATHOLOGICAL NARCISSISM

Although it is difficult to anticipate how a particular therapist will react to a particular patient, some common themes regarding boundary crossings and maintenance have emerged in the clinical literature and pertain specifically to work with patients with narcissistic pathology. Because the potential for difficulty in maintaining boundaries with narcissistic patients exists specifically because of identification and counteridentification, it is important to highlight areas or indicators of boundary crossings that might exist or appear in therapy (Ivey, 1995). . . .

Overinvesting in Caretaking or Overinvesting in Rejection: The Misuse of Empathy

Patients with vulnerable narcissism are challenging because they tend to pull from therapists approval, advice, soothing, caretaking, and overinvolvement that ultimately affects the therapeutic process and the boundary between patient and therapist (Wolf, 1988). Therefore, the pull to bolster the self-esteem of the patient with vulnerable narcissism may involve a misuse of empathy; the therapist may erroneously believe that empathy entails "doing something good for the patient" (Wolf, 1988, p. 132) and performing acts of kindness (Gabbard, 2009). For example, the therapist, in an effort to reduce negative reactions in the patient, may attempt to emphasize positive aspects of the relationship (e.g., progress, closeness) and deemphasize any negative aspects (e.g., failure, ruptures) that may be affecting the therapeutic relationship (Miller, 1997). . . .

Attempting to Engender Closeness or Attempting to Engender Distance

Closeness to and "tranquil union" (Shulman, 1986, p. 146) with patients is a common experience when working with vulnerable narcissistic patients (Shulman, 1986). Therapists are drawn to patients who appear selfless, weak, and helpless, and vulnerable narcissistic patients often implicitly communicate fantasies of rescue and merger (Wolf, 1988). Although attraction to and interest in patients are expected and understandable phenomena, overinvestment in how close therapists feel toward patients may limit authenticity in treatment. The closeness that therapists feel toward their patients may limit therapeutic flexibility and an awareness of negative countertransferential reactions. . . .

Devaluing and Criticizing or Idealizing and Praising: The Role of Therapist Self-Focus

Vulnerable narcissistic patients "respond to their falling short by feeling inherently flawed rather than forgivably human" (McWilliams, 1994, p. 174). Therapists might misinterpret the patient's internal experience of devaluation as a therapeutic failure; their constant criticism of themselves is likely to set the stage for a multitude of difficulties that can compromise the therapeutic relationship and the treatment itself. These difficulties may include being less responsive, more hesitant, less attentive, and more doubtful about accomplishments, therapeutic gain, and therapeutic ability. . . .

A significant trap that therapists can easily fall into when working with patients who display grandiose narcissistic tendencies is identification with the patient's grandiose and inflated sense of self (Coen, 2007; McWilliams, 1994). Such patients can be charming, extroverted, and attractive, qualities that therapists may aspire to but have difficulty owning and believing apply to themselves. By using these qualities, patients with grandiose narcissism can be very convincing in their attempts to exude greatness and infallibility. Therapists can easily be drawn to patients' grandiose presentations and collude with them in believing in their greatness and also begin to identify with this illusion (Gabbard, 2009). . . .

Taking Responsibility or Avoiding Responsibility

Vulnerable narcissistic patients tend to attribute too much error to their own behavior; they feel that they must perfectly attend to others or be rejected and left without purpose. In turn, they may create in therapists the wish to protect, increasing the therapist's susceptibility to taking too much responsibility for lack of progress and difficulty in the therapeutic relationship. Because patients with vulnerable narcissism come across as selfless, eager to assist, giving, agreeable, and caretaking, therapists may feel guilty when they become aware of a lack of improvement or change. For example, therapists may take responsibility for blame too easily or too often when patients express self-blame or fault in terms of lack of progress. Therapists who excessively admit fault and vulnerability may inadvertently reinforce self-devaluation and self-blame to vulnerable narcissistic patients. . . .

Patients who exhibit grandiose narcissistic characteristics challenge therapists to admit vulnerabilities, fallibilities, and mistakes, the same fears that exist for the patient. grandiose narcissistic patients pull therapists to disown their own sense of responsibility and blame the patient for the lack of progress, for difficulty establishing a therapeutic relationship, and for negative countertransference feelings (e.g., anger). In turn, the therapist's inability to accept responsibility may limit the ability of patients to accept their own fallibility, denying them self-expression and subjective experience. For example, a therapist may communicate that patients are "responsible for their own change" while thinking that patients' lack of change is "not my responsibility."

Unconditionally Accepting or Competing and Arguing

The patient with vulnerable narcissistic tendencies often attempts to demonstrate to the therapist his or her capacity to provide constant affection and admiration. As a result, the therapist may feel obligated to unconditionally accept the patient and return the experience of admiration and affection (especially if the therapist struggles with similar difficulties). Boundary transgressions of a more implicit nature can occur as a result of the wish to provide unconditional acceptance (and at its most extreme, love) of the patient. For example, the psychotherapist may frequently and persistently attempt to actively soothe the patient, potentially compromising boundaries because of the motivation and wish to be the perfect parent who is capable of providing unconditional love to the child (Gabbard & Lester, 1995). . . .

Making Connections or Withholding Intervention

The selfless and helpless qualities of patients with vulnerable narcissistic characteristics tend to make them seem needy. Therapists may attempt to gratify the needs of vulnerable narcissistic patients by providing early and frequent interpretations and connections (Gabbard, 2009). Misguided attempts to interpret or intervene may compromise the boundary between therapist and patient (Ogrodniczuk, Piper, Joyce, & McCallum, 1999), as the therapist's attempts to provide for patients may in fact support their pathological belief in their own weakness and helplessness (Miller, 1997). Therapist attempts to further the conscious awareness of patients' past and/or present struggles by constantly attempting to provide greater cognitive and emotional understanding for vulnerable narcissistic patients may recreate past experiences of patients who have never been allowed to engage in self-direction or self-discovery (Gabbard, 2009; Kohut, 1971), thereby supporting feelings of shame and worthlessness. For example, a therapist may be more active than usual in order to feel more helpful and useful (Wolf, 1988), but in doing so may not take into account the vulnerable narcissistic patient's chronic self-doubt and vulnerability. Autonomy, collaboration, and participation might be discouraged (Epstein, 1994), and dependency may be created as the therapist takes on greater responsibility in the relationship by not allowing the patient to confront feelings of weakness and helplessness or confront defenses against guilt and exhibitionistic desires. . . .

Avoiding Termination or Prematurely Terminating

Because patients with vulnerable narcissism tend to be agreeable, giving, accommodating, and pleasing, termination can be a difficult process as therapists are pulled to not relinquish the patient. Avoidance of termination diverts attention away from issues relating to separation, independence, and one's ability to exist separately from others, thereby creating difficulty for the therapist to manage boundaries that aim to support patient growth and development. When vulnerable narcissistic patients (who are adept at recognizing the needs of others) detect therapists' need to remain connected, they are discouraged from ending psychotherapy when termination may be in their best interest. For example, psychotherapists may dissuade patient independence by communicating to patients the importance of remaining in therapy as the only way to maintain change and positive results. . . .

CONCLUSION

Working with patients with pathological narcissism is undeniably challenging. Inherent in the treatment of such patients are difficulties in maintaining therapeutic boundaries. Patients' narcissistic tendencies can incite a variety of reactions in therapists, which have the potential to lead to boundary violations. therapists who themselves possess vulnerable narcissistic traits may be particularly susceptible to experiencing difficulties in maintaining therapeutic boundaries (Luchner et al., 2008). Moreover, therapists who are dealing with environmental struggles (e.g., relational, financial, familial) of their own might be especially challenged by a narcissistic patient's behaviors and find that therapeutic boundaries are threatened (Wolf, 1988). However, all therapists can be expected to face challenges in maintaining therapeutic boundaries with narcissistic patients. Appropriate management of therapeutic boundaries requires a persistent focus on how a patient's narcissistic tendencies are manifesting in treatment and one's own reactions to these manifestations (Coen, 2007). Therefore, awareness of common reactions to narcissistic patients and recognition of deviation from known patterns of relating may be especially important for determining whether boundary crossings have moved away from having a useful place in treatment to impeding treatment by limiting therapist flexibility and autonomy. Training, supervision, and consultation are important to help therapists develop the skills for maintaining appropriate boundaries with narcissistic patients, especially for beginning therapists who may be especially susceptible to the pressure to please others and embarrassment about mistakes (Huprich, 2008). . . .

REFERENCES

American Psychological Association. (2002). Ethical principles of psychologists and code of conduct. *American Psychologist, 57,* 1060–1073. doi:10.1037/0003-066X.57.12.1060

Binder, J. L. (2004). *Key competencies in brief dynamic psychotherapy: Clinical practice beyond the manual.* New York, NY: Guilford Press.

Coen, S. J. (2007). Narcissistic temptations to cross boundaries and how to manage them. *Journal of the American Psychoanalytic Association, 55,* 1169–1190. doi:10.1177/000306510705500404

Dickinson, K. A., & Pincus, A. l. (2003). Interpersonal analysis of grandiose and vulnerable narcissism. *Journal of Personality Disorders, 17,* 188–207. doi:10.1521/pedi.17.3.188.22146

Epstein, R. S. (1994). *Keeping boundaries: Maintaining safety and integrity in the psychotherapeutic process.* Washington, DC: American Psychiatric Press.

Frank, K. A. (2002). The "ins and outs" of enactment: A relational bridge for psychotherapy integration. *Journal of Psychotherapy Integration, 12,* 267–286. doi:10.1037/1053-0479.12.3.267

Gabbard, G. O. (1994). *Psychodynamic psychiatry in clinical practice: The DSM–IV edition.* Washington, DC: American Psychiatric Press.

Gabbard, G. O. (2009). Transference and countertransference: Developments in the treatment of narcissistic personality disorder. *Psychiatric Annals, 39,* 129–136. doi:10.3928/00485713-20090301-03

Gabbard, G. O., & Lester, E. P. (1995). *Boundaries and boundary violations in psychoanalysis.* Washington, DC: American Psychiatric Publishing.

Gelso, C. J., & Hayes, J. A. (1998). *The psychotherapy relationship: Theory, research, and practice.* New York, NY: Wiley.

Glass, L. L. (2003). The gray areas of boundary crossings and violations. *American Journal of Psychotherapy, 57,* 429–444.

Gutheil, T. G., & Gabbard, G. O. (1998). Misuses and misunderstandings of boundary theory in clinical and regulatory settings. *The American Journal of Psychiatry, 155,* 409–414.

Huprich, S. K. (Ed.). (2008). *Narcissistic patients and new therapists: Conceptualization, treatment, and managing countertransference.* London, England: Jason Aronson.

Ivey, G. (1995). Interactional obstacles to empathic relating in the psychotherapy of narcissistic disorders. *American Journal of Psychotherapy, 49,* 350–370.

Kohut, H. (1971). *The analysis of the self.* Madison, CT: International Universities Press.

Kottler, J. A. (2010). *On being a therapist.* San Francisco, CA: Jossey-Bass.

Luchner, A. F., Mirsalimi, H., Moser, C. J., & Jones, R. A. (2008). Maintaining boundaries in psychotherapy: Covert narcissistic personality characteristics and psychotherapists. *Psychotherapy: Theory, Research, Practice, Training, 45*(1), 1–14. doi:10.1037/0033-3204.45.1.1

Masterson, J. F. (1993). *The emerging self: A developmental, self, and object relations approach to the treatment of the closet narcissistic disorder of the self.* New York, NY: Brunner/Mazel.

McWilliams, N. (1994). *Psychoanalytic diagnosis: Understanding personality structure in the clinical process.* New York, NY: Guilford Press.

McWilliams, N. (2004). *Psychoanalytic psychotherapy: A practitioner's guide.* New York, NY: Guilford Press.

Miller, A. (1997). *The drama of the gifted child: The search for the true self* (Rev. ed.). New York, NY: Basic Books.

Ogrodniczuk, J. S., Piper, W. E., Joyce, A. S., & McCallum, M. (1999). Transference interpretations in short-term dynamic psychotherapy. *Journal of Nervous and Mental Disease, 187*, 571–578. doi:10.1097/00005053-199909000-00007

PDM Task Force. (2006). *Psychodynamic diagnostic manual.* Silver Spring, MD: Alliance of Psychoanalytic Organizations.

Shulman, D. G. (1986). Narcissism in two forms: Implications for the practicing psychoanalyst. *Psychoanalytic Psychology, 3*, 133–147. doi:10.1037/0736-9735.3.2.133

Smith, D., & Fitzpatrick, M. (1995). Patient–therapist boundary issues: An integrative review of theory and research. *Professional Psychology: Research and Practice, 26*, 499–506. doi:10.1037/0735-7028.26.5.499

Wink, P. (1991). Two faces of narcissism. *Journal of Personality and Social Psychology, 61*, 590–597. doi:10.1037/0022-3514.61.4.590

Wolf, E. S. (1988). *Treating the self: Elements of clinical self psychology.* New York, NY: Guilford Press.

Zur, O. (2007). *Boundaries in psychotherapy: Ethical and clinical explorations.* Washington, DC: American Psychological Association. doi:10.1037/11563-000

COMMENTARY: Next perhaps to clients/patients with borderline personality disorder, those with pathological narcissism may be the most challenging of all in clinical treatment—and supervision. To what particular extent—or at what preconscious level—can such persons be determined to be reacting to palpable and deep-seated feelings of self-loathing as opposed to a near-delusional belief that they are deserving of special attention and regard? What manner of countertransference is inspired by such issues in a psychological service provider who may be grappling with his or her own questionably appropriate need to be the dominant member of the therapeutic dyad?

The pathologically narcissistic client/patient or supervisee may be all too easy to insult, all too oversensitive to potential challenges, and all too ready to escalate to the level of a lawsuit or professional board complaint grievances that in the instance of a different diagnostic profile would be resolved with comparatively minimal fuss. These circumstances place even more pressure than usual on psychologists to maintain appropriate professional boundaries.

The following references are recommended for those interested in further investigation of the ethical pitfalls that may be inherent in treating and supervising these and other clinically demanding individuals, citing interpersonal processes and the mechanics of termination.

Bhatia, A., & Gelso, C. J. (2017). The termination phase: Therapists' perspective on the therapeutic relationship and outcome. *Psychotherapy, 54,* 76–87. http://dx.doi.org/10.1037/pst0000100

Goode, J., Park, J., Parkin, S., Tompkins, K. A., & Swift, J. K. (2017). A collaborative approach to psychotherapy termination. *Psychotherapy, 54,* 10–14. http://dx.doi.org/10.1037/pst0000085

Gutheil, T. G., & Brodsky, A. (2008). *Preventing boundary violations in clinical practice.* New York, NY: Guilford Press.

Kealy, D., Goodman, G., Rasmussen, B., Weideman, R., & Ogrodniczuk, J. S. (2017). Therapists' perspectives on optimal treatment for pathological narcissism. *Personality Disorders: Theory, Research, and Treatment, 8,* 35–45. http://dx.doi.org/10.1037/per0000164

Wright, A. G. C., Stepp, S. D., Scott, L. N., Hallquist, M. N., Beeney, J. E., Lazarus, S. A., & Pilkonis, P. A. (2017). The effect of pathological narcissism on interpersonal and affective processes in social interactions. *Journal of Abnormal Psychology, 126,* 898–910. http://dx.doi.org/10.1037/abn0000286

5.6. Boundaries, Multiple Roles, and the Professional Relationship

Rita Sommers-Flanagan

. . .

BOUNDARIES AND MORAL PHILOSOPHY

In the world of applied ethics, four or five moral philosophies or positions often are cited, including character ethics; duty-based ethics; utilitarian ethics; principle-based ethics; and feminist ethics, ethics of care, and situation ethics. This section provides a brief summary of each, linking a few of the tenets to the moral considerations related to professional boundaries.

Character Ethics

Aristotle, the founder of what has come to be known as *virtue* or *character* ethics, offered important moral principles to consider in the realm of professional boundaries (Aristotle, trans. 1955). First, his view of the fully self-actualized, virtuous adult human provides good news on at least two fronts. The good news is that humans are built to be virtuous. Aristotle believed that people come into the world with a blueprint that, if followed, will yield a profound sense of satisfaction and happiness, which he called *eudaimonia*. He believed that people have diverse professional callings and gifts to express in the world, but to experience profound happiness, the mature adult must be a virtuous person. Although we have to work at it, we are built to become virtuous. So, according to Aristotle, our calling as psychologists will not be fully satisfying unless we also strive to be virtuous in the way we work.

The second piece of good news, from the perspective of a midlife writer, is that Aristotle (trans. 1955) did not think people become accomplished, virtuous adults all at once—it is a process that requires years and years of training, apprenticeships, practice, and modeling. He did not expect anyone to be ready to assume the mantle of mature, virtuous adulthood until after the age of 50.

Aristotle (trans. 1955) also placed faith in the collective determination of virtue. He might have said something like, "If you want to understand courage, find a person that the community has identified as courageous and see what that person does." Mental health ethics codes addressing professional boundaries

From *APA Handbook of Ethics in Psychology: Vol. 1. Moral Foundations and Common Themes* (pp. 241–277), by S. J. Knapp (Ed.), 2012, Washington, DC: American Psychological Association. Copyright 2012 by the American Psychological Association.

reflect the collective wisdom of virtuous psychologists. A young, still-developing psychotherapist does well to heed this collective wisdom.

Another Aristotelian contribution to our consideration of professional boundaries has to do with moderation. Aristotle (trans. 1955) was the originator of the concept of the golden mean. Real virtue lies in the middle way. It is possible to have too much courage, or too little; too much generosity, or too little. The concept of the golden mean gives modern-day professionals permission to figure out what *too rigid–too loose*, or *too many–too few* might mean when applied to boundaries. I will return to this consideration when applying codes, laws, therapist inclinations, client needs, and theoretical guidelines to the establishment and maintenance of appropriate professional boundaries.

Duty-Based Ethics

Immanuel Kant has the distinction of being considered the founder of *duty-based*, or *deontological* morality (Kant, trans. 1963). This is the morality of absolutes— of doing one's moral duty no matter what the costs, and no matter what the outcome. Kant's *categorical imperative* (unconditional command) can be paraphrased as follows: Act as if you could will your action to become universal law. If the action you are about to take can be generalized to your society, so that all people at all times can choose to do what you are doing, without preconditions or caveats, and your society would be a healthy, happy place to live, then your action is moral. Professionals are expected to do their duty objectively, with client welfare as their highest obligation (R. Sommers-Flanagan & Sommers-Flanagan, 2007).

Kant (trans. 1963) also insisted that we can never justify using other human beings as a means to an end. Human beings are ends in and of themselves. All of our actions must honor this basic moral truth. Of course, humans cannot really apply such selfless, comprehensive, omniscient standards to their actions, but the intent must be there. We can use these imperatives when we are considering either creating or breaking boundaries. Are we building or adhering to a professional boundary system that is just and fair—one that can be applied to all? Could we allow all other psychotherapists to make the same boundary decision we are making, in all times and in all places? Are we defining our professional relationship and ensuring that our boundaries are handled in a way that never veers toward the client as a means to an end? These are the questions one would ask from a deontological moral position. . . .

Utilitarian Ethics

Utilitarian ethics is pragmatically focused on outcome and is sometimes called *consequentialist* or *teleological* ethics. Utilitarians ask, "What will bring about the greatest good for the greatest number?" John Stuart Mill is given credit for articulating this view most fully, and it is a familiar moral position for those who believe in a democratic form of government (Burtness, 1999). We evaluate the morality of a practice, rule, or law by its real or calculated outcome. The moral outcome provides the greatest benefit for the greatest possible number of people. In providing psychotherapy, clients constitute the population of interest, and the greatest good could be defined as effective psychotherapy. If ethical guidelines for boundaries were determined from a utilitarian frame, boundaries should be set and observed that will benefit the highest possible number of our clients as often as possible.

Principle-Based Ethics

In the 1970s, working in the then-new field of bioethics and drawing on the philosophy of W. D. Ross (1930), Beauchamp and Childress (1979) proposed four moral principles to consider when making difficult decisions in medical care. Medical costs had begun their acceleration, while at the same time technology had opened doors to near-miraculous medical possibilities, such as in vitro fertilization and heart transplants. The four principles Beauchamp and Childress (1979) identified were *autonomy, beneficence, nonmaleficence*, and *justice*. Honoring each principle, and reasoning through the lenses they provided, became the task of countless hospital medical ethics boards. These terms should seem quite familiar because in a slightly expanded and rearranged form, they provide the substance for the aspirational portion of the *Ethical Principles of Psychologists and Code of Conduct* (the Ethics Code; American Psychological Association [APA], 2010). The principles are Principle A, Beneficence and Non-maleficence; Principle B, Fidelity and Responsibility; Principle C, Integrity; Principle D, Justice; and Principle E, Respect for People's Rights and Dignity. . . .

All of the principles identified in the Ethics Code are relevant to boundaries in psychotherapy. Each can contribute a piece of the puzzle as we consider ethical boundaries. They do not provide one clear answer (Beauchamp & Childress, 1994), however, and sometimes adhering to one principle leads to actions that contradict another principle. For instance, a psychologist who discovers that her son has become close friends with a young male client she is seeing might wonder what to do. She might believe that the principle of fidelity guides her to continue to work with the client, working diligently to maintain confidentiality and guard the therapy relationship. When the client begins to reveal information about the therapist's son's drug-experimentation behavior, and she realizes that her client someday will find out that this friend is her son, beneficence might argue for disclosure or referral.

Feminist Ethics, Ethics of Care, and Situation Ethics

Although distinct from each other, each of the philosophical stances in this section demands that we consider the context and the particulars in a given situation to determine the moral course of action. Feminist theory includes a critique of power, and the Feminist Therapy Institute (1999) offers a code of ethics that explicitly guides feminist psychotherapists in addressing power and boundaries related to power in the professional relationship (Brown, 2008). In U.S. culture, professional relationships have an imbalance of power, in that someone is seeking, and often paying for, the expertise of someone else. Certainly, the seeker has power, too, but the professional sought out for assistance is imbued with a greater degree of authority. *Feminist ethics* guide professionals in the careful and conscious use of this power, with the main objective being to empower the seeker.

Ethics of care (Gilligan, 1993) and *situation ethics* (Fletcher, 1966) place central importance on the specific context and relationship at hand. Placing the relationship in the center, as care ethics does, provides an alternative to an overemphasis on individual notions of fairness and justice. Care ethics, however, is not exclusively centered on the immediate relationship but also on the "web of relationships that extends beyond immediate personal relationships to people of other races and nations and to all living things" (Taylor, 1995, p. 2).

Fletcher's (1966) situation ethics calls for moral decisions to be based on selflessness. The moral action is the most loving, correct, or healing action possible in each situation. Similar to Aristotle (trans. 1955), Fletcher believed that humans are born with the potential to behave in highly moral ways but that we need training as well. We must use our reasoning, our training, and our hearts to make the best moral decisions. . . .

Maintaining Boundaries

Ethically speaking, even for the most evolved, intelligent, empathic psychologist, flying by the seat of one's pants in determining healthy boundaries is inadvisable. Establishing and maintaining boundaries in the professional relationship cannot be safely done at an intuitive level. The moral philosophies described in this section provide an excellent starting point for the wise professional. In the best scenario, the philosophical basis is used in combination with the Ethics Code, good consultation and supervision practices, and the guidance provided in the remainder of this chapter to create a safe, predictable professional relationship, whether this relationship is between therapist and client, supervisor and supervisee, professor and student, or researcher and participant.
. . .

Using the APA Ethical Principles to Guide Crisis Work

Psychologists volunteering in crisis situations are obligated to the Ethics Code. The code has general, but not specific, applicability to crisis work. When volunteering for organizations that have codes of conduct, such as the Code of Conduct for the International Red Cross and Red Crescent (International Federation of Red Cross and Red Crescent Societies and the ICRC, n.d.) the professional becomes obligated to uphold the additional code as well. The relationship between helper and survivor can seem less professional because it might involve voluntary (uncompensated) professional work and clients who have very few choices in their lives because of the disaster or crisis. However, for psychologists volunteering as psychologists, professional boundaries should be firmly in place (APA, 2008).

Principle A, Beneficence and Nonmaleficence

Principle A is really two principles, so each will be considered separately. Beneficence refers to promoting good for others, not allowing one's own self-interest to override. It might seem that volunteering to help in a crisis situation is by definition beneficent. However, nothing is ever that straightforward. Motives, skill levels, and the ability to take care of oneself all interact with beneficent work.

Motives. Assessing our motives for helping is a challenging assignment, even in ordinary conditions. Of course, in offering therapy in crisis situations, the dominant motive should be a desire to be of help. Other motives that might be in play include self-aggrandizing, a wish to add some interest to one's life, a desire to express outrage or indignation at the unfairness of the disaster or the horrid motives of the perpetrators, or an unspoken hope to impose one's perceived higher values or beliefs on vulnerable people. Having any of these motives as a predominant force in choosing to help is a violation of the core boundaries protecting any professional relationship.

Necessary skills. To be of effective professional help, training, supervision, and extra readings or coursework most likely will be necessary (Smith, 2002). Although the training involved in becoming a psychologist is long and broad, it often does not include specialized training in crisis work. Beneficent professional interventions are based on adequate preparation and knowledge of best practices. Specific knowledge about the psychological aspects of trauma and crisis reactions is essential, and advanced skills are required to help survivors work through their losses and experiences and begin to integrate these into their lives (Collins & Collins, 2005).

Self-care. We have long known that crisis workers can be traumatized by trying to help those devastated by trauma and crises (Pearlman & Mac Ian, 1995). A boundary that may seem quite obvious is that psychologists do not use their clients, or the resources intended for their clients, for their own self-care or betterment. Professional volunteers must monitor themselves so that they do not become so traumatized that the help they offer is ineffective or even damaging. . . .

Let us now consider nonmaleficence. Upholding the principle of nonmaleficence means doing no unjustified harm. The potential for harm is exceptionally high in crisis situations. People are disoriented, and normal delivery systems might be disrupted or damaged. Every resource—physical, social, spiritual, and psychological—is precious. Using any of these resources while having little or nothing to offer is a passive form of harm. However, active harm in the form of misapplication of professional skills or authority is much more damaging (Smith, 2006).

Case conception and diagnosis. The empirical and theoretical battles over personal attributes that contribute to trauma reactions or resiliency are beyond this chapter. However, it is clear that people react and adapt to trauma in individually and culturally diverse ways. Some coping methods might seem more adaptive than others to a psychologist trained within the mores of Western culture. In most situations, a small subset of survivors may develop symptoms that fit a mental health diagnosis, but many will not (Caffo & Belaise, 2005). Even the act of diagnosing could be seen as harmful because it may insinuate the survivor is weak, permanently damaged, or mentally ill (Yehuda & Bierer, 2005). Diagnosing also can create an identity as a sick individual, bringing on further symptoms in a self-fulfilling prophecy (Violanti, 2000).

Cultural concerns. Even volunteering to help with a crisis within your own country can pose cultural challenges. From city to city, and state to state, people who are not part of a defined community are not likely to understand community customs or the deeper concerns of race or culture within the community (Jackson & Cook, 1999). Outsiders can make mistakes by bringing their own assumptions of similarity with them, thereby seeming clueless or insensitive, misunderstanding signals of distress, fear, or even strength. Multicultural awareness and competence is now expected of all mental health professionals (Hays, 2008) and is related to all the principles in the Ethics Code. Hopefully, the basics are in place through graduate training, but being culturally aware and informed is a lifelong task. Under ordinary circumstances, psychologists have time to research, get supervision, and utilize cultural gatekeepers to add knowledge about an unfamiliar community or culture. In crisis situations, there may be little time for this background work. . . .

Principles B and C, Fidelity, Responsibility, and Integrity

In boundary considerations in crisis and trauma work, fidelity, responsibility, and integrity are all closely related. Fidelity speaks to professional loyalty, dependability, and trustworthiness. The concept of responsibility simply underlines the folk assertion "the buck stops here." The professional is responsible for the relationship and holds responsibility to the community and society as well. Integrity has to do with honesty and reliability. Psychologists are expected to provide services and care that do not promise more than actually can be delivered. In volunteering across cultures in disaster situations, these are all especially important duties.

Depending on the nature of the crisis and situation, many customary practices that help establish professional boundaries may be altered or suspended. The informed consent process may be reduced from well-written forms and thoughtful questions and answers to a short verbal exchange providing the essential parameters of therapy. It may even disappear entirely. . . .

Principle D, Justice

The principle of justice implies that psychologists will work to ensure that what they have to offer is equally available to those seeking services. Furthermore, they will work against unjust practices or applications of psychological services. Justice is a high ideal that is difficult to approximate. Individuals have varying levels of need, and resources, such as medical assistance or transplant organs, can be in very short supply (Richard, Rawal, & Martin, 2005). The effort to provide services in a fair and just manner can be most difficult, both practically and emotionally.

Further complicating justice in crisis situations is the fact that such events violate our sense of justice in the world. Terribly unfair things happen to innocent and undeserving people. As we have seen many times in recent history, the least able and the most destitute often are hardest hit by natural or human-caused disasters (Caffo & Belaise, 2005). It can be tempting to choose favorites or to try to obtain goods or services in unfair ways for certain clients. It also can be tempting to be reactive and unfairly withhold time or materials from certain clients in crisis situations. Because we want to believe in a just world, in the face of a disaster, people might be inclined to unfairly level blame at a handy target (Janoff-Bulman, 2004). . . .

Principle E, Respect for People's Rights and Dignity

Honoring this principle involves paying attention to many of the concerns already discussed. Being especially aware of cultural values and of the vulnerabilities inherent in disaster work is essential. This principle also encompasses the principle of autonomy (Beauchamp & Childress, 2001), which asserts that humans should have authority over decisions affecting their health and well-being. . . .

REFERENCES

American Psychological Association. (2008). *Disaster response network member guidelines*. Retrieved from https://www.apa.org/practice/programs/drn/index.aspx

American Psychological Association. (2010). *Ethical principles of psychologists and code of conduct* (2002, Amended June 1, 2010). Retrieved from http://www.apa.org/ethics/code/index.aspx

Aristotle. (1955). *The ethics of Aristotle: The Nichomachean ethics* (Rev. ed.; J. K. Thomson, Trans.). New York, NY: Viking.

Beauchamp, T. L., & Childress, J. F. (1979). *Principles of biomedical ethics*. New York, NY: Oxford University Press.

Beauchamp, T. L., & Childress, J. F. (1994). *Principles of biomedical ethics* (4th ed.). New York, NY: Oxford University Press.

Beauchamp, T. L., & Childress, J. F. (2001). *Principles of biomedical ethics* (5th ed.). New York, NY: Oxford University Press.

Brown, L. S. (2008). *Feminist therapy as a meaning-making practice: Where there is no power, where is the meaning?* New York, NY: Routledge/Taylor & Francis Group.

Burtness, J. H. (1999). *Consequences: Morality, ethics and the future*. Minneapolis, MN: Fortress Press.

Caffo, E., & Belaise, C. (2005). Children and adolescents' psychopathology after trauma: New preventive psychotherapeutic strategies. In K. V. Oxington (Ed.), *Psychology of stress* (pp. 145–163). Hauppauge, NY: Nova Biomedical Books.

Collins, B. G., & Collins, T. M. (2005). *Crisis and trauma: Developmental ecological intervention*. Boston, MA: Lahaska.

Fletcher, J. (1966). *Situation ethics: The new morality*. Philadelphia, PA: Westminster.

Gilligan, C. (1993). *In a different voice: Psychological theory and women's development.* Cambridge, MA: Harvard University Press.

Hays, P. A. (2008). *Addressing cultural complexities in practice: Assessment, diagnosis, and therapy* (2nd ed.). Washington, DC: American Psychological Association. doi:10.1037/11650-000

Jackson, G., & Cook, C. G. (1999). *Disaster mental health: Crisis counseling programs for the rural community.* Washington, DC: U.S. Government Printing Office.

Janoff-Bulman, R. (2004). Posttraumatic growth: Three explanatory models. *Psychological Inquiry, 15,* 30–34.

Kant, I. (1963). *Lectures on ethics* (L. Infield, Trans.). Indianapolis, IN: Hackett.

Pearlman, L. A., & Mac Ian, P. S. (1995). Vicarious traumatization: An empirical study of the effects of trauma work on trauma therapists. *Professional Psychology: Research and Practice, 26,* 558–565. doi:10.1037/0735-7028.26.6.558

Richard, S. A., Rawal, S., & Martin, D. K. (2005, November 30). An ethical framework for cardiac report cards: A qualitative study. *BMC Medical Ethics, 6*(3). doi:10.1186/1472;6939-6-3

Ross, W. D. (1930). *The right and the good.* Oxford, England: Clarendon.

Smith, H. B. (2002). The American Red Cross: How to be part of the solution, rather than part of the problem. In D. D. Bass & R. Yep (Eds.), *Terrorism, trauma, and tragedies: A counselor's guide to preparing and responding* (pp. 37–39). Alexandria, VA: American Counseling Association Foundation.

Smith, H. B. (2006, February 17). Providing mental health services to clients in crisis or disaster situations. *VISTAS Online,* Article 3.

Sommers-Flanagan, R., & Sommers-Flanagan, J. (2007). *Becoming an ethical helping professional: Cultural and philosophical foundations.* Hoboken, NJ: Wiley.

Taylor, K. (1995). *The ethics of caring.* Santa Cruz, CA: Hanford Mead.

Violanti, J. M. (2000). Scripting trauma: The impact of pathogenic intervention. In J. Violanti, D. Paton, & C. Dunning (Eds.), *Posttraumatic stress intervention: Challenges, issues, and perspectives* (pp. 153–165). Springfield, IL: Charles C. Thomas.

Yehuda, R., & Bierer, L. M. (2005). Re-evaluating the link between disasters and psychopathology. In J. J. Lopez-Ibor, G. Christodoulou, M. Maj, N. Sartorius, & A. Okasha (Eds.), *Disasters and mental health* (pp. 65–80). New York, NY: Wiley. doi:10.1002/047002125X.ch4

5.7. The Current State of Sexual Ethics Training in Clinical Psychology: Issues of Quantity, Quality, and Effectiveness

Linda M. Housman and Jayne E. Stake

How do beginning therapists respond when they experience feelings of attraction for their clients? Do today's graduate training programs adequately prepare students to cope with these feelings? Surveys of practicing therapists indicate that many professionals have responded to such feelings of attraction by engaging in sexual relations with their clients. . . . With increased sanctions for sexual misconduct, professionals may have become more hesitant to disclose sexual contact with clients (Williams, 1992). . . .

MEASURES

Student Questionnaire

The student questionnaire comprised four sections: amount of training, program atmosphere, attraction for a client, and sexual ethics training.

Amount of Training

Students reported the number of course work hours in sexual ethics they had completed to date. Course work hours were defined as all hours spent in class and on assignments for class. Students listed the hours separately by course category: ethics courses, psychotherapy courses, sexual ethics courses, course seminars, and other classes. In addition, students reported (a) the number of program workshops–guest lectures in sexual ethics they had attended, (b) whether they had completed a formal ethics course, and (c) whether they had completed all of their program requirements in ethics.

Program Atmosphere

Five items were written for this study to assess perceptions of the quality of the atmosphere of training programs for learning sexual ethics. These questions

From "The Current State of Sexual Ethics Training in Clinical Psychology: Issues of Quantity, Quality, and Effectiveness," by L. M. Housman and J. E. Stake, 1999, *Professional Psychology: Research and Practice*, 30, pp. 302–311. Copyright 1999 by the American Psychological Association.

This article is based on the doctoral dissertation of Linda M. Housman, which was completed under the supervision of Jayne E. Stake.

It is worth noting that this article was published in 1999.

pertained to (1) the adequacy of sexual ethics course work offered in the program, (2) the proportion of faculty and supervisors with whom students would feel comfortable discussing feelings of sexual attraction to a client, (3) the proportion of these educators who provided a safe environment for students to talk about feelings of sexual attraction to clients, (4) the proportion of these educators who are adequate role models for students with respect to sexual ethics, and (5) how well the program prepares students to deal effectively and ethically with sexual dilemmas faced in clinical practice. . . .

Attraction for a Client

Students were asked whether they had ever felt sexually attracted to a client and, if so, to indicate whether they had done any of the following: discussed the attraction with their supervisor, discussed the attraction with the client, or acted on their feelings with the client.

Sexual Ethics Knowledge

Students responded to questions about the following sexual ethics vignette:

> Therapist T has been seeing client C for six months. Client C initially sought therapy for symptoms of anxiety and depression related to personal concerns. Over the course of their working together, therapist T has recognized a developing attraction to client C. Therapist T is almost sure the physical attraction is mutual.

. . .

[See Table 1.]

Training Director Questionnaire

The director questionnaire included measures of amount of training and program atmosphere that paralleled the student measures. In addition, directors were asked to report the amount of experiential training in sexual ethics provided in their program.

TABLE 1. Factor Analysis of Sexual Ethics Knowledge Questions

Item	Factor 1	Factor 2	Factor 3
Knowledge domain			
Sexual feelings for clients			
Therapist attraction okay	.88	−.01	−.01
Therapist attraction common	.86	−.02	−.11
Relations with current clients			
Improve therapeutic alliance	−.11	.80	−.04
Okay for sexual dysfunction	.08	.79	.08
Relations with former clients			
Okay if transferred	.05	−.06	.79
Okay if terminated	.04	.10	.73
Eigenvalues	1.61	1.30	1.09
Commonality	.63	.78	.75
Variance explained (%)	26.8	21.6	18.1

RESULTS

. . .

Amount of Training

Table 2 presents the formal ethics classes and sexual ethics training reported by students and directors. All directors reported sexual ethics training in their programs, and, contrary to previous surveys of psychologists trained earlier, most students (94%) reported they had sexual ethics training in some format during their graduate training. Five percent of student participants reported they had not completed all program requirements relevant to ethics. Given that all directors reported sexual ethics training was available in some format in their programs and 5% of students had not yet completed all program requirements in ethics, it seems that virtually all students will have received sexual ethics training before completing their programs.

The majority of students and directors reported course hours in sexual ethics. Table 2 lists number of hours separately by course type. Means in the table are based on all participants who responded. From the perspective of both students and directors, students averaged about 6 hours of course work in sexual ethics, and most training took place in ethics and psychotherapy classes. Course hours reported by training directors were compared to the mean course hours reported by their respective students in a one-way (directors vs. students) multivariate analysis of variance (MANOVA) with five dependent measures—the reported course hours for each of the five course types. Respondent type (students vs. directors) was treated as a correlated variable because students and directors were reporting on the same program. This comparison between directors and their students did not yield a significant difference. Hence, directors and students

TABLE 2. Sexual Ethics Training Reported by Clinical Graduate Students and Training Directors

Training	Students	Directors
Completed-offer ethics class (%)	83	88
Had-offer sexual ethics training (%)	94	100
Had-offer sexual ethics course hours (%)	73	80
Mean number of sexual ethics course hours		
In ethics course	3.34	3.10
In psychotherapy course	1.55	1.35
In sexual ethics course	0.19	0.16
In course seminars	0.67	0.70
In other classes	0.26	0.56
Total	6.01	5.89
Mean number of workshops–guest lectures	0.43	1.01

Note. Mean values are based on the total number of participants for whom data were available. The number of students varied from 434 to 447 because of missing data; the number of training directors varied from 77 to 84 because of missing data.

were in general agreement on the number of sexual ethics course hours offered in their programs.

Numbers of workshops–guest lectures reported by directors and students were compared in a one-way analysis of variance (ANOVA). Respondent type was again treated as a correlated measure. Directors reported more workshops–guest lectures offered in their programs than students reported they had attended, $F(1, 71) = 5.93$, $p < .05$.

Program Atmosphere

The internal consistency of program atmosphere items was acceptable in the student sample (.76) but low in the director sample (.45). It was therefore appropriate to treat the items as one measure when student responses were analyzed alone but as five individual measures when comparing faculty and student program atmosphere ratings. The faculty–student comparison of program atmosphere ratings was made in a one-way MANOVA in which the five individual program atmosphere items served as the dependent variables and respondent type (director vs. student) served as the independent (correlated) variable. The MANOVA revealed a main effect for respondent type, $F(5, 68) = 16.51$, $p < .0001$. Student ratings of program atmosphere were lower than director ratings ($Ms = 4.09$ vs. 4.91). Thus, in contrast to reports of the amount of sexual ethics course work provided, ratings of the quality of program atmosphere did differ between students and directors.

The mean program atmosphere ratings and results of univariate analyses for each question are presented in Table 3. Student ratings were significantly lower than director ratings ($p < .0001$) for questions pertaining to adequacy of course work and proportion of faculty and supervisors (a) with whom students would feel comfortable discussing sexual attraction to clients, (b) who provide a safe environment to talk about sexual attraction to clients, and (c) who are adequate role models of sexual ethics. Students and directors did not differ in their ratings of how well programs were preparing students for sexual ethics dilemmas. Note that students and directors differed most in their ratings of the proportion of faculty and supervisors who provide a safe environment. The director mean of 5.23 signified that directors, on average, reported almost three fourths

TABLE 3. Student and Director Program Atmosphere Ratings

Item	Students	Directors	F	η^2
Adequacy of course work	3.91	4.53	17.67	.20**
Comfort with faculty	3.58	4.32	20.13	.22**
Faculty provide safe environment	3.87	5.23	70.65	.50**
Faculty are adequate role models	4.97	5.84	22.91	.24**
Program prepares student in sexual ethics	4.14	4.64	3.23	.04[†]

Note. Possible values of program atmosphere ratings ranged from 1 to 7. Results are based on 73 programs.

[†]$p < .10$. **$p < .0001$.

of their faculty and supervisors provided a safe environment to discuss sexual attraction to clients, whereas the student mean of 3.87 indicated that students reported slightly less than half their faculty and supervisors provided a safe environment.

Program atmosphere ratings of female and male students were compared in programs with female and male directors in a 2×2 (gender of student by gender of director) ANOVA. Male students gave slightly higher program atmosphere ratings than female students (4.21 vs. 4.01), but this difference did not reach significance, $F(1, 399) = 3.6$, $p < .06$, $\eta^2 = .03$. Students with female directors did not give significantly different ratings than students with male directors, and the interaction effect was not significant.

Student Attraction and Supervisor Consultation

Slightly more than half (50%) of the student sample reported having had a sexual attraction to a client. Men were more likely than women to report an attraction (73% vs. 38%), and this gender difference was significant, $\chi^2(1, N = 451) = 50.3$, $p < .0001$. Among students who were attracted, 50% discussed their attraction with their supervisor. The proportion of men and women who consulted their supervisors when attracted was not significantly different (51% vs. 49%, respectively). One of the 226 students who were attracted (0.4%) reported acting on the attraction; 9 (4.0%) indicated they discussed the attraction directly with their clients.

Variables associated with supervisor consultation were explored in the sample of students who reported an attraction. The relation between supervisor consultation and completion of an ethics course was tested in a 2×2 chi-square analysis; this relationship was not significant. The relation between supervisor consultation and sexual ethics training was analyzed in a one-way MANOVA in which the set of dependent variables included student program atmosphere scores, total number of sexual ethics course hours reported by students, and number of workshops–guest lectures reported by students. This analysis yielded a significant overall effect, $F(3, 200) = 4.16$, $p < .01$. Univariate analyses revealed that students were more likely to consult their supervisor if they rated their program atmosphere higher ($Ms = 21.15$ vs. 19.59), $F(1, 202) = 3.93$, $p < .05$, $\eta^2 = .02$; had completed more course hours ($Ms = 9.26$ vs. 5.35), $F(1, 202) = 7.58$, $p < .01$, $\eta^2 = .04$; and had attended more program workshops–guest lectures ($Ms = .81$ vs. .34), $F(1, 202) = 6.03$, $p < .05$, $\eta^2 = .03$.

Sexual Ethics Knowledge

Variables associated with students' sexual ethics knowledge were examined by hierarchical regression analyses. Separate analyses were performed for each of the three areas of sexual ethics knowledge. Variables were entered in the regression analysis in the following order: (a) student gender, (b) didactic training in ethics reported by student (i.e., ethics course, number of workshops–

guest lectures, number of course hours), (c) student program atmosphere score, (d) experience of attraction to a client, and (e) discussion of client attraction with a supervisor. Because only 12 directors reported any hours of experiential training, this variable was not included in the analysis. See Table 4 for a summary of results when all variables were entered.

The first three steps of the analysis for knowledge of sexual feelings for clients yielded no significant findings. Significant incremental values were obtained when the sexual attraction variable was entered, $F_{inc}(1, 412) = 32.92$, $p < .001$, $R^2_{inc} = .07$, and when the supervisor consultation variable was entered, $F_{inc}(1, 411) = 8.24$, $p < .01$, $R^2_{inc} = .02$. Students who had experienced an attraction to a client and students who had discussed the attraction with a supervisor were more likely to show knowledge of the acceptability of attraction to clients. The analysis of knowledge scores for relations with current clients yielded no significant findings.

In the analysis of knowledge scores for relations with former clients, gender and didactic training were not significant predictors. The addition of program atmosphere ratings yielded significant incremental values, $F_{inc}(1, 413) = 9.99$, $p < .01$, $R^2_{inc} = .02$. Students who rated their program atmosphere more positively had greater knowledge. The attraction variable was not significant when entered at Step 4; however, supervisor consultation did result in significant incremental values, $F_{inc}(1, 411) = 13.96$, $p < .001$, $R^2_{inc} = .03$, and, once supervisor consultation was added to the equation model, attraction became a significant variable as well ($p < .01$). Students who had experienced attraction to a client showed less knowledge regarding relations with former clients, and students who had discussed the attraction with their supervisor showed more knowledge.

To understand more fully how the experiences of attraction and supervision were related to sexual ethics knowledge, we compared the following groups; (a) students who discussed a client attraction with a supervisor, (b) students who were attracted but did not discuss the attraction with a supervisor, and (c) students who had not experienced a client attraction. See Table 5 for the

TABLE 4. Hierarchical Regression Analysis of Variables Associated With Sexual Ethics Knowledge

	Sexual ethics knowledge area	
Variable	Acceptance of sexual feelings	Relations with former clients
Gender	.02	.08
Ethics didactic training		
Ethics course completed	−.01	.03
Workshops–guest lectures	−.04	.03
Course hours	.07	.06
Program atmosphere	.00	.14*
Sexual attraction to client	.19*	−.17*
Supervisor consultation	.17*	.22*

Note. Table values represent beta weights derived after all variables were entered.

*$p < .01$.

TABLE 5. Student Knowledge of Sexual Ethics by Client Attraction and Supervision Group

	Client attraction			
Sexual ethics knowledge	Discussed with supervisor ($n = 112$)	Not discussed with supervisor ($n = 114$)	No client attraction ($n = 224$)	η^2
Sexual feelings for clients	1.42 (53.2)	1.10 (33.9)	.80 (21.8)	.10**
Relations with current clients	1.92 (92.7)	1.90 (92.0)	1.94 (94.1)	.00
Relations with former clients	1.67 (73.4)	1.28 (49.1)	1.57 (70.5)	.04**

Note. Possible values of knowledge scores ranged from 0 to 2. The percentage of students who responded correctly to both questions is given in parentheses.

**$p < .0001$ in univariate analysis.

knowledge means and percentage of students who correctly answered both items of the knowledge measures in each student group. A one-way MANOVA in which the independent variable was student group and the dependent variables were the three knowledge scores revealed a significant effect of student group, $F(6, 892) = 11.96, p < .0001$. Univariate analyses indicated that the groups differed significantly in knowledge scores for sexual feelings for clients, $F(2, 447) = 25.86, p < .0001, \eta^2 = .10$; and relations with former clients, $F(2, 447) = 9.75, p < .0001, \eta^2 = .04$. All groups had high mean knowledge scores for relations with current clients and did not differ significantly on this measure.

In the case of sexual feelings for clients, all pairwise comparisons between means were significant ($p < .01$) when tested by the Tukey conservative test for unequal numbers per group (Klockars & Sax, 1986). For relations with former clients, the student group that was attracted but did not receive supervision had a significantly lower mean knowledge score than the other two groups ($p < .01$), which did not differ significantly from one another. Overall, the most knowledgeable students were those who had discussed an attraction with a supervisor.

DISCUSSION, IMPLICATIONS, AND RECOMMENDATIONS

From the perspective of training directors and their students, virtually all clinical programs in our sample provided sexual ethics training. Our findings show a marked change from previous studies of program graduates in which many had received no sexual ethics training (Glaser & Thorpe, 1986; Pope et al., 1986; Rodolfa et al., 1994). The difference between this and previous surveys underscores the importance of assessing current students and faculty to achieve an accurate picture of the status of sexual ethics training. The programs in our sample are addressing sexual ethics in much more than a perfunctory manner, with an average of 6 hr devoted to the topic. However, there is continued cause for concern in two respects. First, although our findings appear to be representative of the 105 programs for which some information was obtained, we do not know about the 71 remaining programs. It is likely that directors who were unwilling to respond to our request to distribute questionnaires to students or to complete a questionnaire themselves had less interest or involvement in sexual ethics training. Therefore, some programs are probably not providing this training. The only way to ensure that all programs do so is to add sexual ethics training as a criterion for accreditation. Considering the harm to clients and the profession caused by sexual misconduct and the continued incidence of abuses, an accreditation requirement for sexual ethics training is warranted.

A second cause for concern is that even in the responding programs, many students had not developed an adequate understanding of the principles of sexual ethics. In spite of the training reported by students and corroborated by directors, students showed no more understanding of sexual ethics than practicing professionals in earlier studies who had less sexual ethics training (Borys & Pope, 1989; Herman et al., 1987; Pope et al., 1986). Seven percent of the students in the present study did not know that sex with current clients is always prohibited, 34% did not understand that termination or transfer does not free therapists to have sex with their clients, and 68% did not know that sexual feelings for clients are normal and not unethical. Students who had been attracted to a client and did not discuss the attraction with a supervisor were particularly ill informed. They were therefore at risk for mishandling their feelings of attraction and for making therapeutic errors damaging to themselves and their clients. . . .

REFERENCES

Borys, D. S., & Pope, K. S. (1989). Dual relationships between therapist and client: A national study of psychologists, psychiatrists, and social workers. *Professional Psychology: Research and Practice, 20*, 283–293.

Glaser, R. D., & Thorpe, J. S. (1986). Unethical intimacy. A survey of sexual contact and advances between psychology educators and female graduate students. *American Psychologist, 41*, 43–51.

Herman, J. L., Gartrell, N., Olarte, S., Feldstein, M., & Localio, R. (1987). Psychiatrist–patient sexual contact: Results of a national survey, II: Psychiatrists' attitudes. *American Journal of Psychiatry, 144*, 164–169.

Klockars, A. J., & Sax, G. (1986). *Multiple comparisons.* Newbury Park, CA: Sage.

Pope, K. S., Keith-Spiegel, P., & Tabachnick, B. G. (1986). Sexual attraction to clients. The human therapist and the (sometimes) inhuman training system. *American Psychologist, 41*, 147–158.

Rodolfa, E., Hall, T., Holms, V., Davena, A., Komatz, D., Antunez, M., & Hall, A. (1994). The management of sexual feelings in therapy. *Professional Psychology: Research and Practice, 25*, 168–172.

Williams, M. H. (1992). Exploitation and inference. Mapping the damage from therapist–patient sexual involvement. *American Psychologist, 47*, 412–421.

5.8. Managing Risk When Contemplating Multiple Relationships

Jeffrey N. Younggren and Michael C. Gottlieb

. . .

Professional practice abounds with the potential for multiple relationships, and the circumstances under which these types of relationships occur are quite varied. Although psychologists frequently choose to enter into these types of relationship, many may actually be unavoidable, and in some situations one can even conceptualize the avoidance of the dual relationship not only as unethical but as potentially destructive to treatment itself (Campbell & Gordon, 2003). For example, consider the solo practitioner in a very small community, who must of necessity maintain some multiple relationships with his or her patients by virtue of proximity and living conditions. To avoid all contact with patients in this situation would require the practitioner to lead the life of a virtual hermit. To make matters worse, this type of unusual conduct could raise questions in the minds of other members of the community as to why the practitioner acts in such a manner. A socially isolated practitioner will attract few patients and arguably will serve them less well by failing to integrate himself or herself into the community. Such examples have forced the profession to accept the logical position that not all multiple relationships are unethical per se (American Psychological Association [APA], 2002).

The key considerations for practitioners who are faced with deciding if they should participate in a multiple relationship, or who inadvertently find themselves already in such a relationship, involve thoughtful analysis of potential hazards. our purpose is twofold: First, we focus on how to evaluate and manage such relationships to avoid exploitation of and harm to patients, and second, we discuss how to minimize risk for the practitioner. . . .

ASSUMPTIONS

1. *Engaging in multiple relationships has a high potential for harming patients and, as a general matter, should be avoided* (APA, 1992, 2002). The proscription against multiple relationships has a strong foundation in the prohibition against

From "Managing Risk When Contemplating Multiple Relationships," by J. N. Younggren, and M. C. Gottlieb, 2004, *Professional Psychology: Research and Practice*, 35, pp. 255–260. Copyright 2004 by the American Psychological Association.

We express our appreciation to Gerald Koocher, Edward Nottingham, and Garnett Stokes for the time they took to review earlier versions of this article.

sexual relations with patients. Although sexual misconduct can unquestionably cause harm to patients, plainly constitutes unethical behavior, and violates the law in some states, the concept of multiple relationships extends more broadly and includes many types of nonsexual relationships that possibly may pose danger to patients or risk to the practitioner. These more ambiguous situations establish the need for the following guidelines.

2. *Psychologists have many different types of professional relationships; not all of them involve psychotherapy patients.* The range of potential professional relationships varies so much that we cannot address all such possibilities in this article. Therefore, we confine ourselves to psychotherapy relationships in which the treatment becomes more personal and intense. The issues we address may affect both short- and long-term psychotherapies. . . .

3. *Some multiple relationships are completely unavoidable and even obligatory, such as those that occur in the military* (Barnett & Yutrzenka, 1994). Psychologists can be placed in legally mandated dual relationships by virtue of the roles they occupy. For example, military psychologists are frequently placed in situations in which they are required to engage in administrative evaluations of individuals they treat. Because of frequent personnel limitations, combined with the unique nature of the military mission, psychologists must perform these dual functions or risk being found in violation of the Uniform Code of Military Justice. This paradox is a reality attendant to the unique role of the military psychologist, and it is only through informed consent that psychologists in the military, and others in similar situations, manage these potentially risky conflicts. Although highly problematic, such unique issues reach beyond our intended scope.

4. *Practitioners create risk for themselves and their patients when they make decisions in a vacuum.* We assume that consultation with trusted and knowledgeable colleagues should undergird all steps in the decision-making process. Those who give consideration to entering into a dual relationship should make consultation central to that process.

5. *Good risk management also means providing good care, and these notions are not viewed as mutually exclusive.* This article focuses on providing good care to the patient while also protecting the provider. Although achieving both of these objectives becomes impossible in some circumstances, we believe that they constitute realistic goals in the vast majority of the professional situations practitioners encounter. If one is to assume that good care is generally care that is satisfactory to the patient, we know that satisfied consumers become originators of litigation and disciplinary complaints far less often than those who are disgruntled clients (Hickson et al., 2002).

6. *When adjudicatory panels such as ethics committees or state regulatory boards evaluate cases alleging harmful multiple relationships, they must of necessity focus on the clinician's behavior retrospectively.* When practitioners consider entering multiple relationships, they must think prospectively to consider how professional

bodies might evaluate the complaint retrospectively. Therefore, when considering whether to enter into a multiple relationship, a wise course will involve evaluating how those in the future, in an entirely different setting and circumstance, would react to the present conduct. Although a very difficult task, this commonly used risk-management strategy guides our thinking (APA Insurance Trust [APAIT], 2002a).

QUESTIONS

1. *Is entering into a relationship in addition to the professional one necessary, or should I avoid it?* Psychotherapy, by its very nature, becomes a uniquely complex interpersonal process. Diagnostic formulations may evolve as more information comes to light, causing treatment planning and goals to change. Simply speaking, one cannot know at the outset where the course of treatment will lead. Seemingly straightforward initial clinical presentations may become highly complex and difficult clinical-treatment situations that even the most experienced practitioner could not have predicted. In these circumstances, participating in dual relationships is fraught with unnecessary risk. Therefore, the best interests of the patient and the practitioner generally dictate avoiding dual relationships whenever possible.

2. *Can the dual relationship potentially cause harm to the patient?* A basic principle of biomedical ethics (Beauchamp & Childress, 1994) is that interventions should not harm patients. In addition, if some harm is a necessary component of treatment, an attempt must be made to minimize it. In this connection, any proposed relationship in addition to the therapeutic one must yield to an analysis of risk of harm (Gottlieb, 1993). That is not to say that a professional entering into a dual relationship must anticipate and prevent all risk, but that professional has a fiduciary obligation to anticipate reasonably foreseeable risks and make every effort to avoid, minimize, and manage them. . . .

3. *If harm seems unlikely or avoidable, would the additional relationship prove beneficial? This type of dilemma occurs frequently for those who work in isolated communities.* For example, what should a practitioner do about purchasing a car from the only automobile dealership in a small town when the owner is also a patient? Could making such a purchase enhance the therapeutic alliance by increasing the patient's trust of the therapist and thereby have a positive effect on the therapy? Or, does purchasing the car increase the patient's sense that the therapist trusts him or her? If the practitioner decided to buy the car from the patient, what is to be done regarding negotiating the price? Should the psychologist pay the vehicle's sticker price? Would doing so lead to resentment on the psychologist's part for being forced to pay more than necessary for the vehicle? On the other hand, would purchasing the vehicle elsewhere cause people to wonder why the therapist avoided the local dealership? This might cause particular problems for the practitioner if

strong social pressures exist to support the local economy. In this example, purchasing the car elsewhere not only could raise questions among one's neighbors but also might negatively affect the therapeutic alliance. From this very plausible example, it becomes clear that assessing how patients and practitioners may benefit from additional relationships requires caution, careful thinking, and foresight.

4. *Is there a risk that the dual relationship could disrupt the therapeutic relationship?* This question not only requires careful consideration before treatment but also may require periodic reevaluation throughout the treatment process. Given the need to minimize risk, the practitioner who chooses to enter into a dual relationship with a client must manage the relationships in such a way that the therapeutic relationship is not damaged by the additional one. Whenever possible, the practitioner has an obligation to discuss the issue of potential harm in detail with the patient prior to entering into the additional relationship. Furthermore, both therapist and client should revisit the topic regularly to prevent damage to the therapeutic alliance. In addition, the therapist has the obligation to anticipate the types of situations that could damage the therapeutic alliance, because it seems highly unlikely that the client would recognize them. This type of forethought might even benefit the therapeutic process by offering a starting point for discussion of these types of issues with the client. The client may feel more cared for and protected by the practitioner, and this may lead to enhanced therapeutic effectiveness. . . .

5. *Can I evaluate this matter objectively?* This very difficult question demonstrates a fundamental of good risk management. One must always assume that a compromise in one's objectivity might reach beyond one's awareness. However, when one is confronted with this type of problem, careful self-evaluation is always a good place to start. Standing back from a potential dual relationship and looking at it, oneself, and one's own motivation will surely help lend clarity to the matter. In addition, reviewing the available literature in this area can also improve one's objectivity and could even provide answers to questions about current professional standards of care. . . .

RISK MANAGEMENT

Once a practitioner has addressed the "treatment-oriented" questions above and has decided to proceed with a dual or multiple relationship, he or she should now turn to what we term the "risk-management mode." Because the decision to enter into additional relationships has risk for the patient, the therapy, and the practitioner, he or she must engage in a risk-management strategy that provides protection if charges of unprofessional conduct ever surface as a result of the choice. Although some might see such a strategy as "self-serving," the realities of a litigious society require self-protective conduct. Furthermore, in keeping with our assumptions, we contend that good risk management is also consistent with good clinical and ethical practice. Therefore, when choosing to engage in a dual or multiple relationship, the prudent practitioner should now address the following questions.

1. *Have I adequately documented the decision-making process in the treatment records?* Because the spirit of the law is "If it isn't written down, it did not happen," inadequate documentation can negate the existence and value of the entire decision-making process regardless of how comprehensive and thoughtful it may have been. No matter how well the practitioner may have addressed the questions raised earlier in this article, if the process was not documented, then the protection afforded by having done so is largely lost. Once a complaint or lawsuit is filed, efforts to explain the process without documentation will result in considerable skepticism and will be viewed as self-serving and as an effort to put one's own interests ahead of the patient's. . . .

   More specifically, the record should reflect the process by which the choice evolved and demonstrate full consideration of other alternatives. Creating documentation in this manner produces a record that should lead the reader to reach the same conclusion, or at least to have a good understanding of the practitioner's thinking on the matter. To meet this standard, the practitioner should ensure that the record reflects all consultations and logically explains the rationale for the choices made. . . .

2. *Did the practitioner obtain informed consent regarding the risks of engaging in the dual relationship?* Patients are in relatively less powerful positions with respect to their psychotherapist (Kitchener, 1988). When a practitioner faces a difficult decision that entails the risk of a multiple relationship, he or she should make sure that the client fully understands the issues, the alternatives, and the advantages and disadvantages of each as a matter of informed consent (APA, 1992, 2002; Beauchamp & Childress, 1994). Informed consent, in the era of HIPAA (the Health Insurance Portability and Accountability Act), is increasingly complex, and many consent forms and therapist–patient contracts are currently available commercially, in the published literature, and as part of free risk-management services offered by various organizations (e.g., APAIT, 2002b; APA Practice Organization & APAIT, 2003; Harris & Bennett, 1998). However, the type of informed consent being addressed here would clearly require a detailed addendum to an existing standard form or a separate agreement that clearly sets out the issues addressed in this article. . . .

3. *Does the record show adequate evidence of professional consultation?* In many circumstances, consultation helps to establish that the standard of care was met. Talking with others supports the argument that the decisions made in a given matter were in accordance with the guidance of others who would have behaved in a similar fashion under comparable circumstances. This view of the standard of care can be found in the 2002 APA ethics code, where "reasonable" professional conduct is defined as "the prevailing professional judgment of psychologists engaged in similar activities in similar circumstances given the knowledge the psychologist had or should have had

at the time" (APA, 2002, p. 2). Thus, adequate consultation allows the practitioner to say that he or she did what other reasonable psychologists would do under similar circumstances, creating an additional defense against criticism of his or her conduct that is founded on a violation of the standard of care. . . .

4. *Does the record reflect a patient-oriented decision-making process?* Although not an easy task, making notations that reflect a struggle on the part of the practitioner to protect the patient and to make the right choices for the benefit of the patient become a strong defense in legal and ethical proceedings. Even if the choices are arguably incorrect based on subsequent events, the visibility of the process of seeking the right, patient-oriented answer when confronted with a choice of entering into a dual relationship is a very helpful defense. . . .

5. *Are the sources of consultation credible?* Credibility is difficult to measure as it frequently lies in the eye of the beholder. However, having consulted someone with expertise, not only in the treatment modality being utilized but also in the relevant area of ethics and mental health law, can be a very strong defense. If one does not know how to find such a consultant, contact with local or national professional associations for such a referral can frequently be of great assistance. In addition, these types of consultative services are often provided free of charge to individuals who are members of various organizations, to include the APAIT and the APA Office of Ethics. The individual with whom one consults can be quite important, and, if colleagues of this stature request payment for their consulting services, it is our view that this money is very well spent. Another benefit that comes from practicing in this fashion occurs when the psychologist is sued or his or her license is attacked. Under this circumstance, the consultant can be brought as a witness to testify and, because of being removed from the case and arguably being more objective, may be able to make a stronger argument on behalf of the psychologist than the psychologist could himself or herself.

6. *Do the diagnostic issues matter when considering a dual relationship?* In a word, yes! Logically, entering into a dual relationship with a patient who has a fear of public speaking could be viewed by other professionals as having substantially different risks from those of a patient with a complex borderline personality disorder and a history of childhood sexual abuse. In general, it is our contention that risk is inversely related to the general level of integration of the patient. Multiple relations with patients who are well integrated may present various risks, but these risks are substantially lower than those that occur when a therapist chooses to engage in the same type of relationship with a patient who is seriously emotionally compromised. Multiple relationships in the latter circumstance are almost never a good idea. . . .

7. *Does knowledge of the patient support the establishment of a dual relationship?* How well one knows a patient has a direct impact on the choice to enter into a

dual relationship. Inherent in many of the points made throughout this article is a belief that more, and accurate, information about a patient is helpful in determining whether the choice to enter into a dual relationship is a wise one. Although one might argue that this point relates to the previous one, we believe that not all knowledge impacts diagnosis. Thus, a comprehensive understanding of the patient and the complexity of the patient's life, family, and related issues would be helpful in arriving at the "right choice" in this case. In truth, when faced with the risk (to both client and therapist) that could come from being wrong, logically, more information is always helpful. For example, and simply put, knowing that a patient has a long history of litigious behavior could cause one to pause when considering whether to enter into another relationship with that individual.

8. *Does one's theoretical orientation matter when considering a dual relationship?* Theoretical orientation matters because in some cases it may increase risk. Those who practice from a more traditional, insight-oriented approach are most likely to have patients who develop transferential feelings that must be addressed in therapy. These types of treatment modalities generally call for clear boundaries and, whenever possible, the avoidance of multiple relationships. Conversely, the behavioral modalities could be seen by some as being less prone to the complexities of more traditional treatment relationships.

However, for various reasons, those who practice from a cognitive or behavioral perspective are not immune from the difficulties found in traditional therapies. First, such approaches are not always confined to symptomatic treatment. Second, the treatment itself does not preclude the possibility of perceptual distortions on the part of patients and/or therapists. Third, the type of treatment may be modified as the patient improves and his or her therapeutic needs evolve. . . .

REFERENCES

American Psychological Association. (1992). Ethical principles of psychologists and code of conduct. *American Psychologist, 47,* 1597–1611.

American Psychological Association. (2002). Ethical principles of psychologists and code of conduct. *American Psychologist, 57,* 1060–1073.

American Psychological Association Insurance Trust. (2002a). *Legal and ethical risk management in professional psychological practice—Sequence 1: General risk management strategies* [Workshop presented nationally]. Washington, DC: Author.

American Psychological Association Insurance Trust. (2002b). *Sample Informed Consent Form.* Retrieved July 2003 from http://apait.org/download.asp?item=INF.doc

American Psychological Association Practice Organization & the American Psychological Association Insurance Trust. (2003). *HIPAA for psychologists* [CD-ROM]. Washington, DC: American Psychological Association.

Barnett, J. E., & Yutrzenka, B. A. (1994). Nonsexual dual relationships in professional practice, with special applications to rural and military communities. *The Independent Practitioner, 14,* 243–248.

Beauchamp, T. L., & Childress, J. F. (1994). *Principles of biomedical ethics* (4th ed.). New York: Oxford University Press.

Campbell, C. D., & Gordon, M. C. (2003). Acknowledging the inevitable: Understanding multiple relationships in rural practice. *Professional Psychology: Research and Practice, 34,* 430–434.

Gottlieb, M. C. (1993). Avoiding exploitative dual relationships: A decision making model. *Psychotherapy, 30*, 41–48.

Harris, E. A., & Bennett, B. E. (1998). Sample psychotherapist–patient contract. In G. P Koocher, J. C. Norcross, & S. S. Hill (Eds.), *Psychologists desk reference* (pp. 191–199). New York: Oxford University Press.

Hickson, G. B., Federspiel, C. F., Pichert, J. W., Miller, C. S., Gauld-Jaeger, J., & Bost, P. (2002). Patient complaints and malpractice risk. *Journal of the American Medical Association, 287*, 2951–2957.

Kitchener, K. S. (1988). Dual role relationships: What makes them so problematic? *Journal of Counseling and Development, 67*, 217–221.

COMMENTARY: Among the most confounding aspects of ethical conflicts in psychology is the existence and characterization of the broad category of "multiple relationships." Although some, such as sexual contact with current clients/patients, are clearly nonnegotiable, others can arise without warning and ultimately may even be determined to represent the best available accommodation of an otherwise insolubly complex situation. It is axiomatic in the discourse surrounding contemporary psychological practice that "multiple relationships are not necessarily unethical."

All the more ethically complex may be those circumstances in which the psychologist is not merely attempting to avoid but is actually "contemplating" multiple relationships. Is barter an appropriate form of compensation to be provided by a current client/patient with minimal financial means who nonetheless wishes to shoulder the burden of payment for psychological services? Have all requirements truly been met for the commencement of a more personal relationship with a former client/patient, after the necessary passage of time? To what extent does a scarcity of local professional resources allow for treatment in a situation that might otherwise be deemed to reflect a disqualifying conflict of interest?

The following references are recommended for those interested in further investigation of multiple relationships, their placement on a spectrum ranging from safe acceptability and outright proscription, and how to gain peer support in making related decisions.

Barnett, J. E. (2011). Psychotherapist self-disclosure: Ethical and clinical considerations. *Psychotherapy, 48*, 315–321. http://dx.doi.org/10.1037/a0026056

Campbell, C. D., & Gordon, M. C. (2003). Acknowledging the inevitable: Understanding multiple relationships in rural practice. *Professional Psychology: Research and Practice, 34*, 430–434. http://dx.doi.org/10.1037/0735-7028.34.4.430

Gottlieb, M. C. (2006). A template for peer ethics consultation. *Ethics & Behavior, 16*, 151–162. http://dx.doi.org/10.1207/s15327019eb1602_5

Gottlieb, M. C., Handelsman, M. M., & Knapp, S. (2013). A model for integrated ethics consultation. *Professional Psychology: Research and Practice, 44*, 307–313. http://dx.doi.org/10.1037/a0033541

Oberlander, S. E., & Barnett, J. E. (2005). Multiple relationships between graduate assistants and students: Ethical and practical considerations. *Ethics & Behavior, 15*, 49–63. http://dx.doi.org/10.1207/s15327019eb1501_4

5.9. Remediation for Ethics Violations: Focus on Psychotherapists' Sexual Contact With Clients

Melissa J. Layman and J. Regis McNamara

. . .

Psychologist Impairment

The field of psychology first addressed professional impairment in 1980, when the American Psychological Association (APA) Council formed a task force to examine the issue of providing services to distressed psychologists (Thoreson, 1986). The Committee on Distressed Psychologists presented a final report to the Board of Professional Affairs (Nathan, Thoreson, & Kilburg, 1983); however, unfortunately no specific action was taken because of disagreement over the definition of distress (Thoreson, 1986). The recently revised Ethical Principles of Psychologists (APA, 1992a) mention that "personal problems and conflicts may interfere with [psychologists'] effectiveness" (p. 1601) and state that psychologists should refrain from activity under these conditions. Furthermore, psychologists must "be alert to signs of, and . . . obtain assistance for" their problems at an early stage and take measures such as "obtaining professional consultation or assistance" as well as limiting, suspending, or terminating their duties if necessary (APA, 1992a, p. 1601). The Ethical Principles (APA, 1992a) note the importance of impairment but add little specific information to the issue of formal rehabilitation for impaired colleagues. Practical information about remediation programs was thus lacking until the Advisory Committee on Impaired Psychologists (ACIP) produced a manual to guide state psychological associations in establishing programs to prevent and remediate impairment; this manual was recently revised (Schwebel et al., 1994). The state psychological associations are now moving rapidly to establish programs. A survey conducted under the direction of ACIP (Schwebel et al., 1994) found that 21 states and provinces had functioning programs for impaired psychologists, with 14 having been established in the past 2 years. In addition, 13 more states had programs in development (Schwebel et al., 1994). Seventeen states had no program, an inactive program, or a program on hold (Schwebel et al., 1994). It appears that the field of psychology has made a strong, if recent, commitment to the care of its members. . . .

REMEDIATION

The literature dealing with remediation of ethics violations is scant, and the majority of this work concerns sexual offenses (Pope, 1987; Schoener & Gonsiorek, 1988). As this is arguably the most serious trespass a psychologist can commit, as well as the most common complaint received by ethics committees (APA Ethics Committee, 1991; Pope, Keith-Spiegel, & Tabachnick, 1986; Reaves, 1995; Vasquez, 1988), sexual contact with clients is the ethics violation we emphasize in the remainder of this article. . . .

Research indicates that sexual attraction is common in the therapist–client relationship, and sexual contact does occur within this setting. A recent random survey of university counseling center psychologists revealed that the majority of the sample (88%) had experienced feelings of sexual attraction toward their clients (Rodolfa et al., 1994); this figure is nearly identical to that found by Pope et al. (1986) 8 years earlier. In addition, the number of disciplinary actions taken by state psychology boards specifically for sexual relationships with patients has increased in recent years (Reaves, 1995).

. . .

Specific Options for Remediation

Education and Training

One commonly mentioned solution for ethics violators is additional training in ethics courses, often in the form of continuing education (APA, 1992b; Pope et al., 1986; Reaves, 1995; Schoener & Gonsiorek, 1988; Vasquez, 1988; Welfel & Lipsitz, 1983; Wood et al., 1985). However, researchers have criticized ethics courses for several reasons. The effects of ethics training are rarely studied in professionals or in real therapist–client situations (Welfel & Lipsitz, 1983). Furthermore, the content and efficacy of these courses are not often evaluated (Vasquez, 1988; Welfel, 1992; Welfel & Lipsitz, 1983); when evaluation does occur, it often provides unfavorable results. In terms of content, Vasquez (1988) cited the failure of ethics education to provide specific training in sexual issues. Evaluating the efficacy of ethics training has otherwise failed to reveal positive results. For example, Welfel and Lipsitz (1983) found only weak support for increased awareness of ethical issues following ethics courses, and they reported no data on the usefulness of this awareness with clients. Welfel (1992, p. 186), in a recent critical review, concluded that "the research cannot provide a positive answer" to the question of whether graduate students' ethical judgments or behaviors have improved as a result of ethics education. Ethical sensitivity, or recognizing that a situation involves ethical issues, has a "weak and inconsistent" relationship to ethical training (Welfel, 1992, p. 186). Tennyson and Strom (1986) stated that knowing ethical principles was not enough; psychologists must develop professional responsibleness that cannot be taught in classes. On a more positive note, Wood et al. (1985) did find that ethics training was related to awareness of impaired colleagues, and that those with ethics training were more likely to seek help for themselves or for a colleague. . . .

Punitive Actions

A second specific option for dealing with therapists who commit ethics viola-tions is punitive disciplinary action, such as revocation or suspension of the psychologist's license. The APA Ethics Committee and state psychology boards may initiate such sanctions, ranging from reprimand and censure to stipulated resignation or expulsion from professional membership (APA, 1992b; Reaves, 1995). Pope (1994) discussed the popular, but often invalid, assumption that any exploitative therapist would not be permitted to resume practice. Only a decade ago, as few as 31% of state licensing boards (16 states) considered sexual intimacy with clients as grounds for license revocation, as compared to 96% (48 states and the District of Columbia) that revoked licenses for therapists with drug and alcohol abuse (Laliotis & Grayson, 1985). More recently, 12 states have criminalized sexual abuse of patients by health care providers (Schwebel et al., 1994), and several more states have legislation pending; in addition, this offense is now grounds for license revocation in every jurisdiction (R. Reaves, ASPPB, personal communication, May 16, 1995). Schoener and Gonsiorek (1988) suggested forms of punishment such as censure, loss of license, or loss of job as possible responses to ethical transgressions. Related to this type of response, but less punitive, are options such as practice limitations and change in therapy style (Reaves, 1995; Schoener & Gonsiorek, 1988). The effectiveness of these punitive actions in reducing frequency of future sexual offenses is as yet unknown.

Informal Support Options

In surveying psychologists' attitudes about remedial intervention a decade ago, Wood et al. (1985) found that the least restrictive options were most favored. For example, only 9% of practitioners were in favor of mandatory supervision as a condition of license renewal. In a similar manner, few were supportive of mental health checkups as a prerequisite for license renewal (11%) or for graduate school admission (31%). The majority of therapists (77%) favored intervention in the form of volunteer associations, including Psychologists Helping Psychologists (for chemical dependency) and Volunteers in Psychol-ogy (Thoreson, Nathan, Skorina, & Kilburg, 1983; Wood et al., 1985). Keith-Spiegel and Koocher (1985) further expanded on the idea of informal help for impaired practitioners through support networks in professional associations and mutual support groups for psychologists in stressful settings. . . .

Practice Oversight

There are several options available for overseeing the work of sanctioned pro-fessionals (Reaves, 1995; Schoener & Gonsiorek, 1988; Walzer & Miltimore, 1993). These options include monitoring, or periodic review of service delivery; supervision; consultation; and therapy, which are discussed below. However, disciplining a colleague is a less than palatable task (Walzer & Miltimore, 1993). Furthermore, these tasks are not well-regulated by licensing agencies (Walzer & Miltimore, 1993).

In addition to further ethics education and training, punitive actions, informal support options, and practice oversight, mandatory personal therapy has been suggested as an option for rehabilitation of impaired psychologists and ethics offenders (APA, 1992b; Burton, 1973; V. Hedges, Ohio Board of Psychology, personal communication, May 1995; Laliotis & Grayson, 1985; Lamb et al., 1987; Pope, 1987; R. Reaves, ASPPB, personal communication, May 1995; Schoener & Gonsiorek, 1988). . . .

MANDATED PERSONAL THERAPY AS REMEDIATION

In suggesting mandatory personal therapy as remediation for ethics violations, several variables must be considered. First, what is the field's general opinion of personal therapy for therapists? Second, what special issues have to be taken into account when psychologists are clients? Third, what outcome can be expected from psychologists' personal therapy? Finally, what outcomes can be expected for treatment of sex offenders and mandated psychotherapy in particular? These issues must be considered before conclusions can be drawn about the appropriateness of mandated therapy for ethics transgressions. . . .

Outcome of Sex Offender Treatment

The treatment of the sexually offending therapist cannot accurately be compared with that of other sex offenders, as this latter treatment often focuses on what are considered deviant sexual impulses (i.e., pedophilia, paraphilia) rather than ones that are considered normal but inappropriate for the context. . . .

Hanson, Cox, and Woszcyna (1991) delineated methodological problems inherent in the study of the treatment of sex offenders, including difficulty with using recidivism as an outcome criteria. These problems may include underestimation of reoffending and short follow-up periods (Marshall & Eccles, 1991; Marshall & Pithers, 1994). Several authors (Hanson et al., 1991; Marshall & Pithers, 1994; Schwartz, 1992) have commented that treatment and outcome studies must focus on more indirect risk variables as criteria, such as denial and minimization, sexual activities, sexual interests, and sexual attitudes. . . .

Outcome of Mandated Psychotherapy

As Larke (1985) pointed out, "traditional mental health workers are taught that, for effective treatment to occur, clients must become involved of their own free will" (p. 262). Walzer and Miltimore (1993) noted that mandated therapy is "notoriously unsuccessful . . . because the treatment is perceived as punishment" (p. 578). There is a paucity of empirical investigation concerning the effectiveness of mandated psychotherapy, although court referrals to substance abuse, spouse abuse, and sexual offender programs are increasing and often represent the treatment of choice (Milgram & Rubin, 1992; Rosenfeld,

1992). In fact, the majority of the outcome studies for sex offenders described above involve mandated treatment, and the conclusions may be applicable to this area as well. Attention to this area may be increasing, however, as evidenced by recent additions to the literature (e.g., Group for the Advancement of Psychiatry, 1994). In a recent review of spouse abuse interventions, Rosenfeld (1992) concluded that the existing studies "cast doubt on the assumption that mandatory psychotherapeutic treatments are effective in reducing future incidents of violence between spouses" (p. 205). Furthermore, mandated treatment has not provided clear remediation over and above the effect of traditional deterrent solutions, and it has not resulted in significant reductions in recidivism relative to untreated abusers. Even more damaging evidence against court-ordered treatment was found by Atwood and Osgood (1987), who demonstrated a significant inverse relationship between amount of coercive control and cooperation in treatment for juvenile delinquents. A recent survey of adolescent sex offender program directors indicated that the majority hoped to simply increase the time between offenses and reduce the seriousness of the behavior (Sapp & Vaughn, 1990).

. . .

SUGGESTIONS FOR ALTERNATIVE METHODS OF REMEDIATION

If mandated personal therapy is not an appropriate treatment for ethics violators, what can be done in the way of remediation for these therapists? Future research must be done to evaluate the perpetrators of ethics violations and the reasons for their behavior—vulnerability, situational variables, and so forth (Keith-Spiegel, 1977; Lamb et al., 1987; Welfel & Lipsitz, 1983). As Welfel and Lipsitz (1983) asserted, the profession must commit to the evaluation of unethical behavior in order to make any successful efforts at remediation. . . .

One general suggestion is to carefully identify, monitor, and intervene with therapists at risk for acting on sexual attraction, if possible (Pope, 1987; Schwebel et al., 1994). These therapists may be identified during training or later during their careers by personal characteristics or by the nature of clientele being served, although the chances of accomplishing this scientifically or ethically are low. Given the low base rate of sexual offending, identification on the basis of possible future offenses would be likely to involve a high number of false positives. Pope et al. (1993) suggested a number of conditions for creating an environment for open and appropriate discussion of sexual feelings in therapy. Schwebel et al. (1994) suggested that involving students in committees dealing with impaired psychologists may be an excellent method of introduction during the process of professional socialization. Wood et al. (1985) found through clinician surveys that 26% of therapists were thought to be the targets of their clients' sexual overtures; professionals must therefore be able to apply any skills learned not only to their general clientele but to those who may be sexually provoking. Pope (1987) suggested a therapeutic intervention to prevent sexual contact with clients, including contracting and cognitive-behavioral treatment (self-talk, modeling). Pope (1987) also called for awareness of personal issues of the therapist–client relationship during therapy, as well as working with the therapist–client's strengths (e.g., intellectual abilities, such as reasoning). In this way, the offending therapist learns to view sexual attraction as a useful resource for understanding his or her own clients' dynamics (Pope, 1987). Unfortunately, these suggestions involve interventions that would likely be subject to the same difficulties as would mandated personal therapy (i.e., lack of concern or motivation).

Preventative training specifically aimed at sexual misconduct seems to be a topic of current interest (Schwebel et al., 1994). Vasquez (1988) discussed a prevention program that would be implemented during training, where students would be sensitized to ethical issues surrounding sexuality and sexual contact. In this program, knowledge and self-awareness would be emphasized. Vasquez (1988) felt that "most problems . . . are amenable to amelioration" in counselors-in-training (p. 240); this may, in fact, be an excellent time to identify potential offenders. Another important opportunity for identification of ethics violators is during the internship (Lamb et al., 1987). Lamb et al. indicated that the stresses and situation changes present in transition to full-time clinical practice, concurrent with extensive supervision, present a chance to observe, identify, and treat potential unethical behavior. The training facility has some avenues for prevention in the form of timely evaluation and individualized programs and presentations on such issues as ethics and burnout (Lamb et al., 1987). Furthermore, the program can offer remediation in the form of increased monitoring, reduction of caseload, requirement of specific coursework, and recommendation of a leave of absence or another internship (Lamb et al., 1987). More serious offenses could result in an endorsement for limited practice, failure to successfully complete, recommendation of a career shift, or termination from the program (Lamb et al., 1987). Unfortunately, both Vasquez's and Lamb et al.'s approaches are limited in that a relatively small number of cases of therapist–client sexual contact occur during graduate training or internship. . . .

Another intervention that may prove useful is educating clients about therapy boundaries (Gottlieb, Vasquez, Applebaum, & Jorgenson, 1993; Strasburger, Jorgenson, & Sutherland, 1992), for example, presenting a sexual misconduct brochure to clients before they enter therapy (Thorn, Shealy, & Briggs, 1993). This brochure would inform the client of the unethical nature of therapist sexual misbehavior as well as the right to file a complaint (Thorn et al., 1993). Given that many therapists have encountered a client who was sexually involved with a previous therapist (Pope, 1993; Stake & Oliver, 1991), a brochure of this type may be a useful resource to clients. In addition, the knowledge that a client is aware of sexual inappropriateness and potential legal action may act as an external source of control for the clinician's actions. Thorn et al. (1993) found that exposure to a brochure did change college students' attitudes about therapist–client sexual contact as well as increase their intention to act assertively if such a situation occurred. Therefore, a sexual misconduct brochure may, in fact, be helpful to an impaired therapist. . . .

REFERENCES

American Psychological Association. (1992a). Ethical principles of psychologists. *American Psychologist, 47,* 1597–1611.

American Psychological Association. (1992b). Rules and procedures. *American Psychologist, 47,* 1612–1628.

American Psychological Association Ethics Committee. (1991). Report of the Ethics Committee, 1989 and 1990. *American Psychologist, 46,* 750–757.

Atwood, R. O., & Osgood, D. W. (1987). Cooperation in group treatment programs for incarcerated adolescents. *Journal of Applied Social Psychology, 17,* 969–989.

Burton, A. (1973). The psychotherapist as client. *American Journal of Psychoanalysis, 33,* 94–103.

Gottlieb, M. C., Vasquez, M. J. T., Applebaum, P. S., & Jorgenson, L. (1993). Sexual contact between psychotherapists and clients. In J. A. Mindell (Ed.), *Issues in clinical psychology* (pp. 153–182). Dubuque, IA: Brown & Benchmark/Wm. C. Brown.

Group for the Advancement of Psychiatry. (1994). *Forced into treatment: The role of coercion in clinical practice.* Washington, DC: American Psychiatric Press.

Hanson, R. K., Cox, B., & Woszcyna, C. (1991). Assessing treatment outcome for sexual offenders. *Annals of Sex Research, 4,* 177–208.

Keith-Spiegel, P. (1977). Violation of ethical principles due to ignorance or poor professional judgment versus willful disregard. *Professional Psychology, 8,* 288–296.

Keith-Spiegel, P., & Koocher, G. P. (1985). *Ethics in psychology: Professional standards and cases.* New York: Random House.

Laliotis, D. A., & Grayson, J. H. (1985). Psychologist heal thyself: What is available for the impaired psychologist? *American Psychologist, 40,* 84–96.

Lamb, D. H., Presser, N. R., Pfost, K. S., Baum, M. C., Jackson, V. R., & Jarvis, P. A. (1987). Confronting professional impairment during the internship: Identification, due process, and remediation. *Professional Psychology: Research and Practice, 18,* 597–603.

Larke, J. (1985). Compulsory treatment: Some practical methods of treating the mandated client. *Psychotherapy, 22,* 262–268.

Marshall, W. L., & Eccles, A. (1991). Issues in clinical practice with sex offenders. *Journal of Interpersonal Violence, 6,* 68–93.

Marshall, W. L., & Pithers, W. D. (1994). A reconsideration of treatment outcome with sex offenders. *Criminal Justice and Behavior, 21,* 1027.

Milgram, D., & Rubin, J. S. (1992). Resisting resistance: Involuntary substance abuse group therapy. *Social Work With Groups, 15,* 95–110.

Nathan, P. E., Thoreson, R. W., & Kilburg, R. (1983). *Board of Professional Affairs Steering Committee on Distressed Psychologists: Final report.* Washington, DC: American Psychological Association.

Pope, K. S. (1987). Preventing therapist–patient sexual intimacy: Therapy for a therapist at risk. *Professional Psychology: Research and Practice, 18,* 624–628.

Pope, K. S. (1993). Licensing disciplinary actions for psychologists who have been sexually involved with a client: Some information about offenders. *Professional Psychology: Research and Practice, 24,* 374–377.

Pope, K. S. (1994). *Sexual involvement with therapists: Patient assessment, subsequent therapy, forensics.* Washington, DC: American Psychological Association.

Pope, K. S., Keith-Spiegel, P. C., & Tabachnick, B. (1986). Sexual attraction to clients: The human therapist and the (sometimes) inhuman training system. *American Psychologist, 41,* 147–158.

Pope, K. S., Sonne, J. L., & Holroyd, J. (1993). *Sexual feelings in psychotherapy: Explorations for therapists and therapists-in-training.* Washington, DC: American Psychological Association.

Reaves, R. P. (1995, April). *Top ten reasons for disciplinary action in the U.S. and Canada.* Paper presented at the First International Congress on Licensure, Certification and Credentialing of Psychologists, New Orleans, LA.

Rodolfa, E., Hall, T., Holms, V., Davena, A., Komatz, D., Antunez, M., & Hall, A. (1994). The management of sexual feelings in therapy. *Professional Psychology: Research and Practice, 25*, 168–172.

Rosenfeld, B. D. (1992). Court-ordered treatment of spouse abuse. *Clinical Psychology Review, 12*, 205–226.

Sapp, A. D., & Vaughn, M. S. (1990). Juvenile sex offender treatment at state-operated correctional institutions. *International Journal of Offender Therapy and Comparative Criminology, 34*, 131–146.

Schoener, G. R., & Gonsiorek, J. (1988). Assessment and development of rehabilitation plans for counselors who have sexually exploited their clients. *Journal of Counseling and Development, 67*, 227–232.

Schwartz, B. K. (1992). Effective treatment techniques for sex offenders. *Psychiatric Annals, 22*, 315–319.

Schwebel, M., Skorina, J. K., & Schoener, G. (1994). Assisting impaired psychologists (Rev. ed.). *Program development for state psychological associations.* Washington, DC: American Psychological Association.

Stake, J. E., & Oliver, J. (1991). Sexual contact and touching between therapist and client: A survey of psychologists' attitudes and behavior. *Professional Psychology: Research and Practice, 22*, 297–307.

Strasburger, L. H., Jorgenson, L., & Sutherland, P. (1992). The prevention of psycho-therapist sexual misconduct: Avoiding the slippery slope. *American Journal of Psychotherapy, 46*, 544–555.

Tennyson, W. W., & Strom, S. M. (1986). Beyond professional standards: Developing responsibleness. *Journal of Counseling and Development, 64*, 298–302.

Thoreson, R. W. (1986). Training issues for professionals in distress. In R. R. Kilburg, R. E. Nathan, & R. W. Thoreson (Eds.), *Professionals in distress: Issues, syndromes, and solutions in psychology* (pp. 37–50). Washington, DC: American Psychological Association.

Thoreson, R. W., Nathan, P. E., Skorina, J. K., & Kilburg, R. R. (1983). The alcoholic physician: Issues, problems, and implications for the profession. *Professional Psychology, 14*, 670–684.

Thorn, B. E., Shealy, R. C., & Briggs, S. D. (1993). Sexual misconduct in psychotherapy: Reactions to a consumer-oriented brochure. *Professional Psychology: Research and Practice, 24*, 75–82.

Vasquez, M. J. T. (1988). Counselor-client sexual contact: Implications for ethics training. *Journal of Counseling and Development, 67*, 238–241.

Walzer, R. S., & Miltimore, S. (1993). Mandated supervision, monitoring, and therapy of disciplined health care professionals. *The Journal of Legal Medicine, 14*, 565–596.

Welfel, E. R. (1992). Psychologist as ethics educator: Successes, failures, and unanswered questions. *Professional Psychology: Research and Practice, 23*, 182–189.

Welfel, E. R., & Lipsitz, N. E. (1983). Wanted: A comprehensive approach to ethics research and education. *Counselor Education and Supervision, 22*, 320–332.

Wood, B. J., Klein, S., Cross, H. J., Lammers, C. J., & Elliott, J. K. (1985). Impaired practitioners: Psychologists' opinions about prevalence, and proposals for intervention. *Professional Psychology: Research and Practice, 16*, 843–850.

COMMENTARY: Once a problem has been identified, fault has been established, and discipline has been applied, what is to be done for the psychologist whose transgressions, although undoubtedly significant, have not been deemed so egregious as to warrant permanent expulsion from clinical practice or other professional employment? We and our colleagues do not become psychologists by lottery. Exhaustive classroom instruction, training in applied methods, and monitored, self-directed study—often in the form of mandatory continuing education—have been provided for decades.

How are those who have violated what may be the ultimate professional taboo best assisted in finding their way back? Some combination of collegial supervision, focused literature immersion, and clinical treatment is the typical solution. Mere realization and atonement will not be sufficient. Given that the stakes could scarcely be higher for future clients/patients, students, trainees, subordinates, and other potential affected parties, the impaired psychologist must be provided with a workable framework for avoiding relapses.

The following references are recommended for those interested in further investigation of the availability and efficacy of colleague assistance programs, workplace modification, and other resources at any stage of a professional career.

Barnett, J. E., Baker, E. K., Elman, N. S., & Schoener, G. R. (2007). In pursuit of wellness: The self-care imperative. *Professional Psychology: Research and Practice, 38*, 603–612. http://dx.doi.org/10.1037/0735-7028.38.6.603

Barnett, J. E., & Hillard, D. (2001). Psychologist distress and impairment: The availability, nature, and use of colleague assistance programs for psychologists. *Professional Psychology: Research and Practice, 32*, 205–210. http://dx.doi.org/10.1037/0735-7028.32.2.205

Engle, N. W., Peterson, M., McMinn, M., & Taylor-Kemp, N. (2017). Stressors and resources of psychologists: How are helpers being helped? *North American Journal of Psychology, 19*, 123–137.

Kallaugher, J., & Mollen, D. (2017). Student experiences of remediation in their graduate psychology programs. *Training and Education in Professional Psychology, 11*, 276–282. http://dx.doi.org/10.1037/tep0000175

O'Connor, M. F. (2001). On the etiology and effective management of professional distress and impairment among psychologists. *Professional Psychology: Research and Practice, 32*, 345–350. http://dx.doi.org/10.1037/0735-7028.32.4.345

6

Psychological Assessment

Psychological assessment can be a significantly impactful event at various intervals in the lifespan of the client/patient. A young child may be seeking structured educational opportunities that are tailored to the identified presence of a learning disability. An adolescent may be seeking a differential diagnosis of attention-deficit/hyperactivity disorder versus what could be incipient manifestations of bipolar disorder. A young adult with a family history of psychosis may be seeking to determine whether a single incident of bizarre behavior may signal the coming of a first schizophrenic break. An older adult may be seeking to learn whether increasing memory deficits reflect either dementia or depression. As always, with greater potential impact on clients/patients comes greater potential for ethical conflicts.

Included in the many issues that may arise concerning psychological assessment are the appropriate selection, administration, scoring, interpretation, and reporting of test results. The impaired psychologist may fail to execute any or all of these tasks in a suitably accurate manner. Persons—including student trainees, technical associates, and office staff—to whom these tasks are improperly delegated are prone, of course, to making similar errors. Was an outdated form of the test chosen? Was there a nonstandard administration, raising doubts as to reliability and validity, due to a lack of familiarity with (or even consultation of) the test manual? Was there an error in scoring as a result of undue haste or distraction? Was faulty interpretation provided as a result of insufficient insight into client/patient cultural characteristics? Was a written

http://dx.doi.org/10.1037/0000125-007
Ethical Conflicts in Psychology, Fifth Edition, by E. Y. Drogin

report of findings deficient because results were clumsily and perhaps mislead-ingly conveyed?

Under certain circumstances, psychologists will employ computerized scor-ing and interpretation services to cut down on some of these sources of error. Unfortunately, however, there can be an overreliance on this form of technical support. Every reputable test service includes at least one caveat that tacitly acknowledges what can be the one-size-fits-all nature of "canned" interpreta-tions and that urges the user to take heed of this circumstance. Psychologists—and others—who gain access to these services and who do not undertake to develop an independent understanding of the measures in question can wind up in an ethically compromising situation when misguided or unsupported allegations and recommendations ensue.

Psychological testing was once a near-ubiquitous practice in all manner of clinical settings, during a now-bygone era in which third-party reimbursement for assessment services was routine. Today, those whose careers were largely founded on administering a range of cognitive and personality measures are either compelled to perform this function for little or no pay or to come up with highly detailed justifications for proceeding—situations that can become ethi-cally fraught with respect to cutting corners in either situation.

Among its other features, this chapter addresses the juxtaposition of legal and ethical issues in school psychological assessment, American Psychological Association guidelines for the qualification of persons to use psychological tests, and strategies for private practitioners coping with subpoenas or compelled tes-timony regarding test data or test materials.

6.1. Ethics in Psychological Testing and Assessment

Frederick T. L. Leong, Yong Sue Park, and Mark M. Leach

. . .

Use of Assessments

Psychological testing applies to a wide range of purposes and contexts, which include but are not limited to screening applicants for job placement, diagnosing psychological disorders for mental health treatment, verifying health insurance coverage, conducting focus groups for market research, informing legal decisions and governmental policies, and developing measures to reliably measure personality characteristics (Aiken & Groth-Marnat, 2006; Fisher, 2009). According to the *Eighteenth Mental Measurements Yearbook* (Spies, Carlson, & Geisinger, 2010), there are no less than 19 major categories of psychological tests and assessments.

APA Ethical Standard 9.02 pertains to the proper selection and use of psychological tests and assessments. The first component of this ethical standard stipulates that psychologists administer, adapt, score, interpret, and use psychological testing in the manner and purpose for which the selected tests and assessments were designed to be used as indicated by research (Ethical Standard 9.02a). Furthermore, psychologists should select and use tests or assessments with members of populations for whom adequate reliability and validity of the test scores has been established. If the reliability and validity of the test scores has not been examined or verified for a particular population, psychologists are obligated to describe the strengths and limitations of the interpretations and recommendations derived from the test or assessment results (Ethical Standard 9.02b). The third aspect of this ethical standard obligates psychologists to select tests and assessments that are appropriate to the language preference and competence of the individuals being assessed (Ethical Standard 9.02c).

Test Selection and Usage

Psychologists are responsible for selecting appropriate assessments for the intended purpose of the testing (Ethical Standard 9.02a). To guide the selection of appropriate tests and assessments, psychologists should have adequate knowledge of the theoretical bases and empirical evidence that support the validity and reliability of the tests or assessments; standardized administration and scoring procedures; approaches to interpreting the results; and the populations for which the assessment was normed and designed (Fisher, 2009; see Ethical Standard 9.07, Assessment by Unqualified Persons). Psychologists should also keep themselves updated on the most recent versions of the tests and assessments that they commonly use because testing and assessment procedures and parameters may change in light of theoretical advances and new research (see Ethical Standard 9.08, Obsolete Tests and Outdated Test Results). Finally, psychologists should select tests and assessments that have been empirically validated to be used in the specific contexts and settings in which the testing occurs.

Testing Across Diverse Populations

According to Principles D (Justice) and E (Respect for People's Rights and Dignity) of the APA Ethics Code, psychologists strive to establish fair and equal access to and benefit of psychological contributions for all individuals and populations, which include but are not limited to diversity in age, gender, gender identity, race, ethnicity, culture, national origin, religion, disability, language, and socioeconomic status. Although psychological testing represents a unique contribution of professional psychology to benefiting larger society, ensuring the fair and equal access to and benefit of psychological testing has historically been challenging for the field. According to Reynolds (1982), the reliability and validity of test and assessment scores have predominately been established with White, middle-class samples and may not generalize well to other populations, especially those that represent a minority in the United States. This historical precedence conflicts with Ethical Standard 9.02b, which stipulates the selection and use of assessments that have been found to be adequately valid and reliable for drawing particular inferences for specific populations being assessed. When tests are administered across diverse populations, psychologists are obligated to select and use tests and assessments that have measurement equivalence in that the psychometric properties (i.e., measurement and structural models) have been shown to be equivalent or invariant between members of culturally different populations and those from the reference population for which the test and assessment scores were validated, normed, and found to be reliable (Schmitt, Golubovich, & Leong, 2010).

Testing and Language

APA Ethical Standard 9.02c stipulates that psychologists select tests that are appropriate to be used with the language preferences and levels of competence of the individuals or groups being assessed. Thus, before selecting assessments, it is helpful for psychologists to gather information on examinees' cultural background (e.g., acculturation) and native and English language ability with regard to written, reading, and spoken language proficiencies (Jacob & Hartshorne, 2006; Takushi & Uomoto, 2001). According to Groth-Marnat (2009), literal translation of testing and assessment materials and tools using the commonly implemented method of translation–back-translation may not be adequate because of cross-cultural differences in the conceptual interpretation of items, noncomparable idioms, and within-group differences in dialect and word usage. Furthermore, from an item response theory framework, literal translation of testing and assessment items from one language to another may change the properties of the items' difficulty, which may in turn diminish the measurement equivalence of tests or assessments. For these reasons, the psychometric properties of the original-language version of tests or assessments cannot be assumed to generalize to the alternate-language versions that were developed from a translation–back-translation method. . . .

With regard to testing conducted in person (e.g., interviews) with linguistically different clients, psychologists may consider enlisting the services of a translator for interpretation purposes or consider referring clients to colleagues who have professional proficiency in the clients' language. Professional organizations may be useful resources for identifying and referring clients to professional colleagues with the appropriate linguistic background; for example, the National Association of School Psychologists maintains a directory of bilingual school psychologists that can be found on its website (http://www.nasponline.org/about_nasp/bilingualdirectory.aspx).

. . .

Interpreting Assessment Results

Interpretations of test and assessment results influence the decisions and recommendations that are made in reference to the purpose of the testing (see Ethical Standard 9.02, Use of Assessments), such as diagnosing and informing treatment plans in clinical settings and educational placements in academic settings and determining employment selections and promotions. Interpretations should be based on proper administration of tests and assessments as outlined by the testing manual to ensure the interpretations are in line with the evidence to support the validity and reliability of the test or assessment scores (Fisher, 2009). It is the psychologist's responsibility to ensure that his or her interpretations of test or assessment results are useful and relevant to the purpose of the assessment and take into account various test factors, test taking abilities, and other characteristics of individuals being assessed (Ethical Standard 9.06).

Interpretation of Multiple Sources

Interpretations of test and assessment results should not be derived from a simple, mechanical process that is based solely on the test or assessment scores, score cutoffs, or reliance on automated interpretations (Fisher, 2009; Groth-Marnat, 2009) but that takes into consideration a host of factors, including but not limited to examinees' characteristics, test-taking abilities, styles, issues of fatigue, perceptual and motor impairments, illnesses, language proficiencies, and cultural orientations (Fisher, 2009). Furthermore, Groth-Marnat (2009) recommended that psychologists base their interpretations on multiple sources of data, including behavioral observations, examinee background information, and other assessments. Often, testing is administered using an integrated battery of assessments, and inconsistent findings across the various assessments may result. In these situations, it is the psychologist's responsibility to analyze the contradictions and use his or her clinical and professional judgment to offer the most accurate and relevant interpretation in relation to the purpose of testing (Groth-Marnat, 2009).

Automated Interpretations

There are many well-established, standardized assessments, such as the Minnesota Multiphasic Personality Inventory—2, for which one can receive a computer-generated automated interpretative report. Although these automated interpretations are based on a body of past empirical evidence and theoretical models, it is important to highlight that interpretations are not sophisticated enough to take into account examinees' unique characteristics and test-taking contexts. Thus, psychologists should not base their interpretations solely on automated interpretations but rather use automated interpretations as supplemental resources for integrated interpretations that take into consideration a host of other factors that may influence the testing.

Limitations of Interpretations

According to Ethical Standard 9.06, Interpreting Assessment Results, psychologists are obligated to indicate any significant limitations of their interpretations, especially when the interpretations are not supported by the established validity and reliability of the test or assessment scores in making particular inferences. When interpretation of test or assessment scores is made outside their established validity and reliability, Fisher (2009) recommended that such interpretations be posed as hypotheses, rather than conclusions, to elucidate the limitations of such findings. Another limitation that needs to be indicated is when testing procedures and materials, evidence for validity and reliability, and score cutoffs and norms have become obsolete in the face of new research or changes in the populations for which tests and assessments were designed (see Ethical Standard 9.08, Obsolete Tests and Outdated Test Results).

. . .

Test Scoring and Interpretation Services

APA Ethical Standard 9.09 applies to psychologists who provide test scoring and interpretation services. Within their promotional and other administrative materials (e.g., manuals), these psychologists are obligated to accurately describe the nature and purpose of the assessments, the basis for the standardized norms, and validity and reliability information for their assessment results and interpretations and to specify the qualifications for using the services. When interpretations and recommendations from assessment results are made, psychologists are obligated to provide the theoretical rationale and psychometric evidence for justifying their conclusions and to adequately explain the limitations of their interpretations and recommendations.

Ethical responsibility for the appropriate use of test scoring and interpretation services also applies to psychologists who are consumers of these services. These psychologists are obligated to select services that adequately provide evidence for the validity and reliability of their procedures for administering, scoring, and interpreting test and assessment results. Furthermore, psychologists using these services are obligated to have the qualifications and competence to ensure that the scoring and interpretations made by these services are consistent with APA Ethical Standard 9.06, Interpreting Assessment Results. When these services are used, the HIPAA Notice of Privacy Practices obligates psychologists to inform and obtain authorization from their clients or patients to permit the release of test or assessment information to these services.

Explaining Assessment Results

According to Ethical Standard 9.10, Explaining Assessment Results, psychologists are obligated to provide competent feedback to examinees, or to parents or legal guardians of minors, explaining any interpretations, decisions, and recommendations in relation to the purpose of testing. Groth-Marnat (2009) recommended that the feedback begin with a clear explanation of the rationale for testing, followed by the nature and purpose of the assessment, general conclusions drawn from assessment results, limitations, and common misconceptions or misinterpretations of assessment results. When examinees are minors, psychologists are obligated to provide the feedback to both examinees and their parents or legal guardians.

Sensitivity in the Communication of Assessment Results

The *Standards for Educational and Psychological Tests* (AERA et al., 1999) stipulates that simple, clear, everyday language should be used when providing feedback so that the feedback is readily understood by its recipients. Psychologists should tailor their level of communication to recipients' personal characteristics, such as their educational and linguistic backgrounds, level of knowledge of psychological testing, and possible emotional reactions to the assessment results (Groth-Marnat, 2009). With regard to the possible emotional reactions generated by feedback, it may be helpful for psychologists to make available options for follow-up counseling to facilitate services for examinees who may need support in processing the feedback information. When providing feedback on mental health status, Aiken and Groth-Marnat (2006) recommended that the least stigmatizing label be used to describe the examinees' psychological conditions or diagnoses.

Written Reports

In addition to the oral feedback session, psychologists commonly provide written reports to examinees, or their referral source, regarding the assessment results, interpretations, and recommendations. Written reports should be centered on referral questions and the purpose of the testing and adequately describe the characteristics of the examinees and how they relate to the assessments used and the test situations (Aiken & Groth-Marnat, 2006). According to Jacob and Hartshorne (2006), written reports should be comprehensible to both professionals and nonprofessionals and should be written in a succinct, clear, and comprehensible manner while avoiding overgeneralizations (Aiken & Groth-Marnat, 2006). Psychologists are responsible for signing off on assessment reports only after ensuring the accuracy of the contents contained in the reports.

. . .

REFERENCES

Aiken, L. R., & Groth-Marnat, G. (2006). *Psychological testing and assessment* (12th ed.). Upper Saddle River, NJ: Pearson Education.

American Educational Research Association, American Psychological Association, & National Council on Measurement in Education. (1999). *Standards for educational and psychological testing* (3rd ed.). Washington, DC: American Educational Research Association.

American Psychological Association. (2010). *Ethical principles of psychologists and code of conduct* (2002, amended June 1, 2010). Retrieved from www.apa.org/ethics/code/index.aspx

Fisher, C. B. (2009). *Decoding the ethics code: A practical guide for psychologists* (2nd ed.). Thousand Oaks, CA: Sage.

Groth-Marnat, G. (2009). *Handbook of psychological assessment* (5th ed.). Hoboken, NJ: Wiley.

Jacob, S., & Hartshorne, T. S. (2006). *Ethics and law for school psychologists* (5th ed.). Hoboken, NJ: Wiley.

Reynolds, C. R. (1982). Methods for detecting construct and predictive bias. In R. A. Berk (Ed.), *Handbook of methods for detecting test bias* (pp. 192–227). Baltimore, MD: Johns Hopkins University Press.

Schmitt, N., Golubovich, J., & Leong, F. T. L. (2010). *Impact of measurement invariance on construct correlations, mean differences and relations with external correlates: An illustrative example using Big Five and RIASEC measures. Assessment.* Advance online publication. doi:10.1177/1073191110 373223

Spies, R. S., Carlson, J. F., & Geisinger, K. F. (2010). *Eighteenth mental measurements yearbook.* Lincoln, NE: Buros Institute of Mental Measurements.

Takushi, R., & Uomoto, J. M. (2001). The clinical interview from a multicultural perspective. In L. A. Suzuki, J. G. Ponterotto, & P. J. Meller (Eds.), *Handbook of multicultural assessment* (2nd ed., pp. 47–66). San Francisco, CA: Jossey-Bass.

6.2. Legal Issues in School Psychological Assessments

Matthew K. Burns, David C. Parker, and Susan Jacob

When Binet and Simon published their scale for measuring the intelligence of schoolchildren in 1905, they gave psychology new credibility within the science community and gave birth to psychoeducational assessment. School psychology traces its roots to before mental ability tests were developed (Fagan & Wise, 2007), but assessment has become a defining attribute of the field. The scientific method is the conceptual framework from which school psychology operates, and data-based decision making—an extension of the scientific method—is a foundational competency for school psychologists (Ysseldyke et al., 2006). Psychoeducational assessment of schoolchildren has changed considerably since Binet and Simon conducted their work, as have the potential uses of the assessment results.

The newly revised code of ethics of the National Association of School Psychologists (NASP; 2010) states, "School psychologists are committed to the application of their professional expertise for the purpose of promoting improvement in the quality of life for students, families, and school communities" (p. 2). School-based practitioners must be knowledgeable of legal and ethical issues associated with psychoeducational assessment and the uses of assessment data if they hope to promote supportive social and learning environments for all schoolchildren (NASP, 2010; Reschly & Bersoff, 1999). In this chapter, we discuss legal guidelines for assessment in school-based practice and the three-tier model (TTM) for delivery of comprehensive school psychological assessment and intervention services. We also discuss a contemporary assessment controversy, namely, differing approaches to the identification of students who have a specific learning disability (LD) as defined in the Individuals With Disabilities Education Improvement Act of 2004 (IDEIA) and who are therefore eligible for special education and related services.

LEGAL FRAMEWORK FOR SCHOOL PSYCHOLOGY ASSESSMENT PRACTICES

. . . *School-based practice* is defined as "the provision of school psychological services under the authority of a state, regional, or local educational agency," whether the school psychologist "is an employee of the schools or contracted by the schools on a per-case or consultative basis" (NASP, 2010, p. 3). School-based assessment and intervention practices are highly regulated by law; for this reason, we begin with a brief overview of the legal underpinnings of school-based practice.

The 10th Amendment of the U.S. Constitution has been interpreted as prohibiting the federal government from establishing a nationalized educational system. State governments have assumed the duty and authority to educate youths, which is further delegated by state government to local school boards (Hubsch, 1989). When school psychologists employed by a school board make decisions in their official roles, such acts are seen as an extension of the authority of state government; in legal language, school-based practitioners are considered to be state actors (Jacob, Decker, & Hartshorne, 2011; NASP, 2010; Russo, 2006).

Because education is a state responsibility, for many years the federal government was reluctant to intervene in matters concerning the operation of the public schools. Beginning in the 1950s, however, the federal courts became increasingly involved in public education issues because of school actions that violated the legal rights of students and their parents under the U.S. Constitution. The entitlement to a public education created by state law is a property right protected by the 14th Amendment's equal protection clause. In *Brown v. Board of Education* (1954), the U.S. Supreme Court held that under the 14th Amendment, a state must provide equal educational opportunity to all of its citizens regardless of race. *Brown v. Board of Education* provided the legal reasoning for a subsequent series of "right-to-education" court cases that won access to a public education for students with disabilities (e.g., *Mills v. Board of Education of the District of Columbia*, 1972; *Pennsylvania Association for Retarded Children v. Commonwealth of Pennsylvania*, 1971, 1972). Pertinent to public school assessment practices, the Supreme Court also held that the due process clause of the 14th Amendment protects individuals from arbitrary or unwarranted stigmatization by the state that may interfere with the ability to acquire property (e.g., *Wisconsin v. Constantineau*, 1971). Consequently, a public school may not label a student as having a developmental or cognitive disability without a fair decision-making procedure that includes parental notice of the proposed label and the right to protest the classification.

In addition to the right-to-education court cases that required schools to offer all students with disabilities a free education, a series of court cases beginning in the 1970s challenged whether the assessment practices used by public schools to assign students to "unequal and inferior" classes for students with mental retardation were racially and culturally discriminatory (e.g., *Diana v. State Board of Education*, 1970). These court rulings, together with the right-to-education cases, identified multiple public school responsibilities to students with disabilities that were later incorporated in federal legislation (e.g., the Education for All Handicapped Children Act of 1975).

The U.S. Congress began to pass federal legislation designed to improve the nation's schools in 1965. Congress has the power to shape educational policy and practices by offering monies to states contingent on compliance with federal statutory law. The first major federal law that provided funds to states for education was the Elementary and Secondary Education Act of 1965, passed by Congress to ensure a basic floor of educational opportunity, particularly for students from disadvantaged backgrounds. A series of laws followed that provided funds to states for the education of students with disabilities, including the Education for All Handicapped Children Act of 1975, now known as IDEIA. IDEIA provides funds to states on the condition that states implement a plan to locate and offer a free, appropriate education to all children with disabilities within the state. A portion of IDEIA Part B funds (15%) may be used to provide early intervention services to students who are struggling in the general education curriculum; the remaining funds are to provide special education and related services to students with a disability as defined by the law. A *child with a disability* means a student evaluated in accordance with the procedures outlined in the law who is found to qualify as having a disability in one of 13 categories and who, for that reason, needs special education and related services (34 C.F.R. § 300.8[a]; see also the Assessment of Learning Disability Eligibility section).

To receive funds, each state must have a plan that offers every child with a disability an opportunity to receive special education and related services in conformance with an Individualized Education Program (IEP). The IEP must be developed in accordance with the procedures outlined in the law and provide a special education program that is reasonably designed to confer benefit (*Board of Education of the Hendrick Hudson Central School District v. Rowley*, 1982). A child with a disability must be educated in the least restrictive appropriate environment, namely the educational setting selected from a continuum of alternative placements (ranging from a residential facility to the general education classroom) that is closest to the general education classroom but also meets the child's individual special education needs. Determination of whether a child is eligible for special education under IDEIA is made by a group of people that includes a child's parent (or an adult acting in the place of a parent); if the child is found eligible, the IEP is developed by a team (the IEP team) that includes the parents. Under IDEIA, the parents of children with disabilities (and adult students) have multiple due process protections to safeguard against misclassification, inappropriate evaluation and placement, and failure of the school to provide an IEP reasonably designed to confer benefit. Parents may use administrative remedies outlined in IDEIA (e.g., impartial resolution meetings and due process hearings) to resolve disputes regarding their child's eligibility, classification, placement, or IEP, and they have the right to file a lawsuit against the school if they are not satisfied with the outcome of administrative remedies. Parents may recover the cost of their attorney's fees if they prevail in a court action on any significant issue. Because school–parent disputes under IDEIA are not uncommon, school psychological assessment practices must be legally defensible and documented with enough detail to withstand challenges in due process hearings and court (Jacob et al., 2011).

The U.S. Congress also enacted civil rights legislation that prohibits schools from discriminating against individuals on the basis of race, color, national origin, sex, or disability. Schools must comply with antidiscrimination legislation if they receive any federal funds for any purpose. . . . Section 504 evaluation regulations generally require determination of the following:

1. Is there a physical or mental impairment?
2. Does that impairment substantially limit a major life activity?
3. What kind of accommodations would be needed so that the student will be able to enjoy the benefits of the school program? (Martin, 1992).

Section 504 does not require a specific categorical diagnosis, only the determination of a condition that substantially impairs one or more major life activities at school and requires special accommodation by the school. Under Section 504, schools are required to make accommodations to ensure that pupils with disabilities have equal opportunity to benefit from the schools' programs and activities as their peers without disability.

RELATIONSHIP BETWEEN ETHICAL AND LEGAL ASSESSMENT GUIDELINES

In 1969, NASP was formed to represent school-based psychologists better, particularly non–doctoral-level school psychologists. As described in the previous section, the legal landscape for schools and school psychologists was undergoing rapid change at that time. In 1974, a special issue of NASP's *School Psychology Digest* (now *School Psychology Review*) addressed emerging ethical and legal issues in school psychology (Kaplan, Crisci, & Farling, 1974). Contributors to the special edition recognized that school psychology practitioners needed additional guidance to navigate the legal changes confronting them, and they called for the development of a code of ethics specifically for school psychologists. The American Psychological Association's (APA's) 1963 code of ethics was seen as "either irrelevant or much too vague for operational clarity" for practitioners (Trachtman, 1974, p. 5). Some principles in APA's ethics code conflicted with changing education laws (Ackley, 1974; Bersoff, 1974; Trachtman, 1974). In addition, APA's ethics code did not address issues of growing importance to school-based practitioners such as balancing parent rights with the interests of children (Bersoff, 1974); involving students in decisions affecting their own welfare (Bersoff, 1974; Trachtman, 1974); ensuring fair and valid assessment of students from diverse linguistic and cultural backgrounds; and managing conflicts inherent in the dual roles of child advocate and school employee (Bersoff, 1974; Trachtman, 1974). In 1974, NASP adopted its own code of ethics, the *Principles for Professional Ethics* (PPE). The code was most recently revised in 2010 (see Armistead, Williams, & Jacob, 2011).

School psychology assessment practices are informed by NASP's (2010) PPE and APA's (2010) *Ethical Principles of Psychologists and Code of Conduct.*

The *Standards for Educational and Psychological Testing*, or *Standards* (American Educational Research Association, APA, & National Council on Measurement in Education, 1999), also provides criteria for acceptable assessment practices and has been cited as an authoritative source in court cases challenging assessment practices. Although legal requirements and ethical guidelines for school-based psychoeducational assessment are often similar, at times they result in ambiguity regarding how to address challenging situations. In challenging cases, we recommend that ethical guidelines be considered first because they typically recommend practices that are above and beyond those legally required; however, in situations in which ambiguity remains, legal requirements can be used to determine courses of action. What follows is an integration of ethical and legal standards for school psychological evaluations according to the temporal order of assessment activities.

Before Assessment

Before considering whether a comprehensive psychoeducational assessment of an individual student is needed, school psychologists ensure that appropriate behavioral and instructional practices have been implemented within the student's school environment (NASP PPE II.3.1). . . .

At the outset of establishing a school psychologist–client relationship for the purpose of conducting a psychological assessment with individual students, it is ethically and legally necessary to engage parents and students in the informed consent process (NASP PPE I.1.2). This process ensures that the dignity and rights of the families and students working with school psychologists are respected. Both IDEIA and APA's and NASP's ethics codes provide guidance for how this process should occur. Generally, informed consent is obtained when assessment procedures go beyond normal educational activities (APA Ethical Standard 9.03) and in cases when school psychologists are involved in a student's education to an extensive degree (see NASP PPE I.1.1). When an initial assessment of whether a student has a disability under IDEIA or Section 504 of the Rehabilitation Act of 1973 is under consideration, informed consent is legally required (IDEIA; NASP PPE I.1.2; see also Section 504). An important part of the informed consent process is ensuring that consent is voluntary, ongoing, and informed. The individual providing consent (e.g., a parent or an individual acting in the place of a parent or an adult student) must be given sufficient information to make an informed choice about whether the psychoeducational assessment will be conducted and advised that he or she may revoke consent at any time. Soliciting informed consent involves discussion of the nature and purpose of the assessment, any potential consequences of the assessment results, who will receive information about the outcomes, and the limits of confidentiality (APA Ethical Standard 9.03a; IDEIA; NASP PPE I.1.3). It is ethically permissible to bypass a minor's assent if the service is considered to be of direct benefit to the student or is required by law; however, if a child's assent is not solicited, the school psychologist nevertheless ensures that the child is informed about the nature and purpose of the assessment (NASP PPE I.1.4).

Before beginning an assessment, school psychologists identify instruments and procedures that are technically adequate, valid for the purpose of the assessment, and appropriate for the student who is being assessed (APA Ethical Standard 9.02[b]; NASP PPE II.3.2). If a student is suspected of having a disability under IDEIA, the student must be assessed on the basis of procedures that are multifaceted (based on a variety of assessment tools and strategies), comprehensive (the child is assessed in all areas related to the suspected disability), technically adequate and valid for the purpose used, fair (nondiscriminatory), and useful (provide information that directly assists in determining educational needs; 34 C.F.R. § 300.304; see also Jacob et al., 2011 . . .).

. . .

REFERENCES

Ackley, S. (1974). Psychologists and individual rights. *School Psychology Digest, 3,* 21–25.

American Educational Research Association, American Psychological Association, & National Council on Measurement in Education. (1999). *Standards for educational and psychological testing* (3rd ed.). Washington, DC: American Educational Research Association.

American Psychological Association. (2010). *Ethical principles of psychologists and code of conduct* (2002, amended June 1, 2010). Retrieved from http://www.apa.org/ethics/code/index.aspx

Armistead, L., Williams, B. B., & Jacob, S. (2011). *Professional ethics for school psychologists: A problem-solving model casebook* (2nd ed.). Bethesda, MD: National Association of School Psychologists.

Bersoff, D. N. (1974). The ethical practice of school psychology. *School Psychology Digest, 3,* 16–21.

Board of Education of the Hendrick Hudson Central School District v. Rowley, 458 U.S. 176, 102 S. Ct. 3034 (1982).

Brown v. Board of Education, 347 U.S. 483 (1954).

Diana v. State Board of Education, Civ. Act. No. C-70-37 (N.D. Cal., 1970, further order, 1973).

Education for All Handicapped Children Act of 1975, Pub. L. No. 94-142, 20 U.S.C. § 1400 et seq. renamed the Elementary and Secondary Education Act of 1965, Pub. L. No. 89-313.

Fagan, T. K., & Wise, P. S. (2007). *School psychology: Past, present, and future* (3rd ed.). Bethesda, MD: National Association of School Psychologists.

Hubsch, A. W. (1989). Education and self-government: The right to education under state constitutional law. *Journal of Law and Education, 18,* 93–133.

Individuals With Disabilities Education Act of 1990, Pub. L. 101-476, 20 U.S.C. Ch. 33.

Individuals With Disabilities Education Improvement Act of 2004, Pub. L. No. 108-446, 20 U.S.C. § 1400 et seq.

Jacob, S., Decker, D. M., & Hartshorne, T. S. (2011). *Ethics and law for school psychologists* (6th ed.). Hoboken, NJ: Wiley.

Kaplan, M. S., Crisci, P. E., & Farling, W. (1974). Editorial comment [Special issue on ethical and legal issues]. *School Psychology Digest, 3*(1).

Martin, R. (1992). *Continuing challenges in special education law* [looseleaf notebook]. Urbana, IL: Carle Media.

Mills v. Board of Education of District of Columbia, 348 F. Supp. 866 (1972); contempt proceedings, 551 Educ. of the Handicapped L. Rep. 643 (D.D.C. 1980).

National Association of School Psychologists. (2010). *Principles for professional ethics.* Bethesda, MD: Author. Retrieved from http://www.nasponline.org

Pennsylvania Association for Retarded Children (P.A.R.C.) v. Commonwealth of Pennsylvania, 334 F. Supp. 1257 (D.C.E.D. Pa. 1971), 343 F. Supp. 279 (E.D. Pa. 1972).

Reschly, D. J., & Bersoff, D. N. (1999). Law and school psychology. In C. R. Reynolds & T. B. Gutkin (Eds.), *Handbook of school psychology* (3rd ed., pp. 1077–1112). New York, NY: Wiley.

Russo, C. J. (2006). *Reutter's the law of public education* (5th ed.). New York, NY: Foundation Press.

Trachtman, G. M. (1974). Ethical issues in school psychology. *School Psychology Digest, 3,* 4–5.

Wisconsin v. Constantineau, 400 U.S. 433 (1971).

Ysseldyke, J., Burns, M., Dawson, P., Kelley, B., Morrison, D., Ortiz, S., . . . Telzrow, C. (2006). *School psychology: A blueprint for training and practice III.* Bethesda, MD: National Association of School Psychologists.

6.3. APA's Guidelines for Test User Qualifications: An Executive Summary

Samuel M. Turner, Stephen T. DeMers, Heather Roberts Fox, and Geoffrey M. Reed

A t the direction of the Council of Representatives of the American Psychological Association (APA), the Task Force on Test User Qualifications (TFTUQ) was established in October 1996 to develop guidelines that inform test users and the general public of the qualifications that the APA considers important for the competent and responsible use of psychological tests. The TFTUQ reviewed the relevant literature related to test user qualifications (see, e.g., Eyde, Moreland, Robertson, Primoff, & Most, 1988, and Tyler, 1986), as well as policy statements developed by the APA (1950, 1992) and other groups both national (e.g., American Association for Counseling and Development, 1988; American Educational Research Association [AERA], APA, & National Council on Measurement in Education [NCME], 1999) and international (British Psychological Society, 1995, 1996; International Test Commission, 2000). The task force then developed a set of comprehensive guidelines and solicited comments from numerous individuals and groups involved with test use both within and outside the APA. The final report of the TFTUQ was approved by the APA Council of Representatives in August 2000.

. . .

From "APA's Guidelines for Test User Qualifications: An Executive Summary," by S. M. Turner, S. T. DeMers, H. R. Fox, and G. M. Reed, 2001, *American Psychologist, 56,* pp. 1099–1113. Copyright 2001 by the American Psychological Association.

Editor's Note. This article is an executive summary of a larger report that was adopted by the American Psychological Association's Council of Representatives on August 6, 2000. To obtain a copy of the full *Report of the Task Force on Test User Qualifications,* contact the Science Directorate, American Psychological Association, 750 First Street, NE, Washington, DC 20002-4242; phone number: (202) 336-6000.

The full report was developed by the American Psychological Association (APA) Task Force on Test User Qualifications (TFTUQ). The TFTUQ cochairs were Stephen T. DeMers, EdD, and Samuel M. Turner, PhD. The TFTUQ members included Marcia Andberg, PhD; William Foote, PhD; Leaetta Hough, PhD; Robert Ivnik, PhD; Scott Meier, PhD; Kevin Moreland, PhD (deceased); and Celiane M. Rey-Casserly, PhD. The TFTUQ wishes to acknowledge Stephen DeMers, EdD; Nadine Lambert, PhD; and Leona Aiken, PhD, for their role in the creation of the task force. It was their foresight regarding the need for an official policy on qualifications necessary for the competent use of tests that brought this motion to the APA Council of Representatives. In addition, the TFTUQ extends thanks to Wayne Camara, PhD; Rodney Lowman, PhD; Karen O'Brien, PhD; and many other APA colleagues for the consultation and assistance they gave to this project; to the Board of Professional Affairs, the Board of Scientific Affairs, the Committee on Legal Issues, and especially the Committee on Psychological Tests and Assessment for their kind support; to Dianne Maranto and Dianne Schneider, PhD, for staff support from the Science Directorate; and to Robert Walsh and Georgia Sargeant for staff support from the Practice Directorate.

TEST USER QUALIFICATIONS IN SPECIFIC CONTEXTS

. . .

The sections that follow describe five major contexts in which tests are commonly used: employment, education (both individual and large-scale testing), vocational and career counseling, health care, and forensic assessment. Although there may be other contexts that require specific competencies, the test user qualifications (including appropriate training and supervision) important in the major contexts where tests are used are discussed below.

Employment Context

Many employers use tests as part of the assessment process to develop work-related information and recommendations or decisions about people who work for them or are seeking employment with them. Test users in this context should have not only the qualifications identified as core knowledge and skills but also an understanding of the work setting, the work itself, and the worker characteristics required of the work situation. They should strive to know what skills, abilities, or other individual difference characteristics enable people to perform effectively (as defined in a variety of ways) in a particular work setting. Test users should consider the strengths and weaknesses of different methods for determining the human requirements of the work situation and how to conduct such job, work, or practice analyses. They also should consider and, where appropriate, obtain legal advice about employment law and relevant court decisions (see Dunnette & Hough, 1990, 1991, 1992, 1994; Guion, 1998).
. . .

Educational Context

The results of psychological tests often serve as relevant information to guide educational decisions about both students and programs. Psychological tests are used in a variety of educational settings, including preschools, elementary and secondary schools, higher education, technical schools, business training programs, counseling centers, health and mental health settings that offer educational services, and educational consulting practices. Psychological tests are typically used to acquire information about students to make informed decisions about such issues as student admissions and placement, educational programming, student performance, and teacher or school effectiveness.

On an individual level, psychological tests are often used to describe a student's learning or behavioral strengths and weaknesses. The results may then be used to develop educational interventions, to determine appropriate educational placements (e.g., special education, gifted education, magnet school program, or alternative educational setting), or as part of clinical diagnostic assessment to guide therapeutic services.

Assessment of groups of individuals, often called large-scale testing, typically addresses questions about educational programs or policies. Decision makers may aggregate results from psychological tests and use this information to evaluate program effectiveness and to develop recommendations for changes to educational programs or systems. Test users in these cases may use standardized tests or nonstandardized procedures (e.g., performance events or portfolios of student work) to obtain information about cognitive ability or academic achievement levels of a group of students (Fuchs & Fuchs, 1990).

Test user qualifications that have particular relevance in educational settings include the representativeness of the test sample, attention to language and cultural diversity, and the use of cut scores in selection for special programs. Test users also should understand the cognitive and emotional factors that affect student learning, as well as the social and political factors that affect schools as learning environments. Those who use psychological tests in social institutions like schools should be particularly skilled at communicating the results of testing to many different audiences, including educational decision makers, teachers, students, parents, and the public.

. . .

Career and Vocational Counseling Context

Psychological testing in the career and vocational counseling context is used to help people make appropriate educational, occupational, retirement, and recreational choices and to assess difficulties that impede the career decision-making process. Career and vocational counselors integrate their knowledge of career demands with information about beliefs, attitudes, values, personalities, mental health, and abilities, with the goal of promoting beneficial career development, life planning, and decision making. The individual's self-knowledge about values, strengths, weaknesses, motivation, psychological characteristics, and interests also is relevant.

Testing can provide persons with knowledge about their work-related and avocational interests, their abilities, and their values and can help them understand how these fit into the existing opportunities and requirements of the workplace and into their leisure activities. Test users should strive to understand how individuals' particular interests, values, abilities, and skills relate to their choice of work and leisure activities. Test users also should have substantive knowledge in related areas of psychology, such as adolescent and adult development, personality, and psychopathology, as well as detailed and current knowledge of measurement questions involved with assessing interests, abilities, personality dimensions, and values.

Test users also should make every effort to be knowledgeable about types of work settings, work cultures and values, and the characteristics and requirements of types of jobs. They should strive to integrate the results of multiple measures from a number of different domains with their knowledge of vocational theories (Osipow & Fitzgerald, 1996) and career taxonomies (Holland, 1997; Lowman, 1991).

Test users identify and work with individual difference and systemic variables that may influence the person–environment fit. Such factors include the individual's family system, gender, ethnicity, cultural background, physical ability, SES, and psychological problems. Test users should be able to recognize and work not only with the problems explicitly presented by the test taker but also with other problems, including underlying emotional difficulties or environmental impediments that could affect the way the test taker uses test results.

Often, the person seeking career or leisure counseling is experiencing a life transition that brings additional personal, developmental, and emotional stress. In addition, such individuals may struggle with emotional problems that make deciding on a career difficult. To deal effectively with such complex mixtures of career, developmental, and emotional concerns, vocational test users should have qualifications similar to those required in the health care context (discussed below).

. . .

Health Care Context

Health care is the provision of services aimed at enhancing the physical or mental well-being of individuals or at dealing with behaviors, emotions, or issues that are associated with suffering, disease, disablement, illness, risk of harm, or risk of loss of independence. Health care assessment commonly occurs in private practice, rehabilitation, medical or psychiatric inpatient or outpatient settings, schools, EAPs, and other settings that address health care needs. Psychological tests are used as part of the assessment process to develop health-related information and recommendations or decisions. Those who use tests for this purpose should have thorough grounding both in the core knowledge and skills enumerated earlier and in the specialized knowledge, training, or experience of specific substantive areas of health care.

In the health care context, psychological test data are typically used to augment information gathered from other sources (e.g., patient and collateral interviews, behavioral observations, and laboratory results). Health care providers who use psychological tests should strive to effectively integrate results from multiple tests and sources of information. Psychological test users should strive to understand how the nature of the setting (e.g., psychiatric hospital) and the characteristics of test takers (e.g., those who have a physical illness or disability or who are on medication) might affect the process of test administration, the results, and the interpretation. Test users should strive to communicate the technical aspects of their findings to other professionals as well as to health care consumers in language that is appropriate and understandable to each.

. . .

Forensic Context

In forensic settings, psychological tests are used to gather information and develop recommendations about people who are involved in legal proceedings.

Test users in forensic settings should possess a working knowledge of the functioning of the administrative, correctional, or court system in which they practice. They should strive to be familiar with the statutory, administrative, or case law in the specific legal context where the testing occurs or, where appropriate, obtain legal advice on the pertinent laws. They should strive to communicate test results in a way that is useful for the finder of fact (i.e., the judge, the administrative body, or the jury). This includes communicating verbally with lawyers, writing formal reports, and giving sworn testimony in deposition or court.

This section addresses those who use clinical, rehabilitation, and neuropsychological tests in legal contexts, as well as those who believe that their test data will serve as a foundation for legal consultation or testimony. Thus, in addition to the core qualifications identified earlier, the qualifications described above for test users in health care contexts typically apply to test users in forensic settings. This section does not address test use by those who use psychological tests to conduct research in applied areas of forensics, such as memory, social psychology, or human factors. Nor does it apply to those who use tests in applied areas, such as clinical, rehabilitation, or neuropsychological practice or industrial and organizational or educational psychology, and who may be asked to provide consultation or testimony about work with their clients based on their training, education, or experience.

Those who use tests for forensic purposes should possess substantive knowledge in areas of psychology related to the forensic issues. For example, in correctional or criminal settings, knowledge about violence, criminality, and the relationship of psychopathology to those behaviors and activities is germane. Similarly, when assessing families in child custody or parental rights cases, it is important for test users to understand family dynamics, parenting, and different forms of child custody (APA Committee on Professional Practice and Standards, 1994).

Assessments for forensic purposes often occur in outpatient, inpatient, and correctional settings. Test users should strive to be knowledgeable about the effects of each of these settings on test administration and interpretation.
. . .

A LOOK FORWARD

The psychological testing process has undergone significant technological change over the past few decades. The use of computers to administer tests and to score and interpret test results is already an important part of everyday testing. Emerging technologies of the Internet and other innovations that expand applications across vast distances may significantly alter the relationship of the test user, the test taker, and the consumer of testing results.

Some of the positive changes resulting from these new technologies include wider availability, greater accuracy, and increased accessibility of tests. Continuing improvements in the development of interpretive algorithms and expert systems are leading to diminishing concurrent human oversight of the testing process. This technology will simplify some aspects of the assessment process. As the application of new technology to the testing arena produces improved but more complex testing services, it may become necessary for the knowledge and skills articulated in this article to be supplemented with increased technological sophistication. Ironically, this increased complexity may mandate more extensive education and training in the fundamentals of test use. The knowledge and skills articulated here will become even more important as test users are required to distinguish technology-based style from science-based substance.

REFERENCES

American Association for Counseling and Development. (1988). *Responsibilities of users of standardized tests.* Washington, DC: Author.

American Educational Research Association, American Psychological Association, & National Council on Measurement in Education. (1999). *Standards for educational and psychological testing.* Washington, DC: American Educational Research Association.

American Psychological Association. (1950). Ethical standards for the distribution of psychological tests and diagnostic aids. *American Psychologist, 5,* 620–626.

American Psychological Association. (1992). Ethical principles of psychologists and code of conduct. *American Psychologist, 47,* 1597–1611.

American Psychological Association Committee on Professional Practice and Standards. (1994). Guidelines for child custody evaluations in divorce proceedings. *American Psychologist, 49,* 677–680.

British Psychological Society. (1995). *Certificate statement register—Competencies in occupational testing: General information pack (Level A).* Leicester, England: Author.

British Psychological Society. (1996). *Certificate statement register—Competencies in occupational testing: General information pack (Level B).* Leicester, England: Author.

Dunnette, M. D., & Hough, L. M. (Eds.). (1990). *Handbook of industrial and organizational psychology (Vol. 1).* New York: Rand McNally.

Dunnette, M. D., & Hough, L. M. (Eds.). (1991). *Handbook of industrial and organizational psychology (Vol. 2).* New York: Rand McNally.

Dunnette, M. D., & Hough, L. M. (Eds.). (1992). *Handbook of industrial and organizational psychology (Vol. 3).* New York: Rand McNally.

Dunnette, M. D., & Hough, L. M. (Eds.). (1994). *Handbook of industrial and organizational psychology (Vol. 4).* New York: Rand McNally.

Eyde, L. E., Moreland, K. L., Robertson, G. J., Primoff, E. S., & Most, R. B. (1988). *Test user qualifications: A data-based approached to promoting good test use.* Washington, DC: American Psychological Association.

Fuchs, L. S., & Fuchs, D. (1990). Curriculum-based assessment. In C. R. Reynolds & R. W. Kamphaus (Eds.), *Handbook of psychological and educational assessment of children* (pp. 435–455). New York: Guilford Press.

Guion, R. M. (1998). *Assessment, measurement, and prediction for personnel decisions.* Hillsdale, NJ: Erlbaum.

Holland, J. L. (1997). *Making vocational choices: A theory of vocational personalities and work environments* (3rd ed.). Odessa, FL: Psychological Assessment Resources.

International Test Commission. (2000). *International guidelines for test use: Version 2000.* Retrieved October 18, 2001, from http://cwis.kub.nl/~fsw_1/itc/itcv2000.htm

Lowman, R. L. (1991). *The clinical practice of career assessment.* Washington, DC: American Psychological Association.

Osipow, S. H., & Fitzgerald, L. F. (1996). *Theories of career development*. Boston: Allyn & Bacon.

Tyler, B. (1986). The use of tests by psychologists: Report on a survey of British Psychological Society members. *Bulletin of the International Test Commission, 22*, 7–18.

COMMENTARY: As the various helping professions continue to compete—however decorously, as least on the surface—for their portions of the ever-shrinking mental health dollar, they cast covetous eyes upon functions previously reserved, by law and by custom, to a specific discipline. Thus it was that psychologists embarked upon a quest for what were once called "prescription privileges" and what is now called "prescriptive authority," and that psychiatrists and mental health counselors have attempted to administer, score, and interpret the results of psychological tests.

Just as gains in prescriptive authority for psychologists have opened up new avenues of legal and ethical liability, psychiatrists and mental health counselors are finding, when attempting to conduct psychological testing on their own, that the legal profession is increasingly aware of these issues. Trial attorneys are eyeing standard of practice issues in malpractice lawsuits and board complaints, and fashioning—with the assistance of psychologist trial consultants—ever more technically pointed cross-examination questions to attack test-based forensic testimony in civil and criminal proceedings.

The following references are recommended for those interested in further investigation of how members of other helping professions are attempting to incorporate psychological testing into their own palette of clinical contributions, and the attendant legal and ethical issues.

Baranoski, M. V. (2018). Psychological testing in forensic psychiatry. In L. H. Gold & R. L. Frierson (Eds.), *The American Psychiatric Association Publishing textbook of forensic psychiatry* (3rd ed., pp. 55–74). Arlington, VA: American Psychiatric Association Publishing.

Dattilio, F. M., Sadoff, R. L., Drogin, E. Y., & Gutheil, T. G. (2011). Should forensic psychiatrists conduct psychological testing? *Journal of Psychiatry & Law, 39*, 477–491. http://dx.doi.org/10.1177/009318531103900308

Dattilio, F. M., Tresco, K. E., & Siegel, A. (2007). An empirical survey on psychological testing and the use of the term psychological: Turf battles or clinical necessity? *Professional Psychology: Research and Practice, 38*, 682–689. http://dx.doi.org/10.1037/0735-7028.38.6.682

Neukrug, E., Peterson, C. H., Conner, M., & Lomas, G. I. (2013). A national survey of assessment instruments taught by counselor educators. *Counselor Education and Supervision, 52*, 207–221. http://dx.doi.org/10.1002/j.1556-6978.2013.00038.x

Peterson, C. H., Lomas, G. I., Neukrug, E. S., & Bonner, M. W. (2014). Assessment use by counselors in the United States: Implications for policy and practice. *Journal of Counseling & Development, 92*, 90–98. http://dx.doi.org/10.1002/j.1556-6676.2014.00134.x

6.4. Strategies for Private Practitioners Coping With Subpoenas or Compelled Testimony for Client/Patient Records or Test Data or Test Materials

Committee on Legal Issues

In response to a large number of inquiries by psychologists faced with subpoenas or compelled court testimony concerning Client/Patient records or test data, manuals, protocols, and other test information, the American Psychological Association's (APA) Committee on Legal Issues prepared this article. It identifies legal issues that may arise from such subpoenas and similar legal demands, and it suggests strategies that might be considered in the event such a subpoena or demand is received. This document is not intended to establish any standards of care or conduct for practitioners; rather, it addresses this general question: What strategies may be available to psychologists in private practice for responding to subpoenas or compelled court testimony concerning Client/Patient records, test data, test manuals, test protocols, or other test information?

All citizens are required, as a general principle of law, to provide information necessary for deciding issues before a court. From the perspective of the legal system, the more relevant the available information is to the trier of fact (i.e., judge or jury), the fairer the decision. Statutes, rules of civil and criminal

From "Strategies for Private Practitioners Coping With Subpoenas or Compelled Testimony for Client/Patient Records or Test Data or Test Materials," by the Committee on Legal Issues, 2016, *Professional Psychology: Research and Practice*, 47, pp. 1–11. Copyright 2016 by the American Psychological Association.

Editor's Note. This document does not provide legal advice, nor is it intended to be or to substitute for the advice of an attorney. Relevant law varies substantially from state to state and context to context. Psychologists receiving a subpoena or other legal process that requires or is likely to require revelation of Client/Patient records or test data, manuals, protocols, or other test information are encouraged to consult legal counsel, who can review the pertinent law and facts and provide appropriate legal assistance.

This document was initially published in 1996 and revised in 2006 to provide updated references to the most recent version of the Ethics Code as well as to laws that have come into effect since the first document was published. The current revision was deemed necessary to develop a new section addressing communications with judges and attorneys. The Committee on Legal Issues (COLI) and the Office of General Counsel wish to thank the members of COLI who participated in this revision as well as central office staff for their time and effort in drafting and producing this version of the document. In addition, COLI and the Office of General Counsel wish to extend special appreciation to the representatives from APA's Committee on Professional Practice Standards, the Board of Professional Affairs, the Committee for the Advancement of Professional Practice, the Committee on Psychological Tests and Assessments, and the Ethics Committee for their valuable input and review.

procedure, and rules of evidence have established the procedures for the transmittal of such information. In order to obtain this material, the court may issue *subpoenas* (legal commands to appear to provide testimony) or *subpoenas duces tecum* (legal commands to appear and bring along specific documents). Alternatively, the court may issue a *court order* to provide testimony or produce documents. A subpoena issued by an attorney under court rules, requesting testimony or documents, even if not signed by a judge, requires a timely response, but it may be modified or quashed (i.e., made void or invalid).

It is important to differentiate responding to a subpoena from disclosing confidential information. Unless the issuing attorney or court excuses the psychologist, it will be necessary to respond to a subpoena, that is, to be at a particular place at a particular time (with records if the subpoena is a subpoena duces tecum). Responding to the subpoena, however, does not necessarily entail disclosing confidential information. In order to disclose confidential information, a psychologist will need to ensure that the conditions for disclosing confidential information, such as the Client/Patient's consent or a judge's order or other legal mandate, are met, in addition to having a valid subpoena. Thus, while a subpoena requires a response, a subpoena alone will generally not be sufficient to warrant a disclosure of confidential information. However, once a court order for testimony or documents is issued and any attempt (made in a timely manner) to have the court vacate or modify its order has been unsuccessful, a psychologist may be held in contempt of court if he or she fails to comply.

The demands of the legal system sometimes conflict with the responsibility of psychologists to maintain the confidentiality of Client/Patient records. This responsibility arises from tenets of good clinical practice, ethical standards, professional licensing laws, and other applicable statutes and legal precedent. In many contexts, the Client/Patient material generated in the course of a professional relationship may also fall under an evidentiary privilege, which protects such information from judicial scrutiny. Most state and federal jurisdictions recognize a patient privilege that allows the Client/Patient to prevent confidential material conveyed to a psychologist from being communicated to others in legal settings although there are variations from state to state and between state and federal definitions. In most jurisdictions, the privilege belongs to the Client/Patient, not to the therapist. The psychologist has a responsibility to maintain confidentiality and to assert the psychotherapist–patient privilege unless the Client/Patient has explicitly waived privilege or signed a valid release, unless a legally recognized exception to privilege exists, or unless the court orders the psychologist to turn over the Client/Patient's information.

The clinical record, any separately kept psychotherapy notes, Client/Patient information forms, billing records, and other such information usually may be turned over to the court with appropriate authorization by the Client/Patient or with a court order. (Psychologists who need to comply with HIPAA [Health Insurance Portability and Accountability Act] would need a HIPAA-compliant authorization form to release such information, and a separate authorization for release of psychotherapy notes. The risk of disclosure through subpoena or court order should be disclosed to Client/Patients in the informed consent document and discussion.) Psychological test material and test data can present a more complicated situation. Although a Client/Patient's test data may have to be released in response to a subpoena, the disclosure of test materials (i.e., manuals, instruments, protocols, and test questions) may require the additional safeguard of a court order because the inappropriate disclosure of test materials may seriously impair the security and threaten the validity of the test and its value as a measurement tool.

Psychologists have numerous ethical, professional, and legal obligations that touch on the release of Client/Patient records, test data, and other information in the legal context. Many such obligations may favor disclosure, including, in particular, the general obligation of all citizens to give truthful and complete testimony in courts of law when subpoenaed to do so. But there are often conflicting duties and principles that favor withholding such information. These may include obligations to (a) Client/Patients or other individuals who receive treatment and/or are assessed or administered psychological tests (e.g., privileged or confidential communications that may include Client/Patient responses to test items); (b) the public (e.g., to avoid public dissemination of test items, questions, protocols, or other test information that could adversely affect the integrity and continued validity of tests); (c) test publishers (e.g., contractual obligations between the psychologist and test publishers not to disclose test information; obligations under the copyright laws); and (d) other third parties (e.g., employers). It merits mention that a special type of third-party obligation may arise in forensic contexts: If, for example, a psychologist performed work for an attorney, it is important to investigate whether that work is protected from disclosure under the attorney work product privilege. The aforementioned obligations may, at times, conflict with one another. Psychologists must identify and seek to reconcile their obligations. For more on these obligations, see APA's "Ethical Principles of Psychologists and Code of Conduct" (APA, 2010), hereinafter referred to as the APA Ethics Code. . .

There are specific settings (e.g., educational, institutional, employment) in which the legal or ethical obligations of psychologists as they relate to disclosure of Client/Patient records or test information present special problems. This article does not purport to address disclosure issues in these special contexts, nor does it attempt to resolve dilemmas faced by psychologists in reconciling legal and ethical obligations.

STRATEGIES FOR DEALING WITH SUBPOENAS

Determine Whether the Request for Information Carries the Force of Law

It must first be determined whether a psychologist has, in fact, received a legally valid demand for disclosure of sensitive test data and Client/Patient records. If a demand is not legally enforceable for any reason, then the psychologist has no legal obligation to comply with it and may have no legal obligation even to respond. A subpoena to produce documents generally must allow sufficient time to respond to the demand and provide for some time within which the opposing side may move to quash such a demand. Without this allowed time period, the subpoena may not be valid. Even a demand that claims to be legally enforceable may not be. For example, the court issuing the subpoena may not have jurisdiction over the psychologist or his or her records (e.g., a subpoena issued in one state may not be legally binding on a psychologist residing and working in a different state). Or, the subpoena may not have been properly served on the psychologist (e.g., some states may require service in person or by certified mail or that a subpoena for such records be accompanied by a special court order). It is advisable that a psychologist consult with an attorney in making such a determination.[1]

If the psychologist concludes that the demand is legally valid, then some formal response to the attorney or court will be required—either compliance with or opposition to the demand, in whole or in part. A psychologist's obligations in responding to a valid subpoena are not necessarily the same as those under a court order (see section titled File a Motion to Quash the Subpoena or File a Protective Order). The next step, in most cases, may involve contacting the psychologist's Client/Patient. However, the psychologist may wish to consider grounds for opposing or limiting production of the demanded information before contacting the Client/Patient so that the Client/Patient can more fully understand his or her options (see section titled Possible Grounds for Opposing or Limiting Production of Client/Patient Records or Test Data).

Contact the Client/Patient

The Client/Patient to whom requested records pertain often has a legally protected interest in preserving the confidentiality of the records. If, therefore, a psychologist receives a subpoena or advance notice that he or she may be

---

[1]It is important to recognize that the client's attorney, or the attorney who issues the subpoena, is not the psychologist's attorney and may represent interests different from those of the psychologist. Thus, the psychologist may not be able to rely upon the information provided by that attorney. Psychologists can find attorneys with experience representing psychologists via their states' bar associations, their states' psychological association, colleagues, and local attorneys.

Fees for consultation with or representation by an attorney may be substantial. If consultation with an attorney becomes necessary to protect the interests and privileges of the client, then the practitioner may wish to clarify with his or her client who will be responsible for such legal fees. In some cases, malpractice carriers will authorize legal consultation free of charge. During an initial consultation, psychologists should ask an attorney the following questions before hiring him or her: (a) How many psychologists or other medical professionals has the attorney represented? (b) Is the attorney familiar with the state's psychology licensing statute and ethical code? (c) How many psychologists or other medical professionals has the attorney represented in licensing actions/ethical complaints? (d) Is the attorney familiar with the federal HIPAA law and the state's confidentiality statutes? In addition, the psychologist should not hesitate to ask other relevant questions about fees, retainers, and the like.

required to divulge Client/Patient records or test data, the psychologist may, when appropriate, discuss the implications of the demand with the Client/Patient (or his or her legal guardian). Also when appropriate and with the Client/Patient's valid consent, the psychologist may consult with the Client/Patient's attorney. The discussion with the Client/Patient will inform the Client/Patient which information has been demanded, the purpose of the demand, the entities or individuals to whom the information is to be provided, and the possible scope of further disclosure by those entities or individuals. Following such a discussion, a legally competent Client/Patient or the Client/Patient's legal guardian may choose to consent to production of the data. Generally, it is legally required to have such consent in writing, for clarity and if there is a need for documentation in the future. Written consent may avoid future conflicts or legal entanglements with the Client/Patient over the release of confidential tests or other records pertaining to the Client/Patient. The Client/Patient's consent may not, however, resolve the potential confidentiality claims of third parties (such as test publishers). For more information, see APA Ethics Code, Ethical Standards, Section 4 (APA, 2010), and *Standards for Educational and Psychological Testing* (American Educational Research Association, APA, & National Council on Measurement in Education, 2014).

It also merits emphasis to a Client/Patient that when agreeing to release information requested in a subpoena, he or she cannot specify or limit which information is released, rather, the entire record (e.g., psychotherapy notes, billing records administrative notes) will be available. The scope of the release may be the subject of negotiation among attorneys, however, and if the psychologist believes that a release would harm the Client/Patient, the psychologist should voice his or her concerns and object to the release on that basis.

Negotiate With the Requester

If a Client/Patient does not consent to release of the requested information, the psychologist (often through counsel) may seek to prevent disclosure through discussions with legal counsel for the requesting party. The psychologist's position in such discussions may be bolstered by legal arguments against disclosure, including the psychologist's duties under rules regarding psychotherapist–patient privilege. These rules often allow the psychologist to assert privilege on behalf of the Client/Patient in the absence of a specific release or court order. (Some possible arguments are outlined in the section titled Possible Grounds for Opposing or Limiting Production of Client/Patient Records or Test Data.) Such negotiations may explore whether there are ways to achieve the requesting party's objectives without divulging confidential information, for example, through disclosure of nonconfidential materials or submission of an affidavit by the psychologist disclosing nonconfidential information. Negotiation may also be used as a strategy to avoid compelled testimony in court or by deposition. In short, negotiation can be explored as a possible means of avoiding the wholesale release of confidential test or Client/Patient information—release that may not be in the best interests of the Client/Patient, the public, or the profession and that may not even be relevant to the issues before the court. Such an option could be explored in consultation with the psychologist's attorney or the Client/Patient's attorney.

File a Motion to Quash the Subpoena or File a Protective Order

If negotiation is not successful, it may be necessary to file a motion for relief from the obligations imposed by the demand for production of the confidential records. In many jurisdictions, the possible motions include a motion to quash the subpoena, in whole or in part, or a motion for a protective order. Filing such a motion may require the assistance of counsel, representing either the psychologist or the psychologist's Client/Patient.

Courts are generally more receptive to a motion to quash or a motion for protective order if it is filed by the Client/Patient about whom information sought (who would be defending his or her own interests) rather than a psychologist who, in essence, would be seeking to protect the rights of the client/Patient or other third parties. The psychologist may wish to determine initially whether the Client/Patient's lawyer is inclined to seek to quash a subpoena or to seek a protective order and, if so, may wish to provide assistance to the Client/Patient's attorney in this regard. If the Client/Patient has refused to consent to disclosure of the information, his or her attorney may be willing to take the lead in opposing the subpoena.

A *motion to quash* is a formal application made to a court or judge for purposes of having a subpoena vacated or declared invalid. Grounds may exist for asserting that the subpoena or request for testimony should be quashed, in whole or in part. For example, the information sought may be protected by the therapist–Client/Patient privilege and therefore may not be subject to discovery, or it may not be relevant to the issues before the court (see section titled Possible Grounds for Opposing or Limiting Production of Client/Patient Records or Test Data). This strategy may be used alone or in combination with a motion for a protective order.

A *motion for a protective order* anticipates production of material responsive to the subpoena but seeks an order or decree from the court that protects against the untoward consequences of disclosing information. A protective order can be tailored to meet the legitimate interests of the Client/Patient and other parties such as test publishers and the public. The focus of this strategy first foremost is to prevent or limit those to whom produced information is disclosed and the use of sensitive Client/Patient and test information. The tective order—and the motion—may include any of the elements listed.

Generally, the motion may state that the psychologist is ethically not to produce the confidential records or test data or to testify about unless compelled to do so by the court or with the consent of the Client. It may include a request that the court consider the psychologist's ob to adhere to federal requirements (e.g., the Health Insurance Portabi

Accountability Act of 1996 [HIPAA]) and to protect the interests of the Client/ Patient, the interests of third parties (e.g., test publishers or others), and the public's interest in preserving the integrity and continued validity of the tests themselves. This may help sensitize the court to the potential adverse effects of dissemination. The motion might also attempt to provide suggestions, such as the following, to the court about ways to minimize the adverse consequences of disclosure if the court is inclined to require production at all:

1. Suggest that the court direct the psychologist to provide test data only to another appropriately qualified professional designated by the court or by the party seeking such information. The manual for the test should specify the credentials of the professional who is qualified to use it.

2. Suggest that the court limit the use of Client/Patient records or test data to prevent wide dissemination. For example, the court might order that the information be delivered to the court, be kept under seal, be used solely for the purposes of the litigation, and that all copies of the data be returned to the psychologist under seal after the litigation is terminated. The order might also provide that the requester must prevent or limit the disclosure of the information to third parties.

3. Suggest that the court limit the categories of information that must be produced. For example, Client/Patient records may contain confidential information about a third party, such as a spouse, who may have independent interests in maintaining confidentiality, and such data may be of minimal or no relevance to the issues before the court. The court should limit its production order to exclude such information.

4. Suggest that the court determine for itself, through in camera proceedings (i.e., a nonpublic hearing or a review by the judge in chambers), whether the use of the Client/Patient records or test data is relevant to the issues before the court or whether it might be insulated from disclosure, in whole or in part, by the therapist–Client/Patient privilege or another privilege (e.g., attorney–Client/Patient privilege).

5. Suggest that the court deny or limit the demand because it is unduly burdensome on the psychologist (see, e.g., Federal Rule of Civil Procedure 45(c)).

6. Suggest that the court shield from production "psychotherapy notes" if the psychologist keeps separate psychotherapy notes as defined by the Privacy Rule (see Security and Privacy, 2015). . . .

PSYCHOLOGISTS' TESTIMONY

If a psychologist is asked to disclose confidential information during questioning at a deposition, he or she may refuse to answer the question only if the information is privileged. If there is a reasonable basis for asserting a privilege, the psychologist may refuse to provide test data or Client/Patient records until so ordered by the court. A psychologist who refuses to answer questions without a reasonable basis may be penalized by the court, including the obligation to pay the requesting parties' costs and fees in obtaining court enforcement of the subpoena. For these reasons, it is advisable that a psychologist be represented by his or her own counsel at the deposition. A lawyer may advise the psychologist, on the record, when a question seeks confidential information; such on-the-record advice will help protect the psychologist from the adverse legal consequences of erroneous disclosures or erroneous refusals to disclose.

Similarly, if the request for confidential information arises for the first time during courtroom testimony, the psychologist may assert a privilege and refuse to answer unless directed to do so by the court. The law in this area is somewhat unsettled. Thus, it may be advisable for him or her to consult an attorney before testifying.

POSSIBLE GROUNDS FOR OPPOSING OR LIMITING PRODUCTION OF CLIENT/PATIENT RECORDS OR TEST DATA

The following options may or may not be available under the facts of a particular case and/or a particular jurisdiction for resisting a demand to produce confidential information, records, or test data (see Appendix C):

1. The court does not have jurisdiction over the psychologist, the Client/Patient records, or the test data, or the psychologist did not receive a legally sufficient demand (e.g., improper service) for production of records or test data testimony.

2. The psychologist does not have custody or control of the records or test data that are sought, because, for example, they belong not to the psychologist but to his or her employer.

3. The therapist–Client/Patient privilege insulates the records or test data from disclosure. The rationale for the privilege, recognized in many states, is that the openness necessary for effective therapy requires that Client/Patients have an expectation that all records of therapy, contents of therapeutic disclosures, and test data will remain confidential. Disclosure would be a serious invasion of the Client/Patient's privacy. The psychologist is under an ethical obligation to protect the client's reasonable expectations of confidentiality. See APA Ethics Code, Ethical Standards, Section 4 (APA, 2010). There are important exceptions to this protection that negate the privilege. For example, if the Client/former client is a party to the litigation and has raised his/her mental state as an issue in the proceeding, the client may have waived the psychotherapist–patient privilege. This varies by jurisdiction with most jurisdictions holding a broad patient-litigant exception to privilege, with a few construing the patient-litigant exception much more narrowly.

It is important that the psychologist be aware of the law in the relevant jurisdiction, because this may ultimately control the issue about release of (otherwise) confidential client information.

In this circumstance, the fact that a client who is a party to a legal case does not want to consent to release of information may not ultimately be dispositive on the issue. In such a case, the psychologist should discuss the issue of potential patient-litigant exception with the client's attorney, to determine if the records will need to be turned over due to the exception and to obtain any needed authorizations from the client.[2]

4. The information sought is not relevant to the issues before the court, or the scope of the demand for information is overbroad in reaching information not relevant to the issues before the court, including irrelevant information pertaining to third parties such as a spouse.

5. Public dissemination of test information such as manuals, protocols, and so forth may harm the public interest because it may affect responses of future test populations. This effect could result in the loss of valuable assessment tools to the detriment of both the public and the profession of psychology.

6. Test publishers have an interest in the protection of test information, and the psychologist may have a contractual or other legal obligation (e.g., copyright laws) not to disclose such information. Such contractual claims, coupled with concerns about test data devolving into the public domain and thereby, diminishing its usefulness to the courts, may justify issuance of a protective order against dissemination of a test instrument or protocols.[3]

7. Psychologists have an ethical obligation to protect the integrity and security of test information and data including protecting the intellectual property (copyright) and unauthorized test disclosure, and to avoid misuse of assessment techniques and data. Psychologists are also ethically obligated to take

---

[2] A psychologist's obligation to maintain confidentiality may not apply under certain legally recognized exceptions to the therapist—patient privilege, including, but not limited to, situations such as the following: when child or elder abuse is involved; cases involving involuntary commitment evaluations; court-ordered evaluations; when clients raise their emotional condition as a basis for a legal claim or defense; or when the client presents an imminent danger to himself or herself or the community. Exceptions may depend on jurisdiction and the facts of a particular situation. Thus, the most prudent course of action may be for the psychologist to consult with an attorney.

[3] Most test publishers have policies that address the disclosure of test data and materials. Very often, such policies can be found on a test publisher's website, along with other information such as terms of purchasing psychological tests, the publisher's position on legal aspects of disclosing test data and test materials, and contact information for the test publisher's privacy officer or general counsel. Reviewing a particular test publisher's website can be very helpful when psychologists are considering disclosing test data or test materials, especially when the disclosure potentially involves non-psychologists. Psychologists should be aware that the information on test publisher websites may or may not be consistent with APA policy, may not reflect exceptions that apply in certain states, and APA takes no position on the accuracy of legal statements or claims found on such websites.

reasonable steps to prevent others from misusing such information. See APA Ethics Code, Ethical Standards, Section 2 (APA, 2010).

8. Refer to ethical and legal obligations of psychologists as provided for under ethics codes; professional standards; state, federal, or local laws; or regulatory agencies.

9. Some court rules allow the party receiving the subpoena to object to the subpoena's demand or ask that the demand be limited on the basis that it imposes an undue burden on the recipient (see, e.g., Rule 45(c) of the Federal Rules of Civil Procedure, 2014).

10. Ultimately, the judge's ruling controls in a court. Psychologists who are not violating human rights and who take reasonable steps to follow Standard 1.02 of the Ethics Code and inform the Court of their requirements under the Ethics Code will not be subject to disciplinary procedures for complying with a court order directing to produce information.

APPENDIX C
DISCLOSURE ISSUES

The following steps may be taken, as appropriate:

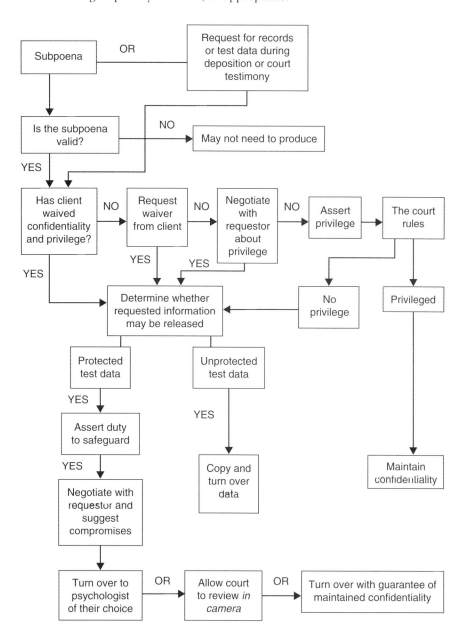

REFERENCES

American Educational Research Association, American Psychological Association, & National Council on Measurement in Education. (2014). *Standards for educational and psychological testing.* Washington, DC: Authors.

American Psychological Association. (2010). *Ethical principles of psychologists and code of conduct* (2002, Amended June 1, 2010). Retrieved from http://www.apa.org/ethics/code/index.aspx

Federal Rules of Civil Procedure, Title VI, Rule 45(c), 28 U.S.C. (2014).

Health Insurance Portability and Accountability Act of 1996, Pub. L. No. 104-191, 110 Stat. 1936.

Security and Privacy, 45 C.F.R. § 164.501 (2015).

COMMENTARY: Requests for records, test data, and test materials are typically precipitated by one or the other of two broad sets of circumstances. "More benign" requests may be filed by such entities as new mental health service providers wishing to better understand clients/patients, social services agencies reviewing an application for benefits, and schools contemplating special education placement or other accommodations pending a determination of disability status.

By contrast, "less benign" requests may be filed by such entities as opposing counsel seeking to undercut a completed forensic psychological evaluation in civil or criminal matters, clients/patients questioning the results of their own evaluations (or hoping to gain an advantage in child custody proceedings based on the results of their children's evaluations), and licensing boards conducting an investigation into the psychologist's adherence to applicable standards of practice. Compliance in some instances is mandatory and virtually automatic, whereas in others, ethical and legal obligations will require a series of stepwise interactions with multiple parties.

The following references are recommended for those interested in further investigation of the fashion in which psychologists may be requested and/or required to disclose client/patient records, test data, or test materials.

Attix, D. K., Donders, J., Johnson-Greene, D., Grote, C. L., Harris, J. G., & Bauer, R. M. (2007). Disclosure of neuropsychological test data: Official position of Division 40 (clinical neuropsychology) of the American Association, Association of Postdoctoral Programs in Clinical Neuropsychology, and American Academy of Clinical Neuropsychology. *The Clinical Neuropsychologist, 21,* 232–238. http://dx.doi.org/10.1080/13854040601042928

Borkosky, B. G. (2016). "Coping with subpoenas": No longer consistent with law, ethics, or social policy. *Professional Psychology: Research and Practice, 47,* 250–251. http://dx.doi.org/10.1037/pro0000091

Bush, S. S., & Martin, T. A. (2006). The ethical and clinical practice of disclosing raw test data: Addressing the ongoing debate. *Applied Neuropsychology, 13,* 115–124. http://dx.doi.org/10.1207/s15324826an1302_6

Committee on Legal Issues. (2016). Committee on Legal Issues (COLI) response to commentary. *Professional Psychology: Research and Practice, 47,* 252–254. http://dx.doi.org/10.1037/pro0000092

Lees-Haley, P. R., Courtney, J. C., & Dinkins, J. P. (2005). Revisiting the need for reform in the disclosure of tests and raw test data to the court: The 2002 APA Ethics Code has not solved our dilemma. *Journal of Forensic Psychology Practice, 5,* 71–81. http://dx.doi.org/10.1300/J158v05n02_05

6.5. The Ethical Practice of School Psychology: A Rebuttal and Suggested Model

Donald N. Bersoff

My article "School Psychology as 'Institutional Psychiatry'" (Bersoff, 1971b) touched responsive chords in at least four people, who raised a number of important issues in their rejoinders. I will discuss the major points brought out by them and then offer a model to help school psychologists, and other clinicians, move toward the ethical practice of their profession.

THE IDEAL AND THE REAL IN SCHOOL PSYCHOLOGY PRACTICE

All of the critics indicated that many of the practices that were likened to "institutional psychiatry" (Szasz, 1970) were not part of the repertoire of most practicing school psychologists. Although the gap between the ideal practice of school psychology as taught by some of our better training programs and the actual behaviors of school psychologists may be narrowing, a relatively wide chasm still exists between good and real practice. MacGregor (1971) suggested that "special class placement should never be involuntary [p. 419]," but it still is involuntary in many schools. Although Tomlinson (1972) asserted that the psychologist "is in the position to counter the effects of . . . labels [p. 27]," many school psychologists still call children retarded, brain damaged, underachieving, and disturbed and, in so doing, use inappropriate procedures, overlooking the fact that the situation within which the child finds himself can be a powerful evoker of behavior. While Kassinove (1971) considered it "good practice to contact the parents of the child to be tested [p. 420]," even this first-order approximation of informed consent is not yet a universal practice.

The fact that naiveté persists in the field despite the attempts of some university training programs to alter the functions and perspectives of the school psychologist is evident in Shohet's (1972) statement that "as a result of testing . . . the psychologist working in the school is able to determine the present status of the youngster to succeed in the tasks expected of him [p. 300]." Individually administered tests are poor indicators of "present status" (Bersoff, 1971a), especially as they reflect classroom performance (Haughton, 1966; Johnson, 1967). There is a growing movement toward systematic observation of behavior as it occurs in the environment to which we actually wish to predict (Bersoff, 1973; see also Mischel, 1968, and Peterson, 1968, for a wider discussion of diagnostic labeling and alternate methods of assessing and conceptualizing persons).

If all school psychologists were operating within the bounds of good practice and legal constraint it would be difficult to explain why they are being sued for incompetence and the misclassification of children, or why Barclay (1971) would conclude that "there is increasing evidence today that school psychology practice has been weighed in the balance and found wanting [p. 257]." Contributing to that judgment, he referred specifically to weaknesses in traditional psychodiagnosis and the inability of school psychologists to develop a repertoire of prescription interventions.

LABELING AS A "LEGAL EXPEDIENCY"

Shohet (1972) supported continued labeling of children, feeling that it is the only way legislatures will continue to vote money for special education. To me, it is indefensible to support labeling on legislative and financial bases alone. While it is recognized that these are the current reasons for maintaining the process of classification and placement in self-contained special classrooms, the theoretical rationale for these activities being sustained appears to have little experimental support. The literature supporting this contention is vast; for a start, the interested reader can look at the *Journal of School Psychology* (1972, Vol. 10, No. 2), which is devoted entirely to school psychology and special education.

Many school psychologists recognize the arguments against labeling, but feel that the money obtained from legislatures for the special education of "handicapped" children through self-contained classrooms far outweighs the disadvantages of labeling. However, there is evidence indicating the long- and short-term negative consequences for those labeled and segregated (Rabkin, 1972), and increasingly those practices are being declared illegal (see Ross, DeYoung, & Cohen, 1971, for a summary of court cases affecting special education practices). The long-range consequences of labeling need particular consideration. It may be "expedient" to place a highly active child who is not learning well in a class for the "neurological handicapped," but it would be helpful to consider the adverse effects that such a label may have on this child in the future (e.g., the inability to obtain certain kinds of insurance because of a childhood diagnosis of brain damage). The fact that "labeling does not begin nor end with school psychologists" (MacGregor, 1971, p. 419; Shohet, 1972) does not in any way obviate our responsibility in the process. In very direct ways we are implicated in it, and we will be held increasingly accountable for our part in those decisions.

In an earlier context (Bersoff, Kabler, Fiscus, & Ankney, 1972) it was suggested that school psychologists need to question whether the remediation of so-called handicapped children is best handled through self-contained classrooms. We saw part of the school psychologist's role as that of investigating workable alternatives to existing ineffectual educational and psychological practices, instituting them on an experimental basis, and attempting to demonstrate their efficacy, a set of behaviors preferable to passively maintaining the dubious role of "institutional school psychologist." That the questioning of ineffectual practices is taking place goes without saying; I am in wholehearted concurrence with MacGregor (1971), who stated that

> the use of labels as a result of testing seems somewhat less common than in the past, chiefly because it is not useful in education. . . . More useful is a description of the child's behavior, a discussion of his interaction with the environment, and suggestions for modification of both [pp. 419–420].

THE SCHOOL AS A NONCONTROLLING INSTITUTION

In debating some of my points, Tomlinson (1972) claimed that there was little analogy between mental institutions and school systems with regard to the amount of control they exercise over their respective clientele. Specifically, Tomlinson said, "Mental institutions maintain extensive control over major sources of reinforcement and punishment, while a school's control over reinforcers and punishers is limited [pp. 26–27]." Such a statement reflects a certain amount of ignorance of the school both as a social institution and as an operant laboratory. Indeed, the school can be viewed in some ways as a giant reinforcement-dispensing machine.

School personnel are continuously engaged in dispensing both positive reinforcement and punishment. Students are allotted privileges ranging from the minor (leading the line, collecting test papers, cleaning the erasers) to the major (receiving good grades, graduating) contingent on performance. Likewise, punishment is distributed regularly. . . . None of those punishments are minor, and they may directly affect the long-range functioning of the children so treated.

In other ways, the school can be considered to be at least as controlling as a mental institution. Attendance is compulsory for a prescribed number of years for the vast majority of children (though this concept is now being reconsidered). School assignment, class placement, and curricular content are all determined by the school. Rarely may a child choose his teacher. He is forced to take tests when the teacher, not the child, feels ready. Parental permission is in almost no case sought when changes in curriculum occur, or when a child is retained, or when he is to undergo statewide achievement tests (contrast all this with the mandatory parental permission sought for physical intervention on a child's body within hospitals).

In addition, the avowed purpose of a mental institution is to enhance the functioning of a patient to the extent that he can function relatively independently outside of the institution. However, the school sees itself as the major transmitter of the American culture and is involved not only in communicating knowledge, but in developing values, attitudes, artistic appreciation, good mental health, impulse control, occupational skills, and so on. In fact, the school is perceived as responsible for molding a child's thinking, believing, behaving, and knowing so that he is unrecognizable at the end of schooling when compared to his entering behavior.

It is only when the real pervasive power of the schools is recognized (Goldman, 1971) that we see the necessity for safeguarding the rights of the individuals within such a powerful institution. Understanding that much of that power may be necessary, that it may have been mandated, and that it may be helpful in the long run, we still need to appreciate that brakes and constraints may be necessary to insure legal and ethical use of that power.

THE DANGER OF CRITICISM

Of all the rebuttals, Shohet's (1972) was the most disconcerting to me, with its attitude of protectionism toward the profession of school psychology as it is, in the main, currently constituted. Such an attitude represents a *genuine* misreading of the contemporary literature. The characterization of the "Institutional Psychiatry" article as irresponsible, ill-informed, and ill-advised seems to imply that the specific criticisms noted had no basis in reality and were, in some way, damaging to school psychology. In fact, other school psychologists have been even more critical. The Barclay (1971) indictment has already been referred to. Clair and Kiraly (1971) have delivered a scathing critique of current practice (and in this case I would agree with their critics that some of the accusations were unfair). More recently, in an article dealing with confidentiality, privacy of student records, and other related issues, Trachtman (1972) did not find it injurious to arouse discontent among his colleagues: "If, on occasion, the comfortable functioning of the psychologist is interrupted, it may be that this is incidental and for the larger good [p. 45]."

The dangers I alluded to in the original article were offered in that spirit, for the larger good. School psychologists' major concern cannot be to protect our profession, no matter which organizational entity we feel deserves our primary loyalty. Rather, as Trachtman (1972) suggested, whatever our persuasion, our common role may be to serve as an "unofficial ombudsman" protecting children from the school when necessary. Recognizing that the following practices are in no way universal, I continue to maintain that in his role as tester (in the sense that he operates as a technician), as one of "society's professional labelers" (Ullman & Krasner, 1969), and sorter of children into self-contained special education classrooms, the school psychologist is acting, not as an ombudsman, but in indefensible and possibly unethical ways.

The use of the term "unethical" is not stated as a dramatic device. There is the very real possibility that many school psychologists are, indeed, not acting in full accordance with the APA Code of Ethics (1963), specifically Principles 7d and 8. As delineated in those sections, psychological assessment proceeds

> only after making certain that the person is fully aware of the purposes of the interview, testing or evaluation and of the ways in which the information may be used [p. 57].

> The psychologist informs his prospective client of the important aspects of the potential relations that might affect the client's decision to enter the relationship [p. 58].

I think that we would admit that these instructions are far from pervasively followed by school psychologists and that on that basis our functioning can be faulted. The next section suggests some ways in which we can alter our behavior to better match that demanded by the Code of Ethics.

A SUGGESTION FOR THE ETHICAL PRACTICE OF SCHOOL PSYCHOLOGY

The following is not meant to be an all-encompassing model, but is limited to the process of assessment. It rests on three assumptions:

1. Test responses are a function not only of the characteristics of the organism to whom the test is administered but also of the stimulus properties of the test and the background or environments (e.g., instructions, setting, nature of the experimenter) in which the test is administered (Fiske, 1967; Hamilton, 1970; Murstein, 1965; Sattler & Theye, 1967).

2. Each person perceives the testing situation differently and thus develops an idiosyncratic style or strategy in responding to test material. Without discerning these strategies, the validity of test interpretation is highly attenuated (Fulkerson, 1965).

3. Parents are at least equally capable as the school staff in deciding what is best for their children (Goldman, 1971).

Accepting these assumptions allows the psychologist to include the client in all aspects of the evaluation. In fact, it makes it imperative that he do so if he wants to obtain data that are not obfuscated by mistrust, misunderstanding, and the inhibition of self-disclosure. Because we have not included the client (both the child and his parents) in the assessment transaction it is possible that most of our test data and their subsequent interpretation may be of doubtful veracity. As Jourard (1971) conjectured,

> the millions of psychometric tests mildewing in agency files might be lies told by untrusting clients and patients to untrustworthy functionaries. If psychologists were serving the interests of bureaucracies, wittingly or unwittingly, in their . . . activities, then it would be quite proper for . . . patients not to trust us; functionaries masquerading as professionals are not to be trusted too far [p. 2],

If we are to achieve intimate, ethical relationships consonant with the empirical data concerning the interactive nature of test productions, it may be necessary to reconceive of the assessment process as one in which there is mutual disclosure. In a series of papers, Fischer (1970, 1971a, 1971b, in press-a, in press-b) detailed both the theoretical foundations and the practical expression of just such a relationship in which tester and client become "coevaluators" (Fischer, 1970). Specifically, the following steps are recommended.

1. *Coadvisement.* This is an expansion of the principle of informed consent. The psychologist tells the child and his parents how he functions; informs them of the identity of the referral agent and the purpose for referral; and describes the nature of the assessment devices he will use, the merits and limitations of those devices, what kinds of information will be put in a report, and who might eventually read the report. The psychologist then asks the child to tell how he perceives the purposes of testing and what he feels the consequences of such an evaluation might be. The psychologist secures agreement from the child and his parents to proceed with the assessment subsequent to full and mutual disclosure concerning the purposes of the evaluation.

2. *Sharing impressions.* Immediately after the administration of the psychometric instruments the psychologist, the child, and his parents engage in a dialogue in which the psychologist gives his interpretation of the child's test behavior as he has just experienced it. By conferring with the child he further attempts to extrapolate from the testing situation to other situations similar to the one represented by the test stimuli. Such a dialogue provides immediate feedback to the child about how others perceive his behavior and enables the assessor to check out hypotheses about how equivalent the test behavior observed is to actual classroom behavior and to develop possible strategies he may use to intervene in the instructional environment (see Fischer, 1970, for an example of how such an interaction might proceed). It also gives the child a chance to disagree with the psychologist's initial interpretations and to offer his perceptions about his own behavior. Rather than assuming that the behavior observed in the testing situation can be extrapolated to all other situations, the psychologist has an opportunity to discover the situations or contexts in which the behavior does occur. Such an approach has been variously called psychosituational (Bersoff, 1971a, 1973; Bersoff & Grieger, 1971) or contextual (Fischer, in press) assessment, but whatever its title, such a method prevents the child from being mislabeled and interpretations of his behavior from being overgeneralized.

3. *Critique of the written evaluation.* This concludes the sequence of mutually disclosing events. After the evaluation is complete and the psychologist has prepared his report, he shows the child and his parents a copy of the written evaluation. This insures that the report will be recorded so that it is understandable to all concerned. In addition, as Fischer (1970) described,

> This procedure also produces a beneficial side effect: Knowing that his client is going to read his report, the psychologist strives all the more to be true to him, to capture his world as well as words allow, and to avoid overstatements, unintended implications, and loose descriptions [p. 74].

Then, the child and his parents are given the opportunity to clarify the points made, to add further material, and, if there is disagreement between the psychologist and the clients, to provide a dissenting view (in writing if warranted).

Finally, the psychologist receives permission to disseminate the report to those whom the child and his parents agree to.

There is no doubt that adopting such an approach requires much rethinking and rebehaving on the part of school psychologists. It may seem idealistic and unworkable (though it is not). Admittedly, there may be some difficulty in implementing the approach fully. Yet, I view movement toward such procedures not as idealistic, but as necessary if we are to function ethically. A comment by Leo Goldman (1971), arguing against psychological secrecy and offering some suggestions for its reduction, may help put the matter in perspective:

> All of this may sound very unappealing to psychologists who would prefer to see themselves as the "good guys" who are there just to help people and make the world a better place. Unfortunately, that just isn't a viable arrangement when one is a member of the staff of a public school serving a community which contains diverse social, ethnic, and political elements. And it certainly is not possible in any pure sense in a setting such as the public schools, where the "clients" are not clients at all but mostly a captive, involuntary audience. We will just have to find a way to work out agreements in each school system . . . so that the professional helpers can do their thing, while the students and their families retain the power to decide whether they will be helped, what personal information they will divulge, and what the school may release to anyone. Although this will undoubtedly cramp our style to some extent, it will on the whole make for a healthier social institution than we now have [p. 11].

The suggestions made in this article for reorienting assessment will hopefully move us toward making the school a healthier social institution. At the very least we will treat the child and his parents as our equals, with the right to participate in the interpretations and decisions that will directly affect their lives. Certainly, the chances of damaging diagnoses and class placements will be lessened. And those diagnoses and placements that are made will have been a "co-constituted" decision, agreed on by those affected, increasing the probability of greater cooperation in making the changes that *all* have deemed appropriate.

REFERENCES

American Psychological Association. (1963). Ethical standards of psychologists. *American Psychologist, 18,* 56–60.

Barclay, J. R. (1971). Descriptive, theoretical, and behavioral characteristics of subdoctoral school psychologists. *American Psychologist, 26,* 257–280.

Bersoff, D. N. (1971a). "Current functioning" myth: An overlooked fallacy in psychological assessment. *Journal of Consulting and Clinical Psychology, 37,* 391–393.

Bersoff, D. N. (1971b). School psychology as "institutional psychiatry." *Professional Psychology, 2,* 266–270.

Bersoff, D. N. (1973). Behavioral approaches to assessment and observation in the school. In J. F. Magary (Ed.), *Handbook of school psychological services.* St. Louis: Mosby.

Bersoff, D. N., & Grieger, R. M. (1971). An interview model for the psychosituational assessment of children's behavior. *American Journal of Orthopsychiatry, 41,* 483–493.

Bersoff, D. N., Kabler, M., Fiscus, E., & Ankney, R. (1972). Effectiveness of special class placement for children labeled neurologically handicapped. *Journal of School Psychology, 10,* 67–73.

Clair, T. N., & Kiraly, J. (1971). Can school psychology survive in the 70's? *Professional Psychology, 2,* 383–388.

Fischer, C. T. (1970). The testee as co-evaluator. *Journal of Counseling Psychology, 17,* 70–76.

Fischer, C. T. (1971a, September). Paradigm changes which allow sharing of "results" with the client. In S. L. Brodsky (Chm.), Shared Results and Open Files with the Client: Professional Responsibility or Effective Involvement. Symposium presented at the annual meeting of the American Psychological Association, Washington, D.C.

Fischer, C. T. (1971b). *Toward the structure of privacy: Implications for psychological assessment.* In A. Giorgi, W. F. Fischer, & R. von Eckartsberg (Eds.), *Duquesne studies in phenomenological psychology.* Pittsburgh: Duquesne University Press.

Fischer, C. T. (in press-a). Contextual approach to assessment. *Journal of Community Mental Health.*

Fischer, C. T. (in press-b). A theme for the child-advocate: Sharable everyday life data of the child-in-the-world. *Journal of Clinical Child Psychology.*

Fiske, D. W. (1967). The subject reacts to tests. *American Psychologist, 22,* 287–296.

Fulkerson, S. C. (1965). Some implications of the new cognitive theory for projective tests. *Journal of Consulting Psychology, 29,* 191–197.

Goldman, L. (1971, September). Psychological secrecy and openness in the public schools. In S. L. Brodsky (Chm.), Shared Results and Open Files with the Client: Professional Responsibility or Effective Involvement. Symposium presented at the annual meeting of the American Psychological Association, Washington, D.C.

Hamilton, J. (1970). Stimulus variables in clinical evaluation. *Professional Psychology, 1,* 151–153.

Haughton, E. (1966, May). Teachers and educational psychology: Grounds for divorce? Paper presented at the annual meeting of the Midwestern Psychological Association, Chicago.

Johnson, N. J. (1967). Daily arithmetic performance compared with teacher ratings, IQ, and achievement tests. Unpublished manuscript, University of Kansas.

Jourard, S. M. (1971, September). Some reflections on a quiet revolution. In S. L. Brodsky (Chm.), Shared Results and Open Files with the Client: Professional Responsibility or Effective Involvement. Symposium presented at the annual meeting of the American Psychological Association, Washington, D.C.

Kassinove, H. (1971). Half-truths. *Professional Psychology, 2,* 420–421.

MacGregor, M. J. (1971). Re: Bersoff and school psychology. *Professional Psychology, 2,* 419–420.

Mischel, W. (1968). *Personality and assessment.* New York: Wiley.

Murstein, B. I. (1965). Assumptions, adaptation level, and projective techniques. In B. I. Murstein (Ed.), *Handbook of projective techniques.* New York: Basic Books.

Peterson, D. R. (1968). *The clinical study of social behavior.* New York: Appleton-Century-Crofts.

Rabkin, J. G. (1972). Opinions about mental illness: A review of the literature. *Psychological Bulletin, 77,* 153–171.

Ross, S. L., DeYoung, H. G., & Cohen, J. S. (1971). Confrontation: Special education and the law. *Exceptional Children, 38,* 5–12.

Sattler, J. M., & Theye, F. (1967). Procedural, situational, and interpersonal variables in individual intelligence testing. *Psychological Bulletin, 68,* 347–361.

Shohet, J. (1972). School psychology as a catalyst for social progress. *Professional Psychology, 3,* 299–301.

Szasz, T. (1970). *The manufacture of madness.* New York: Harper & Row.

Tomlinson, J. R. (1972). Schools and hospitals: A reply to Bersoff. *Professional Psychology, 3,* 25–29.

Trachtman, G. M. (1972). Pupils, parents, privacy and the school psychologist. *American Psychologist, 27*, 37–45.

Ullman, L. P., & Krasner, L. (1969). *A psychological approach to abnormal behavior.* Englewood Cliffs, N.J.: Prentice-Hall.

COMMENTARY: School psychology is a professional service pathway crowded with obstacles. Attempts to provide mental health and other supportive services to students are inevitably going to be complicated by a host of real or perceived obligations to institutions, classmates, and parents. Confidentiality is exceptionally difficult to maintain in an environment in which so much of information derived and advice rendered is destined for eventual disclosure to multiple entities with potentially competing interests.

When it comes to interactions with students themselves, the school psychologist typically contends with situations that may have significant legal—and, often by extension, ethical—ramifications. Bullying, parental neglect, and sexual exploitation are often first discovered in the course of comparatively normal interactions with the school psychologist, who may also be brought in (with scant preparation) almost immediately after such issues have surfaced in another context.

The following references are recommended for those interested in further investigation of the school psychologist's ethical responsibilities concerning such issues as clinical report writing, parenting status, special education needs, and children's rights.

Attard, S., Mercieca, D., & Mercieca, D. P. (2016). Ethics in psychologists' report writing: Acknowledging aporia. *Ethics & Education, 11*, 55–66. http://dx.doi.org/10.1080/17449642.2016.1145488

Flanagan, R., Miller, J. A., & Jacob, S. (2005). The 2002 revision of the American Psychological Association's Ethics Code: Implications for school psychologists. *Psychology in the Schools, 42*, 433–445. http://dx.doi.org/10.1002/pits.20097

Lasser, J., Klose, L. M., & Robillard, R. (2013). Context-sensitive ethics in school psychology. *Contemporary School Psychology, 17*, 119–128.

Nastasi, B. K., & Naser, S. (2013). Child rights as a framework for advancing professional standards for practice, ethics, and professional development in school psychology. *School Psychology International, 35*, 36–49. http://dx.doi.org/10.1177/0143034313512409

Stein, R., & Sharkey, J. (2015). Your hands are (not) tied: School-based ethics when parents revoke special education consent. *Psychology in the Schools, 52*, 168–180. http://dx.doi.org/10.1002/pits.21814

6.6. Utilization Rates of Computerized Tests and Test Batteries Among Clinical Neuropsychologists in the United States and Canada

Laura A. Rabin, Amanda T. Spadaccini, Donald L. Brodale,
Kevin S. Grant, Milushka M. Elbulok-Charcape, and William B. Barr

Subsequent to the introduction of the personal computer in the 1970s, neuropsychologists have utilized computers in research and clinical work to administer, score, and interpret traditional neuropsychological measures (Cernich, Brennana, Barker, & Bleiberg, 2007; Parsey & Schmitter-Edgecombe, 2013; Wild, Howieson, Webbe, Seelye, & Kaye, 2008). Computerized assessment approaches generally fall into one of two categories: translation of existing examiner-administered instruments into computerized administration formats and development of new computerized tests and test batteries. These broad categories can be subdivided into computerized neuropsychological assessment tools that are utilized with diverse clinical populations versus those developed for specific diagnostic subgroups or to address specific referral questions. . . .

TRANSLATION OF EXISTING EXAMINER-ADMINISTERED NEUROPSYCHOLOGICAL INSTRUMENTS INTO COMPUTERIZED ADMINISTRATION FORMATS

Many widely used neuropsychological tests, such as the Wisconsin Card Sorting Test (WCST; Heaton & PAR Staff, 2003), Word Memory Test (Green, 2003; Green, Allen, & Astner, 2000), versions of the Raven's Progressive Matrices (French & Beaumont, 1990; NCS Pearson, 2011), and Category Test (Choca & Morris, 1992) exist in examiner-administered and computerized formats (Hoskins, Binder, Chaytor, Williamson, & Drane, 2010; Schatz & Browndyke, 2002). For

From "Utilization Rates of Computerized Tests and Test Batteries Among Clinical Neuropsychologists in the United States and Canada," by L.A. Rabin, A. T. Spadaccini, D. L. Brodale, K. S. Grant, M. M. Elbulok-Charcape, and W. B. Barr, 2014, *Professional Psychology: Research and Practice, 45*, pp. 368–377. Copyright 2014 by the American Psychological Association.

The authors thank the many members of National Academy of Neuropsychology (NAN) and International Neuropsychological Society (INS) who graciously contributed their time to complete and return the survey. Implementation of the survey instrument was supported, in part, by PSC-CUNY Award 63160–00 41. A portion of this research was presented at the 40th Annual Meeting of the International Neuropsychological Society.

neuropsychologists this offers new possibilities for assessment tools that can complement, or in some cases replace, traditional examiner-administered tests. It is important, however, to first establish correspondence between the computerized and noncomputerized versions to ensure that factors specific to automated administration do not alter test performance. Both experiential equivalence (e.g., demonstration that both versions of the test are measuring the same construct) and psychometric equivalence (e.g., demonstration of statistically similar group means and distributions) should be confirmed before test forms are used interchangeably (Mead & Drasgow, 1993), although this does not always occur (Hoskins et al., 2010).

DEVELOPMENT OF NOVEL COMPUTERIZED NEUROPSYCHOLOGICAL INSTRUMENTS

In addition to translating existing measures into computerized formats, novel computer tests capture aspects of cognition not easily tapped through paper-and-pencil tasks (Schultheis & Rizzo, 2008). Tests such as the Test of Variables of Attention (Dupuy & Cenedela, 2000), Integrated Visual and Auditory Continuous Performance Test (Sandford & Turner, 2004), and Conners Continuous Performance Test II (Conners & MHS Staff, 2000) were developed for computer application. These tests measure complex aspects of attention including vigilance, response inhibition, response sensitivity, and impulsiveness (Strauss, Sherman, & Spreen, 2006). Another example is the Useful Field of View (Ball & Roenker, 1998), a computerized test of visual sensory function, visual processing speed, and visual attention skills, which has significantly predicted driving capacity and crash involvement in older adults and neurologically compromised drivers (Clay et al., 2005; Owsley et al., 1998; Schultheis & Rizzo, 2008). Recently, virtual reality technology that immerses patients in interactive, computer-simulated environments has enabled neuropsychologists to measure cognition and behavior within functionally relevant situations (for review see Parsey & Schmitter-Edgecombe, 2013). Such measures may provide more ecologically valid stimuli than paper-and-pencil measures and elicit more diagnostically relevant responses (Schultheis & Rizzo, 2008).
. . .

COMPUTERIZED ASSESSMENTS GEARED TOWARD SPECIFIC REFERRAL QUESTIONS

In some cases computerized neuropsychological assessment tools are utilized to address a specific referral question or clinical concern. For example, computerized assessments are commonly used in the identification and management of sports-related concussion and return-to-play decisions (Bauer et al., 2012; Maerlender et al., 2010; Schatz & Browndyke, 2002). With computer-based assessment tools, groups of athletes can be screened in a brief period of time and their cognitive deficits tracked longitudinally (Schatz & Browndyke, 2002). The portability of these measures enables them to be used on the field when injuries occur (Collie & Maruff, 2003; Maerlender et al., 2010). Widely used computerized neuropsychological test batteries utilized for concussion screening include CogSport (CogSport, 1999), HeadMinders (Erlanger, Feldman, & Kutner, 1999), and the Immediate Post-Concussion Assessment and Cognitive Testing test system (ImPACT; Lovell, Collins, Podell, Powell, & Maroon, 2000), among others. Although some of these measures are stand-alone software applications, others are administered through a Web browser. . . .

COMPUTERIZED ASSESSMENTS GEARED TOWARD SPECIFIC PATIENT POPULATIONS

A final way to categorize computerized neuropsychological tools is by their use with specific patient populations. For example, several computerized test batteries have been developed for older adult populations, with an eye toward the prospective screening of cognition in the community, early detection of dementia, and longitudinal follow-up (Bauer et al., 2012; Dougherty et al., 2010; Fowler, Saling, Conway, Semple, & Louis, 1997; Inoue, Jinbo, Nakamura, Taniguchi, & Urakami, 2009). Instruments such as the CANTAB, CogState (Fredrickson et al., 2010), and Computer Assessment of Mild Cognitive Impairment (Saxton et al., 2009) have been utilized effectively with older adults (Collerton et al., 2007; Wild et al., 2008; Woo, 2008), and recent research suggests that computerized cognitive tests accurately assess cognition in older adults (Fazeli, Ross, Vance, & Ball, 2013). Utilization of computerized testing for attention deficit hyperactivity disorder (ADHD) is also common. The CANTAB, for example, is known to be sensitive to cognitive dysfunction across multiple domains of ADHD and to the amelioration of cognitive dysfunction through pharmacotherapy (Chamberlain et al., 2011).
. . .

DISCUSSION

The development, use, and potential advantages of computerized neuropsychological assessment techniques have received increased attention in clinical and research settings in recent decades (Bauer et al., 2012; Bilder, 2011; Crook, Kay, & Larrabee, 2009; Vakil, 2012). Current survey results, however, indicate that utilization of computerized neuropsychological tests and emerging technologies is more limited than the literature suggests. . . .

The most endorsed computerized instruments were those used for attention/vigilance/speed of information processing. This is consistent with the widespread development of computerized tests to measure sustained attention and vigilance in numerous clinical populations (Cohen, Malloy, Jenkins, & Paul, 2006; Lezak, Howieson, Loring, Hannay, & Fischer, 2004). In fact, one could make the case that computerized cognitive tests are best suited to assess domains such as attention, vigilance, and speed of information processing, where timing and precision in relation to participant responses are critical (Witt et al., 2013). Given the potential benefits of computerized methods for patients who present with deficits in attention and other cognitive domains that lend themselves to computerized assessment (e.g., visuospatial orientation deficits with visual scanning or virtual reality technology, perceptual deficits with computerized visual field assessment or signal detection tests), the overall low usage rates are surprising.

Possible reasons for the low usage rates include costs associated with computerized tests, lack of appropriate norms for computerized versions of tests, and concerns about aspects of tests' utility or validity. As noted by Witt et al. (2013), in relation to the neuropsychological assessment of patients with epilepsy, there is a dearth of published research documenting the utility of computerized tests for epilepsy patients or evidence for the equivalence of standard paper-pencil and computerized methods addressing identical cognitive domains. Clearly there is a need to garner empirical support for the sensitivity and specificity of computerized tests to clinical disorders and intervention-related variables before they can be integrated into routine neuropsychological assessments (Witt et al., 2013). It is also of interest that no participant reported use of instruments that incorporate computer technologies such as virtual reality, driving simulations, Internet-based assessment, or combined EEG and ERP measurements with neurocognitive computerized tests. Future survey research might inquire about neuropsychologists' knowledge and usage of these assessment approaches. . . .

CONCLUSIONS

Although detailed review of the literature suggests that computerized testing is a highly active area of development, with new tests and findings continuously emerging, our results suggest that there is a proverbial promise not yet fulfilled for computerized testing in neuropsychological practice. Computerized testing barely registers in clinical practice, giving rise to the question of why neuropsychologists choose noncomputerized test formats. Previously mentioned concerns may affect utilization, such as questions about psychometric and experiential equivalency, security and privacy, manufacturer claims of effectiveness, prohibitive cost, loss of qualitative face-to-face information, patient apprehension, cultural differences in patient population, and the infeasibility of computerized assessment with specific clinical populations. It is also possible that lack of exposure to computerized assessment methods or comfort with traditional instruments on which respondents were initially trained contribute to the lack of utilization of computerized tests.

Although additional research is required to determine the array of variables that determine the likelihood of utilization of computerized instruments, results suggest that computerized assessment by neuropsychologists is not influenced by the characteristics of the patients they serve but rather by those of the neuropsychologists themselves. As discussed in the recent joint position paper of the American Academy of Clinical Neuropsychology and the National Academy of Neuropsychology (Bauer et al., 2012), computerized neuropsychological assessment procedures have the potential to bring valid and effective neuropsychological evaluation techniques to underserved populations if designed and used properly by trained professionals. They also have the potential to pair with innovative assessment (Bilder, 2011) and intervention options unavailable with traditional measures (Schultheis & Rizzo, 2008). The realization of the potential benefits of computerized testing may require a more complete understanding of neuropsychologists' familiarity and comfort, as well as the perceived challenges associated with these techniques. Moreover, increased utilization of computerized instruments may require enhanced exposure to such tools at various levels of professional neuropsychological training and development.

REFERENCES

Ball, K., & Roenker, D. (1998). *Useful field of view*. San Antonio, TX: The Psychological Corporation.

Bauer, R. M., Iverson, G. L., Cernich, A. N., Binder, L. M., Ruff, R. M., & Naugle, R. I. (2012). Computerized neuropsychological assessment devices: Joint position paper of the American Academy of Clinical Neuropsychology and the National Academy of Neuropsychology. *Archives of Clinical Neuropsychology*, *27*, 362–373. doi:10.1093/arclin/acs027

Bilder, R. (2011). Neuropsychology 3.0: Evidence-based science and practice. *Journal of the International Neuropsychological Society*, *17*, 7–13. doi:10.1017/S1355617710001396

Cernich, A. N., Brennana, D. M., Barker, L. M., & Bleiberg, J. (2007). Sources of error in computerized neuropsychological assessment. *Archives of Clinical Neuropsychology*, *22*, 39–48. doi:10.1016/j.acn.2006.10.004

Chamberlain, S. R., Robbins, T. W., Winder-Rhodes, S., Muller, U., Sahakian, B. J., Blackwell, A. D., & Barnett, J. H. (2011). Translational approaches to frontostriatal dysfunction in attention-deficit/hyperactivity disorder using a computerized neuropsychological battery. *Biological Psychiatry*, *69*, 1192–1203. doi:10.1016/j.biopsych.2010.08.019

Choca, J. P., & Morris, J. (1992). Administering the category test by computer: Equivalence of results. *Clinical Neuropsychologist*, *6*, 9–15. doi:10.1080/13854049208404112

Clay, O. J., Wadley, V. G., Edwards, J. D., Roth, D. L., Roenker, D. L., & Ball, K. K. (2005). Cumulative meta-analysis of the relationship between useful field of view and driving performance in older adults: Current and future implications. *Optometry and Vision Science*, *82*, 724–731. doi:10.1097/01.opx.0000175009.08626.65

CogSport. (1999). *CogSport*. Parkville, Australia: CogState, Ltd.

Cohen, R. A., Malloy, P. F., Jenkins, M. A., & Paul, R. H. (2006). Disorders of attention. In P. J. Snyder, P. D. Nussbaum, & D. L. Robins (Eds.), *Clinical neuropsychology: A pocket handbook for assessment* (2nd ed., pp. 572–606). Washington, DC: American Psychological Association.

Collerton, J., Collerton, D., Arai, Y., Barrass, K., Eccles, M., Jagger, C., & Kirkwood, T. (2007). A comparison of computerized and pencil-and-paper tasks in assessing cognitive function in community-dwelling older people in the Newcastle 85+ Pilot Study. *Journal of the American Geriatrics Society*, *55*, 1630–1635. doi:10.1111/j.1532-5415.2007.01379.x

Collie, A., & Maruff, P. (2003). Computerised neuropsychological testing. *British Journal of Sports Medicine*, *37*, 2–3. doi:10.1136/bjsm.37.1.2

Conners, C. K., & MHS Staff. (2000). *Conners' Continuous Performance Test (CPT–II) computer programs for Windows™ technical guide and software manual.* North Tonawanda, NY: Multi-Health Systems Inc.

Crook, T. H., Kay, G. G., & Larrabee, G. J. (2009). Computer-based cognitive testing. In I. Grant & K. M. Adams (Eds.), *Neuropsychological assessment of neuropsychiatric and neuromedical disorders* (3rd ed., pp. 84–100). New York, NY: Oxford University Press.

Dougherty, J. H. Jr., Cannon, R. L., Nicholas, C. R., Hall, L., Hare, F., Carr, E., . . . Arunthamakun, J. (2010). The Computerized Self Test (CST): An interactive, internet accessible cognitive screening test for dementia. *Journal of Alzheimer's Disease, 20,* 185–195. doi:10.3233/JAD-2010-1354

Dupuy, T., & Cenedela, M. (2000). *Test of variables of attention: User's guide.* Los Alamitos, CA: Universal Attention Disorders.

Erlanger, D. M., Feldman, D. J., & Kutner, K. (1999). *Concussion resolution index.* New York, NY: HeadMinder, Inc.

Fazeli, P. L., Ross, L. A., Vance, D. E., & Ball, K. (2013). The relationship between computer experience and computerized cognitive test performance among older adults. *The Journals of Gerontology Series B: Psychological Sciences and Social Sciences, 68,* 337–346. doi:10.1093/geronb/gbs071

Fowler, K. S., Saling, M. M., Conway, E. L., Semple, J. M., & Louis, W. J. (1997). Computerized neuropsychological tests in the early detection of dementia: Prospective findings. *Journal of the International Neuropsychological Society, 3,* 139–146.

Fredrickson, J., Maruff, P. P., Woodward, M. M., Moore, L. L., Fredrickson, A. A., Sach, J. J., & Darby, D. D. (2010). Evaluation of the usability of a brief computerized cognitive screening test in older people for epidemiological studies. *Neuroepidemiology, 34,* 65–75. doi:10.1159/000264823

French, C. C., & Beaumont, J. G. (1990). A clinical study of the automated assessment of intelligence by the Mill Hill Vocabulary Test and the Standard Progressive Matrices Test. *Journal of Clinical Psychology, 46,* 129–140. doi:10.1002/1097-4679(199003)46: 2<129::AID-JCLP2270460203>3.0.CO;2-Y

Green, P. (2003). *Green's WordMemory Test for Windows user's manual.* Edmonton, Canada: Green's Publishing.

Green, P., Allen, L. M., III, & Astner, K. (2000). *Word Memory Test (WMT).* Durham, NC: CogniSyst, Inc.

Heaton, R. K., & Psychological Assessment Resources Staff. (2003). *Wisconsin Card Sorting Test computer version 4.* Lutz, FL: Psychological Assessment Resources.

Hoskins, L. L., Binder, L. M., Chaytor, N. S., Williamson, D. J., & Drane, D. L. (2010). Comparison of oral and computerized versions of the Word Memory Test. *Archives of Clinical Neuropsychology, 25,* 591–600. doi:10.1093/arclin/acq060

Inoue, M., Jinbo, D., Nakamura, Y., Taniguchi, M., & Urakami, K. (2009). Development and evaluation of a computerized test battery for Alzheimer's disease screening in community-based settings. *American Journal of Alzheimer's Disease and Other Dementias, 24,* 129–135. doi:10.1177/1533317508330222

Lezak, M. D., Howieson, D. B., Loring, D. W., Hannay, H. J., & Fischer, J. S. (2004). *Neuropsychological assessment* (4th ed.). New York, NY: Oxford University Press.

Lovell, M. R., Collins, M. W., Podell, K., Powell, J., & Maroon, J. (2000). *ImPACT: Immediate Post-Concussion Assessment and Cognitive Testing.* Pittsburgh, PA: NeuroHealth Systems, LLC.

Maerlender, A., Flashman, L. L., Kessler, A. A., Kumbhani, S. S., Greenwald, R. R., Tosteson, T. T., & McAllister, T. T. (2010). Examination of the construct validity of ImPACT™ computerized test, traditional, and experimental neuropsychological measures. *The Clinical Neuropsychologist, 24,* 1309–1325. doi:10.1080/13854046.2010.516072

Mead, A. D., & Drasgow, F. (1993). Equivalence of computerized and paper-and-pencil cognitive ability tests: A meta-analysis. *Psychological Bulletin, 114,* 449–458. doi:10.1037/0033-2909.114.3.449

NCS Pearson. (2011). *Raven's advanced progressive matrices: International technical manual*. London, UK: NCS Pearson, Inc.

Owsley, C., Ball, B., McGwin, G., Jr., Sloane, M. E., Roenker, D. L., White, M. F., & Overley, E. T. (1998). Visual processing impairment and risk of motor vehicle crash among older adults. *Journal of the American Medical Association, 279*, 1083–1088. doi:10.1001/jama.279.14.1083

Parsey, C. M., & Schmitter-Edgecombe, M. (2013). Applications of technology in neuropsychological assessment. *The Clinical Neuropsychologist, 27*, 1328–1361. doi:10.1080/13854046.2013.834971

Sandford, J. A., & Turner, A. (2004). *IVA+Plus™: Integrated Visual and Auditory Continuous Performance Test administration manual*. Richmond, VA: Brain Train, Inc.

Saxton, J., Morrow, L., Eschman, A., Archer, G., Luther, J., & Zuccolotto, A. (2009). Computer assessment in mild cognitive impairment. *Postgraduate Medicine, 121*, 177–185. doi:10.3810/pgm.2009.03.1990

Schatz, P., & Browndyke, J. (2002). Applications of computer-based neuropsychological assessment. *The Journal of Head Trauma Rehabilitation, 17*, 395–410. doi:10.1097/00001199-200210000-00003

Schultheis, M. T., & Rizzo, A. A. (2008). Emerging technologies in practice and research. In J. E. Morgan & J. H. Ricker (Eds.), *Textbook of clinical neuropsychology* (pp. 848–865). New York, NY: Taylor and Francis.

Strauss, E., Sherman, E. M. S., & Spreen, O. (2006). *A compendium of neuropsychological tests: Administration, norms, and commentary* (3rd ed.). New York, NY: Oxford University Press.

Vakil, E. (2012). Neuropsychological assessment: Principles, rationale, and challenges. *Journal of Clinical and Experimental Neuropsychology, 34*, 135–150. doi:10.1080/13803395.2011.623121

Wild, K., Howieson, D., Webbe, F., Seelye, A., & Kaye, J. (2008). The status of computerized cognitive testing in aging: A systematic review. *Alzheimer's & Dementia, 4*, 428–437. doi:10.1016/j.jalz.2008.07.003

Woo, E. (2008). Computerized Neuropsychological Assessments. *CNS Spectrums, 16*, 14–17.

Witt, J.-A., Alpherts, W., & Helmstaedter, C. (2013). Computerized neuropsychological testing in epilepsy: Overview of available tools. *Seizure, 22*, 416–423.

6.7. Psychological Testing on the Internet: New Problems, Old Issues

Jack A. Naglieri, Fritz Drasgow, Mark Schmit, Len Handler,
Aurelio Prifitera, Amy Margolis, and Roberto Velasquez

. . .

Why has Internet testing created so much interest? Internet advocates stress better, faster, and cheaper services and products, and Internet testing provides many good illustrations of this principle. For example, a new test with accompanying translations could be made available around the world almost instantly. Test publishers can download new tests to secure testing sites in a matter of moments, while other test developers can put tests on their Web sites and make them available to anyone with an Internet connection. Updating a test is also much easier. For example, revising a paper-and-pencil test requires printing and distributing new test forms and answer keys and printing new or revised test manuals, an expensive process that may take several months or years. Revisions of a test that appears on the Internet can be downloaded to testing sites around the world in a few minutes at virtually no cost.

In many paper-and-pencil testing and assessment programs, examinees typically receive their scores and interpretive reports a month or two after they take a test. Their answer sheets must first be mailed to the test publisher, where they are scanned and scored, and perhaps interpreted. Then reports are created, printed, and mailed back to the examinees. In an Internet setting, responses are recorded in computer files as examinees answer each item. Software that computes test scores and generates interpretive reports can be run as soon as the last item is answered, with examinees receiving feedback within a few seconds of completing the test.

Internet testing is more scalable than paper-and-pencil testing. In the language of the Internet, *scalable* means that adding volume results in very little additional cost. Therefore, over the course of a year, the number of times people who visit a Web site and respond to a test may increase, for example, from 5,000 per month to 10,000, but the test publisher does not incur the costs associated with printing, distributing, and scoring 5,000 additional paper-based tests. Of course, eventually an additional server may be required, but additional test administrations are much lower in cost in an Internet setting compared with paper-and-pencil administration. Additionally, because of the minimal costs involved, tests and assessments could be made available at no cost to

---

respondents. For example, researchers may put tests and assessments on their Web pages hoping that people will complete the assessment in order to receive a score report. In exchange, the researcher obtains the data provided by the respondents. Test publishers sometimes put free assessments on their Web sites as a means of attracting potential customers. . . .

Benefits of Internet Testing

The benefits of Internet testing are speed, cost, and convenience. Testing over the Internet provides rapid communication of findings to clients, patients, researchers, and the public. It also allows researchers to collect data rapidly, conveniently, and at lower costs than in face-to-face research settings. Internet testing is cheaper and more efficient; it saves valuable time and provides results more rapidly and easily compared with face-to-face testing. Benefits of Internet testing also include sensitization and familiarization of testing to potential clients and the presentation of test materials in a consistent, uniform manner. The more that potential clients become familiarized with these procedures, the more comfortable their approach to the tests can be, reducing spurious sensitization and situational effects.

Internet testing is also beneficial in that it allows patients in rural settings to be tested, where it would be difficult or impossible to travel to a testing center or to the office of a testing professional. Internet testing is of value to patients who lack transportation to such sites or to those who cannot travel because of physical limitations. In addition, tests may be presented in a precise manner or in interesting and novel ways, so that the client's attention to the testing task is enhanced, compared with face-to-face administration. . . .

ETHICAL AND PROFESSIONAL ISSUES

. . .

Our discussion is framed by the current APA *Ethical Principles of Psychologists and Code of Conduct* (American Psychological Association, 2002), specifically Section 9, Assessment, which covers most of the issues surrounding Internet testing. . . .

9.02 Use of Assessments

(a) Psychologists administer, adapt, score, interpret, or use assessment techniques, interviews, tests, or instruments in a manner and for purposes that are appropriate in light of the research on or evidence of the usefulness and proper application of the techniques.

(b) Psychologists use assessment instruments whose validity and reliability have been established for use with members of the population tested. When such validity or reliability has not been established, psychologists describe the strengths and limitations of test results and interpretation.

(c) Psychologists use assessment methods that are appropriate to an individual's language preference and competence, unless the use of an alternative language is relevant to the assessment issues. (American Psychological Association, 2002)

Internet testing, in many cases, has been simply a process of putting paper-and-pencil or computerized tests onto a new medium. However, although research has explored the equivalence of some forms of computerized and paper-and-pencil tests (e.g., Mead & Drasgow, 1993), very little research has been conducted on the equivalence of Internet testing with these other formats. This may call into question the evidence for the usefulness of these tools. Further, tests that may have been developed and researched in a proctored setting are now often being used in an unproctored context that is facilitated by the Internet and its widening accessibility. This approach calls into question the proper application of the techniques. The effects of both the medium and the context require additional research to ensure appropriate use of tests and assessment on the Internet.

As noted earlier, an advantage to using the Internet to deliver tests is that it may provide greater accessibility and reach than an approach that requires an individual to be at a certain place, at a particular time. This advantage can also create a challenge. Wider access may cause a difference in the populations for which the test was developed versus the ultimate population that has access. For example, a preemployment test may be specifically developed and researched for a management population. Under more traditional conditions, applicants for these management positions may be required to test at a specific location where a significant effort and commitment is involved. However, the Internet may provide easy access to a different population where a nonqualified candidate could decide that he or she might just take the test on the off chance that he or she might gain entry to an otherwise inaccessible position.

Normative issues are also a related concern for Internet test delivery. With good intentions, a test may be placed on a Web site by a psychologist in the United States, but someone in China may have access to it and complete the test. Feedback may be based only on U.S. norms. An inadvertent, but inappropriate, use of norms is the result. This is clearly an area of great potential for the inappropriate use of tests and associated norms. Psychologists will need to make substantial efforts to collect demographic information prior to testing and to provide feedback only to individuals in groups for which normative data are available. . . .

The interpretation of Internet test results poses some unique ethical considerations. The relevant ethical principle is as follows:

9.06 Interpreting Assessment Results

When interpreting assessment results, including automated interpretations, psychologists take into account the purpose of the assessment as well as the various test factors, test-taking abilities, and other characteristics of the person being assessed, such as situational, personal, linguistic, and cultural differences, that might affect psychologists' judgments or reduce the accuracy of their interpretations. They indicate any significant limitations of their interpretations. (American Psychological Association, 2002)

Internet testing will often be conducted in unproctored and in variable environments. Test takers will likely be in unstandardized settings (e.g., home, library, school), and psychologists will have little or no way of knowing exactly what conditions might exist that could influence or limit interpretations. This problem may be alleviated to some extent by the use of instructions to test takers, but it is likely that this will only reduce a small amount of irrelevant variability in scores. Further, when tests are completed in unmonitored situations, there is currently no way to guarantee the true identity of the test taker (Schmit, 2001). Thus, psychologists will need to weigh carefully the importance they place on tests administered over the Internet. Confirmatory methods, administration of equivalent forms, or gathering of data through additional methods will almost always be necessary before making anything other than preliminary evaluations, diagnostic, or predictive decisions.

Gaining an understanding of the test-taking skills and specific personal characteristic of the test taker poses an even greater challenge, given the impersonal approach that characterizes most Internet-based testing and assessment. For example, in preemployment testing situations, a provider may have no way of knowing whether an applicant has a particular disability that might affect the test results and invalidate the possible interpretation of those results. Similarly, a test may be posted in English for use in counseling, but the test taker speaks English only as a second language. Unless the test taker is asked about this condition, the interpretation of results will likely be flawed. The point is that psychologists using Internet testing and assessment must make provisions for understanding the unique needs of test takers that may ultimately affect the interpretation of results.

In addition, test takers must be given information that clearly identifies the purpose of the test so that they can determine whether the test is appropriate for their situation. However, this may not be as easy as providing a purpose statement. The test taker will need help understanding whether the test is a fit for his or her situation. There will likely be a need for prescreening the test taker to help him or her understand whether the test or assessment is right for his or her situation. . . .

9.07 Assessment by Unqualified Persons

Psychologists do not promote the use of psychological assessment techniques by unqualified persons, except when such use is conducted for training purposes with appropriate supervision. (American Psychological Association, 2002)

The Internet has made it very easy for anyone to publish any kind of material in the public domain. This freedom has led many to assume that anything published on the Internet is in the public domain and can be copied and used by anyone who chooses to do so. These and other Internet crimes are raising significant challenges for many professions (Reno, 2000). Whole tests, scales, and test items posted on the Internet can be copied and used by unqualified people. It is the responsibility of psychological test publishers and authors to keep their works under tight control and to report copyright violations. Most do this well with customers who use appropriate channels to gain access to the materials. However, publishers and authors must scan the Web for whole and partial elements of tests that require professional training for administration or interpretation. Partial tests are likely to be the most difficult to identify, yet they may be the most damaging, as the original psychometric properties are likely denigrated. . . . It is the duty of the psychology profession to protect the public from unscrupulous vendors who exploit the Internet with tests of others or, worse yet, with bad renditions of the original test.

Principle 9.07 is written in a way that may suggest that psychologists take reactive steps rather than proactive steps in the protection of the profession. However, others have taken more proactive measures to protect the public. For example, a mental health consumer advocacy and education program has stepped up a process for checking credentials of online counselors (Ainsworth, 2002). Online therapists can register with this organization and have their credentials (e.g., education, experience, background) checked. Therapists who pass this check are issued a special icon for posting on their Web site. Clients can go to the advocacy group's Web site to verify the authenticity of the therapist. A similar program could be established by a consortium of test publishers who have or plan to have their psychological test products administered on the Internet. . . .

9.08 Obsolete Tests and Outdated Test Results

(a) Psychologists do not base their assessment or intervention decisions or recommendations on data or test results that are outdated for the current purpose.

(b) Similarly, psychologists do not base such decisions or recommendations on tests and measures that are obsolete and not useful for the current purpose. (American Psychological Association, 2002)

The Internet is full of obsolete and outdated information. Consumers often have difficulty sorting out the current from the outdated pages available on the Internet. Consistent with the discussion of the previous principle, when partial or whole replication of test materials is made through uninformed or fraudulent acts, these tests materials are likely to become obsolete or outdated, because the original publisher updates the materials. Further, it is quite easy for Web publishers to forget about published pages on the Internet that may be updated in different places, yet the old materials remain available to the public. Finally, psychologists who do not closely watch the literature and other materials from test publishers may inadvertently use outdated materials online. Others may resist change and intentionally use outdated materials. As previously noted, test publishers and authors must carefully monitor the Internet for obsolete and outdated materials and take both proactive and reactive steps to curb and eliminate these practices.

Third-party vendors of Internet tests and associated services also have a set of ethical issues to consider. The relevant ethical principle states the following:

9.09 Test Scoring and Interpretation Services

(a) Psychologists who offer assessment or scoring services to other professionals accurately describe the purpose, norms, validity, reliability, and applications of the procedures and any special qualifications applicable to their use.

(b) Psychologists select scoring and interpretation services (including automated services) on the basis of evidence of the validity of the program and procedures as well as on other appropriate considerations.

(c) Psychologists retain responsibility for the appropriate application, interpretation, and use of assessment instruments, whether they score and interpret such tests themselves or use automated or other services. (American Psychological Association, 2002)

The Internet is full of psychological, para-psychological, and pop-psychology tests, as described in earlier sections. Psychologists must find ways to differentiate themselves from the mass of alternatives that do not meet professional standards (American Educational Research Association et al., 1999). Providing the information described in this ethical principle is the first step in overcoming such confusion. Psychologists who provide tools to other trained professionals should go beyond the simple provision of providing basic psychometric information to potential users. Steps could be taken to show the equivalence of Internet testing with traditional forms of the measure (Epstein et al., 2001). Efforts should also be made to provide consultation and training to test users regarding the challenges faced in using tests on the Internet (Barak & English, 2002). The training should be specific to tests and populations that will take the tests. Processional vendors of psychological tests to be used on the Internet may be able to overcome some of the noise of Internet marketing by becoming professional Internet test consultants. Producers of pop-psychology tests should be made to issue more detailed disclaimers, or warnings, describing their tests as entertainment and not as true tests, just as tobacco manufacturers must issue store warnings on cigarette packages. . . .

9.10 Explaining Assessment Results

Regardless of whether the scoring and interpretation are done by psychologists, by employees or assistants, or by automated or other outside services, psychologists take reasonable steps to ensure that explanations of results are given to the individual or designated representative unless the nature of the relationship precludes provision of an explanation of results (such as in some organizational consulting, preemployment or security screenings, and forensic evaluations), and this fact has been clearly explained to the person being assessed in advance. (American Psychological Association, 2002)

Providing feedback to test takers over the Internet is a topic of concern to many psychologists. There are at least three major ethical issues to consider. First, there are limited ways to understand the conditions under which the test taker completed the test. Did the individual complete the test or did someone else help or do it for him or her? Under what environmental conditions was the test taken? These and many other questions should be answered in order to provide accurate feedback. Second, it is very difficult to provide feedback, particularly negative feedback, to a test taker without knowing the person's emotional and mental state. The wrong type of feedback could exacerbate the individual's condition. Third, it is difficult to provide test takers with immediate emotional support in cases where the feedback has traumatic effects on an individual. . . .

REFERENCES

Ainsworth, M. (2002). *Credentials check*. Retrieved January 11, 2002, from http://www.metanoia.org/imhs/identity.htm

American Psychological Association. (2002). Ethical principles of psychologists and code of conduct. *American Psychologist, 47,* 1597–1611. Available from the APA Web site: http://www.apa.org/ethics/code/index.aspx.

Barak, A., & English, N. (2002). Prospects and limitations of psychological testing on the Internet. *Journal of Technology in Human Services, 19,* 65–89.

Epstein, J., Klinkenberg, W. D., Wiley, D., & McKinley, L. (2001). Insuring sample equivalence across Internet and paper-and-pencil assessments. *Computers in Human Behavior, 17,* 339–346.

Mead, A. D., & Drasgow, F. (1993). Equivalence of computerized and paper-and-pencil cognitive ability tests: A meta-analysis. *Psychological Bulletin, 114,* 449–458.

Reno, J. (2000, September). *Statement by the Attorney General. Symposium of the Americas: Protecting intellectual property in the digital age.* Retrieved January 11, 2002, from http://www.usdoj.gov/archive/ag/speeches/2000/91200agintellectualprop.htm

Schmit, M. J. (2001, September). Use of psychological measures for online recruitment and pre-employment selection. In L. Frumkin (Chair), *Internet-based assessment: State of the art in testing.* Symposium conducted at the 109th Annual Conference of the American Psychological Association, San Francisco, CA.

COMMENTARY: With few exceptions, cognitive and personality testing are the exclusive purview of the psychologist. What distinguishes us the most from the other helping professions has undergone steady and impactful change in the course of the past few decades as a result of the advent of increasingly complex cybertechnology. In rough order (with some overlap) came computerized scanning, computerized scoring, real-time computerized data entry, and computerized interpretation.

The field of psychology now faces the circumstance of its unique contribution to mental health care being conducted over the Internet, perhaps without any opportunity for direct, in-person contact with the client/patient in question. How does this affect the reliability and validity of psychological testing, and, in turn, what additional and/or modified legal and ethical obligations will accompany this change in circumstances? Is a test administered via the Internet really the same test at all, even if all of the potential questions and answers are the same?

The following references are recommended for those interested in further investigation of such factors as the absence or alternative provision of proctoring, the specter of cheating (such as covert recourse to off-screen resources in cognitive assessment), and overall validity concerns.

Carstairs, J., & Myors, B. (2009). Internet testing: A natural experiment reveals test score inflation on high-stakes, unproctored cognitive test. *Computers in Human Behavior, 25,* 738–742. http://dx.doi.org/10.1016/j.chb.2009.01.011

Darby, D. G., Fredrickson, J., Pietrzak, R. H., Maruff, P., Woodward, M., & Brodtmann, A. (2014). Reliability and usability of an Internet-based computerized cognitive testing battery in community-dwelling older people. *Computers in Human Behavior, 30,* 199–205. http://dx.doi.org/10.1016/j.chb.2013.08.009

Landers, R. N., & Sackett, P. R. (2012). Offsetting performance losses due to cheating in unproctored internet-based testing by increasing the applicant pool. *International Journal of Selection and Assessment, 20,* 220–228. http://dx.doi.org/10.1111/j.1468-2389.2012.00594.x

Le Corff, Y., Gingras, V., & Busque-Carrier, Mathieu. (2017). Equivalence of unproctored Internet testing and proctored paper-and-pencil testing of the Big Five. *International Journal of Selection and Assessment, 25,* 154–160. http://dx.doi.org/10.1111/ijsa.12168

Lievens, F., & Burke, E. (2011). Dealing with the threats inherent in unproctored Internet testing of cognitive ability: Results from a large-scale operational test program. *Journal of Occupational and Organizational Psychology, 84,* 817–824. http://dx.doi.org/10.1348/096317910X522672

6.8. Practical and Ethical Issues in Teaching Psychological Testing

Patricia A. Rupert, Neal F. Kozlowski, Laura A. Hoffman, Denise D. Daniels, and Jeanne M. Piette

Graduate students in professional psychology spend many hours practicing how to administer, score, and interpret psychological tests. Although such practice is essential to the process of developing competency in the use of complex assessment tools, providing opportunities for this practice raises both practical problems and ethical concerns. With whom should students practice—clients in need of service, undergraduate volunteers, friends, relatives, classmates? How should "practice" subjects be identified and recruited? What are our responsibilities to practice subjects, particularly in terms of ensuring informed consent, providing feedback, and offering assistance if problems emerge? What should be done with the personal, private information obtained from tests given to practice subjects?

The teaching of psychological testing has a long history in graduate training programs in professional psychology, documented over the years through numerous surveys about what tests are taught or about attitudes of training programs toward particular tests or techniques (e.g., Marlowe, Wetzler, & Gibbings, 1992; Piotrowski & Keller, 1984, 1992; Shemberg & Keeley, 1970; Watkins, 1991). These surveys have consistently demonstrated that psychological testing plays a critical role in both the training and practice of psychologists and that tests most frequently taught include complex tests such as the Wechsler scales, the Minnesota Multiphasic Personality Inventory (MMPI), and the Rorschach (see Watkins, 1991). Furthermore, the teaching of child testing has received increased attention over the years (e.g., Elbert, 1984; Elbert & Holden, 1987). However, there has been relatively little focus on "how" testing is taught. We thus have no systematic information about how instructors handle the important ethical questions raised above or about the specific ethical challenges and problems they encounter in their efforts to provide appropriate training experiences for their students.

From "Practical and Ethical Issues in Teaching Psychological Testing," by P. A. Rupert, N. F. Kozlowski, L. A. Hoffman, D. D. Daniels, and J. M. Piette, 1999, *Professional Psychology: Research and Practice, 30*, pp. 209–214. Copyright 1999 by the American Psychological Association.

Portions of these data were presented in two poster presentations, one on issues in teaching adult testing and one on use of child volunteers, at the 104th Annual Convention of the American Psychological Association in Toronto, Ontario, Canada, August 1996. The authors wish to thank Drs. Grayson Holmbeck and Karen Wills for their comments on early versions of the surveys, and Ms. Galena Shabadasli for her valuable assistance in coding data.

The *Ethical Principles of Psychologists and Code of Conduct* (American Psychological Association [APA], 1992; hereinafter referred to as APA Ethics Code) includes detailed standards related to Assessment (Section 2) and Teaching and Training Supervision (Section 6), but it does not specifically address issues involved in testing for training purposes. The code stresses the importance of competence in all professional activities (Principle A and Standard 1.04) and in assessment techniques specifically (Standard 2.02). The code further emphasizes the importance of providing feedback (Standard 2.09) to the person assessed, of maintaining confidentiality in all professional relationships (Standard 5.02), and of contributing to the welfare of others (Principle E). However, when a child or adult is tested by a novice graduate student and the primary goal is to advance the training of the graduate student, all of these standards may be challenged. The APA Ethics Code acknowledges the importance of providing proper training and supervision (Standard 1.22) in order to protect the welfare of others. Beyond that, however, it offers little guidance for dealing with the tensions that invariably exist between the training needs of students and the professional responsibilities we have to those who serve as practice subjects.

THE "PRACTICE" TESTING TRAINING SURVEYS

The present surveys were conducted to understand how testing instructors in professional psychology doctoral programs deal with the ethical issues raised in teaching graduate students to conduct psychological testing. Attention was paid to five areas which have particular relevance to the welfare of practice subjects: student competency and preparation, access to appropriate practice subjects, feedback issues, confidentiality and data handling issues, and consent issues.

A survey packet was sent to training directors of 275 APA-accredited (in 1993) doctoral programs in clinical, counseling, and school psychology. Each survey packet contained a cover letter explaining the project and asking for the director's cooperation in forwarding the surveys to appropriate faculty members. Each packet also contained two envelopes with questionnaires, one for child testing and one for adult testing. Reminder postcards were sent approximately 3 weeks after the initial mailing.

Overall, 162 out of a possible 550 forms were returned, for a response rate of 30%. Eighty-nine of the adult assessment surveys were returned, but 13 of these simply contained a notation that no introductory assessment course was offered. This left a total of 76 usable "adult" surveys (56 from clinical, 15 from counseling, and 5 from school psychology programs). Seventy-three of the child assessment surveys were returned, but 11 of these were returned with a notation that no child assessment course was offered. This left a total of 62 usable "child" surveys (44 from clinical, 6 from counseling, and 12 from school psychology programs).

The survey form asked respondents to provide information about the initial skill building course in their adult or child testing sequence. Basic data about the course (e.g., information about the instructor, assistant, students, tests administered, preparation prior to testing) and specific information about the procedures for practice test administrations for both nonclient volunteers and actual clients (e.g., methods for obtaining testing subjects, informed consent procedures, feedback procedures) were sought. Information about student supervision and storage or handling of test data was also sought. Finally, an open-ended question asked respondents to describe any ethical dilemmas or concerns they had encountered while teaching the testing course. They were encouraged to give a description of the problem and to indicate how they approached or resolved the problem (and 92 of the 162 respondents described one or more problems). A total of 154 problem descriptions (79 from adult and 75 from child testing instructors) were coded to provide insight into problems experienced in the five areas examined in the present study.

Because of the modest response rate, we must be cautious about generalizing the data. Nonetheless, our findings offer initial information about how some instructors deal with areas of ethical concern in the teaching of psychological testing and about the problems programs have encountered in these areas. This information is presented here in order to highlight key concerns and guide recommendations. . . .

Tests Taught

The actual tests taught in the "initial skill building" courses varied considerably. Respondents to the adult survey listed 79 tests, including intelligence, neuropsychological, personality, projective, achievement, and occupational tests. Tests most frequently listed were the Weschler Adult Intelligence Scale—Revised (WAIS–R; 59 respondents), the MMPI or MMPI–II (28), the Weschler Intelligence Scale for Children—Revised (WISC–R) or WISC–III (26), the Rorschach (21) and the Thematic Apperception Test (TAT; 20).

Respondents to the child survey listed 49 tests, including intelligence tests, achievement tests, projective tests, and infant development scales. Intelligence tests were by far the most frequently taught, with the WISC–R or WISC–III listed by 48 respondents, followed by the Stanford–Binet Intelligence Scale (24), the Weschler Preschool and Primary Scale of Intelligence (WPPSI) (17), and the WAIS–R (14). The only other tests listed by 10 or more respondents were the Kaufman Assessment Battery for Children (19), Bender–Gestalt (11), and the Rorschach (10).

Student Competency and Preparation

In a class that provides the first practical experience with testing, careful preparation and supervision are critical, not only for building competency but also for protecting the welfare of individuals being tested. Instructors of both adult and child testing courses relied heavily on the use of nonclient volunteers as practice subjects. Overall, for adult testing, 66 respondents reported using volunteers and 25 reported using actual clients; for child testing, 59 respondents reported using nonclient child volunteers and 20 included child clients. When clients were tested, it was nearly always after students had prepared by practicing on nonclient volunteers; only two adult instructors and one child instructor reported using solely clients as practice subjects.

Prior to testing nonclient volunteers, students in both adult and child testing courses engaged in a number of preparatory activities. Most commonly, they practiced with fellow students, observed the instructor test a classmate or volunteer, or observed videotapes.

Student testing activities were supervised in a variety of ways. Of the 67 adult testing instructors and 60 child instructors providing information about supervision, nearly all (over 90%) reported that test protocols and reports were reviewed. In addition, over half indicated that live supervision was provided, and close to half of the child instructors and one third of adult instructors reported that observation of taped testing sessions was provided.

Despite the apparent emphasis on preparation and supervision, problems did occur in this area. In fact, problems related to student competency and preparation were second in frequency in the open-ended problem descriptions of both adult and child testing instructors; adult instructors described 25 problems and child instructors described 20 that were coded in this area. The majority of these problems involved direct concerns about student competency to administer and interpret tests (e.g., students not following appropriate procedures, not scoring tests properly). With children, an additional concern was raised about students who lacked experience in relating to children. A number of the problems in this area also overlapped with other areas and were thus coded in two areas (e.g., students giving feedback inappropriately or poorly, students violating recruitment policies, students violating confidentiality policies or using data inappropriately, and students not following consent procedures).

The wide range of problems in this area highlights the breadth of preparation that is required in order to safeguard the well-being of practice subjects. Beyond basic test administration procedures, students need to be carefully instructed in policies and procedures related to recruiting subjects, seeking consent, and handling test data. In child testing courses, students may also require instruction and practice in interacting with children at various age levels.

Access to Practice Subjects

Instructors of both adult and child testing courses seemed to turn to a number of sources to find appropriate practice subjects. Of the 64 adult instructors who provided information about sources of nonclient volunteers, a large number reported use of university contacts such as a departmental subject pool (over 50% reported use), university classes (about 42%), or friends of students and faculty (over 50%). The community-at-large (about 31%) and community organizations (about 13%) were also reported as sources of volunteers. Of the 59 child testing instructors who provided information about nonclient child volunteers, many reported use of community resources, including the community at large (about 42%), schools (about 36%), day care centers (about 31%), and community organizations (about 22%). By far, however, the most frequently used source for child volunteers was friends (over 80%).

The use of actual clients as testing subjects was less frequent, perhaps because of the potential tensions between service and training needs plus the difficulty finding clients who may be suitable for beginning level students to test. Interestingly, for both adult (24 instructors reporting) and child (21 instructors reporting) courses, university in-house training clinics were the most frequently noted source of clients (about 63% of adult instructors and about 57% of child instructors reported use). In addition, adult clients were secured from inpatient units (about 42% reported use), outpatient clinics (about 29%), and residential centers (about 17%), and child clients were secured from school system referrals (about 48%), outpatient treatment centers (about 29%), residential centers (about 29%), and inpatient centers (about 24%).

Problems in this area were reported with some frequency; 19 problems described by adult testing instructors and 15 by child testing instructors were coded as being related to this area. These problems seemed to relate primarily to access to appropriate nonclient volunteers. With both adults and children, many problems involved multiple relationship concerns (i.e., testing children of friends or relatives or adults who are known to students through other personal contacts or professional roles) or problems in finding individuals who do not have serious problems, who are not in therapy, or who will not need to be tested at a later time (particularly with children).

These data highlight a number of ethical issues that must be considered in finding appropriate practice subjects. First, the issue of multiple relationships is of concern, particularly given the heavy reliance on friends or university sources. In this regard, the procedure of having students recruit their own volunteers through personal contacts seems especially problematic; in such instances, student create multiple role situations where the potential for breaches of confidentiality and conflicting responsibilities is high. To avoid such problems, it seems important to have a system for securing volunteers that does not rely on students to find their own testing subjects.

To obtain practice subjects, the instructor or program needs to establish contacts necessary to secure appropriate testing subjects. Our data suggest that, for adult volunteers, contacts may be readily established through the use of a departmental subject pool or university classes. To secure child volunteers, contacts with day care centers, schools, and community organizations may be helpful. As an extra safeguard, it is important to educate graduate students about the ethical issues and potential dangers associated with dual relationships. In this regard, a beginning level testing course provides an excellent opportunity for students to learn to establish and maintain appropriate professional boundaries.

A second ethical issue relates to the freedom of "volunteers" to actually choose to serve as "practice" test subjects. In particular, the use of friends and personal or professional contacts to secure volunteers may result in subtle pressure to say yes to help out a colleague or friend. Children may be especially vulnerable if parents feel such pressure. Eliminating the use of personal contacts to secure volunteers should greatly reduce this problem.

The third ethical concern arises in the tension between the training situation and the needs of volunteers who may be in distress or encountering some difficulty that may require future evaluation and service. Given concerns about student competence and potential harm to volunteers, it seems important that recruitment procedures consider ways to minimize the possibility that an adult or child volunteer requires service. Careful selection of nonclinical settings as sources for volunteers (e.g., classes, schools, agencies that serve individuals in the normal range of functioning) may be an important first step in this regard. Beyond that, a brief screening process through telephone interview or questionnaire may provide a way of identifying individuals who are inappropriate practice subjects and directing them to appropriate services. The content of screening questions, of course, depends on the nature of the population and the practice tests to be given; for example, in screening child volunteers for cognitive or intellectual testing, it might be important to ask parents about such issues as developmental concerns or school problems.

Feedback

Feedback policies and procedures varied depending on whether nonclient volunteers or clients were being tested. With nonclient volunteers, only a small percentage of respondents reported giving feedback; about 26% of adult testing instructors and 30% of child testing instructors reported giving feedback on a routine basis. When given, feedback was almost always verbal.

With clients, feedback was much more frequently given on a routine basis; 79% of adult instructors ($n = 24$) and 100% of child instructors ($n = 20$) gave feedback to clients or their parents. With adult clients, feedback was most often verbal (67%), whereas with children, it was most often both written and verbal (59%). With child clients, 50% also reported giving feedback to the child in addition to the parent.

The tension surrounding this area was apparent in the number and types of problems encountered here. Problems related to feedback were the most frequently reported by both adult (34 described problems in this area) and child testing instructors (29 described problems here). In nearly all instances, these problems involved nonclient volunteers, and most centered around no feedback policies. As the data indicated, the majority of instructors adopt no feedback policies when volunteers are tested. In other words, these volunteers are truly seen as "practice" subjects and, given concerns about the validity of testing plus the expectation that these volunteers are relatively intact, results of testing are not shared with the testing subject, parents, or any outside agencies. However, two types of problems were reported with some frequency by both adult and child instructors: (a) volunteers or their parents pressure for feedback, and (b) testing reveals a problem that may require intervention. With adult volunteers, such problems generally took the form of severe distress or psychopathology and suicidal risk. With children, suspected child abuse or learning problems were also noted. A number of problems in this area were also coded as being related to student competency issues; for example, students giving feedback when they had been told not to, giving feedback poorly or insensitively, or forgetting to give feedback that was supposed to be given.

These data highlight two ethical concerns related to the rights and well-being of the practice subjects in testing courses. First, in terms of subjects' rights, the issue of feedback must be considered carefully, and very clear policies must be established and communicated to both students and testing subjects. The APA Ethics Code (Standard 2.09; APA, 1992) states that an explanation of assessment results must be given unless the nature of the assessment precludes such an explanation, and this is clearly explained in advance. When beginning level students are testing nonclient volunteers, two aspects of the testing situation would seem to justify a policy of no feedback: (a) the "subject" is not seeking and, one hopes, does not need, clinical services; and (b) the validity of test results is questionable. Such a policy seems both responsible and ethical if communicated in writing in advance for volunteers. When clients are tested and the need and expectation of services exist, however, feedback must be given. In these instances, adequate preparation and supervision of students is critical to ensure that test results are valid and that feedback is given in a sensitive, helpful manner. If students are giving feedback, role playing with the instructor, assistant, or classmates may be introduced to prepare them for this important function.

Second, even when nonclient volunteers are tested and there is no expectation of feedback, the data underscore that we cannot ignore the well-being of practice subjects. The problem descriptions of our respondents indicate that, even with nonclients, situations occur that challenge the purely "training" nature of the testing and may require some response (e.g., a testing subject expresses suicidal ideation or a child provides evidence of abuse). Thus, a feedback policy must establish criteria for identifying, and procedures for dealing with, emergency situations. These must also be clearly communicated to both students and testing subjects.

Confidentiality and Data Handling

Both child and adult testing instructors indicated that raw test data was reviewed by a number of people. Of the 64 adult instructors and 58 child instructors who provided information about test data from nonclient volunteers, most indicated that test protocols were reviewed by the instructor (about 90% for adult and about 95% for child). Protocols were also frequently reviewed by graduate assistants (about 80% for adult and about 69% for child) and occasionally reviewed by other students in the class (about 27% for adults, about 22% for child). A similar pattern of review was reported when actual clients were tested.

Most respondents seemed sensitive to the confidentiality concerns, particularly with nonclient volunteers. Of the 64 adult instructors and the 57 child instructors providing information about nonclient volunteers, over 80% reported removing names of volunteers from the raw test data and from case presentation materials, and slightly over 90% removed names from test reports. With clients (*n* = 25 for adult and 19 for child testing), names were less frequently removed from both test data and test reports (approximately 50% of adult instructors and approximately 30% of child instructors reported removal). They were more likely to be removed for case presentations, particularly with children (64% for adult and about 84% for child).

Sixty-six adult and 60 child instructors provided information regarding what happened to raw test data when the process of testing and supervision was completed. Some respondents checked more than one option, and this often seemed to be due to the different policies that existed for nonclient volunteers and actual clients. Although these different policies were not assessed, it appeared that data for clients were often placed in clinical records, whereas volunteer data were more likely to be kept by the student (about 50% of instructors checked this) or destroyed (about 25–30% checked this). Only a small number of respondents reported storing data for research purposes (under 15% for both adult and child instructors) and about 15–18% indicated "other" policies (which typically involved the data being kept by the instructor, field supervisor, or department).

Problems related to confidentiality, privacy, or handling of data were reported with some frequency; 12 problems reported by adult instructors and 12 reported by child instructors were coded in this area. Some of these have already been mentioned because they involved other issues: suspected child abuse which raised issues related to feedback and confidentiality, students not following instructions or appropriate procedures related to maintaining data, and using volunteers whose identity could not be disguised. Problems coded solely in this area involved such things as concern about the use of electronic mail to exchange report drafts, inappropriate use of data by parents, and the requirement that students take tests and thus reveal information about themselves to the instructor or classmates. One somewhat unusual problem involved nonclient volunteers requesting test data after time had elapsed (6 months to 1 year) for court purposes.

The APA Ethics Code (Standard 5; APA, 1992) clearly states our "primary obligation" to protect the privacy and confidentiality of those with whom we work. In training settings, special attention to the confidentiality of nonclient volunteers is important; because volunteers and their families may be known to class members through personal or other professional contacts, the potential for unnecessary invasions of privacy or damaging revelations of sensitive information is high. Thus, it is important that data gathered during testing be protected, not only during the training process, but also after training functions have been completed.

More attention may need to be given to what happens to test data and information once training purposes have been served. Obviously, if testing has been done for clinical purposes, test data and reports belong in appropriately managed clinical files. However, if test data are not needed for clinical purposes or if copies of clinical data exist, it seems important that this information either be destroyed or that clear policies be established to guard against careless release of confidential information.

In addition to confidentiality of testing subjects, problem descriptions suggested that instructors must also be concerned about confidentiality of graduate students taking testing courses when these students take tests themselves or test fellow students to gain practice. This was reported as a very common method of providing students with testing experience and seems to be a sound way of introducing students to test administration procedures before asking them to test nonclient volunteers. However, when the testing procedures require students to reveal sensitive information about themselves to their peers or the instructor, this procedure raises ethical concerns about dual roles (Keith-Spiegel & Koocher, 1985). In fact, two of the ethical problems reported involved students revealing information about themselves or classmates in write-ups of practice tests. Although practicing with classmates may play an important role in preparing students to administer complex tests, it is important that instructors be aware of the ethical issues involved and institute safeguards to avoid placing students in quasi-client situations that require them to reveal personal information. Such safeguards may include having students practice only parts of tests or setting up the testing situation as a role play in which the student being tested is asked to play a specific role rather than reveal information about himself or herself.

Consent

Formal consent procedures were routinely followed with nonclient volunteers and clients or their parents and guardians. Of the 63 instructors providing information about consent with nonclient adult volunteers, 63% reported that they used written consent, 22% used verbal consent, 6% used a combination of written and verbal, and only 3% reported that they did not have a formal consent procedure. Similarly, of the 59 instructors providing information about child volunteers, 71% secured written consent of the parent or guardian, 19% secured verbal consent, 8% used a combination of written and verbal, and only 1 instructor did not have a formal consent procedure. With actual clients, particularly child clients, consent procedures seemed more formalized. All 20 instructors who provided information about child clients reported securing formal consent from a parent or guardian; 80% used written consent and 20% used a combination of written and verbal. With adult clients (25 instructors), 60% used a written format, 20% used a combination of written and verbal, and 20% obtained only verbal consent.

With children, an additional ethical issue concerns the child's involvement in the consent process. Both child volunteers and clients were included in the consent process most often by securing their verbal assent to testing; with volunteers, only 25% reported using written consent and, with clients, only 21%.

The concept of informed consent requires that individuals have information necessary to make an informed decision about participation. Respondents were asked to indicate what type of information was provided in the consent process for both adult and child volunteers and clients. Information included most frequently (by at least 80% of the respondents) in the consent process for all included test procedures, confidentiality, how data are used, and feedback policy. Interestingly, freedom to withdraw was also mentioned by at least 80% of the respondents, except with adult clients where only 64% reported covering this. With parents of child clients, risks and benefits were covered by at least 80% of respondents; however, with parents of child volunteers and with adults (either volunteers or clients), they were covered by only 50–60% of the respondents.

Only a small number of problems that seemed to relate directly to the consent process were reported and of these, several related to other ethical areas as well (e.g., students not getting proper consent, difficulties getting subjects to consent when no feedback policies are explained).

Although the APA Ethics Code (APA, 1992) does not explicitly state that informed consent is required for testing, Canter, Bennett, Jones, and Nagy (1994) noted that such a requirement seems inherent in several standards (e.g., Standards 2.01, 1.14, and 4.02). Obviously, when dealing with minor children, it is the consent of the parent or guardian that must be secured (see Standard 4.02). Most respondents seemed sensitive to the importance of obtaining and documenting such consent, particularly when actual clients are tested. However, it should be noted that a substantial number of instructors reported obtaining only verbal consent with adult clients and with nonclient volunteers or their parents. Given the training nature of the experience, a formal written procedure seems advisable when dealing with all practice subjects. In fact, a written consent procedure that very clearly covers the nature of the test situation, ways in which data will be used, and feedback policy might help minimize problems encountered in these areas. If testing data are to be used for research purposes, then procedures for consent to research should be closely followed (see Standard 6.11).

An additional consent issue with children involves the participation of the child in the consent process. As discussed by Gustafson and McNamara (1987), there is considerable research evidence that children can participate in at least some types of treatment decisions. Indeed, the APA Ethics Code highlights the importance of informing individuals who are legally incapable of giving consent about interventions or procedures and seeking their assent (see Standards 4.02 and 6.11). It was thus encouraging to note that a very high percentage of respondents reported involving the child in the consent process, generally by obtaining the child's verbal assent. Such assent may be particularly important with child volunteers who are not being tested because of any identified need and who have nothing to gain from the testing. To avoid exploiting these children for our training purposes, special efforts need to be made to ensure their willingness to participate and protect their well-being throughout the testing process.

SUMMARY AND CONCLUSIONS

Obtaining "practice" subjects for beginning graduate students in psychological testing courses is both a practical problem and one which raises ethical issues. These issues center around the ongoing tension between the training needs of students in our testing classes and the needs, rights, and well-being of persons with whom they practice. The tension may be reduced by preparing students carefully and providing opportunities for them to practice with individuals who are not in need of service and whose well-being is not at high risk. However, such practice subjects are not easily identified. Furthermore, once we identify appropriate practice subjects, we must be careful not to exploit them or infringe on their rights. Careful attention must be given to recruitment policies, consent procedures, confidentiality rights, and policies for handling information obtained during the testing process and for dealing with problems that emerge. . . .

Adequate preparation and supervision of beginning level students are important, not only in terms of test administration and interpretation but also in handling issues surrounding consent, feedback, confidentiality, and relationships with testing subjects. Whether students test volunteers or clients, they are learning skills and attitudes that will be a critical part of their professional lives. As a result, for the benefit of students' professional education as well as the protection of those on whom they practice, it is important that students develop an understanding of ethical concerns such as dual relationships, informed consent, and confidentiality and that they begin to develop sound ethical practices related to these concerns.

REFERENCES

American Psychological Association. (1992). Ethical principles of psychologists and code of conduct. *American Psychologist, 47*, 1597–1611.

Canter, M. B., Bennett, B. E., Jones, S. E., & Nagy, T. F. (1994). *Ethics for psychologists: A commentary on the APA Ethics Code*. Washington, DC: American Psychological Association.

Elbert, J. C. (1984). Training in child diagnostic assessment: A survey of clinical psychology graduate programs. *Journal of Clinical Child Psychology, 13*, 122–133.

Elbert, J. C., & Holden, E. W. (1987). Child diagnostic assessment: Current training practices in clinical psychology internships. *Professional Psychology: Research and Practice, 18*, 587–596.

Gustafson, K. E., & McNamara, J. R. (1987). Confidentiality with minor clients: Issues and guidelines for therapists. *Professional Psychology: Research and Practice, 18*, 503–508.

Keith-Spiegel, P., & Koocher, G. (1985). *Ethics in psychology*. New York: Random House.

Marlowe, D. B., Wetzler, S., & Gibbings, E. N. (1992). Graduate training in psychological assessment: What Psy.D.'s and Ph.D.'s must know. *The Journal of Training and Practice in Professional Psychology, 6*, 9–18.

Piotrowski, C., & Keller, J. W. (1984). Psychodiagnostic testing in APA-approved clinical psychology programs. *Professional Psychology: Research and Practice, 15*, 450–456.

Piotrowski, C., & Keller, J. W. (1992). Psychological testing in applied settings: A literature review from 1982–1992. *The Journal of Training and Practice in Professional Psychology, 6,* 74–82.

Shemberg, K., & Keeley, S. (1970). Psychodiagnostic training in the academic setting: Past and present. *Journal of Consulting and Clinical Psychology, 34,* 205–211.

Watkins, C. E., Jr. (1991). What have surveys taught us about the teaching and practice of psychological assessment? *Journal of Personality Assessment, 56,* 426–437.

7

Therapy and Other Forms of Intervention

ocusing at first on individual psychotherapy, it is the psychologist–client/
patient dyad that is the most intimate relationship—in the ethically appropriate sense of this term—forged in all of clinical service provision. Over what
may be a considerable period of time, vast amounts of highly personal and
detailed information are conveyed, to an extent that the client/patient may
never have experienced at any other time in his or her life. Ethical lapses in this
regard are particularly likely to inspire consternation on the part of the client/
patient.

Themes no less embarrassing or consequential can surface in group psychotherapy, and under these circumstances, of course, confidences are being
shared with a broader audience. Complicating this situation still further is the
fact that the presence of additional parties is considered in many jurisdictions
to erode the invocation of legal privilege—a critical issue when attempts are
made to obtain records from the psychologist in the course of criminal and
civil proceedings.

"Other forms of intervention" can include psychologists' increasing involvement in a broad range of integrated, multidisciplinary health care settings.
Whether it be prescribing psychoactive or other forms of medication, supplementing the efforts of a surgical team to sedate or otherwise calm a preoperative
client/patient, or advising families on potential outcomes to a specific medical
procedure, expanding roles mean increased pressure on psychologists to expand
their knowledge bases in order to inform and keep pace with an evolving standard of practice.

http://dx.doi.org/10.1037/0000125-008
Ethical Conflicts in Psychology, Fifth Edition, by E. Y. Drogin

A desire to be helpful must be tempered with a sense of limitations that can extend beyond matters of technical skill and mastery of the professional literature to those of what is best described as "cultural competence." Open-mindedness and acceptance, although admittedly prerequisites to successful engagement in service provision to members of diverse populations, are ultimately no substitute for the development of true insight into the commonly shared goals, struggles, priorities, and preferences of the cultural cohort in question.

Psychotherapy in the modern age is no longer restricted—to the extent it ever really was—to the examining room. Services are now routinely provided at distances of hundreds or even thousands of miles, both domestically and overseas. Following close upon the upgrading of these technically enhanced options have been attendant concerns regarding licensure, jurisdictionally determined ethical standards, and arrangements for emergency coverage. Even when psychotherapy is conducted under traditional circumstances, it has been common for several years now to augment these experiences with adjunct practice resources designed to supplement therapeutic gains. To what extent must the use of these materials be monitored?

Among its other features, this chapter addresses currently accepted standards for informed consent, strategies for tracking ethical obligations in the dynamically charged atmosphere of couple and family therapy, and American Psychological Association guidelines for conducting psychotherapy with—among others—gay, lesbian, and bisexual as well as transgender and gender nonconforming clients/patients.

7.1. Seeking an Understanding of Informed Consent

Jeffrey E. Barnett

Regardless of the nature of the professional relationship, be it psychotherapy, assessment, research, clinical supervision, consultation, or some other professional role, psychologists are ethically and legally bound to begin these relationships only after initiating a process of informed consent (American Psychological Association [APA], 2002; Knapp & VandeCreek, 2006). *Informed consent* is a shared decision-making process in which the professional communicates sufficient information to the other individual so that she or he may make an informed decision about participation in the professional relationship. In general, clients, supervisees, research participants, and others trust psychologists and depend on them to protect their best interests and to ensure that all risks for harm or adverse outcomes are minimized. Additionally, this dependence on the professional is accentuated by the expert status of the psychologist. Professionals have knowledge, skills, and expertise that others seek out for assistance. But, as all professional services bring with them some risk of adverse impact, however small it may be, prospective participants need adequate information at the outset to help them weigh the potential benefits and risks of both participation and lack of participation.

Unfortunately, informed consent is not uniformly applied, and confusion appears to exist concerning the specifics of informed consent. Challenges for psychologists include knowing just which information to share and in how much detail, deciding in what form it should be shared, knowing how to ensure the prospective participant's understanding of the information, knowing when this process should occur, and the like. These and other challenges relevant to the informed-consent process are addressed, questions for consideration are raised, and recommendations for ethical and effective practice are made.

HISTORICAL PERSPECTIVE

Informed consent has a long history in the health professions, beginning in medicine, and has evolved substantially over the years through case law. Initially, physicians could be seen as benevolent authoritarians who very paternalistically directed each patient's assessment and treatment. Through the 19th and into the 20th century, physicians generally did not first obtain their patients' consent prior to providing services to them and were not seen as under any widely accepted ethical or legal mandate to do so (Grisso & Applebaum, 1998). This model has been described as the "doctor-knows-best system," in which patients were passive recipients of services (Welfel, 2006). There was little sharing of information, collaboration, or patient involvement in decision making, and as a result, patients may be seen as having been more vulnerable to abuse or harm. Overall, the doctrine of informed consent changed this practice to require that health professionals share information about anticipated treatments sufficient to allow the patient to make an informed decision about participation.

A foundation for informed consent seen in case law is *Schloendorf v. Society of New York Hospital* (1914), in which Judge Cardozo stated that "every human being of adult years and sound mind has a right to determine what shall be done with his own body" (as cited in Stromberg et al., 1988, p. 446). Then, over a number of years beginning in the 1950s, a series of malpractice cases ruled on issues of alleged harm to patients by health care professionals. In a number of these cases, rulings specifically addressed issues of harm to patients as a result of how this evolving process of informed consent was addressed by the professional. Each of these legal rulings has contributed to the accepted professional standards for informed consent. It is interesting to note and important to emphasize that prior to these legal rulings, the issue addressed in each had not been part of prevailing professional standards.

In *Salgo v. Stanford* (1957), the California Court of Appeals ruled that a patient must fully comprehend the information shared and that risks and benefits associated with participation must be included in that consent for it to be considered valid. In the landmark case of *Canterbury v. Spence* (1972), it was ruled that merely answering patients' questions is insufficient and that all information necessary must be shared that patients need "for an intelligent decision" (p. 783) regarding participation and that it must be presented in terms that can be understood by the individual. This is a significant step forward from the previous standard of sharing what health professionals determined patients needed to know to make their decisions. In *Truman v. Thomas* (1980), the California Supreme Court ruled that patients must also be informed of the risks associated with refusing treatment, not just the risks associated with acceptance of the proposed treatment. And, more recently, the case of *Osheroff v. Chestnut Lodge* (1985), although settled out of court, established the precedent that patients must also be informed of reasonably available alternatives and their relative risks and benefits as well. Those familiar with informed-consent standards included in the APA's *Ethical Principles of Psychologists and Code of Conduct* (referred to as the APA ethics code; APA, 2002) will see many of the currently accepted elements of informed consent above in this brief review of its chronological development.

GOALS OF INFORMED CONSENT

Although informed consent is rooted in the medical field and originally concerned specific discrete procedures, it has become widely accepted as an essential aspect of each client's participation in the psychotherapy process as well as in all other services psychologists provide. Authors such as Beahrs and Gutheil (2001) defined informed consent as "the process of sharing information with patients that is essential to their ability to make rational choices among multiple options" (p. 4). But informed consent brings with it several other important benefits, including "promoting client autonomy and self-determination, minimizing the risk of exploitation and harm, fostering rational decision-making, and enhancing the therapeutic alliance" (Snyder & Barnett, 2006, p. 37). Although the psychologist's theoretical orientation may affect one's view of informed consent, in general it can be seen as consistent with psychologists' general goal of establishing a collaborative relationship that is built on trust, openness, and respect. Additionally, the provision of information necessary to make an informed choice also promotes the sharing of decision-making power in the professional relationship, which enhances the professional collaboration, reduces risks of exploitation and harm (Meisel, Roth, & Lidz, 1977), and encourages trust, openness, and sharing in the relationship (Snyder & Barnett, 2006).

Informed consent should be viewed as a process, not as a single event that occurs at the outset of treatment (or supervision, research, or any other professional relationship). It is best implemented if integrated into the professional relationship from its outset through its completion. The APA ethics code (APA, 2002) states that psychologists should begin the informed-consent process "as early as is feasible in the therapeutic relationship" (p. 1072), but psychologists should not consider their obligation met at that point. It is important to update the informed-consent agreement throughout the course of the professional relationship as circumstances warrant, such as any proposed significant changes to the treatment to be offered and, thus, changes to the original informed-consent agreement.

With regard to treatment services, the APA ethics code (APA, 2002) requires psychologists to include in each informed-consent agreement information about "the nature and anticipated course of therapy, fees, involvement of third parties, and limits of confidentiality" (p. 1072) as well as reasonable alternatives available, their relative risks and benefits, and the right to refuse or withdraw from treatment. Additional requirements are also included for informed consent to supervision, research, assessment, and other services provided by psychologists. Studies (e.g., Sullivan, Martin, & Handelsman, 1993) have found that consumers value having detailed information provided to them at the outset of the professional relationship and even rate those psychologists who engage in an informed-consent process as more expert and trustworthy than those who do not. But just how that information is provided to them can significantly affect the specific information they request (Braaten, Otto, & Handelsman, 1993). Whether informed consent should be provided through use of written documents, verbally, or in combination is unclear, yet many professionals suggest a combination approach. The use of an appropriate written consent agreement can augment all verbal consent discussions. It helps ensure that clients understand what they are agreeing to, provides clients with a written document they may refer to and review over the course of the professional relationship, and allows the psychologist to refer to it as well should there be any confusion or misunderstandings later.

IS THE CONSENT TRULY INFORMED?

Legally, three conditions must be met for informed consent to be considered valid. The client must understand the information presented, the consent must be given voluntarily, and the client must be competent to give consent (Gross, 2001). It is not sufficient to just present the information to the client "using appropriate language understandable to that person" (APA, 2002, p. 1065). In addition, psychologists must actively ensure each client's understanding of the information presented and of that to which he or she is agreeing. Merely asking if clients understand or if they have any questions would not be seen as meeting this obligation. For example, having clients explain their understanding of information shared and of specific agreements would better demonstrate their understanding than simply asking questions as described above. Written informed-consent agreements may be seen as useful in allowing the client to have something to refer to later, and they provide a tangible record of agreements between both parties. But even in conjunction with a verbal review, written informed-consent agreements should be developed with attention to reading level and ease of comprehension. In one study of informed-consent forms used in 114 U.S. medical schools, results found the forms to be written on average at the 10.6 grade level, despite these schools' own requirements for a readability level of 2.8 grade levels lower (Paasche-Orlow, Taylor, & Brancati, 2003). In the popular media, examples of perhaps even greater concern are seen in a review of the readability of notice of privacy forms from a number of prominent health care facilities: percentage of patient privacy forms that in a test were shown to be as easy to read as comics (0%), percentage as easy to read as J. K. Rowling's *Harry Potter and the Sorcerer's Stone* (1%), percentage as easy to read as H. G. Wells's *The War of the Worlds* (8%), and percentage as easy to read as professional medical literature or legal contracts (91%; "The Numbers Game," 2005).

Just how much information to include in the informed-consent process is unclear. Certainly, it is possible to overwhelm a client with too much information, and this could be inimical to the previously stated goals of the informed-consent process. Studies of psychologists' informed-consent practices have found a wide range of variability in the breadth and depth of information shared with clients (e.g., Dsubanko-Obermayr & Baumann, 1998; Otto, Ogloff, & Small,

1991). Certain issues must always be included in informed consent, as has been described earlier. A careful review of issues such as limits to confidentiality is essential, because clients may have very different expectations of the psychologist's obligations in this regard. For example, Miller and Thelen (1986) found that 69% of consumers surveyed believed and expected that all information shared in psychotherapy would be kept confidential, and 74% stated that there should be no exception to this rule. Finally, 96% expressed wanting to know about any possible limits to confidentiality prior to beginning the psychotherapy relationship. Pomerantz and Handelsman (2004) recommended including issues such as insurance and managed-care details and psychopharmacology, among others. These authors also made recommendations regarding the format for presenting informed-consent information. They offered a written question format that includes a number of questions clients may ask their psychologist to help gather important information relevant to the informed-consent process. They did not suggest one set of questions to be addressed by all clients in all psychotherapy situations. Rather, they offered this as guidance for what Pope (1991) described as a dynamic process that can be tailored to best address each individual client's needs and circumstances.

ISSUES TO CONSIDER

Informed consent is an important aspect of the psychotherapy process and psychotherapy relationship as well as for all professional relationships in which psychologists participate. Whereas standards exist for the minimal information to be included in the informed-consent process, no specific standard exists for when to limit this information and when to know if one is sharing too much. The extent and specificity of information that should be included in this process— as well as how to decide what to include or not to include and how best to present this information—remain unclear. Dilemmas exist regarding competence, understanding, and voluntariness to include obtaining consent from minors, inpatients, prisoners, those with cognitive impairment, and others and knowing when to share information, how much information to share, and when this process may be counterproductive. It is also important to know how best to present the information, be it verbally, through a written document, or in combination. Psychologists should also consider and understand the potential impact of diversity on this process, such as the role that language, age (and developmental level), cultural background, and other factors may play in affecting the informed-consent process. Clinical work with individuals, couples, families, and groups each presents unique challenges with regard to informed consent, as do third-party requests for services, clinical supervision, research, and teaching. Knowing how best to address these challenges is of great importance for protecting clients' rights, promoting their autonomy, and working to achieve the best possible outcomes in the professional relationships we form with them.

REFERENCES

American Psychological Association (APA). (2002). Ethical principles of psychologists and code of conduct. *American Psychologist, 57,* 1060–1073.

Beahrs, J. O., & Gutheil, T. G. (2001). Informed consent in psychotherapy. *American Journal of Psychiatry, 158,* 4–10.

Braaten, E. B., Otto, S., & Handelsman, M. M. (1993). What do people want to know about psychotherapy? *Psychotherapy, 30,* 565–570.

Canterbury v. Spence, 464 F.2d 772 (D.C. Cir. 1972).

Dsubanko-Obermayr, K., & Baumann, U. (1998). Informed consent in psychotherapy: Demands and reality. *Psychotherapy Research, 8,* 231–247.

Grisso, T., & Applebaum, P. S. (1998). *Assessing competence to consent to treatment: A guide for physicians and other health professionals.* New York: Oxford University Press.

Gross, B. H. (2001). Informed consent. *Annals of the American Psychotherapy Association, 4,* 24.

Knapp, S. J., & VandeCreek, L. D. (2006). *Practical ethics for psychologists: A positive approach.* Washington, DC: American Psychological Association.

Meisel, A., Roth, L. H., & Lidz, C. W. (1977). Toward a model of the legal doctrine of informed consent. *American Journal of Psychiatry, 134,* 285–289.

Miller, D. J., & Thelen, M. H. (1986). Knowledge and beliefs about confidentiality in psychotherapy. *Professional Psychology: Research and Practice, 17,* 15–19.

Osheroff v. Chestnut Lodge, 490 A.2d 720 (Md. App. 1985).

Otto, R. K., Ogloff, J. R., & Small, M. A. (1991). Confidentiality and informed consent in psychotherapy: Clinicians' knowledge and practices in Florida and Nebraska. *Forensic Reports, 4,* 379–389.

Paasche-Orlow, M. K., Taylor, H. A., & Brancati, F. L. (2003). Readability standards for informed-consent forms as compared with actual readability. *New England Journal of Medicine, 348,* 721–726.

Pomerantz, A. M., & Handelsman, M. M. (2004). Informed consent revisited: An updated written question format. *Professional Psychology: Research and Practice, 35,* 201–205.

Pope, K. S. (1991). Informed consent: Clinical and legal considerations. *Independent Practitioner, 11,* 36–41.

Salgo v. Leland Stanford Jr. Univ. Bd. of Trustees, 154 Cal. App. 2d 560, 317 P.2d 170 (1957).

Schloendorf v. Society of New York Hospital, 211 N.Y. 125, 105 N.E. 92 (1914).

Snyder, T. A., & Barnett, J. E. (2006). Informed consent and the process of psychotherapy. *Psychotherapy Bulletin, 41,* 37–42.

Stromberg, C. D., Haggarty, D. J., Leibenluft, R. F., McMillian, M. H., Mishkin, B., Rubin, B. L., & Trilling, H. R. (1988). *The psychologist's legal handbook.* Washington, DC: Council for the National Register of Health Service Providers in Psychology.

Sullivan, T., Martin, W. L., & Handelsman, M. M. (1993). Practical benefits of an informed-consent procedure: An empirical investigation. *Professional Psychology: Research and Practice, 24,* 160–163.

The numbers game. (April 12, 2005). *The Washington Post,* p. F3.

Truman v. Thomas, 611 P.2d 902 (Cal. 1980).

Welfel, E. R. (2006). *Ethics in counseling and psychotherapy: Standards, research, and emerging issues.* Belmont, CA: Thomson Brooks/Cole.

COMMENTARY: How can there ever be "too much" informed consent? The answer lies not in the underlying principle of this core aspect of a person's introduction to both clinical service and research participation, but rather in the practical demands of conveying information to certain populations in certain settings, in a fashion that truly fosters understanding and legitimate acceptance, as opposed to burying clients/patients and research participants in paper while stirring up a potent combination of anxiety, confusion, boredom, and even resentment concerning the procedures in question and the psychologists seeking to administer them.

In this process, psychologists need to draw on a critical ability that is an indispensable component of their professional skill set: efficient and effective teaching. It may not always be the case that "less is more," but with some individuals and under some conditions, a tailored approach that boils down certain matters to their relevant essence may be advisable. Psychologists do not want to dilute the reliability and validity of clinical interventions and research findings by introducing environmentally determined sources of error into the mix.

The following references are recommended for those interested in further investigation of optimal methods for obtaining properly informed consent, from persons with cognitive impairment, or from persons who otherwise merit a particularized approach for induction.

Fields, L. M., & Calvert, J. D. (2015). Informed consent procedures with cognitively impaired patients: A review of ethics and best practices. *Psychiatry and Clinical Neurosciences, 69,* 462–471. http://dx.doi.org/10.1111/pcn.12289

Harris, S. E., & Robinson Kurpius, S. E. (2014). Social networking and professional ethics: Client searches, informed consent, and disclosure. *Professional Psychology: Research and Practice, 45,* 11–19. http://dx.doi.org/10.1037/a0033478

Mangual Figueroa, A. (2016). Citizenship, beneficence, and informed consent: The ethics of working in mixed-status families. *International Journal of Qualitative Studies in Education, 29,* 66–85. http://dx.doi.org/10.1080/09518398.2014.974722

Pipes, R. B., Blevins, T., & Kluck, A. (2008). Confidentiality, ethics, and informed consent. *American Psychologist, 63,* 623–624. http://dx.doi.org/10.1037/0003-066X.63.7.623

Verdú, F., Francès, F., & Castelló, A. (2012). Learning ethics through everyday problems: Informed consent. *Advances in Health Sciences Education, 17,* 161–164. http://dx.doi.org/10.1007/s10459-009-9213-z

7.2. Ethics and Values
[*Couple and Family Therapy*]

Jay L. Lebow

Couple and family therapy is both an evidence-informed set of strategies for effective intervention and an ethical context for practice. Although the former set of clinical strategies consumes the vast majority of writing, presentations, and discussion, ethics and values are equally important aspects of practice (Grunebaum, 2006). Couple and family therapy is a complex endeavor, and the boundaries between effective strategies and ethics and values often blur. Because ethics and values are interwoven into the fabric of couple and family therapy, it is essential that therapists be able to deconstruct what is about effective practice from what is about personal values, and clearly understand when and where their own values become part of the treatment.

. . .

POTENTIAL ETHICAL CHALLENGES

Couple and family therapy also has an accompanying set of ethical procedures for practice (Gottlieb, Lasser, & Simpson, 2008). Ethical practice in couple and family therapy includes the broader mandates for practice within professional ethical codes of conduct, but include additional foci that are different from those in individual therapy. This section identifies the special issues that emerge in couple and family therapy. Practitioners are advised to become familiar with the relevant guidelines that inform ethical practice in the field: e.g., the American Psychological Association's (2010) *Ethical Principles of Psychologists and Code of Conduct* (and especially the standards and principles related to informed consent, confidentiality, therapy involving couples or families, and working with multiple relationships) and relevant principles in the *Code of Ethics* of the American Association for Marriage and Family Therapy (2012). Discussion of broader codes of conduct is provided in Barnett and Johnson (2008); L. Campbell, Vasquez, Behnke, and Kinscherff (2010); Knapp, Gottlieb, Handelsman, and VandeCreek (2012); and Nagy (2011).

Fairness and Balance

Couple and family therapists must recognize the existence of multiple understandable and valid positions in relation to the family issues that are debated

---

in this tumultuous and transitional era. They need to engage in ongoing self-examination about their own positions about these issues and if and how their own feelings affect the families they treat. It is expected that therapists will hold positions of their own about these issues and, at times, articulate those positions to clients, but it is essential to separate personal opinion from professional knowledge. ultimately, of course, therapists need to help family members find their own positions on these issues.

Multipartial Alliance

Boszormenyi-Nagy (1987) described the creation of a multipartial alliance that is fair and balanced toward all family members. Beyond pointing to the strategic value of forming good alliances with all family members, Boszormenyi-Nagy emphasized the ethical obligation involved: that each person in the family is entitled to have the therapist understand and be able to incorporate his or her position. The therapist may move from neutrality about specific issues but always with a basis of understanding and responding to each individual's concerns and view of the universe. Finding such a position of multipartiality is an essential skill for couple and family therapists.

Therapeutic Contract

The elements of the therapeutic contract described in Chapter 7 concerned with ethics need to be clearly stated and understood. Most important, there needs to be clarity about who is the client in therapy. In contrast with the simple world of individual therapy, in which the person appearing is clearly the client, couple and family therapies present great complexity in terms of this issue. Two parents may present for therapy with their son because they are concerned about his behavior. Who is the client? Is the son less the client in the three-person family therapy than the parents, such that his concerns are less important than those of the parents or are all concerns equal? A shared understanding needs to evolve as to who has what say about the therapy and its goals.

Direct and Indirect Client Systems

Pinsof (1995) distinguished the direct patient system consisting of the family members who come to treatment from the indirect patient system of those affected by the treatment who do not actively participate in the therapy. Implicit in a systems viewpoint is that treatment affects others and the needs of those others also must be part of the landscape of the therapy. Following this logic, the meanings of actions such as infidelity need to be considered not only in term of the well-being of the clients in therapy but the others in the clients' world. Yet, the contract is arrived at only with the people attending therapy not those others. The special commitment of the therapist to the clients who engage in treatment needs to be considered in helping them chart their course while holding some vision of how this will be experienced by intimate others in the outside world.

Competing Views of Clients

All clients in family therapy have equal status as clients. This can make for complexities in treatment when family members have different ideas about the value of treatment or different goals. Levels of alliance or client behavior may make it easier for therapists to empathize with some family members than others. nonetheless, all family members are entitled to the same rights as clients. It is expected that it is the therapist's role to occasionally side with one family member's vision, especially when that view is more consistent with the body of knowledge about effective relationship life. However, when such siding becomes repetitive and fixed, therapists need to be wary of cocreating split alliances. Focus in that situation best shifts to repair and rebalancing around alliance issues.

Secrets

The place of secrets between family members and the couple or family therapist is the subject of much debate. If clients are entitled to equal treatment, does this mean an equal ability to share secrets or to be free of the possibility that another family member will share a secret with the therapist? The issue is further complicated because clients rarely announce to other family members that they want to discuss a secret with the therapist. Instead, they find ways to share the presence of the secret away from other family members.

Most couple and family therapists explicitly rule out holding secrets, explaining that such sharing undermines the treatment. Pragmatically, it is relatively easy to ensure that there will not be secrets. Most skillful therapists limit most conversations with family members to occasions when everyone is assembled. When there is individual contact and information about matters such as an affair or a plan to take action that has not been shared with the family begins to emerge, these therapists quickly remind the confiding family member that if they share information with the therapist then the therapist will have to share that information with the other family members in treatment. Such a procedure virtually guarantees that there will be no sharing of secrets.

However, some couple and family therapists are more open to holding secrets, arguing that in not being willing to hear them they limit vital information that can help in the work with a family. These therapists suggest that the best way to help the family deal with secrets is to allow for confidentiality about such matters so that the issue can emerge and be worked through (Scheinkman & Werneck, 2010).

Each position toward secrets has merit. each therapist must arrive at a position on the costs and benefits involved in holding client secrets. not allowing secrets makes it easier for therapists to maintain neutrality and alliances with all parties and avoids the problematic situation and, often, sense of betrayal that occur when the secret emerges and the other family members learn that the therapist knew of it. In contrast, sharing a secret allows the therapist the opportunity to work with the secret material and avoid what often is an insurmountable block in treatment (e.g., progress in couples therapy is highly unlikely when one party has a secret involvement), and help the secret eventually emerge. Regardless of the path chosen, it is essential for therapists to be clear with clients about their position about such secrets and to maintain fairness and balance in terms of private exchanges with family members. A caveat here is that holding secrets certainly is not for the beginning therapist: The more conservative and far safer strategy is to set a policy of not allowing secrets.

Goals

Working with different client goals may even be more complex than working with secrets. At a practical level, the skill of helping clarify client goals and mold them into superordinate couple and family goals is an essential skill for couple and family therapists. Whereas some families begin with all family members having the same ultimate goals (e.g., to reduce anger and increase closeness), many families are radically split about goals. one partner wants to divorce, whereas the other wants to save the marriage, or some family members want to confront an older mother, whereas others don't want to disturb her. To a large extent, skillful couple and family therapy consists of finding ways to bring parties together toward a shared agenda. Therapists draw on their tool kits (see Chapters 5 and 6) to find a working agenda that can incorporate these multiple viewpoints.

However, what to do when skillful efforts to this end still leaves a wide gap? Whose goals are more important in the treatment? There is little in the way of consensus here. Those at the postmodern end of the spectrum mostly speak to all parties having an equal voice in the conversation and to the therapist limiting imposing any structure on this set of differences, although they make an exception in providing more room for the voice of the less powerful. Cognitive-behavioral and feminist therapists, among others, are far more inclined to intervene on one side, particularly when one position is identified with a skill deficit or a gendered view.

My own position about such differences again separates the "therapeutic" role of the therapist from the "ethical." I believe that if the matter is one about which the therapist has professional expertise, then it makes sense to share that position and side with the vantage point of one family member. To not do so is to leave the partner of the substance abuser feeling unsupported in his or her position and to create the distinct possibility that the substance abuser will point to the therapist's lack of agreement about the issue. However, when encountering what simply are differences in worldview or priorities (to have children or not, to divorce or not, to connect with a difficult family member or not), therapists do far better to remain on the family's side, maintaining a multi-partial stance in conversation about everything except for the need to work something out (and leaving the possibility to simply accept there is a difference in position and develop a plan on that basis). Also, as narrative therapists suggest, I believe it is particularly important to be sure that less powerful voices are heard and assume equal importance in these conversations.

CONCLUSION

Ethics and values receive insufficient attention in couple and family therapy. Issues concerned with values are often the focus of treatment and, even when not, easily become an unstated subtext. Because conflicts over these issues typically do not have right or wrong answers, the best role for couple and family therapists is to understand their own positions about these issues and work to help the family locate and resolve their own positions, while providing relevant psychoeducation to help inform family decisions. Couple and family therapists also need to understand and respond to the special ethical challenges involved in this work.

REFERENCES

American Association for Marriage and Family Therapy. (2012). *Code of ethics.* Retrieved from http://www.aamft.org/imis15/Content/Legal_Ethics/ Code_of_Ethics.aspx

American Psychological Association. (2010). *Ethical principles of psychologists and code of conduct (2002, Amended June 1, 2010).* Retrieved from http://www.apa.org/ ethics/code/index.aspx

Barnett, J. E., & Johnson, W. B. (2008). *Ethics desk reference for psychologists.* Washington, DC: American Psychological Association.

Boszormenyi-Nagy, I. (1987). *Foundations of contextual therapy: Collected papers of Ivan Boszormenyi-Nagy, M.D.* Philadelphia, PA: Brunner/Mazel.

Campbell, L., Vasquez, M., Behnke, S., & Kinscherff, R. (2010). *APA Ethics Code commentary and case illustrations.* Washington, DC: American Psychological Association.

Gottlieb, M. C., Lasser, J., & Simpson, G. L. (2008). Legal and ethical issues in couple therapy. In A. S. Gurman (Ed.), *Clinical handbook of couple therapy* (4th ed., pp. 698–717). New York, NY: Guilford Press.

Grunebaum, H. (2006). On wisdom. *Family Process, 45,* 117–132. doi:10.1111/ j.1545-5300.2006.00084.x

Knapp, S. J., Gottlieb, M. C., Handelsman, M. M., & VandeCreek, L. D. (2012). *APA handbook of ethics in psychology: Vol. 2. Practice, teaching, and research.* Washington, DC: American Psychological Association.

Nagy, T. F. (2011). A brief history and overview of the APA Ethics Code. In *Essential ethics for psychologists: A primer for understanding and mastering core issues* (pp. 29–48). Washington, DC: American Psychological Association. doi:10.1037/12345-002

Pinsof, W. M. (1995). *Integrative problem-centered therapy: A synthesis of family, individual, and biological therapies.* New York, NY: Basic Books.

Scheinkman, M., & Werneck, D. (2010). Disarming jealousy in couples relationships: A multidimensional approach. *Family Process, 49,* 486–502. doi:10.1111/ j.1545-5300.2010.01335.x

COMMENTARY: The psychologist as couple and family therapist is a primary target for emergent issues of an ethically and legally fraught nature. Whether divorce/separation represents either a failure of clinical intervention or its inevitable and indeed clinically advisable outcome, the emotional and economic fallout of divorce/separation can leave one or even all parties resentful and eager to lay blame on someone outside the underlying relationship. Such concerns can be exacerbated dramatically when a struggle regarding child custody and visitation is also in the offing.

Couple and family therapy is an exceptionally active form of service provision, and action incurs risk. Boundaries can be highly difficult to maintain, especially when the psychologist is engaging in a form of service provision that itself is largely consumed with the identification, exploration, and confrontation of boundary problems in the first place. All of this becomes more complex when it transpires that it is not just the relationship/family but one or more of the clients/patients themselves who are psychologically compromised.

The following references are recommended for those interested in further investigation of the unique ethical and legal challenges that accompany couple and family therapy, viewed from varying clinical treatment perspectives.

Bellesheim, K. R. (2016). Ethical challenges and legal issues for mental health professionals working with family caregivers of individuals with serious mental illness. *Ethics & Behavior, 26*, 607–620. http://dx.doi.org/10.1080/10508422.2015.1130097

Caldwell, B. E., & Stone, D. J. (2016). Using scaling to facilitate ethical decision-making in family therapy. *American Journal of Family Therapy, 44*, 198–210. http://dx.doi.org/10.1080/01926187.2016.1150797

Hecker, L. L. (2015). Ethical, legal, and professional issues in marriage and family therapy. In J. L. Wetchler & L. L. Hecker (Eds.), *An introduction to marriage and family therapy* (2nd ed., pp. 505–545). New York, NY: Routledge/Taylor & Francis.

Hodgson, J., & Gaff, C. (2013). Enhancing family communication about genetics: Ethical and professional dilemmas. *Journal of Genetic Counseling, 22*, 16–21. http://dx.doi.org/10.1007/s10897-012-9514-x

Kaslow, F. W., & Benjamin, G. A. H. (2015). Ethical wills: The positives and the perils for the family. *Journal of Family Psychotherapy, 26*, 163–177. http://dx.doi.org/10.1080/08975353.2015.1067530

7.3. National Survey of Ethical Practices Across Rural and Urban Communities

Craig M. Helbok, Robert P. Marinelli, and Richard T. Walls

Do rural psychologists encounter more ethical dilemmas than their urban counterparts? The present study examined potential differences in ethical practices across rural and urban communities. The goal was to identify whether there are unique ethical problems that arise while practicing psychology in rural communities. Much of the previous literature on rural practice has been anecdotal. Our objective was to quantify differences across communities by gathering baseline data on actual practices.

Ethical problems or dilemmas may arise in rural communities because of limited population density as well as geographical isolation. Rural communities are complex interrelated systems of formal and informal social and political units (Hargrove, 1986). Relationships among community members are interdependent and complex, and may have deep historical, social, political, and familial roots (Hargrove, 1986; Sundet & Mermelstein, 1983). Members of the community often have multiple roles within the community, tend to rely on each other and on kinship ties, and prefer to take care of their own problems rather than place any trust in outsiders (Stockman, 1990).

Compared with urban areas, rural communities tend to have scarce resources, high rates of poverty, lack of access to employment, lack of higher formal education, higher illiteracy rates, inadequate health services, limited insurance coverage, higher rates of disabilities, and fewer mental health resources (Murray & Keller, 1991; Reed, 1992; Wagenfeld, 1988; Wilcoxon, 1989). Persons who live in these communities tend to have strong family ties, avoid conflict and discussion of feelings, have limited tolerance for diversity, have high religious involvement, possess fatalistic and stoic attitudes, and are less likely to seek mental health services because of the stigma associated with seeking such services and the lack of understanding of what such services entail (Cook, Copans, & Schetky, 1998; Stockman, 1990).

There is considerable evidence that there is a greater prevalence of social and health problems in rural areas than in urban areas (Wagenfeld & Buffum, 1983). Research has shown that rural residents experience mood and anxiety disorders, trauma, and cognitive, developmental, and psychotic disorders at rates as least as high as residents of urban areas (Roberts, Battaglia, & Epstein, 1999). Suicide rates in rural areas have been higher than in urban areas for the last 20 years; rural areas have high rates of chronic illness, alcohol abuse, and disability (Roberts et al., 1999; Wagenfeld, 1988).

Most psychologists are trained according to an urban model of psychology, with most of their research performed and practical experience gained at universities in urban areas, where there is access to many services. Urban-based practice tends to take for granted services such as day treatment centers, public transportation, community centers, and easy access to self-help groups (Cook et al., 1998). Because rural areas generally have limited resources, psychologists must be creative and flexible and must make use of existing natural resources such as kin, churches, and other nonprofessional supports (Reed, 1992). Murray and Keller (1991) stated that "there has been a consensus in the literature that this urban model of mental health service delivery is inappropriate to meet the special needs of rural communities" (p. 225). These same authors pointed out the relative dearth of studies concerned with rural practice. Rural providers often feel that ethics codes, texts, and other literature are so urban biased, or culturally incongruent, that they are not helpful (Roberts et al., 1999). Whether rural practice is distinct from urban practice is an empirical question, one which we hope this study begins to address.

. . .

Participants

A computer-generated, randomized list of 1,000 psychologists was obtained from the APA. This list was stratified, with 500 psychologists practicing in urban communities and 500 in nonurban areas, as designated by their zip codes. All participants were members of the APA. The APA Research Office suggested using two variables to identify those psychologists whose primary work is therapy. The first variable was that the psychologists are licensed in their state to practice psychology; the second was the special assessment fee from the APA's Practice Directorate.

. . .

Survey Instrument

The final survey instrument consisted of demographic items plus 120 questions related to the practice of psychology. The survey instrument is based on previous surveys of ethical practices, although questions were added and deleted to address issues specific to the practice of psychology in rural areas (Ackerly et al., 1988; Baer & Murdock, 1995; Borys & Pope, 1989; Gibson & Pope, 1993; Haas, Malouf, & Mayerson, 1986; Hines, Ader, Chang, & Rundell, 1998; Lamb & Catanzaro, 1998; Percival & Striefel, 1994; Pope et al., 1987, 1988; Pope & Vetter, 1992; Rae & Worchel, 1991; Shore & Golann, 1969; Tubbs & Pomerantz, 2001).

Results for the Primary Research Question

. . .

As predicted, psychologists in small town/rural areas appeared to encounter significantly more multiple relationship behaviors and situations than did those in urban/suburban areas. Although there are significant differences between some behaviors, they still may not occur frequently. For example, one question asked about socializing with clients after terminating therapy. More small town/rural practitioners (57.5% responded "never") engaged in this behavior than did urban/suburban practitioners (77.2% responded "never"); however, within the small town/rural group, only 5.3% did so "sometimes or more." With some behaviors, however, such as engaging in a romantic relationship with a client or going into business with a client, the fact that it does occur at all may be a concern. Other behaviors, such as loaning books to a client, may occur sometimes or more often but may not be as much of a concern. Surprisingly, a high percentage of psychologists from all communities encounter clients at parties or social gatherings. Approximately 36% of urban/suburban psychologists and 58.4% of small town/rural practitioners run into clients sometimes or more often. Only 22% and 15%, respectively, reported never running into clients at social gatherings or parties. . . .

As predicted, therapists in small towns and rural communities may be more likely to feel they are therapists 24 hours a day, to run into clients in the community, and to participate in activities in which clients are also participating. These results also tend to confirm the reports in the review of the rural literature that a therapist has to be willing to be known as a person in rural communities and that clients are likely to know a great deal about the therapist, whether the therapist is comfortable with this or not. . . .

We had predicted that psychologists from small towns and rural areas would have difficulty maintaining their competency and that they would struggle with having to take patients who are beyond their scope of training. This was not the case, however, at least according to self-report. Although therapists did not endorse items that concerned their own competency, they were much more likely to be concerned about their colleagues' competency, though this held true across types of community. . . .

Contrary to predictions, small town and rural psychologists did not endorse more items indicative of burnout. In fact, psychologists from both urban/suburban and small town/rural communities endorsed items suggesting that they enjoy their work, feel they have control over their work environment, have autonomy, and find their work professionally and personally satisfying. Urban psychologists appear to be more likely to seek counseling from another therapist, but we cannot determine if this is due to different value systems or to the availability of the resources. . . .

Urban/suburban therapists are more likely to discuss their work or their clients with friends, colleagues, and other professionals. On the open-ended question at the end of the survey, several respondents emphasized that when discussing clients with others, they do not use client identifying information. As expected, small town/rural psychologists are more likely to prepare their clients for chance encounters, and they are more likely to learn information about the client from sources other than the client.

. . .

Implications for Rural Practitioners

From a review of the rural literature, we had expected that rural practitioners would experience more multiple relationships, struggle to maintain competency, have difficulty maintaining confidentiality, experience more visibility in the community, and experience more burnout as a result of the characteristics of rural communities. Results of the statistical analyses support some of these hypotheses. It appears that rural practitioners encounter significantly more multiple relationships than do their urban counterparts. For the multiple relationships items, 19 questions showed a significant difference between the two groups of psychologists. These multiple relationships range from incidental contacts, such as purchasing goods or services from a client, to more intensive relationships, such as providing therapy to a client with whom one has had a previous social relationship or becoming social friends with a former client. . . .

CONCLUSIONS

The purpose of this study was to empirically examine the question of whether there are unique ethical dilemmas when practicing psychology in rural communities. Findings suggest that rural psychologists are more likely to encounter specific types of ethical dilemmas, particularly related to multiple relationships. Rural psychologists also struggle with maintaining client confidentiality and issues related to being so highly visible in the community, such as having some clients know a great deal about the psychologist's personal life. These potential ethical dilemmas are likely to have an impact on clinical practice and clinical decision making. We believe it is imperative to have a forum for rural psychologists to discuss the issues related to their practice. Furthermore, the issues raised in this study apply to nonrural psychologists as well—for example, practitioners who work with a narrowly defined client population within an urban area. The present study was intended to be a broad national study, but the limitation of such a study is that many aspects of working in specific rural communities may have been unaddressed. It is hoped that this study will generate more empirical research pertinent to the practice of psychology in rural communities, such as studying the impact of these dilemmas on both clients and psychologists, as well as encourage discussion of methods to cope with ethical and clinical issues that are unique to rural environments.

REFERENCES

Ackerly, G. D., Burnell, J., Holder, D. C., & Kurdek, L. A. (1988). Burnout among licensed psychologists. *Professional Psychology: Research and Practice, 19,* 624–631.

Baer, B. E., & Murdock, N. L. (1995). Nonerotic dual relationships between therapists and clients: The effects of sex, theoretical orientation, and interpersonal boundaries. *Ethics & Behavior, 5,* 131–145.

Borys, D. S., & Pope, K. S. (1989). Dual relationships between therapist and client: A national study of psychologists, psychiatrists, and social workers. *Professional Psychology: Research and Practice, 20,* 283–293.

Cook, A. D., Copans, S. A., & Schetky, D. H. (1998). Psychiatric treatment of children and adolescents in rural communities. *Child and Adolescent Psychiatric Clinics of North America, 7,* 673–690.

Gibson, W. T., & Pope, K. S. (1993). The ethics of counseling: A national survey of certified counselors. *Journal of Counseling & Development, 71,* 330–336.

Haas, L. J., Malouf, J. L., & Mayerson, N. H. (1986). Ethical dilemmas in psychological practice: Results of a national survey. *Professional Psychology: Research and Practice, 17,* 316–321.

Hargrove, D. S. (1986). Ethical issues in rural mental health practice. *Professional Psychology: Research and Practice, 17,* 20–23.

Hines, A. H., Ader, D. N., Chang, A. S., & Rundell, J. R. (1998). Dual agency, dual relationships, boundary crossings and associated boundary violations: A survey of military and civilian psychiatrists. *Military Medicine, 163,* 826–833.

Lamb, D. H., & Catanzaro, S. J. (1998). Sexual and nonsexual boundary violations involving psychologists, clients, supervisees, and students: Implications for professional practice. *Professional Psychology: Research and Practice, 29,* 498–503.

Murray, J. D., & Keller, P. A. (1991). Psychology and rural America: Current status and future directions. *American Psychologist, 46,* 220–231.

Percival, G., & Striefel, S. (1994). Ethical beliefs and practices of AAPB members. *Biofeedback and Self-Regulation, 19,* 67–93.

Pope, K. S., Tabachnick, B. G., & Keith-Spiegel, P. (1987). Ethics of practice: The beliefs and behaviors of psychologists as therapists. *American Psychologist, 42,* 993–1006.

Pope, K. S., Tabachnick, B. G., & Keith-Spiegel, P. (1988). Good and poor practices in psychotherapy: National survey of beliefs of psychologists. *Professional Psychology: Research and Practice, 19,* 547–552.

Pope, K. S., & Vetter, V. A. (1992). Ethical dilemmas encountered by members of the American Psychological Association: A national survey. *American Psychologist, 47,* 397–411.

Rae, W. A., & Worchel, F. F. (1991). Ethical beliefs and behaviors of pediatric psychologists: A survey. *Journal of Pediatric Psychology, 16,* 727–745.

Reed, D. A. (1992). Adaptation: The key to community psychiatric practice in the rural setting. *Community Mental Health Journal, 28,* 141–150.

Roberts, L. W., Battaglia, J., & Epstein, R. S. (1999). Frontier ethics: Mental health care needs and ethical dilemmas in rural communities. *Psychiatric Services, 50,* 497–503.

Shore, M. F., & Golann, S. E. (1969). Problems of ethics in community mental health: A survey of community psychologists. *Community Mental Health Journal, 5,* 452–460.

Stockman, A. F. (1990). Dual relationships in rural mental health practice: An ethical dilemma. *Journal of Rural Community Psychology, 11,* 31–45.

Sundet, P. A., & Mermelstein, J. (1983). The meaning of community in rural mental health. *International Journal of Mental Health, 12,* 25–44.

Tubbs, P., & Pomerantz, A. M. (2001). Ethical behaviors of psychologists: Changes since 1987. *Journal of Clinical Psychology, 57,* 395–399.

Wagenfeld, M. O. (1988). Rural mental health and community psychology in the post community mental health era: An overview and introduction to the special issue. *Journal of Rural Community Psychology, 9,* 5–11.

Wagenfeld, M. O., & Buffum, W. E. (1983). Problems in, and prospects for, rural mental health services in the United States. *International Journal of Mental Health, 12,* 89–107.

Wilcoxon, S. A. (1989). Leadership behavior and therapist burnout: A study of rural agency settings. *Journal of Rural Community Psychology, 10,* 3–13.

7.4. Guidelines for Psychological Practice With Girls and Women

American Psychological Association

These guidelines were approved as APA policy by the APA Council of Representatives on February 16, 2007. They were developed by an interdivisional task force of APA Divisions 17 (Society of Counseling Psychology) and 35 (Society for the Psychology of Women). The task force co-chairs were Roberta L. Nutt, Joy K. Rice, and Carolyn Z. Enns, who were appointed in 2000 by Nadya Fouad, then President-Elect of Division 17, and Janice Yoder, President-Elect of Division 35. Task force members and consultants at various stages of development included Julie Ancis, Martha Bergen, Kathleen Bieschke, Michele Boyer, Laura Boykin, Mary Brabeck, Sara Bridges, Redonna Chandler, Madonna Constantine, Carmen Cruz, Donna Davenport, Amanda Dickson, Ruth Fassinger, Laura Forrest, Linda Forrest, Lisa Frey, Deborah Gerrity, Glenn Good, Barbara Gormley, Michael Gottlieb, Kris Hancock, Nancy Downing Hansen, Michele Harway, Danica Hays, Misty Hook, Kathy Hotelling, Rachel Latta, Karen Lese, Don-David Lusterman, Jim Mahalik, Connie Matthews, Dinah Meyer, Debra Mollen, Cassie Nichols, Laura Palmer, Adrienne Paulson, Randy Pipes, Beverly Pringle, Jill Rader, Faye Reimers, Pam Remer, Rory Remer, Christina Rodriguez, Holly Savoy, Anne Scott, Susan Seem, Elizabeth Skowron, Stacey Smoot, Dawn Szymanski, Virginia Theo-Steelman, Ellen Tunnell, Melba Vasquez, Heather Weiner, Ashley Williams, Libby Nutt Williams, Kacey Wilson, Judy Worell, and Karen Wyche. Twenty doctoral students from eight programs were included in this process.

The development of these guidelines depended on the earlier foundation of such historical precedents as APA's (1978) "Guidelines for Therapy With Women: Task Force on Sex Bias and Sex Role Stereotyping in Psychotherapeutic Practice," APA's (1979) Division 17 "Principles Concerning the Counseling and Psychotherapy of Women," APA Division 35's First National Conference on Education and Training in Feminist Practice in 1993 and its resulting book (Worell & Johnson, 1997), APA's 1998 Division 17 Section for the Advancement of Women Michigan conference on the integration of feminism and multiculturalism, and the ongoing work of APA's Committee on Women in Psychology. Participants were determined to produce guidelines that honored the complexity of the lives of girls and women in their multicultural contexts.

The comments and suggestions garnered from various APA boards and committees, APA divisions, and state and territorial psychological associations added immensely to the richness and utility of the document. The members of the groups may also be considered as consultants and contributors. The authors are particularly indebted to Sarah Jordan for keeping oversight of the complex APA review process in the final stages.

This document is scheduled to expire as APA policy in eight years (2015). After this date, users are encouraged to contact the Practice Directorate, American Psychological Association, to confirm that this document remains in effect or is under revision.

Author's Note: This article excerpts the Introduction and 11 Guidelines from the original report issued in the December 2007 issue of the *American Psychologist*. The guidelines were approved as APA policy by the APA Council of Representatives on February 16, 2007. Full text is available at http://www.apa.org/about/policy/girls-and-women-archived.pdf

uring recent decades, women and girls of diverse ethnicities, social classes, sexual orientations, and life experiences have encountered dramatic and complex changes in education, health, work, reproductive and caregiving roles, and personal relationships. Although many of these changes have resulted in increased equality, opportunity, and quality of life, girls and women are also at risk for a variety of health concerns and life stresses (*National Healthcare Disparities Report*, 2005). Stressors in the lives of women and girls include interpersonal victimization and violence, unrealistic media images of girls and women, discrimination and oppression, devaluation, limited economic resources, role overload, relationship disruptions, and work inequities. Violence against girls and women is often predicated in sexism, racism, classism, and homophobia (Glick & Fiske, 1997; Koss, Heise, & Russo, 1994; West, 2002). Salient mental health statistics reveal that women are two times more likely than men to be depressed, and girls are seven times more likely than boys to be depressed (Lewinsohn, Rhode, Seeley, & Baldwin, 2001). Women who are subject to group and individual discrimination are even more likely to experience depression (Klonis, Endo, Crosby, & Worell, 1997). Girls and women are also roughly nine times more likely to have eating disorders than boys and men (Stice & Bearman, 2001; Stice, Burton, & Shaw, 2004). Compared with men, women are two to three times more likely to experience many types of anxiety disorders (U.S. Department of Health and Human Services, Office on Women's Health, 2001). The abuse and violence in U.S. society (e.g., abuse, battering, rape) may contribute to the development of dysfunctional behaviors, such as eating disorders, depression, anxiety, and suicidal behavior, whereas discrimination against women and girls of color can result in lowered self-expectations, anxiety, depression, and negative attitudes toward self (Keith, Jackson, & Gary, 2003). In general, the physical and mental health concerns of women and girls are related to complex and diverse economic, biological, developmental, psychological, and sociocultural environments. The concerns, behaviors, values, attitudes, and feelings of women and girls also arise from myriad interactions among their multiple identities related to age, race, ethnicity, class, sexual orientation, marital, partnership and parental status, gender identity, ability, culture, immigration, geography, and other life experiences (Sparks & Park, 2000; Stewart & McDermott, 2004).

Although many psychologists and members of the general public may believe that women's issues in psychology were dealt with and resolved in the 1970s and 1980s, the changing and increasingly complex life experiences of girls and women and the intersection of their gender roles with ethnicity, sexual orientation, ability, socioeconomic status (SES), and so forth demonstrate compelling evidence and need for professional guidance for helping psychologists (a) avoid harm in psychological practice with girls and women; (b) improve research, teaching, consultation, and psychotherapeutic and counseling training and practice; and (c) develop and enhance treatment efforts, research, prevention, teaching, and other areas of practice that will benefit women and girls. In addition, although blatant forms of sexism and racism have decreased over time (J. D. Campbell, Schellenberg, & Senn, 1997), researchers have noted the continuing presence of more subtle forms of sexist and racist bias (e.g., ambivalent, symbolic, or unintentional racism/sexism; Glick & Fiske, 1997; Swim & Cohen, 1997). Given that the majority of those seeking mental health services continue to be female (e.g., Rhodes, Goering, To, & Williams, 2002), special attention to the unique treatment needs of girls and women of diverse backgrounds is warranted (Trimble, Stevenson, Worell, & the American Psychological Association [APA] Commission on Ethnic Minority Recruitment, Retention, and Training Task Force Textbook Initiative Work Group, 2003). The majority of those seeking treatment remain women and girls, and the demographics of the U.S. population are rapidly changing, resulting in more diversity among the women and girls needing psychological services. Improved treatment not only reduces potential harm, but will also likely benefit women and girls, particularly through the greater awareness, education, and prevention fostered by guidelines for psychological practice with girls and women.

. . .

DIVERSITY, SOCIAL CONTEXT, AND POWER

Guideline 1: Psychologists strive to be aware of the effects of socialization, stereotyping, and unique life events on the development of girls and women across diverse cultural groups.

Rationale

One of the most consistent patterns documented in research on gender socialization is that traditional roles related to gender and sexuality may be reinforced through the differential treatment of boys and girls and may also be enacted without self-awareness or conscious intention (APA, 2004b; Bem, 1993; Crawford & Unger, 2004). Females may be devalued relative to their male counterparts and socialized into patterns of nurturance, passivity, helplessness, and preoccupation with appearance. The presentation of women and girls as sexual objects, which begins in childhood and extends through adulthood, is promulgated by the media and emphasizes the role of appearance and beauty (J. D. Brown, Steele, & Walsh-Childers, 2002; Calvert, 1999). The internalization of stereotypes about the abilities and social roles of women and girls (e.g., less competent, dependent) has been shown to produce decrements in their performance and aspirations (Davies, Spencer, & Steele, 2005; Lesko & Corpus, 2006).

. . .

Guideline 2: Psychologists are encouraged to recognize and utilize information about oppression, privilege, and identity development as they may affect girls and women.

Rationale

Because girls and women have multiple personal and social group memberships, they may simultaneously belong to both socially privileged and disempowered groups (e.g., White, heterosexual, lower SES, and female) or to multiple socially oppressed groups (e.g., African American, female, lesbian, disabled; Ancis & Ladany, 2001; Greene & Sanchez-Hucles, 1997; Suyemoto & Kim, 2005). Numerous authors have documented the stress of managing multiple identities associated with oppression, which is sometimes labeled *double jeopardy* or *triple jeopardy* (Banks & Marshall, 2004; Espín, 1993; Greene, 1997a; T. L. Robinson & Howard-Hamilton, 2000). Saliency of a particular identity is determined by several factors, including socialization experiences (Cross & Vandiver, 2001) and the amount of social support received in a particular situation (Wyche & Rice, 1997). For example, coming out as a lesbian, gay, or bisexual person may be more complicated or less acceptable within some racial/ethnic groups because of the complexity of balancing issues of racism, ethnic discrimination, and homophobia (APA, 2000b; Greene, 1997a; McCarn & Fassinger, 1996).

. . .

Guideline 3: Psychologists strive to understand the impact of bias and discrimination on the physical and mental health of those with whom they work.

Rationale

Bias and discrimination are embedded in and driven by organizational, institutional, and social structures. These dynamics legitimize and foster inequities, influence personal relationships, and affect the perception and treatment of a person's mental and behavioral problems. Discrimination has been shown to contribute more to women's perceptions of their psychiatric and physical symptoms than any other environmental stressor (Klonoff et al., 2000; Moradi & Subich, 2002). . . . Violence against women is often predicated in sexism, racism, classism, and homophobia (Glick & Fiske, 1997; Koss, Heise, & Russo, 1994).

. . .

PROFESSIONAL RESPONSIBILITY

Guideline 4: Psychologists strive to use gender sensitive and culturally sensitive, affirming practices in providing services to girls and women.

Rationale

As discussed in the introductory section of these guidelines, assessment, diagnostic, and psychotherapy practices can represent important sources of bias against girls and women. In addition, models and practices implying that the typical experiences of middle-class White women are normative for all girls and women have the potential to marginalize or exclude the experiences and concerns of other girls and women (Reid, 1993; Reid & Kelly, 1994; Saris & Johnston-Robledo, 2000). Women of color, lesbian women, and women with disabilities may be especially vulnerable to misdiagnosis and other forms of bias (APA, 2000b; Banks & Kaschak, 2003; Leigh & Huff, 2006; *National Healthcare Disparities Report*, 2005).

. . .

Guideline 5: Psychologists are encouraged to recognize how their socialization, attitudes, and knowledge about gender may affect their practice with girls and women.

Rationale

The practice of psychologists is likely to be influenced by their culture, values, biases, socialization, and experiences of privilege and oppression or disempowerment. Limited self-knowledge may contribute to subtle belief systems that can be potentially harmful to girls and women with diverse social identities. For example, studies have revealed that psychotherapists may engage in subtle forms of differential treatment of male and female clients (e.g., Friedlander, Wildman, Heatherington, & Skowron, 1994; Werner-Wilson et al., 1997) and thereby may be at risk for reinforcing views about gender, sexual orientation, culture, and family life that may be detrimental to girls and women. Similar results have been reported for evidence of personal bias related to culture and/or sexual orientation in other APA practice guidelines (APA, 2000b, 2003).

. . .

PRACTICE APPLICATIONS

Guideline 6: Psychologists are encouraged to use interventions and approaches that have been found to be effective in the treatment of issues of concern to girls and women.

Rationale

The practice of psychologists is enhanced by knowledge about the challenges, strengths, social contexts, and identities of girls and women as well as about interventions that are associated with positive outcomes. In the case of psychotherapy, positive outcomes are consistently associated with the therapeutic alliance and common curative psychotherapy factors (e.g., Lambert & Bergin, 1994; Wampold, 2001), such as client expectations and openness, therapist sensitivity and expertise in implementing interventions, length of treatment, and the similarity of the client's and psychologist's worldviews (Fischer, Jome, & Atkinson, 1998; Kopta, Lueger, Saunders, & Howard, 1999). If evidence-based interventions are not used, there is the danger of not being helpful or even causing harm (Werner-Wilson et al., 1997; Woolley, 2000).

. . .

Guideline 7: Psychologists strive to foster therapeutic relationships and practices that promote initiative, empowerment, and expanded alternatives and choices for girls and women.

Rationale

Symptoms of depression, disturbed body image and eating disorders, and dependency in girls and women can emerge in a context of powerlessness (Enns, 2004; Mazure et al., 2002). Fear of rape and other forms of violence and coercion may limit girls' and women's full participation in society and can contribute to passivity and learned helplessness (APA, 2005; Gutek & Done, 2001; Koss, 1993). These issues may be compounded by the impact of their intersection with social class, race/ethnicity, sexual orientation, physical illness, and physical ability (Harway & O'Neil, 1999; Koss et al., 1994; Neville & Heppner, 1999). Gender roles related to the giving and receiving of caregiving and social support are relevant to empowerment (Harway & Nutt, 2006). The experience of giving and receiving social support is often a major emotional resource for women and is strongly related to women's life satisfaction (Diener & Fujita, 1995). Under some conditions, however, gender roles of girls and women (e.g., caregiving) can also contribute to the depletion of emotional resources and to a lack of self-development, independence, and personal choice (Farran, Miller, Kaufman, Donner, & Fogg, 1999).

. . .

Guideline 8: Psychologists strive to provide appropriate, unbiased assessments and diagnoses in their work with girls and women.

Rationale

Psychologists have identified gender bias in the following areas of assessment and diagnosis: clinical judgment, theoretical foundations of assessment, diagnostic processes, psychological assessment measures, and the conceptualization of developmental experiences (e.g., APA, 2000c, 2003, 2004b; Marecek, 2001). For example, an element of women's normal development that is often viewed as problematic, rather than normative, is menopause. Some cultural stereotypes of menopause associate this period with loss and depression, but many women feel happier and more energized during menopause (Apter, 1996; Rostosky & Travis, 2000; Sherwin, 2001). Some societies view menopause as a time of freedom from menstruation, pregnancy, and social limitations on appropriate female behavior, with postmenopausal women viewed as wise and valuable (Beyene, 1992; Lamb, 2002; G. Robinson, 2002).

. . .

Guideline 9: Psychologists strive to consider the problems of girls and women in their sociopolitical context.

Rationale

As discussed in Guideline 3, sociocultural variables, oppressive environments, and power differentials may precipitate and maintain problematic issues for women and girls, limit their access to resources, or contribute to blaming girls and women for their problems (Martinez, Davis, & Dahl, 1999). Social statuses of women and girls, such as gender, ethnicity, disability, age, sexual orientation, and culture, may influence their development, behavior, and symptom presentation. As an example, it is normative in some cultural contexts for women to be physically coerced within marriage. Psychologists' perceptions of the social roles and identities of women and girls, as well as psychologists' personal biases, values, and social identities, may also have an impact on their understanding and ratings of the adjustment, traits, symptoms, and assumptions about future behavior of girls and women (Becker & Lamb, 1994; Porter, 1995). A psychologist with a traditional gender-role orientation, for example, might perceive exaggerations of the traditional female gender role as markers of a personality disorder rather than considering the full range of sociopolitical factors that may contribute to a client's problems.

. . .

Guideline 10: Psychologists strive to acquaint themselves with and utilize relevant mental health, education, and community resources for girls and women.

Rationale

The APA ethics code (APA, 2002b) principle of fidelity and responsibility states that "Psychologists consult with, refer to, or cooperate with other professionals and institutions to the extent needed to serve the best interests of those with whom they work" (p. 3). Gaining information about the availability of community resources has also been identified as a culturally and sociopolitically relevant factor in a client's history . . . Complex psychological problems with multiple causes are likely to be best addressed by collaborative approaches that draw on personal, interpersonal, educational, and community resources. Community-based, culturally competent, collaborative systems of care can complement or enhance therapeutic, educational, and research efforts. These resources include women's self-help groups; women's centers, shelters, and safe houses; psycho-educational experiences for girls and women; work/training experiences; and public assistance resources. . . .

Guideline 11: Psychologists are encouraged to understand and work to change institutional and systemic bias that may impact girls and women.

Rationale

As directed by the APA ethics code (APA, 2002b) psychologists "recognize that fairness and justice entitle all persons to have access to and benefit from the contributions of psychology and to equal quality in the processes, procedures, and services being conducted by psychologists" (p. 1062). In addition,

> psychologists are aware of and respect cultural, individual, and role differences, including those based on age, gender, gender identity, race, ethnicity, culture, national origin, religion, sexual orientation, disability, language, and socioeconomic status, and consider these factors when working with members of such groups. (APA, 2002b, p. 1063). . . .

REFERENCES

American Psychological Association. (1978). Guidelines for therapy with women: Task Force on Sex Bias and Sex Role Stereotyping in Psychotherapeutic Practice. *American Psychologist, 33*, 1122–1123.

American Psychological Association. (1979). Principles concerning the counseling and psychotherapy of women. *Counseling Psychologist, 8,* 21.

American Psychological Association. (2000b). Guidelines for psychotherapy with lesbian, gay, and bisexual clients. *American Psychologist, 55,* 1440–1451.

American Psychological Association. (2000c). *Resolution on poverty and socioeconomic status,* Washington, DC: Author.

American Psychological Association. (2002b). Ethical principles of psychologists and code of conduct. *American Psychologist, 57,* 1060–1073.

American Psychological Association. (2003). Guidelines on multicultural education, training, research, practice, and organizational change for psychologists. *American Psychologists, 58,* 377–402.

American Psychological Association. (2004b). *Resolution on culture and gender awareness in international psychology.* Washington, DC: Author.

American Psychological Association. (2005). *Resolution on male violence against women.* Washington, DC: Author.

Ancis, J. R., & Ladany, N. (2001). A multicultural framework for counselor supervision. In L. J. Bradley & N. Ladany (Eds.), *Counselor supervision: Principles, process, and practice* (3rd ed., pp. 63–90). Philadelphia: Brunner-Routledge.

Apter, T. (1996). Path of development in midlife women. *Feminism and Psychology, 6,* 557–562.

Becker, D., & Lamb, S. (1994). Sex bias in the diagnosis of borderline personality disorder and post traumatic stress disorder. *Professional Psychology: Research and Practice, 25,* 56–61.

Banks, M. E., & Kaschak, E. (2003). *Women with visible and invisible disabilities: Multiple intersections, multiple issues, multiple therapies.* New York: Haworth.

Banks, M. E., & Marshall, C. (2004). Beyond the "triple whammy": Social class as a factor in discrimination against persons with disabilities. In J. L. Chin (Ed.), *The psychology of prejudice and discrimination: Combating prejudice in all forms of discrimination: Vol. 4. Disability, religion, physique, and other traits* (pp. 95–110). Westport, CT: Praeger.

Bem, S. L. (1993). *The lenses of gender: Transforming the debate on sexual inequality.* New Haven, CT: Yale University Press.

Beyene, Y. (1992). Menopause: A biocultural event. In A. J. Dan & L. L. Lewis (Eds.), *Menstrual health in women's lives* (pp. 169–177). Chicago: University of Illinois Press.

Brown, J. D., Steele, J. R., & Walsh-Childers, K. (Eds.). (2002). *Sexual teens, sexual media: Investigating media's influence on adolescent sexuality.* Mahwah, NJ: Erlbaum.

Calvert, S. L. (1999). *Children's journeys through the information age.* New York: McGraw-Hill.

Campbell, J. D., Schellenberg, E. G., & Senn, C. Y. (1997). Evaluating measures of contemporary sexism. *Psychology of Women Quarterly, 21,* 89–102.

Crawford, M., & Unger, R. (2004). *Women and gender: A feminist psychology* (4th ed.). New York: McGraw-Hill.

Cross, W. E., Jr., & Vandiver, B. J. (2001). Nigrescence theory and measurement: Introducing the Cross Racial Identity Scale (CRIS). In J. G. Ponterotto, J. M. Casas, L. M. Suzuki, & C. M. Alexander (Eds.), *Handbook of multicultural counseling* (2nd ed., pp. 371–393). Thousand Oaks, CA: Sage.

Davies, P. G., Spencer, S. J., & Steele, C. M. (2005). Clearing the air: Identity safety moderates the effects of stereotype threat on women's leadership aspirations. *Journal of Personality and Social Psychology, 88,* 276–287.

Diener, E., & Fujita, F. (1995). Resources, personal strivings, and subjective well-being: A nomothetic and ideographic approach. *Journal of Personality and Social Psychology, 68,* 926–935.

Enns, C. Z. (2004). *Feminist theories and feminist psychotherapies: Origins, themes, and diversity* (2nd ed.). Binghamton, NY: Haworth.

Espín, O. M. (1993). Issues of identity in the psychology of Latina lesbians. In L. D. Garnets & D. C. Kimmel (Eds.), *Psychological perspectives on lesbian and gay male experiences* (pp. 348–363). New York: Columbia University Press.

Farran, C. J., Miller, B. H., Kaufman, J. E., Donner, E., & Fogg, L. (1999). Finding meaning through caregiving: Development of an instrument for family caregivers of persons with Alzheimers' disease. *Journal of Clinical Psychology, 55,* 1107–1125.

Fischer, A. R., Jome, L. M., & Atkinson, D. R. (1998). Reconceptualizing multicultural counseling: Universal healing conditions in a culturally specific context. *Counseling Psychologist, 26,* 525–588.

Friedlander, M. L., Wildman, J., Heatherington, L., & Skowron, E. A. (1994). What we do and don't know about the process of family therapy. *Journal of Family Psychology, 8,* 390–416.

Glick, P., & Fiske, S. T. (1997). Hostile and benevolent sexism: Measuring ambivalent sexist attitudes toward women. *Psychology of Women Quarterly, 21,* 119–136.

Greene, B. (1997a). Lesbian woman of color: Triple jeopardy. *Journal of Lesbian Studies, 1,* 109–147.

Greene, B., & Sanchez-Hucles, J. B. (1997). Diversity: Advancing an inclusive feminist psychology. In J. Worell & N. G. Johnson (Eds.), *Shaping the future of feminist psychology: Education, research, and practice* (pp. 173–202). Washington, DC: American Psychological Association.

Gutek, B. A., & Done, R. S. (2001). Sexual harassment. In R. K. Unger (Ed.), *Handbook of the psychology of women and gender* (pp. 358–366). New York: Wiley.

Harway, M., & O'Neil, J. M. (Eds.). (1999). *What causes men's violence against women?* Thousand Oaks, CA: Sage.

Harway, M., & Nutt, R. L. (2006). Women and giving. In J. Worell & C. R. Goodheart (Eds.), *Handbook of girls' and women's psychological health: Gender and well-being across the lifespan* (pp. 200–207). New York: Oxford.

Keith, V. M., Jackson, J. S., & Gary, L. E. (2003). (Dis)respected and (dis)regarded: Experiences in racism and psychological distress. In D. R. Brown & V. M. Keith (Eds.), *In and out of our right minds: The mental health of African American women* (pp. 83–98). New York: Columbia University Press.

Klonis, S., Endo, J., Crosby, F. J., & Worell, J. (1997). Feminism as a life raft. *Psychology of Women Quarterly, 21,* 333–346.

Klonoff, E. A., Landrine, H., & Campbell, R. (2000). Sexist discrimination may account for well-known gender differences in psychiatric symptoms. *Psychology of Women Quarterly, 24,* 93–99.

Kopta, S. M., Lueger, R. J., Saunders, S. M., & Howard, K. I. (1999). Individual psychotherapy outcome and process research: Challenges leading to greater turmoil or a positive transition? *Annual Review of Psychology, 50,* 441–470.

Koss, M. (1993). Rape: Scope, impact, interventions, and public policy responses. *American Psychologist, 48,* 1062–1069.

Koss, M. P., Heise, L., & Russo, N. F. (1994). The global health burden of rape. *Psychology of Women Quarterly, 18,* 509–537.

Lamb, S. (2002). Women, abuse, and forgiveness: A special case. In S. Lamb & J. G. Murphy (Eds.), *Before forgiving: Cautionary view of forgiveness in psychotherapy* (pp. 155–171). New York: Oxford.

Lambert, J. J., & Bergin, A. E. (1994). The effectiveness of psychotherapy. In A. E. Bergin & S. L. Garfield (Eds.), *Handbook of psychotherapy and behavior change* (4th ed., pp. 143–189). New York: Wiley.

Leigh, W. A., & Huff, D. (2006). *Women of color health data book: Adolescents to seniors* (3rd ed., NIH Publication No. 06–4247). Bethesda, MD: Office of Research on Women's Health, National Institutes of Health.

Lesko, A. C., & Corpus, J. H. (2006). Discounting the difficult: How high math-identified women respond to stereotype threat. *Sex Roles, 54,* 113–125.

Lewinsohn, P. M., Rhode, P., Seeley, J., & Baldwin, C. (2001). Gender differences in suicide attempts from adolescence to young adulthood. *Journal of the American Academy for Child & Adolescent Psychiatry, 40*, 427–434.

Marecek, J. (2001). Disorderly constructs: Feminist frameworks for clinical psychology. In R. K. Unger (Ed.), *Handbook of the psychology of women and gender* (pp. 303–316). New York: Wiley.

Martinez, L. J., Davis, K. C., & Dahl, B. (1999). Feminist ethical challenges in supervision: A trainee perspective. *Women and Therapy, 22*(4), 35–54.

Mazure, C. M., Keita, G. P., & Blehar, M. C. (2002). *Summit on women and depression: Proceedings and recommendations.* Washington, DC: American Psychological Association.

McCarn, S. R., & Fassinger, R. E. (1996). Revisioning sexual minority identity formation: A new model of lesbian identity and its implications for counseling and research. *Counseling Psychologist, 24*, 508–534.

Moradi, B., & Subich, L. M. (2002). Perceived sexist events and feminist identity development attitudes: Links to women's psychological distress. *Counseling Psychologist, 30*, 44–65.

National healthcare disparities report, 2005. (2005). Rockville, MD: Agency for Healthcare Research and Quality. Retrieved June 28, 2007, from http://www.ahrq.gov/qual/nhdr05/nhdr05.htm

Neville, H. A., & Heppner, M. J. (1999). Contextualizing rape: Reviewing sequelae and proposing a culturally inclusive ecological model of sexual assault recovery. *Applied and Preventive Psychology, 3*, 41–62.

Porter, N. (1995). Supervision of psychotherapists: Integrating anti-racist, feminist, and multicultural perspectives. In H. Landrine (Ed.), *Bringing cultural diversity to feminist psychology: Theory, research, and practice* (pp. 163–176). Washington, DC: American Psychological Association.

Reid, P. T. (1993). Poor women in psychological research: Shut up and shut out. *Psychology of Women Quarterly, 17*, 133–150.

Reid, P. T., & Kelly, E. (1994). Research on women of color: From ignorance to awareness. *Psychology of Women Quarterly, 18*, 477–486.

Rhodes, A. E., Goering, P. N., To, T., & Williams, J. I. (2002). Gender and outpatient mental health service use. *Social Science and Medicine, 54*, 1–10.

Robinson, G. (2002). Cross-cultural perspectives on menopause. In A. E. Hunter & C. Forden (Eds.), *Readings in the psychology of gender* (pp. 140–149). Boston: Allyn & Bacon.

Robinson, T. L., & Howard-Hamilton, M. F. (2000). *The convergence of race, ethnicity, and gender: Multiple identities in counseling.* Upper Saddle River, NJ: Merrill.

Rostosky, S. S., & Travis, C. B. (2000). Menopause and sexuality: Ageism and sexism unite. In C. B. Travis & J. W. White (Eds.), *Sexuality, society, and feminism* (pp. 181–209). Washington, DC: American Psychological Association.

Saris, R. N., & Johnston-Robledo, I. (2000). Poor women are still shut out of mainstream psychology. *Psychology of Women Quarterly, 24*, 233–235.

Sherwin, B. B. (2001). Menopause: Myths and realities. In N. Stotland & D. E. Stewart (Eds.), *Psychological aspects of women's health care* (2nd ed., pp. 241–259). Washington, DC: American Psychiatric Press.

Sparks, E. E., & Park, A. H. (2000). The integration of feminism and multiculturalism: Ethical dilemmas at the border. In M. M. Brabeck (Ed.), *Practicing feminist ethics in psychology* (pp. 203–224). Washington, DC: American Psychological Association.

Stewart, A., & McDermott, C. (2004). Gender in psychology. *Annual Review of Psychology, 55*, 519–544.

Stice, E., & Bearman, S. K. (2001). Body-image and eating disturbances prospectively predict increases in depressive symptoms in adolescent girls: A growth curve analysis. *Developmental Psychology, 37*, 597–607.

Stice, E., Burton, E. M., & Shaw, H. (2004). Prospective relations between bulimic pathology, depression, and substance abuse: Unpacking comorbidity in adolescent girls. *Journal of Consulting and Clinical Psychology, 72*, 62–71.

Suyemoto, K. L., & Kim, G. S. (2005). Journeys through diverse terrains: Multiple identities and social contexts in individual therapy. In M. P. Mirkin, K. L. Suyemoto, & B. F. Okun (Eds.), *Psychotherapy with women: Exploring diverse contexts and identities* (pp. 9–41). New York: Guilford.

Swim, J. K., & Cohen, L. L. (1997). Overt, covert, and subtle sexism. *Psychology of Women Quarterly, 21*, 103–118.

Trimble, J. E., Stevenson, M. R., Worell, J. P., & the APA Commission on Ethnic Minority Recruitment, Retention, and Training Task Force Textbook Initiative Work Group. (2003). *Toward an inclusive psychology: Infusing the introductory psychology textbook with diversity content*. Washington, DC: American Psychological Association.

U.S. Department of Health and Human Services, Office on Women's Health. (2001). *Women's health issues: An overview*. Washington, DC: National Women's Health Information Center.

Wampold, B. E. (2001). *The great psychotherapy debate*. Mahwah, NJ: Erlbaum.

Werner-Wilson, R., Price, S., Zimmerman, T. S., & Murphy, M. (1997). Client gender as a process variable in marriage and family therapy: Are women clients interrupted more than men clients? *Journal of Family Psychology, 11*, 373–377.

West, C. (2002). *Violence in the lives of Black women: Battered, Black, and blue*. Binghamton, NY: Haworth Press.

Woolley, S. (2000). Gender biases and therapists' conceptualizations of couple difficulties. *American Journal of Family Therapy, 28*, 181–192.

Worell, J., & Johnson, N. G. (Eds.). (1997). *Shaping the future of feminist psychology: Education, research, and practice*. Washington, DC: American Psychological Association.

Wyche, K. F., & Rice, J. K. (1997). Feminist therapy: From dialogue to tenets. In J. Worell & N. G. Johnson (Eds.), *Shaping the future of feminist psychology: Education, research, and practice* (pp. 57–71). Washington, DC: American Psychological Association.

7.5. Guidelines for Psychological Practice With Lesbian, Gay, and Bisexual Clients

American Psychological Association

The "Guidelines for Psychological Practice With Lesbian, Gay, and Bisexual Clients" provide psychologists with (a) a frame of reference for the treatment of lesbian, gay, and bisexual clients[1] and (b) basic information and further references in the areas of assessment, intervention, identity, relationships, diversity, education, training, and research. These practice guidelines are built

---

[1]Throughout this document, the term *clients* refers to individuals across the life span, including youth, adult, and older adult lesbian, gay, and bisexual clients. There may be issues that are specific to a given age range, and, when appropriate, the document identifies these groups.

From "Guidelines for Psychological Practice With Lesbian, Gay, and Bisexual Clients," by the American Psychological Association, 2012, *American Psychologist, 67*, pp. 10–42. Copyright 2012 by the American Psychological Association.

These guidelines were adopted by the APA Council of Representatives, February 18–20, 2011, and replace the original "Guidelines for Psychotherapy With Lesbian, Gay, and Bisexual Clients," which were adopted February 26, 2000, and expired at the end of 2010. These revised and updated guidelines were developed by the Division 44/Committee on Lesbian, Gay, Bisexual, and Transgender Concerns Guidelines Revision Task Force. The task force included Kristin Hancock (chair) and members Laura Alie, Armand Cerbone, Sari Dworkin, Terry Gock, Douglas Haldeman, Susan Kashubeck-West, and Glenda Russell. The task force thanks Glenn Ally, Laura Brown, Linda Campbell, Jean Carter, James Croteau, Steven David, Randall Ehbar, Ruth Fassinger, Beth Firestein, Ronald Fox, John Gonsiorek, Beverly Greene, Lisa Grossman, Christine Hall, Tania Israel, Corey Johnson, Jennifer Kelly, Christopher Martell, Jonathan Mohr, David Pantalone, Mark Pope, and Melba Vasquez for their thoughtful contributions. The task force also acknowledges the long-standing support of Clinton Anderson, director of APA's Lesbian, Gay, Bisexual, and Transgender Concerns Office, and APA staff liaisons Sue Houston (Board for the Advancement of Psychology in the Public Interest) and Mary Hardiman (Board of Professional Affairs) for their assistance.

Each of the 21 new guidelines provides an update of the psychological literature supporting it, includes sections on rationale and application, and expands upon the original guidelines to provide assistance to psychologists in areas such as religion and spirituality, the differentiation of gender identity and sexual orientation, socioeconomic and workplace issues, and the use and dissemination of research on lesbian, gay, and bisexual issues. The guidelines are intended to inform the practice of psychologists and to provide information for the education and training of psychologists regarding lesbian, gay, and bisexual issues. The revision was funded by Division 44 (Society for the Psychological Study of Lesbian, Gay, and Bisexual Issues) of the American Psychological Association (APA) and the APA Board of Directors.

This document is scheduled to expire as APA policy in 10 years (2020). After this date, users are encouraged to contact the APA Public Interest Directorate to confirm that this document remains in effect or is under revision.

upon the "Guidelines for Psychotherapy With Lesbian, Gay, and Bisexual Clients" (Division 44/Committee on Lesbian, Gay, and Bisexual Concerns Joint Task Force on Guidelines for Psychotherapy with Lesbian, Gay, and Bisexual Clients, 2000) and are consistent with the American Psychological Association (APA) "Criteria for Practice Guideline Development and Evaluation" (APA, 2002a).

. . .

ATTITUDES TOWARD HOMOSEXUALITY AND BISEXUALITY

Guideline 1. Psychologists strive to understand the effects of stigma (i.e., prejudice, discrimination, and violence) and its various contextual manifestations in the lives of lesbian, gay, and bisexual people.

Rationale

Living in a heterosexist society inevitably poses challenges to people with non-heterosexual orientations. Many lesbian, gay, and bisexual people face social stigma, heterosexism, violence, and discrimination (Herek, 1991b, 2009; Mays & Cochran, 2001; I. H. Meyer, 2003). Stigma is defined as a negative social attitude or social disapproval directed toward a characteristic of a person that can lead to prejudice and discrimination against the individual (VandenBos, 2007). . . . These challenges may precipitate a significant degree of minority stress for lesbian, gay, and bisexual people, many of whom may be tolerated only when they are "closeted" (DiPlacido, 1998). Minority stress can be experienced in the form of ongoing daily hassles (e.g., hearing antigay jokes) and more serious negative events (e.g., loss of employment, housing, custody of children, physical and sexual assault; DiPlacido, 1998).

. . .

Guideline 2. Psychologists understand that lesbian, gay, and bisexual orientations are not mental illnesses.

Rationale

No scientific basis for inferring a predisposition to psychopathology or other maladjustment as intrinsic to homosexuality or bisexuality has been established. . . [S]tudies have continued to show no differences between heterosexual groups and homosexual groups on measures of cognitive abilities (Tuttle & Pillard, 1991). . . .

At the present time, efforts to repathologize nonheterosexual orientations persist on the part of advocates for conversion or reparative therapy (APA, 2009b; Haldeman, 2002). Nevertheless, major mental health organizations . . . have affirmed that homosexuality and bisexuality are not mental illnesses.

. . .

Guideline 3. Psychologists understand that same-sex attractions, feelings, and behavior are normal variants of human sexuality and that efforts to change sexual orientation have not been shown to be effective or safe.

Rationale

Therapeutic efforts to change sexual orientation have increased and become more visible in recent years (Beckstead & Morrow, 2004). Therapeutic interventions intended to change, modify, or manage unwanted nonheterosexual orientations are referred to as "sexual orientation change efforts" (SOCE; APA, 2009b). The majority of clients who seek to change their sexual orientation do so through so-called ex-gay programs or ministries (Haldeman, 2004; Tozer & Hayes, 2004). Most contexts in which SOCE occur derive from the religion-based ex-gay movement (Haldeman, 2004), although several psychotherapeutic approaches also exist.

. . .

Guideline 4. Psychologists are encouraged to recognize how their attitudes and knowledge about lesbian, gay, and bisexual issues may be relevant to assessment and treatment and seek consultation or make appropriate referrals when indicated.

Rationale

The APA Ethics Code urges psychologists to eliminate the effect of biases on their work (APA, 2002b, Principle E). To do so, psychologists strive to evaluate their competencies and the limitations of their expertise, especially when offering assessment and treatment services to people who share characteristics that are different from their own (e.g., lesbian, gay, and bisexual clients). Without a high level of awareness about their own beliefs, values, needs, and limitations, psychologists may impede the progress of a client in psychotherapy (Corey, Schneider-Corey, & Callanan, 1993). This is particularly relevant when providing assessment and treatment services to lesbian, gay, and bisexual clients.

. . .

Guideline 5. Psychologists strive to recognize the unique experiences of bisexual individuals.

Rationale

Bisexual persons are affected by negative individual and societal attitudes toward bisexuality that are expressed by both heterosexual and gay/lesbian people (Bradford, 2004a; Eliason, 2001; Evans, 2003; Herek, 2002; Mulick & Wright, 2002). In addition, bisexuality may not be regarded as a valid sexual orientation (Dworkin, 2001) but instead be viewed as a transitional state between heterosexual and homosexual orientations (Eliason, 2001; Herek, 2002; G. M. Russell & Richards, 2003; Rust, 2000a). Bisexual individuals also may be viewed as promiscuous, developmentally arrested, or psychologically impaired (Fox, 1996; T. Israel & Mohr, 2004; Mohr, Israel, & Sedlacek, 2001; Oxley & Lucius, 2000). Visibility of sexual identity may be particularly challenging for bisexual persons, as others may assume they are lesbian or gay if in a same-sex relationship or heterosexual if they are in a mixed-sex relationship (Bradford, 2004a; Keppel & Firestein, 2007; Rust, 2007).

. . .

Guideline 6. Psychologists strive to distinguish issues of sexual orientation from those of gender identity when working with lesbian, gay, and bisexual clients.

Rationale

Sexual orientation and gender identity are distinct characteristics of an individual (APA, 2006). A common error is to see gay men and lesbians as particularly likely to manifest gender-nonconforming behavior and/or to be transgender (Fassinger & Arseneau, 2007; Helgeson, 1994; Kite, 1994; Kite & Deaux, 1987; Martin, 1990). Similarly, gender nonconformity may result in an individual being perceived as lesbian or gay, independent of that person's actual sexual orientation. Because gender nonconformity is likely to be stigmatized, gender nonconformity itself can result in prejudice and discrimination, regardless of sexual orientation (J. Green & Brinkin, 1994; Lombardi, 2001). For example, some research in schools indicates that gender nonconformity (regardless of sexual orientation) evokes at least as much antipathy among high school students as does a lesbian, gay, or bisexual orientation alone (e.g., Horn, 2007).

. . .

RELATIONSHIPS AND FAMILIES

Guideline 7. Psychologists strive to be knowledgeable about and respect the importance of lesbian, gay, and bisexual relationships.

Rationale

Lesbian, gay, and bisexual couples are both similar to and different from heterosexual couples (Peplau, Veniegas, & Campbell, 1996). They form relationships for similar reasons (Herek, 2006), express similar satisfactions with their relationships (Kurdek, 1995; Peplau & Cochran, 1990), and follow developmental patterns similar to heterosexual couples (Clunis & Green, 1988; McWhirter & Mattison, 1984). The differences are derived from several factors, including different patterns of sexual behavior, gender role socialization (Hancock, 2000; Herek, 1991b; Ossana, 2000), and the stigmatization of their relationships (Garnets & Kimmel, 1993).

. . .

Guideline 8. Psychologists strive to understand the experiences and challenges faced by lesbian, gay, and bisexual parents.

Rationale

Research has indicated that lesbian, gay, and bisexual parents are as capable as heterosexual parents (cf. Armesto, 2002; Erich, Leung, & Kindle, 2005; Herek, 2006; Patterson, 2000, 2004; Perrin, 2002; Tasker, 1999). . . . Such findings are important to note, given the context of discrimination that lesbian, gay, and bisexual parents face (e.g., legal barriers to foster parenting and same-sex and second-parent adoption, the threat of loss of custody of children, prohibitions against living with one's same-sex partner, the lack of legal rights of one of the parents; ACLU Lesbian and Gay Rights Project, 2002; Appell, 2004; Patterson, Fulcher, & Wainwright, 2002). In becoming parents, lesbian, gay, and bisexual people face challenges not required of heterosexual people, such as stressors related to alternative insemination and surrogacy (Gifford, Hertz, & Doskow, 2010).

. . .

Guideline 9. Psychologists recognize that the families of lesbian, gay, and bisexual people may include people who are not legally or biologically related.

Rationale

For a significant number of lesbian, gay, and bisexual individuals, nondisclosure of sexual orientation and/or lack of acknowledgement of their intimate relationships may result in emotional distancing from their family of origin (Patterson, 2007). Even when families are accepting, this acceptance often may be tolerance rather than true acceptance (R. J. Green, 2004). For many lesbian, gay, and bisexual people, a network of close friends may constitute an alternative family structure—one that may not be based on legal and/or biological relationships. These families of choice provide social connections and familial context for lesbian, gay, and bisexual individuals (R. J. Green, 2004) and may be more significant than the individual's family of origin (Kurdek, 1988). Such family structures can mitigate the effects of discrimination and the absence of legal or institutional recognition (Weston, 1992).

. . .

Guideline 10. Psychologists strive to understand the ways in which a person's lesbian, gay, or bisexual orientation may have an impact on his or her family of origin and the relationship with that family of origin.

Rationale

There are many responses a family can have upon learning that one of its members is lesbian, gay, or bisexual (Patterson, 2007; Savin-Williams, 2003). Some families of origin may be unprepared to accept a lesbian, gay, or bisexual child or family member because of familial, ethnic, or cultural norms; religious beliefs; or negative stereotypes (Buxton, 2005; Chan, 1995; Firestein, 2007; Greene, 2000; Matteson, 1996). For these families, this awareness may precipitate a family crisis that can result in profound distancing from or expulsion of the lesbian, gay, or bisexual family member; rejection of the parents and siblings by that family member; parental guilt and self-recrimination; or conflicts within the parents' relationship (Dickens & McKellen, 1996;

Griffin, Wirth, & Wirth, 1996; Savin-Williams, 2003; Savin-Williams & Dube, 1998; Strommen, 1993). On the other hand, there are families of origin in which acceptance of their lesbian, gay, or bisexual member is unconditional or without crisis (Patterson, 2007; Savin-Williams, 2003). Research does suggest, however, that even supportive families may experience an adjustment period upon learning that a family member is lesbian, gay, or bisexual (Jennings & Shapiro, 2003; Pallotta-Chiarolli, 2005).

. . .

ISSUES OF DIVERSITY

. . .

Guideline 11. Psychologists strive to recognize the challenges related to multiple and often conflicting norms, values, and beliefs faced by lesbian, gay, and bisexual members of racial and ethnic minority groups.

Rationale

Lesbian, gay, and bisexual individuals who are members of racial, ethnic, and cultural minority groups must negotiate the norms, values, and beliefs regarding homosexuality and bisexuality of both mainstream and minority cultures (Chan, 1992, 1995; Greene, 1994b; Manalansan, 1996; Rust, 1996a). There is some evidence to suggest that cultural variation in these norms, values, beliefs, and attitudes can be a significant source of psychological stress that affects the health and mental health of lesbians, gay men, and bisexual women and men (Díaz, Ayala, Bein, Henne, & Marin, 2001; Harper & Schneider, 2003; I. H. Meyer, 2003). Recently, however, there is evidence to suggest that lesbian, gay, and bisexual individuals from diverse racial, ethnic, and cultural backgrounds may have lower rates of mental health problems (e.g., Cochran, Mays, Alegria, Ortega, & Takeuchi, 2007; Kertzner, Meyer, Frost, & Stirratt, 2009; I. H. Meyer, Dietrich, & Schwartz, 2008). It may be that the skills learned in negotiating one stigmatized aspect of identity may actually assist the individual in dealing with and protect the individual from other forms of stigmatization.

. . .

Guideline 12. Psychologists are encouraged to consider the influences of religion and spirituality in the lives of lesbian, gay, and bisexual persons.

Rationale

The influence of religion and spirituality in the lives of lesbian, gay, and bisexual persons can be complex, dynamic, and a source of ambivalence. Such is the case because their experience, especially with organized religion, is varied and diverse. Although some religious and spiritual belief systems are relatively neutral about diverse sexual orientations (e.g., Buddhism and Hinduism), others historically have been more condemnatory (e.g., Christianity, Judaism, and Islam). Even within religious traditions that have been historically disapproving of nonheterosexual orientations, there has been an emerging and growing theological paradigm in the past 20 to 30 years that accepts and supports diverse sexual orientations (Borg, 2004).

. . .

Guideline 13. Psychologists strive to recognize cohort and age differences among lesbian, gay, and bisexual individuals.

Rationale

Lesbian, gay, and bisexual individuals may differ substantially based on the effects of cohort and age. Cohort influences are broad historical forces that shape the context of development; for lesbian, gay, and bisexual people, the time period in which one has lived and/or come out can profoundly shape such developmental tasks as claiming identity labels, identity disclosure, parenting, and political involvement (Fassinger & Arseneau, 2007). Examples of factors influencing generational differences include changing societal attitudes toward sexuality; the effects of HIV/AIDS on sexual minority communities; changing religious and spiritual attitudes and practices; the women's, gay, and civil rights movements; advancements in reproductive technologies and changes in ideologies about families; and changes in conceptualizations of sexual and gender identity, including identity labels.

. . .

Guideline 14. Psychologists strive to understand the unique problems and risks that exist for lesbian, gay, and bisexual youths.

Rationale

Navigating the cognitive, emotional, and social developmental changes of adolescence while simultaneously integrating the emergence of a lesbian, gay, or bisexual identity can be challenging for youths (D'Augelli, 2006). Lesbian, gay, bisexual, and questioning youths may be at increased risk for difficulties not experienced by their heterosexual counterparts (cf. D'Augelli, 2002; Espelage et al., 2008; Lasser, Tharinger, & Cloth, 2006; Thomas & Larrabee, 2002), such as homelessness (Urbina, 2007), prostitution (Savin-Williams, 1994), and sexually transmitted diseases (Solorio, Milburn, & Weiss, 2006). Lesbian, gay, bisexual, and questioning youths who do not conform to gender norms may experience increased difficulties in peer relationships (D'Augelli et al., 2002; Wilson, Griffin, & Wren, 2005). Decisions about coming out may pose even greater difficulties for lesbian, gay, and bisexual youths of color, for whom family and community may be a vital source of support for dealing with racism (see Guideline 11). Lesbian, gay, and bisexual youths often have problems in school that are related to their sexual orientation (Cooper-Nicols, 2007), such as social alienation (Sullivan & Wodarski, 2002) and bullying (E. J. Meyer, 2009). These factors may increase the risk of substance abuse (Jordan, 2000) or have long-term consequences, such as posttraumatic stress (Rivers, 2004).

. . .

Guideline 15. Psychologists are encouraged to recognize the particular challenges that lesbian, gay, and bisexual individuals with physical, sensory, and cognitive–emotional disabilities experience.

Rationale

Lesbian, gay, and bisexual individuals with disabilities may encounter a wide range of particular challenges related to the social stigma associated both with disability and with sexual orientation (Saad, 1997). They also may experience the sense of invisibility that is associated with the intersection of same-sex orientation and physical, cognitive–emotional, and/or sensory disability (Abbott & Burns, 2007; Lofgren-Martenson, 2009), due to prevailing societal views of people with disabilities as nonsexual and alone.

. . .

Guideline 16. Psychologists strive to understand the impact of HIV/AIDS on the lives of lesbian, gay, and bisexual individuals and communities.

Rationale

Because HIV/AIDS and sexual orientation have been conflated, people living with the disease are stigmatized (Herek, Capitanio, & Widaman, 2002). Additional factors that contribute to the prejudice and discrimination faced by people living with HIV/AIDS include misunderstanding of or misinformation about the virus (Ritieni, Moskowitz, & Tholandi, 2008), general homophobia and racism (Brooks, Etzel, Hinojos, Henry, & Perez, 2005), and the fact that the virus is spread through behavior that some individuals or groups condemn as objectionable (Kopelman, 2002). Although an AIDS diagnosis was initially a death sentence, significant medical advances in the treatment of HIV/AIDS have resulted in its reconceptualization as a chronic disease (Pierret, 2007).

. . .

ECONOMIC AND WORKPLACE ISSUES

Guideline 17. Psychologists are encouraged to consider the impact of socioeconomic status on the psychological well-being of lesbian, gay, and bisexual clients.

Rationale

Data indicate that lesbian, gay, and bisexual men and women are often at economic disadvantage in contrast to their heterosexual counterparts. . . . Research has also shown that gay men living in same-sex relationships earn less than men in heterosexual marriages (Allegretto & Arthur, 2001; Klawitter & Flatt, 1998). . . . Although gay men and lesbians tend to be more highly educated than their heterosexual counterparts (Carpenter, 2005; Rothblum, Balsam, & Mickey, 2004), they continue to earn less money (Egan, Edelman, & Sherrill, 2008; Factor & Rothblum, 2007; Fassinger, 2008). . . . Lesbian, gay, and bisexual individuals have been fired, denied promotion, given negative performance evaluations, and received unequal pay and benefits on the basis of their sexual orientation (Badgett, Lau, Sears, & Ho, 2007).

. . .

Guideline 18. Psychologists strive to understand the unique workplace issues that exist for lesbian, gay, and bisexual individuals.

Rationale

There are unique difficulties and risks faced by lesbian, gay, and bisexual individuals in the workplace, particularly the impact of sexual stigma (Herek, 2007; Herek, Gillis, & Cogan, 2009) on vocational decision making, choice, implementation, adjustment, and achievement (Croteau et al., 2008; Fassinger, 2008; Pope et al., 2004). Barriers to the vocational development and success of lesbian, gay, and bisexual individuals include employment discrimination (Fassinger, 2008; Kirby, 2002); wage discrimination (Badgett, 2003; Elmslie & Tebaldi, 2007); lack of benefits (e.g., family medical leave, bereavement leave, child care, same-sex partner benefits; Fassinger, 2008); hostile workplace climates (Ragins & Cornwell, 2001; Ragins, Singh, & Cornwell, 2007); job stereotyping (Chung, 2001; Keeton, 2002); occupational restrictions (e.g., military, clergy; Fassinger, 2008); the interactive effects of bias based upon gender, race and ethnicity, disability, and other aspects of marginalized status (Bieschke et al., 2008; Van Puymbroeck, 2002); and compromised career assessment (M. Z. Anderson, Croteau, Chung, & DiStefano, 2001; Pope et al., 2004).

. . .

EDUCATION AND TRAINING

Guideline 19. Psychologists strive to include lesbian, gay, and bisexual issues in professional education and training.

Rationale

Despite the rising emphasis on diversity training during graduate education and internship, studies have shown that graduate students in psychology and early career psychologists report inadequate education and training in lesbian, gay, and bisexual issues (Matthews, Selvidge, & Fisher, 2005; Pilkington & Cantor, 1996) and feel unprepared to work with these groups (Allison, Crawford,

Echemendia, Robinson, & Knepp, 1994; Phillips & Fischer, 1998). . . . Students may describe their attitudes as more affirmative than these actually are if examined more deeply. Training has been shown to clarify negative attitudes about nonheterosexual orientations (Boysen & Vogel, 2008; T. Israel & Hackett, 2004). Identification as lesbian, gay, or bisexual does not necessarily confer expertise in practice with lesbian, gay, and bisexual clients.

. . .

Guideline 20. Psychologists are encouraged to increase their knowledge and understanding of homosexuality and bisexuality through continuing education, training, supervision, and consultation.

Rationale

Although the study of diverse populations has received more attention in recent years, many practicing psychologists may not have received basic information pertaining to working with lesbian, gay, and bisexual clients. APA's Ethics Code (APA, 2002b) urges psychologists to "undertake ongoing efforts to develop and maintain their competence" (p. 1064). Unfortunately, the education, training, practice experience, consultation, and/or supervision that psychologists receive regarding lesbian, gay, and bisexual issues often have been inadequate, outdated, or unavailable (Morrow, 1998; J. A. Murphy, Rawlings, & Howe, 2002; Pilkington & Cantor, 1996; Sherry, Whilde, & Patton, 2005). Studies historically have revealed psychotherapist prejudice and insensitivity in working with lesbian, gay, and bisexual people (Garnets et al., 1991; Liddle, 1996; Nystrom, 1997; Winegarten et al., 1994).

. . .

RESEARCH

Guideline 21. In the use and dissemination of research on sexual orientation and related issues, psychologists strive to represent results fully and accurately and to be mindful of the potential misuse or misrepresentation of research findings.

Rationale

Just as bias can influence the conduct of research, it also can influence the interpretations of research by others and the uses to which research results are put. Sound research findings about any stigmatized group represent an important contribution to the discipline of psychology and to society in general. However, research about lesbian, gay, and bisexual people has been misused and misrepresented to the detriment of lesbian, gay, and bisexual individuals (Herek, 1998; Herek, Kimmel, Amaro, & Melton, 1991; G. M. Russell & Kelly, 2003).

. . .

REFERENCES

Abbott, D., & Burns, J. (2007). What's love got to do with it? Experiences of lesbian, gay, and bisexual people with intellectual disabilities in the United Kingdom and views of the staff who support them. *Sexuality Research and Social Policy, 4*, 27–39. doi:10.1525/srsp.2007.4.1.27

ACLU Lesbian and Gay Rights Project. (2002). *Too high a price: The case against restricting gay parenting.* New York, NY: American Civil Liberties Union.

Allegretto, S. A., & Arthur, M. M. (2001). An empirical analysis of homosexual/heterosexual male earnings differentials: Unmarried and unequal? *Industrial and Labor Relations Review, 54*, 631–646. doi:10.2307/2695994

Allison, K. W., Crawford, I., Echemendia, R., Robinson, L., & Knepp, D. (1994). Human diversity and professional competence: Training in clinical and counseling psychology revisited. *American Psychologist, 49*, 792–796. doi:10.1037/0003-066X.49.9.792

American Psychological Association. (2002a). Criteria for practice guideline development and evaluation. *American Psychologist, 57*, 1048–1051. doi:10.1037/0003-066X.57.12.1048

American Psychological Association. (2002b). Ethical principles of psychologists and code of conduct. *American Psychologist, 57*, 1060–1073. doi:10.1037/0003-066X.57.12.1060

American Psychological Association. (2006). *Answers to your questions about transgender individuals and gender identity.* Retrieved from http://www.apa.org/topics/transgender.html

American Psychological Association. (2009b). *Report of the APA Task Force on Appropriate Therapeutic-Responses to Sexual Orientation.* Retrieved from http://www.apa.org/pi/lgbt/resources/therapeutic-response.Pdf

Anderson, M. Z., Croteau, J. M., Chung, Y. B., & DiStefano, T. M. (2001). Developing an assessment of sexual identity management for lesbian and gay workers. *Journal of Career Assessment, 9*, 243–260. doi:10.1177/106907270100900303

Appell, A. R. (2004). Recent developments in lesbian and gay adoption law. *Adoption Quarterly, 7*, 73–84. doi:10.1300/J145v07n01_06

Armesto, J. C. (2002). Developmental and contextual factors that influence gay fathers' parental competence: A review of the literature. *Psychology of Men & Masculinity, 3*, 67–78. doi:10.1037/1524-9220.3.2.67

Badgett, M. V. L. (2003). *Money, myths, and change: The economic lives of lesbians and gay men.* Chicago, IL: University of Chicago Press.

Badgett, M. V. L., Lau, H., Sears, B., & Ho, D. (2007). *Bias in the workplace: Consistent evidence of sexual orientation and gender identity discrimination.* Retrieved from https://williamsinstitute.law.ucla.edu/wp-content/uploads/Badgett-Sears-Lau-Ho-Bias-in-the-Workplace-Jun-2007.pdf

Beckstead, A. L., & Morrow, S. L. (2004). Mormon clients' experiences of conversion therapy: The need for a new treatment approach. *Counseling Psychologist, 32*, 651–690. doi:10.1177/0011000004267555

Bieschke, K. J., Hardy, J. A., Fassinger, R. E., & Croteau, J. M. (2008). Intersecting identities of gender-transgressive sexual minorities: Toward a new paradigm of affirmative psychology. In B. Walsh (Ed.), *Biennial review of counseling psychology* (Vol. 1, pp. 177–207). New York, NY: Routledge/Taylor & Francis Group.

Borg, M. J. (2004). *The heart of Christianity: Rediscovering a life of faith.* San Francisco, CA: Harper.

Boysen, G. A., & Vogel, D. L. (2008). The relationship between level of training, implicit bias, and multicultural competency among counselor trainees. *Training and Education in Professional Psychology, 2*, 103–110. doi:10.1037/1931-3918.2.2.103

Bradford, M. (2004a). The biscxual experience: Living in a dichotomous culture. *Journal of Bisexuality, 4*(1–2), 7–23. doi:10.1300/J159v04n01_02

Brooks, R. A., Etzel, M. A., Hinojos, E., Henry, C. L., & Perez, M. (2005). Preventing HIV among Latino and African American gay and bisexual men in a context of

HIV-related stigma, discrimination, and homophobia: Perspectives of providers. *AIDS Patient Care and STDs, 19*, 737–744. doi:10.1089/apc.2005.19.737

Buxton, A. P. (2005). A family matter: When a spouse comes out as gay, lesbian, or bisexual. *Journal of GLBT Family Studies, 1*(2), 49–70. doi:10.1300/J461v01n02_04

Carpenter, C. S. (2005). Self-reported sexual orientation and earnings: Evidence from California. *Industrial and Labor Relations Review, 58*, 258–273.

Chan, C. (1992). Asian-American lesbians and gay men. In S. Dworkin & F. Gutierrez (Eds.), *Counseling gay men and lesbians: Journey to the end of the rainbow* (pp. 115–124). Alexandria, VA: American Association for Counseling and Development.

Chan, C. (1995). Issues of sexual identity in an ethnic minority: The case of Chinese American lesbians, gay men, and bisexual people. In A. D'Augelli & C. Patterson (Eds.), *Lesbian, gay, and bisexual identities over the lifespan: Psychological perspectives* (pp. 87–101). New York, NY: Oxford University Press.

Chung, Y. B. (2001). Work discrimination and coping strategies: Conceptual frameworks for counseling lesbian, gay, and bisexual clients. *Career Development Quarterly, 50*, 33–44.

Clunis, D. M., & Green, G. D. (1988). *Lesbian couples.* Seattle, WA: Seal Press.

Cochran, S. D., Mays, V. M., Alegria, M., Ortega, A. N., & Takeuchi, D. (2007). Mental health and substance use disorders among Latino and Asian American lesbian, gay, and bisexual adults. *Journal of Consulting and Clinical Psychology, 75*, 785–794. doi:10.1037/0022-006X.75.5.785

Cooper-Nicols, M. (2007). Exploring the experiences of gay, lesbian, and bisexual adolescents in school: Lessons for school psychologists. *Dissertation Abstracts International: Section B. Sciences and Engineering, 67*(7), 4131.

Corey, G., Schneider-Corey, M., & Callanan, P. (1993). *Issues and ethics in the helping professions* (4th ed.). Belmont, CA: Brooks/Cole.

Croteau, J. M., Bieschke, K. J., Fassinger, R. E., & Manning, J. L. (2008). Counseling psychology and sexual orientation: History, selective trends, and future directions. In S. D. Brown & R. W. Lent (Eds.), *Handbook of counseling psychology* (4th ed., pp. 194–211). New York, NY: Wiley.

D'Augelli, A. R. (2002). Mental health problems among lesbian, gay, and bisexual youths ages 14–21. *Clinical Child Psychology and Psychiatry, 7*, 433–456.

D'Augelli, A. R. (2006). Developmental and contextual factors and mental health among lesbian, gay, and bisexual youths. In A. M. Omoto & H. S. Kurtzman (Eds.), *Sexual orientation and mental health: Examining identity and development in lesbian, gay, and bisexual people* (pp. 37–53). Washington, DC: American Psychological Association.

D'Augelli, A. R., Pilkington, N. W., & Hershberger, S. L. (2002). Incidence and mental health impact of sexual orientation victimization of lesbian, gay, and bisexual youths in high school. *School Psychology Quarterly, 17*, 148–167. doi:10.1521/scpq.17.2.148.20854

Díaz, R. M., Ayala, G., Bein, E., Henne, J., & Marin, B. V. (2001). The impact of homophobia, poverty, and racism on the mental health of gay and bisexual Latino men: Findings from 3 US cities. *American Journal of Public Health, 91*, 927–932. doi:10.2105/AJPH.91.6.927

Dickens, J., & McKellen, I. (1996). *Family outing: Guide for parents of gay, lesbian, and bisexual people.* London, England: Dufour Editions.

DiPlacido, J. (1998). Minority stress among lesbians, gay men, and bisexuals: A consequence of heterosexism, homophobia, and stigmatization. In G. Herek (Ed.), *Psychological perspectives on lesbian and gay issues: Vol. 4. Stigma and sexual orientation: Understanding prejudice against lesbians, gay men, and bisexuals* (pp. 138–159). Thousand Oaks, CA: Sage.

Division 44/Committee on Lesbian, Gay, and Bisexual Concerns Joint Task Force on Guidelines for Psychotherapy with Lesbian, Gay, and Bisexual Clients. (2000). Guidelines for psychotherapy with lesbian, gay, and bisexual clients. *American Psychologist, 55*, 1440–1451.

Dworkin, S. H. (2001). Treating the bisexual client. *Journal of Clinical Psychology, 57*, 671–680. doi:10.1002/jclp.1036

Egan, P. J., Edelman, M. S., & Sherrill, K. (2008). *Findings from the Hunter College Poll of lesbians, gays, and bisexuals: New discoveries about identity, political attitudes, and civic engagement.* Retrieved from http://www.hrc.org//documents/Hunter_college_report.pdf

Eliason, M. (2001). Bi-negativity: The stigma facing bisexual men. *Journal of Bisexuality, 1*(2–3), 137–154. doi:10.1300/J159v01n02_05

Elmslie, B., & Tebaldi, E. (2007). Sexual orientation and labor market discrimination. *Journal of Labor Research, 28*, 436–453. doi:10.1007/s12122-007-9006-1

Erich, S., Leung, P., & Kindle, P. (2005). A comparative analysis in adoptive family functioning with gay, lesbian, and heterosexual parents and their children. *Journal of GLBT Family Studies, 1*, 43–60. doi:10.1300/J461v01n04_03

Espelage, D. L., Aragon, S. R., Birkett, M., & Koenig, B. W. (2008). Homophobic teasing, psychological outcomes, and sexual orientation among high school students: What influence do parents and school have? *School Psychology Review, 37*, 202–216.

Evans, T. (2003). Bisexuality: Negotiating lives between two cultures. *Journal of Bisexuality, 3*(2), 91–108. doi:10.1300/J159v03n02_06

Factor, R. J., & Rothblum, E. D. (2007). A study of transgender adults and their non-transgender siblings on demographic characteristics, social support, and experiences of violence. *Journal of LGBT Health Research, 3*, 11–30.

Fassinger, R. E. (2008). Workplace diversity and public policy: Challenges and opportunities for psychology. *American Psychologist, 63*, 252–268. doi:10.1037/0003-066X.63.4.252

Fassinger, R. E., & Arseneau, J. R. (2007). "I'd rather get wet than be under that umbrella": Differentiating the experiences and identities of lesbian, gay, bisexual, and transgender people. In K. J. Bieschke, R. M. Perez, & K. A. DeBord (Eds.), *Handbook of counseling and psychotherapy with lesbian, gay, bisexual, and transgender clients* (2nd ed., pp. 19–49). Washington, DC: American Psychological Association.

Firestein, B. (2007). Cultural and relational contexts of bisexual women: Implications for therapy. In B. A. Firestein (Ed.), *Becoming visible: Counseling bisexuals across the lifespan* (pp. 127–152). New York, NY: Columbia University Press.

Fox, R. (1996). Bisexuality in perspective: A review of theory and research. In B. A. Firestein (Ed.), *Bisexuality: The psychology and politics of an invisible minority* (pp. 3–50). Thousand Oaks, CA: Sage.

Garnets, L., Hancock, K., Cochran, S., Goodchilds, J., & Peplau, L. (1991). Issues in psychotherapy with lesbians and gay men: A survey of psychologists. *American Psychologist, 46*, 964–972. doi:10.1037/0003-066X.46.9.964

Garnets, L., & Kimmel, D. (1993). Lesbian and gay male dimensions in the psychological study of human diversity. In L. Garnets & D. Kimmel (Eds.), *Psychological perspectives on lesbian and gay male experiences* (pp. 1–51). New York, NY: Columbia University Press.

Gifford, D., Hertz, F., & Doskow, E. (2010). *A legal guide for lesbian and gay couples.* Berkeley, CA: Nolo.

Green, J., & Brinkin, L. (1994). *Investigations into discrimination against transgender people.* San Francisco, CA: San Francisco Human Rights Commission.

Green, R. J. (2004). Risk and resilience in lesbian and gay couples: Comment on Solomon, Rothblum, and Balsam (2004). *Journal of Family Psychology, 18*, 290–292. doi:10.1037/0893-3200.18.2.290

Greene, B. (1994b). Lesbian and gay sexual orientations: Implications for clinical training, practice, and research. In B. Greene & G. Herek (Eds.), *Psychological perspectives on lesbian and gay issues: Vol. 1. Lesbian and gay psychology: Theory, research, and clinical applications* (pp. 1–24). Thousand Oaks, CA: Sage.

Greene, B. (2000). African American lesbian and bisexual women. *Journal of Social Issues, 56*, 239–249. doi:10.1111/0022-4537.00163

Griffin, C. W., Wirth, M. J., & Wirth, A. G. (1996). *Beyond acceptance: Parents of lesbians and gays talk about their experiences.* New York, NY: St. Martin's Press.

Haldeman, D. C. (2002). Gay rights, patient rights: The implications of sexual orientation conversion therapy. *Professional Psychology: Research and Practice, 33,* 260–264. doi:10.1037/0735-7028.33.3.260

Haldeman, D. C. (2004). When sexual and religious orientations collide: Considerations in working with conflicted same-sex attracted male clients. *Counseling Psychologist, 32,* 691–715. doi:10.1177/0011000004267560

Hancock, K. A. (2000). Lesbian, gay, and bisexual lives: Basic issues in psychotherapy training and practice. In B. Greene & G. L. Croom (Eds.), *Psychological perspectives on lesbian and gay issues: Vol. 5. Education, research, and practice in lesbian, gay, bisexual, and transgendered psychology: A resource manual* (pp. 91–130). Thousand Oaks, CA: Sage.

Harper, G. W., & Schneider, M. (2003). Oppression and discrimination among lesbian, gay, bisexual, and transgendered people and communities: A challenge for community psychology. *American Journal of Community Psychology, 31,* 243–252. doi:10.1023/A:1023906620085

Helgeson, V. S. (1994). Prototypes and dimensions of masculinity and femininity. *Sex Roles, 31,* 653–682. doi:10.1007/BF01544286

Herek, G. M. (1991b). Stigma, prejudice, and violence against lesbians and gay men. In J. Gonsiorek & J. Weinrich (Eds.), *Homosexuality: Research implications for public policy* (pp. 60–80). Newbury Park, CA: Sage.

Herek, G. M. (1998). Bad science in the service of stigma: A critique of the Cameron group's survey studies. In G. M. Herek (Ed.), *Stigma and sexual orientation: Understanding prejudice against lesbians, gay men, and bisexuals* (pp. 223–255). Thousand Oaks, CA: Sage.

Herek, G. M. (2002). Heterosexuals' attitudes toward bisexual men and women in the United States. *Journal of Sex Research, 39,* 264–274. doi:10.1080/00224490209552150

Herek, G. M. (2006). Legal recognition of same-sex relationships in the United States. *American Psychologist, 61,* 607–621. doi:10.1037/0003-066X.61.6.607

Herek, G. M. (2007). Confronting sexual stigma and prejudice: Theory and practice. *Journal of Social Issues, 63,* 905–925. doi:10.1111/j.1540-4560.2007.00544.x

Herek, G. M. (2009). Hate crimes and stigma-related experiences among sexual minority adults in the United States: Prevalence estimates from a national probability sample. *Journal of Interpersonal Violence, 24,* 54–74. doi:10.1177/0886260508316477

Herek, G. M., Capitanio, J. P., & Widaman, K. F. (2002). HIV-related stigma and knowledge in the United States: Prevalence and trends, 1991–1999. *American Journal of Public Health, 92,* 371–377. doi:10.2105/AJPH.92.3.371

Herek, G. M., Gillis, J. R., & Cogan, J. C. (2009). Internalized stigma among sexual minority adults: Insights from a social psychological perspective. *Journal of Counseling Psychology, 56,* 32–43. doi:10.1037/a0014672

Herek, G. M., Kimmel, D. C., Amaro, H., & Melton, G. B. (1991). Avoiding heterosexist bias in psychological research. *American Psychologist, 46,* 957–963. doi:10.1037/0003-066X.46.9.957

Horn, S. S. (2007). Adolescents' acceptance of same-sex peers based on sexual orientation and gender expression. *Journal of Youth and Adolescence, 36,* 363–371. doi:10.1007/s10964-006-9111-0

Israel, T., & Hackett, G. (2004). Counselor education on lesbian, gay, and bisexual issues: Comparing information and attitude exploration. *Counselor Education and Supervision, 43,* 179–191.

Israel, T., & Mohr, J. (2004). Attitudes toward bisexual women and men: Current research, future directions. *Journal of Bisexuality, 4*(1–2), 117–134.

Jennings, K., & Shapiro, P. (2003). *Always my child: A parent's guide to understanding your gay, lesbian, bisexual, transgendered, or questioning son or daughter.* New York, NY: Simon & Schuster.

Jordan, K. (2000). Substance abuse among gay, lesbian, bisexual, transgender, and questioning adolescents. *School Psychology Review, 29*, 201–206.

Keeton, M. D. (2002). Perceptions of career-related barriers among gay, lesbian, and bisexual individuals. *Dissertation Abstracts International: Section B. Sciences and Engineering, 63*(2), 1075.

Keppel, B., & Firestein, B. (2007). Bisexual inclusion in addressing issues of GLBT aging: Therapy with older bisexual women and men. In B. A. Firestein (Ed.), *Becoming visible: Counseling bisexuals across the lifespan* (pp. 164–185). New York, NY: Columbia University Press.

Kertzner, R. M., Meyer, I. H., Frost, D. M., & Stirratt, M. J. (2009). Social and psychological well-being in lesbians, gay men, and bisexuals: The effects of race, gender, age, and sexual identity. *American Journal of Orthopsychiatry, 79*, 500–510. doi:10.1037/a0016848

Kirby, K. M. (2002). Gay, lesbian, and bisexual employee issues in the workplace. In D. S. Sandhu (Ed.), *Counseling employees: A multifaceted approach* (pp. 169–184). Alexandria, VA: American Counseling Association.

Kite, M. E. (1994). When perceptions meet reality: Individual differences in reactions to gay men and lesbians. In B. Greene & G. Herek (Eds.), *Psychological perspectives on lesbian and gay issues: Vol. 1. Lesbian and gay psychology: Theory, research, and clinical applications* (pp. 25–53). Thousand Oaks, CA: Sage.

Kite, M. E., & Deaux, K. (1987). Gender belief systems: Homosexuality and the implicit inversion theory. *Psychology of Women Quarterly, 11*, 83–96. doi:10.1111/j.1471-6402.1987.tb00776.x

Klawitter, M., & Flatt, V. (1998). The effects of state and local antidiscrimination policies for sexual orientation. *Journal of Policy Analysis and Management, 17*, 658–686. doi:10.1002/(SICI)1520-6688(199823)17: 4_658::AID-PAM4_3.0.CO;2-P

Kopelman, L. M. (2002). If HIV/AIDS is punishment, who is bad? *Journal of Medicine & Philosophy, 27*, 231–243. doi:10.1076/jmep.27.2.231.2987

Kurdek, L. (1988). Perceived social support in gays and lesbians in cohabiting relationships. *Journal of Personality and Social Psychology, 54*, 504–509. doi:10.1037/0022-3514.54.3.504

Kurdek, L. A. (1995). Lesbian and gay couples. In A. D'Augelli & C. Patterson (Eds.), *Lesbian, gay, and bisexual identities over the lifespan: Psychological perspectives* (pp. 243–261). New York, NY: Oxford University Press.

Lasser, J., Tharinger, D., & Cloth, A. (2006). Gay, lesbian, and bisexual youth. In G. G. Bear & K. M. Minke (Eds.), *Children's needs III: Development, prevention, and intervention* (pp. 419M–430). Washington, DC: National Association of School Psychologists.

Liddle, B. (1996). Therapist sexual orientation, gender, and counseling practices as they relate to ratings of helpfulness by gay and lesbian clients. *Journal of Counseling Psychology, 43*, 394–401. doi:10.1037/0022-0167.43.4.394

Lofgren-Martenson, L. (2009). The invisibility of young homosexual women and men with intellectual disabilities. *Sexuality and Disability, 27*, 21–26. doi:10.1007/s11195-008-9101-0

Lombardi, E. (2001). Enhancing transgender health care. *American Journal of Public Health, 91*, 869–872. doi:10.2105/AJPH.91.6.869

Manalansan, M. (1996). Double minorities: Latino, Black, and Asian men who have sex with men. In R. Savin-Williams & K. Cohen (Eds.), *The lives of lesbians, gays, and bisexuals: Children to adults* (pp. 393–415). Fort Worth, TX: Harcourt Brace.

Martin, C. L. (1990). Attitudes and expectations about children with nontraditional and traditional gender roles. *Sex Roles, 22*, 151–165. doi:10.1007/BF00288188

Matteson, D. (1996). Counseling and psychotherapy with bisexual and exploring clients. In B. A. Firestein (Ed.), *Bisexuality: The psychology and politics of an invisible minority* (pp. 185–213). Thousand Oaks, CA: Sage.

Matthews, C. R., Selvidge, M., & Fisher, K. (2005). Addictions counselors' attitudes and behaviors toward gay, lesbian, and bisexual clients. *Journal of Counseling & Development, 83,* 57–65.

Mays, V. M., & Cochran, S. D. (2001). Mental health correlates of perceived discrimination among lesbian, gay, and bisexual adults in the United States. *American Journal of Public Health, 91,* 1869–1876. doi:10.2105/

McWhirter, D., & Mattison, A. M. (1984). *The male couple.* Englewood Cliffs, NJ: Prentice-Hall.

Meyer, E. J. (2009). *Gender, bullying, and harassment.* New York, NY: Teacher's College Press.

Meyer, I. H. (2003). Prejudice, social stress, and mental health in lesbian, gay, and bisexual populations: Conceptual issues and research evidence. *Psychological Bulletin, 129,* 674–697. doi:10.1037/0033-2909.129.5.674

Meyer, I. H., Dietrich, J., & Schwartz, S. (2008). Lifetime prevalence of mental disorders and suicide attempts in diverse lesbian, gay, and bisexual populations. *American Journal of Public Health, 98,* 1004–1006. doi:10.2105/AJPH.2006.096826

Mohr, J. J., Israel, T., & Sedlacek, W. E. (2001). Counselors' attitudes regarding bisexuality as predictors of counselors' clinical responses: An analogue study of a female bisexual client. *Journal of Counseling Psychology, 48,* 212–222. doi:10.1037/0022-0167.48.2.212

Morrow, S. L. (1998). Toward a new paradigm in counseling psychology training and education. *Counseling Psychologist, 26,* 797–808. doi:10.1177/0011000098265007

Mulick, P. S., & Wright, L. W., Jr. (2002). Examining the existence of biphobia in the heterosexual and homosexual populations. *Journal of Bisexuality, 2*(4), 45–64. doi:10.1300/J159v02n04_03

Murphy, J. A., Rawlings, E. I., & Howe, S. R. (2002). A survey of clinical psychologists on treating lesbian, gay, and bisexual clients. *Professional Psychology: Research and Practice, 33,* 183–189. doi:10.1037/0735-7028.33.2.183

Nystrom, N. (1997, February). *Mental health experiences of gay men and lesbians.* Paper presented at the meeting of the American Association for the Advancement of Science, Houston, TX.

Ossana, S. M. (2000). Relationship and couples counseling. In R. M. Perez, K. A. DeBord, & K. J. Bieschke (Eds.), *Handbook of counseling and psychotherapy with lesbian, gay, and bisexual clients* (pp. 275–302). Washington, DC: American Psychological Association.

Oxley, E., & Lucius, C. A. (2000). Looking both ways: Bisexuality and therapy. In C. Neal & D. Davies (Eds.), *Issues in therapy with lesbian, gay, bisexual, and transgender clients* (pp. 115–127). Buckingham, England: Open University Press.

Pallotta-Chiarolli, M. (2005). *When our children come out: How to support gay, lesbian, bisexual and transgendered young people.* Lane Cove, New South Wales, Australia: Finch.

Patterson, C. J. (2000). Family relationships of lesbians and gay men. *Journal of Marriage and Family, 62,* 1052–1069. doi:10.1111/j.1741-3737.2000.01052.x

Patterson, C. J. (2004). Gay fathers. In M. E. Lamb (Ed.), *The role of the father in child development* (4th ed., pp. 397–416). New York, NY: Wiley.

Patterson, C. J. (2007). Lesbian and gay family issues in the context of changing legal and social policy environments. In K. J. Bieschke, R. M. Perez, & K. A. DeBord (Eds.), *Handbook of counseling and psychotherapy with lesbian, gay, bisexual, and transgender clients* (2nd ed., pp. 359–377). Washington, DC: American Psychological Association.

Patterson, C. J., Fulcher, M., & Wainwright, J. (2002). Children of lesbian and gay parents: Research, law, and policy. In B. L. Bottoms, M. B. Kovera, & B. D. McAuliff (Eds.), *Children, social science, and the law* (pp. 176–200). New York, NY: Cambridge University Press.

Peplau, L. A., & Cochran, S. D. (1990). A relational perspective on homosexuality. In D. McWhirter, S. A. Sanders, & J. M. Reinisch (Eds.), *Homosexuality/heterosexuality: Concepts of sexual orientation* (pp. 321–349). New York, NY: Oxford University Press.

Peplau, L. A., Veniegas, R. C., & Campbell, S. M. (1996). Gay and lesbian relationships. In R. C. Savin-Williams & K. M. Cohen (Eds.), *The lives of lesbians, gays, and bisexuals: Children to adults* (pp. 250–273). Fort Worth, TX: Harcourt Brace.

Perrin, E. C. (2002). *Sexual orientation in child and adolescent health care.* New York, NY: Kluwer Academic.

Phillips, J. C., & Fischer, A. (1998). Graduate students' training experiences with lesbian, gay, and bisexual issues. *Counseling Psychologist, 26,* 712–734. doi:10.1177/0011000098265002

Pierret, J. (2007). An analysis over time (1990–2000) of the experiences of living with HIV. *Social Science & Medicine, 65,* 1595–1605. doi:10.1016/j.socscimed.2007.06.017

Pilkington, N., & Cantor, J. (1996). Perceptions of heterosexual bias in professional psychology programs: A survey of graduate students. *Professional Psychology: Research and Practice, 27,* 604–612. doi:10.1037/0735-7028.27.6.604

Pope, M., Barret, B., Szymanski, D. M., Chung, Y. B., McLean, R., Singaravelu, H., & Sanabria, S. (2004). Culturally appropriate career counseling with gay and lesbian clients. *Career Development Quarterly, 53,* 158–177.

Ragins, B. R., & Cornwell, J. M. (2001). Pink triangles: Antecedents and consequences of perceived workplace discrimination against gay and lesbian employees. *Journal of Applied Psychology, 86,* 1244–1261. doi:10.1037/0021-9010.86.6.1244

Ragins, B. R., Singh, R., & Cornwell, J. M. (2007). Making the invisible visible: Fear and disclosure of sexual orientation at work. *Journal of Applied Psychology, 92,* 1103–1118. doi:10.1037/0021-9010.92.4.1103

Ritieni, A., Moskowitz, J., & Tholandi, M. (2008). HIV/AIDS misconceptions among Latinos: Findings from a population-based survey of California adults. *Health Education & Behavior, 35,* 245–259. doi:10.1177/1090198106288795

Rivers, I. (2004). Recollections of bullying at school and their long-term implications for lesbians, gay men, and bisexuals. *Crisis: The Journal of Crisis Intervention and Suicide Prevention, 25,* 169–175. doi:10.1027/0227-5910.25.4.169

Rothblum, E. D., Balsam, K. F., & Mickey, R. M. (2004). Brothers and sisters of lesbians, gay men, and bisexuals as a demographic comparison group: An innovative research methodology to examine social change. *Journal of Applied Behavioral Science, 40,* 283–301. doi:10.1177/0021886304266877

Russell, G. M., & Kelly, N. H. (2003). *Subtle stereotyping: The media, homosexuality, and the priest sexual abuse scandal.* Retrieved from http://drglendarussell.com/wp-content/uploads/2013/05/MediaStereotype.pdf

Russell, G. M., & Richards, J. A. (2003). Stressor and resilience factors for lesbians, gay men, and bisexuals confronting antigay politics. *American Journal of Community Psychology, 31,* 313–328. doi:10.1023/A:1023919022811

Rust, P. (1996a). Managing multiple identities: Diversity among bisexual women and men. In B. A. Firestein (Ed.), *Bisexuality: The psychology and politics of an invisible minority* (pp. 53–83). Thousand Oaks, CA: Sage.

Rust, P. C. (2000a). Popular images and the growth of bisexual community and visibility. In P. C. Rust (Ed.), *Bisexuality in the United States: A social science reader* (pp. 537–553). New York, NY: Columbia University Press.

Rust, P. C. (2007). The construction and reconstruction of bisexuality: Inventing and reinventing the self. In B. A. Firestein (Ed.), *Becoming visible: Counseling bisexuals across the lifespan* (pp. 3–27). New York, NY: Columbia University Press.

Saad, C. (1997). Disability and the lesbian, gay man, or bisexual individual. In M. Sipski & S. C. Alexander (Eds.), *Sexual function in people with disability and chronic illness: A health professional's guide* (pp. 413–427). Gaithersburg, MD: Aspen.

Savin-Williams, R. C. (1994). Verbal and physical abuse as stressors in the lives of lesbian, gay male, and bisexual youths: Associations with school problems, running away, substance abuse, prostitution, and suicide. *Journal of Consulting and Clinical Psychology, 62,* 261–269. doi:10.1037/0022-006X.62.2.261

Savin-Williams, R. C. (2003). Lesbian, gay, and bisexual youths' relationships with their parents. In L. D. Garnets & D. C. Kimmel (Eds.), *Psychological perspectives on lesbian, gay, and bisexual experiences* (2nd ed., pp. 299–326). New York, NY: Columbia University Press.

Savin-Williams, R., & Dube, E. (1998). Parental reactions to their child's disclosure of gay/lesbian identity. *Family Relations, 47,* 7–13. doi:10.2307/584845

Sherry, A., Whilde, M. R., & Patton, J. (2005). Gay, lesbian, and bisexual training competencies in American Psychological Association accredited graduate programs. *Psychotherapy: Theory, Research, Practice, Training, 42,* 116–120. doi:10.1037/0033-3204.42.1.116

Solorio, M. R., Milburn, N. G., & Weiss, R. E. (2006). Newly homeless youth STD testing patterns over time. *Journal of Adolescent Health, 39,* 443.e9–443.e16. doi:10.1016/j.jadohealth.2005.12.017

Strommen, E. (1993). "You're a what?": Family member reactions to the disclosure of homosexuality. In L. Garnets & D. Kimmel (Eds.), *Psychological perspectives on lesbian and gay male experiences* (pp. 248–266). New York, NY: Columbia University Press.

Sullivan, M., & Wodarski, J. S. (2002). Social alienation in gay youth. *Journal of Human Behavior in the Social Environment, 5*(1), 1–17. doi:10.1300/J137v05n01_01

Tasker, F. (1999). Children in lesbian-led families: A review. *Clinical Child Psychology and Psychiatry, 4,* 153–166. doi:10.1177/1359104599004002003

Thomas, S. R., & Larrabee, T. G. (2002). Gay, lesbian, bisexual, and questioning youth. In J. Sandoval (Ed.), *Handbook of crisis counseling, intervention, and prevention in the schools* (2nd ed., pp. 301–322). Mahwah, NJ: Erlbaum.

Tozer, E. E., & Hayes, J. A. (2004). Why do individuals seek conversion therapy? The role of religiosity, internalized homonegativity, and identity development. *Counseling Psychologist, 32,* 716–740. doi:10.1177/0011000004267563

Tuttle, G. E., & Pillard, R. C. (1991). Sexual orientation and cognitive abilities. *Archives of Sexual Behavior, 20,* 307–318. doi:10.1007/BF01541849

Urbina, I. (2007, May 17). Gay youths find place to call home in specialty shelters. *The New York Times.* Retrieved from http://www.nytimes.com/2007/05/17/us/17homeless.html

VandenBos, G. R. (Ed.). (2007). *APA dictionary of psychology.* Washington, DC: American Psychological Association.

Van Puymbroeck, C. M. (2002). Career development of lesbian, gay, and bisexual undergraduates: An exploratory study. *Dissertation Abstracts International: Section B. Sciences and Engineering, 62*(12), 5982.

Weston, K. (1992). *Families we choose.* New York, NY: Columbia University Press.

Wilson, I., Griffin, C., & Wren, B. (2005). The interaction between young people with atypical gender identity organization and their peers. *Journal of Health Psychology, 10,* 307–315. doi:10.1177/1359105305051417

Winegarten, B., Cassie, N., Markowski, K., Kozlowski, J., & Yoder, J. (1994, August). *Aversive heterosexism: Exploring unconscious bias toward lesbian psychotherapy clients.* Paper presented at the meeting of the American Psychological Association, Los Angeles, CA.

7.6. Guidelines for Psychological Practice With Transgender and Gender Nonconforming People

American Psychological Association

. . . Within the last two decades, there has been a significant increase in research about [transgender and gender nonconforming] TGNC people. This increase in knowledge, informed by the TGNC community, has resulted in the development of progressively more trans-affirmative practice across the multiple health disciplines involved in the care of TGNC people (Bockting, Knudson, & Goldberg, 2006; Coleman et al., 2012). Research has documented the extensive experiences of stigma and discrimination reported by TGNC people (Grant et al., 2011) and the mental health consequences of these experiences across the life span (Bockting, Miner, Swinburne Romine, Hamilton, & Coleman, 2013), . . .

. . . Psychologists and other mental health professionals who have limited training and experience in TGNC-affirmative care may cause harm to TGNC people (Mikalson, Pardo, & Green, 2012; Xavier et al., 2012).

. . .

From "Guidelines for Psychological Practice With Transgender and Gender Non-conforming People," by the American Psychological Association, 2015, *American Psychologist, 70*, pp. 832–864. Copyright 2015 by the American Psychological Association.

The American Psychological Association's (APA's) Task Force on Guidelines for Psychological Practice With Transgender and Gender Nonconforming People developed these guidelines. lore m. dickey, Louisiana Tech University, and Anneliese A. Singh, The University of Georgia, served as chairs of the Task Force. The members of the Task Force included Walter O. Bockting, Columbia University; Sand Chang, Independent Practice; Kelly Ducheny, Howard Brown Health Center; Laura Edwards-Leeper, Pacific University; Randall D. Ehrbar, Whitman Walker Health Center; Max Fuentes Fuhrmann, Independent Practice; Michael L. Hendricks, Washington Psychological Center, P.C.; and Ellen Magalhaes, Center for Psychological Studies at Nova Southeastern University and California School of Professional Psychology at Alliant International University.

The Task Force is grateful to BT, Robin Buhrke, Jenn Burleton, Theo Burnes, Loree Cook-Daniels, Ed Delgado-Romero, Maddie Deutsch, Michelle Emerick, Terry S. Gock, Kristin Hancock, Razia Kosi, Kimberly Lux, Shawn MacDonald, Pat Magee, Tracee McDaniel, Edgardo Menvielle, Parrish Paul, Jamie Roberts, Louise Silverstein, Mary Alice Silverman, Holiday Simmons, Michael C. Smith, Cullen Sprague, David Whitcomb, and Milo Wilson for their assistance in providing important input and feedback on drafts of the guidelines. The Task Force is especially grateful to Clinton Anderson, Director, and Ron Schlittler, Program Coordinator, of APA's Office on LGBT Concerns, who adeptly assisted and provided counsel to the Task Force throughout this project. The Task Force would also like to thank liaisons from the APA Committee on Professional Practice and Standards (COPPS), April Harris-Britt and Scott Hunter, and their staff support, Mary Hardiman. Additionally, members of the Task Force would like to thank the staff at the Phillip Rush Center and Agnes Scott College Counseling Center in Atlanta, Georgia, who served as hosts for face-to-face meetings.

This document will expire as APA policy in 2022. After this date, users should contact the APA Public Interest Directorate to determine whether the guidelines in this document remain in effect as APA policy.

FOUNDATIONAL KNOWLEDGE AND AWARENESS

Guideline 1. Psychologists understand that gender is a nonbinary construct that allows for a range of gender identities and that a person's gender identity may not align with sex assigned at birth.

Rationale

Gender identity is defined as a person's deeply felt, inherent sense of being a girl, woman, or female; a boy, a man, or male; a blend of male or female; or an alternative (Bethea & McCollum, 2013; Institute of Medicine [IOM], 2011). In many cultures and religious traditions, gender has been perceived as a binary construct, with mutually exclusive categories of male or female, boy or girl, man or woman (Benjamin, 1966; Mollenkott, 2001; Tanis, 2003). These mutually exclusive categories include an assumption that gender identity is always in alignment with sex assigned at birth (Bethea & McCollum, 2013). For TGNC people, gender identity differs from sex assigned at birth to varying degrees, and may be experienced and expressed outside of the gender binary (Harrison, Grant, & Herman, 2012; Kuper, Nussbaum, & Mustanski, 2012).

. . .

Guideline 2. Psychologists understand that gender identity and sexual orientation are distinct but interrelated constructs.

Rationale

The constructs of gender identity and sexual orientation are theoretically and clinically distinct, even though professionals and nonprofessionals frequently conflate them. Although some research suggests a potential link in the development of gender identity and sexual orientation, the mechanisms of such a relationship are unknown (Adelson & American Academy of Child and Adolescent Psychiatry [AACAP] Committee on Quality Issues [CQI], 2012; APA TFGIGV, 2009; A. H. Devor, 2004; Drescher & Byne, 2013). *Sexual orientation* is defined as a person's sexual and/or emotional attraction to another person (Shively & De Cecco, 1977), compared with *gender identity*, which is defined by a person's felt, inherent sense of gender. For most people, gender identity develops earlier than sexual orientation. Gender identity is often established in young toddlerhood (Adelson & AA-CAP CQI, 2012; Kohlberg, 1966), compared with awareness of same-sex attraction, which often emerges in early adolescence (Adelson & AACAP CQI, 2012; D'Augelli & Hershberger, 1993; Herdt & Boxer, 1993; Ryan, 2009; Savin-Williams & Diamond, 2000).

. . .

Guideline 3. Psychologists seek to understand how gender identity intersects with the other cultural identities of TGNC people.

Rationale

Gender identity and gender expression may have profound intersections with other aspects of identity (Collins, 2000; Warner, 2008). These aspects may

include, but are not limited to, race/ethnicity, age, education, socioeconomic status, immigration status, occupation, disability status, HIV status, sexual orientation, relational status, and religion and/or spiritual affiliation. Whereas some of these aspects of identity may afford privilege, others may create stigma and hinder empowerment (Burnes & Chen, 2012; K. M. de Vries, 2015). In addition, TGNC people who transition may not be prepared for changes in privilege or societal treatment based on gender identity and gender expression. To illustrate, an African American trans man may gain male privilege, but may face racism and societal stigma particular to African American men. An Asian American/Pacific Islander trans woman may experience the benefit of being perceived as a cisgender woman, but may also experience sexism, misogyny, and objectification particular to Asian American/Pacific Islander cisgender women.
. . .

Guideline 4. Psychologists are aware of how their attitudes about and knowledge of gender identity and gender expression may affect the quality of care they provide to TGNC people and their families.

Rationale

Psychologists, like other members of society, come to their personal understanding and acceptance of different aspects of human diversity through a process of socialization. Psychologists' cultural biases, as well as the cultural differences between psychologists and their clients, have a clinical impact (Israel, Gorcheva, Burnes, & Walther, 2008; Vasquez, 2007). The assumptions, biases, and attitudes psychologists hold regarding TGNC people and gender identity and/or gender expression can affect the quality of services psychologists provide and their ability to develop an effective therapeutic alliance (Bess & Stabb, 2009; Rachlin, 2002). In addition, a lack of knowledge or training in providing affirmative care to TGNC people can limit a psychologist's effectiveness and perpetuate barriers to care (Bess & Stabb, 2009; Rachlin, 2002). Psychologists experienced with lesbian, gay, or bisexual (LGB) people may not be familiar with the unique needs of TGNC people (Israel, 2005; Israel et al., 2008). In community surveys, TGNC people have reported that many mental health care providers lack basic knowledge and skills relevant to care of TGNC people (Bradford, Xavier, Hendricks, Rives, & Honnold, 2007; Xavier, Bobbin, Singer, & Budd, 2005).
. . .

STIGMA, DISCRIMINATION, AND BARRIERS TO CARE

Guideline 5. Psychologists recognize how stigma, prejudice, discrimination, and violence affect the health and well-being of TGNC people.

Rationale

Many TGNC people experience discrimination, ranging from subtle to severe, when accessing housing, health care, employment, education, public assistance, and other social services (Bazargan & Galvan, 2012; Bradford, Reisner, Honnold, & Xavier, 2013; Dispenza, Watson, Chung, & Brack, 2012; Grant et al., 2011). Discrimination can include assuming a person's assigned sex at birth is fully aligned with that person's gender identity, not using a person's preferred name or pronoun, asking TGNC people inappropriate questions about their bodies, or making the assumption that psychopathology exists given a specific gender identity or gender expression (Nadal, Rivera, & Corpus, 2010; Nadal, Skolnik, & Wong, 2012). Discrimination may also include refusing access to housing or employment or extreme acts of violence (e.g., sexual assault, murder). TGNC people who hold multiple marginalized identities are more vulnerable to discrimination and violence. TGNC women and people of color disproportionately experience severe forms of violence and discrimination, including police violence, and are less likely to receive help from law enforcement (Edelman, 2011; National Coalition of Anti-Violence Programs, 2011; Saffin, 2011).

. . .

Guideline 6. Psychologists strive to recognize the influence of institutional barriers on the lives of TGNC people and to assist in developing TGNC-affirmative environments.

Rationale

Antitrans prejudice and the adherence of mainstream society to the gender binary adversely affect TGNC people within their families, schools, health care, legal systems, workplaces, religious traditions, and communities (American Civil Liberties Union National Prison Project, 2005; Bradford et al., 2013; Brewster et al., 2014; Levy & Lo, 2013; McGuire, Anderson, & Toomey, 2010). TGNC people face challenges accessing gender-inclusive restrooms, which may result in discomfort when being forced to use a men's or women's restroom (Transgender Law Center, 2005). In addition to the emotional distress the forced binary choice that public restrooms may create for some, TGNC people are frequently concerned with others' reactions to their presence in public restrooms, including potential discrimination, harassment, and violence (Herman, 2013)

. . .

Guideline 7: Psychologists understand the need to promote social change that reduces the negative effects of stigma on the health and well-being of TGNC people.

Rationale

The lack of public policy that addresses the needs of TGNC people creates significant hardships for them (Taylor, 2007). Although there have been major advances in legal protections for TGNC people in recent years (Buzuvis, 2013; Harvard Law Review Association, 2013), many TGNC people are still not afforded protections from discrimination on the basis of gender identity or expression (National LGBTQ Task Force, 2013; Taylor, 2007). For instance, in many states, TGNC people do not have employment or housing protections and may be fired or lose their housing based on their gender identity. Many policies that protect the rights of cisgender people, including LGB people, do not protect the rights of TGNC people (Currah & Minter, 2000; Spade, 2011a).

. . .

LIFE SPAN DEVELOPMENT

Guideline 8. Psychologists working with gender-questioning[1] and TGNC youth understand the different developmental needs of children and adolescents, and that not all youth will persist in a TGNC identity into adulthood.

Rationale

Many children develop stability (constancy across time) in their gender identity between Ages 3 to 4 (Kohlberg, 1966), although gender consistency (recognition that gender remains the same across situations) often does not occur until Ages 4 to 7 (Siegal & Robinson, 1987). Children who demonstrate gender nonconformity in preschool and early elementary years may not follow this trajectory (Zucker & Bradley, 1995). Existing research suggests that between 12% and 50% of children diagnosed with gender dysphoria may persist in their identification with a gender different than sex assigned at birth into late adolescence and young adulthood (Drummond, Bradley, Peterson-Badaali, & Zucker, 2008; Steensma, McGuire, Kreukels, Beekman, & Cohen-Kettenis, 2013; Wallien & Cohen-Kettenis, 2008). However, several research studies categorized 30% to 62% of youth who did not return to the clinic for medical intervention after initial assessment, and whose gender identity may be unknown, as "desisters" who no longer identified with a gender different than sex assigned at birth (Steensma et al., 2013; Wallien & Cohen-Kettenis, 2008; Zucker, 2008a). As a result, this research runs a strong risk of inflating estimates of the number of youth who do not persist with a TGNC identity.

. . .

Guideline 9. Psychologists strive to understand both the particular challenges that TGNC elders experience and the resilience they can develop.

Rationale

Little research has been conducted about TGNC elders, leaving much to be discovered about this life stage for TGNC people (Auldridge, Tamar-Mattis, Kennedy, Ames, & Tobin, 2012). Socialization into gender role behaviors and

---

[1] Gender-questioning youth are differentiated from TGNC youth in this section of the guidelines. Gender-questioning youth may be questioning or exploring their gender identity but have not yet developed a TGNC identity. As such, they may not be eligible for some services that would be offered to TGNC youth. Gender-questioning youth are included here because gender questioning may lead to a TGNC identity.

expectations based on sex assigned at birth, as well as the extent to which TGNC people adhere to these societal standards, is influenced by the chronological age at which a person self-identifies as TGNC, the age at which a person comes out or socially and/or medically transitions (Birren & Schaie, 2006; Bockting & Coleman, 2007; Cavanaugh & Blanchard-Fields, 2010; Nuttbrock et al., 2010; Wahl, Iwarsson, & Oswald, 2012), and a person's generational cohort (e.g., 1950 vs. 2010; Fredriksen-Goldsen et al., 2011).

. . .

ASSESSMENT, THERAPY, AND INTERVENTION

Guideline 10. Psychologists strive to understand how mental health concerns may or may not be related to a TGNC person's gender identity and the psychological effects of minority stress.

Rationale
TGNC people may seek assistance from psychologists in addressing gender-related concerns, other mental health issues, or both. Mental health problems experienced by a TGNC person may or may not be related to that person's gender identity and/or may complicate assessment and intervention of gender-related concerns. In some cases, there may not be a relationship between a person's gender identity and a co-occurring condition (e.g., depression, PTSD, substance abuse). In other cases, having a TGNC identity may lead or contribute to a co-occurring mental health condition, either directly by way of gender dysphoria, or indirectly by way of minority stress and oppression (Hendricks & Testa, 2012; I. H. Meyer, 1995, 2003).

. . .

Guideline 11. Psychologists recognize that TGNC people are more likely to experience positive life outcomes when they receive social support or trans-affirmative care.

Rationale
Research has primarily shown positive treatment outcomes when TGNC adults and adolescents receive TGNC-affirmative medical and psychological services (i.e., psychotherapy, hormones, surgery; Byne et al., 2012; R. Carroll, 1999; Cohen-Kettenis, Delemarre-van de Waal, & Gooren, 2008; Davis & Meier, 2014; De Cuypere et al., 2006; Gooren, Giltay, & Bunck, 2008; Kuhn et al., 2009), although sample sizes are frequently small with no population-based studies. In a meta-analysis of the hormone therapy treatment literature with TGNC adults and adolescents, researchers reported that 80% of participants receiving trans-affirmative care experienced an improved quality of life, decreased gender dysphoria, and a reduction in negative psychological symptoms (Murad et al., 2010).

. . .

Guideline 12. Psychologists strive to understand the effects that changes in gender identity and gender expression have on the romantic and sexual relationships of TGNC people.

Rationale

Relationships involving TGNC people can be healthy and successful (Kins, Hoebeke, Heylens, Rubens, & De Cuyprere, 2008; Meier, Sharp, Michonski, Babcock, & Fitzgerald, 2013). . . . A study of successful relationships between TGNC men and cisgender women found that these couples attributed the success of their relationship to respect, honesty, trust, love, understanding, and open communication (Kins et al., 2008). Just as relationships between cisgender people can involve abuse, so can relationships between TGNC people and their partners (Brown, 2007), with some violent partners threatening to disclose a TGNC person's identity to exact control in the relationship (FORGE, n.d.). . . .

Guideline 13. Psychologists seek to understand how parenting and family formation among TGNC people take a variety of forms.

Rationale

Psychologists work with TGNC people across the life span to address parenting and family issues (Kenagy & Hsieh, 2005). There is evidence that many TGNC people have and want children (Wierckx et al., 2012). Some TGNC people conceive a child through sexual intercourse, whereas others may foster, adopt, pursue surrogacy, or employ assisted reproductive technologies, such as sperm or egg donation, to build or expand a family (De Sutter, Kira, Verschoor, & Hotimsky, 2002). Based on a small body of research to date, there is no indication that children of TGNC parents suffer long-term negative impacts directly related to parental gender change (R. Green, 1978, 1988; White & Ettner, 2004). TGNC people may find it both challenging to find medical providers who are willing to offer them reproductive treatment and to afford the cost (Coleman et al., 2012). Similarly, adoption can be quite costly, and some TGNC people may find it challenging to find foster care or adoption agencies that will work with them in a nondiscriminatory manner. Current or past use of hormone therapy may limit fertility and restrict a TGNC person's reproductive options (Darnery, 2008; Wierckx et al., 2012). Other TGNC people may have children or families before coming out as TGNC or beginning a gender transition. . . .

Guideline 14. Psychologists recognize the potential benefits of an interdisciplinary approach when providing care to TGNC people and strive to work collaboratively with other providers.

Rationale

Collaboration across disciplines can be crucial when working with TGNC people because of the potential interplay of biological, psychological, and social factors in diagnosis and treatment (Hendricks & Testa, 2012). The challenges of living with a stigmatized identity and the need of many TGNC people to transition, socially and/or medically, may call for the involvement of health professionals from various disciplines, including psychologists, psychiatrists, social workers, primary health care providers, endocrinologists, nurses, pharmacists, surgeons, gynecologists, urologists, electrologists, speech therapists, physical therapists, pastoral counselors and chaplains, and career or educational counselors. Communication, cooperation, and collaboration will ensure optimal coordination and quality of care.

. . .

RESEARCH, EDUCATION, AND TRAINING

Guideline 15. Psychologists respect the welfare and rights of TGNC participants in research and strive to represent results accurately and avoid misuse or misrepresentation of findings.

Rationale

Historically, in a set of demographic questions, psychological research has included one item on either sex or gender, with two response options—male and female. This approach wastes an opportunity to increase knowledge about TGNC people for whom neither option may fit their identity, and runs the risk of alienating TGNC research participants (IOM, 2011). For example, there is little knowledge about HIV prevalence, risks, and prevention needs of TGNC people because most of the research on HIV has not included demographic questions to identify TGNC participants within their samples. Instead, TGNC people have been historically subsumed within larger demographic categories (e.g., men who have sex with men, women of color), rendering the impact of the HIV epidemic on the TGNC population invisible (Herbst et al., 2008).

. . .

Guideline 16. Psychologists seek to prepare trainees in psychology to work competently with TGNC people.

Rationale

The *Ethical Principles of Psychologists and Code of Conduct* (APA, 2010) include gender identity as one factor for which psychologists may need to obtain training, experience, consultation, or supervision in order to ensure their competence (APA, 2010). In addition, when APA-accredited programs are required to demonstrate a commitment to cultural and individual diversity, gender identity is specifically included (APA, 2015). Yet surveys of TGNC people suggest that many mental health care providers lack even basic knowledge and skills required to offer trans-affirmative care (Bradford et al., 2007; O'Hara, Dispenza, Brack, & Blood, 2013; Xavier et al., 2005). . . . Only 52% percent of psychologists and graduate students who responded to a survey conducted by an APA Task Force reported having had the opportunity to learn about TGNC issues in school; of those respondents, only 27% reported feeling adequately familiar with gender concerns ($n = 294$; APA TFGIGV, 2009).

. . .

REFERENCES

Adelson, S. L., & The American Academy of Child and Adolescent Psychiatry (AACAP) Committee on Quality Issues (CQI). (2012). Practice parameter on gay, lesbian, or bisexual sexual orientation, gender nonconformity, and gender discordance in children and adolescents. *Journal of the American Academy of Child & Adolescent Psychiatry, 51*, 957–974. http://download.journals.elsevierhealth.com/pdfs/journals/0890-8567/PIIS089085671200500X.pdf. http://dx.doi.org/10.1016/j.jaac.2012.07.004

American Civil Liberties Union National Prison Project. (2005). *Still in danger: The ongoing threat of sexual violence against transgender prisoners.* Washington, DC: Author. Retrieved from https://justdetention.org/wp-content/uploads/2015/10/Still-In-Danger-The-Ongoing-Threat-of-Sexual-Violence-against-Transgender-Prisoners.pdf

American Psychological Association. (2010). *Ethical principles of psychologists and code of conduct* (2002, amended June 1, 2010). Retrieved from http://www.apa.org/ethics/code/principles.pdf

American Psychological Association. (2015). *Standards of accreditation for health service psychology.* Retrieved from http://www.apa.org/ed/accreditation/about/policies/standards-of-accreditation.pdf

American Psychological Association Task Force on Gender Identity and Gender Variance. (2009). *Report of the APA task force on gender identity and gender variance.* Washington, DC: Author. Retrieved from http://www.apa.org/pi/lgbt/resources/policy/gender-identity-report.pdf

Auldridge, A., Tamar-Mattis, A., Kennedy, S., Ames, E., & Tobin, H. J. (2012). *Improving the lives of transgender older adults: Recommendations for policy and practice.* New York, NY: Services and Advocacy for LGBT Elders & Washington, DC: National Center for Transgender Equality. Retrieved from https://www.issuelab.org/resource/improving-the-lives-of-transgender-older-adults-recommendations-for-policy-and-practice.html

Bazargan, M., & Galvan, F. (2012). Perceived discrimination and depression among low-income Latina male-to-female transgender women. *BMC Public Health, 12*, 663–670. http://dx.doi.org/10.1186/1471-2458-12-663

Benjamin, H. (1966). *The transsexual phenomenon.* New York, NY: Warner.

Bess, J. A., & Stabb, S. D. (2009). The experiences of transgendered persons in psychotherapy: Voices and recommendations. *Journal of Mental Health Counseling, 31*, 264–282. http://dx.doi.org/10.17744/mehc.31.3.f62415468l133w50

Bethea, M. S., & McCollum, E. E. (2013). The disclosure experiences of male-to-female transgender individuals: A Systems Theory perspective. *Journal of Couple & Relationship Therapy, 12*, 89–112. http://dx.doi.org/10.1080/15332691.2013.779094

Birren, J. E., & Schaie, K. W. (2006). *Handbook of the psychology of aging* (6th ed.). Burlington, MA: Elsevier Academic.

Bockting, W. O., & Coleman, E. (2007). Developmental stages of the transgender coming-out process. In R. Ettner, S. Monstrey, & A. Eyler (Eds.), *Principles of transgender medicine and surgery* (pp. 185–208). New York, NY: Haworth.

Bockting, W. O., Knudson, G., & Goldberg, J. M. (2006). Counseling and mental health care for transgender adults and loved ones. *International Journal of Transgenderism, 9*, 35–82. http://dx.doi.org/10.1300/J485v09n03_03

Bockting, W. O., Miner, M. H., Swinburne Romine, R. E., Hamilton, A., & Coleman, E. (2013). Stigma, mental health, and resilience in an online sample of the US transgender population. *American Journal of Public Health, 103*, 943–951. http://dx.doi.org/10.2105/AJPH.2013.301241

Bradford, J., Reisner, S. L., Honnold, J. A., & Xavier, J. (2013). Experiences of transgender-related discrimination and implications for health: Results from the Virginia Transgender Health Initiative Study. *American Journal of Public Health, 103*, 1820–1829. http://dx.doi.org/10.2105/AJPH.2012.300796

Bradford, J., Xavier, J., Hendricks, M., Rives, M. E., & Honnold, J. A. (2007). The health, health-related needs, and lifecourse experiences of transgender Virginians. *Virginia Transgender Health Initiative Study Statewide Survey Report*. Retrieved from http://www.vdh.virginia.gov/content/uploads/sites/10/2016/01/THISFINALREPORTVol1.pdf

Brewster, M. E., Velez, B. L., Mennicke, A., & Tebbe, E. (2014). Voices from beyond: A thematic content analysis of transgender employees' workplace experiences. *Psychology of Sexual Orientation and Gender Diversity*, *1*, 159–169. http://dx.doi.org/10.1037/sgd0000030

Brown, N. (2007). Stories from outside the frame: Intimate partner abuse in sexual-minority women's relationships with transsexual men. *Feminism & Psychology*, *17*, 373–393.

Burnes, T. R., & Chen, M. M. (2012). The multiple identities of transgender individuals: Incorporating a framework of intersectionality to gender crossing. In R. Josselson & M. Harway (Eds.), *Navigating multiple identities: Race, gender, culture, nationality, and roles* (pp. 113–128). New York, NY: Oxford University Press. http://dx.doi.org/10.1093/acprof:oso/9780199732074.003.0007

Buzuvis, E. (2013). "On the basis of sex": Using Title IX to protect transgender students from discrimination in education. *Wisconsin Journal of Law, Gender & Society*, *28*, 219–347.

Byne, W., Bradley, S. J., Coleman, E., Eyler, A. E., Green, R., Menvielle, E. J., . . . & American Psychiatric Association Task Force on Treatment of Gender Identity Disorder. (2012). Report of the American Psychiatric Association Task Force on Treatment of Gender Identity Disorder. *Archives of Sexual Behavior*, *41*, 759–796. http://dx.doi.org/10.1007/s10508-012-9975-x

Carroll, R. (1999). Outcomes of treatment for gender dysphoria. *Journal of Sex Education & Therapy*, *24*, 128–136.

Cavanaugh, J. C., & Blanchard-Fields, F. (2010). *Adult development and aging* (5th ed.). Belmont, CA: Wadsworth/Thomson Learning.

Cohen-Kettenis, P. T., Delemarre-van de Waal, H. A., & Gooren, L. J. G. (2008). The treatment of adolescent transsexuals: Changing insights. *Journal of Sexual Medicine*, *5*, 1892–1897. http://dx.doi.org/10.1111/j.1743-6109.2008.00870.x

Coleman, E., Bockting, W., Botzer, M., Cohen-Kettenis, P., DeCuypere, G., Feldman, J., . . . Zucker, K. (2012). Standards of care for the health of trans-sexual, transgender, and gender nonconforming people, 7th version. *International Journal of Transgenderism*, *13*, 165–232. http://dx.doi.org/10.1080/15532739.2011.700873

Collins, P. H. (2000). *Black feminist thought: Knowledge, consciousness, and the politics of empowerment* (2nd ed.). New York, NY: Routledge.

Currah, P., & Minter, S. P. (2000). *Transgender equality: A handbook for activists and policymakers*. San Francisco, CA: National Center for Lesbian Rights; New York, NY: The Policy Institute of the National Gay & Lesbian Task Force. Retrieved from http://www.thetaskforce.org/static_html/downloads/reports/reports/TransgenderEquality.pdf

Darnery, P. D. (2008). Hormonal contraception. In H. M. Kronenberg, S. Melmer, K. S. Polonsky, & P. R. Larsen (Eds.), *Williams textbook of endocrinology* (11th ed., pp. 615–644). Philadelphia, PA: Saunders.

D'Augelli, A. R., & Hershberger, S. L. (1993). Lesbian, gay, and bisexual youth in community settings: Personal challenges and mental health problems. *American Journal of Community Psychology*, *21*, 421–448. http://dx.doi.org/10.1007/BF00942151

Devor, A. H. (2004). Witnessing and mirroring: A fourteen-stage model of transsexual identity formation. *Journal of Gay & Lesbian Psychotherapy*, *8*, 41–67.

Davis, S. A., & Meier, S. C. (2014). Effects of testosterone treatment and chest reconstruction surgery on mental health and sexuality in female-to-male transgender
people. *International Journal of Sexual Health, 26,* 113–128. http://dx.doi.org/10.1080/
19317611.2013.833152

De Cuypere, G., Elaut, E., Heylens, G., Van Maele, G., Selvaggi, G., T'Sjoen, G., . . .
Monstrey, S. (2006). Long-term follow-up: Psychosocial outcome of Belgian transsexuals after sex reassignment surgery. *Sexologies, 15,* 126–133. http://dx.doi.org/
10.1016/j.sexol.2006.04.002

De Sutter, P., Kira, K., Verschoor, A., & Hotimsky, A. (2002). The desire to have children
and the preservation of fertility in transsexual women: A survey. *International Journal
of Transgenderism, 6*(3), 215–221.

de Vries, K. M. (2015). Transgender people of color at the center: Conceptualizing
a new intersectional model. *Ethnicities, 15,* 3–27. http://dx.doi.org/10.1177/
1468796814547058

Dispenza, F., Watson, L. B., Chung, Y. B., & Brack, G. (2012). Experience of career-
related discrimination for female-to-male transgender persons: A qualitative
study. *Career Development Quarterly, 60,* 65–81. http://dx.doi.org/10.1002/
j.2161-0045.2012.00006.x

Drescher, J., & Byne, W. (Eds.). (2013). *Treating transgender children and adolescents:
An interdisciplinary discussion.* New York, NY: Routledge.

Drummond, K. D., Bradley, S. J., Peterson-Badaali, M., & Zucker, K. J. (2008).
A follow-up study of girls with gender identity disorder. *Developmental Psychology,
44,* 34–45. http://dx.doi.org/10.1037/0012-1649.44.1.34

Edelman, E. A. (2011). "This area has been declared a prostitution free zone": Discursive formations of space, the state, and trans "sex worker" bodies. *Journal of
Homosexuality, 58,* 848–864. http://dx.doi.org/10.1080/00918369.2011.581928

FORGE. (n.d.). *Trans-specific power and control tactics.* Retrieved from http://forge-
forward.org/wp-content/docs/power-control-tactics-categories_FINAL.pdf

Fredriksen-Goldsen, K. I., Kim, H., Emlet, C. A., Muraco, A., Erosheva, E. A.,
Hoy-Ellis, C. P., . . . Petry, H. (2011). *The aging and health report: Disparities
and resilience among lesbian, gay, bisexual and transgender older adults.* Retrieved
from http://www.age-pride.org/wordpress/wp-content/uploads/2011/05/
Full-Report-FINAL-11-16-11.pdf

Gooren, L. J., Giltay, E. J., & Bunck, M. C. (2008). Long-term treatment of transsexuals
with cross-sex hormones: Extensive personal experience. *Journal of Clinical Endocrinology & Metabolism: Clinical and Experimental, 93,* 19–25. http://dx.doi.org/10.1210/
jc.2007-1809

Grant, J. M., Mottet, L. A., Tanis, J., Harrison, J., Herman, J. L., & Kiesling, M. (2011).
Injustice at every turn: A report of the national transgender discrimination survey.
Washington, DC: National Center for Transgender Equality & National Gay and
Lesbian Task Force. Retrieved from http://endtransdiscrimination.org/PDFs/
NTDS_Report.pdf

Green, R. (1978). Sexual identity of 37 children raised by homosexual and transsexual
parents. *American Journal of Psychiatry, 135,* 692–697. http://dx.doi.org/10.1176/
ajp.135.6.692

Green, R. (1988). Transsexuals' children. *International Journal of Transgendersim, 2*(4).

Harrison, J., Grant, J., & Herman, J. L. (2012). A gender not listed here: Genderqueers,
gender rebels and otherwise in the National Transgender Discrimination Study.
LGBT Policy Journal at the Harvard Kennedy School, 2, 13–24. Retrieved from
http://isites.harvard.edu/icb/icb.do?keyword_k78405&pageid_icb.page497030

Harvard Law Review Association. (2013). Recent case: Employment law: Title VII:
EEOC affirms protections for transgender employees: Macy v. Holder. *Harvard Law
Review, 126,* 1731–1738.

Hendricks, M. L., & Testa, R. J. (2012). A conceptual framework for clinical work with transgender and gender nonconforming clients: An adaptation of the minority stress model. *Professional Psychology: Research and Practice, 43*, 460–467. http://dx.doi.org/10.1037/a0029597

Herbst, J. H., Jacobs, E. D., Finlayson, T. J., McKleroy, V. S., Neumann, M. S., & Crepaz, N. (2008). Estimating HIV prevalence and risk behaviors of transgender persons in the United States: A systemic review. *AIDS & Behavior, 12*, 1–17. http://dx.doi.org/10.1007/s10461-007-9299-3

Herdt, G., & Boxer, A. (1993). *Children of horizons: How gay and lesbian teens are leading a new way out of the closet.* Boston, MA: Beacon Press.

Herman, J. L. (2013). Gendered restrooms and minority stress: The public regulation of gender and its impact on transgender people's lives. *Journal of Public Management and Social Policy, 19*, 65–80.

Institute of Medicine. (2011). *The health of lesbian, gay, bisexual, and transgender people: Building a foundation for better understanding.* Washington, DC: National Academy of Sciences.

Israel, T. (2005). . . . and sometimes T: Transgender issues in LGBT psychology. *Newsletter of the Society for the Psychological Study of Lesbian, Gay, and Bisexual Issues, 21*, 16–18.

Israel, T., Gorcheva, R., Burnes, T. R., & Walther, W. A. (2008). Helpful and unhelpful therapy experiences of LGBT clients. *Psychotherapy Research, 18*, 294–305. http://dx.doi.org/10.1080/10503300701506920

Kenagy, G. P., & Hsieh, C. (2005). Gender differences in social service needs of transgender people. *Journal of Social Service Research, 31*, 1–21.

Kins, E., Hoebeke, P., Heylens, G., Rubens, R., & De Cuyprere, G. (2008). The female-to-male transsexual and his female partner versus the traditional couple: A comparison. *Journal of Sex and Marital Therapy, 34*, 429–438. http://dx.doi.org/10.1080/00926230802156236

Kohlberg, L. (1966). A cognitive-developmental analysis of children's sex-role concepts and attitudes. In E. E. Maccoby (Ed.), *The development of sex differences* (pp. 82–173). Stanford, CA: Stanford University.

Kuhn, A., Brodmer, C., Stadlmayer, W., Kuhn, P., Mueller, M. D., & Birkhauser, M. (2009). Quality of life 15 years after sex reassignment surgery for transsexualism. *Fertility and Sterility, 92*, 1685–1689. http://dx.doi.org/10.1016/j.fertnstert.2008.08.126

Kuper, L. E., Nussbaum, R., & Mustanski, B. (2012). Exploring the diversity of gender and sexual orientation identities in an online sample of transgender individuals. *Journal of Sex Research, 49*, 244–254. http://dx.doi.org/10.1080/00224499.2011.596954

Levy, D. L., & Lo, J. R. (2013). Transgender, transsexual, and gender queer individuals with a Christian upbringing: The process of resolving conflict between gender identity and faith. *Journal of Religion & Spirituality in Social Work: Social Thought, 32*, 60–83. http://dx.doi.org/10.1080/15426432.2013.749079

McGuire, J. K., Anderson, C. R., & Toomey, R. B. (2010). School climate for transgender youth: A mixed method investigation of student experiences and school responses. *Journal of Youth and Adolescence, 39*, 1175–1188. http://dx.doi.org/10.1007/s10964-010-9540-7

Meier, S. C., Sharp, C., Michonski, J., Babcock, J. C., & Fitzgerald, K. (2013). Romantic relationships of female-to-male trans men: A descriptive study. *International Journal of Transgenderism, 14*, 75–85. http://dx.doi.org/10.1080/15532739.2013.791651

Meyer, I. H. (1995). Minority stress and mental health in gay men. *Journal of Health and Social Behavior, 36*, 38–56. http://dx.doi.org/10.2307/2137286

Meyer, I. H. (2003). Prejudice, social stress, and mental health in lesbian, gay, and bisexual populations: Conceptual issues and research evidence. *Psychological Bulletin, 129*, 674–697. http://dx.doi.org/10.1037/0033-2909.129.5.674

Mikalson, P., Pardo, S., & Green, J. (2012). *First do no harm: Reducing disparities for lesbian, gay, bisexual, transgender, queer, and questioning populations in California.*

Retrieved from https://lhc.ca.gov/sites/lhc.ca.gov/files/Reports/225/ReportsSubmitted/CRDPLGBTQReport.pdf

Mollenkott, V. (2001). *Omnigender: A trans-religious approach*. Cleveland, OH: Pilgrim Press.

Murad, M. H., Elamin, M. B., Garcia, M. Z., Mullan, R. J., Murad, A., Erwin, P. J., & Montori, V. M. (2010). Hormonal therapy and sex reassignment: A systemic review and meta-analysis of quality of life and psychosocial outcomes. *Clinical Endocrinology*, *72*, 214–231. http://dx.doi.org/10.1111/j.1365-2265.2009.03625.x

Nadal, K. L., Rivera, D. P., & Corpus, M. J. H. (2010). Sexual orientation and transgender microaggressions in everyday life: Experiences of lesbians, gays, bisexuals, and transgender individuals. In D. W. Sue (Ed.), *Microaggressions and marginality: Manifestation, dynamics, and impact* (pp. 217–240). New York, NY: Wiley.

Nadal, K. L., Skolnik, A., & Wong, Y. (2012). Interpersonal and systemic microaggressions toward transgender people: Implications for counseling. *Journal of LGBT Issues in Counseling*, *6*, 55–82. http://dx.doi.org/10.1080/15538605.2012.648583

National Coalition of Anti-Violence Programs. (2011). *Hate violence against lesbian, gay, bisexual, transgender, queer, and HIV-affected communities in the United States in 2011: A report from the National Coalition of Anti-Violence Programs*. New York, NY: Author. Retrieved from https://avp.org/ncavp-report-hate-violence-lesbian-gay-bisexual-transgender-queer-hiv-affected-communities-released-today/

National LGBTQ Task Force. (2013). *Hate crimes laws in the U.S.* Washington, DC: Author. Retrieved from http://www.thetaskforce.org/hate-crimes-laws-map/

Nuttbrock, L., Hwahng, S., Bockting, W., Rosenblum, A., Mason, M., Macri, M., & Becker, J. (2010). Psychiatric impact of gender-related abuse across the life course of male-to-female transgender persons. *Journal of Sex Research*, *47*, 12–23. http://dx.doi.org/10.1080/00224490903062258

O'Hara, C., Dispenza, F., Brack, G., & Blood, R. A. (2013). The preparedness of counselors in training to work with transgender clients: A mixed methods investigation. *Journal of LGBT Issues in Counseling*, *7*, 236–256. http://dx.doi.org/10.1080/15538605.2013.812929

Rachlin, K. (2002). Transgender individuals' experience of psychotherapy. *International Journal of Transgenderism, 6*(1).

Ryan, C. (2009). *Supportive families, healthy children: Helping families with lesbian, gay, bisexual & transgender children*. San Francisco, CA: Family Acceptance Project, Marian Wright Edelman Institute, San Francisco State University. Retrieved from http://familyproject.sfsu.edu/files/FAP_English%20Booklet_pst.pdf

Saffin, L. A. (2011). Identities under siege: Violence against transpersons of color. In E. A. Stanley & N. Smith (Eds.), *Captive genders: Transembodiment and the prison industrial complex* (pp. 141–162). Oakland, CA: AK Press.

Savin-Williams, R. C., & Diamond, L. M. (2000). Sexual identity trajectories among sexual-minority youths: Gender comparisons. *Archives of Sexual Behavior*, *29*, 607–627. http://dx.doi.org/10.1023/A:1002058505138

Shively, M. G., & De Cecco, J. P. (1977). Component of sexual identity. *Journal of Homosexuality*, *3*, 41–48. http://dx.doi.org/10.1300/J082v03n01_04

Siegal, M., & Robinson, J. (1987). Order effects in children's gender constancy responses. *Developmental Psychology*, *23*, 283–286. http://dx.doi.org/10.1037/0012-1649.23.2.283

Spade, D. (2011a). *Normal life: Administrative violence, critical trans politics, and the limits of the law*. Brooklyn, NY: South End.

Steensma, T. D., McGuire, J. K., Kreukels, B. P., Beekman, A. J., & Cohen-Kettenis, P. T. (2013). Factors associated with desistence and persistence of childhood Gender Dysphoria: A quantitative follow-up study. *Journal of the American Academy of Child and Adolescent Psychiatry*, *52*, 582–590. http://dx.doi.org/10.1016/j.jaac.2013.03.016

Tanis, J. E. (2003). *Trans-gendered: Theology, ministry, and communities of faith*. Cleveland, OH: Pilgrim.

Taylor, J. K. (2007). Transgender identities and public policy in the United States: The relevance for public administration. *Administration & Society, 39*, 833–856.

Transgender Law Center. (2005). *Peeing in peace: A resource guide for transgender activists and allies.* San Francisco, CA: Author. Retrieved from http://transgenderlawcenter.org/issues/public-accomodations/peeing-in-peace

Vasquez, M. J. T. (2007). Cultural difference and the therapeutic alliance: An evidence-based analysis. *American Psychologist, 62*, 878–885. http://dx.doi.org/10.1037/0003-066X.62.8.878

Wahl, H. W., Iwarsson, S., & Oswald, F. (2012). Aging well and the environment: Toward an integrative model and research agenda for the future. *The Gerontologist, 52*, 306–316. http://dx.doi.org/10.1093/geront/gnr154

Wallien, M. S. C., & Cohen-Kettenis, P. T. (2008). Psychosexual outcome of gender-dysphoric children. *Journal of the American Academy of Child and Adolescent Psychiatry, 47*, 1413–1423. http://dx.doi.org/10.1097/CHI.0b013e31818956b9

Warner, L. R. (2008). A best practices guide to intersectional approaches in psychological research. *Sex Roles: A Journal of Research, 59*, 454–463.

White, T., & Ettner, R. (2004). Disclosure, risks and protective factors for children whose parents are undergoing a gender transition. *Journal of Gay and Lesbian Psychotherapy, 8*, 129–147.

Wierckx, K., Van Caenegem, E., Pennings, G., Elaut, E., Dedecker, D., Van de Peer, F., . . . T'Sjoen, G. (2012). Reproductive wish in transsexual men. *Human Reproduction, 27*, 483–487. http://dx.doi.org/10.1093/humrep/der406

Xavier, J., Bobbin, M., Singer, B., & Budd, E. (2005). A needs assessment of trans-gendered people of color living in Washington, DC. *International Journal of Transgenderism, 8*, 31–47. http://dx.doi.org/10.1300/J485v08n02_04

Xavier, J., Bradford, J., Hendricks, M., Safford, L., McKee, R., Martin, E., & Honnold, J. A. (2012). Transgender health care access of Virginia: A qualitative study. *International Journal of Transgenderism, 14*, 3–17. http://dx.doi.org/10.1080/15532739.2013.689513

Zucker, K. J. (2008a). Children with gender identity disorder. Is there a best practice? *Neuropsychiatrie de l'Enfance et de l'Adolescence, 56*, 358–364. http://dx.doi.org/10.1016/j.neurenf.2008.06.003

Zucker, K. J., & Bradley, S. J. (1995). *Gender identity disorder and psychosexual problems in children and adolescents.* New York, NY: Guilford Press.

COMMENTARY: Many a psychologist will initially be unprepared to identify and meet the individual mental health needs of transgender and gender nonconforming people. An insidious aspect of naive but well-intentioned therapy and counseling services with this population is that the psychologist may plunge into the treatment relationship with a greater—and, indeed, ultimately patronizing—reliance on "acceptance" than on fully realized clinical acumen. There is no reason to presume, absent specific clarification, that transgender and gender nonconforming people are seeking services because of or for reasons discernibly related to this particular status.

Fortunately, there is considerable support available for psychologists' ethically informed attempts to walk that fine line between acknowledging situationally influenced other population-related factors and concluding that these somehow define the client/patient. The available literature in this area has grown significantly, and with the recent advent of practice guidelines promulgated by the American Psychological Association, the road to effective clinical services can now be paved with much more than simply good intentions.

The following references are recommended for those interested in further investigation of ethical issues germane to treatment of transgender and gender nonconforming people, reflecting specifically upon the needs of children and families as well as individual adults.

Bernal, A. T., & Coolhart, D. (2012). Treatment and ethical considerations with transgender children and youth in family therapy. *Journal of Family Psychotherapy, 23,* 287–203. http://dx.doi.org/10.1080/08975353.2012.735594

Bidell, M. P. (2017). Mind our professional gaps: Competent lesbian, gay, bisexual and transgender mental health services. *Counselling Psychology Review, 31,* 67–76.

Kessler, L. E., & Waehler, C. A. (2005). Addressing multiple relationships between clients and therapists in lesbian, gay, bisexual, and transgender communities. *Professional Psychology: Research and Practice, 36,* 66–72. http://dx.doi.org/10.1037/0735-7028.36.1.66

Martin, J. (2003). Applying ethical standards to research and evaluations involving lesbian, gay, bisexual, and transgender populations. *Journal of Gay & Lesbian Social Services: Issues in Practice, Policy & Research, 15,* 181–201. http://dx.doi.org/10.1300/J041v15n01_12

Murphy, T. F. (2010). The ethics of helping transgender men and women have children. *Perspectives in Biology and Medicine, 53,* 46–60. http://dx.doi.org/10.1353/pbm.0.0138

Singh, A., & dickey, l. m. (2017). *Affirmative counseling and psychological practice with transgender and gender nonconforming clients.* Washington, DC: American Psychological Association.

7.7. Multicultural Guidelines: An Ecological Approach to Context, Identity, and Intersectionality

American Psychological Association

. . .

INTRODUCTION

. . .

The current *Multicultural Guidelines: An Ecological Approach to Context, Identity, and Intersectionality, 2017* (i.e., *Multicultural Guidelines*) are conceptualized from a need to reconsider diversity and multicultural practice within professional psychology at a different period in time, with intersectionality as its primary purview. The 2017 version of the *Multicultural Guidelines* encourages psychologists

From "Multicultural Guidelines: An Ecological Approach to Context, Identity, and Intersectionality," by the American Psychological Association, 2017. Retrieved from http://www.apa.org/about/policy/multicultural-guidelines.pdf. Copyright 2017 by the American Psychological Association.

Multicultural Guidelines: An Ecological Approach to Context, Identity, and Intersectionality, 2017 is an update of the *2002 Guidelines on Multicultural Education, Training, Research, Practice, and Organizational Change for Psychologists (Multicultural Guidelines)*.

The *2017 Guidelines* were developed by a five-member *Task Force on Re-envisioning the Multicultural Guidelines for the 21st Century*, appointed by the Board for the Advancement of Psychology in the Public Interest (BAPPI), and adopted by the Council of Representatives in August 2017.

Members of the Task Force included: Caroline S. Clauss-Ehlers, Rutgers, The State University of New Jersey (Chair); David A. Chiriboga, University of South Florida; Scott J. Hunter, University of Chicago; Gargi Roysircar-Sodowsky, Antioch University New England; and Pratyusha Tummala-Narra, Boston College.

The Task Force gratefully acknowledges the earlier pioneering work of multiple individuals, whose steadfast commitment over several years and extensive knowledge of history and subject matter made this work possible. BAPPI liaisons April Harris-Britt and Gayle Skawennio Morse provided vital guidance and invaluable collaboration. Sincere appreciation is extended to Renato Alarcón, William D. Parham, and Terrence Roberts for their willingness to contribute their invaluable knowledge, encouragement, and assistance. Roy Sainsbury, Sally Pulleyn, and the Social Research Policy Unit at the University of York are acknowledged for the support provided during a sabbatical leave.

The Task Force appreciates BAPPI's consistent support, extensive reviews, and substantive feedback. Task Force members also express their appreciation to the individuals and groups who provided insightful feedback during the public review process.

Appreciation is extended to Clinton W. Anderson, Interim Executive Director of the APA Public Interest Directorate, for his support in bringing this document to fruition, and to Sue Houston, who was responsible for assisting the Task Force in its work and who played an instrumental role in shepherding the document through the final approval process. The Task Force is also grateful for the contributions of students Cara Lomaro and Noël Su.

This document will expire as APA policy in 10 years (2027).

to consider how knowledge and understanding of identity develops from and is disseminated within professional psychological practice. Endemic to this understanding is an approach that incorporates developmental and contextual antecedents of identity and how they can be acknowledged, addressed, and embraced to engender more effective models of professional engagement. The *Multicultural Guidelines* incorporate broad reference group identities (e.g., Black/African American/Black American, White/White American, and Asian/Asian American/Pacific Islander) to acknowledge within-group differences and the role of self-definition in identity.

With the *Multicultural Guidelines*, APA and its members are presented with an opportunity to participate directly, as professional psychologists, in engaging a fuller understanding of diversity and its considerations within practice, research, consultation, and education (including supervision) to directly address how development unfolds across time and intersectional experiences and identities; and to recognize the highly diverse nature of individuals and communities in their defining characteristics, despite also sharing many similarities by virtue of being human. Our conscious awareness of what it means to think, feel, regulate, behave, and create meaning has been enhanced by advances in research and clinical scholarship affording us a contemporary consideration of psychology that incorporates human differences across their varied elements.

. . .

PURPOSE

The purpose of the *Multicultural Guidelines* is to provide psychologists with a framework from which to consider evolving parameters for the provision of multiculturally competent services. Services include practice, research, consultation, and education, all of which benefit from an *appreciation for, understanding of,* and *willingness to learn about* the multicultural backgrounds of individuals, families, couples, groups, research participants, organizations, and communities. To simplify the presentations that follow, the *Multicultural Guidelines* often refer to the client when in fact speaking not only of the recipient of clinical services, but also the student, research participant, or consultee. With the exception of the case studies presented in Appendix B, the guidelines use nonbinary pronouns. The current *Multicultural Guidelines* also advocate for a more diverse and inclusive population of psychologists.

. . .

Guideline 1. Psychologists seek to recognize and understand that identity and self-definition are fluid and complex and that the interaction between the two is dynamic. To this end, psychologists appreciate that intersectionality is shaped by the multiplicity of the individual's social contexts.

. . .

Psychologists are encouraged to consider the relationship between various layers of an individual's ecological contexts and identity development and the implications of this relationship for experiences of privilege and oppression, well-being, access to resources, and barriers from and access to appropriate, quality care.

Psychologists strive to recognize the need to move beyond stereotypes when working with clients, research participants, students, and consultees. They seek to avoid overgeneralized or simplistic categories and labels of sociocultural groups. Such categorization has been described through the concept of *ethnic gloss*, that refers to an illusion of homogeneity among diverse groups that minimizes important distinctions among ethnic groups within a broader racial category; for example, American Indian, Latino/Hispanic/Latinx, Asian/Asian American/Pacific Islander, Black/African American/Black American, and White/White American (Trimble & Dickson, 2005).

. . .

Guideline 2. Psychologists aspire to recognize and understand that as cultural beings, they hold attitudes and beliefs that can influence their perceptions of and interactions with others as well as their clinical and empirical conceptualizations. As such, psychologists strive to move beyond conceptualizations rooted in categorical assumptions, biases, and/or formulations based on limited knowledge about individuals and communities.

. . .

Psychologists' worldviews are rooted in their professional knowledge, personal life experiences, and interactions with others across their ecological contexts, and these worldviews influence their empirical and clinical conceptualizations and approaches. Multicultural and feminist scholars have emphasized that people are cultural beings whose beliefs, attitudes, and life histories influence their clinical and research conceptualizations (APA, 2003; Arredondo et al., 1996; Brown, 2010; Fouad & Brown, 2000; Jernigan, Green, Helms, Perez-Gualdron, & Henze, 2010; Kelly & Greene, 2010; Sue & Sue, 2016). Socialization concerning age, sex, gender, race, ethnicity, sexual orientation, religion and spirituality, social class, and disability has important implications for psychologists' conscious and unconscious preferences and inclinations when formulating diagnoses, analyzing and interpreting research data, and planning interventions (Greenwald & Banaji, 1995; Saewyc, 2011; Sue, Arredondo, & McDavis, 1992).

. . .

Guideline 3. Psychologists strive to recognize and understand the role of language and communication through engagement that is sensitive to the lived experience of the individual, couple, family, group, community, and/or organizations with whom they interact. Psychologists also seek to understand how they bring their own language and communication to these interactions.

. . .

Psychologists are encouraged to consider the role of language in their professional relationships as well as within the context of the client's experience within school, work, family, and community contexts. Language refers to the verbal and nonverbal symbols used to communicate with others (Guo et al., 2009; Javier, 2007). Through language, the individual, group, couple, family, community, and/or organization share an aspect of self and experience with someone else. Language embodies the culture and values in which is it spoken (Chen, 2015). For instance, in Spanish the word "yo" means "I" but is not capitalized as in the English language (Clauss-Ehlers, 2006). This difference reflects the focus on the collective or the larger group in many Spanish-speaking countries. This is in contrast to the frequent focus on the individual as reflected in many English-speaking cultures.

. . .

Guideline 4. Psychologists endeavor to be aware of the role of the social and physical environment in the lives of clients, students, research participants, and/or consultees.

. . .

The psychologist is aware that the resources available in the immediate environment provide many of the tools by which individuals can build their lives. These resources combine into what is sometimes called social capital, and include factors such as the overall wealth and safety of the neighborhood, the quality of schools, pollution and other environmental hazards, the quality and accessibility of healthcare and transportation systems, and the availability of nutritious food. A resource-rich environment can maximize the potential for a quality life, while a resource-poor environment can create barriers to self-actualization. Unfortunately, individuals from disadvantaged backgrounds are disproportionately represented in resource-poor environments (Krieger et al., 2016; Olkin, 2002; Reardon, Fox, & Townsend, 2015). The psychologist may therefore wish to pay special attention to resources available to clients, including barriers to healthcare services, the quality of such services, and other social and physical environmental factors that might either impede or facilitate interventions. In the healthcare community, the term "social determinants of health" has been defined by Healthy People 2020 (2017) to include neighborhood and built environment, health and health care, social and community context, education, and economic stability.

. . .

Guideline 5. Psychologists aspire to recognize and understand historical and contemporary experiences with power, privilege, and oppression. As such, they seek to address institutional barriers and related inequities, disproportionalities, and disparities of law enforcement, administration of criminal justice, educational, mental health, and other systems as they seek to promote justice, human rights, and access to quality and equitable mental and behavioral health services.

. . .

At the macro level, oppression (Essed, 2002) in its various forms such as racism (Du Bois, 1903/1996; Franklin, 2004); cultural imperialism (Mohawk,

2004; Speight, 2007); classism (Liu, 2012); ableism (Goodley & Runswick-Cole, 2011; Olkin & Pledger, 2003); ageism (Lamont et al., 2015); English-only injunction (Lynch, 2006); and stigma about minority status (Hatzenbuehler, 2016; Meyer, 2003) hinder access to societal resources, which results in disparities. Ample research has indicated that people from oppressed groups experience limited access to, less utilization of, and diminished quality of health care (Institute of Medicine, 2003; USDHHS, 2001).

If psychologists focus only on individual functioning, they may not include in their understanding structural oppression embedded in institutional practices that produce inequities and disproportionalities, resulting in negative psychosocial outcomes for underserved individuals, couples, families, and communities (Aldarondo, 2007; Liu, Pickett, & Ivey, 2007). With regard to racism, psychologists are encouraged to challenge their color-blind racial attitudes and beliefs that the world is just and fair (cf., Neville et al., 2013). Psychologists are also encouraged to observe an ongoing self-reflective process of their own social position, exploring and owning their privilege when interacting with clients and the possibility of their clients' less privileged position (Ancis & Szymanski, 2001; Roysircar, 2004b, 2008).

. . .

Guideline 6. Psychologists seek to promote culturally adaptive interventions and advocacy within and across systems, including prevention, early intervention, and recovery.

. . .

Psychologists endeavor to recognize that culture's relevance to mental health treatment, intervention, prevention, and service delivery is well established (Bernal & Sáez-Santiago, 2006). With this recognition comes the need to understand the multicultural aspects of personal and organizational experience. The term "culture-centered interventions" (APA, 2003; Pederson, 1997) refers to those intervention efforts that view the integration of culture and language as central to the delivery of services. Culture-centered interventions commonly exhibit an awareness of culture; knowledge concerning cultural aspects of an individual, group, couple, family, community, or organizational experience; an understanding of the difference between culture and pathology; and an ability to integrate the aforementioned points within the context of service delivery (Zayas, Torres, Malcolm, & DesRosiers, 1996).

Related work has considered the role of the culturally centered psychologist as a tool in the provision of culturally and linguistically relevant clinical services (Aldarondo, 2007; Hall, Ibaraki, Huang, Marti, & Stice, 2016); the development of rapport from a cross-cultural framework (Hays, 2016; Toporek, Gerstein, Fouad, Roysircar, & Israel, 2006); and social justice efforts to decrease health disparities through the provision of culturally centered service delivery and development of more culturally competent infrastructures. Perception and acceptance of help seeking is likely to vary across cultures. Research has found significant differences across communities in terms of access and utilization of

services (USDHHS, 2001). The role of mental health stigma may be a factor that decreases help-seeking behavior. For instance, research has identified a relationship between stigma and low functioning among patients with bipolar disorder who were recruited from Latin America (Vázquez et al., 2011). Stigma can also affect the individual's decision to continue to engage in ongoing care.
. . .

Guideline 7. Psychologists endeavor to examine the profession's assumptions and practices within an international context, whether domestically or internationally based, and consider how this globalization has an impact on the psychologist's self-definition, purpose, role, and function.

. . .

Globalization, international geopolitics, and digital technologies have drawn the United States into a global satellite, where a complexity of social, business, and military encounters and ensuing intersectional identities are experienced at individual, local, and universal levels. A resultant dynamic interaction of local, national, and cross-national psychologies enhances understanding of indigenous, culture-specific, and common, as well as unique, aspects of behavior and identity development. Multilateral and horizontal dialogues among psychology professionals working collaboratively on cross-national projects can address the question of what it means to be human, universal, local, indigenous, communal, and individualistic so that psychology can be practiced broadly in global contexts. In addition, psychologists, as upholders of social justice, strive to develop coalition building with practitioners across nationalities to stop oppression, disempowerment, and crimes against humanity.

One traumatic event in one city in one part of the world, such as the violence of domestic terrorists in London or Paris, reverberates across the globe to the United States, and thus psychologists, while acting locally, aspire to think globally and understand human conditions in broad contexts. By recognizing that international psychology represents a postmodern form of consciousness, psychologists can theorize about universal conditions of trauma, resilience, oppression, empowerment, and human rights and dignity, while also operationalizing culture-specific manifestations of a universal experience.
. . .

Guideline 8. Psychologists seek awareness and understanding of how developmental stages and life transitions intersect with the larger biosociocultural context, how identity evolves as a function of such intersections, and how these different socialization and maturation experiences influence worldview and identity.

. . .

The life cycle of individuals is heavily influenced not only by the immediate social and physical environment but also by current societal trends and the historical period. For example, wars and economic depressions affect the life cycle at all levels. The psychologist seeks ways to remain aware of how a client's personal experience and development has been influenced by these dynamic forces.

As discussed in several other guidelines, people often have multiple identifications. These identifications may have their own developmental cycles, as well as emerging and engaging across the full developmental cycle of the individuals psychologists consult with and treat. An individual who identified as a Black/African American/Black American activist and champion of the poor at one stage of life may transition into the Chief Executive Officer (CEO) position of a large corporation at another. A multiracial person may identify with a singular, multiple, or no racial category (Rockquemore, Brunsma, & Delgado, 2009), and these identifications may change from childhood through older adulthood. A gay preadolescent with myotonic muscular dystrophy may transition to a community activist leading the fight for disability rights upon entry to adulthood. The historical period one lives through may also affect how individuals perceive themselves. Growing up during the Great Depression had a lifelong effect on the lives of those in later adolescence at the time, but only a minimal effect on those who were younger (Elder, 1974, 1998). Some historical periods have a lasting influence, such as the continuing impact of America's period of slavery and the infamous Tuskegee experiments. For these reasons, psychologists seek to develop and sustain an awareness of how an individual's identity has changed over time and how their identities, and the importance of each, are affected by the historical period, and the concurrent immediate developmental, social, and familial contexts in which the individual is situated.

. . .

Guideline 9. Psychologists strive to conduct culturally appropriate and informed research, teaching, supervision, consultation, assessment, interpretation, diagnosis, dissemination, and evaluation of efficacy. . . .

The several levels of the model that inform the present guidelines all exert an influence on both the client and the psychologist. When dealing with clients and research participants who present with complex intersectional identities, these multiple lines of influence add to the usual challenges faced by the psychologist engaged in assessment, selection of appropriate intervention strategies, and research and consultation.

The psychologist therefore recognizes that assessment tools, and nearly all clinical interventions, have the potential to mischaracterize or even miss the behavioral health needs of racial/ethnic and other identity groups. The reasons include cultural and regional differences, stigma, literacy (including health literacy), the unique presentation of symptoms, explanations of psychological distress, distrust of providers and authority in general, and many other factors (Sue & Sue, 2016). When the fit of a particular therapy or assessment tool to a particular group is unclear, further research may be called for. In that case, focus groups and community involvement are forms of qualitative research that may be most helpful in the early stages of cultural adaptation (Hall, Yip, & Zárate, 2016; Ramos & Alegría, 2014).

. . .

Guideline 10. Psychologists actively strive to take a strength-based approach when working with individuals, families, groups, communities, and organizations that seeks to build resilience and decrease trauma within the sociocultural context.

. . .

Resilience is one aspect of the strength-based approach. Resilience refers to the "process, capacity or outcome of successful adaptation despite challenges or threatening circumstances . . . good outcomes despite high risk status, sustained competence under threat and recovery from trauma" (Masten, Best, & Garmezy, 1990, p. 426). The concept of resilience has been deeply considered throughout the psychological literature (Masten, 2014), with a research and practice trajectory largely influenced by Rutter's study of how children cope with adversity (Cicchetti, 2013; Garmezy, 1991; Luthar, 2006; Rutter, 1985).

A focus on human strengths and resilience is found in positive psychology. Positive psychology is a framework that emphasizes mental health, adaptive functioning, and human strengths (Chang, Downey, Hirsch, & Lin, 2016). The focus shifts from exploring psychopathology to understanding how human beings achieve optimal well-being (Seligman & Csikszentmihalyi, 2000). Positive psychology emphasizes individual qualities such as hope and optimism, capacity for love and vocation, perseverance, and courage over external and contextual sources of resilience. While it is important for psychologists to recognize the role of individual factors that determine resilience, psychologists are also encouraged to consider the role of contextual level factors and how they intersect with individual level factors in resilience.

. . .

REFERENCES

Aldarondo, E. (Ed.). (2007). *Advancing social justice through clinical practice.* New York, NY: Routledge.

American Psychological Association. (2003). Guidelines on multicultural education, training, research, practice, and organizational change for psychologists. *American Psychologist, 58,* 377–402.

Ancis, J. R., & Szymanski, D. (2001). Awareness of White privilege among White counseling trainees. *The Counseling Psychologist, 29*(4), 548–569.

Arredondo, P., Toporek, R., Brown, S. P., Jones, J., Locke, D., Sanchez, J., & Stadler, H. (1996). Operationalization of the multicultural counseling competencies. *Journal of Multicultural Counseling and Development, 24,* 42–78.

Bernal, G., & Sáez-Santiago, E. (2006). Culturally centered psychosocial interventions. *Journal of Community Psychology, 34*(2), 121–132.

Brown, L. S. (2010). *Feminist therapy.* Washington, DC: American Psychological Association.

Chang, E. C., Downey, C. A., Hirsch, J. K., & Lin, N. J. (2016). *Positive psychology in racial and ethnic groups: Theory, research, and practice.* Washington, DC: American Psychological Association.

Chen, S. X. (2015). Toward a social psychology of bilingualism and biculturalism. *Asian Journal of Social Psychology, 18,* 1–11.

Cicchetti, D. (2013). Resilient functioning in maltreated children: Past, present, and future perspectives. *Journal of Child Psychology and Psychiatry, 54,* 402–422.

Clauss-Ehlers, C. S. (2006). Bilingualism. In Y. Jackson (Ed.), *Encyclopedia of multicultural psychology* (pp. 70–71). Newbury Park, CA: Sage.

Du Bois, W. E. B. (1903/1996). *The souls of Black folk.* New York, NY: Penguin Books.

Elder, G. H. (1974). *Children of the Great Depression: Social change in life experience.* Chicago, IL: University of Chicago Press.

Elder, G. (1998). The life course as development theory. *Child Development, 69,* 1–12.

Essed, P. (2002). Everyday racism. In D. T. Goldberg & J. Solomos (Eds.), *A companion to racial and ethnic studies* (pp. 202–216). Malden, MA: Blackwell.

Fouad, N. A., & Brown, M. T. (2000). The role of race and class in development: Implications for counseling psychology. In S. D. Brown & R. W. Lent (Eds.), *Handbook of counseling psychology* (3rd ed., pp. 379–408). New York, NY: Wiley.

Franklin, A. J. (2004). *From brotherhood to manhood: How Black men rescue their dreams and relationships from the invisibility syndrome.* New York, NY: Wiley.

Garmezy, N. (1991). Resilience in children's adaptation to negative life events and stressed environments. *Pediatric Annals, 20,* 459–460, 463–466.

Goodley, D., & Runswick-Cole, K. (2011). The violence of disablism. *Sociology of Health & Illness, 33*(4), 602–617.

Greenwald, A. G., & Banaji, M. R. (1995). Implicit social cognition: Attitudes, self-esteem, and stereotypes. *Psychological Review, 102,* 4–27.

Guo, J., Lieven, E., Budwig, N., Ervin-Tripp, S., Nakamura, K., & Özçalişkan, Ş. (2009). *Crosslinguistic approaches to the psychology of language: Research in the tradition of Dan Isaac Slobin.* New York, NY: Psychology Press, Taylor & Francis.

Hall, G. C. N., Ibaraki, A. Y., Huang, E. R., Marti, C. N., & Stice, E. (2016). A meta-analysis of cultural adaptations of psychological interventions. *Behavior Therapy, 47,* 993–1014.

Hall, G. C. N., Yip, T., & Zárate, M. A. (2016). On becoming multicultural in a mono-cultural research world: A conceptual approach to studying ethnocultural diversity. *American Psychologist, 71,* 40–51.

Hatzenbuehler, M. L. (2016). Structural stigma: Research evidence and implications for psychological science. *American Psychologist, 71*(8), 742–751.

Hays, P. A. (2016). Understanding clients' identities and contexts. *Addressing cultural complexities in practice: Assessment, diagnosis, and therapy* (3rd ed.). Washington, DC: American Psychological Association.

Healthy People 2020. (2017). *Social determinants of health.* Office of Disease Prevention and Health Promotion, U.S. Department of Health and Human Services. Retrieved from https://www.healthypeople.gov/2020/topics-objectives/topic/social-determinants-of-health

Institute of Medicine. (2003). *Unequal treatment: Confronting racial and ethnic disparities in healthcare.* Washington, DC: National Academies Press.

Javier, R. A. (2007). *The bilingual mind: Thinking, feeling, and speaking in two languages.* New York, NY: Springer.

Jernigan, M. M., Green, C. E., Helms, J. E., Perez-Gualdron, L., & Henze, K. (2010). An examination of people of color supervision dyads: Racial identity matters as much as race. *Training and Education in Professional Psychology, 4*(1), 62–73.

Kelly, J. F., & Greene, B. (2010). Diversity within African American, female therapists: Variability in clients' expectations and assumptions about the therapist. *Psychotherapy: Theory, Research, Practice, Training, 47*(2), 186–197.

Krieger, N., Waterman, P. D., Spasojevic, J., Li, W., Maduro, G., & Van Wye, G. (2016). Public health monitoring of privilege and deprivation with the index of concentration at the extremes. *American Journal of Public Health, 106*(2), 256–263.

Lamont, R. A., Swift, H. J., & Abrams, D. (2015). A review and meta-analysis of age-based stereotype threat: Negative stereotypes, not facts, do the damage. *Psychology and Aging, 30*(1), 180–193.

Liu, W. M. (2012). *Social class and classism in the helping professions: Research, theory, and practice.* Thousand Oaks, CA: Sage.

Liu, W. M., Pickett, T., Jr., & Ivey, A. E. (2007). White middle-class privilege: Social class bias and implications for training and practice. *Journal of Multicultural Counseling and Development, 35*(4), 194–206.

Luthar, S. S. (2006). Resilience in development: A synthesis of research across five decades. In D. Cicchetti & D. J. Cohen (Eds.), *Developmental psychopathology: Risk, disorder, and adaptation* (2nd ed., Vol. 3, pp. 739–795). Hoboken, NJ: Wiley.

Lynch, W. (2006). A Nation established by immigrants sanctions employers for requiring English to be spoken at work: English-only work rules and national origin discrimination, *Temple Political and Civil Rights Law Review, 16*(1), 65–102.

Masten, A. S. (2014). Global perspectives on resilience in children and youth. *Child Development, 85*(1), 6–20.

Masten, A. S., Best, K. M., & Garmezy, N. (1990). Resilience and development: Contributions from the study of children who overcome adversity. *Development and Psychopathology, 2,* 425–444.

Meyer, I. H. (2003). Prejudice, social stress, and mental health in lesbian, gay, and bisexual populations: Conceptual issues and research evidence. *Psychological Bulletin, 129,* 674–697.

Mohawk, J. (2004). The tragedy of colonization. *Indian Country Media Network.* Retrieved from https://newsmaven.io/indiancountrytoday/archive/mohawk-the-tragedy-of-colonization-r0EUAcsOG02ey3VavG8ONQ/

Neville, H. A., Awad, G. H., Brooks, J., Flores, M. P., & Bluenel, J. (2013). Color-blind racial ideology: Theory, training, and measurement implications. *American Psychologist, 68,* 455–466.

Olkin, R. (2002). Could you hold the door for me? Including disability in diversity. *Cultural Diversity & Ethnic Minority Psychology, 8*(2), 130–137.

Olkin, R., & Pledger, C. (2003). Can disability studies and psychology join hands? *American Psychologist, 58*(4), 296–304.

Pederson, P. B. (1997). *Culture-centered counseling interventions: Striving for accuracy.* Thousand Oaks, CA: Sage.

Ramos, Z., & Alegría, M. (2014). Cultural adaptation and health literacy refinement of a brief depression intervention for Latinos in a low-resource setting. *Cultural Diversity and Ethnic Minority Psychology, 20*(2), 293–301.

Reardon, S. F., Fox, L., & Townsend, J. (2015). Neighborhood income composition by household race and income, 1990–2009. *The Annals of the American Academy of Political and Social Science, 660*(1), 78–97.

Rockquemore, K. A., Brunsma, D. L., & Delgado, D. J. (2009). Racing to theory or retheorizing race? Understanding the struggle to build a multiracial identity theory. *Journal of Social Issues, 65*(1), 13–34.

Roysircar, G. (2004b). Cultural self-awareness assessment: Practice examples from psychology training. *Professional Psychology: Research and Practice, 35,* 658–666.

Roysircar, G. (2008). Social privilege: Counselors' competence with systemically determined inequalities. *Journal for Specialists in Group Work, 33*(4), 377–384.

Rutter, M. (1985). Resilience in the face of adversity: protective factors and resistance to psychiatric disorder. *British Journal of Psychiatry, 147,* 598–611.

Saewyc, E. M. (2011). Research on adolescent sexual orientation: Development, health disparities, stigma, and resilience. *Journal of Research on Adolescence, 21*(1), 256–272.

Seligman, M., & Csikszentmihalyi, M. (2000). Positive psychology: An introduction. *American Psychologist, 55*(1), 5–14.

Speight, S. L. (2007). Internalized racism: One more piece of the puzzle. *The Counseling Psychologist, 35*(1), 126–134.

Sue, D. W., Arredondo, P., & McDavis, R. (1992). Multicultural counseling competencies and standards: A call to the profession. *Journal of Counseling and Development, 70,* 477–486.

Sue, D. W., & Sue, D. (2016). *Counseling the culturally diverse: Theory and practice* (7th ed.). Hoboken, NJ: John Wiley & Sons.

Toporek, R. L., Gerstein, L. H., Fouad, N. A., Roysircar, G., & Israel, T. (Eds.). (2006). *Handbook for social justice in counseling psychology: Leadership, vision, and action.* Thousand Oaks, CA: Sage.

Trimble, J. E., & Dickson, R. (2005). Ethnic gloss. In C. B. Fisher & R. M. Lerner (Eds.), *Encyclopedia of applied developmental science* (Vol. 1, pp. 412–415). Thousand Oaks, CA: Sage.

U.S. Department of Health and Human Services. (2001). *Mental health: Culture, race and ethnicity—A supplement to mental health: A report of the Surgeon General.* Rockville, MD: U.S. Department of Health and Human Services, Public Health Office, Office of the Surgeon General. Retrieved from http://health-equity.lib.umd.edu/866/1/sma-01-3613.pdf

Vázquez, G. H., Kapczinski, F., Magalhaes, P. V., Córdoba, R., Jaramillo, C. L., Rosa, A. R., Sanchez de Carmona, M., Tohen, M., & The Ibero-American Network on Bipolar Disorders (IAN-BD) Group. (2011). Stigma and functioning in patients with bipolar disorder. *Journal of Affective Disorders, 130*(1–2), 323–327.

Zayas, L. H., Torres, L. R., Malcolm, J., & DesRosiers, F. S. (1996). Clinicians' definitions of ethnically sensitive therapy. *Professional Psychology: Research and Practice, 27,* 78–82.

COMMENTARY: Psychology as a profession has achieved its most significant institutional enshrinement and its most influential scientific advances in a country specifically intended as an experiment in multicultural cooperation; however, that does not, of course, translate into a guarantee of multicultural insight and competency on the part of all who choose to practice here. Fortunately, in recent years, there has been a virtual explosion of social scientific literature on this topic, and the American Psychological Association has provided guidelines for education, training, research, practice, and organizational change concerning multicultural issues.

Language can be one factor complicating service delivery, and psychologists need to remain aware of the differences between "interpretation" and "translation" (and the strikingly different forms these means of support can assume) before attempting to scale the Tower of Babel in pursuit of effective treatment. Reflexive referral of potential clients/patients to providers with similar cultural affiliation is its own none-too-subtle form of discrimination.

The following references are recommended for those interested in further investigation of available resources, common challenges, and occasionally clashing schools of thought regarding ethically charged multicultural issues.

Frame, M. W., & Williams, C. B. (2005). Issues and insights: A model of ethical decision making from a multicultural perspective. *Counseling and Values, 49,* 165–179. http://dx.doi.org/10.1002/j.2161-007X.2005.tb01020.x

Jason, L. A. (2015). Ethical and diversity challenges in ecologically sensitive systems-oriented interventions. *American Psychologist, 70,* 764–775. http://dx.doi.org/10.1037/a0039642

Knapp, S., & VandeCreek, L. (2007). When values of different cultures conflict: Ethical decision making in a multicultural context. *Professional Psychology: Research and Practice, 38,* 660–666. http://dx.doi.org/10.1037/0735-7028.38.6.660

Nelson, J. K., Poms, L. W., & Wolf, P. P. (2012). Developing efficacy beliefs for ethics and diversity management. *Academy of Management Learning & Education, 11,* 46–98. http://dx.doi.org/10.5465/amle.2009.0115

Sadeghi, M., Fischer, J. M., & House, S. G. (2003). Ethical dilemmas in multicultural counseling. *Journal of Multicultural Counseling and Development, 31,* 179–191. http://dx.doi.org/10.1002/j.2161-1912.2003.tb00542.x

7.8. Guidelines for Psychological Practice With Older Adults

American Psychological Association

. . .

Unquestionably, the demand for psychologists with a substantial understanding of later-life wellness, cultural, and clinical issues will expand in future years as the older population grows and becomes more diverse and as cohorts of middle-aged and younger individuals who are receptive to psychological services move into old age (Karel, Gatz, & Smyer, 2012). However, psychologist time devoted to care of older adults does not and likely will not meet the anticipated need (Karel, Gatz, & Smyer, 2012; Qualls, Segal, Norman, Niederehe, & Gallagher-Thompson, 2002). Indeed, across professions, the geriatric mental health care workforce is not adequately trained to meet the health and mental health needs of the aging population (Institute of Medicine, 2012).

Older adults are served by psychologists across subfields including clinical, counseling, family, geropsychology, health, industrial/organizational, neuropsychology, rehabilitation, and others. The 2008 APA Survey of Psychology Health Service Providers found that 4.2% of respondents viewed older adults as their primary focus and 39% reported that they provided some type of

From "Guidelines for Psychological Practice With Older Adults," by the American Psychological Association, 2014, *American Psychologist, 69*, pp. 34–65. Copyright 2014 by the American Psychological Association.

This revision of the 2003 "Guidelines for Psychological Practice With Older Adults" was completed by the Guidelines for Psychological Practice With Older Adults Revision Working Group and approved as APA policy by the APA Council of Representatives in August 2013. Members of the Guidelines for Psychological Practice With Older Adults Revision Working Group were Gregory A. Hinrichsen (chair), Icahn School of Medicine at Mount Sinai; Adam M. Brickman, Columbia University; Barry Edelstein, West Virginia University; Tammi Vacha-Haase, Colorado State University; Kimberly Hiroto, Puget Sound Health Care System, U.S. Department of Veterans Affairs; and Richard Zweig, Yeshiva University.

The Guidelines Revision Working Group is thankful to the APA Committee on Aging for convening the group and to Division 20 (Adult Development and Aging) and Division 12 Section II (Society of Clinical Geropsychology) and the APA Council of Representatives for providing financial support for the revision. APA Office on Aging Director Deborah DiGilio and Administrative Coordinator Martha Randolph provided outstanding administrative support.

The literature cited herein does not reflect a systematic meta-analysis or review of the literature but rather was selected by the working group to emphasize clinical best practices. Care was taken to avoid endorsing specific products, tools, or proprietary approaches.

These guidelines are scheduled to expire as APA policy in February 2023. After this date, users are encouraged to contact the Office on Aging, APA Public Interest Directorate to determine whether this document remains in effect.

psychological services to older adults (APA, Center for Workforce Studies, 2008). Relatively few psychologists, however, have received formal training in the psychology of aging. Fewer than one third of APA-member practicing psychologists who conducted some clinical work with older adults reported having had any graduate coursework in geropsychology, and fewer than one in four received any supervised practicum or internship experience with older adults (Qualls et al., 2002). Many psychologists may be reluctant to work with older adults because they feel they do not possess the requisite knowledge and skills. In the practitioner survey conducted by Qualls et al., a high proportion of the respondents (58%) reported that they needed further training in professional work with older adults, and 70% said that they were interested in attending specialized education programs in clinical geropsychology. In two small surveys of psychology students, over half of those surveyed desired further education and training in this area, and 90% expressed interest in providing clinical services to older adults (Hinrichsen, 2000; Zweig, Siegel, & Snyder, 2006). . . .

COMPETENCE IN AND ATTITUDES TOWARD WORKING WITH OLDER ADULTS

Guideline 1. Psychologists are encouraged to work with older adults within their scope of competence.

Training in professional psychology provides general skills that can be applied for the potential benefit of older adults. Many adults have presenting issues similar to those of other ages and generally respond to the repertoire of skills and techniques possessed by all professional psychologists. For example, psychologists are often called upon to evaluate and/or assist older adults with life stress or crisis (Brown, Gibson, & Elmore, 2012) and adaptation to late-life issues (e.g., chronic medical problems affecting daily functioning; Qualls & Benight, 2007). Psychologists play an equally important role in facilitating the maintenance of healthy functioning, accomplishment of new life-cycle developmental tasks, and/or achievement of positive psychological growth in the later years (King & Wynne, 2004). Given some commonalities across age groups, considerably more psychologists may want to work with older adults, as many of their already existing skills can be effective with these clients (Molinari et al., 2003). . . .

Guideline 2. Psychologists are encouraged to recognize how their attitudes and beliefs about aging and about older individuals may be relevant to their assessment and treatment of older adults, and to seek consultation or further education about these issues when indicated.

Principle E of the APA Ethics Code (APA, 2002a, 2010a) urges psychologists to respect the rights, dignity, and welfare of all people and eliminate the effect of cultural and sociodemographic stereotypes and biases (including ageism) on their work. In addition, the APA Council of Representatives passed a resolution opposing ageism and committing the Association to its elimination as a matter of APA policy (APA, 2002c). . . .

Negative stereotypes can become self-fulfilling prophecies and adversely affect health care providers' attitudes and behaviors toward older adult clients. For example, stereotypes can lead health care providers to misdiagnose disorders (Mohlman et al., 2011), inappropriately lower their expectations for the improvement of older adult clients . . . , and delay preventive actions and treatment (Levy & Myers, 2004). Providers may also misattribute older adults' report of treatable depressive symptoms (e.g., lethargy, decreased appetite, anhedonia) to aspects of normative aging. Some psychologists unfamiliar with facts about aging may assume that older adults are too old to change (Ivey et al., 2000; Kane, 2004) or are less likely than younger adults to benefit from psychosocial therapies (Gatz & Pearson, 1988). What may seem like discriminatory behavior by some health providers toward older adults may be more a function of lack of familiarity with aging issues than discrimination based solely on age (James & Haley, 1995). . . .

GENERAL KNOWLEDGE ABOUT ADULT DEVELOPMENT, AGING, AND OLDER ADULTS

Guideline 3. Psychologists strive to gain knowledge about theory and research in aging.

APA-supported training conferences have recommended that psychologists acquire familiarity with the biological, psychological, cultural, and social content and contexts associated with normal aging as part of their knowledge base for working clinically with older adults (Knight et al., 2009; Knight, Teri, Wohlford, & Santos, 1995; Santos & VandenBos, 1982). Most practicing psychologists will work with clients, family members, and caregivers of diverse ages. Therefore, a rounded preparatory education for anyone delivering services to older adults encompasses training with a life-span developmental perspective for which knowledge of a range of age groups including older adults is very useful (Abeles et al., 1998). APA accreditation criteria now require that students be exposed to the current body of knowledge in human development across the life span (APA, Commission on Accreditation, 2008, Section C). . . .

Guideline 4. Psychologists strive to be aware of the social/psychological dynamics of the aging process.

As part of the broader developmental continuum of the life span, aging is a dynamic process that challenges the aging individual to make continuing behavioral adaptations (Labouvie-Vief, Diehl, Jain, & Zhang, 2007). Just as younger individuals' developmental pathways are shaped by their ability to adapt to normative early life transitions, so are older individuals' developmental trajectories molded by their ability to contend successfully with normative later life transitions such as retirement (Sterns & Dawson, 2012), residential relocations, changes in relationships with partners or in sexual functioning (Hillman, 2012; Levenson, Carstensen, & Gottman, 1993; Matthias, Lubben, Atchison, & Schweitzer, 1997), and bereavement and widowhood (Kastenbaum, 1999), as well as non-normative experiences such as traumatic events (Cook & Elmore, 2009; Cook & O'Donnell, 2005) and social isolation and loneliness. Clinicians who work with older adults strive to be knowledgeable of issues specific to later life, including grandparenting (Hayslip & Kaminski, 2005), adaptation to typical age-related physical changes such as health problems and disability (Aldwin, Park, & Spiro, 2007; Schulz & Heckhausen, 1996), and a need to integrate or come to terms with one's personal lifetime of aspirations, achievements, and failures (R. N. Butler, 1969). . . .

Guideline 5. Psychologists strive to understand diversity in the aging process, particularly how sociocultural factors such as gender, race, ethnicity, socioeconomic status, sexual orientation, disability status, and urban/rural residence may influence the experience and expression of health and of psychological problems in later life.

The older adult population is highly diverse and is expected to become even more so in coming decades (Administration on Aging, 2011). The heterogeneity among older adults surpasses that seen in other age groups (Cosentino, Brickman, & Manly, 2011; Crowther & Zeiss, 2003). Psychological issues experienced by older adults may differ according to factors such as age cohort, gender, race, ethnicity and cultural background, sexual orientation, rural/frontier living status, education and socioeconomic status, and religion. It should be noted that age may be a weaker predictor of outcomes than factors such as demographic characteristics, physical health, functional ability, or living situation (Lichtenberg, 2010). For example, clinical presentations of symptoms and syndromes may reflect interactions among these factors and type of clinical setting or living situation (Gatz, 1998; Knight & Lee, 2008). . . .

Guideline 6. Psychologists strive to be familiar with current information about biological and health-related aspects of aging.

In working with older adults, psychologists are encouraged to be informed about the normal biological changes that accompany aging. Though there are considerable individual differences in these changes, with advancing age the older adult almost inevitably experiences changes in sensory acuity, physical appearance and body composition, hormone levels, peak performance capacity of most body organ systems, and immunological responses and increased susceptibility to illness (Masoro & Austad, 2010; Saxon, Etten, & Perkins, 2010). Disease accelerates age-related decline in sensory, motor, and cognitive functioning, whereas lifestyle factors may mitigate or moderate the effects of aging on functioning. Such biological aging processes may have significant hereditary or genetic components (McClearn & Vogler, 2001), about which older adults and their families may have concerns. Adjusting to age-related physical change is a core task of the normal psychological aging process (Saxon et al., 2010). Fortunately, lifestyle changes, psychological interventions, and the use of assistive devices can often lessen the burden of some of these changes. When older clients discuss concerns about their physical health, most often they involve memory impairment, vision, hearing, sleep, continence, and energy levels or fatigability.

. . .

CLINICAL ISSUES

Guideline 7. Psychologists strive to be familiar with current knowledge about cognitive changes in older adults.

. . . From a clinical perspective, one of the greatest challenges facing practitioners who work with older adults is knowing when to attribute subtle observed cognitive changes to an underlying neurodegenerative condition versus normal developmental changes. Further, several moderating and mediating factors contribute to age-associated cognitive changes within and across individuals.

For most older adults, age-associated changes in cognition are mild and do not significantly interfere with daily functioning. The vast majority of older adults continue to engage in longstanding pursuits, interact intellectually with others, actively solve real-life problems, and achieve new learning. Cognitive functions that are better preserved with age include aspects of language and vocabulary, wisdom, reasoning, and other skills that rely primarily on stored information and knowledge (P. B. Baltes, 1993). Older adults remain capable of new learning, though typically at a somewhat slower pace than younger individuals. . . .

Guideline 8. Psychologists strive to understand the functional capacity of older adults in the social and physical environment.

Most older adults maintain high levels of functioning, suggesting that factors related to health, lifestyle, and the match between functional abilities and environmental demands more powerfully determine performance than does age (P. B. Baltes, Lindenberger, & Staudinger, 2006; Lichtenberg, 2010). Functional ability and related factors weigh heavily in decisions older adults make about employment, health care, relationships, leisure activities, and living environment. For example, many older adults may wish or need to remain in the work force (Sterns & Dawson, 2012). However, the accumulation of health problems and their effect on functioning may make that difficult for some older adults. Changes in functional abilities may impact other aspects of older adults' lives. Intimate relationships may become strained by the presence of health problems in one or both partners. Discord among adult children may be precipitated or exacerbated because of differing expectations about how much care each child should provide to the impaired parent (Qualls & Noecker, 2009). Increasing needs for health care can be frustrating for older adults because of demands on time, finances, transportation, and lack of communication among care providers. . . .

Guideline 9. Psychologists strive to be knowledgeable about psychopathology within the aging population and cognizant of the prevalence and nature of that psychopathology when providing services to older adults.

Most older people have good mental health. However, prevalence estimates suggest that approximately 20%–22% of older adults may meet criteria for some form of mental disorder, including dementia (Jeste et al., 1999; Karel, Gatz, & Smyer, 2012). Older women have higher rates of certain mental disorders (e.g., depression) than do men (Norton et al., 2006), with research continuing to support a slightly lower subjective well-being for older women when compared to their male counterparts, most likely due to disadvantages older women experience in regard to health, socioeconomic status, and widowhood (Pinquart & Sörensen, 2001). For those living in a long-term care setting during their later years, estimates are much higher, with almost 80% suffering from some form of mental disorder (Conn, Herrmann, Kaye, Rewilak, & Schogt, 2007). Older adults may present a broad array of psychological issues for clinical attention. These issues include almost all of the problems that affect younger adults. In addition, older adults may seek or benefit from psychological services when they experience challenges specific to late life, including developmental issues and social changes. Some problems that rarely affect younger adults, notably, dementias due to degenerative brain diseases and stroke, are much more common in old age. . . .

ASSESSMENT

Guideline 10. Psychologists strive to be familiar with the theory, research, and practice of various methods of assessment with older adults, and knowledgeable of assessment instruments that are culturally and psychometrically suitable for use with them.

Relevant methods for assessment of older adults may include clinical interviewing, use of self-report measures, cognitive performance testing, direct behavioral observation, role play, psychophysiological techniques, neuroimaging, and use of informant data. Psychologists should aspire to have familiarity with contemporary biological approaches for differential diagnosis or disease characterization and with how this information can contribute to the assessment process and outcome, even if they do not apply these techniques themselves.

A thorough geriatric assessment is preferably an interdisciplinary one, focusing on both strengths and weaknesses, determining how problems interrelate, and taking account of contributing factors. In evaluating older adults it is useful to ascertain the possible influence of medications and medical disorders, since, for example, medical disorders sometimes mimic psychological disorders. Other possible influences to review include immediate environmental factors on the presenting problem(s) and the nature and extent of the individual's familial or other social support. In many contexts, particularly hospital and outpatient care settings, psychologists are frequently asked to evaluate older adults with regard to depression, anxiety, cognitive impairment, sleep disturbance, suicide risk factors, psychotic symptoms, decision-making capacity, and the management of behavior problems associated with these and other disorders. . . .

Guideline 11. Psychologists strive to develop skill in accommodating older adults' specific characteristics and the assessment contexts.

At times the practitioner may face the challenge of adapting assessment procedures to accommodate the particular impairments or living contexts of older adults (Edelstein et al., 2012). For example, with older adults who have sensory or communication problems, elements of the evaluation process may include assessing the extent of these impediments, modifying other assessments to work around such problems, and taking these modifications into account when interpreting the test findings. In particular, clinicians would not want to confuse cognitive impairment with sensory deficits.

The effects of vision deficits can be attenuated to some degree through oral presentation of assessment questions and encouragement of the use of corrective lenses, nonglare paper, and bright light in the testing environment. To be useful, self-administered assessment forms may have to be reprinted in a larger font (e.g., 16 point) or enlarged if administered by computer. The effects of hearing deficits can be attenuated through the use of hearing aids and other assistive listening devices (e.g., headset with amplifier). Hearing difficulties in older adults tend to be worse at higher frequencies, and thus it can be helpful for female psychologists, in particular, to lower the pitch of their voices. When making accommodations in the assessment process, psychologists strive to be knowledgeable about how such accommodations may influence/alter the specific cognitive demands of the task. To reduce the influence of sensory problems, it may also be useful to modify the assessment environment in various ways (e.g., avoid glaring lights, and lower the background noise, which may tend to be especially distracting; National Institute on Deafness and Other Communication Disorders, 2010). . . .

Guideline 12. Psychologists strive to develop skill at conducting and interpreting cognitive and functional ability evaluations.

Quite commonly, when evaluating older adults, psychologists may use specialized procedures to help determine the nature of and bases for cognitive difficulties, functional impairment, or behavioral disturbances (Attix & Welsh-Bohmer, 2006; Cosentino et al., 2011; Lichtenberg, 2010). Psychologists are often asked to characterize an older adult's current cognitive profile and determine whether it represents a significant change from an earlier time and, if so, whether the observed problems are due to a specific neurodegenerative process, a psychiatric issue, and/or other causes (Morris & Brookes, 2013). Assessments can range from a brief cognitive screening to in-depth diagnostic evaluation. Cognitive screening typically involves use of brief instruments to identify global impairment with high sensitivity but with relatively low diagnostic specificity. Diagnostic evaluations include more comprehensive assessment than screening instruments and can be used to characterize the nature and extent of cognitive deficits. Assessment of cognition may be appropriate for older adults who are at risk for dementia or have suspected cognitive decline due to an underlying neurodegenerative disorder, mental disorder, or medical condition. Federal legislation provides for screening for cognitive impairment during annual wellness visits for Medicare beneficiaries (Patient Protection and Affordable Care Act, 2010). . . .

INTERVENTION, CONSULTATION, AND OTHER SERVICE PROVISION

Guideline 13. Psychologists strive to be familiar with the theory, research, and practice of various methods of intervention with older adults, particularly with current research evidence about their efficacy with this age group.

Psychologists have been adapting their treatments and doing psychological interventions with older adults over the entire history of psychotherapy (Knight, Kelly, & Gatz, 1992; Molinari, 2011). As different theoretical approaches have emerged, each has been applied to older adults, including psychodynamic psychotherapy, behavior modification, cognitive therapy, interpersonal psychotherapy, and problem-solving therapy. In addition, efforts have been made to use the knowledge base from research on adult development and aging to inform intervention efforts with older adults in a way that draws upon psychological and social capacities built during the individual's life span (Anderson et al., 2012; Knight, 2004).

Evidence documents that older adults respond well to a variety of forms of psychotherapy and can benefit from psychological interventions to a degree comparable with younger adults (APA, 2012d; Pinquart & Sörensen, 2001; Scogin, 2007; Zarit & Knight, 1996). . . .

Guideline 14. Psychologists strive to be familiar with and develop skill in applying culturally sensitive, specific psychotherapeutic interventions and environmental modifications with older adults and their families, including adapting interventions for use with this age group.

Such interventions may include individual, group, couples, and family therapies. Examples of interventions that may be unique to older adults or that are very commonly used with this population include reminiscence and life review; grief therapy; psychotherapy focusing on developmental issues and behavioral adaptations in late life; expressive therapies for those with communication difficulties; methods for enhancing cognitive function in later years; and psychoeducational programs for older adults, family members, and other caregivers (APA, Presidential Task Force on Caregivers, 2011; Gallagher-Thompson & Coon, 2007; Qualls, 2008). No single modality of psychological intervention is preferable for all older adults. The selection of the most appropriate treatments and modes of delivery depends on the nature of the problem(s) involved, clinical goals, the immediate situation, and the individual patient's characteristics, preferences, gender, cultural background (Gum et al., 2006; Landreville, Landry, Baillargeon, Guerette, & Matteau, 2001), and place on the continuum of care . . . , and, as noted earlier, on the availability of an evidence-based practice. . . .

Guideline 15. Psychologists strive to understand and address issues pertaining to the provision of services in the specific settings in which older adults are typically located or encountered.

Psychologists often work with older adults in a variety of settings, reflecting the continuum of care along which most services are delivered (APA, Presidential Task Force on Integrated Health Care for an Aging Population, 2008). These service delivery sites encompass various community settings where older people are found, including community-based and in-home care settings (e.g., senior centers, their own homes or apartments . . .); outpatient settings (e.g., mental health or primary care clinics, independent practitioner offices, or outpatient group programs); day programs (such as adult day care centers, psychiatric partial hospitalization programs) serving older adults with multiple or complex problems; inpatient medical or psychiatric hospital settings; and long-term care settings (such as nursing homes, assisted living, hospice, and other congregate care sites). . . .

Guideline 16. Psychologists strive to recognize and address issues related to the provision of prevention and health promotion services with older adults.

Psychologists may contribute to the health and well-being of older adults by helping to provide psychoeducational programs (e.g., Alvidrez, Areán, &

Stewart, 2005) and by involvement in broader prevention efforts and other community-oriented interventions. Related efforts include advocacy within health care and political legal systems (Hartman-Stein, 1998; Hinrichsen, Kietzman, et al., 2010; Karel, Gatz, & Smyer, 2012; Norris, 2000). In such activities, psychologists integrate their knowledge of clinical problems and techniques with consultation skills, strategic interventions, and preventive community or organizational programming to benefit substantial numbers of older adults (Cohen et al., 2006). Such work may entail becoming familiar with outreach, case finding, referral, and early intervention, as these relate to particular groups of at-risk older adults (Berman & Furst, 2011). An important aspect of these efforts is for psychologists to understand the strengths and limitations of local community resources relative to their domains of practice, or the risk factors affecting the older adult group of concern. . . .

Guideline 17. Psychologists strive to understand issues pertaining to the provision of consultation services in assisting older adults.

Psychologists who work with older adults are frequently asked to provide consultation on aging-related issues to a variety of groups and individuals. Many psychologists possess a complement of knowledge and skills that are especially valuable in the provision of consultation, including in the areas of social psychology, developmental psychology, diversity, group dynamics, communications, program design and evaluation, and others. Psychologists who work with older adults possess such knowledge and skills with specific relevance to the older adult age group (APA, Presidential Task Force on Integrated Health Care for an Aging Population, 2008). Psychologists frequently consult with family members of older relatives who have mental health problems, especially those with dementia. Given the anticipated dearth of aging specialists as the size of the older population rapidly grows, psychologists with aging expertise will likely play important roles in educating other professionals about aging (Institute of Medicine, 2012). . . .

Guideline 18. In working with older adults, psychologists are encouraged to understand the importance of interfacing with other disciplines, and to make referrals to other disciplines and/or to work with them in collaborative teams and across a range of sites, as appropriate.

In their work with older adults, psychologists are encouraged to be cognizant of the importance of a coordinated care approach and may collaborate with other health, mental health, or social service professionals who are responsible for and/or provide particular forms of care to the same older individuals. As most older adults suffer from chronic health problems for which medications have been prescribed, coordination with the professionals prescribing them to the older adult is often very useful. Other disciplines typically involved in coordinated care, either as part of a team or to which referrals may be appropriate, include physicians, nurses, social workers, pharmacists, and associated others such as direct care workers, clergy, and lawyers. Psychologists can help a group of professionals become an interdisciplinary team rather than function as a multidisciplinary one by generating effective strategies for integration and coordination of services provided by the various team members (Zeiss, 2003; Zeiss & Karlin, 2008; see *Blueprint for Change: Achieving Integrated Healthcare for an Aging Population*, APA, Presidential Task Force on Integrated Health Care for an Aging Population, 2008). . . .

Guideline 19. Psychologists strive to understand the special ethical and/or legal issues entailed in providing services to older adults.

It is important for psychologists to strive to ensure the right of older adults with whom they work to direct their own lives. Conflicts sometimes arise among family members, formal caregivers, and physically frail or cognitively impaired older adults because some concerned individuals may believe that these older adults do not possess the ability to make decisions about their own lives that can affect their safety and well-being. Psychologists are sometimes called upon to evaluate one or more domains of capacity of older adults (e.g., medical, financial, contractual, testamentary, or independent living decision making; Moye, Marson, & Edelstein, 2013). . . . Psychologists working with older adults are encouraged to be prepared to work through difficult ethical dilemmas in ways that balance considerations of the ethical principles of beneficence and autonomy—that is, guarding the older adult's safety and well-being as well as recognizing the individual's right to make his or her own decisions to the extent possible (Karel, 2011; Marson et al., 2011; Moye & Marson, 2007). . . .

PROFESSIONAL ISSUES AND EDUCATION

Guideline 20. Psychologists strive to be knowledgeable about public policy and state and federal laws and regulations related to the provision of and reimbursement for psychological services to older adults and the business of practice.

With the recent passage of the Affordable Care Act, the health care landscape continues to change. Psychologists who serve older adults are encouraged to be alert to changes in health care policy and practice that will impact their professional work, including practice establishment, state laws that govern practice, potential for litigation, and reimbursement for services.

Medicare (the federal health insurance program for persons 65 years of age and older and for younger persons with disabilities) is a chief payer for mental health services for older adults. Psychologists were named as independent providers under Medicare in 1989, and the regulations that govern provision of services as well as reimbursement rules and regulations have evolved in the intervening years (Hinrichsen, 2010). Therefore, it is important for those who provide psychological services to older adults to be knowledgeable of the structure of the Medicare program and the rules that govern provision of and reimbursement for services billed to Medicare (Hartman-Stein & Georgoulakis, 2008). . . .

Guideline 21. Psychologists are encouraged to increase their knowledge, understanding, and skills with respect to working with older adults through training, supervision, consultation, and continuing education.

As the need for psychological services grows in the older population, additional health care providers will be required, especially those with knowledge and skills in working with older adults (Institute of Medicine, 2012). Practitioners often work competently with older adults who have issues similar to those of younger clients. With increasing problem complexity, psychological practice with older adults benefits from the acquisition and application of specialized knowledge and skills (Knight et al., 2009). For example, older adults can present with a range of unique, life-stage challenges, including adjustment to retirement, aging with acquired and congenital disabilities, chronic illnesses, progressive cognitive impairment, and end-of-life issues that most young and middle-aged adults encounter less frequently. . . .

REFERENCES

Abeles, N., Cooley, S., Deitch, I. M., Harper, M. S., Hinrichsen, G., Lopez, M. A., & Molinari, V. A. (1998). *What practitioners should know about working with older adults.* Retrieved from http://www.apa.org/pi/aging/resources/guides/practitioners-should-know.aspx

Administration on Aging. (2011). *Minority aging.* Retrieved from https://acl.gov/aging-and-disability-in-america/data-and-research/minority-aging

Aldwin, C. M., Park, C. L., & Spiro, A. (Eds.). (2007). *Handbook of health psychology and aging.* New York, NY: Guilford Press.

Alvidrez, J., Areán, P. A., & Stewart, A. L. (2005). Psychoeducation to increase psychotherapy entry for older African Americans. *American Journal of Geriatric Psychiatry, 13*(7), 554–561. doi:10.1097/00019442-200507000-00003

American Psychological Association. (2002a). Ethical principles of psychologists and code of conduct. *American Psychologist, 57*(12), 1060–1073. doi:10.1037/0003-066X.57.12.1060

American Psychological Association. (2002c). *Guidelines on multicultural education, training research, practice, and organizational change for psychologists.* Retrieved from http://www.apa.org/pi/oema/resources/policy/multicultural-guidelines.aspx

American Psychological Association. (2010a). *Ethical principles of psychologists and code of conduct including 2010 amendments.* Retrieved from http://www.apa.org/ethics/code/index.aspx

American Psychological Association. (2012d). *Resolution on the recognition of psychotherapy effectiveness*. Retrieved from http://www.apa.org/about/policy/resolution-psychotherapy.aspx

American Psychological Association, Center for Workforce Studies. (2008). *2008 APA Survey of Psychology Health Service Providers*. Retrieved from http://www.apa.org/workforce/publications/08-hsp/index.aspx

American Psychological Association, Commission on Accreditation. (2008). *Policy statements & implementing regulations*. Retrieved from http://www.apa.org/ed/accreditation/about/policies/implementing-regs.pdf

American Psychological Association, Presidential Task Force on Caregivers. (2011). *APA Family Caregiver Briefcase*. Retrieved from http://www.apa.org/pi/about/publications/caregivers/index.aspx

American Psychological Association, Presidential Task Force on Integrated Health Care for an Aging Population. (2008). *Blueprint for change: Achieving integrated health care for an aging population*. Retrieved from http://www.apa.org/pi/aging/programs/integrated/integrated-healthcare-report.pdf

Anderson, M. L., Goodman, J., & Schlossberg, N. K. (2012). *Counseling adults in transition: Linking Scholossberg's theory with practice in a diverse world*. New York, NY: Springer.

Attix, D. K., & Welsh-Bohmer, K. A. (Eds.). (2006). *Geriatric neuropsychology: Assessment and intervention*. New York, NY: Guilford Press.

Baltes, P. B. (1993). The aging mind: Potential and limits. *The Gerontologist, 33*(5), 580–594. doi:10.1093/geront/33.5.580

Baltes, P. B., Lindenberger, U., & Staudinger, U. M. (2006). Theoretical models of human development. In R. M. Lerner & W. Damon (Eds.), *Life span theory in developmental psychology. Handbook of child psychology* (6th ed., Vol. 1, pp. 569–664). Hoboken, NJ: Wiley.

Berman, J., & Furst, L. M. (2011). *Depressed older adults: Education and screening*. New York, NY: Springer.

Brown, L. M., Gibson, M., & Elmore, D. (2012). Disaster behavioral health and older adults: American and Canadian readiness and response. In J. L. Framingham & M. L. Teasley (Eds.), *Behavioral health response to disasters* (pp. 159–174). Boca Raton, FL: CRC. doi:10.1201/b11954-14

Butler, R. N. (1969). Ageism: Another form of bigotry. *The Gerontologist, 9*, 243–246.

Cohen, G. D., Perlstein, S., Chapline, J., Kelly, J., Firth, K., & Simmens, S. (2006). The impact of professionally conducted cultural programs on the physical health, mental health, and social functioning of older adults. *The Gerontologist, 46*(6), 726–734. doi:10.1093/geront/46.6.726

Conn, D., Herrmann, N., Kaye, A., Rewilak, D., & Schogt, B. (Eds.). (2007). *Practical psychiatry in the long-term care home* (3rd ed.). Boston, MA: Hogrefe & Huber.

Cook, J. M., & Elmore, D. L. (2009). Disaster mental health in older adults: Symptoms, policy and planning. In Y. Neria, S. Galea, & F. Norris (Eds.), *Mental health consequences of disasters* (pp. 233–263). New York, NY: Cambridge University Press. doi:10.1017/CBO9780511730030.014

Cook, J. M., & O'Donnell, C. (2005). Assessment and psychological treatment of post-traumatic stress disorder in older adults. *Journal of Geriatric Psychiatry and Neurology, 18*(2), 61–71. doi:10.1177/0891988705276052

Cosentino, S. A., Brickman, A. M., & Manly, J. J. (2011). Neuropsychological assessment of the dementias of late life. In K. W. Schaie & S. L. Willis (Eds.), *Handbook of the psychology of aging* (7th ed., pp. 339–352). San Diego, CA: Elsevier Academic Press. doi:10.1016/B978-0-12-380882-0.00022-X

Crowther, M. R., & Zeiss, A. M. (2003). Aging and mental health. In J. S. Mio & G. Y. Iwamasa (Eds.), *Culturally diverse mental health: The challenge of research and resistance* (pp. 309–322). New York, NY: Brunner-Routledge.

Edelstein, B. A., Martin, R. R., & Gerolimatos, L. A. (2012). Assessment in geriatric settings. In J. R. Graham & J. A. Naglieri (Eds.), *Handbook of psychology: Assessment psychology* (pp. 425–448). Hoboken, NJ: Wiley. doi:10.1002/9781118133880.hop210017

Gallagher-Thompson, D., & Coon, D. W. (2007). Evidence-based psychological treatments for distress in family caregivers of older adults. *Psychology and Aging, 22*, 37–51. doi:10.1037/0882-.7974.22.1.37

Gatz, M. (1998). Towards a developmentally-informed theory of mental disorder in older adults. In J. Lomranz (Ed.), *Handbook of aging and mental health* (pp. 101–120). New York, NY: Plenum Press.

Gatz, M., & Pearson, C. G. (1988). Ageism revised and the provision of psychological services. *American Psychologist, 43*(3), 184–189. doi:10.1037/0003-066X.43.3.184

Gum, A. M., Areán, P. A., Hunkeler, E., Tang, L., Kanton, W., Hitchcock, P., . . . Unützer, J. (2006). Depression treatment preferences in older primary care patients. *The Gerontologist, 46*(1), 14–22. doi:10.1093/geront/46.1.14

Hartman-Stein, P. E. (1998). Hope amidst the behavioral healthcare crisis. In P. E. Hartman-Stein (Ed.), *Innovative behavioral healthcare for older adults* (pp. 201–214). San Francisco, CA: Jossey-Bass.

Hartman-Stein, P. E., & Georgoulakis, J. M. (2008). How Medicare shapes behavioral health practice with older adults in the U.S.: Issues and recommendations for practitioners. In D. G. Gallagher-Thompson, A. M. Steffen, & L. W. Thompson (Eds.), *Handbook of behavioral and cognitive therapies with older adults* (pp. 323–334). New York, NY: Springer. doi:10.1007/978-0-387-72007-4_21

Hayslip, B., & Kaminski, P. L. (2005). Grandparents raising their grandchildren: A Review of the literature and suggestions for practice. *The Gerontologist, 45*(2), 262–269. doi:10.1093/geront/45.2.262

Hillman, J. (2012). *Sexuality and aging: Clinical perspectives*. New York, NY: Springer.

Hinrichsen, G. A., Kietzman, K. G., Alkema, G. E., Bragg, E. J., Hensel, B. K., Miles, T. P., . . . Zerzan, J. (2010). Influencing public policy to improve the lives of older Americans. *The Gerontologist, 50*(6), 735–743. doi:10.1093/geront/gnq034

Hinrichsen, G. A. (2000). Knowledge of and interest in geropsychology among psychology trainees. *Professional Psychology: Research and Practice, 31*, 442–445. doi:10.1037/0735-7028.31.4.442

Hinrichsen, G. A. (2010). Public policy and the provision of psychological services to older adults. *Professional Psychology: Research and Practice, 41*(2), 97–103. doi:10.1037/a0018643

Institute of Medicine. (2012). *The mental health and substance use workforce for older adults: In whose hands?* Retrieved from http://www.iom.edu/Reports/2012/The-Mental-Health-and-Substance-Use-Workforce-for-Older-Adults.aspx

Ivey, D. C., Wieling, E., & Harris, S. M. (2000). Save the young—the elderly have lived their lives: Ageism in marriage and family therapy. *Family Process, 39*(2), 163–175. doi:10.1111/j.1545-5300.2000.39202.x

James, J. W., & Haley, W. E. (1995). Age and health bias in practicing clinical psychologists. *Psychology and Aging, 10*, 610–616. doi:10.1037//0882-7974.10.4.610

Jeste, D. V., Alexopoulos, G. S., Bartels, S. J., Cummings, J. L., Gallo, J. J., Gottlieb, G. L., . . . Lebowitz, B. D. (1999). Consensus statement on the upcoming crisis in geriatric mental health: Research agenda for the next 2 decades. *Archives of General Psychiatry, 56*(9), 848–853. doi:10.1001/archpsyc.56.9.848

Kane, M. N. (2004). Ageism and intervention: What social work students believe about treating people differently because of age. *Educational Gerontology, 30*(9), 767–784. doi:10.1080/03601270490498098

Karel, M. J. (2011). Ethics. In V. Molinari (Ed.), *Specialty competencies in geropsychology* (pp. 115–142). New York, NY: Oxford University Press.

Karel, M. J., Gatz, M., & Smycr, M. A. (2012). Aging and mental health in the decade ahead: What psychologists need to know. *American Psychologist, 67*, 184–198. doi:10.1037/a0025393

Kastenbaum, R. (1999). Dying and bereavement. In J. C. Cavanaugh & S. K. Whitbourne (Eds.), *Gerontology: An interdisciplinary perspective* (pp. 155–185). New York, NY: Oxford University Press.

King, D. A., & Wynne, L. C. (2004). The emergence of "family integrity" in later life. *Family Process, 43*(1), 7–21. doi:10.1111/j.1545-5300.2004.04301003.x

Knight, B. G. (2004). *Psychotherapy with older adults* (3rd ed.). Thousand Oaks, CA: Sage.

Knight, B. G., & Lee, L. O. (2008). Contextual adult lifespan theory for adapting psychotherapy. In K. Laidlaw & B. Knight (Eds.), *Handbook of emotional disorders in later life: Assessment and treatment* (pp. 59–88). New York, NY: Oxford University Press.

Knight, B. G., Karel, M. J., Hinrichsen, G. A., Qualls, S. H., & Duffy, M. (2009). Pikes Peak model for training in professional geropsychology. *American Psychologist, 64*(3), 205–214. doi:10.1037/a0015059

Knight, B. G., Kelly, M., & Gatz, M. (1992). Psychotherapy and the older adult: An historical review. In D. K. Freedheim (Ed.), *History of psychotherapy: A century of change* (pp. 528–551). Washington, DC: American Psychological Association.

Knight, B. G., Teri, L., Wohlford, P., & Santos, J. (Eds.). (1995). *Mental health services for older adults: Implications for training and practice in geropsychology*. Washington, DC: American Psychological Association. doi:10.1037/10184-000

Labouvie-Vief, G., Diehl, M., Jain, E., & Zhang, F. (2007). Six-year change in affect optimization and affect complexity across the adult life span: A further examination. *Psychology and Aging, 22*(4), 738–751. doi:10.1037/0882-7974.22.4.738

Landreville, P., Landry, J., Baillargeon, L., Guerette, A., & Matteau, E. (2001). Older adults' acceptance of psychological and pharmacological treatments for depression. *Journals of Gerontology, Series B: Psychological Sciences and Social Sciences, 56*(5), 285–291. doi:10.1093/geronb/56.5.P285

Levenson, R. W., Carstensen, L. L., & Gottman, J. M. (1993). Long-term marriage: Age, gender, and satisfaction. *Psychology and Aging, 8*(2), 301–313. doi:10.1037/0882-7974.8.2.301

Levy, B. R., & Myers, L. M. (2004). Preventive health behaviors influenced by self-perceptions of aging. *Preventive Medicine, 39*(3), 625–629. doi:10.1016/j.ypmed.2004.02.029

Lichtenberg, P. A. (Ed.). (2010). *Handbook of assessment in clinical gerontology* (2nd ed.). New York, NY: Wiley.

Marson, D. C., Hebert, K., & Solomon, A. C. (2011). Assessing civil competencies in older adults with dementia: Consent capacity, financial capacity, and testamentary capacity. In G. J. Larrabee (Ed.), *Forensic neuropsychology. A scientific approach* (pp. 334–377). New York, NY: Oxford University Press.

Masoro, E. J., & Austad, S. N. (Eds.). (2010). *Handbook of the biology of aging* (7th ed.). San Diego, CA: Academic Press.

Matthias, R. E., Lubben, J. E., Atchison, K. A., & Schweitzer, S. O. (1997). Sexual activity and satisfaction among very old adults: Results from a community-dwelling Medicare population survey. *The Gerontologist, 37*(1), 6–14. doi:10.1093/geront/37.1.6

McClearn, G. E., & Vogler, G. P. (2001). The genetics of behavioral aging. In J. E. Birren & K. W. Schaie (Eds.), *Handbook of the psychology of aging* (5th ed., pp. 109–131). San Diego, CA: Academic Press.

Mohlman, J., Sirota, K. G., Papp, L. A., Staples, A. M., King, A., & Gorenstein, E. E. (2011). Clinical interviewing with older adults. *Cognitive and Behavioral Practice, 19*, 89–100. doi:10.1016/j.cbpra.2010.10.001

Molinari, V. (2011). Professional identification. In V. Molinari (Ed.), *Specialty competencies in geropsychology* (pp. 1–13). New York, NY: Oxford University Press.

Molinari, V., Karel, M., Jones, S., Zeiss, A., Cooley, S., Wray, L., . . . Gallagher-Thompson, D. (2003). Recommendations about the knowledge and skills required of psychologists working with older adults. *Professional Psychology: Research and Practice, 34*, 435–443. doi:10.1037/0735-7028.34.4.435

Morris, R. G., & Brookes, R. L. (2013). Neuropsychological assessment of older adults. In L. H. Goldstein & J. E. McNeil (Eds.), *Clinical neuropsychology: A practical guide to assessment and management for clinicians* (2nd ed., pp. 347–374). Hoboken, NJ: Wiley.

Moye, J., & Marson, D. C. (2007). Assessment of decision-making capacity in older adults: An emerging area of practice and research. *Journals of Gerontology, Series B: Psychological Sciences and Social Sciences, 62*(1), P3–P11. doi:10.1093/geronb/62.1.P3

Moye, J., Marson, D. C., & Edelstein, B. (2013). Assessment of capacity in an aging society. *American Psychologist, 68*(3), 158–171. doi:10.1037/a0032159

National Institute on Deafness and Other Communication Disorders. (2010). *Healthy People 2010 hearing health progress review*. Retrieved from http://www.nidcd.nih.gov/health/healthyhearing/what_hh/pages/progress_review_04.aspx

Norris, M. P. (2000). Public policy and the delivery of mental health care to older adults. In V. Molinari (Ed.), *Professional psychology in long-term care: A comprehensive guide* (pp. 425–443). New York, NY: Hatherleigh Press.

Norton, M. C. Skoog, I., Toone, L., Corcoran, C., Tschanz, J. T., Lisota, R. D., . . . Cache County Investigators. (2006). Three-year incidence of first-onset depressive syndrome in a population sample of older adults: The Cache County Study. *American Journal of Geriatric Psychiatry, 14*(3), 237–245. doi:10.1097/01.JGP.0000196626.34881.42

Patient Protection and Affordable Care Act, 42 C.F.R. § 410.15(a) (2010). Retrieved from http://www.gpo.gov/fdsys/pkg/CFR-2011-title42-vol2/pdf/CFR-2011-title42-vol2-sec410-15.pdf

Pinquart, M., & Sörensen, S. (2001). How effective are psychotherapeutic and other psychosocial interventions with older adults? A meta-analysis. *Journal of Mental Health and Aging, 7*, 207–243.

Qualls, S. H. (2008). Caregiver family therapy. In B. Knight & K. Laidlaw (Eds.), *Handbook of emotional disorders in older adults* (pp. 183–209). Oxford, England: Oxford University Press.

Qualls, S. H., & Benight, C. C. (2007). The role of clinical health geropsychology in the health care of older adults. In C. M. Aldwin, C. L. Park, & A. Spiro (Eds.), *Handbook of health psychology and aging* (pp. 367–389). New York, NY: Guilford Press.

Qualls, S. H., & Noecker, T. L. (2009). Caregiver family therapy for conflicted families. In S. H. Qualls & S. H. Zarit (Eds.), *Aging families and caregiving* (pp. 155–188). Hoboken, NJ: Wiley.

Qualls, S. H., Segal, D., Norman, S., Niederehe, G., & Gallagher-Thompson, D. (2002). Psychologists in practice with older adults: Current patterns, sources of training, and need for continuing education. *Professional Psychology: Research and Practice, 33*, 435–442. http://dx.doi.org/10.1037/0735-7028.33.5.435

Santos, J. F., & VandenBos, G. R. (Eds.). (1982). *Psychology and the older adult: Challenges for training in the 1980s*. Washington, DC: American Psychological Association.

Saxon, S. V., Etten, M. J., & Perkins, E. A. (2010). *Physical change and aging: A guide for the helping professions*. New York, NY: Springer.

Schulz, R., & Heckhausen, J. (1996). A life span model of successful aging. *American Psychologist, 51*, 702–714. doi:10.1037//0003-066X.51.7.702

Scogin, F. (2007). Introduction to the special section on evidence-based psychological treatments for older adults. *Psychology and Aging, 22*, 1–3. doi:10.1037/0882-7974.22.1.1

Stcrns, H. L., & Dawson, N. T. (2012). Emerging perspectives on resilience in adulthood and later life: Work, retirement, and resilience. *Annual Review of Gerontology and Geriatrics, 32*(1), 211–230. doi:10.1891/0198-8794.32.211

Zarit, S. H., & Knight, B. G. (Eds.). (1996). *A guide to psychotherapy and aging: Effective clinical interventions in a life-stage context.* Washington, DC: American Psychological Association.

Zeiss, A. M. (2003). Providing interdisciplinary geriatric team care: What does it really take? *Clinical Psychology: Science and Practice, 10,* 115–119. doi:10.1093/clipsy.10.1.115

Zeiss, A. M., & Karlin, B. E. (2008). Integrating mental health and primary care services in the Department of Veterans Affairs health care system. *Journal of Clinical Psychology in Medical Settings, 15*(1), 73–78. doi:10.1007/s10880-008-9100-4

Zweig, R. A., Siegel, L., & Snyder, R. (2006). Doctoral gero-psychology training in primary care: Preliminary findings from a clinical training project. *Journal of Clinical Psychology in Medical Settings, 13,* 19–28. doi:10.1007/s10880-005-9010-7

7.9. Guidelines for Assessment of and Intervention With Persons With Disabilities

American Psychological Association

. . .

To work effectively with people who have disabilities, psychologists need to become familiar with how disability influences a client's psychological well-being and functioning. Psychologists should also become aware of how their own attitudes, reactions, conceptions of disability, and possible biases may

From "Guidelines for Assessment of and Intervention With Persons With Disabilities," by the American Psychological Association, 2012, *American Psychologist*, 67, pp. 43–62. Copyright 2011 by the American Psychological Association.

These guidelines were developed by the American Psychological Association's (APA's) Task Force on Guidelines for Assessment and Treatment of Persons With Disabilities. The task force members included Kurt F. Geisinger (University of Nebraska, Lincoln); Kay Kriegsman (independent practice, Bethesda, Maryland); Irene W. Leigh (Gallaudet University); Elina Manghi (Adler School of Professional Psychology, University of Illinois at Chicago); Izabela Z. Schultz (University of British Columbia, Canada); Tom Seekins (University of Montana, Missoula); and Greg Taliaferro (Cincinnati Psychoanalytic Institute). Izabela Z. Schultz and Greg Taliaferro were the task force co-chairs.

The task force wishes to acknowledge Izabela Schultz for her foresight regarding the need for guidelines and for initiating their careful development. In addition, the task force is grateful to Rosemarie Alvaro, Thomas Bartlett, Jim Butcher, Susan Drumheller, Michael Dunn, Stephen Flamer, Alan Goldberg, Virginia Gutman, Dara Hamilton, Roger Heller, Tamar Heller, Rosemary Hughes, William Kachman, Monica Kurylo, Kurt Metz, Sharon Nathan, Rhoda Olkin, Sara Palmer, Diana Pullin, Jeff Rosen, Cheryl Shigaki, David Smith, Martha Thurlow, Michael Wehmeyer, Julie Williams, and Gerry Young for their assistance in providing important feedback on several drafts of the guidelines; to Diana Spas (University of Montana, Missoula) for her thorough and thoughtful review and editorial suggestions; to APA's governance groups who reviewed this document and provided valuable feedback and suggestions; and to myriad other individuals for their careful review and comments. The task force is especially grateful to Anju Khubchandani, director of APA's Office on Disability Issues, who adeptly assisted and provided counsel to the task force throughout this project, and to her administrative coordinators, Sara Laney and Mara Lunaria. Greg Taliaferro wished to thank the Research Fund of the Cincinnati Psychoanalytic Institute for its support.

The late Greg Taliaferro served as a member and co-chair of this task force. Greg made an indelible impression not only with his professionalism and determination but with his grace, his courage, and his puckish sense of humor.

This document will expire as APA policy in February 2021. After this date, users should contact the APA Practice Directorate to determine whether the guidelines in this document remain in effect as APA policy.

affect their professional relationships with clients who have disabilities. Further, it is important for psychologists to learn the best "barrier-free" psychological practices for clients with disabilities, including provision of reasonable accommodations and appropriate integration of disability-related issues into assessment and intervention. . . .

The goal of these "Guidelines for Assessment of and Intervention With Persons With Disabilities" is to help psychologists conceptualize and implement more effective, fair, and ethical psychological assessments and interventions with persons with disabilities. The guidelines provide suggestions on ways psychologists can make their practices more accessible and disability-sensitive and on how they might enhance their working relationships with clients with disabilities. Additionally, the guidelines provide information on how psychologists can obtain more education, training, and experience with disability-related matters. . . .

DISABILITY AWARENESS, TRAINING, ACCESSIBILITY, AND DIVERSITY

Guideline 1. Psychologists strive to learn about various disability paradigms and models and their implications for service provision.

The term *disability* is not easily defined, yet the effects of its definition are far-reaching. For example, different legal definitions have implications for obtaining services and benefits. Generally, disabilities are physical, mental, and/or sensory characteristics that affect a person's ability to engage in activities of daily life (U.S. Department of Health and Human Services, 2005). The Americans With Disabilities Act (ADA) Amendments Act of 2008 defines disability as a physical or mental impairment that substantially limits a major life activity, or having a record of such impairment, or being regarded as having such impairment because of an actual or perceived physical or mental impairment. This holds even with the use of equipment designed to mitigate the disability. So, for example, a person with a hearing impairment that interferes with most social interactions would be considered as having a disability even if the use of an augmentative communication device significantly improves his or her ability to engage in conversations. . . .

Guideline 2. Psychologists strive to examine their beliefs and emotional reactions toward various disabilities and determine how these might influence their work.

Research suggests psychologists and other mental health professionals often lack sufficient knowledge of disability issues and have limited experience in working with clients who have disabilities (Leigh et al., 2004; Strike et al., 2004). With little understanding of disability experience, a psychologist may feel anxious, repulsed, fearful, and vulnerable when working with a client who has disabilities (Olkin, 1999a). Lack of experience may lead to erroneous assumptions about clients with disabilities. . . .

Research suggests psychologists tend to believe problems experienced by clients with intellectual disabilities are attributable to their disability as opposed to psychological conditions, such as depression (Mason & Scior, 2004; Nezu & Nezu, 1994; Reiss, Levitan, & Szyszko, 1982). This misperception is an example of *diagnostic overshadowing*, that is, overemphasizing or mistakenly focusing on a client's disability while ignoring important aspects of his or her life, such as life events, capabilities and strengths, and other issues related to the client's presenting problems (Jopp & Keys, 2001; Kemp & Mallinckrodt, 1996; Mason, 2007; Reiss et al., 1982; White, Nichols, Cook, & Spengler, 1995). . . .

Guideline 3. Psychologists strive to increase their knowledge and skills about working with individuals with disabilities through training, supervision, education, and expert consultation.

A psychologist's competence in the area of disability affects the fairness and validity of assessments and interventions. Even highly trained and experienced professionals need continuing education in assessing persons with disabilities, accommodations, evolving technology, and federal and local laws governing disability issues (Holzbauer & Berven, 1999). Continuing education may include division/state association workshops, academic disability studies and rehabilitation psychology courses and certificate programs, re-specialization programs, postdoctoral fellowships, self-study, disability-related coursework, working with a mentor, and/or seeking supervision. . . .

Guideline 4. Psychologists strive to learn about federal and state laws that support and protect people with disabilities.

The goal of laws that protect the rights of individuals with disabilities is to ensure their freedom to participate fully in all aspects of society (Crawford, Jackson, & Godbey, 1991; Pullin, 2002). Three primary federal laws affect individuals with disabilities: Sections 503 and 504 of the Rehabilitation Act of 1973; the Americans With Disabilities Act of 1990 (ADA); and the Individuals With Disabilities Education Act (IDEA; 1975).

Sections 503 and 504 of the Rehabilitation Act of 1973 (Public Law 93-122) prohibit disability-based discrimination by federally funded institutions. This law has increasingly been used in schools to provide services for children who do not qualify under IDEA. . . .

Guideline 5. Psychologists strive to provide a barrier-free physical and communication environment in which clients with disabilities may access psychological services.

An accessible office facilitates service delivery for clients with disabilities. As an alternative, a psychologist may conduct sessions in a mutually convenient accessible location or refer the client to an appropriate psychologist with similar or greater qualifications whose workspace is more easily accessible. Accessibility encompasses the following:

Clients with disabilities need accessible transportation services in order to get to a psychologist's office. An office location with nearby accessible public transportation enhances access to services for clients with disabilities. However, at times, public transportation may entail effort, time, and cost. It is also helpful to be aware of other accessible transportation options, such as wheelchair-accessible van services. . . .

Guideline 6. Psychologists strive to use appropriate language and respectful behavior toward individuals with disabilities.

One way to respect the dignity and worth of all people (Principle E of the "Ethical Principles of Psychologists and Code of Conduct"; APA, 2002) is to support the use of disability-sensitive language. APA's *Publication Manual* cautions against using language which equates individuals with their conditions (e.g., "the disabled" or "the psychotic") or demeans such individuals. Such language may bias diagnostic and intervention processes (Simeonsson & Scarborough, 2001).

Language may reveal our attitudes toward people with disabilities (Hauser, Maxwell-McCaw, Leigh, & Gutman, 2000). Excessively positive language (e.g., "heroic," "despite his disability," or references to "overcoming disability") or excessively negative language (e.g., "afflicted with," "suffering from," or "confined to a wheelchair") regarding people with disabilities focuses on stereotypes, rather than individuals (Katz, Hass, & Bailey, 1988). . . .

Guideline 7. Psychologists strive to understand both the common experiences shared by persons with disabilities and the factors that influence an individual's personal disability experience.

The presence of a disability reveals little about a person (Dunn & Dougherty, 2005; Olkin, 1999b). In addition to their own disability experiences, and those experiences which they share with other people who have disabilities, individuals with disabilities have unique life histories. Becoming acquainted with the experience of living with a disability increases empathy and understanding and thus enhances assessments and interventions.

Daily hassles are a common disability experience. A person who uses a wheelchair may need a friend to verify that a restaurant has an accessible bathroom before deciding to eat there. A student with a visual impairment must make arrangements to obtain an alternative format (e.g., large print, electronic version) of a textbook or secure the services of a reader. A person with a brain injury may need to use special mnemonic devices or procedures to complete errands or juggle medical appointments. Such added challenges can be frustrating, exhausting, and time-consuming. . . .

Guideline 8. Psychologists strive to recognize social and cultural diversity in the lives of persons with disabilities.

The intersection between multiple identities impacts any person's experience and social opportunities. To work effectively with clients who have disabilities, it is important for psychologists to consider how a client's disability-related issues interact with his or her other cultural and social identities and experiences.

In the United States, African American, American Indian, and Latina/o adults are more likely to have a disability than are their non-Latina/o, White, and Asian/Pacific Islander counterparts. Higher rates of disability in people of color are related to several factors, including disproportionately high levels of poverty and unemployment and disproportionately low levels of formal education and access to health care (e.g., Flack et al., 1995). . . .

Guideline 9. Psychologists strive to learn how attitudes and misconceptions, the social environment, and the nature of a person's disability influence development across the life span.

Individuals with disabilities face the same developmental tasks and milestones as anyone, such as forming friendships with peers, pursuing an education, developing a cohesive identity, becoming sexual and establishing intimate relationships, getting a job, conceiving and raising children, and dealing with advancing age. For individuals with disabilities, the ability to achieve developmental goals often depends less on the nature of their disabilities than on their personal relationships with family, significant others, and friends and systemic interactions with their schools, employers, healthcare providers, and communities (Goodley & Lawthom, 2006; Olkin, 1999b; Reeve, 2000; Woolfson, 2004). For example, to transition successfully into adulthood, a high school student with a learning disability needs an encouraging and supportive family and a school that provides appropriate academic and vocational preparation. To negotiate aging successfully, a person with a spinal cord injury may need accessible community supports, personal assistance services, and assistive technology.

Societal attitudes and biases may also restrict an individual's opportunities for typical development (Murray, 2006; Woolfson, 2004). . . .

Guideline 10. Psychologists strive to recognize that families of individuals with disabilities have strengths and challenges.

Families of individuals with disabilities often face additional challenges and stresses. Families spend extra time helping a member with self-care needs, researching a family member's disability, keeping frequent medical and therapy appointments, dealing with social services, making plans for the future, and often bearing extra financial burdens (Ainbinder et al., 1998; Dobson & Middleton, 1998; Powers, 1993; Singer & Powers, 1993; Turnbull & Turnbull, 1991). Along with these stressors, family members may feel frustrated, angry, confused, exhausted, and sad (Rolland & Walsh, 2006).

Despite these issues, most families of people with disabilities are resilient. They meet these challenges and enjoy a quality family life by realigning their priorities, balancing the needs of all family members, and deciding what is important in life (Goodley & Tregaskis, 2006; Rosenthal, Kosciulek, Lee, Frain, & Ditchman, 2009; Wilgosh, Nota, Scorgie, & Soresi, 2004; Wilgosh & Scorgie, 2006). . . .

Guideline 11. Psychologists strive to recognize that people with disabilities are at increased risk for abuse and address abuse-related situations appropriately.

People with disabilities are often vulnerable to violence and abuse (Hassouneh-Phillips & Curry, 2002; Horner-Johnson & Drum, 2006; Hughes, 2005; Sullivan & Knutson, 1998). Compared to youth without disabilities, children and adolescents with disabilities may be three to ten times more likely to be abused or neglected (Sullivan & Knutson, 2000), particularly those with behavior disorders, intellectual disabilities, communication disorders, or multiple disabilities (Sullivan & Knutson, 1998). Women with disabilities, especially older women, are at elevated risk of abuse (Brownridge, 2006; Martin, Rey, Serte-Alvarez, Kepper, Meracco, & Prickers, 2006; Smith, 2008), and they experience abuse for longer durations than women without disabilities (Nosek, Foley, Hughes, & Howland, 2001). Although men with disabilities experience similar types of abuse, society often fails to recognize this (Saxton, McNeff, Powers, Curry, & Limont, 2006). People with disabilities are at risk for abuse because they are perceived to be powerless, easily exploited, and may be physically helpless, socially isolated, emotionally deprived, and/or sexually naïve. . . .

Guideline 12. Psychologists strive to learn about the opportunities and challenges presented by assistive technology.

Assistive technology is defined as equipment, products, or systems that improve the functional capabilities of people with disabilities. Assistive technology includes ventilators that help people breathe; robotics to facilitate limb movement; vans with ramps or lifts for transporting people who use manual and power wheelchairs and scooters; baby-care equipment; adaptive eating utensils; hearing devices and text pagers; reading technology (e.g., JAWS computer screen-reading software; the Kurzweil Reader, which converts text to speech) for people with visual or learning disabilities; and programs to simplify written language for individuals with neurodevelopmental disabilities (Vensand, Rogers, Tuleja, & DeMoss, 2000; Wehmeyer, 2006; Wehmeyer, Smith, & Davies, 2005). Computers with touch- and/or voice-activated programs and assistive devices allow users with communication disabilities to use a laser wand (usually attached to the person's head) to choose symbols or spell words, construct sentences, and "speak" with a synthesized voice (Beukelman & Mirenda, 2005; Wehmeyer et al., 2005). . . .

TESTING AND ASSESSMENT

Guideline 13. In assessing persons with disabilities, psychologists strive to consider disability as a dimension of diversity together with other individual and contextual dimensions.

When conducting psychological assessments in clinical settings, it is essential to consider the interaction between the individual with a disability and his or her environment. The dimensions of this interaction include how the individual functions over time, in varied situations, and in response to changing environmental demands (Bruyère & Peterson, 2005; Bruyère et al., 2005; Peterson, 2005; Radnitz, Bockian, & Moran, 2000; Reed et al., 2005; Scherer, 1998; Simeonsson & Rosenthal, 2001). Considering the central role of contexts in assessing a person's psychological functioning is consistent with the *International Classification of Functioning, Disability and Health* (ICF) integrative model of disability (WHO, 2001). For example, understanding co-workers' attitudes, family members' responses, classroom design elements, or the effect of school or work accommodations is important in assessing individuals with disabilities (Bruyère & Peterson, 2005; Bruyère et al., 2005; Chan et al., 2009; Hurst, 2003; Peterson, 2005; Reed et al., 2005; Szymanski, 2000). . . .

Guideline 14. Depending on the context and goals of assessment and testing, psychologists strive to apply the assessment approach that is most psychometrically sound, fair, comprehensive, and appropriate for clients with disabilities.

. . . The label test is ordinarily reserved for instruments on which responses are evaluated for their correctness or quality. Assessment is a broader term, commonly referring to a process that integrates test information with information from other sources. Psychological assessment involves solving problems or answering questions (Vanderploeg, 2000) and, in addition to reviewing test results, may incorporate multiple data collection methods: behavioral observation, an interview with client(s), collateral interviews, and reviews of case records (Vanderploeg, 2000). . . .

Guideline 15. Psychologists strive to determine whether accommodations are appropriate for clients to yield a valid test score.

A testing accommodation is a change in a test format or content, or some aspect of test administration, which makes the test accessible to individuals who might otherwise be unable to complete the measure but does not alter the construct being measured. Making accommodations will help a psychologist test and assess clients with varying levels of ability. Scientists have carefully scrutinized the validity of accommodation measures in certain educational settings (Koenig & Bachman, 2004; Sireci, Scarpati, & Li, 2005; Willingham, Ragosta, Bennett, Rock, & Powers, 1988). It is expected that for many kinds of tests, an accommodated measure would yield more valid results than the same measure without such accommodations. . . . For example, a student with a visual disability using a large-print format reading test may need additional time to accommodate turning pages (i.e., to refer between the reading selection and the test questions). Without extra time in addition to the large-print format, the student's score may be less valid than if the appropriate additional time were granted. In many educational tests, it has been found that the general norms work well for people with disabilities receiving accommodations, but each such application needs to be validated before this is implemented. . . .

Guideline 16. Consistent with the goals of the assessment and disability-related barriers to assessment, psychologists in clinical settings strive to appropriately balance quantitative, qualitative, and ecological perspectives and articulate both the strengths and limitations of assessment.

. . . In assessing a client with a disability in a clinical setting, a psychologist can conduct an integrated, semi-structured interview about the client's relevant disability-related issues, their relative importance among various personal concerns, and how they interact with other psychological issues (Mohr & Beutler, 2003). When appropriate in the context of the assessment's goals, the psychologist may ask about the client's type and origin of disability; the client's perception of disability-related strengths and limitations; the functional impact of the client's disability; the reactions of others to the client's disability; required aids, accommodations, treatments, and medications; and necessary lifestyle modifications (Olkin, 1999b; Vane & Motta, 1987).

It is important for the psychologist to watch not only external manifestations of the client's disability, such as behavioral mannerisms, speech difficulties, and medical symptoms or physical anomalies, but also a wide range of other functional domains (e.g., level of arousal, language, psychomotor and motor functions, cooperation, interpersonal skills, cognition, mood, affect and emotional state, frustration tolerance, coping, and insight; Vanderploeg, 2000). . . .

Guideline 17. Psychologists in clinical settings strive to maximize fairness and relevance in interpreting assessment data of clients who have disabilities by applying approaches which reduce potential bias and balance and integrate data from multiple sources.

Psychologists attempt to recognize any personal conceptions of and reactions to disability that may bias their interpretation of assessment data. Involving clients in a collaborative feedback process in regard to the results of assessments (Farley, Bolton, & Parkerson, 1992; Finn & Tonsager, 1997) and using multiple independent information sources (Holzbauer & Berven, 1999; Vanderploeg, 2000; Vane & Motta, 1987) may help to safeguard against bias-related problems.

The literature on fairness in psychological assessment suggests a number of strategies for removing or minimizing bias. . . .

Overall, psychologists should attempt to balance the consideration of social, clinical, and psychometric disability-related issues with other intra-individual factors (such as sociodemographic background, motivation, strengths, resources, or coping skills) and environmental factors such as attitudes and reactions of others, context of assessment, and various societal systems (Mackelprang & Salsgiver, 1999; Olkin, 1999b). . . .

INTERVENTIONS

Guideline 18. Psychologists strive to recognize that there is a wide range of individual response to disability, and collaborate with their clients who have disabilities, and when appropriate, with their clients' families to plan, develop, and implement psychological interventions.

Psychologists provide interventions with persons with disabilities in a variety of settings including outpatient and inpatient facilities, schools, work, social service agencies, and disaster sites. In working with clients who have disabilities, a psychologist does not automatically assume that certain treatment modalities, interventions, and theoretical orientations are appropriate or inappropriate according to the individual's type of disability. For example, a psychologist would not assume that a client with an intellectual disability could not benefit from individual psychotherapy (Butz, Bowling, & Bliss, 2000; Mason, 2007; Nezu & Nezu, 1994). Critical aspects of psychological interventions include establishing a secure working relationship, understanding the client's unique life and disability-related experiences, determining the client's treatment needs, and collaborating to develop an intervention plan and goals. A client's disability may make this process more complex.

Disability issues may or may not relate to why a person with a disability seeks psychological services. Concerns of persons who have disabilities may be related to other issues, such as interpersonal difficulties with a significant other (Blotzer & Ruth, 1995; Olkin, 1999b; Wilson, 2003). . . .

Guideline 19. Psychologists strive to be aware of the therapeutic structure and environment's impact on their work with clients with disabilities.

Persons with disabilities are the ultimate authority on their own needs. To support individual freedom and choice, the psychologist should attempt to provide a hospitable environment for psychological intervention (Banks & Kaschak, 2003), to understand how the individual's environment affects the disability, and to work with the client to ensure that the therapeutic environment accommodates a client's disability. . . .

Guideline 20. Psychologists strive to recognize that interventions with persons with disabilities may focus on enhancing well-being as well as reducing distress and ameliorating skill deficits.

. . .

It is increasingly recognized that people with disabilities, like everyone else, have unique strengths (e.g., Shogren, Wehmeyer, Reese, & O'Hara, 2006). A client whose strengths are recognized and enhanced has a more positive self-image and ability to deal with life issues (Dunn & Dougherty, 2005; Dykens, 2006; Olkin, 1999b). Personal strengths include education, personality traits, creativity and talent, social relationships, and access to necessary supports. . . .

Guideline 21. When working with systems that support, treat, or educate people with disabilities, psychologists strive to keep the clients' perspectives paramount and advocate for client self-determination, integration, choice, and least restrictive alternatives.

Many community agencies and systems influence the lives and psychological well-being of individuals with disabilities and their families (DeJong, 1979, 1983; Heinemann, 2005; Hernandez, Balcazar, Keys, Hidalgo, & Rosen, 2006). The psychologist who works with organizations that serve individuals with disabilities promotes inclusive environments and supports clients with disabilities by consulting with individuals and groups, working with collaborative teams, and creating beneficial adaptations, accommodations, as well as enabling environments. A psychologist may advocate for persons with disabilities and family members to participate in agency leadership roles. . . .

Guideline 22. Psychologists strive to recognize and address health promotion issues for individuals with disabilities.

Psychologists recognize that disability is not synonymous with disease or illness. In fact, individuals with disabilities often lead healthy and independent lives but may have a smaller margin of health and be at increased risk for preventable and/or manageable secondary health conditions that may affect their well-being and participation in community life (Kinne, Patrick, & Doyle, 2004; Pope & Tarlov, 1991; Ravesloot, Seekins, & White, 2005; WHO, 2001). Given that physical and mental health are intimately related, psychologists can help clients with disabilities understand how maintaining health and preventing secondary conditions can help them achieve life goals. For example, maintaining an exercise program and diet might prevent Type II diabetes and help clients to obtain their goals more easily. When appropriate, psychologists learn about their clients' health issues, help their clients understand the relationship between health and well-being, and encourage clients to practice healthy lifestyles that prevent both primary and secondary health problems (Gill & Brown, 2002; Heller, Hsieh, & Rimmer, 2002; Heller & Marks, 2002). . . .

REFERENCES

Ainbinder, J. G., Blanchard, L. W., Singer, G. H. S., Sullivan, M. E., Powers, L. K., Marquis, J. G., . . . the Consortium to Evaluate Parent to Parent. (1998). A qualitative study of Parent to Parent support for parents of children with special needs. *Journal of Pediatric Psychology, 23*(2), 99–109. doi:10.1093/jpepsy/23.2.99

American Psychological Association. (2002). Ethical principles of psychologists and code of conduct. *American Psychologist, 57*(12), 1060–1073. doi:10.1037/0003-066X.57.12.1060

Banks, M. E., & Kaschak, E. (2003). *Women with visible and invisible disabilities: Multiple intersections, multiple issues, multiple therapies.* New York, NY: Haworth Press.

Beukelman, D. R., & Mirenda, P. (2005). *Augmentative & alternative communication: Supporting children & adults with complex communication needs* (3rd ed.). Baltimore, MD: Paul H. Brookes.

Blotzer, M. A., & Ruth, R. (1995). *Sometimes you just want to feel like a human being: Case studies of empowering psychotherapy with people with disabilities.* Baltimore, MD: Paul H. Brookes.

Brownridge, D. A. (2006). Partner violence against women with disabilities: Prevalence, risk, and explanations. *Violence Against Women, 12*(9), 805–822. doi:10.1177/1077801206292681

Bruyère, S. M., & Peterson, D. B. (2005). Introduction to the special section on the International Classification of Functioning, Disability, and Health: Implications for rehabilitation psychology. *Rehabilitation Psychology, 50*(2), 103–104. doi:10.1037/0090-5550.50.2.103

Bruyère, S. M., Van Looy, S. A., & Peterson, D. B. (2005). The International Classification of Functioning, Disability and Health: Contemporary literature overview. *Rehabilitation Psychology, 50*(2), 113–121. doi:10.1037/0090-5550.50.2.113

Butz, M. R., Bowling, J. B., & Bliss, C. A. (2000). Psychotherapy with the mentally retarded: A review of the literature and the implications. *Professional Psychology: Research and Practice, 31*(1), 42–47. doi:10.1037/0735-7028.31.1.42

Chan, F., Gelman, J. S., Ditchman, N., Kim, J.-H., & Chiu, C.-Y. (2009). The World Health Organization ICF model as a conceptual framework of disability. In F. Chan, E. Da Silva Cardoso, & J. A. Chronister (Eds.), *Understanding psychosocial adjustment to chronic illness and disability* (pp. 23–50). New York, NY: Springer.

Crawford, D. W., Jackson, E. L., & Godbey, G. (1991). A hierarchical model of leisure constraints. *Leisure Sciences, 13*(4), 309–320. doi:10.1080/01490409109513147

DeJong, G. (1979). *The movement for independent living: Origins, ideology, and implications for disability research* (Occasional Paper No. 2). East Lansing: University Centers for International Rehabilitation, Michigan State University. Reprinted in A. Brechin, P. Liddiard, & J. Swain (Eds.), *Handicap in a social world: A reader* (pp. 239–248), 1981, Milton Keynes, England: Hodder & Stoughton in association with the University Press.

DeJong, G. (1983). Defining and implementing the independent living concept. In N. M. Crewe & I. K. Zola (Eds.), *Independent living for physically disabled people* (pp. 4–27). San Francisco, CA: Jossey-Bass.

Dobson, B., & Middleton, S. (1998). *Paying to care: The cost of childhood disability.* New York, NY: Joseph Rowntree Foundation.

Dunn, D. S., & Dougherty, S. B. (2005). Prospects for a positive psychology of rehabilitation. *Rehabilitation Psychology, 50*(3), 305–311. doi:10.1037/0090-5550.50.3.305

Dunn, D. S., & Dougherty, S. B. (2005). Prospects for a positive psychology of rehabilitation. *Rehabilitation Psychology, 50*(3), 305–311. doi:10.1037/0090-5550.50.3.305

Dykens, E. M. (2006). Toward a positive psychology of mental retardation. *American Journal of Orthopsychiatry, 76*, 185–193. doi:10.1037/0002-9432.76.2.185

Farley, R. C., Bolton, B., & Parkerson, S. (1992). Effects of client involvement in assessment on vocational development. *Rehabilitation Counseling Bulletin, 35*(3), 146–153.

Finn, S. E., & Tonsager, M. E. (1997). Information-gathering and therapeutic models of assessment: Complementary paradigms. *Psychological Assessment, 9*(4), 374–385. doi:10.1037/1040-3590.9.4.374

Flack, J. M., Amaro, H., Jenkins, W., Kunitz, S., Levy, J., Mixon, M., & Yu, E. (1995). Panel I: Epidemiology of minority health. *Health Psychology, 14*(7), 592–600. doi:10.1037/0278-6133.14.7.592

Gill, C. J., & Brown, A. (2002). Health and aging issues for women in their own voices. In P. H. Walsh & T. Heller (Eds.), *Health of women with intellectual disabilities* (pp. 139–153). Oxford, England: Blackwell. doi:10.1002/9780470776162.ch9

Goodley, D., & Lawthom, R. (2006). *Disability and psychology.* London, England: Palgrave.

Goodley, D., & Tregaskis, C. (2006). Storying disability and impairment: Retrospective accounts of disabled family life. *Qualitative Health Research, 16*(5), 630–646. doi:10.1177/1049732305285840

Hassouneh-Phillips, D., & Curry, M. A. (2002). Abuse of women with disabilities: State of the science. *Rehabilitation Counseling Bulletin, 45*(2), 96–104. doi:10.1177/003435520204500204

Hauser, P. C., Maxwell-McCaw, D. L., Leigh, I. W., & Gutman, V. A. (2000). Internship accessibility issues for deaf and hard-of-hearing applications: No cause for complacency. *Professional Psychology: Research and Practice, 31*(5), 569–574. doi:10.1037/0735-7028.31.5.569

Heinemann, A. W. (2005). Putting outcome measurement in context: A rehabilitation psychology perspective. *Rehabilitation Psychology, 50*(1), 6–14. doi:10.1037/0090-5550.50.1.6

Heller, T., Hsieh, K., & Rimmer, J. (2002). Barriers and supports for exercise participation among adults with Down syndrome. *Journal of Gerontological Social Work, 38*(1–2), 161–178. doi:10.1300/J083v38n01_03

Heller, T., & Marks, B. (2002). Health promotion for women with intellectual disabilities. In P. H. Walsh & T. Heller (Eds.), *Health of women with intellectual disabilities* (pp. 170–189). Oxford, England: Blackwell.

Hernandez, B., Balcazar, F., Keys, C., Hidalgo, M., & Rosen, J. (2006). Taking it to the streets: Ethnic minorities with disabilities seek community inclusion. *Community Development: Journal of the Community Development Society, 37*(3), 13–25. doi:10.1080/15575330.2006.10383104

Holzbauer, J. J., & Berven, N. L. (1999). Issues in vocational evaluation and testing related to the Americans With Disabilities Act. *VEWAA (Vocational Evaluation & Work Adjustment Association) Journal, 32*(2), 83–96.

Horner-Johnson, W., & Drum, C. E. (2006). Prevalence of maltreatment of people with intellectual disabilities: A review of recently published research. *Mental Retardation and Developmental Disabilities Research Reviews, 12*(1), 57–69. doi:10.1002/mrdd.20097

Hughes, R. B. (2005). Violence against women with disabilities: Urgent call for action. *The Community Psychologist, 38,* 28–30.

Hurst, R. B. (2003). The international disability rights movement and the ICF. *Disability & Rehabilitation, 25,* 572–576. doi:10.1080/0963828031000137072

Individuals With Disabilities Education Act, Pub. L. No. 94–142. (1975). (Individuals With Disabilities Education Act Amendments of 1997, Pub. L. No. 105-17).

Jopp, D. A., & Keys, C. B. (2001). Diagnostic overshadowing reviewed and reconsidered. *American Journal on Mental Retardation, 106*(5), 416–433. doi:10.1352/0895-8017(2001)106_0416:DORAR_2.0.CO;2

Katz, I., Hass, R. G., & Bailey, J. (1988). Attitudinal ambivalence and behavior toward people with disabilities. In H. E. Yuker (Ed.), *Attitudes toward persons with disabilities* (pp. 47–57). New York, NY: Springer.

Kemp, N. T., & Mallinckrodt, B. (1996). Impact of professional training on case conceptualization of clients with a disability. *Professional Psychology: Research and Practice, 27*(4), 378–385. doi:10.1037/0735-7028.27.4.378

Kinne, S., Patrick, D. L., & Doyle, D. L. (2004). Prevalence of secondary conditions among people with disabilities. *American Journal of Public Health, 94,* 443–445. doi:10.2105/AJPH.94.3.443

Koenig, J. A., & Bachman, L. F. (2004). *Keeping score for all: The effects of inclusion and accommodation policies on large-scale educational assessment.* Retrieved from http://www.nap.edu/catalog/.php?record_id_11029

Leigh, I. W., Powers, L., Vash, C., & Nettles, R. (2004). Survey of psychological services to clients with disabilities: The need for awareness. *Rehabilitation Psychology, 49*(1), 48–54. doi:10.1037/0090-5550.49.1.48

Mackelprang, R. W., & Salsgiver, R. O. (1999). *Disability: A diversity model approach in human service practice.* Pacific Grove, CA: Brooks/Cole.

Martin, S. L., Rey, N., Serte-Alvarez, D., Kepper, L. L., Meracco, R. E., & Prickers, P. A. (2006). Physical and sexual assault of women with disabilities. *Violence Against Women, 12,* 823–837. doi:10.1177/1077801206292672

Mason, J. (2007). The provision of psychological therapy to people with intellectual disabilities: An investigation into some of the relevant factors. *Journal of Intellectual Disability Research, 51*(3), 244–249. doi:10.1111/j.1365-2788.2006.00867.x

Mason, J., & Scior, K. (2004). 'Diagnostic overshadowing' amongst clinicians working with people with intellectual disabilities in the UK. *Journal of Applied Research in Intellectual Disabilities, 17*(2), 85–90. doi:10.1111/j.1360-2322.2004.00184.x

Mohr, D., & Beutler, L. E. (2003). The integrative clinical interview. In L. E. Beutler & G. Groth-Marnat (Eds.), *Integrative assessment of adult personality* (2nd ed., pp. 82–122). New York, NY: Guilford Press.

Murray, P. (2006). Being in school? Exclusion and the denial of psychological reality. In D. Goodley & R. Lawthom (Eds.), *Disability and psychology* (pp. 34–41). London, England: Palgrave.

Nezu, C. M., & Nezu, A. M. (1994). Outpatient psychotherapy for adults with mental retardation and concomitant psychopathology: Research and clinical imperatives. *Journal of Consulting and Clinical Psychology, 62*(1), 34–42. doi:10.1037/0022-006X.62.1.34

Nosek, M. A., Foley, C. C., Hughes, R. B., & Howland, C. A. (2001). Vulnerabilities for abuse among women with disabilities. *Sexuality and Disability, 19*(3), 177–189. doi:10.1023/A:1013152530758

Olkin, R. (1999a). The personal, professional and political when clients have disabilities. *Women & Therapy, 22*(2), 87–103. doi:10.1300/J015v22n02_07

Olkin, R. (1999b). *What psychotherapists should know about disability.* New York, NY: Guilford Press.

Peterson, D. B. (2005). International Classification of Functioning, Disability and Health: An introduction for rehabilitation psychologists. *Rehabilitation Psychology, 50*(2), 105–112. doi:10.1037/0090-5550.50.2.105

Pope, A. M., & Tarlov, A. R. (1991). *Disability in America: Toward a national agenda for prevention.* Washington, DC: National Academy Press.

Powers, L. E. (1993). Disability and grief: From tragedy to challenge. In G. H. S. Singer & L. E. Powers (Eds.), *Families, disability, and empowerment: Active coping skills and strategies for family interventions* (pp. 119–149). Baltimore, MD: Paul H. Brookes.

Pullin, D. (2002). Testing individuals with disabilities: Reconciling social science and social policy. In R. B. Ekstrom & D. Smith (Eds.), *Assessing individuals with disabilities in educational, employment, and counseling settings* (pp. 11–31). Washington, DC: American Psychological Association. doi:10.1037/10471-001

Radnitz, C. L., Bockian, N., & Moran, A. I. (2000). Assessment of psychopathology and personality in people with physical disabilities. In R. G. Frank & T. R. Elliott (Eds.), *Handbook of rehabilitation psychology* (pp. 287–309). Washington, DC: American Psychological Association. doi:10.1037/10361-013

Ravesloot, C., Seekins, T., & White, G. (2005). Living well with a disability health promotion intervention: Improved health status for consumers and lower costs for health care policymakers. *Rehabilitation Psychology, 50*(3), 239–245. doi:10.1037/0090-5550.50.3.239

Reed, G. M., Lux, J. B., Bufka, L. F., Trask, C., Peterson, D. B., Stark, S., . . . Hawley, J. A. (2005). Operationalizing the International Classification of Functioning, Disability and Health in clinical settings. *Rehabilitation Psychology, 50*(2), 122–131. doi:10.1037/0090-5550.50.2.122

Reeve, D. (2000). Oppression within the counseling room. *Disability & Society, 15*(4), 669–682. doi:10.1080/09687590050058242

Reiss, S., Levitan, G. W., & Szyszko, J. (1982). Emotional disturbance and mental retardation: Diagnostic overshadowing. *American Journal of Mental Deficiency, 86*(6), 567–574.

Rolland, J. S., & Walsh, F. (2006). Facilitating family resilience with childhood illness and disability. *Current Opinions in Pediatrics, 18*(5), 527–538. doi:10.1097/01.mop.0000245354.83454.68

Rosenthal, D. A., Kosciulek, J., Lee, G. K., Frain, M., & Ditchman, N. (2009). Family and adaptation to chronic illness and disability. In F. Chan, E. Da Silva Cardoso, & J. A. Chronister (Eds.), *Understanding psychosocial adjustment to chronic illness and disability* (pp. 185–207). New York, NY: Springer.

Saxton, M., McNeff, E., Powers, L., Curry, M., & Limont, M. (2006). We're all little John Waynes: A study of disabled men's experience of abuse by personal assistants. *The Journal of Rehabilitation, 72*, 3–13.

Scherer, M. J. (1998). The impact of assistive technology on the lives of people with disabilities. In D. B. Gray, L. A. Quatrano, & M. L. Lieberman (Eds.), *Designing and using assistive technology: The human perspective* (pp. 99–115). Baltimore, MD: Paul H. Brookes.

Shogren, K. A., Wehmeyer, M. L., Reese, R. M., & O'Hara, D. (2006). Promoting self-determination in health and medical care: A critical component of addressing health disparities in people with intellectual disabilities. *Journal of Policy and Practice in Intellectual Disabilities, 3*(2), 105–113. doi:10.1111/j.1741-1130.2006.00061.x

Simeonsson, R. J., & Rosenthal, S. L. (2001). Clinical assessment of children: An overview. In R. J. Simeonsson & S. L. Rosenthal (Eds.), *Psychological and developmental assessment: Children with disabilities and chronic conditions* (pp. 1–14). New York, NY: Guilford Press.

Simeonsson, R. J., & Scarborough, A. (2001). Issues in clinical assessment. In R. J. Simeonsson & S. L. Rosenthal (Eds.), *Psychological and developmental assessment: Children with disabilities and chronic conditions* (pp. 17–31). New York, NY: Guilford Press.

Singer, G. H. S., & Powers, L. E. (1993). Contributing to resilience in families: An overview. In G. H. S. Singer & L. E. Powers (Eds.), *Families, disability, and empowerment: Active coping skills and strategies for family interventions* (pp. 1–25). Baltimore, MD: Paul H. Brookes.

Sireci, S. G., Scarpati, S. E., & Li, S. (2005). Test accommodations for students with disabilities: An analysis of the interaction hypothesis. *Review of Educational Research, 75*(4), 457–490. doi:10.3102/00346543075004457

Smith, D. L. (2008). Disability, gender, and intimate partner violence: Relationships from the Behavioral Risk Factor Surveillance System. *Sexuality and Disability, 26,* 15–28. doi:10.1007/s11195-007-9064-6

Strike, D. L., Skovholt, T. M., & Hummel, T. J. (2004). Mental health professionals' disability competence: Measuring self-awareness, perceived knowledge, and perceived skills. *Rehabilitation Psychology, 49*(4), 321–327. doi:10.1037/0090-5550.49.4.321

Sullivan, P. M., & Knutson, J. F. (1998). The association between child maltreatment and disabilities in a hospital-based epidemiological study. *Child Abuse & Neglect, 22*(4), 271–288. doi:10.1016/S0145-2134(97)00175-0

Sullivan, P. M., & Knutson, J. F. (2000). Maltreatment and disabilities: A population-based epidemiological study. *Child Abuse & Neglect, 24*(10), 1257–1273. doi:10.1016/S0145-2134(00)00190-3

Szymanski, E. M. (2000). Disability and vocational behavior. In R. G. Frank & T. R. Elliot (Eds.), *Handbook of rehabilitation psychology* (pp. 499–517). Washington, DC: American Psychological Association. doi:10.1037/10361-023

Turnbull, A. P., & Turnbull, H. R., III. (1991). Understanding families from a systems perspective. In J. M. Williams & T. Kay (Eds.), *Head injury: A family matter* (pp. 37–63). Baltimore, MD: Paul H. Brookes.

U.S. Department of Health and Human Services. (2005). *The surgeon general's call to action to improve the health and wellness of persons with disabilities.* Retrieved from https://www.cdc.gov/ncbddd/disabilityandhealth/pdf/whatitmeanstoyou508.pdf

Vanderploeg, R. D. (2000). The interpretation process. In R. D. Vanderploeg (Ed.), *Clinician's guide to neuropsychological assessment* (pp. 111–154). Mahwah, NJ: Erlbaum.

Vane, J. R., & Motta, R. W. (1987). Basic issues in psychological evaluation. In V. B. Van Hasselt & M. Hersen (Eds.), *Psychological evaluation of the developmentally and physically disabled* (pp. 19–39). New York, NY: Plenum Press.

Vensand, K., Rogers, J., Tuleja, C., & DeMoss, A. (2000). *Adaptive baby care equipment: Guidelines, prototypes and resources.* Berkeley, CA: The Looking Glass.

Wehmeyer, M. L. (2006). Universal design for learning, access to the general education curriculum and students with mild mental retardation. *Exceptionality, 14*(4), 225–235. doi:10.1207/s15327035ex1404_4

Wehmeyer, M. L., Smith, S. J., & Davies, D. (2005). Technology use and students with intellectual disability: Universal design for all students. In D. Edyburn, K. Higgins, & R. Boone (Eds.), *Handbook of special education technology research and practice* (pp. 309–323). Whitefish Bay, WI: Knowledge by Design.

White, M. J., Nichols, C. N., Cook, R. S., & Spengler, P. M. (1995). Diagnostic over-shadowing and mental retardation: A meta-analysis. *American Journal on Mental Retardation, 100*(3), 293–298.

Wilgosh, L., Nota, L., Scorgie, K., & Soresi, S. (2004). Effective life management in parents of children with disabilities: A cross-national extension. *International Journal for the Advancement of Counselling, 26*(3), 301–312. doi:10.1023/B:ADCO.0000035532.45759.fe

Wilgosh, L., & Scorgie, K. (2006). Theoretical model for conceptualizing cross-cultural applications and intervention strategies for parents of children with disabilities. *Journal of Policy and Practice in Intellectual Disabilities, 3*(4), 211–218. doi:10.1111/j.1741-1130.2006.00082.x

Willingham, W. W., Ragosta, M., Bennett, R. E., Rock, D. A., & Powers, D. E. (1988). *Testing handicapped people.* Needham Heights, MA: Allyn & Bacon.

Wilson, S. (2003). *Disability, counseling, and psychotherapy.* London, England: Palgrave.

Woolfson, L. (2004). Family well-being and disabled children: A psychosocial model of disability-related child behaviour problems. *British Journal of Health Psychology, 9*(1), 1–13. doi:10.1348/135910704322778687

World Health Organization. (2001). *The world health report—mental health: New understanding, new hope.* Geneva, Switzerland: World Health Organization.

7.10. Practice Guidelines Regarding Psychologists' Involvement in Pharmacological Issues

American Psychological Association

Several factors have converged that will inevitably increase psychologists' involvement in the medication management of the individuals they serve. One is the increasing use of psychotropic medications for the treatment of psychological disorders, a clinical practice which is referred to as *pharmacotherapy* in this document. A national survey of physician records suggested that the proportion of the population using antidepressants increased from 6.7% in 1990 to 15.1% in 1998, an increase of 125.4% even after adjusting for population growth (Skaer, Sclar, Robison, & Galin, 2000). According to VandenBos and Williams (2000), practicing psychologists, on average, estimated that 43% of their current patients were using psychotropic medications. Another factor is the movement for prescriptive authority within psychology. Appropriately trained psychologists are now eligible for prescriptive authority in two states (Louisiana and New Mexico) as well as in the military. With similar legislative agendas emerging in a number of other

From "Practice Guidelines Regarding Psychologists' Involvement in Pharmacological Issues," by the American Psychological Association, 2011, *American Psychologist*, 66, pp. 835–849. Copyright 2011 by the American Psychological Association.

These guidelines were developed by the American Psychological Association (APA) Division 55 (American Society for the Advancement of Pharmacotherapy) Task Force on Practice Guidelines. The task force was chaired by Robert E. McGrath. Task force members included Stanley Berman, Elaine LeVine, Elaine Mantell, Beth Rom-Rymer, Morgan Sammons, and James Quillin. Additional input on the guidelines was provided by Robert Ax, representing Division 18 (Psychologists in Public Service). None of the individuals involved in the development of this document has any personal investment in pharmaceutical products of any kind, nor did the developers receive any financial support for its creation.

The task force anticipates that these guidelines may deserve reconsideration in a relatively brief time frame, given anticipated changes in psychologists' role in pharmacotherapy as well as changes in the perceptions and use of psychotropic medications. In particular, it is the belief of the members of the task force that future efforts should include consideration of whether some elements of the enclosed guidelines merit elevation to the level of practice standards. Accordingly, this document is scheduled to expire as APA policy in August 2014, five years after the date of its approval and adoption by the APA Council of Representatives. After this date, users are encouraged to contact the APA Practice Directorate to confirm whether this document remains in effect.

states, the number of states offering prescriptive authority to psychologists will inevitably increase further.

. . .

GENERAL

Guideline 1. Psychologists are encouraged to consider objectively the scope of their competence in pharmacotherapy and to seek consultation as appropriate before offering recommendations about psychotropic medications.

Rationale

Ethical Standard 2.01 of the APA (2002b) Ethics Code indicates psychologists provide services within the boundaries of their competence. Two factors complicate psychologists' efforts to comply with this standard in the context of pharmacotherapy. The first factor is pressure exerted on psychologists to serve in a collaborative or information-providing role. Patients or family members who find it difficult or uncomfortable to request information from the prescriber may look to the psychologist with whom they have established a therapeutic relationship for specific advice. Primary care physicians and other prescribers with limited specialized training in psychological disorders and their treatment, or who do not know the patient as well as the psychologist does, sometimes look to the psychologist for input on the choice of medication.

. . .

Guideline 3. Psychologists involved in prescribing or collaborating are sensitive to the developmental, age and aging, educational, sex and gender, language, health status, and cultural/ethnicity factors that can moderate the interpersonal and biological aspects of pharmacotherapy relevant to the populations they serve.

Rationale

Principle E of the Ethics Code (APA, 2002b) focuses on the importance of considering cultural and personal variables in the populations served. This standard takes on additional implications in the context of pharmacotherapy, because individual differences can affect the interpersonal aspects of medication management, the effectiveness of treatment, and its side-effect profile. . . .

[T]he number and variety of person variables that can potentially moderate the process or outcome of pharmacotherapy is daunting, and no one person can be expected to be familiar with all the potential moderators. Psychologists who prescribe or collaborate strive to educate themselves on those factors that are particularly relevant for the populations of individuals they serve on a regular basis and are sensitive to the possible role of such factors in the psychopharmacological treatment of other groups as well. . . .

EDUCATION

Guideline 4. Psychologists are urged to identify a level of knowledge concerning pharmacotherapy for the treatment of psychological disorders that is appropriate to the populations they serve and the type of practice they wish to establish, and to engage in educational experiences as appropriate to achieve and maintain that level of knowledge.

Rationale

Where Guideline 1 focused on practicing within one's scope of competence, this practice guideline focuses on involvement in continuing education activities that are appropriate for providing optimal care to one's patients. Various studies suggest most doctoral programs in professional psychology offer training in psychopharmacological interventions, but the educational requirements are fairly limited in scope (Collins, 2000; Monti, Wallander, & Delancey, 1983; Smyer et al., 1993). For the psychologist with prescriptive authority, state legislation will ultimately establish the minimum criteria for basic and continuing education and the boundaries of acceptable practice. The psychologist who at times plays a collaborative or information-providing role operates under more ambiguous expectations about the appropriate degree of continuing education.
. . .

Guideline 5. Psychologists strive to be sensitive to the potential for adverse effects associated with the psychotropic medications used by their patients.

Rationale

Adverse effects of medication are widespread and in some studies represent the most common reason cited for premature termination of pharmacotherapy (e.g., Ashton, Jamerson, Weinstein, & Wagoner, 2005; Brambilla, Cipriani, Hotopf, & Barbui, 2005; Kampman & Lehtinen, 1999). Iatrogenic medication effects can arise from a number of sources, including the patient's reaction to a medication protocol, the ill-advised use of polypharmacy, use of excessive dosages (Antonuccio, Burns, & Danton, 2002), a drug–drug interaction, a drug–diet interaction, a known or undiagnosed medical condition, or poor patient adherence with the medication schedule or dosing (Brown, Frost, Ko, & Woosley, 2006). Often, low-probability adverse effects do not become evident until well after the medication has been approved by the Food and Drug Administration (Lasser et al., 2002). The possibility even exists that effects may not emerge until many years later, particularly in developmentally immature patients.
. . .

Guideline 6. Psychologists involved in prescribing or collaborating are encouraged to familiarize themselves with the technological resources that can enhance decision making during the course of treatment.

Rationale

The practice of pharmacotherapy is undergoing rapid change as information is gathered about the positive and negative effects of various medications. Mastery of the relevant literature is difficult to achieve and maintain, especially when one considers such issues as drug–drug and drug–diet interactions. A range of electronic resources has emerged in recent years that many prescribing professionals find indispensable in their daily practice.

Implications

Psychologists with prescriptive authority and direct collaborators are urged to familiarize themselves with available technological and expert resources . . . that offer critically evaluated, evidence-based, synthesized information about the effective practice of pharmacotherapy. In terms of daily practice, psychologists with prescriptive authority and psychologists who directly collaborate in medication decision making are well served by products now available for computers and/or personal digital assistants that offer extensive and frequently updated information about pharmaceutical agents. . . .

ASSESSMENT

Guideline 7. Psychologists with prescriptive authority strive to familiarize themselves with key procedures for monitoring the physical and psychological sequelae of the medications used to treat psychological disorders, including laboratory examinations and overt signs of adverse or unintended effects.

Rationale

Methods of assessing medication effects and indications, both positive and negative, represent a body of knowledge that is distinct from the literature devoted to the medications themselves. The psychologist with prescriptive authority strives to remain current in both bodies of literature as a means of ensuring optimal patient care.

. . .

Guideline 8. Psychologists with prescriptive authority regularly strive to monitor the physiological status of the patients they treat with medication, particularly when there is a physical condition that might complicate the response to psychotropic medication or predispose a patient to experience an adverse reaction.

Rationale

When serving as a prescriber, a psychologist is participating in the medical treatment of the patient at a level previously unparalleled in the history of psychology. A thorough medical history, including prior adverse responses to a medication or a combination of medications, represents an important starting point for optimal medical care and for avoiding adverse reactions.

. . .

Guideline 9. Psychologists are encouraged to explore issues surrounding patient adherence and feelings about medication.

Rationale

Adherence rates in pharmacotherapy are quite poor. . . . Patients do not or cannot adhere with treatment for many reasons including lack of access to a prescribing provider; the financial and organizational challenges involved in seeing multiple health providers, only one of whom would be the prescriber; ambivalence or fears about the medication; distressing side effects; misinformation about the latency of the therapeutic effect; shame or self-consciousness about taking psychoactive medications; the perception (which can be valid but is sometimes mistaken) that the treatment is ineffective or insufficiently effective; and concerns about medication changing their behavior, their ways of thinking, or, more profoundly, their fundamental personality style. As a result, many patients receive less than optimal benefit from their medication (Mitchell, 2006). The frequent contact between psychologist and patient that characterizes traditional psychological treatment provides a setting for monitoring patient feelings about the medication and willingness to continue.

. . .

INTERVENTION AND CONSULTATION

Guideline 10. Psychologists are urged to develop a relationship that will allow the populations they serve to feel comfortable exploring issues surrounding medication use.

Rationale

This guideline is intended to complement the previous one. A sizeable proportion of patients who terminate medication treatment prematurely do so without informing the prescribing professional of this decision and may even report continued use of the medication to the prescriber (e.g., Maddox, Levi, & Thompson, 1994). Research consistently demonstrates the communication style of the provider is a significant predictor of adherence to medication (Bultman & Svarstad, 2000; DiMatteo, 2003). Whether the psychologist serves as a prescriber, collaborator, or information provider, the effectiveness of monitoring attitudes concerning and adherence to prescribed medications depends on the degree to which the patient perceives the relationship with the psychologist as one that allows for such discussion.

Implications

In any exchange concerning medication, the psychologist may want to consider the potential impact of moderating factors that can interfere with the free flow of information, such as intellectual, developmental, emotional, interpersonal, gender, or cultural factors. . . .

Guideline 11. To the extent deemed appropriate, psychologists involved in prescribing or collaboration adopt a biopsychosocial approach to case formulation that considers both psychosocial and biological factors.

Rationale

The biopsychosocial model for the understanding of human health (Engel, 1977) represents the dominant model in the health care disciplines. At a minimum, this model suggests that psychosocial factors (including interpersonal, intrapersonal, gender, cultural, spiritual, and socioeconomic variables) play an important role in the etiology of and response to medical conditions as well as the recognition that psychoeducational and psychological services can be essential in coping with and recovering from illness. Within this broad perspective, there is much room for variation in the degree to which these different perspectives are considered important for understanding the nature of psychological disorders.
. . .

Guideline 12. The psychologist with prescriptive authority is encouraged to use an expanded informed consent process to incorporate additional issues specific to prescribing.

Rationale

The APA (2002b) Ethics Code requires psychologists to obtain informed consent before any professional interaction whenever possible. The decision to prescribe medication for a patient optimally results from collaboration between that patient and the psychologist, rather than from a unilateral decision by the prescriber. A collaborative decision depends upon appropriate education of the patient about alternative treatments and full informed consent.
. . .

Guideline 13. When making decisions about the use of psychological treatments, pharmacotherapy, or their combination, the psychologist with prescriptive authority considers the best interests of the patient, current research, and when appropriate, the needs of the community.

Rationale

As noted previously, combined psychotherapy and pharmacotherapy can be superior to either treatment alone, at least in some circumstances. The therapeutic relationship, characterized by empathic interaction with the patient and the enhancement of awareness, often provides the optimal framework for focal interventions including medication. However, the situational factors that predict which treatment option to select remain largely unknown. In the absence of clear guidelines, personal preferences for one approach or the other can become predominant in a practitioner's decision making rather than an individualized analysis of the best course of action. For example, given psychologists' traditional reliance on psychotherapy as a primary treatment, it would not be surprising to find some psychologists with prescriptive authority elect never to prescribe except in the context of a psychotherapeutic relationship.

. . .

Guideline 14. Psychologists involved in prescribing or collaborating strive to be sensitive to the subtle influences of effective marketing on professional behavior and the potential for bias in information in their clinical decisions about the use of medications.

Rationale

A substantial literature indicates the pharmaceutical industry potentially influences decision making about medications in at least four ways. First is through its role in research and journal publications. A recent comparison of seven meta-analyses published with pharmaceutical industry support versus parallel meta-analyses published under the auspices of the independent Cochrane Collaboration found every one of the former recommended the medication without reservations while none of the latter did, even though mean effect sizes reported were similar (Jørgensen, Hilden, & Gøtzsche, 2006). Panels created for the development of treatment guidelines often consist largely or exclusively of researchers receiving funding from the pharmaceutical industry (Choudhry, Stelfox, & Detsky, 2002). However, even relatively independent analyses of the literature must rely on primary research that is heavily funded by pharmaceutical companies, and such studies tend to support the superiority of the funder's products (e.g., Heres et al., 2006; Lexchin, Bero, Djulbegovic, & Clark, 2003; Rising, Bacchetti, & Bero, 2008; Turner, Matthews, Linardatos, Tell, & Rosenthal, 2008).

. . .

Guideline 15. Psychologists with prescriptive authority are encouraged to use interactions with the patient surrounding the act of prescribing to learn more about the patient's characteristic patterns of interpersonal behavior.

Rationale

The patient's characteristic patterns of interpreting interpersonal situations inevitably play a role in the desire for medication, the reaction to the recommendation of medication, and compliance with the treatment regimen (e.g., Brockman, 1990; O'Neill & Bornstein, 2001).

. . .

RELATIONSHIPS

Guideline 16. Psychologists with prescriptive authority are sensitive to maintaining appropriate relationships with other providers of psychological services.

Rationale

There are already various circumstances in which one mental health professional may refer to a psychologist for specialized services, referral for assessment perhaps being the most common. The emergence of the psychologist with prescriptive authority will undoubtedly produce circumstances in which mental health professionals refer to a psychologist for purposes of medication consultation only. Within this division of labor there exists the potential for miscommunication, differences in interpretation of the patient's problems, and differences in beliefs about optimal interventions. Rivalry can also develop between clinicians, with unintended iatrogenic effects.

. . .

Guideline 17. Psychologists are encouraged to maintain appropriate relationships with providers of biological interventions.

Rationale

Ethical Standard 3.09 of the APA (2002b) Ethics Code highlights the importance of cooperation with other professionals in service to patients. Psychologists who prescribe, collaborate, or provide information on pharmacotherapy will at times find they are working together with other health care professionals, a category that in some cases will include traditional healers offering complementary medical treatments. Collaborating and information-providing psychologists by definition work in conjunction with prescribing professionals, most of whom are not psychologists at this point, though they increasingly may be. Prescribing, collaborating, and information-providing psychologists are often dealing with patients who demonstrate comorbid medical conditions. Given the potential for drug–drug interactions and medical complications in such situations, collaboration with other health care providers actively involved in treating the patient can be particularly important.

. . .

REFERENCES

American Psychological Association. (2002b). Ethical principles of psychologists and code of conduct. *American Psychologist, 57*, 1060–1073. doi:10.1037/0003-066X.57.12.1060

Antonuccio, D. O., Burns, D. D., & Danton, W. G. (2002). Antidepressants: A triumph of marketing over science? *Prevention & Treatment, 5*, Article 25. doi:10.1037/1522-3736.5.1.525c

Ashton, A. K., Jamerson, B. D., Weinstein, W. L., & Wagoner, C. (2005). Antidepressant-related adverse effects impacting treatment compliance: Results of a patient survey. *Current Therapeutic Research: Clinical and Experimental, 66*, 96–106. doi:10.1016/j.curtheres.2005.04.006

Brambilla, P., Cipriani, A., Hotopf, M., & Barbui, C. (2005). Side-effect profile of fluoxetine in comparison with other SSRIs, tricyclic and newer antidepressants: A meta-analysis of clinical trial data. *Pharmacopsychiatry, 38*, 69–77. doi:10.1055/s-2005-837806

Brockman, R. (1990). Medication and transference in psychoanalytically oriented psychotherapy of the borderline patient. *Psychiatric Clinics of North America, 13*, 287–295.

Brown, M., Frost, R., Ko, Y., & Woosley, R. (2006). Diagramming patients' views of root causes of adverse drug events in ambulatory care: An online tool for planning education and research. *Patient Education and Counseling, 62*, 302–315. doi:10.1016/j.pec.2006.02.007

Bultman, D. C., & Svarstad, B. L. (2000). Effects of physician communication style on client medication beliefs and adherence with antidepressant treatment. *Patient Education and Counseling, 40,* 173–185. doi:10.1016/S0738-3991(99)00083-X

Choudhry, N. K., Stelfox, H. T., & Detsky, A. S. (2002). Relationships between authors of clinical practice guidelines and the pharmaceutical industry. *Journal of the American Medical Association, 287,* 612–617. doi:10.1001/jama.287.5.612

Collins, W. J. (2000). Licensed psychologists: Psychopharmacology training. *Dissertation Abstracts International, 61*B, 2750.

DiMatteo, M. R. (2003). Future directions in research on consumer-provider communication and adherence to cancer prevention and treatment. *Patient Education and Counseling, 50,* 23–26. doi:10.1016/S0738-3991(03)00075-2

Engel, G. L. (1977). The need for a new medical model: A challenge for biomedicine. *Science, 196,* 129–136. doi:10.1126/science.847460

Heres, S., Davis, J., Maino, K., Jetzinger, E., Kissling, W., & Leucht, S. (2006). Why olanzapine beats risperidone, risperidone beats quetiapine, and quetiapine beats olanzapine: An exploratory analysis of head-to-head comparison studies of second-generation antipsychotics. *American Journal of Psychiatry, 163,* 185–194. doi:10.1176/appi.ajp.163.2.185

Jørgensen, A. W., Hilden, J., & Gøtzsche, P. C. (2006, October 6). Cochrane reviews compared with industry supported meta-analyses and other meta-analyses of the same drugs: Systematic review. *British Medical Journal, 333,* 782. doi:10.1136/bmj.38973.444699.0B

Kampman, O., & Lehtinen, K. (1999). Compliance in psychoses. *Acta Psychiatrica Scandinavica, 100,* 167–175. doi:10.1111/j.1600-0447.1999.tb10842.x

Lasser, K. E., Allen, P. D., Woolhandler, S. J., Himmelstein, D. U., Wolfe, S. M., & Bor, D. H. (2002). Timing of new black box warnings and withdrawals for prescription medications. *Journal of the American Medical Association, 287,* 2215–2220. doi:10.1001/jama.287.17.2215

Lexchin, J., Bero, L. A., Djulbegovic, B., & Clark, O. (2003). Pharmaceutical industry sponsorship and research outcome and quality: Systematic review. *British Medical Journal, 326,* 1167–1170. doi:10.1136/bmj.326.7400.1167

Maddox, J. C., Levi, M., & Thompson, C. (1994). The compliance with antidepressants in general practice. *Journal of Psychopharmacology, 8,* 48–52. doi:10.1177/026988119400800108

Mitchell, A. J. (2006). Depressed patients and treatment adherence. *Lancet, 367,* 2041–2043. doi:10.1016/S0140-6736(06)68902-2

Monti, P. M., Wallander, J. L., & Delancey, A. L. (1983). Seminar training in APA-approved internship programs: Is there a core curriculum? *Professional Psychology: Research and Practice, 14,* 490–496. doi:10.1037/0735-7028.14.4.490

O'Neill, R. M., & Bornstein, R. F. (2001). The dependent patient in a psychiatric inpatient setting: Relationship of interpersonal dependency to consultation and medication frequencies. *Journal of Clinical Psychology, 57,* 289–298. doi:10.1002/jclp.1012

Rising, K., Bacchetti, P., & Bero, L. (2008). Reporting bias in drug trials submitted to the Food and Drug Administration: Review of publication and presentation. *PLoS Med, 5,* e217. doi:10.1371/journal.pmed.0050217

Skaer, T. L., Sclar, D. A., Robison, L. M., & Galin, R. S. (2000). Trend in the use of antidepressant pharmacotherapy and diagnosis of depression in the US: An assessment of office-based visits 1990 to 1998. *CNS Drugs, 14,* 473–481. doi:10.2165/00023210-200014060-00005

Smyer, M. A., Balster, R. L., Egli, D., Johnson, D. L., Kilbey, M. M., Lieth, N. J., & Puente, A. E. (1993). Summary of the Report of the Ad Hoc Task Force on Psychopharmacology of the American Psychological Association. *Professional Psychology: Research and Practice, 24,* 394–403. doi:10.1037/0735-7028.24.4.394

Turner, E. H., Matthews, A. M., Linardatos, E., Tell, R. A., & Rosenthal, R. (2008). Selective publication of antidepressant trials and its influence on apparent efficacy. *New England Journal of Medicine, 358,* 252–260. doi:10.1056/NEJMsa065779

VandenBos, G. R., & Williams, S. (2000). Is psychologists' involvement in the prescribing of psychotropic medication really a new activity? *Professional Psychology: Research and Practice, 31,* 615–618. doi: 10.1037/0735-7028.31.6.615

COMMENTARY: "Involvement in psychopharmacological issues" is an exquisitely apt characterization of the task with which all psychologists are now faced, irrespective of their personal or professional perspectives on the increasingly visible phenomenon of full or partial "prescriptive authority." Regardless of who ultimately wields the prescription pad, there is no denying the steady move toward integrated clinical services in this country, and it is a strangely rarified private practice indeed that would allow a psychologist to treat solely those clients/patients whose needs would never involve medication for mental health issues.

The most salient ethical obligation in this context—as in so many others—is to ensure that one's advice on psychopharmacological issues never outstrips one's relevant and up-to-date knowledge and objectively demonstrable credentials for offering such advice. It is clear to see, given the irreparable and easily quantifiable harm that can be occasioned by medication errors, how quickly and easily ethical concerns could evolve into legal ones as well.

The following references are recommended for those interested in further investigation of the potential ethical ramifications of involvement in psychopharmacological issues, including the political as well as scientific forces shaping debates on utility and appropriateness.

Cox, D. E., & Ellis, J. B. (2003). Prescriptive authority for clinical psychologists: A review of the debate. *Social Behavior and Personality, 31,* 275–282. http://dx.doi.org/10.2224/sbp.2003.31.3.275

DeLeon, P. H., Robinson Kurpius, S. E., & Sexton, J. L. (2001). Prescriptive authority for psychologists: Law, ethics, and public policy. In M. T. Sammons & N. B. Schmidt (Eds.), *Combined treatment for mental disorders: A guide to psychological and pharmacological interventions* (pp. 33–52). Washington, DC: American Psychological Association.

Gutheil, T. G. (2012). Reflections on ethical issues in psychopharmacology: An American perspective. *International Journal of Law and Psychiatry, 35,* 387–391. http://dx.doi.org/10.1016/j.ijlp.2012.09.007

Rinaldi, A. P. (2013). Prescriptive authority and counseling psychology: Implications for practitioners. *The Counseling Psychologist, 41,* 1213–1228. http://dx.doi.org/10.1177/0011000012461956

Storlie, C. A., Woo, H., Dipeolu, A., & Duenvas, D. (2015). Infusing ethics in psychopharmacology course design. *Journal of Creativity in Mental Health, 10,* 507–521. http://dx.doi.org/10.1080/15401383.2015.1044682

7.11. Guidelines for the Practice of Telepsychology

Joint Task Force for the Development of Telepsychology
Guidelines for Psychologists

These guidelines are designed to address the developing area of psychological service provision commonly known as telepsychology. *Telepsychology* is defined, for the purpose of these guidelines, as the provision of psychological services using telecommunication technologies, as expounded in the Definition of Telepsychology section of these guidelines. The expanding role of technology in the provision of psychological services and the continuous development of new technologies that may be useful in the practice of psychology present unique opportunities, considerations, and challenges to practice. With the advancement of technology and the increased number of psychologists using technology in their practices, these guidelines have been prepared to educate and guide them. . . .

The practice of telepsychology involves consideration of legal requirements, ethical standards, telecommunication technologies, intra- and interagency policies, and other external constraints, as well as the demands of the particular professional context. In some situations, one set of considerations may suggest a different course of action than another, and it is the responsibility of the psychologist to balance them appropriately. These guidelines aim to assist psychologists in making such decisions. In addition, it will be important for psychologists to be cognizant of and compliant with laws and regulations that govern independent practice within jurisdictions and across jurisdictional and international borders.

From "Guidelines for the Practice of Telepsychology," by the Joint Task Force for the Development of Telepsychology Guidelines for Psychologists, 2013, *American Psychologist*, *68*, pp. 791–800. Copyright 2013 by the American Psychological Association.

The "Guidelines for the Practice of Telepsychology" were developed by the Joint Task Force for the Development of Telepsychology Guidelines for Psychologists established by the following three entities: the American Psychological Association (APA), the Association of State and Provincial Psychology Boards (ASPPB), and the APA Insurance Trust (APAIT). The "Guidelines for the Practice of Telepsychology" were approved as APA policy by the APA Council of Representatives on July 31, 2013. The co-chairs of the joint task force were Linda Campbell and Fred Millan. Additional members of the task force included the following psychologists: Margo Adams Larsen, Sara Smucker Barnwell, Bruce E. Crow, Terry S. Gock, Eric A. Harris, Jana N. Martin, Thomas W. Miller, and Joseph S. Rallo. APA staff (Ronald S. Palomares, Deborah Baker, Joan Freund, and Jessica Davis) and ASPPB staff (Stephen DeMers, Alex M. Siegel, and Janet Pippin Orwig) provided direct support to the joint task force.

These guidelines are scheduled to expire as APA policy 10 years from July 31, 2013 (the date of their adoption by the APA Council of Representatives). After this date, users are encouraged to contact the APA Practice Directorate to determine whether this document remains in effect.

This is particularly true when providing telepsychology services. Where a psychologist is providing services from one jurisdiction to a client/patient located in another jurisdiction, the law and regulations may differ between the two jurisdictions. Also, it is the responsibility of the psychologists who practice telepsychology to maintain and enhance their level of understanding of the concepts related to the delivery of services via telecommunication technologies. Nothing in these guidelines is intended to contravene any limitations set on psychologists' activities based on ethical standards, federal or jurisdictional statutes or regulations, or for those psychologists who work in agencies and public settings.

. . .

COMPETENCE OF THE PSYCHOLOGIST

Guideline 1. Psychologists who provide telepsychology services strive to take reasonable steps to ensure their competence with both the technologies used and the potential impact of the technologies on clients/patients, supervisees, or other professionals.

Rationale

Psychologists have a primary ethical obligation to provide professional services only within the boundaries of their competence based on their education, training, supervised experience, consultation, study, or professional experience. As with all new and emerging areas in which generally recognized standards for preparatory training do not yet exist, psychologists utilizing telepsychology aspire to apply the same standards in developing their competence in this area. Psychologists who use telepsychology in their practices assume the responsibility for assessing and continuously evaluating their competencies, training, consultation, experience, and risk management practices required for competent practice.

. . .

STANDARDS OF CARE IN THE DELIVERY OF TELEPSYCHOLOGY SERVICES

Guideline 2. Psychologists make every effort to ensure that ethical and professional standards of care and practice are met at the outset and throughout the duration of the telepsychology services they provide.

Rationale

Psychologists delivering telepsychology services apply the same ethical and professional standards of care and professional practice that are required when providing in-person psychological services. The use of telecommunication technologies in the delivery of psychological services is a relatively new and rapidly evolving area, and therefore psychologists are encouraged to take particular care to evaluate and assess the appropriateness of utilizing these technologies prior to engaging in, and throughout the duration of, telepsychology practice to determine if the modality of service is appropriate, efficacious, and safe.

Telepsychology encompasses a breadth of different psychological services using a variety of technologies (e.g., interactive videoconferencing, telephone, text, e-mail, Web services, and mobile applications). The burgeoning research in telepsychology suggests that certain types of interactive telepsychological interventions are equal in effectiveness to their in-person counterparts (specific therapies delivered over videoteleconferencing and telephone). Therefore, before psychologists engage in providing telepsychology services, they are urged to conduct an initial assessment to determine the appropriateness of the telepsychology service to be provided for the client/patient. Such an assessment may include the examination of the potential risks and benefits of providing telepsychology services for the client's/patient's particular needs, the multicultural and ethical issues that may arise, and a review of the most appropriate medium (video teleconference, text, e-mail, etc.) or best options available for the service delivery. It may also include considering whether comparable in-person services are available and why services delivered via telepsychology are equivalent or preferable to such services. In addition, it is incumbent on the psychologist to engage in a continual assessment of the appropriateness of providing telepsychology services throughout the duration of the service delivery.

. . .

INFORMED CONSENT

Guideline 3. Psychologists strive to obtain and document informed consent that specifically addresses the unique concerns related to the telepsychology services they provide. When doing so, psychologists are cognizant of the applicable laws and regulations, as well as organizational requirements, that govern informed consent in this area.

Rationale
The process of explaining and obtaining informed consent, by whatever means, sets the stage for the relationship between the psychologist and the client/patient. Psychologists make reasonable efforts to offer a complete and clear description of the telepsychology services they provide, and they seek to obtain and document informed consent when providing professional services (APA Ethics Code, Standard 3.10). In addition, they attempt to develop and share the policies and procedures that will explain to their clients/patients how they will interact with them using the specific telecommunication technologies involved.

It may be more difficult to obtain and document informed consent in situations where psychologists provide telepsychology services to their clients/patients who are not in the same physical location or with whom they do not have in-person interactions. Moreover, there may be differences with respect to informed consent between the laws and regulations in the jurisdictions where a psychologist who is providing telepsychology services is located and those in the jurisdiction in which this psychologist's client/patient resides. Furthermore, psychologists may need to be aware of the manner in which cultural, linguistic, and socioeconomic characteristics and organizational considerations may impact a client's/patient's understanding of, and the special considerations required for, obtaining informed consent (such as when securing informed consent remotely from a parent/guardian when providing telepsychology services to a minor).

. . .

CONFIDENTIALITY OF DATA AND INFORMATION

Guideline 4. Psychologists who provide telepsychology services make reasonable efforts to protect and maintain the confidentiality of the data and information relating to their clients/patients and inform them of the potentially increased risks of loss of confidentiality inherent in the use of the telecommunication technologies, if any.

Rationale

The use of telecommunications technologies and the rapid advances in technology present unique challenges for psychologists in protecting the confidentiality of clients/patients. Psychologists who provide telepsychology learn about the potential risks to confidentiality before utilizing such technologies. When necessary, psychologists obtain the appropriate consultation with technology experts to augment their knowledge of telecommunication technologies in order to apply security measures in their practices that will protect and maintain the confidentiality of data and information related to their clients/patients.

Some of the potential risks to confidentiality include considerations related to uses of search engines and participation in social networking sites. Other challenges in this area may include protecting confidential data and information from inappropriate and/or inadvertent breaches to established security methods the psychologist has in place, as well as boundary issues that may arise as a result of a psychologist's use of search engines and participation on social networking sites. In addition, any Internet participation by psychologists has the potential of being discovered by their clients/patients and others and thereby potentially compromising a professional relationship.

. . .

SECURITY AND TRANSMISSION OF DATA AND INFORMATION

Guideline 5. Psychologists who provide telepsychology services take reasonable steps to ensure that security measures are in place to protect data and information related to their clients/patients from unintended access or disclosure.

Rationale

The use of telecommunication technologies in the provision of psychological services presents unique potential threats to the security and transmission of client/patient data and information. These potential threats to the integrity of data and information may include computer viruses, hackers, theft of technology devices, damage to hard drives or portable drives, failure of security systems, flawed software, ease of accessibility to unsecured electronic files, and malfunctioning or outdated technology. Other threats may include policies and practices of technology companies and vendors, such as tailored marketing derived from e-mail communications. Psychologists are encouraged to be mindful of these potential threats and to take reasonable steps to ensure that security measures are in place for protecting and controlling access to client/patient data within an information system. In addition, they are cognizant of relevant jurisdictional and federal laws and regulations that govern electronic storage and transmission of client/patient data and information, and they develop appropriate policies and procedures to comply with such directives. When developing policies and procedures to ensure the security of client/patient data and information, psychologists may include considering the unique concerns and impacts posed by both intended and unintended use of public and private technology devices, active and inactive therapeutic relationships, and the different safeguards required for different physical environments, different staffs (e.g., professional vs. administrative staff), and different telecommunication technologies.

. . .

DISPOSAL OF DATA AND INFORMATION AND TECHNOLOGIES

Guideline 6. Psychologists who provide telepsychology services make reasonable efforts to dispose of data and information and the technologies used in a manner that facilitates protection from unauthorized access and accounts for safe and appropriate disposal.

Rationale

Consistent with the APA "Record Keeping Guidelines" (American Psychological Association, 2007), psychologists are encouraged to create policies and procedures for the secure destruction of data and information and the technologies used to create, store, and transmit the data and information. The use of telecommunication technologies in the provision of psychological services poses new challenges for psychologists when they consider the disposal methods to utilize in order to maximally preserve client confidentiality and privacy. Psychologists are therefore urged to consider conducting an analysis of the risks to the information systems within their practices in an effort to ensure full and complete disposal of electronic data and information, plus the technologies that created, stored, and transmitted the data and information.

. . .

TESTING AND ASSESSMENT

Guideline 7. Psychologists are encouraged to consider the unique issues that may arise with test instruments and assessment approaches designed for in-person implementation when providing telepsychology services.

Rationale

Psychological testing and other assessment procedures are an area of professional practice in which psychologists have been trained, and they are uniquely qualified to conduct such tests. While some symptom screening instruments are already frequently being administered online, most psychological test instruments and other assessment procedures currently in use were designed and developed originally for in-person administration. Psychologists are thus encouraged to be knowledgeable about, and account for, the unique impacts of such tests, their suitability for diverse populations, and the limitations on test administration and on test and other data interpretations when these psychological tests and other assessment procedures are considered for and conducted via telepsychology. Psychologists also strive to maintain the integrity of the application of the testing and assessment process and procedures when using telecommunication technologies. In addition, they are cognizant of the accommodations for diverse populations that may be required for test administration via telepsychology. . . .

INTERJURISDICTIONAL PRACTICE

Guideline 8. Psychologists are encouraged to be familiar with and comply with all relevant laws and regulations when providing telepsychology services to clients/patients across jurisdictional and international borders.

Rationale

With the rapid advances in telecommunication technologies, the intentional or unintentional provision of psychological services across jurisdictional and international borders is becoming more of a reality for psychologists. Such service provision may range from the psychologists or clients/patients being temporarily out of state (including split residence across states) to psychologists offering their services across jurisdictional borders as a practice modality to take advantage of new telecommunication technologies. Psychological service delivery systems within such institutions as the U.S. Department of Defense and the Department of Veterans Affairs have already established internal policies and procedures for providing services within their systems that cross jurisdictional and international borders.

. . .

CONCLUSION

It is important to note that it is not the intent of these guidelines to prescribe specific actions, but rather, to offer the best guidance available at present when incorporating telecommunication technologies in the provision of psychological services. Because technology and its applicability to the profession of psychology constitute a dynamic area with many changes likely ahead, these guidelines also are not inclusive of all other considerations and are not intended to take precedence over the judgment of psychologists or applicable laws and regulations that guide the profession and practice of psychology. It is hoped that the framework presented will guide psychologists as the field evolves.

REFERENCE

American Psychological Association. (2007). Record keeping guidelines. *American Psychologist, 62,* 993–1004. doi:10.1037/0003-066X.62.9.993

COMMENTARY: Telepsychology was an inevitable development; after a fashion, it has existed since the roughly contemporaneous introduction of modern psychotherapy and the first public telephone systems. Psychologists have always been in touch with clients/patients by telephone to set appointments, deal with sudden crises, and offer occasional encouragement and support between sessions. Now, however, advances in Internet technology—and that technology's ubiquity in other commonplace contexts—have made it easier than ever to conceive of telepsychology as an appropriate medium for therapy and counseling sessions themselves.

The arrival of new or greatly enhanced media almost always occasions changes in standards of practice and attendant ethical considerations. Much is typically gained from the ability to see clients/patients in the flesh; are such data no longer relevant or required for certain forms of diagnosis or treatment? Is the session being recorded? By whom? Who else is present—in person just outside the frame, or electronically? Are the client/patient's responses to certain questions literally coming from a script? Of one thing we can be sure: Internet technology and related professional guidelines will continue to evolve in tandem.

The following references are recommended for those interested in further investigation of updated ethical requirements and proscriptions, and—as has so often been the case—the ways in which rural service provision has continued to spur policy innovations.

Campbell, L. F., Millan, F., & Martin, J. N. (2018). *A telepsychology casebook: Using technology ethically and effectively in your professional practice.* Washington, DC: American Psychological Association. http://dx.doi.org/10.1037/0000046-000

Fleming, D. A., Edison, K. E., & Pak, H. (2009). Telehealth ethics. *Telemedicine and e-Health, 15,* 797–803. http://dx.doi.org/10.1089/tmj.2009.0035

Graff, C. A., & Hecker, L. L. (2010). E-therapy: Developing an ethical online practice. In L. L. Hecker (Ed.), *Ethics and professional issues in couple and family therapy* (pp. 243–255). New York, NY: Routledge/Taylor & Francis.

Hertlein, K. M., Blumer, M. L. C., & Mihaloliakos, J. H. (2015). Marriage and family counselors' perceived ethical issues related to online therapy. *The Family Journal, 23,* 5–12. http://dx.doi.org/10.1177/1066480714547184

Reed, G. M., McLaughlin, C. J., & Milholland, K. (2000). Ten interdisciplinary principles for professional practice in telehealth: Implications for psychology. *Professional Psychology: Research and Practice, 31,* 170–178. http://dx.doi.org/10.1037/0735-7028.31.2.170

Schopp, L. H., Demiris, G., & Glueckauf, R. L. (2006). Rural backwaters or front-runners? Rural telehealth in the vanguard of psychology practice. *Professional Psychology: Research and Practice, 37,* 165–173. http://dx.doi.org/10.1037/0735-7028.37.2.165

8

Academia, Research, Teaching, and Supervision

Much has been made in earlier portions of this volume of the critical importance of instilling ethical values at regular, coordinated intervals in the course of university-based professional training. This having been noted, failure to provide such guidance is not the only ethical concern that looms over our understanding of the formative years of a psychological career. Sins of commission exist as well, including a host of inappropriate multiple relationships, such as exploitation of student labor, plagiarism or other misappropriation of student research, compelled personal disclosure in the context of student supervisory experiences that may adopt the contours of unwanted and contextually unwarranted psychotherapy, and romantic and sexual boundary violations.

Many such concerns bridge the chronological and experiential gap between student teaching and supervision on the one hand and interactions with insufficiently empowered junior research colleagues on the other. Contributions to published works must be credited, with authors listed in the order of their contributions to the book, chapter, article, or other resource in question. When an impasse is reached concerning the direction of an ongoing writing project, who "owns" the contributions that have already been made, when one party feels so strongly about the divisive issue that he or she views withdrawal as the only viable option? This situation becomes all the more consequential when the seemingly abandoned party has been relying on a successful conclusion to this project for continued academic employment, academic promotion, or tenure.

http://dx.doi.org/10.1037/0000125-009
Ethical Conflicts in Psychology, Fifth Edition, by E. Y. Drogin

What are the requisite parameters of clinical supervision? Are student trainees gaining only minimal exposure to needed opportunities because the supervisor—be it due to liability concerns, control issues, or inadvertence—insists upon conducting all psychotherapeutic and assessment services without allowing any more participation than passive observation? Alternatively, are supervisees being left, in effect, unsupervised, making critical therapeutic decisions and conducting complex psychological testing without their work truly being subjected to meaningful critique, and if necessary, correction?

Less easy in many settings to detect, substantiate, and ultimately prove are failures to provide opportunities for institutional advancement, perhaps because of a senior faculty member's acknowledged antipathy toward—or simple, personally unexamined neglect of—colleagues whose age, gender, cultural background, sexual orientation, or other observable or imputed characteristics are the basis for such neglect. Distinct from what may be the evidentiary underpinnings of legally founded grievances, how much does it matter for purposes of ethical saliency if this sort of lapse is motivated by bias or prejudice as opposed to simple inadvertence?

Among its other features, this chapter addresses ethics in research and publication, criticism and promotion of institutional review boards, the role of deception in research, laboratory animal research ethics, ethical boundaries of research conducted online, and the optimal content of undergraduate instruction on research ethics.

8.1. Ethics in Research and Publication

Thomas F. Nagy

Dr. Bell planned to use telephone interviews to gather data about the health history of older men and women from low socioeconomic positions. His rationale was that the phone typically offers greater privacy than face-to-face interviews, and research participants are likely to be more self-disclosing with the anonymity provided by this medium (Sieber, 1992). He had rejected using the Internet for gathering data because he concluded that this population would be less likely to be familiar with computers and his sampling would therefore be less representative.

He did not know that people from low socioeconomic groups usually do not live alone or have privacy from their families or caretakers when they use the phone (Sieber, 1992). He was also unaware that this population often keeps health secrets from their own family members and, therefore, would be less likely to freely disclose to a researcher information that they would not reveal to a family member who was within earshot. If he had conducted a pilot study or consulted an experienced investigator familiar with the characteristics of this group, he would have known that his methodology was flawed, and he could have made the necessary changes before proceeding.

INTRODUCTION

Although the first American Psychological Association (APA) Ethics Code (1953a) devoted many more standards to clinical than research matters, it at least introduced the topic of conducting the science of psychology within an ethical framework. The research section consisted of three parts: (a) Maintaining Standards of Research, (b) Protecting Welfare of Research Subjects, and (c) Reporting Research Results. These parts addressed such topics as preserving privacy, informed consent, harmful aftereffects, suppressing data, and humane treatment of animals—all present in the 2002 Ethics Code.

The first Ethics Code also addressed publication matters, in a section titled Writing and Publishing. This included how to list coauthors when there are multiple investigators, a decision rule for identifying who should be listed as the lead author, and acknowledging published and unpublished material that has influenced the research or writing (i.e., not mentioning plagiarism per se but addressing the topic in a general way).

The current ethical regulations about research and publication incorporate all of these original concepts and more. They have matured into a comprehensive tutorial comprising more ethical standards than any other section in the entire code. In this chapter, I first examine seven ethical areas concerning research, beginning with institutional review boards, and then four areas addressing publication matters.

INSTITUTIONAL REVIEW BOARDS

When contemplating research, psychologists must obtain approval from institutions where the research is conducted before proceeding (universities, schools, prisons, hospitals, the military, or any other setting). They must also submit their research proposal to the institutional review board (IRB) associated with their place of employment. In reviewing research proposals, the IRB considers institutional commitments and regulations, applicable laws, and standards of professional conduct and practice to safeguard the rights and welfare of people who volunteer to participate in the study.

According to federal rules, the IRB must include at least five members of varying backgrounds and diversity, including race, gender, and cultural matters, who are sensitive to community attitudes (Institutional Review Boards, 1991). Rules of membership are quite clear: include a diversity of professionals (e.g., psychologist, psychiatrist), at least one member whose primary concerns are in the scientific area, at least one member whose primary concerns are in non-scientific areas, at least one member who is not otherwise affiliated with the institution and is not related to a family member of a person affiliated with the institution, and no member who has a conflict of interest with any project under review. If the IRB reviews proposals involving vulnerable subjects, such as children, older people, hospitalized HIV patients, prisoners, pregnant women, or those who are mentally disabled (inpatients or outpatients), then the board must include someone who is knowledgeable about these populations.

Many investigators rely on federal grants for funding, and they must comply with federal rules and regulations, as articulated by the National Institutes of Health's Office of Research Integrity. For the most part these regulatory standards are clear and straightforward, and the investigator can learn which steps to take and what to avoid in protecting the welfare of research participants. These include such topics as minimizing risk to participants, providing thorough informed consent in advance, debriefing, and the like. If investigators are engaged in animal research, they must be well versed in the animal welfare principles as articulated by the federal rules and regulations, such as the Animal Welfare Act (2007), to be discussed in the section that follows.

PLANNING RESEARCH

Investigators are obligated to do research on topics with which they already have some familiarity so as to minimize the likelihood of harm to individuals. No matter how sophisticated investigators may be in their own specialty area, they may be relatively uninformed about a different area of study for a variety of reasons (e.g., type of population, the milieu, research design). If they are completely naive about a topic or a population, they must obtain some training or consult with others who are knowledgeable so as to optimize the research protocol and minimize the possibility of harm.

The psychologist who is researching alcoholism in an American Indian population but who has never directly observed the Indian culture should work with a coinvestigator or consultant who is familiar and skilled with this population. Likewise, an investigator using the Internet as a means of gathering data on patients with major depressive disorder would do well to consult with someone familiar with this medium first to better address informed consent, minimize potential harm to online participants who might be suicidal, and conduct long-term follow-up. By being familiar with the population and milieu, researchers will minimize invasiveness and be able to fine-tune protocols so as to choose procedures that might be more palatable to the research participants without compromising the study.

INFORMED CONSENT FOR RESEARCH PARTICIPANTS

Researchers must provide informed consent to individuals considering participating in research, disclosing information sufficient in scope and depth to help them formulate a decision about participating in the study.

Vulnerable Groups

When recruiting minors, investigators must obtain informed consent from parents or legal guardians and must obtain assent from the children (i.e., their agreement, regardless of how much the child understands of the research); direct appeals should never be offered directly to a child (Scott-Jones, 2000). An IRB would expect extra measures to be taken when recruiting members of other vulnerable groups, such as American Indians, high school equivalency students, those lacking financial resources (e.g., the homeless), those living in institutions (e.g., prisoners, residents of assisted living settings), those experiencing social stigmas (e.g., due to ethnicity, race, sexual orientation, physical disability), those in poor health (e.g., hospitalized patients), or those with mental limitations (e.g., serious mental illnesses, developmental disabilities, or dementias; Knapp & VandeCreek, 2006).

An example of an extra measure might be assessing a candidate's mental competency to understand informed consent in a study involving experimental treatment by using an instrument such as the MacArthur Competence Assessment Tool for Treatment (Grisso & Appelbaum, 1998). Examples of potential risk to a vulnerable group are examining the ethicality of assigning someone with suicidal ideation to a placebo group or allowing a participant exhibiting the beginning symptoms of mania to continue as a member of the control group. Another example is recruiting someone with dementia for a study involving deception.

Although the rationale and general concepts of informed consent are discussed in Chapter 5, it is useful to examine the specific ethical requirements as they appear in the 2002 Ethics Code. Standard 8.02, Informed Consent to Research, requires psychologists to

> inform prospective participants about (1) the purpose of the research, expected duration, and procedures; (2) their right to decline to participate and to withdraw from the research once it has begun; (3) the foreseeable consequences of declining or withdrawing; (4) reasonably foreseeable factors that may be expected to influence their willingness to participate such as potential risks, discomfort, or adverse effects; (5) any prospective research benefits; (6) limits of confidentiality; (7) incentives for participation; and (8) whom to contact for questions about the research and research participants' rights.

They must also provide the opportunity for participants to ask questions and receive answers.

The Stanford Prison Experiment was conducted in 1971 by Phil Zimbardo for the purpose of examining the psychological effects of assuming the role of a prisoner or prison guard (Haney, Banks, & Zimbardo, 1973). It is an excellent example of psychological research going awry and what the investigator ultimately did to protect the participants. The investigators paid 24 college students $15 per day to participate in the research. The students were screened for mental disorders and history of criminal activity and randomized into two groups, prisoners and guards, in a carefully designed "prison" setting in the basement of a building at Stanford University. What was intended to be a 2-week study had to be ended prematurely after 6 days because of the mental deterioration of the participants; the "guards" became sadistic, and the "prisoners" showed signs of extreme stress.

The primary investigator acknowledged that he had become so engaged in his role that he initially failed to appreciate the harm that his experiment could have on the participants. However, to his credit, he subsequently used the experiment for teaching ethical concepts for decades following the research. His website contains interesting video clips of the original study and is narrated by the author himself (http://www.prisonexp.org/).

Intervention research examines the use of experimental treatments and strategies with those experiencing clinical symptoms (e.g., obsessive-compulsive disorder, chemical dependency, or major depression), and psychologists must always proceed cautiously to protect patients and clients from harm. They must clarify the following to these prospective participants at the outset:

- the experimental nature of the treatment;

- the services that will or will not be available to the control group, if appropriate (i.e., if symptoms become worse during participation and a participant had been randomly assigned to a control group, what can that person expect by way of support or crisis intervention);

- the means by which assignment to treatment and control groups will be made;

- available treatment alternatives if one does not wish to participate in the research or decides to withdraw after the study has begun; and

- compensation for or monetary costs of participating, including whether third-party reimbursement will be sought (e.g., health insurance, Medicare).

. . .

Dispensing With Informed Consent

There are situations in which informed consent may be omitted, such as when the research would not be assumed to create distress or harm and confidentiality is protected. The following situations are described in Standard 8.05, Dispensing With Informed Consent for Research, of the 2002 Ethics Code as meeting the criteria for dispensing with informed consent: (a) studying normal educational practices, curricula, or classroom management methods conducted in educational settings; (b) anonymous questionnaires, naturalistic observations, or archival research (e.g., using anonymous patient data in hospitals) for which disclosure of responses would not place participants at risk of criminal or civil liability or damage their financial standing, employability, or reputation; and (c) the study of factors related to job or organization effectiveness conducted in organizational settings for which there is no risk to participants' employability.

The U.S. Department of Health and Human Services discusses the circumstances under which informed consent may be omitted in its *Code of Federal Regulations*, under Title 45, Public Welfare, Part 46, Protection of Human Subjects. It states that an IRB may rule to dispense with informed consent when (a) the research presents no more than minimal risk to participants and involves no procedures for which written consent is normally required outside of the research context and (b) the only record linking the subject and the research is the consent document itself, and the principal risk would be potential harm resulting from a breach of confidentiality (Protection of Human Subjects, 1991, amended 2005). To satisfy the second condition, each subject would be asked whether he or she wants documentation linking him or her with the research, and these wishes would govern. The term *minimal risk* means that the probability and magnitude of harm or discomfort anticipated in the research are not greater in and of themselves than those ordinarily encountered in daily life or during the performance of routine physical or psychological examinations or tests (Protection of Human Subjects, 1991, amended 2005).

Researchers may dispense with informed consent when audio- and videotaping under two conditions: (a) if the research consists solely of naturalistic observations in public places, and it is not anticipated that the recording will be used in a way that could cause personal identification or harm or (b) the research design includes deception, and consent for the use of the recording is obtained during the debriefing stage, after the participant's involvement with the protocol has ended (i.e., the participant may choose to delete the recording at that point).

Protecting the Welfare of Subordinate Research Participants Who Decline or Withdraw

When conducting research with those in a subordinate relationship, such as patients or students, investigators must exercise additional caution to protect the prospective subjects' rights if they decline to participate or withdraw after data gathering has begun. If a patient or student refuses to participate in the study or withdraws after it has begun, he or she is entitled to receive referrals to competent therapists uninvolved with the research protocol who are able to accept new patients. The investigator must be neither coercive regarding participating at the outset nor punitive if the individual withdraws. And if students are required to participate in research as part of a course requirement or for extra credit, they must also be given the option of an equitable alternative if they decline to engage in the investigation.

OFFERING INDUCEMENTS FOR PARTICIPATING IN RESEARCH

Investigators commonly offer incentives to prospective participants, such as money, medication, didactic experiences, or therapeutic interventions (e.g., meditation, hypnosis, individual or group therapy). These can be powerful motivating factors for the vulnerable groups mentioned earlier (students, those who lack financial resources, and those who are stigmatized, institutionalized, or physically or mentally ill).

> In an attempt to increase response rate, a researcher planned to offer elementary school children a decorative pencil as a reward for returning a signed parental permission form. The researcher devised this strategy because the school did not give permission to mail forms directly to parents; instead, the school requested that forms be sent home with the children. The researcher emphasized that all children who returned a signed form would receive the pencil, including those children whose parents declined to participate as well as those whose parents agreed. At its initial review, the IRB objected to the pencil as an inducement, asserting that such a reward was coercive. On appeal, however, the IRB reversed its decision, acknowledging that the magnitude of this reward was modest and was unlikely to be coercive. In addition, the reward was given to children for returning the signed permission form, regardless of parents' decision to agree or decline to participate (Scott-Jones, 2000).

If offering clinical services as an inducement, investigators must provide information about the nature of the services, risks and obligations, and limitations. For example, when offering individual psychotherapy to research participants, the investigator must clarify if there is an option to continue in treatment with the same therapist after the protocol has ended. Also, the investigator must clarify if there would be any cost for the treatment, either during the course of data gathering or afterward, and if there is a limit to the number of therapy sessions afterward.

Investigators must avoid taking advantage of prospective participants, exploiting, or coercing them in any way as a means of increasing their sample size. The investigator must carefully consider the value of an inducement with a particular vulnerable group within the local geographical area. Offering too great an inducement diminishes the participant's freedom of choice in weighing risks and benefits (Scott-Jones, 2000). Coercion can occur whenever an individual feels that he or she cannot afford to avoid participating in the investigation because there is so much to gain from the inducement that is offered. A homeless person, prisoner, or someone experiencing panic attacks might feel that the inducements of money, privileges, or clinical intervention would far outweigh any potential adverse experiences that might be inherent in the research. They may give a cursory glance at the risks section of the consent form and make a premature decision to join the study, regardless of personal inconvenience, time required, psychological stress, or other negative factors to be encountered as part of the study. When investigators have questions about the nature of an inducement to offer, they should consult with peers, their IRB overseeing the study, and stakeholders in the study. Even if they are not affiliated with an institution with an IRB, they may seek a review of their protocol with another institution's IRB that is authorized to evaluate external research proposals.

DECEPTION IN RESEARCH

Deception in research consists of either providing false information to participants about the purpose or goals of an investigation at the outset or deliberately misrepresenting facts or information during the course of the experiment. It remains a controversial topic among psychologists even in this day and age. Questions (Eyde, 2000) to consider are as follows:

- What responsibilities does an investigator have when considering using deception in research?

- How might participants be harmed by the deceptive information about the nature of the experiment?

- Which populations are at the greatest risk of experiencing this harm?

- To what extent are self-reports of no adverse impact by the deception judged to be expected and desirable responses to the experimenter (at the debriefing session)?

- What might researchers do to counteract potential negative consequences of deception?

On deontological grounds it can be argued that it is inherently unethical and undesirable to ever deliberately deceive people. This is consistent with the Principle C: Integrity: "Psychologists seek to promote accuracy, honesty, and truthfulness in the science, teaching, and practice of psychology. In these activities psychologists do not steal, cheat, or engage in fraud, subterfuge, or *intentional misrepresentation of fact*" [italics added]. Principle B: Fidelity and

Responsibility reminds psychologists that "psychologists establish relationships of trust with those with whom they work." Lying about the purpose of an experiment or providing erroneous data during its course would seem to violate this principle.

On teleological grounds it can be argued that acts of deception by researchers result in undesirable consequences for the research participant, individual investigator, the public perception of psychologists, and ultimately the science of psychology (Kimmel, 1998; Ortmann & Hertwig, 1997). It undermines individual's trust in psychologists, alters the behavior of future participants in the same experimental protocol (the *spillover effect* whereby future participants are contaminated by learning of past participants' experiences and expect to be deceived), thereby possibly affecting data collection and the ultimate findings of the investigation.

A commonly cited experiment. . . was conducted by Stanley Milgram, who published his controversial investigation titled "Behavioral Study of Obedience" in 1963. Milgram studied *destructive obedience* by recruiting 40 participants ("teachers") to administer electric shocks to "learners" (confederates in another room pretending to suffer with each jolt) whenever they made an error. The primary dependent variable was the maximum shock (30 levels of intensity) that the teacher was willing to deliver before refusing to continue. Of the group, 26 participants obeyed all commands, administering the maximum intensity of shock even while hearing screams of anguish from learners; 14 participants broke off the experiment at some point after the victim protested and refused to provide further answers. The procedure created extreme levels of nervous tension in some teachers, including profuse sweating, trembling, stuttering, and nervous laughter. Extensive debriefing followed the experiment, whereby teachers and confederates were allowed to interact with each other, disclose the deception, and process their emotional reaction. Milgram argued that the social benefit of his study outweighed any adverse effects to the participants.

To be sure, Milgram's notorious investigation revealed useful data about the willingness of people to comply with authority, as did Zimbardo's Stanford prison experiment 8 years later. However, neither of these investigations would likely be approved by an IRB by today's standards because the risk of harm to participants would be considered too great, and the use of nondeceptive techniques or lower risk designs might be able to be substituted to attain the same results (e.g., virtual reality settings created on the computer).

There is a fundamental rule against deceiving participants in a research experiment: If the same research can be carried out without deception, then it should be. However, if the prospective value of the research necessitates having some degree of deception in the course of the study, then this is acceptable as long as adequate debriefing occurs so that participants do not feel duped, manipulated, betrayed, or otherwise harmed. Standard 8.07, Deception in Research, of the 2002 Ethics Code sums up the four criteria to be met before an investigator may use deception: (a) Deceptive techniques must be justified by the study's significant prospective scientific, educational, or applied value and only if nondeceptive strategies are not feasible; (b) there must be no deception about the infliction of physical pain or severe emotional distress; (c) the deception must be revealed and participants debriefed as early as feasible—preferably at the end of their participation, but no later than at the end of data collection; and (d) participants must be permitted to withdraw their data after being debriefed. The last three criteria are straightforward and could unambiguously be met by an investigator; however, the first one can be a major hurdle to overcome because it consists of the investigator's personal judgment about the prospective value of the study and is therefore subject to bias.

The *prospective scientific value* of an investigation consists of its significance as a contribution to the knowledge base. The *prospective educational value* of an investigation refers to its benefit to individuals or to society. And the *prospective applied value* refers to industrial and organizational settings, environmental psychology, or direct implications for the ways in which psychologists intervene in the lives of others (Nagy, 2005). Before the investigator proceeds, it is his or her ethical duty to make an objective appraisal of the prospective value of the research using available resources, such as consulting with peers who have addressed similar hypotheses in their research, review of the scientific literature, and seeking advice from the local IRB. The investigator should consider deception to be a last resort, an acceptable choice only after exploring all reasonable options for testing the hypotheses without using deception.

DEBRIEFING

Investigators must provide a prompt opportunity for participants to learn about the nature, results, and conclusions of the research as well as correct any misconceptions that participants may have concerning the investigation. They may delay or withhold this feedback if scientific or humane values justify such a step. For example, as mentioned, it may be important to avoid contaminating the subject pool of future participants by delaying debriefing, and in research with participants with diminished capacity or who are moribund and unable to comprehend the debriefing, it may be more humane to withhold it (Canter et al., 1994).

Debriefing can mollify the effects of research using deception or creating aversive reactions. Certainly the creative measures taken by Milgram, allowing participant and confederate to interact at the conclusion of the study and revealing the true nature of the research, and Zimbardo, ending the experiment after only 6 days and evaluating the participants, helped reverse any long-term negative effects. If investigators discover that being involved in research has harmed a participant, they must take steps to minimize the harm at the end of data collection.

> In a study designed to test the effect of negative emotions on memory, participants were asked to take a psychological test to measure anxiety and depression and then randomized into two groups. One group was given true feedback about test results, and one was given exaggerated false negative feedback results intended to elevate anxiety in the participants. Participants were then asked to memorize a list

of paired words, given a distraction cognitive task, and then tested on their memory for the paired-words list.

Immediately following the data collection the experimenter provided an open-ended, extensive debriefing to those who were deceived by having an individual face-to-face meeting. The experimenter explained that participants were given false results and apologized for misleading them. The experimenter asserted a preference for conducting the study without deception but stated that it was essential to create cognitive dissonance in one group by providing falsely elevated anxiety and depression scores and then noting how their performance differed from the other group. The experimenter then showed the participants a bell-shaped curve and explained, in lay terms, what the participants' true scores were on depression and anxiety controlled for age and gender. She monitored the participants' emotional reactions during the debriefing session and encouraged participants to ask questions and seek clarification in an unhurried manner.

The experimenter explained that there still was a possibility that the effects of negative feedback might persist and that people sometimes have a tendency to discount information that is presented during debriefing that is inconsistent with the deceptive negative feedback received during the experiment (Ross, Lepper, & Hubbard, 1975). Simply being aware of this possibility helps dispel the effect. The experimenter assured the participants that pilot testing had been done to ascertain that the deception was believable and that participants were not gullible and should not feel shameful or foolish. The experimenter again apologized for the subterfuge, and on closing the interview, provided a name, telephone number, and e-mail address for any questions or concerns that might surface later. The experimenter asked permission to telephone participants for follow-up after 1 week to check on their frame of mind and make sure that they were feeling all right about the experiment (Eyde, 2000).

The importance of debriefing and removing misconceptions cannot be over-emphasized. In a marketing study, participants had been told that a fast-food chain had been rumored to be using red-worm meat in its hamburgers. At the conclusion of the study, one group of participants received a conventional debriefing but continued to hold significantly less positive attitude toward the fast-food chain. The other group received explicit debriefing and did not hold a statistically different attitude toward the chain than the control group, which had not been told of the red-worm rumor (Misra, 1992). Misconceptions can linger for an indefinite period of time, possibly forever, and affect former participants in a variety of ways, even without conscious awareness.

ANIMAL RESEARCH

More than 90% of animal research involves the use of rodents (rats and mice) or birds (usually pigeons); use of dogs and cats by experimenters is rare (Knapp & VandeCreek, 2006). Supporters of animal research argue that humans benefit from animal experimentation and that animals do not experience discomfort or restriction of freedom in the same way as humans. Detractors argue that there is limited generalizability from animal research to humans, that animals do experience pain and suffering, that they have rights that should be protected, and that investigators have a duty to protect those rights (Beauchamp, 1997).

Although the first Ethics Code (1953a) contained no specific standards on animal welfare, it referred readers to a separate document, *Rules Regarding Animals*, that was published by the APA Committee on Precautions in Animal Experimentation (1949). The 2002 Ethics Code presents seven standards for the humane care and use of animals: (a) investigators must comply with federal, state, and local laws when acquiring, caring for, maintaining, using, and disposing of animals; (b) investigators must be trained in research methods and supervise all procedures, ensuring comfort, health, and humane treatment; (c) investigators must ensure adequate instruction to those under their supervision in the proper maintenance and handling of the species being used; (d) investigators must minimize discomfort, infection, illness, and pain; (e) investigators must never use a procedure subjecting animals to pain, stress, or privation unless there are no alternative procedures that address the same hypothesis and the goal is justified by its prospective scientific, educational, or applied value (see previous standards); (f) when performing surgical procedures, investigators must always use appropriate anesthesia and follow procedures to avoid infection and minimize pain during and after surgery; and (g) when terminating an animal's life, investigators must proceed rapidly, attempting to minimize pain, in accordance with accepted procedures. The APA Board of Scientific Affairs' Committee on Animal Research and Ethics has also produced videos and other educational materials, among them *Guidelines for Ethical Conduct in the Care and Use of Animals* (1996; http://www.apa.org/science/leadership/care/guidelines.aspx). Institutions that support animal research have an institutional animal care and use committee that oversees the conduct of all researchers and assistants who maintain, use, and care for the animals.

Federal laws constitute another resource for animal experimenters. Regulations of the U.S. Department of Agriculture were signed into law as The Animal Welfare Act in 1966, with the most recent amendment in 2007, and this law describes specific responsibilities and obligations of researchers for the humane treatment of the animals they use (Animal Welfare Act, 1996, amended 2007). And the Institute of Laboratory Animal Resources, Commission on Life Sciences, and the National Research Council, under the auspices of the National Academy of Sciences, published the *Guide for the Care and Use of Laboratory Animals* (1996). In addition, there is a private nonprofit organization, the American Association for the Accreditation of Laboratory Animal Care, that educates researchers about the minimum legal requirements and provides advice to researchers when needed (http://www.aaalac.org/about/index.cfm).

REPORTING RESEARCH RESULTS

Fair and accurate reporting of scientific research has been an ethical duty since the very first Ethics Code in 1953, which required psychologists interpreting the science of psychology to do so "fairly and accurately," without "exaggeration, sensationalism, superficiality, and premature reporting of new developments." Since then a number of ethical rules have been developed to guide investigators reporting on their research in individual or collaborative efforts. Original research is generally reported first in professional journals and later released to the media—Internet, radio or television, newspapers, and popular magazines—as journalists become aware of innovative studies. The primary directive in reporting research results is to do so accurately, avoiding deceptive or false statements. Psychologists must never fabricate data—that is, they must never change the reported sample sizes, delete data that did not support the research hypothesis, misrepresent the nature of the independent variables, falsify participants' ratings or reactions, lie about the characteristics of the participants, make false claims about the methodology of the investigation (report on interventions that never occurred, claim that randomized trials occurred when in fact they did not), alter statistical findings (levels of statistical significance, correlation coefficients, analysis of variance findings, chi square results), or misrepresent or distort any aspect of the protocol design or implementation. Also, if they discover significant errors in their published results, they must take reasonable steps to correct them, generally in the form of a printed correction, retraction, erratum, or other means.

One safeguard for preserving the integrity of authors is the peer-monitoring system whereby investigators are obliged to release their research data for verification by others. Researchers must release their data after the results have been published to any competent professional who wishes to verify the substantive claims by reanalyzing the data. However, they may not then use the data for research of their own unless consent is secured from the original investigator.

The Office of Research Integrity (ORI), a branch of the U.S. Department of Health and Human Services (http://ori.hhs.gov), publishes a quarterly newsletter reporting on scientific misconduct at institutions where federally funded research has occurred. Examples from this publication follow; they are taken from the 2006 ORI Annual Report:

> Based on the report of an investigation conducted by the University of Wisconsin-Madison (UWM) and additional analysis conducted by the Office of Research Integrity in its oversight review, PHS found that Ms. ____, former graduate student, UWM, engaged in research misconduct by fabricating data in thirty-nine (39) questionnaires of sibling human subjects associated with an autism study. The research was supported by National Institute on Aging (NIA), National Institutes of Health (HIN), grant# _____.

It is particularly sad when a graduate student begins a career in psychology by falsifying research for her doctoral degree, as in the following case.

> Based on an investigation conducted by the University of California at Los Angeles (UCLA) and additional analysis conducted by the Office of Research Integrity (ORI) in its oversight review, ORI found that Ms. _____, former graduate student, Department of Psychology, UCLA, engaged in research misconduct by falsifying or fabricating data and statistical results for up to nine pilot studies on the impact of vulnerability on decision-making from the fall 2000 to winter 2002 as a basis for her doctoral thesis research. The falsified or fabricated data were included in a manuscript submitted to *Psychological Science*, in National Institutes of Mental

Health (NIMH), National Institutes of Health (NIH), grant application #_____, and in NIMH, NIH, pre-doctoral training grant#_____.

It is noteworthy that even students and researchers carrying out studies at excellent academic institutions still commit research fraud, sometimes falling prey to publication pressures that are a common aspect of academia, as in this excerpt from a 1999 ORI Newsletter.

> ORI found that Ms. _____, a former research assistant, Department of Psychiatry at the UIC [University of Illinois at Chicago], engaged in scientific misconduct in clinical research supported by a grant from NIMH by fabricating data in the records of 41 patients, including dates on which she claimed to have conducted interviews in certain clinics, fabricating patient consent forms and questionnaires from patients participating in the project; and submitting false information in "Study Daily Logs" that recorded each day's events. For 3 years beginning December 7, 1998, Ms. _____ is prohibited from serving in any advisory capacity to the PHS, and her participation any PHS-funded research is subject to supervision requirements.

Students are not the only ones who can run afoul of the rules. In 2000, a promising young psychology professor from Harvard University published a research paper in the *Personality and Social Psychology Bulletin* that was based on data that she had fabricated. The fraud was revealed when a colleague asked to see her original data, and she admitted to having used invalid data. The professor's lamentable actions resulted in, among other things, being excluded from U.S. government agency grants, contracts, and cooperative agreements for 5 years (http://grants.nih.gov/grants/guide/notice-files/NOT-OD-02-020.html).

Plagiarism and Duplicate Publication of Data

Psychologists must never present portions of another's work or data as their own. Whether using a verbatim quote or paraphrasing another, whether published or unpublished, authors must always acknowledge their sources, including personal communications such as discussions, correspondence, e-mail, or other significant contributing bases for their remarks. Even plagiarizing from oneself is considered unethical. This occurs if an author publishes his original data as seminal research on more than one occasion, such as publishing one's research about using positron emission tomography technology in developing a treatment protocol for those with Tourette's disorder in a psychological journal in 2009 and then again in a psychiatry or neurology journal in 2010 without citing the original publication.

Plagiarism is not restricted to those doing research. Clinicians who do psychological assessment may send a personality test such as the Millon Clinical Multiaxial Inventory-III to a computerized scoring service and receive a narrative report in return. It may be common practice for a psychologist performing an evaluation to include the results of the scoring and even copy complete sentences or paragraphs of the computerized printout for use in the psychological report; however the psychologist must still cite the source, such as Consulting Psychologists Press or Psychological Assessment Resources. These materials are clearly labeled "copyrighted," and plagiarizing them is not only unethical but also illegal under federal law and extending to citizens in most countries of the world.

A relatively recent form of plagiarism involves academic fraud, a student's use of online resources, or "paper mills" for meeting course requirements. Obviously these sources would never be cited, and additional ethical rules beyond avoiding plagiarizing would also be involved.

Publication Credit: A Gray Area

Attributing authorship in a joint venture is usually decided in advance and based on the relative scientific or professional contributions of the individuals involved, regardless of their status (e.g., professor, graduate student). Minor contributions to the research or writing are acknowledged in other ways, such as in footnotes or an introductory section. Usually a student is listed as the primary author in a multiple-authored article if it is substantially based on the student's doctoral dissertation.

However, ambiguities sometimes present themselves, such as when a friendly, informal discussion between professionals about psychological topics results in one of the parties deciding to proceed with developing a research hypothesis and designing a protocol for examining the question. Should the colleague in the original discussion then be cited, footnoted, or recognized in some other way when the article is published in a professional journal? Remedies for this sort of dilemma can usually be rectified by consulting with the colleague early on and seeking his or her input on resolving it. Problems can also occur when an initial agreement for collaborative work is not honored and disputes for principal authorship result. . . .

CONFIDENTIALITY IN PEER REVIEW

Psychologists who review material that is submitted for presentation, publication, grant, or research proposal review must preserve the confidentiality and proprietary rights of the author. They must not only treat as confidential the substance and content of material but also refrain from using it in any way. Discussing or revealing the contents with anyone not specifically involved with the review process is prohibited, as is using or discussing the information with colleagues, students, the media, over the Internet, or in any other personal or professional forum.

It is fair to say that the science of psychology and most of what psychologists do in delivering their services to consumers rests solidly on research that ultimately is published in peer-reviewed professional journals and books. And that very research serves the profession and humanity well when it is carried out in an unhurried, well-planned manner that is consistent with professional, ethical, and legal guidelines for the benefit of all. Students, trainees, and their teachers and mentors depend on the integrity of those doing research in learning and teaching applied psychology. . . .

REFERENCES

American Psychological Association, Committee on Precautions in Animal Experimentation. (1949). *Rules regarding animals.* Washington, DC: Author.

American Psychological Association. (1953a). *Ethical standards of psychologists.* Washington, DC: Author.

American Psychological Association. (2010). *Ethical principles of psychologists and code of conduct* (2002, Amended June 1, 2010). Retrieved from http://www.apa.org/ethics/code/index.aspx

Animal Welfare Act, 7 U.S.C. § 2131–2156. (1966, amended 2007). Retrieved from http://www.nal.usda.gov/awic/legislat/awa.htm

Beauchamp, T. (1997). Opposing views of animal experimentation: Do animals have rights? *Ethics & Behavior, 7,* 113–121. doi:10.1207/s15327019eb0702_3

Canter, M., Bennett, B., Jones, S., & Nagy, T. (1994). *Ethics for psychologists: A commentary on the APA ethics code.* Washington, DC: American Psychological Association. doi:10.1037/10162-000

Eyde, L. (2000). Other responsibilities to participants. In B. Sales & S. Folkman (Eds.), *Ethics in research with human participants* (pp. 61–73). Washington, DC: American Psychological Association.

Grisso, T., & Appelbaum, P. (1998). *Assessing competence to consent to treatment: A guide for physicians and other health professionals.* New York, NY: Oxford University Press.

Haney, C., Banks, W. C., & Zimbardo, P. G. (1973). Interpersonal dynamics in a simulated prison. *International Journal of Criminology and Penology, 1,* 69–97.

Institute of Laboratory Animal Resources, Commission on Life Sciences, & National Research Council. (1996). *Guide for the care and use of laboratory animals.* Retrieved from http://www.nap.edu/openbook.php?record_id=5140

Institutional Review Boards, Subpart B: Organization and Personnel, 21 C.F.R. 56.107, IRB membership (1991).

Kimmel, A. (1998). In defense of deception. *American Psychologist, 53,* 803–804. doi:10.1037/0003-066X.53.7.803

Knapp, S. J., & VandeCreek, L. D. (2006). *Practical ethics for psychologists: A positive approach.* Washington, DC: American Psychological Association.

Milgram, S. (1963). Behavioral study of obedience. *Journal of Abnormal and Social Psychology, 67,* 371–378. doi:10.1037/h0040525

Misra, S. (1992). Is conventional debriefing adequate? An ethical issue in consumer research. *Journal of the Academy of Marketing Science, 20,* 269–273. doi:10.1007/BF02723415

Nagy, T. (2005). *Ethics in plain English: An illustrative casebook for psychologists.* Washington, DC: American Psychological Association.

Ortmann, A., & Hertwig, R. (1997). Is deception acceptable? *American Psychologist, 52,* 746–747. doi:10.1037/0003-066X.52.7.746

Protection of Human Subjects, 45, C.F.R., Pt. 46 § 46.107 (1991, amended 2005).

Ross, L., Lepper, M. R., & Hubbard, M. (1975). Perseverance in self-perception and social perception: Biased attributional processes in the debriefing paradigm. *Journal of Personality and Social Psychology, 32,* 880–892. doi:10.1037/0022-3514.32.5.880

Scott-Jones, D. (2000). Recruitment of research participants. In B. Sales & S. Folkman (Eds.), *Ethics in research with human participants* (pp. 27–34). Washington, DC: American Psychological Association.

Sieber, J. E. (1992). *Planning ethically responsible research.* Newbury Park, CA: Sage.

COMMENTARY: Ethical issues regarding research and publication receive considerably less attention than those that involve clinical matters—in the annals of our various state licensing boards and in the pages of the American Psychological Association's (2017) *Ethical Principles of Psychologists and Code of Conduct* ("APA Ethics Code"). This is not to suggest that the stakes for those conducting studies and contributing to the professional literature are any less impactful or that discerning the right form of collegial comportment is any less complex a matter. The amount of ink devoted to an ethical topic is no reliable measure of its relevance.

Failures to adhere to ethical principles in this area do a disservice to the vital intellectual and scientific wellspring of psychology as a discipline. Researchers and other authors can be dissuaded from following this career path altogether if their published works are plagiarized, or if they do not receive proper credit for their contributions. Looming over all of this, of course, is the potential for harm to human and nonhuman research subjects—the focus of institutional review boards, the activities of which have far-reaching ethical implications.

The following references are recommended for those interested in further investigation of research and publication ethics from the point of view of academic contributors and science journal editors alike.

American Psychological Association. (2017). *Ethical principles of psychologists and code of conduct* (2002, Amended June 1, 2010 and January 1, 2017). Retrieved from http://www.apa.org/ethics/code/index.aspx

Klein, D. F., & Glick, I. D. (2008). Conflict of interest, journal review, and publication policy. *Neuropsychopharmacology, 33*, 3023–3026. http://dx.doi.org/10.1038/npp.2008.109

Laflin, M. T., Glover, E. D., & McDermott, R. J. (2005). Publication ethics: An examination of authorship practices. *American Journal of Health Behavior, 29*, 579–587. http://dx.doi.org/10.5993/AJHB.29.6.12

Poster, E., Pearson, G. S., & Pierson, C. (2012). Publication ethics: Its importance to readers, authors, and the profession. *Journal of Child and Adolescent Psychiatric Nursing, 25*, 1–2. http://dx.doi.org/10.1111/j.1744-6171.2011.00317.x

Price, J. H., Dake, J. A., & Islam, R. (2001). Selected ethical issues in research and publication: Perceptions of health education faculty. *Health Education & Behavior, 28*, 51–64. http://dx.doi.org/10.1177/109019810102800106

Wager, E., Fiack, S., Graf, C., Robinson, A., & Rowlands, I. (2009). Science journal editors' views on publication ethics: Results of an international survey. *Journal of Medical Ethics, 35*, 348–353. http://dx.doi.org/10.1136/jme.2008.028324

8.2. Asking Too Much of Institutional Review Boards

Gregory A. Miller

Consider some premises: (1) Unfettered inquiry is fundamentally important to scholarship and to the many public benefits that quality scholarship brings. (2) Ethical treatment of subjects in human research is imperative, common, and sometimes inconvenient. (3) Serious abuse happens but is very rare. (4) Detecting nonsalient events, with high sensitivity and high specificity, can be more difficult when base rates are low. On these grounds alone, we know that we will have a difficult time establishing procedures for scholars, and for those who regulate them, that both maximize protection of subjects and minimize interference with scholarship. It is quite likely that we will create rules and procedures that most of the time appear to be a waste of resources—regulating common, innocuous activities in order to prevent or detect uncommon, harmful activities. Indeed, if Institutional Review Board (IRB) efforts routinely revealed unethical scholarship, something would be terribly wrong. That most IRB-related work appears unnecessary is ethically very reassuring.

Work on clinical decision-making tells us that judges will (and probably should) alter their decision thresholds based on perceptions of base rates. Thus, a sense that federal regulators have become more willing to "invoke the death penalty" (shutting down virtually all human research indefinitely at an institution found to have hosted seriously noncompliant projects, jeopardizing not

From "Asking Too Much of Institutional Review Boards," by G. A. Miller, 2007, APA Division 12, Society of Clinical Psychology, Section III Society for a Science of Clinical Psychology, *Winter 2007*, pp. 6–9. Copyright 2007 by the American Psychological Association.

I appreciate Dan Klein's invitation to comment on the recent crescendo in debates about the scope of IRB regulation of scholarship. I thank my fellow members of the University of Illinois Center for Advanced Study Steering Committee: E. M. Bruner, N. C. Burbules, L. Dash, M. Finkin, J. P. Goldberg, W. T. Greenough, C. K. Gunsalus (chair), & M. G. Pratt. Also due thanks are Stephen Breckler and Ivor Pritchard for insightful consultation. Some of the points made here draw from the collective work of the Steering Committee:

Gunsalus, C. K., Bruner, E. M., Burbules, N. C., Dash, L., Finkin, M., Goldberg, J. P., Greenough, W. T., Miller, G. A., Pratt, M. G., Iriye, M., & Aronson, D. (2005). The Illinois White Paper—Improving the system for protecting human subjects: Counteracting IRB "Mission Creep." In C.K. Gunsalus (Ed.), *Human subject protection regulations and research outside the biomedical sphere*. Urbana, IL: University of Illinois Center for Advanced Study, available at http://www.law.uiuc.edu/conferences/whitepaper/whitepaper.pdf.

Gunsalus, C. K., Bruner, E. M., Burbules, N. C., Dash, L., Finkin, M., Goldberg, J. P., Greenough, W. T., Miller, G. A., & Pratt, M. G. (2006). Mission creep in the IRB world. *Science, 312*, 1441.

only careers but millions of dollars in research grants) has spooked scholars and IRBs alike. One result is that many feel that IRBs are suffering from "mission creep," with the implicit assumption that more regulation of more scholarly activity will improve protection of subjects, scholars, and the universities, hospitals, and other institutions that house them.

Widespread perceptions that IRBs are extending their reach beyond their mandates and beyond their resources are fostering considerable discussion about the nature of research, the proper scope of IRBs, and the principles and mechanics of IRB operation. I have participated in conferences sponsored by the University of Illinois Center for Advanced Study (2003, 2005) and the American Psychological Association (2006) as well as in a series of study groups at the University of Illinois advising campus administration on the nature and operation of our IRB. The resulting advice is cheap and not to date generally followed, but the issues are coming more into focus. Some issues of definition and scope are particularly clear and far from resolved.

A central issue concerns the nature and scope of scholarly activity that IRBs should routinely review and regulate. This issue turns on both a policy question (should IRBs regulate "all research" or only certain kinds of research?) and an abstract question (what counts as "research?"). On the policy question, a university might decide to require that its IRB review "all research." Federal regulators do not require that, but the buzz has been that the feds do unofficially encourage it, putting unstated pressure on institutions to go that route. Anecdotal evidence suggests that the tide has shifted, however, with more institutions opting for what is called a "limited assurance" agreement with federal regulators, with full-blown IRB review covering only federally funded research, rather than a "general assurance," covering all research at the institution regardless of funding source, in part because of issues discussed below about the appropriateness of conventional IRB criteria and procedures for many kinds of scholarly activity.

Given an assumption that IRB regulation is an ethical good, the policy decision that all research should be regulated to IRB standards is appealing. How could one possibly defend applying lower ethical standards to research simply because it does not have federal funding? But the devil is in the assumptions—here, that IRB standards are in some sense higher than those applied in the absence of IRB oversight. There are at least two problems with this. First, the implication is that a single dimension of ethical judgment exists and applies feasibly and sufficiently to all types of research. Second, IRB standards are not the only basis of ethical judgments. Psychologists are generally familiar with the American Psychological Association Ethics Code. It happens that other disciplines have developed formal ethics codes as well, including disciplines not historically seen as within IRB purview, such as ethnography and journalism, appropriate to their diverse research contexts. So the argument should not be about whether it is OK to apply to lower standards to unfunded research. A starting point for a good argument would be: what sorts of ethical issues arise in a particular discipline, and how should ethical treatment of human subjects ensue?

Thus, a focus of the current debate about IRBs is whether a single set of standards should apply to all disciplines under IRB purview. Modern IRBs are a recent invention, growing out of the Belmont Report on biomedical and behavioral research, based in part on the Nuremberg Code. . . . What came to be known as the Belmont Principles (respect for persons, beneficence toward them, and justice for them) are laudable, but their operationalization might sensibly vary considerably in different contexts. It has been widely noted that the Belmont process never undertook to address types of activity that are quite different from laboratory research, such as anthropology or journalism. Substantial portions of psychology arguably fall outside that tradition as well. The point is not that non-biomedical disciplines are immune from ethical issues but that the culture that has developed around modern IRBs is fundamentally foreign to those disciplines. Predictably, then, recent attempts to bring them under IRB purview have been highly problematic—hence, mission creep is meeting more and more resistance.

This policy question, of whether a single set of review criteria and mechanisms should subsume all research, presupposes a clear answer to the more abstract question of what counts as research. It could be the case, but it is not the case, that relevant federal regulations provide clear guidance on what is research (Title 45 Part 46 of the Code of Federal Regulations, section 102, www.hhs.gov/ohrp/humansubjects/guidance/45cfr46.htm):

"(d) Research means a systematic investigation, including research development, testing and evaluation, designed to develop or contribute to generalizable knowledge. Activities which meet this definition constitute research for purposes of this policy, whether or not they are conducted or supported under a program which is considered research for other purposes. For example, some demonstration and service programs may include research activities.

"(e) Research subject to regulation, and similar terms are intended to encompass those research activities for which a federal department or agency has specific responsibility for regulating as a research activity. . ."

Paragraph (e) says roughly that relevant terms apply to whatever federal regulators regulate, which is a bit circular and begs the question of what falls within what is to be regulated. Paragraph (d) sounds more promising, defining research as "a systematic investigation . . . designed to develop or contribute to generalizable knowledge." Sometimes this stance is summarized in terms of a scholar's intentions rather than "design" of a project. That is, the design follows from the scholar's goals. In any case, this statement is notoriously difficult to operationalize. What are the bounds on the intent of an individual or on the design of a project? For example, when does an intention or a design form? A friend of mine, an ethnomusicologist, studies the role of music in Hispanic culture in the southwest, particularly the role of and implications for young Latinas, of public performances by family-based musical groups. My friend is also a folksinger in her own right, composing and performing music. An important entree into the families she studies is playing music with them. Does she need IRB approval to play music? To play music with people of a certain ethnicity, simply because she has a relevant research interest and might someday channel her experiences into a research product? Does she need IRB approval to make entries in a private journal? To draw on that journal for her published scholarship? These questions might warrant different answers under different circumstances. Part of the difficulty in this example is that there is a continuum from traditional laboratory psychology research, into community psychology, and out beyond psychology altogether.

A particularly important example is journalism. A journalist might or might not be interested in "generalizable knowledge," and that interest might change as an investigation unfolds. Does this activity fall under IRB purview? IRBs sometimes insist on oversight of journalism faculty doing the same work that journalists based outside the academy are not subject to. Among other issues, how does the concept of informed consent play out in journalism? Is a journalist to be stopped from investigating people who do not consent to being investigated? Furthermore, a journalist, like a community psychologist or an ethnographer, may be trying to understand a neighborhood, not an individual. The primary ethical duty may be to the public, rather than to an individual from whom or about whom the journalist is gathering information. That is simply what it means to do journalism. For an IRB to insist otherwise is not merely to bring journalism under its purview, it is to preclude journalism altogether (not a good thing for a free society). This example does not imply that there are no ethical dilemmas regarding protection of individual subjects, but professional journalism has its own code of ethics, painstakingly developed. It is not apparent that IRB culture ought to trump that.

Turning to a clinical example, the Food and Drug Administration approves specific drugs for specific uses but allows physicians to prescribe approved drugs for uses other than those approved, called off-label prescribing. My impression is that physicians generally consider off-label drug administration to their patients to be entirely within the realm of clinical practice, not research in an IRB sense. One could argue that the goal is to treat the patient, not to produce generalizable knowledge. But if the physician tries something, and it works, so she tries it on 3 other patients, and it works, she might want to publicize her observations. In fact at some point it might unethical for her not to publicize it. The moment she publicizes it, or plans to, does it become research? Does it fall under IRB review? Reasonable people could agree on some examples of such a case, where the answer is "yes" in some cases and "no" in other cases. But in some cases agreement would be difficult, with physicians claiming that the intrusion of an IRB would amount to the IRB practicing medicine, rather than the physician conducting research of the sort that IRBs ought to monitor. There may be ways for an IRB to assert control over such things, but the premise that research has a specific beginning point defined by the intention of the researcher or the design of the research, when publishable research may not have been the initial goal at all, is not viable.

As an example closer to home for SSCP: What if, having seen clients for decades, and having supervised many dozens of others' cases, I decide to write a scholarly paper or book about therapy? Arguably, the clients might suddenly be considered research subjects. Although the book might or might not include some quotes or vignettes for individual clients, let us assume that there would be no identifying information. Even without such material, anything I would say would be influenced by my clients. This would happen in ways that in many cases would not be assignable to specific clients—not only due to my imperfect memory, but due to my perspective being an emergent property of countless clinical experiences. Where does research begin in this scenario? If and when I choose to write about my experiences as a clinician? Or when I began seeing clients years ago? Does it matter whether the book talks explicitly about real individual cases? What if just about composites based on real cases? Based partially on my own cases, partially on hypothetical cases, partially on cases discussed by other authors? Where is the boundary between my work as a clinical scientist doing therapy and my work as a clinical scientist writing about therapy? When should the IRB pass judgment on my work? Federal regulations could be read to mean that the answer is: at the time my intention to attempt to contribute to generalizable knowledge was formed. But it happens that there was no specific moment that it formed and that I had a notion of contributing to the therapy literature before there were modern, post-Belmont IRBs. For a psychotherapist reflecting on decades of professional work, simply writing up those thoughts is not the bulk of the "research"—most of the research was being done when I was working with those clients, my own supervisors and supervisees, and the colleagues I consulted with all those years. The present claim is not that the IRB has no role in such work but that simply that the federal definition of "research" is not viable as a basis for determining IRB purview.

Although the diverse activities of a clinical scientist may not pose as fundamental a challenge to current IRB culture as does journalism, the harsh distinction between research and non-research activities that IRBs try to make does not make sense in clinical science. The claim here is not that IRBs should disappear altogether—only that a sensible application of current policy is not an option. The implication is not that all the activities of clinical psychologists, community psychologists, journalists, anthropologists, or medical clinicians ought to be exempt from IRB review. But different disciplines have different constraints on ethical responsibility, different notions of what constitutes research, and different boundaries, if any, between research and other aspects of the discipline. IRBs cannot allow every discipline to write its own rules, but IRBs have to come to grips with the culture of each discipline, the meaning of research in each, and the relevant ethics. A single standard is not only unappealing, it is not an option.

A tension in philosophy of science is whether one should offer an articulation of some ideal notion of how to do science vs. offer a characterization of how scientists actually do their work. Large portions of scholarly endeavor do not unfold as current IRB culture assumes. The stipulation that, in effect, IRB purview begins when the scholar forms an intention to study human subjects is unworkable in the general case. A scholar typically has a general intention spanning years or decades and may entertain numerous research designs that evolve in parallel, usually based heavily on prior research. There may be no precise starting point for a project. The argument here is not that these factors make IRB purview impossible—only that basing IRB purview on assumptions that do not apply to some types of research creates an unworkable scenario.

Although one of the central debates about IRBs is often framed in terms of whether all research should be subject to IRB review, this is actually not worth arguing about. For reasons just reviewed, a policy that "all research" should be reviewed is simply not meaningful and not workable. In the absence of clear, shared definitions of crucial terms, IRBs will necessarily operate inconsistently, and scholars will necessarily run afoul of what IRBs request. This is not a function of bureaucratic perfidy or scholarly immorality. It is entirely predictable, and unavoidable, despite the best of intentions on all sides.

The IRB should not try to protect my client from the future risk of ending up with a few of his words spoken in therapy appearing in my book someday, nor to protect Aristotle from discussion by a classical scholar, nor to protect Richard Nixon from the *Washington Post*. Possibly issues of consent and IRB oversight arise when I write the book, but not when I am doing the therapy. Even regarding the book, I could argue that the unit of analysis is not an individual client, but a particular type of psychopathology I faced in a number of clients, or a dynamic that arose sometimes between client and therapist, or an issue I repeatedly confronted about the role of a therapist. If my focus is not on individual clients, if that is not the unit of analysis, who could I meaningfully get consent from?

The expansion of IRB reach beyond biomedical research into fields not on the table when relevant principles and practices were developed brings great burdens not only on researchers but on IRBs, diverting resources from oversight of research that does warrant close scrutiny. The same damage is caused by the expansion of the types of judgments IRBs are now being asked to make, such as about the value of the research, which in most cases IRBs lack the expertise and time to do. Having sat on a campus IRB and having chaired a departmental review committee, I have seen how a shortage of staff resources, in the face of escalating and sometimes inappropriate performance demands, undermines an operation that, as argued above, is already not viable on a priori grounds. Understandable institutional temptations to centralize and standardize are exactly the wrong strategy. We need clearer definitions (not only of "research" but of "harm" and "risk," for example, which are not defined in 45 CFR 46) and better appreciation for the differentiation of disciplines potentially relevant to IRB oversight. That has to be achieved at a national level, not left to each IRB to fumble with.

Most ironically, there is virtually no research available on the actual behavior of IRBs. We know very little about how IRBs set thresholds for "minimal risk" or "discomfort"; about typical numbers of protocols reviewed, turnaround time, approval rates; or especially how effective the IRB system actually is in protecting subjects. Recent national conferences have sounded the alarm. . . . The *Journal of Empirical Research on Human Research Ethics* (http://www.jerhre.org) is a very promising new venue.

The temptation for the individual scholar is to see this problem of IRB mission creep as merely an isolated hassle with which one can hopefully minimize engagement. But if we do not jump in and contribute, there is little chance that the results of other forces in this continuing evolution will be favorable to our work or to our subjects. For example, there is some talk of universities and medical centers outsourcing IRB review to commercial entities. It is difficult to imagine that that would be an advance for academic freedom. It is essential that active scholars participate on IRBs and work to improve them, from inside and outside.

COMMENTARY: Institutional review boards (IRBs) frequently find themselves in the crosshairs. As the most important guardians of ethical research practices next to researchers themselves, they are subjected to the closest scrutiny by host academic bodies and government oversight agencies. At the same time—in some cases rightly, and in some cases wrongly (or with undue force)—they draw the ire of researchers for alleged shortcomings that can include poor grounding in specialty scientific areas, excessive paperwork requirements, and unsuitably prolonged turnaround times for ultimate decisions—be they in one direction or the other.

The key to successful navigation of IRBs is an understanding of the boards themselves—an approach that, for psychologists, should not be an unnatural path to enlightenment. What may seem at first blush like petty distinctions and obsessive rituals can make considerably more sense with a fresh perspective, and in time the most effective methods for clearing regulatory hurdles will become apparent.

The following references are recommended for those interested in further investigation of the role and functioning of institutional review boards, including bureaucratic mandates, regulatory obligations, and the potential consequences of a research participant's complaint.

Bozeman, B., Slade, C., & Hirsch, P. (2009). Understanding bureaucracy in health science ethics: Toward a better institutional review board. *American Journal of Public Health, 99*, 1549–1556. http://dx.doi.org/10.2105/AJPH.2008.152389

Clapp, J. T., Gleason, K. A., & Joffe, St. (2017). Justification and authority in institutional review board decision letters. *Social Science & Medicine, 194*, 25–33. http://dx.doi.org/10.1016/j.socscimed.2017.10.013

DeMeo, S. D., Nagler, A., & Heflin, M. T. (2016). Development of a health professions education research-specific institutional review board template. *Academic Medicine, 91*, 229–232. http://dx.doi.org/10.1097/ACM.0000000000000987

Masters, K. S. (2009). Milgram, stress research, and the Institutional Review Board. *American Psychologist, 64,* 621–622. http://dx.doi.org/10.1037/a0017110

Motil, K. J., Allen, J., & Taylor, A. (2004). When a research subject calls with a complaint, what will the institutional review board do? *IRB: Ethics & Human Research, 26,* 9–13. http://dx.doi.org/10.2307/3563581

8.3. Deception in Research

Allan J. Kimmel

. . .

Why Deceive?

When social psychologist Stanley Milgram (1963, 1974) carried out his well-known series of experiments on obedience to authority at Yale University between 1960 and 1964, deception had not yet become a common fixture in psychological research laboratories. Yet Milgram's project, perhaps more than any other, aroused initial concerns about the ethicality of using deception to satisfy research objectives and gave impetus to the development of internal standards regulating the use of deception within the discipline of psychology (Benjamin & Simpson, 2009). Other controversial deception studies, such as the Stanford prison experiment in psychology, the "tearoom trade" research in sociology, and the Tuskegee syphilis study in biomedicine also greatly contributed to a rise in sensitivities and stimulated debate about deception in research (see Bok, 1978; Diener & Crandall, 1978; Kelman, 1967; Kimmel, 2007). Milgram (1963) misled his volunteer participants into believing that they were administering dangerous electric shocks to an innocent victim, an experimental confederate who was portrayed as an ordinary research participant. The central deception in the obedience studies involved presenting the experiment as one pertaining to the effects of punishment on learning, with the volunteers instructed to deliver increasingly stronger electric shocks (up to 450 volts) each time the learner–confederate made a mistake on a simple memory task. In actuality, the learner did not receive shocks, but made a number of preplanned mistakes and feigned pain on receiving the punishment. The goal was to observe the extent to which participants obeyed the authority of the experimenter, who ordered them to proceed with the procedure despite their protests and the confederate's apparent agony.

Milgram received high praise for his ingenious experiments, which in a broader sense were intended to shed light on the Nazi atrocities committed in obedience to the commands of malevolent authorities during World War II, and his research continues to resonate to this day (e.g., a 2009 special issue of *American Psychologist* was devoted to the obedience research). But the research

From *APA Handbook of Ethics in Psychology: Vol. 2. Practice, Teaching, and Research* (pp. 401–421), by S. J. Knapp (Ed.), 2012, Washington, DC: American Psychological Association. Copyright 2012 by the American Psychological Association.

eventually became the target of scathing attacks (e.g., Baumrind, 1964; Kelman, 1967), which centered on the potential adverse outcomes stemming from the deceptive methodology; specifically, that Milgram had subjected participants to extreme levels of stress and guilt as a result of their believing that they harmed innocent victims, that he should have terminated the experiment at the first indications of participant discomfort, and that he alienated participants from future participation in research and harmed their image of the discipline. These points typify some of the common ethical arguments against the use of deception in psychological research, which, in one form or another, suggest that because it involves lying and deceit, its employment in research is morally reprehensible and may have potentially harmful effects on each of the parties involved in the research or implicated by it (Bassett, Basinger, & Livermore, 1992; Christensen, 1988; Kimmel & Smith, 2001; Ortmann & Hertwig, 1997). In short, critics of deception have decried its use on moral, methodological, and disciplinary grounds:

1. Regardless of the anticipated research ends, it is morally wrong to mislead research participants because deception is a clear violation of the individual's basic right to informed consent and undermines the trust inherent in the implicit contractual relationship between the researcher and participant.

2. Deceptive procedures could harm research participants by lowering their self-esteem (via embarrassment or "inflicted insight"—i.e., undesirable self-revelations) and impairing their relationships with others, or by serving as a model for deceptive behavior in participants' subsequent actions.

3. Deception places participants in a subservient, powerless role in the research context and ultimately may help shape a negative attitude toward research participation.

4. The use of deception may prove to be self-defeating to the extent that its use increases the suspicions of future research participants about investigators and the research process, thereby exhausting the pool of naive participants.

5. Deceptive techniques reduce the public's trust in social scientists and give the research professions a poor reputation, thereby jeopardizing community and financial support for the research enterprise and public trust in expert authorities.

. . .

The following arguments reflect those typically posited as justification for deceptive research procedures (e.g., Bonetti, 1998; Bortolotti & Mameli, 2006; Kimmel, 1988, 1998; Pittenger, 2002):

1. Deception enables the researcher to increase the impact of a laboratory setting, such that the experimental situation becomes more realistic, thereby enhancing the study's internal validity.

2. Deception can reduce the effects of participants' motives and role-playing behavior in the experimental situation.

3. Certain significant areas of human life cannot be experimentally studied in an otherwise ethical manner; that is, deception can create a reasonable facsimile of the topic of interest without placing individuals in compromising or dangerous real-life situations for achieving research objectives.

4. Potential negative effects resulting from deception (e.g., threats to self-esteem, guilt, embarrassment) can be reduced through intensive prescreening of participants or removed through careful postexperimental procedures, such as debriefing.

5. Participation in deceptive research can serve as an involving learning experience for participants, by providing insight into their own or others' behavior, as well as the research process.

Clearly, there are compelling arguments both for and against the use of deception in psychological research. Although the argument can be made that deception in research—whether by omission or commission—represents a serious violation of human rights and is never morally justifiable (Baumrind, 1971, 1975), it generally is understood that the application of such a position would preclude research on certain essential topics, such as placebo effects or social attitudes, and thus would provide a significant barrier to scientific advance within the discipline. The recognition that deception may have beneficial or harmful consequences for participants, society, and the scientific discipline of psychology has moved much of the ethical debate away from the question of whether deception should be allowed at all to a focus on the circumstances under which its use could be considered ethically acceptable (Kimmel, 2003, 2006; Smith et al., 2009).

TREATMENT OF DECEPTION BY INSTITUTIONAL REVIEW BOARDS AND ETHICAL CODES

Decision making regarding the propriety of using deception in a research investigation usually comes down to the weighing of potential costs and benefits, with the decision to proceed contingent on a preponderance of likely beneficial consequences, assuming no alternative approaches could be utilized to satisfy research objectives. Although not formally grounded in theories of moral philosophy, this cost–benefit approach is consistent with consequentialist (e.g., utilitarian) theories, which hold that the morally right action would be the one that produces at least as good a ratio of good to bad consequences (e.g., in terms of welfare or utility) as any other course of action, including not carrying out the action at all (Pittenger, 2002). Nonconsequentialist (e.g., deontological) theories maintain that the ethical evaluation of an action generally would reflect an assessment of its consistency with binding moral rules or duties—such as to always tell the truth—and consequences are not of primary importance. Such an approach would preclude the use of any deception in research because to deceive would violate an overriding obligation always to be completely honest with participants.

The cost–benefit approach derived from consequentialist theories is incorporated within the procedures utilized by most ethics review committees and provides a framework for the standards and guidelines that appear in human participant ethical codes worldwide (Kimmel, 2007). In short, deception in research is considered to be morally permissible to the extent that it is consistent with certain principles. In some respects, this position is analogous to how lying is treated in everyday life. Although lying generally is considered to be wrong, most people prefer to live in a world where some lying is permissible, such as white lies, lies to certain kinds of people (children, the dying), and lies to avoid greater harms. In these situations, it is important for the persons telling the lies to be able to justify their actions, if only to themselves. In the research context, a similar logic prevails, where the researcher's justification for deception is guided by ethical standards, governmental regulations, and external review.

. . .

The American Psychological Association's Ethical Standards

The current *Ethical Principles of Psychologists and Code of Conduct* (the Ethics Code; American Psychological Association [APA], 2010) is the result of a more than 50-year history of development and revision, including substantial strengthening of its research guidelines in the wake of debate about the use of deception in controversial studies (cf. Kelman, 1967). The research guidelines emphasize voluntary participation and informed consent as fundamental prerequisites for research with human participants, ethical requirements that date back to the 1947 Nuremberg Code, a general set of standards formulated to prevent atrocities like those perpetrated by Nazi researchers, and the forerunner to all subsequent guidelines governing experimentation with human participants (Schuler, 1982). Ethics Code Standard 8.07, Deception in Research, dictates that deception should be used only if (a) effective, nondeceptive alternative procedures are not feasible, (b) the research is not likely to cause physical pain or severe emotional distress, (c) deceptions that are integral features of the study's design are explained to participants as early as possible during a debriefing, and (d) a study's results are likely to be sufficiently important (because of "the study's significant prospective scientific, educational, or applied value"). Standard 8.01, Institutional Approval, acknowledges that investigators may be required to obtain institutional approval through their IRB before conducting research.

Standard 8.07 is built on an ethical dilemma, one that brings into conflict two of the profession's core values, the value of advancing the science of psychology through research (as explicated in APA's, 2009, Vision Statement and in Principle B, Fidelity and Responsibility, in the Ethics Code, the latter of which emphasizes psychologists' "scientific responsibilities to society") and the promotion of truthfulness (as spelled out in the Ethics Code's Principle C, Integrity, which maintains that "psychologists seek to promote accuracy, honesty, and truthfulness in the science . . . of psychology"; Behnke, 2009). Although the standard incorporates a utilitarian approach for resolving this dilemma, it does not clarify how it can be determined that the results of a study are "sufficiently important" to adequately justify the use of deception. In fact, the various criteria spelled out for the use of deception in the Ethics Code have fueled extensive debate regarding interpretation of the principles and their implementation (Kimmel, 2007; Schuler, 1982) and, despite obtaining feedback from researchers before the adoption of new versions of the code, APA members never reached consensus as to the specific wording of the standards for research or how to apply them. (A separate code of ethics for members of the Association for Psychological Science [APS] currently does not exist. The APS board of directors approved a brief, general statement of principle that is consistent with the society's interests in scientific and personal integrity but that does not put APS in the position of judging the conduct of its members. The statement requires APS members to adhere to all relevant codes of ethical behavior and legal and regulatory requirements.)

Despite its various limitations, the APA guidelines have served as a model for other professional associations, including the Australian Psychological Society, the Canadian Psychological Association, and the British Psychological Society (cf. Kimmel, 2007; Leach & Harbin, 1997). The criteria for the use of deception in research in the current code of the American Sociological Association (ASA, 1999) are nearly identical to those of the APA (2010). The ASA utilizes the same cost–benefit approach, although it does allow a broader interpretation of harm and requires IRB (or equivalent) approval. Because sociologists commonly use nonexperimental methodologies, the code acknowledges that informed consent may not always be possible or appropriate and suggests that it should not be an absolute requirement for all sociological research. Like psychology, the field has abundant examples of controversial deception studies (Allen, 1997; Reynolds, 1982).

. . .

REFERENCES

Allen, C. (1997, November). Spies like us: When sociologists deceive their subjects. *Lingua Franca*, pp. 31–39.

American Psychological Association. (2010). *Ethical principles of psychologists and code of conduct (2002, Amended June 1, 2010)*. Retrieved from http://www.apa.org/ethics/code/index.aspx

American Sociological Association. (1999). *American Sociological Association code of ethics*. Retrieved from http://www.asanet.org

Bassett, R. L., Basinger, D., & Livermore, P. (1992). Lying in the laboratory: Deception in human research from psychological, philosophical, and theological perspectives. *Journal of the American Scientific Affiliation, 34*, 201–212.

Baumrind, D. (1964). Some thoughts on ethics of research: After reading Milgram's "Behavioral study of obedience." *American Psychologist, 19*, 421–423.

Baumrind, D. (1971). Principles of ethical conduct in the treatment of subjects: Reaction to the draft report of the Committee on Ethical Standards in Psychological Research. *American Psychologist, 26*, 887–896.

Baumrind, D. (1975). Metaethical and normative considerations governing the treatment of human subjects in the behavioral sciences. In E. C. Kennedy (Ed.), *Human rights and psychological research: A debate on psychology and ethics* (pp. 37–68). New York, NY: Thomas Y. Crowell.

Baumrind, D. (1985). Research using intentional deception: Ethical issues revisited. *American Psychologist, 40,* 165–174.

Behnke, S. (2009, April). Reading the Ethics Code more deeply. *Monitor on Psychology, 40*(4), 66–67.

Benjamin, L. T., & Simpson, J. A. (2009). The power of the situation: The impact of Milgram's obedience studies on personality and social psychology. *American Psychologist, 64,* 12–19.

Bok, S. (1978). *Lying: Moral choice in public and private life.* New York, NY: Pantheon.

Bonetti, S. (1998). Experimental economics and deception. *Journal of Economic Psychology, 19,* 377–395.

Bortolotti, L., & Mameli, M. (2006). Deception in psychology: Moral costs and benefits of unsought self-knowledge. *Accountability in Research, 13,* 259–275.

Christensen, L. (1988). Deception in psychological research: When is its use justified? *Personality and Social Psychology Bulletin, 14,* 664–675.

Diener, E., & Crandall, R. (1978). *Ethics in social and behavioral research.* Chicago, IL: University of Chicago Press.

Kelman, H. C. (1967). Human use of human subjects: The problem of deception in social psychological experiments. *Psychological Bulletin, 67,* 1–11.

Kimmel, A. J. (1988). *Ethics and values in applied social research.* Newbury Park, CA: Sage.

Kimmel, A. J. (1998). In defense of deception. *American Psychologist, 53,* 803–805.

Kimmel, A. J. (2003). Ethical issues in social psychology research. In C. Sansone, C. C. Morf, & A. T. Panter (Eds.), *The Sage handbook of methods in social psychology* (pp. 45–70). Thousand Oaks, CA: Sage.

Kimmel, A. J. (2006). From artifacts to ethics: The delicate balance between methodological and moral concerns in behavioral research. In D. Hantula (Ed.), *Advances in theory and methodology in social and organizational psychology* (pp. 113–140). Mahwah, NJ: Erlbaum.

Kimmel, A. J. (2007). *Ethical issues in behavioral research: Basic and applied perspectives.* Cambridge, MA: Blackwell.

Kimmel, A. J., & Smith, N. C. (2001). Deception in marketing research: Ethical, methodological, and disciplinary implications. *Psychology and Marketing, 18,* 663–689.

Leach, M. M., & Harbin, J. J. (1997). Psychological ethics codes: A comparison of twenty-four countries. *International Journal of Psychology, 32,* 181–192.

Milgram, S. (1963). Behavioral study of obedience. *Journal of Abnormal and Social Psychology, 67,* 371–378.

Milgram, S. (1974). *Obedience to authority: An experimental view.* New York, NY: Harper & Row.

Ortmann, A., & Hertwig, R. (1997). Is deception acceptable? *American Psychologist, 52,* 746–747.

Pittenger, D. J. (2002). Deception in research: Distinctions and solutions from the perspective of utilitarianism. *Ethics and Behavior, 12*(2), 117–142.

Reynolds, P. D. (1982). *Ethics and social science research.* Englewood Cliffs, NJ: Prentice Hall.

Schuler, H. (1982). *Ethical problems in psychological research.* New York, NY: Academic Press.

Smith, N. C., Kimmel, A. J., & Klein, J. G. (2009). Social contract theory and the ethics of deception in consumer research. *Journal of Consumer Psychology, 19,* 486–496.

COMMENTARY: To many, "deception" is a fancy word for "lying." Making false misrepresentations may cut very much against the personal and professional grain for those whose entire discipline has at its core an unflinching commitment to ethical principles—and whose very ability to continue to practice and conduct scientific studies may be at the mercy of institutional interpretations of a morally grounded ethics code. Despite waning applications of this technique in recent years, there are many who will continue to argue that certain avenues of inquiry can only be satisfied by at least temporarily misleading participants in psychological research.

Deceptive techniques are still discernible in mainstream psychological research. If a deception-based study, having cleared the relevant institutional review board, will seek the participation of persons with disabilities—or of those who find themselves operating under stressful or otherwise distracting circumstances—then naturally the researcher's harm reduction procedures and debriefing strategies will receive even greater emphasis than usual.

The following references are recommended for those interested in further investigation of deception in research, focusing in particular on its use in different settings, the true nature of a "placebo," and the participation of children and other specialized populations.

Fisher, C. B. (2005). Deception research involving children: Ethical practices and paradoxes. *Ethics & Behavior, 15,* 271–287. http://dx.doi.org/10.1207/s15327019eb1503_7

Justman, S. (2013). Placebo: The lie that comes true? *Journal of Medical Ethics, 39,* 243–248. http://dx.doi.org/10.1136/medethics-2012-101057

Kimmel, A. J., & Smith, N. C. (2001). Deception in marketing research: Ethical, methodological and disciplinary implications. *Psychology & Marketing, 18,* 663–689. http://dx.doi.org/10.1002/mar.1025

Miller, F. G., & Kaptchuk, T. J. (2008). Deception of subjects in neuroscience: An ethical analysis. *The Journal of Neuroscience, 28,* 4841–4843. http://dx.doi.org/10.1523/JNEUROSCI.1493-08.2008

Sommers, R., & Miller, F. G. (2013). Forgoing debriefing in deceptive research: Is it ever ethical? *Ethics & Behavior, 15,* 271–287.

8.4. Laboratory Animal Research Ethics: A Practical, Educational Approach

Jennifer L. Perry and Nancy K. Dess

ngaging in research of any kind is a privilege that carries with it weighty ethical responsibilities and opportunities. Laboratory ("lab") animal research is a scholarly enterprise that has played an important role in the development of psychology as a science, including the development of its ethical dimensions. Much has been written on the subject, and a thorough review is beyond the scope of this chapter. Here, we articulate a practical, educational approach to the ethical care and use of lab animals in psychology in the United States. The usefulness of our suggestions will vary depending on readers' prior knowledge, as well as on the nature of her or his past, current, and prospective relationship to lab animal research as scholar, practicing scientist, teacher, and citizen. In addition to helping ensure that lab animal research is carried out ethically, this approach should elevate the discourse about research ethics and yield skills in reasoning transferable to other domains.

. . .

THE CONTEMPORARY LANDSCAPE

The world has changed dramatically in the 200 years since European animal activists protested experimentation on horses and dogs without anesthesia. Lab animal research has changed. Anesthesia and analgesia are available and cheap and their use is standard practice. Lab animal research has been institutionalized in diverse academic departments, government agencies, and the private sector. It has expanded across levels of organization from subcellular to social. Although the entire enterprise remains a referent for the term *(anti)vivisection*, much research is non- or minimally invasive, especially in psychology. The relevance of psychological research with lab animals has grown as interest in evolution and neuroscience has exploded and as chronic conditions from cardiovascular disease to depression have supplanted infectious diseases as the leading causes of human death and disability worldwide. Vastly more lab animal research is done, in more countries. Recent estimates (*Fifth Report*, 2005; Taylor, Gordon, Langley, & Higgins, 2008) put the total number of live nonhuman vertebrates used at 58 to 115 million, with about 17 million in the

From *APA Handbook of Ethics in Psychology: Vol. 2. Practice, Teaching, and Research* (pp. 423–440), by S. J. Knapp (Ed.), 2012, Washington, DC: American Psychological Association. Copyright 2012 by the American Psychological Association.

United States and 11 to 12 million each in Japan and the European Union. More mice and rats (85%–90%) are used than other rodents, birds, fishes, or reptiles; larger mammals (e.g., nonhuman primates, dogs, rabbits, cats, marine mammals) each account for less than 1%. Many more invertebrates (e.g., nematodes, insects, mollusks) than vertebrates are used.

. . .

BEYOND COMPLIANCE: ETHICAL DECISION MAKING

At its best, oversight improves lab animal research. Prudent leadership in agencies, IACUCs, departments, and labs creates a coeducational climate from which good science, practices that promote animal welfare, and protections for personnel emerge. Researchers do well to foster such a climate by engaging constructively with USDA, OLAW, and their IACUC. In so doing, rather than merely being subject to oversight, researchers participate in shaping effective, efficient policies and practices. They also model responsible research for collaborators and students and enjoy indemnification and other forms of community support.

Researchers also do well to guard against a possible unintended consequence of oversight—letting oversight compliance overshadow ethical decision making. Rule following can fall short as a guide to day-to-day ethical conduct. Consider, for instance, a scenario: A monkey caretaker leaves a housing area and removes her personal protective equipment. Through a window she sees that a knife used to cut fruit was left within a monkey's reach. A monkey is reaching for it. She has time to retrieve the knife and prevent serious harm to one or more monkeys—if she does not gown up. Policy requires her to protect monkeys from imminent danger. It also prohibits her from entering without gowning up. It does not specify which rule trumps the other. What should she do?

At such a moment, behavior could be governed by impulse, anxiety, or indecision. Alternatively, it could be guided by quick, principled decision making. The latter does not require the person to be a moral philosopher, any more than other professionals with weighty responsibilities—physicians, pilots, child care providers, and so on—have to be philosophers to behave ethically. Instruction in oversight obligations, however, will not suffice. Oversight can enhance the quality of lab animal care and use, and it is informed by values. It does not in itself, however, prepare researchers to make ethical decisions, and it does not prepare anyone to develop an informed ethical position on lab animal research. Ethical decision making and position taking require practical ethics education. Many people are familiar with the idea that what is *legal* is not necessarily *ethical*, that laws can be just or unjust. Elaboration on that idea yields basic distinctions between morality, ethics, justice, and laws (Ray, 1996). Whereas morality involves first-order beliefs about good and evil, ethics involves second-order reflective deliberation of moral matters. Ethics adds to judgment of an action's rectitude an explanation, or moral theory, of why the action is right or wrong.

As Hinman (2002) explained, *morality* is to music as *ethics* is to musicology. Justice specifically concerns whether an action advances fairness. Finally, morality, ethics, and justice can be distinguished from law. Although laws, regulations, and such symbolize the values of a moral community, they are a means of aversively motivating individuals' actions and thus are fundamentally coercive. By definition, delivering lists of dos and don'ts, exhortations, and threats does not constitute an ethics education.

McCarthy (1999) noted, "There is at present no widely accepted, comprehensive moral theory pertaining to research involving laboratory animals." A more coherent framework prevails for human research (per the *Belmont Report*; National Commission for the Protection of Human Subjects of Biomedical and Behavioral Research, 1979), which likely will remain the case given the more diverse nature of research with nonhuman animals. An achievable goal may be ethics education that provides people with "a basis for creating, embracing, or enriching the moral framework that governs their attitudes and behavior toward laboratory animals" (McCarthy, 1999). Fostering inquirers' identity as moral agents whose decision making is mindful and open to change may not make up a comprehensive moral theory, but it does include a feasible metaethic.

The Ethics Cascade

Lab animal research is not *an* ethical issue. It is a complex enterprise to which many ethical issues apply. Dess and Foltin (2005) outlined an *ethics cascade* composed of questions that progress from general—who has moral authority—to specific—whether a particular procedure with a particular species is ethical. Using such an approach will encourage consideration of broad *contextual* values (what should be studied, when, by whom) as well as narrower *constitutive* values (what methods are best, what protections are appropriate, etc.) relevant to lab animal research (see Rooney, 1992).

In the cascade, the omnibus question of whether lab animal research is an ethical enterprise is considered about midway, in more or less the same context as the question of whether research with human participants is an ethical enterprise. Although research with humans and nonhuman animals are not the same issue, both ought to be regarded as scientific endeavor taking place in larger contexts in which such issues as who has power and agency, what questions matter and to whom, and so on should be pondered before broaching a distinction between the populations involved or specific methodologies.

Some people have an abolitionist posture toward lab animal research, but surveys of the public, students, and psychologists show that most people distinguish different levels in the cascade when given the opportunity to do so (Hagelin et al., 2003). Normative nuance accounts in part for their finding that surveys including various versions of a yes or no question about support for lab animal research yielded a range of 27% to 100% for "yes" responses and a range of 0% to 68% "no" responses. The cascade can help people locate their own views with some specificity and identify bases of agreement and disagreement with others (Saucier & Cain, 2006). Such discussions also present instructional opportunities to psychology teachers and research mentors. If students support lab animal research because they tend toward facile generalization across species or do not believe lab animals experience pain, such reasoning can be corrected (see the section Pain and Stress later in this chapter). If students oppose it because they believe that it is mostly replication or has not played a significant role in psychology, such reasoning can be corrected (Compton, Dietrich, & Smith, 1995; Domjan & Purdy, 1995).

Framing Matters

Ethics lessons get off to a bad start if strong framing effects occur. Negative framing of lab animal research is common. Sometimes it transparently attempts to persuade. A 2003 People for the Ethical Treatment of Animals survey, for instance, queried,

> Before reading this mailing, were you aware of the vast numbers of animals who suffer and perish every year in American research laboratories? Did you realize that the vast majority of painful animal experimentation has no relation at all to human survival or the elimination of disease?

Yet lessons by well-meaning people can have a similar effect. An example is labeling lab animal ethics as "a controversy" (Herzog, 2005; Richmond, Engelmann, & Krupka, 1990). Human research can carry serious risks, and many aspects are controversial, yet its ethics are not introduced as "the human research controversy." Such framing compromises full and fair consideration of the ethical issues.

Similarly, introducing lab animal research as a "debate" implies that it is a unitary issue with discrete, mutually exclusive sides. In McGraw-Hill's *Taking Sides* series, complex issues are "thoughtfully framed" as a debate to "stimulate student interest and develop critical thinking skills." In two 2007 volumes, sections appear with the titles "Should Animal Research in Psychology Be Eliminated?" (McGraw-Hill Higher Education, 2007b) and "Should Animal Experimentation Be Permitted?" (McGraw-Hill Higher Education, 2007a), each with "Yes" and "No" essays. Disclaimers that the issue is complex may do little to countermand the categorical thinking primed by binary organization; that this approach endorses "taking sides" and normalizes conflict as a discursive mode ("clashing views") is too plain. It is a disservice to psychology for research to be presented as a moral minefield, for side-choosing or opting out to seem so attractive as to foreclose deep thinking.

An alternative, affirmative, balanced pedagogy involves scaffolding ethical issues from the general to the particular (see the section The Ethics Cascade; also see O'Donnell, Francis, & Mahurin, 2008). It encourages inquirers to engage the issues seriously and to embrace the responsibilities that come with being a serious scholar. They should ponder not only potential pitfalls and debates but also the shared positive values and moral aspirations of those who do lab animal research and the possible costs of *not* doing the research, which might be less salient (Hearst, 1991) but no less important than costs of doing the research.

Rubrics for Ethical Decision Making

Ethical decision making involves consideration of values, stakeholders, development of alternative courses of action, evaluation of the "pros" and "cons" of possible actions, consulting others, and reflecting on decisions in their aftermath. (More information on these topics and the ethical theories that inform the decision-making process can be found in Volume 1, Chapters 1 and 4, this handbook.) A few issues that can be explored in the context of laboratory animal research:

- *Determining stakeholders* presents an opportunity to discuss who potentially benefits from the research: Which species? Only humans? Only some humans?

- *Developing alternative courses of action* presents an opportunity to discuss the option of doing nothing (is that ethically "neutral"?), alternatives to live animal research (in vitro methods, simulations, disenfranchised humans), sample size, and power.

- *Consulting others* presents an opportunity to talk about responsibilities that researchers have regarding oversight and also about IACUC, OLAW, and other valuable resources. It also provides a context for discussing the reach of personal ethics: If a person judges an action to be unethical, should she or he insist that everyone refrain from it?

- *Postdecisional reflection* presents an opportunity to teach that ethical decision making should be iterative and ongoing. One can make a sound ethical decision that should be revised going forward, for instance, because of new knowledge about the species under study.

The prevailing model for ethical review of psychological research—weighing cost–risks against benefits—conforms to consequentialism. However, consideration of consequences as a step in a decision-making rubric can include whether a course of action would be consistent with the actor's dearest values or moral theory. Teachers and mentors can use that step to provide a primer on moral theory, to revisit and critically discuss the conventional cost–risk:benefit approach in that light, and to connect the "pros" and "cons" of lab animal research to models of human–nonhuman relationships.

Normalizing the 3 Rs

An important advantage of using a domain-general rubric for ethical decision making about lab animal research is that it helps to reframe the "3 Rs" of refinement (minimal invasiveness-aversiveness), reduction (minimizing the number of animals used), and replacement (using alternatives to live animal methods; Animal Welfare Information Center, n.d.). Being minimally impactful, collecting data from as many individuals as suffices, and involving live creatures only when necessary are principles that should constrain all research. The history of the development of the 3 Rs links them to lab animal research, an unfortunate

association that carries with it a "necessary evil" implication. The teaching community would do well to socialize the 3 Rs as part of basic research ethics.
. . .

CONCLUSION

Ethics involves thinking through the moral dimensions of actions. Most lab animal researchers are vested with oversight compliance responsibilities, and fulfilling those responsibilities has moral value. We have argued, however, that the ethical conduct of lab animal research is not synonymous with oversight compliance or with actions taken on the basis of unexamined instincts about what is nice versus what is unpleasant. Inquirers should learn about the distinctions among these bases of judgment. They then can engage the process of ethical decision making with confidence, critical thought, and an appropriate measure of trepidation. This chapter hopefully will be helpful to students and their mentors who engage that process.

For lab animal researchers, redoubling efforts at ethics education will take time and courage. Time, often in short supply, must be found. On the positive side, the effort is timely. For reasons ranging from devastating financial scandals and student plagiarism to high-profile research misconduct cases and huge new societal challenges related to bioethics, ethics are in the news. Oversight on ethics education is growing, too. Effective January 2010, the National Science Foundation (NSF) increased requirements for research ethics training for all grant beneficiaries. A silver lining to these trends is that they have opened a window to funding opportunities. Several federal agencies (e.g., NIH, NSF, Department of Energy, Office of Research Integrity) make funding available for research ethics education. Examples include NIH's Short-Term Courses in Research Ethics (T15) program and enhancements to NSF Research Experiences for Undergraduates grants. College and university administrators also may make funds available to faculty with good proposals for enhancing ethics education in undergraduate, graduate, and postdoctoral curricula and research programs through course development, sabbaticals, brown bag seminars, or other activities.

Courage must be mustered to promote open discussion of ethics in an era in which animal extremists have destroyed laboratories and harassed and threatened researchers and their families. Enhanced protections—for instance, the Animal Enterprise Terrorism Act of 2006—and the knowledge that violent extremists are few offer a measure of comfort. Yet, researchers may hesitate to increase their visibility on these issues when the climate makes it acceptable for a critic to testify before the U.S. Senate that murdering researchers to save lab animals is morally justifiable, defending the chilling statement, "I don't think you'd have to kill, assassinate too many. I think for five lives, ten lives, fifteen human lives, we could save a million, two million, or ten million non-human lives" (J. Vlasak, before the U.S. Senate Committee on Environment and Public

Works, 2005). Resolve to overcome that reasonable reluctance can flow from commitments to maintaining high ethical standards in the laboratory, to increasing students' sophistication in thinking about the issues, and to cultivating public confidence in the enterprise. . . .

REFERENCES

Compton, D. M., Dietrich, K. L., & Smith, J. S. (1995). Animal rights activism and animal welfare concerns in the academic setting: Levels of activism and the perceived importance of research with animals. *Psychological Reports*, 76(1), 23–31.

Dess, N. K., & Foltin, R. W. (2005). The ethics cascade. In C. K. Akins, S. Panicker, & C. L. Cunningham (Eds.), *Laboratory animals in research and teaching: Ethics, care, and methods* (pp. 31–39). Washington, DC: American Psychological Association.

Domjan, M., & Purdy, J. E. (1995). Animal research in psychology: More than meets the eye of the general psychology student. *American Psychologist*, 50, 496–503. doi:10.1037/0003-066X.50.7.496

Fifth Report from the Commission to the Council and the European Parliament on the statistics on the number of animals used for experimental and other scientific purposes in the member states of the European Union. (2005). Retrieved from http://eur-lex.europa.eu/LexUriServ/LexUriServ.do?uri=CELEX:52007DC0675:EN:NOT

Hagelin, J., Carlsson, H-E., & Hau, J. (2003). An overview of surveys on how people view animal experimentation: Some factors that may influence the outcome. *Public Understanding of Science (Bristol, England)*, 12(1), 67–81. doi:10.1177/0963662503012001247

Hearst, E. (1991). Psychology and nothing. *American Scientist*, 79, 432–443.

Herzog, H. A. (2005). Dealing with the animal research controversy. In C. K. Akins, S. Panicker, & C. L. Cunningham (Eds.), *Laboratory animals in research and teaching: Ethics, care, and methods* (pp. 31–39). Washington, DC: American Psychological Association.

Hinman, L. M. (2002). *Ethics: A pluralistic approach to ethical theory* (3rd ed.). Belmont, CA: Wadsworth. Retrieved from http://ethics.sandiego.edu/LMH/E2/Glossary.asp

McCarthy, C. R. (1999). Introduction: Toward a coherent ethic of research involving laboratory animals. *ILAR Journal*, 40(1).

McGraw-Hill Higher Education. (2007a). *Taking sides: Clashing views on bioethical issues* (12th ed.). Retrieved from http://highered.mcgraw-hill.com/sites/0076667771/student_view0/bioethical_issues/12e/table_of_contents.html

McGraw-Hill Higher Education. (2007b). *Taking sides: Clashing views on psychological issues* (15th ed.).

National Commission for the Protection of Human Subjects of Biomedical and Behavioral Research. (1979). *The Belmont report: Ethical principles and guidelines for the protection of human subjects of research.* Washington, DC: U.S. Department of Health, Education, and Welfare.

O'Donnell, S. L., Francis, A. L., & Mahurin, S. L. (2008). Critical thinking on contemporary issues. In D. S. Dunn, J. S. Halonen, & R. A. Smith (Eds.), *Teaching critical thinking in psychology: A handbook of best practices* (pp. 117–126). Malden, MA: Blackwell. doi:10.1002/9781444305173.ch10

Ray, T. T. (1996). Differentiating the related concepts of ethics, morality, law, and justice. *New Directions for Teaching and Learning*, 1996(66), 47–53. doi:10.1002/tl.37219966609

Richmond, G., Engelmann, M., & Krupka, L. R. (1990). The animal research controversy: Exploring student attitudes. *The American Biology Teacher*, 52(8), 467–471.

Rooney, P. (1992). On values in science: Is the epistemic/non-epistemic distinction useful? *Proceedings of the Biennial Meeting of the Philosophy of Science Association*, 1, 13–22.

Saucier, D. A., & Cain, M. E. (2006). The foundations of attitudes about animal research. *Ethics and Behavior*, 16(2), 117–133. doi:10.1207/s15327019eb1602_3

Taylor, K., Gordon, N., Langley, G., & Higgins, W. (2008). Estimates for worldwide laboratory animal use in 2005. *Alternatives to Laboratory Animals, 36*, 327–342.

U.S. Senate Committee on Environment and Public Works. (2005, October 26). *Second hearing on ecoterrorism specifically examining Stop Huntington Animal Cruelty ("SHAC")*. Retrieved from http://www.naiaonline.org/pdfs/Oct.%2026,%202005%20 eco-terrorism%20transcript.pdf; video archived at http://epw.senate.gov/ epwmultimedia/epwmultimedia.htm

COMMENTARY: Animal research remains one of the most controversial avenues of scientific investigation—not just for psychologists but for adherents of all laboratory-based disciplines. Unintended lapses and incidents of outright abuse make occasional headlines and inflame passions accordingly. An increasingly organized resistance to animal research of any sort has even resulted, in extreme cases, in the targeting and harassment of researchers themselves.

The American Psychological Association's (APA's; 2017) *Ethical Principles of Psychologists and Code of Conduct* ("APA Ethics Code") devotes more detailed attention to animal welfare than it does to any other aspect of scientific inquiry, and this has recently been supplemented by *Guidelines for Ethical Conduct in the Care and Use of Nonhuman Animals in Research* (APA, Committee on Animal Research and Ethics, 2012), which draws on not only the experiences of psychologists in this area but also legal regulations as well as codes and guidelines promulgated by other professions. The professional literature on this topic extends beyond critical moral imperatives to detailed investigations of what scientific studies truly require and what alternatives are truly available.

The following references are recommended for those interested in further investigation of laboratory animal research ethics. Political and moral as well as scientific perspectives are addressed, with contributions from other disciplines in additional to institutional psychology.

American Psychological Association. (2017). *Ethical principles of psychologists and code of conduct* (2002, Amended June 1, 2010 and January 1, 2017). Retrieved from http://www.apa.org/ethics/code/index.aspx

American Psychological Association, Committee on Animal Research and Ethics. (2012). *Guidelines for ethical conduct in the care and use of nonhuman animals in research*. Retrieved from http://www.apa.org/science/leadership/care/guidelines.aspx

Hom, H. L., Jr., & Kaiser, D. L. (2016). Role of hindsight bias, ethics, and self–other judgments in students' evaluation of an animal experiment. *Ethics & Behavior, 26*, 1–13. http://dx.doi.org/10.1080/10508422.2014.963223

Marks, J. (2013). Animal abolitionism meets moral abolitionism: Cutting the Gordian knot of applied ethics. *Journal of Bioethical Inquiry, 10*, 445–455. http://dx.doi.org/10.1007/s11673-013-9482-3

Peggs, K., & Smart, B. (2017). Nonhuman animal suffering: Critical pedagogy and practical animal ethics. *Society & Animals: Journal of Human-Animal Studies, 25*, 181–198. http://dx.doi.org/10.1163/15685306-12341445

Timm, S. C. (2016). Moral intuition or moral disengagement? Cognitive science weighs in on the animal ethics debate. *Neuroethics, 9*, 225–234. http://dx.doi.org/10.1007/s12152-016-9271-x

Tulloch, G. (2011). Animal ethics: The capabilities approach. *Animal Welfare, 20*(1), 3–10.

8.5. Guidelines for Ethical Conduct in the Care and Use of Nonhuman Animals in Research

American Psychological Association

A s a field of study, psychology examines a broad range of research and applied areas. Important parts of such work are teaching and research on the behavior of nonhuman animals, which contribute to the understanding of basic principles underlying behavior and to advancing the welfare of both human and nonhuman animals. While psychologists must conduct their teaching and research in a manner consonant with relevant laws and regulations, ethical concerns further mandate that psychologists consider the costs and benefits of procedures involving animals before proceeding with these activities.

The following guidelines were developed by the American Psychological Association (APA) for use by psychologists working with nonhuman animals. They are informed by Section 8.09 of the *Ethical Principles of Psychologists and Code of Conduct* (APA, 2010). . . .

I. JUSTIFICATION OF THE RESEARCH

A. Research should be undertaken with a clear scientific purpose. There should be a reasonable expectation that the research will a) increase knowledge of the process underlying the evolution, development, maintenance, alteration, control, or biological significance of behavior; b) determine the replicability and generality of prior research; c) increase understanding of the species under study; or d) provide results that benefit the health or welfare of humans or other animals.

B. The scientific purpose of the research should be of sufficient potential significance to justify the use of nonhuman animals. In general, psychologists should act on the assumption that procedures that are likely to produce pain in humans may also do so in other animals, unless there is species-specific evidence of pain or stress to the contrary.

C. In proposing a research project, the psychologist should be familiar with the appropriate literature, consider the possibility of non-animal alternatives,

From *Guidelines for Ethical Conduct in the Care and Use of Nonhuman Animals in Research* (pp. 1–14), by the American Psychological Association, 2012, Washington, DC: Author. Retrieved from http://www.apa.org/science/leadership/care/guidelines.aspx

These guidelines are scheduled to expire 10 years from February 24, 2012 (the date of adoption by the APA Council of Representatives). After this date users are encouraged to contact the APA Science Directorate to determine if this document remains in effect.

and use procedures that minimize the number of nonhuman animals in research. If nonhuman animals are to be used, the species chosen for the study should be the best suited to answer the question(s) posed.

D. Research on nonhuman animals may not be conducted until the protocol has been reviewed by an appropriate animal care committee; typically, an Institutional Animal Care and Use Committee (IACUC), to ensure that the procedures are appropriate and humane.

E. The psychologist(s) should monitor the research and the subjects' welfare throughout the course of an investigation to ensure continued justification for the research.

II. PERSONNEL

A. Psychologists should ensure that personnel involved in their research with nonhuman animals be familiar with these guidelines.

B. Research procedures with nonhuman animals should conform to the Animal Welfare Act (7 U.S.C. §2131 et. seq.) and applicable federal regulations, policies, and guidelines, regarding personnel, supervision, record keeping, and veterinary care.

C. As behavior is not only the focus of study of many experiments but also a primary source of information about an animal's health and well-being, psychologists and their assistants should be informed about the behavioral characteristics of their nonhuman animal subjects. Awareness of the difference between unusual behaviors and normal, species-specific behaviors may allow for earlier assessment and treatment of health problems.

D. Psychologists should assume it their responsibility that all individuals who work with nonhuman animals under their supervision receive explicit instruction in experimental methods and in the care, maintenance, and handling of the species being studied. The activities that any individuals are allowed to engage in must not exceed their respective competencies, training, and experience in either the laboratory or the field setting.

III. CARE AND HOUSING OF LABORATORY ANIMALS

As a scientific and professional organization, APA recognizes the complexities of defining psychological well-being for both human and non-human animals. APA does not provide specific guidelines for the maintenance of psychological well-being of research animals, as procedures that are appropriate for a particular species may not be for others. Psychologists who are familiar with the species, relevant literature, federal guidelines, and their institution's research facility context should consider the appropriateness of measures such as enrichment to maintain or improve psychological well-being of those species.

A. The facilities housing laboratory animals should meet or exceed current regulations and guidelines (USDA, 1990, 1991; NIH, 2002) and are required to be inspected twice a year (USDA, 1989, NIH, 2002).

B. All procedures carried out on nonhuman animals are to be reviewed by an institutional animal care and use committee (IACUC) to ensure that the procedures are appropriate and humane. The committee must have representation from within the institution and from the local community. In event that it is not possible to constitute an appropriate IACUC in the psychologist's own institution, psychologists should seek advice and obtain review from a corresponding committee of a cooperative institution.

C. Laboratory animals are to be provided with humane care and healthful conditions during their stay in any facilities of the institution. Responsibilities for the conditions under which animals are kept, both within and outside of the context of active experimentation or teaching, rests with the psychologist under the supervision of the IACUC (where required by federal regulations) and with individuals appointed by the institution to oversee laboratory animal care.

IV. ACQUISITION OF LABORATORY ANIMALS

A. Laboratory animals not bred in the psychologist's facility are to be acquired lawfully. The USDA and local ordinances should be consulted for information regarding regulations and approved suppliers.

B. Psychologists should make every effort to ensure that those responsible for transporting the nonhuman animals to the facility provide adequate food, water, ventilation, space, and impose no unnecessary stress on the animals (NRC, 2006).

C. Nonhuman animals taken from the wild should be trapped in a humane manner and in accordance with applicable federal, state, and local regulations.

D. Use of endangered, threatened or imported nonhuman animals must only be conducted with full attention to required permits and ethical concerns. Information and permit applications can be obtained from the Fish and Wildlife Service website at http://www.fws.gov/.

V. EXPERIMENTAL PROCEDURES

Consideration for the humane treatment and well-being of the laboratory animal should be incorporated into the design and conduct of all procedures involving such animals, while keeping in mind the primary goal of undertaking the specific procedures of the research project—the acquisition of sound, replicable data. The conduct of all procedures is governed by Guideline I (Justification of Research) above.

A. Observational and other noninvasive forms of behavioral studies that involve no aversive stimulation to, or elicit no sign of distress from the nonhuman animal are acceptable.

B. Whenever possible behavioral procedures should be used that minimize discomfort to the nonhuman animal. Psychologists should adjust the parameters of aversive stimulation to the minimal levels compatible with the aims of the research. Consideration should be given to providing the research animals control over the potential aversive stimulation whenever it is consistent with the goals of the research. Whenever reasonable, psychologists are encouraged to first test the painful stimuli to be used on nonhuman animal subjects on themselves.

C. Procedures in which the research animal is anesthetized and insensitive to pain throughout the procedure, and is euthanized (AVMA, 2007) before regaining consciousness are generally acceptable.

D. Procedures involving more than momentary or slight aversive stimulation, which is not relieved by medication or other acceptable methods, should be undertaken only when the objectives of the research cannot be achieved by other methods.

E. Experimental procedures that require prolonged aversive conditions or produce tissue damage or metabolic disturbances require greater justification and surveillance by the psychologist and IACUC. A research animal observed to be in a state of severe distress or chronic pain that cannot be alleviated and is not essential to the purposes of the research should be euthanized immediately (AVMA, 2007).

F. Procedures that employ restraint must conform to federal regulations and guidelines.

G. Procedures involving the use of paralytic agents without reduction in pain sensation require particular prudence and humane concern. Use of muscle relaxants or paralytics alone during surgery, without anesthesia, is unacceptable.

H. Surgical procedures, because of their invasive nature, require close supervision and attention to humane considerations by the psychologist. Aseptic (methods that minimize risks of infection) techniques must be used on laboratory animals whenever possible.

1. All surgical procedures and anesthetization should be conducted under the direct supervision of a person who is trained and competent in the use of the procedures.

2. Unless there is specific justification for acting otherwise, research animals should be maintained under anesthesia until all surgical procedures are ended.

3. Postoperative monitoring and care, which may include the use of analgesics and antibiotics, should be provided to minimize discomfort, prevent infection and promote recovery from the procedure.

4. In general, laboratory animals should not be subjected to successive survival surgical procedures, except as required by the nature of the research, the nature of the specific surgery, or for the well-being of the animal. Multiple surgeries on the same animal must be justified and receive approval from the IACUC.

I. To minimize the number of nonhuman animals used, multiple research uses of individual animals should be considered. Such uses must be compatible with the goals of the research, sound scientific practice, and the welfare of the animal.

J. To ensure their humane treatment and well-being, laboratory animals generally may not be released from institutional facilities. Nonhuman animals reared in the laboratory must not be released into the wild because, in most cases, they cannot survive or they may survive by disrupting the natural ecology. Return of any wild-caught animal to the field also carries risks, both to the formerly captive animals and to the ecosystem.

K. When euthanasia is appropriate, either as a requirement of the research or because it constitutes the most humane form of disposition of a nonhuman animal at the conclusion of the research:

1. Euthanasia must be accomplished in a humane manner, appropriate for the species and age, and in such a way as to ensure immediate death, and in accordance with procedures outlined in the latest version of the "AVMA (American Veterinary Medical Association) Guidelines on Euthanasia (2007)," available from https://olaw.nih.gov/sites/default/files/Euthanasia2007.pdf.

2. Disposal of euthanized laboratory animals must be conducted in accord with all relevant legislation, consistent with health, environmental, and aesthetic concerns, and as approved by the IACUC. No animal shall be discarded until its death is verified.

VI. FIELD RESEARCH

Field research that carries a risk of materially altering the behavior of nonhuman animals and/or producing damage to sensitive ecosystems is subject to IACUC approval. Field research, if strictly observational, may not require animal care committee approval (USDA, 2000).

A. Psychologists conducting field research should disturb their populations as little as possible, while acting consistent with the goals of the research. Every effort should be made to minimize potential harmful effects of the study on the population and on other plant and animal species in the area.

B. Research conducted in populated areas must be done with respect for the property and privacy of the inhabitants of the area.

C. Such research on endangered species should not be conducted unless IACUC approval has been obtained and all requisite permits are obtained (see IV.D of this brochure.)

VII. EDUCATIONAL USE OF NONHUMAN ANIMALS

Laboratory exercises as well as classroom demonstrations involving live animals are of great value as instructional aids. Psychologists are encouraged to include instruction and discussion of the ethics and values of nonhuman animal research in all relevant courses.

A. Nonhuman animals may be used for educational purposes only after review by an IACUC or committee appropriate to the institution.

B. Consideration should be given to the possibility of using non-animal alternatives. Some procedures that can be justified for research purposes may not be justified for educational purposes.

It is important to recognize that this document constitutes "guidelines," which serve a different purpose than "standards." Standards, unlike guidelines, require mandatory compliance, and may be accompanied by an enforcement mechanism. This document is meant to be aspirational in intent, and to provide recommendations for the professional conduct of specified activities. These guidelines are not intended to be mandatory, exhaustive, or definitive and should not take precedence over the judgment of individuals who have competence in the subject addressed.

APA has adopted separate guidelines for the use of nonhuman animals in research and teaching at the pre-college level. . . .

REFERENCES

American Psychological Association. (2010). *Ethical principles of psychologists and code of conduct* (2002, Amended June 1, 2010). Retrieved September 19, 2011 from http://www.apa.org/ethics/code/index.aspx

American Veterinary Medical Association. (2007). *AVMA guidelines on euthanasia*. Retrieved April 8, 2010 from http://www.avma.org/issues/animal_welfare/euthanasia.pdf

Animal Welfare Act 7 U.S.C. § 2131 et seq. Retrieved April 8, 2010 from http://awic.nal.usda.gov/nal_display/index.php?info_center=3&tax_level=3&tax_subject=182&topic_id=1118&level3_id=6735

National Institutes of Health Office of Laboratory Animal Welfare. (2002). *Public Health Service policy on the humane care and use of laboratory animals*. Bethesda, MD: NIH. Retrieved September 27, 2011 from http://grants.nih.gov/grants/olaw/references/phspol.htm

National Research Council. (2006). *Guidelines for the humane transportation of research animals*. Washington, DC: The National Academies Press.

U.S. Department of Agriculture. (1989). Animal welfare; Final Rules. Federal Register, 54(168), (Aug 31, 1989), 36112–36163.

U.S. Department of Agriculture. (1990). Guinea pigs, hamsters, and rabbits; Final Rule. Federal Register, 55(136), (July 16, 1990), 28879–28884.

U.S. Department of Agriculture. (1991). Animal welfare; Standards; Part 3, Final Rule. Federal Register, 55(32), (Feb 15, 1991), 6426–6505.

U.S. Department of Agriculture. (2000). Field study; Definition; Final Rule. Federal Register, 65(27), (Feb 9, 2000), 6312–6314.

. . .

8.6. Psychological Research Online: Report of Board of Scientific Affairs' Advisory Group on the Conduct of Research on the Internet

Robert Kraut, Judith Olson, Mahzarin Banaji, Amy Bruckman, Jeffrey Cohen, and Mick Couper

. . .

CHALLENGES OF INTERNET RESEARCH: PROTECTION OF HUMAN SUBJECTS

In addition to potentially affecting data quality, conducting research online can affect human subjects and the actions that researchers must take to protect their welfare. We believe that online research poses no more risk to human subjects than comparable research conducted through other means, but conducting research online changes the nature of the risks and investigators' ability to assess it. Some of the challenges arise because fundamental concepts that underlie federal regulation for the protection of human subjects, such as the concept of minimal risk and public behavior, change or become ambiguous when research is conducted online. Other challenges arise because it is more difficult to assess subjects' identities or their reactions to the research experience online.

The basic ethical principles underlying research involving human subjects—respect for persons, beneficence, and justice—are contained in the Belmont Report (National Commission for the Protection of Human Subjects of Biomedical and Behavioral Research, 1979). These principles have been formalized into the Federal Policy for the Protection of Human Subjects (known as the *Common Rule*).[1] The regulation sets standards for assessing the degree of risk to

---

[1] Federal regulations are published in the Code of Federal Regulations (C.F.R.). Each of the federal agencies and departments that has adopted the Common Rule has published it with different C.F.R. numbers (e.g., the Department of Health and Human Services' regulations are published as 45 C.F.R. pt. 46, 1999). The content is identical for each. In referring to sections of the Common Rule in this document, we will use the notation C.R. § 102(b), where the C.R. stands for the document (i.e., the Common Rule) and the code following the § stands for a part number and letter subsection. The Office of Human Subjects Protections posts a copy of the Common Rule at http://ohrp.osophs.dhhs.gov/humansubjects/guidance/45cfr46.htm

human subjects and trade-offs between risk and benefit; for establishing and documenting voluntary, informed consent before people participate in research; and for the treatment of minors and other vulnerable populations. It established an oversight process called the IRB system, which assists those conducting research involving human subjects to comply with the spirit and the letter of the regulation.

Ambiguities in Key Concepts When Research Is Conducted Online

Both the broad ethical principles articulated by the Belmont Report and the detailed federal regulations about the protection of human subjects depend on key concepts, such as minimum risk, expectations of privacy, the notion of pre-existing records, and anonymity, whose complex meanings are affected when research is conducted online. . . . This decision [whether the researcher needs to obtain and document informed consent from a research subject] involves determining:

- whether individuals are identifiable or anonymous,
- whether behavior is public or involves reasonable expectations of privacy,
- whether individuals expected that records were being created or expected that their behavior was ephemeral,
- whether subjects expected that records about them would be made public or kept private,
- and the degree of risk associated with the research experience.

Each of these determinations is likely to change when the research is conducted online, rather than through a more conventional mode. We consider these issues in more detail below.

Identifiable Versus Anonymous Information

Determining whether an individual is identifiable or anonymous has implications for the risks subjects are exposed to, whether the research is exempt from federal human-subjects regulations, and whether the research is even defined as involving human subjects at all. According to the federal regulations (C.R. § 102(f)), research involves human subjects only if data are collected through interaction with a subject or if it collects "identifiable private information." Observations of public behavior, in which individuals cannot be identified directly or indirectly, are exempt from the federal regulations protecting human subjects (C.R. § 101(b)).

As we will discuss, the greatest risk associated with online research centers on breaches of confidentiality, in which private, identifiable information is disclosed outside of the research context. In the case of online survey and experimental research, the researcher can often reduce this risk by explicitly not asking for identifying information or by recording personal identifiers separately from the research data.

In observations of naturally occurring online behavior, however, anonymity is more difficult to achieve, and the very nature of anonymity versus identifiability becomes ambiguous. Suppose one wishes to quote statements made in an online forum. One cannot assume that pseudonyms, often used by individuals to simultaneously mask and express their identities online, render their conversations anonymous, because posters may choose pseudonyms that contain part or all of their real names or disclose information that publicly links their pseudonyms to their real identities (see Bassett & O'Riordan, 2002, for a fuller discussion). Even seemingly anonymous snippets of text posted in an online diary (known as a Web log or blogs) or online forum may be traced back to individual posters through the use of Internet search engines. Therefore, to preserve anonymity, researchers should disguise pseudonyms and alter quoted text.

Public Versus Private Behavior

Some have argued that scientists can record public Internet-based communication without the knowledge or consent of subjects, because this constitutes observation of public behavior (Herring, 1996). Many online communication forums have unrestricted membership, allowing anyone who comes by to participate in conversation or observe it. For example, lurkers (individuals who read messages but don't post them) represent well over 50% of subjects in many e-mail distribution lists (Nonnecke & Preece, 2000). In such cases, we believe that people who post in these groups should have no reasonable expectation of privacy, and researchers and IRBs should be able to treat online communication in them as public behavior.

There are, however, important caveats about when online communication should be treated as public behavior. The federal regulation bases its definition of private information on the expectation of privacy. Whether a person conversing online can reasonably expect the communication to be private depends on legal regulation, social norms, and specific details of implementation, all of which are changing. Implementation details include such features of the online settings as the number of people who subscribe, whether membership is restricted or open, whether membership is static or rapidly changing, whether conversations are ephemeral or archived, whether the presence of lurkers is visible, and whether the forum has posted explicit recording policies. Researchers and IRBs need to take considerations such as these into account on a case-by-case basis when deciding about the status of online communications among individuals on an electronic distribution list (e.g., Baym, 1993) or an Internet chat room (e.g., Bull & McFarlane, 2000).

The ethical considerations should be influenced by relevant legislation, but the laws about the privacy of computer-based electronic communication are still evolving. The Electronic Communications Privacy Act (1986) states that it is illegal to intercept electronic communications. Private e-mail and instant messaging exchanged between individuals are considered protected communication. However, this protection does not include most group-oriented communication, such as bulletin boards, public distribution lists, and chat rooms, even ones where members must enter a password before participating, if the person recording the information is considered a "party to the communication." The communication is also not protected if "the electronic communication system . . . is configured so that such electronic communication is readily accessible to the general public" (Electronic Communications Privacy Act, 1986, 18 U.S.C. § 2511(2)(g)(I)).

Whether behavior should be considered public or private also depends on changing features of technology. For example, many Web sites automatically create logs showing the IP address of the machines that visit the site. When a person has exclusive use of a personal computer with a fixed IP address, knowing the IP address is tantamount to knowing the identity of its user. However, dynamic IP addresses, in which one of a fixed number of addresses is assigned to a machine on the fly, do not translate into individual identifiers. In the case of dynamic IP addresses, tracing the address only identifies the machine pool, not the individual machine or its user.

Preexisting Public Records

Research is exempt from human-subjects regulations if it involves collecting preexisting public data, documents, and records (C.R. § 46.101(b)(4)). We addressed the ambiguity in the definition of *public* previously. The concept of preexisting is also ambiguous. In order to be preexisting, all of the data must exist prior to the beginning of the research, such as research on archives of online discussions. Data that are generated during the course of the research, such as postings to a blog (i.e., a Web log or online diary posted for public consumption and comment) or to a live discussion group would not be considered preexisting. Such research would qualify for expedited review: "Research involving materials (data, documents, records, or specimens) that have been collected, or will be collected solely for nonresearch purposes" (Categories of Research That May Be Reviewed by the Institutional Review Board [IRB] Through an Expedited Review Procedure, 1998). Under expedited review, the requirements for informed consent must be considered, but the expedited reviewer can waive those requirements if the regulatory criteria are met.

RISK TO SUBJECTS FROM INTERNET RESEARCH

Both general ethical principles and federal regulation require that the risks to subjects from participating in research be minimized. Although few psychological studies involve physical risk, they can involve social, psychological, economic, and legal outcomes that may have harmful effects. According to the federal regulations, research has minimal risk when "the probability and magnitude of harm or discomfort anticipated in the research are not greater in and of themselves than those ordinarily encountered in daily life" (C.R. § 102(i)).

Internet research involves two potential sources of risk:

- harm resulting from direct participation in the research (e.g., emotional reactions to questions or experimental manipulations) and

- harm resulting from breach of confidentiality.

Harm as a Consequence of Participation in Online Research

Much online research involves minimal risk. It exposes subjects to innocuous questions and benign or transient experiences with little lasting impact. In general, online surveys, experiments, or observations are no more risky than any of their offline counterparts. In some respects, they may be less risky, because the reduced social pressure (Sproull & Kiesler, 1991) in online surveys or experiments makes it easier for subjects to quit whenever they feel discomfort. This freedom to withdraw is no trivial benefit, given the strong pressures to continue in face-to-face studies (e.g., Milgram, 1963) and even telephone calls.

Although risk in online settings is typically low, the actual risk depends on the specifics of the study. For example, some questions in a survey or feedback from an experiment may cause subjects to reflect on unpleasant experiences or to learn something unpleasant about themselves (e.g., Nosek et al.'s, 2002b, research on automatic stereotyping). Experiments that deliberately manipulate a subject's sense of self-worth, reveal a lack of cognitive ability, challenge deeply held beliefs or attitudes, or disclose some other real or perceived characteristic may result in mental or emotional harm to some subjects. The concern in online research is not that some subjects are at risk. Risks can be justified if the potential benefits of the research are substantial enough and the cost–benefit analysis is no different in evaluating online research than in medical research or in traditional psychological research. Rather, the special concern is that researchers may have a diminished ability to monitor subjects in online research and remediate any harm caused by the research.

Although not explicitly covered in the Common Rule, research subjects may be harmed if the welfare of the online groups in which they participate is damaged by the research. Consider online social-support groups, where people who confront a common health or other problem share information, empathy, and advice. King (1996) quoted a member of an online support group who wrote that she was not going to participate actively because of a researcher's presence in the group: "When I joined this I thought it would be a *support* group, not a fishbowl for a bunch of guinea pigs" (p. 122; see Eysenbach & Till, 2001, for similar concerns). When conducting cost–benefit analysis for research, investigators and IRBs alike must consider these subtle consequences of their decisions.

Debriefing

American Psychological Association (2002) ethical guidelines call for debriefing subjects—providing an explanation of the nature, results, and conclusions of the research—as soon after their participation as practical. If deception was involved, the researcher needs to explain the value of the research results and why deception was necessary. If investigators become aware during the debriefing that research procedures have caused harm to a subject, they are to take steps to ameliorate the harm.

When conducting research online, researchers can post debriefing materials at a Web site, can automatically update these material as new results become available, and can tailor debriefing materials to particular experimental conditions or even individual subjects. There are even methods to provide debriefing materials to those who leave before completing the research (Nosek, Banaji, & Greenwald, 2002a). For example, researchers can deliver debriefing material through a link to a "leave the study" button or through a pop-up window, which executes when a subject leaves a defined Web. As suggested earlier, however, appropriate debriefing in online research may be difficult. The absence of a researcher in the online setting makes it difficult to assess a subject's state and therefore to determine whether an individual has been upset by an experimental procedure or understands feedback received.

Breach of Confidentiality

We believe that a greater risk of harm in online research comes from possible disclosure of identifiable private information outside of the research context, not from the experience of participating in the research itself. The identifying information can include records of statements, attitudes, or behaviors coupled with names, e-mail addresses, partially disguised pseudonyms, or other identifying information. Researchers must ensure adequate provisions to protect the privacy of subjects and to maintain the confidentiality of data.

Identifying information may be inadvertently disclosed either as the data are being collected or, more commonly, when they are stored on a networked computer connected to the public Internet. Data in transit are vulnerable, for example, if a subject or automated process sends data to the investigator by e-mail. The store-and-forward nature of e-mail means that the message may rest in temporary directories on intervening computers before it is finally delivered to the addressee. The danger is less for data collected through automated Web surveys, although "sniffing" programs can eavesdrop on data in transit to search for known patterns, such as social security numbers, credit card numbers, or e-mail addresses. These risks can be avoided by not collecting identifying information or by separating these data from other research data. Although analogous risks can occur with paper forms, they are higher when data are shipped over the Internet, because of the openness of the networks and the possibility of automated pattern detection.

Greater risks to confidentiality result from outsiders gaining access to stored data files, either through deliberate hacking or because researchers mistakenly distributed them. This risk is not unique to online research but is a challenge for all data stored on networked computers. The standard approach to dealing with problems of confidentiality is to separate personal identifiers from other data describing subjects. Thus, one should keep identifying information, such as names and addresses, in one file and data in a second, with an arbitrary code number to link the two. Tourangeau, Couper, and Steiger (2003) illustrated some techniques used to maintain separation of identity from data in survey research involving sensitive data.

Maintaining the confidentiality of data stored on computer systems may require psychologists to become more sophisticated about computer technology than many currently are. Researchers should configure their computers so that only those with a need to know have access to directories containing research data and should regularly check the permissions. They should routinely keep abreast of the security alerts issued by their vendors and apply security updates when these are released. For sensitive data, directories can be password protected, and sensitive files can be encrypted. Many investigators, however, fail to take these precautions to protect their data.

A special complication in maintaining a subject's anonymity arises when an investigator conducting online research must match different pieces of information from the same respondent. For example, the hypertext markup language (HTML) protocol, in which most Web surveys are authored, does not keep history from one page view to another and link responses from a single respondent. There are a variety of ways to keep track of a respondent's answers across several Web pages without compromising anonymity, such as session cookies, which are stored in memory; hidden values embedded in the HTML; or environment variables such as IP address.

Paying online subjects for their participation may also link subjects' responses to their identities when sending a payment requires a mailing address or accounting regulations require a social security number. Some researchers have severed this link by buying gift certificates from online retailers, such as Amazon.com, and displaying the unique certificate number to a respondent at the completion of a questionnaire. Thus, subjects can redeem their certificates without revealing their identity.

The degree of concern over confidentiality and steps taken to ensure it should be directly related to the sensitivity of the data being collected. One is less concerned when subjects are anonymous or when the information about them is innocuous (i.e., its revelation would bring no harm or embarrassment to subjects). Many online surveys and experiments fall into one or both of these categories. In these cases, use of passwords, encryption, or strong assurance to research subjects is not needed and may harm the research. For example, as Singer, Hippler, and Schwarz (1992) demonstrated, overly elaborate assurances of confidentiality may actually heighten rather than diminish respondents' concern, causing subjects to be less willing to provide sensitive information. Strong security measures (e.g., using secure socket layer protocols) may prohibit some research subjects from participating.

However, when subjects are identifiable and the research involves data that place them at risk of criminal or civil liability or that could damage their financial standing, employability, insurability, reputation, or could be stigmatizing, investigators must be especially concerned about breaches of confidentiality. Under these circumstances, standard security measures in place for electronic commerce, such as encryption and secure protocols, are likely to be suffi-cient. Numerous tutorials outline the options (e.g., Garfinkel, Spafford, & Russell, 2002).

Informed Consent

Investigators must typically obtain and document voluntary informed consent from research subjects, in which subjects freely agree to participate after they understand what the research involves and its risks and benefits (C.R. § 116). Federal human-subjects regulation also requires that informed consent be documented by the use of a "written consent form approved by the IRB and signed by the subject" (C.R. § 117). It is difficult to obtain legally binding signa-tures online. However, IRBs can waive the requirements for written documen-tation of informed consent for minimal-risk research either when the research would not require informed consent outside a research context or when the documentation is the only link between the research data and a subject's identity (C.R. § 117(c)). In the case of much online research involving adults, these conditions for waiving documentation of informed consent are met, and we recommend that IRBs should waive the document and allow a procedure in which subjects click a button on an online form to indicate they have read and understood the consent form.

As we have indicated earlier, the lack of interactivity in online research means that the investigator often cannot tell whether a subject understood the informed consent statement. As a result, online research may require more pretesting of these statements than research conducted in other venues. Researchers can increase the likelihood that subjects are granting truly informed consent by requiring feedback from subjects about their level of understanding, for example, by requiring a "click to accept" for each element in an informed consent statement or even administering short quizzes to establish that a sub-ject understood. As with efforts to protect confidentiality, however, these extra efforts to ensure informed consent may reduce response rates, increase non-response to sensitive items (Singer, 1978), and possibly produce biased data (Trice, 1987). Therefore, these techniques are recommended only for research involving more than minimal risk to the subject.

These simple procedures for research involving competent adults may not be appropriate for online research involving children and other vulnerable groups, such as the mentally handicapped. According to federal regulation, these populations are not empowered to give consent for themselves. Their parent or guardian must consent, and the child may optionally be asked to assent. Here the inability to establish the subjects' identity is especially prob-lematic, because researchers cannot easily determine whether online subjects are revealing their true age and because children can easily pretend to be their parents. Researchers can institute procedures to more reliably distinguish chil-dren from adults by having subjects enter information that is generally avail-able only to adults (e.g., credit card numbers) or by requiring that they register with a trusted authority, such as VeriSign (http://www.verisign.com/products/asb/). Depending on the risk involved, the researcher and IRB must either accept the possibility that unidentified minors participated in the research or that they forged parental consent or insist that a legally verified signature accompany the consent form, by conducting the research offline. Note that researchers working with children online are subject not only to human-subjects regulations, but also to the Children's Online Privacy Protection Act (1998; see http://www.ftc.gov/ogc/coppa1.htm). Researchers are prohibited from collecting personal information from a child without posting notices about how the information will be used and without getting verifiable parental consent.

. . .

REFERENCES

American Psychological Association. (2002). *Ethical principles of psychologists and code of conduct, Draft 7.* Washington, DC: Author.

Bassett, E. H., & O'Riordan, K. (2002). Ethics of Internet research: Contesting the human subjects model. *Journal of Ethics and Information Technology, 4,* 233–247.

Baym, N. (1993). Interpreting soap operas and creating community: Inside a computer-mediated fan culture. *Journal of Folklore Research, 30,* 143–176.

Bull, S., & McFarlane, M. (2000). Soliciting sex on the Internet: What are the risks for sexually transmitted diseases and HIV? *Sexually Transmitted Diseases, 27,* 545–550.

Categories of Research That May Be Reviewed by the Institutional Review Board (IRB) Through an Expedited Review Procedure, 63 Fed. Reg. 60364–60367 (Nov. 9, 1998)

Children's Online Privacy Protection Act, 13 U.S.C. §§ 1301–1308 (1998).

Electronic Communications Privacy Act, 18 U.S.C. § 2511 (1986).

Eysenbach, G., & Till, J. E. (2001). Ethical issues in qualitative research on Internet communities. *British Medical Journal, 323,* 103–105.

Garfinkel, S., Spafford, G., & Russell, D. (2002). *Web security, privacy and commerce.* Cambridge, MA: O'Reilly & Associates.

Herring, S. (1996). Linguistic and critical analysis of computer-mediated communication: Some ethical and scholarly considerations. *The Information Society, 12,* 153–168.

King, S. (1996). Researching Internet communities: Proposed ethical guidelines for the reporting of results. *The Information Society, 12,* 119–127.

Milgram, S. (1963). Behavioral study of obedience. *Journal of Abnormal and Social Psychology, 67,* 371–378.

National Commission for the Protection of Human Subjects of Biomedical and Behavioral Research. (1979, April 18). *Belmont report: Ethical principles and guidelines for the protection of human subjects of research.* Retrieved, November 2, 2003, from https://www.hhs.gov/ohrp/sites/default/files/the-belmont-report-508c_FINAL.pdf

Nonnecke, B., & Preece, J. (2000). Lurker demographics: Counting the silent. *CHI 2000, ACM Conference on Human Factors in Computing Systems, CHI Letters, 4*(1), 73–80.

Nosek, B. A., Banaji, M. R., & Greenwald, A. G. (2002a). E-research: Ethics, security, design, and control in psychological research on the Internet. *Journal of Social Issues, 58,* 161–176.

Nosek, B. A., Banaji, M., & Greenwald, A. G. (2002b). Harvesting implicit group attitudes and beliefs from a demonstration web site. *Group Dynamics, 6,* 101–115.

Singer, E. (1978). Informed consent: Consequences for response rate and response quality in social surveys. *American Sociological Review, 43,* 144–162.

Singer, E., Hippler, H., & Schwarz, N. (1992). Confidentiality assurances in surveys: Reassurance or threat? *International Journal of Public Opinion Research, 4,* 256–268.

Sproull, L., & Kiesler, S. (1991). *Connections: New ways of working in the networked organization.* Cambridge, MA: MIT Press.

Tourangeau, R., Couper, M. P., & Steiger, D. M. (2003). Humanizing self-administered surveys: Experiments on social presence in Web and IVR surveys. *Computers in Human Behavior, 19,* 1–24.

Trice, A. D. (1987). Informed consent: VIII. Biasing of sensitive self-report data by both consent and information. *Journal of Social Behavior and Personality, 2,* 369–374.

COMMENTARY: Internet-based research enables psychologists to reach the deepest possible pool of research participants, with hitherto unforeseen speed and efficiency, and across vast geographical and cultural divides. With this freedom of recruitment options comes, of course, a concomitant lack of control. Under what circumstances are questionnaires being endorsed? Who is actually providing informed consent? How many times is an individual participant seeking to contribute? For what reasons has participation been terminated?

With hindsight, it is apparent that the increasing prevalence of this mode of data collection was as inevitable as telepsychology in clinical practice—another innovation that grew out of a natural tendency to keep pace with advances in everyday communications capabilities. Now psychologists must keep pace in another fashion: with threats to the integrity and products of research design and to the safety of vulnerable populations. Although much of what we prize and take for granted is confirmed and enhanced by the utilization of new media, we also face new challenges that will continue to challenge long-held assumptions.

The following references are recommended for those interested in further investigation of Internet-based research, with attention paid to such factors as the function of Institutional Review Boards and the recruitment—wittingly or otherwise—of minor participants.

Gosling, S. D., & Mason, W. (2015). Internet research in psychology. *Annual Review of Psychology, 66,* 877–902. http://dx.doi.org/10.1146/annurev-psych-010814-015321

Graber, M. A., & Graber, A. (2013). Internet-based crowdsourcing and research ethics: The case for IRB review. *Journal of Medical Ethics, 39,* 115–118.

McKee, H. A., & Porter, J. E. (2009). *The ethics of Internet research: A rhetorical, case-based process.* New York: Peter Lang.

McKellar, K., & Toth, N. (2016). Ethical considerations in face-to-face and internet-mediated research with teenage populations. In L. Little, D. Fitton, B. T. Bell, & N. Toth (Eds.), *Perspectives on HCI research with teenagers* (pp. 29–59). Cham, Switzerland: Springer International.

Whitehead, L. C. (2007). Methodological and ethical issues in Internet-mediated research in the field of health: An integrated review of the literature. *Social Science & Medicine, 65,* 782–791. http://dx.doi.org/10.1016/j.socscimed.2007.03.005

8.7. What and When Should Undergraduates Learn About Research Ethics?

Blaine F. Peden and Allen H. Keniston

Acting ethically is a desirable and important outcome of student learning (American Psychological Association [APA], 2007; APA, Board of Educational Affairs, 2008). Because ethics permeates every topic in psychology, questions often arise regarding how to teach about the responsible conduct of research. In this chapter, we present a developmentally appropriate model that ensures "every psychology student is (or should be) presented with a range of ethical considerations as part of his or her undergraduate education" (Landrum et al., 2010, p. 158). Our "scope and sequence" agenda assumes that teaching ethically requires instructors to learn and teach ethics throughout their careers.

Our suggestions for teaching about research ethics across the undergraduate curriculum derive from several sources. The APA (2007) student learning outcomes include objectives specific to teaching ethics. Additional resources include the developmentally coherent curriculum (APA, Board of Educational Affairs, 2008), discussions of ethical acculturation (e.g., Handelsman, Gottlieb, & Knapp, 2005), and guidelines for conducting ethical research (e.g., Aguinis & Henle, 2002; Kimmel, 2007). . . .

TEACHING RESEARCH ETHICS IN THE FIRST YEAR

Introductory psychology courses should produce a basic understanding of research ethics in all students (Dunn, Beins, McCarthy, & Hill, 2010). Student learning outcomes regarding the ethical knowledge, skills, and values for undergraduate psychology majors can be found in the APA *Guidelines for the Undergraduate Psychology Major* (APA, 2007). Teachers may impart information about psychology-specific learning objectives using textbooks, lectures, and demonstrations and by having undergraduates participate in research. Subsequent learning objectives should be addressed later in students' educational careers.

During the first year of students' experience, educators should also introduce the APA *Ethical Principles of Psychologists and Code of Conduct* (hereinafter referred to as the Ethics Code; APA, 2010). Instructors should explain that ethics applies to psychologists working as helping professionals, teachers, and

From *Teaching Ethically: Challenges and Opportunities* (pp. 151–160), by R. E. Landrum and M. A. McCarthy (Eds.), 2012, Washington, DC: American Psychological Association. Copyright 2012 by the American Psychological Association.

researchers. Teachers should explain that psychologists formally adopted their first professional code of conduct in the 1950s and have revised it regularly since then. Instructors should also emphasize that the Ethics Code applies to students. For example, student affiliates of the APA must agree to adhere to the Ethics Code. Finally, first-year students should understand that the APA Ethics Code dictates the conduct of research and fosters thinking critically about research.

Beyond the usual discussion about the Milgram (1963) study of obedience, several authors (Fisher & Kuther, 1997; Handelsman, 2002; Korn, 1984) have offered ways to introduce ethical topics into beginning courses. For example, teachers can promote understanding of the APA Ethics Code, the requirement to follow the Ethics Code in the treatment of human and nonhuman participants, recognition of the necessity of ethical behavior in the science and practice of psychology, the use of information and technology ethically and responsibly, and the regular display of personal integrity with others, all in the students' first year.

Faculty can also help first-year students gain a basic level of ethical proficiency by making a distinction between classroom demonstrations and psychological research intended to produce new knowledge. Demonstrations of obedience (e.g., Lucas & Lidstone, 2000), discussions of Milgram's (1963) original study and the replication by Burger (2009), and assessment of students' opinions and concerns about these materials can be beneficial in helping students learn the basics of research ethics (Harcum & Friedman, 1991). Engaging students in the classroom demonstration and discussing the accompanying classic article (Milgram, 1963) along with the commentaries on the Burger (2009) article from *American Psychologist* should prompt students to think critically about relevant ethical issues and ethically complex situations. Moreover, discussion about the recent replication of the Milgram procedure allows instructors to raise interesting questions about the use of alternative procedures (Slater et al., 2006).

First-year students can also learn about research ethics by participating in research. . . . Instructors can and, perhaps should, use videos to enhance student interest and participation in research (Sacco & Bernstein, 2010). Most important, teachers must ensure students' understanding of their roles, rights, and responsibilities in psychological research (Korn, 1988). . . .

Student participants should expect ethical treatment by researchers; however, participants should also act ethically. Kimble (1987) provided syllabus language that instructors could use to promote responsible research participation by first-year students and thereby help to ensure quality scientific research. First, Kimble argued that a syllabus should state that participating in research provides experience with experimental procedures that is otherwise unavailable. Second, psychologists do research to find behavioral solutions to real social problems. Third, future students benefit from today's research in the same way that students now benefit from earlier research. Finally, students should have equitable alternatives to participating in research in accord with

Standard 8.04, Client/Patient, Student, and Subordinate Research Participants, of the Ethics Code (APA, 2010).

Korn (1988) further described how first-year courses might provide opportunities for teachers to educate their students about how to be high-quality research participants and, at the same time, to educate students on their rights as participants. Korn (1984) emphasized that beginning students should learn about their rights as research participants because they are the largest group of individuals participating in academic research today. Instructors who use syllabus language adapted from Kimble (1987) enhance their students' ability to make informed decisions about starting and finishing a psychological study.

Another way to promote teaching and learning about research ethics is to have students be experimenters. First-year students can learn about psychological research by serving as research assistants. Students might read articles on a topic (selected by the instructor), engage in data collection and analysis (using procedures and instructions provided by the instructor), and write reports about the research as a way to learn about the research enterprise. These experiences allow students to engage in multiple levels of the research process. . . .

TEACHING RESEARCH ETHICS IN THE SECOND YEAR

Undergraduates typically take statistics prior to research methods in their second college year (Peden & Carroll, 2009; Stoloff et al., 2010). In second-year courses, the student learning outcomes generally should move beyond retention and comprehension to analysis and application of proficiencies. Although statistics instructors usually do not focus on ethical practices, they nevertheless should convey Vardeman and Morris's (2003) advice that doing statistics is an inherently ethical endeavor. Their emphasis on personal integrity and the necessity of ethical behavior in all aspects of practice, research, and teaching echoes more advanced learning objectives. For example, statistics instructors can review ethical concerns regarding plagiarism presented in first-year courses and then discuss fabrication and falsification of data. All three concepts apply to statistics homework and real data. Students in a more advanced statistics course should use their knowledge about the roles, rights, and responsibilities of research participants when they volunteer to serve in research (Korn, 1988) as well as use their new knowledge about measurement, sampling issues, and experimental design. Statistics students should be inclined and able to ask questions during the informed consent or debriefing processes and receive clear and reasonable answers.

The research methods course allows psychology students to apply knowledge about both ethics and statistics during the design, planning, and analysis phases of research. More advanced methods courses provide additional venues to teach about ethical guidelines for the design and implementation of research (Aguinis & Henle, 2002; Kimmel, 2007). Students should receive training about the steps involved in obtaining approval to conduct research. More important, students should learn that ensuring ethical treatment of participants is at the heart of the institutional review board (IRB) process. Students with a developing level of understanding about the ethical treatment of research participants should be able to identify ethical issues that arise at each point in the research process. In the second stage of the research process, researchers are focused on securing a sufficiently large and representative sample, which requires methodological competence and ethical sensitivities. At this point students should learn about controversies associated with recruiting participants through subject pools (for a complete review of issues, see Chastain & Landrum, 1999; Dalziel, 1996; Diamond & Reidpath, 1994).

Discussions of recruitment also prompt researchers to consider whether inducements (e.g., extra credit in a class, money, food) unduly influence (i.e., coerce) students to participate in a given study. Evaluating the level of inducement may prove troublesome for student researchers because students have a unique perspective. For example, Miller and Kreiner (2008) demonstrated that members of IRBs regard inducements as much more coercive than do students. Teaching ethically requires educators to understand students' viewpoints and help them resolve contradictory opinions. It is only later in the sequence of educational training that students are in a position to fully realize the complexity associated with current practices in the recruitment of research participants. Undergraduates typically have some knowledge about conducting research from their own experience as participants. We believe that students can benefit from participating again when they are further along in the major. By serving again as participants, student researchers perceive research and responsible conduct in a different light.

Students who are early in their educational careers may be taught about plagiarism at an introductory level. Although these students may learn that plagiarism is unethical, they may be insensitive to subtle ethical issues regarding authorship (e.g., order of listing), misrepresenting their own or the research of others, and censoring data or ideas. It is likely that students will not fully grasp these subtleties until they are in their third or fourth year and can more directly experience "real life" authorship.

TEACHING RESEARCH ETHICS IN THE THIRD AND FOURTH YEARS

Successful completion of the second-year curriculum prepares students for third- and fourth-year courses. Students are apprentices and may possess skills beyond analysis and application of research, developing their own projects. These student researchers now have the potential to do "real" research that meaningfully contributes to the literature. There are two primary venues for this level of training: advanced content courses and independent work with faculty on research projects. In either case, we recommend that students and faculty discuss a range of ethical issues (Dunn, 2010; Goodyear, Crego, & Johnston, 1992).

One approach to communicating research ethics involves infusing the content into the fabric of the course (Carroll, Keniston, & Peden, 2008). In typical content courses, students may write research proposals and even conduct their own research. Students must delve into the literature to learn about the logic and design of specific paradigms. Reviewing the literature should help to make students aware of the ethical challenges and opportunities inherent in specific research designs. For example, studying incidental recall may require deception because participants must recall material they did not expect to remember (e.g., instructions often suggest that the experiment is about something other than remembering). However, the Ethics Code (APA, 2010) generally proscribes the use of deception (see Standard 8.07, Deception in Research); therefore, students now must learn to make more refined, careful, and sophisticated ethical judgments. Less sophisticated ethical reasoning must give way to more complex solutions.

Instructors of content courses should be conversant with the range of methodological and ethical issues related to student research projects. Faculty may scaffold the learning so that students develop a research project, but faculty must help students prepare IRB protocols. Students must learn about appropriate recruitment, informed consent, and debriefing.

A second approach to communicating research ethics is an apprenticeship in which a student may work as a research assistant for a faculty member. In this context, students learn how to conduct a literature search, master a research paradigm, and become skillful at collecting and analyzing data. Professors can and should model the ethical practices. Students might review prior IRB protocols to learn the rationale and procedures for the study.

Educators should convey that the process of planning a study, recruiting participants, conducting the study, and publishing an article often takes years rather than months. Hence, students who become members of a real research team must understand that they now have ethical obligations to the members of the team, to the profession, and to science that extend to the completion of the project. In other words, abandoning a study because the semester ends is ethically unacceptable.

Students who have become competent researchers in upper level coursework are now literate citizens of the psychological research community. At this point, they may begin to train and supervise other students new to the laboratory group. The final level of learning typically occurs in a capstone course or a faculty–student collaborative research project. In a capstone course, a student may refine and conduct research proposed in an earlier course or propose a new project. The capstone course should require students to demonstrate what they have learned about well-conceived, competently executed, and ethically responsible research. At this level, supervising professors act less as guides and more as evaluators of these three components. Educators also help students find financial resources to support the work and possibly provide proof of oversight. Students doing research for capstone courses must demonstrate that they can design research projects and address the ethical issues on their own. Their success provides a final indication of individual and institutional accomplishment. Success in a capstone course documents a psychology program's ability to develop and acculturate its students as academic psychologists (Handelsman et al., 2005).

Students may also become fully empowered collaborators working with professors on research programs. Experienced student collaborators may be able to propose new studies with the promise of results worth presenting at research conferences or publishing in peer-reviewed journals. In addition to mastering the methodological and ethical necessities of their research, students must become knowledgeable about the ethics of publication and collaboration. Failures of academic integrity threaten their coinvestigators. Thus, students must avoid plagiarism or citation errors and must discover such errors in the work of others on a research team. Students may have major responsibility for research protocols submitted to IRBs and must expertly evaluate the ethical concerns raised by their research. They must participate fully in decisions about authorship that fairly represent the relative contributions of all members of the research team. Serving as a coresearcher implies a leadership role in the research.

Undergraduate psychology students who complete the sequence of development required to become ethical researchers become full members of the academic community. They become models and teachers of ethical research practice who demonstrate conceptual and methodological expertise. After presenting or publishing their work, these advanced undergraduates may begin to identify with an even larger community defined by the individuals and institutions integral to their research. These students are ready for the transition to the next stages of their training as teachers, researchers, or applied researchers. The ultimate test of their training will be understanding that ethical standards are not static and therefore require commitment to further study and reflection. New or revised ethical standards require willing and cooperative accommodation of research practices to the new standards. We hope that students will adapt to changing ethical climates and cultures and make their own contributions to psychologists' evolving understanding about how best to teach and learn ethically.

. . .

REFERENCES

Aguinis, H., & Henle, C. A. (2002). Ethics in research. In S. G. Rogelberg (Ed.), *Handbook of research methods in industrial and organizational psychology* (pp. 34–56). Malden, MA: Blackwell.

American Psychological Association. (2007). *APA guidelines for the undergraduate psychology major.* Retrieved from http://www.apa.org/ed/precollege/about/psymajor-guidelines.pdf

American Psychological Association. (2010). *Ethical principles of psychologists and code of conduct* (Amended June 1, 2010). Retrieved from http://www.apa.org/ethics/code/index.aspx

American Psychological Association, Board of Educational Affairs. (2008). *Teaching, learning, and assessing in a developmentally coherent curriculum.* Retrieved from http://www.apa.org/ed/governance/bea/curriculum.pdf

Burger, J. M. (2009). Replicating Milgram: Would people still obey today? *American Psychologist, 64,* 1–11. doi:10.1037/a0010932

Carroll, D. W., Keniston, A. H., & Peden, B. F. (2008). Integrating critical thinking with course content. In D. S. Dunn, J. S. Halonen, & R. A. Smith (Eds.), *Teaching critical thinking in psychology: A handbook of best practices* (pp. 99–115). Malden, MA: Wiley-Blackwell. doi:10.1002/9781444305173.ch9

Chastain, G., & Landrum, R. E. (Eds.). (1999). *Protecting human subjects: Departmental subject pools and institutional review boards.* Washington, DC: American Psychological Association. doi:10.1037/10322-000

Dalziel, J. R. (1996). Students as research subjects: Ethical and educational issues. *Australian Psychologist, 31,* 119–123. doi:10.1080/00050069608260190

Diamond, M. R., & Reidpath, D. D. (1994). Are students really human? Observations on institutional ethics committees. *Australian Psychologist, 29,* 145–146. doi:10.1080/00050069408257339

Dunn, D. S. (2010). *The practical researcher: A student guide to conducting psychological research* (2nd ed.). Malden, MA: Wiley-Blackwell.

Dunn, D. S., Beins, B. B., McCarthy, M. A., & Hill, G. W., IV. (2010). *Best practices for teaching beginnings and endings in the psychology major: Research, cases, and recommendations.* New York, NY: Oxford University Press.

Fisher, C. B., & Kuther, T. L. (1997). Integrating research ethics into the introductory psychology course curriculum. *Teaching of Psychology, 24,* 172–175. doi:10.1207/s15328023top2403_4

Goodyear, R., Crego, C. A., & Johnston, M. W. (1992). Ethical issues in the supervision of student research: A study of critical incidents. *Professional Psychology: Research and Practice, 23,* 203–210. doi:10.1037/0735-7028.23.3.203

Handelsman, M. M. (2002, Fall). Where are the ethics in introductory psychology? *Psychology Teacher Network, 12*(3), pp. 1, 3.

Handelsman, M. M., Gottlieb, M. C., & Knapp, S. (2005). Training ethical psychologists: An acculturation model. *Professional Psychology: Research and Practice, 36,* 59–65. doi:10.1037/0735-7028.36.1.59

Harcum, E. R., & Friedman, H. (1991). Students' ethics ratings of demonstrations in introductory psychology. *Teaching of Psychology, 18,* 215–218. doi:10.1207/s15328023top1804_3

Kimble, G. A. (1987). The scientific value of undergraduate research participation. *American Psychologist, 42,* 267–268. doi:10.1037/0003-066X.42.3.267.b

Kimmel, A. J. (2007). *Ethical issues in behavioral research: Basic and applied perspectives* (2nd ed.). Malden, MA: Blackwell.

Korn, J. H. (1984). Coverage of research ethics in introductory and social psychology textbooks. *Teaching of Psychology, 11,* 146–149.

Korn, J. H. (1988). Students' roles, rights, and responsibilities as research participants. *Teaching of Psychology, 15,* 74–78. doi:10.1207/s15328023top1502_2

Landrum, R. E., Beins, B. C., Bhall, M., Brakke, K., Briihl, D. S., & Curl-Langager, R. M., . . . Van Kirk, J. J. (2010). Desired outcomes of an undergraduate education in psychology from departmental, student, societal perspectives. In D. F. Halpern (Ed.), *Undergraduate education in psychology: A blueprint for the future of the discipline* (pp. 145–160). Washington, DC: American Psychological Association.

Lucas, K. B., & Lidstone, J. G. (2000). Ethical issues in teaching about research ethics. *Evaluation and Research in Education, 14,* 53–64. doi:10.1080/09500790008666961

Milgram, S. (1963). Behavioral study of obedience. *Journal of Abnormal and Social Psychology, 67,* 371–378. doi:10.1037/h0040525

Miller, W. E., & Kreiner, D. S. (2008). Student perception of coercion to participate in psychological research. *North American Journal of Psychology, 10,* 53–64.

Peden, B. F., & Carroll, D. W. (2009). Historical trends in teaching research methods by psychologists in the United States. In M. Garner, C. Wagner, & B. Kawulich (Eds.), *Teaching research methods in the social sciences* (pp. 23–34). Farnham, Surrey, England: Ashgate.

Sacco, D. F., & Bernstein, M. J. (2010). A video introduction to psychology: Enhancing research interest and participation. *Teaching of Psychology, 37,* 28–31. doi:10.1080/00986280903425995

Slater, M., Antley, A., Davison, A., Swapp, D., Guger, C., Barker, C., . . . Sanchez-Vivez, M. V. (2006). A virtual reprise of the Stanley Milgram obedience experiments. *PLoS ONE, 1,* e39. doi:10.1371/journal.pone.0000039

Stoloff, M., McCarthy, M. A., Keller, L., Varfolomeeva, V., Lynch, J., Makara, K., . . . Smiley, W. (2010). The undergraduate psychology major: An examination of structure and sequence. *Teaching of Psychology, 37,* 4–15. doi:10.1080/00986280903426274

Vardeman, S. B., & Morris, M. D. (2003). Statistics and ethics: Some advice for young statisticians. *The American Statistician, 57,* 21–26. doi:10.1198/0003130031072

COMMENTARY: Immersion in research ethics should not be required only of those psychology students whose declared intention is to pursue a career in the laboratory sciences. Budding clinicians, too, will benefit overwhelmingly in this regard, for two distinct but related reasons. The first of these is to become critical consumers of the research that forms the empirical basis for their efforts in providing psychotherapy and counseling. The second is to gain an understanding that ethical concerns permeate every aspect of their chosen discipline.

Involvement in on-campus investigative studies—if only as "Psychology 101" research participants—is a common experience for college undergraduates and is often the defining factor in their decision to pursue applied psychology as an attractive career option. An appreciation for ethics must be a part of this introduction to the field. Also, to the extent that psychology students are assuming an ancillary role in actually conducting research, their predictable lack of grounding in ethical obligations must be remedied as quickly as feasible.

The following references are recommended for those interested in further investigation of what undergraduates are taught about research ethics. Included here is information about diversity-oriented recruitment, student empowerment, and multidisciplinary perspectives on education.

Carpi, A., Ronan, D. M., Falconer, H. M., & Lents, N. H. (2017). Cultivating minority scientists: Undergraduate research increases self-efficacy and career ambitions for underrepresented students in STEM. *Journal of Research in Science Teaching, 54,* 169–194. http://dx.doi.org/10.1002/tea.21341

Johnson, W. B., Behling, L. L., Miller, P., & Vandermaas-Peeler, M. (2015). Undergraduate research mentoring: Obstacles and opportunities. *Mentoring & Tutoring: Partnership in Learning, 23,* 441–453. http://dx.doi.org/10.1080/13611267.2015.1126167

Morales, D. X., Grineski, S. E., & Collins, T. W. (2017). Faculty motivation to mentor students through undergraduate research programs: A study of enabling and constraining factors. *Research in Higher Education, 58,* 520–544. http://dx.doi.org/10.1007/s11162-016-9435-x

Moyer, A., & Franklin, N. (2011). Strengthening the educational value of undergraduate participation in research as part of a psychology department subject. *Journal of Empirical Research on Human Research Ethics, 6,* 75–82. http://dx.doi.org/10.1525/jer.2011.6.1.75

Segarra, I., & Gomez, M. (2014). A learning activity to introduce undergraduate students to bioethics in human clinical research: A case study. *Journal of Empirical Research on Human Research Ethics, 9,* 56–63. http://dx.doi.org/10.1177/1556264614557238

8.8. Ethics in Teaching, Training, and Supervision

Thomas F. Nagy

Dr. Branden agreed to supervise Cheryl as a psychological assistant in his private practice for 1 year prior to her sitting for the Examination for the Professional Practice of Psychology. After 2 months, unfortunately, Dr. Branden developed chronic pain in his back requiring physical therapy. His medical needs and busy clinical schedule demanded so much of his waning energy that he began to reduce the frequency of his clinical supervision with Cheryl. Instead of weekly face-to-face meetings, as required by the state licensing board, he only had time for brief meetings every other week, supplemented by e-mail and telephone conversations.

Although Cheryl was a competent therapist, she was not adequately trained to treat a 16-year-old girl who had begun cutting herself with a razor blade. When the girl presented for a second session with additional cuts on her arm, Cheryl, feeling uneasy about the self-mutilation, ignored the cuts and, instead, focused the session on the girl's learning disability and study skills. Later that day, when her mother discovered the new cuts, she telephoned Cheryl to terminate therapy because she felt that she was not competent to treat her daughter. This was unfortunate because Dr. Branden was skilled at treating adolescents and could have helped Cheryl in treating her if he had only taken the time to provide adequate supervision.

INTRODUCTION

Recent editions of the American Psychological Association (APA) Ethics Code have devoted a variety of ethical standards and even entire sections to education and training, and many of these standards were rooted in the original Ethics Code (APA, 1953a, 1981, 1992, 2002, 2010). The 1953 Ethics Code devoted an entire section to Teaching of Psychology, with four long paragraphs: (a) General Responsibilities, (b) Safeguarding Students' Rights, (c) Instructing in Clinical Techniques, and (d) Advising Students. Topics included objectivity in teaching, free expression of criticism and support for various approaches to psychology, students' right to privacy, exploitation of students, competent supervision in assessment, informed consent, multiple relationships, and dealing with the impaired student.

Complaints against teachers and supervisors are relatively rare, ranging from 0% to 5% of all complaints against psychologists, according to the annual reports of the APA Ethics Committee. Examples of typical complaints are absence of timely evaluations and improper termination with a patient while under clinical supervision (APA, Ethics Committee, 2002, 2005). Although a patient may initially bring a complaint against her therapist–trainee, it is ultimately the clinical supervisor who will be the subject of the complaint because the supervisor is the one who is responsible for all professional conduct of the supervisee.

GENERAL PRINCIPLES AND TRAINING

The general principles provide guidance for teachers at every level, from high school to postgraduate training. The aspirational values described in Principle A: Beneficence and Nonmaleficence guide teachers to safeguard the welfare of their students and trainees and never behave in a way that would harm them. The high school teacher who compels students to publicly participate in discussing sensitive topics, such as their sexual experience or history of physically or emotionally abusive experiences in their family, harms them by exposing them to the judgment of others and also demonstrates poor respect for their right of privacy.

Principle B: Fidelity and Responsibility guides teachers to establish trusting relationships with students and uphold professional standards of conduct. Teachers must also clarify their roles and obligations and manage conflicts of interest. The professor who chairs a graduate student's dissertation committee bears an obligation to protect the student's research from unauthorized use. Plagiarizing the student's work and using it as a part of the professor's own research or publishing it without permission or citation would be exploitative and harmful.

Principle C: Integrity as applied to teaching involves keeping commitments; avoiding unnecessary deception; and promoting accuracy, honesty, and truthfulness in the role of professor or supervisor. Lapses in integrity are demonstrated by the teacher who is careless about accuracy in presenting psychological information to students or the supervisor who abrogates his or her responsibilities for careful monitoring of a student therapist because the supervisor has become too busy with other matters.

Principle E: Respect for People's Rights and Dignity includes educators' respect for the worth of all people and their rights to privacy, confidentiality, and autonomy. Educators respect cultural, individual, and role differences, including those based on age, gender, ethnicity, and other factors that may add to a student's vulnerability. A White male teacher who is openly sarcastic with a Latina student for pursuing a valid culture-based theoretical orientation that differs from his own demonstrates a lack of respect by humiliating her. This is a harmful act that detracts from her self-esteem as well as the learning experience for other students. It also exploits the White male privilege that is bestowed by the construction of gender, race, and ethnicity in society as well as the power bestowed by his role as teacher.

ETHICAL STANDARDS ABOUT EDUCATION AND TRAINING

It is noteworthy that there are fewer standards concerning teaching activities per se than any other aspect of education and training. Only three topics are examined—designing education and training programs, accuracy in teaching, and assessing academic performance—whereas the remaining four standards pertain to informed consent matters (e.g., describing the curriculum or course requirements in advance) and multiple-role relationships (e.g., prohibiting sex with students, prohibiting engaging in the professor–therapist role concurrently).

Designing Education and Training Programs

Teaching in a secondary school, college, graduate school, or even at the postgraduate level requires careful planning to ensure that course content reflects stated educational goals, as discussed under the sections on competence and informed consent in Chapters 4 and 5. A professor who is teaching an introductory course in theories of psychotherapy must make a good faith effort to broadly represent the variety of treatment approaches, rather than focus predominantly on his personal favorites.

Above and beyond ethical requirements, a psychology department within a university that is regionally accredited (e.g., New England Association of Schools and Colleges) must comply with rigorous standards in providing a learning environment for students.[1] If a training program is accredited by the APA (doctoral programs, predoctoral internships, and postdoctoral residencies), it must meet additional standards of quality developed by this association as well, and graduate students are well advised to seek educational experiences that have this accreditation (http://www.apa.org/ed/accreditation/).

The Ethics Code requires those teaching and supervising advanced graduate or postdoctoral students to include course content and educational experiences that meet requirements for state licensure or certification, consistent with claims made in descriptive materials or brochures. Even psychologists teaching workshops to experienced clinicians must include topics and experiences that qualify for certification or meet continuing education requirements if they are APA-sponsored events.

---

[1] These standards include using research-based knowledge about teaching and learning, using assessment for evaluating student learning, and promoting standards-based curriculum development, to name a few of the requirements (http://www.acswasc.org/).

Accuracy in Teaching

Teachers and supervisors are ethically bound to inform students at the outset about the process of assessing and grading their work and providing timely feedback as needed. And teachers and supervisors must base evaluations of actual performance on program requirements, appraising their students and supervisees on objective criteria, regardless of personal feelings of friendship or animosity. The professor who plays favorites and allows friendly feelings to influence grading of a particular student, regardless of the student's performance, behaves unfairly and conveys the idea that personal friendships can trump knowledge and skills in academia.

Standard 7.03, Accuracy in Teaching, grounded in Principle C: Integrity, requires accuracy of course syllabi regarding the subject matter to be covered, the basis for evaluating progress, and the nature of course experiences. It also requires those engaged in teaching or training at any level to present psychological information accurately. It is useful to consider the psychotherapist who successfully used a clinical intervention with an adolescent who compulsively played computer games 9 hours each day. The psychotherapist may have had good results with this single patient using a specific therapeutic intervention, but in teaching graduate students, the psychotherapist should present this clinical intervention as experimental rather than evidence based because results attained with one therapist on a single patient would not necessarily qualify as a statistically significant finding.

> Dr. Lernit, a young professor, taught a graduate level course in chemical dependency. She herself was a recovering alcoholic and had been sober for 4 years. Partway into the semester she had the creative idea that an experiential component would be an excellent way for students to understand the nature of addiction and its treatment. She gave the following assignment: Each student was to attend three different 12-step open meetings (e.g., Alcoholics Anonymous, Nar-Anon, Nicotine Anonymous), visit two unfamiliar bars at night to observe those who were intoxicated, and walk or drive during the daytime through a part of town that was notorious for drug dealing.
>
> Some of the students welcomed this nondidactic part of the course and eagerly began to carry out the assignment. However, others voiced objections to it on several grounds. The part of town where drug dealing occurred was also notorious for carjackings and other violent crimes. Even though the daytime drive-through was not considered as dangerous as nighttime excursions, there was still some risk of harm. Other students objected on the grounds that the additional time required to visit the bars and 12-step meetings was excessive and that this was never described in the course catalogue or even the syllabus at the beginning of the semester.
>
> Dr. Lernit listened carefully to her students' objections and began to understand that her last-minute assignment would inflict hardships on most of them even though it may have had merit as a learning experience. She withdrew the requirement and placed it in the course catalogue description for the following semester with suggested modifications.

Mandatory Individual or Group Therapy

Some training programs require undergraduate or graduate students to have individual psychotherapy, group therapy, or other therapeutic experience as a part of training. Students must be apprised of this before entering the program and must be given the option of selecting a therapist who is not affiliated with the university or professional school.

Faculty who are or will be responsible for teaching or evaluating students must not, themselves, be the ones who provide the therapy. In this way those in teaching or supervisory positions avoid creating a multiple-role relationship, that of teacher–therapist. The student who is struggling to fulfill course requirements with Dr. Brown or feels that he or she received an unfair evaluation on a project for the class on Monday will likely not feel comfortable confiding in Dr. Brown on Tuesday at the weekly therapy session. And the transparency, self-disclosure, humor, and personal opinions and traits revealed by a teacher in the classroom may well conflict with the somewhat more detached persona of the therapist involved in administering psychotherapy. For example, if the teacher in class expresses a critical view of an antiabortion prolife political candidate yet is providing psychotherapy to one of the students in the class who holds strongly opposing religious convictions on the subject, the teacher will appear disingenuous in therapy while trying to be accepting of the student's values when the student already knows of the strength of the teacher's beliefs to the contrary. In this example the expectations for the two different roles diverge and conflict, as is often the case in multiple-role relationships.

SUPERVISION

After successfully completing the doctoral degree the therapist-trainee must then complete face-to-face supervision with a licensed psychologist as a postdoctoral intern, fellow, or employee. This is the final hurdle for aspiring psychologists before taking the licensing exam, and it is rapidly becoming a specialty unto itself (Falender & Shafranske, 2004; Haynes, Corey, & Moulton, 2002; Thomas, 2010). Clinical supervision is considered so beneficial that state licensing boards have begun requiring ongoing formal training for supervisors as a prerequisite for accepting their documented supervised clinical hours of trainees.

The process of finding an internship site where trainees will have supervised clinical experience, usually at hospitals and clinics, is facilitated by the Association of Psychology Postdoctoral and Internship Centers (APPIC), which is responsible for matching individuals with internship settings. The APPIC is an educational nonprofit organization that maintains a website for practical use by psychology intern applicants, psychology postdoctoral students, trainers of psychologists, and psychology faculty members (http://www.appic.org/). In recent years there has been an increase in graduate students seeking clinical supervision and a shortage of available internship cites. A total of 3,598 students sought internship positions at 3,051 APA-accredited internship cites for the 2009–2010 academic year (http://www.appic.org/).

Guidelines for Practicum Experience

Guidelines for the supervision of doctoral, nondoctoral, and uncredentialed individuals who provide psychological services in the United States and Canada have been published by the Association of State and Provincial Psychology Boards (ASPPB, 2003). This organization has also developed other important information, such as guidelines for continuing education for licensed psychologists. Their website can be accessed at http://www.asppb.org/ (ASPPB, 2003).

Although the ASPPB recognizes that there are no explicit criteria for practicum experiences, it has developed seven guidelines for practicum settings that can be used as a basis for developing standards to be used by training programs and possibly incorporated into state licensing board requirements. These guidelines are not currently incorporated into the APA Ethics Code, but it is possible that they might inform future standards concerning training and supervision. The general topics covered are (a) organized sequence of training, (b) breadth and depth of training, (c) hour requirement, (d) supervision, (e) supervisor qualifications, (f) training sequence, and (g) setting. The ASPPB guidelines are available online (http://www.asppb.net/i4a/pages/index.cfm?pageid=3531).

Characteristics of Competent Supervision

The competent supervisor should also be a skilled practitioner in the areas in which that person supervises. This includes having knowledge of clinical matters, current information about ethical and legal issues, and sufficiently robust mental health to endure the daily stresses of carrying out the professional responsibilities involved in supervision and practice.

Rodolfa (2001) summarized the desirable qualities of a supervisor as follows: assumes responsibility for what happens in the clinical and supervisory settings, develops congruent goals with the supervisee, is able to teach the artistry of psychotherapy and also enhance the trainee's creativity, is understanding and nonjudgmental, maintains a suitable balance between support and challenge, encourages disclosure of feelings and thoughts, is self-disclosing, has capacities for intimacy and imagination, respects supervisees' autonomy, and can acknowledge individual differences between supervisor and supervisee. The latter includes tolerance of theoretical differences and awareness, understanding, and valuing of gender differences and multicultural issues. Multicultural factors include a tolerance for (a) variations in definitions of mental health, (b) differing worldviews, (c) relative emphasis on individual versus family, (d) concepts of independence versus dependence as they bear on mental health, and (e) subjective awareness of cultural bias and prejudice that leads to stereotyping clients and patients. Supervisors are ethically obliged to avoid discriminating against supervisees on the basis of other attributes as well, such as religion, disability, age, socioeconomic status, national origin, or any basis proscribed by law.

> Dr. Handle sent a letter of agreement to her new psychological assistant, Don, explaining how supervision would proceed and gave details about the nature of

the patient population to anticipate (largely Latino), the use of one-way mirrors for observation, documentation responsibilities, and other useful information about the upcoming training experience. Don adjusted well to the new setting, and he valued Dr. Handle's weekly supervision, particularly her gentle way of providing feedback about his therapy skills.

Don had one patient who was quite engaging—Carmen, a 26-year-old Mexican woman with anxiety disorder. She seemed friendly and appreciative; it was her habit to stand quite close to him on entering and leaving the office, and after the second session she gave him a kiss on the cheek "out of gratitude" for all the help he had provided. Don felt uncomfortable with her forwardness and hoped that it would not happen again. At the end of the next session Carmen announced that her anxiety was suddenly gone, and she wondered if it would be all right to "treat" her therapist at a nearby Starbucks. This offer took him by surprise, but he agreed to meet her at the end of the day following his last patient.

Don promptly telephoned Dr. Handle to discuss both the kiss on the cheek from several days before and her invitation of today. Dr. Handle explained that Carmen may indeed feel grateful and that the boundaries in the Latin culture are more fluid and allow for more familiarity, even in professional settings. Don had wondered whether Carmen's behavior might suggest a personality disorder or at least poor personal boundaries. Dr. Handle indicated that she saw Carmen's invitation as more likely related to cultural factors. Further, perhaps, her naiveté about the therapist–patient relationship and possible interest in Don as a single male might account for her "flight into health" in feeling anxiety-free and possibly enabling her, now, to explore a personal relationship with him.

Dr. Handle pointed out that the two of them had never processed the kiss at the end of the previous session and that Don's avoidance was likely interpreted as tacit approval by Carmen to initiate the next logical step in the relationship. She also pointed out that Carmen may desire more therapy in the future and that even an innocent cup of coffee at Starbucks, where the discussion would likely be more social and self-disclosing on Don's part, could change the relationship irrevocably. Furthermore, there had been no actual termination session discussing progress, exploring new goals, processing her therapy experience, and making any formal recommendations for the future.

Don admitted to Dr. Handle that he did find Carmen attractive, but he was well aware of the prohibition against developing a relationship with a patient. He welcomed the opportunity to safely explore his feelings with Dr. Handle as he was simultaneously processing the breaking of his engagement to be married several months before he moved to begin his internship.

He decided to refrain from meeting Carmen for coffee and contacted her by cell phone to cancel, while inviting her to return for one more therapy session. At the next session they discussed the kiss, boundaries, their professional relationship, and additional therapeutic goals of Carmen's that surfaced in that session.

Problems Encountered in Supervision

Some of the problems trainees encounter include supervisors' attitudes and behaviors that result in incompetent supervision. Rodolfa (2001) described the *problem supervisor* as one who may exhibit the following characteristics: lacking knowledge or competence, authoritarian, self-doubting, overly active or passive, poor at listening and communicating (e.g., sarcastic, dismissive, avoidant of important issues), unclear or ambiguous about expectations, focusing only on content (i.e., not process or the therapy relationship), not trusting or engendering trust, tolerating a negative feeling between supervisor and supervisee without addressing it, having personality conflicts or rivalry with the supervisee, or being prone to boundary violations. The latter can contaminate the supervisory relationship if the supervisor is too self-disclosing to the trainee, gives inappropriate gifts, allows for extra supervisory contact to gratify his or her own needs, gives unwanted touches or hugs, or is flirtatious. Other supervisory behaviors that can damage the relationship are being overly inquisitive about the trainee's private life (e.g., family of origin, sexual history) or encouraging the supervision to transcend the normal boundaries and transition into individual psychotherapy (Thomas, 2010).

The lessons learned from teachers, professors, supervisors, and mentors can last a lifetime. The content and knowledge absorbed from classroom, experiential setting, and one-to-one supervision are as important as what the trainee learns by observing the behavior of those who are in teaching positions. The professor or supervisor who manifests poor boundaries by being seductive does not help that trainee toward professional maturation. Rather, the professor or supervisor models a poor example for the trainee to follow when the trainee is in a similar professional relationship. Conversely, the supervisor who openly acknowledges that an interpersonal problem may exist with the trainee or copes with his or her own sexual attraction to the trainee by consulting an experienced colleague or his or her own therapist stands a better chance of modeling ethical and professional adult boundaries and behavior.

Teaching at any level in academia or supervising at any stage of the trainee's professional development can be a gratifying experience for all involved, dispensing a contagion for the love of learning and personal development and growth. The good teacher is aware that there is always more to discover from the science of psychology, and he or she bears a certain humility about the current state of scientific knowledge and curiosity about what may lie ahead. In a larger sense, the quintessential teacher is also aware that there is always more to learn about oneself and that this ultimately may be the origin of the quest as well as the reward provided for entering such a fulfilling, demanding, and richly diverse career as psychology.

REFERENCES

American Psychological Association. (1953a). *Ethical standards of psychologists.* Washington, DC: Author.

American Psychological Association. (1981). Ethical standards of psychologists. *American Psychologist, 36,* 633–638. doi:10.1037/0003-066X.36.6.633

American Psychological Association. (1992). Ethical principles of psychologists and code of conduct. *American Psychologist, 47,* 1597–1611.

American Psychological Association. (2002). Ethical principles of psychologists and code of conduct. *American Psychologist, 57,* 1060–1073. doi:10.1037/0003-066X.57.12.1060 (Also available from http://www.apa.org/ethics/code/index.aspx)

American Psychological Association. (2010). *Ethical principles of psychologists and code of conduct* (2002, Amended June 1, 2010). Retrieved from http://www.apa.org/ethics/code/index.aspx

American Psychological Association, Ethics Committee. (2002). Report of the Ethics Committee, 2001. *American Psychologist, 57*, 646–653. doi:10.1037/0003-066X.57.8.646

American Psychological Association, Ethics Committee. (2005). Report of the Ethics Committee, 2004. *American Psychologist, 60*, 523–528.

Association of State and Provincial Psychology Boards. (2003). *Guidelines for supervision of doctoral level candidates for licensure.* Retrieved from http://www.asppb.org

Falender, C., & Shafranske, E. (2004). *Clinical supervision: A competency-based approach.* Washington, DC: American Psychological Association. doi:10.1037/10806-000

Haynes, R., Corey, G., & Moulton, P. (2002). *Clinical supervision in the helping professions: A practical guide.* Pacific Grove, CA: Brooks/Cole.

Rodolfa, E. (2001, September). *Workshop on supervision: Process, issues dilemmas.* Workshop presented at the California School of Professional Psychology, Alameda.

Thomas, J. T. (2010). *The ethics of supervision and consultation: Practical guidance for mental health professionals.* Washington, DC: American Psychological Association.

9

Forensic Settings

Particularly in jurisdictions that still support capital punishment, the outcome of a forensic psychological evaluation can literally be a matter of life or death. Psychologists seeking to sign on for this particular form of litigation have a special obligation that is relevant to parties on both sides of the aisle. If the psychologist is opposed to capital punishment, prosecutors and some judges may view assessment findings as dubious. If the psychologist endorses capital punishment, the suspicions of the defense bar are heightened, as are those of some judges. Practice in this singular environment calls for particular self-scrutiny so that psychologists can remain sure—and can reassure others—that forensic assessment outcomes and their interpretation will remain unaffected by one's either self-acknowledged or latent biases and prejudices.

Ethical conflicts are difficult to resolve under comparatively normal circumstances, but forensic practice occurs against the backdrop of an adversarial system in which counsel for either side—in criminal and civil matters alike—is invariably angling for the most client-friendly outcome possible from a forensic psychological evaluation. At first blush, this might seem unethical, but what it actually represents is a different ethical obligation: that of what attorneys term *zealous advocacy*. Clients do not hire an attorney for his or her dedication to the scientific method and to the clinical autonomy of mental health professionals. They hire an attorney to win their case. Counsel's role stops short of intimidating witnesses, suborning perjury, or tampering with evidence, but if there is any chance that a testifying expert is willing to convey results in a helpful fashion, that chance will be explored with what psychologists may view as astonishing and distasteful rigor.

http://dx.doi.org/10.1037/0000125-010
Ethical Conflicts in Psychology, Fifth Edition, by E. Y. Drogin

With forensic cases come forensic guidelines. Guidelines do not carry the same authority and enforceability as the American Psychological Association's (APA's; 2017) *Ethical Principles of Psychologists and Code of Conduct*, its only mandatory source of professional instruction. Nonetheless, psychologists functioning in the legal arena are likely to be accosted by attorneys for whom everything is, if not a "rule," at the very least evidence of a standard of practice with which testifying experts may not be complying. Another complicating factor in terms of ethics is the large sums of money that can change hands in forensic matters. Psychologists may be earning many times their purely "clinical" hourly rate, and there will always be those who seek to infer bias from this circumstance.

A perennial concern in forensic practice is the extent to which a testifying expert has actually conducted key aspects of an underlying evaluation—or, in some cases, whether that expert has actually met with the litigant at all. Sometimes the testing and interviewing have been performed by an unaccompanied student trainee, whose contributions will likely be dismissed as constituting "someone learning at the expense of my client's interests."

Among its other features, this chapter addresses attempts to reconcile impartiality with advocacy, the APA's ethical guidelines concerning forensic psychological practice in general and child custody evaluations in particular, and ethical parameters of forensic risk assessment.

REFERENCE

American Psychological Association. (2017). *Ethical principles of psychologists and code of conduct* (2002, Amended June 1, 2010 and January 1, 2017). Retrieved from http://www.apa.org/ethics/code/index.aspx

9.1. Ethical Challenges in Forensic Psychology Practice

Michael C. Gottlieb and Alicia Coleman

. . .

ETHICAL ISSUES

Those who practice forensic psychology navigate complex waters because they must adhere to state regulatory board rules and regulations in their jurisdiction, professional ethical standards (APA, 2010), specialty guidelines (Committee on Ethical Guidelines for Forensic Psychologists, 1991), and relevant legal requirements and procedures. At times, reconciling these demands can be challenging. Therefore, it is incumbent on forensic psychologists to be extremely familiar with the ethical guidelines of their specialty and to make every effort to follow overarching ethical principles or virtues in light of these obligations (e.g., Handelsman, Knapp, & Gottlieb, 2002). In the following sections, we highlight those obligations that are most salient.

Who Is the Client?

A client is someone to whom the psychologist is primarily obligated (Monahan, 1980). Most psychologists understand this concept well in the clinical context, but in the legal arena, the definition of the client may require more careful definition. Typically, forensic psychologists work for the court or an attorney, but these matters are not always so clear-cut, and in some cases, psychologists work for litigants directly.

Working for the Court

Forensic psychologists often function under court orders. Sometimes, these orders are standard and unambiguous, such as court-ordered competency or sanity evaluations. . . . In this case, the forensic psychologist is working for the court and must inform the defendant of that relationship before proceeding (see Packer, 2009). A similar situation arises when courts appoint child custody evaluators are asked to make recommendations regarding a child's best interest.

From *APA Handbook of Ethics in Psychology: Vol. 2. Practice, Teaching, and Research* (pp. 91–123), by S. J. Knapp (Ed.), 2012, Washington, DC: American Psychological Association. Copyright 2012 by the American Psychological Association.

Unfortunately, the role of court-appointed evaluator is not readily understood by all and oftentimes may require more extensive explanation as a matter of informed consent. . . .

Working for an Attorney

When working for an attorney, forensic psychologists may play a variety of roles. Regardless of the specific role psychologists play, they still are required to adhere to appropriate professional standards. For example, in a consulting role, one must inform the lawyer that no science exists to answer a particular question. Or when asked, a consultant must be clear that there is little science regarding the selection of potential jurors who will be favorable to a lawyer's case (see Wrightsman, 2005) and that selection often is based on inaccurate social stereotypes. Being honest with the lawyer in this case is a matter of fidelity (Kitchener, 1984); the consultant has an obligation to scientific responsibility (Standard 2.04, Bases of Scientific or Professional Judgments) even at the risk of upsetting the lawyer and losing future referrals from him or her. Consider the following example.

Case Example 4

Dr. Karen Knows Herstuff was hired by a criminal defense lawyer to evaluate the defendant for possible mitigation testimony at trial. The attorney had provided Dr. Herstuff with a number of legal theories that she hoped to pursue and wanted to know which would be scientifically supportable. After evaluating the defendant, Dr. Herstuff reported that none of the theories the lawyer had proposed could be scientifically supported because she concluded that the defendant was a psychopath, and she was unable to testify at mitigation.

This certainly is not information the attorney had hoped for because she now must construct a different legal theory to present in mitigation. We do not know from the example whether Dr. Herstuff was tempted to modify test scores, interpret information in ways more favorable to the lawyer's case, or ignore certain information, but it is hard to imagine that she found it easy to deliver such unwelcome news. Furthermore, our example does not tell us what happened next. How much did the lawyer pressure Dr. Herstuff to "find a way to help because the entire case rests on your testimony." Unfortunately, scenarios such as these are not rare, and it is hard to withstand such impassioned appeals. Nevertheless, we presume that Dr. Herstuff stood her ground because she understood that aside from doing the best she could for her client within the confines of her professional ethical standards (e.g., Standard 2.04, Bases for Scientific and Professional Judgment), she had an overarching obligation to the court to tell the whole truth (Gutheil et al., 2003).

Pro Se Litigants

A *pro se* litigant (or *pro per* in some states) is one who represents him- or herself. Such individuals are rare in criminal matters in which the government must provide an attorney for those who cannot afford one. This is not the case in civil and family law matters where forensic psychologists may be approached for assistance directly by litigants. We are unaware of any ethical standard or guideline that specifically prohibits accepting such assignments, but doing so generally is considered ill advised. The primary reason for refusing such assignments is the risk of entering into a potentially harmful multiple relationship (Standard 3.05, Multiple Relationships) in which the forensic psychologists risk playing the roles of independent evaluator, strategy consultant, and even therapist with someone who does not appreciate the need for such distinctions.

Regardless of whom the client may be, a forensic psychologist ultimately must balance the obligations to one's client with those to one's profession. As we have noted, limit setting in such cases often is necessary not only as a matter of good ethical practice but also as a matter of maintaining respect for the profession.

Finally, even though forensic psychologists have a primary obligation to one party, such as an attorney, this does not mean that they have no aspirational obligations to others. For example, one should act in ways that reduce harm to litigants by conscientiously explaining the nature of the evaluation, striving to ensure that a party has a chance to present his or her case, and carefully writing reports to avoid unnecessary pain.

Informed Consent

The contemporary notion of informed consent originated in part as a result of the Nuremberg trials after World War II. (For a detailed discussion, see Beauchamp & Childress, 2009. More information on this topic can be found in Volume 1, Chapter 12, this handbook, and Chapter 16, this volume.) In the 21st century, psychologists have a fundamental obligation to provide informed consent to those with whom they work (Standard 3.10, Informed Consent, and Standard 9.03, Informed Consent in Assessments; Committee on Ethical Guidelines for Forensic Psychologists, 1991, IV.E.1). Such issues are relatively clear-cut in clinical work, but they can be quite different in forensic contexts. For example, a person can be evaluated for competency to stand trial, pursuant to a court order, without informed consent, but a conscientious and ethical forensic psychologist would take steps to help ensure that the party being evaluated understood the nature of the evaluation (Standards 3.10c, Informed Consent; Standard 3.07, Third-Party Requests for Services; and Standard 9.03(a), Informed Consent in Assessments).

When Parties Can Consent

Following is a hypothetical example illustrating when parties can consent.

Case Example 5

Harriet Hapless sued her former employer for sexual harassment. Because she was claiming psychological damages as a result of her experience, her lawyer referred her for evaluation to Dr. Simon Straightarrow. At their first meeting, Dr. Straightarrow informed Ms. Hapless that he was working for her attorney, and after the evaluation, he would provide feedback to her lawyer based on the best science available. As a result, he could not guarantee Hapless results she would necessarily find favorable. Hapless became infuriated and stormed out of Straightarrow's office. As she left, he heard her say, "Whose side are you on anyway?"

We acknowledge that this example is a bit exaggerated, but it illustrates the point that Ms. Hapless is not required to use the services of an expert that her attorney chooses for her. Even if the lawyer knew Dr. Straightarrow well, and that he would do an excellent job in assisting with the case, Ms. Hapless still has the right, as a matter of respect for her rights and dignity (Principle E of the Ethics Code) to refuse Dr. Straightarrow's services.

Dr. Straightarrow was wise to begin his first meeting with Ms. Hapless by reviewing relevant matters of informed consent. The issues to be discussed vary based on the context of the evaluation, such as civil versus criminal matters, but most generally, informed consent procedures contain the following basic elements: definition of the client, the purpose of the evaluation, the procedures that will be used, limitations to confidentiality, to whom information will be provided and under what circumstances, reporting only findings that can be supported by psychological science, inability to guarantee favorable results, discussion of possible outcomes, and fee arrangements. In some cases, an explanation of these matters can be accomplished expeditiously, and the assessment may proceed, but this is not always the case. Sometimes, litigants will not have been prepared sufficiently by their lawyers, and more time will be needed to explain these issues. In other situations, litigants may be intellectually challenged or too emotionally distraught to appreciate what they are being told (Jeste & Saks, 2006). When any of these circumstances occur, the forensic psychologist is wise to take as much time as is necessary to explain this material and ensure that the litigant appreciates what she or he is being told. (For further reading, see Beauchamp & Childress, 2009, Chapter 4.) If after one's best effort, the litigant still does not seem to understand, it may be best to adjourn and contact the attorney.

When Parties Cannot Consent

FMHAs often are conducted under court order for matters such as competency to stand trial and insanity. In such cases, defendants are not free to consent. Nevertheless, it remains the forensic psychologist's obligation to provide the examinee with much the same information as included when parties can consent, take into consideration the person's preference, and make reasonable efforts to seek his or her assent (Standard 3.10(b), Informed Consent). Even when defendants do not have a choice in the matter, they generally appreciate the time taken to explain these issues. On the other hand, at times, defendants may refuse to participate. This decision can leave the examiner in a difficult situation. Should she or he submit a report based on what was learned from the meeting nonetheless, or is doing so unethical? We know of no resolution to this issue but find the recommendations of Melton et al. (2007) helpful. They have suggested that the examiner advise the defendant of any known sanctions that may be imposed by refusing, arrange for the individual to seek guidance from his or her attorney, inform the person that a report will be sent nonetheless (assuming that is the examiner's decision), explain how the refusal may reduce the validity of the report's findings, avoid frightening the defendant to avoid coercion (Melton et al., 2007, p. 97), and "make bona fide efforts to assist the defendant in understanding the parameters of the evaluation and to obtain his or her assent to proceed" (Melton et al., 2007, p. 158). (For further reading, see Packer, 2009.) In the spirit of positive ethics (Handelsman et al., 2002), when a party's ability to understand the nature of the evaluation appears compromised, the evaluator may try innovative ways to explain the process, such as multiple explanations or suggest to the attorney the possibility of involving family members as intermediaries. Barriers to informed assent also may arise in civil contexts, such as child custody evaluations. Consider the following example.

Case Example 6

Dr. Midell O'The Road was performing a child custody evaluation. The parents were both deeply wounded and furious with each other. Dr. Road made it clear at the outset that she was working under the court's order and that it was her job to make recommendations based on what was in their child's best interest rather than the preferences of either parent. Nevertheless, she found herself spending a great deal of time reexplaining her neutral role to both parents who did not seem to understand why she was not on their side.

In this example, one could argue that because the parties were court ordered to be evaluated by Dr. Road, it was not necessary for her to provide the same information repeatedly simply because the parties did not like, or did not chose to accept, what they had been told. Furthermore, we are unaware of any legal requirement that Dr. Road should do so. But, the fact that no rule requires such repeated explanations does not mean that doing so is a bad idea. Rather, it is the forensic psychologist's ethical responsibility to make bona fide efforts. It is also a matter of sound risk management.

Confidentiality and Privilege

Practicing psychologists of all varieties are well schooled in the requirement to maintain confidentiality in their professional work (Standard 4.01, Maintaining Confidentiality). (More information on this topic can be found in Volume 1, Chapter 13, this handbook.) In legal matters, this issue becomes more complex.

As we have noted, forensic psychologists sometimes consult with attorneys. When doing so, they often work under the attorney-work product rule, and if asked, must refuse to disclose their involvement in the case. This issue becomes more complex when attorneys ask forensic psychologists to evaluate their clients. For example, forensic psychologists often are asked to evaluate defendants in anticipation that testimony will be required for mitigation during the punishment phase of a criminal trial, but explaining this process to defendants can be challenging. Consider the following example.

Case Example 7

Always N. Trouble was being tried for capital murder. Worried that her client would be convicted, Trouble's lawyer requested a forensic evaluation to determine whether mitigating evidence could be presented during the punishment phase of the trial. She retained Dr. Lives-In-The Jail and reminded him that he was working under the work product rule until she decided whether his testimony could be helpful.

When Dr. Jail meets Trouble for an initial interview, he must explain the differences between privacy, confidentiality, privilege, and disclosure. Specifically, he must inform Trouble that he is going to be interviewing him and will be asking for a great deal of personal information, which normally would be private. He can assure Trouble that because the attorney is Dr. Jail's client, his information will not be revealed to anyone other than his lawyer, and if in the lawyer's judgment, the data collected are not helpful to his case, the attorney–work product rule will prevent disclosure of any information Trouble provides. But, if the lawyer believes that Dr. Jail's testimony will be helpful at trial, he must inform Trouble that whatever he tells him cannot be protected.

In this example, Dr. Jail has two obligations. First, he must meet his ethical obligation as a matter of informed consent to explain these distinctions before beginning his interview with Trouble (Standard 9.03, Informed Consent in Assessments). Second, Dr. Jail must assess Trouble's understanding of these issues and their distinctions. If he has a reason to believe that Trouble does not "appreciate" these matters, he must make every reasonable effort to see that he does. If after reasonable efforts, Dr. Jail believes that Trouble still does not understand these matters, he would be well advised to discontinue the interview and consult with Trouble's lawyer before proceeding.

As we have noted, the third prong of FMHAs is collateral sources of information. Typically, FMHAs entail collecting as much independent information as possible to corroborate data provided by defendants or litigants. A second issue regarding confidentiality can arise here in a number of ways. First, it is typical to request information from a variety of professional sources, such as physicians, mental health professionals, or schools. Because these people or institutions are obligated to maintain confidentiality, information can be obtained only when the defendant or litigant executes a valid release. . . . Note that schools are covered by the Family Educational Rights and Privacy Act of 1974 (FERPA) rather than the Health Insurance Portability and Accountability Act of 1996 (HIPAA), but releases still are required.

A more complex problem arises when forensic psychologists seek to interview persons who may have direct knowledge regarding the facts of the case. Consider the following example.

Case Example 8

I've Got No Control was being sued for divorce by his wife Should'ot Picked'em Better. Among other concerns, Better alleged that the children would not be safe with Control because of his history of domestic violence. Unfortunately for Better, she could recall no one who ever witnessed Control harming her, and therefore, her allegations could not be substantiated. Later, she recalled that a neighbor had witnessed at least one of these instances and provided the child custody evaluator with the person's name.

Given this new information, the custody evaluator should contact the neighbor in an effort to verify or refute Better's allegations. In doing so, and as a matter of transparency, she must explain that the witness is not legally required to speak with her, the information to be provided is not confidential, and she could be called to court to testify regarding what she saw. Although providing this information may discourage the witness from disclosing what she knows, it is the forensic psychologist's obligation to explain both her role and the relevant aspects of the legal process.

Another issue with regard to confidentiality surrounds protecting testing materials. In legal contexts, it is common for attorneys to request a litigant's or defendant's entire file from a forensic psychologist. Because psychological testing is a fundamental element of FMHAs, test results typically are included in the file. But, psychologists are expected to maintain test security as both an ethical (Standard 9.11, Maintaining Test Security) and a legal matter under copyright law. Therefore, when a file is requested, a forensic psychologist has an obligation to determine what if any proprietary material must be protected and therefore not provided to the attorney. This decision must be made within the context of the Ethics Code, state law, and the state regulatory board rules and regulations in his or her jurisdiction. (For example, in California, there are legal procedures that if followed would allow the psychologist to provide this information.) We recommend that when test materials are withheld, a notice to the attorney be included with the file citing the relevant ethical principle or state board ruling governing disclosure. (More information on testing can be found in Chapter 4 of this volume.) When such efforts are not successful, it is wise to consult a local attorney familiar with the issues to determine what other measures might be considered to protect the information.

Issues regarding confidentiality can arise in less obvious ways. Forensic psychologists should be well grounded in clinical skills such as interviewing and observations, psychological testing, and relationship establishment; that is, forensic psychologists should be good clinicians. We assume that these skills contribute to eliciting greater and more detailed information, and when interviews go well, interviewees become more relaxed and tend to reveal more about themselves. At the same time, interviewees may lose sight of the purpose of the interview and begin to treat it as more of a therapeutic encounter. While doing so is certainly understandable, forensic psychologists remain mindful that, at times, it may be necessary to remind evaluees of the purpose of the meeting and that what they are disclosing cannot be protected. This issue is less problematic when forensic psychologists work under the attorney–work product rule. But, when forensic psychologists work for the court, such information cannot be protected. In those cases, forensic psychologists must decide whether to interrupt interviewees and remind them of this matter before proceeding.

Finally, the forensic psychologist always should determine whether a criminal defendant has been instructed by his or her attorney not to discuss information related to the crime or to reveal information that could bear on his or her guilt to avoid self-incrimination. Forensic psychologists query defense attorneys regarding whether such information is to be withheld before initiating interviews with the defendant.

Competence

We have noted that there are many paths to achieving competence in forensic psychology. Although formal training is increasingly available to students, informal and self-directed methods remain the norm. For those who pursue the latter course, there is no overarching authority available to evaluate one's performance. Furthermore, lawyers often are not the best ones to make such decisions for us. Consider the following example.

Case Example 9

Ima Newbie was a young attorney who accepted a variety of cases. One day, she was in court attending a hearing on temporary orders in a family law matter when the court appointed a custody evaluator. When asked whom she would prefer to fill this role, she immediately mentioned Dr. Reck T'Tude, whom she recently had retained successfully in a criminal matter. Knowing that Dr. T'Tude was a respected forensic psychologist, Newbie presumed that he would be competent to accept this assignment as well. When Dr. T'Tude received the order appointing him, he called Newbie to explain, much to her chagrin, that he did not accept such assignments because he had never performed such an evaluation and was not competent to do so.

The law requires that experts have the requisite education, training, and experience (Testimony by Experts, 2000) to perform forensic roles, especially if one is to testify, but lawyers are seldom in a good position to appropriately evaluate those whom they wish to retain. Such decisions often are made on the basis of reputation, word of mouth, and, increasingly, recommendations from professional listservs. Because such means are highly imperfect, it remains the forensic psychologist's ethical obligation to accurately represent his or her qualifications (Standard 5.01, Avoidance of False or Deceptive Statements) and to function within his or her boundaries of competence (Standard 2.01, Boundaries of Competence). If they wish to enter new practice areas, they "undertake relevant education, training, supervised experience, consultation or study" (Standard 2.01(c), Boundaries of Competence) to ensure that they offer competent services.

Unfortunately, some colleagues find adhering to these standards challenging, especially when attorneys are highly persuasive and offer large retainers. Potential consultants must be wary of accepting such tempting assignments, especially when they pose potential conflicts of interest (Standard 3.06, Conflict of Interest; Standard 3.05(c), Multiple Relationships). Sadly, the literature is replete with examples of those who failed to do so (e.g., Eisner, 2010). Not only does such behavior bring discredit to the profession, but it risks causing harm (Principle A. . .).

. . .

REFERENCES

American Psychological Association. (2010). *Ethical principles of psychologists and code of conduct* (2002, Amended June 1, 2010). Retrieved from http://www.apa.org/ ethics/code/index.aspx

Beauchamp, T. L., & Childress, J. F. (2009). *Principles of biomedical ethics* (6th ed.). New York, NY: Oxford.

Committee on Ethical Guidelines for Forensic Psychologists. (1991). Specialty guidelines for forensic psychologists. *Law and Human Behavior, 15,* 655–665. doi:10.1007/ BF01065858

Eisner, D. A. (2010). Expert witness mental health testimony: Handling deposition and trial traps. *American Journal of Forensic Psychology, 28,* 47–65. doi:10.1037/a0012767

Gutheil, T. G., Hauser, M., White, M. S., Spruiell, G., & Strassburger, L. H. (2003). "The whole truth" versus "the admissible truth": An ethics dilemma for expert witnesses. *Journal of the American Academy of Psychiatry and Law, 31,* 422–427.

Handelsman, M. M., Knapp, S. J., & Gottlieb, M. C. (2002). Positive ethics. In C. R. Snyder and S. J. Lopez (Eds.), *Handbook of positive psychology* (pp. 731–744). New York, NY: Oxford University Press.

Jeste, D. V., & Saks, E. (2006). Decisional capacity in mental illness and substance use disorders: Empirical database and policy implications. *Behavioral Sciences and the Law, 24,* 607–628. doi:10.1002/bsl.707

Kitchener, K. S. (1984). Intuition, critical evaluation and ethical principles: The foundation for ethical decisions in counseling psychology. *The Counseling Psychologist, 12,* 43–55. doi:10.1177/0011000084123005

Melton, G. B., Petrila, J., Poythress, N. G., & Slobogin, C. (2007). *Psychological evaluation for the courts* (3rd ed.). New York, NY: Guilford Press.

Monahan, J. (Ed.). (1980). *Who is the client? The ethics of psychological intervention in the criminal justice system.* Washington, DC: American Psychological Association. doi:10.1037/10051-000

Packer, I. K. (2009). *Evaluation of criminal responsibility.* New York, NY: Oxford University Press.

Testimony by Experts, Fed. R. Evid., Rule 702 (2000).

Wrightsman, L. S. (2005). *Trial consulting.* New York, NY: Oxford University Press.

COMMENTARY: Forensic psychologists should not, despite their typical sophistication in legal matters, be presumed to possess deeper insight into ethical obligations than their nonforensic colleagues. Law and ethics, although often similar in focus and intent, are neither equivalent nor interchangeable notions. Ethical challenges in forensic practice are exacerbated by the fact that the contributions of psychologists to criminal and civil proceedings occur in the context of an adversarial system that imposes its own unique array of pressures and demands.

Missteps in ethical adherence are often all the more consequential for the forensic psychologist because there are always those who stand to gain in a very direct fashion from opportunities to minimize the impact of assessment practices, report writing, and testimony and who would not hesitate to institute licensing board complaints or supplemental lawsuits to press an advantage. Similarly, harm to examinees may be exacerbated by the fact that adverse legal consequences can accompany and inflate already negative personal reactions.

The following references are recommended for those interested in further investigation of ethical challenges in forensic psychology practice, featuring advice proffered by forensic psychologists, forensic psychiatrists, and attorneys alike.

Borkosky, B. (2014). Who is the client and who controls release of records in a forensic evaluation? A review of ethics codes and practice guidelines. *Psychological Injury and Law, 7,* 264–289. http://dx.doi.org/10.1007/s12207-014-9199-6

Bush, S. S., & Morgan, J. E. (2017). Ethical practice in forensic neuropsychology. In S. S. Bush, G. J. Demakis, & M. L. Rohling (Eds.). *APA handbook of forensic neuropsychology* (pp. 23–37). Washington, DC: American Psychological Association.

Candilis, P. J., & Neal, T. M. S. (2014). Not just welfare over justice: Ethics in forensic consultation. *Legal and Criminological Psychology, 19,* 19–29. http://dx.doi.org/10.1111/lcrp.12038

Morse, S. J. (2008). The ethics of forensic practice: Reclaiming the wasteland. *Journal of the American Academy of Psychiatry and the Law, 36,* 206–217.

Pirelli, G., Beattey, R. A., & Zapf, P. A. (Eds.). (2017). *The ethical practice of forensic psychology: A casebook.* New York, NY: Oxford University Press.

9.2. The Expert Witness, the Adversary System, and the Voice of Reason: Reconciling Impartiality and Advocacy

Daniel W. Shuman and Stuart A. Greenberg

. . .

THE ROLES THAT EXPERTS PLAY

Tension in the roles that experts are expected to play is fundamental to the way in which experts are used in the legal system. Yet their use has become routine and, in some cases, almost unavoidable: "Expert testimony often adds an aura of reliability to a party's theories and claims. Many cases could not be tried without expert witnesses to testify as to the applicable standard of care, the reconstruction of accidents, or the value of a plaintiff's damages" (Richmond, 2000, p. 909).

It is often assumed that the major role problem presented by expert testimony is the conflict between serving therapeutic and forensic functions for the same client (Greenberg & Shuman, 1997; Heilbrun, 1995; Simon, 1995; Strasburger et al., 1997). It is easy to ignore the problems of intrarole conflicts and assume that each role is clear and manageable in its own right. However, the forensic expert is beholden to multiple masters. Integrating the demands of these masters is inherently complex. This requires reconciliation of a system of mental health professional regulation that demands impartiality and a system of legal dispute resolution that demands partisanship.

Attorneys are ethically required to be diligent advocates for their clients. Implicitly, all aspects of an attorney's conduct, including the presentation of experts, should further that role of diligent advocacy rather than disinterested neutrality. Most attorneys "would go into a lawsuit with an objective uncommitted independent expert about as willingly as [they] would occupy a foxhole with a couple of noncombatant soldiers" (Jensen, 1993, p. 192).

From "The Expert Witness, the Adversary System, and the Voice of Reason: Reconciling Impartiality and Advocacy," by D. W. Shuman and S. A. Greenberg, 2003, *Professional Psychology: Research and Practice, 34*, pp. 219–224. Copyright 2003 by the American Psychological Association.

We wish to thank William Bender, Andrew Benjamin, Carl Edwards, William Foote, David Martindale, J. Randall Price, Kirk Heilbrun, and John Zervopolous, who provided insightful comments on an earlier version of this article.

This concern is all the more powerful for those who work full time as forensic experts. Experts are aware that they are retained to assist in partisan advocacy that their ethics appear to prohibit. Experts are also aware that those who criticize the use of partisan experts complain that, for the right price, it is almost always possible to retain an expert to testify favorably in a case, regardless of the consensus of professional opinion on an issue.

Is there a role dictated by the "voice of reason" for the retained expert who responds to the demands of the adversary system yet still fulfills the expert's obligations to the court to be neutral? How can a retained testifying expert, operating within the constraints of these tensions, satisfy the adversarial imperatives, avoid malpractice liability, provide testimony that meets the highest standards of the profession, and be regularly employed?

LICENSURE AND ETHICAL JEOPARDY

Psychologists' behavior while providing expert testimony is governed by their professional ethical rules and guidelines. Violations of these rules and guidelines may result in exclusion of their testimony or a breach of contract or malpractice action (*Murphy v. A. A. Mathews*, 1992). However, experts are often granted immunity from civil claims for their conduct as experts. Nonetheless, no state extends that immunity to proceedings before state licensing boards or professional ethics committees (*Budwin v. American Psychological Association*, 1994). In two cases of first impression, Washington and Pennsylvania courts declined to extend immunity to ethical complaints lodged with state licensing boards for the actions of health care professionals while serving as expert witnesses. The Washington Supreme Court refused to extend the broad grant of immunity it recognized for expert witnesses from civil liability to disciplinary proceedings (*Deatherage v. Examining Board of Psychology*, 1997). The court reasoned that the threat of professional discipline is an important check on the conduct of professionals who are otherwise immune from civil liability. In *Huhta v. State Board of Medicine* (1998), a Pennsylvania appellate court also held that immunity from civil liability for expert witnesses is not a defense in disciplinary proceedings before the State Board of Medicine because it would hamper the licensing board's fulfilling its responsibility to ensure the competence and fitness of physicians to practice medicine (Trimmer, 1999).

The grant of immunity from civil liability while retaining liability for professional disciplinary actions leaves experts subject to substantial risk. The necessity of defending oneself before a licensing board or ethics committee carries dire consequences for experts that are similar to those involved in the defense of a civil suit. Prevailing in either forum may nonetheless leave the expert's reputation tainted. Experts can and should carry insurance against a licensing board complaint in addition to insurance against a civil claim for damages arising out of their forensic activities. However, the economic costs of legal and professional sanctions are borne by the licensee. Lost income as the result of the suspension or revocation of a license or the harm to reputation suffered with a tort malpractice judgment remains a cost to be borne by the professional.

. . .

BEYOND COMPETENCY: IMPARTIALITY AS THE BEST ADVOCACY

Expert witnesses face evidentiary demands imposed by courts, ethical demands imposed by professional licensing agencies, liability demands imposed by disgruntled litigants, and economic demands imposed by the attorneys who employ them. How should experts respond to these demands, which seem to ask them to play both neutral and partisan roles? Our proposal, *impartiality as the best advocacy*, does not ask experts to choose between these roles but offers guidance on how to fulfill both roles simultaneously. The crucial assumption that guides this proposal is that an expert's credibility is an essential component of being an effective advocate and that credibility derives from the expert's impartiality. An expert's absence of impartiality is fatal not only for its impact on neutrality but also for its impact on advocacy.

In the sections that follow, we address the question of how to reconcile these demands. Our message is that properly understood, these different forces can be harmonized to arrive at a consistent set of behaviors to guide the expert's behavior. We suggest the application of five principles to integrate these demands: competence, relevance, perspective, balance, and candor. Our principles are not an attempt to supplant or modify the Ethical Principles of Psychologists and Code of Conduct or the Specialty Guidelines for Forensic Psychologists. We begin where they end.

Competence

The application of the Ethical Principles of Psychologists and Code of Conduct (APA, 2002) and the Specialty Guidelines for Forensic Psychologists (APA, 1991) in a world that seems hostile to them emphasizes what we regard as their core concern: "Forensic psychologists [should] provide services only in areas of psychology in which they have specialized knowledge, skill, experience, and education" (APA, 1991, p. 658). Unlike the clinical setting in which the psychologist's competence may be an issue that forms a part of the process of informed consent, forensic psychological services are imposed on individuals who do not necessarily consent or accede to the psychologist's competence. The competence of psychologists to provide forensic services is issue specific and contextual. Experts are pressured by advocates to offer opinions beyond the bounds of their competence. The tensions of the context, however, are never a basis for experts to offer opinions on subjects about which they are not competent. For example, notwithstanding the tensions that exist in child sexual abuse prosecutions, no expert should offer an opinion that abuse did occur because of the presence of behavioral indicators or that it did not occur because of the presence of suggestive questioning of the child. The state of the knowledge that would serve as the basis for such professional expertise is such that it does not provide answers to either of these questions to an adequate degree of certainty.

. . .

Relevance

The rules of evidence define relevant evidence as "evidence having any tendency to make the existence of any fact that is of consequence to the determination of the action more probable than it would be without the evidence" (Fed. R. Evid. 401). We speak here of a narrower concept of relevance to the opinion that the expert has been asked to address that is more tailored to Rule 705, which addresses the disclosure of the "facts or data underlying expert opinion" (Fed. R. Evid. 705). This principle applies to any evidence that has any tendency to add or subtract weight from the expert's opinion.

When testifying, experts should attempt to disclose to the parties all information relevant to their proffered opinion testimony on those questions, even when the issues change during the course of trial. Conversely, although they must answer all questions asked fully and truthfully, we maintain that experts have no obligation to attempt to disclose information that is not relevant to the issues questioned, whether that information or those opinions might be relevant to other legal issues in the case or not. We suggest that this careful selection and omission of opinion testimony by the attorney and the retained expert is both a legitimate and an effective means of advocacy. Although experts may be compelled by the court to disclose nonprivileged information that is relevant to the case whether or not they were initially requested to address that issue, we maintain that to integrate the role of neutrality and advocacy, the expert's unilateral obligation of disclosure only applies to information relevant to issues on which the expert's opinions have been sought.

. . .

Perspective

To integrate neutrality and advocacy effectively, experts have an obligation to test their opinions on the issues they have been asked to address from the perspective of the parties' competing versions of the case, without insulation from opposing views. Any case has at least two conflicting perspectives on some relevant question or it would have been resolved. To be effective, experts must require the attorneys who retain them to provide, at minimum, the pleadings and legal memorandums describing the competing versions of the case, as well as all reports of other experts. Balancing the demands of lawyers, litigants, judges, and licensing boards requires that forensic experts maintain a realistic appreciation of the adversarial context in which forensic examinations occur. This realistic perspective requires experts to identify the evidence that might support or refute each party's perspective. An expert witness who is uninformed of the parties' differing perspectives can hardly be expected to be a credible witness.

. . .

Balance

Having identified each perspective, the expert has an obligation to assign a fair weight to each, not to engage in confirmatory or hindsight bias, and not to allow the inherent pressures of the situation to influence this decision making. The expert's approach to the litigants' differing perspectives on the relevance issue is critical to integrating neutrality and advocacy effectively. Experts who fail to balance the parties' perspectives fairly are unlikely to help the fact finder reach accurate conclusions on the issues they have been asked to address, and the fact finder is unlikely to perceive them as credible. Looking at issues disproportionately from the perspective of the litigant who hired the expert violates this principle because this absence of balance renders the expert an ineffective advocate for whatever opinions the expert reaches.

Experts are obligated to weigh all perspectives fairly. By this we mean that they must consider the rival hypotheses in an evenhanded manner. Experts and attorneys are familiar with the tendency to invoke a bunker mentality in which their side's perspective is given greater weight and the other side's perspective is minimized. Failing to provide appropriate weight to the perspective of each litigant violates this principle.

. . .

Candor

By *candor* we refer to the forthrightness with which psychological experts present their analysis. Experts who selectively disclose relevant information about an opinion to aid or disadvantage a party frustrate the search for accuracy and impair their own credibility. Thus, having identified the issues they have been asked to address and having considered them fairly from the perspective of all parties, experts have an obligation to present all perspectives considered candidly and explain the weight assigned to each in presenting their findings.

In our discussions of the first four principles, we considered the way in which experts should go about reaching an opinion. But in any legal proceeding there is much filtering of the facts and opinions. Aside from the well-recognized phenomenon of "wood shedding," or, more politely phrased, "negotiating opinions" (Gutheil, 2001), attorneys formulate questions to which experts have no legal right to object or demand that supplemental questions be asked. Nonetheless, experts have certain latitude in responding to the questioning process (Brodsky, 1991). We contend that experts should, to the maximum extent provided by law, candidly present the results of their fact finding and analysis, as described previously. The role of the expert is not to deliver favorable testimony as a matter of contract. The obligation is to render services at the relevant professional standard of care (*Panitz v. Behrend*, 1993). One clear benefit of this approach is that it is exactly what courts expect of witnesses—candid and forthright testimony.

. . .

CONCLUSION

What is the value of our principles in resolving these potential conflicts? Although the APA Ethics Code addresses forensic issues and describes ethical standards that govern the behavior of psychologists when testifying, our principles explain how psychologists can integrate the idealistic Ethics Code in the rough-and-tumble adversary system. The APA Ethics Code and the Specialty Guidelines for Forensic Psychologists appear to direct psychologists to a standard of behavior that is destined to collide with the reality of the judicial world. Attorneys are ethically obligated to advocate for their clients while experts are ethically obligated to examine issues objectively and advocate accordingly. Our principles reconcile these conflicts and offer psychologists a path that is both ethical and practicable to provide assistance to the courts.

. . .

REFERENCES

American Psychological Association. (2002). Ethical principles of psychologists and code of conduct. Retrieved October 18, 2002, from http://www.apa.org/ethics/code2002.html

American Psychological Association, Committee on Ethical Guidelines for Forensic Psychologists. (1991). Specialty guidelines for forensic psychologists. *Law and Human Behavior, 15*, 655–665.

Brodsky, S. L. (1991). *Testifying in court: Guidelines and maxims for the expert witness.* Washington, DC: American Psychological Association.

Budwin v. American Psychological Association, 29 Cal. Rptr. 2d 453 (1994).

Deatherage v. Examining Board of Psychology, 948 P. 2d 828 (Wash. 1997).

Fed. R. Evid. 401.

Fed. R. Evid. 705.

Greenberg, S. A., & Shuman, D. W. (1997). Irreconcilable conflict between therapeutic and forensic roles. *Professional Psychology: Research and Practice, 28*, 50–57.

Gutheil, T. G. (2001). Adventures in the twilight zone: Empirical studies of the attorney–expert relationship. *Journal of the American Academy of Psychiatry and the Law, 29*, 13–17.

Heilbrun, K. (1995). Child custody evaluation: Critically assessing mental health experts and psychological tests. *Family Law Quarterly, 29*, 63–78.

Huhta v. State Board of Medicine, 706 A. 2d 1275 (Pa. Commw. Ct. 1998), appeal denied 727 A. 2d 1124 (Pa. 1998).

Jensen, E. (1993). When "hired guns" backfire: The witness immunity doctrine and the negligent expert witness. *University of Missouri at Kansas City Law Review, 62*, 185–207.

Murphy v. A. A. Mathews, 841 S.W. 2d 671 (Mo. 1992).

Panitz v. Behrend, 632 A. 2d 562 (Pa. Super. 1993).

Richmond, D. R. (2000). Expert witness conflicts and compensation. *Tennessee Law Review, 67,* 909–948.

Simon, R. I. (Ed.). (1995). Toward the development of guidelines in the forensic psychiatric examination of posttraumatic stress disorder claims. In R. Simon (Ed.), *Post-traumatic stress disorder in litigation: Guidelines for forensic assessment* (pp. 31–34). Washington, DC: American Psychiatric Publishing.

Strasburger, L. H., Gutheil, T. G., & Brodsky, A. (1997). On wearing two hats: Role conflict in serving as both psychotherapist and expert witness. *American Journal of Psychiatry, 154,* 448–456.

Trimmer, M. A. (1999). Annual survey of Pennsylvania administrative law: Survey of selected court decisions: Licensing: Huhta v. State Board of Medicine. *Widener Journal of Public Law, 8,* 843–855.

9.3. Specialty Guidelines for Forensic Psychology

American Psychological Association

In the past 50 years forensic psychological practice has expanded dramatically. The American Psychological Association (APA) has a division devoted to matters of law and psychology (APA Division 41, the American Psychology–Law Society), a number of scientific journals devoted to interactions between psychology and the law exist (e.g., *Law and Human Behavior*; *Psychology, Public Policy, and Law*; *Behavioral Sciences & the Law*), and a number of key texts have been published and undergone multiple revisions (e.g., Grisso, 1986, 2003; Melton, Petrila, Poythress, & Slobogin, 1987, 1997, 2007; Rogers, 1988, 1997, 2008). In addition, training in forensic psychology is available in predoctoral, internship, and postdoctoral settings, and APA recognized forensic psychology as a specialty in 2001, with subsequent recertification in 2008.

. . .

The goals of these Specialty Guidelines for Forensic Psychology ("the Guidelines") are to improve the quality of forensic psychological services; enhance the practice and facilitate the systematic development of forensic psychology; encourage a high level of quality in professional practice; and encourage forensic practitioners to acknowledge and respect the rights of those they serve.

. . .

From "Specialty Guidelines for Forensic Psychology," by the American Psychological Association, 2013, *American Psychologist*, 68, pp. 7–19. Copyright 2012 by the American Psychological Association.

These Specialty Guidelines for Forensic Psychology were developed by the American Psychology–Law Society (Division 41 of the American Psychological Association [APA]) and the American Academy of Forensic Psychology. They were adopted by the APA Council of Representatives on August 3, 2011.

The previous version of the Guidelines ("Specialty Guidelines for Forensic Psychologists"; Committee on Ethical Guidelines for Forensic Psychologists, 1991) was approved by the American Psychology–Law Society (Division 41 of APA) and the American Academy of Forensic Psychology in 1991. The current revision, now called the "Specialty Guidelines for Forensic Psychology" (referred to as "the Guidelines" throughout this document), replaces the 1991 "Specialty Guidelines for Forensic Psychologists."

These guidelines are scheduled to expire August 3, 2021. After this date, users are encouraged to contact the American Psychological Association Practice Directorate to confirm that this document remains in effect.

1. RESPONSIBILITIES

Guideline 1.01: Integrity

Forensic practitioners strive for accuracy, honesty, and truthfulness in the science, teaching, and practice of forensic psychology and they strive to resist partisan pressures to provide services in any ways that might tend to be misleading or inaccurate.

Guideline 1.02: Impartiality and Fairness

When offering expert opinion to be relied upon by a decision maker, providing forensic therapeutic services, or teaching or conducting research, forensic practitioners strive for accuracy, impartiality, fairness, and independence (EPPCC Standard 2.01). Forensic practitioners recognize the adversarial nature of the legal system and strive to treat all participants and weigh all data, opinions, and rival hypotheses impartially.

. . .

Guideline 1.03: Avoiding Conflicts of Interest

Forensic practitioners refrain from taking on a professional role when personal, scientific, professional, legal, financial, or other interests or relationships could reasonably be expected to impair their impartiality, competence, or effectiveness, or expose others with whom a professional relationship exists to harm (EPPCC Standard 3.06).

. . .

2. COMPETENCE

Guideline 2.01: Scope of Competence

When determining one's competence to provide services in a particular matter, forensic practitioners may consider a variety of factors including the relative complexity and specialized nature of the service, relevant training and experience, the preparation and study they are able to devote to the matter, and the opportunity for consultation with a professional of established competence in the subject matter in question. Even with regard to subjects in which they are expert, forensic practitioners may choose to consult with colleagues.

Guideline 2.02: Gaining and Maintaining Competence

Competence can be acquired through various combinations of education, training, supervised experience, consultation, study, and professional experience. Forensic practitioners planning to provide services, teach, or conduct research involving populations, areas, techniques, or technologies that are new to them are encouraged to undertake relevant education, training, supervised experience, consultation, or study.

. . .

Guideline 2.03: Representing Competencies

Consistent with the EPPCC, forensic practitioners adequately and accurately inform all recipients of their services (e.g., attorneys, tribunals) about relevant aspects of the nature and extent of their experience, training, credentials, and qualifications, and how they were obtained (EPPCC Standard 5.01).

Guideline 2.04: Knowledge of the Legal System and the Legal Rights of Individuals

Forensic practitioners recognize the importance of obtaining a fundamental and reasonable level of knowledge and understanding of the legal and professional standards, laws, rules, and precedents that govern their participation in legal proceedings and that guide the impact of their services on service recipients (EPPCC Standard 2.01).

. . .

Guideline 2.05: Knowledge of the Scientific Foundation for Opinions and Testimony

Forensic practitioners seek to provide opinions and testimony that are sufficiently based upon adequate scientific foundation, and reliable and valid principles and methods that have been applied appropriately to the facts of the case.

. . .

Guideline 2.06: Knowledge of the Scientific Foundation for Teaching and Research

Forensic practitioners engage in teaching and research activities in which they have adequate knowledge, experience, and education (EPPCC Standard 2.01), and they acknowledge relevant limitations and caveats inherent in procedures and conclusions (EPPCC Standard 5.01).

Guideline 2.07: Considering the Impact of Personal Beliefs and Experience

Forensic practitioners recognize that their own cultures, attitudes, values, beliefs, opinions, or biases may affect their ability to practice in a competent and impartial manner. When such factors may diminish their ability to practice in a competent and impartial manner, forensic practitioners may take steps to correct or limit such effects, decline participation in the matter, or limit their participation in a manner that is consistent with professional obligations.

Guideline 2.08: Appreciation of Individual and Group Differences

When scientific or professional knowledge in the discipline of psychology establishes that an understanding of factors associated with age, gender, gender identity, race, ethnicity, culture, national origin, religion, sexual orientation, disability, language, socioeconomic status, or other relevant individual and cultural differences affects implementation or use of their services or research, forensic practitioners consider the boundaries of their expertise, make an appropriate referral if indicated, or gain the necessary training, experience, consultation, or supervision (EPPCC Standard 2.01; APA, 2003, 2004, 2011c, 2011d, 2011e).
. . .

Guideline 2.09: Appropriate Use of Services and Products

Forensic practitioners are encouraged to make reasonable efforts to guard against misuse of their services and exercise professional discretion in addressing such misuses.

3. DILIGENCE

Guideline 3.01: Provision of Services

Forensic practitioners are encouraged to seek explicit agreements that define the scope of, time-frame of, and compensation for their services. In the event that a client breaches the contract or acts in a way that would require the practitioner to violate ethical, legal or professional obligations, the forensic practitioner may terminate the relationship. . . .

Guideline 3.02: Responsiveness

Forensic practitioners seek to manage their workloads so that services can be provided thoroughly, competently, and promptly. They recognize that acting with reasonable promptness, however, does not require the forensic practitioner to acquiesce to service demands not reasonably anticipated at the time the service was requested, nor does it require the forensic practitioner to provide services if the client has not acted in a manner consistent with existing agreements, including payment of fees.

Guideline 3.03: Communication

Forensic practitioners strive to keep their clients reasonably informed about the status of their services, comply with their clients' reasonable requests for information, and consult with their clients about any substantial limitation on their conduct or performance that may arise when they reasonably believe that their clients expect a service that is not consistent with their professional obligations. Forensic practitioners attempt to keep their clients reasonably informed regarding new facts, opinions, or other potential evidence that may be relevant and applicable.

Guideline 3.04: Termination of Services

The forensic practitioner seeks to carry through to conclusion all matters undertaken for a client unless the forensic practitioner–client relationship is terminated. When a forensic practitioner's employment is limited to a specific matter, the relationship may terminate when the matter has been resolved, anticipated services have been completed, or the agreement has been violated.

4. RELATIONSHIPS

. . .

Guideline 4.01: Responsibilities to Retaining Parties

Most responsibilities to the retaining party attach only after the retaining party has requested and the forensic practitioner has agreed to render professional services and an agreement regarding compensation has been reached. Forensic practitioners are aware that there are some responsibilities, such as privacy, confidentiality, and privilege, that may attach when the forensic practitioner agrees to consider whether a forensic practitioner–retaining party relationship shall be established. Forensic practitioners, prior to entering into a contract, may direct the potential retaining party not to reveal any confidential or privileged information as a way of protecting the retaining party's interest in case a conflict exists as a result of preexisting relationships.

. . .

Guideline 4.02: Multiple Relationships

A multiple relationship occurs when a forensic practitioner is in a professional role with a person and, at the same time or at a subsequent time, is in a different role with the same person; is involved in a personal, fiscal, or other relationship with an adverse party; at the same time is in a relationship with a person closely associated with or related to the person with whom the forensic practitioner has the professional relationship; or offers or agrees to enter into another relationship in the future with the person or a person closely associated with or related to the person (EPPCC Standard 3.05).

. . .

Guideline 4.02.01: Therapeutic–Forensic Role Conflicts

Providing forensic and therapeutic psychological services to the same individual or closely related individuals involves multiple relationships that may impair objectivity and/or cause exploitation or other harm. Therefore, when requested or ordered to provide either concurrent or sequential forensic and therapeutic services, forensic practitioners are encouraged to disclose the potential risk and make reasonable efforts to refer the request to another qualified provider. If referral is not possible, the forensic practitioner is encouraged to consider the risks and benefits to all parties and to the legal system or entity likely to be impacted, the possibility of separating each service widely in time, seeking judicial review and direction, and consulting with knowledgeable colleagues. When providing both forensic and therapeutic services, forensic practitioners seek to minimize the potential negative effects of this circumstance (EPPCC Standard 3.05).

Guideline 4.02.02: Expert Testimony by Practitioners Providing Therapeutic Services

Providing expert testimony about a patient who is a participant in a legal matter does not necessarily involve the practice of forensic psychology even when that testimony is relevant to a psycholegal issue before the decision maker. . . .

Guideline 4.02.03: Provision of Forensic Therapeutic Services

Although some therapeutic services can be considered forensic in nature, the fact that therapeutic services are ordered by the court does not necessarily make them forensic.

In determining whether a therapeutic service should be considered the practice of forensic psychology, psychologists are encouraged to consider the potential impact of the legal context on treatment, the potential for treatment to impact the psycholegal issues involved in the case, and whether another reasonable psychologist in a similar position would consider the service to be forensic and these Guidelines to be applicable.

. . .

Guideline 4.03: Provision of Emergency Mental Health Services to Forensic Examinees

When providing forensic examination services an emergency may arise that requires the practitioner to provide short-term therapeutic services to the examinee in order to prevent imminent harm to the examinee or others. In such cases the forensic practitioner is encouraged to limit disclosure of information and inform the retaining attorney, legal representative, or the court in an appropriate manner. Upon providing emergency treatment to examinees, forensic practitioners consider whether they can continue in a forensic role with that individual so that potential for harm to the recipient of services is avoided (EPPCC Standard 3.4)

5. FEES

Guideline 5.01: Determining Fees

When determining fees forensic practitioners may consider salient factors such as their experience providing the service, the time and labor required, the novelty and difficulty of the questions involved, the skill required to perform the service, the fee customarily charged for similar forensic services, the likelihood that the acceptance of the particular employment will preclude other employment, the time limitations imposed by the client or circumstances, the nature and length of the professional relationship with the client, the client's ability to pay for the service, and any legal requirements.

Guideline 5.02: Fee Arrangements

Forensic practitioners are encouraged to make clear to the client the likely cost of services whenever it is feasible, and make appropriate provisions in those cases in which the costs of services is greater than anticipated or the client's ability to pay for services changes in some way.

. . .

Guideline 5.03: Pro Bono Services

Forensic psychologists recognize that some persons may have limited access to legal services as a function of financial disadvantage and strive to contribute a portion of their professional time for little or no compensation or personal advantage (EPPCC Principle E).

6. INFORMED CONSENT, NOTIFICATION, AND ASSENT

Because substantial rights, liberties, and properties are often at risk in forensic matters, and because the methods and procedures of forensic practitioners are complex and may not be accurately anticipated by the recipients of forensic services, forensic practitioners strive to inform service recipients about the nature and parameters of the services to be provided (EPPCC Standards 3.04, 3.10).

Guideline 6.01: Timing and Substance

Forensic practitioners strive to inform clients, examinees, and others who are the recipients of forensic services as soon as is feasible about the nature and extent of reasonably anticipated forensic services.

. . .

Guideline 6.02: Communication With Those Seeking to Retain a Forensic Practitioner

As part of the initial process of being retained, or as soon thereafter as previously unknown information becomes available, forensic practitioners strive to disclose to the retaining party information that would reasonably be anticipated to affect a decision to retain or continue the services of the forensic practitioner.

. . .

Guideline 6.03: Communication With Forensic Examinees

Forensic practitioners inform examinees about the nature and purpose of the examination (EPPCC Standard 9.03; American Educational Research Association, American Psychological Association, & National Council on Measurement in Education [AERA, APA, & NCME], in press). Such information may include the purpose, nature, and anticipated use of the examination; who will have access to the information; associated limitations on privacy, confidentiality, and privilege including who is authorized to release or access the information contained in the forensic practitioner's records; the voluntary or involuntary nature of participation, including potential consequences of participation or nonparticipation, if known; and, if the cost of the service is the responsibility of the examinee, the anticipated cost.

Guideline 6.03.01: Persons Not Ordered or Mandated to Undergo Examination

If the examinee is not ordered by the court to participate in a forensic examination, the forensic practitioner seeks his or her informed consent (EPPCC Standards 3.10, 9.03). If the examinee declines to proceed after being notified of the nature and purpose of the forensic examination, the forensic practitioner may consider postponing the examination, advising the examinee to contact his or her attorney, and notifying the retaining party about the examinee's unwillingness to proceed.

Guideline 6.03.02: Persons Ordered or Mandated to Undergo Examination or Treatment

If the examinee is ordered by the court to participate, the forensic practitioner can conduct the examination over the objection, and without the consent, of the examinee (EPPCC Standards 3.10, 9.03). If the examinee declines to proceed after being notified of the nature and purpose of the forensic examination, the forensic practitioner may consider a variety of options including postponing the examination, advising the examinee to contact his or her attorney, and notifying the retaining party about the examinee's unwillingness to proceed. . . .

Guideline 6.03.03: Persons Lacking Capacity to Provide Informed Consent

Forensic practitioners appreciate that the very conditions that precipitate psychological examination of individuals involved in legal proceedings can impair their functioning in a variety of important ways, including their ability to understand and consent to the evaluation process.

. . .

Guideline 6.03.04: Evaluation of Persons Not Represented by Counsel

Because of the significant rights that may be at issue in a legal proceeding, forensic practitioners carefully consider the appropriateness of conducting a forensic evaluation of an individual who is not represented by counsel. Forensic practitioners may consider conducting such evaluations or delaying the evaluation so as to provide the examinee with the opportunity to consult with counsel.

Guideline 6.04: Communication With Collateral Sources of Information

Forensic practitioners disclose to potential collateral sources information that might reasonably be expected to inform their decisions about participating that may include, but may not be limited to, who has retained the forensic practitioner; the nature, purpose, and intended use of the examination or other procedure; the nature of and any limits on privacy, confidentiality, and privilege; and whether their participation is voluntary (EPPCC Standard 3.10).

Guideline 6.05: Communication in Research Contexts

When engaging in research or scholarly activities conducted as a service to a client in a legal proceeding, forensic practitioners attempt to clarify any anticipated use of the research or scholarly product, disclose their role in the resulting research or scholarly products, and obtain whatever consent or agreement is required.

. . .

7. CONFLICTS IN PRACTICE

. . .

Guideline 7.01: Conflicts With Legal Authority

When their responsibilities conflict with law, regulations, or other governing legal authority, forensic practitioners make known their commitment to the EPPCC, and take steps to resolve the conflict. In situations in which the EPPCC or the Guidelines are in conflict with the law, attempts to resolve the conflict are made in accordance with the EPPCC (EPPCC Standard 1.02). . . .

Guideline 7.02: Conflicts With Organizational Demands

When the demands of an organization with which they are affiliated or for whom they are working conflict with their professional responsibilities and obligations, forensic practitioners strive to clarify the nature of the conflict and, to the extent feasible, resolve the conflict in a way consistent with professional obligations and responsibilities (EPPCC Standard 1.03).

Guideline 7.03: Resolving Ethical Issues With Fellow Professionals

When an apparent or potential ethical violation has caused, or is likely to cause, substantial harm, forensic practitioners are encouraged to take action appropriate to the situation and consider a number of factors including the nature and the immediacy of the potential harm; applicable privacy, confidentiality, and privilege; how the rights of the relevant parties may be affected by a particular course of action; and any other legal or ethical obligations (EPPCC Standard 1.04). . . .

8. PRIVACY, CONFIDENTIALITY, AND PRIVILEGE

. . .

Guideline 8.01: Release of Information

Forensic practitioners are encouraged to recognize the importance of complying with properly noticed and served subpoenas or court orders directing release of information, or other legally proper consent from duly authorized persons, unless there is a legally valid reason to offer an objection. When in doubt about an appropriate response or course of action, forensic practitioners may seek assistance from the retaining client, retain and seek legal advice from their own attorney, or formally notify the drafter of the subpoena or order of their uncertainty.

Guideline 8.02: Access to Information

If requested, forensic practitioners seek to provide the retaining party access to, and a meaningful explanation of, all information that is in their records for the matter at hand, consistent with the relevant law, applicable codes of ethics and professional standards, and institutional rules and regulations. Forensic examinees typically are not provided access to the forensic practitioner's records without the consent of the retaining party. . . .

Guideline 8.03: Acquiring Collateral and Third Party Information

Forensic practitioners strive to access information or records from collateral sources with the consent of the relevant attorney or the relevant party, or when otherwise authorized by law or court order.

Guideline 8.04: Use of Case Materials in Teaching, Continuing Education, and Other Scholarly Activities

Forensic practitioners using case materials for purposes of teaching, training, or research strive to present such information in a fair, balanced, and respectful manner. They attempt to protect the privacy of persons by disguising the confidential, personally identifiable information of all persons and entities who would reasonably claim a privacy interest; using only those aspects of the case available in the public domain; or obtaining consent from the relevant clients, parties, participants, and organizations to use the materials for such purposes (EPPCC Standard 4.07; also see Guidelines 11.06 and 11.07 of these Guidelines).

9. METHODS AND PROCEDURES

Guideline 9.01: Use of Appropriate Methods

Forensic practitioners strive to utilize appropriate methods and procedures in their work. When performing examinations, treatment, consultation, educational activities, or scholarly investigations, forensic practitioners seek to maintain integrity by examining the issue or problem at hand from all reasonable perspectives and seek information that will differentially test plausible rival hypotheses.

Guideline 9.02: Use of Multiple Sources of Information

Forensic practitioners ordinarily avoid relying solely on one source of data, and corroborate important data whenever feasible (AERA, APA, & NCME, in press). When relying upon data that have not been corroborated, forensic practitioners seek to make known the uncorroborated status of the data, any associated strengths and limitations, and the reasons for relying upon the data.

Guideline 9.03: Opinions Regarding Persons Not Examined

Forensic practitioners recognize their obligations to only provide written or oral evidence about the psychological characteristics of particular individuals when they have sufficient information or data to form an adequate foundation for those opinions or to substantiate their findings (EPPCC Standard 9.01). Forensic practitioners seek to make reasonable efforts to obtain such information or data, and they document their efforts to obtain it. When it is not possible or feasible to examine individuals about whom they are offering an opinion, forensic practitioners strive to make clear the impact of such limitations on the reliability and validity of their professional products, opinions, or testimony.

. . .

10. ASSESSMENT

Guideline 10.01: Focus on Legally Relevant Factors

Forensic examiners seek to assist the trier of fact to understand evidence or determine a fact in issue, and they provide information that is most relevant to the psycholegal issue. In reports and testimony, forensic practitioners typically provide information about examinees' functional abilities, capacities, knowledge, and beliefs, and address their opinions and recommendations to the identified psycholegal issues (American Bar Association & American Psychological Association, 2008; Grisso, 1986, 2003; Heilbrun, Marczyk, DeMatteo, & Mack-Allen, 2007).

. . .

Guideline 10.02: Selection and Use of Assessment Procedures

Forensic practitioners use assessment procedures in the manner and for the purposes that are appropriate in light of the research on or evidence of their usefulness and proper application (EPPCC Standard 9.02; AERA, APA, & NCME, in press). This includes assessment techniques, interviews, tests, instruments, and other procedures and their administration, adaptation, scoring, and interpretation, including computerized scoring and interpretation systems.

. . .

Guideline 10.03: Appreciation of Individual Differences

When interpreting assessment results, forensic practitioners consider the purpose of the assessment as well as the various test factors, test-taking abilities, and other characteristics of the person being assessed, such as situational, personal, linguistic, and cultural differences that might affect their judgments or reduce the accuracy of their interpretations (EPPCC Standard 9.06). Forensic practitioners strive to identify any significant strengths and limitations of their procedures and interpretations.

. . .

Guideline 10.04: Consideration of Assessment Settings

In order to maximize the validity of assessment results, forensic practitioners strive to conduct evaluations in settings that provide adequate comfort, safety, and privacy.

Guideline 10.05: Provision of Assessment Feedback

Forensic practitioners take reasonable steps to explain assessment results to the examinee or a designated representative in language they can understand (EPPCC Standard 9.10). In those circumstances in which communication about assessment results is precluded, the forensic practitioner explains this to the examinee in advance (EPPCC Standard 9.10).

. . .

Guideline 10.06: Documentation and Compilation of Data Considered

Forensic practitioners are encouraged to recognize the importance of documenting all data they consider with enough detail and quality to allow for reasonable judicial scrutiny and adequate discovery by all parties. This documentation includes, but is not limited to, letters and consultations; notes, recordings, and transcriptions; assessment and test data, scoring reports and interpretations; and all other records in any form or medium that were created or exchanged in connection with a matter.

. . .

Guideline 10.07: Provision of Documentation

Pursuant to proper subpoenas or court orders, or other legally proper consent from authorized persons, forensic practitioners seek to make available all documentation described in Guideline 10.05, all financial records related to the matter, and any other records including reports (and draft reports if they have been provided to a party, attorney, or other entity for review), that might reasonably be related to the opinions to be expressed.

Guideline 10.08: Record Keeping

Forensic practitioners establish and maintain a system of record keeping and professional communication (EPPCC Standard 6.01; APA, 2007), and attend to relevant laws and rules. When indicated by the extent of the rights, liberties, and properties that may be at risk, the complexity of the case, the amount and legal significance of unique evidence in the care and control of the forensic practitioner, and the likelihood of future appeal, forensic practitioners strive to inform the retaining party of the limits of record keeping times. If requested to do so, forensic practitioners consider maintaining such records until notified that all appeals in the matter have been exhausted, or sending a copy of any unique components/aspects of the record in their care and control to the retaining party before destruction of the record.

11. PROFESSIONAL AND OTHER PUBLIC COMMUNICATIONS

Guideline 11.01: Accuracy, Fairness, and Avoidance of Deception

Forensic practitioners make reasonable efforts to ensure that the products of their services, as well as their own public statements and professional reports and testimony, are communicated in ways that promote understanding and avoid deception (EPPCC Standard 5.01).

. . .

Guideline 11.02: Differentiating Observations, Inferences, and Conclusions

In their communications, forensic practitioners strive to distinguish observations, inferences, and conclusions. Forensic practitioners are encouraged to explain the relationship between their expert opinions and the legal issues and facts of the case at hand.

Guideline 11.03: Disclosing Sources of Information and Bases of Opinions

Forensic practitioners are encouraged to disclose all sources of information obtained in the course of their professional services, and to identify the source of each piece of information that was considered and relied upon in formulating a particular conclusion, opinion, or other professional product.

Guideline 11.04: Comprehensive and Accurate Presentation of Opinions in Reports and Testimony

Consistent with relevant law and rules of evidence, when providing professional reports and other sworn statements or testimony, forensic practitioners strive to offer a complete statement of all relevant opinions that they formed within the scope of their work on the case, the basis and reasoning underlying the opinions, the salient data or other information that was considered in forming the opinions, and an indication of any additional evidence that may be used in support of the opinions to be offered. The specific substance of forensic reports is determined by the type of psycholegal issue at hand as well as relevant laws or rules in the jurisdiction in which the work is completed.

. . .

Guideline 11.05: Commenting Upon Other Professionals and Participants in Legal Proceedings

When evaluating or commenting upon the work or qualifications of other professionals involved in legal proceedings, forensic practitioners seek to represent their disagreements in a professional and respectful tone, and base them on a fair examination of the data, theories, standards, and opinions of the other expert or party.

. . .

Guideline 11.06: Out of Court Statements

Ordinarily, forensic practitioners seek to avoid making detailed public (out-of-court) statements about legal proceedings in which they have been involved. However, sometimes public statements may serve important goals such as educating the public about the role of forensic practitioners in the legal system, the appropriate practice of forensic psychology, and psychological and legal issues that are relevant to the matter at hand. When making public statements, forensic practitioners refrain from releasing private, confidential, or privileged information, and attempt to protect persons from harm, misuse, or misrepresentation as a result of their statements (EPPCC Standard 4.05).

Guideline 11.07: Commenting Upon Legal Proceedings

Forensic practitioners strive to address particular legal proceedings in publications or communications only to the extent that the information relied upon is part of a public record, or when consent for that use has been properly obtained from any party holding any relevant privilege (also see Guideline 8.04).

. . .

REFERENCES

American Bar Association & American Psychological Association. (2008). *Assessment of older adults with diminished capacity: A handbook for psychologists.* Washington, DC: American Bar Association and American Psychological Association.

American Educational Research Association, American Psychological Association, & National Council on Measurement in Education. (in press). *Standards for educational and psychological testing* (3rd ed.). Washington, DC: Authors.

American Psychological Association. (2003). Guidelines on multicultural education, training, research, practice, and organizational change for psychologists. *American Psychologist, 58,* 377–402. doi:10.1037/0003-066X.58.5.377

American Psychological Association. (2004). Guidelines for psychological practice with older adults. *American Psychologist, 59,* 236–260. doi:10.1037/0003-066X.59.4.236

American Psychological Association. (2007). Record keeping guidelines. *American Psychologist, 62,* 993–1004. doi:10.1037/0003-066X.62.9.993

American Psychological Association. (2011c). *Guidelines for the evaluation of dementia and age related cognitive change.* Washington, DC: Author. (*American Psychologist,* 2012, *67,* 1–9. doi:10.1037/a0024643)

American Psychological Association. (2011d). *Guidelines for assessment of and intervention with persons with disabilities.* Washington, DC: Author. (*American Psychologist,* 2012, *67,* 43–62. doi:10.1037/a0025892)

American Psychological Association. (2011e). *Guidelines for psychological practice with lesbian, gay, and bisexual clients.* Washington, DC: Author. (*American Psychologist,* 2012, *67,* 10–42. doi:10.1037/a0024659)

Grisso, T. (1986). *Evaluating competencies: Forensic assessments and instruments.* New York, NY: Plenum.

Grisso, T. (2003). *Evaluating competencies: Forensic assessments and instruments* (2nd ed.). New York, NY: Kluwer/Plenum.

Heilbrun, K., Marczyk, G., DeMatteo, D., & Mack-Allen, J. (2007). A principles-based approach to forensic mental health assessment: Utility and update. In A. M. Goldstein (Ed.), *Forensic psychology: Emerging topics and expanding roles* (pp. 45–72). Hoboken, NJ: Wiley.

Melton, G., Petrila, J., Poythress, N., & Slobogin, C. (1987). *Psychological evaluations for the courts: A handbook for mental health professionals and lawyers.* New York, NY: Guilford Press.

Melton, G., Petrila, J., Poythress, N., & Slobogin, C. (1997). *Psychological evaluations for the courts: A handbook for mental health professionals and lawyers* (2nd ed.). New York, NY: Guilford Press.

Melton, G., Petrila, J., Poythress, N., & Slobogin, C. (2007). *Psychological evaluations for the courts: A handbook for mental health professionals and lawyers* (3rd ed.). New York, NY: Guilford Press.

Rogers, R. (Ed.). (1988). *Clinical assessment of malingering and deception.* New York, NY: Guilford Press.

Rogers, R. (Ed.). (1997). *Clinical assessment of malingering and deception* (2nd ed.). New York, NY: Guilford Press.

Rogers, R. (Ed.). (2008). *Clinical assessment of malingering and deception* (3rd ed.). New York, NY: Guilford Press.

9.4. Guidelines for Child Custody Evaluations in Family Law Proceedings

American Psychological Association

INTRODUCTION

Family law proceedings encompass a broad range of issues, including custody, maintenance, support, valuation, visitation, relocation, and termination of parental rights. The following guidelines address what are commonly termed *child custody* evaluations, involving disputes over decision making, caretaking, and access in the wake of marital or other relationship dissolution. The goal of these guidelines is to promote proficiency in the conduct of these particular evaluations. This narrowed focus means that evaluations occurring in other contexts (e.g., child protection matters) are not covered by these guidelines. In addition, the guidelines acknowledge a clear distinction between the forensic evaluations described in this document and the advice and support that psychologists provide to families, children, and adults in the normal course of psychotherapy and counseling.

Although some states have begun to favor such terms as *parenting plan, parenting time,* or *parental rights and responsibilities* over the term *custody* (American

From "Guidelines for Child Custody Evaluations in Family Law Proceedings," by the American Psychological Association, 2010, *American Psychologist, 65,* pp. 863–867. Copyright 2010 by the American Psychological Association.

This revision of the 1994 "Guidelines for Child Custody Evaluations in Divorce Proceedings" (American Psychological Association, 1994) was completed by the Committee on Professional Practice and Standards (COPPS) and approved as APA policy by the APA Council of Representatives on February 21, 2009. Members of COPPS during the development of this document were Lisa Drago Piechowski (chair, 2009), Eric Y. Drogin (chair, 2007–2008), Mary A. Connell (chair, 2006), Nabil El-Ghoroury (Board of Professional Affairs [BPA] liaison, 2007–2008), Michele Galietta, Terry S. W. Gock, Larry C. James (BPA liaison, 2004–2006), Robert Kinscherff, Stephen J. Lally, Gary D. Lovejoy, Mary Ann McCabe, Bonnie J. Spring, and Carolyn M. West. COPPS is grateful for the support and guidance of the BPA and particularly to BPA Chairs Cynthia A. Sturm (2009), Jaquelyn Liss Resnick (2008), Jennifer F. Kelly (2007), and Kristin Hancock (2006). COPPS also acknowledges the consultation of APA Practice Directorate staff Shirley A. Higuchi and Alan Nessman. COPPS extends its appreciation to the APA Practice Directorate staff who facilitated both the work of COPPS and the revision efforts: Lynn F. Bufka, Mary G. Hardiman, Omar Rehman, Geoffrey M. Reed, Laura Kay-Roth, Ernestine Penniman, and Ayobodun Bello.

Expiration: These guidelines are scheduled to expire 10 years from February 21, 2009 (the date of their adoption by the APA Council of Representatives). After this date, users are encouraged to contact the APA Practice Directorate to determine whether this document remains in effect.

Law Institute, 2000, pp. 131–132), the substantial majority of legal authorities and scientific treatises still refer to *custody* when addressing the resolution of decision-making, caretaking, and access disputes. In order to avoid confusion and to ensure that these guidelines are utilized as widely as possible, these guidelines apply the term custody to these issues generically, unless otherwise specified. It is no longer the default assumption that child custody proceedings will produce the classic paradigm of sole custodian versus visiting parent. Many states recognize some form of joint or shared custody that affirms the decision-making and caretaking status of more than one adult. The legal system also recognizes that the disputes in question are not exclusively marital and therefore may not involve divorce per se. Some parents may never have been married and perhaps may never even have lived together. In addition, child custody disputes may arise after years of successful co-parenting when one parent seeks to relocate for work-related or other reasons. These guidelines apply the term *parents* generically when referring to persons who seek legal recognition as sole or shared custodians.

Parents may have numerous resources at their disposal, including psychotherapy, counseling, consultation, mediation, and other forms of conflict resolution. When parents agree to a child custody arrangement on their own—as they do in the overwhelming majority (90%) of cases (Melton, Petrila, Poythress, & Slobogin, 2007)—there may be no dispute for the court to decide. However, if parties are unable to reach such an agreement, the court must intervene in order to allocate decision making, caretaking, and access, typically applying a "best interests of the child" standard in determining this restructuring of rights and responsibilities (Artis, 2004; Elrod, 2006; Kelly, 1997).

Psychologists render a valuable service when they provide competent and impartial opinions with direct relevance to the "psychological best interests" of the child (Miller, 2002). The specific nature of psychologists' involvement and the potential for misuse of their influence have been the subject of ongoing debate (Grisso, 1990, 2005; Krauss & Sales, 1999, 2000; Melton et al., 2007). The acceptance and thus the overall utility of psychologists' child custody evaluations are augmented by demonstrably competent forensic practice and by consistent adherence to codified ethical standards.

These guidelines are informed by the American Psychological Association's (APA's) "Ethical Principles of Psychologists and Code of Conduct" (hereinafter referred to as the Ethics Code; APA, 2002). The term *guidelines* refers to statements that suggest or recommend specific professional behavior, endeavors, or conduct for psychologists. Guidelines differ from *standards* in that standards are mandatory and may be accompanied by an enforcement mechanism. Guidelines are aspirational in intent. They are intended to facilitate the continued systematic development of the profession and to help facilitate a high level of practice by psychologists. Guidelines are not intended to be mandatory or exhaustive and may not be applicable to every professional situation. They are not definitive, and they are not intended to take precedence over the judgment of psychologists.

I. ORIENTING GUIDELINES: PURPOSE OF THE CHILD CUSTODY EVALUATION

1. The purpose of the evaluation is to assist in determining the psychological best interests of the child.

Rationale

The extensive clinical training of psychologists equips them to investigate a substantial array of conditions, statuses, and capacities. When conducting child custody evaluations, psychologists are expected to focus on factors that pertain specifically to the psychological best interests of the child, because the court will draw upon these considerations in order to reach its own conclusions and render a decision.

. . .

2. The child's welfare is paramount.

Rationale

Psychologists seek to maintain an appropriate degree of respect for and understanding of parents' practical and personal concerns; however, psychologists are mindful that such considerations are ultimately secondary to the welfare of the child.

. . .

3. The evaluation focuses upon parenting attributes, the child's psychological needs, and the resulting fit.

Rationale

From the court's perspective, the most valuable contributions of psychologists are those that reflect a clinically astute and scientifically sound approach to legally relevant issues. Issues that are central to the court's ultimate decision-making obligations include parenting attributes, the child's psychological needs, and the resulting fit. The training of psychologists provides them with unique skills and qualifications to address these issues.

. . .

II. GENERAL GUIDELINES: PREPARING FOR THE CUSTODY EVALUATION

4. Psychologists strive to gain and maintain specialized competence.

Rationale

Laws change, existing methods are refined, and new techniques are identified. In child custody evaluations, general competence in the clinical assessment of children, adults, and families is necessary but is insufficient in and of itself. The court will expect psychologists to demonstrate a level of expertise that reflects contextual insight and forensic integration as well as testing and interview skills.

. . .

5. Psychologists strive to function as impartial evaluators.

Rationale

Family law cases involve complex and emotionally charged disputes over highly personal matters, and the parties are often deeply invested in a specific outcome. The volatility of this situation is often exacerbated by a growing realization that there may be no resolution that will completely satisfy every person involved. In this contentious atmosphere, it is crucial that evaluators remain as free as possible of unwarranted bias or partiality.

. . .

6. Psychologists strive to engage in culturally informed, nondiscriminatory evaluation practices.

Rationale

Professional standards and guidelines articulate the need for psychologists to remain aware of their own biases, and those of others, regarding age, gender, gender identity, race, ethnicity, national origin, religion, sexual orientation, disability, language, culture, and socioeconomic status. Biases and an attendant lack of culturally competent insight are likely to interfere with data collection and interpretation and thus with the development of valid opinions and recommendations.

. . .

7. Psychologists strive to avoid conflicts of interest and multiple relationships in conducting evaluations.

Rationale

The inherent complexity, potential for harm, and adversarial context of child custody evaluations make the avoidance of conflicts of interest particularly important. The presence of such conflicts will undermine the court's confidence in psychologists' opinions and recommendations and in some jurisdictions may result in professional board discipline and legal liability.

. . .

III. PROCEDURAL GUIDELINES: CONDUCTING THE CHILD CUSTODY EVALUATION

8. Psychologists strive to establish the scope of the evaluation in a timely fashion, consistent with the nature of the referral question.

Rationale

The scope of a child custody evaluation will vary according to the needs of a particular case and the specific issues psychologists are asked to address. Referral questions may vary in the degree to which they specify the desired parameters of the evaluation. Failure to ensure in a timely fashion that an evaluation is appropriately designed impairs the utility and acceptance of the resulting opinions and recommendations.

. . .

9. Psychologists strive to obtain appropriately informed consent.

Rationale

Obtaining appropriately informed consent honors the legal rights and personal dignity of examinees and other individuals. This process allows persons to determine not only whether they will participate in a child custody evaluation but also whether they will make various disclosures during the course of an examination or other request for information.

. . .

10. Psychologists strive to employ multiple methods of data gathering.

Rationale

Multiple methods of data gathering enhance the reliability and validity of psychologists' eventual conclusions, opinions, and recommendations. Unique as well as overlapping aspects of various measures contribute to a fuller picture of each examinee's abilities, challenges, and preferences.

. . .

11. Psychologists strive to interpret assessment data in a manner consistent with the context of the evaluation.

Rationale

The context in which child custody evaluations occur may affect the perceptions and behavior of persons from whom data are collected, thus altering both psychological test responses and interview results. Unreliable data result in decreased validity, a circumstance that enhances the potential for erroneous conclusions, poorly founded opinions, and misleading recommendations.

. . .

12. Psychologists strive to complement the evaluation with the appropriate combination of examinations.

Rationale

Psychologists provide an opinion of an individual's psychological characteristics only after they have conducted an examination of the individual adequate to support their statements and conclusions (Ethics Code, Standard 9.01(b)). The only exception to this rule occurs in those particular instances of record review, consultation, or supervision (as opposed, in each case, to evaluations) in which an individual examination is not warranted or necessary for the psychologist's opinion (Ethics Code, Standard 9.01(c)). The court typically expects psychologists to examine both parents as well as the child.

. . .

13. Psychologists strive to base their recommendations, if any, upon the psychological best interests of the child.

Rationale

Not every child custody evaluation will result in recommendations. Psychologists may conclude that this is an inappropriate role for a forensic evaluator or that available data are insufficient for this purpose. If a recommendation is provided, the court will expect it to be supportable on the basis of the evaluations conducted.

. . .

14. Psychologists create and maintain professional records in accordance with ethical and legal obligations.

Rationale

Legal and ethical standards describe requirements for the appropriate development, maintenance, and disposal of professional records. The court expects psychologists providing child custody evaluations to preserve the data that inform their conclusions. This enables other professionals to analyze, understand, and provide appropriate support for (or challenges to) psychologists' forensic opinions.

. . .

REFERENCES

American Law Institute. (2000). *Principles of the law of family dissolution: Analysis and recommendations.* Newark, NJ: Mathew Bender.

American Psychological Association. (1994). Guidelines for child custody evaluations in divorce proceedings. *American Psychologist, 49,* 677–680. doi:10.1037/0003-066X.49.7.677

American Psychological Association. (2002). Ethical principles of psychologists and code of conduct. *American Psychologist, 57,* 1060–1073. doi:10.1037/0003-066X.57.12.1060

Artis, J. E. (2004). Judging the best interests of the child: Judges' accounts of the tender years doctrine. *Law and Society Review, 38,* 769–806. doi:10.1111/j.0023-9216.2004.00066.x

Elrod, L. D. (2006). A move in the right direction? Best interests of the child emerging as the standard for relocation cases. *Journal of Child Custody, 3,* 29–61. doi:10.1300/J190v03n03_03

Grisso, T. (1990). Evolving guidelines for divorce/custody evaluations. *Family and Conciliation Courts Review, 28,* 35–41. doi:10.1111/j.174-1617.1990.tb01228.x

Grisso, T. (2003). *Evaluating competencies: Forensic assessments and instruments* (2nd ed.). New York, NY: Kluwer Academic/Plenum.

Grisso, T. (2005). Commentary on "Empirical and ethical problems with custody recommendations": What now? *Family Court Review, 43*, 223–228. doi:10.1111/j.1744-1617.2005.00020.x

Kelly, J. B. (1997). The best interests of the child: A concept in search of meaning. *Family and Conciliation Courts Review, 35*, 377–387. doi:10.1111/j.174-1617.1997.tb00480.x

Krauss, D. A., & Sales, B. (1999). The problem of "helpfulness" in applying Daubert to expert testimony: Child custody determinations in family law as an exemplar. *Psychology, Public Policy, and Law, 5*, 78–99. doi:10.1037/1076-8971.5.1.78

Krauss, D. A., & Sales, B. D. (2000). Legal standards, expertise, and experts in the resolution of contested child custody cases. *Psychology, Public Policy, and Law, 6*, 843–879. doi:10.1037/1076-8971.6.4.843

Melton, G., Petrila, J., Poythress, N., & Slobogin, C. (2007). *Psychological evaluations for the courts: A handbook for mental health professionals and lawyers* (3rd ed.). New York, NY: Guilford Press.

Miller, G. H. (2002). The psychological best interest of the child is not the legal best interest. *Journal of the American Academy of Psychiatry and Law, 30*, 196–200.

COMMENTARY: Forensic psychologists contemplating engagement in family law proceedings often pause when reminded of the twin practical realities of this specialty area. The first of these is that in almost every instance, there exists a person who is convinced that the psychologist has failed grievously to reach a justifiable conclusion in the matter at hand. The second of these is that this person already has an attorney.

In this most overtly combative of legal contexts, guidelines for child custody evaluations may wind up constituting a justification of standard evaluative procedures as much as a template for ethical conduct—with the latter, of course, providing the most appropriate basis for both promulgation and adherence. Key among ethical considerations in this mode of forensic service provision will always be the issue of bias. Courts and litigants in child custody matters will often clamor for decisions that draw heavily on the evaluator's personal judgment—and will not hesitate to cite bias as a reason for rejecting that judgment.

The following references are recommended for those interested in further investigation of the ethical dimensions of child custody evaluations. Given the increasing employment in amply funded proceedings of consultants as well as evaluators, both roles are addressed.

Ackerman, M. J., & Pritzl, T. B. (2011). Child custody evaluation practices: A 20-year follow-up. *Family Court Review, 49*, 618–628. http://dx.doi.org/10.1111/j.1744-1617.2011.01397.x

Barth, L. (2011). Consultant conduct in anticipation of a child custody evaluation: Ethical and social dilemmas and the need for neutral parent education. *Family Court Review, 49*, 155–169. http://dx.doi.org/10.1111/j.1744-1617.2010.01359.x

Bucky, S. F. (2014). Introduction to the special issue: Ethical issues relevant to the child custody evaluation process. *Journal of Child Custody: Research, Issues, and Practices, 11*, 77–80. http://dx.doi.org/10.1080/15379418.2014.923239

Ellis, E. M. (2010). Should participation in a child custody evaluation compel the release of psychotherapy records? *Journal of Child Custody: Research, Issues, and Practices, 7,* 138–154. http://dx.doi.org/10.1080/15379418.2010.508265

Fuhrmann, G., & Zibbell, R. A. (2013). Evaluation for child custody. In R. Roesch & P. A. Zapf (Eds.), *Forensic assessments in criminal and civil law: A handbook for lawyers* (pp. 207–221). New York, NY: Oxford University Press.

9.5. Irreconcilable Conflict Between Therapeutic and Forensic Roles

Stuart A. Greenberg and Daniel W. Shuman

With increasing frequency, psychologists, psychiatrists, and other mental health professionals are participating as forensic experts in litigation on behalf of their patients. Factors such as tightened insurance reimbursement rules, a growing market for forensic mental health professionals, and zealous patient advocacy by therapists have combined to induce many therapists, including those who once zealously avoided the judicial system, to appear, often willingly, as forensic expert witnesses on behalf of their patients. Although therapists' concerns for their patients and for their own employment is understandable, this practice constitutes engaging in dual-role relationships and often leads to bad results for patients, courts, and clinicians.

Although there are explicit ethical precepts about psychologists and psychiatrists engaging in these conflicting roles, they have not eliminated this conduct. One important factor contributing to this continued conduct is that psychologists and psychiatrists have not understood why these ethical precepts exist and how they affect the behavior of even the most competent therapists. When the reasons for the ethical precepts are understood, it is clear why no psychologist, psychiatrist, or other mental health professional is immune from the concerns that underlie them.

. . .

ROLE CONFLICT

In most jurisdictions, a properly qualified therapist testifies as a fact witness for some purposes, as he or she is expected to testify to information learned first hand in therapy, and as an expert witness for some purposes, as he or she is permitted to testify to opinions about mental disorder that a layperson would not be permitted to offer. Thus, a therapist may, if requested to do so by a patient or ordered to do so by a court, properly testify to facts, observations, and clinical opinions for which the therapy process provides a trustworthy basis. This testimony may include the history as provided by a patient; the clinical diagnosis; the care provided to a patient; the patient's response to that treatment; the patient's prognosis; the mood, cognitions, or behavior of the patient

From "Irreconcilable Conflict Between Therapeutic and Forensic Roles," by S. A. Greenberg and D. W. Shuman, 1997, *Professional Psychology: Research and Practice, 28,* pp. 50–57. Copyright 1997 by the American Psychological Association.

at particular times; and any other statements that the patient made in treatment. A therapist may properly testify, for example, that Ms. Jones reported the history of a motor vehicle accident (MVA) 2 weeks prior to the start of therapy and that the therapist observed the patient to be bruised, bandaged, tearful, and extremely anxious. The therapist may properly testify that he or she observed, and that Ms. Jones reported, symptoms that led to a diagnosis of posttraumatic stress disorder (PTSD). The therapist may also describe the particular type of treatment used, the patient's response to that treatment, and her prognosis. The therapist may properly testify that the primary focus for the therapy was the MVA, or the PTSD secondary to the MVA. The therapist may even properly testify that, for treatment purposes, the operating assumption was that the MVA rather than her impending divorce or recent job termination or the death of a family member was what caused the patient's distress.

To be admissible, an expert opinion must be reliable and valid to a reasonable degree of scientific certainty (a metric for scrutinizing the certainty of expert testimony as a condition of its admissibility). It is improper for the therapist to offer an expert opinion that the MVA was the proximate cause of her impairments rather than the divorce, job termination, or bereavement. This is true for two reasons. First, the type and amount of data routinely observed in therapy is rarely adequate to form a proper foundation to determine the psycholegal (as opposed to the clinically assumed) cause of the litigant's impairment, nor is therapy usually adequate to rule out other potential causes. Second, such testimony engages the therapist in conflicting roles with the patient. Common examples of this role conflict occur when a patient's therapist testifies to the psycholegal issues that arise in competency, personal injury, worker's compensation, and custody litigation.

These concerns do not apply when the treating expert witness stays within the boundaries of facts and opinions that can be reliably known by the treating professional. Indeed, the treating therapist can be compelled to testify to information perceived during the therapeutic process and to opinions previously formed for the purpose of therapy but cannot be compelled to do a forensic examination or analysis (Shuman, 1983). Clinical, ethical, and legal concerns arise when the treating expert offers psycholegal assessment—an assessment for which the treating expert does not have adequate professional basis, for which there are inherent role conflicts, and for which there will almost certainly be negative implications for continued therapy.

. . .

WAIVING THE DUAL-ROLE CONFLICT

These role differences are not merely artificial distinctions but are substantial differences that make inherently good sense. Unless these distinctions are respected, not only are both the therapeutic and forensic endeavors jeopardized for the patient–litigant but as well the rights of all parties who are affected by this erroneous and conflictual choice. Unlike some conflicts of interest, this role conflict is not one that the plaintiff can waive, because it is not the exclusive province of the plaintiff's side of the case. The conflict affects not only the plaintiff but also the defense and the court. This conflict not only poses therapeutic risks to the patient–litigant but also risks of inaccuracy and lack of objectivity to the court's process and to all of the litigants.

EXISTING PROFESSIONAL GUIDELINES

On the basis of these concerns, both psychological and psychiatric organizations have sought to limit these situations when dual functions are performed by a single psychologist or psychiatrist. In increasing detail and specificity, professional organizations have discouraged psychologists and psychiatrists from engaging in conflicting dual professional roles with patient-litigants. As the Ethical Guidelines for the Practice of Forensic Psychiatry, adopted by the American Academy of Psychiatry and the Law (AAPL) in 1989, note:

> A treating psychiatrist should generally avoid agreeing to be an expert witness or to perform an evaluation of his patient for legal purposes because a forensic evaluation usually requires that other people be interviewed and testimony may adversely affect the therapeutic relationship.

In a very similar vein, the Specialty Guidelines for Forensic Psychologists indicate the following:

> Forensic psychologists avoid providing professional services to parties in a legal proceeding with whom they have personal or professional relationships that are inconsistent with the anticipated relationship.
>
> When it is necessary to provide both evaluation and treatment services to a party in a legal proceeding (as may be the case in small forensic hospital settings or small communities), the forensic psychologist takes reasonable steps to minimize the potential negative effects of these circumstances on the rights of the party, confidentiality, and the process of treatment and evaluation. (Committee on Ethical Guidelines for Forensic Psychologists, 1991, p. 659)

The Committee on Psychiatry and Law of the Group for the Advancement of Psychiatry (GAP, 1991) concluded in 1991 that "While, in some areas of the country with limited number of mental health practitioners, the therapist may have the role of forensic expert thrust upon him, ordinarily, it is wise to avoid mixing the therapeutic and forensic roles" (p. 44). Similarly, the Ethical Principles of Psychologists and Code of Conduct of the American Psychological Association (APA, 1992) admonishes that "In most circumstances, psychologists avoid performing multiple and potentially conflicting roles in forensic matters" (p. 1610). Finally, the most recent and the most specific of these codes, the American Psychological Association's (1994) guidelines for conducting child custody evaluations, concluded the following:

> Psychologists generally avoid conducting a child custody evaluation in a case in which the psychologist served in a therapeutic role for the child or his or her

immediate family or has had other involvement that may compromise the psychologist's objectivity. This should not, however, preclude the psychologist from testifying in the case as a fact witness concerning treatment of the child. In addition, during the course of a child custody evaluation, a psychologist does not accept any of the involved participants in the evaluation as a therapy client. Therapeutic contact with the child or involved participants following a child custody evaluation is undertaken with caution.

A psychologist asked to testify regarding a therapy client who is involved in a child custody case is aware of the limitations and possible biases inherent in such a role and the possible impact on the ongoing therapeutic relationship. Although the court may require the psychologist to testify as a fact witness regarding factual information he or she became aware of in a professional relationship with a client, that psychologist should decline the role of an expert witness who gives a professional opinion regarding custody and visitation issues (see Ethical Standard 7.03) unless so ordered by the court, (p. 678)

. . .

WHERE THEN SHOULD THE LINE BE DRAWN?

As stated earlier, psychologists and psychiatrists may appropriately testify as treating experts (subject to privilege, confidentiality, and qualifications) without risk of conflict on matters of the reported history as provided by the patient; mental status; the clinical diagnosis; the care provided to the patient and the patient's response to it; the patient's prognosis; the mood, cognitions, or behavior of the patient; and any other relevant statements that the patient made in treatment. These matters, presented in the manner of descriptive "occurrences" and not psycholegal opinions, do not raise issues of judgment, foundation, or historical truth. Therapists do not ordinarily have the requisite database to testify appropriately about psycholegal issues of causation (i.e., the relationship of a specific act to claimant's current condition) or capacity (i.e., the relationship of diagnosis or mental status to legally defined standards of functional capacity). These matters raise problems of judgment, foundation, and historical truth that are problematic for treating experts.

When faced with issues that seem to fall between these guideposts, it is useful to ask whether each opinion is one that could or should have been reached in therapy. Thus, if the legal system did not exist, would therapists be expected to reach these sorts of conclusions on their own? Would doing so ordinarily be considered an aspect of the therapy process? In doing so, would the opinion be considered exploratory, tentative, and speculative, or instead as providing an adequate basis for guiding legal action outside of therapy? Is the therapist generating hypotheses to facilitate treatment or is he or she reasonably scientifically certain that this opinion is accurate? Is it based on something substantially more than, "My patient said so," "My patient would have no reason to lie," or "My patient would not lie to me"?

. . .

REFERENCES

American Academy of Psychiatry and the Law. (1989). *Ethical guidelines for the practice of forensic psychiatry. In Membership directory of American Academy of Psychiatry and the Law* (pp. x–xiii). Bloomfield, CT: Author.

American Psychological Association. (1992). Ethical principles of psychologists and code of conduct. *American Psychologist, 47,* 1597–1611.

American Psychological Association. (1994). Guidelines for child custody evaluations in divorce proceedings. *American Psychologist, 49,* 677–680.

Committee on Ethical Guidelines for Forensic Psychologists. (1991). Specialty guidelines for forensic psychologists. *Law and Human Behavior, 15,* 655–665.

Committee on Psychiatry and Law, Group for the Advancement of Psychiatry. (1991). *The mental health professional and the legal system* (Rep. No. 131). New York: Brunner/ Mazel.

Shuman, D. W. (1983). Testimonial compulsion: The involuntary medical expert witness. *Journal of Legal Medicine, 4,* 419–446.

COMMENTARY: This seminal article was the first—from the perspective of forensic psychology as opposed to forensic psychiatry—to illuminate in a substantial and impactful fashion the potential consequences of what is now commonly recognized as a critical role conflict: the simultaneous or sequential provision of nonforensic and court-related services. The central tenet espoused by Drs. Greenberg and Shuman is that a clinician who is already dedicated to the welfare of a client/patient cannot reasonably or ethically be required or expected to offer what should be an unbiased, unconflicted forensic opinion on that person's legally relevant mental status.

Less recognized but no less relevant are ethical concerns regarding the inversion of the classic clinician-to-expert transformation. It is often the practice of personal injury attorneys, for example, to encourage favorably inclined forensic evaluators to provide follow-up treatment to civil litigants, usually out of a desire to portray the provider at some later date as that person's own "doctor" as opposed to a "hired gun." The forensic psychologist's conflict of interest here is no less palpable, to the potential detriment of all involved.

The following references are recommended for those interested in further investigation of conflicts between therapeutic and forensic roles, reflecting an attempt to identify authors who express varying degrees of concern over the practices in question.

Blackburn, L. B. (2005). The evolution of a forensic case: A transition from treating clinician to expert witness. In R. L. Heilbronner (Ed.), *Forensic neuropsychology casebook* (pp. 185–204). New York, NY: Guilford Press.

Greenberg, S. A., & Shuman, D. W. (2007). When worlds collide: Therapeutic and forensic roles. *Professional Psychology: Research and Practice, 38,* 129–132. http:// dx.doi.org/10.1037/0735-7028.38.2.129

Gutheil, T. G., & Hilliard, J. T. (2001). The treating psychiatrist thrust into the role of expert witness. *Psychiatric Services, 52,* 1526–1527. http://dx.doi.org/10.1176/ appi.ps.52.11.1526

Heltzel, T. (2007). Compatibility of therapeutic and forensic roles. *Professional Psychology: Research and Practice, 38,* 122–128. http://dx.doi.org/10.1037/0735-7028.38.2.122

Iverson, G. L. (2000). Dual relationships in psycholegal evaluations: Treating psychologists serving as expert witnesses. *American Journal of Forensic Psychology, 18,* 79–87.

9.6. Conducting Risk Evaluations for Future Violence: Ethical Practice Is Possible

Anton O. Tolman and Andrea L. Rotzien

. . .

CONDUCTING ETHICAL RISK EVALUATIONS

. . . The goal of ethical practice is to provide the court with information on risk factors, describe whether or not those factors apply in the current context, describe and elaborate the person's history of previous violent behaviors and relate those previous contexts to the person's current and reasonably estimated future situations, and suggest strategies to reduce risk. Ethical and effective risk evaluations are highly responsive to the legal context in which the evaluation is performed (e.g., sentencing evaluations vs. release evaluations in a forensic hospital), consistent with the review by Heilbrun (1997). Ethical practice in this area is based on competent and relevant forensic assessment using modern instruments and methods; education of legal decision makers, if necessary, regarding the elements of the report; careful delineation of the limits of our technology and knowledge; and effective use of scientific reasoning. The role of the risk evaluator as a neutral party and educator for the court on risk issues is consistent with the role of an expert witness and appears to be one of the defining characteristics of forensic evaluators versus clinicians (Tolman & Mullendore, 2003). As an example, there is evidence that judges often may confuse distinct terms such as *psychopath* with *psychosis* and may need assistance in interpreting the risk factors that are present (Tolman & Buehmann, 2004).

It seems obvious to recommend that a mental health professional be competent in the field of risk assessment before stepping into a courtroom, but unfortunately there is evidence that professionals become involved in these cases without adequate preparation (Haag, 2006; Tolman, 2001; Tolman & Mullendore, 2003). Given that the field of risk assessment is rapidly developing and changing, any professional practicing in this field must stay abreast of the evolving guidelines and methods of evaluation. For professionals conducting forensic evaluations, ethical standards have existed for some time, as reflected in the Specialty Guidelines (Committee on Ethical Guidelines for Forensic Psychologists, 1991). These guidelines are currently under revision, but they originally built on and supported the American Psychological Association's Ethical Standards at the time. They emphasize competence, understanding of legal standards and contexts, protection of the legal rights of evaluees, maintenance of objectivity in practice, clarification regarding the boundaries of testimony or reports, and preservation of scientific knowledge regarding one's specialized area of practice. Other professional standards of practice for risk assessments exist such as for evaluating sexual offenders (Association for the Treatment of Sexual Abusers, 2005); these standards have been debated in professional circles and are published and available. Heilbrun (2001) described a set of general principles that apply to most forensic evaluations, depending on the evaluation context. Heilbrun, Marczyk, and DeMatteo (2002) also gave examples of how specific principles apply to risk assessment, including use of relevance and reliability as guides for seeking information and data sources, use of scientific reasoning in assessing the causal connection between clinical condition and functional abilities, identification of relevant forensic issues, clarification of one's role with an attorney, and use of nomothetic evidence in reaching conclusions. Ethical forensic evaluations emphasize the role of the psychologist as an objective evaluator, not an advocate, regardless of which side retained the expert. Practicing psychologists should be aware of and adhere to these ethical principles in conducting evaluations (see also American Educational Research Association, 1999; American Psychological Association, 2002).

Apart from ethical standards, practitioners should be aware that even a cursory review of the scientific risk assessment literature indicates some broad areas of agreement on practice standards for ethical risk evaluations. First, there is almost universal agreement that unstructured clinical techniques are insufficient (e.g., Monahan, 1981). Second, given the strength and stability of the relationship between psychopathy and recidivism, this is a factor that should probably be assessed when evaluating a person's risk for future violence, using an instrument designed for that purpose (e.g., Hare, 2003) and after having received training in its use (see also Gacono, 2000; Hart, 1998; Monahan et al., 2001). Antisocial traits such as poor self-regulation (Hanson & Morton-Bourgon, 2005) have also been linked to violent recidivism. Specific to sexual violence, there is evidence that sexual deviance is strongly related to recidivism (Hanson & Morton-Bourgon, 2005). Miller, Amenta, and Conroy (2005) noted that assessment devices for sexual deviance are limited; however, Hanson and Morton-Bourgon (2005) found that many experts use clinical interviews and self-report measures to diagnose pedophilia or paraphilias. Although some clinicians may shy away from self-report measures with offenders, a recent meta-analysis by Walters (2006) indicated that self-report measures and standardized risk appraisal measures performed equally in predicting institutional adjustment and recidivism. According to Walters, the self-report measures that tap into issues directly related to recidivism (e.g., criminal attitudes) perform better than more general instruments such as personality inventories. In addition, most actuarial measures designed for evaluating sexual offenders include items for assessing sexual deviance. Walters also found that self-report measures and risk appraisal measures account for unique variance in outcomes. This provides some support for combining these methods.

Third, risk evaluations should review other known risk factors related to the context of the evaluation (e.g., Hanson & Bussiere, 1998; Harris et al., 2003; Quinsey et al., 1998), a task that is enhanced through the use of actuarial (e.g., Quinsey et al., 1998) and guided clinical instruments (e.g., Webster et al., 1997) and not rely solely on traditional clinical instruments and techniques. Earlier we provided several comprehensive resources for more information on these instruments.

Fourth, an expert should consider dynamic risk factors as well as potential protective factors and base rates (Douglas & Skeem, 2005; Rogers, 2000; Webster, Hucker, & Bloom, 2002) in evaluating risk; it should be noted that the guided clinical instruments such as the HCR–20 already enjoin consideration of dynamic factors as part of the instrument. The impact of treatment on dynamic factors and consequently recidivism is not yet clear (Miller et al., 2005). However, Douglas and Skeem (2005) provided an excellent review of the most promising dynamic factors with regard to violence risk assessment.

Fifth, forensic evaluators should make use of collateral data sources and assess multiple domains of functioning, as well as address issues of risk management and risk reduction (e.g., Hart, 2001). We acknowledge that integrating these sources and variables can be difficult. We have found Heilbrun (2001), Heilbrun et al. (2002), and Gacono (2000) particularly helpful with regard to synthesizing report information.

CONCLUSION

The debate about the nature and ethics of conducting risk evaluations has been going on for more than two decades and will continue. We note that the issue of admissibility of risk evaluations under *Daubert v. Merrell Dow Pharmaceuticals*, or even the older *Frye v. United States* (1923) standard, is not a psychological determination. The trial judges, as monitored by the appellate courts, determine what proffered evidence or testimony will be admitted under *Frye* or *Daubert*. Preliminary evidence (Tolman & Rhodes, 2005) suggests that 96% of cases involving the PCL–R (Hare, 2003) and 93% of cases involving the Static–99 (Harris et al., 2003) in at least 23 jurisdictions were found by U.S. federal and state courts to be admissible either explicitly or implicitly. In addition, the number of articles, books, and conference talks dedicated to issues of risk management would certainly suggest that the practice is generally accepted.

The real-world context of risk evaluations is that courts want and need information about individuals' potential risk of engaging in future violence to make crucial decisions on a regular basis. The reality of risk evaluations is that substantial and compelling progress (e.g., Hanson, 2005) has been made in our identification of risk factors known to be linked to violence and in the development of both actuarial and guided clinical instruments to assist practitioners in reducing bias, ensuring adequate review of key known risk factors, and improving consistency in their reports compared with the past. The practical reality for many involved with the justice system would be that without state-of-the-art risk assessment and management information, decisions would be made about their future and their liberty based on prejudice, bias, social myths, and irrelevant contextual factors. The real world of risk evaluations is that a decision on whether these evaluations are ethical or not hinges on the context in which the evaluations occur and in the degree of knowledge, competence, and proficiency of the examiner.

We suggest that it is time to move beyond simple black-and-white questions of whether risk evaluations are ethical or not. Psychologists involved in training and continuing education programs need to more clearly define the boundary lines between forensic and clinical practice (e.g., Greenberg & Shuman, 1997; Tolman & Mullendore, 2003) and should develop and implement explicit empirical and theoretical models for teaching psychologists about issues related to risk factors, dangerousness, and ethical assessment (e.g., Tolman, 2001). Practicing psychologists should become involved in educational innovation and interdisciplinary efforts between psychology and law to enhance the understanding of the legal system among psychologists and to enhance attorneys' and judges' abilities to recognize unethical and improper evaluations when they see them. Research psychologists should continue research into understanding how to improve the ability to predict and manage violence risk based on dynamic and protective factors (e.g., Douglas, Webster, Hart, Eaves, & Ogloff, 2001). The literature base needs to be expanded in contexts in which there is relatively little current information (e.g., risk evaluations in spousal abuse cases, stalking, custody). Further clarification and consensus building regarding a more specific standard of practice for risk evaluations would enhance psychologists' standing in the courts and in our profession.

REFERENCES

American Educational Research Association. (1999). *Standards for educational and psychological testing*. Washington, DC: Author.

American Psychological Association. (2002). Ethical principles of psychologists and code of conduct. *American Psychologist, 57*, 1052–1059.

Association for the Treatment of Sexual Abusers. (2005). *Practice standards for the evaluation, treatment and management of adult sexual abusers*. Beaverton, OR: Author.

Committee on Ethical Guidelines for Forensic Psychologists. (1991). Specialty guidelines for forensic psychologists. *Law and Human Behavior, 15*, 655–665.

Daubert v. Merrell Dow Pharmaceuticals, Inc., 509 U.S. 579 (1993).

Douglas, K. S., & Skeem, J. L. (2005). Violence risk assessment: Getting specific about being dynamic. *Psychology, Public Policy, and Law, 11*, 347–383.

Douglas, K. S., Webster, C. D., Hart, S. D., Eaves, D., & Ogloff, J. R. P. (Eds.). (2001). *HCR–20 violence risk management companion guide*. Burnaby, British Columbia, Canada: Simon Fraser University, Mental Health, Law, and Policy Institute.

Frye v. United States, 293 F. 1013 (D.C. Cir. 1923).

Gacono, C. B. (Ed.). (2000). *The clinical and forensic assessment of psychopathy: A practitioner's guide*. Mahwah, NJ: Erlbaum.

Greenberg, S. A., & Shuman, D. W. (1997). Irreconcilable conflict between therapeutic and forensic roles. *Professional Psychology: Research and Practice, 28,* 50–57.

Haag, A. M. (2006). Ethical dilemmas faced by correctional psychologists in Canada. *Criminal Justice and Behavior, 33,* 93–109.

Hanson, R. K. (2005). Twenty years of progress in violence risk assessment. *Journal of Interpersonal Violence, 20,* 212–217.

Hanson, R. K., & Bussiere, M. T. (1998). Predicting relapse: A meta-analysis of sexual offender recidivism studies. *Journal of Consulting and Clinical Psychology, 66,* 348–362.

Hanson, R. K., & Morton-Bourgon, K. E. (2005). The characteristics of persistent sexual offenders: A meta-analysis of recidivism studies. *Journal of Consulting and Clinical Psychology, 73,* 1154–1163.

Hare, R. D. (2003). *Psychopathy Checklist—Revised (2nd ed.) technical manual.* Toronto, Ontario, Canada: Multi-Health Systems.

Harris, A. J. R., Phenix, A., Hanson, R. K., & Thornton, D. (2003). *Static–99 coding rules revised.* Ottawa, Canada: Office of Public Safety and Emergency Preparedness. Retrieved November 8, 2005, from http://www.sgc.gc.ca/corrections/publications_e.asp#2003

Hart, S. D. (1998). Psychopathy and the risk for violence. In D. J. Cooke, A. E. Forth, & R. D. Hare (Eds.), *Psychopathy: Theory, research, and implications for society* (pp. 355–373). Dordrecht, the Netherlands: Kluwer Academic.

Hart, S. D. (2001). Assessing and managing violence risk. In K. S. Douglas, C. D. Webster, S. D. Hart, D. Eaves, & J. R. P. Ogloff (Eds.), *HCR–20 violence risk management companion guide* (pp. 13–26). Burnaby, British Columbia: Simon Fraser University, Mental Health, Law, and Policy Institute.

Heilbrun, K. (1997). Prediction versus management models relevant to risk assessment: The importance of legal decision-making context. *Law and Human Behavior, 21,* 347–359.

Heilbrun, K. (2001). *Principles of forensic mental health assessment.* New York: Kluwer Academic/Plenum.

Heilbrun, K., Marczyk, G. R., & DeMatteo, D. (2002). *Forensic mental health assessment: A casebook.* Oxford, England: Oxford University Press.

Miller, H. A., Amenta, A. E., & Conroy, M. A. (2005). Sexually violent predator evaluations: Empirical evidence, strategies for professionals, and research directions. *Law and Human Behavior, 29,* 29–54.

Monahan, J. (1981). *The clinical prediction of violent behavior. In Crime and delinquency issues: A monograph series* (Publication No. ADM 81-921). Washington, DC: U.S. Government Printing Office.

Monahan, J., Steadman, H. J., Silver, E., Appelbaum, P. S., Robbins, P. C., Mulvey, E. P., et al. (2001). *Rethinking risk assessment: The MacArthur Study of Mental Disorder and Violence.* Oxford, England: Oxford University Press.

Quinsey, V. L., Harris, G. T., Rice, M. E., & Cormier, C. A. (1998). *Violent offenders: Appraising and managing risk.* Washington, DC: American Psychological Association.

Rogers, R. (2000). The uncritical acceptance of acceptance of risk assessment in forensic practice. *Law and Human Behavior, 24,* 595–605.

Tolman, A. O. (2001). Clinical training and the duty to protect. *Behavioral Sciences and the Law, 19,* 387–404.

Tolman, A. O., & Buehmann, E. (2004, June). *Judicial perceptions of expert risk assessment.* Paper presented at the Fourth Annual Conference of the International Association of Forensic Mental Health Services, Stockholm, Sweden.

Tolman, A. O., & Mullendore, K. B. (2003). Risk evaluations for the courts: Is service quality a function of specialization? *Professional Psychology: Research and Practice, 34,* 225–232.

Tolman, A. O., & Rhodes, J. (2005, March). *The admissibility of actuarial risk instruments in federal and state courts: Current status.* Paper presented at the annual conference of the American Psychology-Law Society, San Diego, CA.

Walters, G. D. (2006). Risk appraisal versus self-report in the prediction of criminal justice outcomes: A meta-analysis. *Criminal Justice and Behavior, 33,* 279–304.

Webster, C. D., Douglas, K. S., Eaves, D., & Hart, S. D. (1997). *HCR–20: Assessing risk for violence* (Version 2). Burnaby, British Columbia, Canada: Simon Fraser University, Mental Health, Law, and Policy Institute.

Webster, C. D., Hucker, S. J., & Bloom, H. (2002). Transcending the actuarial versus clinical polemic in assessing risk for violence [Special issue: Risk assessment]. *Criminal Justice and Behavior, 29,* 659–665.

COMMENTARY: The oft-cited perspective that forensic psychologists cannot conclusively predict the occurrence or nonoccurrence of future violent behavior for a given individual has led many to question whether we should allow ourselves to be inveigled into such evaluations in the first place. Undoubtedly, it was in recognition of such concerns that Drs. Tolman and Rotzien chose to emphasize that ethical practice is "possible" instead of simply laying out ethical requirements for optimal professional conduct in this context.

As difficult as reaching a scientifically supportable conclusion in such cases is conveying to courts, institutions, and other relevant parties just how certain that conclusion should be regarded to be. Risk evaluations—formerly termed dangerousness evaluations but relabeled for just such reasons—are often highly prized by a legal decision-maker less because of a belief in their validity than a desire to find someone willing to shoulder the responsibility for addressing what all involved tacitly recognize as an insoluble dilemma.

The following references are recommended for those interested in further investigation of the ethical ramifications of conducting risk evaluations for future violence, with a focus on different populations and settings and the validity of statistically influenced decisions.

Desmarais, S. L., Nicholls, T. L., Read, J. D., & Brink, J. (2010). Confidence and accuracy in assessments of short-term risks presented by forensic psychiatric patients. *Journal of Forensic Psychiatry & Psychology, 21*(1), 1–22. http://dx.doi.org/10.1080/14789940903183932

McGuire, J. (2004). Minimising harm in violence risk assessment: Practical solutions to ethical problems? *Health, Risk & Society, 6,* 327–345. http://dx.doi.org/10.1080/13698570412331323225

Olver, M. E., & Jung, S. (2017). Incremental prediction of intimate partner violence: An examination of three risk measures. *Law and Human Behavior, 41,* 440–453. http://dx.doi.org/10.1037/lhb0000251

Russo, A. C. (2013). Ethical, legal and risk management considerations in the neuropsychological assessment of veterans. *Psychological Injury and Law, 6*(1), 21–30.

Viljoen, J. L., McLachlan, K., & Vincent, G. M. (2010). Assessing violence risk and psychopathy in juvenile and adult offenders: A survey of clinical practices. *Assessment, 17,* 377–395. http://dx.doi.org/10.1177/1073191109359587

9.7. Law, Ethics, and Competence

David Breiger, Kristen Bishop, and G. Andrew H. Benjamin

All children ages 3 to 21 who have a mental, physical, or emotional impairment that affects the ability to learn are entitled to additional support and services to help them access a meaningful education. The federally funded Early Intervention Program (Part C of the Individuals With Disabilities Education Improvement Act of 2004) also provides special education services for children younger than 3 years. The legal rights of children with disabilities include evaluation, an appropriate educational program, and due process protections. Both federal and state laws protect the educational rights of students with disabilities. Although state laws differ among the 50 jurisdictions, and the different districts within each jurisdiction may interpret and implement the laws somewhat differently (Lai & Berkeley, 2012; MacFarlane & Kanaya, 2009), the federal laws have raised standards across the jurisdictions. Nevertheless, differences do exist:

> By examining the legal code, we found wide variability in eligibility criteria between the states. It is important to recognize that this variability has the largest impact on children who are clinically diagnosed with [an autism-spectrum disorder] (e.g., Asperger's disorder). An ASD child would qualify for Autism services in a state that includes ASDs in their eligibility but may fail to do so in a state that requires a clinical diagnosis of Autism. In these latter cases, children with ASDs will likely be placed into "Other Health Impairment" or "Emotional Disturbance." (MacFarlane & Kanaya, 2009, p. 667)

Psychologists who work in this arena should obtain the written standards and procedures of the school district and the department of education in the state or territory where they will practice (for a directory of the state and territory education agencies, see http://wdcrobcolp01.ed.gov/programs/erod/org_list.cfm?category_ID=SEA).

Significant differences exist among legal, psychological, and educational professionals in the ways they approach data collection and the synthesis of information in the educational context. Legal professionals must frame their work within the pertinent judicial and legal standards. Psychologists gather information from semistructured clinical interviews, psychological testing, self-report measurement, third party collateral reports, and relevant records.

These data are transformed into a cohesive summary that guides recommendations about how to promote child adjustment. Educational professionals depend more on functional and academic information about the child, including that culled from in-class assessments (often called *curriculum-based measures*) that are completed by the general education teacher.

These differences translate into important practical considerations for psychologists conducting educational evaluations. Application of scientific values (e.g., arriving at a conclusion only after multiple-measure corroboration) in psychological assessment is one of the highest priorities in evaluations, yet it is important to ensure that the information gathered for these assessments is obtained within the constraints of the legal rules and will have practical usefulness within the educational context: "Recommendations are much more likely to be integrated into the [individualized education plan] when they address needs specific to the school environment" (Ernst, Pelletier, & Simpson, 2008, p. 968). Access to and use of data must both meet the ethical standards for psychologists as well as the constraints of legal rules. It is critical that psychologists incorporate into their assessment process an understanding of the prevailing legal standards (e.g., obtaining the local school district and state standards and procedures that flesh out the federal law; American Psychological Association, 2002, 2010). The more psychologists use the terms of the substantive law to organize their recitation of the evaluation's findings, the more likely it is that legal and educational professionals will find the discussion of psychological reports useful. Indeed, psychology's ethical guidelines call for the exercise of such knowledge: "When assuming forensic roles, psychologists are or become reasonably familiar with the judicial or administrative rules governing their roles" (American Psychological Association, 2010, Standard 2.01f; http://www.apa.org/ethics/code/index.aspx?item=5).

To facilitate an understanding of the primary legal and scientific considerations in conducting evaluations, in this chapter we highlight both the legally crafted standards used in educational cases and the scientific considerations in conducting evaluations in school settings.

EVALUATION FOR SERVICES UNDER THE EDUCATION LAWS

. . . Section 504 of the Rehabilitation Act of 1973 (Nondiscrimination on the Basis of Handicap, 34 C.F.R. § 104 (2010)) and IDEIA have created the legal framework that prevents states from allowing school districts to exclude children with disabilities.

Requests for evaluations (a referral for a special education evaluation used to be called a *focus of concern*) typically are made by parents. School districts will expect a written referral, and no action will occur unless such a referral is made. District policy will also specify whether the referral goes to the school principal or a specific district representative.

Requests should urge that the school evaluate the child in all areas related to the specific concerns about the child under both Section 504 and IDEIA, because the child may not be eligible for special education under the more narrow standards of IDEIA. Psychologists can assist parents in formulating a sufficient request by urging them to submit supporting records from the health care providers who have evaluated or treated the child, delineate concrete examples based on their own observations about the specific concerns, and integrate the corroborating evidence from the health care records and observations about the specific concerns in their request.

The school district should confirm that the request for evaluation was received and provide written notification of the decision about whether the child's concerns will be evaluated after a review of the school's records and the parents' request occurs. Although no evaluation timelines are established in Section 504, IDEIA specifies that once the parents provide consent, an initial evaluation to determine whether the child has a disability shall be conducted within 60 days (20 U.S.C. § 1414(a)(1)(C)(i)(I)). State laws typically will establish a timeline for notification and content of the notification.

Legal Process if the School Agrees to Evaluate or Decides to Pursue an Evaluation

Before the district conducts any evaluation of the child, the parents must consent. The district may pursue a hearing if the parents refuse to provide consent (20 U.S.C. § 1414(a)(1)(D)(ii)). Once consent has been obtained to evaluate the child for special education eligibility, an initial evaluation is conducted to determine whether the child has a disability (20 U.S.C. § 1414(a)(1)(C)(i)(I)). State laws typically specify the time frame within which the district must complete the evaluation and determine whether the child needs special education services. It is possible for the district and parents to decide on another timeline, although such a decision should be documented.

Under the law, assessment in all areas of suspected disability must occur. If the district has stopped the evaluation once a student is found eligible for special education in a particular area, and has not addressed the other concerns raised by the parents, the parents have the right to insist on a comprehensive evaluation in all areas of concern (20 U.S.C. § 1414(b)(3)(B)).

Relevant functional, developmental, and academic data about the student must be collected using a variety of assessment approaches (20 U.S.C. § 1414(b)(2)(A)). Evaluation tests cannot discriminate on the basis of race, culture, or gender; any testing must be conducted in the student's native language or other mode of communication, such as American Sign Language (20 U.S.C.§ 1414(b)(3)(A)). Although district staff will conduct most of the assessment, they must seek external expertise if particular assessment skills are outside of the scope of their training. This is often the point at which psychologists become involved in the process. If the district seeks further clarification by engaging outside expertise, it is their responsibility to fund the evaluation. Sometimes the district may ask a family to use its insurance benefits or other sources of funding, but if the family refuses, the district must pay for any outside evaluations.

An eligibility-determination group will focus on the evaluation to determine whether the student has a disability and if so, how the disability affects the student's progress in school and what services would likely address his or her individual needs. Before such a team meeting, the parents may request the evaluation results. That way, if the results do not address the parents' concerns, they will be better prepared to insist on an independent educational evaluation (IEE) and have such a request granted if other, contradictory data suggest that the school district's evaluation is insufficient. The parents should seek outside consultation from a psychologist to help them organize the contradictory data into a compelling narrative. Note that the law does not preclude the parents' consultant from interacting with the appropriate school personnel before and during the eligibility-determination group's meeting.

School districts must identify one person in each district to coordinate their efforts to comply with Section 504. Under the law, each district must identify the procedures and the name of the person designated as a Section 504 compliance officer (Designation of Responsible Employee, 34 C.F.R § 104.7 (2010)). Before the eligibility-determination group meets, parents should request that the district's Section 504 program representative participate as part of the group. If the student is deemed to not be eligible for special education under IDEIA, services may still be provided under Section 504. In most states, parents must be given notice of the meeting; they have the right to attend it, and parents should request to be a part of the eligibility-determination team. However, recent research findings suggest that the procedures for implementing Section 504 differ markedly from district to district:

> There is a disturbing inconsistency related to how students are determined to be eligible under Section 504 . . . only 54% of the respondents indicated that a disability must be diagnosed for a student to be eligible to receive Section 504 services. Likewise, only 61% indicated that a significant impairment to a major life function must be established for a student to be eligible to receive Section 504 services. (Madaus & Shaw, 2007, p. 374)

Parents will be provided a copy of the evaluation report and documentation about the district's decision regarding eligibility.

Most states' laws include a time frame within which the eligibility decision for special education must be announced and another time frame within which an individualized education program (IEP) is designed. A specialized team crafts the IEP, which details the instruction and services a student with disabilities should receive. The IEP team usually is made up of the following people (20 U.S.C.§ 1414(d)(1)(B)):

- parent or guardian;

- at least one of the child's general education teachers;

- at least one of the child's special education teachers or, where appropriate, special education provider;

- a district representative, such as a director of special education;

- an individual who can interpret the evaluation data;

- the child (if appropriate); and

- transition service providers (e.g., vocational specialists or someone from an outside agency, such as a representative from the state's Office of Developmental Disabilities).

The team is not limited to the people in this list. IDEIA specifically allows others who "have knowledge or special expertise regarding the child" to participate on the IEP team. The team certainly could include a consulting psychologist hired by the parents. Both the district and the parent have the right to decide who has the expertise regarding the child and to suggest who else should serve on the team. Most states require that the district notify the parents of the purpose of the IEP meeting, its time and location, and who will be attending. If necessary, meetings can occur by telephone or videoconference (20 U.S.C. § 1414(f)).

Sometimes members of the IEP team may have to miss one or more IEP meetings. The parents and the school district may agree in writing to excuse a team member from a meeting, even if the meeting involves a discussion regarding the team member's specialization. The IEP team member who is excused, though, must submit written input about the development of the IEP to the parents and the school district before the meeting (20 U.S.C. §§ 1414(d)(1)(B)–(C)).

The mandatory contents of an IEP should guide the psychologist as to how to arrange the psychological evidence under the concrete categories within the Impressions section of the final report (see Chapter 5, this volume). The IEP must include the following (20 U.S.C. § 1414(d) (1)(A)):

- a statement about the child's current levels of education and functional performance;

- annual educational goals;

- a statement about how the child's progress will be measured and when periodic reports in the child's progress should be provided;

- descriptions of all services a child will receive, both in the general education classroom setting and in a special education setting;

- a description of "related services" the student will receive, such as speech and language therapy, psychotherapy, and so on;

- a description of all program modifications to be provided, such as modified reading materials, a reader for examinations and other assignments, and tape recorder for lectures;

- a determination of whether the child needs assistive technology devices and services (i.e., equipment that enhances or maintains the capabilities of the student, e.g., a computer or custom keyboard);

- a decision about eligibility for adaptive physical education and, if the student is eligible, how this will be provided;

- a description of how the student will participate in general education classes and activities and if not, why;

- any accommodations the student will have for taking state or district achievement tests;

- extended school year services, if determined necessary by the IEP team;

- aversive interventions, if any, required for the student;

- the location, duration, and frequency of the services to be delivered;

- dates on which services will begin; and

- transition services that would begin no later than the IEP.

To be in effect when the student turns 16 (or younger, if determined appropriate by the IEP team), two specific services must be provided to prepare the child for an adult life to promote movement from school to postschool activities, including college, vocational training programs, independent living programs, and supported employment (20 U.S.C. § 1414(d)(1)(A)(i)(vIII)): (a) appropriate measurable postsecondary goals and (b) specific transition services needed to assist the student in reaching those goals.

Before an IEP is implemented, the parents must agree to the services. A school district cannot override the parents' refusal to consent to the initiation of special education services (20 U.S.C.§ 1414(a)(1)(D)(ii)). However, if the child is found eligible for special education and an IEP is never implemented because of lack of parental consent, it is possible that services under Section 504 can be provided.

IEPs are supposed to be reviewed annually, but if a review does not occur, that district must continue to follow the existing plan. An IEP meeting can be requested before the annual review to delineate what services identified in the IEP are being delivered, what behaviors of the child have not changed, and how the placement of the child should change. The revised IEP should anticipate a child's changing needs and incorporate new information that has emerged during the provision of services up to that point. A request of any team member, or a change of circumstances, can lead to an IEP team meeting review. Written documentation, without a meeting, can change the child's IEP if the parents and district agree to the changes (20 U.S.C. § 1414(d)(3)(D)).

Comprehensive reevaluations, with testing, of the child must occur once every 3 years (20 U.S.C. § 1414(a)(2)(B)(ii)). If the school district determines that the educational service needs of the child warrant a reevaluation, or if the parent or teacher requests a reevaluation, the comprehensive reevaluation must be done (20 U.S.C. § 1414(a)(2)(A)).

Legal Process if the School Declines to Evaluate the Child or Denies Eligibility

Parents can challenge the district's decision if the school declines to evaluate the child or the child is denied eligibility for special education services. In some instances, the district's evaluation methodology will not reveal subtle neuro-psychological conditions that affect learning; some neurocognitive and sensori-motor deficits will avoid identification with the psychoeducational methodology used by school district personnel (Ernst et al., 2008).

Parents can request an IEE at the district's expense by a qualified person who is not an employee of the district (Independent Educational Evaluation, 34 C.F.R. § 300.502(a)(3)(i) (2010)). The parents can request an IEE if concerns arise about the school's decision or the results of the district's evaluation; such a request may be necessary for the district to fully involve the parents in the planning and implementation of services (Schrank, Miller, Caterino, & Desrochers, 2006). Although school districts typically have a list of the evaluators who can perform IEEs (Independent Educational Evaluation, 34 C.F.R § 300.502(a)(2) (2010)), they can be done by someone who is not on the district's list (Independent Educational Evaluation, 34 C.F.R § 300.502(a)(3)(i) (2010)). unless the school district objects to the IEE, the district must pay for it (Independent Educational Evaluation, 34 C.F.R § 300.502(b)(2) (2010)). At a hearing that must occur without unnecessary delay, if the hearing officer determines that the district's evaluation is appropriate, the family still has a right to an independent evaluation, at the parents' expense (Independent Educational Evaluation, 34 C.F.R § 300.502(b)(3) (2010)). Parents are entitled to one IEE at public expense each time the district conducts an evaluation with which the parents disagree (Independent Educational Evaluation, 34 C.F.R § 300.502(b)(5) (2010)).

If the district balks at paying for the IEE, the parents, in consultation with their psychologist, should attempt to negotiate with the school district about the IEE parameters. A district will be less likely to force the matter into a hearing if it believes that the parents are acting reasonably. Parents should consider making the following suggestions to the district (Ernst et al., 2008; TeamChild, 2008):

- suggest three independent evaluators with whom the district has worked before and with whom the school district appears to have developed good working relationships;

- identify a cap for the cost of the IEE or agree to split the cost in some way; and

- delineate the specific school district input, in addition to a thorough records review, by identifying in advance the collateral interviews that would occur with the teacher, principal (or his or her representative), and the district evaluation specialist.

If no compromise can be arranged quickly, the district must move forward and either request a hearing or fund the IEE. Evidence of the parents attempting to act reasonably with the district in light of its flat refusal to fund the evaluation will carry some weight with the hearing officer.

. . .

SECTION 504 OF THE REHABILITATION ACT

All programs that receive federal funding, including schools, must not discriminate against people on the basis of disability. Congress intended that the Rehabilitation Act of 1973 would remove barriers so that people with disabilities could fully participate in activities such as school (Definitions, 34 C.F.R. § 104.3(k)(2) (2010)). Section 504 of this law defines a disability as an impairment that substantially limits a major life activity (Definitions, 34 C.F.R. § 104.3(j)(1)(i) (2010)). As we have noted, Section 504 establishes a broader definition of disability than does IDEIA, and thus many more children qualify for services under the former legislation than the latter. School districts are financially more at risk for not complying with Section 504 than with IDEIA:

> When civil rights violations of students with disabilities is demonstrated, any federal funds can be pulled, whereas under IDEIA, only those specific IDEIA funds will be revoked for violations . . . a [lawsuit] from a civil rights violation could potentially affect a school district at a much broader level, including within general education itself. (Schraven & Jolly, 2010, p. 429)

Under Section 504, school districts are required to identify students who may have disabilities and evaluate the extra support those students might need in order to obtain an education. School districts must use valid assessment tools that are administered by trained people and tailored to test the specific questions at hand so that the results accurately reflect the child's needs (Evaluation and Placement, 34 C.F.R. § 104.35(a) (2010)). No specific timelines for the district to finish the evaluation are established by law. Parents and other education advocates may initiate the evaluation for Section 504 services. Parental consent is not required to conduct an initial Section 504 evaluation.

Section 504 requires periodic reevaluation of the children who receive services under that law, although reevaluation has to occur only once every 3 years (Evaluation and Placement, 34 C.F.R. § 104.35(a) (2010)). Section 504 also requires a reevaluation if the school district proposes significant changes to the child's services. Unfortunately, Section 504 fails to require that the plan be established in writing. Nor is there clarity about the membership of the team that makes decisions regarding placement and services, based on the evaluation data, and the resources that may be available within the district. Parents and consulting psychologists are not precluded from being part of the 504 team (Evaluation and Placement, 34 C.F.R. § 104.35(c)(3) (2010)). The plan may include a broad range of services (Nonacademic Services 34 C.F.R. §§ 104.37, 104.43–104.47 (2010)). Unless an IEP or Section 504 plan requires that services be rendered in another setting, the child must be educated in the school that he or she would attend if not disabled, and he or she must be incorporated into mainstream classroom activities (Educational Setting, 34 C.F.R. § 104.34(a) (2010)).

Section 504 requires that school districts develop dispute-resolution procedures, such as notice, an opportunity for parents to examine relevant records, an impartial hearing with the opportunity for participation by parents and representation by counsel, and a review procedure (Procedural Safeguards,

34 C.F.R. § 104.36 (2010)). As we noted earlier, each district must have a written set of its procedures and an identified Section 504 coordinator.

CONCLUSION

An understanding of the laws governing special education is necessary to ensure that an evaluation used to help determine a child's eligibility for special education services or accommodations meets the criteria set forth by federal and state statutes. These laws—Section 504 of the Rehabilitation Act of 1973 (Nondiscrimination on the Basis of Handicap, 34 C.F.R. § 104 (2010)) and IDEIA—define concepts such as disability as they pertain to educational settings and set forth the requirements to protect children from discrimination. It is important for psychologists to be familiar with not only the definitions of key concepts but also the processes used to determine eligibility and to manage disagreements between families and schools. Psychologists who are familiar with the laws that govern special education, the processes used to determine eligibility, and how to work within the school environment are in a good position to conduct useful and helpful evaluations. Such evaluations can facilitate the work of the school team and family as they collaborate in developing an environment in which the child will be successful.

REFERENCES

American Psychological Association. (2002). Ethical principles of psychologists and code of conduct. *American Psychologist*, 57, 1060–1073.

American Psychological Association. (2010). 2010 amendments to the 2002 "Ethical Principles of Psychologists and Code of Conduct." *American Psychologist*, 65, 493.

Definitions, 34 C.F.R. § 104.3 (2010).

Designation of Responsible Employee and Adoption of Grievance Procedures, 34 C. F. R. § 104.7 (2010).

Educational Setting, 34 CFR 104.34 (2010).

Ernst, W. J., Pelletier, S. L. F., & Simpson, G. (2008). Neuropsychological consultation with school personnel: What clinical neuropsychologists need to know. *The Clinical Neuropsychologist*, 22, 953–976. doi:10 1080/138540407 01676591

Evaluation and Placement, 34 C.F.R. § 104.35 (2010).

Independent Educational Evaluation, 34 C.F.R. § 300.502 (2010).

Individuals With Disabilities Education Improvement Act of 2004, 20 U.S.C. § 1400 *et seq.*

Lai, S. A., & Berkeley, S. (2012). High-stakes test accommodations: Research and practice. *Learning Disability Quarterly*, 35, 158–169.

MacFarlane, J. R., & Kanaya, T. (2009). What does it mean to be autistic? Interstate variation in special education criteria for autism services. *Journal of Child and Family Studies*, 18, 662–669. doi:10.1007/s10826-009-9268-8

Madaus, J. W., & Shaw, S. F. (2007). The role of school professionals in implementing section 504 for students with disabilities. *Educational Policy*, 22, 363–378. doi:10.1177/0895904807307069

Nonacademic Services, 34 C.F.R. § 104.37 (2010).

Nondiscrimination on the Basis of Handicap in Programs or Activities Receiving Federal Financial Assistance, 34 C. F. R. § 104 (2010).

Procedural Safeguards, 34 CFR 104.36 (2010).

Rehabilitation Act of 1973, 29 U.S.C. § 701 *et seq.*

Schrank, F. A., Miller, J. A., Caterino, L. C., & Desrochers, J. (2006). American Academy of School Psychology survey on the independent educational evaluation for a specific learning disability: Results and discussion. *Psychology in the Schools, 43,* 771–780. doi:10.1002/pits.20187

Schraven, J., & Jolly, J. L. (2010). Section 504 in American public schools: An ongoing response to change. *American Educational Historical Journal, 37,* 419–436.

TeamChild. (2008). *Make a difference in a child's life: A manual for helping children and youth get what they need in school.* Retrieved from http://www.dshs.wa.gov/pdf/ca/TeamChildMannual.pdf

COMMENTARY: The psychologist who conducts an evaluation of a child with special needs may not think that he or she is doing so for legally related reasons, but the passage of time almost invariably proves otherwise. Determining appropriate levels of support—and identifying which parties are responsible for the funding and provision of services—are exercises increasingly likely to play out in a court of law. Ethical concerns are heightened when legal involvement looms.

One increasingly observed phenomenon is the extent to which modern schools wind up filing criminal charges against children with disabilities. Conduct that was once considered a predictable by-product of clinically based behavioral dysfunction can assume a vastly different meaning in the context of what may be long-standing battles between families and school districts over placement and benefits. Caught in the middle of such conflicts—with attendant ethical concerns—are forensic evaluators, school psychologists, and external consultants whose typical efforts may wind up having broader implications than previously assumed.

The following references are recommended for those interested in further investigation of ethical dimensions of educational evaluations of children with special needs. Particular emphasis is placed on autism spectrum disorder, bullying, and other contemporary foci.

Fox, M. (2002). The education of children with special educational needs: Evidence or value driven? *Educational and Child Psychology, 19*(3), 42–53.

Freeman, B. W., Thompson, C., & Jaques, C. (2012). Forensic aspects and assessment of school bullying. *Psychiatric Clinics of North America, 35,* 877–900. http://dx.doi.org/10.1016/j.psc.2012.08.007

Kroncke, A. P., Willard, M., & Huckabee, H. (2016). *Assessment of autism spectrum disorder: Critical issues in clinical, forensic, and school settings.* Cham, Switzerland: Springer International.

Petrenko, C. L. M., Culhane, S. E., Garrido, E. F., & Taussig, H. N. (2011). Do youth in out-of-home care receive recommended mental health and educational services following screening evaluations? *Children and Youth Services Review, 33,* 1911–1918. http://dx.doi.org/10.1016/j.childyouth.2011.05.015

Steinnes, J. (2011). The knight of faith: Ethics in special needs education. *Journal of Moral Education, 40,* 457–469. http://dx.doi.org/10.1080/03057240.2011.618777

9.8. Legal and Ethical Pitfalls

Michael Karson and Lavita Nadkarni

Principle: Be humble with respect to rules of evidence, rules of ethics, and the tendency to resolve anxiety by ignoring competing evidence and explanations.

Some laws and regulations just do not make sense. For example, the Sex Offender Management Board in Colorado requires the use of a test that in other jurisdictions is not allowed in court because it fails to meet scientific standards. What is a conscientious practitioner to do? One solution is to ignore the rulings in other jurisdictions; another is to ignore the rule in Colorado. Adopting the former will lead to poor clinical practice when the basis of the rulings in other jurisdictions is not used to discredit or delimit the test results. Adopting the latter solution will lead to professional and possibly civil sanctions. The simple solution is not to conduct evaluations of sex offenders in Colorado, but aside from that possibility, what is needed is due consideration of the regulatory requirements and the criticisms of the test. So the ethical thing to do is to administer the test and to interpret the results in light of criticisms of the test's validity. The point is that you cannot ignore even bad ethical and legal rules any more than you can ignore bad statutes in other areas of life. In this chapter, we cover some common pitfalls by emphasizing the fact that forensic clinicians can use what they know about rule-breakers and apply that knowledge to themselves when they are the potential rule-breakers.

TERMS TO KNOW

A word is in order about the terms *ethical* and *legal*. *Ethical,* at least in professions that have written standards, applies to conduct that comports with the written requirements of one's profession; if there is not a professional rule against one's conduct, it is not unethical. *Legal* applies to conduct that comports with the statutes, common (judge-made) law, and regulations of one's governments (usually state and federal in the United States); if there is not a law against conduct or a law requiring an omitted behavior, it is not illegal. Sometimes, people use the word *ethical* as a substitute for *professional* or *moral,* but properly it should refer to an ethics code (in the context of practicing psychology and writing forensic reports). *Unprofessional* refers to behavior that the

From *Principles of Forensic Report Writing* (pp. 119–128), by M. Karson and L. Nadkarni, 2013, Washington, DC: American Psychological Association. Copyright 2013 by the American Psychological Association.

speaker thinks would be condemned by a substantial majority of the members of the profession in question. *Immoral* refers to behavior that the speaker thinks would be condemned by God. This lexicon leaves no word for behavior that the speaker condemns without reference to the profession, the ethical rules, laws, or God—such behavior can be condemned by saying you disapprove of it.

So when we say that the ethical thing to do in Colorado is to administer the contested test and to interpret it warily, we are referring to the *Ethical Principles of Psychologists and Code of Conduct* (American Psychological Association [APA], 2010a), which applies to members of the APA and which we are using as an example for ethical analysis. Your professional organizations probably impose some similar code on your work, or your legislature does—when it is a legislative imposition, it is correct to describe breaches of the code as illegal, but it also makes sense to call them unethical if the statute is based on a profession's ethical principles. In this case, we were referring to APA Standard 9.02b: "Psychologists use assessment instruments whose validity and reliability have been established for use with members of the population tested. When such validity or reliability has not been established, psychologists describe the strengths and limitations of test results and interpretation." We think that exclusion of a test's results in some jurisdictions raises enough questions about a test's validity (regarding the exact same purpose it was excluded for) to require psychologists to describe that test's strengths and limitations.

COMMON STUMBLING BLOCKS TO LEGAL AND ETHICAL BEHAVIOR

When considering legal and ethical pitfalls, clinicians are in the position of the potential defendant in a criminal case. Forensic clinicians are often anxious because they are involved in important matters with limited tools. One way of managing anxiety is to ignore confusing information. When ignored information constitutes legal and ethical rules, clinicians can find themselves in trouble, having thought like criminals (Walters, 2006, and citations found therein). Like criminals, clinicians tend to examine their conduct in light of their own motives rather than the rules or the effects of their conduct. They tend to view their own motives as just and downplay remote harms that their conduct might inflict on their profession, the justice system, or society at large. They have a tendency to consider the details of their own situations and to let those details override the rules imposed on them by legislative and professional groups that do not know the details. If they can acknowledge their propensity to think like criminals, they can take steps to ensure that they follow the different kinds of rules they operate under. Because of such all-too-human tendencies, clinicians should recognize their vulnerability to certain temptations, such as self-promotion and acting without acknowledging gaps in their competence or authority.

Temptation to Self-Promote

The ethical pitfall of overvaluing your motives and undervaluing the rules of the profession comes up quite often in our experience, even or especially among professionals who would never violate a standard or a law for the usual motivations of money, sex, and power. Few people would sell access to a client's confidential material even if it were quite valuable, as in a high-profile case. But to educate early career professionals or graduate students, to rebut erroneous information purveyed at a cocktail party, or to make a telling clinical point on a Listserv, who has not been tempted? And that temptation rarely includes acknowledgment that the real reason for the breach would have been your interest in the enhanced social status accorded to your proximity to the high-profile case. We are guided (and humbled) by George Bernard Shaw's definition of *virtue*: insufficient temptation. If we are plagued by confirmation bias in our assessments of others, how much more strongly does it operate in our assessments of ourselves? "I am a good person, so whatever I do must be all right." So, unless an injustice will be perpetrated of the sort that might prompt us to civil disobedience, we just obey the rules and hope that the ones we do not like will be revised (possibly with our input).

Thinking You Know More Than You Do

Besides seeing yourself as a good person who does not need to keep an eye out for transgressions, another common context for acting unethically or illegally is thinking you know more than you do. Most clinicians who receive a subpoena, for example, probably react as they used to before specializing in forensic work: panic followed by phone calls to national and local professional organizations, relatives who are attorneys, and former professors. The anxiety of not knowing what to do leads you to find out what to do. But if you already think you know what to do, you will not feel anxious, and if what you think you know is that an official-looking subpoena that "commands" your presence with your client's files has the force of a court order, you might find yourself unethically handing over confidential documents without authority to do so. What you ought to do, of course, is to keep in mind that a subpoena, unlike most court orders, does not relieve you of your confidentiality duties and then call the lawyer who issued it and find out what he or she wants. Further steps depend on whether you can or want to give them what they want.

When you are asked to assess a psycholegal question, you are probably good at recognizing when you do not know what to do, and you seek guidance accordingly. If you are asked to assess multiple psycholegal questions, you may miss the fact that guidance on each question separately is not nearly good enough. For example, whether you are even allowed to assess competence to proceed *and* mental state at the time of the offense varies across jurisdictions, as does whether you have to write two separate reports. If you evaluate both people in a custody dispute, you'd better arrange ways to treat them exactly the same, no matter how clinically sensible your idea might be to give one a Minnesota Multiphasic Personality Inventory—2 and the other a Sixteen Personality Factor Questionnaire. And you'd better figure out beforehand how to report your results in a way that does not breach the confidentiality of one to the attorney of the other. Generally, then, you need to keep in mind that there are a lot of unexpected rules, so periodically read specialized texts and maintain a consultative relationship with an expert (even if you are one yourself) on the pitfalls associated with the area of practice.

USING THE AVAILABILITY HEURISTIC
TO HONE YOUR ETHICAL BEHAVIOR

Cognitive psychology teaches that people are more likely to behave ethically and legally if the rules are easy to retrieve (Kahneman, 2011). One way to take advantage of people's tendency to retrieve information that they have recently been exposed to is to read the rules periodically. Unfortunately, ethical principles and statutes are too long either to keep in mind or to reread with any great frequency. Instead, we recommend reading them all once and then highlighting the parts that you are likely to forget or to want to forget. Then you only have to reread the highlighted parts because the bulk of the code is something you will follow intuitively.

Thus, if you are a nongreedy gossipy know-it-all, you do not have to worry about all the rules related to money because your assessment is that you will not be tempted to overbill, charge for incidentals, or make referrals on commission. On the other hand, you might need a constant reminder not to divulge confidential information (one clinician we know wrote on his bathroom mirror "Keep Your Mouth Shut," but its stimulus value declined after a few months). And you might need to periodically read the section of the ethics code on practicing within your areas of competence and the statute in your jurisdiction on scope of practice. Psychologists who know enough about medications to offer a second opinion and psychiatrists who know enough about psychological tests to interpret them accurately are practicing within their scope of competence but beyond their authority. They could benefit from repeated reminders that they are not authorized to do certain things even if they are good at them.

Similarly, if you like off-the-cuff reports, you can prepare for your future impulsivity by making templates for various reports and sticking to them. This will help you ensure that all the legally required information is in the report. Templates are especially a good idea in jurisdictions that have required contents and required omissions for the type of report you are doing. Required omissions are things you are not allowed to write about, including incriminating information in some jurisdictions in a report on competency to proceed. If you tend to reveal too much information on the phone, you can keep a script near your phone with the relevant citation for the statute or ethical principle and what you want to say. "I'm not sure I'm allowed to answer that question, so I'll have to get back to you on that."

Our point is that most of the ethical rules, like most statutes, are a litany of bad behavior that people have thought to codify only because someone did the things that they outlaw. Rules against behavior that you are not tempted to do need not concern you, but all people are capable of some bad behaviors. In the long run, it would be great to assimilate the reasons for the rules to the point at which they all seem intuitive, but in the short run, the best you can do is to make sure the rule is available to you in the situation.

AVOIDING COMMON PITFALLS

You can get pretty far in clinical work when it comes to ethics just by behaving honorably and paying your insurance premiums. You probably needed to be told that it is unethical to practice on friends and family, to divulge the items of psychological tests, and to mention membership in the APA in your marketing materials. Oh, wait; mentioning APA membership used to be unethical but no longer is (APA, 1967, 1987). The point is that there are rules like these that you cannot intuit, but most of the rules just tell you not to indulge your interest in money, sex, and power at the expense of vulnerable people. There are few ethical problems in clinical work that an honorable approach cannot avoid or fix. An exception to the general rule of just behaving well must be created if you are the type of person to go above and beyond to try to assist someone or make people feel good. Then, you need to keep in mind the sections of the APA ethics Code having to do with dual roles, conflicts of interest, and boundaries of competence. Any time you find yourself going the extra mile, you need consultation on whether you are going too far.

Sharing Information Appropriately

In forensic work, in contrast, there are a few things that you have to get correct from the start, that you cannot go back and fix. One of these is figuring out at the outset who will get your report. The APA (2010a) Ethics Code states,

> **4.02 Discussing the Limits of Confidentiality**
>
> (a) Psychologists discuss with persons (including, to the extent feasible, persons who are legally incapable of giving informed consent and their legal representatives) and organizations with whom they establish a scientific or professional relationship (1) the relevant limits of confidentiality and (2) the foreseeable uses of the information generated through their psychological activities.

In clinical work, if you forget to tell an assessment subject that your report goes to the therapist and not just to the client, you can just get permission later to send it to the therapist. If the client refuses, the therapist does not get the report. In forensic work, if you forget to tell the subject of an assessment that the report goes to the court and not just to the subject's attorney, you cannot fix it if you have a separate obligation to send it to the court.

Sharing information between clinical and forensic systems is also complicated, but it's the kind of ethical problem that you know you have when you have it (because someone asks you for information and you know that is always an ethical issue). Knowing there is an issue, you can take the usual steps to resolve it, consulting ethical help lines, colleagues, attorneys, and the judge on the case you are involved in. You might also want to check what has been written about the problem (e.g., Petrila & Fader-Towe, 2010).

Providing Data for Second Opinions

One of our biggest peeves in forensic work involves clinicians who submit a report that one of the attorneys or the judge wants a second opinion on. It ought to be a simple matter to get the permission of the subject, send the consent form to the report writer, and then obtain the original test results and interview notes so the second opinion can be rendered. But this process often takes weeks or months, even after appropriate permissions are obtained. A surprising number of psychologists think that the APA Ethics Code still requires them to send test data only to other psychologists, but that changed in 2002. (Almost as large a number think that the *Diagnostic and Statistical Manual of Mental Disorders* [4th ed., text revision; American Psychiatric Association, 2000] still forbids diagnosing a personality disorder in children, but that changed in 1994.) Local statutes may override the APA ethics Code on this issue, but even when the recipient of information is another psychologist, the report writer is often dilatory in supplying information.

It seems to us that a clinician conducting an assessment in a disputed psycholegal matter is obliged to produce a record of the assessment that can be examined by another clinician (or by an attorney). Illegible notes and response records cannot be reviewed independently. If your hand-writing is hard to read, this is easy to fix when the material is requested by creating an audio file of you reading your notes aloud, and this file can be transmitted with the handwritten notes. When the record is requested with due authorization, it should not come as a surprise to a forensic clinician that the assessment will be reviewed by other experts.

Following Mandatory Reporting Statutes

Another problem that cannot be fixed has to do with mandatory reporting statutes regarding disclosures of child abuse. In many states, the clinician has a legal obligation to report child abuse, and the lawyer has a legal obligation not to. When the clinician is on the legal team, non-disclosure requirements fall on the clinician just as they do on the lawyer's secretary, paralegal, and private investigator. However, the clinician cannot thereby be relieved of the obligation to disclose, which falls on the clinician independently because of his or her own profession (Hall, 2006). The only way out is to inform an attorney for whom you are working, and to inform the attorney's client as well, that you will disclose child abuse, imminent threats of homicide or suicide, and if relevant in your jurisdiction, elder abuse. If you do not do this at the outset, you cannot fix it later without either breaching your obligations under the attorney's umbrella or your obligations as a member of your profession.

CONCLUSION

Our ongoing effort to identify with the subjects of our forensic assessments led us to conceptualize our potential for breaking rules in terms of criminal psychology. Criminal thinking is not a characteristic of a group of people but of all people when they break rules. We seek conversation with other experts not only to check the currency of our practice ideas but also to ensure that we are participating in a culture that promotes legal and ethical conduct, partly by constantly bringing up the topic. There are a few extraordinary instances in which we endorsed a breach of the ethics Code in fact if not in spirit. For example, one of us overstepped the bounds of the role to prevent a little girl from undergoing a clitorectomy. A lawyer we know cheerfully decided to throw away his career if need be by breaking confidentiality and turning in a serial killer. Generally, though, we soothe ourselves with the belief that our profession is smarter than we are, and we just follow its rules.

. . .

REFERENCES

American Psychiatric Association. (2000). *Diagnostic and statistical manual of mental disorders* (4th ed., text revision). Washington, DC: Author.

American Psychological Association. (1967). *Casebook on ethical standards of psychologists.* Washington, DC: Author.

American Psychological Association. (1987). *Casebook on ethical principles of psychologists.* Washington, DC: Author.

American Psychological Association. (2010a). *Ethical principles of psychologists and code of conduct (2002, Amended June 1, 2010).* Retrieved from http://www.apa.org/ethics/code/index.aspx

Hall, S. R. (2006). Child abuse reporting law and attorney-client privilege: Ethical dilemmas and practical suggestions for the forensic psychologist. *Journal of Forensic Psychology Practice, 6*(4), 55–68. doi:10.1300/J158v06n04_04

Kahneman, D. (2011). *Thinking fast and slow.* New York, NY: Farrar, Straus & Giroux.

Petrila, J., & Fader-Towe, H. (2010). *Information sharing in criminal justice–mental health collaborations: Working with HIPAA and other privacy laws.* Retrieved from https://www.bja.gov/Publications/CSG_CJMH_Info_Sharing.pdf

Walters, G. D. (2006). Appraising, researching, and conceptualizing criminal thinking: A personal view. *Criminal Behaviour and Mental Health, 16,* 87–99. doi:10.1002/cbm.50

COMMENTARY: In the context of legal proceedings, it seems at times that everyone has an opinion on forensic reports—how long they should be, what they should (or should not) contain, and the explicitness and far-ranging nature of their conclusions. Not surprisingly, retaining counsel may adopt a particular perspective on these issues in one case, and then adopt a strikingly different one in another. As an ethical matter, of course, the final decision on such matters is the psychologist's alone, but this does not prevent retaining counsel from attempting to influence that decision with the needs of a particular client in mind.

Forensic psychologists will not typically receive much guidance in the formatting of such reports from professional codes or guidelines, but some states have begun to impose their own standards as a quality control measure. Awareness of the existence of these standards—and of the ethical implications of attempted modification or compliance—is of critical importance, especially when one is temporarily or newly admitted to practice in the jurisdiction in question.

The following references are recommended for those interested in further investigation of ethical concerns regarding principles of forensic report writing. Different disciplines and specialty areas tend to prize different attributes and champion varying requirements.

Ackerman, M. J. (2006). Forensic report writing. *Journal of Clinical Psychology, 62,* 59–72. http://dx.doi.org/10.1002/jclp.20200

Meharg, S. S. (2017). Forensic neuropsychological reports. In S. S. Bush, G. J. Demakis, & M. L. Rohling (Eds.), *APA handbook of forensic neuropsychology* (pp. 397–411). Washington, DC: American Psychological Association.

Resnick, P. J., & Soliman, S. (2012). Planning, writing, and editing forensic psychiatric reports. *International Journal of Law and Psychiatry, 35,* 412–417. http://dx.doi.org/10.1016/j.ijlp.2012.09.019

van Gorp, W. G., & Kalechstein, A. (2005). Threats to the validity of the interpretation and conveyance of forensic neuropsychological results. *Journal of Forensic Neuropsychology, 4,* 67–77. http://dx.doi.org/10.1300/J151v04n03_05

Young, G. (2016). Psychiatric/psychological forensic report writing. *International Journal of Law and Psychiatry, 49*(Part B), 214–220. http://dx.doi.org/10.1016/j.ijlp.2016.10.008

10

The Business of Psychology

It may be that "the business of America is business," but the business of psychology is often a poor excuse for business at all. In many cases, it is a burgeoning disaffection regarding matters of materiality and commerce that propelled a college student down the road toward a career in the social sciences in the first place. This does not, of course, provide any sort of justification for ethical lapses when the practical end of a psychological practice has fallen into neglectful disrepair.

One ethically charged by-product of substandard business conduct may be billing irregularities—errors sometimes inspired by a genuine mistake or by a self-serving confabulation of fee totals when the psychologist truly possesses no idea of how much money is actually owed. The psychologist is not the only party who stands to be disadvantaged by the consequences of this form of bookkeeping inadequacy. The client/patient may be tarred fiscally by association with such concerns, and in any event needed assessment or treatment services may wind up being delayed as a result.

Born typically of ignorance rather than mendacity, another complication may involve the psychologist's attempt to ease the financial burden for a client/patient by agreeing to receive as compensation only that portion of psychotherapy fees that would normally be covered by insurance—for example, if the stated hourly cost of treatment is $100 per hour and a source of third-party reimbursement has agreed to pay 80% of that cost, then the client/patient would simply pay $80 per hour to the psychologist. It often comes as a surprise to psychologists that such an accommodation is considered unethical, but what

http://dx.doi.org/10.1037/0000125-011
Ethical Conflicts in Psychology, Fifth Edition, by E. Y. Drogin

the insurance company has actually agreed to provide is not $80 per hour, but rather 80% of what the psychologist is willing to accept. Thus, the appropriate reimbursement in this instance would instead be $64.

Another ethically challenging facet of the business of psychology is the need to preserve appropriate boundaries between the roles of clinical service providers and office staff. Receptionists, secretaries, and other persons associated with a psychological practice often enjoy considerable contact with clients/patients. This is how appointments are set, paperwork is kept up-to-date, and a host of other day-to-day considerations are managed. The fashion in which office staff is obligated to maintain patient/client confidentiality is a focus of considerable attention when it comes to the Health Insurance Portability and Accountability Act. Less obvious may be other boundary issues—for example, the inappropriateness of office staff administering even the most basic of psychological tests or conducting what amount to clinical interviews as opposed to standard requests for demographic information.

Among its other features, this chapter addresses American Psychological Association guidelines for record-keeping, ethically proper techniques for bill collection and for the construction of alternative financial arrangements, and ethical ramifications of compliance with managed care requirements.

10.1. Record Keeping Guidelines

American Psychological Association

INTRODUCTION

These guidelines are designed to educate psychologists and provide a framework for making decisions regarding professional record keeping. State and federal laws, as well as the American Psychological Association's (APA, 2002b) "Ethical Principles of Psychologists and Code of Conduct" (hereafter referred to as the Ethics Code), generally require maintenance of appropriate records of psychological services. The nature and extent of the record will vary depending upon the purpose, setting, and context of the psychological services. Psychologists should be familiar with legal and ethical requirements for record keeping in their specific professional contexts and jurisdictions. These guidelines are not intended to describe these requirements fully or to provide legal advice.

Records benefit both the client[1] and the psychologist through documentation of treatment plans, services provided, and client progress. Record keeping documents the psychologist's planning and implementation of an appropriate course of services, allowing the psychologist to monitor his or her work. Records may be especially important when there are significant periods of time between contacts or when the client seeks services from another professional. Appropriate

---

[1] The term *client* is used throughout this document to refer to the child, adolescent, adult, older adult, family, group, organization, community, or other population receiving psychological services. Although it is recognized that the client and the recipient of services may not necessarily be the same entity (APA Ethics Code, Standard 3.07), for economy the term *client* is used in place of *service recipient*.

From "Record Keeping Guidelines," by the American Psychological Association, 2007, *American Psychologist, 62*, pp. 993–1004. Copyright 2007 by the American Psychological Association.

This revision of the 1993 "Record Keeping Guidelines" was completed by the Board of Professional Affairs (BPA) Committee on Professional Practice and Standards (COPPS). Members of COPPS during the development of this document were Eric Y. Drogin (Chair, 2007), Mary A. Connell (Chair, 2006), William E. Foote (Chair, 2005), Cynthia A. Sturm (Chair, 2004), Kristin A. Hancock (Chair, 2003), Armand R. Cerbone, Victor de la Cancela, Michele Galietta, Larry C. James (BPA liaison, 2004–2006), Leigh W. Jerome (BPA liaison, 2003), Sara J. Knight, Stephen Lally, Gary D. Lovejoy, Bonnie J. Spring, Carolyn M. West, and Philip H. Witt. COPPS is grateful for the support and guidance of the BPA, particularly to BPA Chairs Kristin A. Hancock (2006), Rosie Phillips Bingham (2005), and Jalie A. Tucker (2004). COPPS also acknowledges the consultation of Lisa R. Grossman, Stephen Behnke, Lindsay Childress-Beatty, Billie Hinnefeld, and Alan Nessman. COPPS extends its appreciation to the APA staff members who facilitated the work of COPPS: Lynn F. Bufka, Mary G. Hardiman, Laura Kay-Roth, Ernestine Penniman, Geoffrey M. Reed, and Omar Rehman.

records can also help protect both the client and the psychologist in the event of legal or ethical proceedings. Adequate records are generally a requirement for third-party reimbursement for psychological services.

. . .

Guideline 1—Responsibility for Records: Psychologists generally have responsibility for the maintenance and retention of their records.

Rationale

Psychologists have a professional and ethical responsibility to develop and maintain records (Ethics Code, Standard 6.01). The psychologist's records document and reflect his or her professional work. In some circumstances, the records are the only way that the psychologist or others may know what the psychologist did and the psychologist's rationale for those actions. As a consequence, the psychologist aspires to create records that are consistent with high-quality professional work. If the psychologist is later questioned about services or billing, the availability of accurate records facilitates explanation and accountability.

. . .

Guideline 2—Content of Records: A psychologist strives to maintain accurate, current, and pertinent records of professional services as appropriate to the circumstances and as may be required by the psychologist's jurisdiction. Records include information such as the nature, delivery, progress, and results of psychological services, and related fees.

Rationale

The Ethics Code (Standard 6.01) sets forth reasons why psychologists create and maintain records. Based on various provisions in the Ethics Code, in decision making about content of records, a psychologist may determine what is necessary in order to (a) provide good care; (b) assist collaborating professionals in delivery of care; (c) ensure continuity of professional services in case of the psychologist's injury, disability, or death or with a change of provider; (d) provide for supervision or training if relevant; (e) provide documentation required for reimbursement or required administratively under contracts or laws; (f) effectively document any decision making, especially in high-risk situations; and (g) allow the psychologist to effectively answer a legal or regulatory complaint.

. . .

Guideline 3—Confidentiality of Records: The psychologist takes reasonable steps to establish and maintain the confidentiality of information arising from service delivery.

Rationale

Confidentiality of records is mandated by law, regulation, and ethical standards (Ethics Code, Standards 4.01 and 6.02). The assurance of confidentiality is critical for the provision of many psychological services. Maintenance of confidentiality preserves the privacy of clients and promotes trust in the profession of psychology.

. . .

Guideline 4—Disclosure of Record Keeping Procedures: When appropriate, psychologists inform clients of the nature and extent of record keeping procedures (including a statement on the limitations of confidentiality of the records; Ethics Code, Standard 4.02).

Rationale

Informed consent is part of the ethical and legal basis of professional psychology procedures (Ethics Code, Standards 3.10, 8.02, 9.03, and 10.01), and disclosure of record keeping procedures may be a part of this process.

. . .

Guideline 5—Maintenance of Records: The psychologist strives to organize and maintain records to ensure their accuracy and to facilitate their use by the psychologist and others with legitimate access to them.

Rationale

The usefulness of psychological service records often depends on the records being systematically updated and logically organized. Organization of client records in a manner that allows for thoroughness and accuracy of records, as well as efficient retrieval, both benefits the client and permits the psychologist to monitor ongoing care and interventions. In the case of the death or disability of the psychologist or of an unexpected transfer of the client's care to another professional, current, accurate, and organized records allow for continuity of care (see Guideline 13).

. . .

Guideline 6—Security: The psychologist takes appropriate steps to protect records from unauthorized access, damage, and destruction.

Rationale

Psychologists proceed with respect for the rights of individuals to privacy and confidentiality (Ethics Code, Principle E). Appropriate security procedures protect against the loss of or unauthorized access to the record, which could have serious consequences for both the client and psychologist.[2] Access to the records is limited in order to safeguard against physical and electronic breaches of the

---

[2] For psychologists who are subject to HIPAA and keep electronic records, the HIPAA Security Rule requires a detailed analysis of the risk of loss of, or unauthorized access to, electronic records and detailed policies and procedures to address those risks (for more details regarding the Security Rule, see Health Insurance Reform: Security Standards, 2003).

confidentiality of the information. Advances in technology, especially in electronic record keeping, may create new challenges for psychologists in their efforts to maintain the security of their records (see Guideline 9).

. . .

Guideline 7—Retention of Records: The psychologist strives to be aware of applicable laws and regulations and to retain records for the period required by legal, regulatory, institutional, and ethical requirements.

Rationale
A variety of circumstances (e.g., requests from clients or treatment providers, legal proceedings) may require release of client records after the psychologist's termination of contact with the client. Additionally, it is beneficial for the psychologist to retain information concerning the specific nature, quality, and rationale for services provided. The retention of records may serve not only the interests of the client and the psychologist but also society's interests in a fair and effective legal dispute resolution and administration of justice, when those records are sought to illuminate some legal issue such as the nature of the treatment provided or the psychological condition of the client at the time of services.

. . .

Guideline 8—Preserving the Context of Records: The psychologist strives to be attentive to the situational context in which records are created and how that context may influence the content of those records.

Rationale
Records may have a significant impact on the lives of clients (and prior clients). At times, information in a client's record is specific to a given temporal or situational context (e.g., the time frame and situation in which the services were delivered and the record was created). When that context changes over time, the relevance and meaning of the information may also change. Preserving the context of the record protects the client from the misuse or misinterpretation of those data in a way that could prejudice or harm the client.

. . .

Guideline 9—Electronic Records: Electronic records, like paper records, should be created and maintained in a way that is designed to protect their security, integrity, confidentiality, and appropriate access, as well as their compliance with applicable legal and ethical requirements.

Rationale
The use of electronic methods and media compels psychologists to become aware of the unique aspects of electronic record keeping in their particular

practice settings. These aspects include limitations to the confidentiality of these records, methods to keep these records secure, measures necessary to maintain the integrity of the records, and the unique challenges of disposing of these records. In many cases, psychologists who maintain electronic records will be subject to the HIPAA [Health Insurance Portability and Accountability Act] Security Rule, which requires a detailed analysis of the risks associated with electronic records. Conducting that risk analysis may be advisable even for psychologists who are not technically subject to HIPAA. . .

. . .

Guideline 10—Record Keeping in Organizational Settings: Psychologists working in organizational settings (e.g., hospitals, schools, community agencies, prisons) strive to follow the record keeping policies and procedures of the organization as well as the APA Ethics Code.

Rationale

Organizational settings may present unique challenges in record keeping. Organizational record keeping requirements may differ substantially from procedures in other settings. Psychologists working in organizational settings may encounter conflicts between the practices of their organization and established professional guidelines, ethical standards, or legal and regulatory requirements. Additionally, record ownership and responsibility is not always clearly defined. Often, multiple service providers access and contribute to the record. This potentially affects the degree to which the psychologist may exercise control of the record and its confidentiality.

. . .

Guideline 11—Multiple Client Records: The psychologist carefully considers documentation procedures when conducting couple, family, or group therapy in order to respect the privacy and confidentiality of all parties.

Rationale

In providing services to multiple clients, issues of record keeping may become very complex. Because records may include information about more than one individual client, legitimate disclosure of information regarding one client may compromise the confidentiality of other clients.

. . .

Guideline 12—Financial Records: The psychologist strives to ensure accuracy of financial records.

Rationale

Accurate and complete financial record keeping helps to ensure accuracy in billing (Ethics Code, Standards 6.04 and 6.06). A fee agreement or policy, although not explicitly required for many kinds of psychological services such as preemployment screening under agency contract or emergency counseling services at a disaster site, provides a useful starting point in most service delivery contexts for documenting reimbursement of services. Accurate financial records not only assist payers in assessing the nature of the payment obligation but also provide a basis for understanding exactly which services have been billed and paid. Up-to-date record keeping can alert the psychologist and the client to accumulating balances that, left unaddressed, may adversely affect the professional relationship.

. . .

Guideline 13—Disposition of Records: The psychologist plans for transfer of records to ensure continuity of treatment and appropriate access to records when the psychologist is no longer in direct control, and in planning for record disposal, the psychologist endeavors to employ methods that preserve confidentiality and prevent recovery.[3]

Rationale

Client records are accorded special treatment in times of transition (e.g., separation from work, relocation, death). A record transfer plan is required by both the Ethics Code (Standard 6.02), and by laws and regulations governing health care practice in many jurisdictions. Such a plan provides for continuity of treatment and preservation of confidentiality. Additionally, the Ethics Code (Standards 6.01 and 6.02) requires psychologists to dispose of records in a way that preserves their confidentiality.

. . .

CONCLUSION

These "Record Keeping Guidelines" provide a framework for keeping, maintaining, and providing for the disposition of records and what is contained in them. They discuss special situations: electronic records, organizational settings, and multiple clients. They are intended to benefit both the psychologist and the client by facilitating continuity and evaluation of services, preserving the client's privacy, and protecting the psychologist and client in legal and ethical proceedings.

. . .

---

[3] See the HIPAA Security Rule.

REFERENCES

American Psychological Association. (2002b). Ethical principles of psychologists and code of conduct. *American Psychologist, 57,* 1060–1073.

Health Insurance Reform: Security Standards; Final Rule, 45 C.F.R. Parts 160, 162, and 164 (2003). Retrieved December 9, 2006, from http://www.cms.hhs.gov/SecurityStandard/Downloads/securityfinalrule.pdf

COMMENTARY: The steady transition from paper-based to electronic mental health records has done much for the quick retrieval and transmission of client/patient information, and physical storage space is no longer at such a premium, although expenditures of time and money to keep up with technological requirements and related professional standards have eroded the overall positive effect of such windfalls.

Access to psychological records can be characterized, without resorting to histrionics, as a matter of life and death when eligibility for critical benefits is at issue and in those jurisdictions that continue to use the death penalty as a sentencing option in criminal proceedings. Much has also been written, with less dramatic stakes, of the economic liability, social stigma, and other potential consequences of poorly preserved and improperly disclosed psychological records. All of this continues to place considerable ethical pressure on psychologists to tend to these documents with appropriate care at every stage—from creation through disposal.

The following references are recommended for those interested in further investigation of ethically oriented guidelines for psychological record keeping, citing recent technological advances and the requirements of institutional as opposed to private practice settings.

Devereaux, R. L., & Gottlieb, M. C. (2012). Record keeping in the cloud: Ethical considerations. *Professional Psychology: Research and Practice, 43,* 627–632. http://dx.doi.org/10.1037/a0028268

Drogin, E. Y., & Armontrout, J. A. (2017). Recordkeeping in private practice. In S. Walfish, J. E. Barnett, & J. Zimmerman (Eds.), *Handbook of private practice: Keys to success for mental health practitioners* (pp. 66–77). New York, NY: Oxford University Press.

Fisher, M. A. (2012). Confidentiality and record keeping. In S. J. Knapp, M. C. Gottlieb, M. M. Handelsman, & L. D. VandeCreek (Eds.), *APA handbooks in psychology. APA handbook of ethics in psychology, Vol. 1. Moral foundations and common themes* (pp. 333–375). Washington, DC: American Psychological Association.

Knapp, S. J., VandeCreek, L. D., & Fingerhut, R. (2017). Confidentiality, privileged communications, and record keeping. In S. J. Knapp, L. D. VandeCreek, & R. Fingerhut, *Practical ethics for psychologists: A positive approach* (pp. 125–147). Washington, DC: American Psychological Association.

Purves, D. (2015). The ethics and responsibilities of record keeping and note taking. In R. Tribe & J. Morrissey (Eds.), *Handbook of professional and ethical practice for psychologists, counsellors and psychotherapists* (pp. 82–92). New York, NY: Routledge/Taylor & Francis Group.

10.2. The American Psychological Association's Revised "Record Keeping Guidelines": Implications for the Practitioner

Eric Y. Drogin, Mary Connell, William E. Foote, and Cynthia A. Sturm

The American Psychological Association (APA) has revised its 1993 "Record Keeping Guidelines" (RKG) in a fashion "designed to educate psychologists and provide a framework for making decisions regarding professional record keeping" (APA, 2007, p. 993). Since their publication in December 2007, the revised RKG have received minimal attention in the professional literature and virtually no critical review. They were reproduced in their entirety in the most recent edition of one standard text on psychological ethics (Bersoff, 2008), and Fisher (2008) briefly outlined their contents in the most recent edition of another, commenting that revised RKG provisions for documentation of billing and fees merited "special attention" (p. 171). Richards (2009) acknowledged the relevance of the revised RKG to proper utilization of Electronic Medical Records (EMR). According to Barnett and Kannankeril (2008), the revised RKG bibliography contains "helpful references and resources" (p. 59). The slight recognition afforded the revised RKG makes it all the more important to place this document in context, identifying problems that may arise and how psychologists can anticipate and solve them.

Promulgation and revision of practice-oriented guidelines is the responsibility of the APA's Committee on Professional Practice and Standards (COPPS). As the former COPPS chairpersons during whose tenure the revised RKG was developed, we are grateful for the opportunity to provide a detailed review of the implications of this document for psychological practitioners, with reference to applicable portions of the "Ethical Principles of Psychologists and Code of Conduct" (Ethics Code) mandated by the APA (2002).

. . .

DISCLOSURE OF RECORD KEEPING PROCEDURES

The revised RKG suggest that "when appropriate, psychologists inform clients of the nature and extent of record keeping procedures" (APA, 2007, p. 997). Although simple enough on its surface, this particular guideline becomes more complex when psychologists attempt to determine just when and how to apply it.

First of all, what is meant by the term "when appropriate"? One potential interpretation is that psychologists provide this information in *cases* for which such disclosure is appropriate, while another is that psychologists do so at the appropriate *juncture*, in most or all cases. Psychologists might also reason that "when appropriate" means "when not inappropriate," and if this is the approach they take, they will be hard pressed to identify many cases—if any—in which it would *not* be appropriate to share the information in question.

Embedded in this guideline is a specific reference to the Ethics Code, with which compliance is of course mandatory, not optional. Ethics Code Standard 4.02, Discussing Limits of Confidentiality (APA, 2002) directs psychologists to provide not merely disclosure—or, as this guideline suggests, a "statement"—but actually to "discuss" the "relevant limitations of confidentiality" as well as "the foreseeable uses of the information" (p. 1066).

Despite the Ethics Code's mandatory direction and the similarly exacting nature of some state laws regarding psychologists' record keeping procedures, the "Application" section of this guideline conveys a pointedly permissive perspective on this issue, advising that "in some circumstances, when it is anticipated that the client might want or need to know how records will be maintained, this process may include the disclosure of record keeping procedures," and that "this may be especially relevant when record keeping procedures are likely to have an impact upon confidentiality or when the client's expressed expectations regarding record keeping differ from the required procedures" (APA, 2007, p. 997).

"Some," "might," "may," "may," "may," "likely"—psychologists reading this particular guideline without a copy of the Ethics Code in their laps could easily be forgiven for concluding that disclosure of record keeping procedures is being assigned a relatively low priority. When they read a bit further, however, psychologists learn that they are actually "encouraged" to inform clients about situations in which record keeping "may potentially affect the client in ways that may be unanticipated by the client"—including events such as transfer of records from one treating professional to another and public access to court transcripts (APA, 2007, p. 997).

Faced with a revised RKG recommendation that is directive in its formal wording but conveys contrasting levels of urgency regarding essentially similar functions, psychologists can play it safe—particularly given the interwoven presence of Ethics Code requirements, with potentially stiff penalties for non-compliance—by simply incorporating some oral reference to the record keeping procedures into their initial interaction with clients as well as into standardized consent forms. What might the creation and storage these "records" involve? What might they contain? How are they kept? Where could they go? Why, and when? What might this mean for the client at some point in the future?

MAINTENANCE OF RECORDS

The revised RKG offer the following advice in this regard: "Psychologists strive to organize and maintain records to ensure their accuracy and to facilitate their use by the psychologist and others with legitimate access to them" (APA, 2007, p. 997). Several purposes are served by this relatively brief suggestion.

The first purpose is to promote the notion that proper organization and maintenance will serve to keep records more "accurate." At first blush, psychologists might wonder how a record can be made more valid and precise simply by virtue of the way in which it is subsequently handled. The answer lies in the ability to supplement the record over the course of ongoing or resumed treatment—essentially, when we can find the client's file and make sense of it when faced with the complex demands and rushed circumstances of a typical daily schedule, we stand a better chance of capturing the client's progress in appropriately full detail.

The revised RKG further refer to "use by the psychologist *and others*" (APA, 2007, p. 1067), thus affirming the requirement under Ethics Code Standard 6.01, Documentation of Professional and Scientific Work and Maintenance of Records (APA, 2002)—although not identifying it by its source—that psychologists "maintain, disseminate, store, retain, and dispose of records" in order to "facilitate provision of services later by them or by other professionals" (APA, 2007, p. 1067). The unarticulated paradigm is that a subsequent treatment provider would be able to undertake the case with a minimum of duplicative effort and essentially pick up where the previous clinician left off. In addition, records conveyed by the current treatment provider would facilitate adjunctive treatment—such as, for example, medication management or couples psychotherapy—and serve the client's interests in legal proceedings, employment applications, benefits applications, and other secondary contexts.

In addition to its relevance to Electronic Health Records (EHR)—addressed in detail below—this guideline's reference to "legitimate access" raises the specter of "test security" as addressed in Ethics Code Standard 9.11, Maintaining Test Security (APA, 2002), which directs psychologists to "make reasonable efforts to maintain the integrity and security of test materials and other assessment techniques consistent with the law and contractual obligations" (p. 1072). Psychologists who distribute test materials and test data haphazardly throughout a client record may wind up releasing test materials—including computerized test stimuli protected by copyright—in a hurried attempt to comply with a signed release or subpoena, or they may find such references difficult or impossible to redact when the deadline looms to forward records to clients, the courts, or other treatment providers whose own adherence to standards of test security may be questionable. Optimal handling of test materials and test data is additionally addressed in other sources of professional guidance (Behnke, 2004; Bush & Martin, 2006; Chadda & Stein, 2005; Committee on Legal Issues, 2006; Committee on Psychological Tests and Assessment, 1996; Erard, 2004; Lees-Haley & Courtney, 2000; Rapp, Ferber, & Bush, 2008).

The revised RKG provide an unusual amount of practice advice for adherence in this regard; for example, the development of a "logical file labeling system," the provision of advance notice to clients who may wish to challenge the release of records, and the physical division of client files into multiple sections to accommodate such contents as psychotherapy notes, client-generated data, and contributions from third parties (APA, 2007, pp. 997–998). To this list, we now suggest adding another measure: the purchase or development of an overall electronic tracking system that is searchable by client name, date of initiation of services, and physical file location. This could be as simple and easy as compiling a word processing document—with appropriate password protection—to which the clinician adds an accounting of each file as it is either opened or sent away to long-term storage.

SECURITY

The revised RKG indicate that "the psychologist takes appropriate steps to protect records from unauthorized access, damage, and destruction" (APA, 2007, p. 998). Just what is "appropriate" in this context will depend upon the storage medium—for example, paper versus electronic—as well as upon the practical limitations to what psychologists can do without making their own access to records too time-consuming and prohibitively costly.

Unauthorized access to paper records can be prevented by what the revised RKG describe as "storing files in locked cabinets or other containers housed in locked offices or storage rooms" (APA, 2007, p. 998). Following this advice in too literal-minded a fashion could, however, lead to problems. Psychologists should not seize upon the fact that the phrasing of this passage suggests an "either–or" solution to unauthorized access by presuming that they have been handed a license to store records however they wish, as long as the rooms holding the containers are locked. Locked offices become unlocked when clients visit, when office staff persons arrive to commence the day's operations, and when maintenance contractors perform their duties in the evening. When psychologists are not themselves present in the room with client records, who else can obtain access and how? The answer to this question will assist psychologists in determining the potential need for "locked cabinets."

Preventing unauthorized access to electronic records may include encryption and typically involves the use of passwords—ideally, "smart" or "alphanumeric" passwords of sufficient length that involve both letters and numbers, as opposed to the psychologist's first name, birth year, or the digits "1234." In some states, encryption is now required by law; psychologists should investigate such requirements for each jurisdiction in which they practice. Laptop computers are attractive to thieves whether they contain sensitive patient data or not and merely locking such equipment into a docking station will do little to deter those happy to purloin both the computer and the cradle that contains it. Personal Data Assistants (PDAs) and mobile phones often contain client data, such as names, numbers, and appointment times, and should be secured when not under the psychologist's direct control. Care should be taken to store backup media as carefully as the original files themselves, instead of leaving disks, tapes, and flash drives out in the open as reminders to duplicate records before the end of the workday.

The principal distinction to be drawn between "damage" and "destruction" in this context involves not the degree of impairment but rather the specific means by which harm occurs. "Damage" as described in the revised RKG involves fire, water, mold, and even infestation regarding paper records, while power surges and computer viruses are viewed as primary threats to the integrity of electronic records. When archiving paper records, psychologists should determine whether storage units are "climate controlled" and should request location on a higher floor when available. Psychologists should also make it a point to scan electronic records for the presence of computer viruses and other flaws *prior* to backup, in order to avoid an infection that could compromise the file in question and potentially spread to other preserved data as well.

"Destruction" refers in this context of the revised RKG to the deliberate or accidental trashing of an entire patient record. Multiple backups may be impractical in the case of paper records but are a relatively inexpensive option for electronic records. If possible, multiple backups should be stored at sites that are geographically diverse as well as secure.

Maintaining a separate electronic file that lists stored records by last date of service—and updating that electronic file in the event of unexpected resumption of care—will assist in making the data destruction process a more orderly and predictable one. Alternatively, the list might include a "destroy by" date—calculated by determining how many years after the termination of services destruction is advisable, with due consideration for state and federal laws (including HIPAA)—to alert the psychologist or designee to the date when it would be legally and ethically justifiable to dispose of the file. Although paper records can be shredded, technical consultation may be necessary to ensure that electronically stored information can no longer be accessed from the device or medium in question.

RETENTION OF RECORDS

Regarding records retention, the revised RKG state the following: "The psychologist strives to be aware of applicable laws and regulations and to retain records for the period required by legal, regulatory, institutional, and ethical requirements" (APA, 2007, p. 999). What this language does not convey, however, is the one piece of advice that has come to define the original and revised RKG and is perhaps—although, for example, the Association of State and Provincial Psychology Boards (ASPPB) has not published any data on retention-based licensure complaints—the primary reason psychologists consult the RKG in the first place. Buried in this particular guideline's "Application" section is the following statement: "In the absence of a superseding requirement, psychologists may consider retaining full records until 7 years after the last date of service delivery for adults or until 3 years after a minor reaches the age of majority, whichever is later" (APA, 2007, p. 999).

This recommendation stands in striking contrast to the one found in original RKG, in which psychologists were told that absent any superseding legal authority, "complete records are maintained for a minimum of three years after the last contact with the client," that "records, or a summary, are then maintained for an additional 12 years before disposal," and that "if the client is a minor, the record period is extended until 3 years after the age of minority" (APA, 1993, p. 985).

Despite the revised RKG's description of various factors that psychologists are free to take into account, its "may consider" paradigm means that no psychologist can be penalized for running afoul of it, and indeed, this document goes so far as to observe that under some circumstances—such as documentation of "demeaning or embarrassing" behavior on the part of a minor—"the client may be served by the disposal of the record as soon as allowed" (APA, 2007, p. 999). Here, in effect, retention under some circumstances is actually being discouraged.

Psychologists will note that the revised RKG have also dispensed with the distinction between "full" and "summary" records. Those who do elect to destroy records at the professionally justifiable time may, of course, maintain discharge summaries, reports, or other such documents for which the cost-benefit analysis for retention argues in favor of it. It may also be advisable to review contracts with insurance companies for supervening contractual obligations and to address specific deadlines for record retention in such agreements.
. . .

REFERENCES

American Psychological Association. (1993). Record keeping guidelines. *American Psychologist, 48*, 984–986.

American Psychological Association. (2002). Ethical principles of psychologists and code of conduct. *American Psychologist, 57*, 1060–1073.

American Psychological Association. (2007). Record keeping guidelines. *American Psychologist, 62*, 993–1004.

Barnett, J. E., & Kannankeril, C. A. (2008). Documentation, record keeping, and the APA Record Keeping Guidelines. *Psychotherapy Bulletin, 43*(1), 55–59.

Behnke, S. (2004). Release of test data and the new ethics code. *Monitor on Psychology, 35*(10), 90–91.

Bersoff, D. N. (2008). *Ethical conflicts in psychology* (4th ed.). Washington, DC: American Psychological Association.

Bush, S. S., & Martin, T. A. (2006). The ethical and clinical practice of disclosing raw test data: Addressing the ongoing debate. *Applied Neuropsychology, 13*, 115–124.

Chadda, R., & Stein, S. J. (2005). Test publisher's perspective: Release of test data to non-psychologists. *Journal of Forensic Psychology Practice, 5*, 59–69.

Committee on Legal Issues. (2006). Strategies for private practitioners coping with subpoenas or compelled testimony for client records or test data. *Professional Psychology: Research and Practice, 37*, 215–222.

Committee on Psychological Tests and Assessment. (1996). Statement on the disclosure of test data. *American Psychologist, 51,* 644–648.

Erard, R. E. (2004). Release of test data under the 2002 ethics code and the HIPAA privacy rule: A raw deal or just a half-baked idea? *Journal of Personality Assessment, 82,* 23–30.

Fisher, C. B. (2008). *Decoding the ethics code: A practical guide for psychologists* (2nd ed.). Thousand Oaks, CA: Sage.

Lees-Haley, P. R., & Courtney, J. C. (2000). Disclosure of tests and raw test data to the courts: A need for reform. *Neuropsychology Review, 10,* 169–174.

Rapp, D. L., Ferber, P. S., & Bush, S. S. (2008). Unresolved issues about release of raw test data and test materials. In A. M. Horton, Jr. & D. Wedding (Eds.), *The neuropsychology handbook* (3rd ed., pp. 469–497). New York, NY: Springer.

Richards, M. M. (2009). Electronic medical records: Confidentiality issues in the time of HIPAA. *Professional Psychology: Research and Practice, 40,* 550–556.

10.3. HIPAA: Federal Regulation of Healthcare Records

Donald N. Bersoff

The record-keeping landscape has changed materially as a result of promulgation by the U.S. Department of Health and Human Services of rules implementing the Health Insurance Portability and Accountability Act (HIPAA) of 1996. There are three major rules: (a) the transaction rule, which focuses on creating a standard format for electronic transactions related to health care claims, plan eligibility, and plan coverage; (b) the security rule, which focuses on the health care provider's physical infrastructure to ensure confidentiality of patient information; and (c) most relevant for psychologists, the privacy rule, which focuses on policies, procedures, and business service agreements used to control access to patient information. The privacy rule took effect in April 2003, for most large health plans; those with less than $5 million in annual receipts had 1 additional year to comply (see 45 CFR part 160 and Subparts A & E of Part 164).

The HIPAA privacy rule applies to data called Protected Health Information (PHI), defined as information, whether oral, written, typed, or electronic, that relates to the past, present, or future physical or mental health condition of an identifiable individual; the provision of health care to such an individual; and the past, present, or future payment for the provision of health care to such an individual.

The privacy rule is triggered when a covered entity (e.g., a health care provider) transmits PHI in electronic form (e.g., Internet, CDs, faxes) in connection with health care claims for reimbursement, payments, enrollment in health plans, and status, among other transactions. Once triggered, however, the privacy rule applies to psychologists' entire operation, not solely to information in electronic form. With certain limited exceptions the rule protects PHI regardless of whether the patient is dead or alive. Only those involved (a) directly with patient care, (b) with record keeping or billing, and (c) with quality assurance and training are permitted access to PHI.

Originally, the privacy rule required patient consent prior to using PHI to carry out treatment, payment, and health care operations. But this requirement was eliminated as too burdensome and disruptive of patient care. As a substitute all patients must be provided a Notice of Disclosure informing them "about what information is designated as personally identifiable, how their

From *Ethical Conflicts in Psychology* (4th ed., pp. 543–545), by D. N. Bersoff, 2008, Washington, DC: American Psychological Association. Copyright 2008 by the American Psychological Association.

private health information will be protected, and how disclosures will be made" (Benefield, Ashkanazi, & Rozensky, 2006, p. 274). A signed copy of this Notice is then placed in the patient's record. Patients may request access to their records, review their records, ask for them to be duplicated, and amend records to correct any perceived inaccuracies.

The notice requirement does not pertain, however, to psychotherapy notes. The psychologist must obtain additional authorization for process notes to be released to third parties. The authorization must define specifically the information to be disclosed, indicate to whom the information is going and for what purpose, specify an expiration date, and inform patients that they have a right to refuse authorization or revoke authorization once given. In that light, it is highly recommended that clinicians keep psychotherapy process notes in a secure file separate from more routine PHI, such as diagnoses, prognosis, and treatment plan, to which third-party payors have legitimate access. The regulations, in fact, contain a provision that will gladden the hearts of therapists who must deal with managed care companies (see material later in this chapter). Such companies and other third-party payors are barred from conditioning eligibility for, or payments of, benefits on the disclosure of psychotherapy notes.

With regard to children receiving psychological services, in general, parents, as their personal representatives, have the right of access to their minors' mental health records unless state law permits minors access without parental consent, a court authorizes someone other than parents to make health care decisions for a minor, or a parent agrees to confidentiality between the child and the psychologist.

As defined in regulations adopted in March 2006, there are three escalating penalties for failing to comply with HIPAA. At present, DHHS may take administrative action; the psychologist may be fined up to $100 for each violation with a cap of $25,000 per year; and for wrongful disclosure of PHI there may be fines up to $250,000 and/or imprisonment for up to 10 years. Readers should note that as of the date of the regulations, DHHS received close to 19,000 HIPAA compliance complaints, most from patients of private health entities.

Finally, the privacy rule merely establishes a minimum set of mandates for the protection of PHI. It takes precedence over state law only when it is more stringent than state law. But, when state law is more protective of PHI, then state law takes precedence.

This is but a brief educational summary of the major requirements under privacy rule regulations. Because the operations of all practitioners and the facilities within which they work (and some researchers who use PHI, see Fisher, 2004), are affected, it is helpful to obtain formal legal advice, review the regulations in the *Federal Register* (December 28, 2000), and gain access to the American Psychological Association's (APA's) Practice Organization material referenced in the Commentary that follows to be better informed about its nuances and to apply successfully all the regulations. Although under Standard 1.02 of the Ethics Code (APA, 2002), psychologists can attempt to resolve conflicts between the code and the law, as the standard also indicates, "if the conflict is unresolvable via such means, psychologists may adhere to the requirements of the law, regulations, or other governing legal authority."

REFERENCES

American Psychological Association. (2002). Ethical principles of psychologists and code of conduct. *American Psychologist, 57,* 1060–1073.

Benefield, H., Ashkanazi, G., & Rozensky, R. H. (2006). Communication and records: HIPPA [sic] issues when working in health care settings. *Professional Psychology: Research and Practice, 37,* 273–277.

Fisher, C. B. (2004). Informed consent and clinical research involving children and adolescents: Implications of the revised APA ethics code and HIPAA. *Journal of Clinical Child and Adolescent Psychology, 33,* 832–839.

COMMENTARY: Since its inception more than 20 years ago, HIPAA has been accompanied by a cottage industry that has terrorized managers, clinicians, and office personnel with the prospect of dire consequences for failure to adhere to what has typically been advertised as an impenetrably dense chunk of federal regulatory code. In fact, as such mandates go, HIPAA—as amended—is comparatively straightforward and accessible, but the myth of its incomprehensibility has continued to swell with the passage of time.

HIPAA is, of course, a source of legal as opposed to ethical guidance, but it connects directly to such core ethical concerns as confidentiality and adequate record keeping. Complicating its impact is an ongoing disagreement between well-regarded commentators concerning the extent to which it actually applies in some contexts, such as forensic psychological evaluations. Psychologists are best advised to err on the side of caution when attempting to determine—with recourse to legal advice—the extent to which HIPAA requirements pertain in a given situation.

The following references are recommended for those interested in further investigation of HIPAA and related ethical concerns. Obligations may vary, as addressed by these sources, depending on different physical settings and the specific media by which communications are conveyed.

Barraza, L., Collmer, V., Meza, N., & Penunuri, K. (2015). The legal implications of HIPAA privacy and public health reporting for correctional facilities. *Journal of Correctional Health Care, 21,* 213–221. http://dx.doi.org/10.1177/1078345815585050

Borkosky, B. G., Pellett, J. M., & Thomas, M. S. (2014). Are forensic evaluations "health care" and are they regulated by HIPAA? *Psychological Injury and Law, 7*(1), 1–8. http://dx.doi.org/10.1007/s12207-013-9158-7

Gomez, A., & Knight, S. C. (2013). Disclosure of mental health records in court-mandated outpatient treatment proceedings and the Health Insurance Portability and Accountability Act (HIPAA). *Journal of the American Academy of Psychiatry and the Law, 41,* 460–461.

Hecker, L. (2017). HIPAA 101 for the private practitioner. In S. Walfish, J. E. Barnett, & J. Zimmerman (Eds.), *Handbook of private practice: Keys to success for mental health practitioners* (pp. 477–491). New York: Oxford University Press.

Luxton, D. D., Kayl, R. A., & Mishkind, M. C. (2012). mHealth data security: The need for HIPAA-compliant standardization. *Telemedicine and e-Health, 18,* 284–288. http://dx.doi.org/10.1089/tmj.2011.0180

10.4. The Ethics of Billing, Collecting, and Financial Arrangements: A Working Framework for Clinicians

Jeffrey E. Barnett and Steven Walfish

The reality of being in private practice is that our clients pay our salaries. It is only by generating fees and effectively collecting them that we can keep our practices viable. Yet our attempts to maximize profits occur in the context of a therapeutic relationship. How we balance the business and clinical aspects of our practice in an ethical manner is an essential concern for all clinicians.

A focus on ethical practice is a hallmark of our work, and the ethics codes of each of the mental health professions are built on a group of underlying principles (Beauchamp & Childress, 1994; Kitchener, 1984) that provide guidance in all areas of professional practice. These underlying ethical principles include the following:

- Beneficence: To help those we serve and to be guided by their best interests in all we do.

- Nonmaleficence: To avoid or prevent exploitation and harm of those we serve.

- Fidelity: Exercising faithfulness in our obligations to others.

- Autonomy: Promoting others' independence of us over time and not creating needless dependence on us.

- Integrity: Being truthful and honest; keeping all agreements and promises made.

- Justice: Being fair in all interactions and ensuring equal access to high-quality services for all individuals.

These principles form the basis of the specific ethical standards that comprise each mental health profession's ethics code. Areas of practice typically emphasized in these standards include a comprehensive informed-consent process, as well as competence in clinical practice to include multicultural competence, confidentiality, boundaries and multiple relationships, termination and abandonment, advertising and public statements, media presentations, assessment, research and publishing, supervision, and teaching, among others (see American Counseling Association [ACA], 2005; American Psychological Association [APA], 2010a; National Association of Social Workers [NASW], 1999).

In addition to ethical standards directly relevant to the clinical services that clinicians provide, standards exist that emphasize the business aspects of mental

From *Billing and Collecting for Your Mental Health Practice: Effective Strategies and Ethical Practice* (pp. 7–25), by J. E. Barnett and S. Walfish, 2012, Washington, DC: American Psychological Association. Copyright 2012 by the American Psychological Association.

health practice. The Ethical Principles of Psychologists and Code of Conduct (APA Ethics Code; APA, 2010a) addresses these issues in Standards 6.04, Fees and Financial Arrangements; 6.05, Barter With Clients/Patients; 6.06, Accuracy in Reports to Payors and Funding Sources; 6.07, Referrals and Fees; and 6.03, Withholding Records for Nonpayment. Similar standards are found in the American Counseling Association's Code of Ethics (ACA, 2005) to include Standard A.10, Fees and Bartering (which includes Accepting Fees From Agency Clients, Establishing Fees, Nonpayment of Fees, Bartering, and Receiving Gifts), and Standard C.6.b., Reports to Third Parties. Similarly, the NASW Code of Ethics (NASW, 1999) includes Standards 1.13, Payment for Services; 2.06, Referral for Services; 3.05, Billing; 4.04, Dishonesty, Fraud, and Deception; and 4.06, Misrepresentation.

Thus, it is clear that the ethics codes of the mental health professions apply not only to clinical aspects of practice but also to billing, fees, and financial arrangements. Additionally, as will be addressed, specific laws and regulations exist that affect the fee and billing activities of clinicians. Knowledge of ethical standards, laws, and regulations relevant to fees, billing, and financial arrangements is essential for the appropriate and ethical conduct of clinicians.

In this chapter, we discuss several aspects of the billing and collections process as it intersects with ethical practice. These include (a) integrating financial issues into the informed-consent process, (b) understanding informed consent as an ongoing process rather than a solitary event, (c) anticipating financial limitations that may affect clients' ability to pay for services, (d) the role that non-insurance third parties may play in the billing and collections process, (e) how to ethically and appropriately raise fees, (f) how to respond when clients do not pay agreed-on fees, (g) negotiating the use of alternative methods to pay for services, (h) referrals and fees, (i) the need for accurate billing, and (j) how to prevent fraudulent billing.

OVERVIEW OF INFORMED CONSENT

Informed consent is described by Barnett, Wise, Johnson-Greene, and Bucky (2007) as "a shared decision-making process in which the professional communicates sufficient information to the other individual so that she or he may make an informed decision about participation in the professional relationship" (p. 179). Other authors have added to this definition of informed consent, such as Beahrs and Gutheil (2001) who described informed consent as "the process of sharing information with patients that is essential to their ability to make rational choices among multiple options" (p. 4). The fact that various clinicians may have different fees, financial policies, and financial arrangements makes the sharing of this information especially relevant. Failure to do so could be seen as severely limiting the client's ability to make an informed decision about entering treatment with a particular clinician. The fact that third party payors (e.g., insurance companies) are often involved in the payment of some part of the fees on behalf of the client can serve to complicate the financial disclosure process. By sharing sufficient information with clients, they are better able to choose from among the many options available to them for mental health services.

A number of financial matters should be addressed as part of the informed-consent process. These include the discussion of the client's financial limitations as well as an accurate explanation of fees, financial policies and arrangements, charges for various services to be provided, and what reasonably to anticipate with regard to insurance coverage and reimbursement. Furthermore, whether the clinician participates in specific insurance and managed care plans, is an in-network provider for certain insurance companies, or solely follows a fee-for-service model should all be discussed. It is each clinician's responsibility to ensure that clients understand the information presented and their implications with regard to the services the client is seeking (Barnett, Wise, et al., 2007).

When clients are using their health insurance benefits for reimbursement of the fees for services provided, it is important for clinicians to clarify the limits of each client's insurance coverage from the outset. Pomerantz (2005) offered a number of questions clients may have that should be answered during the informed-consent process. These include the following:

- How much does psychotherapy cost?

- Do you accept my insurance?

- How much does my insurance company pay (percentage, total)?

- What forms of payment do you accept (cash, credit cards, check)?

- How often will I need to pay?

- Can fees go up at some point?

- What information will my insurance company be given?

- What information will my employer be given? (p. 355)

Important pieces of information to clarify also include the following:

- Are there any limits to coverage, such as a maximum number of treatment sessions per year?

- Is there a deductible before insurance benefits are paid?

- Are there certain disorders or diagnoses (e.g., parent–child communication problem, learning disabilities, partner-communication problem, obesity) that are not covered?

It is clear that clients will want and need to know what portion of fees charged will be their responsibility and what portion will be covered by their insurance. If this cannot be determined before an initial insurance claim is processed, this fact should be clarified with the client from the outset. Clients will also want to know whether you will file the insurance claim and wait to be reimbursed or whether they must pay for the session up front and wait to be reimbursed by their insurance company. Additionally, it is especially important that clients are informed of one's policy on canceled and missed appointments, because most insurers will only provide reimbursement for services actually rendered. Furthermore, as Knapp and VandeCreek (2008) recommended, fees for all nonclinical services such as letter or report writing and fees for time spent on telephone calls or e-mails, with either clients or collateral contacts, should be fully addressed as well and should comport with contractual obligations with insurers.

Accuracy and honesty in the setting of fees and in how information about them is shared with clients is essential. Standard 6.04(c), Fees and Financial Arrangements, of the APA (2010a) Ethics Code clearly states that "Psychologists do not misrepresent their fees." Similarly, Standard 4.04, Dishonesty, Fraud, and Deception, of the NASW (1999) Code of Ethics states that "Social workers should not participate in, condone, or be associated with dishonesty, fraud, or deception." Thus, all information provided to clients should be presented accurately, both verbally and in a written financial agreement to which the client can refer back over time. The use of a written financial agreement and open discussion during the informed-consent procedure also helps ensure that clients have realistic expectations of the clinician and about treatment from the outset. It is important to minimize the risk of misunderstandings that may have an adverse impact on the professional relationship and the clinical services provided.

INFORMED CONSENT AS AN ETHICAL MANDATE

Snyder and Barnett (2006) emphasized that benefits of the informed consent process include "promoting client autonomy and self-determination, minimizing the risk of exploitation and harm, fostering rational decision-making, and enhancing the therapeutic alliance" (p. 37). Only by fulfilling our informed-consent obligations with clients can we achieve these goals. Failure to provide clients with the information needed to make an informed decision about participation in the professional relationship, including policies and procedures for billing and collecting fees, can jeopardize each of these goals. This point is well made in a study by Sullivan, Martin, and Handelsman (1993) in which they surveyed potential consumers of mental health services about the use of informed consent. These researchers found that consumers rated those professionals who engaged in an informed-consent process with clients as more expert and trustworthy. Furthermore, these clients would be more likely to refer friends to these professionals and to use the professionals themselves compared with clients with mental health professionals who did not provide informed consent.

The inclusion of fees, financial policies, and financial arrangements in every client's informed-consent agreement is consistent with the dictates of the ethics codes of the mental health professions. The APA (2010a) Ethics Code includes these issues as essential elements required in Standard 10.01, Informed Consent to Therapy. Content that must be addressed in each client's informed-consent agreement include "the nature and course of therapy, *fees*, involvement of third parties, and limits of confidentiality" (emphasis added). Further, in Standard 6.04, Fees and Financial Arrangements, the APA Ethics Code requires that at the earliest time possible, psychologists and those to whom they provide professional services "reach an agreement specifying compensation and billing arrangements."

The NASW (2008) Ethics Code identifies informed consent as essential for helping to promote each client's self-determination (Standard 1.02, Self-Determination). In Standard 1.03, Informed Consent, the NASW Ethics Code includes "limits to services because of the requirements of a third party payer" and "relevant costs" as essential elements of each client's informed-consent agreement (para. 25). The ACA (2005) Code of Ethics similarly mandates inclusion of fees and billing arrangements in each client's informed consent and requires that "counselors take steps to ensure that clients understand the implications of . . . fees and billing arrangements" (p. 4). Principal 7.2 of the American Association of Marriage and Family Therapists Ethics Code (AAMFT; 2001) states that

> prior to entering into the therapeutic relationship marriage and family therapists clearly disclose and explain to clients all financial arrangements and fees related to professional services, including charges for canceled or missed appointments, use of collection agencies, and the procedure for obtaining payment from the client, if payment is denied by a third party payor. (para. 66)

Thus, it can be seen that there is wide agreement in the ethics codes of the mental health professions that these issues must be openly and thoughtfully addressed in each client's informed consent.

As is true with other important informed-consent issues, fees and financial arrangements should not be discussed on a single occasion but should be reviewed over time throughout the professional relationship (Barnett, Wise, et al., 2007; C. B. Fisher & Oransky, 2008). There are two important reasons to address informed consent from a process model approach (Pomerantz, 2005). First, clients are presented with a significant amount of information that they need to absorb and understand, and when this information is shared at the beginning of the professional relationship, the client is frequently in an emotionally charged state, if not in emotional crisis. The likelihood of clients concentrating on, and fully understanding, the implications of all information shared with them under these circumstances is not great. Second, situations change over the course of treatment. For example, clients' insurance coverage or their ability to afford treatment may change; the clinician may discontinue participation in an insurance network or raise the fees charged. Thus, revisiting informed-consent issues over the course of the professional relationship is viewed as essential for meeting our ethical obligations to clients.

WHEN SHOULD THE INFORMED-CONSENT PROCESS BEGIN?

The ethics codes of the mental health professions advise that informed consent be provided as soon as is feasible in the professional relationship. As Pomerantz (2005) has highlighted, this may mean that different issues are discussed at different points in time. However, one should not assume that as early as is feasible begins during the first session with a new client. Instead, it is recommended that informed consent related to financial matters first be addressed even before the initial appointment with clients. Potential clients have the right to know the fees they will be expected to pay, whether insurance is accepted, how payment is expected, and the like before the initial session. Such information is so important to many individuals that it may be a deciding factor whether they will be able to seek the services of a particular clinician.

Referrals to clinicians come from many sources. These may include primary care physicians, other mental health professionals who are colleagues or who may know of the mental health professional by reputation, schools, friends or colleagues of past clients, and others. These referral sources may not be aware of a particular clinician's fees, payment and billing practices, financial policies, or participation in insurance and managed care. Ensuring that every potential referral source in one's local area has such up-to-date information is not likely to be feasible.

Potential clients may be referred to you with every intention of working with you because of a strong personal recommendation received from an individual whose opinions they trust. However, the recommendation about the types of clients you work with and the fine job you did previously are not the only information potential clients will need. Many may be greatly limited by financial restrictions such as the need to work with a clinician who is an in-network provider for their insurance company. Thus, making information about fees and financial policies and arrangements available to potential clients is of great importance (rather than their finding this out during the initial session) and should be seen as the first step in the informed-consent process.

One way to begin sharing information with potential clients to assist them in making informed decisions about with whom to enter treatment is the use of a professional website. In addition to basic information such as your name, degree, licensure status, areas of professional expertise, office location, and *the like*, information on the website can include the following:

- Fees for each type of service provided: Do you charge different fees for the initial evaluation session, for psychotherapy versus psychological testing, for forensic services, etc.?

- How payment is accepted: Do you only accept cash or personal checks? Do you accept credit card payments, and if so, what type?

- When payment is expected: Is payment expected at the beginning of each appointment, at the end of each appointment, monthly? If payment is not expected at each appointment, do you bill the client?

- Participation in insurance or managed care: For which insurance and managed care plans are you an in-network provider? Does the potential client need to obtain preauthorization before the first appointment, and if so, how is this done? If you are an out-of-network provider, for which insurance plans does this apply and how does this affect coverage of professional services provided by you for the client?

Thus, sharing information about fees and financial policies and expectations should begin before the first appointment with a new client. This is important because such knowledge could affect the potential client's decision about seeking professional services from you and because of the need for some clients to contact their insurer to obtain preauthorization before the first appointment to have it covered by their insurance. Finding out after the first appointment that it was not covered by the insurer is not a surprise clients will be pleased to receive, and it is not a good way to begin the professional relationship.

SETTING FEES

When you set fees, a number of matters should be considered thoughtfully and proactively. These include prevailing fees charged by clinicians in your area, your level of experience and expertise, how many other clinicians in the local area provide comparable services, and the population you plan to serve, together with the likely ability of members of that population to pay for needed services. This is in keeping with Standard 1.13(a), Payment for Services, of the NASW (1999) Code of Ethics, which states: "When setting fees, social workers should ensure that the fees are fair, reasonable, and commensurate with the services provided. Consideration should be given to the clients' ability to pay."

As mentioned previously, fees should be set before one's first contact with a new client. It would be inappropriate to inform clients of the fees for services after the service is provided. Informing clients of the fees after seeing how they dress or what car they drive and basing the fee on your perception of their level of affluence would be patently unethical. Discussions of fees, payment options, and the like should be set in written office policies, they should be included in each client's informed-consent process, and this information should be shared with potential clients before the first session. Clinicians with websites often put their policies and forms online for clients to print and fill out before their first appointment. These suggestions are in keeping with the APA (2010a) Ethics Code's Standard 6.04(a), Fees and Financial Arrangements, which states: "As early as is feasible in a professional or scientific relationship, psychologists and recipients of psychological services reach an agreement specifying compensation and billing arrangements."

Because relationships with clients are built on trust, it is vital that the formation of this trusting relationship begin even before the first in-person contact. Furthermore, by sharing needed information with clients, to include fees, financial policies, and financial arrangements, we actively assist them to make informed decisions about participation in the professional relationship, helping to promote their autonomous functioning.

ANTICIPATING A CLIENT'S FINANCIAL LIMITATIONS

In keeping with a focus on each client's best interests, the initial assessment of clients should not be limited solely to their clinical needs. Clients' financial situation should be openly discussed so that any financial limitations that might have an impact on their ability to participate in treatment may be addressed from the outset. Although all possible situations and circumstances can never be fully anticipated, having such a discussion with clients may also sensitize clients to these issues and highlight to them the need to be proactive should any change in their finances occur during the course of treatment.

Standard 6.04(d), Fees and Financial Arrangements, of the APA (2010a) Ethics Code makes this clear in stating: "If limitations to services can be anticipated because of limitations in financing, this is discussed with the recipient of services as early as is feasible." This discussion should address the nature of the anticipated financial difficulties, whether it is likely to be temporary or permanent, and whether there are other options to consider that might help make it easier for the client to afford treatment. Similarly, Standard A.10.b., Establishing Fees, of the ACA (2005) Code of Ethics includes the following statement:

> In establishing fees for professional counseling services, counselors consider the financial status of clients and locality. In the event that the established fee structure is inappropriate for the client, counselors assist clients in attempting to find comparable services of acceptable cost.

Financial limitations should be assessed in the initial session, and an appropriate treatment plan that takes these financial limitations into consideration should be developed (Knapp & VandeCreek, 2006). For example, developing a plan for 9 to 12 months of weekly psychotherapy sessions for an individual who can only afford 9 to 12 psychotherapy sessions would be inappropriate. When you perceive that the client's treatment needs exceed her or his financial resources, other options and treatment alternatives need to be discussed openly. The result of this discussion may be that the client is referred to another professional or program that is better able to work within his or her financial limitations, you could provide treatment to the client but with more limited treatment goals, or you might provide treatment to the client, making alternative financial arrangements so that he or she can afford to participate in treatment.

The pros and cons of each option should be openly discussed during the informed-consent process with each client. Furthermore, it is recommended that clinicians discuss fees and insurance participation during the first telephone contact with the prospective client. Insurance benefits may need to be verified ahead of time so that you know (or can estimate) what the client's financial liability will be.

WORKERS COMPENSATION

Clients who experience an injury on the job may find that their treatment is not covered through their health insurance. Rather, it may be expected that the employer's workers compensation coverage will be responsible for any mental health care that is needed as a result of the injury. Each state has different workers compensation rules, and it is necessary for the clinician to be aware of these rules as they apply to the provision and reimbursement of services. Such services must be preauthorized, traditional confidentiality rules may not apply (e.g., in many states, treatment records are part of an "open system"), certain requirements must be met to be reimbursed (e.g., submission of treatment records with each invoice), fees may be set by a state agency or regulatory commission, clients may not be charged any co-pays or be billed for cancellations or no-shows, and care may only be authorized for curative treatment and not for palliative care. In addition, once it has been determined that the client has reached "maximum medical improvement," authorization (and payment) for services may cease immediately (with no sessions allowed for the termination process). Those working in this system must understand these policies so that each may be fully explained to the client. If care is to be continued past when it is authorized, discussions must take place regarding how the client will pay for this care.

THE ROLE OF NONINSURANCE THIRD PARTIES

During the informed-consent process, the role of any third parties should be made clear because they may have an impact on the treatment relationship. Third parties may include (a) parents or guardians who plan to pay for a client's treatment or whose insurance will be used to help cover the costs of the mental health services or (b) government agencies or legal authorities if treatment is mandated or required by law or the courts.

It is essential that the role and level of involvement in the mental health services to be provided is clarified from the outset and included in the informed-consent agreement. At times, the individual receiving the mental health service is not the one who accepts responsibility for payment for these services. However, as with all treatment agreements, it is best to have all parties sign a written agreement that specifies their roles and responsibilities, before the professional services being provided. It is recommended that verbal promises from the client about who will pay for treatment not be used. Statements such as "My stepdad said you should just bill him. He'll take care of everything" have no legal bearing and are not enforceable. When providing professional services to children of divorced parents, it may be important to review the settlement agreement to determine which parent is actually responsible for fees and to have a signed agreement with that parent.

There are times when treatment is for a diagnosis that ordinarily would be covered by an individual's insurance policy but the request for services came from a third party, such as the justice system. For example, although a client may have a diagnosis of intermittent explosive disorder, treatment may not be reimbursed if the counseling was court-ordered, such as the result of an arrest for a road-rage incident. Another example may be court-ordered alcohol abuse counseling following an arrest for driving while intoxicated. Insurance companies often do not consider these treatments "medically necessary" but to be forensically related. Clients have a right to be aware of reimbursement matters before initiating treatment.

When a third party requests or mandates mental health services for one's client, it is important that each party's responsibilities be fully discussed and documented from the outset. This should include responsibility for payment as well as access to treatment information. At times, a third party that accepts financial responsibility for an individual's treatment will assume that this brings with it certain rights or privileges, such as access to confidential treatment information or even the right to influence treatment planning and goal setting. As the ACA (2005) Code of Ethics states in Standard B.3.d., Third Party Payers, "Counselors disclose information to third party payers only when clients have authorized such disclosure" (p. 8). Carefully addressing these matters in the informed-consent process and ensuring each party's understanding of agreed-on roles and responsibilities before the services are provided will help prevent misunderstandings and untoward effects as the professional relationship proceeds.

This informed-consent process becomes especially complicated when the identified patient is an adolescent. Barnett (2010) discussed ethical and legal aspects of working with this patient population and suggests that the way confidential information will be shared with parents be highlighted at the beginning of treatment. In certain jurisdictions, parents may have full access to their adolescent's treatment records, and in other jurisdictions no access at all. For example, in several states, adolescents aged over 14 years have the right to consent to their own treatment and thus to make treatment decisions to include regulating confidentiality; in other states, those aged 16 and older have this right. This can result in a situation in which an adolescent is admitted to a treatment program that is being paid for through the parent's insurance (with parents paying for the portion not covered by the insurance) but the professional staff is not allowed to share any information with the parents because the adolescent declines to provide this authorization. Although the therapeutic merits of such a system can be debated, the point is that it is important for treating professionals to provide informed consent about treatment and billing to all of the relevant parties so they understand their rights, obligations, and responsibilities from the outset.

RAISING FEES

Like all others in business, mental health professionals have a range of expenses that may have an impact on their ability to remain viable and to earn a reasonable living. Expenses such as rent, utilities, telephone, insurance, and staff salaries are each likely to increase over time. Accordingly, mental health professionals will periodically need to increase the fees they charge. The possibility of such increases should be included in the informed-consent agreement so that clients will be able to factor these potential increased costs into their financial planning. For example, clinicians may include in the informed-consent agreement that all fees charged increase by 10% on January 1 of each year.

An alternative approach is to increase fees on an as-needed basis and to provide clients with advanced notice of doing so. Advanced notice is vital because some clients may not be able to afford increased fees. For these clients, the extra time may be used to consider other treatment options and to make alternative arrangements. We generally recommend 60 days notice, but this may be affected by factors that include the length of the client's treatment thus far and the client's financial situation. Furthermore, this should be fully discussed with the client and documented in his or her treatment record.

Mental health professionals certainly may increase their fees periodically, but they must remember to do so in a manner that is not exploitative of clients. Furthermore, in keeping with Standard 6.04(c), Fees and Financial Arrangements, of the APA (2010a) Ethics Code, "Psychologists do not misrepresent their fees." Accordingly, it would never be appropriate to charge one fee when a client enters treatment and then as soon as the treatment relationship is developed, dramatically increase the fee without notice.

WHEN CLIENTS DO NOT PAY AGREED-ON FEES

In addition to having a clear policy in place that addresses charges for missed appointments and charges for treatment sessions cancelled without adequate notice, it is also important to address the issue of unpaid bills with clients. The APA (2010a) Ethics Code states in Standard 6.04(e) that

> if the recipient of services does not pay for services as agreed, and if psychologists intend to use collection agencies or legal measures to collect the fees, psychologists first inform the person that such measures will be taken and provide that person an opportunity to make prompt payment.

Similar guidance is provided in the ACA (2005) Code of Ethics in Standard A.10.c., Nonpayment of Fees, which states,

> if counselors intend to use collection agencies or take legal measures to collect fees from clients who do not pay for services as agreed upon, they first inform clients of intended actions and offer clients the opportunity to make payment.

However, the prudent mental health professional will endeavor to use a preventive approach to addressing payment concerns rather than allow a client to build up a large outstanding balance owed. The first step is to address fees and payment requirements in the initial informed-consent discussion and include it in the written financial agreement. It is also recommended that a maximum allowable outstanding balance be specified in this agreement. For example, the clinician may inform clients that the maximum outstanding balance allowed is the equivalent of three sessions. Should the client's balance begin to grow, the clinician needs to remind the client of this agreement and discuss with him or her any difficulties that are present with regard to making payments. If, despite these reminders, that level of outstanding balance is reached, the clinician should openly discuss relevant concerns with the client and offer appropriate options. Such options include paying off the balance in full, working out a payment plan agreement, increasing the amount of time between treatment sessions, agreeing to a reduced fee either permanently or for an agreed-on period of time, referring the client to another professional or to a facility that offers a sliding fee scale or pro bono services, or some combination of these (e.g., allowing the client to pay a reduced fee, with the promise of the outstanding balance being paid at a specified rate over time after treatment is completed). Of course, the client's stated reasons for not paying agreed-on fees in a timely manner may affect the clinician's decision making on the best course of action. For example, one may respond quite differently to a client who recently lost her job and her health insurance than to a client who keeps forgetting his checkbook and makes continued promises to pay the fees owed but fails to do so.

Some clinicians may view these possible options with skepticism because of concerns about being accused of abandoning clients. It is important that mental health professionals understand that their obligation is to take actions to reasonably ensure that their clients' treatment needs are adequately addressed, not that they must personally provide ongoing treatment to a client indefinitely, even if the client is not paying for services as had been agreed-on in the informed-consent process.

As the ACA (2005) Code of Ethics states in Standard A.11.c., Appropriate Termination, "Counselors may terminate a counseling relationship when . . . clients do not pay fees as agreed upon." Further, Standard A.11.a., Abandonment Prohibited, states that "Counselors do not abandon or neglect clients in counseling. Counselors assist in making appropriate arrangements for the continuation of treatment . . . following termination."

Further guidance is found in the NASW (1999) Code of Ethics in Standard 1.16(c), Termination of Services, which states,

> Social workers in fee-for-service settings may terminate services to clients who are not paying an overdue balance if the financial contractual arrangements have been made clear to the client, if the client does not pose an imminent danger to self or others, and if the clinical and other consequences of the current nonpayment have been addressed and discussed with the client.

Additionally, Standard 1.16(d) states, "Social workers who anticipate the termination or interruption of services to clients should notify clients promptly and seek the transfer, referral, or continuation of services in relation to the clients' needs and preferences."

These standards support the ability of clinicians to make alternative arrangements when clients do not pay for treatment as had been agreed on, when done in keeping with ethical standards, and with attention to the client's ongoing treatment needs. However, it is clear that mental health professionals should never abruptly terminate clients' treatment when they are in crisis; clinical needs must be placed before financial gain. Addressing each client's ongoing clinical needs in a manner consistent with our obligation to "First, do no harm" (see Principle A: Beneficence and Nonmaleficence, APA, 2010a) can be done while ensuring that one does not have to provide clinical services indefinitely without being appropriately compensated (Younggren & Gottlieb, 2008).

When considering the option of using a collection agency or a small claims court, it is important for the mental health professional to remain cognizant of each client's particular circumstances. At times, clients may lose their ability to afford ongoing treatment. For example, clients may lose their jobs or health insurance benefits, or they may have unexpected expenses, such as those due to an illness or accident. Although all mental health professionals have the right to be fairly compensated for all services provided, they must at the same time be sensitive to their clients' financial circumstances.

Furthermore, mental health professionals should never terminate treatment solely for financial reasons. Clinical need must always be considered when making such decisions (Younggren & Gottlieb, 2008). Although no mental health professional is required to meet each client's every need, we are required to take reasonable steps to ensure that clients' treatment requirements are appropriately met and that clients are not abandoned (Vasquez, Bingham, & Barnett, 2008).

Should one wish to use a small claims court or collection agency to collect fees owed by a client, it is best to first discuss this with him or her and try to work out a mutually agreeable plan. If one decides to take this route, the client must first be informed of this possibility (in addition to the initial informed consent) and be offered options for making restitution in a reasonable and agreed-on time period. If this does not prove effective, the client is then informed of the action to be taken.

Although Standard 6.04(b), Fees and Financial Arrangements, of the APA (2010a) Ethics Code allows for the use of collection agencies and the use of small claims courts to collect fees owed by clients, risk management specialists have emphasized that the use of these means of collecting fees is often seen as antagonistic by clients and former clients (Bennett et al., 2006). These authors highlighted that clients who were previously pleased with the treatment received suddenly can find fault with it and file a malpractice suit or a complaint through a licensing board when they receive notice of a collections proceeding or of a legal action against them. In these cases, the amount of money spent defending oneself against these complaints typically far exceeds the amount one was trying to recover. Thus, prevention is deemed a much better approach for addressing fees owed by clients. However, should a collection agency be used, it is important to ensure that all requirements of one's ethics code are met, that the process be openly discussed with the client in advance of taking this action, that all such discussions be documented, that these discussions be followed up with written correspondence with copies kept in the treatment record, and that the collection agency is informed of acceptable and unacceptable practices. Furthermore, each client's confidentiality should be protected. The only information that should be shared with a collection agency is the client's name, the dates of service, and the fees owed.

ALTERNATIVE PAYMENT METHODS

When clients are not able to pay for their needed treatment, mental health clinicians who still desire to provide the treatment have several options available to them. These include providing services on a pro bono basis, a sliding-scale basis, or through bartering.

Pro Bono Services

Pro bono, or free, services are an option for all mental health professionals. Although this practice is not mandated in any of the mental health professions' ethics codes, it is encouraged when possible. The APA (2010a) Ethics Code Principle B: Fidelity and Responsibility includes the statement that "psychologists strive to contribute a portion of their professional time for little or no compensation or personal advantage." Similarly, in the introduction to Section A: The Counseling Relationship, the ACA (2005) Code of Ethics advises that "counselors are encouraged to contribute to society by devoting a portion of their professional activity to services for which there is little or no financial return (pro bono publico)" (p. 4). In its discussion of the value, Service, the NASW (2008) Ethics Code advises that "social workers are encouraged to volunteer some portion of their professional skills with no expectation of significant financial return (pro bono service)" (para. 20).

These suggestions are aspirational in nature. Mental health professionals must each decide if they can offer pro bono services, and if so, to how many clients and for what period of time, on the basis of their own unique financial circumstances. There is no ethical mandate to provide clients with services free of charge, but it is one option to consider for assisting clients experiencing significant financial hardship and who are in need of ongoing treatment. We also have a colleague who has found that doing an occasional pro bono forensic case has significantly enhanced his exposure and created significant goodwill in the courthouse, resulting in many additional referrals.

Sliding Fee Scale

A similar issue is that of a sliding fee scale: charging fees of varying amounts to clients on the basis of their ability to pay. Similar to pro bono services, this practice is never mandated but is an aspirational ideal that may be considered to enable clients to receive needed mental health services that they might not otherwise be able to afford. A sliding fee scale may be considered in situations in which clients who previously had paid the full fee for services are no longer able to afford this fee or whose insurance previously had provided coverage for treatment and no longer will do so. It also may be used as the initial payment method for clients in one's practice so that clients of limited means may be able to receive needed services.

When considering the use of a sliding fee scale, it is best to include the specific parameters of its use in a financial agreement that is included as part of the informed-consent process. Additionally, it is best if a consistent method for determining clients' fees is included in this agreement. For example, specific fees may be associated with certain reported household incomes. This practice may prove more effective than making individual determinations and decisions with every client who requests this fee option. The agreement should also specify any documentation of earnings or expenses that the clinician would want to review before making a fee determination. Finally, it is recommended that the issue of changes in the client's financial status be included in this financial agreement as well. Should the client no longer be in financial need and be able to afford a higher fee or even the full fee, that expectation should be clearly articulated in the agreement as well. Most clinicians will not be pleased to hear about a client's upcoming vacation to Disney World or see a client drive up in a new luxury car when providing services in good faith for a greatly reduced fee. It has been mentioned that the professional relationship is one that is built on trust, something that is relevant to both sides of the relationship.

Barter

At times, the only way a client is able to afford needed mental health services is through the use of barter, payment in the form of goods or services by the client in exchange for the professional services. Although engaging in barter is not unethical per se, each of the mental health professions' ethics codes recommends caution when participating in it. These ethics codes do acknowledge that there are times when there may be no other way for clients to access needed treatment services, and there may be settings, such as some rural communities or with certain ethnic groups, where the use of barter is consistent with prevailing community standards.

As with other fee and payment arrangements, the use of barter should be discussed in detail in the informed-consent agreement. All barter arrangements should be discussed on an ongoing basis to ensure that neither party is feeling taken advantage of or exploited (Zur, 2007). Any difficulties experienced should be discussed openly as they arise. Furthermore, a specific written policy on barter is recommended to help ensure that it is applied consistently and to help prevent confusion or an adverse impact on the treatment relationship or process. It is also recommended that goods with an agreed-on value be chosen over the provision of services, for which disagreement over the quality and value could arise (Knapp & VandeCreek, 2008), and in situations in which an inappropriate multiple-relationship situation between the client and clinician may arise.

It is each mental health professional's ethical obligation to ensure that clients are not exploited by a barter arrangement. As the NASW (2008) Code of Ethics states, social workers may only engage in barter when it is "considered to be essential for the provision of services, negotiated without coercion, and entered into at the client's initiative and with the client's informed consent" (para. 75).

Similarly, psychologists may only engage in barter with clients when "it is not clinically contraindicated" and "the resulting arrangement is not exploitative" (APA, 2010a, 6.05). The ACA (2005) Code of Ethics provides similar guidance and also adds that "counselors consider the cultural implications of bartering and discuss relevant concerns with clients and document such agreements in a clear written contract" (p. 6). The AAMFT (2001) Ethics Code calls for the establishment of a clear, written agreement and that there be an assurance that the professional relationship is not distorted as a result of the bartering arrangement.

Mental health professionals who engage in barter should also remember that they are receiving income (although it is not cash) for the services they are providing. As such, they are legally obligated to include the fair market value of the goods or services received in their income that is reported to the Internal Revenue Service and to pay taxes on what has been received. Failure to do so may bring with it significant tax and legal consequences.

REFERRALS AND FEES

The process of making a referral of a client to another professional should always be motivated by the client's best interests. Referral decisions should be made based on the client's specific treatment needs and how well it appears that the new professional can meet those needs. A referral should not be motivated by the benefit of the referring professional. For example, the APA (2010a) Ethics Code in Standard 6.07, Referrals and Fees, states,

> When psychologists pay, receive payment from, or divide fees with another professional, other than in an employer–employee relationship, the payment to each is based on the services provided (clinical, consultative, administrative, or other) and is not based on the referral itself.

It is important that referrals not be motivated by possible financial gain for the referring practitioner but be based solely on the client's clinical and financial needs and interests. The payment or receipt of a fee for making or receiving a referral is considered a conflict of interest and not in keeping with the ethical standards of the mental health professions.

CONCLUSION

It is important that clinicians develop a working framework for billing and collecting of ethical practices that falls within legal guidelines. In developing procedures for this aspect of their business, we think it is important that clinicians attend to each of the following:

- Be familiar with the ethical principles and standard of their profession.

- Understand that informed consent applies not only to clinical issues but also to financial issues of paying for services.

- Be prepared to begin the financial portion of the informed-consent process as early as possible, even before treatment begins.

- Anticipate, if possible, financial limitations of the client's being able to pay for treatment.

- Be able to communicate adequately, both verbally and in writing, all financial aspects of treatment, including what role an insurance company may play in paying for all or part of services provided.

- Have a set policy that is communicated to clients regarding possible increases in fees.

- Have a set policy that is communicated to clients about what will occur if they do not pay for fees that are owed for services provided.

- Consider, within ethical guidelines, alternative payment methods such as accepting a sliding fee or bartering, when appropriate.

- Understand that when making referrals on behalf of clients, the overarching concern is the client's best interest and not any financial or professional gain for making the referral.

REFERENCES

American Association of Marital and Family Therapy. (2001). *AAMFT code of ethics.* Retrieved from https://www.aamft.org/Legal_Ethics/Code_of_Ethics.aspx

American Counseling Association. (2005). *ACA code of ethics.* Retrieved from http://www.counseling.org/Resources/CodeOfEthics/TP/Home/CT2.aspx

American Psychological Association. (2010a). *Ethical principles of psychologists and code of conduct.* Retrieved from http://www.apa.org/ethics/code/index.aspx

Barnett, J. E. (2010). Adolescent and (vs.) parent: Clinical, ethical, and legal issues for practitioners. *The Independent Practitioner, 30,* 77–80.

Barnett, J. E., Wise, E. H., Johnson-Greene, D., & Bucky, S. F. (2007). Informed consent: Too much of a good thing? Or not enough? *Professional Psychology: Research and Practice, 38,* 179–186. doi:10.1037/0735-7028.38.2.179

Beahrs, J. O., & Gutheil, T. G. (2001). Informed consent in psychotherapy. *The American Journal of Psychiatry, 158,* 4–10. doi:10.1176/appi.ajp.158.1.4

Beauchamp, T. L., & Childress, J. F. (1994). *Principles of biomedical ethics* (4th ed.). New York: Oxford University Press.

Bennett, B., Bricklin, P., Harris, E., Knapp, S., VandeCreek, L., & Younggren, J. (2006). *Assessing and managing risk in psychological practice: An individual approach.* Rockville, MD: American Psychological Association Insurance Trust.

Fisher, C. B., & Oransky, M. (2008). Informed consent to psychotherapy: Protecting the dignity and respecting the autonomy of patients. *Journal of Clinical Psychology, 64,* 576–588.

Kitchener, K. S. (1984). Intuition, critical evaluation and ethics principles: The foundation for ethical decisions in counseling psychology. *The Counseling Psychologist, 12,* 43–55. doi:10.1177/0011000084123005

Knapp, S., & VandeCreek, L. (2006). *Practical ethics for psychologists: A positive approach.* Washington, DC: American Psychological Association. doi:10.1037/11331-000

Knapp, S., & VandeCreek, L. (2008). The ethics of advertising, billing, and finances in psychotherapy. *Journal of Clinical Psychology, 64,* 613–625.

National Association of Social Workers. (1999). *NASW code of ethics*. Retrieved from http://www.socialworkers.org/pubs/code/default.asp

National Association of Social Workers. (2008). *The code of ethics of the National Association of Social Workers*. Retrieved from http://www.naswdc.org/pubs/code/code.asp

Pomerantz, A. M. (2005). Increasingly informed consent: Discussing distinct aspects of psychotherapy at different points in time. *Ethics & Behavior, 15*, 351–360. doi:10.1207/s15327019eb1504_6

Snyder, T. A., & Barnett, J. E. (2006). Informed consent and the psychotherapy process. *Psychotherapy Bulletin, 41*, 37–42.

Sullivan, T., Martin, W. L., & Handelsman, M. M. (1993). Practical benefits of an informed consent procedure: An empirical investigation. *Professional Psychology: Research and Practice, 24*, 160–163. doi:10.1037/0735-7028.24.2.160

Vasquez, M. J. T., Bingham, R. P., & Barnett, J. E. (2008). Psychotherapy termination: Clinical and ethical responsibilities. *Journal of Clinical Psychology, 64*, 653–665.

Younggren, J. N., & Gottlieb, M. C. (2008). Termination and abandonment: History, risk, and risk management. *Professional Psychology: Research and Practice, 39*, 498–504. doi:10.1037/0735-7028.39.5.498

Zur, O. (2007). *Boundaries in psychotherapy: Ethical and clinical explorations*. Washington, DC: American Psychological Association. doi:10.1037/11563-000

COMMENTARY: Psychologists went to school to study science, not accounting. Whatever facility they once enjoyed with statistical analysis—and some, of course, vow never to reflect on such matters again once they pass their licensing examinations—billing draws on a clearly distinct skill set. As a result of these and other considerations, psychologists often attempt to outsource the business end of their practices to the extent ethically feasible, and their judgment may also be affected by administrative and financial pressures unique to an era of managed care.

Billing is greatly complicated for clinical as opposed to other business concerns for two related reasons. The first of these is the confidential nature of the services in question; the second is the potential emotional vulnerability—and potential retaliation in the form of licensing board complaints—of persons subjected to collection proceedings in this context. Billing may present unique personnel-related issues as well because it is the activity least likely to conducted with day-to-day oversight on the part of the psychologist.

The following references are recommended for those interested in further investigation of billing, collection, and financial arrangements and associated ethical considerations, with relevance to private, multidisciplinary, and institutional practices.

Barnett, J. E., & Walfish, S. (2012). Ethical lapses by clinicians in the billing process. In J. E. Barnett & S. Walfish, *Billing and collecting for your mental health practice: Effective strategies and ethical practice* (pp. 79–86). Washington, DC: American Psychological Association.

Datz, G., & Bruns, D. (2015). Billing psychological services for patients with chronic pain. In T. R. Deer, M. S. Leong, & A. L. Ray (Eds.), *Treatment of chronic pain by integrative approaches: The American Academy of Pain Medicine textbook on patient management* (pp. 101–113). New York, NY: Springer Science+Business Media.

Hutton, R. E. (2009). Practical considerations when beginning to practice: Ethics, billing, insurance. In S. F. Davis, P. J. Giordano, & C. A. Licht (Eds.), *Your career in psychology: Putting your graduate degree to work* (pp. 163–174). Hoboken, NJ: Wiley-Blackwell.

Knapp, S., & VandeCreek, L. (2008). The ethics of advertising, billing, and finances in psychotherapy. *Journal of Clinical Psychology, 64,* 613–625. http://dx.doi.org/10.1002/jclp.20475

Kozak, T. M., & Miller, A. K. (2017). Effective billing and collecting. In S. Walfish, J. E. Barnett, & J. Zimmerman (Eds.), *Handbook of private practice: Keys to success for mental health practitioners* (pp. 250–264). New York, NY: Oxford University Press.

10.5. Practicing Psychology in the Era of Managed Care: Implications for Practice and Training

Lisa M. Sanchez and Samuel M. Turner

. . .

New Patterns in Service Delivery and Organizational Structure

Because the majority of the American insured population is under a managed behavioral health care plan, many practitioners have been forced to work with managed care companies (Hayes et al., 1999). In a 1996 national survey of APA Division 42 (Psychologists in Independent Practice; $N = 1,000$, respondents = 442), 84% of the respondents indicated they were members of HMO or PPO panels (Murphy, DeBernardo, & Shoemaker, 1998). The modal number of panel memberships was in the category of nine or more. In response to demands imposed by this new relationship, many mental health care providers have been forced to reorganize their practice and methods for treating patients in order to maintain profits.

Prior to managed care, most clinicians in private practice carried a relatively small caseload and treated each patient over a long period of time (Shore & Beigel, 1996). Generally, patients who had indemnity insurance and who pursued long-term therapy were young, educated, and affluent persons who sought help for problems in living (Cummings et al., 1998). Cummings et al. (1998) noted that during the peak of solo fee-for-service practice, 20% of patients accounted for 70% of the total mental health care expenditures. In the current system, session limits often are imposed by the managed care organization, and the goal of treatment is functional improvement and symptom reduction in the context of short-term therapy (Bedell, Hunter, & Corrigan, 1997; Shore & Beigel, 1996).

Previously, the individual clinician attracted patients on the basis of reputation, visibility, or advertising (Drum, 1995). In contrast, providers are now more obliged to recruit patients and secure referrals by competing for membership on managed care panels. Currently, most mental health benefits are provided only if patients receive treatment from a clinician on their insurance plan panel of providers. Benefits for treatment received by an out-of-network provider will typically be denied or subject to higher copayments. Therefore, those who offer

effective services at lower prices can more successfully bid for panel membership and obtain a secure referral base (Hayes et al., 1999). This competition for
patients has resulted in reduced fees because, as previously noted, managed
care organizations reimburse services at lower rates (Hayes et al., 1999). One
interpretation of this shift is that managed care is requiring the field to acknowledge its finite resources and examine how resources are best distributed to the
overall population. Although no specific data support this assertion, there is an
impression that mental health providers must treat a larger and more hetero-
geneous population in order to maintain previous levels of income (Hayes et al.,
1999). It can be argued that with fewer people using up the bulk of mental
health resources, services have the potential for being more broadly delivered.
The issue of access to and utilization of mental health services is revisited as a
quality-of-care concern in subsequent sections.

In addition to changing patterns of service delivery, managed care policies
also have impacted the organization of clinician practices. The survey of APA
Division 42 members (Murphy et al., 1998) revealed that 21% of the respondents had moved from solo practice to a larger integrated network, and an
additional 23% anticipated joining a group or network in the future. Because
clinicians have more administrative responsibilities in the current system,
many have reduced their clinical hours or have added salaried clerical staff to
manage administrative tasks. Therefore, one change in practice patterns as a
result of managed care is increased attention to administrative responsibilities
and, as a result, the shift toward larger networks of providers with support staff.

A second change in practice patterns relates to treatment outcome and efficacy. Utilization reviewers typically require documentation of treatment efficacy
before offering reimbursement. One strategy adopted by practitioners for dealing with these requirements has been the increased use of outcome measures.
A 1995 national survey of all APA members who had been billed for special
practice assessment as part of their APA dues ($N = 47,119$, respondents = 15,918)
revealed a small but consistent trend for more recently licensed providers to use
outcome measures in clinical practice (Phelps, Eisman, & Kohout, 1998). Twenty-
three percent of those licensed through 1969 reported using outcome measures,
compared with 27% licensed in 1970–1979 and 31% licensed in 1990–1995.
This trend likely reflects the increasing need of providers to be accountable for
treatment efficacy and to offer inexpensive services in order to retain managed
care referrals and be reimbursed for services.

Similarly, new reimbursement requirements may have fostered increased
use of and adherence to practice guidelines. In response to the need to prove
treatment efficacy and greater accountability, in the late 1980s, the federal government sought the construction of clinical practice guidelines (Hayes et al.,
1999). *Best practice standards* are now typically part of the utilization review process, and providers may be dropped from managed care panels and subject to
legal action if they are not followed. Although some consider the guidelines to
create more uniformity in services delivered and provide an empirical basis for
assessing and treating mental health problems, others view psychotherapy as

too complex and individualized to be subjected to standardized interventions. Again, it is unclear what effect guidelines have had on treatment outcome.

Finally, social workers and other master's-level clinicians have assumed a more prominent role in the current behavioral health care market (Cummings, 1995). Eighty-three percent of respondents in the 1995 national survey of APA members indicated they believed ("to a great extent") that managed care has led to an increased use of non–doctoral-level providers, such as social workers, for service delivery (Phelps et al., 1998). It has been argued that the delivery of services by less trained and less educated practitioners results in poorer standards of care. However, this has yet to be subjected to empirical study.

It is important to note that managed care may have been among the factors contributing to the increasing privatization of the public sector delivery of behavioral health care. Severely mentally ill patients, who in the past would have been treated in long-term public mental hospitals, are now largely treated on an outpatient basis or in community settings such as nursing homes, supervised residences, or board and care homes (Mechanic, McAlpine, & Olfson, 1998). Private nonprofit hospitals increasingly treat those with managed care insurance. In response, states continue to downsize public mental hospitals and transfer long-term patients to community residences and general hospitals. Data from the National Hospital Discharge Survey and the Inventory of Mental Health Organizations indicate that between 1988 and 1994, rates of discharge from public mental health hospitals decreased by 20% and rates of discharge from general hospitals increased by 35% (Mechanic et al., 1998). A significant portion of the cost reductions achieved for mental health services are due to reductions in days of inpatient care (Leslie & Rosenheck, 1999). Although this movement began prior to managed care and involved a host of social, political, and legal issues, managed care likely accelerated this trend, as hospital-based care historically has been the highest source of behavioral health care cost. As cited in Richardson and Austad (1991), 75% of mental health care costs can be attributed to residential and inpatient treatment. Therefore, managed care organizations and states clearly benefit financially from limiting the use of hospitals for delivery of care. It is not yet clear how this change has impacted quality of care for patients.

In summary, managed behavioral health care has fostered a system of rewards for those who address specific behavioral symptoms and use short-term, empirically based treatments. Long-term treatment in public hospitals now has limited third-party financial support. There also is an increased market for less educated and less costly practitioners, such as master's-level clinicians. According to results from survey data (Murphy et al., 1998), in response to the new financial and administrative responsibilities brought on by managed care, an increasing number of clinicians are leaving solo practice to join integrated networks. As another strategy for coping with financial constraints, less costly formats, such as group therapy, may become more prevalent. It has yet to be determined what the impact of these changes will be on treatment outcome or quality of care.

Quality of Behavioral Health Care
in the Managed Care Environment

The quality of mental health care in the context of managed care is arguably one of the most important and fiercely debated issues in the psychological literature as well as in the popular media. In the past, individual clinicians and patients made decisions regarding length of therapy and type of treatment. However, decisions regarding many aspects of treatment, including access to professional mental health services and type and length of treatment delivered, is currently dictated by managed care policies. Because the clinician is widely considered to base treatment decisions on the best interest of the patient, whereas managed care organizations are considered to base treatment decisions solely on profit, concerns have arisen regarding quality of care provided in this new environment. To explore the veracity of such misgivings, we will review research examining the quality of psychological treatment in terms of consumer access, sufficiency of services, appropriateness of services, accuracy of detection, and treatment outcome in the managed care environment.

One of the ways the managed care system has altered patient access to psychological services is by requiring primary care physicians to authorize a mental health referral. In a 1986 national survey of all operating HMOs, 75% ($N = 473$, respondents = 286) indicated that the approval of a patient's primary care physician was required for any mental health service to be obtained (Shadle & Christianson, 1988). One concern with respect to the increasing reliance on primary care physicians for the detection of and referral for mental health problems is that patients will be deflected from mental health settings to primary care settings and treated primarily pharmacologically. The influx of patients into the primary care setting also is feared to promote the conceptualization of mental disorders in an overly biological and reductionistic manner (Dana et al., 1996). There is some evidence to support this concern. For example, in recently created clinical practice guidelines for depression, there is a strong emphasis on pharmacological treatment (American Psychiatric Association, 1993; Barlow, 1996). In addition, in a national survey of 1,350 randomly selected primary care physicians (Williams et al., 1999), the most common form of treatment reported for depression was antidepressant medication (72.5%); the second most common form of treatment was a mental health referral (38.4%).

This practice may be cause for concern in light of other data indicating that most physicians diagnosed depression without using the *Diagnostic and Statistical Manual of Mental Disorders* (4th edition; *DSM–IV*; American Psychiatric Association, 1994) criteria, during a 13-minute visit wherein an average of six problems were discussed (Schappert, 1994). Also, although medication reduces acute symptoms of depression (e.g., Hirschfeld, 1994), personality and situational factors that maintain depressive symptoms often are not addressed and may be related to a higher relapse rate (Dana et al., 1996). Impressive data attest to the effectiveness of psychological interventions for depression as well as other conditions. For example, in a review of 302 studies examining psychological treatment outcome (for a variety of diagnosable disorders), more than

85% of the effect sizes were .20 or larger, and the mean treatment effect size over all studies was .50 (Lipsey & Wilson, 1993). This positive trend was present even when controlling for placebo artifacts and bias resulting from increased availability of published versus unpublished studies. Therefore, relying on medication as the sole form of treatment for depression is contrary to empirical evidence demonstrating that psychological interventions can be as effective or even more effective than pharmacotherapy, and the efficacy of medication is often increased when used in conjunction with psychological treatment (Barlow, 1996). However, because researchers examining mental health treatment in general medical settings have focused largely on depression, the conclusion that there is a general increase in the medicalization of mental health conceptualization and treatment should be interpreted with caution.

A second issue pertains to the accuracy of physician detection and treatment. In the 1987 RAND Medical Outcomes Study, survey information from over 22,000 adults in Boston, Chicago, and Los Angeles was collected to examine quality of care in different practice settings and among different specialty groups. This study focused on outcomes for patients with one or more of four chronic conditions (depression, congestive heart failure, hypertension, and diabetes). The methodology is described in detail elsewhere (e.g., Rogers, Wells, Meredith, Sturm, & Burnam, 1993). Using these data, Sturm and Wells (1995) examined treatment utilization and functional status of 424 severely depressed patients over the course of two years. Results indicated that depression was almost twice as likely to be correctly detected by psychiatrists than by general medical practitioners. In addition, the probability that the patient received appropriate antidepressant medication and/or counseling was significantly higher for those who visited psychiatrists than for those who visited other physicians ($p < .05$). Of course, because patients were not randomized to conditions, it is possible that those who saw general physicians represented a subgroup of people who were more difficult to diagnose, possibly because of the complexity of comorbid medical conditions. However, researchers conducting other studies also have reported a low rate of accurate detection of depression, from 30% to 50%, among general physicians (e.g., Gerber et al., 1989; Simon & VonKorff, 1995). Therefore, concerns regarding the adequacy and appropriateness of physician (gatekeeper) referrals may be warranted.

Perhaps the chief concern regarding the quality of treatment provided in a managed care system is related to the imposition of third-party payers into the traditional dual relationship between patient and clinician. Specifically, these concerns relate to the increasing control of managed care companies in determining treatment decisions and limiting the supply of services available to enrollees. Data from the RAND Health Insurance Study, in which patients were randomized into an HMO or one of several fee-for-service plans, indicated that patients in fee-for-service plans incurred 2.8 times more cost that did those in HMO plans ($p < .05$). The cost differential primarily was due to fewer visits per enrollee, greater reliance on group versus individual therapy, and increased use of non-doctoral-level providers (Wells, Manning, & Benjamin, 1986). It has been argued that such cost-cutting strategies, which focus on service reduction and the use of less educated clinicians, adversely impact treatment outcome.

In addition, the results of several surveys suggest that treatment may be terminated prematurely as a result of managed care practices. In a Colorado survey of 223 responding psychologists, 64% reported incidents of managed care companies discontinuing treatment prematurely (Hipp, Atkinson, & Pelc, 1994). In a national survey of psychologists in APA Division 39 (Psychoanalysis; $N = 3,956$, respondents = 718), 49% reported that their patients experienced adverse consequences due to treatment delay or denial (Tucker & Lubin, 1994). Adverse outcomes included the need for hospitalization, suicidal or homicidal ideation and behavior, medical illness, severe anxiety and depression, and increased rates of relapse. However, it was not specified what percentage of patients experienced these outcomes, and it is not clear that such outcomes were the direct result of treatment delay or denial. Furthermore, these data reflected opinion and were not the result of systematic empirical study.

This cost-driven system may also adversely impact quality by relying on utilization reviewers, who typically have less knowledge and education than do the providers, to authorize or deny treatment (I. J. Miller, 1996). In the Tucker and Lubin (1994) survey, 79% of the responding psychologists expressed dissatisfaction with the utilization reviewer's knowledge and expertise, and 90% reported that reviewers interfered with treatment plans that the responding psychologist considered to be in the patient's best interest. However, in interpreting these results, one must be cognizant of the survey respondents' investment in being reimbursed for long-term therapy, given their psychoanalytic orientation, and the likelihood that they would not be highly trained in short-term treatment techniques.

In summary, on the basis of these survey data, it has been concluded that outpatient therapy is becoming too focused on crisis intervention and transient symptom reduction with insufficient coverage for preventative services (e.g., Dana et al., 1996), and those in need are often denied access to appropriate diagnosis and treatment because of gatekeeping practices that prevent them from being evaluated and treated by more highly trained specialists (I. J. Miller, 1996). Again, it is important to recognize the potential bias stemming from the interest and theoretical orientation of the researchers collecting the data on which this conclusion was based. Thus, there is a need for better studies with clinicians of varied theoretical backgrounds.

. . .

Confidentiality of Patient Information in the Managed Care Environment

Another primary concern for psychologists, particularly those in independent practice, is the extent to which the informational requirements of managed care interfere with the confidential relationship of psychotherapy. During utilization review, managed care staff collect patient information from the therapist to authorize treatment and payment. One concern is that this intrusion may impact the quality of the therapeutic relationship. Analogue studies examining confidentiality have found that patients prefer conditions of absolute confidentiality over conditions of limited confidentiality. Under conditions of limited confidentiality, subjects report they are less willing to self-disclose (Haut & Muehleman, 1986; Nowell & Spruill, 1993).

In a second study, Kremer and Gesten (1998) compared the impact of three different descriptions of therapeutic confidentiality on students' and therapy patients' self-reported willingness to disclose. Results indicated that patients and students in the managed care condition were significantly less willing to disclose than were subjects in the standard limits or rationale conditions ($p < .05$; see Kremer & Gesten, 1998). The effect size of the managed care condition versus the standard limits condition was especially large for psychotherapy patients ($n = 92$, $d = .93$). These data suggest that limits to confidentiality imposed by managed care companies can reduce patients' willingness to self-disclose.

To date, there are limited data on the impact of less self-disclosure on treatment outcome. However, the implication is that patients' reluctance to disclose sensitive and potentially therapeutically relevant information will adversely affect treatment by resulting in improper or inadequate diagnosis and treatment (Kremer & Gesten, 1998; McGuire, Toal, & Blau, 1985). In addition, the quality of the therapeutic relationship is widely considered to be a major factor in treatment outcome (e.g., Beutler, Machado, & Neufeldt, 1994), and managed care informational requirements may interfere with this relationship by introducing an element of distrust. Ambivalence regarding managed care limits to confidentiality may even prevent patients from pursuing treatment in the first place. Then again, it is not clear that self-disclosure as a global construct in psychotherapy is specifically related to clinical outcome. Thus, arguments have been based on the a priori notion that self-disclosure is important to treatment outcome, but in reality this is a complex variable that needs to be examined in a more specific fashion.

In addition, the aforementioned study (Kremer & Gesten, 1998) may be limited in external validity because in practice, many psychologists do not provide full disclosure of limits to confidentiality (e.g., Baird & Rupert, 1987), and most clients expect that confidentiality in psychotherapy is absolute (D. J. Miller & Thelen, 1986). Also, although a consent form must be signed prior to the collection of information, this often takes the form of a blanket statement, presented on signing up for coverage, that permits the managed care company to inspect all medical records. Therefore, it may be possible that at least some patients may be unaware of managed care reporting requirements and that the analogue populations used in these studies may not be entirely representative of actual practice populations.

A second issue relating to confidentiality is the extent to which the managed care environment affects clinicians' reporting practices. In a survey of APA Division 42 practitioners in 1996, 75% of the 442 respondents indicated that concerns regarding confidentiality and reimbursement have compromised patient confidentiality and reporting practices (Murphy et al., 1998). Fifty-three percent strongly disagreed that the vast majority of managed care companies would keep their patients' information confidential, and 63% felt that there was a high potential that information provided to managed care companies could be used to harm patients. These concerns apparently have resulted in some rather disturbing developments. For example, 63% of clinicians in this survey believed that to a large extent, psychologists alter diagnoses or Current Procedural Terminology codes to protect patients' confidentiality, future employment, or future medical insurance. Sixty-one percent believed that psychologists submit the lowest level of diagnosis that is reimbursable and leave off an Axis II diagnosis if a patient has a reimbursable Axis I diagnosis. In addition to the ethical and legal implications of misreporting, this behavior may result in the collection of inaccurate information on the epidemiology of treated disorders and outcome of treatment. If this were to occur, it could result in the development of inaccurate treatment guidelines that could subsequently affect the treatment of patients.

In conclusion, the policy of obtaining confidential information from patients to authorize treatment seems to have impacted the nature and quality of the therapeutic relationship. Evidence indicates that patients who know about limits to confidentiality are less willing to disclose therapeutically relevant information. It remains unclear if this adversely affects treatment outcome, but, at the very least, the process of assessment and intervention is more difficult if the patient is not forthcoming about his or her difficulties. Possibly for this reason, evidence indicates that a large number of practitioners have misreported information to managed care companies to protect their patients' confidentiality. As a result, information on the epidemiology of disorders and outcome of treatment may be inaccurate and might ultimately lead to poorly developed practice guidelines.

. . .

SUMMARY AND CONCLUSIONS

The economics of the current health care system have greatly impacted the practice of behavioral health care. The cost-conscious managed care environment has favored time-limited, symptom-focused, outpatient behavioral health care services. This environment has produced dramatic changes in the way psychological services are delivered and consumed by the population. The changes most frequently cited in the literature include the shift of treatment decision-making power from the behavioral health care provider to policy-makers, reduction in income, concerns regarding quality of care and patient confidentiality, increase in the number of non-doctoral-level providers in the marketplace, emergence of practice guidelines, focus on short-term therapeutic approaches in lieu of long-term therapy, and the need for empirical outcome evidence. Unfortunately, the literature to date focuses primarily on the impact of managed care on independent practice, perhaps because this segment of the field is most directly affected by the new system. It would be interesting for future research efforts to focus on the impact of managed care on other domains of psychology, including academia and research.

Given all the changes in the field, which seem to be perceived negatively, it is striking that an estimated half of mental health care providers are spending at least three quarters of their time in independent practice settings (Phelps et al., 1998). Also, only 6% of responding APA Division 42 members reported leaving practice for other employment or that they anticipated doing so in the future (Murphy et al., 1998). Therefore, it would seem that clinicians in independent practice have successfully adapted to new demands in the marketplace. Perhaps, as noted by Feldman (1992), the emotion involved in the managed care debate has less to do with the issues discussed here and more to do with the managed care threat to professional prerogatives, power, and autonomy, things that are valued highly by most mental health professionals.

Similarly, it is plausible that information regarding adverse outcomes is simply not being disseminated within the professional literature, as clinicians do not typically generate or publish large-scale outcome research. This is a good example of the difficulties created when a strong division and a lack of communication between researchers and practitioners exist, as unfortunately is the case within the field of mental health care. It is striking how little empirical data there are regarding treatment outcome and efficacy following the health reform movement. With the exception of a few published papers based on data collected from the RAND Medical Outcomes and Health Insurance studies (e.g., Rogers et al., 1993; Wells et al., 1986), virtually no research has evaluated comparative outcomes. Therefore, although we have information regarding organizational and assessment shifts in the field, there are not enough data to judge the impact these changes have had on quality of care and treatment outcome. Thus, it is fair to say that the current assessment of the impact of these changes is based more on emotional reaction than on empirical data. If patients are to be optimally treated and the new initiatives of managed care evaluated, it is essential that additional research be conducted on the impact of changes in the field brought about by managed care.

To achieve high-quality patient care in the context of limited resources, it appears that the development of integrated networks, production of outcome research, advocacy within the legal system, and diversification of professional services will be important components in behavioral health care. Recently, there has been a movement toward the integrated combination of mental health and physical health, and it appears initial attempts to integrate primary care and behavioral health care have been successful. If integration were to occur on a more widespread level, the need for psychologists to obtain prescription privileges would not seem to be a critical priority. Again, it will be essential that outcome research be conducted as this system continues to evolve so that effectiveness and efficiency in integrated versus nonintegrated systems can be evaluated.

As the profession continues to evolve and be influenced by the managed care environment, it is likely that the role of the psychologist will continue to change in coming years. The scientist–practitioner may be best prepared to function in the managed care environment because this model, with its focus on integrating scientific and clinical knowledge, best prepares the doctoral-level clinician to educate utilization reviewers, evaluate effectiveness and efficiency of treatment through outcome research, design and manage integrated networks, develop and evaluate clinical practice guidelines, supervise nondoctoral providers, and deliver empirically based treatments. Perhaps the ultimate irony, as noted by Seligman (1998), is that managed care may serve as the impetus to establish the scientific foundations of training and practice in clinical psychology as originally conceived at the 1949 Boulder conference.

REFERENCES

American Psychiatric Association. (1993). Practice guideline for major depressive disorder in adults. *American Journal of Psychiatry, 150*(4, Suppl. 1), 1–26.

American Psychiatric Association. (1994). *Diagnostic and statistical manual of mental disorders* (4th ed.). Washington, DC: Author.

Baird, K. A., & Rupert, P. A. (1987). Clinical management of confidentiality: A survey of psychologists in seven states. *Professional Psychology: Research and Practice, 18*, 347–352.

Barlow, D. H. (1996). Health care policy, psychotherapy research, and the future of psychotherapy. *American Psychologist, 51*, 1050–1058.

Bedell, J. R., Hunter, R. H., & Corrigan, P. W. (1997). Current approaches to assessment and treatment of persons with serious mental illness. *Professional Psychology: Research and Practice, 28*, 217–228.

Beutler, L. E., Machado, P. P., & Neufeldt, S. A. (1994). Therapist variables. In A. E. Bergin & S. L. Garfield (Eds.), *Handbook of psychotherapy and behavior change* (4th ed., pp. 243–244). New York: Wiley.

Cummings, N. A. (1995). Unconscious fiscal connivance. *Psychotherapy in Private Practice, 14*, 23–28.

Cummings, N. A., Budman, S. H., & Thomas, J. L. (1998). Efficient psychotherapy as a viable response to scarce resources and rationing of treatment. *Professional Psychology: Research and Practice, 29*, 460–469.

Dana, R. H., Conner, M. G., & Allen, J. (1996). Quality of care and cost-containment in managed mental health: Policy, education, research, advocacy. *Psychological Reports, 79*, 1395–1422.

Drum, D. D. (1995). Changes in the mental health service delivery and finance systems and resulting implications for the National Register. *Register Report, 20*, 4–10.

Feldman, S. (1992). *Managed mental health services.* Springfield, IL: Charles C Thomas.

Gerber, P. D., Barrett, J., Barrett, J., Manheimer, E., Whiting, R., & Smith, R. (1989). Recognition of depression by internists in primary care: A comparison of internist and "gold standard" psychiatric assessments. *Journal of General Internal Medicine, 4*, 7–13.

Haut, M. W., & Muehleman, T. (1986). Informed consent: The effects of clarity and specificity on disclosure in a clinical interview. *Psychotherapy, 23*(1), 93–101.

Hayes, S. C., Barlow, D. H., & Nelson-Gray, R. O. (1999). *The scientist practitioner: Research and accountability in the age of managed care.* Boston: Allyn & Bacon.

Hipp, M. L., Atkinson, C., & Pelc, R. (1994). *Colorado Psychological Association legislative survey.* Denver: Colorado Psychological Association.

Hirschfeld, R. M. A. (1994). Guidelines for the long-term treatment of depression. *Journal of Clinical Psychiatry, 55*(Suppl. 12), 59–67.

Kremer, T. G., & Gesten, E. L. (1998). Confidentiality limits of managed care and clients' willingness to self-disclose. *Professional Psychology: Research and Practice, 29*, 553–558.

Leslie, D. L., & Rosenheck, R. (1999). Shifting to outpatient care? Mental health care use and cost under private insurance. *American Journal of Psychiatry, 156*, 1250–1257.

Lipsey, M. W., & Wilson, D. B. (1993). The efficacy of psychological, educational, and behavioral treatment: Confirmation from meta-analysis. *American Psychologist, 48*, 1181–1209.

McGuire, J., Toal, P., & Blau, B. (1985). The adult client's conception of confidentiality in the therapeutic relationship. *Professional Psychology: Research and Practice, 16*, 375–384.

Mechanic, D., McAlpine, D. D., & Olfson, M. (1998). Changing patterns of psychiatric inpatient care in the United States, 1988–1994. *Archives of General Psychiatry, 55*, 785–791.

Miller, D. J., & Thelen, M. H. (1986). Knowledge and beliefs about confidentiality in psychotherapy. *Professional Psychology: Research and Practice, 17*, 15–19.

Miller, I. J. (1996). Managed care is harmful to outpatient mental health services: A call for accountability. *Professional Psychology: Research and Practice, 27*, 349–363.

Murphy, M. J., DeBernardo, C. R., & Shoemaker, W. E. (1998). Impact of managed care on independent practice and professional ethics: A survey of independent practitioners. *Professional Psychology: Research and Practice, 29*, 43–51.

Nowell, D., & Spruill, J. (1993). If it's not absolutely confidential, will information be disclosed? *Professional Psychology: Research and Practice, 16*, 385–397.

Phelps, R., Eisman, E. J., & Kohout, J. (1998). Psychological practice and managed care: Results of the CAPP practitioner survey. *Professional Psychology: Research and Practice, 29*, 31–36.

Richardson, L. M., & Austad, C. S. (1991). Realities of mental health practice in managed-care settings. *Professional Psychology: Research and Practice, 22*, 52–59.

Rogers, W. H., Wells, K. B., Meredith, L. S., Sturm, R., & Burnam, A. (1993). Outcomes for adult outpatients with depression under prepaid or fee-for-service financing. *Archives of General Psychiatry, 50*, 517–525.

Schappert, S. M. (1994). National ambulatory medical care survey: 1991 summary. *Vital Health Statistics, 13*, 1–110.

Seligman, M. E. P. (1998). The effectiveness of therapy. *APA Monitor, 29*, 2.

Shadle, M., & Christianson, J. B. (1988). Organization of mental health care delivery in HMOs. *Administration in Mental Health, 15*, 201–225.

Shore, M. F., & Beigel, A. (1996, January 11). The challenges posed by managed behavioral health care. *New England Journal of Medicine, 334*(2), 116–119.

Simon, G. E., & VonKorff, M. (1995). Recognition, management, and outcomes of depression in primary care. *Archives of Family Medicine, 4*, 99–105.

Sturm, R., & Wells, K. B. (1995, June 21). How can care for depression become more cost-effective? *JAMA, 273*, 51–58.

Tucker, L., & Lubin, W. (1994). *National survey of psychologists* (Report from Division 39, American Psychological Association). Washington, DC: American Psychological Association.

Wells, K. B., Manning, W. G., & Benjamin, B. (1986). Use of outpatient mental health service in HMO and fee-for-service plans: Results from a randomized controlled trial. *Health Services Research, 21*, 453–474.

Williams, J. W., Rost, K., Dietrich, A. J., Ciotti, M. C., Zyzanski, S. J., & Cornell, J. (1999). Primary care physicians' approach to depressive disorders. *Archives of Family Medicine, 8*, 58–67.

COMMENTARY: The phenomenon of managed care has been met with an out-pouring of vitriol on the part of clinical psychologists that is matched in volume and intensity only by the reactions of their research colleagues to the alleged dep-redations of institutional review boards (IRBs). What was once viewed as a sudden and perhaps reversible plague has now, after the passage of more than a quarter of a century, been grudgingly acknowledged—if not exactly accepted—as a perma-nent fixture of the externally funded mental health landscape.

Now, the focus on ethical issues regarding managed care has shifted from a debate over whether it is acceptable to participate in such plans at all to an explora-tion of ways in which doing so can be accomplished with the least ostensible harm to clients/patients. Of particular note from an ethical perspective is that service recipients can suffer significant consequences occasioned by the activities of psy-chologists who have agreed to conduct psychotherapy or counseling within this scheme but who fail to accommodate its contractual requirements.

The following references are recommended for those interested in further inves-tigation of ethical concerns regarding the phenomenon of managed care, including its optimal accommodation in various contexts and a recognition of the distinct needs of different vulnerable populations.

Bowers, A., Owen, R., & Heller, T. (2017). Care coordination experiences of people with disabilities enrolled in Medicaid managed care. *Disability and Rehabilitation: An International, Multidisciplinary Journal, 39,* 2207–2214. http://dx.doi.org/10.1080/09638288.2016.1219773

Dugan, J. (2015). Trends in managed care cost containment: An analysis of the managed care backlash. *Health Economics, 24,* 1604–1618. http://dx.doi.org/10.1002/hec.3115

Gibbons, H. M., Owen, R., & Heller, T. (2016). Perceptions of health and healthcare of people with intellectual and developmental disabilities in Medicaid Managed Care. *Intellectual and Developmental Disabilities, 54,* 94–105. http://dx.doi.org/10.1352/1934-9556-54.2.94

Marton, J., Yelowitz, A., Shores, M., & Talbert, J. C. (2016). Does Medicaid managed care help equalize racial and ethnic disparities in utilization? *Health Services Research, 51,* 872–891. http://dx.doi.org/10.1111/1475-6773.12396

Morelock, J. C. (2016). Bureaucratically distorted communication: The case of managed mental health care. *Social Theory & Health, 14,* 436–457. http://dx.doi.org/10.1057/s41285-016-0015-0

10.6. Considerations for Ethical Practice in Managed Care

Catherine Acuff, Bruce E. Bennett, Patricia M. Bricklin, Mathilda B. Canter, Samuel J. Knapp, Stanley Moldawsky, and Randy Phelps

Marketplace changes, including the advent of and high level of market penetration by managed care, have caused an upheaval in the practice community. What dilemmas do practitioners face when working in, or contracting with, organized systems of care? What should practitioners be doing to maintain both ethical standards and high-quality services in this era of managed care? What concerns are there regarding the ethics of such systems themselves? In this article we explore these issues.

The business emphasis in the current health care marketplace on "units of work" (therapy hours) and "commodity prices" (fees) by the "provider" (psychologist) represents a language and set of values that are alien to many practitioners. Many psychologists experience considerable discomfort over their professional roles and organizational expectations when business standards and incentives conflict with professional values and ethics.

Reactions among psychologists to these marketplace changes have been mixed, but are frequently intense. Some psychologists have welcomed the emphasis on financial accountability and the opportunities for personal advancement. Many psychologists have continued to try to work ethically and competently within organized systems of care, including managed care organizations (MCOs). However, some have rejected managed care entirely and eschewed all things related to it. Still others have seized entrepreneurial opportunities and have become managers for, leaders in, or owners of MCOs. In addition, many psychologists have expressed deep concern about the future of professional psychology.

Regardless of the individual's current level of involvement or concern, psychologists feel distress whenever patient care is compromised and should be

From "Considerations for Ethical Practice in Managed Care," by C. Acuff, B. E. Bennett, P. M. Bricklin, M. B. Canter, S. J. Knapp, S. Moldawsky, and R. Phelps, 1999, *Professional Psychology: Research & Practice, 30*, pp. 563–575. Copyright 1999 by the American Psychological Association.

The opinions expressed in this article are the authors' own and do not represent an official statement by the APA Ethics Committee or the APA Office of Ethics. Statements made neither add to nor reduce requirements of the APA Ethics Code, nor can they be definitively relied on as interpretations of the meaning of the Ethics Code standards or their application to particular situations. The opinions expressed by Catherine Acuff are solely hers. No official support or endorsement by the Substance Abuse and Mental Health Services Administration is intended or should be inferred.

We gratefully acknowledge the assistance of the following persons in the preparation of this material: Shirley A. Higuchi, Elizabeth A. Cullen, Cherie Jones, Billie Hinnefeld, and Anthony E. Chuukwu.

concerned about the impact of business practices on the quality and accessibility of psychological services. This concern predates managed care but is more manifest for many psychologists working with or for MCOs. Because many of the ethical dilemmas psychologists face as a result of managed care are systemic in nature, there is a limit on the ability of any single psychologist to affect the current health care marketplace. Therefore, advocacy efforts, both by individual psychologists and the profession as a whole, are needed.

. . .

The task force reviewed issues of ethical service delivery in organized care settings and submitted an internal report to CAPP in June, 1998. Our focus was on the process involved in ethical decision making and problem solving in the current era of managed care. Our review of the issues suggested that overall, the APA Ethics Code (APA, 1992) and other APA documents generally provide adequate guidance for individual psychologists when managed care presents ethical challenges. Indeed, most, if not all, of the issues created by managed care policies (such as limited treatment reimbursement and threats to confidentiality) have been faced before by psychologists in other settings and contexts. However, managed care seems to have greatly increased the frequency with which psychologists encounter these issues, as well as their intensity.

In the current article, we review general considerations in ethical decision making and problem solving. In addition, we discuss the need for sustained and organized advocacy efforts to ensure patient access to quality health care, the impact of managed care systems on professional relationships, both among psychologists and between psychologists and other professionals, and the need for a systematic approach to ethical decision making. We also examine four areas, or domains, in which ethical dilemmas most commonly arise for psychologists working in or with organized systems of care: informed consent, confidentiality, abandonment, and utilization management–utilization review. Hypothetical examples are provided to illustrate many of the issues and dilemmas encountered in the managed care environment.

GENERAL CONSIDERATIONS

Many practitioners are experiencing dilemmas or are raising questions about their ethical obligations because some MCOs deny authorization for needed treatment, fail to respect patient privacy, restrict communications between psychologists and their patients, or are perceived as attempting to intimidate psychologists through the use of "no cause termination" clauses. Although these practices are not engaged in by every MCO, they are clearly problematic when they occur. In addition, psychologists who are increasingly entering into capitated contrasts or working on a case-rate basis face the problem of delivering quality health care services within a very limited budget. And, one impact of marketplace changes in general, and of managed care in particular, has been to curtail drastically the availability of psychological assessment and long-term therapy, two of psychology's most significant modalities. Finally, the competitiveness embodied in the managed care marketplace has changed the tenor of professional relationships within the health care industry. Psychologists face competing demands as they try to meet their ethical obligations while providing services in a changing environment.

The following vignette illustrates a dilemma regarding the competing demands of capitation and one way in which a hypothetical group of psychologists may deal with these demands.

VIGNETTE 1

Situation

The Acme Psychological Center, a private corporation owned by 10 psychologists, has just been awarded a large capitated contract, which starts in 1 month. When the new plan takes effect, 30% of the Center's patient caseload will be either entirely self-pay or under fee-for-service insurance, 30% will be under other managed care plans, and 40% will be under the new capitated plan.

Issue

The owners, being ethical psychologists, are concerned that they do not put profits above patient welfare in the capitated contract. They have assigned one of the practice partners, Dr. Anne Ethical, to propose internal procedures to ensure that patient welfare will not be compromised.

Discussion and Response

Dr. Ethical wants to ensure that the recommendations will reduce the temptation to compromise patient care. In the proposal she sent to the other group members, Dr. Ethical recommended that (a) all patients will be given access to an internal utilization review process if they are dissatisfied with the treatment plan or services offered to them. The utilization review process includes input from a respected outside psychologist who has no financial ties to the group practice; (b) the informed consent brochure given to incoming patients informs them of the potential for conflict of interest and of the internal utilization review process; (c) the practice will develop an internal monitoring system that looks at the length of patient care in the nonmanaged care and managed care (capitated) reimbursement systems. The owners will monitor their behavior to ensure that the capitated patients are not subjected to a systematic downgrading of their treatment; (d) outcome measures and satisfaction forms will be used for both the capitated and noncapitated patient populations; and (e) the owners will agree that the sharing of profits depends, in part, on the results of the outcomes and patient satisfaction data.

A CRITICAL DISTINCTION

The terms *ethics* and *ethical* can have various connotations depending on the context in which they are used. For example, the term *ethical* may refer to overarching moral principles, such as autonomy, beneficence (doing good for others), nonmaleficence (doing no harm), fidelity, and justice.

In a more narrow sense, the term *ethical* may refer to the "APA Ethical Principles of Psychologists and Code of Conduct" (APA, 1992) or to codes of ethics adopted by state boards of psychology. These codes of conduct mandate or prohibit specific actions and they may have the force of law. MCOs' actions often seem to offend the "ethics" of many practitioners and the public in the first sense of the term; that is, they are seen as morally outrageous. In this article we evaluate psychologists' ethical questions in the second sense of the word; that is, in the context of managed care in accordance with the APA Ethics Code.

No code of ethics, however well written, can anticipate all of the various situations in which psychologists may confront ethical dilemmas, and no code of ethics may be able to specify concrete actions for the psychologist to follow in all situations. Consequently, some of the possible ethical conflicts faced by psychologists have no clear solution and require psychologists to engage in an ethical decision process involving the balancing of competing ethical standards. The challenges presented by MCOs make it more important than ever for psychologists to familiarize themselves with the APA Ethics Code and relevant state laws.

Several studies reveal that a majority of practitioners believe managed care has created ethical dilemmas for most psychologists (Murphy, DeBernardo, & Shoemaker, 1998; Phelps, Eisman, & Kohout, 1998; Rothbaum, Bernstein, Haller, Phelps, & Kohout, 1998). Despite these beliefs, our task force found, on the basis of our own survey of state licensing boards and state association ethics committees, that there have been few adjudicated cases dealing specifically with alleged violations arising from psychological practice related to managed care. This suggests that psychologists who participate in managed care arrangements may use the term *ethics* to refer to their personal moral outrage toward the rules and limitations imposed by the managed care system, rather than to actual violations of the APA Ethics Code. In other words, an MCO's requirements may create limitations for the client and difficult situations for the psychologist, but these problems may not always rise to the level of an actual violation of the APA Ethics Code.

Nonetheless, although an actual violation of the code may not be involved, current health care practices that limit access to quality health care are of concern to psychologists. In addition to individual efforts by psychologists to grapple with practice dilemmas in this era of managed care, the profession as a whole is engaged in a variety of efforts to support ethical practice. Active involvement by all psychologists in the APA, its divisions, and the state psychological associations will further these efforts.

The following example addresses some of the issues and frustrations psychologists may experience in attempting to provide treatment in the context of managed care requirements and procedures.

VIGNETTE 2

Situation

Dr. F. Russ Stration is working with a patient who consulted him following an initial panic attack. At the first session, as part of his normal consent procedure, Dr. Stration reviewed with the patient her MCO benefit. He informed her that this particular MCO requires treatment reports every third session, which might include disclosure of his session notes and treatment summaries. He developed a treatment plan that he reviewed with the patient before submitting it to the MCO.

Several days before the second session, Dr. Stration called the MCO about the status of his request for approval of the treatment plan. The MCO case manager explained that the normal response time for nonemergent care approval was 2 weeks but that he would try to have an answer for Dr. Stration as soon as possible. By the time of the second session, Dr. Stration still had not heard from the MCO and found himself unable to tell the patient whether their third session would be the last under her benefit or whether additional sessions would be allowed. As of the third session, the patient appeared to be benefiting from the treatment interventions; she reported no further panic attacks and said she felt an increased sense of well-being. Dr. Stration told her he would call her when he heard from the MCO, scheduled a tentative fourth session contingent on plan approval, and discussed with her the availability of a local support group should further treatment be denied.

Issue

Dr. Stration was angry over this situation and feared that the uncertainty of further treatment would be detrimental to therapy. Although he felt that he had done all he could for this patient, he believed that the MCO case manager was acting unethically and he was outraged.

Discussion

Dr. Stration's feelings of distress over this situation may be familiar to many psychologists. Despite these feelings, Dr. Stration has dealt effectively with the ethical issues that could have arisen. By conducting an extensive discussion with the patient at the outset of therapy, Dr. Stration has met his obligation in structuring the relationship (Standard 4.01), providing informed consent to treatment (Standard 4.02), explaining the limits of confidentiality (Standard 5.01), and disclosing information appropriately (Standard 5.05). He has also planned for facilitating care in the event that psychological services are interrupted (Standard 4.08), and offered an appropriate alternative (Standard 4.09) should treatment terminate because of the MCO's refusal to authorize continued care.

Response

Dr. Stration should review his contract with the MCO regarding response time for treatment requests. If the MCO has violated the contract, he could protest the lack of timely response, as well as support the patient in protesting to her employer's benefits manager. Otherwise, his response to the MCO's procedures may best be categorized as moral outrage, and one course of action may be to engage in advocacy efforts to make known his feelings to legislators and others who can affect managed care policies and procedures.

SYSTEMIC ADVOCACY

Psychology is both a science and a profession, with a long heritage of working to improve public welfare by providing quality health care services. The ethical aspirations of professional psychologists include an obligation to work in sustained and meaningful activities that ensure public access to quality health care services. Psychologists seek to develop organizational policies and laws that increase access to needed services. This means working to address organizational policies or laws that restrict such access, interfere with or limit informed consent, result in patient abandonment or other inappropriate treatment of patients, or compromise patient confidentiality.

Such activities constitute an awareness that some dilemmas cannot be solved by actions at the level at which they occur. For example, an individual psychologist who has experienced a retaliatory termination from a panel may be unable to successfully challenge or change this action on the part of the MCO. However, such retaliatory terminations may be legally actionable. A few successful legal and legislative challenges along those lines may provide more opportunity for psychologists to successfully advocate for them at the MCO level. For example, the APA Practice Directorate is currently supporting several lawsuits that have the potential to change the way some MCOs operate. Changes occurring as a result of successful resolution of these suits will assist the individual psychologist in advocating for his or her patients. Thus, the psychologist is urged to use a problem-solving approach, either singly or in concert with organized psychology.

Although the obligation to engage in advocacy does not represent an enforceable standard, it does represent a goal to which all psychologists should aspire. Professional advocacy is not restricted to the psychologist's individual concerns but also may extend to systemic policies that negatively impact quality care. Furthermore, advocacy efforts should focus on the needs of the public. Advocacy can be accomplished individually or collectively through organizations such as APA and its divisions, the Association for the Advancement of Psychology, state or provincial psychological associations, and through multidisciplinary and consumer groups. Psychologists can also participate in disseminating information to the public (such as through APA's Public Education Campaign) about the benefits of psychological services.

Psychologists can actively support governmental advocacy efforts to ensure basic patient protections in all managed care policies. This can be done through direct lobbying at the state or national level, and by supporting the state and national political action committees that advocate on behalf of psychologists. Psychologists can also consider running for office themselves. They can support consumer advocacy efforts that are consistent with the ethics and aspirations of the profession. Additionally, psychologists can advocate directly with the purchasers of insurance or MCOs to improve access to quality care and can develop alternative models of service delivery. Finally, and to the extent allowed by their individual MCO contract, psychologist providers can disseminate information regarding the MCOs' policies, particularly those that compromise patient care. Vignettes 3 and 4 provide examples of such advocacy activities at various levels.

VIGNETTE 3

Situation

Dr. R. E. Search evaluates a 10-year old hyperactive boy with behavioral problems in school. He also interviews the parents. Dr. Search then recommends therapy for the child, a referral for evaluation of specific medication as an adjunct to treatment, and adjunctive therapy for the parents. The parents agree to the plan. During utilization review, the MCO's reviewer states that medication should be prescribed for the boy and that psychotherapy will not be authorized.

Issue

Dr. Search is faced with a denial of the treatment plan that, in his professional judgment, is in the best interest of the patient.

Discussion

Dr. Search has an ethical obligation to his patient within the context of the professional relationship that has been established. The highest aspirational goals of the profession call him to act according to the patient's welfare (Principle E). To the extent that he believes the MCO's recommended treatment will harm the patient, Standard 1.14 is applicable.

Response

Dr. Search's response may include any of the following: (a) submitting a written appeal to the MCO, (b) presenting literature to the reviewer indicating that medication without psychotherapy is not as effective as combined therapy, (c) explaining to the parents that he does not agree with the reviewer's recommendation and that the parents may wish to appeal the decision as well, and (d) engaging in advocacy efforts such as writing a letter to the editor of a newspaper, calling the MCO to task for just trying to save costs and not attending to the quality care needed for the patient.

If the MCO's utilization reviewer is a psychologist, he or she should review the relevant data and information regarding appropriate treatment for the described disorder. The issue is whether the recommendation to prescribe medication only would be considered to be below the prevailing "standard of care." If so, then the reviewer is behaving unethically by recommending a treatment plan that is below the standard and not supported by the professional literature or community.

VIGNETTE 4

Situation

Dr. Thoughtful is the only Spanish-speaking member of a managed care provider panel. She has been working for several months with Mr. Newcomer to deal with depression related to a recent move from El Salvador. Additional issues include his new job, extended family conflict associated with the move, and stresses of acculturation. Mr. Newcomer's sister, who works for the same company and is covered under the same managed care plan, contacts Dr. Thoughtful seeking therapy as well. Like her brother, she needs a Spanish-speaking therapist who is familiar with cultural and acculturation issues in El Salvadoran families.

Issue

On the basis of her work with Mr. Newcomer, Dr. Thoughtful is aware that conflicts between his and his sister's immediate families contribute to Mr. Newcomer's depression. Dr. Thoughtful concludes that it would be clinically contraindicated at this time to accept the sister as a client. However, she is also aware that the managed care plan has no other bilingual providers on their panel, although there are other culturally competent providers in the area. Nor do they provide for competent translation services. Additionally, the telephone call from the sister has convinced her that the situation is acute and calls for immediate assistance.

Discussion

Dr. Thoughtful is very attuned to issues of cultural competence in providing psychological services to ethnically diverse populations. She understands the potential new client's need for psychotherapy services to be provided in her own language and recognizes as well that ethnicity and culture are significant parameters in understanding psychological processes (Principle D of the APA's "Guidelines for Providers of Psychological Services to Ethnic, Linguistic, and

Culturally Diverse Populations," 1990). She is also concerned that the acuteness of the situation will not permit sufficient time to complete Mr. Newcomer's treatment before accepting the sister as a client. However, she is not prepared to risk premature termination and abandonment of her current client (Standard 4.09). On the other hand, Dr. Thoughtful is concerned about the welfare of her client's sibling, and given the seriousness of the situation, she wants to assist the sister in obtaining treatment as soon as possible (Principle E).

Response

Dr. Thoughtful could appeal to the clinical director of the MCO on behalf of the potential client to authorize a referral to a culturally competent, bilingual colleague who is not on the existing provider panel. This will often resolve the issue; but, if not, she could press the MCO to provide a competent mental health translator for therapy work with a non-Spanish-speaking member of the panel, although one who is fluent in dealing with mental health and acculturation issues in El Salvadoran families. Translators add a different dimension to therapy and should only be utilized if the first option does not work out.

BUSINESS RELATIONSHIPS

One of the more problematic impacts of marketplace changes has been in the area of psychologists' professional relationships. Although there is no longer a specific standard in the APA Ethics Code such as the one in the 1963 code entitled "Interprofessional Relations," the sentiment it expressed is still valued by psychologists. It read, "a psychologist acts with integrity in regard to colleagues in psychology and in other professions" (APA, 1963).

Because of the increased emphasis on the business of health care delivery, the proliferation of corporate groups that compete for beneficiaries and for health care contracts, and the effects of closed or closing panels on psychologists who have historically practiced in the same communities, there is concern that, as psychologists, we may lose our heritage of collegiality.

For some, managed care has brought about a competitive mindset that was not previously present, and psychologists may find themselves divided from those with whom they have had long, productive relationships. For example, proprietary information about one's practice group or current activities in contract negotiations will separate us out of business necessity. These situations are foreign to many psychologists even though they are a reality of the marketplace. We must learn that business competitors do not necessarily need to have noncollegial relationships. We urge psychologists to seek out venues where common bonds can continue to be forged. Active membership in state and regional psychological associations, involvement in advocacy coalitions, and participation in professional activities with other psychologists are recommended.

AN ETHICAL DECISION-MAKING PROCESS

The drastic change in the context of psychological practice over the past decade has made it necessary for psychologists to renew their familiarity with the APA Ethics Code and to use a deliberative process in applying it to current dilemmas. However, ethical dilemmas all too often lack clear-cut right or wrong answers. In fact, different solutions, all of them appropriate to the individual circumstances, may well be arrived at by different people at different times.

Moreover, there are times when, after a search for answers in the Ethics Code, professional guidelines, and related documents, and through consultation with colleagues, no clear resolution to a dilemma is apparent. This is one reason for developing decision-making processes for ethical problem solving. The literature on ethics in psychology contains many examples of such processes. Haas and Malouf (1995) and Kitchener (1984) are among those who have written in some detail on the importance of such decision making in the resolution of ethical dilemmas or even when deciding whether a dilemma is an ethical one. They have provided valuable models for psychologists facing such dilemmas.

It is beyond the scope of this article to review in detail the models presented elsewhere. However, such a decision-making process often includes an examination of the psychologist's personal ethics relative to the issue and an examination of the psychologist's initial intuitive responses. The resulting subjective affective awareness is usually followed by a series of questions, the answers to which permit the rational examination of relevant ethical issues, the stakeholders, applicable ethical and legal codes, and the generation of possible courses of action.

Because decision making is so important, below are a series of questions that a psychologist facing a managed care dilemma of ethical dimensions might ask himself or herself and their answers, which may help the psychologist to decide on a possible course of action.

1. What are my personal ethics on similar issues?

2. What is my gut-level opinion on a possible course of action? Awareness of personal ethics and understanding of gut-level or intuitive responses to any given situation are necessary before the psychologist can proceed to examine rationally the next seven questions.

3. Is this truly an ethical dilemma, or is it a business, technical, or other problem?

4. Is this a dilemma that I cannot resolve? Does it require systems change and/or organizational advocacy, or legal or legislative action? The answer to these questions may direct the psychologist to the importance of consultation and group advocacy in resolving many dilemmas of managed care. This question is particularly important in managed care settings. If the psychologist's answer to this question is yes, then the recognition that this is not a dilemma the psychologist alone can solve is helpful and frees

the psychologist to consult or participate in advocacy or other actions more likely to lead to resolution of the dilemmas.

5. If it is an ethical dilemma, who are the persons who have a legitimate stake in the resolution of the dilemma?

6. What are the relevant ethical standards or principles?

7. Is a psychological or legal consultation needed?

8. Are there compelling reasons to deviate from the ethical standard?

9. What are the overarching ethical principles involved (e.g., patient autonomy, doing good for others, doing no harm, justice or fidelity)? See Haas and Malouf (1995) and Kitchener (1984) for more elaborate discussions of similar decision-making processes. It is at this point that prioritization of those major principles is critical: the patient's rights to make autonomous decisions versus a psychologist's belief about what is good for the patient versus issues of trust, confidentiality, and truthfulness versus the overriding "above all, do no harm."

Depending on the answers to these questions, the final steps involve generating possible courses of action, evaluating, and choosing among them. At this point the psychologist asks two questions: Is this plan of action ethical and Is it implementable? Above all, psychologists must recognize which dilemmas are beyond the power of an individual acting alone.

The reader may wish to apply the above series of decision-making questions to each of the vignettes in order to illustrate for himself or herself how well a systematic decision-making process may work and to determine its helpfulness in arriving at courses of action.

DOMAINS

We have identified four domains in which ethical dilemmas most commonly arise for psychologists working in or with organized systems of care: (1) informed consent, (2) confidentiality, (3) abandonment, and (4) utilization management.

Informed Consent

Managed care organizations contract or subcontract with employer groups to provide or manage health care benefit programs and with health care providers to deliver services to the subscriber group. For mental health care, these contracts generally contain provisions that limit the type of therapy and related psychological services available to patients. They may also restrict access to certain providers or provider groups. Patients generally do not appreciate the extent of these limitations until the need for services arises. It is only at that critical moment that potentially crucial inadequacies in the mental health care plan become apparent.

In addition, the cost containment incentives embodied in managed care arrangements may require precertification of specific treatments, as well as initial and ongoing authorizations for therapy. The manner in which these utilization procedures are implemented by some MCOs may be overly intrusive and thereby disrupt the therapeutic process. The MCO may limit the primary therapist's ability to refer to specialists, require release of confidential patient information in excess of that needed to process claims, authorize reimbursement for fewer sessions than the number stated in the health care plan, or impose other conditions that a patient would not generally anticipate.

The patient's confidence and trust in the psychologist constitute an essential component of successful psychotherapy. In this context, it is not surprising that confusion on the part of the patient may easily lead to dissatisfaction and anger. Misunderstandings and miscommunications between the psychologist and the patient may interfere with the course of therapy and may lead the patient to develop ill feeling toward the psychologist.

Regardless of the type of health care service provided—or the setting in which the service is delivered—informed consent is an essential aspect of modern-day practice. Informed consent is such a fundamental part of health care that it is now required by APA Ethics Code (Standard 4.02). Because some MCOs do not provide full, complete, and accurate information to their subscribers, many patients are not fully aware of the complexities of managed care arrangements and how these arrangements affect their benefits and rights. Psychologists must be especially attentive to informed consent issues when working with these patients. However, individual psychologists cannot be held accountable for the array of managed care arrangements in the current marketplace. Psychologists may need to turn to APA or their state organizations for advocacy to ensure that benefits provided by an MCO are those that are publicly declared in the patient's contracts.

On the basis of the experiences of the authors and the feedback given from other psychologists, three areas of particular importance (fees and other types of financial arrangements, role clarification, and confidentiality) will be discussed in the context of informed consent.

Informed Consent, Fees, and Financial Arrangements

To avoid confusion or misunderstanding, it is important that the psychologist reach an agreement with the patient specifying the compensation and the billing arrangements to be used (Standard 1.25[a]). The agreement should address the psychologist's billing practices for ancillary services, such as testing, report writing, professional consultation, voluntary or required court appearances, and other related procedures that may be provided by the psychologist.

The psychologist is also required by the Ethics Code to discuss any limitation on services that may be anticipated due to limitations in financing (Standard 1.25[e]). Such limitations may result from contractual obligations in the patient's managed care program. It is helpful for psychologists to understand and be able to convey to their patients such information as: (1) the MCO's provisions related to the number of authorized sessions, (2) the method and timing of utilization review, (3) the nature of the information required by the MCO to authorize services, (4) the amount of reimbursement provided, (5) the patient's share of any expenses (deductible or copayment), (6) the services that are covered or excluded, (7) the responsibility for payment if the MCO determines that a particular service is not covered under the patient's plan, and (8) any other foreseeable financial matters.

Informed Consent and Role Clarification

Frequently, psychologists find themselves in conflicting roles when providing professional services, especially in a managed care setting. For example, psychologists who provide services under a capitated arrangement may feel increased pressure to limit treatment in order to sustain profits. When such conflicts occur or are foreseeable, the psychologist should attempt to clarify the situation with the parties involved and delineate the role(s) that the psychologist can and cannot perform. These role clarification issues take on greater significance when providing couples, marital, or family therapy because of the increased complexity when multiple parties are involved (Standards 1.21, 4.03, and 7.03).

Informed Consent and Confidentiality

Confidentiality is an essential ingredient in the therapeutic relationship. It is important that the patient be fully informed about professional and legal obligations that may require the psychologist to release sensitive patient information to the MCO as a part of utilization review or for determination of necessity of treatment (Standard 5.05). If it is foreseeable that the information obtained in the course of delivering services may be used for these or other purposes, the patient should be made aware of this fact. The discussion of confidentiality should occur at the initial stages of treatment and thereafter as new issues arise in therapy. Special confidentiality provisions are involved when the psychologist is providing couples, marital, family, or group therapy (Standard 5.01).

Informed Consent Recommendations

The following are specific recommendations regarding informed consent. Standards of the APA Ethics Code are referenced where appropriate.

1. Psychologists should be aware that informed consent is an ethical requirement (Standard 4.02).

2. Psychologists should provide informed consent, which, at a minimum, includes (a) information regarding fees and other potential costs of services (Standard 1.25); (b) responsibility for payment (Standard 1.25); (c) type of service and anticipated number of sessions (Standards 1.07 and 4.01); (d) any contractual limitations on the services provided (Standard 1.25[e]); (e) record keeping, including electronic storage and transfer, release of information, and

confidentiality (Standards 1.24 and 5.01); and (f) the roles that the psychologist can and cannot play (Standards 1.17, 1.21, and 4.03).

3. When working with a patient who is part of a managed care arrangement, the psychologist should review with the patient any information that will be provided to the MCO for purposes of utilization review or quality assurance (Standard 5.05).

4. Because informed consent is an ongoing process, issues should be addressed at the onset of services and thereafter, as appropriate. For example, the patient should be informed if his or her MCO requires reauthorization information.

5. Psychologists may want to consider using a written document for establishing informed consent. An example is the "Psychotherapist–Patient Informed Consent Contract" (Harris & Bennett, 1998). Psychologists are advised to consult with an attorney prior to using such a document to ensure that it is in compliance with local and state statutes.

Confidentiality

Confidentiality and trust are critical to most effective health care treatments and particularly to mental health care. *Confidentiality* is the ethical and legal duty imposed on therapists to protect sensitive information obtained in the delivery of professional services from disclosure to third parties. Without assurance of confidentiality many individuals will not seek treatment, and those in treatment may withhold crucial information. The atmosphere of safety provided by confidentiality is critical to effective treatment.

Exceptions to confidentiality have always existed. For decades, even under indemnity arrangements, insurance companies have required the psychologist to provide the patient's diagnosis and, at times, the treatment plan prior to paying for the service. The legal system similarly places limits on confidentiality to serve the interests of justice and the public welfare. For example, mandatory child-abuse-reporting statutes are found in all states. Nevertheless, the strong demand for patient information inherent in managed care systems far exceeds these previous provisions and threatens the confidentiality of the psychologist–patient relationship, potentially reducing the quality of patient care.

MCOs, for example, may require patients to reveal sensitive and affect-laden information to case managers or intake workers before authorizing initial or additional treatment, or when transferring a patient from one provider to another. It is not unheard of for an MCO to require a practitioner to submit all treatment records before payment is made. More often, MCOs use standard forms that may solicit more information than is typically required for the development of an effective treatment plan. Some MCO policies require certain information from all patients on the premise that they need access to this information to monitor patient care. This requirement may lead psychologists reluctantly to place more information in the records than may be necessary.

It is assumed that the patient has consented to release this type of information because insureds will typically have signed release forms when first enrolled in the managed care plan (except in the case where the MCO requires the provider to obtain the release). However, the insured rarely understands the extent to which the release permits private information to be shared, so it is incumbent on the psychologist to inform the patient in this regard. Unless the release is revoked by the patient, it will probably be effective, so the psychologist may release the information if required by law. Psychologists should be aware of the applicable confidentiality laws specific to their state.

MCOs sometimes demand inspection of a psychologists' records of non-beneficiaries before they will credential the psychologist as a member of the MCO panel. Although psychologists risk exclusion from panels for failure to comply with this standard, there are no exceptions to confidentiality that allow client information to be revealed without written consent under these circumstances. In this situation, redacted records should be acceptable to the MCO. If not, the psychologist may want to pursue other alternatives with the MCO, such as challenging the request on ethical grounds, offering to provide a fictitious sample record, or offering to share an MCO's patient record after becoming a member of the MCO panel and receiving the referral, following patient consent.

Some MCO contracts state that the MCO owns the patient's records. The psychologist is advised to review all managed care contracts related to record ownership. Again, the psychologist should be aware of applicable state confidentiality laws.

With ongoing buyouts and mergers in the health care industry, no one has assurances regarding the ultimate disposition of confidential patient information. Information that a psychologist might have once been able to hold in confidence may now be open to review or entry into databases. The mental health information may be comingled with other health care information. The disclosure of mental health information may be more problematic than the disclosure of general health information because of the risk of greater stigmatization.

Confidentiality Recommendations

The following are specific recommendations regarding confidentiality. Standards of the APA Ethics Code are referenced where appropriate.

1. Psychologists should inform patients as soon as feasible at the outset of treatment about the relevant limits of confidentiality under their managed care policy. Patients should be made aware that psychologists have no control over confidential information after it leaves their offices (Standards 4.01, 4.02, and 5.01).

2. It may not be clinically indicated or feasible in all situations for psychologists to share with patients all information that will be released to the MCO.

However, the usual rule of thumb is that patients should know generally what is being released. There should be appropriate consent prior to the release of this information (Standards 4.02 and 5.05).

3. Because of the potential for abuses of confidential information by MCOs, psychologists need to consider what they place in clinical records. Psychologists can obtain guidance on record keeping from the APA's "Record Keeping Guidelines" (APA, 1993), regulations from their state boards of psychology, or various ethics texts and articles (Standards 5.03 and 5.07).

4. Psychologists who perform utilization reviews are held to the same ethical standards as psychologists who provide direct treatment. They may not share patient information without written consent and are entitled only to as much information as is necessary to fulfill their professional duties (Standards, 1.03, 5.03, and 5.06).

5. Psychologists should be aware of and make accommodations for the threats to confidentiality inherent in newer modes of information transmission and storage such as fax and electronic mail communication, computerized databases, and so forth (Standards 5.04 and 5.07).

6. Psychologists should read managed care contracts carefully to determine their obligations related to confidential information including who, under the terms of the contract, owns the records and has control over their release. Psychologists also should be aware of the limits on confidentiality governed by applicable state laws (Standards 5.09 and 5.10).

7. Without written permission from the patient, psychologists may not allow MCOs to inspect patient records (Standard 5.05). Psychologists should be aware that the patient may have signed a waiver to permit records inspection by the MCO.

VIGNETTE 5

Situation

Dr. Show's application to become a member of an MCO panel is contingent on a site visit to her office. As part of the visit, the MCO staff member plans to review several current patient records. After Dr. Show points out that she has no patients insured by that particular MCO, the company requests that she share files from any of her current patients. When Dr. Show points out that to do so would be a violation of patient confidentiality, the MCO requests access to former patient files from an MCO that has been bought out by the current company. Dr. Show refuses to comply on the grounds that these patients did not authorize the release of their files to the current company, and she is subsequently denied membership to the MCO panel.

Issue

The primary issue is one of protecting confidential patient information. There are secondary issues about access due to the increasing mergers and acquisitions of some MCOs by other MCOs. Finally, a situation such as this has an impact on the psychologist's ability to practice.

Discussion

Releasing nonmember patient records to the MCO without informed and written consent likely would be a violation of the ethical obligation to preserve the confidentiality of her patient's records, as well as a likely violation of applicable law. In a similar way, releasing former MCO patient records would also likely be an ethical violation, unless it is apparent that these patients had given informed and written consent to this procedure in the event of a sale of one MCO to another. This instance highlights the need for psychologists to be actively involved in advocacy efforts aimed at influencing managed care policies that cannot be fulfilled by the psychologist without violating the APA Ethics Code.

Response

Dr. Show has behaved appropriately by not allowing disclosure of records without the informed consent of her patients. She could consider appealing through the MCO's clinical director the decision to deny her membership and may be able to negotiate a review of redacted records. She may also wish to contact her state licensing board for assistance in documenting to the MCO that she is being asked to violate state law.

ABANDONMENT

Abandonment, the abrupt or unwanted discontinuation of treatment during a time of need, is a potential ethical and legal cause of action and may lead to harm of the patient. Although current marketplace trends limiting treatment may affect continuity of care, thereby increasing the potential for abandonment, it should be noted that the issue of abandonment also predates managed care. Abandonment can include the precipitous termination of a patient in crisis because of nonpayment for services. Abandonment may also arise if psychologists do not have sufficient coverage during weekends, out-of-office hours, vacations, or educational leaves. The APA Ethics Code provides guidance on these issues (Standards 4.08 and 4.09).

Although the cost containment practices of MCOs are not inherently unethical, they have led to increased concerns about patient abandonment. Psychologists working in organized systems of care are often concerned that the institution or the MCO's session limit will necessitate termination with patients who need more treatment. Psychologists are also concerned that such terminations may be violations of legal and ethical standards that prohibit patient abandonment. Moreover, many MCOs have closed panels, and psychologists face dilemmas when their patients change health care coverage to a company in which the psychologist is not an impaneled provider. And, as companies consolidate or as new MCOs enter the market, psychologists must be concerned about disruption of treatment with existing patients.

Unfortunately, the industrialization of health care has created financial incentives to limit treatment even when, in the psychologist's opinion, treatment is clinically indicated and the patient desires more treatment. These arrangements may limit the ability of psychologists and patients to work collaboratively to complete treatment successfully within a realistic time frame. Overly restrictive limits on sessions or benefits may result in the interruption of needed services to a particular patient. These incentives to limit care may occur when (a) MCOs contract directly with psychologists as providers, (b) MCOs limit the ability of psychologists to contract independently with patients covered under the MCO contract, or (c) psychologists work under a capitated contract with an MCO.

MCOs Contract Directly With Psychologists

Even when psychologists have directly contracted as providers for MCOs, they should only accept patients whom they believe they can benefit. That decision may depend on the match between the needs of the patient and the expertise of the psychologist (Standards 1.04 and 1.05), as well as the ability of the patient (or the patient's insurer) to meet the financial requirements of the treatment. One factor to consider is whether the benefit will allow the psychologist sufficient time to diagnose and treat the problem or otherwise benefit the patient. Such decisions may be difficult because the primary issue for which the person sought treatment may not turn out to be the primary focus of therapy. External stressors may lead to a precipitous decline in the functioning of the patient, or the true nature of the problem may not be discernible until therapy has been underway for some time. Nevertheless, to the extent feasible, the psychologist and patient need to discuss the anticipated needs of the patient and the ability of the MCO or the patient to pay for needed services.

Even after a patient is accepted into therapy, an MCO may discontinue reimbursement for a variety of reasons. At these times, if in the psychologist's opinion the patient still needs treatment, the psychologist may be obligated to appeal, or to encourage a patient to appeal, those decisions (see section on Utilization Management–Utilization Review).

When patients without financial resources require additional treatment, psychologists may refer them to public agencies or self-help groups, develop a deferred or reduced payment plan, schedule sessions less frequently or of shorter duration if clinically appropriate, or use other strategies to ensure access to care. Bartering may also be a consideration, but psychologists should be familiar with Standard 1.18 of the APA Ethics Code. The exact nature of the psychologist's recommendations involves both clinical and financial considerations.

Regarding coverage situations, an MCO contract may not permit the psychologist a full range of colleagues to use for coverage while the psychologist is absent. For example, coverage arrangements may be restricted to the MCO's provider panel. In that instance, arranging coverage can be particularly challenging when a psychologist's caseload consists of patients from several MCOs. Psychologists need to consider this possible issue when deciding to sign a managed care contract.

Prohibition on Private Fee Arrangements

Most MCOs permit psychologists who are network providers to enter into private fee arrangements with patients for noncovered services. However, some do not. Psychologists should look for these clauses in MCO contracts and should consider them when making long-term plans for the care of patients.

Psychologists Directly Hold Capitated Contracts

Some MCOs hire psychologists and other mental health professionals on a fee-for-service basis. Other MCOs may "carve out" behavioral health care services through capitated arrangements with subcontractors, including group practices in which psychologists have a personal financial risk that may depend, in part, on the type and length of treatment provided patients. The very nature of these arrangements places the psychologist in a potential conflict of interest with his or her patients because the psychologist's business interests may be advanced to the detriment of the patient through the withholding of care. Psychologists should inform patients when they are involved in any financial arrangements that might serve as an incentive to potentially limit care (see earlier section on *Informed Consent*).

Abandonment Recommendations

The following are specific recommendations regarding abandonment. Standards of the APA Ethics Code are referenced where appropriate.

1. Patients should not be abandoned during periods of crisis (Standards 4.08 and 4.09).

2. Psychologists are aware that emergency, weekend, or afterhours coverage may be required for some patients (Standards 1.07, 4.01, 4.02, 4.08, and 4.09), and they should make necessary arrangements for this coverage. Particularly for managed care patients, it may be necessary to consider other impaneled providers when making coverage arrangements.

3. When patients without financial resources need more treatment, psychologists should attempt to help them find alternative ways to receive the needed treatment (Standards 1.18, 1.20, and 4.09).

4. Psychologists should read MCO contracts carefully to understand any limits on coverage. They should also be aware of the appeal mechanism(s) in the contract and pay attention to any other clauses that could limit patient care (Standards 1.02, 4.01, 4.02, and 8.030).

5. Psychologists should inform patients if the contract includes financial incentives to limit care. Although capitation arrangements are not inherently unethical, psychologists with financial incentives to deny care are advised to develop quality control mechanisms that minimize the likelihood that patient welfare would be compromised (Standards 1.13, 1.14, and 1.15). (See Vignette 1 for examples.)

VIGNETTE 6

Situation

Dr. Greatheart and her patient are close to reaching their therapy goals when the patient is diagnosed as having breast cancer and becomes emotionally distraught. The therapist requests authorization for additional sessions, but the MCO denies the request because the patient's benefits have been exhausted. The patient suggests that Dr. Greatheart continue to see her by naming her husband as the patient, because he had not used his benefits at all.

Issue

Dr. Greatheart knows that continued psychological treatment could make a significant difference for the patient during this difficult time and is aware that the APA Ethics Code makes it clear that psychologists may not abandon patients in crisis (Standard 4.09). The issue for Dr. Greatheart is how to meet her ethical and professional responsibilities to her patient given the MCO's denial.

Discussion

Initially, Dr. Greatheart is frustrated with the MCO, but she realizes that the denial of additional sessions is based on her patient reaching the contractual benefit limit. This is a different situation than one where an MCO denies sessions for other reasons (e.g., additional treatment does not meet their definition of *medical necessity*) and is an issue that psychologists have faced many times in the past (e.g., with uninsured patients or when patients with indemnity insurance reached the benefit limit). Therefore, the situation is not limited to managed care arrangements.

Even though the benefit is exhausted, it is possible that an appeal may be successful, and Dr. Greatheart may wish to consider this option. MCO's often have a multistage appeals process, ranging from the utilization reviewer to a clinical peer or equivalent and finally to the clinical director.

If the MCO contract permits, Dr. Greatheart could also consider seeing the patient on a private basis at her usual and customary fee, a reduced fee, or on a pro bono basis. She may also consider making a referral to an appropriate community resource for therapy. Additionally, she may refer the patient to the local American Cancer Society chapter for assistance and available peer support groups. In the absence of community resources, she may involve herself in advocacy efforts within her state or local psychological association or other community groups (e.g., United Way, city council, and other arenas) for funding for the development of appropriate community resources.

Response

In this situation, Dr. Greatheart should make arrangements to see that the patient's needs for continuity of care are considered to the extent feasible. Psychologists should not falsify information in the interests of providing patient care. This patient's suggestion that the psychologist continue to see her, but name her husband as the patient, is not acceptable. For Dr. Greatheart to collude in this fashion could be considered fraud.

UTILIZATION MANAGEMENT–UTILIZATION REVIEW

Utilization management (UM), in the broadest sense and under different names, is not new to psychology. Psychologists have been making UM decisions ethically and professionally for decades. UM involves making decisions regarding types of treatment, setting, and treatment duration in the delivery of professional services, and has occurred in both the public and the private sectors. UM also involves other such clinical functions as supervision, consultation, case staffing, peer review, and case studies.

Utilization review (UR), one form of UM, is in and of itself neither ethical nor unethical. In the past, the primary focus of utilization management was to serve the best interests of the patient or client. For years, public mental health agencies have engaged in heroic efforts to provide quality services to patients with limited budgets and serious financial restrictions. Today, there is a legitimate need to control health care costs, and some MCOs are interested in the quality of care provided while being responsive to this need. However, the high profits awarded CEOs of some MCOs and the emphasis on earnings within the for-profit MCOs suggest that the normal outrage of many psychologists who decry UR does have some rational basis. Also, some psychologists working as utilization reviewers within managed care systems may face a built-in conflict-of-interest as pressures for cost containment and profit motives compete with, and may well override, quality of care priorities in their decision making.

The applicability of the APA Ethics Code to UM-UR functions depends on the financial incentives involved and the issues to be considered in the decision-making process. When psychologist–reviewers exercise professional judgment in performing UR services they may be performing a health care procedure as opposed to a benefits management procedure. Thus, the type of service performed (e.g., health care vs. benefits decisions) will determine the ethical obligations of the psychologist. When professional judgment is required, and the psychologist is free to exercise discretion determining the number of sessions allowed—as opposed to purely routine administrative functions such as determining the number of sessions remaining in the plan benefit—ethical obligations to the patient ensue.

Psychologist–reviewers and providers are in the most precarious situation when the UR procedures provide financial incentives to deny treatment (e.g., in capitated arrangements or when the reviewer is employed by an MCO where the primary goal of the UR may be cost saving, rather than quality service provision). If the employer's benefit package limits the benefit to a specific number of sessions, the psychologist–provider should offer the best service possible, given the limits of the benefit.

On the other hand, if the design of the benefit is unlimited, or the limit of benefits has not yet been reached when UR is instituted, the psychologist–reviewer is exercising professional judgment in authorizing or denying treatment. Whereas containing costs may be one of the MCO's objectives, it is only one of many criteria that should guide the reviewer's decision to deny or continue care. Patient needs should remain paramount, though they should be met in a cost-effective manner.

Recommendations for Psychologists Performing Utilization Management and Review

As noted earlier, UR may involve a primarily administrative function, such as determining if a particular service is covered by the MCO contract. However, UR often requires psychologists to exercise professional judgment to determine if the treatment is "medically necessary," or to determine the type of service or number of sessions needed to help the patient. Such clinical decision making in UR is a professional service and is subject to ethical standards and requirements for ethical practice. Relevant sections of the Ethics Code include all under Standard 1.0, particularly 1.14, Avoiding Harm.

1. Psychologists are advised to be cautious about entering into employment with MCOs that appear to base UR decisions primarily or solely on cost containment or profit motives, rather than on quality of care.

2. Prior to accepting employment with an MCO, psychologists are advised to read carefully both their contracts and the MCO's UR-UM policies. They are also cautioned to review renewal contracts and policy changes (Standards 1.02 and 8.03).

3. When psychologists who are functioning as utilization reviewers respond to requests for additional care of patients, they should be flexible in applying criteria for continuing care. Their decisions should be based on patient

needs within the framework of the benefits stipulated in the contract (Standards 1.14, 1.15, and 1.25[b]).

4. When performing UR that requires professional judgment and allows discretion, psychologists may be providing professional services. They should perform these services within the boundaries of their competence. Because the reviewer is called on to make clinical judgments without having direct contact with the patient, it is particularly important to attend to the basis on which "medical necessity" is determined in reaching these decisions (Standards 1.04, 1.05, 1.06, and 2.02).

The following three vignettes illustrate dilemmas faced by psychologists working as utilization reviewers for MCOs and some possible responses to those dilemmas.

VIGNETTE 7

Situation

Dr. Bill Payer has been offered a job in an MCO's utilization review department.

Issue

Is it unethical for Dr. Payer to work for a managed care company?

Discussion

Although many psychologists decry the changes in practice brought about by managed care, there is nothing in the APA Ethics Code that prohibits Dr. Payer from employment within this industry. As with any potential position, Dr. Payer will need to evaluate the job responsibilities involved and his competence to fulfill these responsibilities, with particular attention to his obligations to the APA Ethics Code and state laws and regulations.

Response

Dr. Payer may wish to review Principles A–F of the APA Ethics Code as he considers this position, as well as specific standards that will be applicable to his work (Standard 8.01). In addition, Dr. Payer should carefully review the employment contract and the company's UM policies. Standard 1.03 requires Dr. Payer to provide services only in the "context of a defined professional . . . role," and he is advised to clarify this role at the outset. He should evaluate the job demands in terms of the professional judgments he will be required to make and refer to Standards 1.06, 1.15, and 1.16 in this regard. Dr. Payer may wish to consult with others as he considers the position (Standard 8.02). Standard 8.03 may be useful in guiding his preemployment discussions with the company.

VIGNETTE 8

Situation

After taking a job with the MCO, Dr. M. Ployee learns that the president of the company, Ms. Ivanna Profit, has recently implemented an employment contract for utilization reviewers that provides incentives to pay specific attention to issues of cost containment. The incentives include gifts, vacations, and other financial rewards. Important features of the contract are year-end bonuses for reviewers and the implementation of an employer-sponsored incentive plan based on the company's overall profitability and performance.

Issue

Dr. Ployee is now confronted with a potentially significant conflict of interest: His overall income will increase as a direct function of the total amount of care he denies to insureds. Further, because the overall bonuses or incentives are distributed among the reviewers in the department, each reviewer is subject to strong peer pressure to deny care.

Discussion

Dr. Ployee must be extremely vigilant in the performance of his job duties. Attention should be given to Standard 1.15 of the APA Ethics Code (1992), which states in part that psychologists, "are alert to and guard against personal, financial, social, organizational, or political factors that might lead to misuse of their influence." In addition Dr. Ployee needs to pay particular attention to Standard 1.16(a), which prohibits psychologists from participating "in activities in which it appears likely that their skills or data will be misused by others, unless corrective mechanisms are available."

Response

Fortunately, Standard 8.03 provides guidance for Dr. Ployee. On the basis of standard, Dr. Ployee should bring to Ms. Profit's attention the apparent or real conflicts between the company's incentive program, his job responsibilities and the Ethics Code. Dr. Ployee should "clarify the nature of the conflict, make known [his] commitment to the Ethics Code and, to the extent feasible, seek to resolve the conflict in a way that permits the fullest adherence to the Ethics Code."

VIGNETTE 9

Situation

Mr. Lonely, a 65-year-old divorced white male, with a diagnosis of substance abuse and major depression, has chronic suicidal ideation, but no clear current suicide plan of action. Dr. Helper, the psychologist–reviewer for the MCO that provides Mr. Lonely's health benefit, is being asked by the treating psychologist to authorize additional treatment for the patient. The MCO's policy is to authorize additional sessions above the standard limit only when there are life-endangering conditions. These conditions include being "actively suicidal," which is defined by the MCO as having a clear and imminent plan of action.

Issue

The conflict faced by Dr. Helper is that the patient may be at serious risk for self-harm. She has reviewed the treating psychologist's report and treatment plan, and she believes that the decision tree used by the company fails to identify all of the factors that should be considered for potential self-harm.

Discussion

Dr. Helper must consider whether she is making a competent assessment of the lethality of this patient if she uses the MCO decision tree and whether the MCO's organizational demands conflict with her obligations to the welfare of the patient.

Response

Dr. Helper should consult with the treating psychologist to determine if she has enough information to judge the likelihood of suicide and the benefits of authorizing additional services. Depending on the situation, she may request more information. If the patient's presenting problems fall outside of Dr. Helper's area of expertise, she may request consultation with knowledgeable peers. The Ethics Code requires psychologists to identify when organizational demands force them to compromise their obligations under the Code and to seek to change those policies when appropriate (Standard 8.03). This may require the psychologist to request a formal review of the MCO's definition of *actively suicidal*, as well as the procedures used to review these difficult cases.

Recommendations for Psychologists Delivering Professional Services Subject to Utilization Review

Many psychologists are not employed by MCOs but have contracted to provide professional services to patients with health care benefits administered by MCOs. The following specific recommendations are provided for these psychologists. Standards of the APA Ethics Code are referenced where appropriate.

1. When an MCO denies needed care, psychologists should assist the patient in trying to obtain the needed services. This may require working with the patient to appeal the decision or writing to the clinical director to notify the MCO of the potential adverse consequences to the patient. It may also involve

exploring other options available outside of the MCO (Standards 1.14, 1.15, 4.02, 4.08, 4.09, and 5.0).

2. When psychologists believe that an MCO's authorization for treatment is less than appropriate care, they should consider other available options and possible consequences for the patient's welfare and should act in the best interests of the patient within their ethical obligations. It is important to inform and discuss with the patient the implications of any decisions being made. The decision may be to appeal the MCO's decision or to accept the UR determination and proceed with the authorized treatment. Of course, it is essential that the treating psychologist has an adequate clinical basis for the appeal. Whatever the psychologist and patient decide to do, it should be based on helping and not harming the patient (Standards 1.14, 4.02, and 4.08).

SUMMARY

As psychological practice has undergone changes brought about by managed care's increasingly high level of market penetration, practitioners have raised many questions about the ethics of working in or with managed care organizations. Although many of these questions are framed in the context of concerns about the ethics of such systems themselves, others address particular dilemmas that arise during the day-to-day conduct of practice. Many of these dilemmas involve the clash of two different points of view.

When considering an issue exclusively from a cost-driven perspective, business ethics (which do exist) prevail. When considering the same issue from a care-driven perspective, psychological ethics prevail. The juxtaposition of these opposing alternatives creates "catch-22" situations and is the key to many of the dilemmas psychologists face in the current marketplace. Decisions to terminate treatment or whether a given intervention is "medically necessary" may be cost driven, care driven, or some balance of the two. In making a determination about the ethics of any specific situation, psychologists must also be clear about the meaning of the terms *ethics* and *ethical,* which can have various connotations depending on the context in which they are used.

In the broadest sense, the term *ethical* may refer to overarching moral principles, such as autonomy, beneficence (doing good for others), nonmaleficence (doing no harm), fidelity, and justice. In this article we have used the term *ethical* in a more narrow sense, referring to the APA's "Ethical Principles of Psychologists and Code of Conduct" (APA, 1992), or to codes of ethics adopted by state boards of psychology. Although MCOs' actions often offend the ethics of many practitioners in the first sense of the term (e.g., they are seen as morally outrageous), these actions may not always rise to the level of an actual violation of the APA Ethics Code.

In trying to sort out whether there is an actual or potential violation of the APA Ethics Code, the individual psychologist will have to seek his or her answer through careful application of a systematic problem-solving and decision-making process, including consultation with peers who are knowledgeable about the Code. The psychologist should acknowledge that there is no mandated "right" course of action in many circumstances and that there may be more than one possible appropriate solution. In fact, different solutions, all of them appropriate to the individual circumstances, may well be arrived at by different people at different times.

Finally, psychologists facing managed care dilemmas must recognize which of them are beyond the power of an individual acting alone. This is one reason that the recurrent recommendation that consultation with knowledgeable colleagues should be sought, and for our belief that all psychologists should be involved in systemic advocacy.

REFERENCES

American Psychological Association. (1963). Ethical standards of psychologists. *American Psychologist, 18*, 56–60.

American Psychological Association. (1992). Ethical principles of psychologists and code of conduct. *American Psychologist, 47*, 1597–1611.

American Psychological Association. (1993). Record keeping guidelines. *American Psychologist, 48*, 984–986.

American Psychological Association, Board of Ethnic Minority Affairs, Task Force on the Delivery of Services to Ethnic Minority Population. (1990). *Guidelines for providers of psychological services to ethnic, linguistic, and culturally diverse populations.* Washington, DC: Author.

Haas, L. J., & Malouf, J. L. (1995). *Keeping up the good work: A practitioner's guide to mental health ethics* (2nd ed.). Sarasota, FL: Professional Resource Exchange.

Harris, E., & Bennett, B. E. (1998). Sample psychotherapist–patient contract. In G. P. Koocher, J. C. Norcross, & S. S. Hill (Eds.), *Psychologist's desk reference* (pp. 191–196). London: Oxford University Press.

Kitchener, K. S. (1984). Intuition, critical evaluation and ethical principles: The foundation for ethical decision-making in counseling psychology. *The Counseling Psychologist, 12*, 43–55.

Murphy, M. J., DeBemardo, C. R., & Shoemaker, W. E. (1998). Impact of managed care on independent practice and professional ethics: A survey of independent practitioners. *Professional Psychology: Research and Practice, 29*, 43–51.

Phelps, R., Eisman, E. J., & Kohout, J. (1998). Psychological practice and managed care: Results of the CAPP practitioner survey. *Professional Psychology: Research and Practice, 29*, 31–36.

Rothbaum, P. A., Bernstein, D. M., Haller, O., Phelps, R., & Kohout, J. (1998). New Jersey psychologists report on managed mental health care. *Professional Psychology: Research and Practice, 29*, 37–42.

INDEX

ABOUT THE AUTHOR

Eric Y. Drogin, JD, PhD, ABPP, is a Fellow of the American Psychological Association (APA), a Fellow of the American Academy of Forensic Psychology, and a Diplomate and former president of the American Board of Forensic Psychology. Dr. Drogin holds faculty appointments with the Harvard Medical School and the BIDMC Harvard Psychiatry Residency Training Program and is a member of the Program in Psychiatry & the Law at the Massachusetts Mental Health Center. Additional roles have included chair of the APA's Committee on Professional Practice and Standards, and Chair of the APA's Committee on Legal Issues. Dr. Drogin is a Life Fellow of the American Bar Foundation and an American Bar Association (ABA) appointee to the National Conference of Lawyers and Scientists. Additional legally related roles have included chair of the ABA's Section of Science and Technology Law, chair of the ABA's Committee on the Rights and Responsibilities of Scientists, and commissioner of the ABA's Commission on Mental and Physical Disability Law. Dr. Drogin teaches on the adjunct faculty of the University of New Hampshire School of Law, as an instructor in the Harvard Law School Trial Advocacy Workshop, and as an honorary professor for the Aberystwyth Law School, *Prifysgol Aberystwyth* (formerly University of Wales). He has authored or coauthored over 250 scientific and legal publications to date, including *Mental Disability Law, Evidence, and Testimony* (2007), *Science for Lawyers* (2008), *Evaluation for Guardianship* (2010), *Handbook of Forensic Assessment* (2011), and *The Mental Health Professional in Court* (2013).